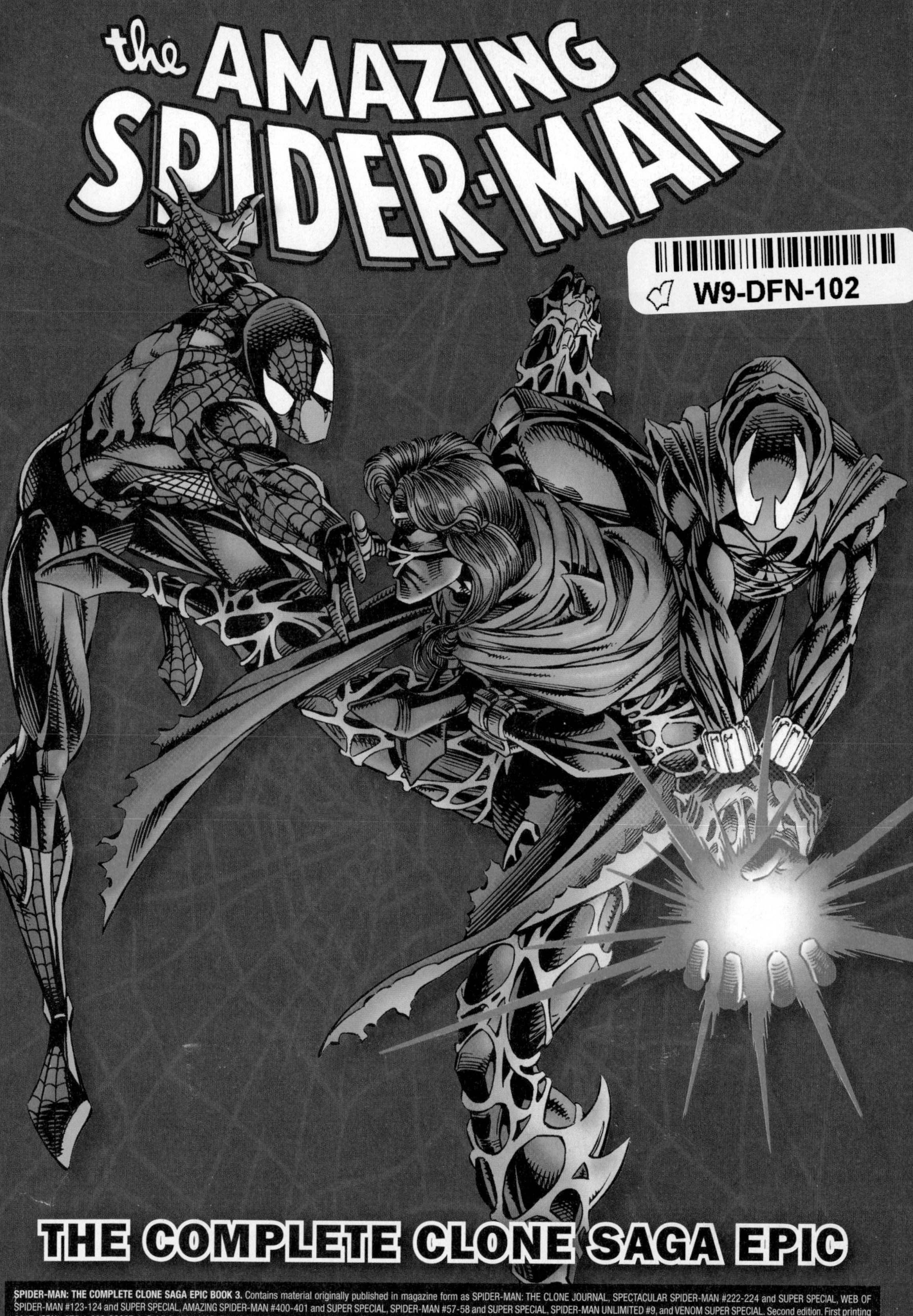

the AMAZING SPIDER-MAN

THE COMPLETE CLONE SAGA EPIC

SPIDER-MAN: THE COMPLETE CLONE SAGA EPIC BOOK 3. Contains material originally published in magazine form as SPIDER-MAN: THE CLONE JOURNAL, SPECTACULAR SPIDER-MAN #222-224 and SUPER SPECIAL, WEB OF SPIDER-MAN #123-124 and SUPER SPECIAL, AMAZING SPIDER-MAN #400-401 and SUPER SPECIAL, SPIDER-MAN #57-58 and SUPER SPECIAL, SPIDER-MAN UNLIMITED #9, and VENOM SUPER SPECIAL. Second edition. First printing 2017. ISBN# 978-1-302-90367-1. Published by MARVEL WORLDWIDE, INC., a subsidiary of MARVEL ENTERTAINMENT, LLC. OFFICE OF PUBLICATION: 135 West 50th Street, New York, NY 10020. Copyright © 2017 MARVEL No similarity between any of the names, characters, persons, and/or institutions in this magazine with those of any living or dead person or institution is intended, and any such similarity which may exist is purely coincidental. **Printed in the U.S.A.** DAN BUCKLEY, President, Marvel Entertainment; JOE QUESADA, Chief Creative Officer; TOM BREVOORT, SVP of Publishing; DAVID BOGART, SVP of Business Affairs & Operations, Publishing & Partnership; C.B. CEBULSKI, VP of Brand Management & Development, Asia; DAVID GABRIEL, SVP of Sales & Marketing, Publishing; JEFF YOUNGQUIST, VP of Production & Special Projects; DAN CARR, Executive Director of Publishing Technology; ALEX MORALES, Director of Publishing Operations; SUSAN CRESPI, Production Manager; STAN LEE, Chairman Emeritus. For information regarding advertising in Marvel Comics or on Marvel.com, please contact Vit DeBellis, Integrated Sales Manager, at vdebellis@marvel.com. For Marvel subscription inquiries, please call 888-511-5480. **Manufactured between 2/3/2017 and 3/7/2017 by LSC COMMUNICATIONS INC., SALEM, VA, USA.**

10 9 8 7 6 5 4 3 2 1

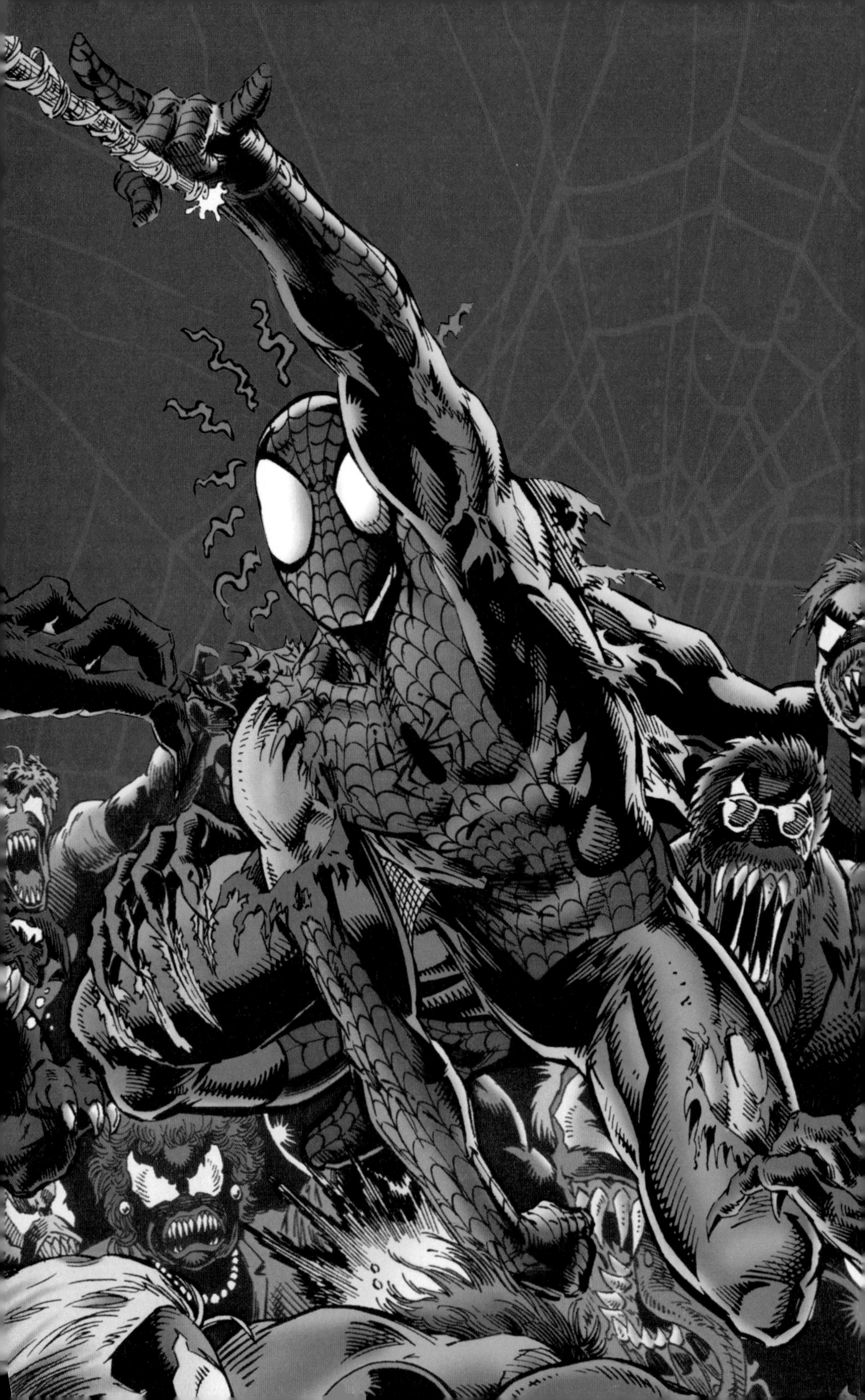

the AMAZING SPIDER-MAN

THE COMPLETE CLONE SAGA EPIC
BOOK 3

WRITERS
Tom DeFalco, J.M. DeMatteis,
Terry Kavanagh, Tom Lyle,
Stan Lee, Howard Mackie &
David Michelinie

PENCILERS
Mark Bagley, Robert Brown,
Sal Buscema, Steve Butler,
Ron Garney, Tom Grummett,
Dave Hoover, Kyle Hotz,
Steve Lightle, Ron Lim,
Tom Lyle, Darick Robertson,
John Romita Jr., Tod Smith &
Joe St. Pierre

INKERS
Greg Adams, Ralph Cabrera,
Sam De La Rosa, Randy Emberlin,
Armando Gil, Scott Hanna,
Don Hudson, Klaus Janson,
Larry Mahlstedt, Al Milgrom,
Tom Palmer, Jimmy Palmiotti,
George Pérez, Joe Rubinstein,
Bill Sienkiewicz, Arne Starr
& Tim Tuohy

COLORISTS
Chia-Chi Wang,
Randy Emberlin, John Kalisz,
Marianne Lightle, Malibu,
Tom Smith, Kevin Tinsley &
Wolf Pack with
Salvador Mancha

LETTERERS
John Costanza, Steve Dutro,
Loretta Krol, Bill Oakley, N.J.Q.,
Clem Robins, Joe Rosen &
Richard Starkings & Comicraft

EDITORS
Mark Bernardo, Tom Brevoort,
Eric Fein, Danny Fingeroth &
Mark Powers

WITH THANKS TO
Todd DeZago, Phil Gosier &
Mike Manley

Front Cover Artist: Joe St. Pierre
Front Cover Colorist: Thomas Mason

Spider-Man created by Stan Lee & Steve Ditko

Collection Editor: Mark D. Beazley
Assistant Editor: Caitlin O'Connell
Associate Managing Editor: Kateri Woody
Senior Editor, Special Projects: Jennifer Grünwald
VP Production & Special Projects: Jeff Youngquist
SVP Print, Sales & Marketing: David Gabriel
Research: Jeph York
Production: ColorTek & M. Hands
Book Designer: Arlene So

Editor In Chief: Axel Alonso
Chief Creative Officer: Joe Quesada
President: Dan Buckley
Executive Producer: Alan Fine

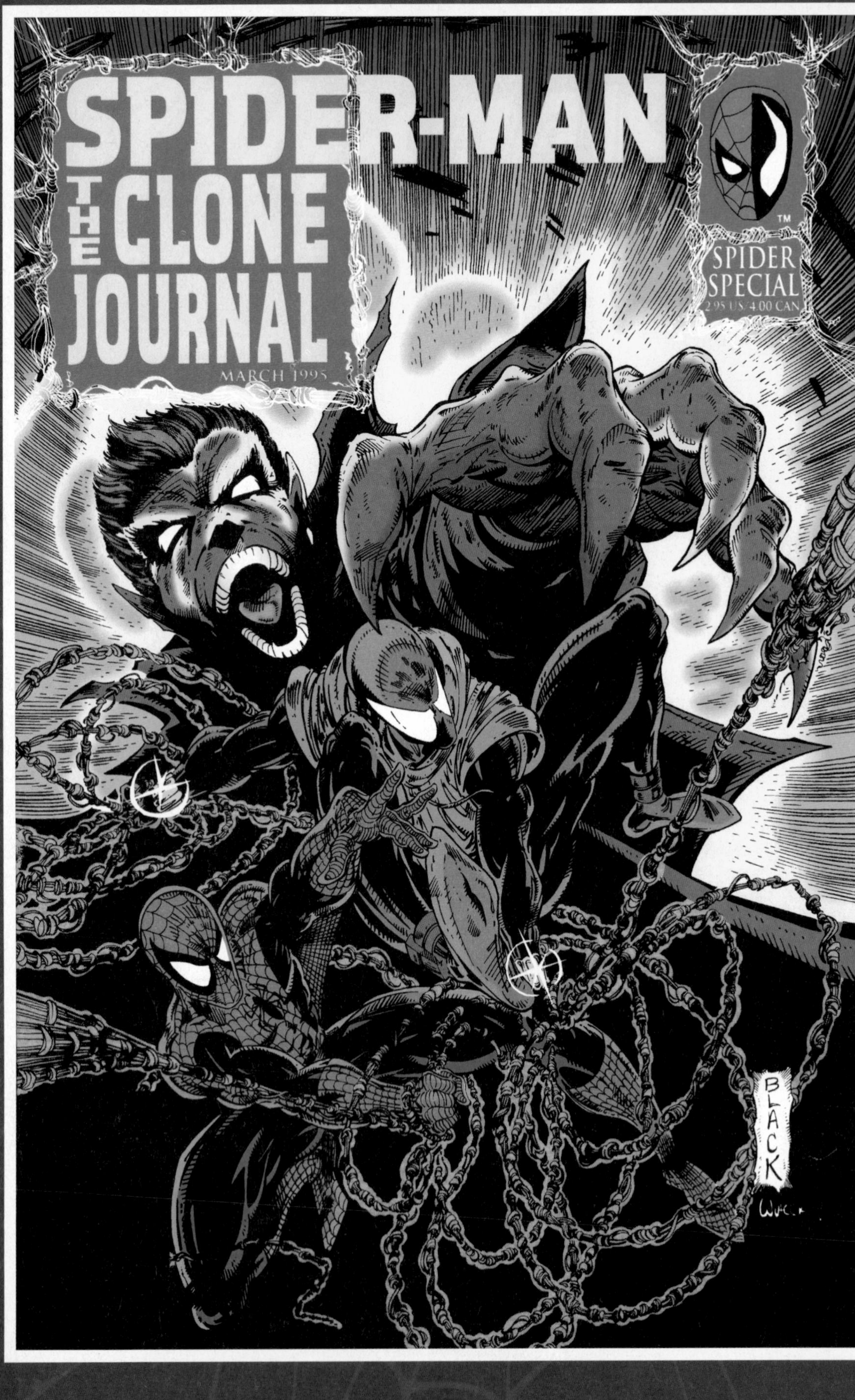
SPIDER-MAN
THE CLONE JOURNAL
MARCH 1995
TM
SPIDER SPECIAL
2.95 US/4.00 CAN
BLACK

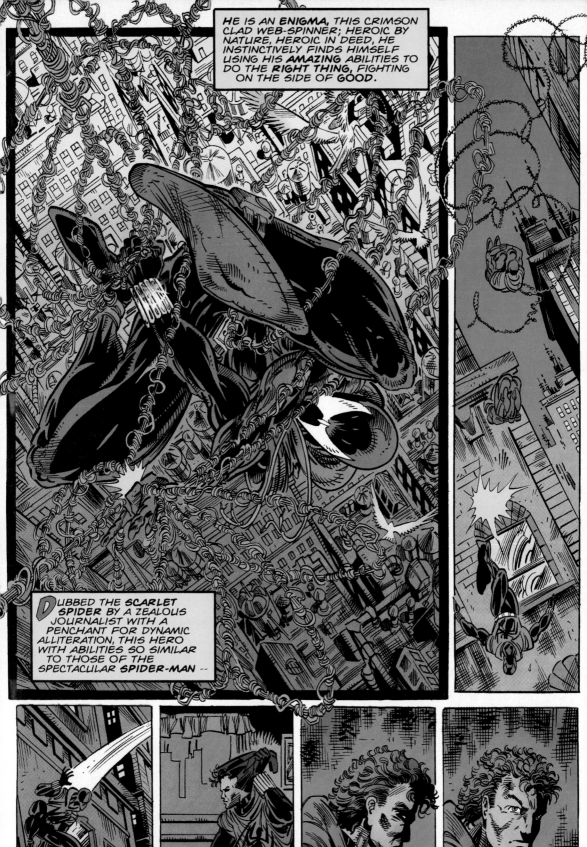

HE IS AN ENIGMA, THIS CRIMSON CLAD WEB-SPINNER; HEROIC BY NATURE, HEROIC IN DEED, HE INSTINCTIVELY FINDS HIMSELF USING HIS AMAZING ABILITIES TO DO THE RIGHT THING, FIGHTING ON THE SIDE OF GOOD.

DUBBED THE SCARLET SPIDER BY A ZEALOUS JOURNALIST WITH A PENCHANT FOR DYNAMIC ALLITERATION, THIS HERO WITH ABILITIES SO SIMILAR TO THOSE OF THE SPECTACULAR SPIDER-MAN --

-- REMAINS A PARADOX -- A RIDDLE --

-- A MYSTERY.

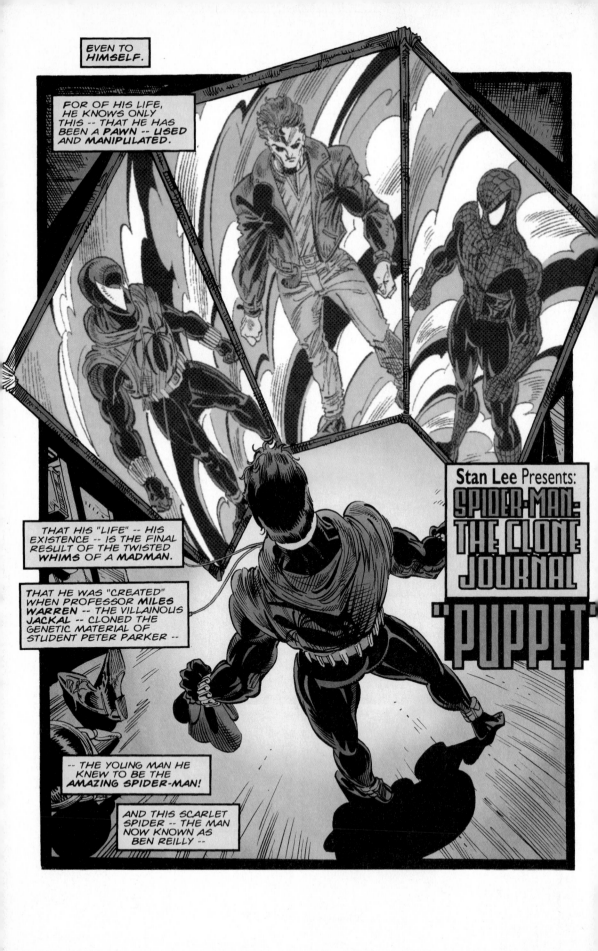

EVEN TO HIMSELF.

FOR OF HIS LIFE, HE KNOWS ONLY THIS -- THAT HE HAS BEEN A *PAWN* -- USED AND *MANIPULATED.*

THAT HIS "LIFE" -- HIS EXISTENCE -- IS THE FINAL RESULT OF THE TWISTED *WHIMS* OF A *MADMAN.*

THAT HE WAS "CREATED" WHEN PROFESSOR *MILES WARREN* -- THE VILLAINOUS *JACKAL* -- CLONED THE GENETIC MATERIAL OF STUDENT *PETER PARKER* --

-- THE YOUNG MAN HE KNEW TO BE THE AMAZING *SPIDER-MAN!*

AND THIS SCARLET SPIDER -- THE MAN NOW KNOWN AS *BEN REILLY* --

Stan Lee Presents:
SPIDER-MAN: THE CLONE JOURNAL
"PUPPET"

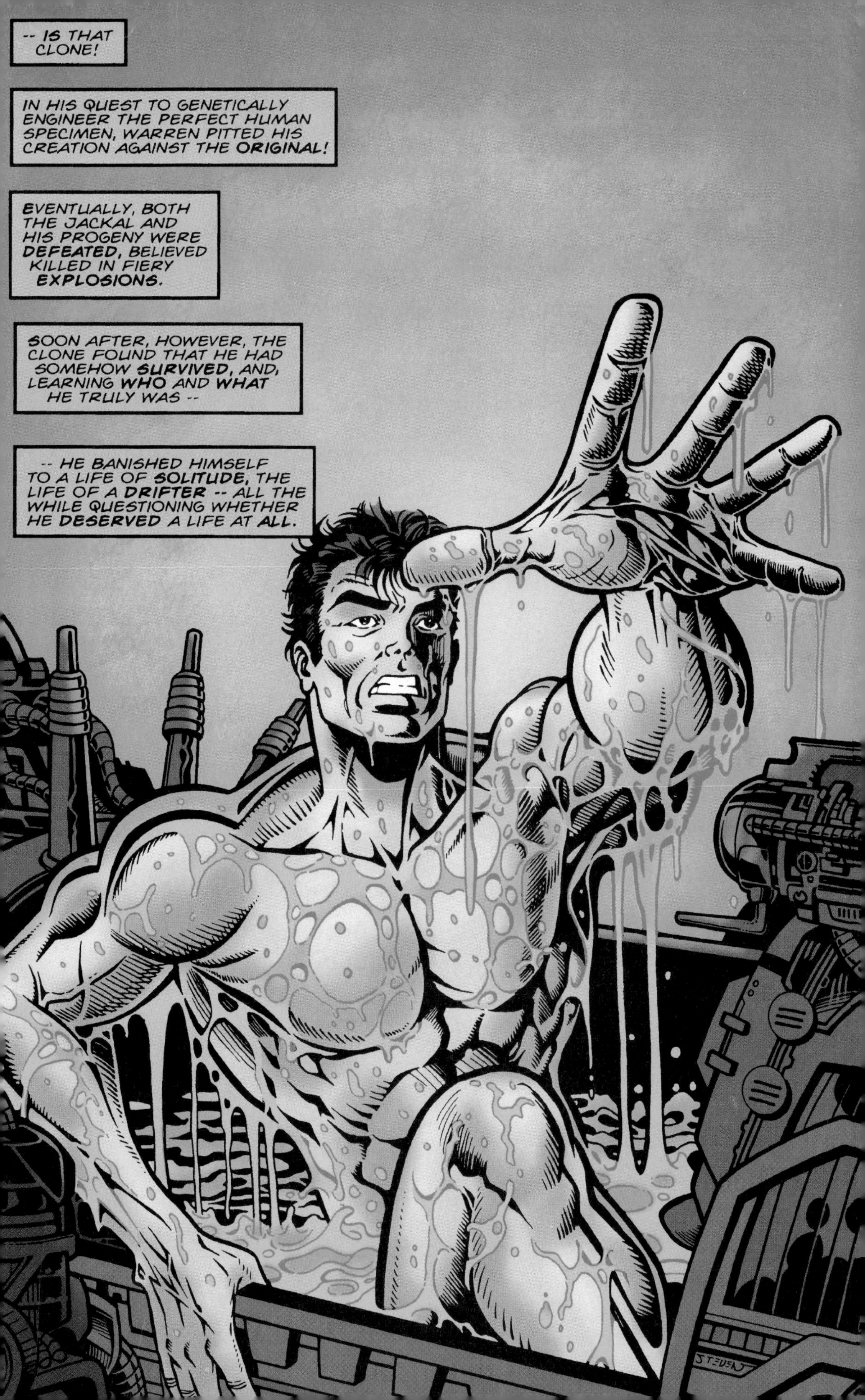
-- IS THAT CLONE!
IN HIS QUEST TO GENETICALLY ENGINEER THE PERFECT HUMAN SPECIMEN, WARREN PITTED HIS CREATION AGAINST THE ORIGINAL!
EVENTUALLY, BOTH THE JACKAL AND HIS PROGENY WERE DEFEATED, BELIEVED KILLED IN FIERY EXPLOSIONS.
SOON AFTER, HOWEVER, THE CLONE FOUND THAT HE HAD SOMEHOW SURVIVED, AND, LEARNING WHO AND WHAT HE TRULY WAS --
-- HE BANISHED HIMSELF TO A LIFE OF SOLITUDE, THE LIFE OF A DRIFTER -- ALL THE WHILE QUESTIONING WHETHER HE DESERVED A LIFE AT ALL.

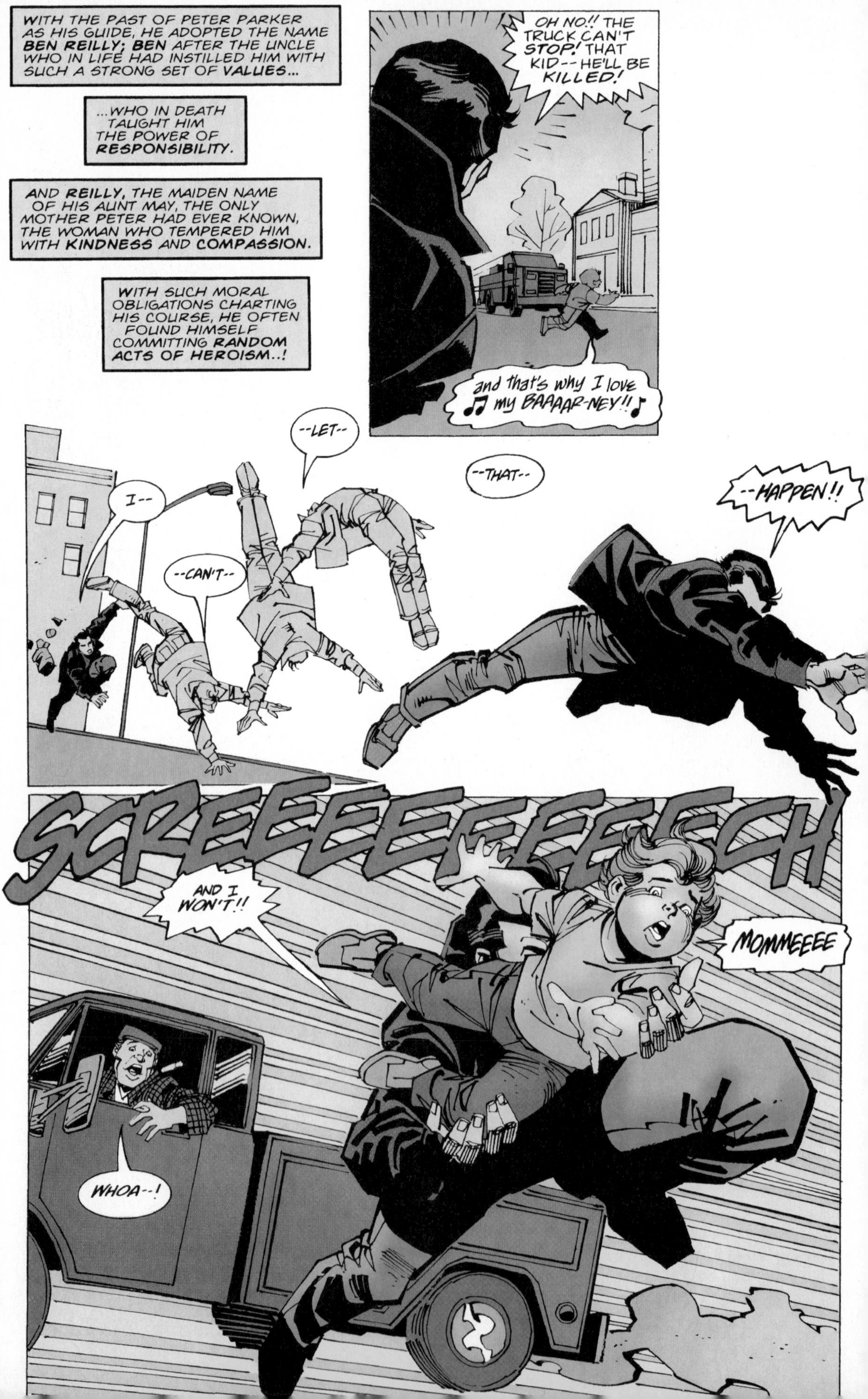
WITH THE PAST OF PETER PARKER AS HIS GUIDE, HE ADOPTED THE NAME BEN REILLY; BEN AFTER THE UNCLE WHO IN LIFE HAD INSTILLED HIM WITH SUCH A STRONG SET OF VALUES...
...WHO IN DEATH TAUGHT HIM THE POWER OF RESPONSIBILITY.
AND REILLY, THE MAIDEN NAME OF HIS AUNT MAY, THE ONLY MOTHER PETER HAD EVER KNOWN, THE WOMAN WHO TEMPERED HIM WITH KINDNESS AND COMPASSION.
WITH SUCH MORAL OBLIGATIONS CHARTING HIS COURSE, HE OFTEN FOUND HIMSELF COMMITTING RANDOM ACTS OF HEROISM..!
OH NO!! THE TRUCK CAN'T STOP! THAT KID-- HE'LL BE KILLED!
and that's why I love my BAAAAR-NEY!!
I--
--CAN'T--
--LET--
--THAT--
--HAPPEN!!
SCREEEEEEEEECH
AND I WON'T!!
MOMMEEEE
WHOA--!

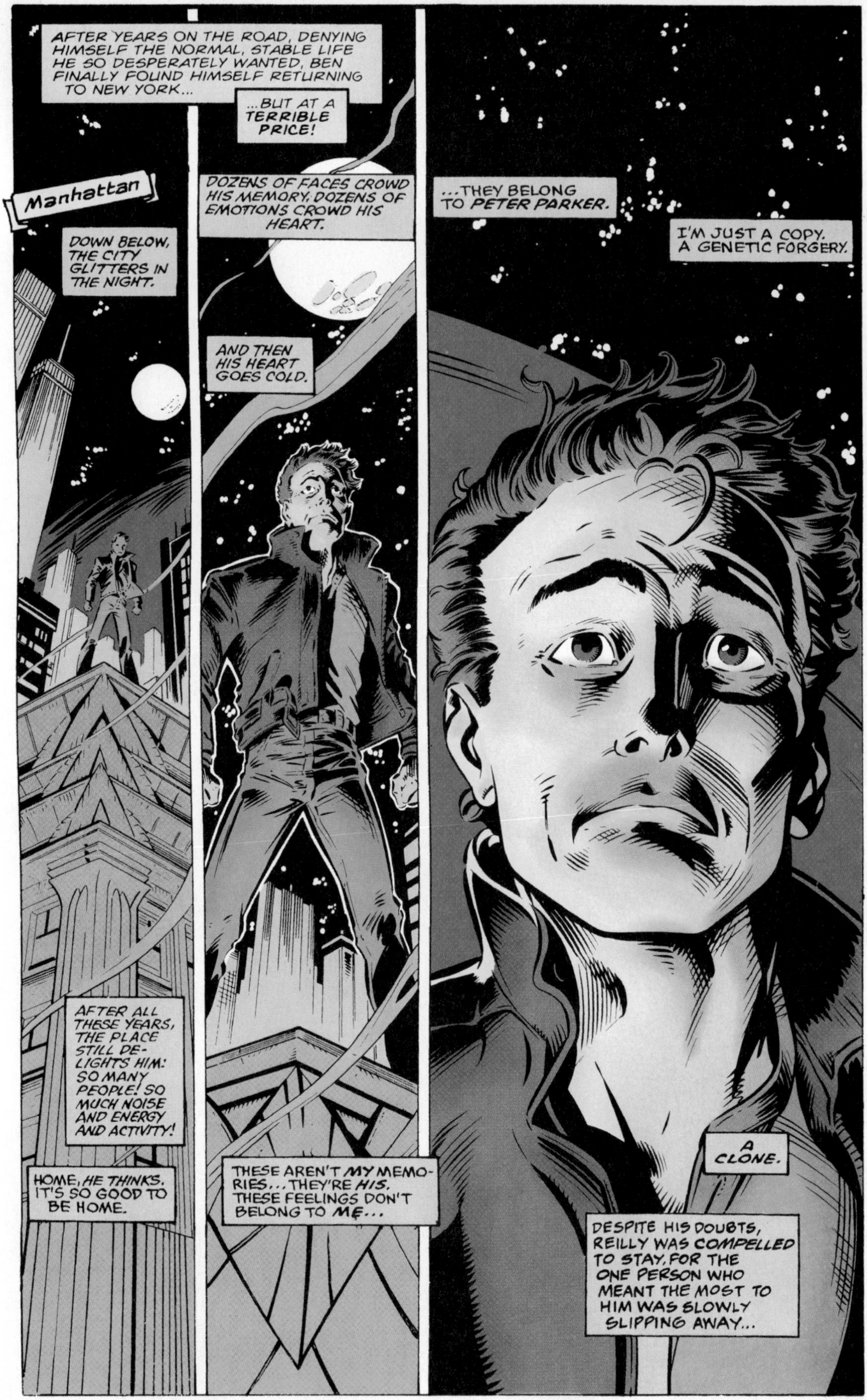
AFTER YEARS ON THE ROAD, DENYING HIMSELF THE NORMAL, STABLE LIFE HE SO DESPERATELY WANTED, BEN FINALLY FOUND HIMSELF RETURNING TO NEW YORK...
...BUT AT A TERRIBLE PRICE!
Manhattan
DOWN BELOW, THE CITY GLITTERS IN THE NIGHT.
AFTER ALL THESE YEARS, THE PLACE STILL DE-LIGHTS HIM: SO MANY PEOPLE! SO MUCH NOISE AND ENERGY AND ACTIVITY!
HOME, HE THINKS. IT'S SO GOOD TO BE HOME.
DOZENS OF FACES CROWD HIS MEMORY, DOZENS OF EMOTIONS CROWD HIS HEART.
AND THEN HIS HEART GOES COLD.
THESE AREN'T MY MEMO-RIES... THEY'RE HIS. THESE FEELINGS DON'T BELONG TO ME...
...THEY BELONG TO PETER PARKER.
I'M JUST A COPY. A GENETIC FORGERY.
A CLONE.
DESPITE HIS DOUBTS, REILLY WAS COMPELLED TO STAY, FOR THE ONE PERSON WHO MEANT THE MOST TO HIM WAS SLOWLY SLIPPING AWAY...

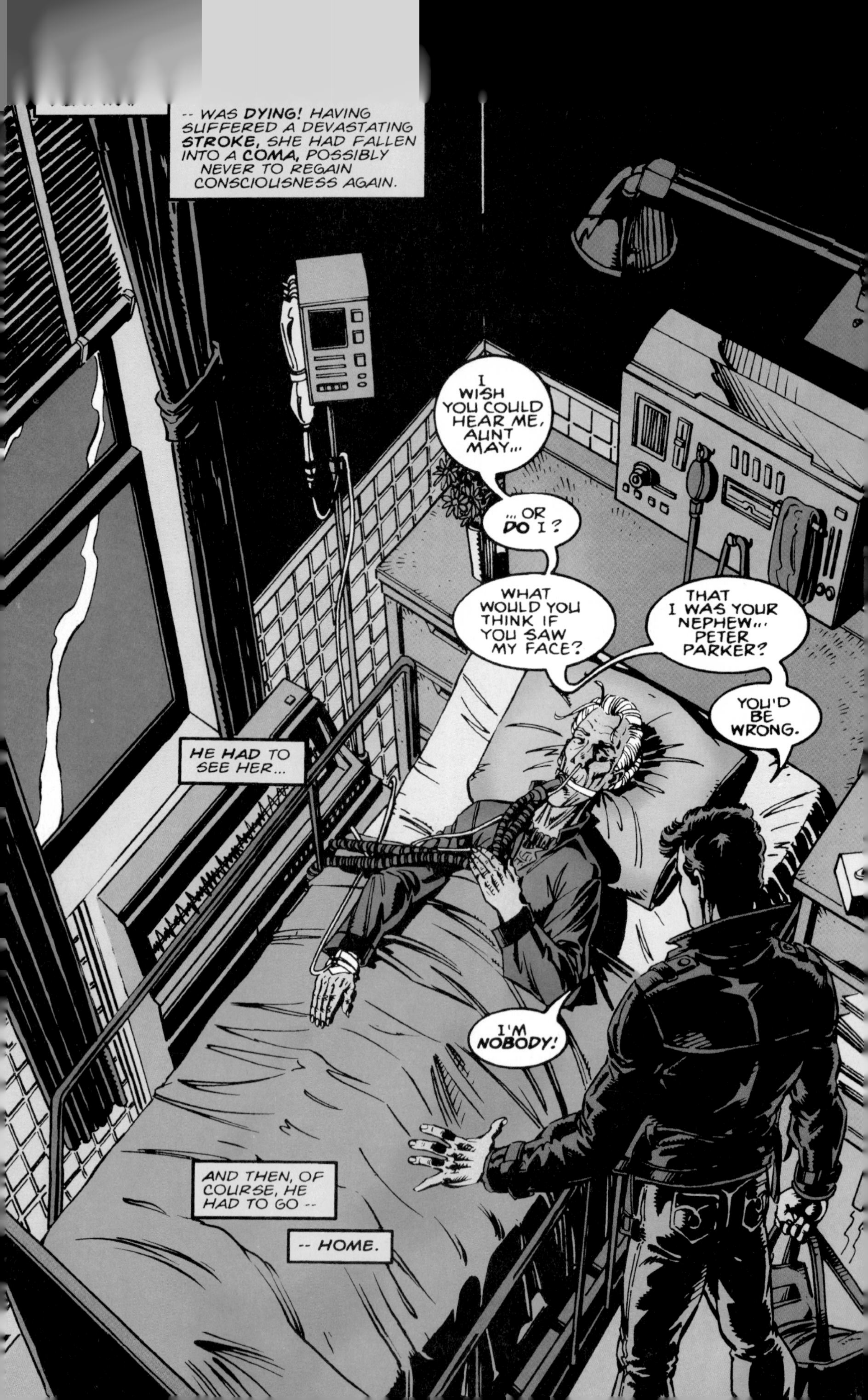
-- WAS DYING! HAVING SUFFERED A DEVASTATING STROKE, SHE HAD FALLEN INTO A COMA, POSSIBLY NEVER TO REGAIN CONSCIOUSNESS AGAIN.
I WISH YOU COULD HEAR ME, AUNT MAY...
...OR DO I?
WHAT WOULD YOU THINK IF YOU SAW MY FACE?
THAT I WAS YOUR NEPHEW... PETER PARKER?
YOU'D BE WRONG.
HE HAD TO SEE HER...
I'M NOBODY!
AND THEN, OF COURSE, HE HAD TO GO --
-- HOME.

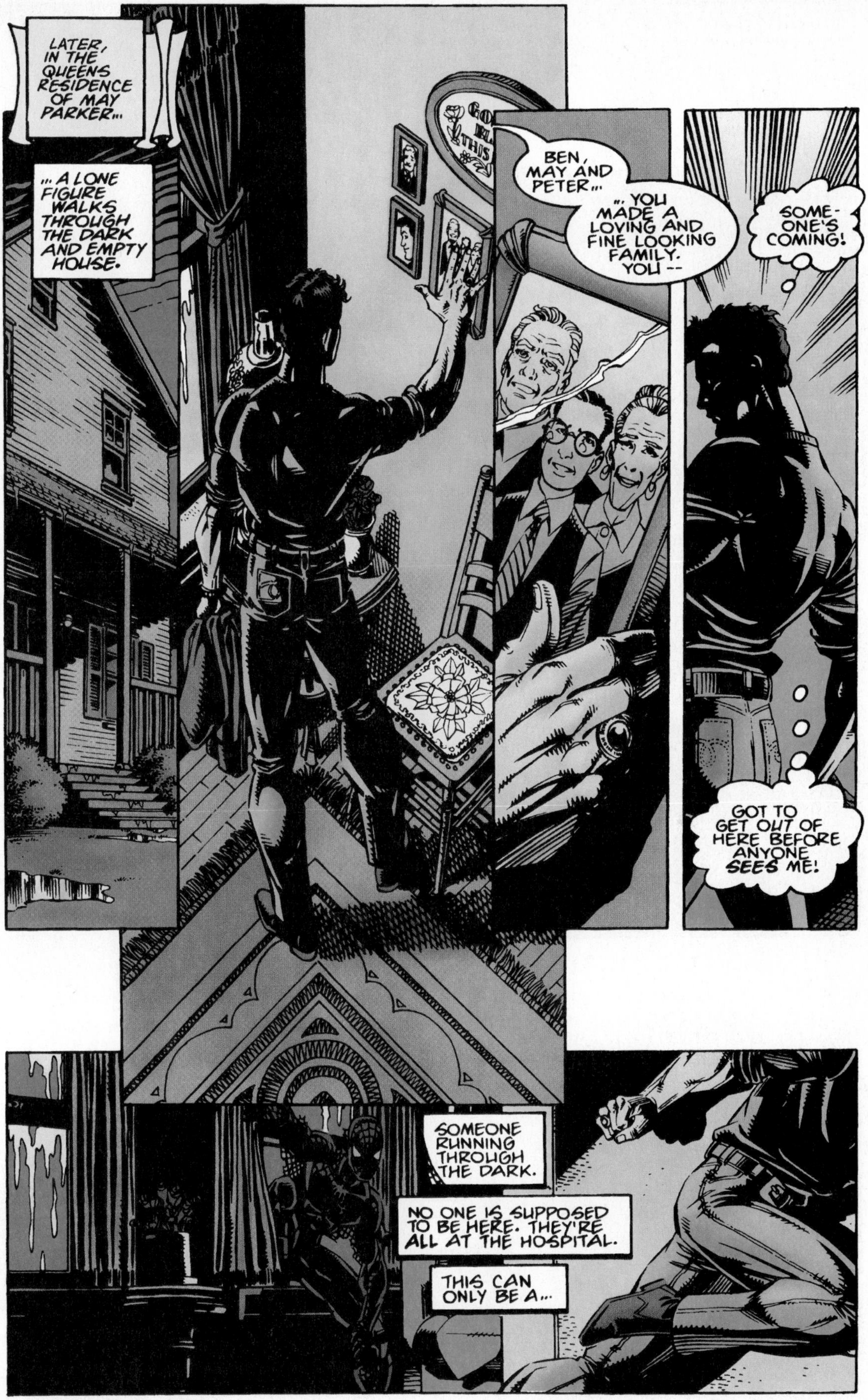
LATER, IN THE QUEENS RESIDENCE OF MAY PARKER...
...A LONE FIGURE WALKS THROUGH THE DARK AND EMPTY HOUSE.
BEN, MAY AND PETER...
...YOU MADE A LOVING AND FINE LOOKING FAMILY. YOU --
SOME-ONE'S COMING!
GOT TO GET OUT OF HERE BEFORE ANYONE SEES ME!
SOMEONE RUNNING THROUGH THE DARK.
NO ONE IS SUPPOSED TO BE HERE. THEY'RE ALL AT THE HOSPITAL.
THIS CAN ONLY BE A...

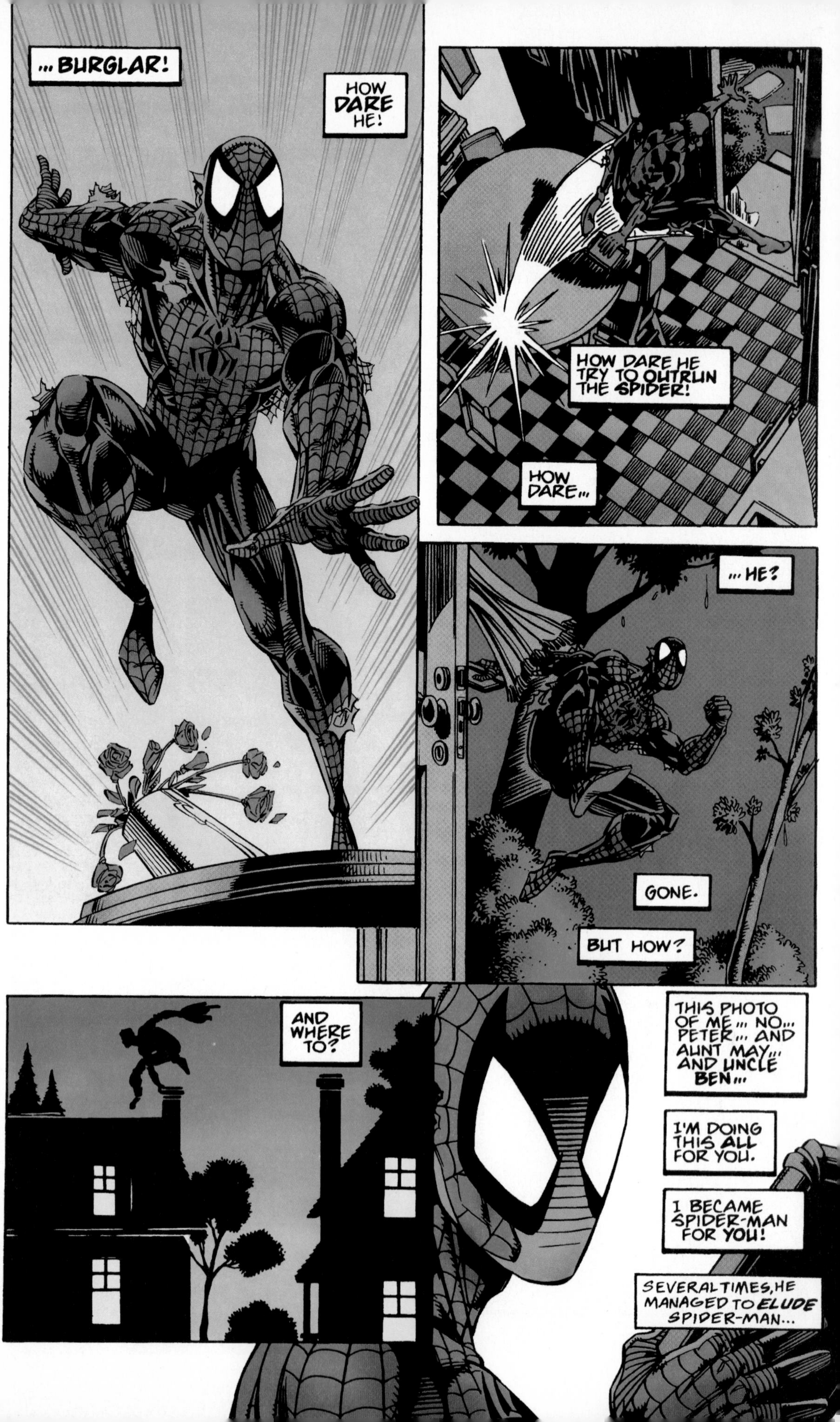
...BURGLAR!
HOW DARE HE!
HOW DARE HE TRY TO OUTRUN THE SPIDER!
HOW DARE...
...HE?
GONE.
BUT HOW?
AND WHERE TO?
THIS PHOTO OF ME... NO... PETER... AND AUNT MAY... AND UNCLE BEN...
I'M DOING THIS ALL FOR YOU.
I BECAME SPIDER-MAN FOR YOU!
SEVERAL TIMES, HE MANAGED TO ELUDE SPIDER-MAN...

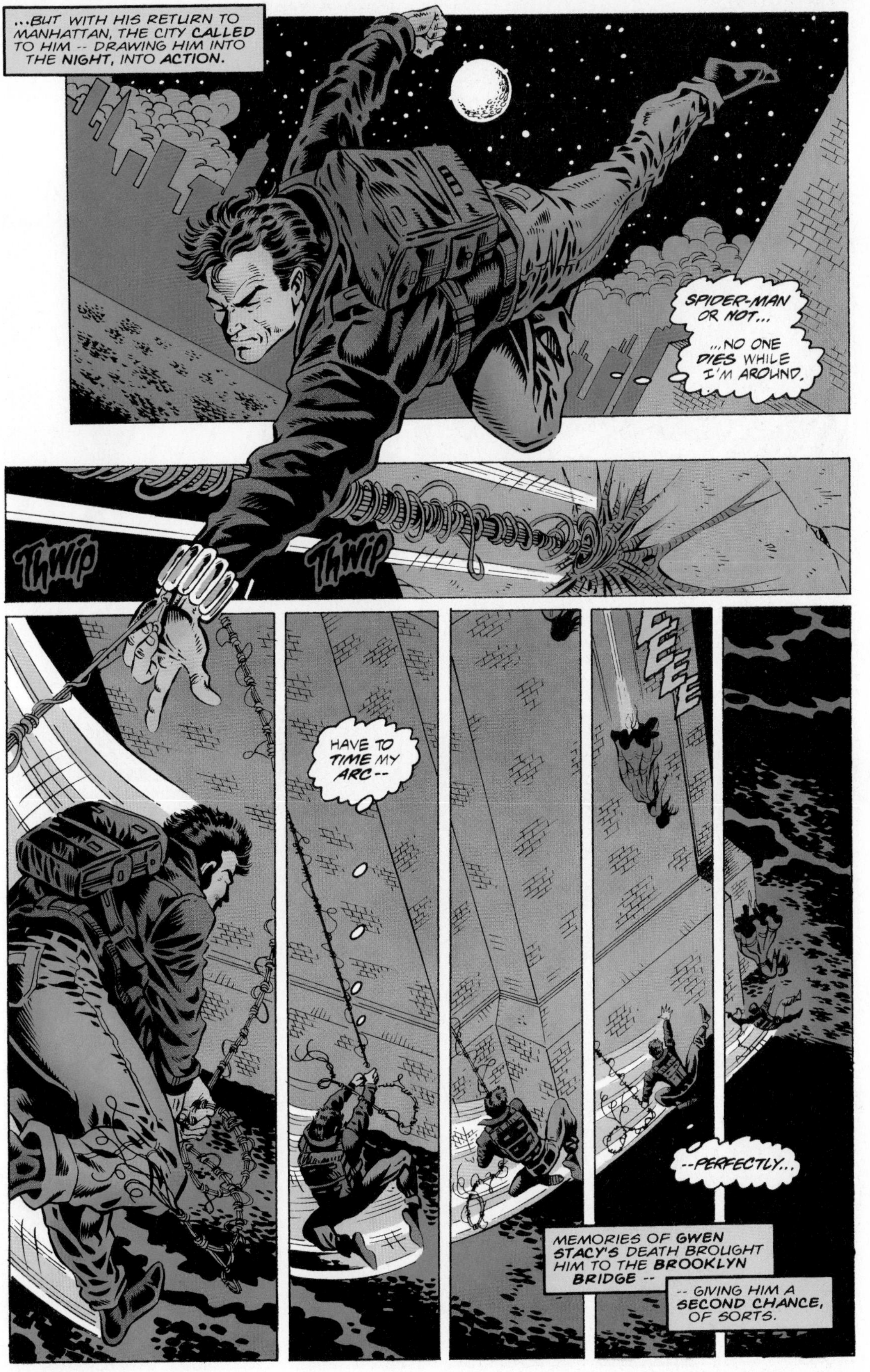
...BUT WITH HIS RETURN TO MANHATTAN, THE CITY CALLED TO HIM -- DRAWING HIM INTO THE NIGHT, INTO ACTION.
SPIDER-MAN OR NOT...
...NO ONE DIES WHILE I'M AROUND.
THWIP
THWIP
HAVE TO TIME MY ARC--
--PERFECTLY...
MEMORIES OF GWEN STACY'S DEATH BROUGHT HIM TO THE BROOKLYN BRIDGE --
-- GIVING HIM A SECOND CHANCE, OF SORTS.

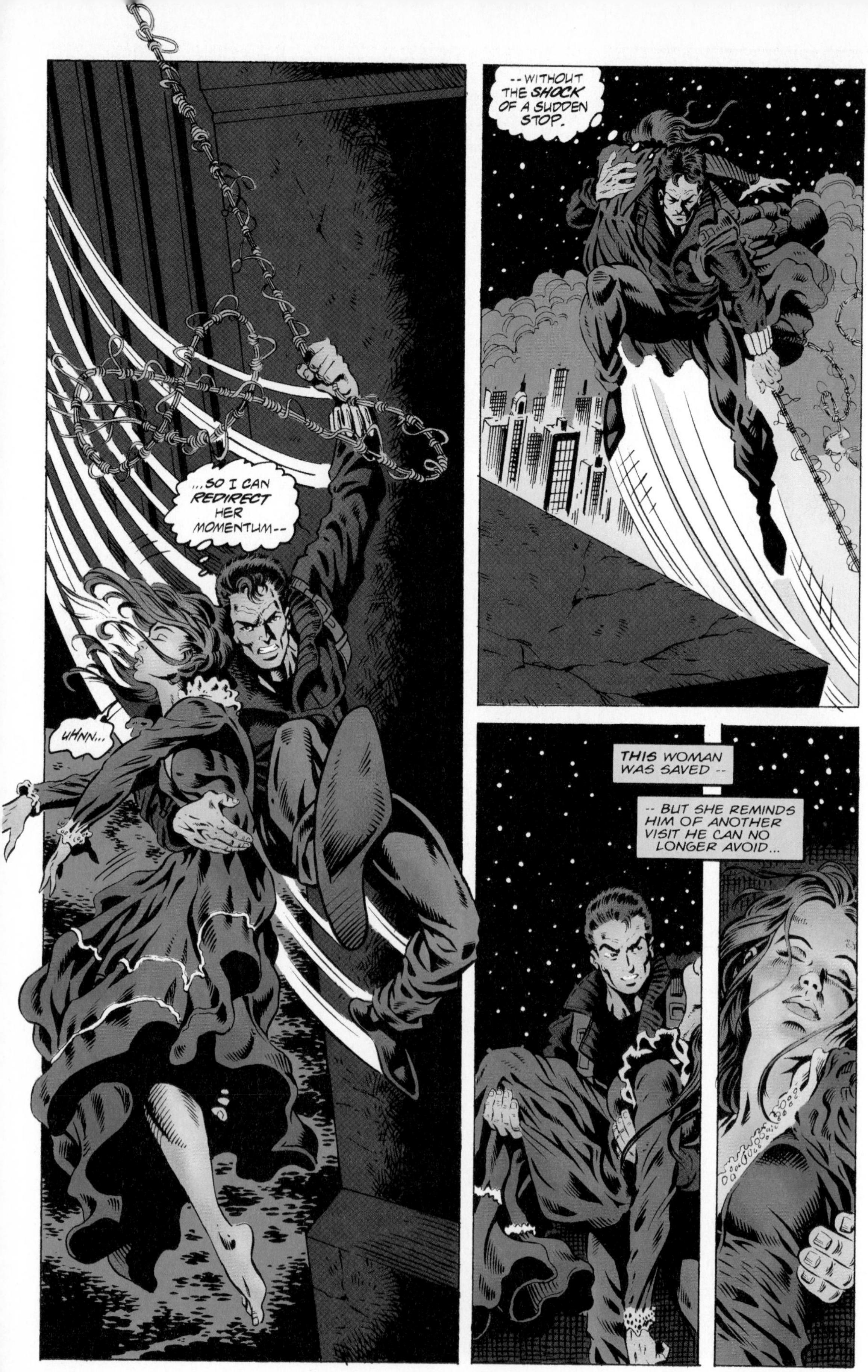
...SO I CAN REDIRECT HER MOMENTUM--
UHNN...
--WITHOUT THE SHOCK OF A SUDDEN STOP.
THIS WOMAN WAS SAVED --
-- BUT SHE REMINDS HIM OF ANOTHER VISIT HE CAN NO LONGER AVOID...

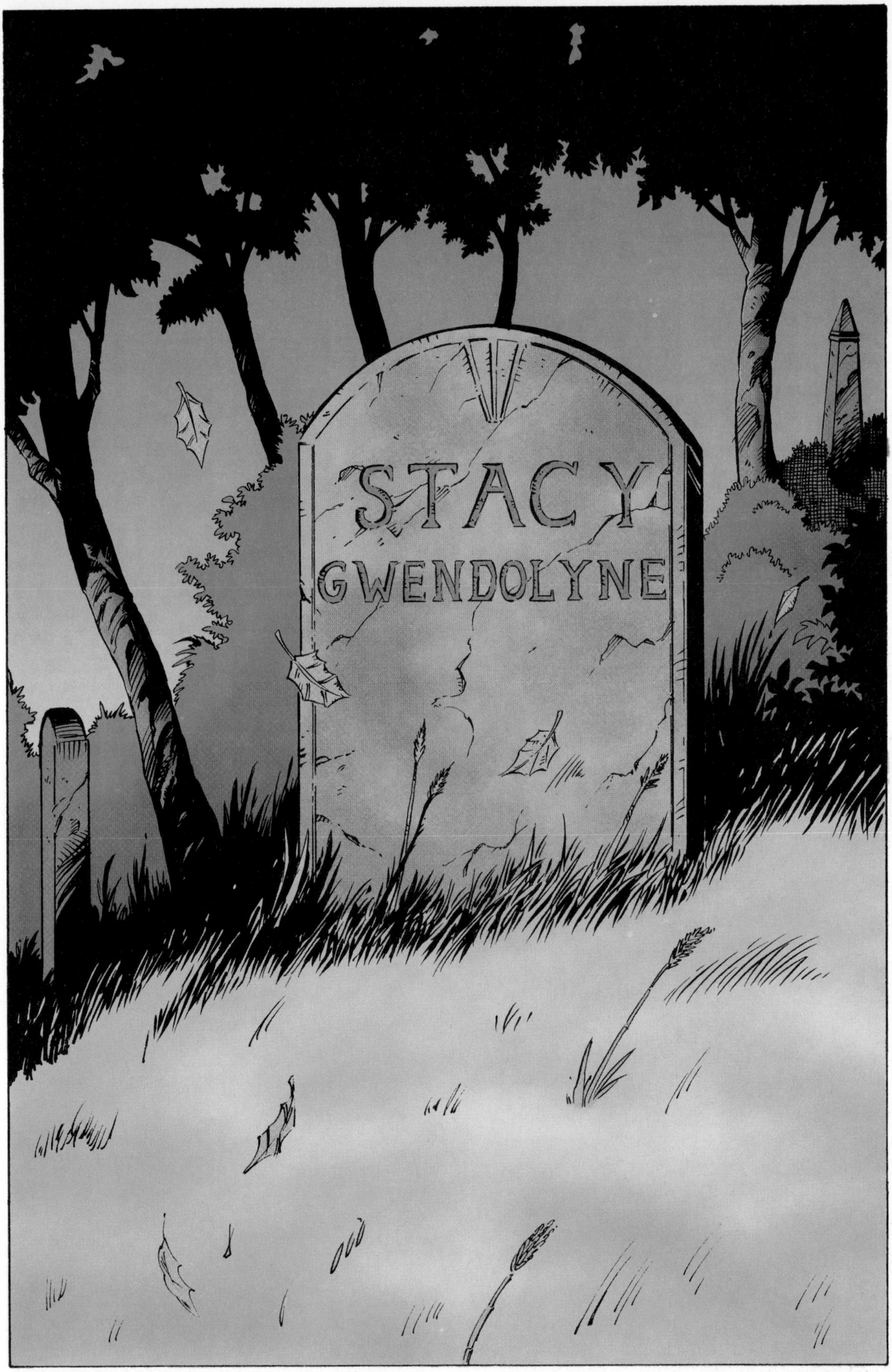
STACY
GWENDOLYNE

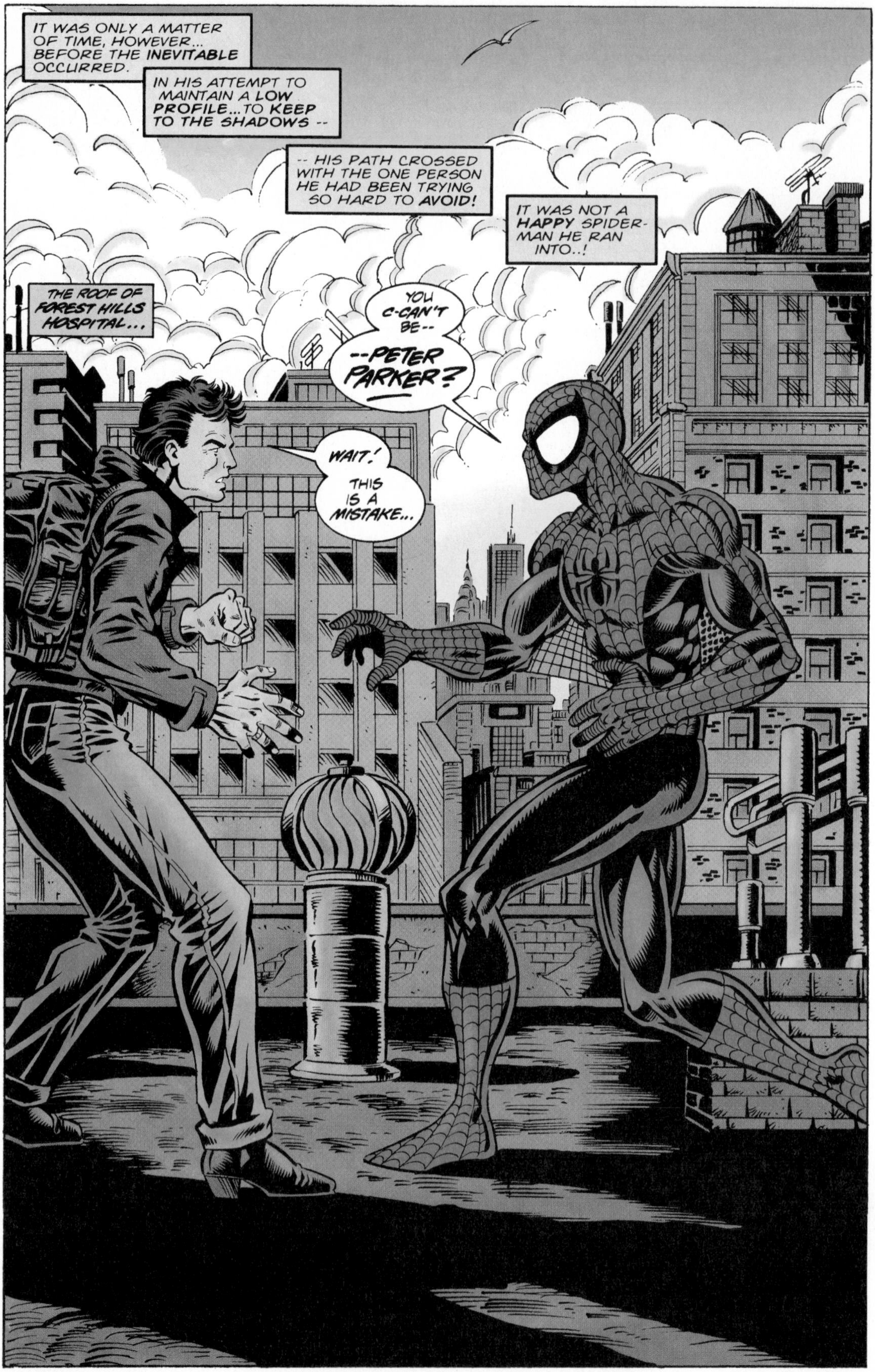
IT WAS ONLY A MATTER OF TIME, HOWEVER... BEFORE THE INEVITABLE OCCURRED.
IN HIS ATTEMPT TO MAINTAIN A LOW PROFILE...TO KEEP TO THE SHADOWS --
-- HIS PATH CROSSED WITH THE ONE PERSON HE HAD BEEN TRYING SO HARD TO AVOID!
IT WAS NOT A HAPPY SPIDER-MAN HE RAN INTO..!
THE ROOF OF FOREST HILLS HOSPITAL...
YOU C-CAN'T BE-- --PETER PARKER?
WAIT! THIS IS A MISTAKE...

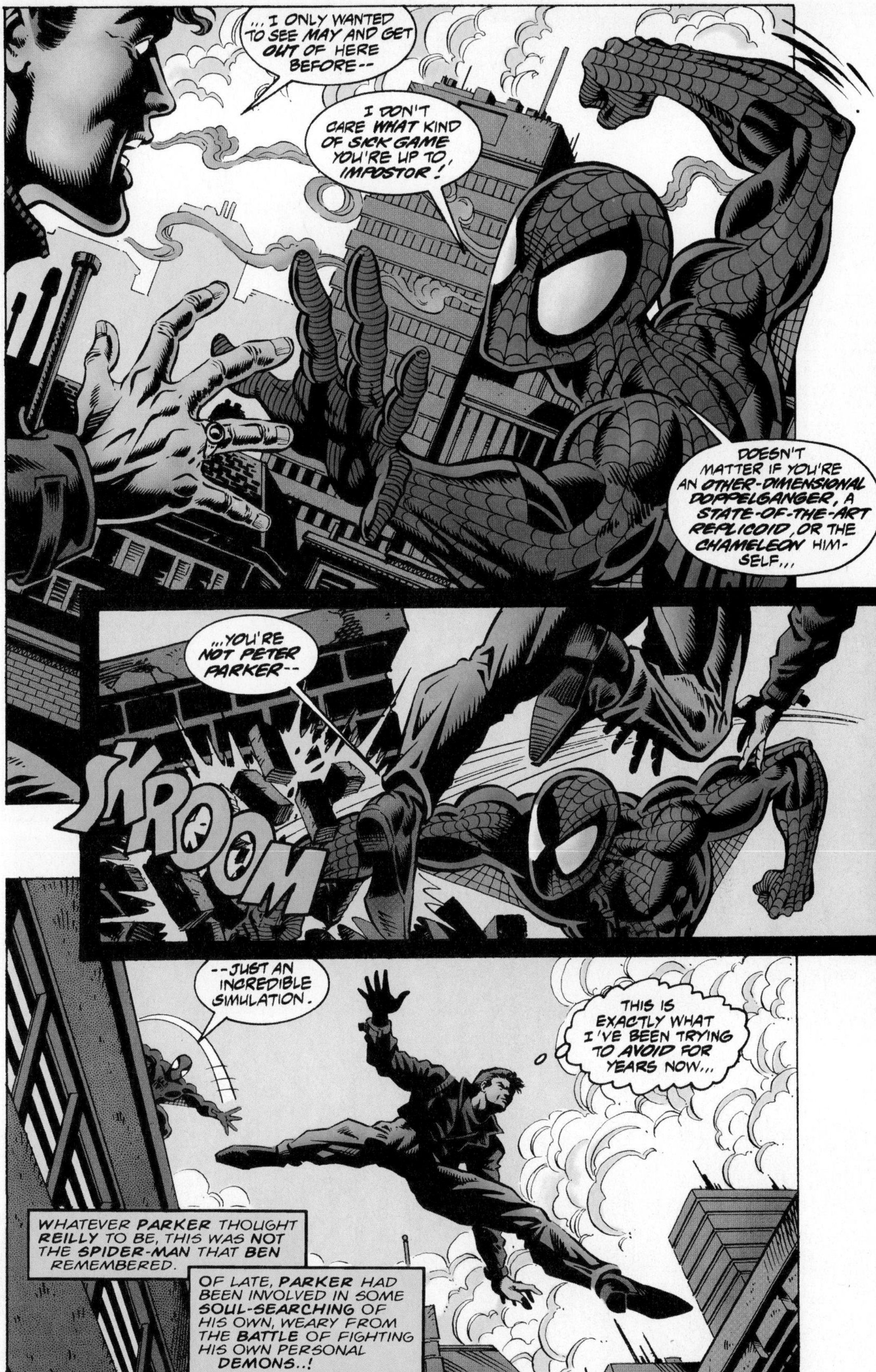
...I ONLY WANTED TO SEE MAY AND GET OUT OF HERE BEFORE--
I DON'T CARE WHAT KIND OF SICK GAME YOU'RE UP TO, IMPOSTOR!
DOESN'T MATTER IF YOU'RE AN OTHER-DIMENSIONAL DOPPELGANGER, A STATE-OF-THE-ART REPLICOID, OR THE CHAMELEON HIM-SELF...
...YOU'RE NOT PETER PARKER--
SKROOM
--JUST AN INCREDIBLE SIMULATION.
THIS IS EXACTLY WHAT I'VE BEEN TRYING TO AVOID FOR YEARS NOW...
WHATEVER PARKER THOUGHT REILLY TO BE, THIS WAS NOT THE SPIDER-MAN THAT BEN REMEMBERED.
OF LATE, PARKER HAD BEEN INVOLVED IN SOME SOUL-SEARCHING OF HIS OWN, WEARY FROM THE BATTLE OF FIGHTING HIS OWN PERSONAL DEMONS..!

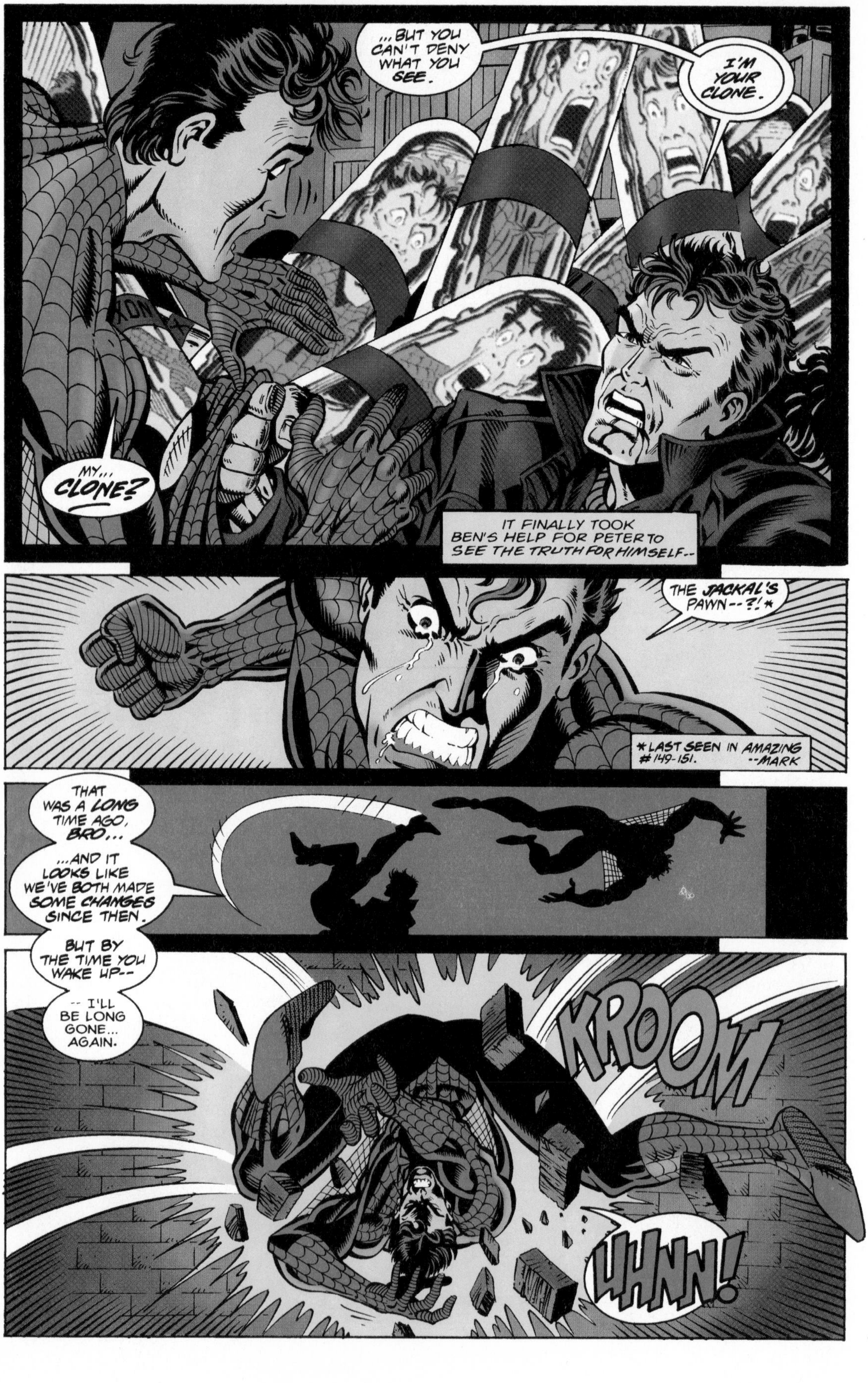
...BUT YOU CAN'T DENY WHAT YOU SEE.
I'M YOUR CLONE.
MY... CLONE?
IT FINALLY TOOK BEN'S HELP FOR PETER TO SEE THE TRUTH FOR HIMSELF--
THE JACKAL'S PAWN--?!*
*LAST SEEN IN AMAZING #149-151. --MARK
THAT WAS A LONG TIME AGO, BRO...
...AND IT LOOKS LIKE WE'VE BOTH MADE SOME CHANGES SINCE THEN.
BUT BY THE TIME YOU WAKE UP--
-- I'LL BE LONG GONE... AGAIN.
KROOM
UHNN!

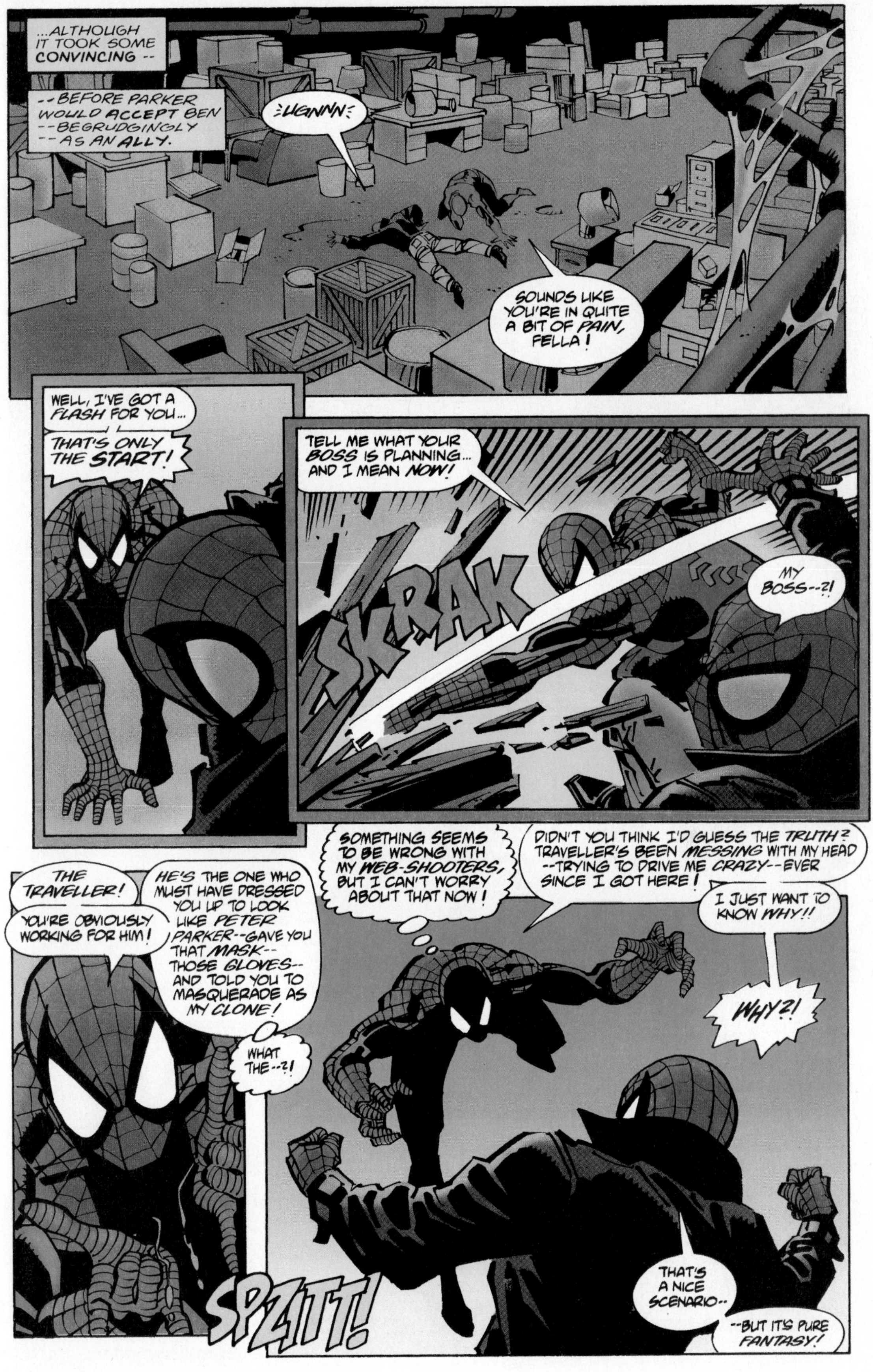
...ALTHOUGH IT TOOK SOME CONVINCING --
--BEFORE PARKER WOULD ACCEPT BEN --BEGRUDGINGLY --AS AN ALLY.
UGNNN
SOUNDS LIKE YOU'RE IN QUITE A BIT OF PAIN, FELLA!
WELL, I'VE GOT A FLASH FOR YOU...
THAT'S ONLY THE START!
TELL ME WHAT YOUR BOSS IS PLANNING... AND I MEAN NOW!
SKRAK
MY BOSS--?!
THE TRAVELLER!
YOU'RE OBVIOUSLY WORKING FOR HIM!
HE'S THE ONE WHO MUST HAVE DRESSED YOU UP TO LOOK LIKE PETER PARKER--GAVE YOU THAT MASK-- THOSE GLOVES-- AND TOLD YOU TO MASQUERADE AS MY CLONE!
WHAT THE--?!
SPZITT!
SOMETHING SEEMS TO BE WRONG WITH MY WEB-SHOOTERS, BUT I CAN'T WORRY ABOUT THAT NOW!
DIDN'T YOU THINK I'D GUESS THE TRUTH? TRAVELLER'S BEEN MESSING WITH MY HEAD --TRYING TO DRIVE ME CRAZY--EVER SINCE I GOT HERE!
I JUST WANT TO KNOW WHY!!
WHY?!
THAT'S A NICE SCENARIO--
--BUT IT'S PURE FANTASY!

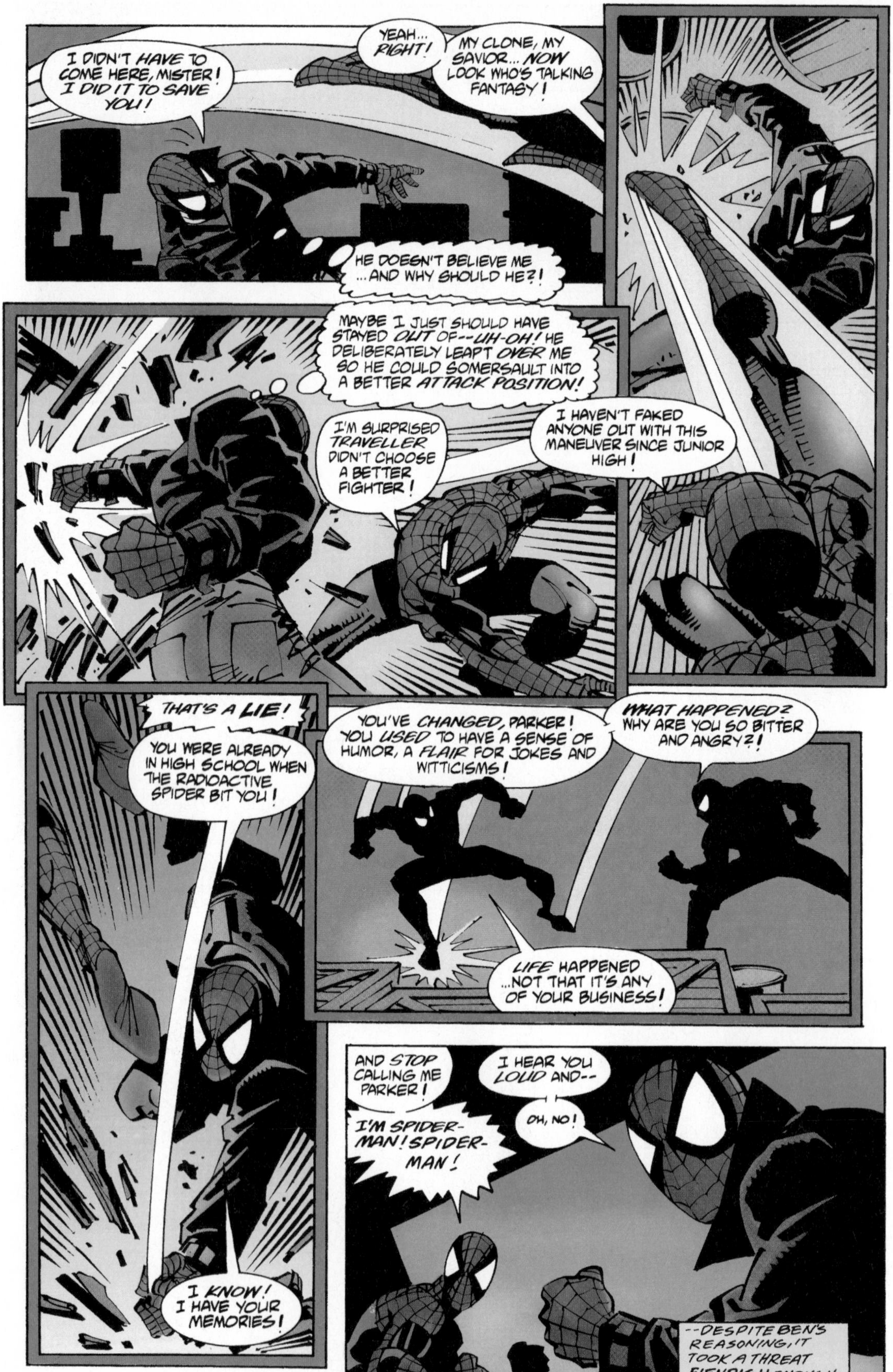
I DIDN'T HAVE TO COME HERE, MISTER! I DID IT TO SAVE YOU!
YEAH... RIGHT!
MY CLONE, MY SAVIOR... NOW LOOK WHO'S TALKING FANTASY!
HE DOESN'T BELIEVE ME ...AND WHY SHOULD HE?!
MAYBE I JUST SHOULD HAVE STAYED OUT OF--UH-OH! HE DELIBERATELY LEAPT OVER ME SO HE COULD SOMERSAULT INTO A BETTER ATTACK POSITION!
I'M SURPRISED TRAVELLER DIDN'T CHOOSE A BETTER FIGHTER!
I HAVEN'T FAKED ANYONE OUT WITH THIS MANEUVER SINCE JUNIOR HIGH!
THAT'S A LIE!
YOU WERE ALREADY IN HIGH SCHOOL WHEN THE RADIOACTIVE SPIDER BIT YOU!
I KNOW! I HAVE YOUR MEMORIES!
YOU'VE CHANGED, PARKER! YOU USED TO HAVE A SENSE OF HUMOR, A FLAIR FOR JOKES AND WITTICISMS!
WHAT HAPPENED? WHY ARE YOU SO BITTER AND ANGRY?!
LIFE HAPPENED ...NOT THAT IT'S ANY OF YOUR BUSINESS!
AND STOP CALLING ME PARKER!
I'M SPIDER-MAN! SPIDER-MAN!
I HEAR YOU LOUD AND--
OH, NO!
--DESPITE BEN'S REASONING, IT TOOK A THREAT FIENDISH ENOUGH...

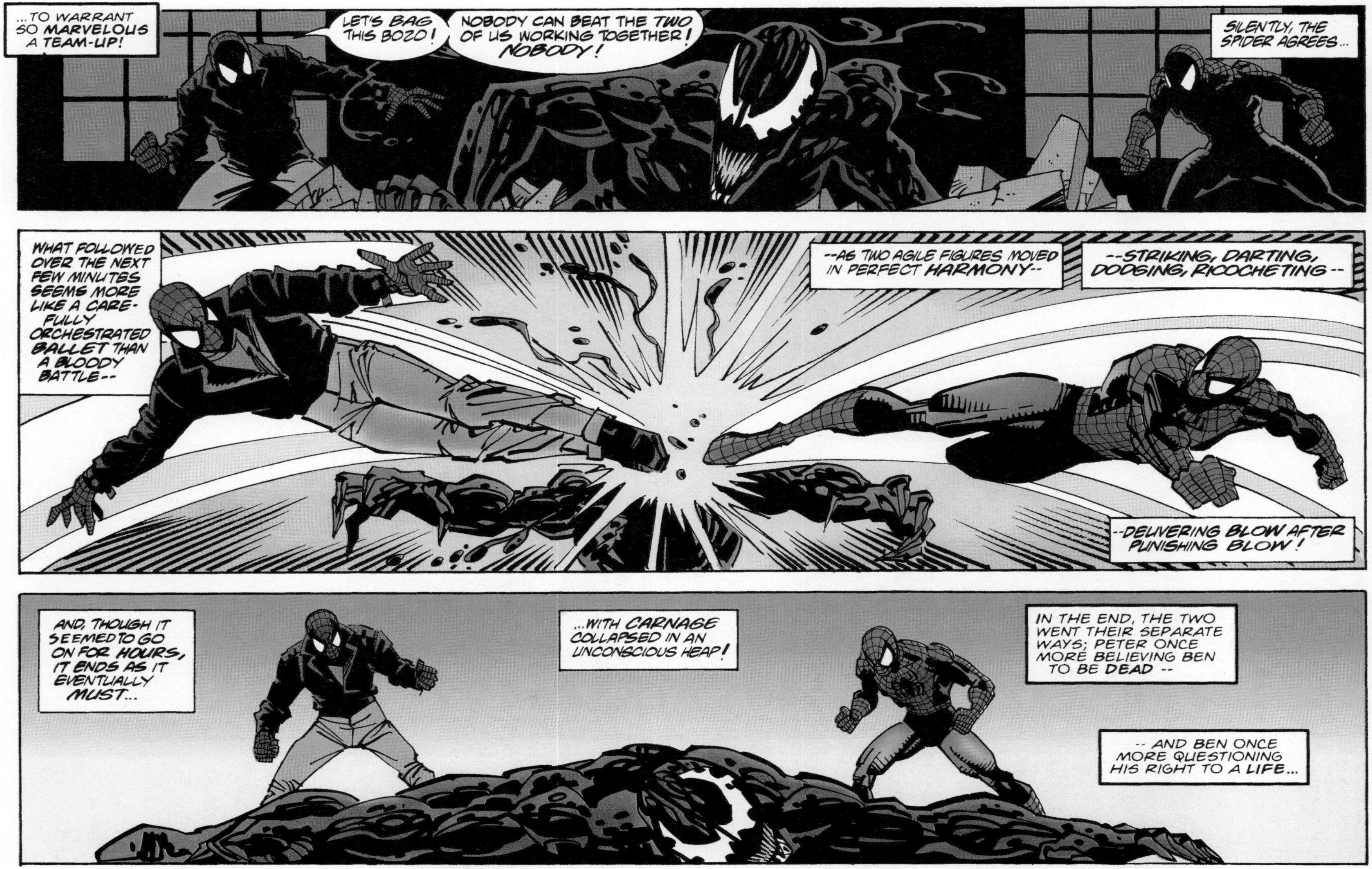
...TO WARRANT SO MARVELOUS A TEAM-UP!
LET'S BAG THIS BOZO!
NOBODY CAN BEAT THE TWO OF US WORKING TOGETHER! NOBODY!
SILENTLY, THE SPIDER AGREES...
WHAT FOLLOWED OVER THE NEXT FEW MINUTES SEEMS MORE LIKE A CARE-FULLY ORCHESTRATED BALLET THAN A BLOODY BATTLE--
--AS TWO AGILE FIGURES MOVED IN PERFECT HARMONY--
--STRIKING, DARTING, DODGING, RICOCHETING--
--DELIVERING BLOW AFTER PUNISHING BLOW!
AND, THOUGH IT SEEMED TO GO ON FOR HOURS, IT ENDS AS IT EVENTUALLY MUST...
...WITH CARNAGE COLLAPSED IN AN UNCONSCIOUS HEAP!
IN THE END, THE TWO WENT THEIR SEPARATE WAYS; PETER ONCE MORE BELIEVING BEN TO BE DEAD --
-- AND BEN ONCE MORE QUESTIONING HIS RIGHT TO A LIFE...

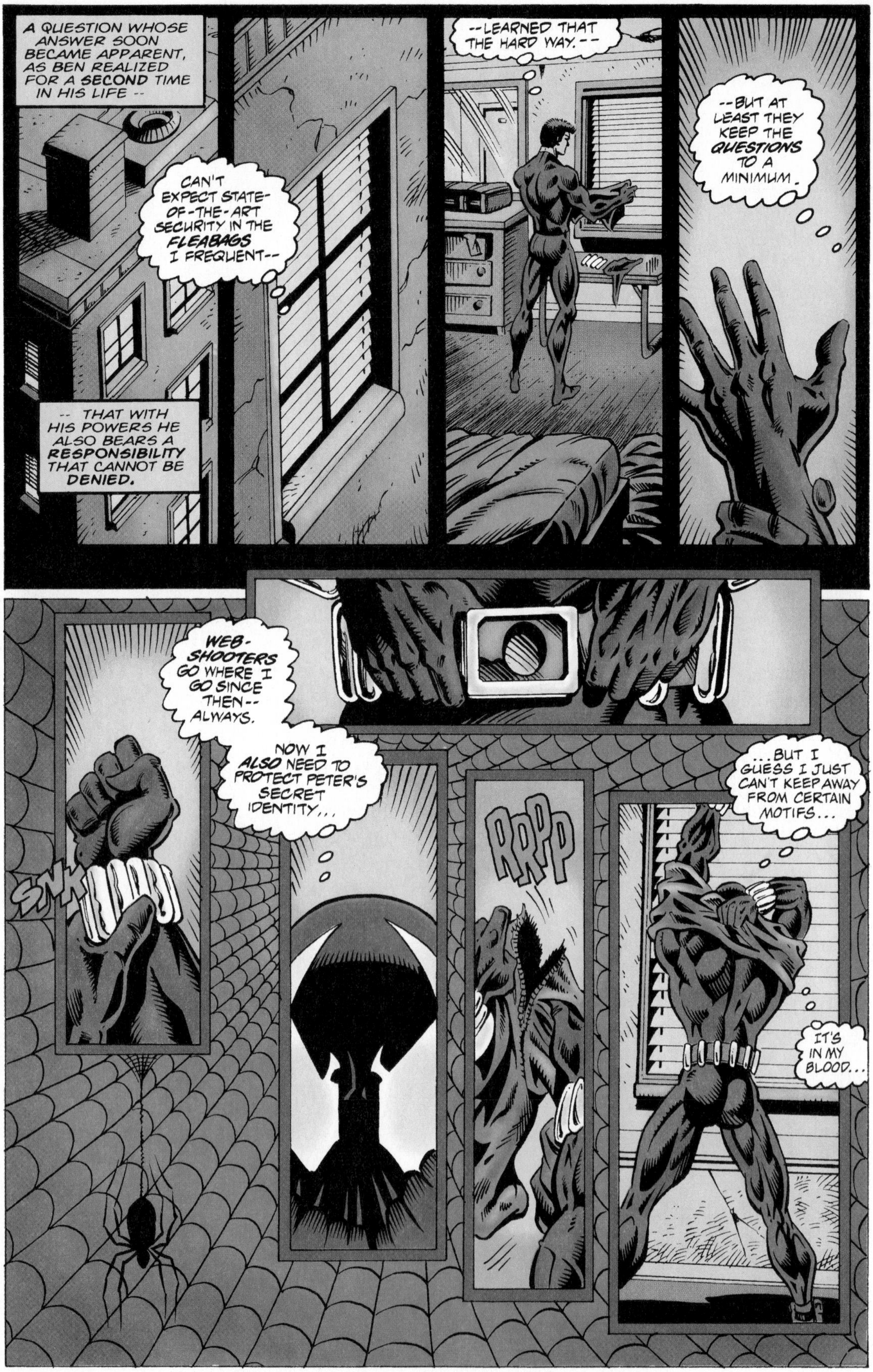
A QUESTION WHOSE ANSWER SOON BECAME APPARENT, AS BEN REALIZED FOR A SECOND TIME IN HIS LIFE --
CAN'T EXPECT STATE-OF-THE-ART SECURITY IN THE FLEABAGS I FREQUENT--
-- THAT WITH HIS POWERS HE ALSO BEARS A RESPONSIBILITY THAT CANNOT BE DENIED.
--LEARNED THAT THE HARD WAY.--
--BUT AT LEAST THEY KEEP THE QUESTIONS TO A MINIMUM.
WEB-SHOOTERS GO WHERE I GO SINCE THEN-- ALWAYS.
SNK
NOW I ALSO NEED TO PROTECT PETER'S SECRET IDENTITY...
RRPP
...BUT I GUESS I JUST CAN'T KEEP AWAY FROM CERTAIN MOTIFS...
IT'S IN MY BLOOD...

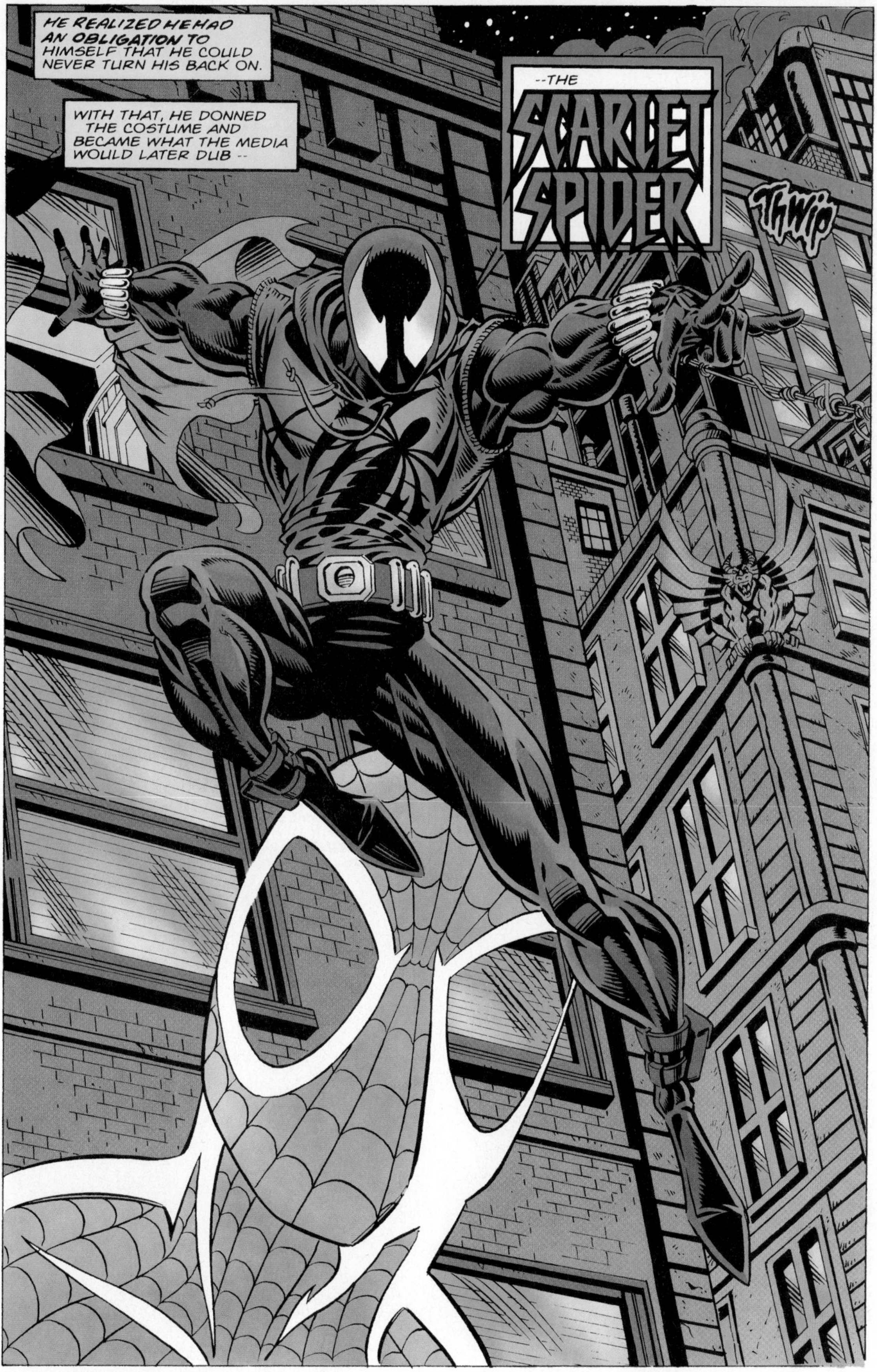
HE REALIZED HE HAD AN OBLIGATION TO HIMSELF THAT HE COULD NEVER TURN HIS BACK ON.
WITH THAT, HE DONNED THE COSTUME AND BECAME WHAT THE MEDIA WOULD LATER DUB --
--THE
SCARLET SPIDER
THWIP

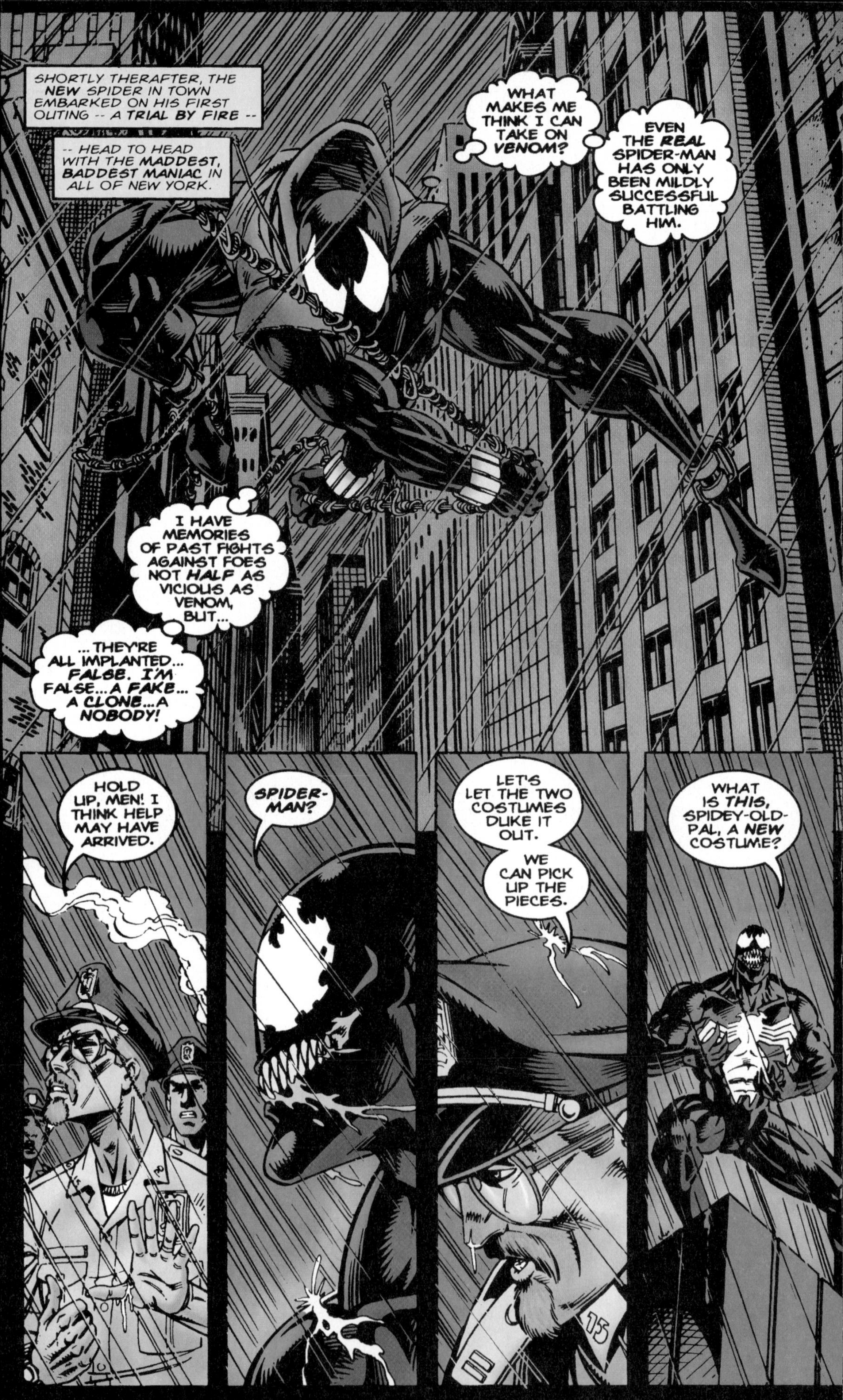
SHORTLY THERAFTER, THE NEW SPIDER IN TOWN EMBARKED ON HIS FIRST OUTING -- A TRIAL BY FIRE --
-- HEAD TO HEAD WITH THE MADDEST, BADDEST MANIAC IN ALL OF NEW YORK.
WHAT MAKES ME THINK I CAN TAKE ON VENOM?
EVEN THE REAL SPIDER-MAN HAS ONLY BEEN MILDLY SUCCESSFUL BATTLING HIM.
I HAVE MEMORIES OF PAST FIGHTS AGAINST FOES NOT HALF AS VICIOUS AS VENOM, BUT...
... THEY'RE ALL IMPLANTED... FALSE. I'M FALSE... A FAKE... A CLONE... A NOBODY!
HOLD UP, MEN! I THINK HELP MAY HAVE ARRIVED.
SPIDER-MAN?
LET'S LET THE TWO COSTUMES DUKE IT OUT.
WE CAN PICK UP THE PIECES.
WHAT IS THIS, SPIDEY-OLD-PAL, A NEW COSTUME?

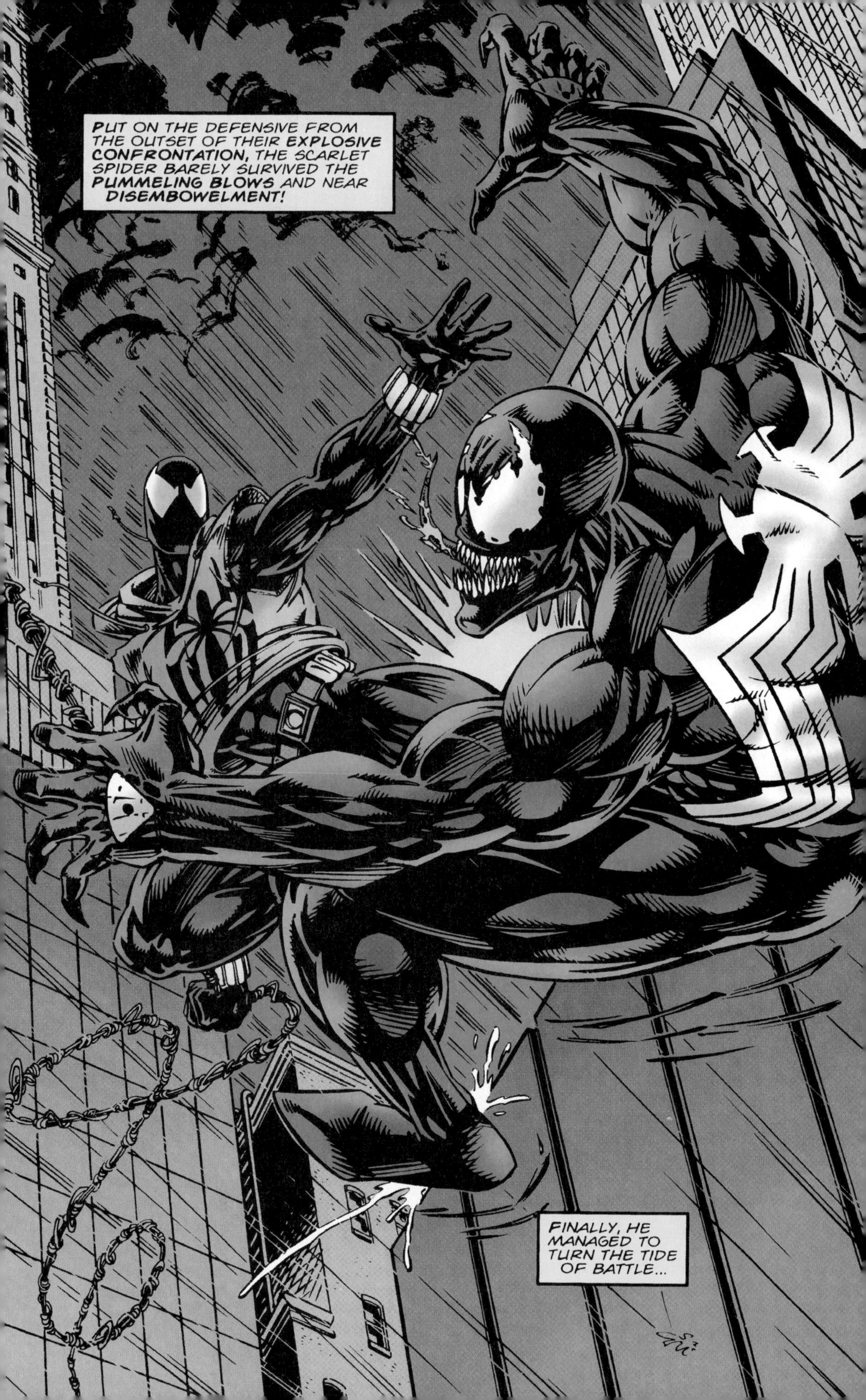
PUT ON THE DEFENSIVE FROM THE OUTSET OF THEIR EXPLOSIVE CONFRONTATION, THE SCARLET SPIDER BARELY SURVIVED THE PUMMELING BLOWS AND NEAR DISEMBOWELMENT!
FINALLY, HE MANAGED TO TURN THE TIDE OF BATTLE...

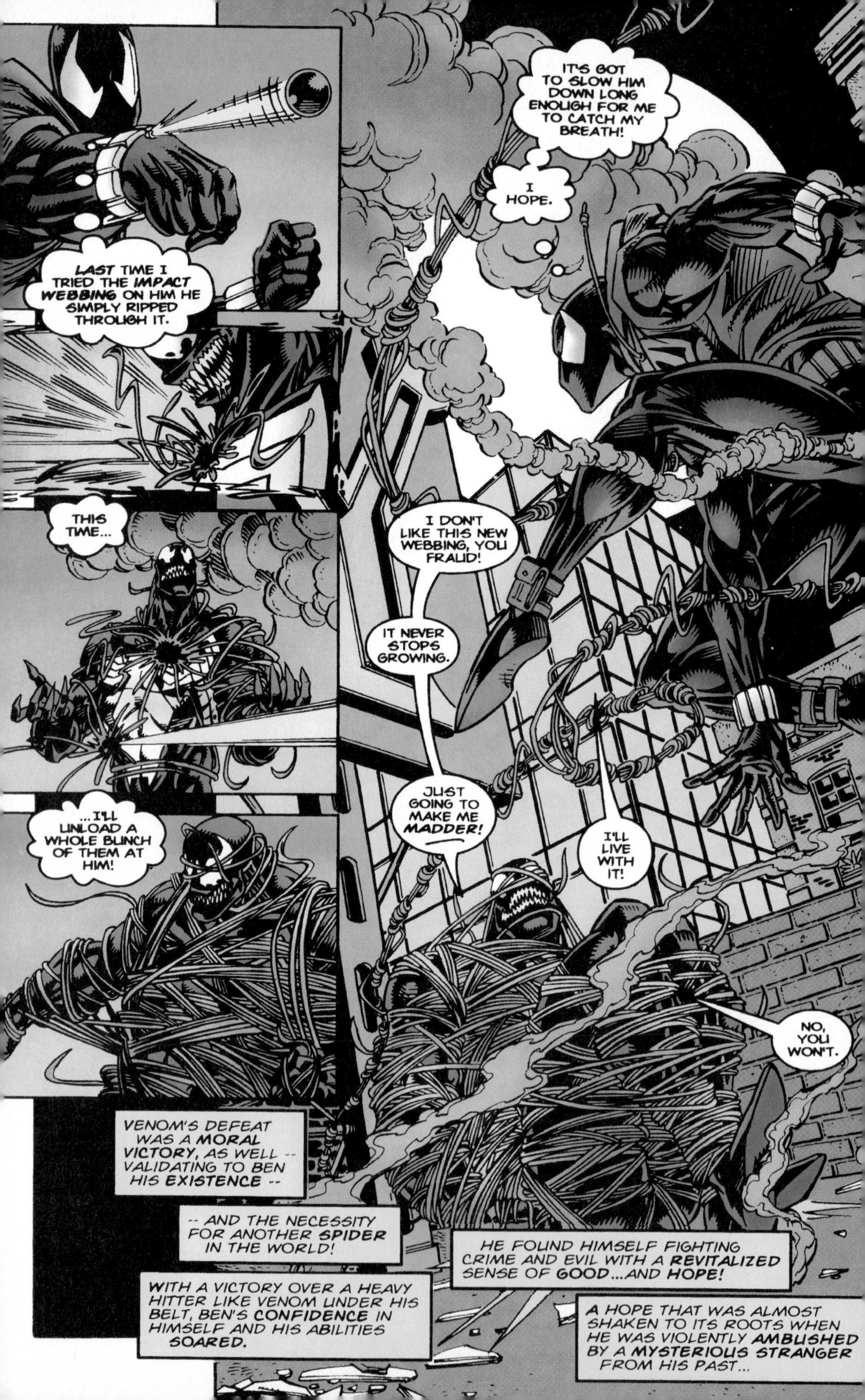

LAST TIME I TRIED THE IMPACT WEBBING ON HIM HE SIMPLY RIPPED THROUGH IT.
THIS TIME...
...I'LL UNLOAD A WHOLE BUNCH OF THEM AT HIM!
IT'S GOT TO SLOW HIM DOWN LONG ENOUGH FOR ME TO CATCH MY BREATH!
I HOPE.
I DON'T LIKE THIS NEW WEBBING, YOU FRAUD!
IT NEVER STOPS GROWING.
JUST GOING TO MAKE ME MADDER!
I'LL LIVE WITH IT!
NO, YOU WON'T.
VENOM'S DEFEAT WAS A MORAL VICTORY, AS WELL -- VALIDATING TO BEN HIS EXISTENCE --
-- AND THE NECESSITY FOR ANOTHER SPIDER IN THE WORLD!
WITH A VICTORY OVER A HEAVY HITTER LIKE VENOM UNDER HIS BELT, BEN'S CONFIDENCE IN HIMSELF AND HIS ABILITIES SOARED.
HE FOUND HIMSELF FIGHTING CRIME AND EVIL WITH A REVITALIZED SENSE OF GOOD...AND HOPE!
A HOPE THAT WAS ALMOST SHAKEN TO ITS ROOTS WHEN HE WAS VIOLENTLY AMBUSHED BY A MYSTERIOUS STRANGER FROM HIS PAST...

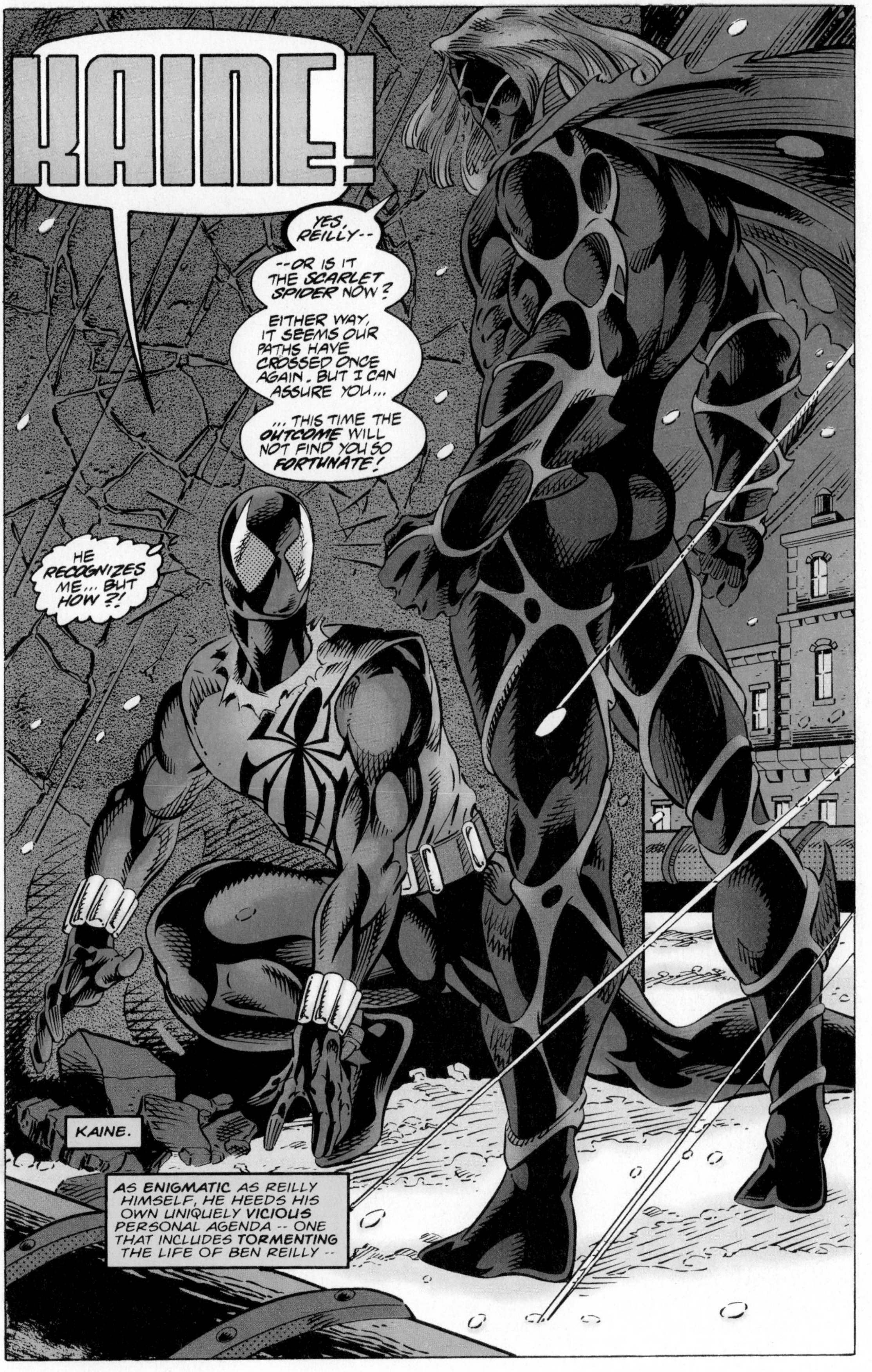
KAINE!
YES, REILLY--
--OR IS IT THE SCARLET SPIDER NOW?
EITHER WAY, IT SEEMS OUR PATHS HAVE CROSSED ONCE AGAIN. BUT I CAN ASSURE YOU...
...THIS TIME THE OUTCOME WILL NOT FIND YOU SO FORTUNATE!
HE RECOGNIZES ME... BUT HOW?!
KAINE.
AS ENIGMATIC AS REILLY HIMSELF, HE HEEDS HIS OWN UNIQUELY VICIOUS PERSONAL AGENDA -- ONE THAT INCLUDES TORMENTING THE LIFE OF BEN REILLY --

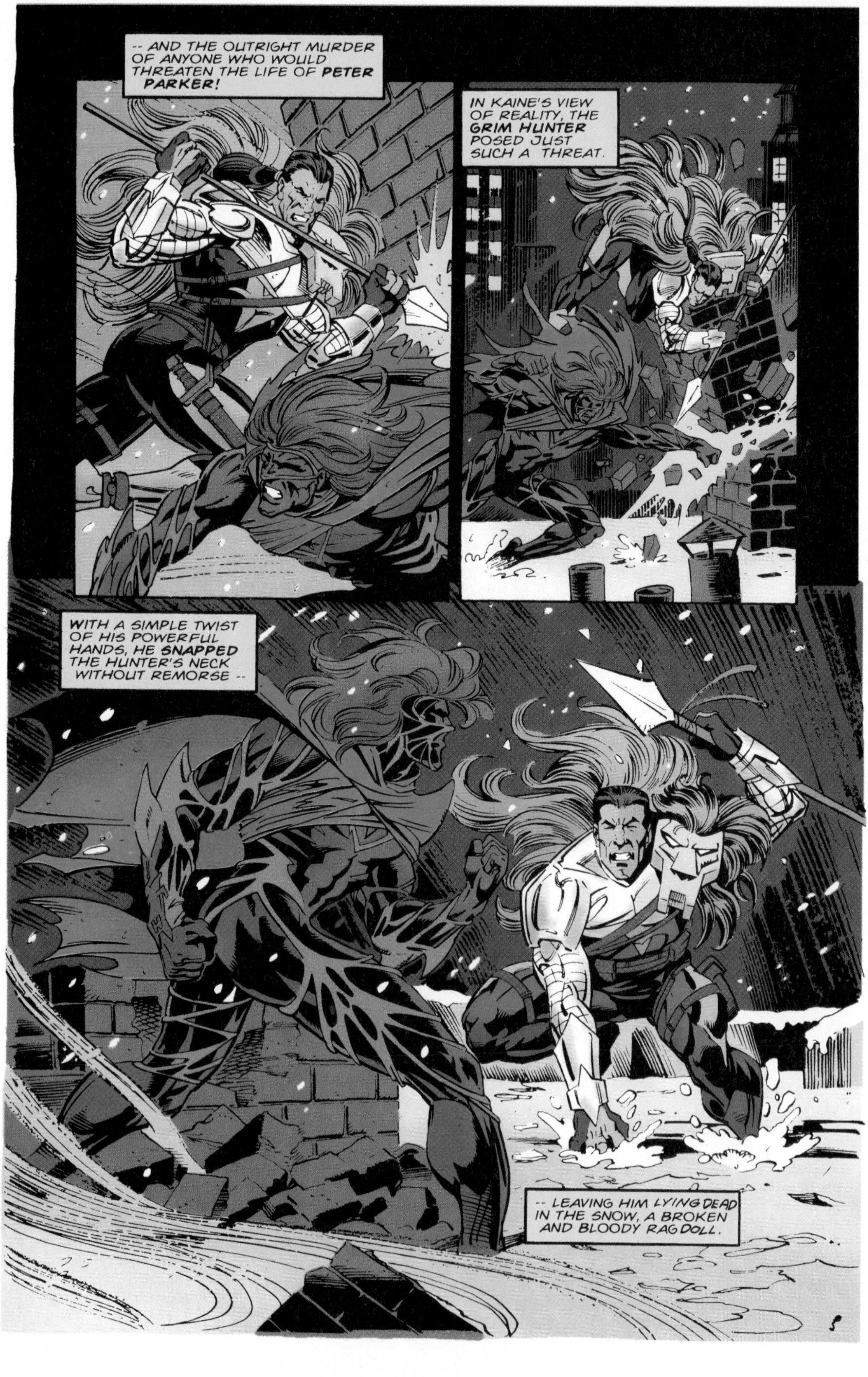
-- AND THE OUTRIGHT MURDER OF ANYONE WHO WOULD THREATEN THE LIFE OF PETER PARKER!
IN KAINE'S VIEW OF REALITY, THE GRIM HUNTER POSED JUST SUCH A THREAT.
WITH A SIMPLE TWIST OF HIS POWERFUL HANDS, HE SNAPPED THE HUNTER'S NECK WITHOUT REMORSE --
-- LEAVING HIM LYING DEAD IN THE SNOW, A BROKEN AND BLOODY RAG DOLL.

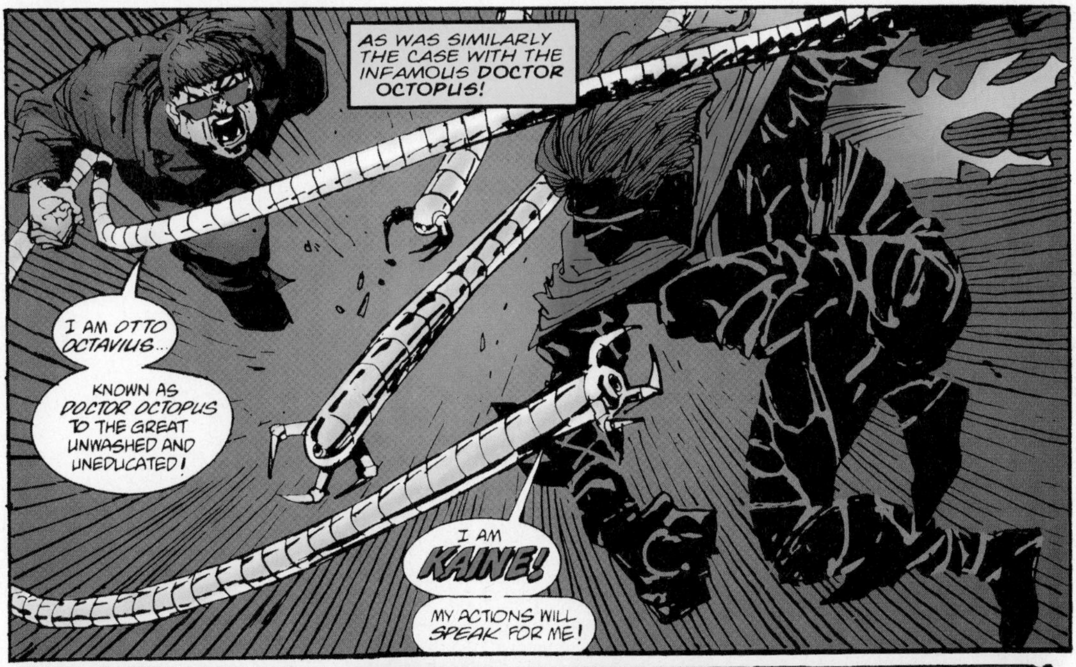
AS WAS SIMILARLY THE CASE WITH THE INFAMOUS DOCTOR OCTOPUS!
I AM OTTO OCTAVIUS...
KNOWN AS DOCTOR OCTOPUS TO THE GREAT UNWASHED AND UNEDUCATED!
I AM KAINE!
MY ACTIONS WILL SPEAK FOR ME!

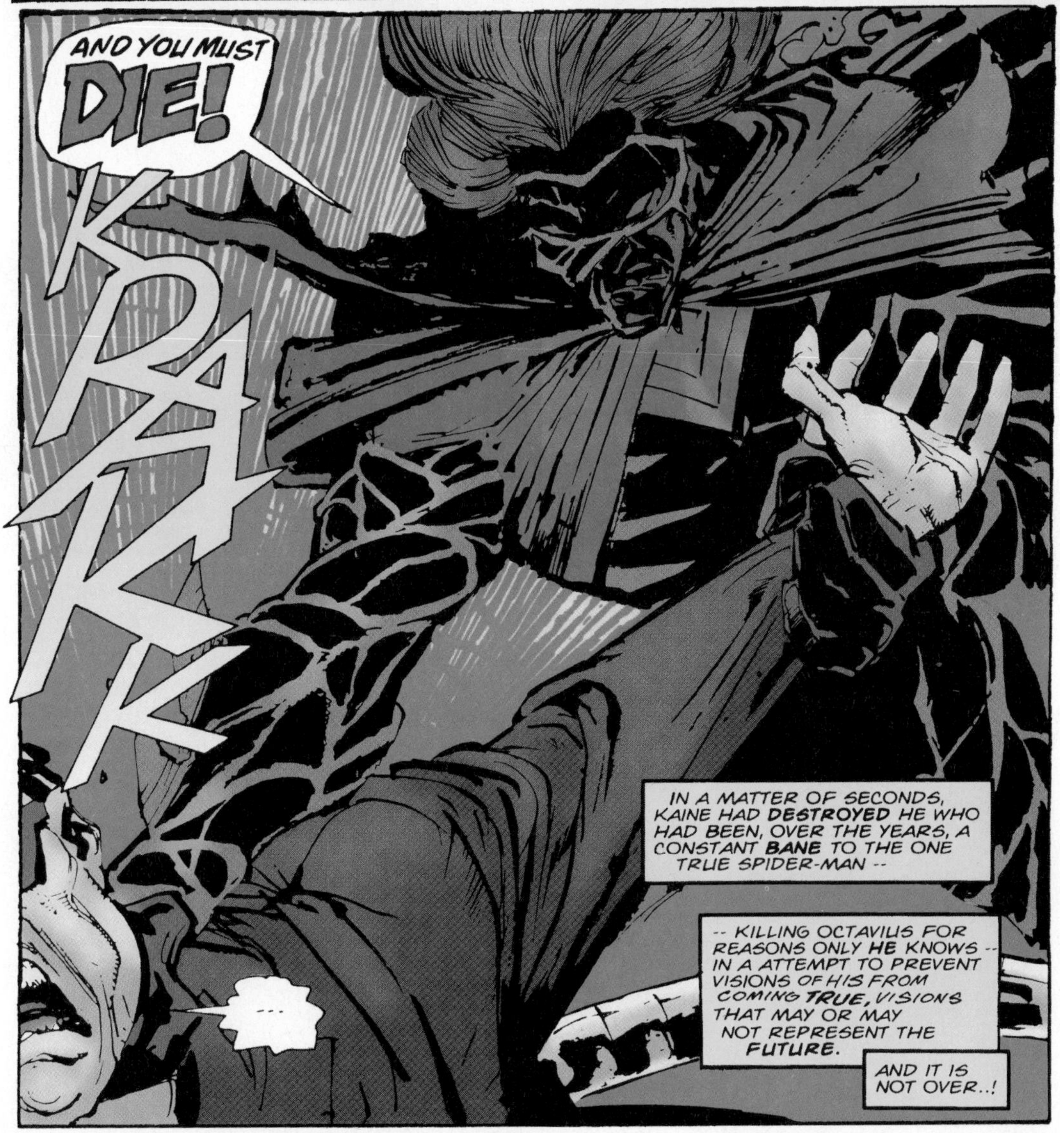
AND YOU MUST DIE!
KRAKKK
IN A MATTER OF SECONDS, KAINE HAD DESTROYED HE WHO HAD BEEN, OVER THE YEARS, A CONSTANT BANE TO THE ONE TRUE SPIDER-MAN --
...
-- KILLING OCTAVIUS FOR REASONS ONLY HE KNOWS -- IN A ATTEMPT TO PREVENT VISIONS OF HIS FROM COMING TRUE, VISIONS THAT MAY OR MAY NOT REPRESENT THE FUTURE.
AND IT IS NOT OVER..!

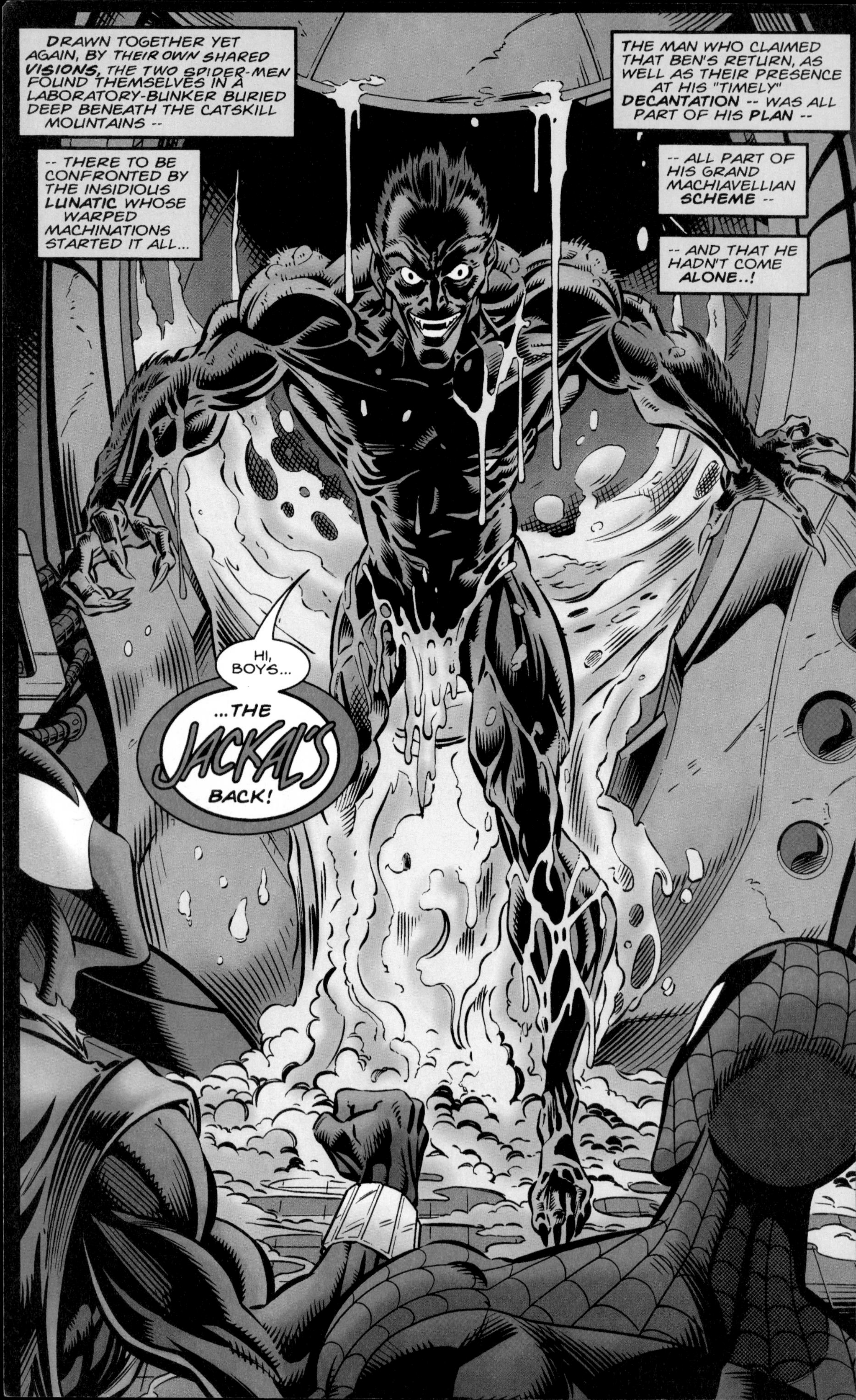
DRAWN TOGETHER YET AGAIN, BY THEIR OWN SHARED VISIONS, THE TWO SPIDER-MEN FOUND THEMSELVES IN A LABORATORY-BUNKER BURIED DEEP BENEATH THE CATSKILL MOUNTAINS --
-- THERE TO BE CONFRONTED BY THE INSIDIOUS LUNATIC WHOSE WARPED MACHINATIONS STARTED IT ALL...
THE MAN WHO CLAIMED THAT BEN'S RETURN, AS WELL AS THEIR PRESENCE AT HIS "TIMELY" DECANTATION -- WAS ALL PART OF HIS PLAN --
-- ALL PART OF HIS GRAND MACHIAVELLIAN SCHEME --
-- AND THAT HE HADN'T COME ALONE..!
HI, BOYS...
...THE JACKAL'S BACK!

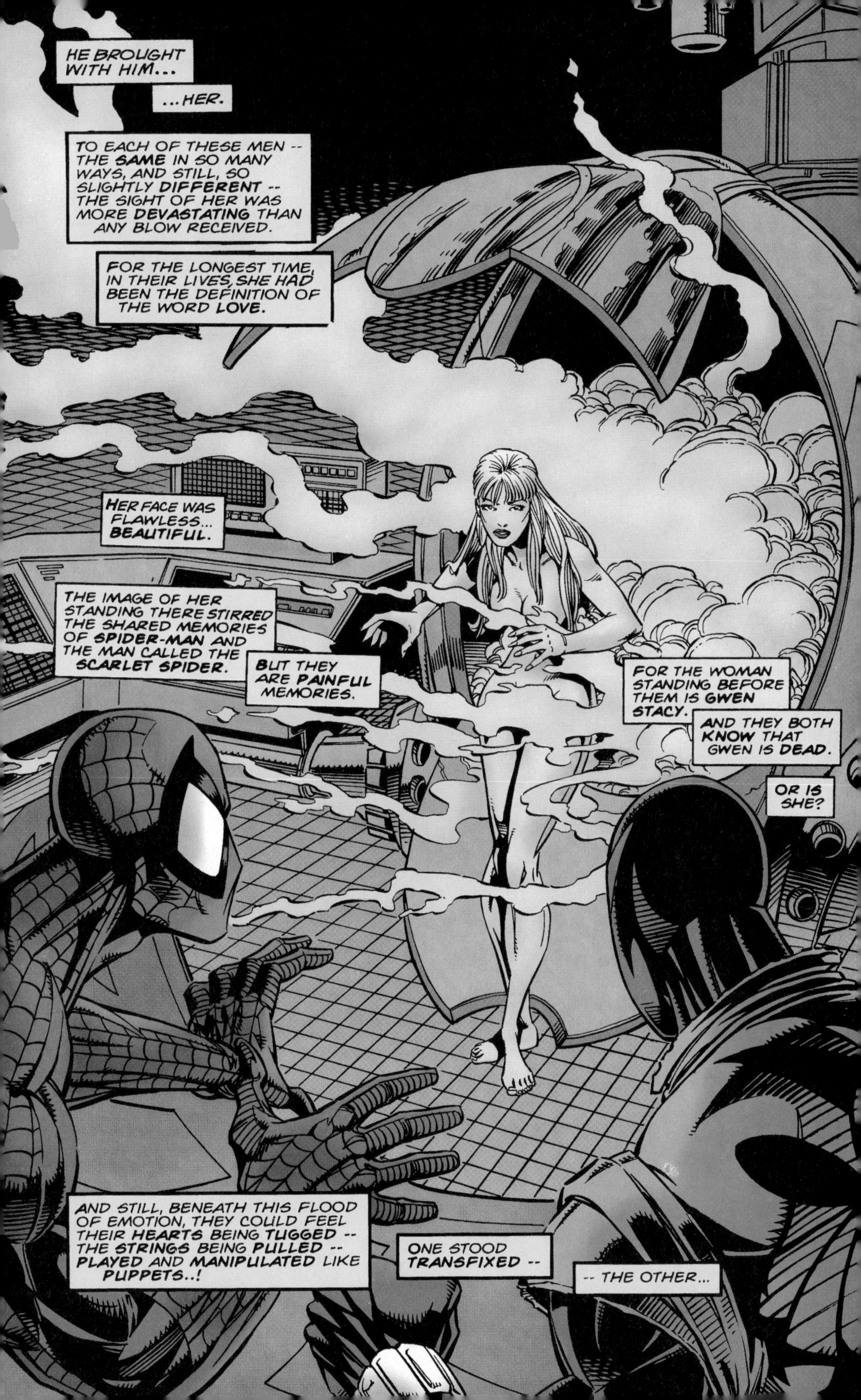
HE BROUGHT WITH HIM...
...HER.
TO EACH OF THESE MEN -- THE SAME IN SO MANY WAYS, AND STILL, SO SLIGHTLY DIFFERENT -- THE SIGHT OF HER WAS MORE DEVASTATING THAN ANY BLOW RECEIVED.
FOR THE LONGEST TIME, IN THEIR LIVES, SHE HAD BEEN THE DEFINITION OF THE WORD LOVE.
HER FACE WAS FLAWLESS... BEAUTIFUL.
THE IMAGE OF HER STANDING THERE STIRRED THE SHARED MEMORIES OF SPIDER-MAN AND THE MAN CALLED THE SCARLET SPIDER.
BUT THEY ARE PAINFUL MEMORIES.
FOR THE WOMAN STANDING BEFORE THEM IS GWEN STACY.
AND THEY BOTH KNOW THAT GWEN IS DEAD.
OR IS SHE?
AND STILL, BENEATH THIS FLOOD OF EMOTION, THEY COULD FEEL THEIR HEARTS BEING TUGGED -- THE STRINGS BEING PULLED -- PLAYED AND MANIPULATED LIKE PUPPETS..!
ONE STOOD TRANSFIXED --
-- THE OTHER...

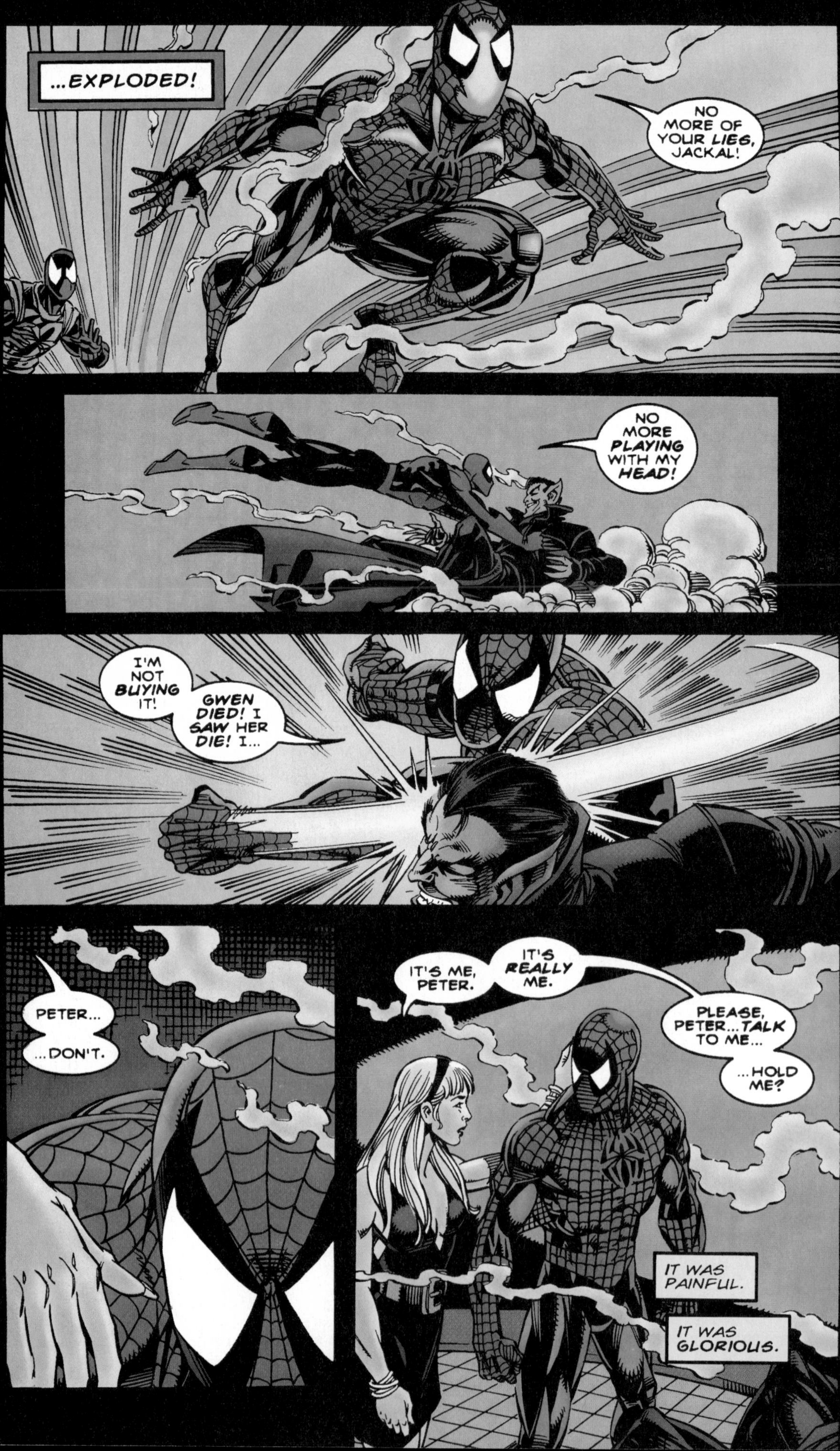
...EXPLODED!
NO MORE OF YOUR LIES, JACKAL!
NO MORE PLAYING WITH MY HEAD!
I'M NOT BUYING IT!
GWEN DIED! I SAW HER DIE! I...
PETER...
...DON'T.
IT'S ME, PETER.
IT'S REALLY ME.
PLEASE, PETER... TALK TO ME...
...HOLD ME?
IT WAS PAINFUL.
IT WAS GLORIOUS.

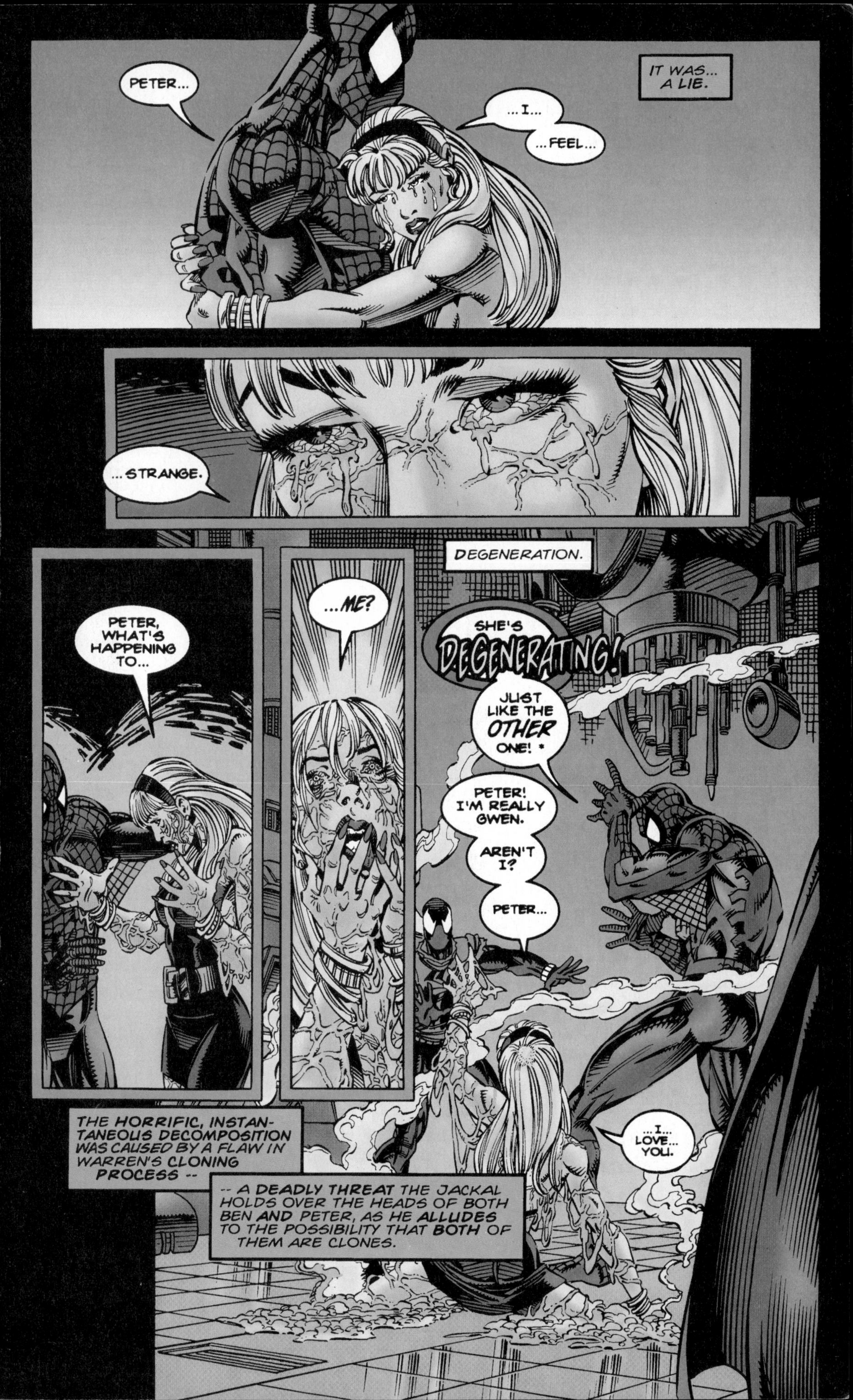
IT WAS... A LIE.
PETER...
...I...
...FEEL...
...STRANGE.
DEGENERATION.
PETER, WHAT'S HAPPENING TO...
...ME?
SHE'S DEGENERATING!
JUST LIKE THE OTHER ONE! *
PETER! I'M REALLY GWEN.
AREN'T I?
PETER...
...I... LOVE... YOU.
THE HORRIFIC, INSTANTANEOUS DECOMPOSITION WAS CAUSED BY A FLAW IN WARREN'S CLONING PROCESS --
-- A DEADLY THREAT THE JACKAL HOLDS OVER THE HEADS OF BOTH BEN AND PETER, AS HE ALLUDES TO THE POSSIBILITY THAT BOTH OF THEM ARE CLONES.

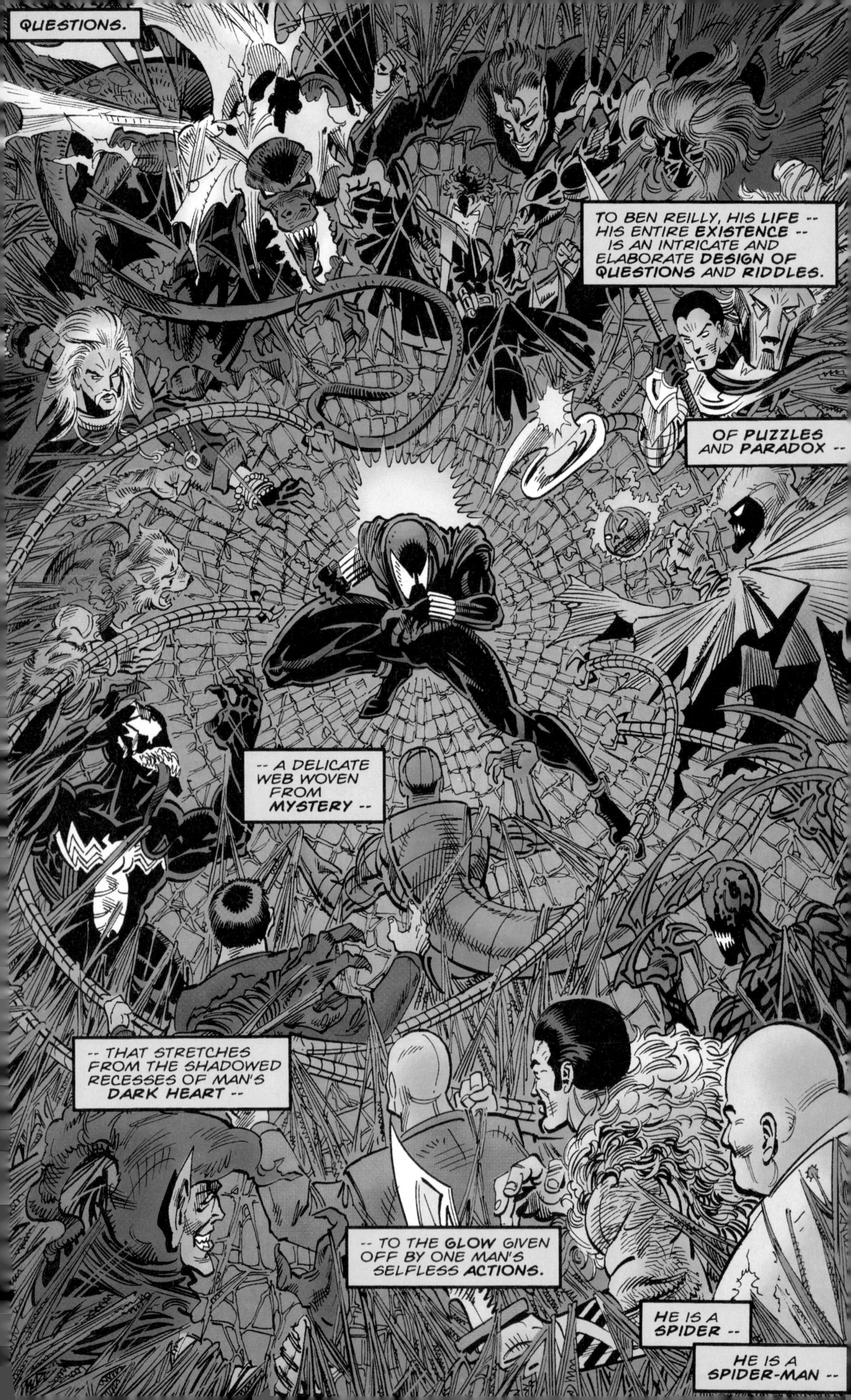
QUESTIONS.
TO BEN REILLY, HIS LIFE -- HIS ENTIRE EXISTENCE -- IS AN INTRICATE AND ELABORATE DESIGN OF QUESTIONS AND RIDDLES.
OF PUZZLES AND PARADOX --
-- A DELICATE WEB WOVEN FROM MYSTERY --
-- THAT STRETCHES FROM THE SHADOWED RECESSES OF MAN'S DARK HEART --
-- TO THE GLOW GIVEN OFF BY ONE MAN'S SELFLESS ACTIONS.
HE IS A SPIDER --
HE IS A SPIDER-MAN --

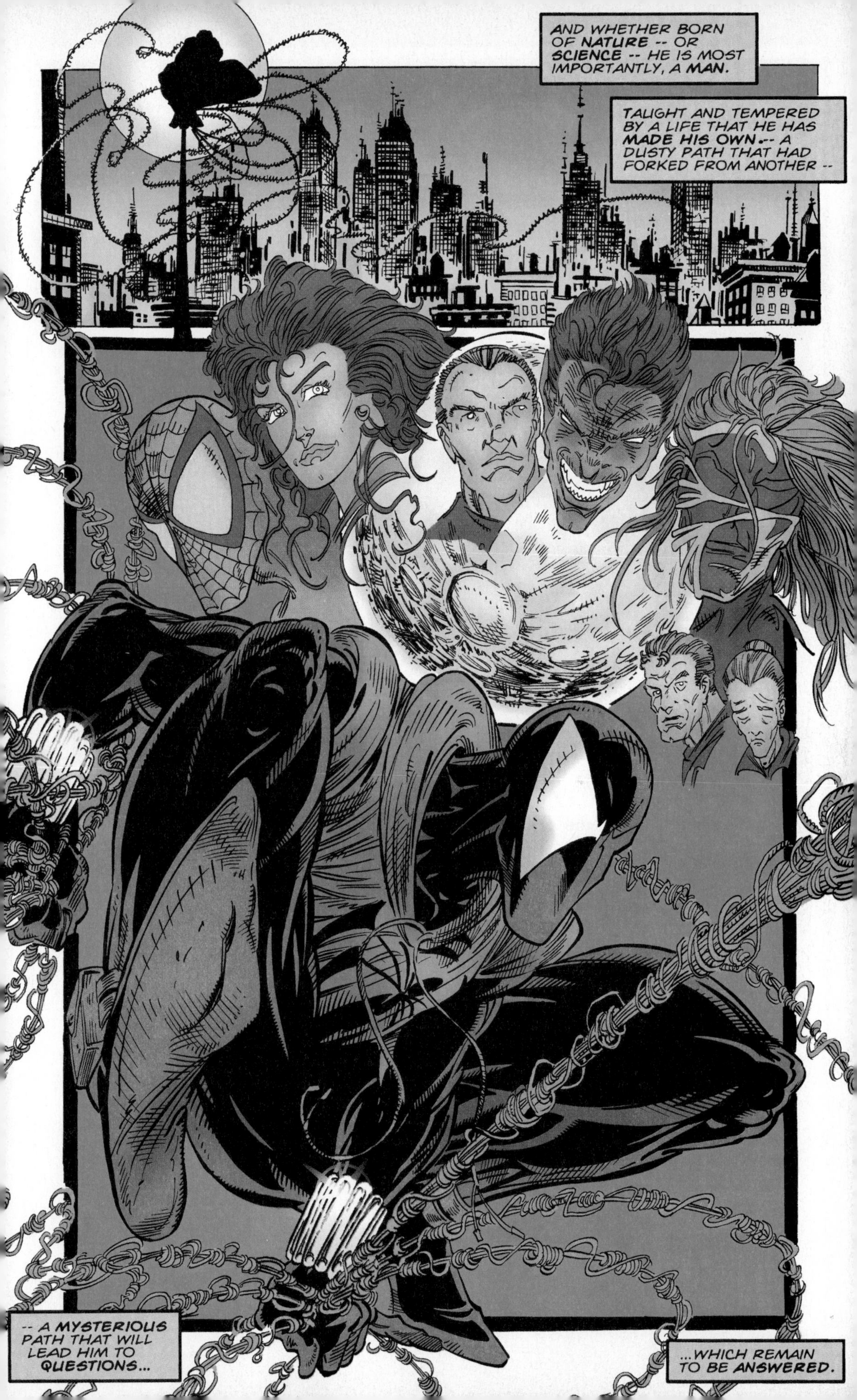
AND WHETHER BORN OF NATURE -- OR SCIENCE -- HE IS MOST IMPORTANTLY, A MAN.
TAUGHT AND TEMPERED BY A LIFE THAT HE HAS MADE HIS OWN -- A DUSTY PATH THAT HAD FORKED FROM ANOTHER --
-- A MYSTERIOUS PATH THAT WILL LEAD HIM TO QUESTIONS...
...WHICH REMAIN TO BE ANSWERED.

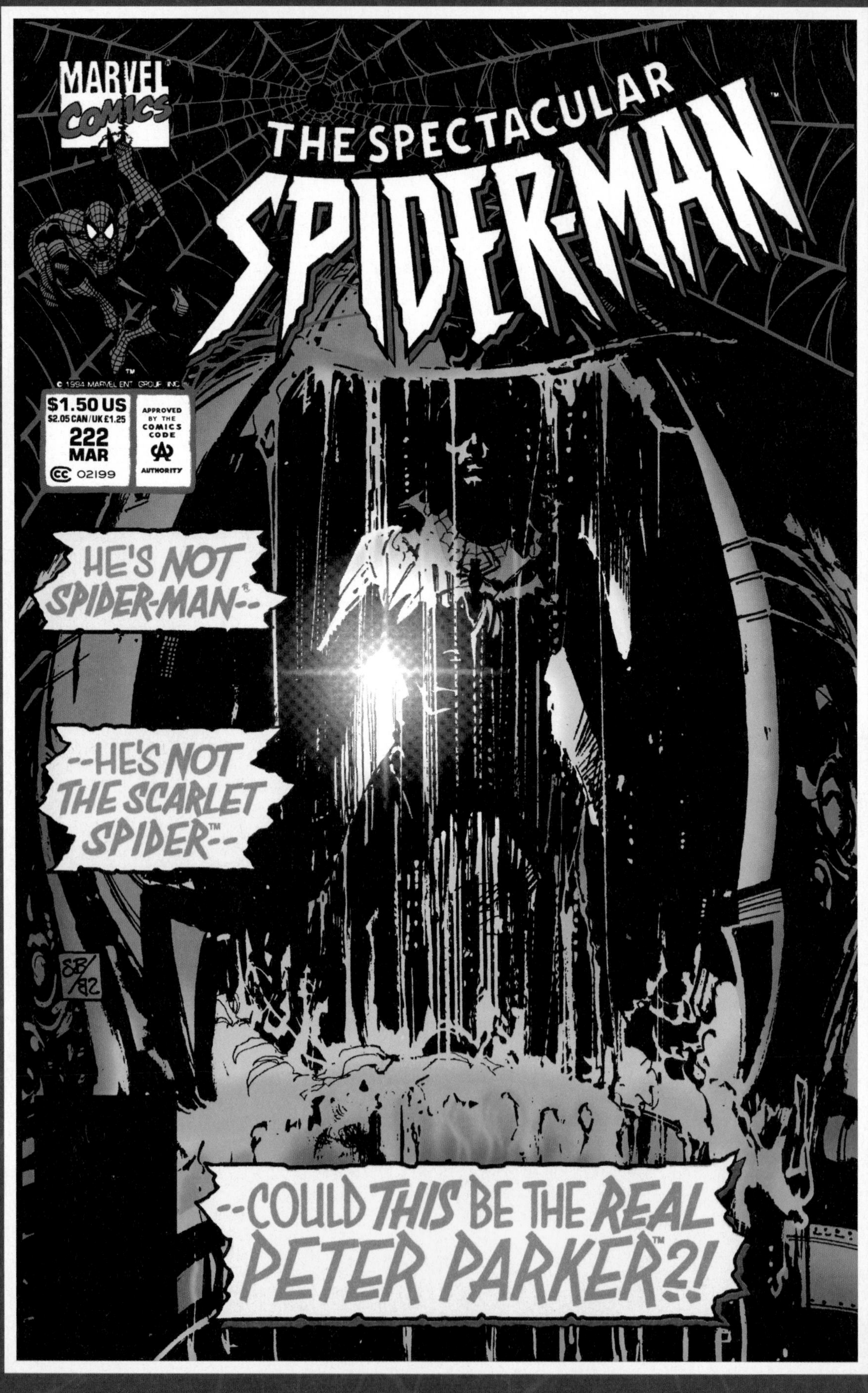
MARVEL COMICS
THE SPECTACULAR SPIDER-MAN
© 1994 MARVEL ENT. GROUP, INC.
$1.50 US
$2.05 CAN/UK £1.25
222
MAR
02199
APPROVED BY THE COMICS CODE AUTHORITY
HE'S NOT SPIDER-MAN--
--HE'S NOT THE SCARLET SPIDER--
--COULD THIS BE THE REAL PETER PARKER?!

BITTEN BY A RADIOACTIVE SPIDER, STUDENT PETER PARKER GAINED THE PROPORTIONATE STRENGTH AND AGILITY OF AN ARACHNID! ARMED WITH HIS WONDROUS WEB-SHOOTERS, THE RELUCTANT SUPER HERO STRUGGLES WITH SINISTER SUPER-VILLAINS, MAKING ENDS MEET, AND MAINTAINING SOME SEMBLANCE OF A NORMAL LIFE!

STAN LEE PRESENTS: **THE SPECTACULAR SPIDER-MAN!**

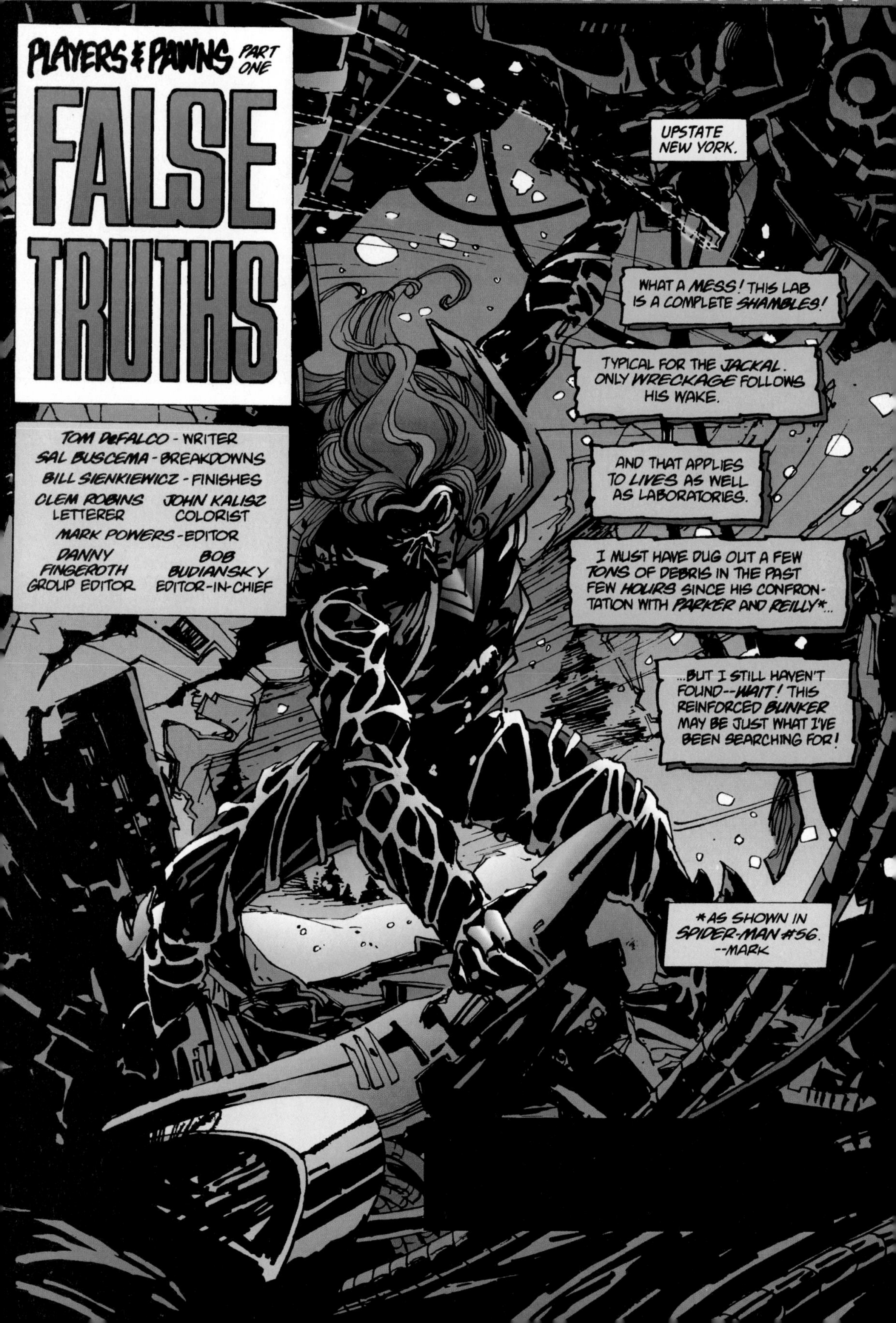

PLAYERS & PAWNS PART ONE
FALSE TRUTHS
TOM DeFALCO - WRITER
SAL BUSCEMA - BREAKDOWNS
BILL SIENKIEWICZ - FINISHES
CLEM ROBINS LETTERER
JOHN KALISZ COLORIST
MARK POWERS - EDITOR
DANNY FINGEROTH GROUP EDITOR
BOB BUDIANSKY EDITOR-IN-CHIEF
UPSTATE NEW YORK.
WHAT A MESS! THIS LAB IS A COMPLETE SHAMBLES!
TYPICAL FOR THE JACKAL. ONLY WRECKAGE FOLLOWS HIS WAKE.
AND THAT APPLIES TO LIVES AS WELL AS LABORATORIES.
I MUST HAVE DUG OUT A FEW TONS OF DEBRIS IN THE PAST FEW HOURS SINCE HIS CONFRONTATION WITH PARKER AND REILLY*...
...BUT I STILL HAVEN'T FOUND--WAIT! THIS REINFORCED BUNKER MAY BE JUST WHAT I'VE BEEN SEARCHING FOR!
*AS SHOWN IN SPIDER-MAN #56. --MARK
[redacted]

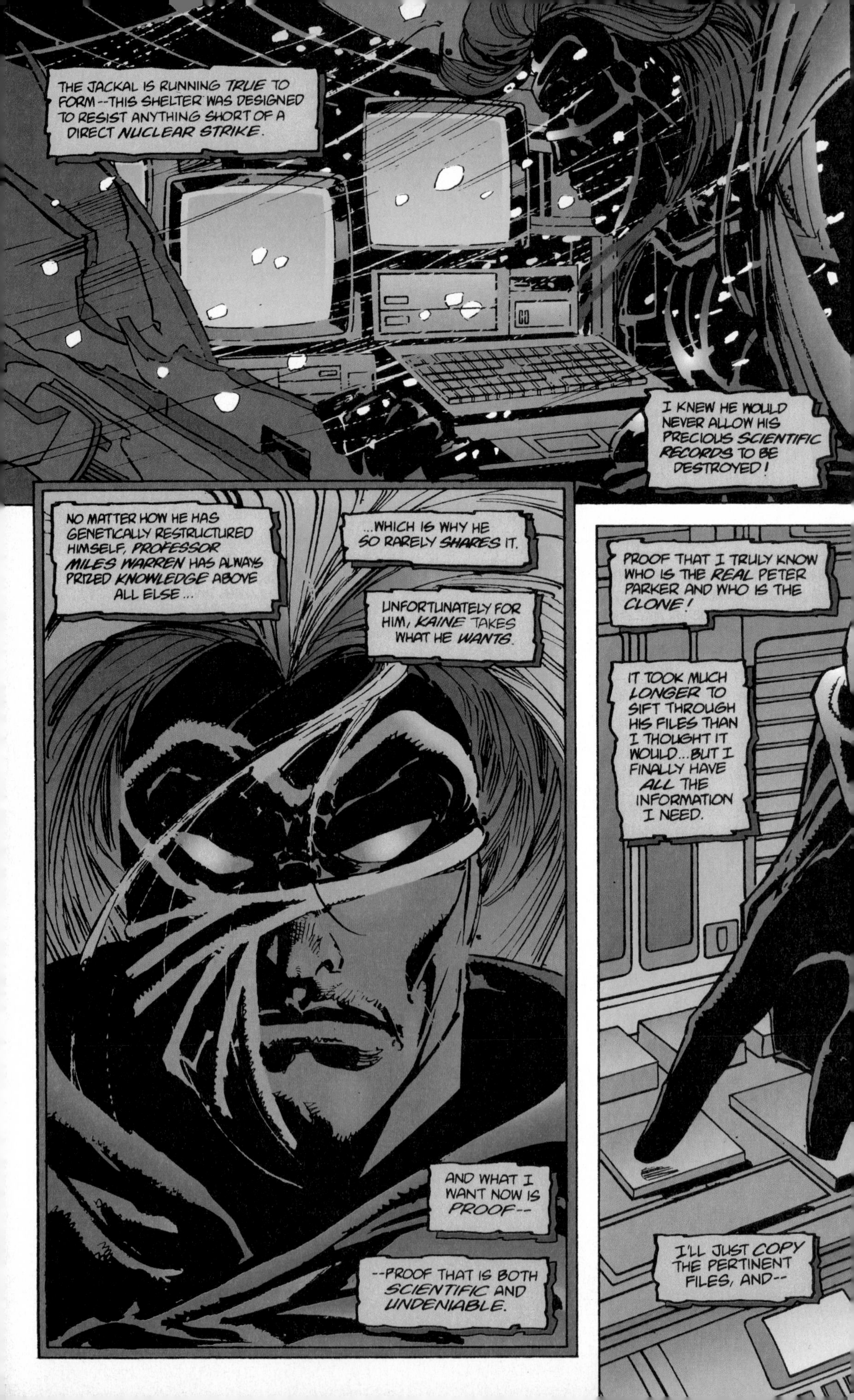
THE JACKAL IS RUNNING TRUE TO FORM--THIS SHELTER WAS DESIGNED TO RESIST ANYTHING SHORT OF A DIRECT NUCLEAR STRIKE.
I KNEW HE WOULD NEVER ALLOW HIS PRECIOUS SCIENTIFIC RECORDS TO BE DESTROYED!
NO MATTER HOW HE HAS GENETICALLY RESTRUCTURED HIMSELF, PROFESSOR MILES WARREN HAS ALWAYS PRIZED KNOWLEDGE ABOVE ALL ELSE...
...WHICH IS WHY HE SO RARELY SHARES IT.
UNFORTUNATELY FOR HIM, KAINE TAKES WHAT HE WANTS.
AND WHAT I WANT NOW IS PROOF--
--PROOF THAT IS BOTH SCIENTIFIC AND UNDENIABLE.
PROOF THAT I TRULY KNOW WHO IS THE REAL PETER PARKER AND WHO IS THE CLONE!
IT TOOK MUCH LONGER TO SIFT THROUGH HIS FILES THAN I THOUGHT IT WOULD...BUT I FINALLY HAVE ALL THE INFORMATION I NEED.
I'LL JUST COPY THE PERTINENT FILES, AND--

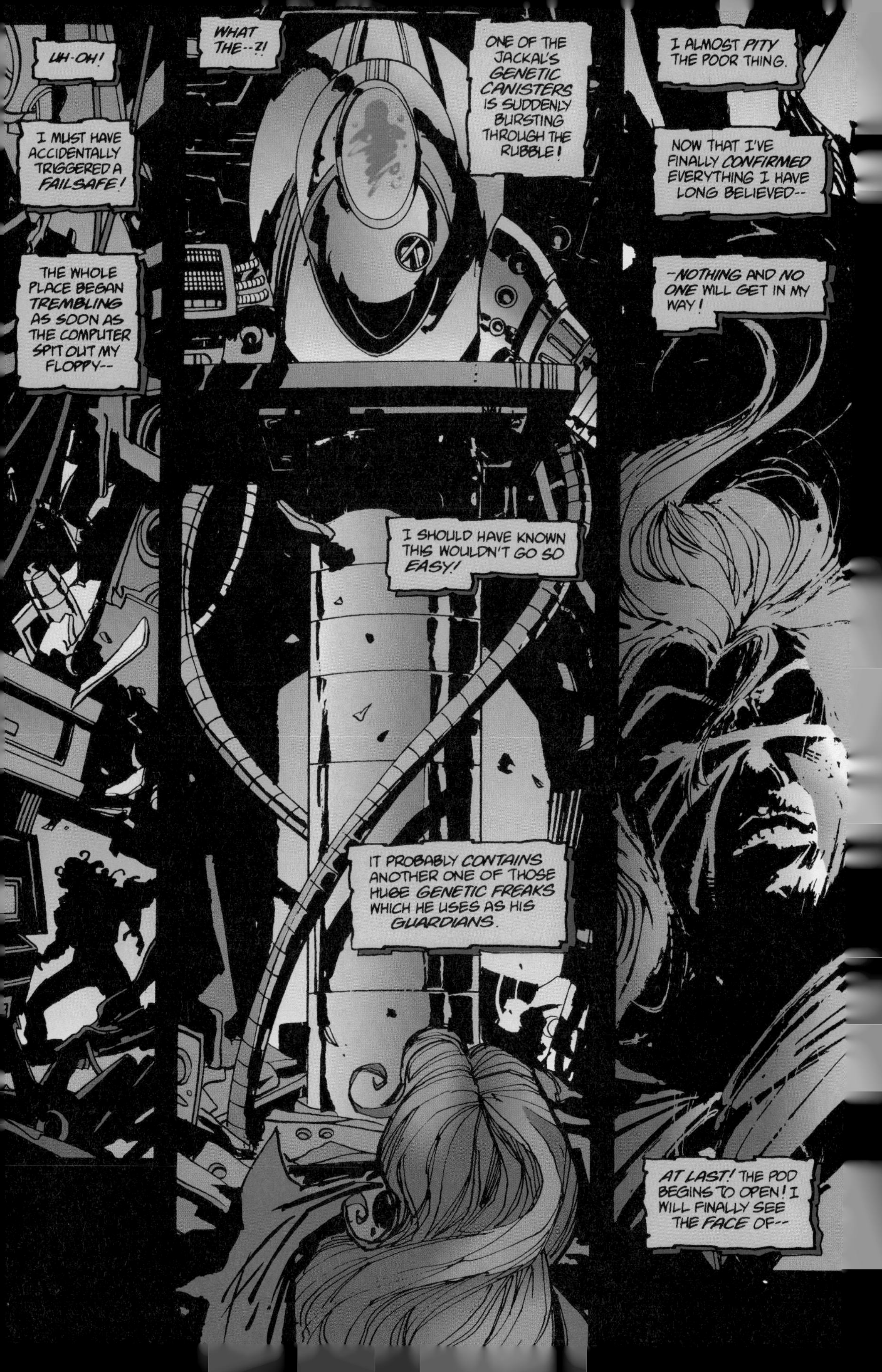
UH-OH!
I MUST HAVE ACCIDENTALLY TRIGGERED A FAILSAFE!
THE WHOLE PLACE BEGAN TREMBLING AS SOON AS THE COMPUTER SPIT OUT MY FLOPPY--
WHAT THE--?!
ONE OF THE JACKAL'S GENETIC CANISTERS IS SUDDENLY BURSTING THROUGH THE RUBBLE!
I SHOULD HAVE KNOWN THIS WOULDN'T GO SO EASY!
IT PROBABLY CONTAINS ANOTHER ONE OF THOSE HUGE GENETIC FREAKS WHICH HE USES AS HIS GUARDIANS.
I ALMOST PITY THE POOR THING.
NOW THAT I'VE FINALLY CONFIRMED EVERYTHING I HAVE LONG BELIEVED--
--NOTHING AND NO ONE WILL GET IN MY WAY!
AT LAST! THE POD BEGINS TO OPEN! I WILL FINALLY SEE THE FACE OF--

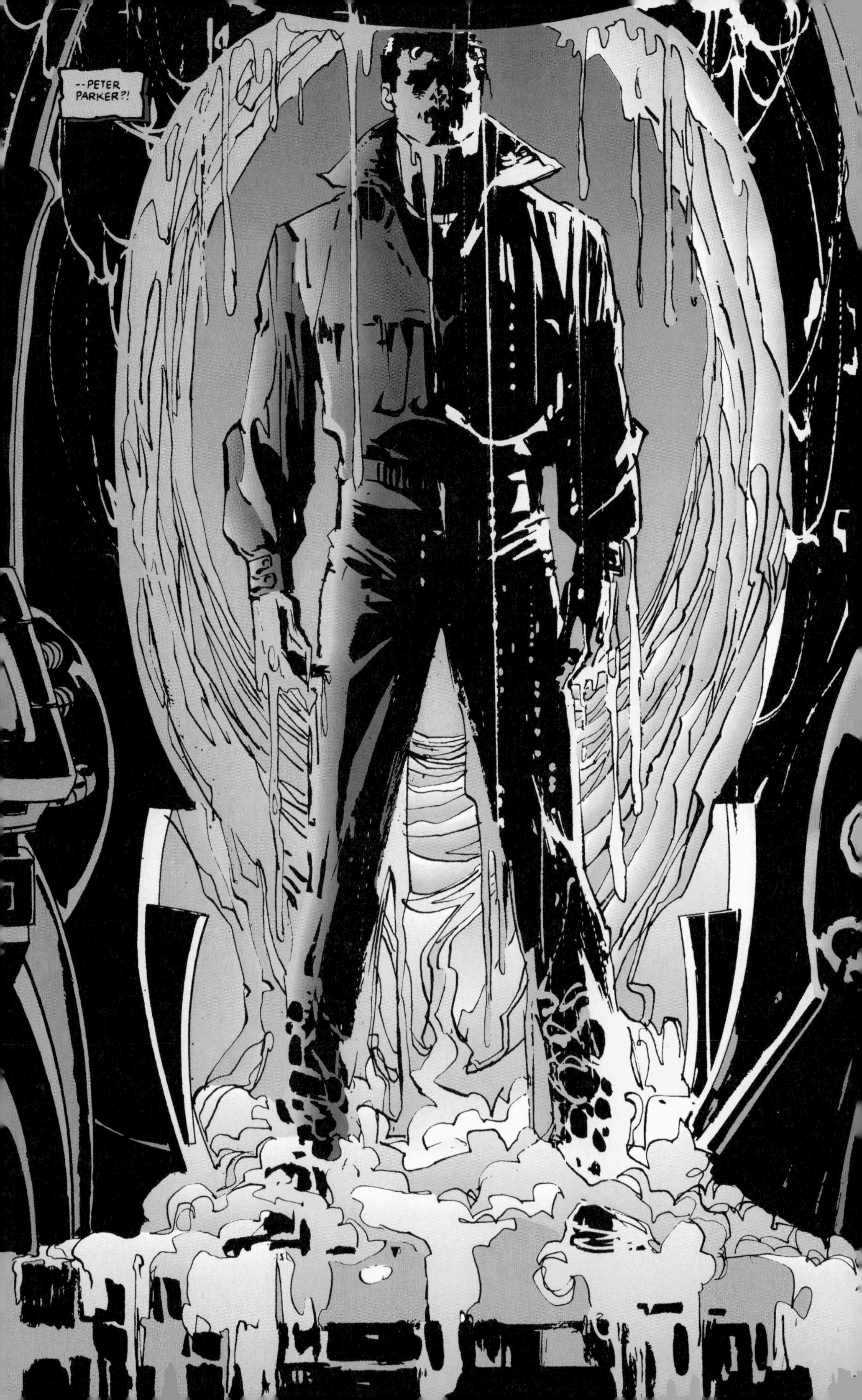
--PETER PARKER?!

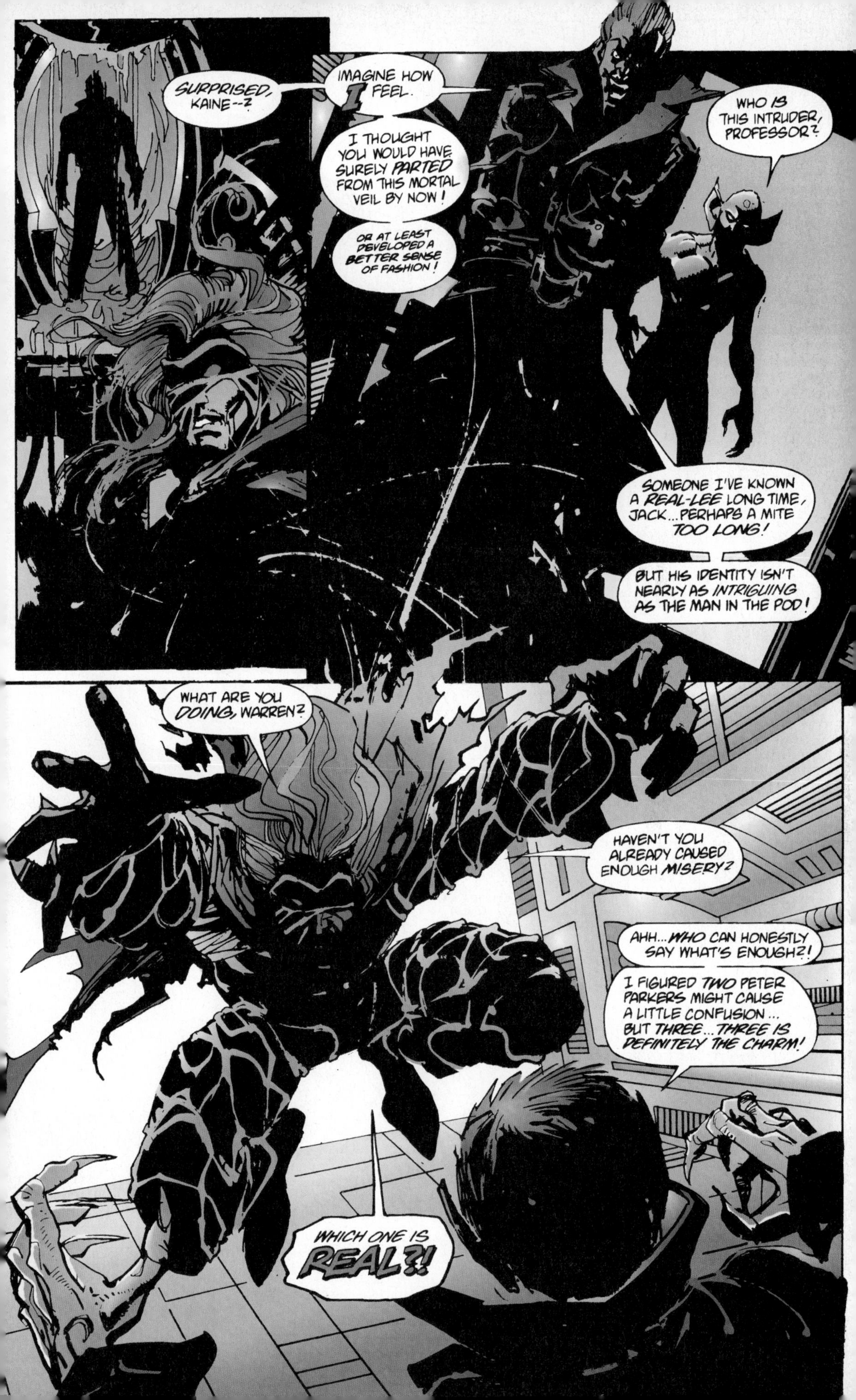
SURPRISED, KAINE--?
IMAGINE HOW I FEEL.
I THOUGHT YOU WOULD HAVE SURELY PARTED FROM THIS MORTAL VEIL BY NOW!
OR AT LEAST DEVELOPED A BETTER SENSE OF FASHION!
WHO IS THIS INTRUDER, PROFESSOR?
SOMEONE I'VE KNOWN A REAL-LEE LONG TIME, JACK...PERHAPS A MITE TOO LONG!
BUT HIS IDENTITY ISN'T NEARLY AS INTRIGUING AS THE MAN IN THE POD!
WHAT ARE YOU DOING, WARREN?
HAVEN'T YOU ALREADY CAUSED ENOUGH MISERY?
AHH...WHO CAN HONESTLY SAY WHAT'S ENOUGH?!
I FIGURED TWO PETER PARKERS MIGHT CAUSE A LITTLE CONFUSION... BUT THREE... THREE IS DEFINITELY THE CHARM!
WHICH ONE IS REAL?!

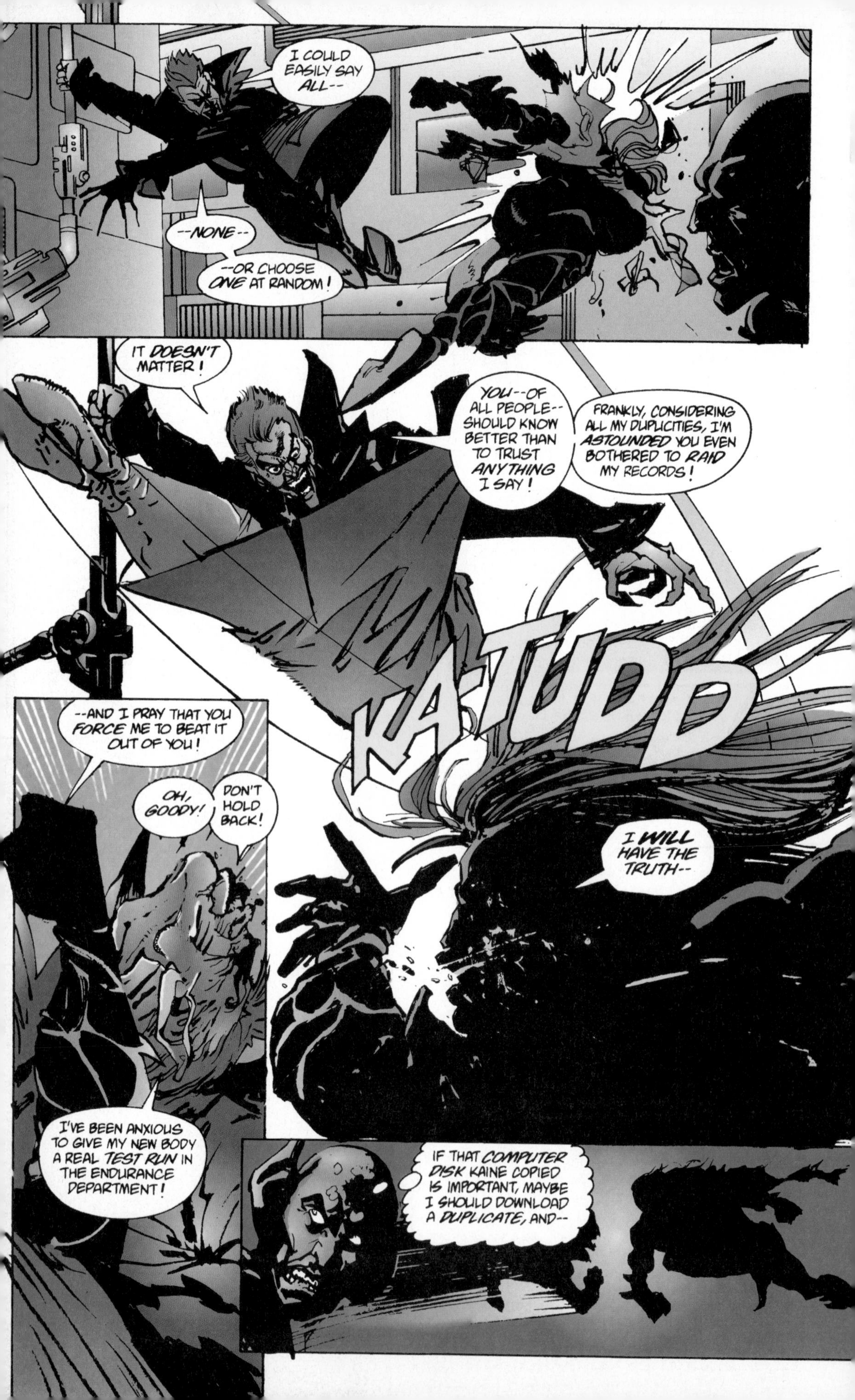
I COULD EASILY SAY ALL--
--NONE--
--OR CHOOSE ONE AT RANDOM!
IT DOESN'T MATTER!
YOU--OF ALL PEOPLE--SHOULD KNOW BETTER THAN TO TRUST ANYTHING I SAY!
FRANKLY, CONSIDERING ALL MY DUPLICITIES, I'M ASTOUNDED YOU EVEN BOTHERED TO RAID MY RECORDS!
KA-TUDD
I WILL HAVE THE TRUTH--
--AND I PRAY THAT YOU FORCE ME TO BEAT IT OUT OF YOU!
OH, GOODY!
DON'T HOLD BACK!
I'VE BEEN ANXIOUS TO GIVE MY NEW BODY A REAL TEST RUN IN THE ENDURANCE DEPARTMENT!
IF THAT COMPUTER DISK KAINE COPIED IS IMPORTANT, MAYBE I SHOULD DOWNLOAD A DUPLICATE, AND--

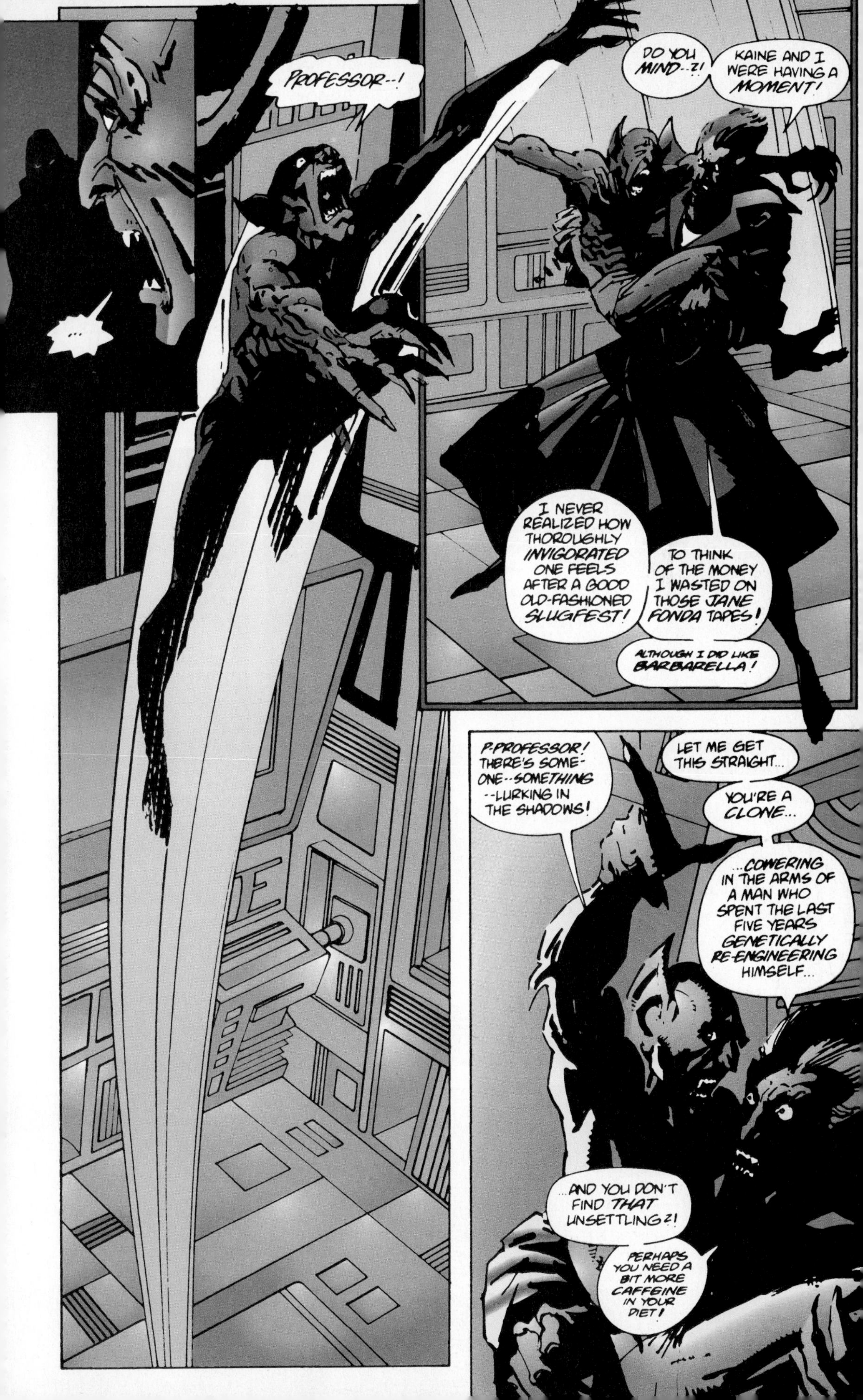

PROFESSOR--!
...
DO YOU MIND--?!
KAINE AND I WERE HAVING A MOMENT!
I NEVER REALIZED HOW THOROUGHLY INVIGORATED ONE FEELS AFTER A GOOD OLD-FASHIONED SLUGFEST!
TO THINK OF THE MONEY I WASTED ON THOSE JANE FONDA TAPES!
ALTHOUGH I DID LIKE BARBARELLA!
P-PROFESSOR! THERE'S SOME-ONE--SOMETHING--LURKING IN THE SHADOWS!
LET ME GET THIS STRAIGHT...
YOU'RE A CLONE...
...COWERING IN THE ARMS OF A MAN WHO SPENT THE LAST FIVE YEARS GENETICALLY RE-ENGINEERING HIMSELF...
...AND YOU DON'T FIND THAT UNSETTLING?!
PERHAPS YOU NEED A BIT MORE CAFFEINE IN YOUR DIET!

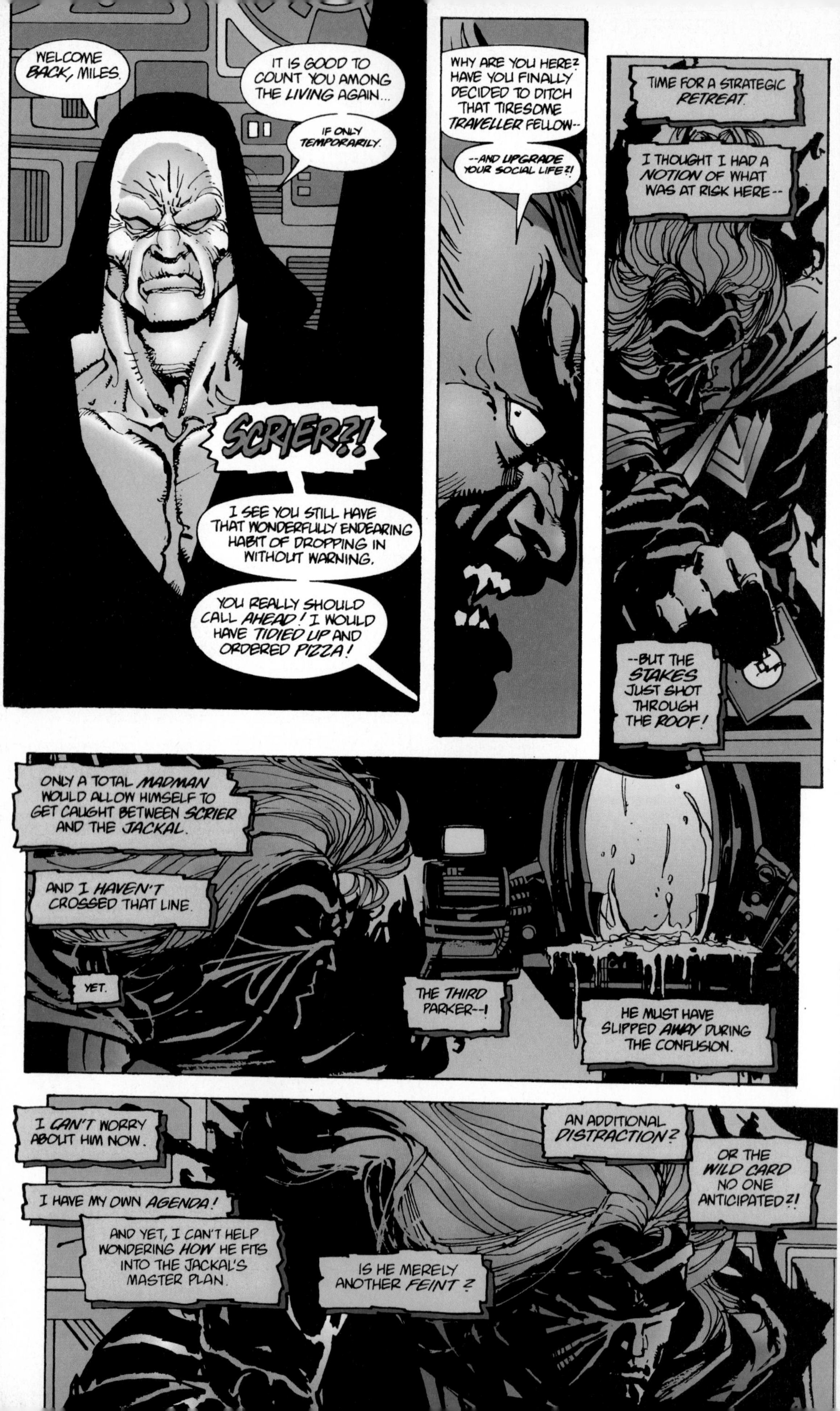

WELCOME BACK, MILES.
IT IS GOOD TO COUNT YOU AMONG THE LIVING AGAIN...
IF ONLY TEMPORARILY.
SCRIER?!
I SEE YOU STILL HAVE THAT WONDERFULLY ENDEARING HABIT OF DROPPING IN WITHOUT WARNING.
YOU REALLY SHOULD CALL AHEAD! I WOULD HAVE TIDIED UP AND ORDERED PIZZA!
WHY ARE YOU HERE? HAVE YOU FINALLY DECIDED TO DITCH THAT TIRESOME TRAVELLER FELLOW--
--AND UPGRADE YOUR SOCIAL LIFE?!
TIME FOR A STRATEGIC RETREAT.
I THOUGHT I HAD A NOTION OF WHAT WAS AT RISK HERE--
--BUT THE STAKES JUST SHOT THROUGH THE ROOF!
ONLY A TOTAL MADMAN WOULD ALLOW HIMSELF TO GET CAUGHT BETWEEN SCRIER AND THE JACKAL.
AND I HAVEN'T CROSSED THAT LINE.
YET.
THE THIRD PARKER--!
HE MUST HAVE SLIPPED AWAY DURING THE CONFUSION.
I CAN'T WORRY ABOUT HIM NOW.
I HAVE MY OWN AGENDA!
AND YET, I CAN'T HELP WONDERING HOW HE FITS INTO THE JACKAL'S MASTER PLAN.
IS HE MERELY ANOTHER FEINT?
AN ADDITIONAL DISTRACTION?
OR THE WILD CARD NO ONE ANTICIPATED?!

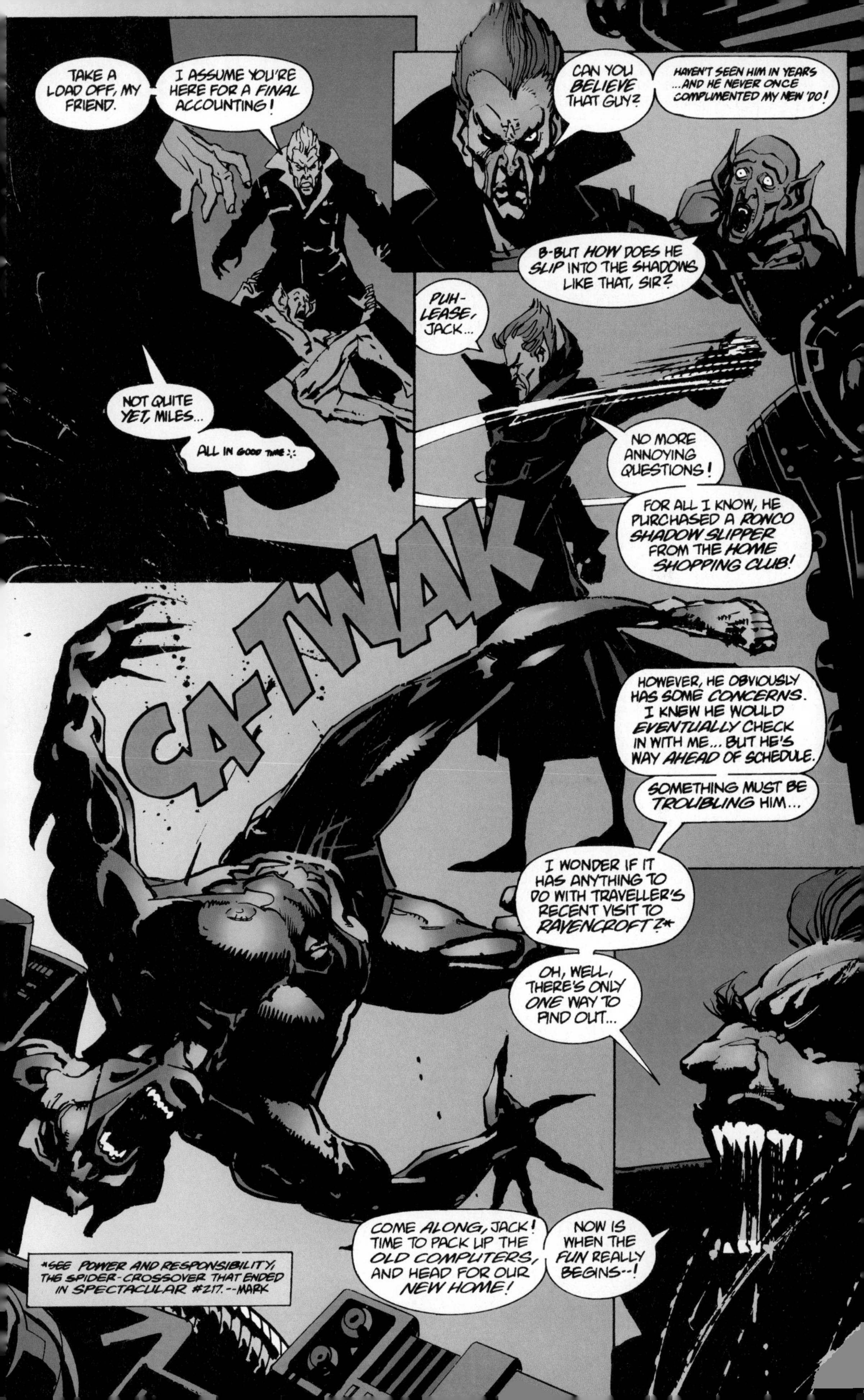
TAKE A LOAD OFF, MY FRIEND.
I ASSUME YOU'RE HERE FOR A FINAL ACCOUNTING!
CAN YOU BELIEVE THAT GUY?
HAVEN'T SEEN HIM IN YEARS ...AND HE NEVER ONCE COMPLIMENTED MY NEW 'DO!
B-BUT HOW DOES HE SLIP INTO THE SHADOWS LIKE THAT, SIR?
PUH-LEASE, JACK...
NOT QUITE YET, MILES...
ALL IN GOOD TIME...
NO MORE ANNOYING QUESTIONS!
FOR ALL I KNOW, HE PURCHASED A RONCO SHADOW SLIPPER FROM THE HOME SHOPPING CLUB!
CA-TWAK
HOWEVER, HE OBVIOUSLY HAS SOME CONCERNS. I KNEW HE WOULD EVENTUALLY CHECK IN WITH ME... BUT HE'S WAY AHEAD OF SCHEDULE.
SOMETHING MUST BE TROUBLING HIM...
I WONDER IF IT HAS ANYTHING TO DO WITH TRAVELLER'S RECENT VISIT TO RAVENCROFT?*
OH, WELL, THERE'S ONLY ONE WAY TO FIND OUT...
*SEE POWER AND RESPONSIBILITY, THE SPIDER-CROSSOVER THAT ENDED IN SPECTACULAR #217. --MARK
COME ALONG, JACK! TIME TO PACK UP THE OLD COMPUTERS, AND HEAD FOR OUR NEW HOME!
NOW IS WHEN THE FUN REALLY BEGINS--!

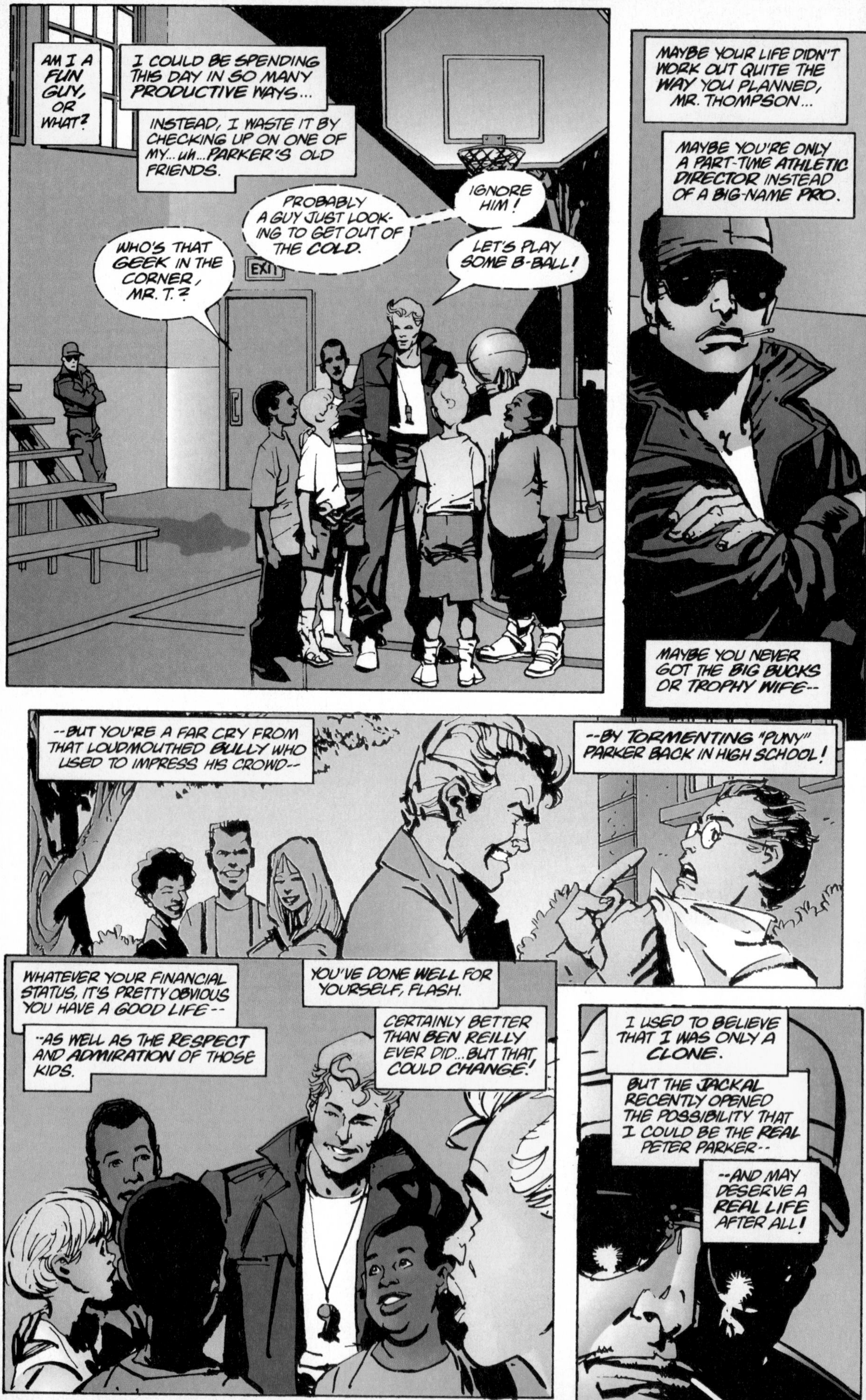

AM I A FUN GUY, OR WHAT?
I COULD BE SPENDING THIS DAY IN SO MANY PRODUCTIVE WAYS...
INSTEAD, I WASTE IT BY CHECKING UP ON ONE OF MY... uh... PARKER'S OLD FRIENDS.
WHO'S THAT GEEK IN THE CORNER, MR. T.?
PROBABLY A GUY JUST LOOKING TO GET OUT OF THE COLD.
IGNORE HIM!
LET'S PLAY SOME B-BALL!
EXIT
MAYBE YOUR LIFE DIDN'T WORK OUT QUITE THE WAY YOU PLANNED, MR. THOMPSON...
MAYBE YOU'RE ONLY A PART-TIME ATHLETIC DIRECTOR INSTEAD OF A BIG-NAME PRO.
MAYBE YOU NEVER GOT THE BIG BUCKS OR TROPHY WIFE--
--BUT YOU'RE A FAR CRY FROM THAT LOUDMOUTHED BULLY WHO USED TO IMPRESS HIS CROWD--
--BY TORMENTING "PUNY" PARKER BACK IN HIGH SCHOOL!
WHATEVER YOUR FINANCIAL STATUS, IT'S PRETTY OBVIOUS YOU HAVE A GOOD LIFE--
--AS WELL AS THE RESPECT AND ADMIRATION OF THOSE KIDS.
YOU'VE DONE WELL FOR YOURSELF, FLASH.
CERTAINLY BETTER THAN BEN REILLY EVER DID... BUT THAT COULD CHANGE!
I USED TO BELIEVE THAT I WAS ONLY A CLONE.
BUT THE JACKAL RECENTLY OPENED THE POSSIBILITY THAT I COULD BE THE REAL PETER PARKER--
--AND MAY DESERVE A REAL LIFE AFTER ALL!

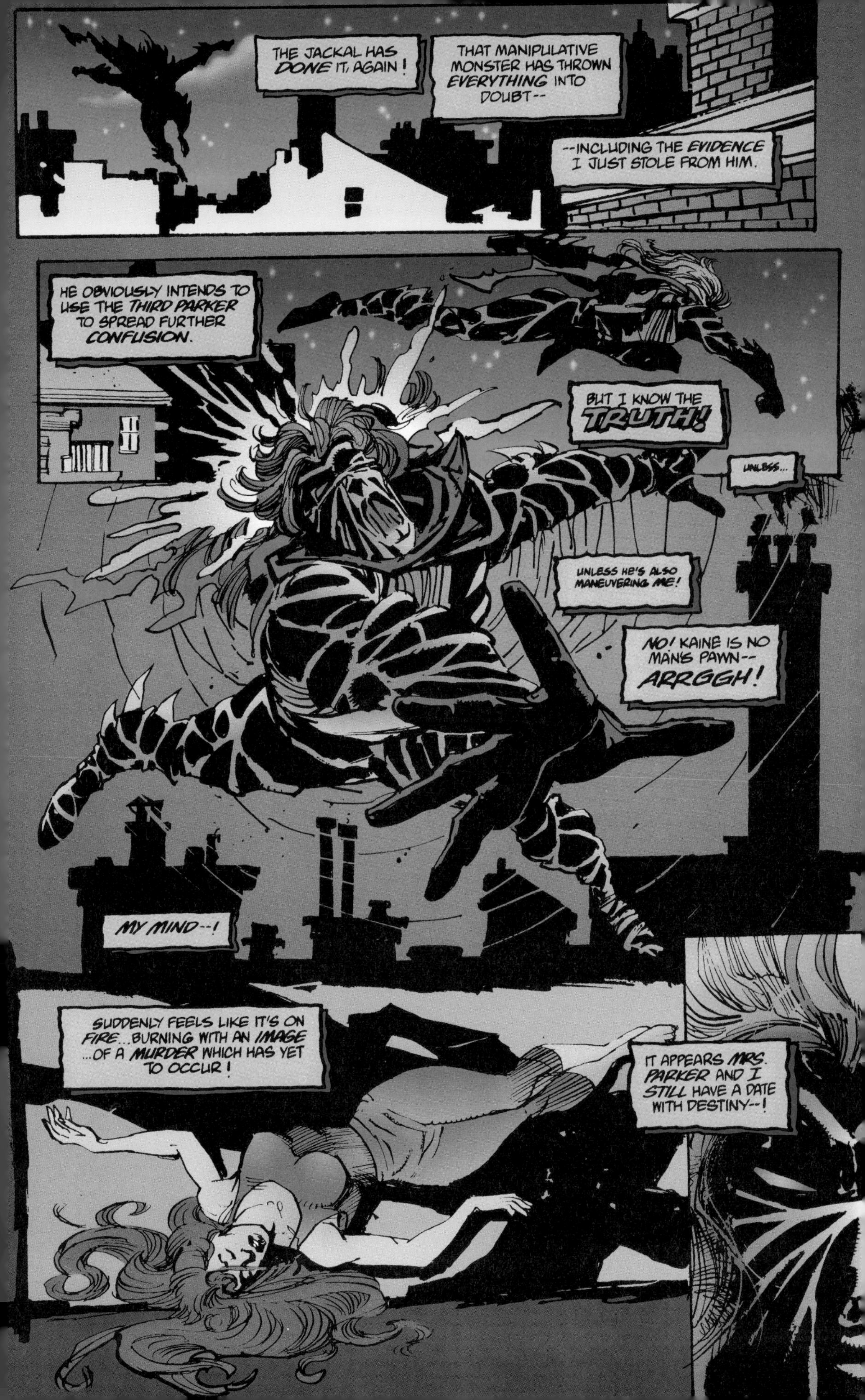
THE JACKAL HAS DONE IT, AGAIN!
THAT MANIPULATIVE MONSTER HAS THROWN EVERYTHING INTO DOUBT--
--INCLUDING THE EVIDENCE I JUST STOLE FROM HIM.
HE OBVIOUSLY INTENDS TO USE THE THIRD PARKER TO SPREAD FURTHER CONFUSION.
BUT I KNOW THE TRUTH!
UNLESS...
UNLESS HE'S ALSO MANEUVERING ME!
NO! KAINE IS NO MAN'S PAWN-- ARRGGH!
MY MIND--!
SUDDENLY FEELS LIKE IT'S ON FIRE...BURNING WITH AN IMAGE ...OF A MURDER WHICH HAS YET TO OCCUR!
IT APPEARS MRS. PARKER AND I STILL HAVE A DATE WITH DESTINY--!

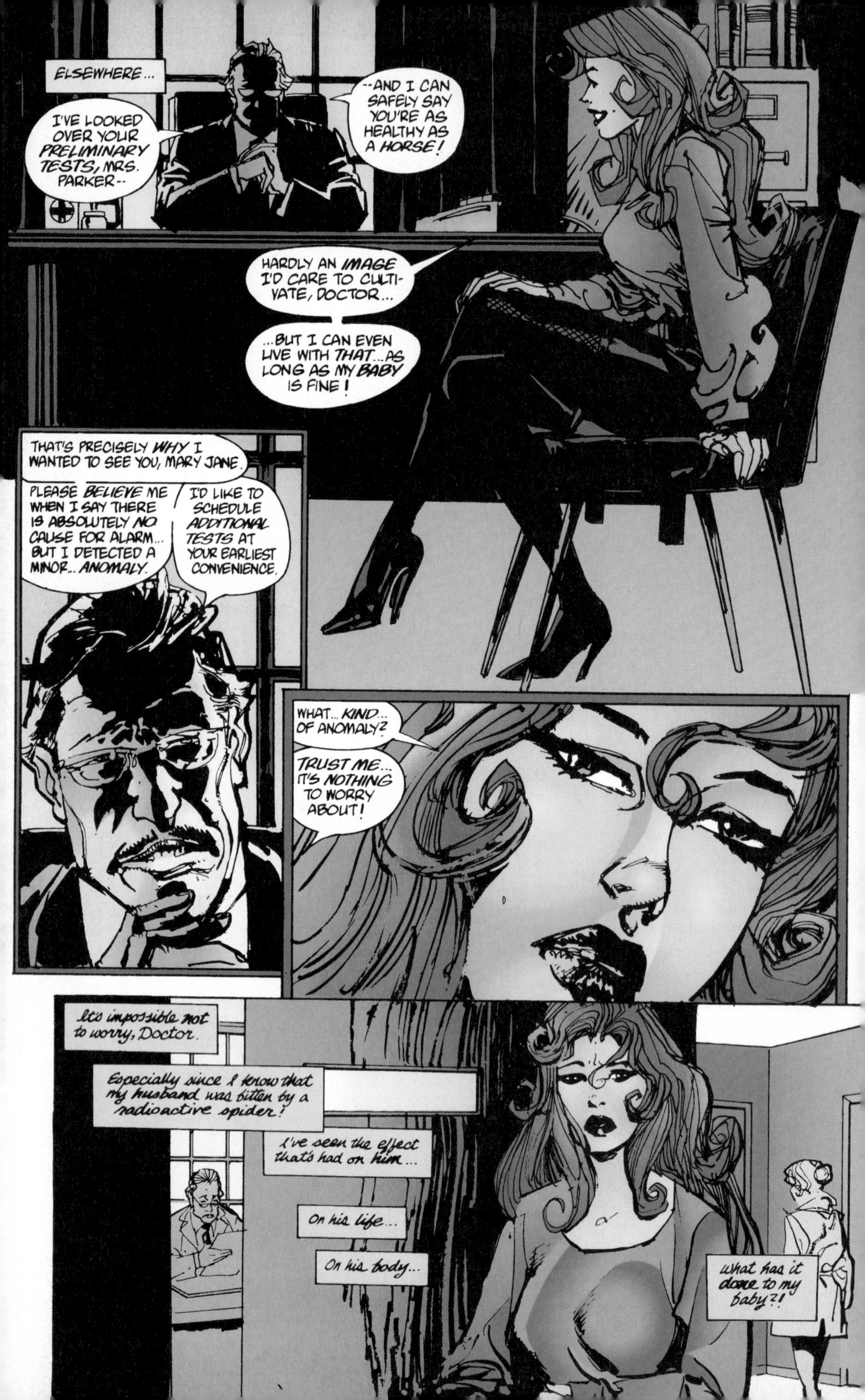
ELSEWHERE...
I'VE LOOKED OVER YOUR PRELIMINARY TESTS, MRS. PARKER--
--AND I CAN SAFELY SAY YOU'RE AS HEALTHY AS A HORSE!
HARDLY AN IMAGE I'D CARE TO CULTI-VATE, DOCTOR...
...BUT I CAN EVEN LIVE WITH THAT...AS LONG AS MY BABY IS FINE!
THAT'S PRECISELY WHY I WANTED TO SEE YOU, MARY JANE.
PLEASE BELIEVE ME WHEN I SAY THERE IS ABSOLUTELY NO CAUSE FOR ALARM... BUT I DETECTED A MINOR... ANOMALY.
I'D LIKE TO SCHEDULE ADDITIONAL TESTS AT YOUR EARLIEST CONVENIENCE.
WHAT... KIND... OF ANOMALY?
TRUST ME... IT'S NOTHING TO WORRY ABOUT!
It's impossible not to worry, Doctor.
Especially since I know that my husband was bitten by a radioactive spider!
I've seen the effect that's had on him...
On his life...
On his body...
What has it done to my baby?!

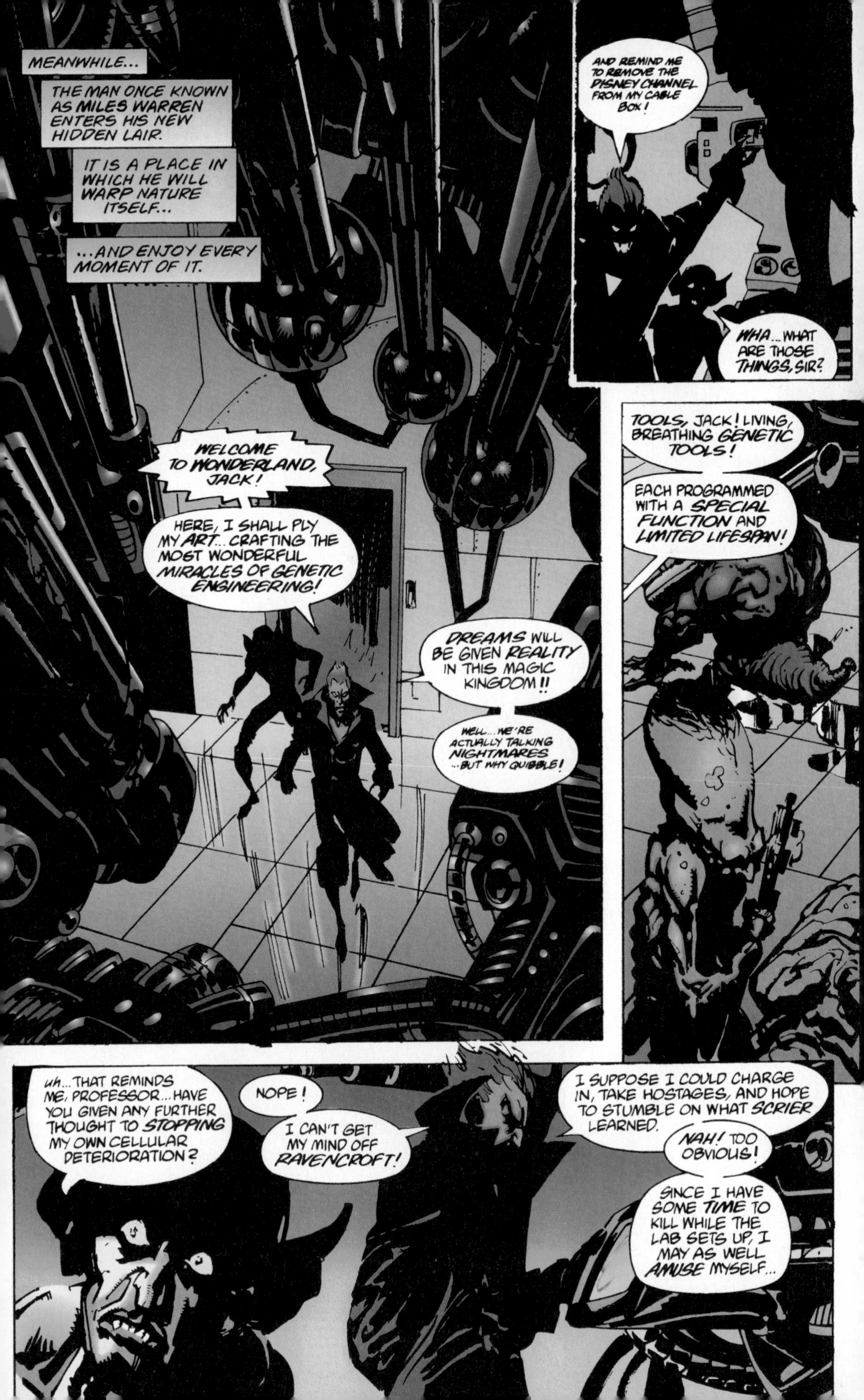
MEANWHILE...
THE MAN ONCE KNOWN AS MILES WARREN ENTERS HIS NEW HIDDEN LAIR.
IT IS A PLACE IN WHICH HE WILL WARP NATURE ITSELF...
...AND ENJOY EVERY MOMENT OF IT.
WELCOME TO WONDERLAND, JACK!
HERE, I SHALL PLY MY ART... CRAFTING THE MOST WONDERFUL MIRACLES OF GENETIC ENGINEERING!
DREAMS WILL BE GIVEN REALITY IN THIS MAGIC KINGDOM!!
WELL... WE'RE ACTUALLY TALKING NIGHTMARES ...BUT WHY QUIBBLE!
AND REMIND ME TO REMOVE THE DISNEY CHANNEL FROM MY CABLE BOX!
WHA... WHAT ARE THOSE THINGS, SIR?
TOOLS, JACK! LIVING, BREATHING GENETIC TOOLS!
EACH PROGRAMMED WITH A SPECIAL FUNCTION AND LIMITED LIFESPAN!
uh... THAT REMINDS ME, PROFESSOR... HAVE YOU GIVEN ANY FURTHER THOUGHT TO STOPPING MY OWN CELLULAR DETERIORATION?
NOPE!
I CAN'T GET MY MIND OFF RAVENCROFT!
I SUPPOSE I COULD CHARGE IN, TAKE HOSTAGES, AND HOPE TO STUMBLE ON WHAT SCRIER LEARNED.
NAH! TOO OBVIOUS!
SINCE I HAVE SOME TIME TO KILL WHILE THE LAB SETS UP, I MAY AS WELL AMUSE MYSELF...

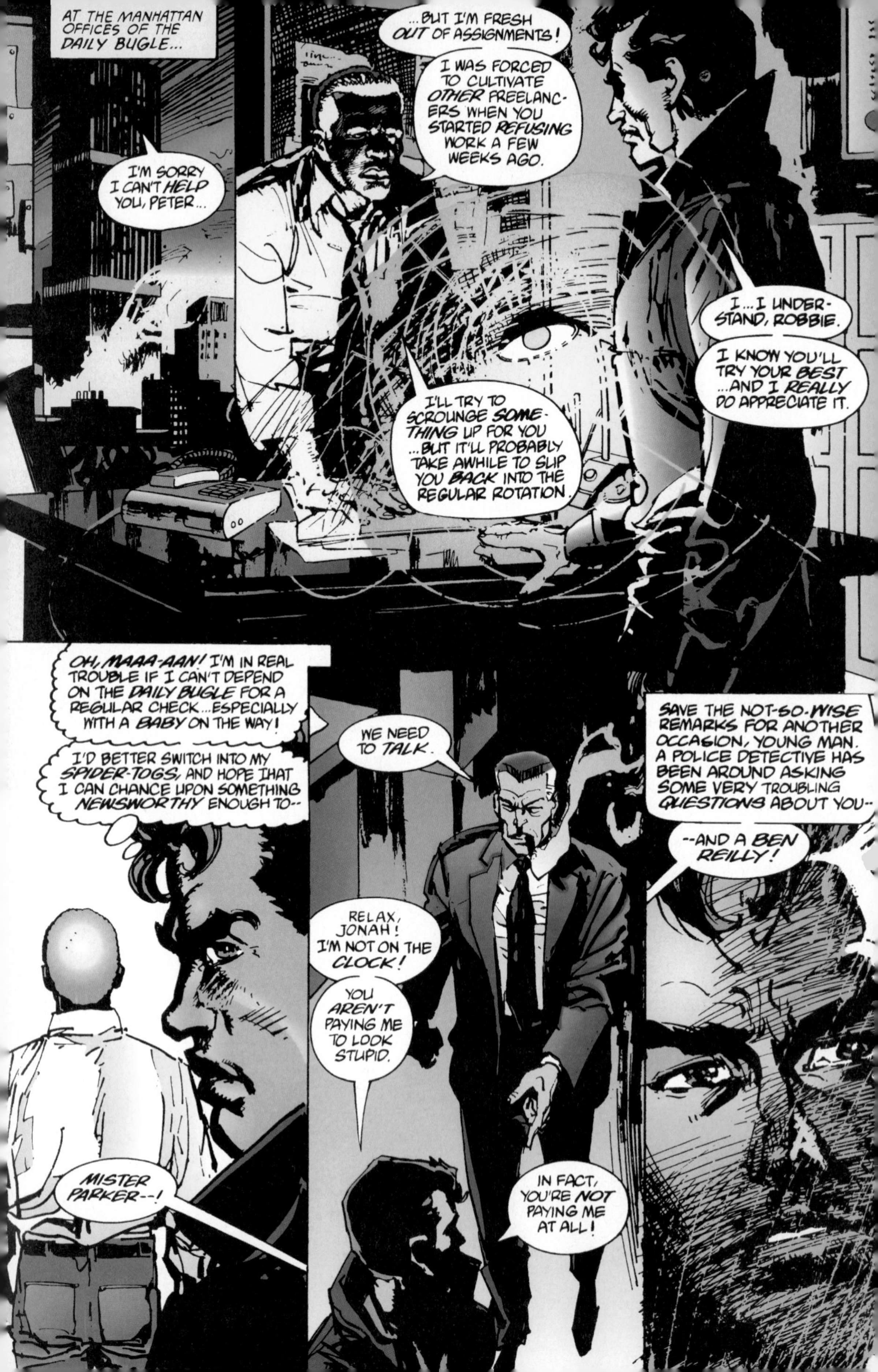
AT THE MANHATTAN OFFICES OF THE DAILY BUGLE...
I'M SORRY I CAN'T HELP YOU, PETER...
...BUT I'M FRESH OUT OF ASSIGNMENTS!
I WAS FORCED TO CULTIVATE OTHER FREELANCERS WHEN YOU STARTED REFUSING WORK A FEW WEEKS AGO.
I'LL TRY TO SCROUNGE SOMETHING UP FOR YOU ...BUT IT'LL PROBABLY TAKE AWHILE TO SLIP YOU BACK INTO THE REGULAR ROTATION.
I...I UNDERSTAND, ROBBIE.
I KNOW YOU'LL TRY YOUR BEST ...AND I REALLY DO APPRECIATE IT.
OH, MAAA-AAN! I'M IN REAL TROUBLE IF I CAN'T DEPEND ON THE DAILY BUGLE FOR A REGULAR CHECK...ESPECIALLY WITH A BABY ON THE WAY!
I'D BETTER SWITCH INTO MY SPIDER-TOGS, AND HOPE THAT I CAN CHANCE UPON SOMETHING NEWSWORTHY ENOUGH TO--
MISTER PARKER--!
WE NEED TO TALK.
RELAX, JONAH! I'M NOT ON THE CLOCK!
YOU AREN'T PAYING ME TO LOOK STUPID.
IN FACT, YOU'RE NOT PAYING ME AT ALL!
SAVE THE NOT-SO-WISE REMARKS FOR ANOTHER OCCASION, YOUNG MAN. A POLICE DETECTIVE HAS BEEN AROUND ASKING SOME VERY TROUBLING QUESTIONS ABOUT YOU--
--AND A BEN REILLY!

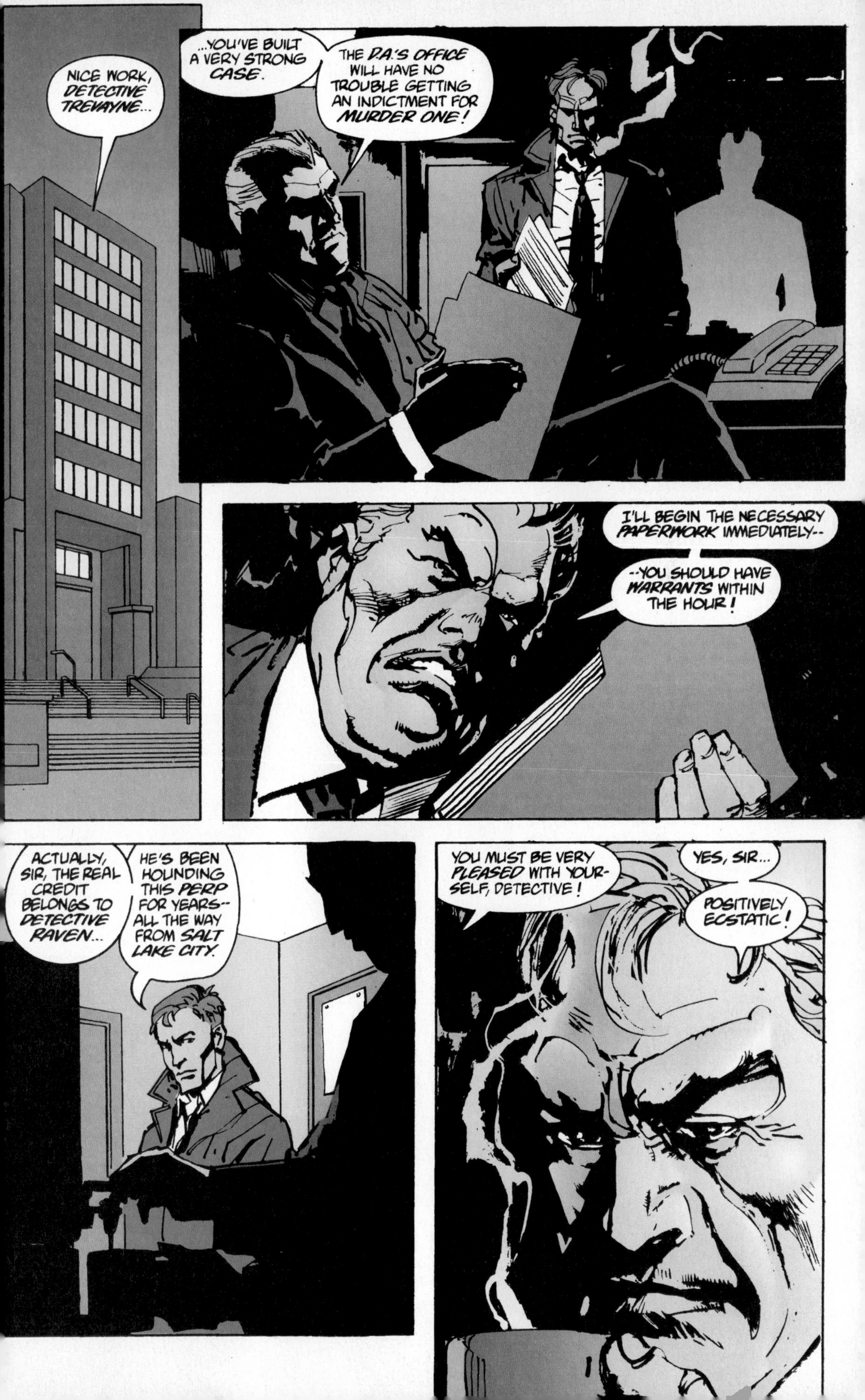
NICE WORK, DETECTIVE TREVAYNE...
...YOU'VE BUILT A VERY STRONG CASE.
THE D.A.'S OFFICE WILL HAVE NO TROUBLE GETTING AN INDICTMENT FOR MURDER ONE!
I'LL BEGIN THE NECESSARY PAPERWORK IMMEDIATELY--
--YOU SHOULD HAVE WARRANTS WITHIN THE HOUR!
ACTUALLY, SIR, THE REAL CREDIT BELONGS TO DETECTIVE RAVEN...
HE'S BEEN HOUNDING THIS PERP FOR YEARS-- ALL THE WAY FROM SALT LAKE CITY.
YOU MUST BE VERY PLEASED WITH YOURSELF, DETECTIVE!
YES, SIR...
POSITIVELY ECSTATIC!

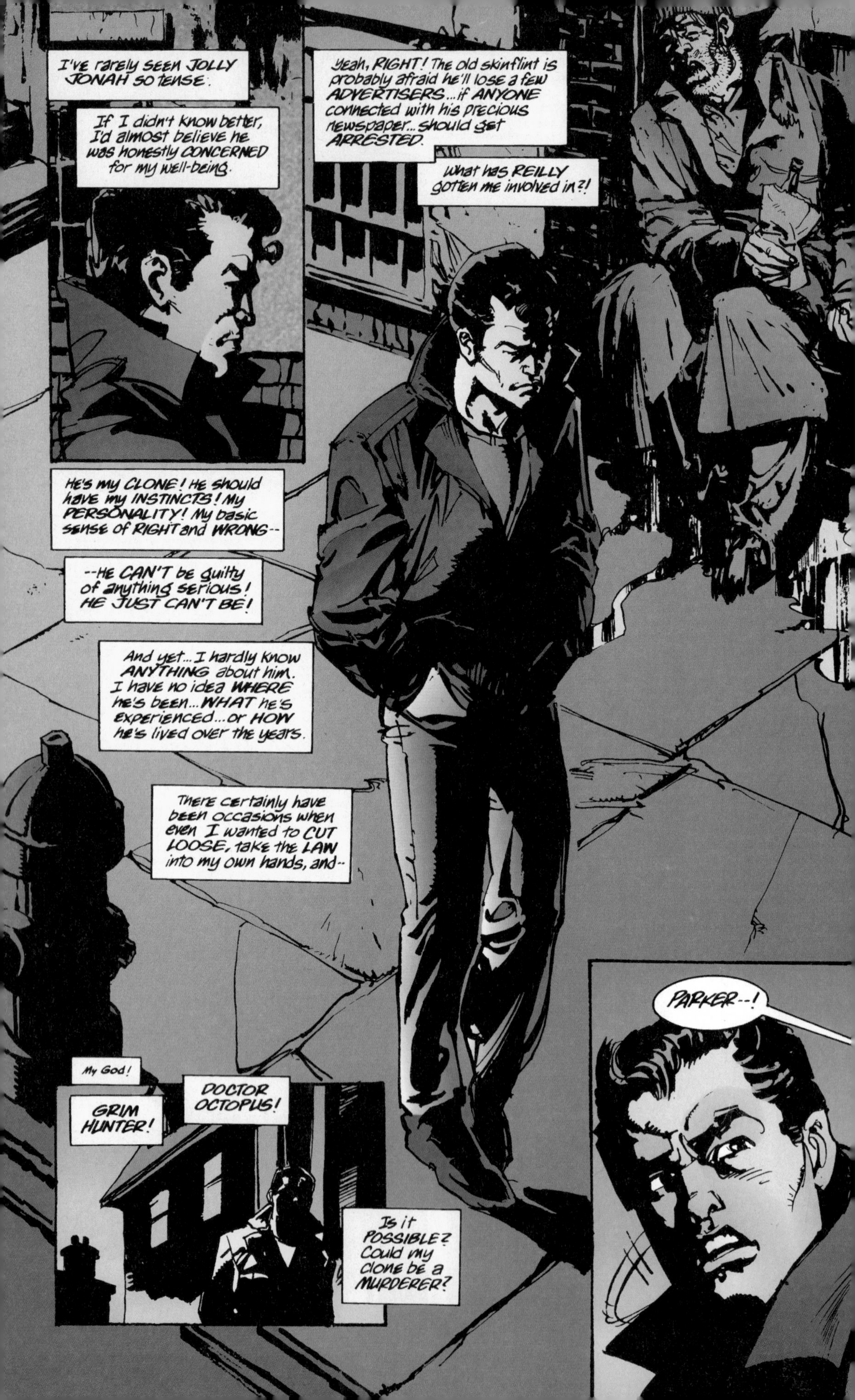
I've rarely seen JOLLY JONAH so tense.
If I didn't know better, I'd almost believe he was honestly CONCERNED for my well-being.
Yeah, RIGHT! The old skinflint is probably afraid he'll lose a few ADVERTISERS...if ANYONE connected with his precious newspaper...should get ARRESTED.
What has REILLY gotten me involved in?!
He's my CLONE! He should have my INSTINCTS! My PERSONALITY! My basic sense of RIGHT and WRONG--
--HE CAN'T be guilty of anything serious! HE JUST CAN'T BE!
And yet...I hardly know ANYTHING about him. I have no idea WHERE he's been...WHAT he's experienced...or HOW he's lived over the years.
There certainly have been occasions when even I wanted to CUT LOOSE, take the LAW into my own hands, and--
My God!
GRIM HUNTER!
DOCTOR OCTOPUS!
Is it POSSIBLE? Could my clone be a MURDERER?
PARKER--!

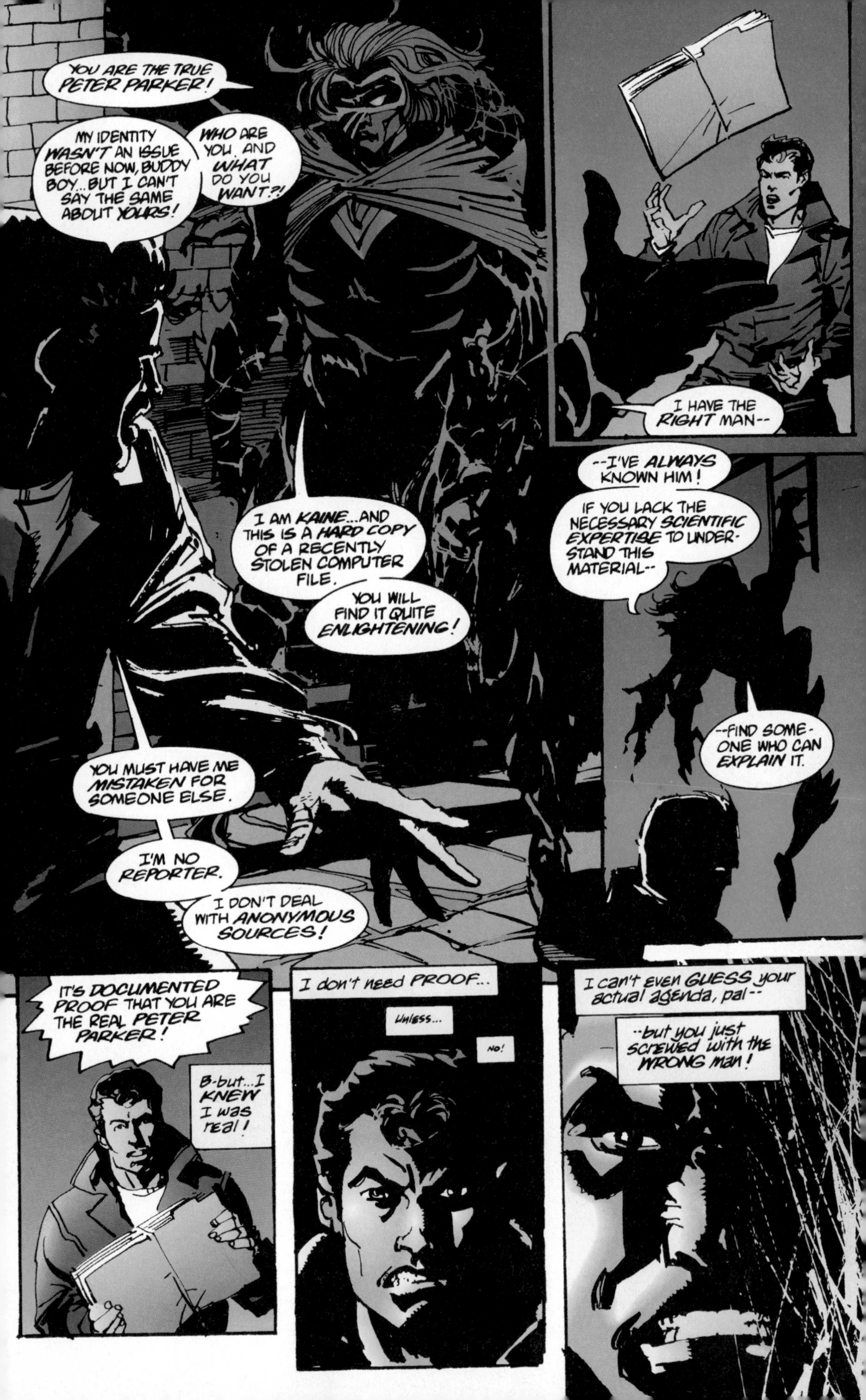
YOU ARE THE TRUE PETER PARKER!
MY IDENTITY WASN'T AN ISSUE BEFORE NOW, BUDDY BOY... BUT I CAN'T SAY THE SAME ABOUT YOURS!
WHO ARE YOU, AND WHAT DO YOU WANT?!
I AM KAINE... AND THIS IS A HARD COPY OF A RECENTLY STOLEN COMPUTER FILE.
YOU WILL FIND IT QUITE ENLIGHTENING!
YOU MUST HAVE ME MISTAKEN FOR SOMEONE ELSE.
I'M NO REPORTER.
I DON'T DEAL WITH ANONYMOUS SOURCES!
I HAVE THE RIGHT MAN--
--I'VE ALWAYS KNOWN HIM!
IF YOU LACK THE NECESSARY SCIENTIFIC EXPERTISE TO UNDERSTAND THIS MATERIAL--
--FIND SOMEONE WHO CAN EXPLAIN IT.
IT'S DOCUMENTED PROOF THAT YOU ARE THE REAL PETER PARKER!
B-but... I KNEW I was real!
I don't need PROOF...
Unless...
No!
I can't even GUESS your actual agenda, pal--
--but you just screwed with the WRONG man!

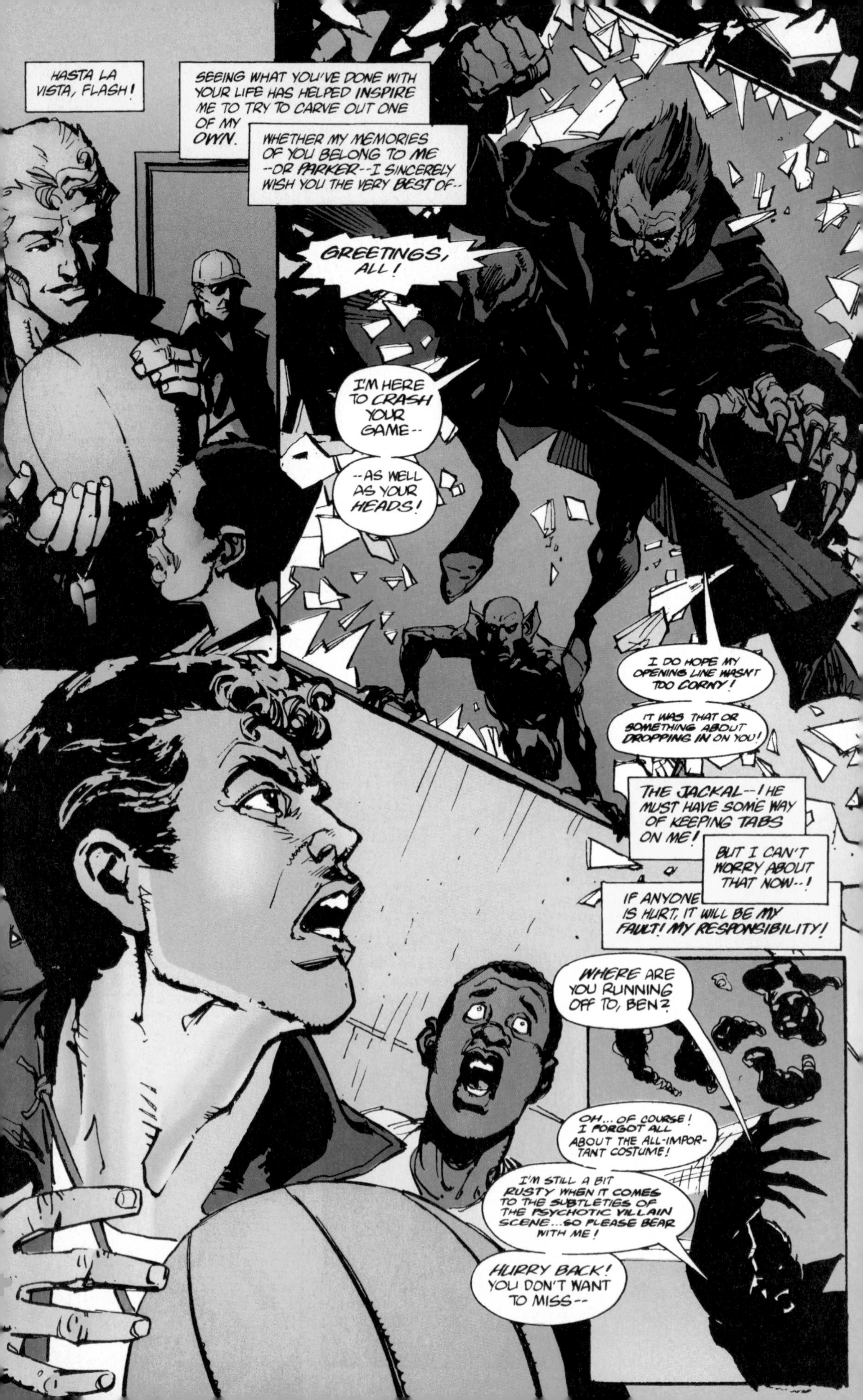
HASTA LA VISTA, FLASH!
SEEING WHAT YOU'VE DONE WITH YOUR LIFE HAS HELPED INSPIRE ME TO TRY TO CARVE OUT ONE OF MY OWN.
WHETHER MY MEMORIES OF YOU BELONG TO ME --OR PARKER--I SINCERELY WISH YOU THE VERY BEST OF--
GREETINGS, ALL!
I'M HERE TO CRASH YOUR GAME--
--AS WELL AS YOUR HEADS!
I DO HOPE MY OPENING LINE WASN'T TOO CORNY!
IT WAS THAT OR SOMETHING ABOUT DROPPING IN ON YOU!
THE JACKAL--! HE MUST HAVE SOME WAY OF KEEPING TABS ON ME!
BUT I CAN'T WORRY ABOUT THAT NOW--!
IF ANYONE IS HURT, IT WILL BE MY FAULT! MY RESPONSIBILITY!
WHERE ARE YOU RUNNING OFF TO, BEN?
OH... OF COURSE! I FORGOT ALL ABOUT THE ALL-IMPORTANT COSTUME!
I'M STILL A BIT RUSTY WHEN IT COMES TO THE SUBTLETIES OF THE PSYCHOTIC VILLAIN SCENE... SO PLEASE BEAR WITH ME!
HURRY BACK! YOU DON'T WANT TO MISS--

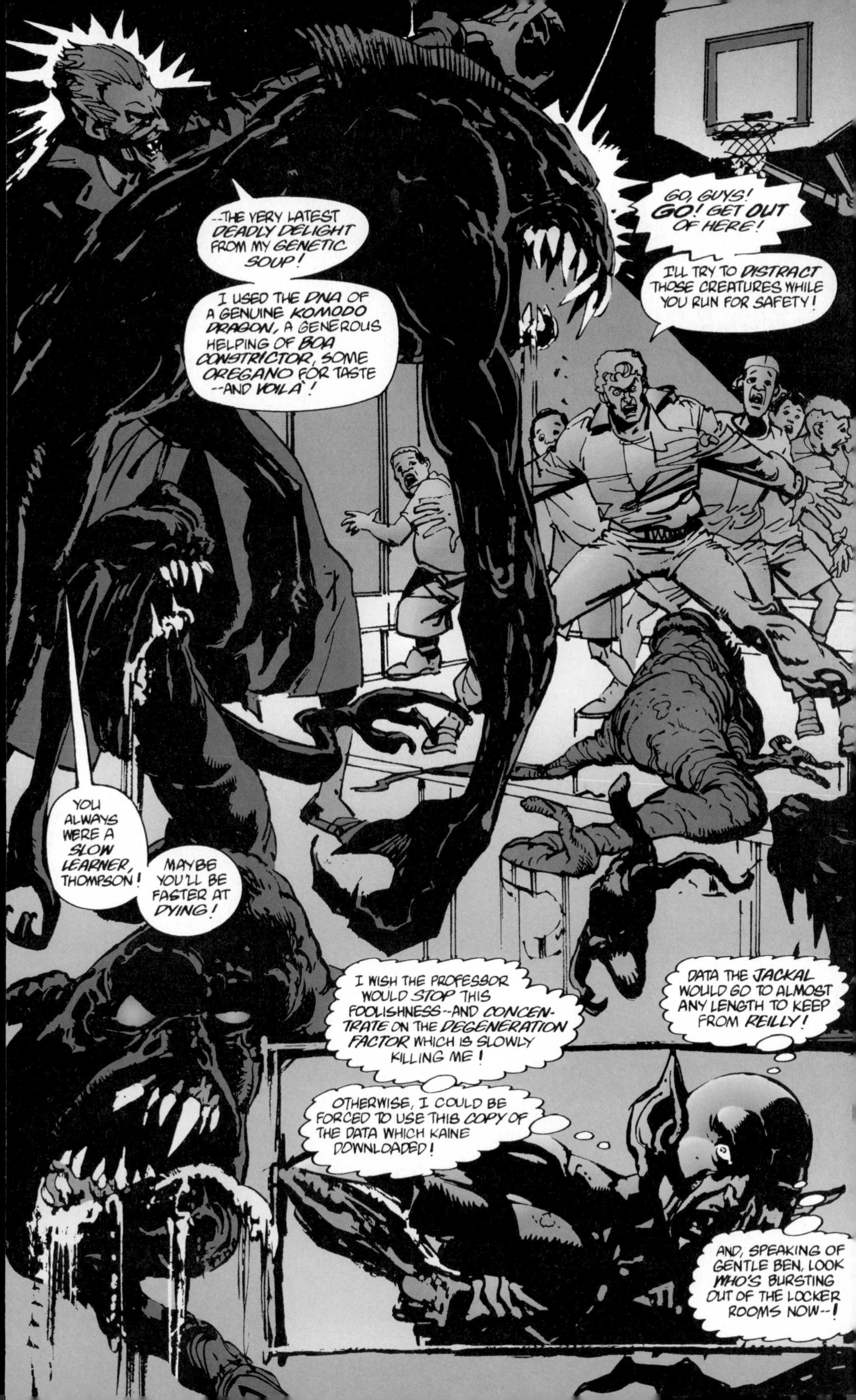
--THE VERY LATEST DEADLY DELIGHT FROM MY GENETIC SOUP!
I USED THE DNA OF A GENUINE KOMODO DRAGON, A GENEROUS HELPING OF BOA CONSTRICTOR, SOME OREGANO FOR TASTE --AND VOILÀ!
GO, GUYS! GO! GET OUT OF HERE!
I'LL TRY TO DISTRACT THOSE CREATURES WHILE YOU RUN FOR SAFETY!
YOU ALWAYS WERE A SLOW LEARNER, THOMPSON!
MAYBE YOU'LL BE FASTER AT DYING!
I WISH THE PROFESSOR WOULD STOP THIS FOOLISHNESS--AND CONCENTRATE ON THE DEGENERATION FACTOR WHICH IS SLOWLY KILLING ME!
DATA THE JACKAL WOULD GO TO ALMOST ANY LENGTH TO KEEP FROM REILLY!
OTHERWISE, I COULD BE FORCED TO USE THIS COPY OF THE DATA WHICH KAINE DOWNLOADED!
AND, SPEAKING OF GENTLE BEN, LOOK WHO'S BURSTING OUT OF THE LOCKER ROOMS NOW--!

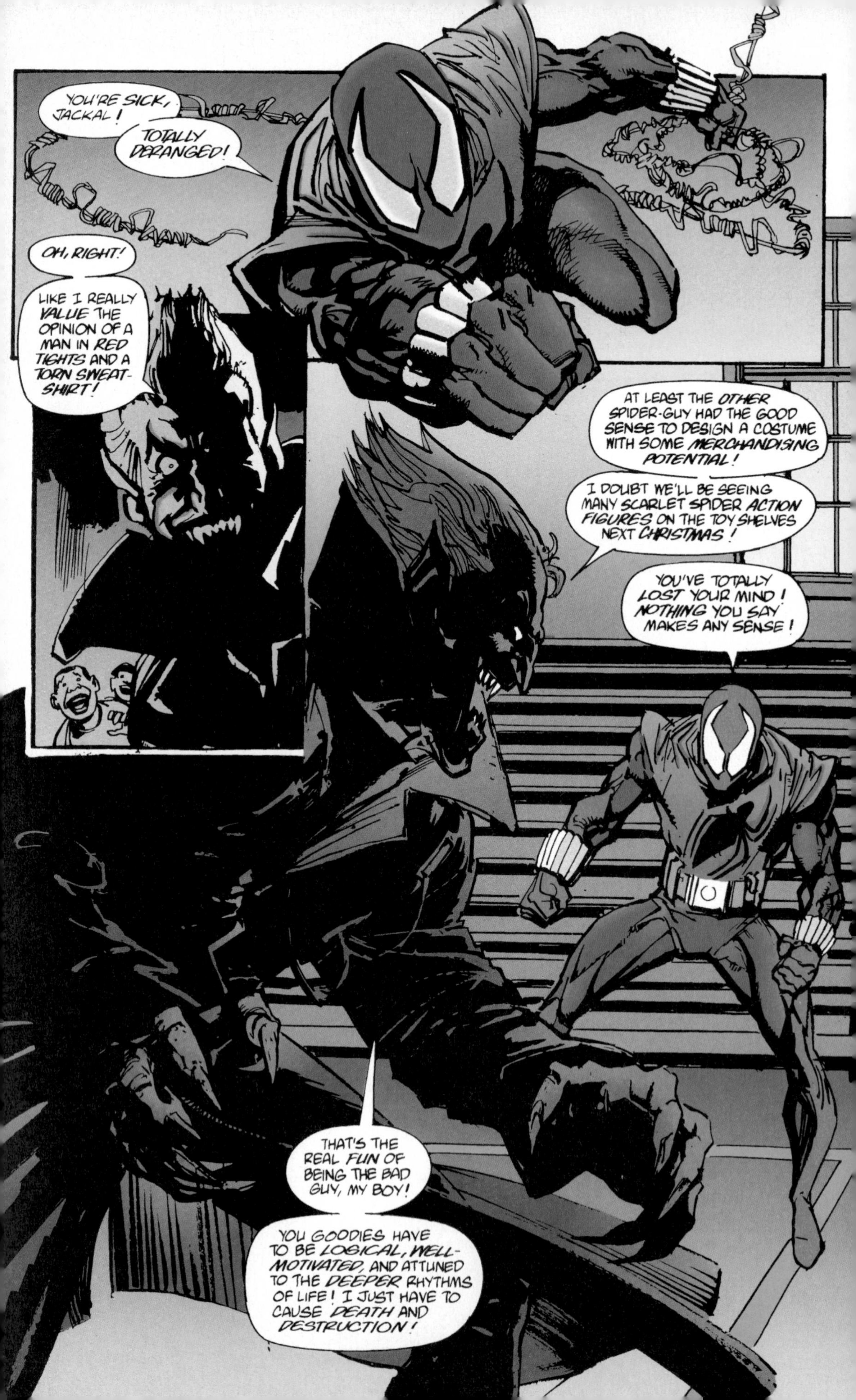
YOU'RE SICK, JACKAL!
TOTALLY DERANGED!
OH, RIGHT!
LIKE I REALLY VALUE THE OPINION OF A MAN IN RED TIGHTS AND A TORN SWEAT-SHIRT!
AT LEAST THE OTHER SPIDER-GUY HAD THE GOOD SENSE TO DESIGN A COSTUME WITH SOME MERCHANDISING POTENTIAL!
I DOUBT WE'LL BE SEEING MANY SCARLET SPIDER ACTION FIGURES ON THE TOY SHELVES NEXT CHRISTMAS!
YOU'VE TOTALLY LOST YOUR MIND! NOTHING YOU SAY MAKES ANY SENSE!
THAT'S THE REAL FUN OF BEING THE BAD GUY, MY BOY!
YOU GOODIES HAVE TO BE LOGICAL, WELL-MOTIVATED, AND ATTUNED TO THE DEEPER RHYTHMS OF LIFE! I JUST HAVE TO CAUSE DEATH AND DESTRUCTION!

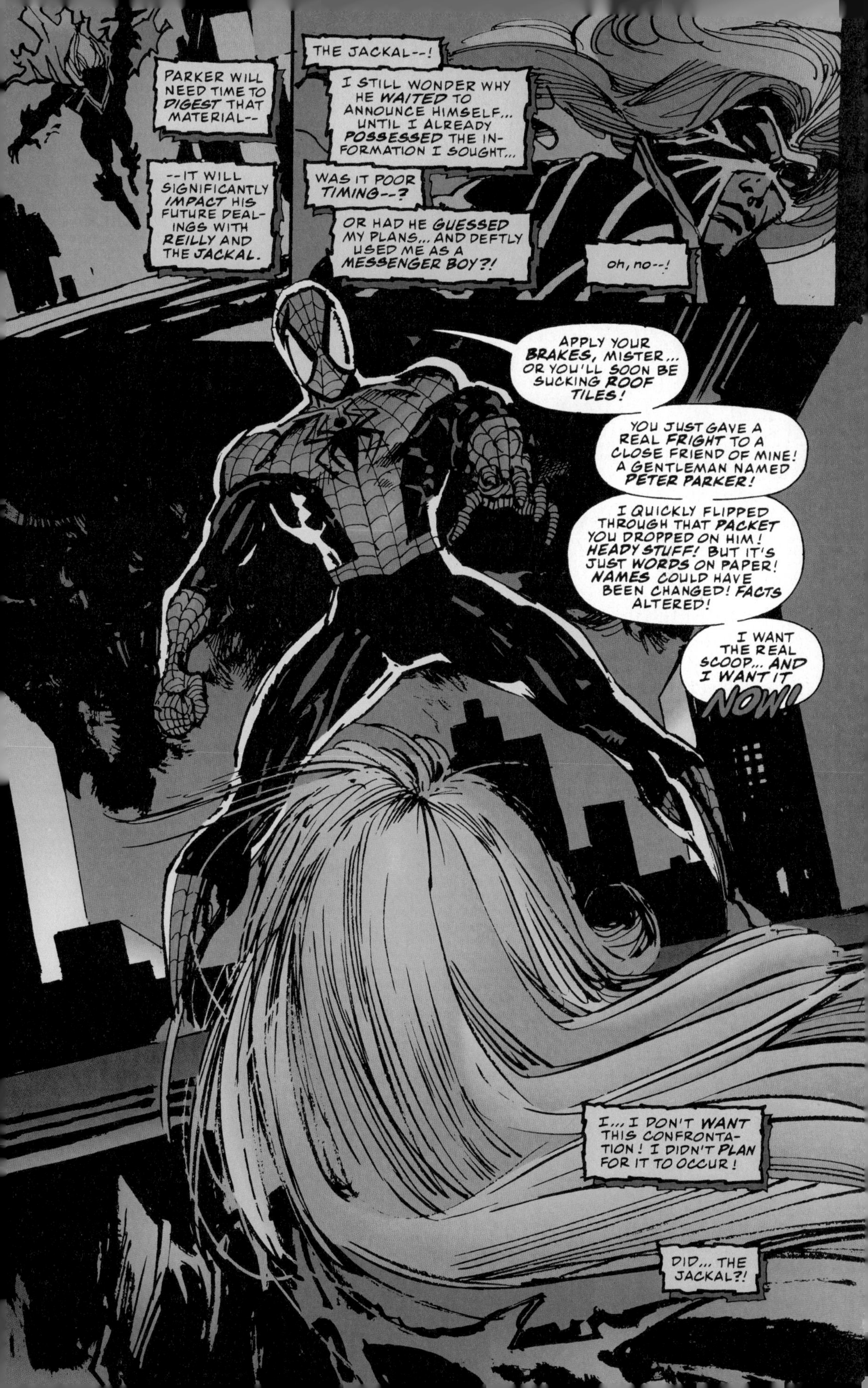
PARKER WILL NEED TIME TO DIGEST THAT MATERIAL--
--IT WILL SIGNIFICANTLY IMPACT HIS FUTURE DEALINGS WITH REILLY AND THE JACKAL.
THE JACKAL--!
I STILL WONDER WHY HE WAITED TO ANNOUNCE HIMSELF... UNTIL I ALREADY POSSESSED THE INFORMATION I SOUGHT...
WAS IT POOR TIMING--?
OR HAD HE GUESSED MY PLANS... AND DEFTLY USED ME AS A MESSENGER BOY?!
oh, no--!
APPLY YOUR BRAKES, MISTER... OR YOU'LL SOON BE SUCKING ROOF TILES!
YOU JUST GAVE A REAL FRIGHT TO A CLOSE FRIEND OF MINE! A GENTLEMAN NAMED PETER PARKER!
I QUICKLY FLIPPED THROUGH THAT PACKET YOU DROPPED ON HIM! HEADY STUFF! BUT IT'S JUST WORDS ON PAPER! NAMES COULD HAVE BEEN CHANGED! FACTS ALTERED!
I WANT THE REAL SCOOP... AND I WANT IT NOW!
I... I DON'T WANT THIS CONFRONTATION! I DIDN'T PLAN FOR IT TO OCCUR!
DID... THE JACKAL?!

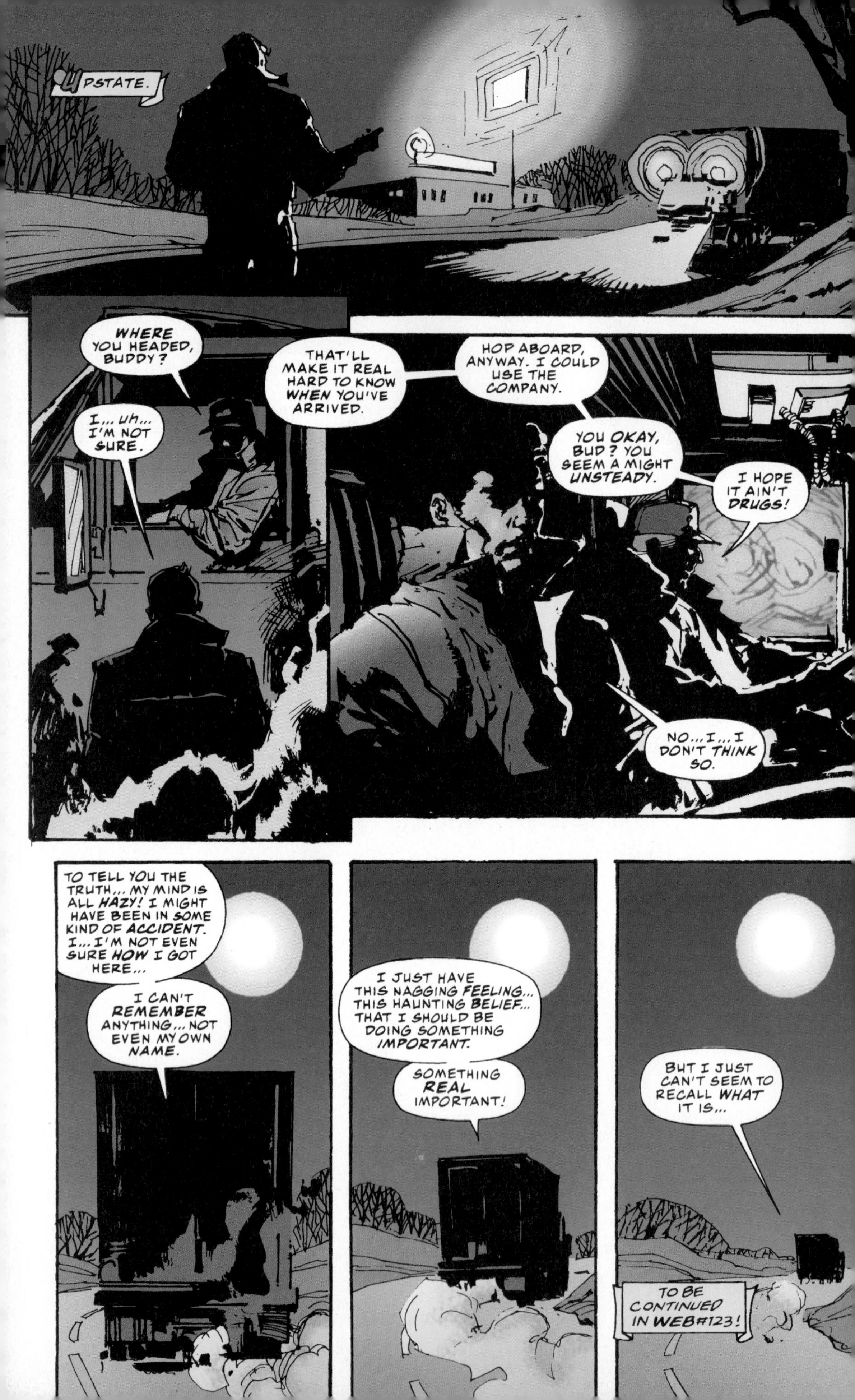
UPSTATE.
WHERE YOU HEADED, BUDDY?
I... uh... I'M NOT SURE.
THAT'LL MAKE IT REAL HARD TO KNOW WHEN YOU'VE ARRIVED.
HOP ABOARD, ANYWAY. I COULD USE THE COMPANY.
YOU OKAY, BUD? YOU SEEM A MIGHT UNSTEADY.
I HOPE IT AIN'T DRUGS!
NO... I... I DON'T THINK SO.
TO TELL YOU THE TRUTH... MY MIND IS ALL HAZY! I MIGHT HAVE BEEN IN SOME KIND OF ACCIDENT. I... I'M NOT EVEN SURE HOW I GOT HERE...
I CAN'T REMEMBER ANYTHING... NOT EVEN MY OWN NAME.
I JUST HAVE THIS NAGGING FEELING... THIS HAUNTING BELIEF... THAT I SHOULD BE DOING SOMETHING IMPORTANT.
SOMETHING REAL IMPORTANT!
BUT I JUST CAN'T SEEM TO RECALL WHAT IT IS...
TO BE CONTINUED IN WEB #123!

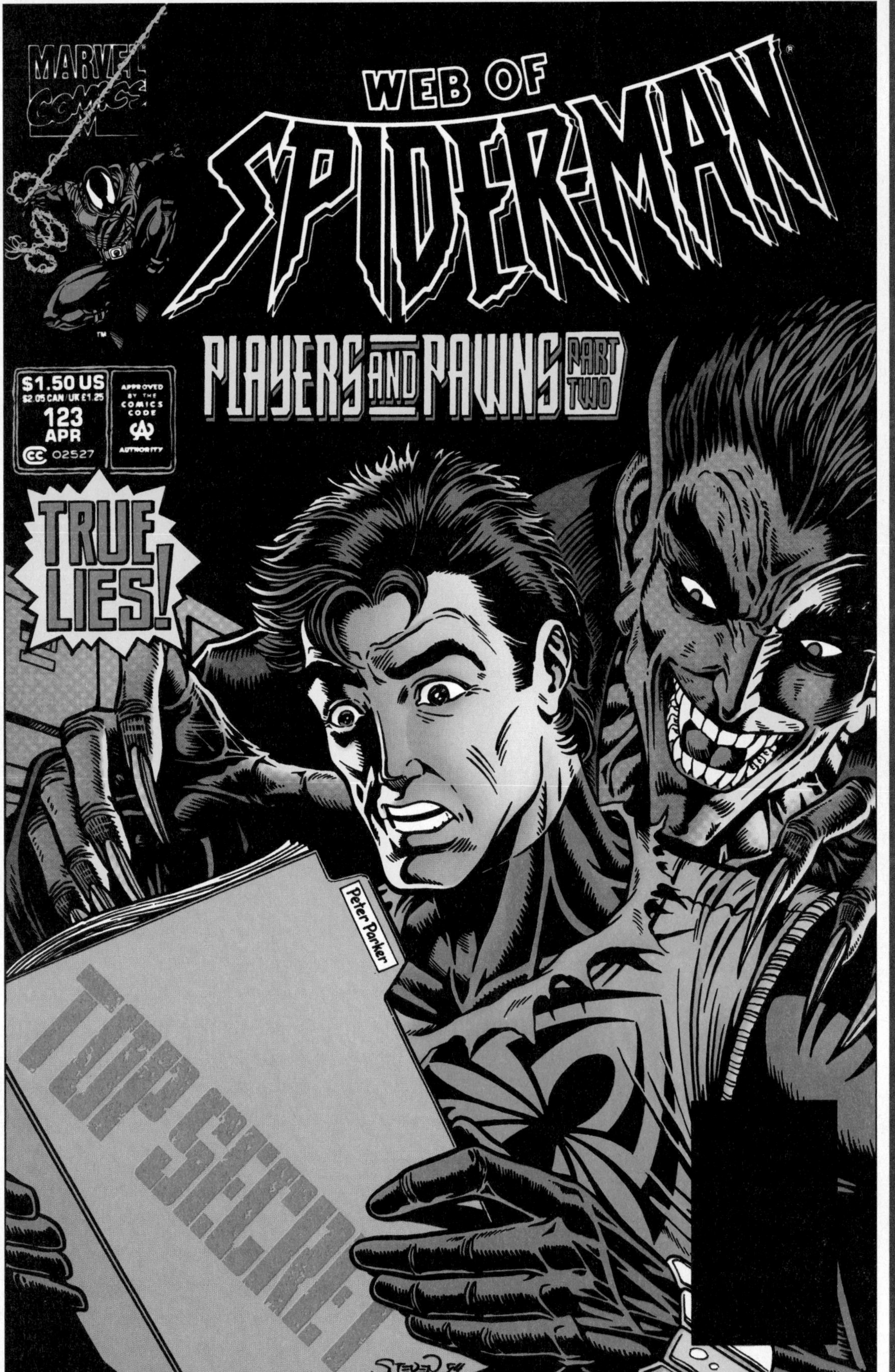

MARVEL COMICS
WEB OF SPIDER-MAN
PLAYERS AND PAWNS PART TWO
$1.50 US
$2.05 CAN / UK £1.25
123
APR
02527
APPROVED BY THE COMICS CODE AUTHORITY
TRUE LIES!
Peter Parker
TOP SECRET
STEVEN '94

STAN LEE
PRESENTS: **SPIDER-MAN AND THE SCARLET SPIDER!**

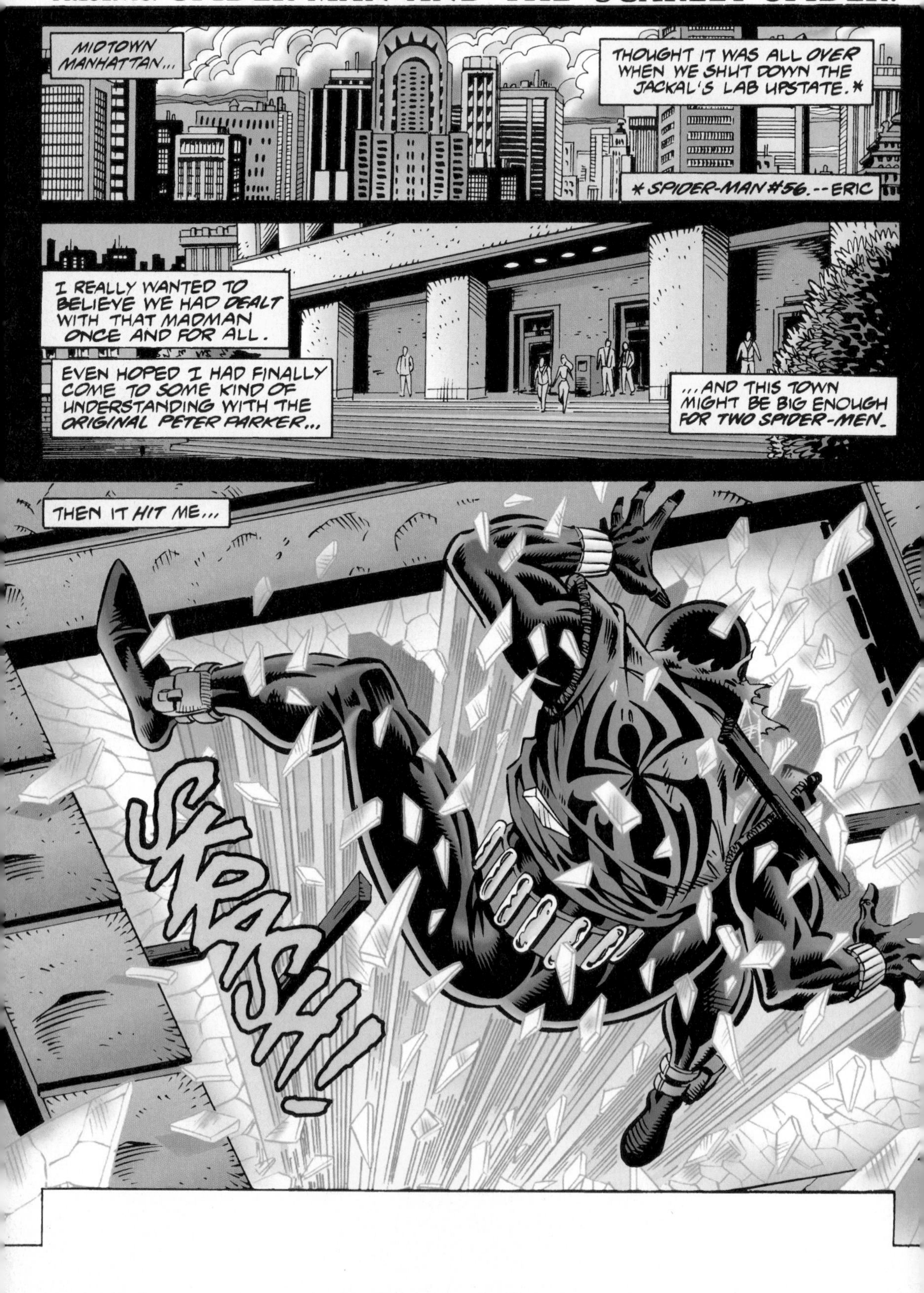

MIDTOWN MANHATTAN...
THOUGHT IT WAS ALL OVER WHEN WE SHUT DOWN THE JACKAL'S LAB UPSTATE.*
* SPIDER-MAN #56.--ERIC
I REALLY WANTED TO BELIEVE WE HAD DEALT WITH THAT MADMAN ONCE AND FOR ALL.
EVEN HOPED I HAD FINALLY COME TO SOME KIND OF UNDERSTANDING WITH THE ORIGINAL PETER PARKER...
...AND THIS TOWN MIGHT BE BIG ENOUGH FOR TWO SPIDER-MEN.
THEN IT HIT ME...
SKRASH!

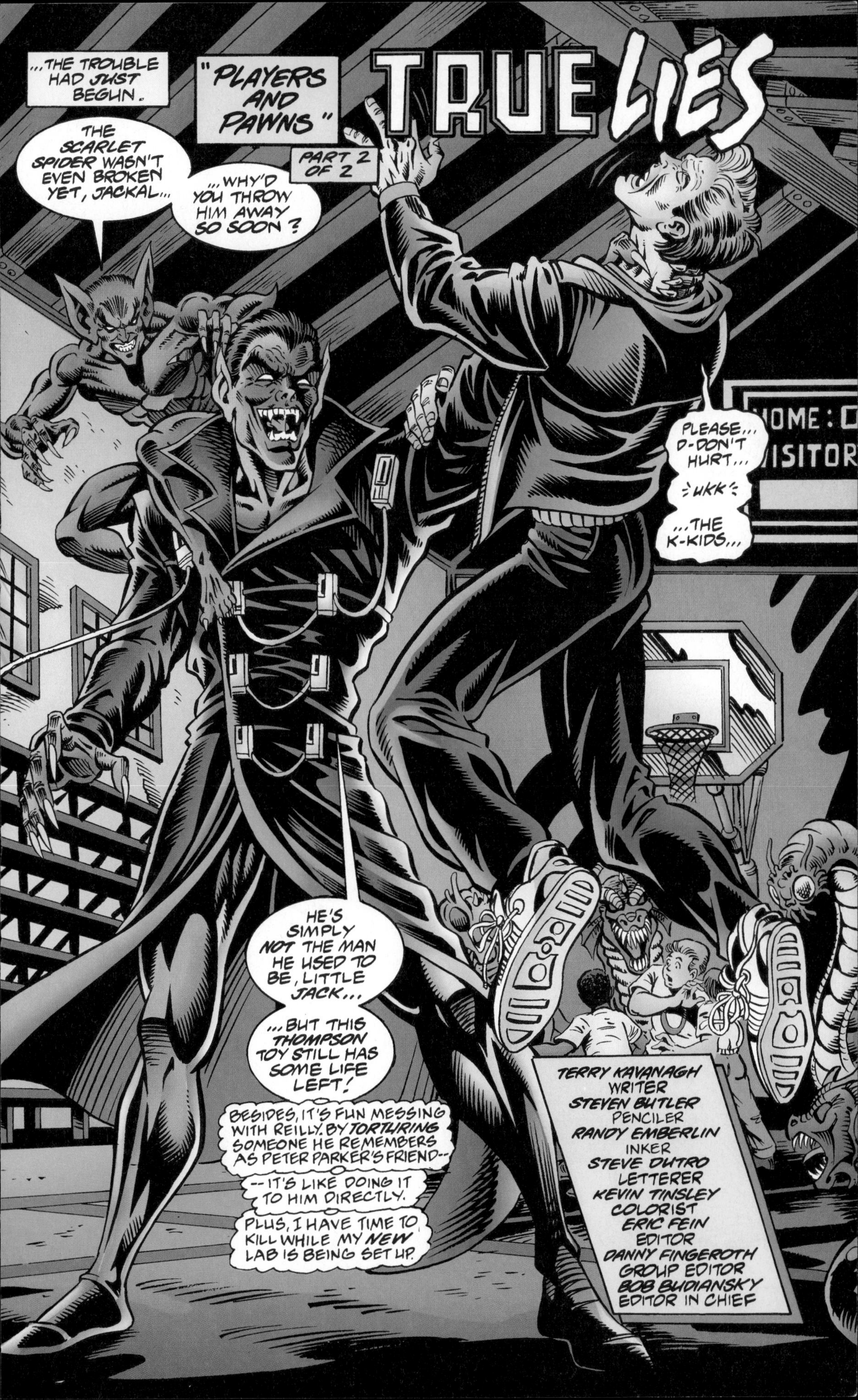
...THE TROUBLE HAD JUST BEGUN.
"PLAYERS AND PAWNS"
TRUE LIES
PART 2 OF 2
THE SCARLET SPIDER WASN'T EVEN BROKEN YET, JACKAL...
...WHY'D YOU THROW HIM AWAY SO SOON?
PLEASE... D-DON'T HURT...
UKK
...THE K-KIDS...
HOME: VISITOR
HE'S SIMPLY NOT THE MAN HE USED TO BE, LITTLE JACK...
...BUT THIS THOMPSON TOY STILL HAS SOME LIFE LEFT!
BESIDES, IT'S FUN MESSING WITH REILLY. BY TORTURING SOMEONE HE REMEMBERS AS PETER PARKER'S FRIEND--
--IT'S LIKE DOING IT TO HIM DIRECTLY.
PLUS, I HAVE TIME TO KILL WHILE MY NEW LAB IS BEING SET UP.
TERRY KAVANAGH WRITER
STEVEN BUTLER PENCILER
RANDY EMBERLIN INKER
STEVE DUTRO LETTERER
KEVIN TINSLEY COLORIST
ERIC FEIN EDITOR
DANNY FINGEROTH GROUP EDITOR
BOB BUDIANSKY EDITOR IN CHIEF

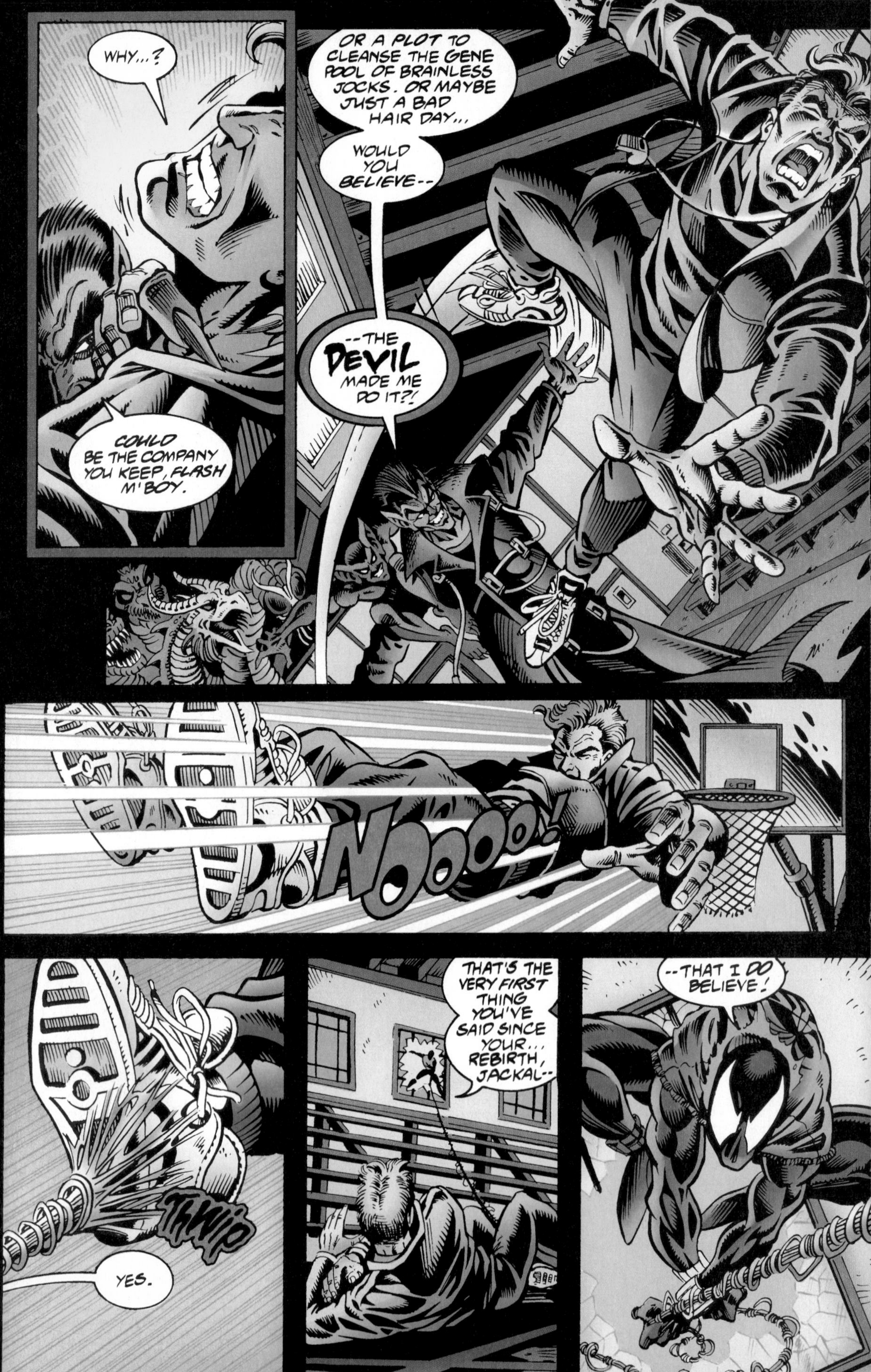
WHY...?
COULD BE THE COMPANY YOU KEEP, FLASH M'BOY.
OR A PLOT TO CLEANSE THE GENE POOL OF BRAINLESS JOCKS. OR MAYBE JUST A BAD HAIR DAY...
WOULD YOU BELIEVE--
--THE DEVIL MADE ME DO IT?!
NOOOOO!
THWIP
YES.
THAT'S THE VERY FIRST THING YOU'VE SAID SINCE YOUR... REBIRTH, JACKAL--
--THAT I DO BELIEVE!

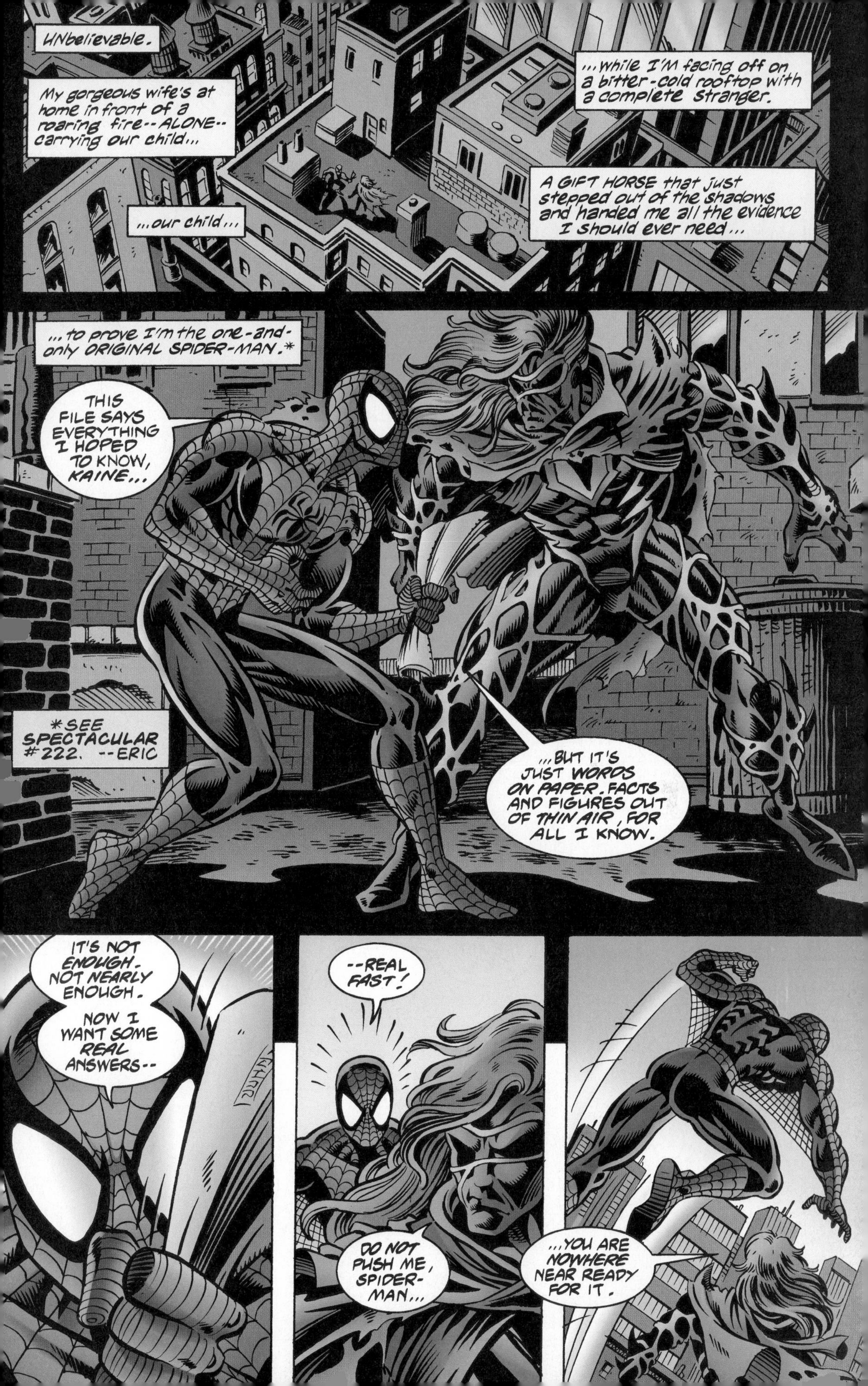
UNbelievable.
My gorgeous wife's at home in front of a roaring fire--ALONE--carrying our child...
...our child...
...while I'M facing off on a bitter-cold rooftop with a complete stranger.
A GIFT HORSE that just stepped out of the shadows and handed me all the evidence I should ever need...
...to prove I'm the one-and-only ORIGINAL SPIDER-MAN.*
THIS FILE SAYS EVERYTHING I HOPED TO KNOW, KAINE...
...BUT IT'S JUST WORDS ON PAPER. FACTS AND FIGURES OUT OF THIN AIR, FOR ALL I KNOW.
*SEE SPECTACULAR #222. --ERIC
IT'S NOT ENOUGH. NOT NEARLY ENOUGH.
NOW I WANT SOME REAL ANSWERS--
--REAL FAST!
DO NOT PUSH ME, SPIDER-MAN...
...YOU ARE NOWHERE NEAR READY FOR IT.

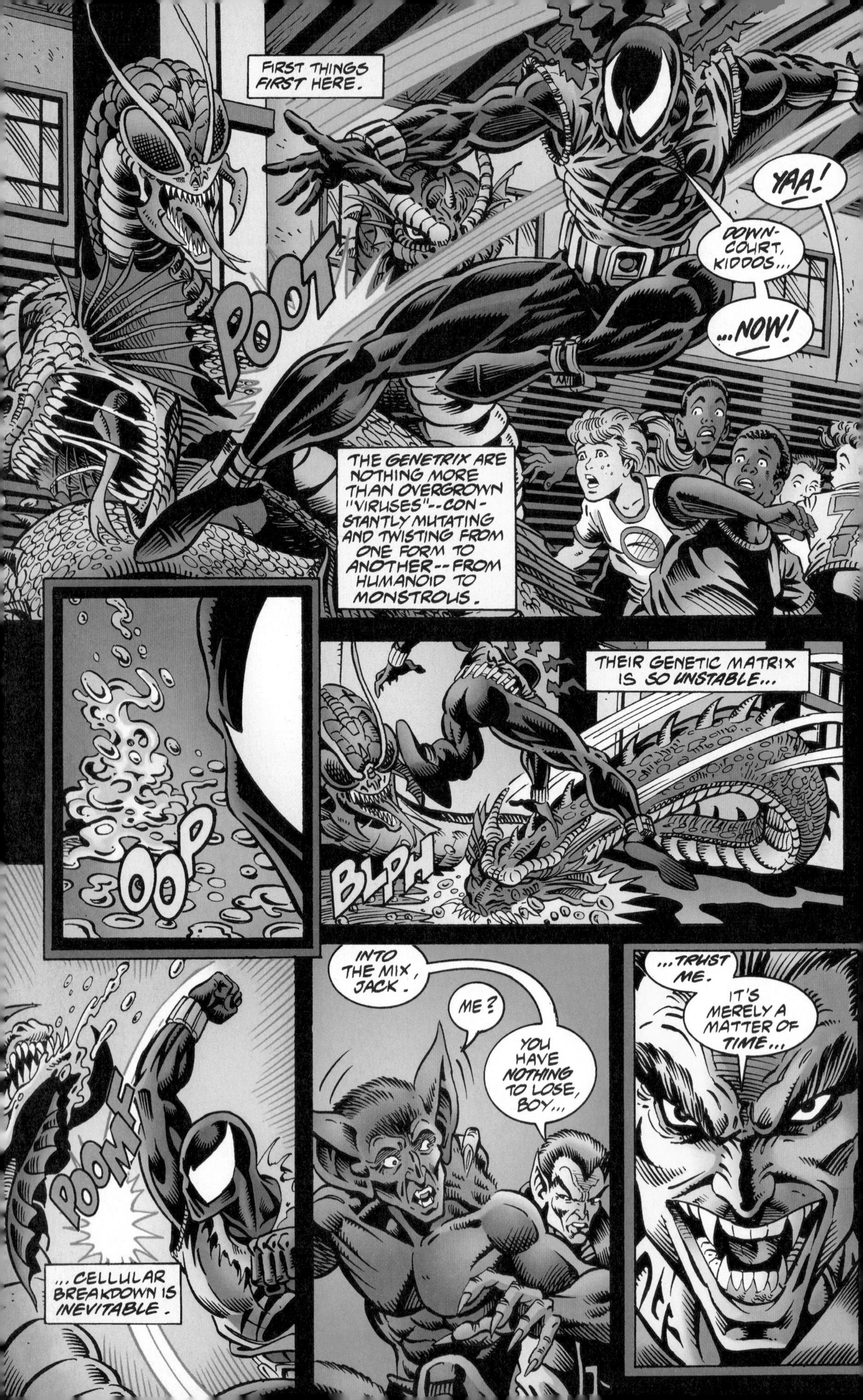
FIRST THINGS FIRST HERE.
POOT
YAA!
DOWN-COURT, KIDDOS...
...NOW!
THE GENETRIX ARE NOTHING MORE THAN OVERGROWN "VIRUSES"--CONSTANTLY MUTATING AND TWISTING FROM ONE FORM TO ANOTHER--FROM HUMANOID TO MONSTROUS.
OOP
THEIR GENETIC MATRIX IS SO UNSTABLE...
BLPH
...CELLULAR BREAKDOWN IS INEVITABLE.
POOMF
INTO THE MIX, JACK.
ME?
YOU HAVE NOTHING TO LOSE, BOY...
...TRUST ME.
IT'S MERELY A MATTER OF TIME...

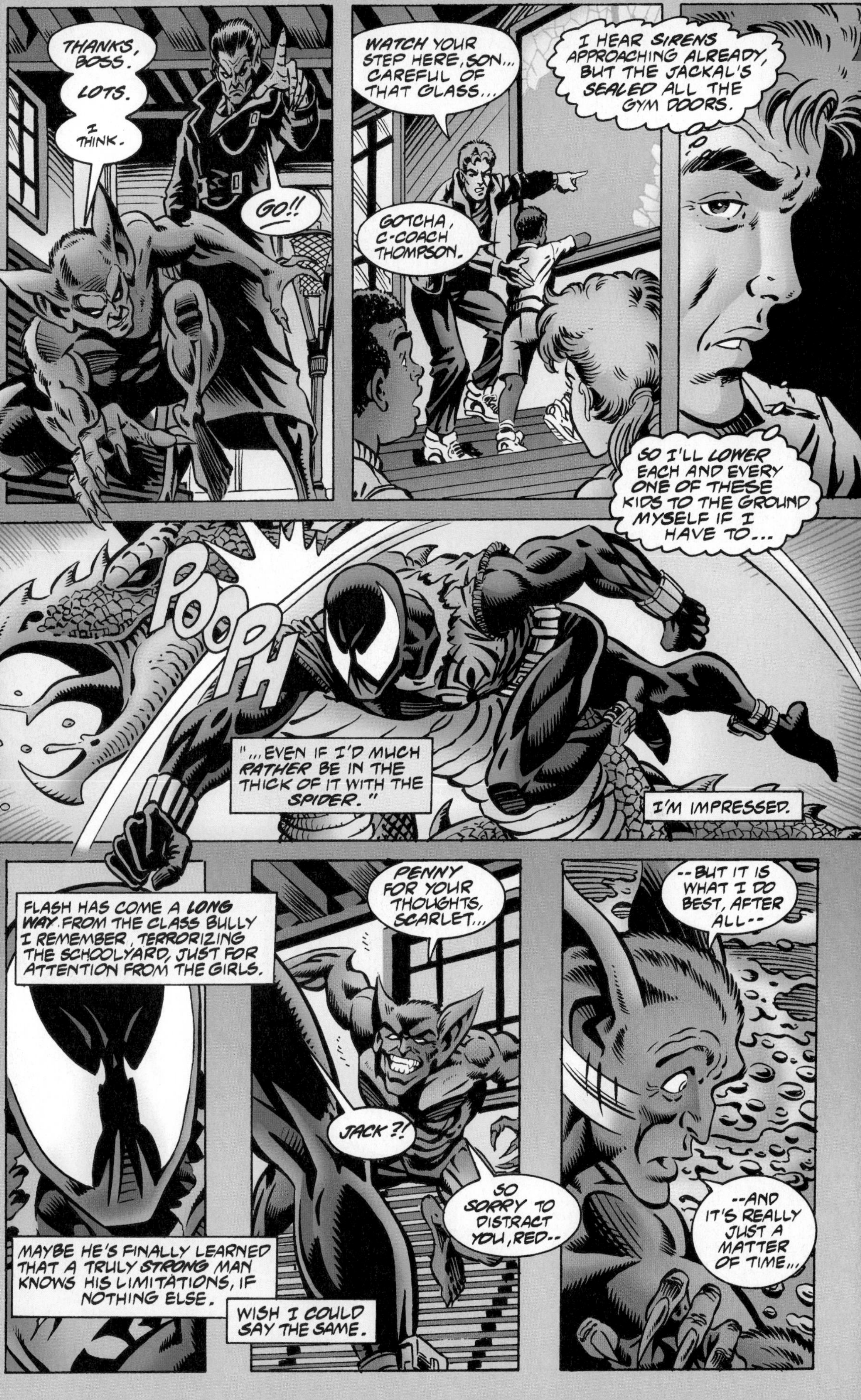
THANKS, BOSS.
LOTS.
I THINK.
GO!!
WATCH YOUR STEP HERE, SON... CAREFUL OF THAT GLASS...
GOTCHA, C-COACH THOMPSON.
I HEAR SIRENS APPROACHING ALREADY, BUT THE JACKAL'S SEALED ALL THE GYM DOORS.
SO I'LL LOWER EACH AND EVERY ONE OF THESE KIDS TO THE GROUND MYSELF IF I HAVE TO...
POOOPH
"...EVEN IF I'D MUCH RATHER BE IN THE THICK OF IT WITH THE SPIDER."
I'M IMPRESSED.
FLASH HAS COME A LONG WAY FROM THE CLASS BULLY I REMEMBER, TERRORIZING THE SCHOOLYARD, JUST FOR ATTENTION FROM THE GIRLS.
MAYBE HE'S FINALLY LEARNED THAT A TRULY STRONG MAN KNOWS HIS LIMITATIONS, IF NOTHING ELSE.
WISH I COULD SAY THE SAME.
PENNY FOR YOUR THOUGHTS, SCARLET...
JACK?!
SO SORRY TO DISTRACT YOU, RED--
--BUT IT IS WHAT I DO BEST, AFTER ALL--
--AND IT'S REALLY JUST A MATTER OF TIME...

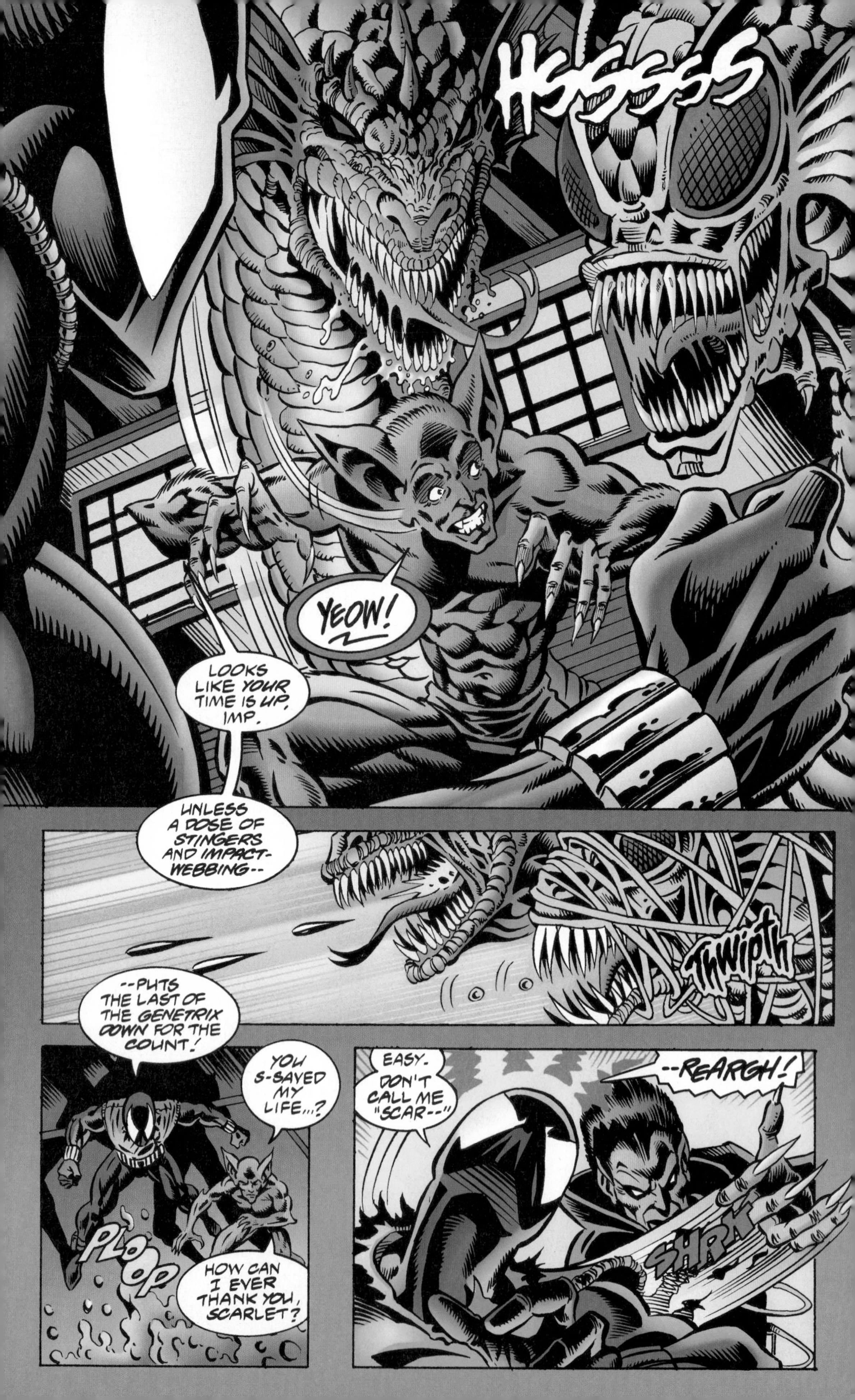
HSSSSS
YEOW!
LOOKS LIKE YOUR TIME IS UP, IMP.
UNLESS A DOSE OF STINGERS AND IMPACT-WEBBING--
THWIPTH
--PUTS THE LAST OF THE GENETRIX DOWN FOR THE COUNT!
YOU S-SAVED MY LIFE...?
PLOOP
HOW CAN I EVER THANK YOU, SCARLET?
EASY. DON'T CALL ME "SCAR--"
--REARGH!
SHRK

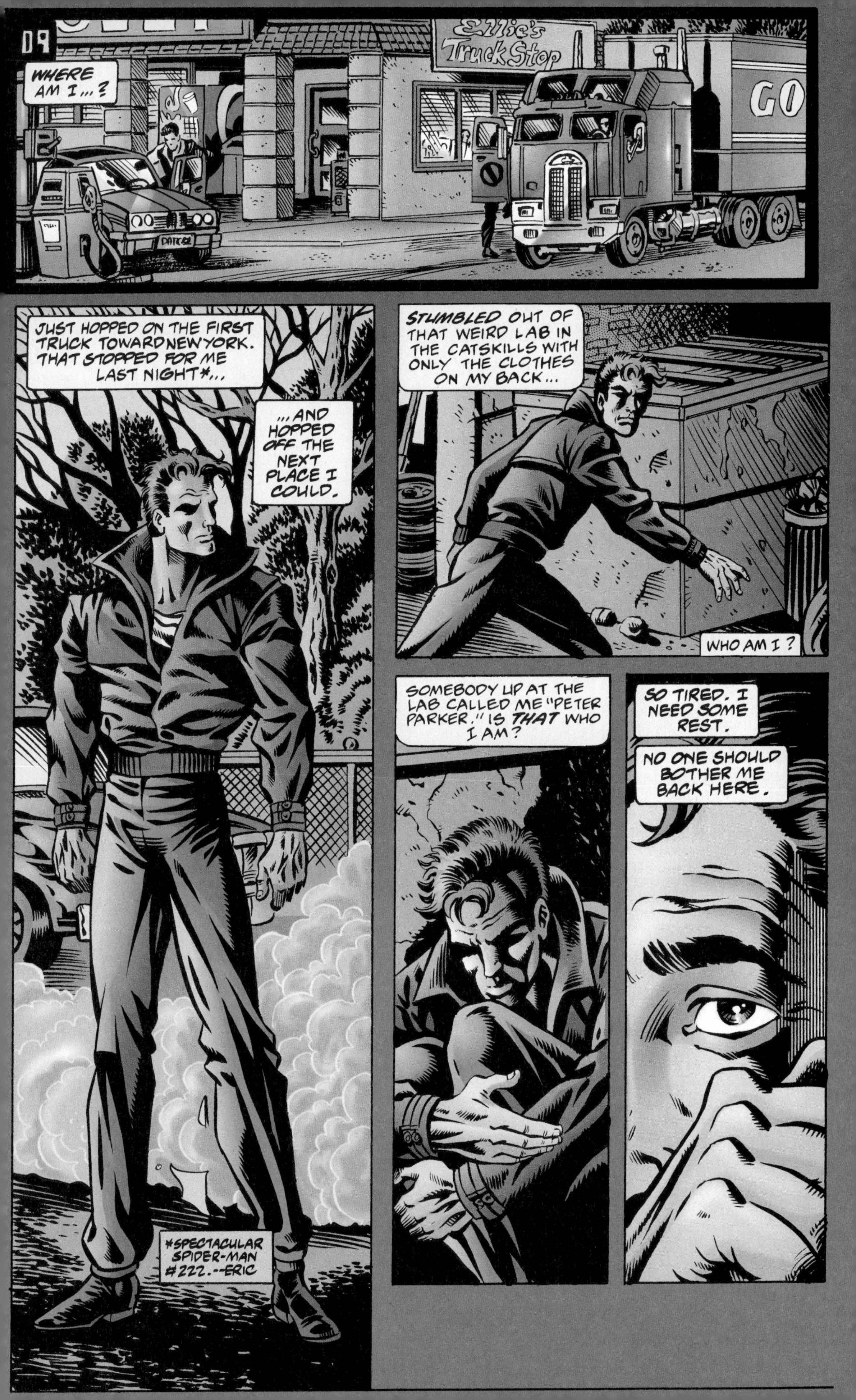

Ellie's Truck Stop
GO
WHERE AM I...?
JUST HOPPED ON THE FIRST TRUCK TOWARD NEW YORK. THAT STOPPED FOR ME LAST NIGHT*...
...AND HOPPED OFF THE NEXT PLACE I COULD.
*SPECTACULAR SPIDER-MAN #222.--ERIC
STUMBLED OUT OF THAT WEIRD LAB IN THE CATSKILLS WITH ONLY THE CLOTHES ON MY BACK...
WHO AM I?
SOMEBODY UP AT THE LAB CALLED ME "PETER PARKER." IS THAT WHO I AM?
SO TIRED. I NEED SOME REST.
NO ONE SHOULD BOTHER ME BACK HERE.

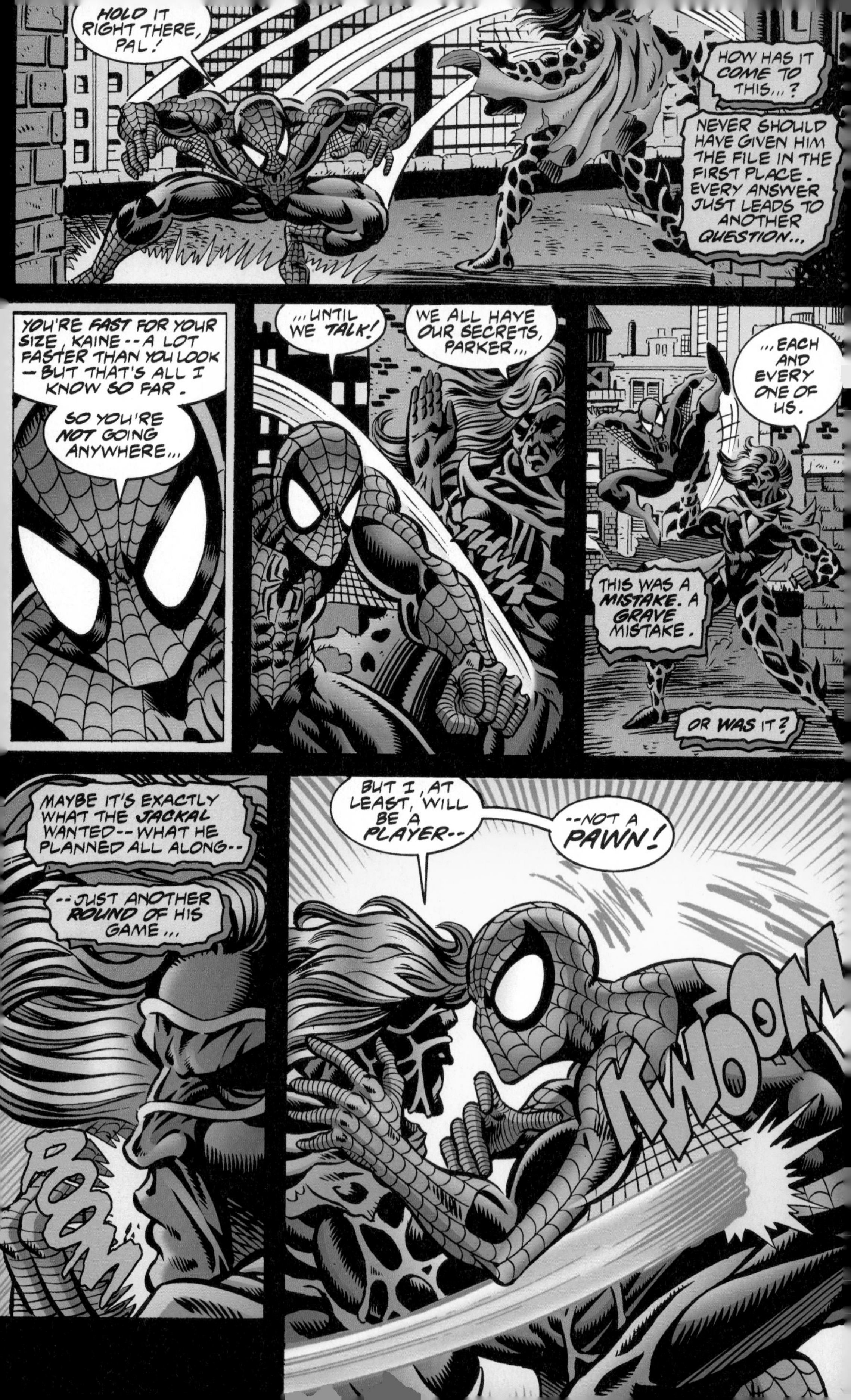
HOLD IT RIGHT THERE, PAL!
HOW HAS IT COME TO THIS...?
NEVER SHOULD HAVE GIVEN HIM THE FILE IN THE FIRST PLACE. EVERY ANSWER JUST LEADS TO ANOTHER QUESTION...
YOU'RE FAST FOR YOUR SIZE, KAINE--A LOT FASTER THAN YOU LOOK --BUT THAT'S ALL I KNOW SO FAR.
SO YOU'RE NOT GOING ANYWHERE...
...UNTIL WE TALK!
WE ALL HAVE OUR SECRETS, PARKER...
THWK
...EACH AND EVERY ONE OF US.
THIS WAS A MISTAKE. A GRAVE MISTAKE.
OR WAS IT?
MAYBE IT'S EXACTLY WHAT THE JACKAL WANTED--WHAT HE PLANNED ALL ALONG--
--JUST ANOTHER ROUND OF HIS GAME...
POOM
BUT I, AT LEAST, WILL BE A PLAYER--
--NOT A PAWN!
KWOOM

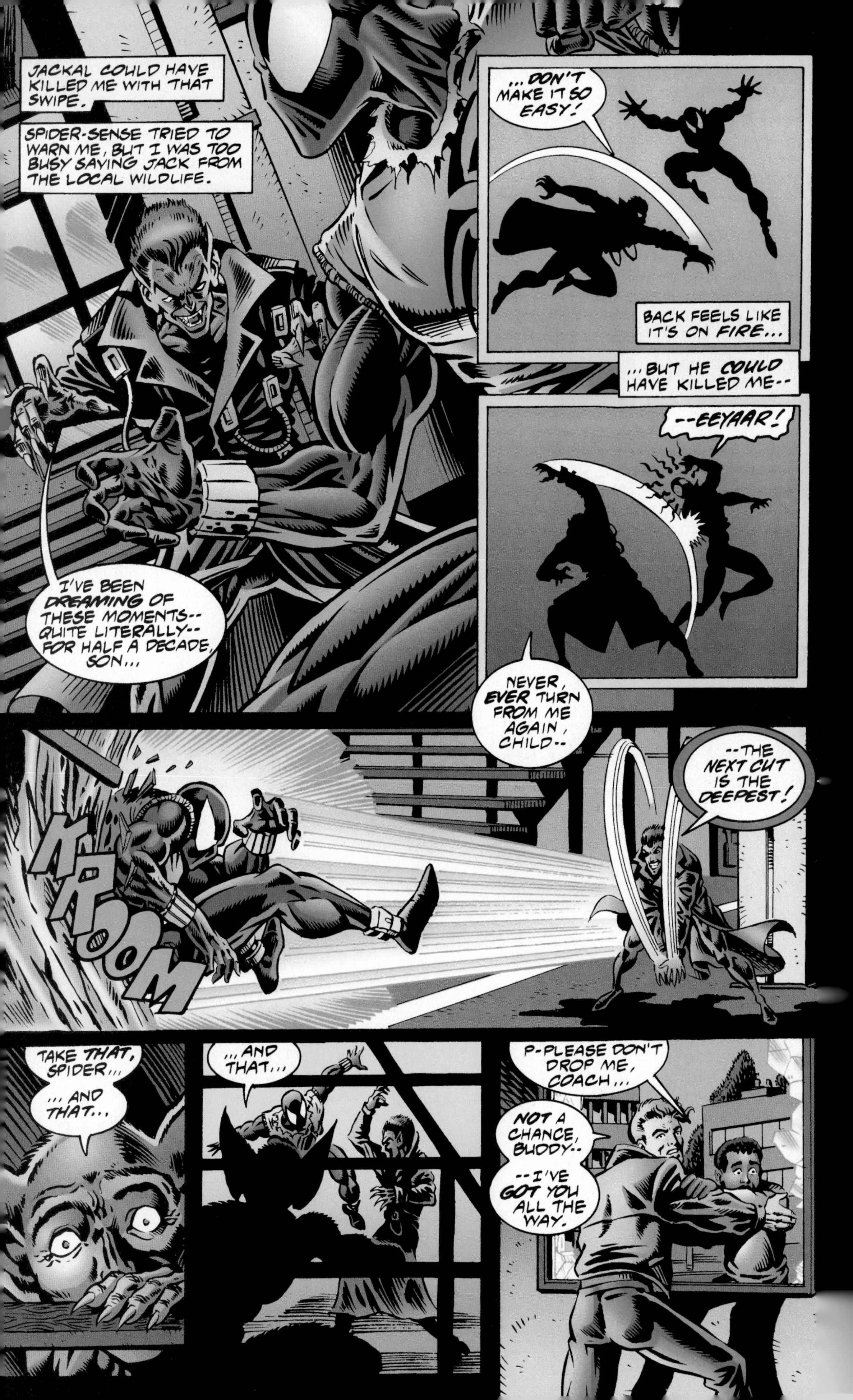
JACKAL COULD HAVE KILLED ME WITH THAT SWIPE.
SPIDER-SENSE TRIED TO WARN ME, BUT I WAS TOO BUSY SAVING JACK FROM THE LOCAL WILDLIFE.
I'VE BEEN DREAMING OF THESE MOMENTS-- QUITE LITERALLY-- FOR HALF A DECADE, SON...
...DON'T MAKE IT SO EASY!
BACK FEELS LIKE IT'S ON FIRE...
...BUT HE COULD HAVE KILLED ME--
--EEYAAR!
NEVER, EVER TURN FROM ME AGAIN, CHILD--
--THE NEXT CUT IS THE DEEPEST!
KROOM
TAKE THAT, SPIDER...
...AND THAT...
...AND THAT...
P-PLEASE DON'T DROP ME, COACH...
NOT A CHANCE, BUDDY--
--I'VE GOT YOU ALL THE WAY.

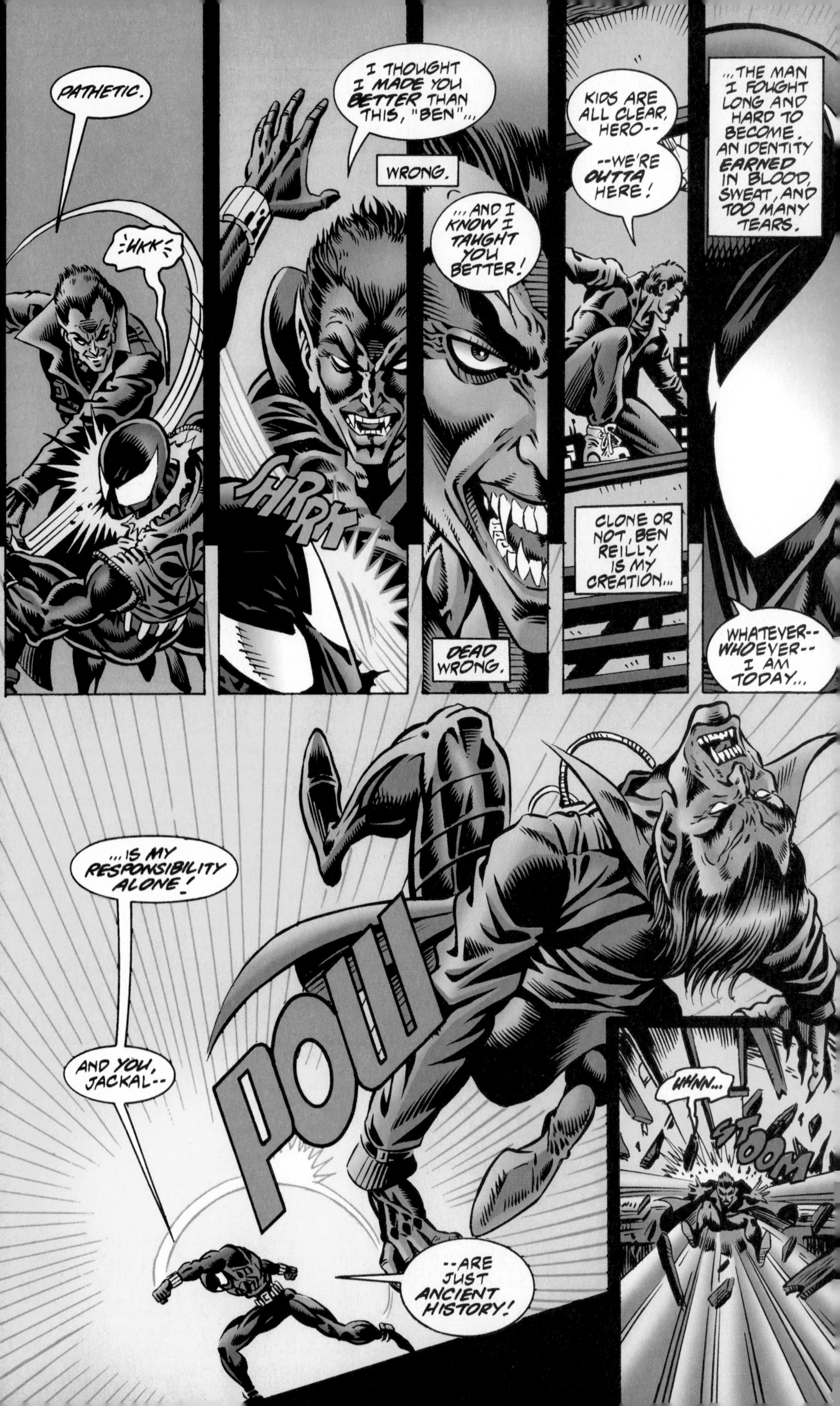

PATHETIC.
:UKK:
I THOUGHT I MADE YOU BETTER THAN THIS, "BEN"...
WRONG.
SHRK
...AND I KNOW I TAUGHT YOU BETTER!
DEAD WRONG.
KIDS ARE ALL CLEAR, HERO--
--WE'RE OUTTA HERE!
CLONE OR NOT, BEN REILLY IS MY CREATION...
...THE MAN I FOUGHT LONG AND HARD TO BECOME. AN IDENTITY EARNED IN BLOOD, SWEAT, AND TOO MANY TEARS.
WHATEVER-- WHOEVER-- I AM TODAY...
...IS MY RESPONSIBILITY ALONE!
AND YOU, JACKAL--
POW
--ARE JUST ANCIENT HISTORY!
UHNN...
STOOM

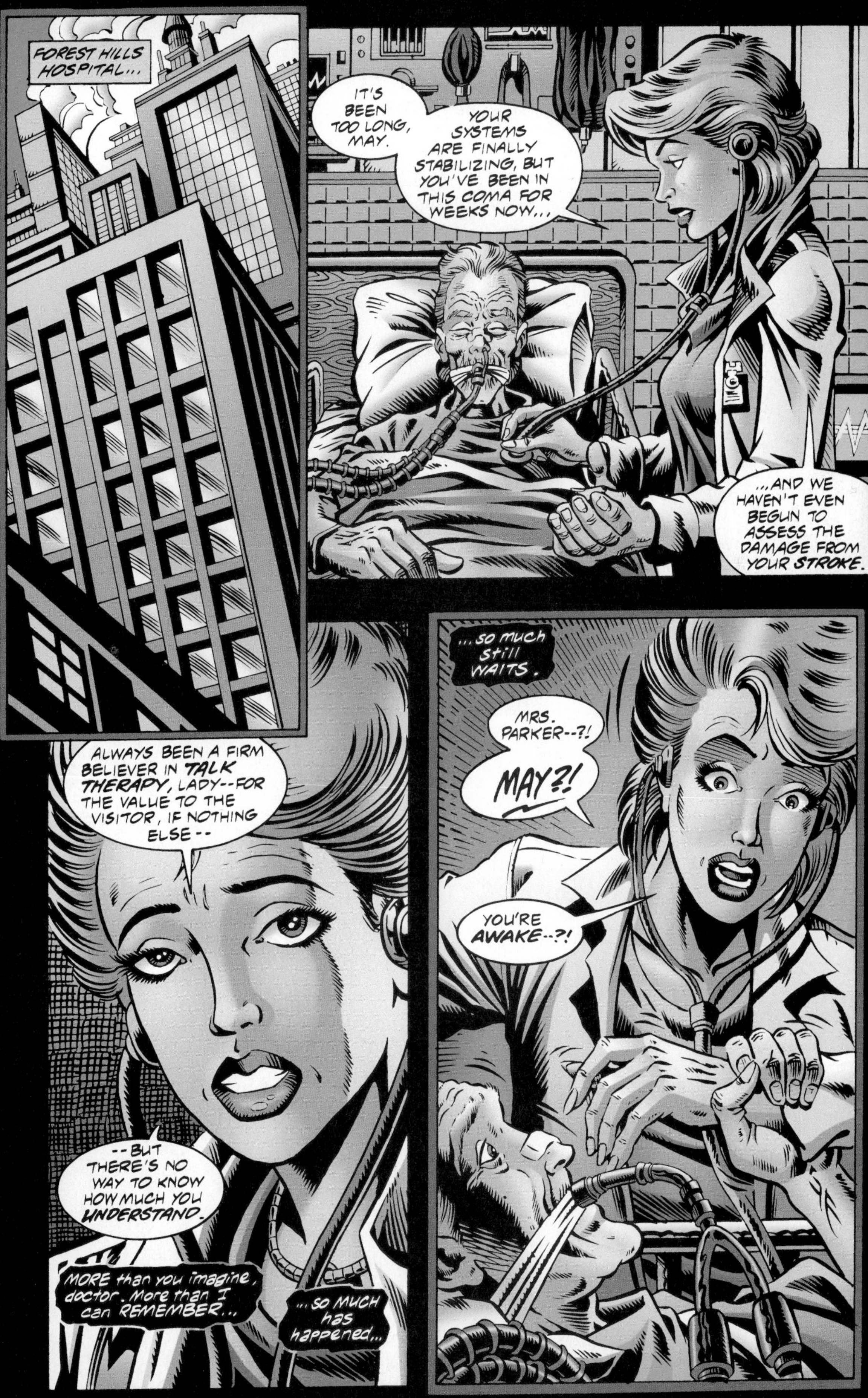
FOREST HILLS HOSPITAL...
IT'S BEEN TOO LONG, MAY.
YOUR SYSTEMS ARE FINALLY STABILIZING, BUT YOU'VE BEEN IN THIS COMA FOR WEEKS NOW...
...AND WE HAVEN'T EVEN BEGUN TO ASSESS THE DAMAGE FROM YOUR STROKE.
ALWAYS BEEN A FIRM BELIEVER IN TALK THERAPY, LADY--FOR THE VALUE TO THE VISITOR, IF NOTHING ELSE--
--BUT THERE'S NO WAY TO KNOW HOW MUCH YOU UNDERSTAND.
MORE than you imagine, doctor. More than I can REMEMBER...
...so MUCH has happened...
...so much still WAITS.
MRS. PARKER--?!
MAY?!
YOU'RE AWAKE--?!

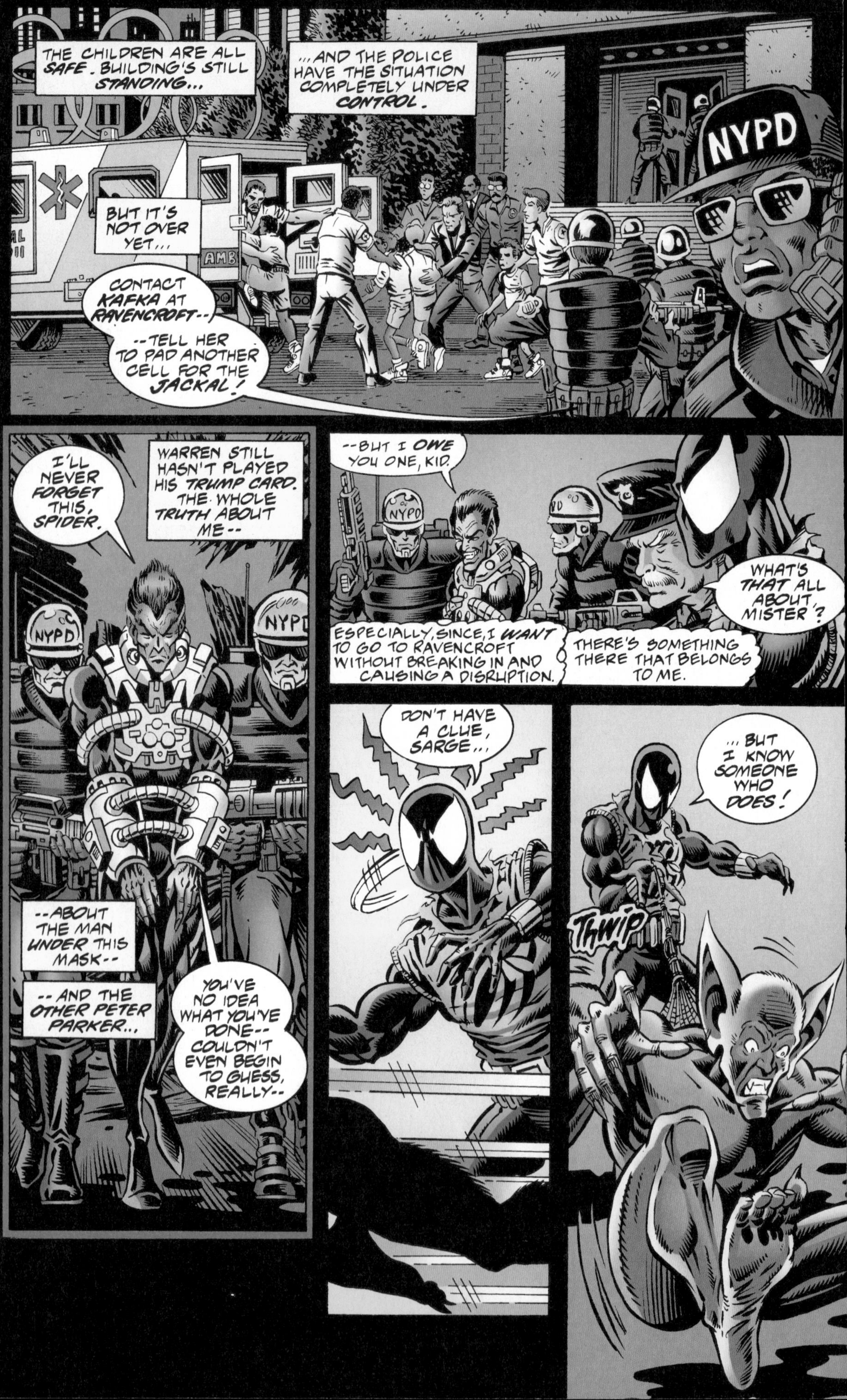
THE CHILDREN ARE ALL SAFE. BUILDING'S STILL STANDING...
...AND THE POLICE HAVE THE SITUATION COMPLETELY UNDER CONTROL.
NYPD
BUT IT'S NOT OVER YET...
CONTACT KAFKA AT RAVENCROFT--
--TELL HER TO PAD ANOTHER CELL FOR THE JACKAL!
I'LL NEVER FORGET THIS, SPIDER.
WARREN STILL HASN'T PLAYED HIS TRUMP CARD. THE WHOLE TRUTH ABOUT ME--
NYPD
NYPD
--ABOUT THE MAN UNDER THIS MASK--
--AND THE OTHER PETER PARKER...
YOU'VE NO IDEA WHAT YOU'VE DONE-- COULDN'T EVEN BEGIN TO GUESS, REALLY--
--BUT I OWE YOU ONE, KID.
NYPD
ESPECIALLY, SINCE, I WANT TO GO TO RAVENCROFT WITHOUT BREAKING IN AND CAUSING A DISRUPTION.
THERE'S SOMETHING THERE THAT BELONGS TO ME.
WHAT'S THAT ALL ABOUT, MISTER?
DON'T HAVE A CLUE, SARGE...
...BUT I KNOW SOMEONE WHO DOES!
THWIP

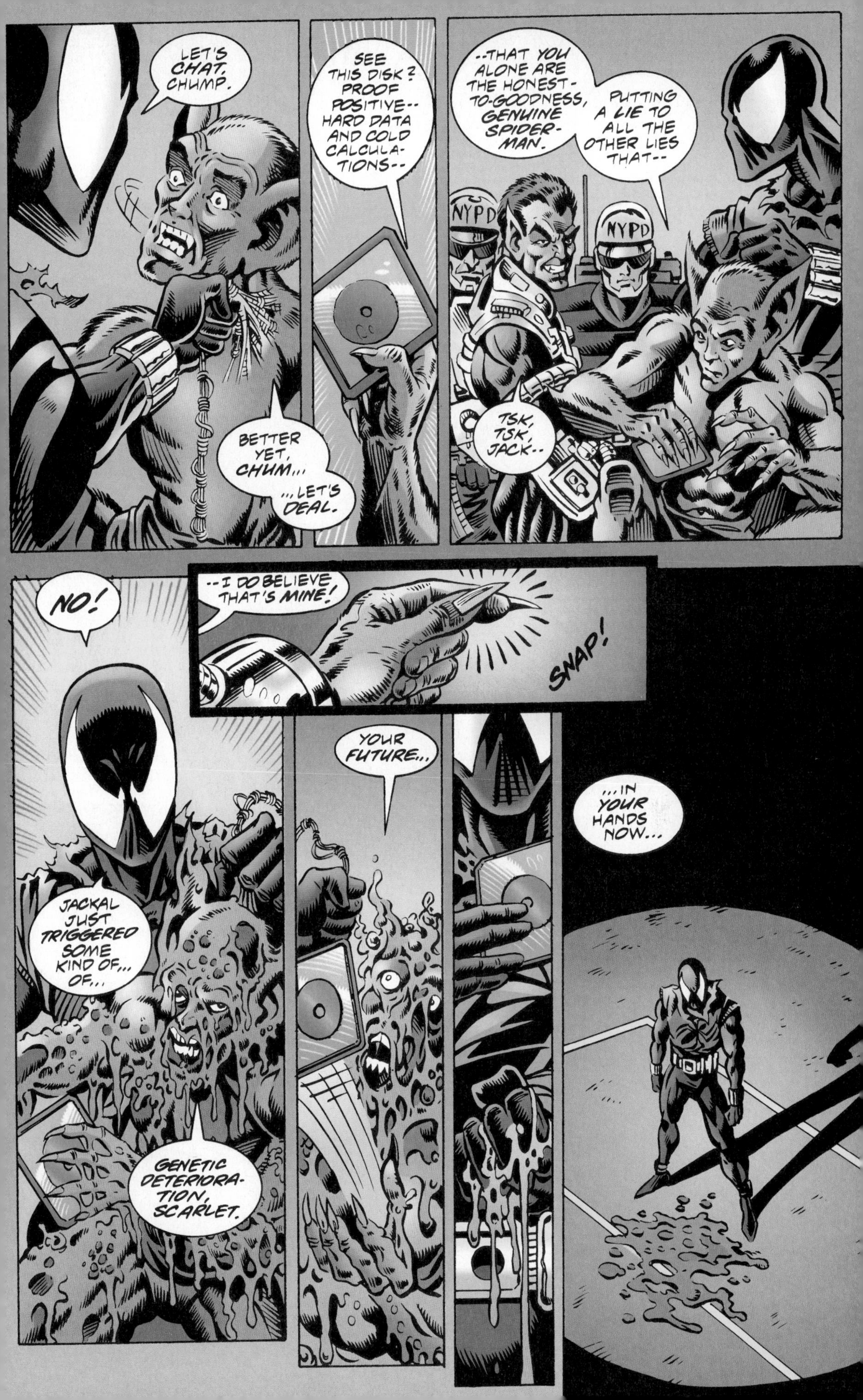
LET'S CHAT, CHUMP.
BETTER YET, CHUM...
...LET'S DEAL.
SEE THIS DISK? PROOF POSITIVE-- HARD DATA AND COLD CALCULATIONS--
--THAT YOU ALONE ARE THE HONEST-TO-GOODNESS, GENUINE SPIDER-MAN.
PUTTING A LIE TO ALL THE OTHER LIES THAT--
TSK, TSK, JACK--
NO!
--I DO BELIEVE THAT'S MINE!
SNAP!
JACKAL JUST TRIGGERED SOME KIND OF... OF...
GENETIC DETERIORATION, SCARLET.
YOUR FUTURE...
...IN YOUR HANDS NOW...

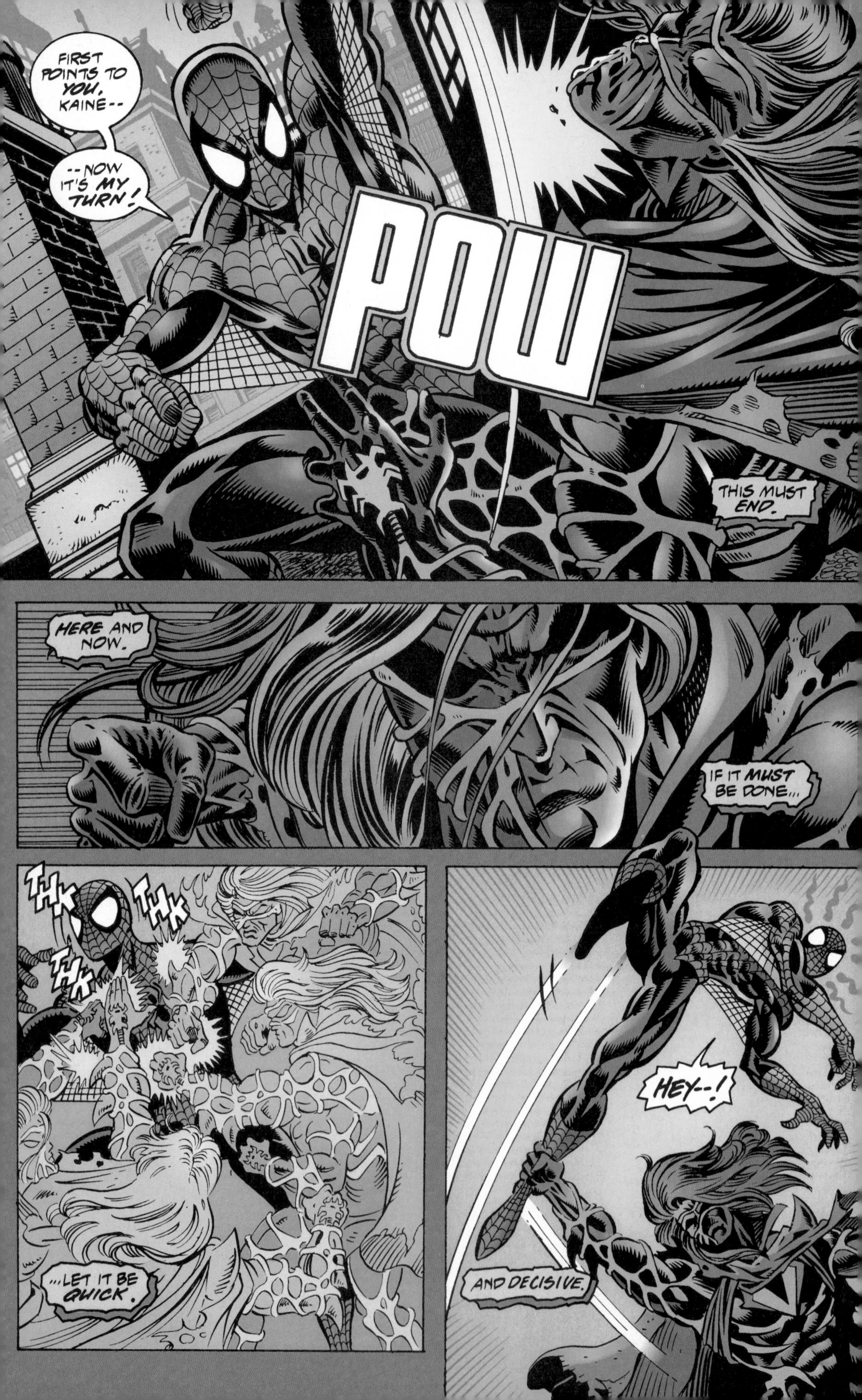
FIRST POINTS TO YOU, KAINE--
--NOW IT'S MY TURN!
POW
THIS MUST END.
HERE AND NOW.
IF IT MUST BE DONE...
THK
THK
THK
...LET IT BE QUICK.
HEY--!
AND DECISIVE.

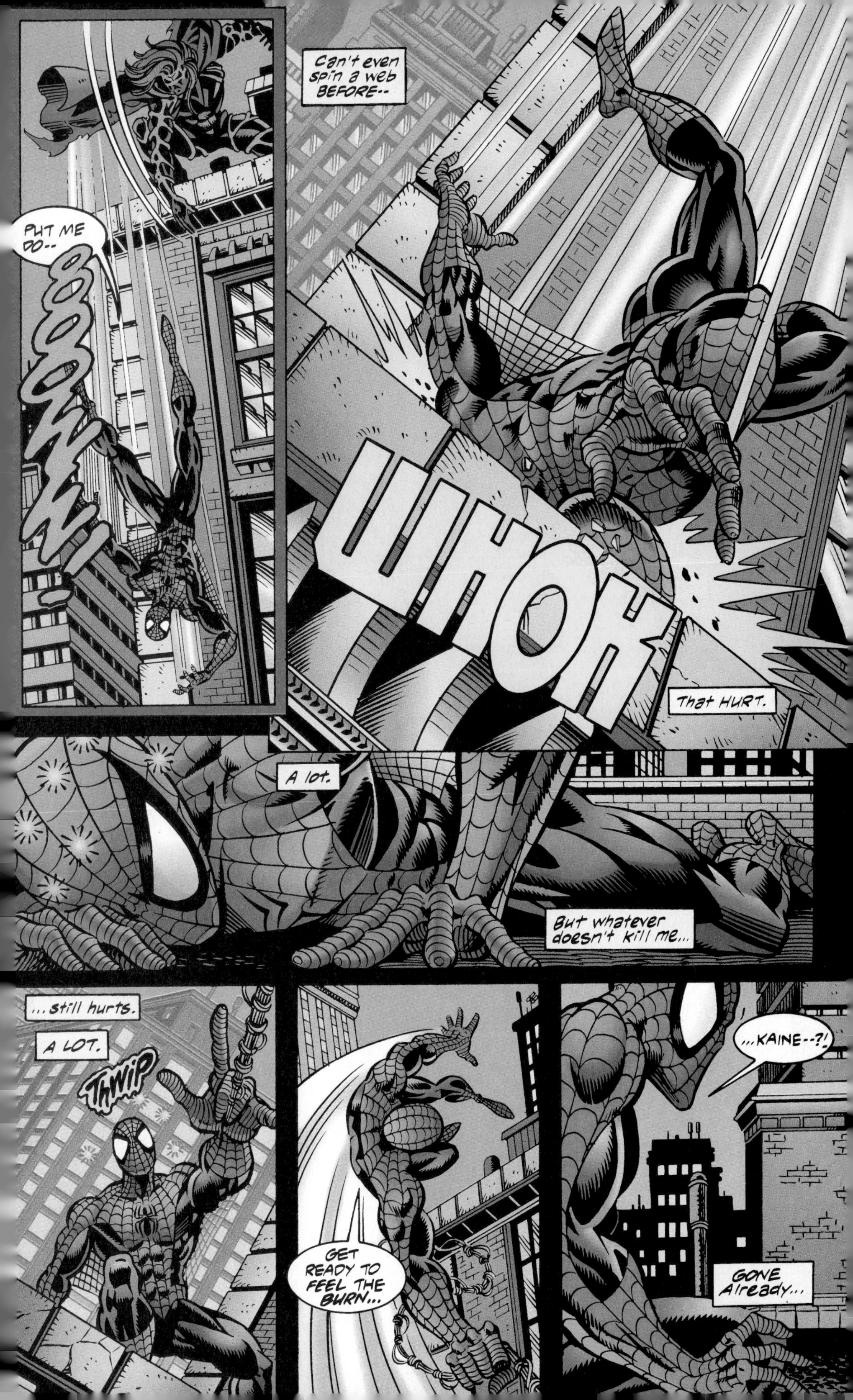
PUT ME DO--
OOOOWN!
Can't even spin a web BEFORE--
WHOH
That HURT.
A lot.
But whatever doesn't kill me...
...still hurts.
A LOT.
THWIP
GET READY TO FEEL THE BURN...
...KAINE--?!
GONE Already...

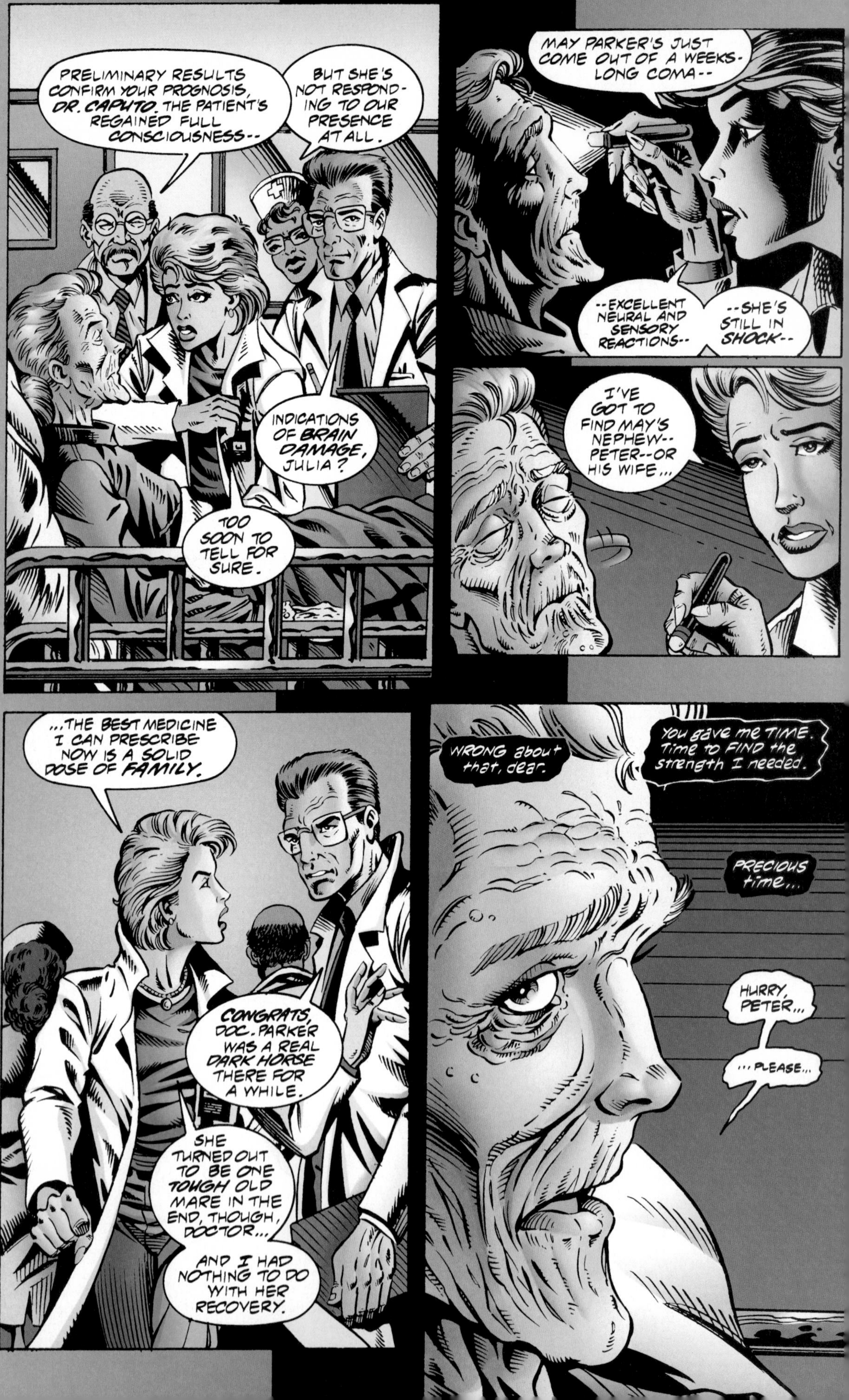
PRELIMINARY RESULTS CONFIRM YOUR PROGNOSIS, DR. CAPUTO. THE PATIENT'S REGAINED FULL CONSCIOUSNESS--
BUT SHE'S NOT RESPONDING TO OUR PRESENCE AT ALL.
INDICATIONS OF BRAIN DAMAGE, JULIA?
TOO SOON TO TELL FOR SURE.
MAY PARKER'S JUST COME OUT OF A WEEKS-LONG COMA--
--EXCELLENT NEURAL AND SENSORY REACTIONS--
--SHE'S STILL IN SHOCK--
I'VE GOT TO FIND MAY'S NEPHEW--PETER--OR HIS WIFE...
...THE BEST MEDICINE I CAN PRESCRIBE NOW IS A SOLID DOSE OF FAMILY.
CONGRATS, DOC. PARKER WAS A REAL DARK HORSE THERE FOR A WHILE.
SHE TURNED OUT TO BE ONE TOUGH OLD MARE IN THE END, THOUGH, DOCTOR...
AND I HAD NOTHING TO DO WITH HER RECOVERY.
WRONG about that, dear.
You gave me TIME. Time to FIND the strength I needed.
PRECIOUS time...
HURRY, PETER...
...PLEASE...

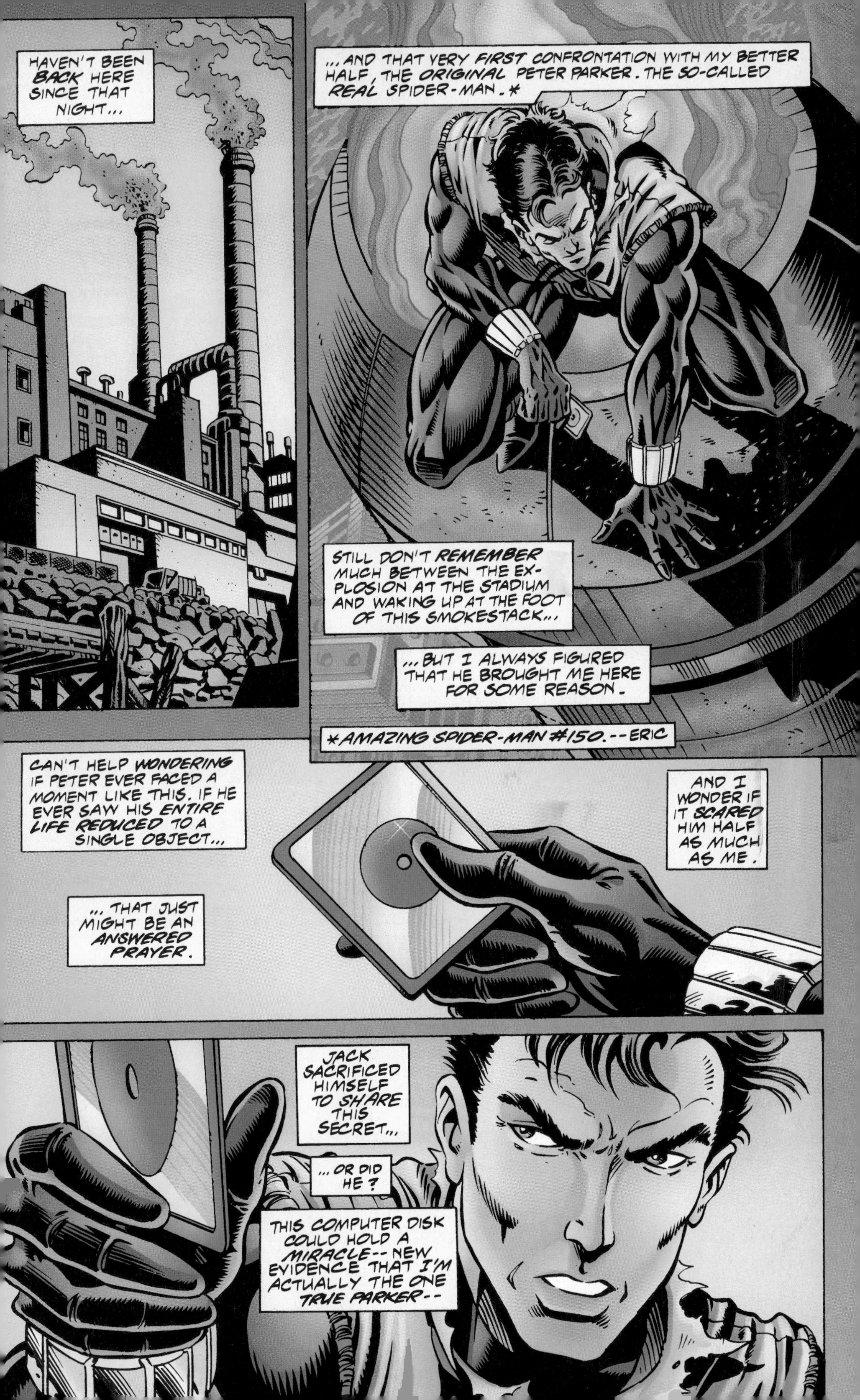

HAVEN'T BEEN BACK HERE SINCE THAT NIGHT...
...AND THAT VERY FIRST CONFRONTATION WITH MY BETTER HALF, THE ORIGINAL PETER PARKER. THE SO-CALLED REAL SPIDER-MAN.*
STILL DON'T REMEMBER MUCH BETWEEN THE EX-PLOSION AT THE STADIUM AND WAKING UP AT THE FOOT OF THIS SMOKESTACK...
...BUT I ALWAYS FIGURED THAT HE BROUGHT ME HERE FOR SOME REASON.
*AMAZING SPIDER-MAN #150.--ERIC
CAN'T HELP WONDERING IF PETER EVER FACED A MOMENT LIKE THIS. IF HE EVER SAW HIS ENTIRE LIFE REDUCED TO A SINGLE OBJECT...
...THAT JUST MIGHT BE AN ANSWERED PRAYER.
AND I WONDER IF IT SCARED HIM HALF AS MUCH AS ME.
JACK SACRIFICED HIMSELF TO SHARE THIS SECRET...
...OR DID HE?
THIS COMPUTER DISK COULD HOLD A MIRACLE-- NEW EVIDENCE THAT I'M ACTUALLY THE ONE TRUE PARKER--

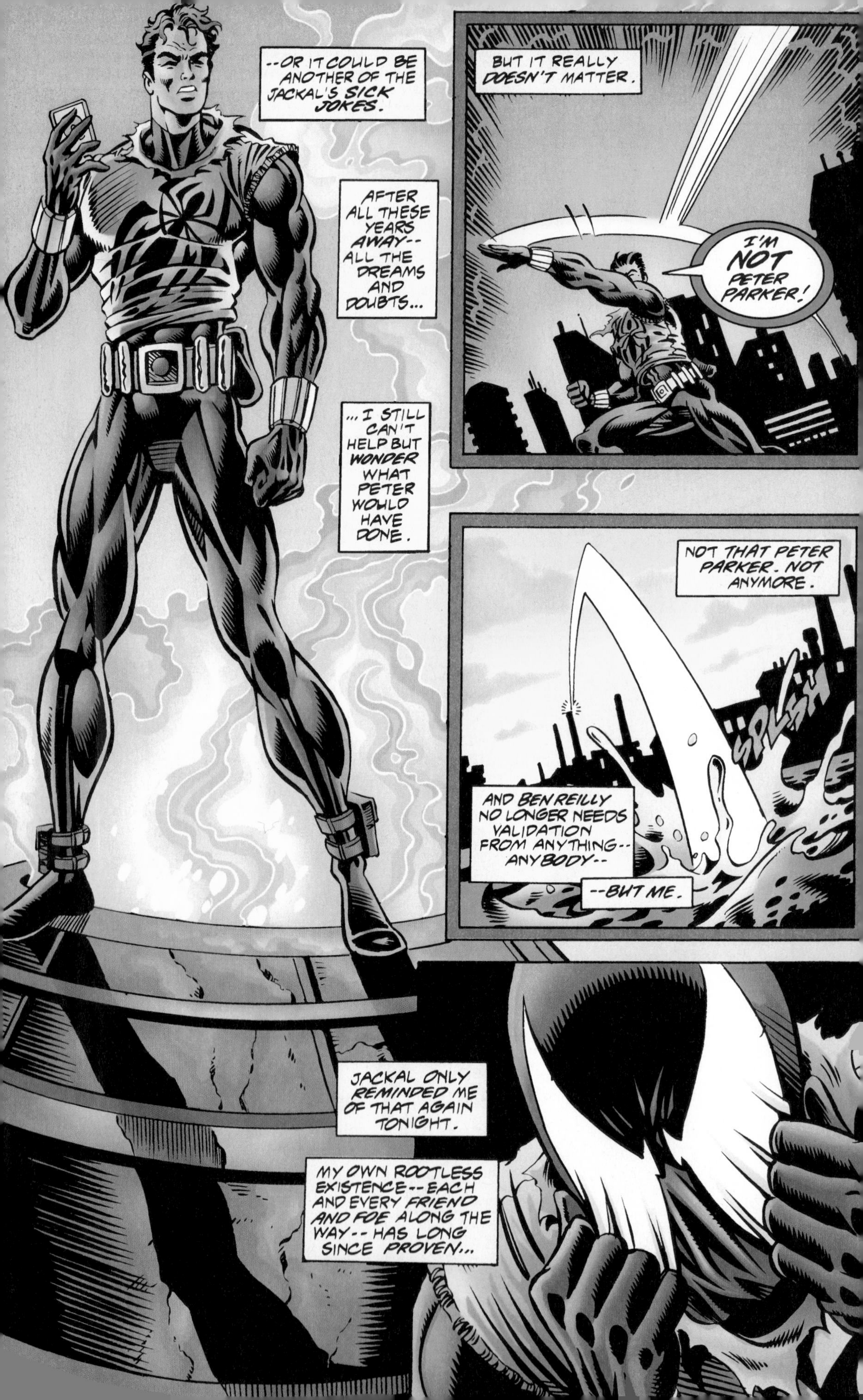
--OR IT COULD BE ANOTHER OF THE JACKAL'S SICK JOKES.
AFTER ALL THESE YEARS AWAY-- ALL THE DREAMS AND DOUBTS...
...I STILL CAN'T HELP BUT WONDER WHAT PETER WOULD HAVE DONE.
BUT IT REALLY DOESN'T MATTER.
I'M NOT PETER PARKER!
NOT THAT PETER PARKER. NOT ANYMORE.
SPLSH
AND BEN REILLY NO LONGER NEEDS VALIDATION FROM ANYTHING-- ANYBODY--
--BUT ME.
JACKAL ONLY REMINDED ME OF THAT AGAIN TONIGHT.
MY OWN ROOTLESS EXISTENCE-- EACH AND EVERY FRIEND AND FOE ALONG THE WAY-- HAS LONG SINCE PROVEN...

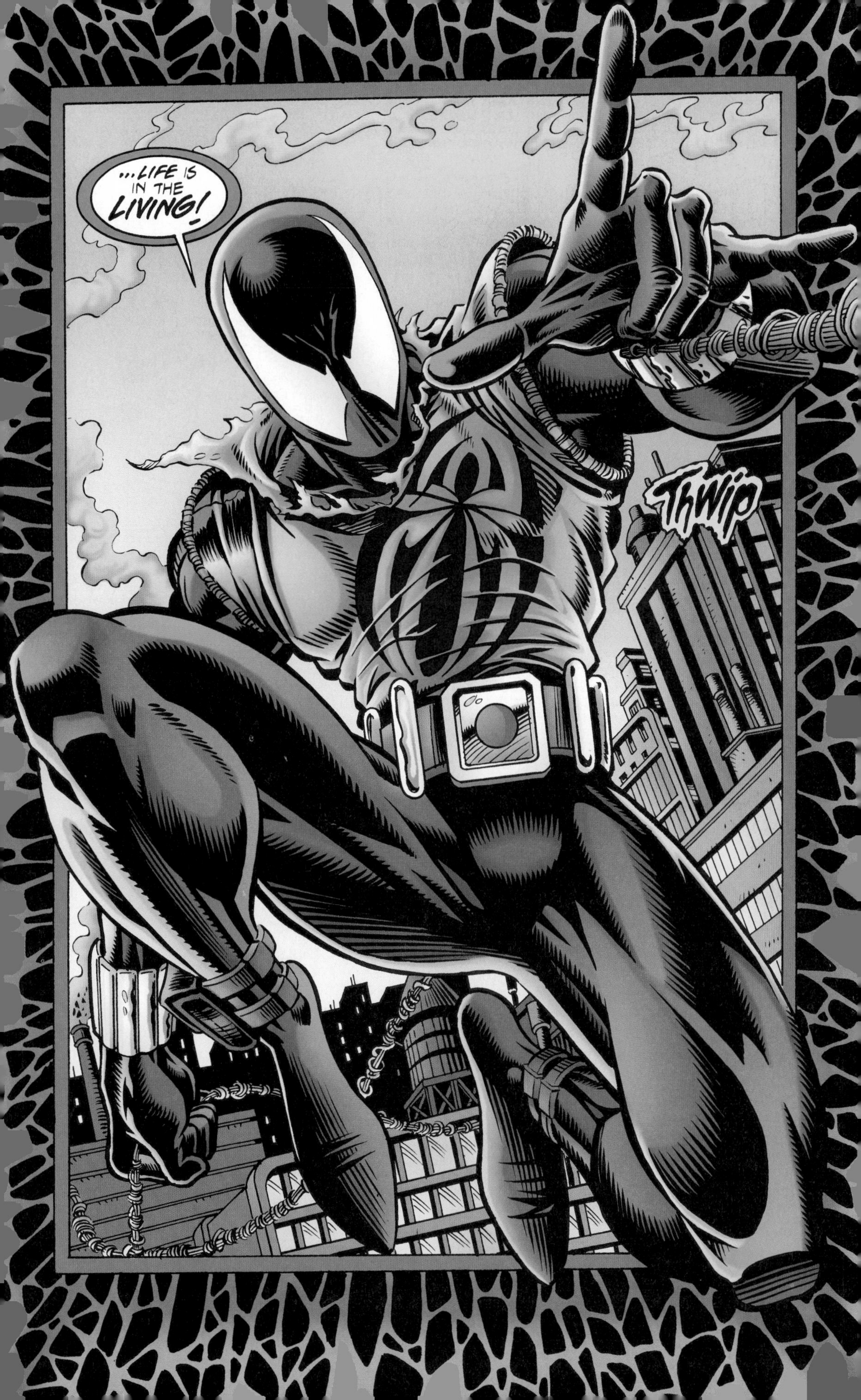
...LIFE IS IN THE LIVING!
THWIP

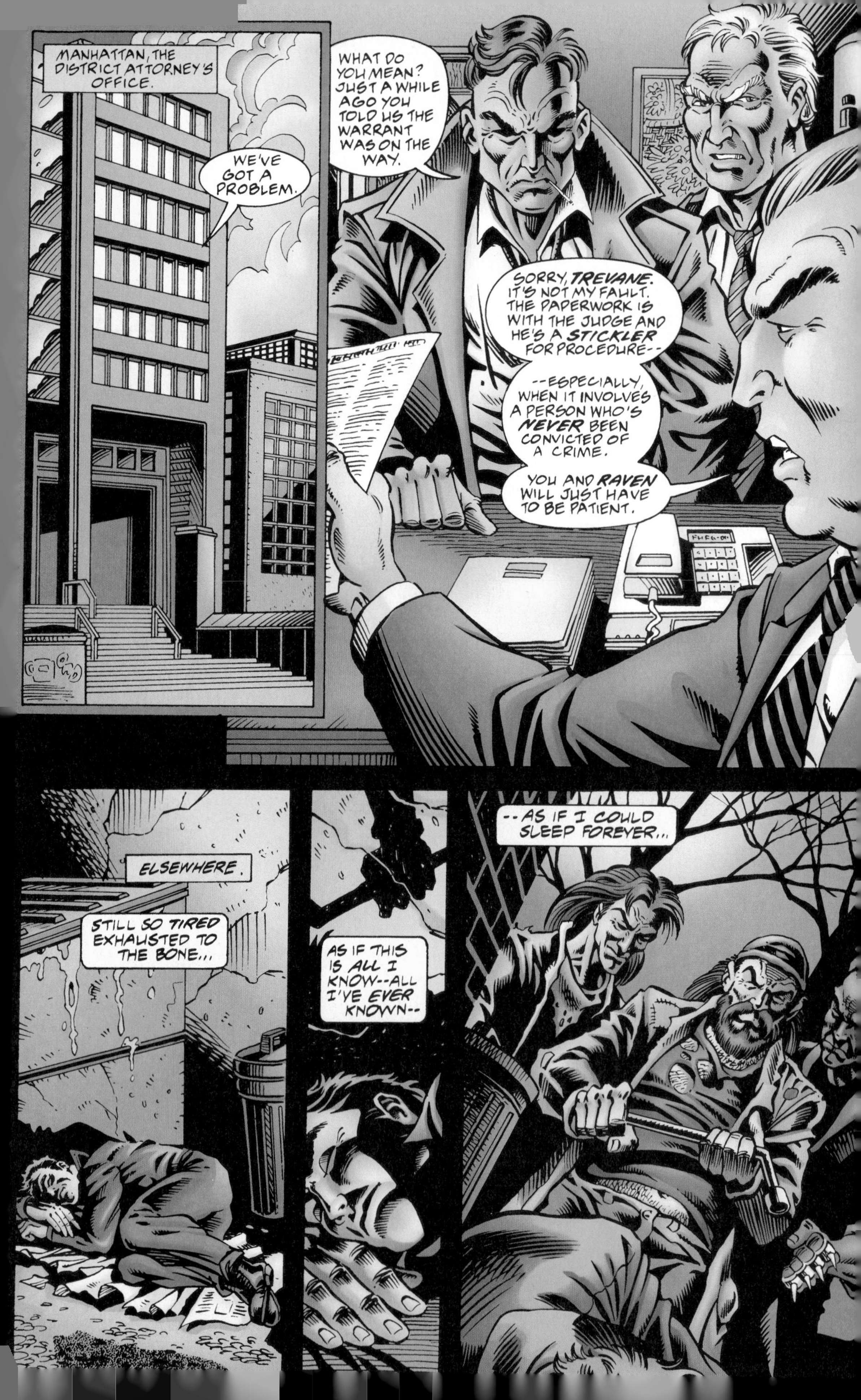
MANHATTAN, THE DISTRICT ATTORNEY'S OFFICE.
WE'VE GOT A PROBLEM.
WHAT DO YOU MEAN? JUST A WHILE AGO YOU TOLD US THE WARRANT WAS ON THE WAY.
SORRY, TREVANE. IT'S NOT MY FAULT. THE PAPERWORK IS WITH THE JUDGE AND HE'S A STICKLER FOR PROCEDURE--
--ESPECIALLY, WHEN IT INVOLVES A PERSON WHO'S NEVER BEEN CONVICTED OF A CRIME.
YOU AND RAVEN WILL JUST HAVE TO BE PATIENT.
ELSEWHERE.
STILL SO TIRED EXHAUSTED TO THE BONE...
AS IF THIS IS ALL I KNOW--ALL I'VE EVER KNOWN--
--AS IF I COULD SLEEP FOREVER...

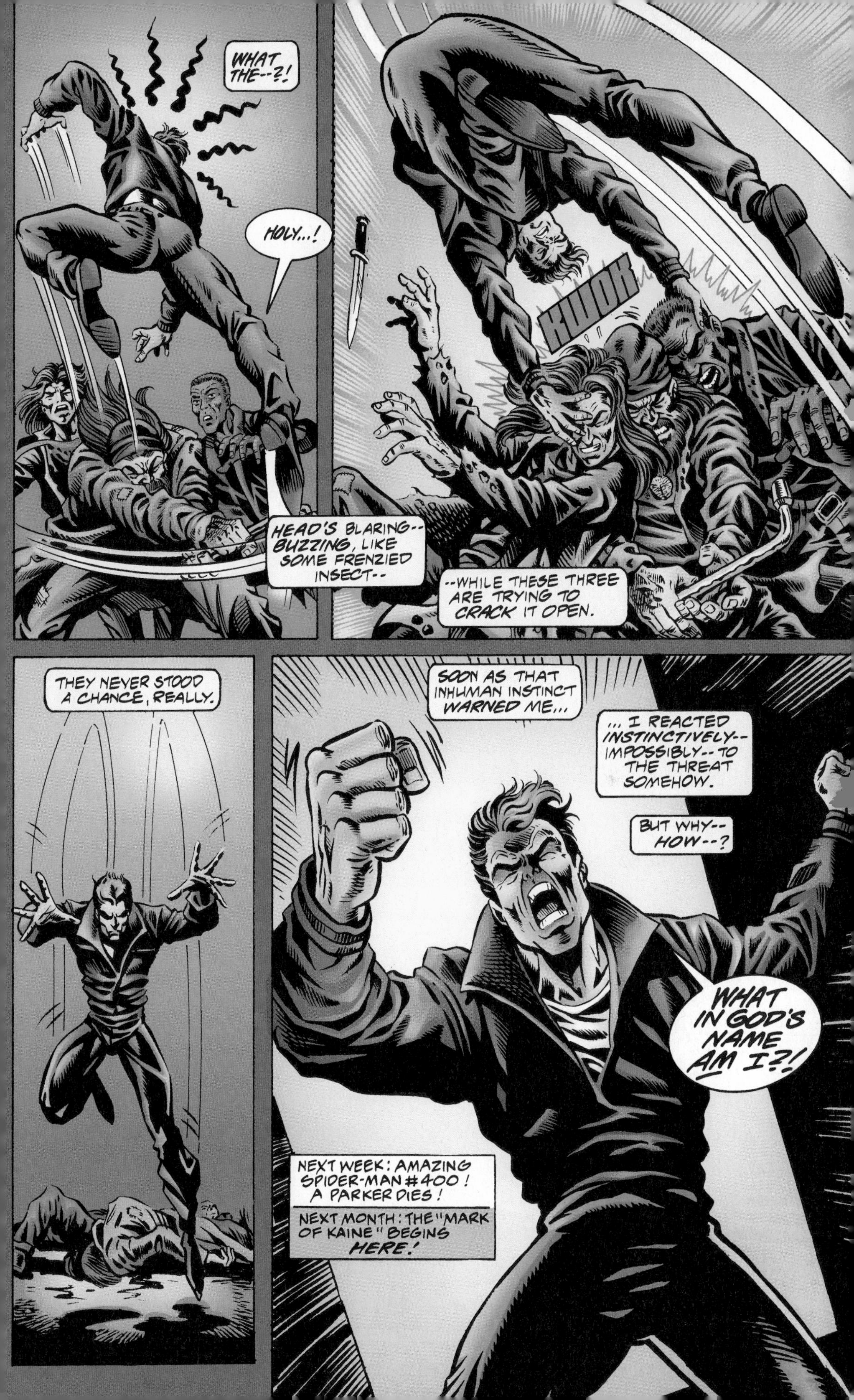
WHAT THE--?!
HOLY...!
HEAD'S BLARING-- BUZZING, LIKE SOME FRENZIED INSECT--
KWOK
--WHILE THESE THREE ARE TRYING TO CRACK IT OPEN.
THEY NEVER STOOD A CHANCE, REALLY.
SOON AS THAT INHUMAN INSTINCT WARNED ME...
... I REACTED INSTINCTIVELY-- IMPOSSIBLY-- TO THE THREAT SOMEHOW.
BUT WHY-- HOW--?
WHAT IN GOD'S NAME AM I?!
NEXT WEEK: AMAZING SPIDER-MAN #400! A PARKER DIES!
NEXT MONTH: THE "MARK OF KAINE" BEGINS HERE!

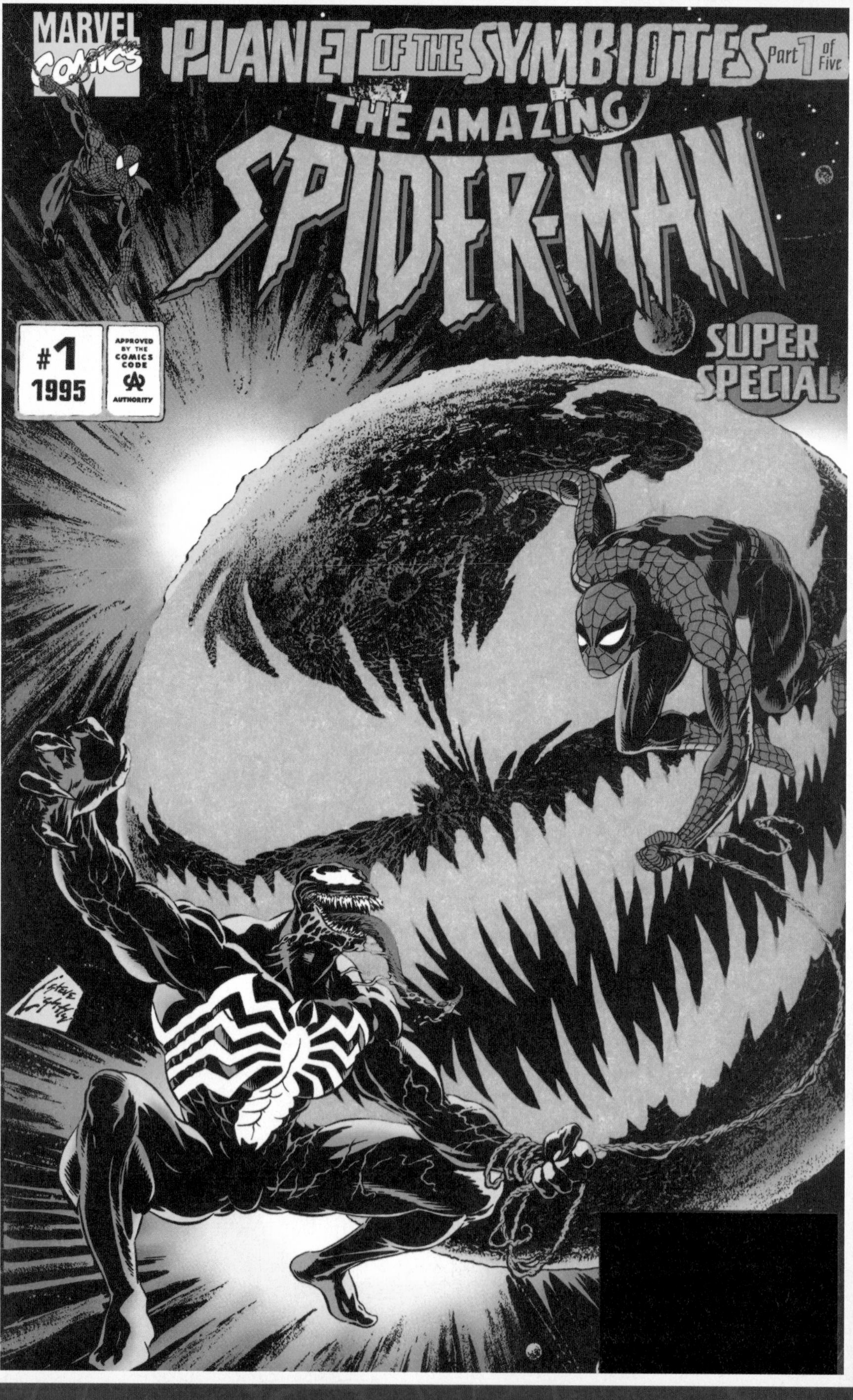
MARVEL COMICS
PLANET OF THE SYMBIOTES Part 1 of Five
THE AMAZING SPIDER-MAN
#1
1995
APPROVED BY THE COMICS CODE AUTHORITY
SUPER SPECIAL

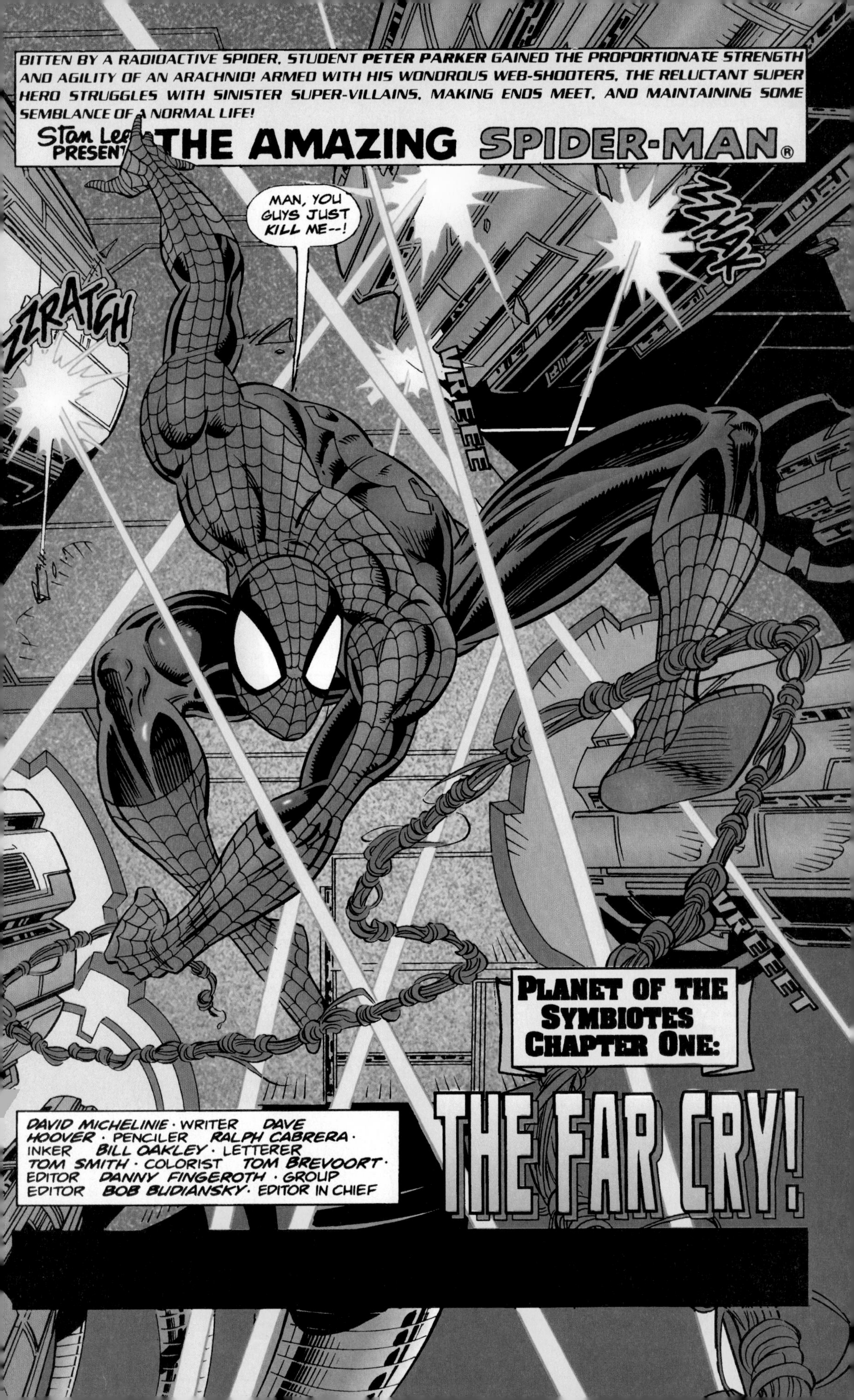
BITTEN BY A RADIOACTIVE SPIDER, STUDENT PETER PARKER GAINED THE PROPORTIONATE STRENGTH AND AGILITY OF AN ARACHNID! ARMED WITH HIS WONDROUS WEB-SHOOTERS, THE RELUCTANT SUPER HERO STRUGGLES WITH SINISTER SUPER-VILLAINS, MAKING ENDS MEET, AND MAINTAINING SOME SEMBLANCE OF A NORMAL LIFE!
Stan Lee PRESENTS THE AMAZING SPIDER-MAN®
MAN, YOU GUYS JUST KILL ME--!
ZZHAK
ZZRATCH
VREEE
VREEET
PLANET OF THE SYMBIOTES CHAPTER ONE:
THE FAR CRY!
DAVID MICHELINIE · WRITER DAVE HOOVER · PENCILER RALPH CABRERA · INKER BILL OAKLEY · LETTERER TOM SMITH · COLORIST TOM BREVOORT · EDITOR DANNY FINGEROTH · GROUP EDITOR BOB BUDIANSKY · EDITOR IN CHIEF
[redacted]

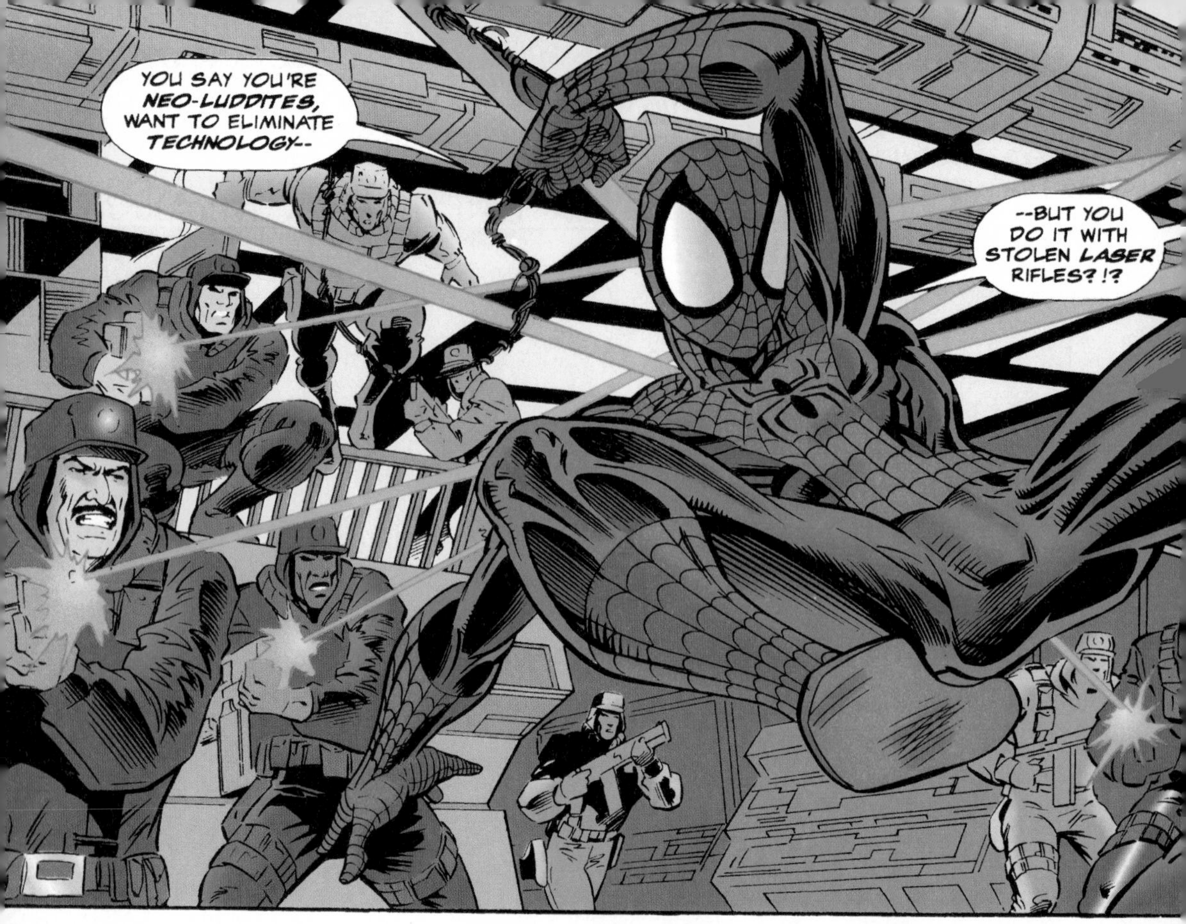
YOU SAY YOU'RE NEO-LUDDITES, WANT TO ELIMINATE TECHNOLOGY--
--BUT YOU DO IT WITH STOLEN LASER RIFLES?!?

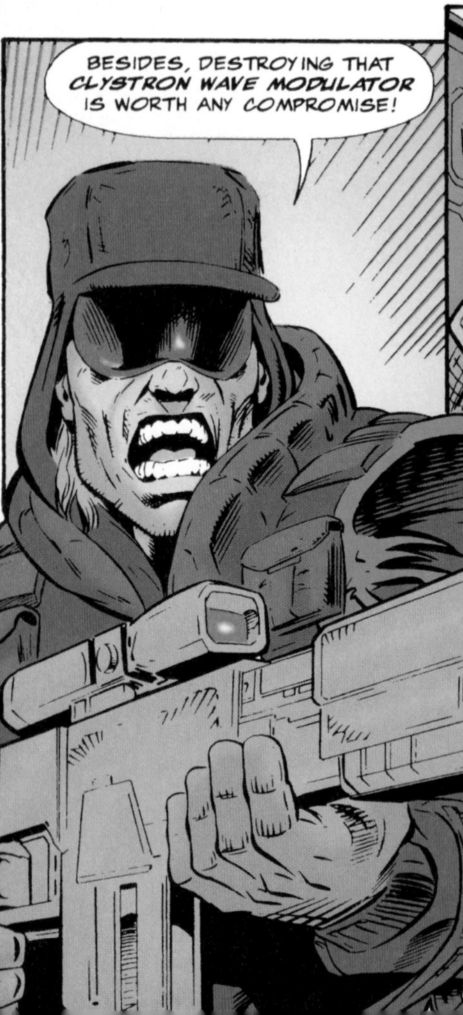
BESIDES, DESTROYING THAT CLYSTRON WAVE MODULATOR IS WORTH ANY COMPROMISE!

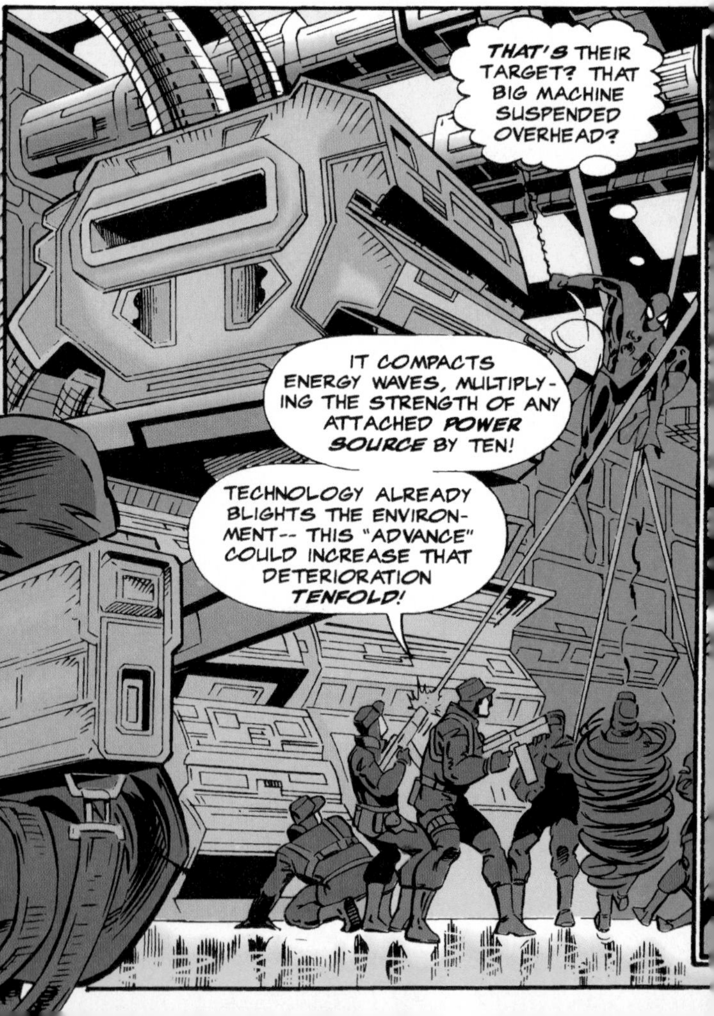
THAT'S THEIR TARGET? THAT BIG MACHINE SUSPENDED OVERHEAD?
IT COMPACTS ENERGY WAVES, MULTIPLY-ING THE STRENGTH OF ANY ATTACHED POWER SOURCE BY TEN!
TECHNOLOGY ALREADY BLIGHTS THE ENVIRON-MENT-- THIS "ADVANCE" COULD INCREASE THAT DETERIORATION TENFOLD!

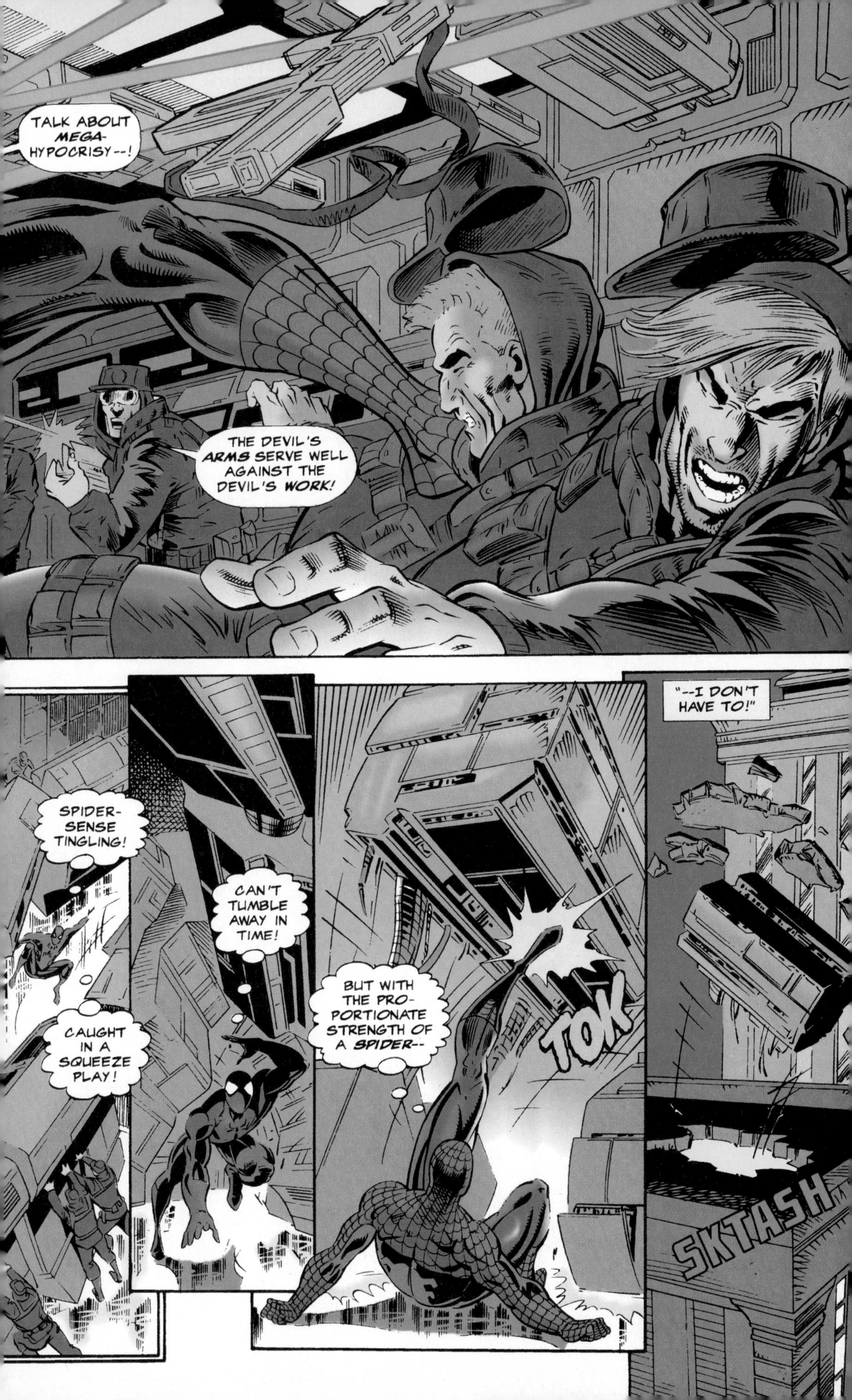
TALK ABOUT MEGA-HYPOCRISY--!
THE DEVIL'S ARMS SERVE WELL AGAINST THE DEVIL'S WORK!
SPIDER-SENSE TINGLING!
CAUGHT IN A SQUEEZE PLAY!
CAN'T TUMBLE AWAY IN TIME!
BUT WITH THE PROPORTIONATE STRENGTH OF A SPIDER--
TOK
"--I DON'T HAVE TO!"
SKTASH

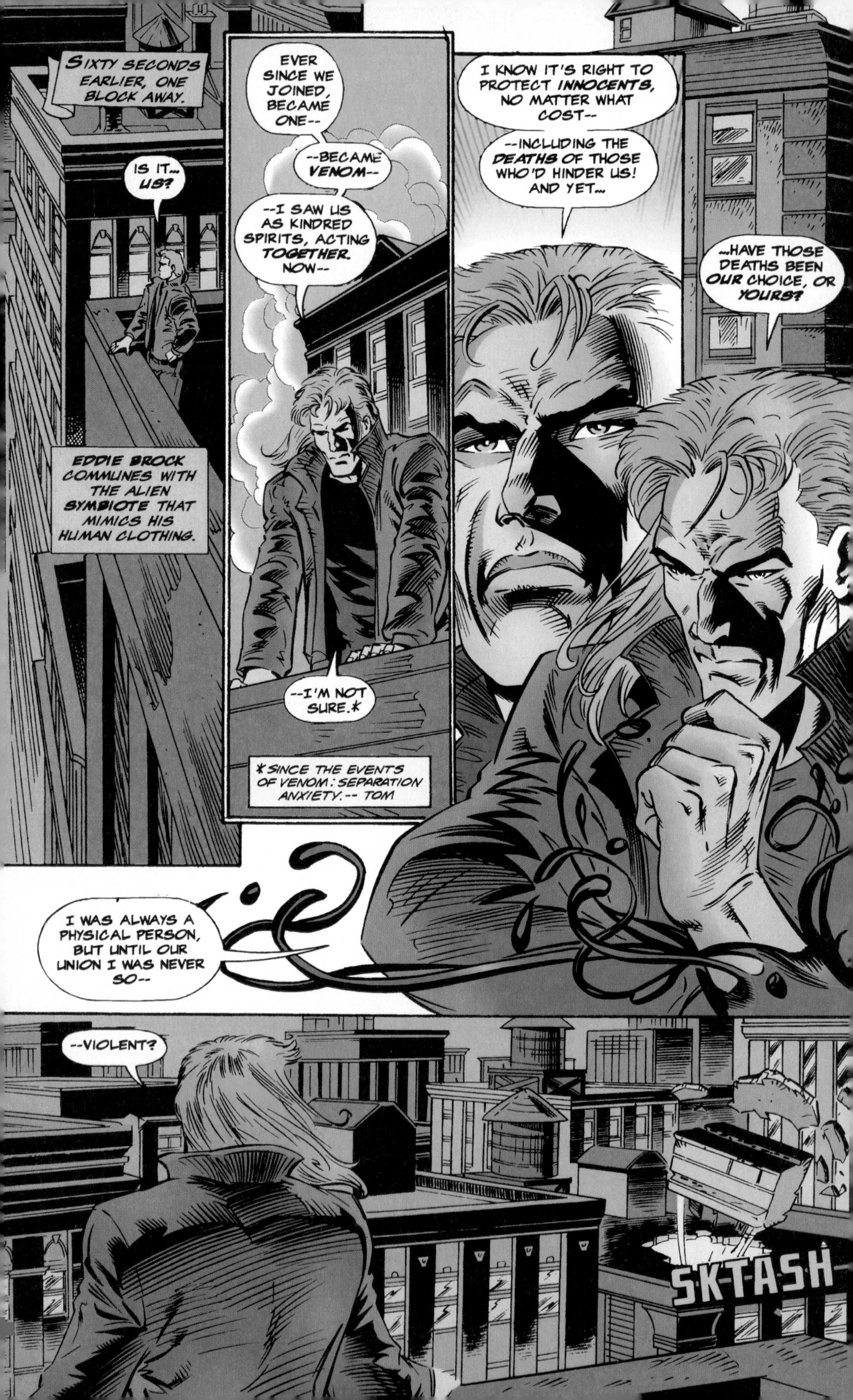
SIXTY SECONDS EARLIER, ONE BLOCK AWAY.
IS IT... US?
EDDIE BROCK COMMUNES WITH THE ALIEN SYMBIOTE THAT MIMICS HIS HUMAN CLOTHING.
EVER SINCE WE JOINED, BECAME ONE--
--BECAME VENOM--
--I SAW US AS KINDRED SPIRITS, ACTING TOGETHER. NOW--
--I'M NOT SURE.*
*SINCE THE EVENTS OF VENOM: SEPARATION ANXIETY. -- TOM
I KNOW IT'S RIGHT TO PROTECT INNOCENTS, NO MATTER WHAT COST--
--INCLUDING THE DEATHS OF THOSE WHO'D HINDER US! AND YET...
...HAVE THOSE DEATHS BEEN OUR CHOICE, OR YOURS?
I WAS ALWAYS A PHYSICAL PERSON, BUT UNTIL OUR UNION I WAS NEVER SO--
--VIOLENT?
SKTASH

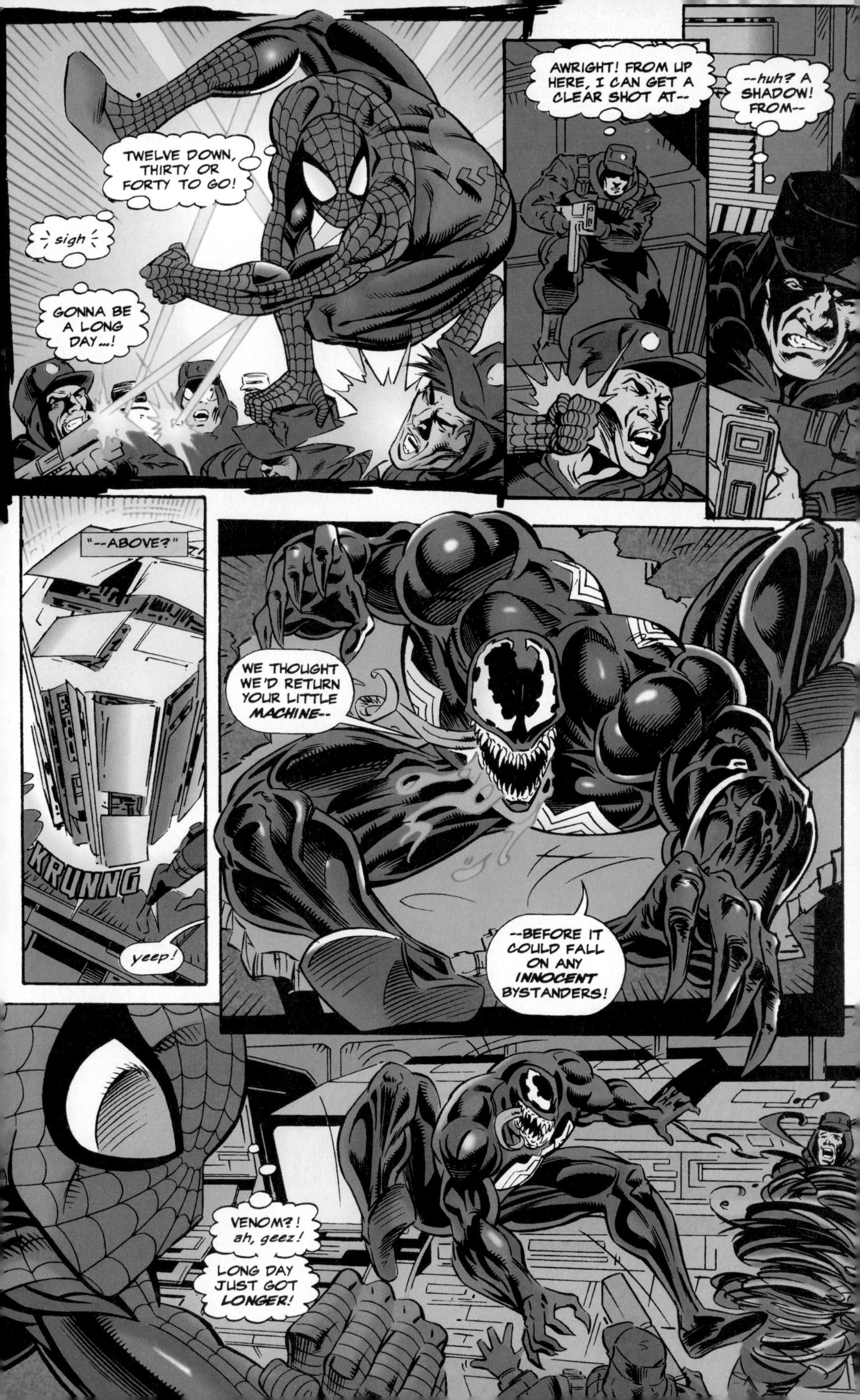
TWELVE DOWN, THIRTY OR FORTY TO GO!
sigh
GONNA BE A LONG DAY...!
AWRIGHT! FROM UP HERE, I CAN GET A CLEAR SHOT AT--
--huh? A SHADOW! FROM--
"--ABOVE?"
KRUNNG
yeep!
WE THOUGHT WE'D RETURN YOUR LITTLE MACHINE--
--BEFORE IT COULD FALL ON ANY INNOCENT BYSTANDERS!
VENOM?! ah, geez!
LONG DAY JUST GOT LONGER!

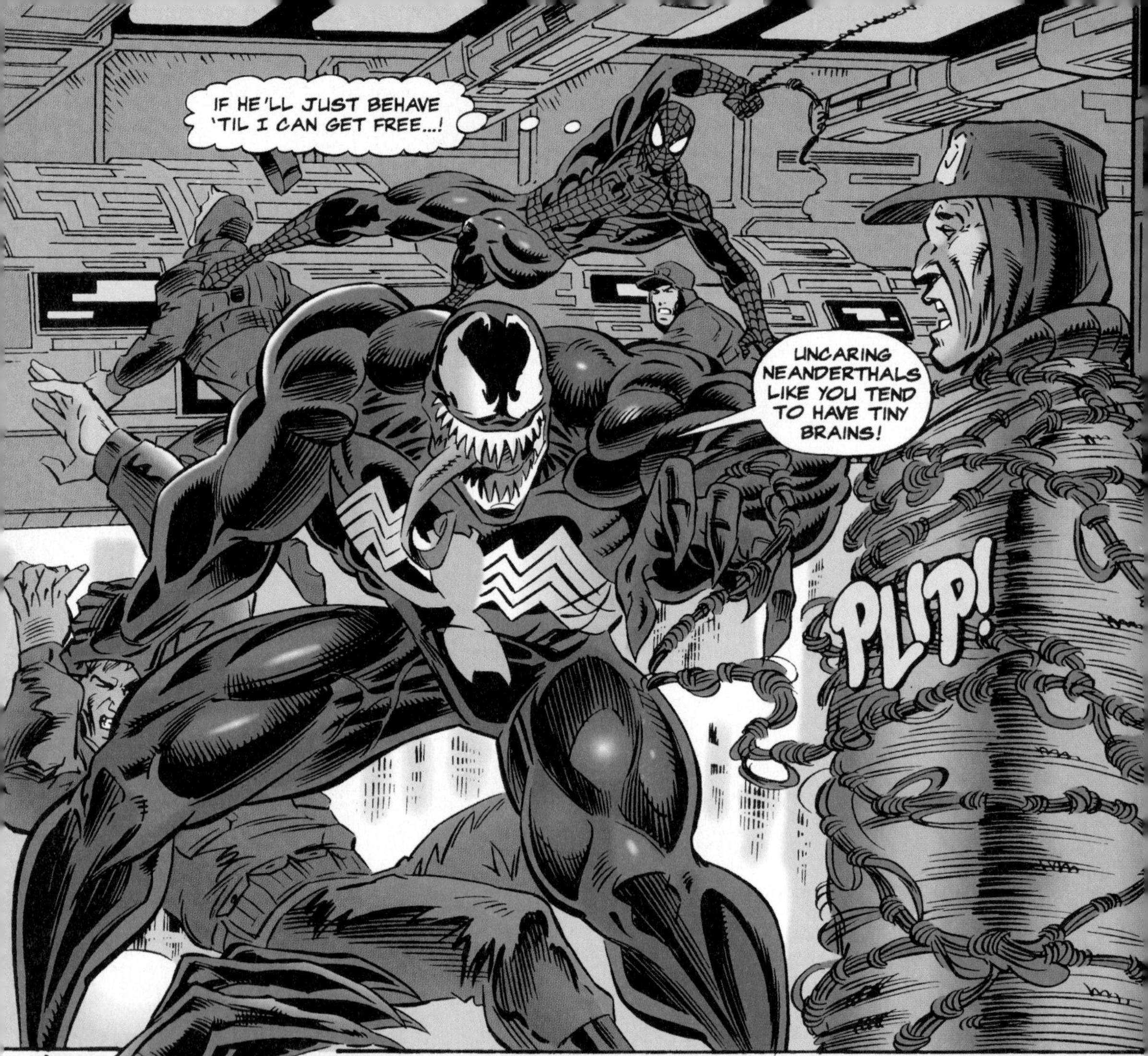
IF HE'LL JUST BEHAVE 'TIL I CAN GET FREE...!
UNCARING NEANDERTHALS LIKE YOU TEND TO HAVE TINY BRAINS!
PLIP!
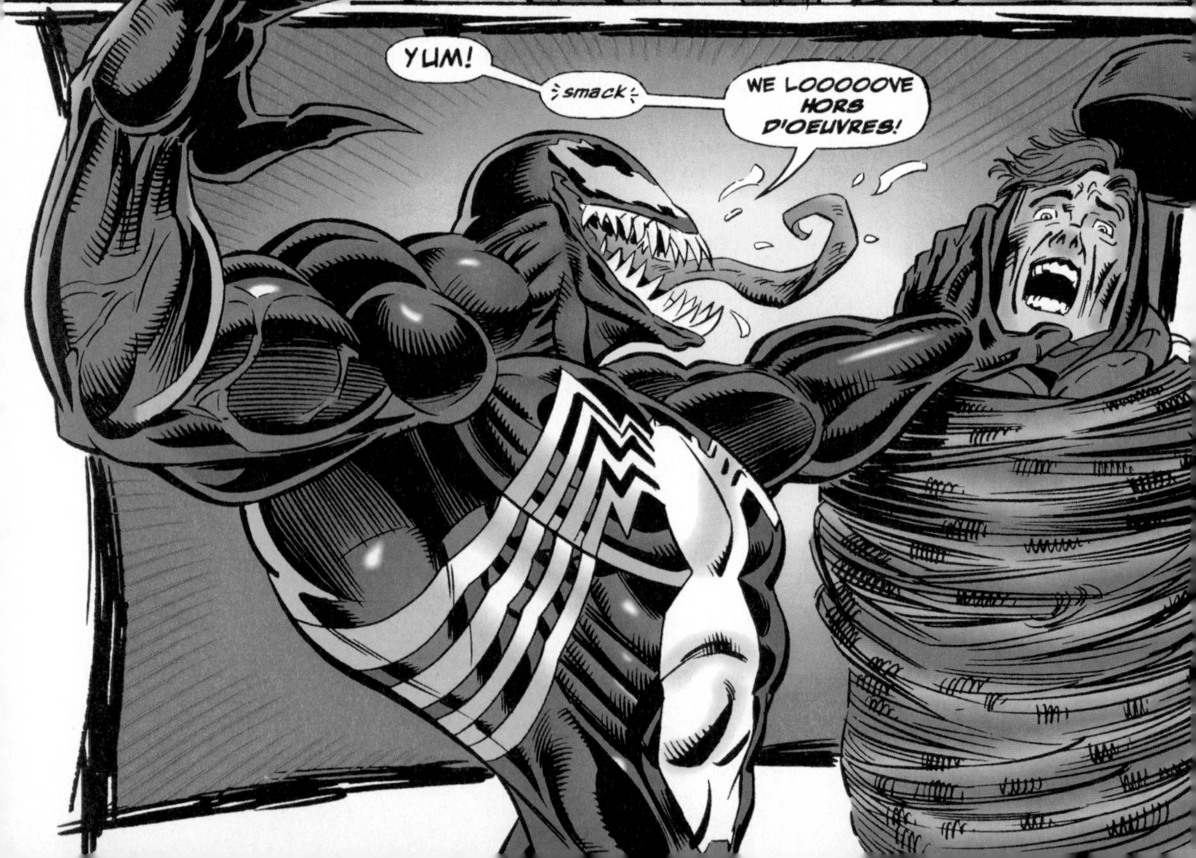
YUM!
smack
WE LOOOOOVE HORS D'OEUVRES!

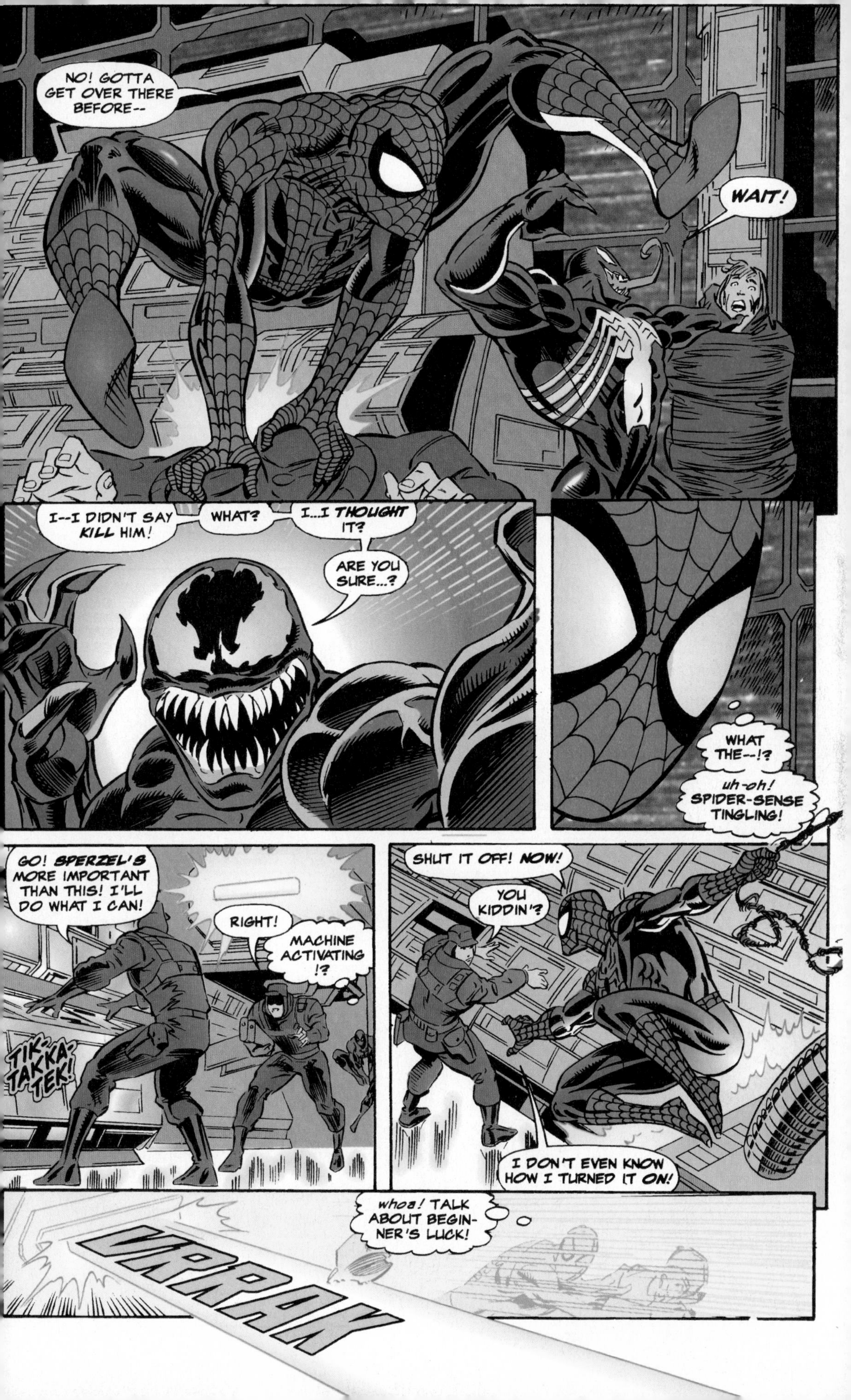

NO! GOTTA GET OVER THERE BEFORE--
WAIT!
I--I DIDN'T SAY KILL HIM!
WHAT?
I...I THOUGHT IT?
ARE YOU SURE...?
WHAT THE--!?
uh-oh! SPIDER-SENSE TINGLING!
GO! SPERZEL'S MORE IMPORTANT THAN THIS! I'LL DO WHAT I CAN!
RIGHT!
MACHINE ACTIVATING !?
TIK-TAKKA-TEK!
SHUT IT OFF! NOW!
YOU KIDDIN'?
I DON'T EVEN KNOW HOW I TURNED IT ON!
whoa! TALK ABOUT BEGIN-NER'S LUCK!
VRRRAK

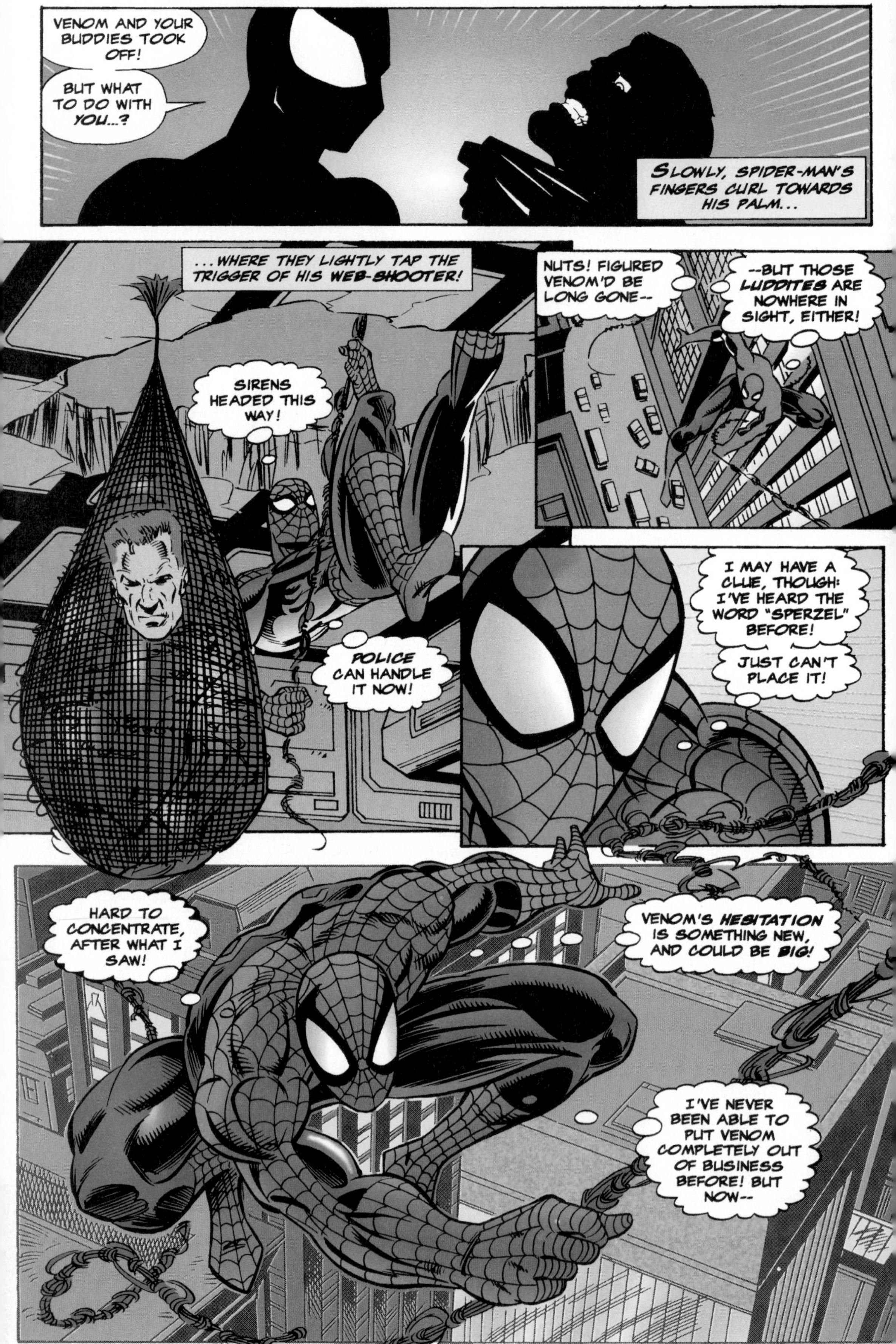
VENOM AND YOUR BUDDIES TOOK OFF!
BUT WHAT TO DO WITH YOU...?
SLOWLY, SPIDER-MAN'S FINGERS CURL TOWARDS HIS PALM...
...WHERE THEY LIGHTLY TAP THE TRIGGER OF HIS WEB-SHOOTER!
SIRENS HEADED THIS WAY!
POLICE CAN HANDLE IT NOW!
NUTS! FIGURED VENOM'D BE LONG GONE--
--BUT THOSE LUDDITES ARE NOWHERE IN SIGHT, EITHER!
I MAY HAVE A CLUE, THOUGH: I'VE HEARD THE WORD "SPERZEL" BEFORE!
JUST CAN'T PLACE IT!
HARD TO CONCENTRATE, AFTER WHAT I SAW!
VENOM'S HESITATION IS SOMETHING NEW, AND COULD BE BIG!
I'VE NEVER BEEN ABLE TO PUT VENOM COMPLETELY OUT OF BUSINESS BEFORE! BUT NOW--

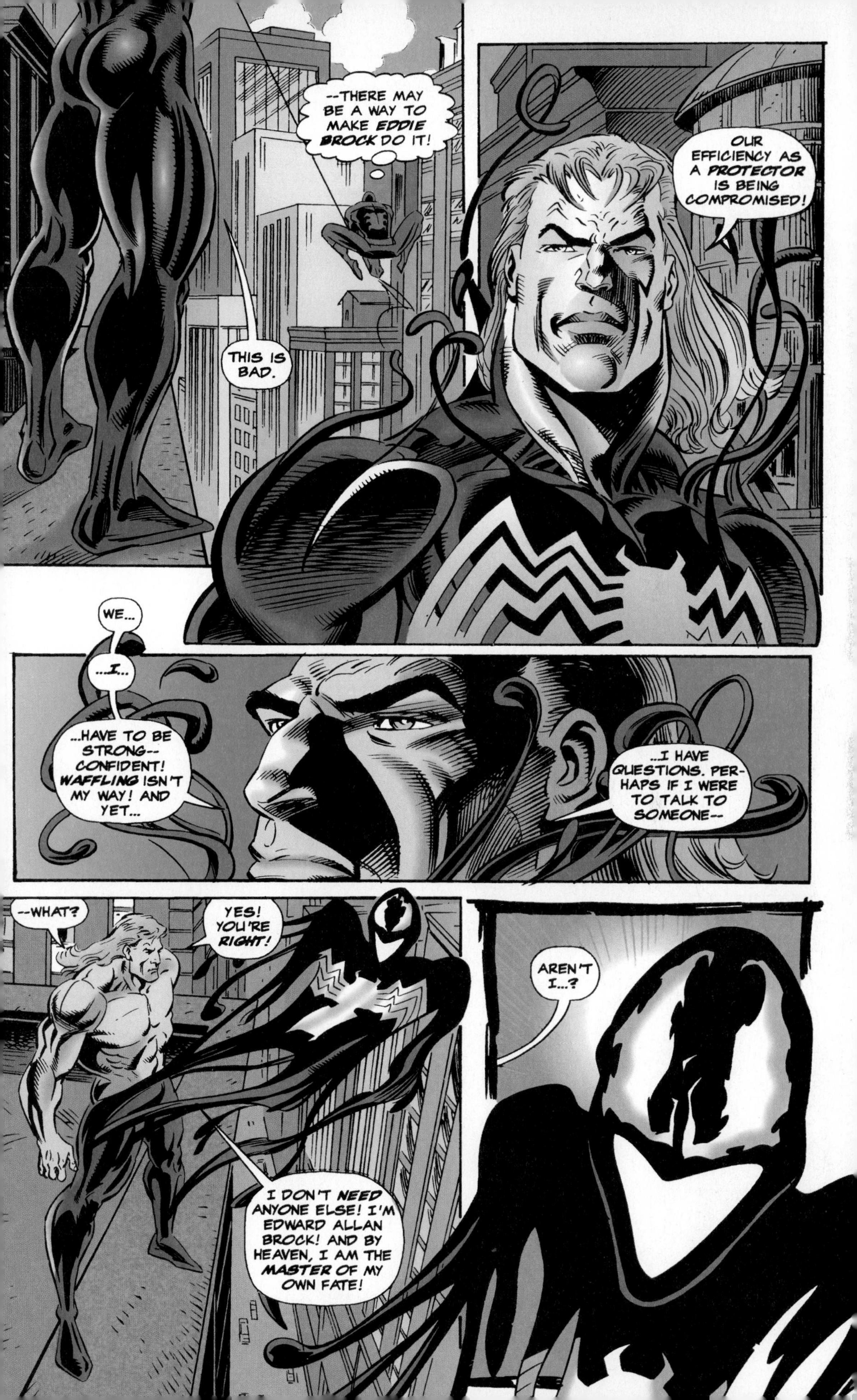
--THERE MAY BE A WAY TO MAKE EDDIE BROCK DO IT!
THIS IS BAD.
OUR EFFICIENCY AS A PROTECTOR IS BEING COMPROMISED!
WE...
...I...
...HAVE TO BE STRONG-- CONFIDENT! WAFFLING ISN'T MY WAY! AND YET...
...I HAVE QUESTIONS. PERHAPS IF I WERE TO TALK TO SOMEONE--
--WHAT?
YES! YOU'RE RIGHT!
I DON'T NEED ANYONE ELSE! I'M EDWARD ALLAN BROCK! AND BY HEAVEN, I AM THE MASTER OF MY OWN FATE!
AREN'T I...?

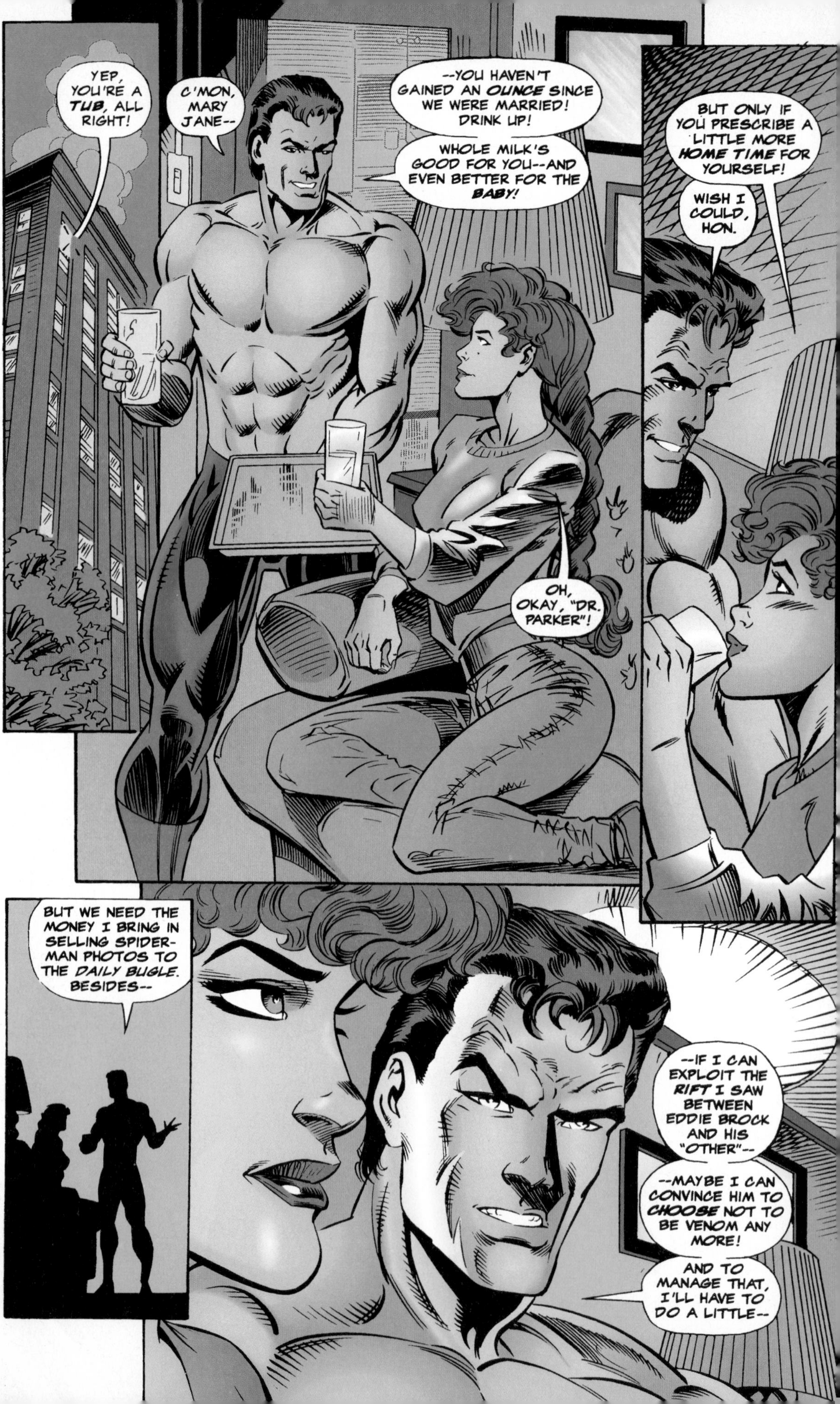
YEP, YOU'RE A TUB, ALL RIGHT!
C'MON, MARY JANE--
--YOU HAVEN'T GAINED AN OUNCE SINCE WE WERE MARRIED! DRINK UP!
WHOLE MILK'S GOOD FOR YOU--AND EVEN BETTER FOR THE BABY!
OH, OKAY, "DR. PARKER"!
BUT ONLY IF YOU PRESCRIBE A LITTLE MORE HOME TIME FOR YOURSELF!
WISH I COULD, HON.
BUT WE NEED THE MONEY I BRING IN SELLING SPIDER-MAN PHOTOS TO THE DAILY BUGLE. BESIDES--
--IF I CAN EXPLOIT THE RIFT I SAW BETWEEN EDDIE BROCK AND HIS "OTHER"--
--MAYBE I CAN CONVINCE HIM TO CHOOSE NOT TO BE VENOM ANY MORE!
AND TO MANAGE THAT, I'LL HAVE TO DO A LITTLE--

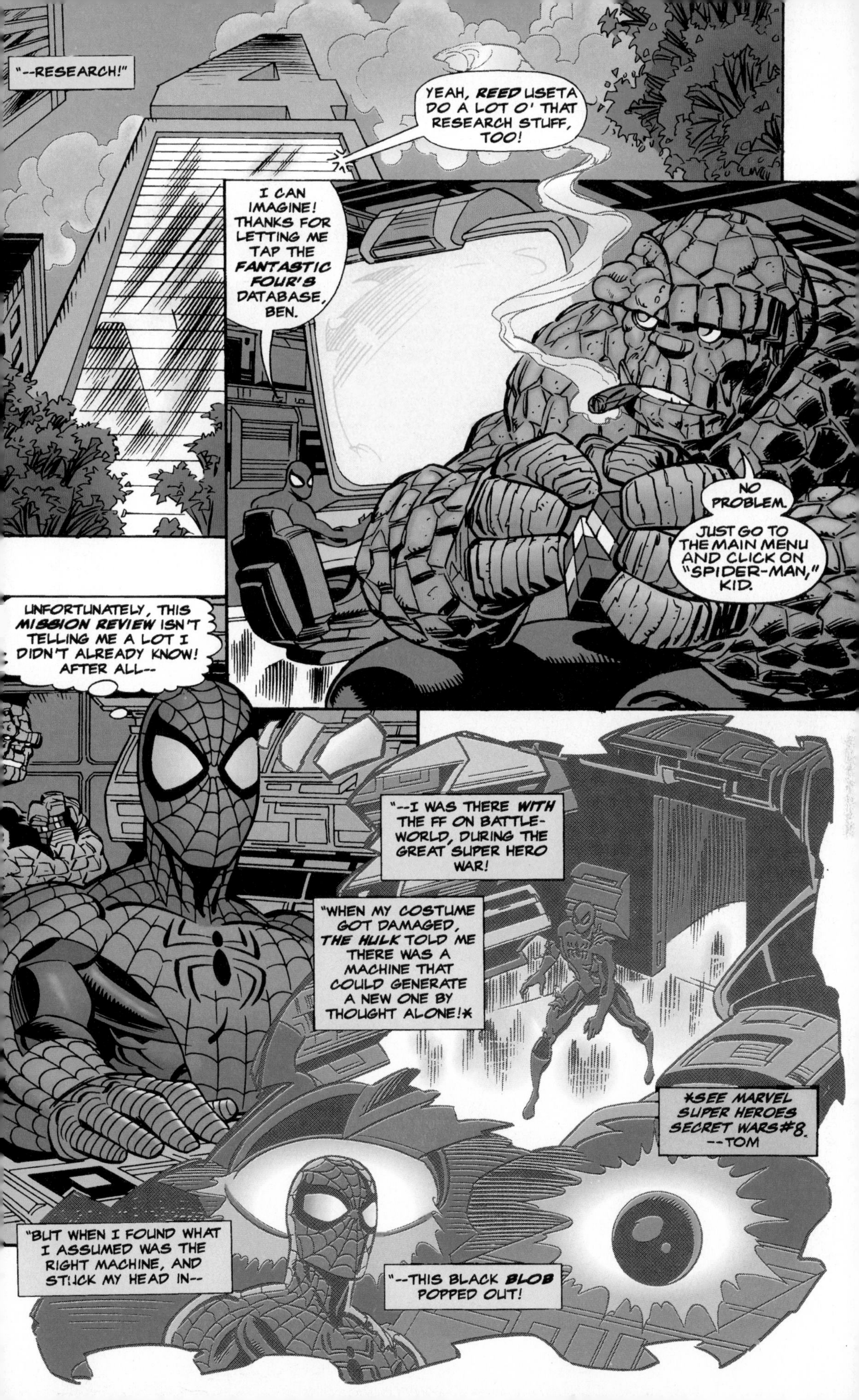
"--RESEARCH!"
YEAH, REED USETA DO A LOT O' THAT RESEARCH STUFF, TOO!
I CAN IMAGINE! THANKS FOR LETTING ME TAP THE FANTASTIC FOUR'S DATABASE, BEN.
NO PROBLEM.
JUST GO TO THE MAIN MENU AND CLICK ON "SPIDER-MAN," KID.
UNFORTUNATELY, THIS MISSION REVIEW ISN'T TELLING ME A LOT I DIDN'T ALREADY KNOW! AFTER ALL--
"--I WAS THERE WITH THE FF ON BATTLE-WORLD, DURING THE GREAT SUPER HERO WAR!
"WHEN MY COSTUME GOT DAMAGED, THE HULK TOLD ME THERE WAS A MACHINE THAT COULD GENERATE A NEW ONE BY THOUGHT ALONE!*
*SEE MARVEL SUPER HEROES SECRET WARS #8. --TOM
"BUT WHEN I FOUND WHAT I ASSUMED WAS THE RIGHT MACHINE, AND STUCK MY HEAD IN--
"--THIS BLACK BLOB POPPED OUT!

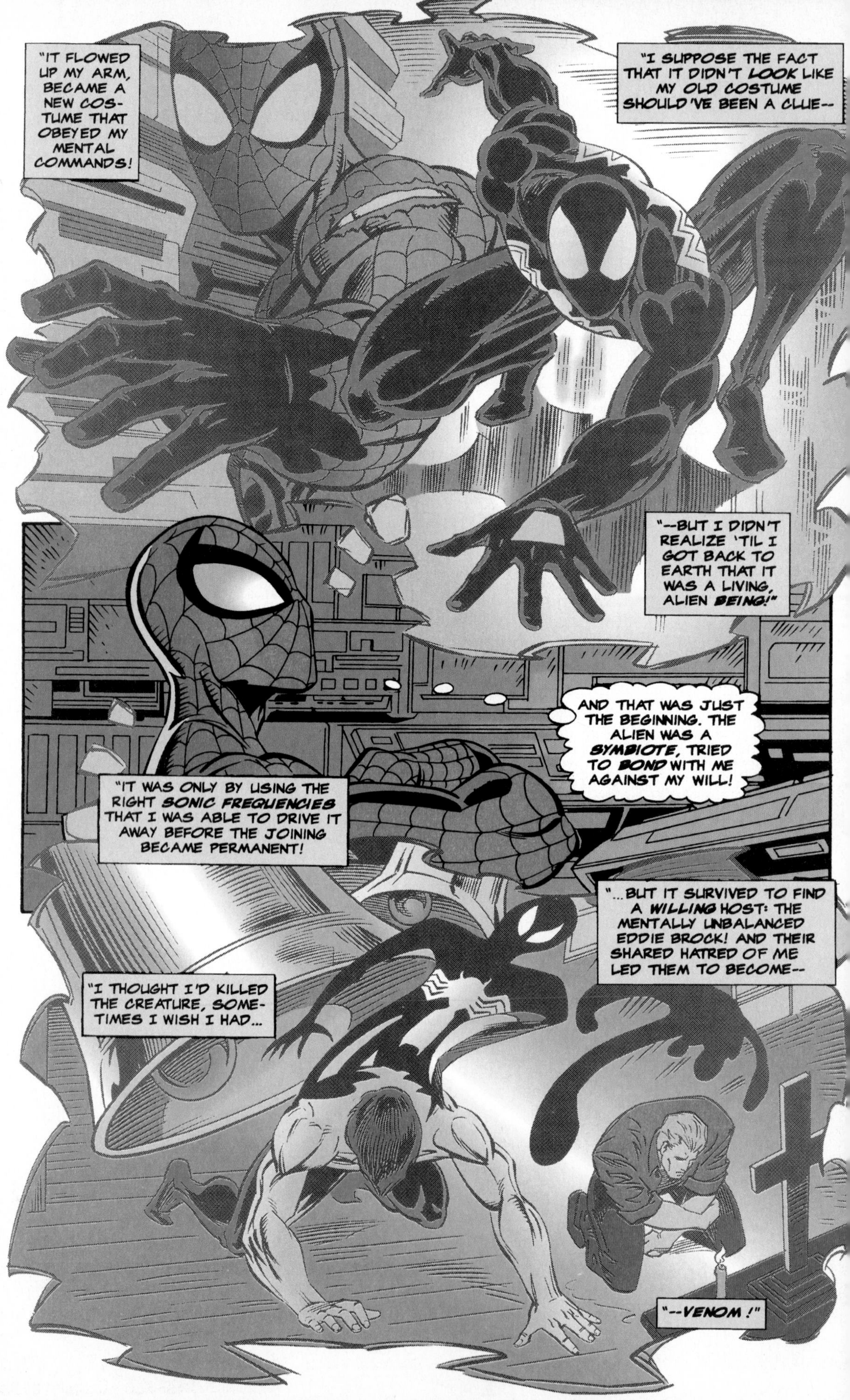
"IT FLOWED UP MY ARM, BECAME A NEW COS-TUME THAT OBEYED MY MENTAL COMMANDS!
"I SUPPOSE THE FACT THAT IT DIDN'T LOOK LIKE MY OLD COSTUME SHOULD'VE BEEN A CLUE--
"--BUT I DIDN'T REALIZE 'TIL I GOT BACK TO EARTH THAT IT WAS A LIVING, ALIEN BEING!"
AND THAT WAS JUST THE BEGINNING. THE ALIEN WAS A SYMBIOTE, TRIED TO BOND WITH ME AGAINST MY WILL!
"IT WAS ONLY BY USING THE RIGHT SONIC FREQUENCIES THAT I WAS ABLE TO DRIVE IT AWAY BEFORE THE JOINING BECAME PERMANENT!
"...BUT IT SURVIVED TO FIND A WILLING HOST: THE MENTALLY UNBALANCED EDDIE BROCK! AND THEIR SHARED HATRED OF ME LED THEM TO BECOME--
"I THOUGHT I'D KILLED THE CREATURE, SOME-TIMES I WISH I HAD...
"--VENOM!"

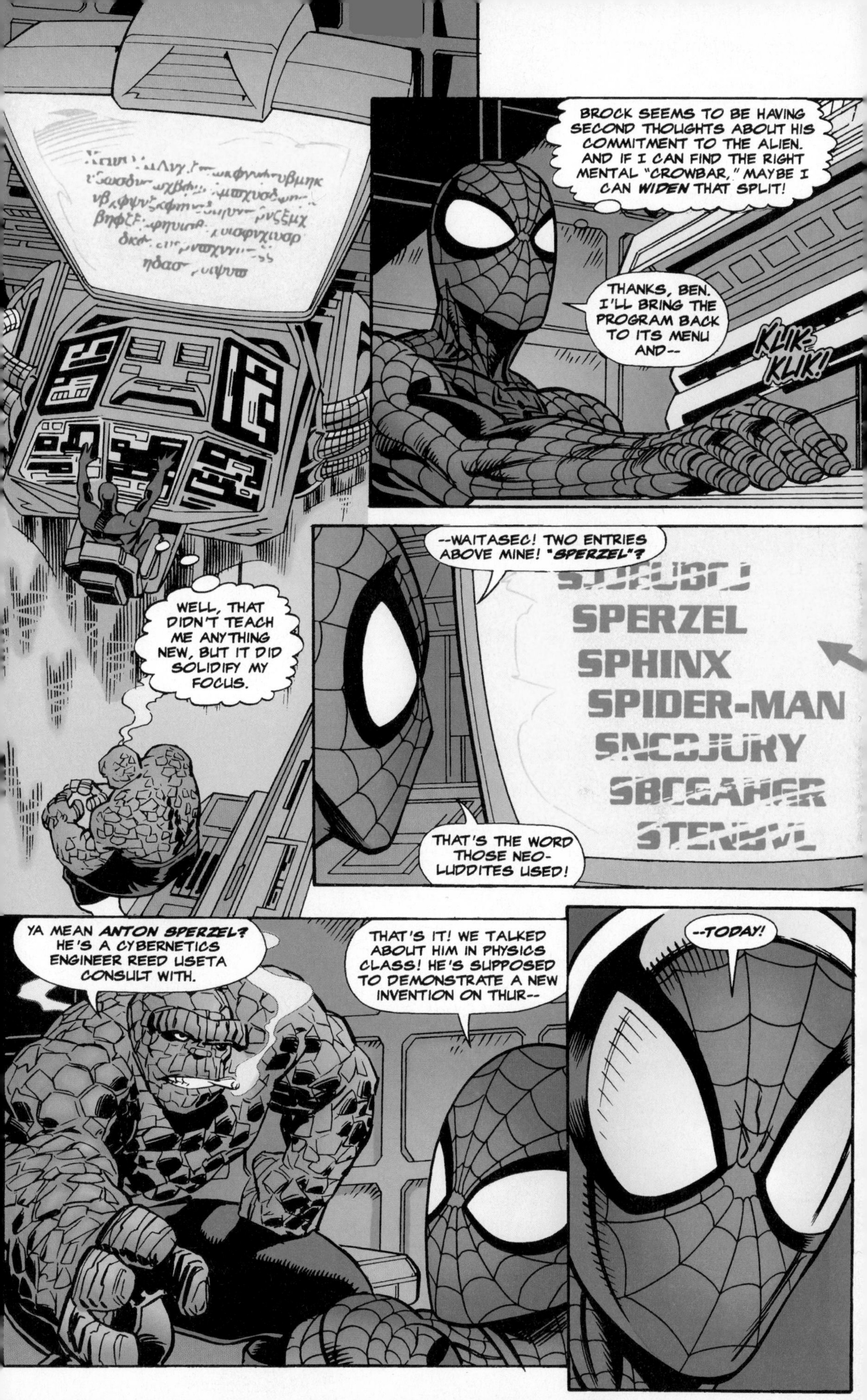
BROCK SEEMS TO BE HAVING SECOND THOUGHTS ABOUT HIS COMMITMENT TO THE ALIEN. AND IF I CAN FIND THE RIGHT MENTAL "CROWBAR," MAYBE I CAN *WIDEN* THAT SPLIT!
THANKS, BEN. I'LL BRING THE PROGRAM BACK TO ITS MENU AND--
KLIK-KLIK!
WELL, THAT DIDN'T TEACH ME ANYTHING NEW, BUT IT DID SOLIDIFY MY FOCUS.
--WAITASEC! TWO ENTRIES ABOVE MINE! "*SPERZEL*"?
SPERZEL
SPHINX
SPIDER-MAN
THAT'S THE WORD THOSE NEO-LUDDITES USED!
YA MEAN *ANTON SPERZEL*? HE'S A CYBERNETICS ENGINEER REED USETA CONSULT WITH.
THAT'S IT! WE TALKED ABOUT HIM IN PHYSICS CLASS! HE'S SUPPOSED TO DEMONSTRATE A NEW INVENTION ON THUR--
--*TODAY!*

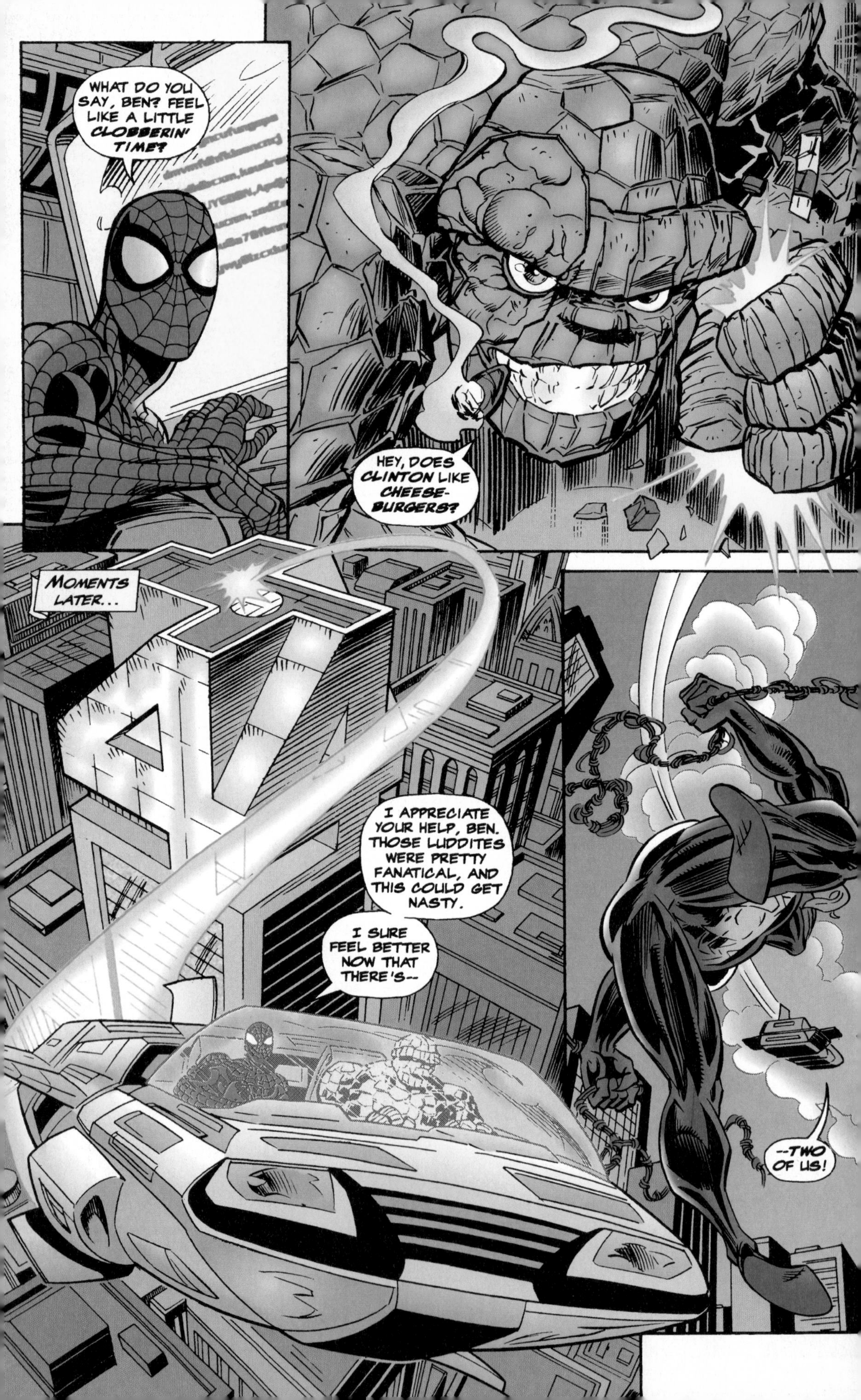
WHAT DO YOU SAY, BEN? FEEL LIKE A LITTLE CLOBBERIN' TIME?
HEY, DOES CLINTON LIKE CHEESE-BURGERS?
MOMENTS LATER...
I APPRECIATE YOUR HELP, BEN. THOSE LUDDITES WERE PRETTY FANATICAL, AND THIS COULD GET NASTY.
I SURE FEEL BETTER NOW THAT THERE'S--
--TWO OF US!

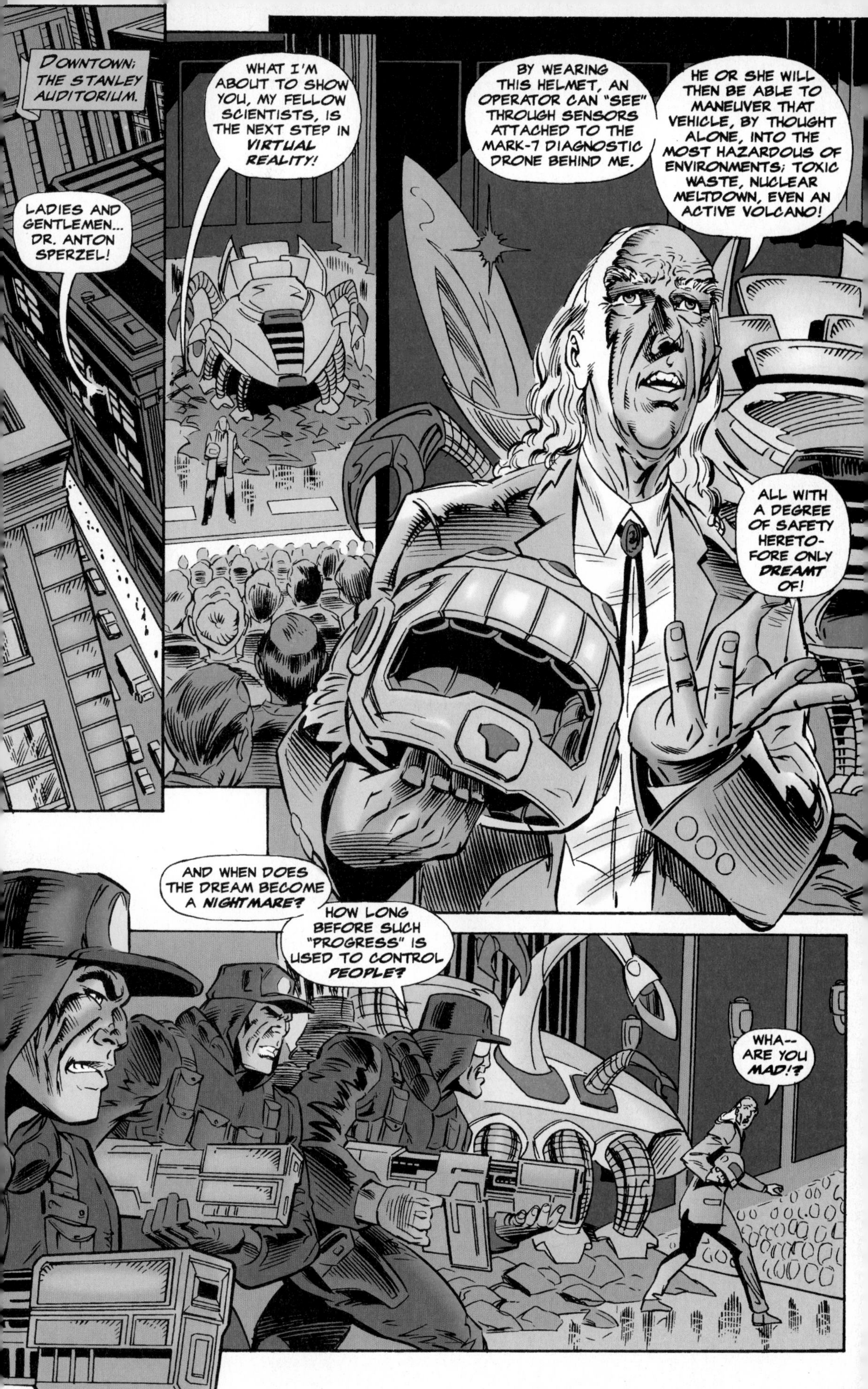
DOWNTOWN: THE STANLEY AUDITORIUM.
LADIES AND GENTLEMEN... DR. ANTON SPERZEL!
WHAT I'M ABOUT TO SHOW YOU, MY FELLOW SCIENTISTS, IS THE NEXT STEP IN VIRTUAL REALITY!
BY WEARING THIS HELMET, AN OPERATOR CAN "SEE" THROUGH SENSORS ATTACHED TO THE MARK-7 DIAGNOSTIC DRONE BEHIND ME.
HE OR SHE WILL THEN BE ABLE TO MANEUVER THAT VEHICLE, BY THOUGHT ALONE, INTO THE MOST HAZARDOUS OF ENVIRONMENTS; TOXIC WASTE, NUCLEAR MELTDOWN, EVEN AN ACTIVE VOLCANO!
ALL WITH A DEGREE OF SAFETY HERETO-FORE ONLY DREAMT OF!
AND WHEN DOES THE DREAM BECOME A NIGHTMARE?
HOW LONG BEFORE SUCH "PROGRESS" IS USED TO CONTROL PEOPLE?
WHA-- ARE YOU MAD!?

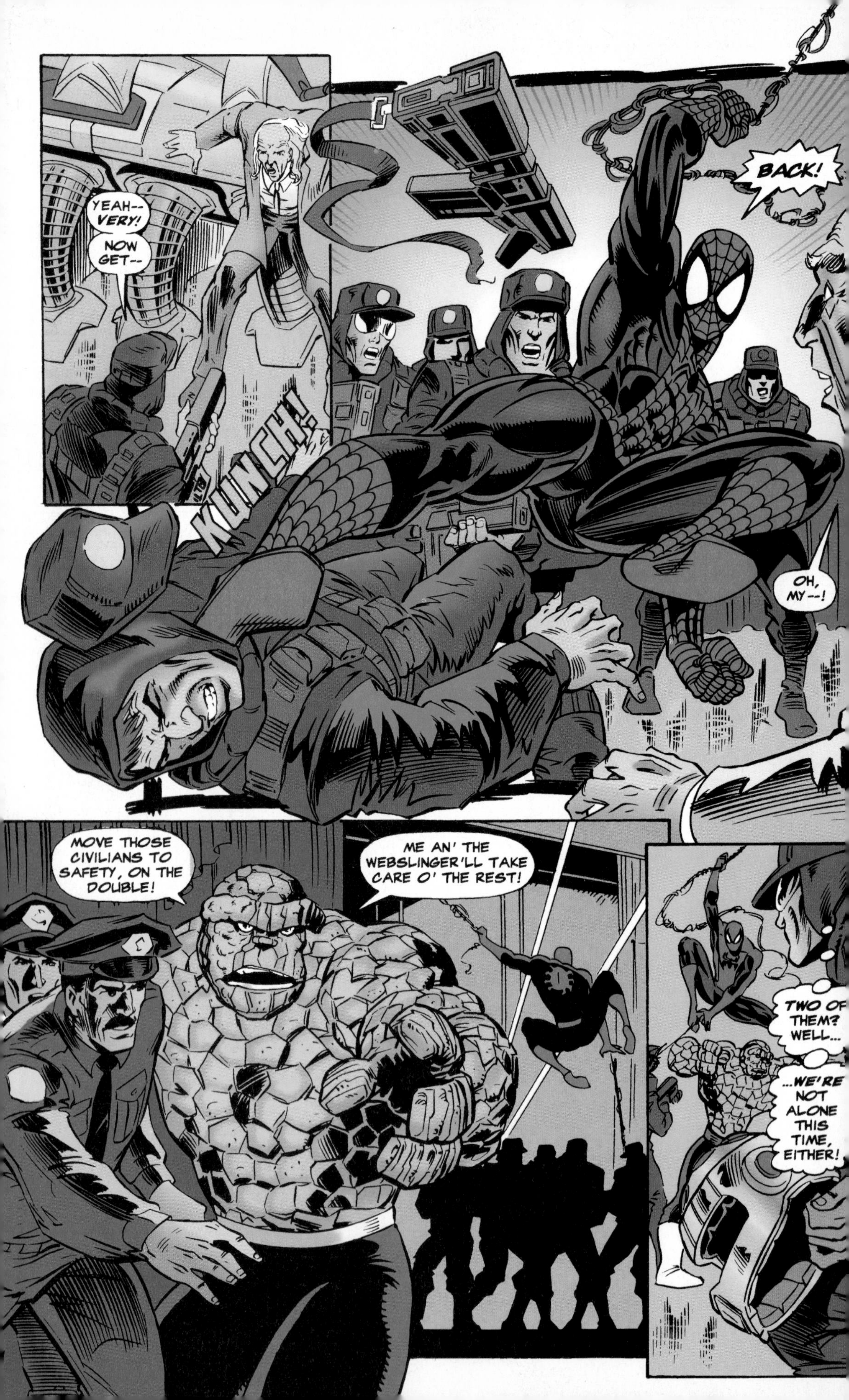
YEAH-- VERY!
NOW GET--
BACK!
KUNCH!
OH, MY--!
MOVE THOSE CIVILIANS TO SAFETY, ON THE DOUBLE!
ME AN' THE WEBSLINGER'LL TAKE CARE O' THE REST!
TWO OF THEM? WELL...
...WE'RE NOT ALONE THIS TIME, EITHER!

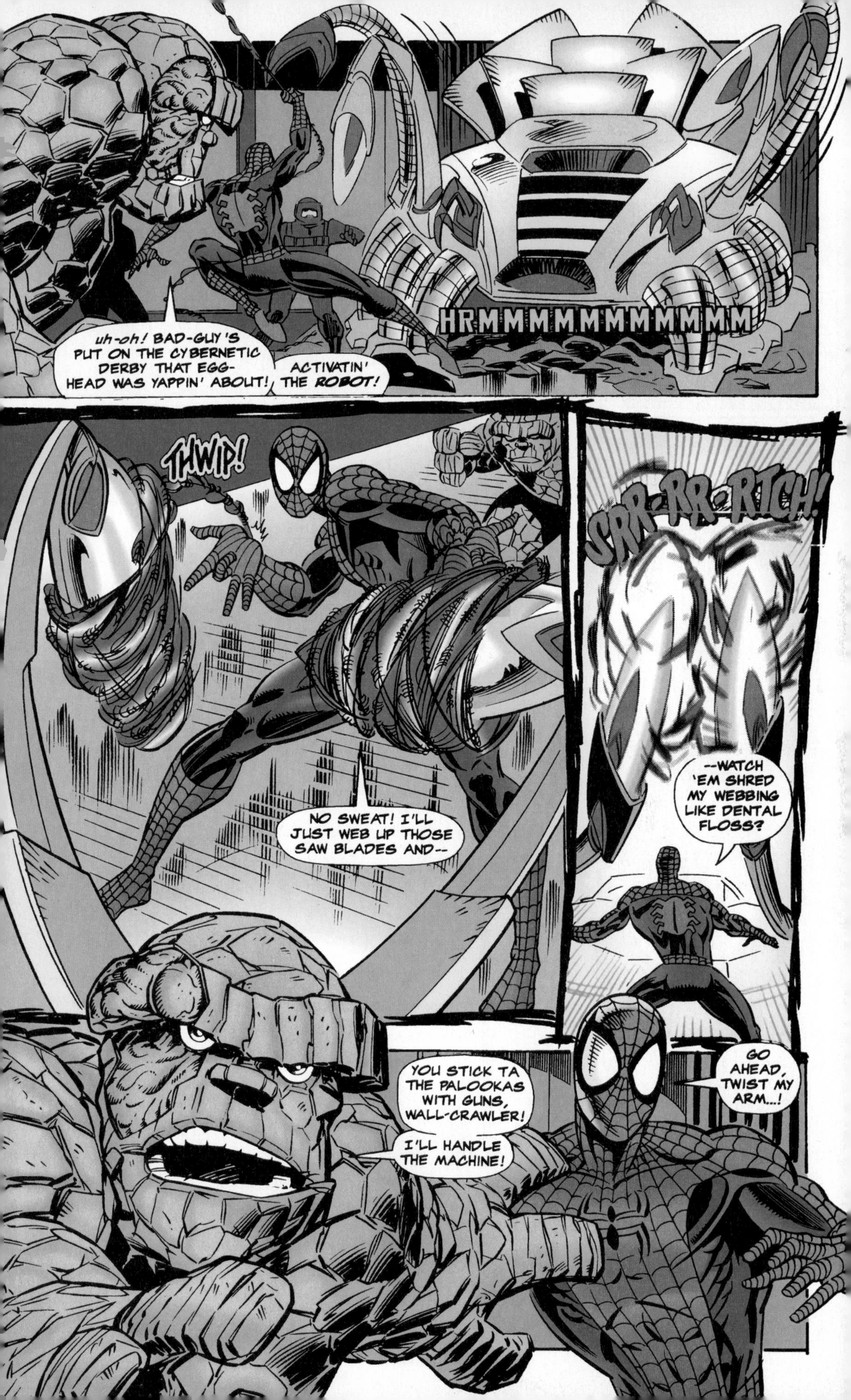
HRMMMMMMMMMMMMM
uh-oh! BAD-GUY'S PUT ON THE CYBERNETIC DERBY THAT EGG-HEAD WAS YAPPIN' ABOUT!
ACTIVATIN' THE ROBOT!
THWIP!
NO SWEAT! I'LL JUST WEB UP THOSE SAW BLADES AND--
SRR-RR-RTCH!
--WATCH 'EM SHRED MY WEBBING LIKE DENTAL FLOSS?
YOU STICK TA THE PALOOKAS WITH GUNS, WALL-CRAWLER!
I'LL HANDLE THE MACHINE!
GO AHEAD, TWIST MY ARM...!

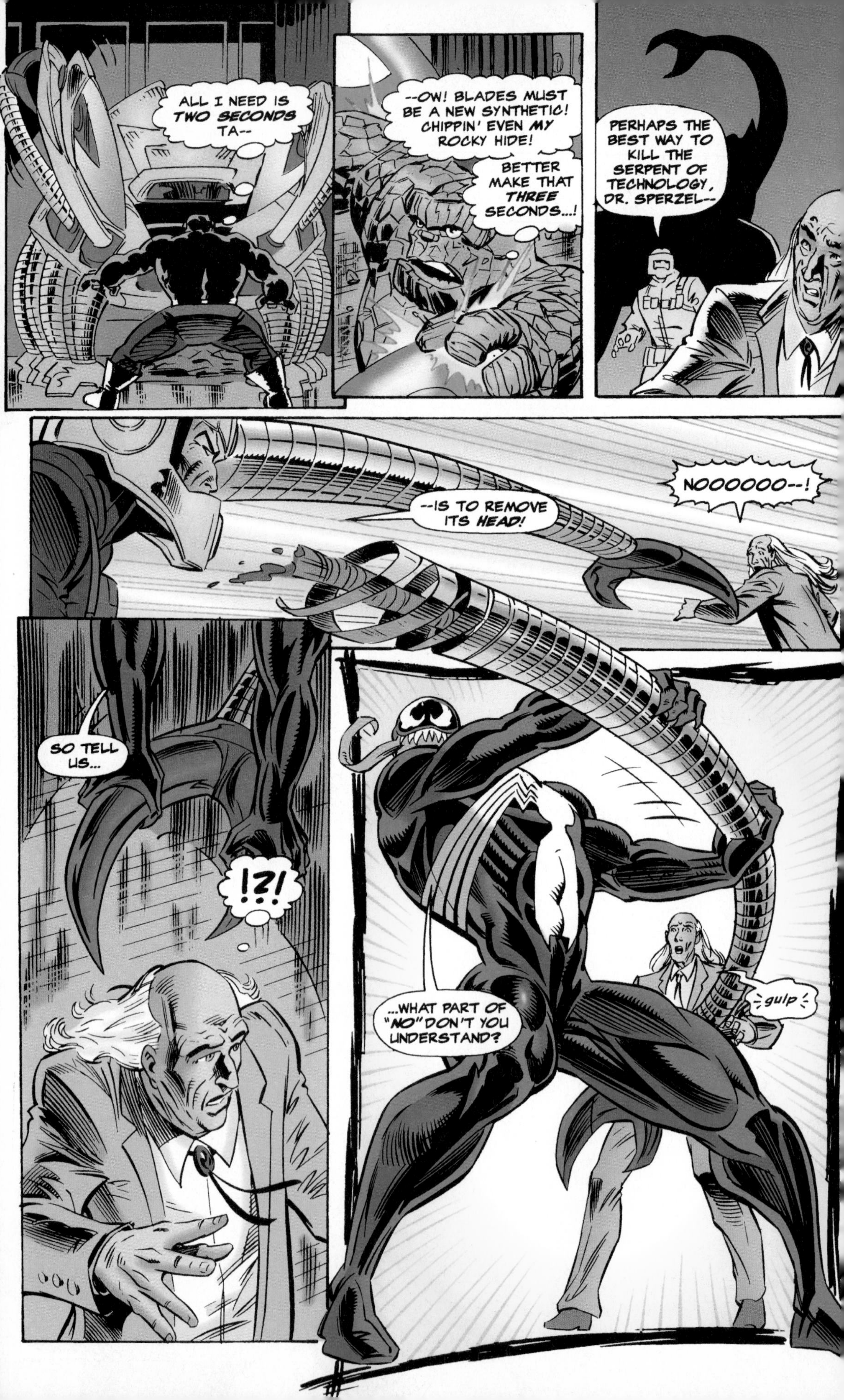
ALL I NEED IS TWO SECONDS TA--
--OW! BLADES MUST BE A NEW SYNTHETIC! CHIPPIN' EVEN MY ROCKY HIDE!
BETTER MAKE THAT THREE SECONDS...!
PERHAPS THE BEST WAY TO KILL THE SERPENT OF TECHNOLOGY, DR. SPERZEL--
--IS TO REMOVE ITS HEAD!
NOOOOOO--!
SO TELL US...
!?!
...WHAT PART OF "NO" DON'T YOU UNDERSTAND?
gulp

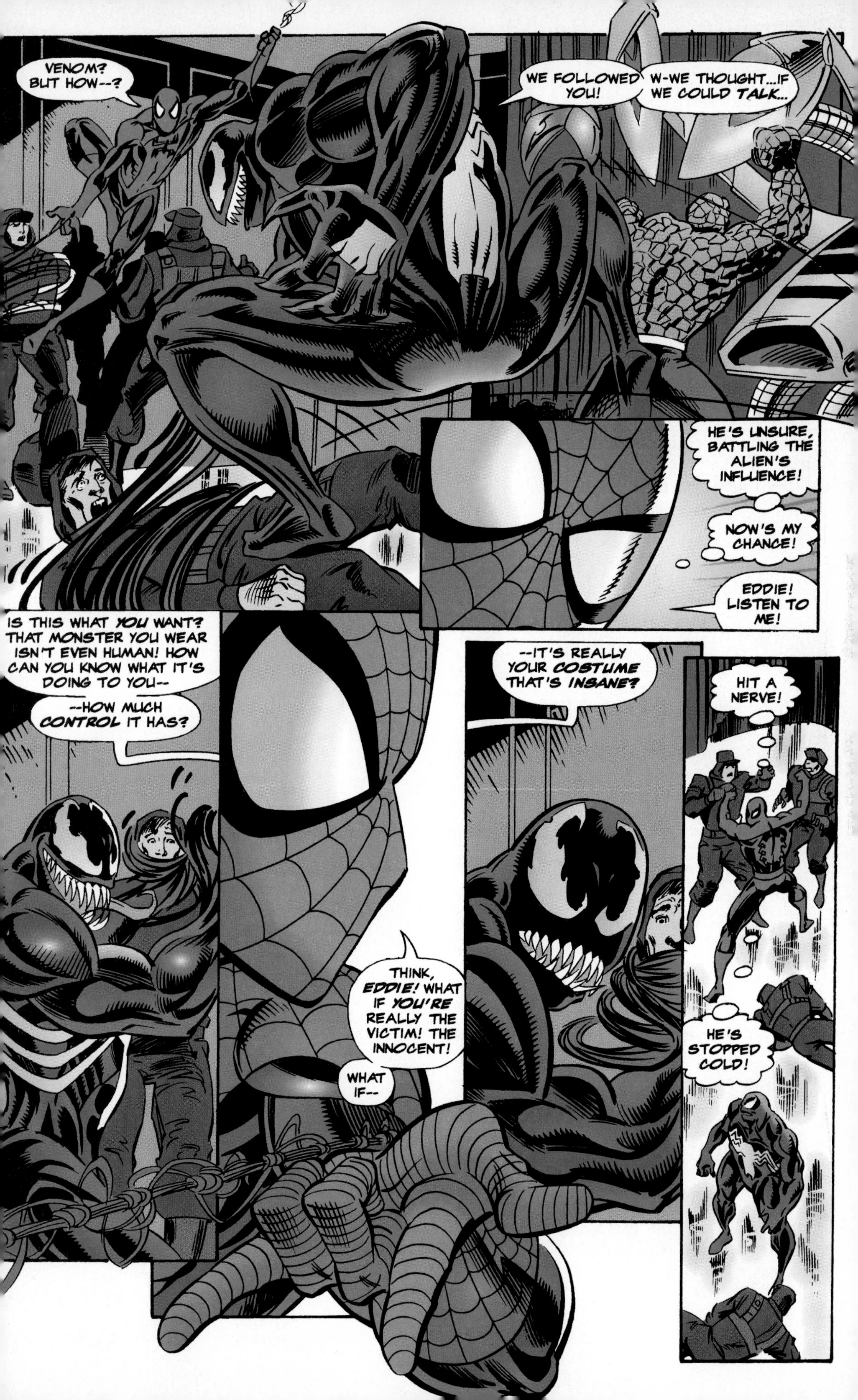
VENOM? BUT HOW--?
WE FOLLOWED YOU!
W-WE THOUGHT...IF WE COULD TALK...
HE'S UNSURE, BATTLING THE ALIEN'S INFLUENCE!
NOW'S MY CHANCE!
EDDIE! LISTEN TO ME!
IS THIS WHAT YOU WANT? THAT MONSTER YOU WEAR ISN'T EVEN HUMAN! HOW CAN YOU KNOW WHAT IT'S DOING TO YOU--
--HOW MUCH CONTROL IT HAS?
THINK, EDDIE! WHAT IF YOU'RE REALLY THE VICTIM! THE INNOCENT!
WHAT IF--
--IT'S REALLY YOUR COSTUME THAT'S INSANE?
HIT A NERVE!
HE'S STOPPED COLD!

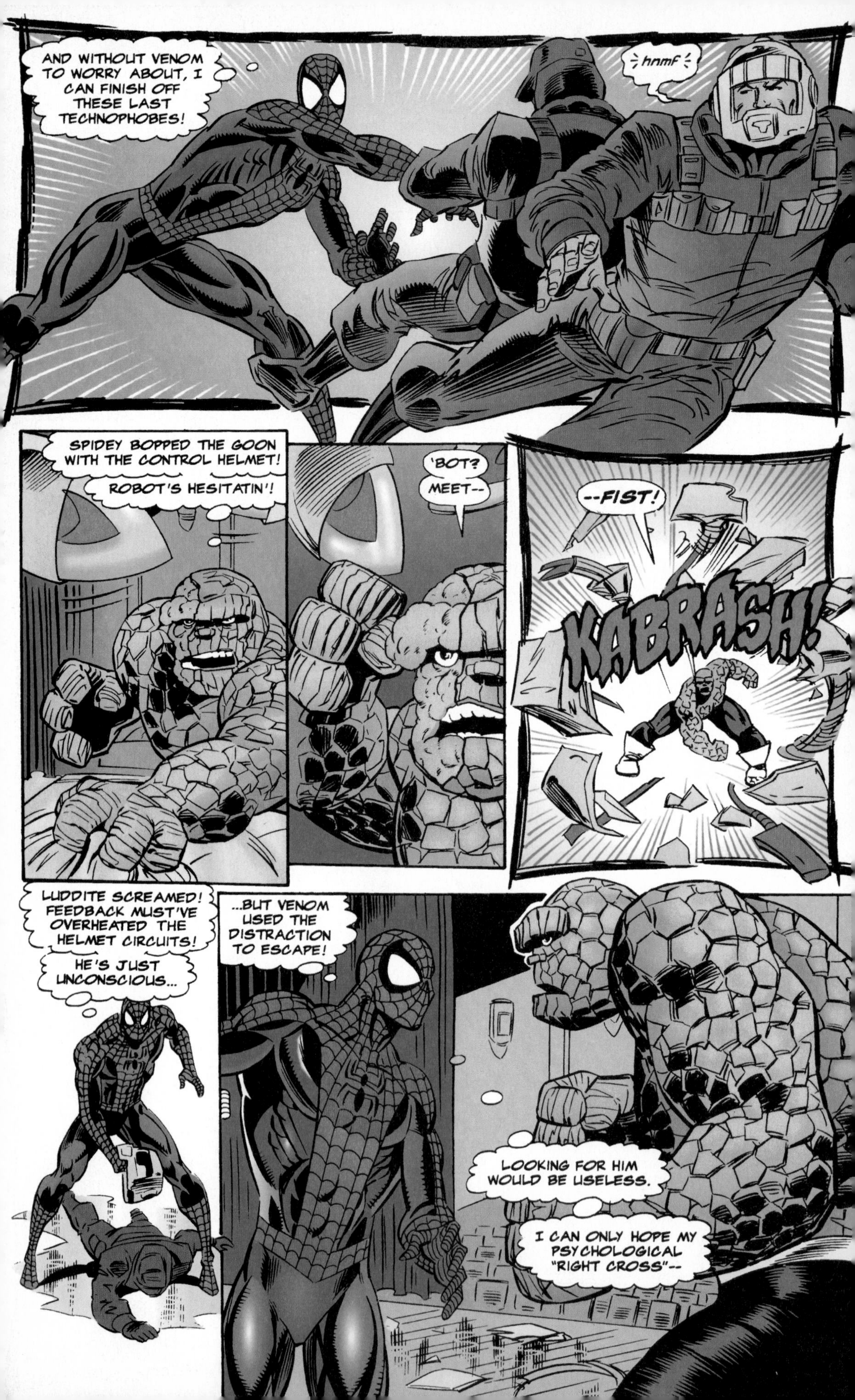
AND WITHOUT VENOM TO WORRY ABOUT, I CAN FINISH OFF THESE LAST TECHNOPHOBES!
hnmf
SPIDEY BOPPED THE GOON WITH THE CONTROL HELMET!
ROBOT'S HESITATIN'!
'BOT? MEET--
--FIST!
KABRASH!
LUDDITE SCREAMED! FEEDBACK MUST'VE OVERHEATED THE HELMET CIRCUITS!
HE'S JUST UNCONSCIOUS...
...BUT VENOM USED THE DISTRACTION TO ESCAPE!
LOOKING FOR HIM WOULD BE USELESS.
I CAN ONLY HOPE MY PSYCHOLOGICAL "RIGHT CROSS"--

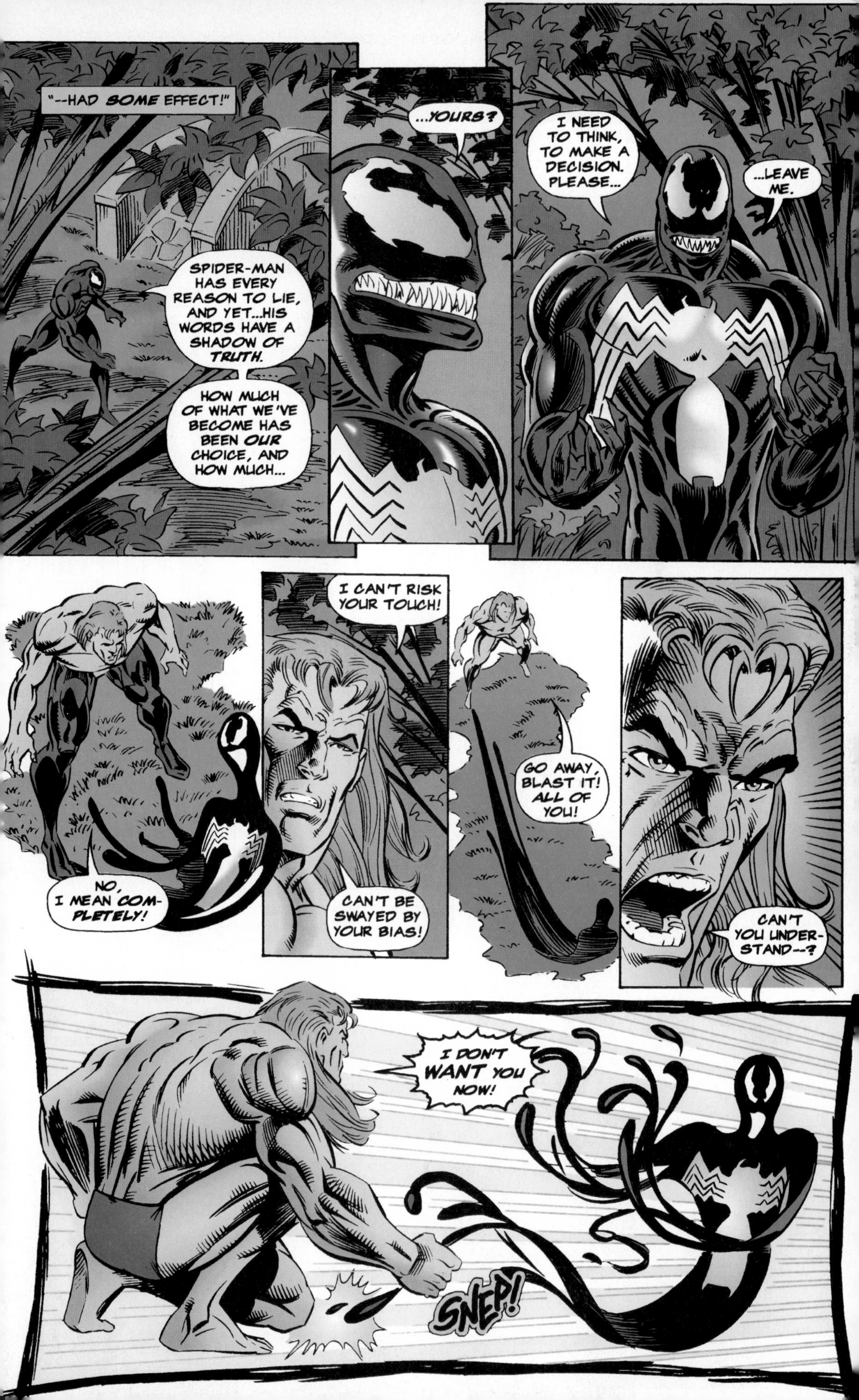
"--HAD SOME EFFECT!"
SPIDER-MAN HAS EVERY REASON TO LIE, AND YET...HIS WORDS HAVE A SHADOW OF TRUTH.
HOW MUCH OF WHAT WE'VE BECOME HAS BEEN OUR CHOICE, AND HOW MUCH...
...YOURS?
I NEED TO THINK, TO MAKE A DECISION. PLEASE...
...LEAVE ME.
NO, I MEAN COMPLETELY!
I CAN'T RISK YOUR TOUCH!
CAN'T BE SWAYED BY YOUR BIAS!
GO AWAY, BLAST IT! ALL OF YOU!
CAN'T YOU UNDERSTAND--?
I DON'T WANT YOU NOW!
SNEP!

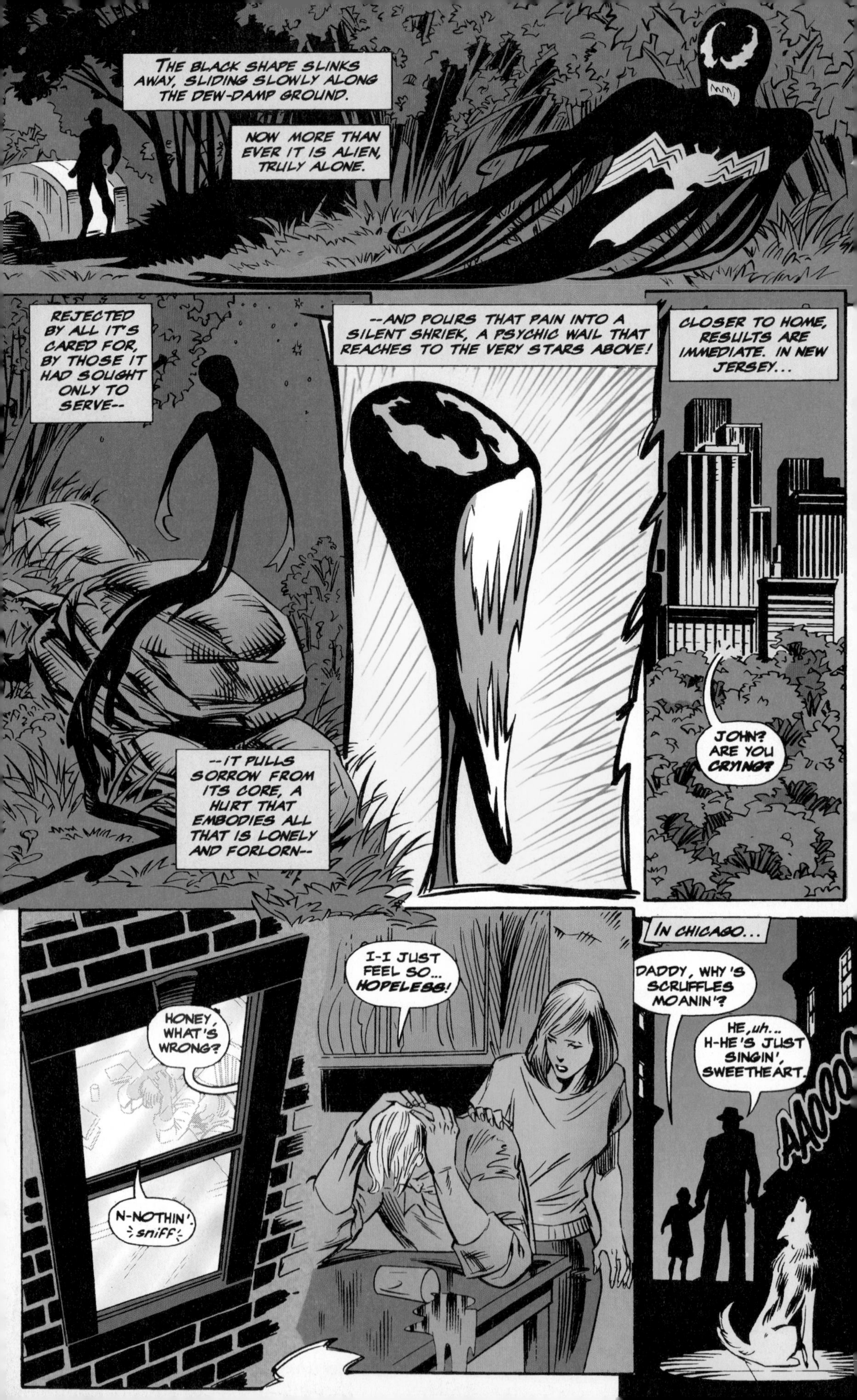
THE BLACK SHAPE SLINKS AWAY, SLIDING SLOWLY ALONG THE DEW-DAMP GROUND.
NOW MORE THAN EVER IT IS ALIEN, TRULY ALONE.
REJECTED BY ALL IT'S CARED FOR, BY THOSE IT HAD SOUGHT ONLY TO SERVE--
--IT PULLS SORROW FROM ITS CORE, A HURT THAT EMBODIES ALL THAT IS LONELY AND FORLORN--
--AND POURS THAT PAIN INTO A SILENT SHRIEK, A PSYCHIC WAIL THAT REACHES TO THE VERY STARS ABOVE!
CLOSER TO HOME, RESULTS ARE IMMEDIATE. IN NEW JERSEY...
JOHN? ARE YOU CRYING?
HONEY, WHAT'S WRONG?
N-NOTHIN'. sniff
I-I JUST FEEL SO... HOPELESS!
IN CHICAGO...
DADDY, WHY'S SCRUFFLES MOANIN'?
HE, uh... H-HE'S JUST SINGIN', SWEETHEART.

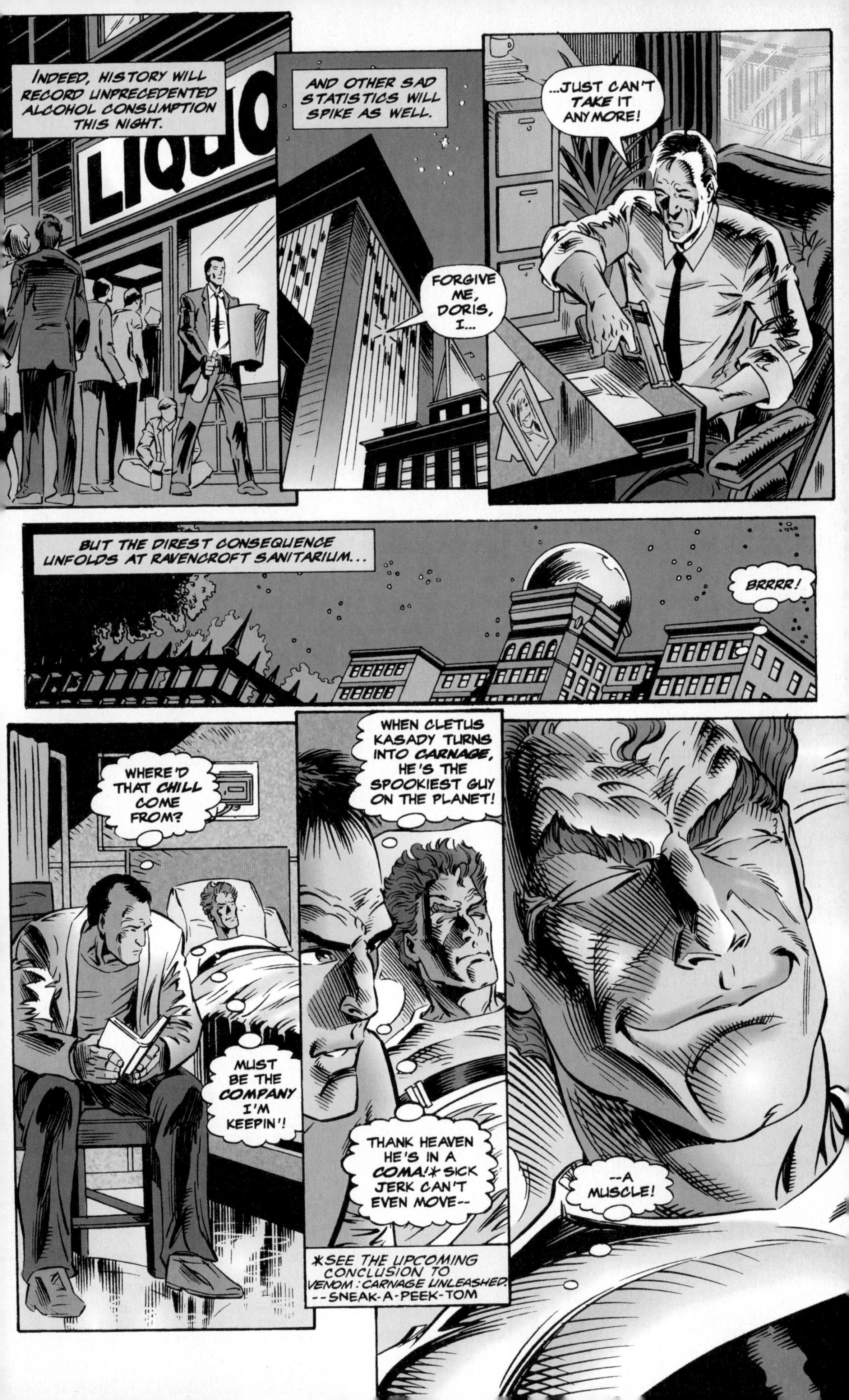
INDEED, HISTORY WILL RECORD UNPRECEDENTED ALCOHOL CONSUMPTION THIS NIGHT.
LIQUO
AND OTHER SAD STATISTICS WILL SPIKE AS WELL.
FORGIVE ME, DORIS, I...
...JUST CAN'T TAKE IT ANYMORE!
BUT THE DIREST CONSEQUENCE UNFOLDS AT RAVENCROFT SANITARIUM...
BRRRR!
WHERE'D THAT CHILL COME FROM?
MUST BE THE COMPANY I'M KEEPIN'!
WHEN CLETUS KASADY TURNS INTO CARNAGE, HE'S THE SPOOKIEST GUY ON THE PLANET!
THANK HEAVEN HE'S IN A COMA!* SICK JERK CAN'T EVEN MOVE--
*SEE THE UPCOMING CONCLUSION TO VENOM: CARNAGE UNLEASHED. --SNEAK-A-PEEK-TOM
--A MUSCLE!

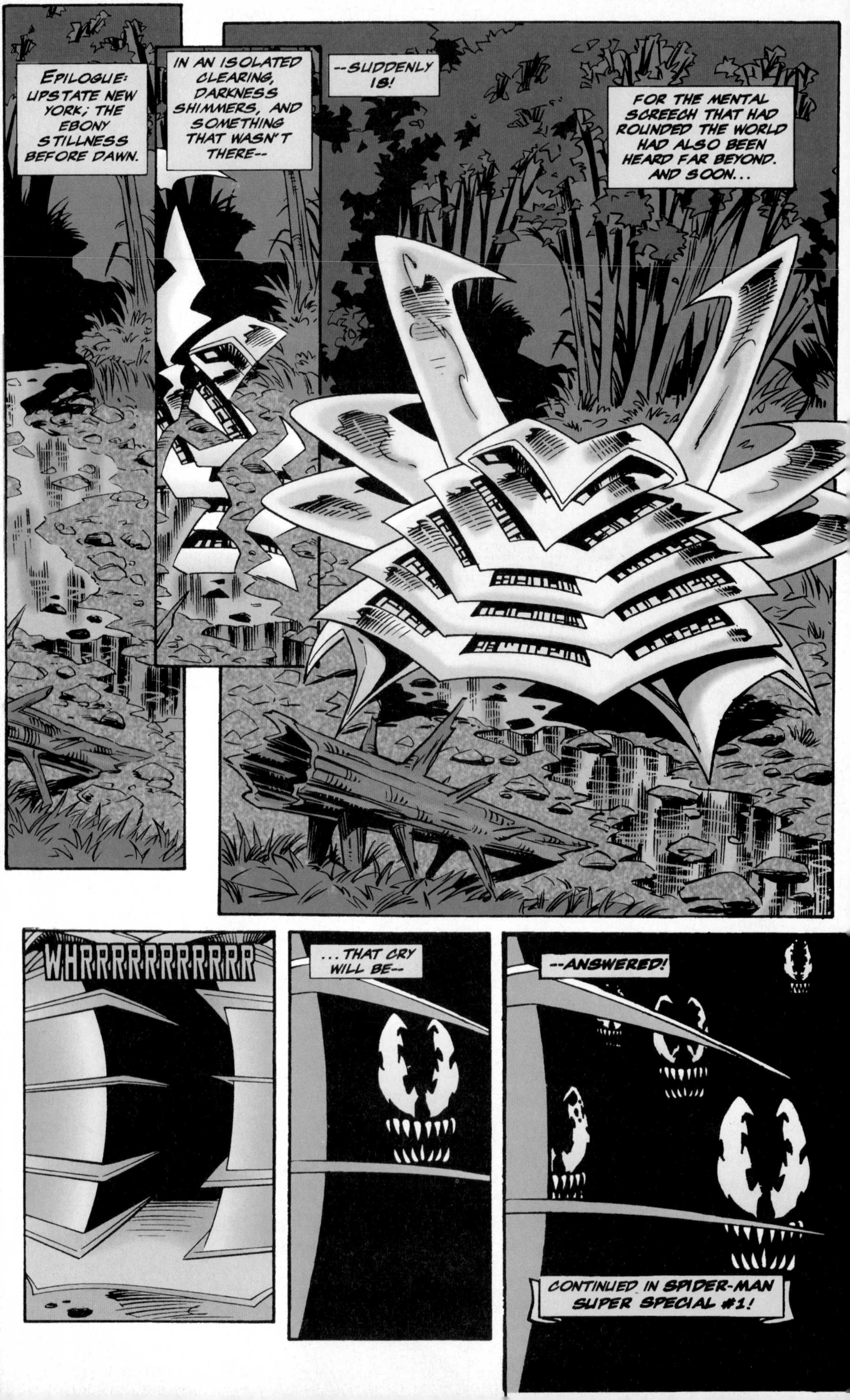

EPILOGUE: UPSTATE NEW YORK; THE EBONY STILLNESS BEFORE DAWN.
IN AN ISOLATED CLEARING, DARKNESS SHIMMERS, AND SOMETHING THAT WASN'T THERE--
--SUDDENLY IS!
FOR THE MENTAL SCREECH THAT HAD ROUNDED THE WORLD HAD ALSO BEEN HEARD FAR BEYOND. AND SOON...
WHRRRRRRRRRRRR
...THAT CRY WILL BE--
--ANSWERED!
CONTINUED IN SPIDER-MAN SUPER SPECIAL #1!

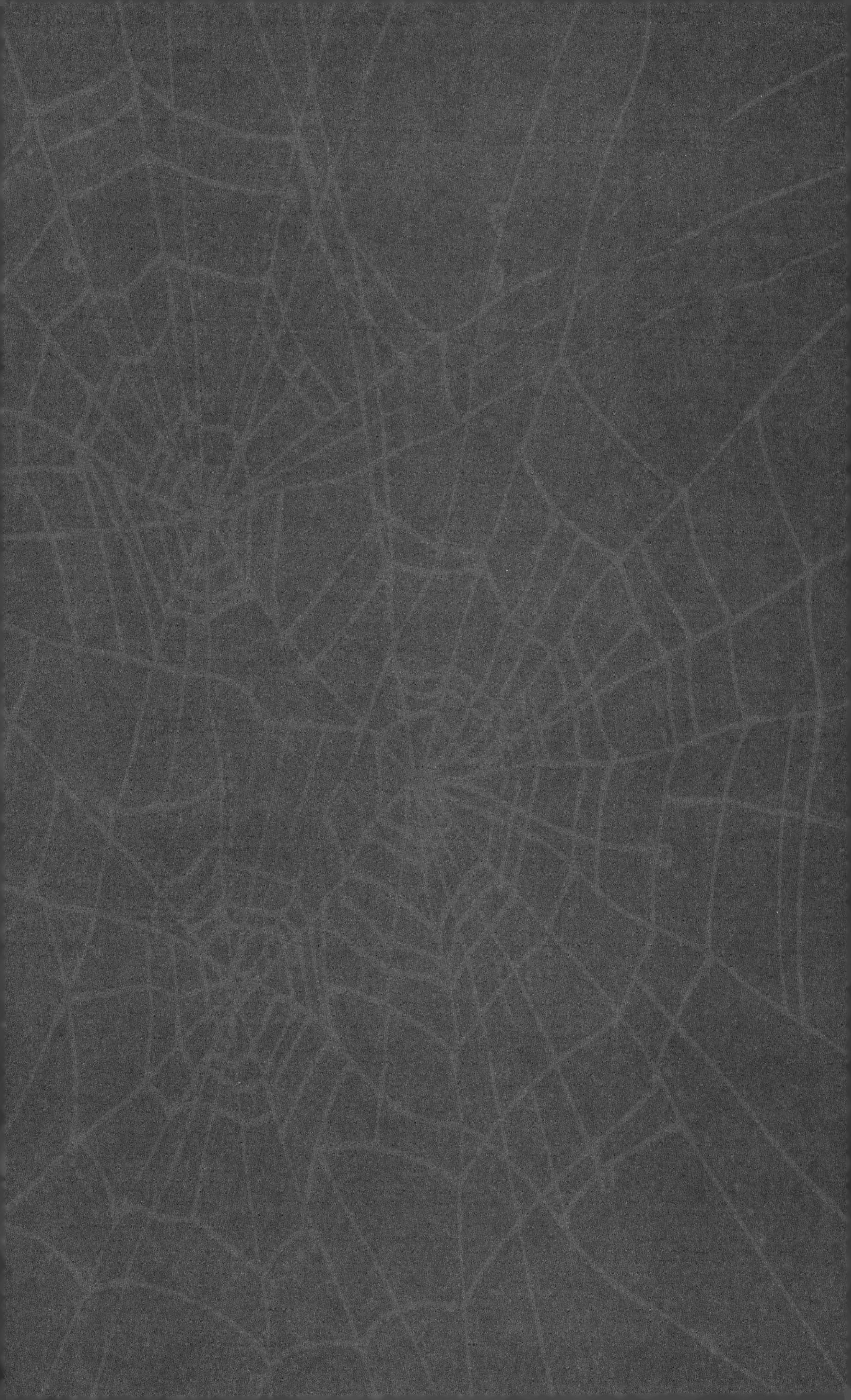

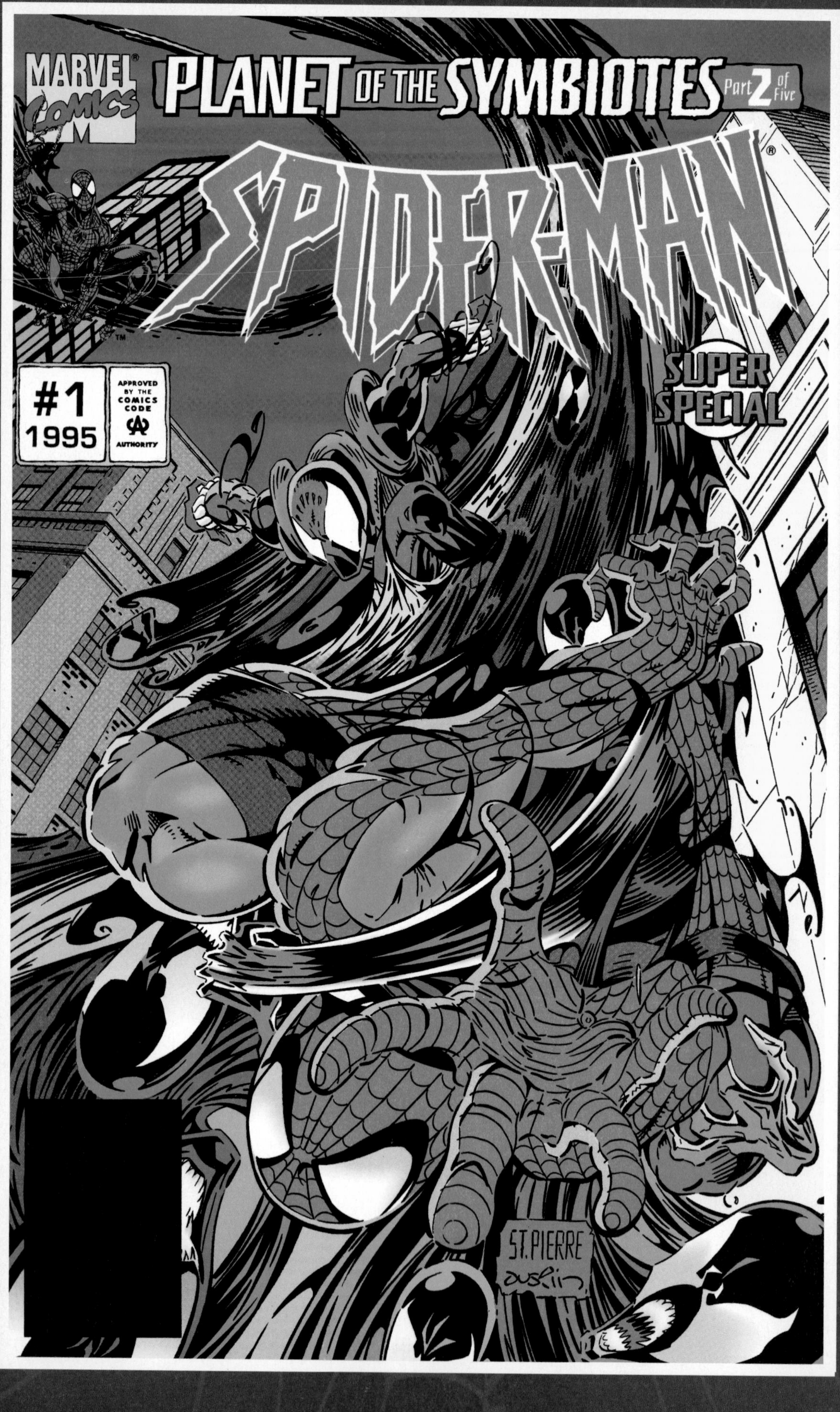
MARVEL COMICS
PLANET OF THE SYMBIOTES Part 2 of Five
SPIDER-MAN
SUPER SPECIAL
#1
1995
APPROVED BY THE COMICS CODE AUTHORITY
ST. PIERRE

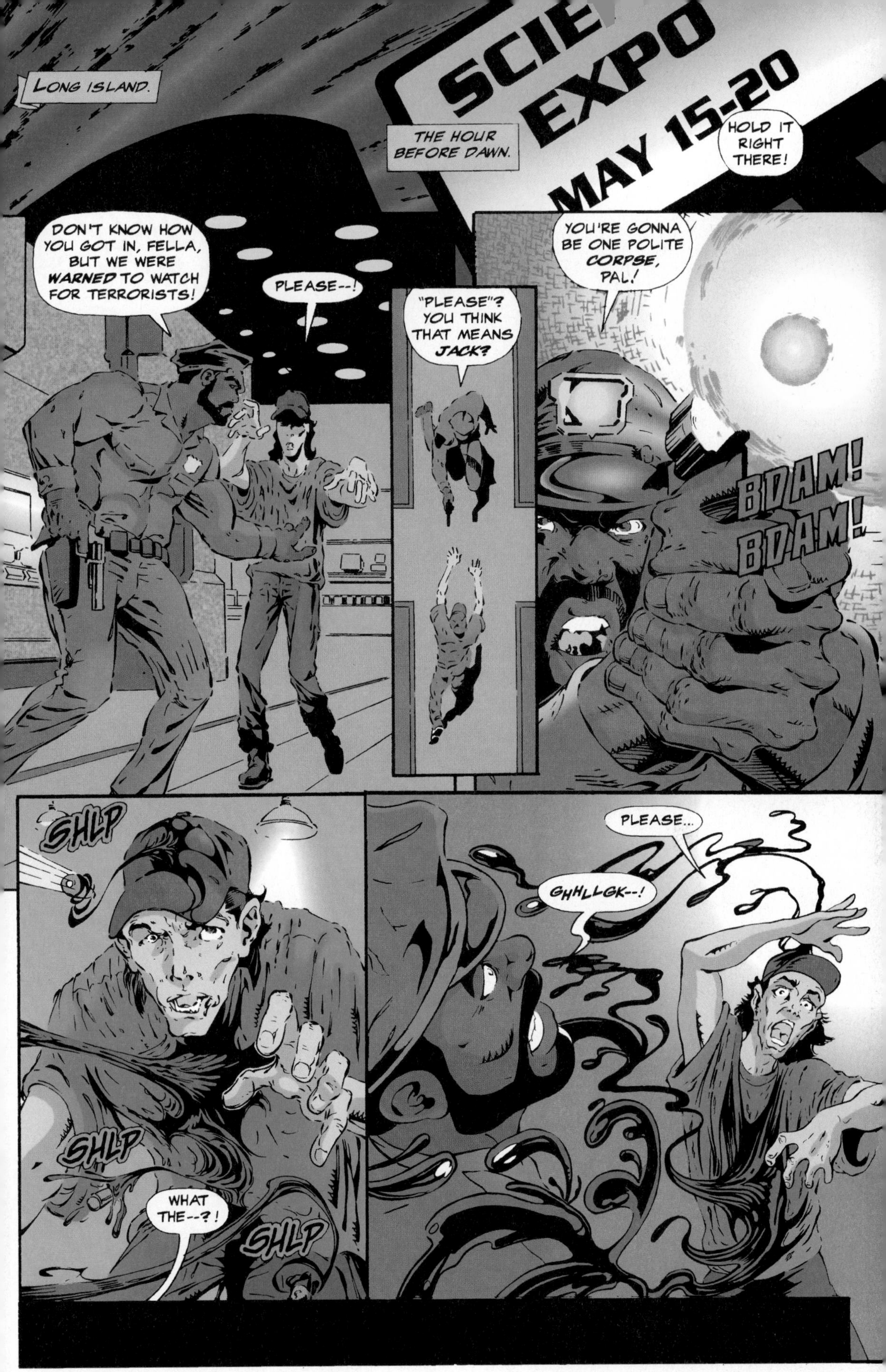
LONG ISLAND.
SCIE
EXPO
MAY 15-20
THE HOUR BEFORE DAWN.
HOLD IT RIGHT THERE!
DON'T KNOW HOW YOU GOT IN, FELLA, BUT WE WERE WARNED TO WATCH FOR TERRORISTS!
PLEASE--!
"PLEASE"? YOU THINK THAT MEANS JACK?
YOU'RE GONNA BE ONE POLITE CORPSE, PAL!
BDAM! BDAM!
SHLP
SHLP
WHAT THE--?!
SHLP
PLEASE...
GHHLLGK--!

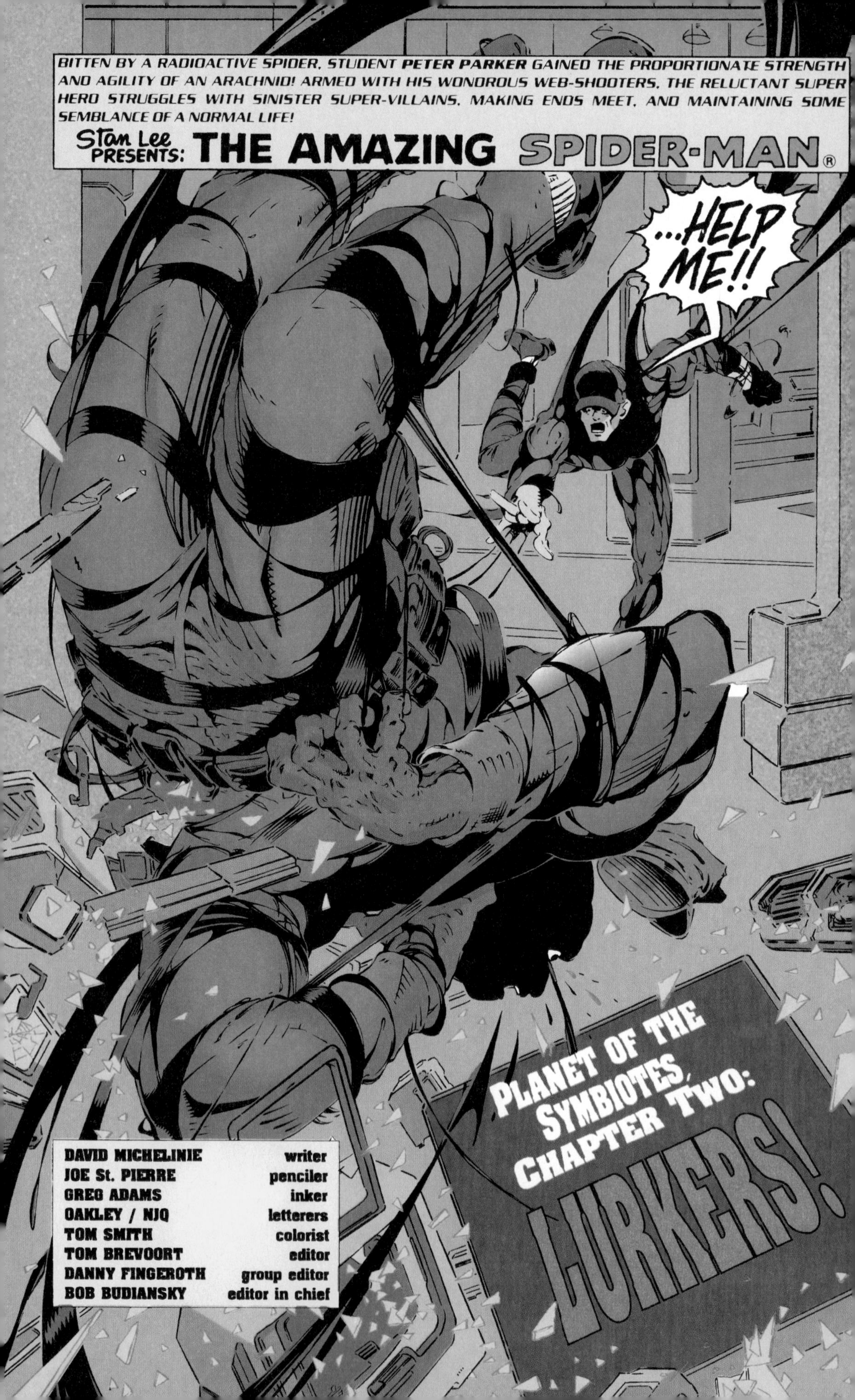
BITTEN BY A RADIOACTIVE SPIDER, STUDENT PETER PARKER GAINED THE PROPORTIONATE STRENGTH AND AGILITY OF AN ARACHNID! ARMED WITH HIS WONDROUS WEB-SHOOTERS, THE RELUCTANT SUPER HERO STRUGGLES WITH SINISTER SUPER-VILLAINS, MAKING ENDS MEET, AND MAINTAINING SOME SEMBLANCE OF A NORMAL LIFE!
Stan Lee PRESENTS: THE AMAZING SPIDER-MAN®
...HELP ME!!
PLANET OF THE SYMBIOTES, CHAPTER TWO:
LURKERS!
DAVID MICHELINIE writer
JOE St. PIERRE penciler
GREG ADAMS inker
OAKLEY / NJQ letterers
TOM SMITH colorist
TOM BREVOORT editor
DANNY FINGEROTH group editor
BOB BUDIANSKY editor in chief

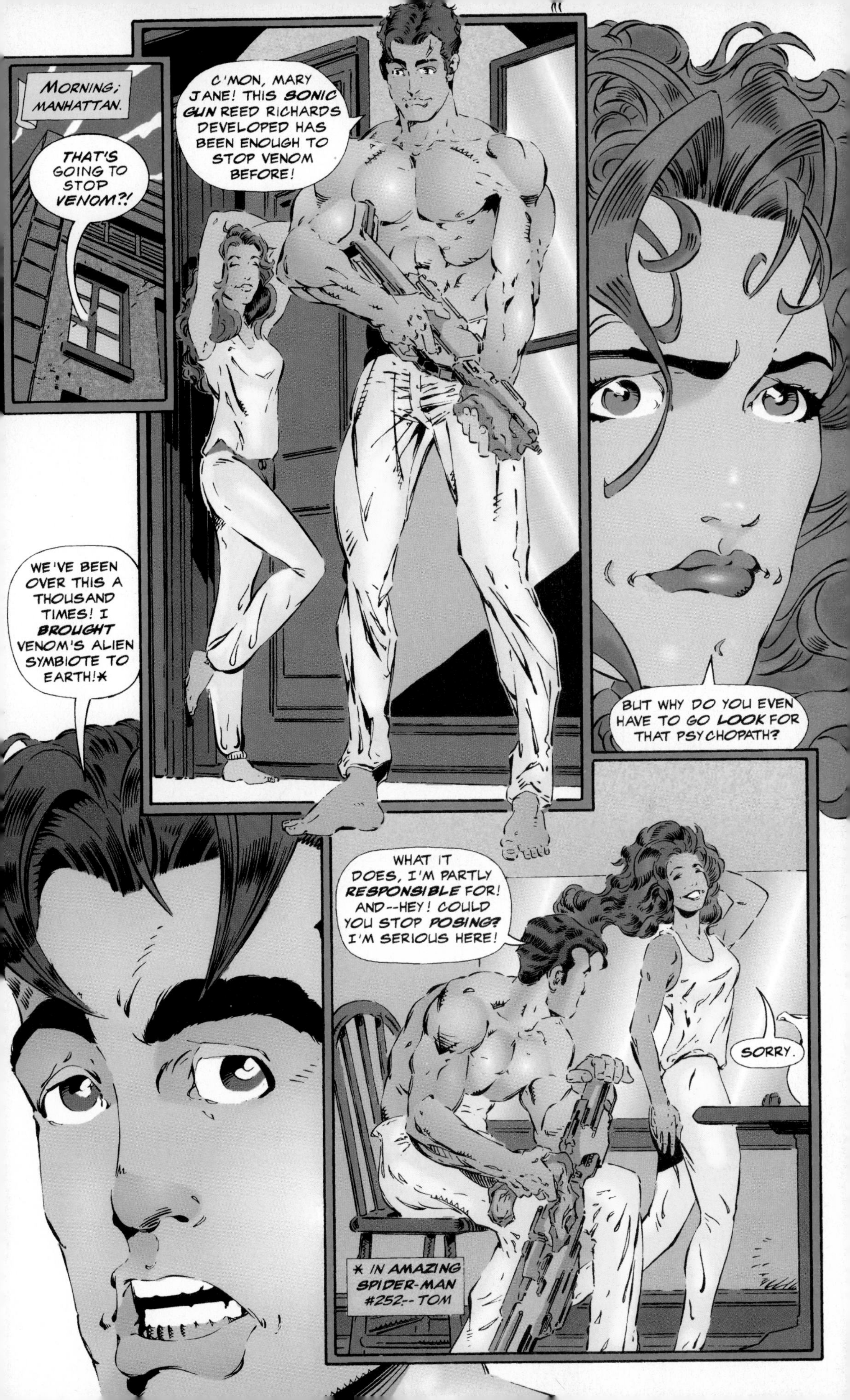
MORNING; MANHATTAN.
THAT'S GOING TO STOP VENOM?!
C'MON, MARY JANE! THIS SONIC GUN REED RICHARDS DEVELOPED HAS BEEN ENOUGH TO STOP VENOM BEFORE!
BUT WHY DO YOU EVEN HAVE TO GO LOOK FOR THAT PSYCHOPATH?
WE'VE BEEN OVER THIS A THOUSAND TIMES! I BROUGHT VENOM'S ALIEN SYMBIOTE TO EARTH!*
WHAT IT DOES, I'M PARTLY RESPONSIBLE FOR! AND--HEY! COULD YOU STOP POSING? I'M SERIOUS HERE!
SORRY.
* IN AMAZING SPIDER-MAN #252.--TOM

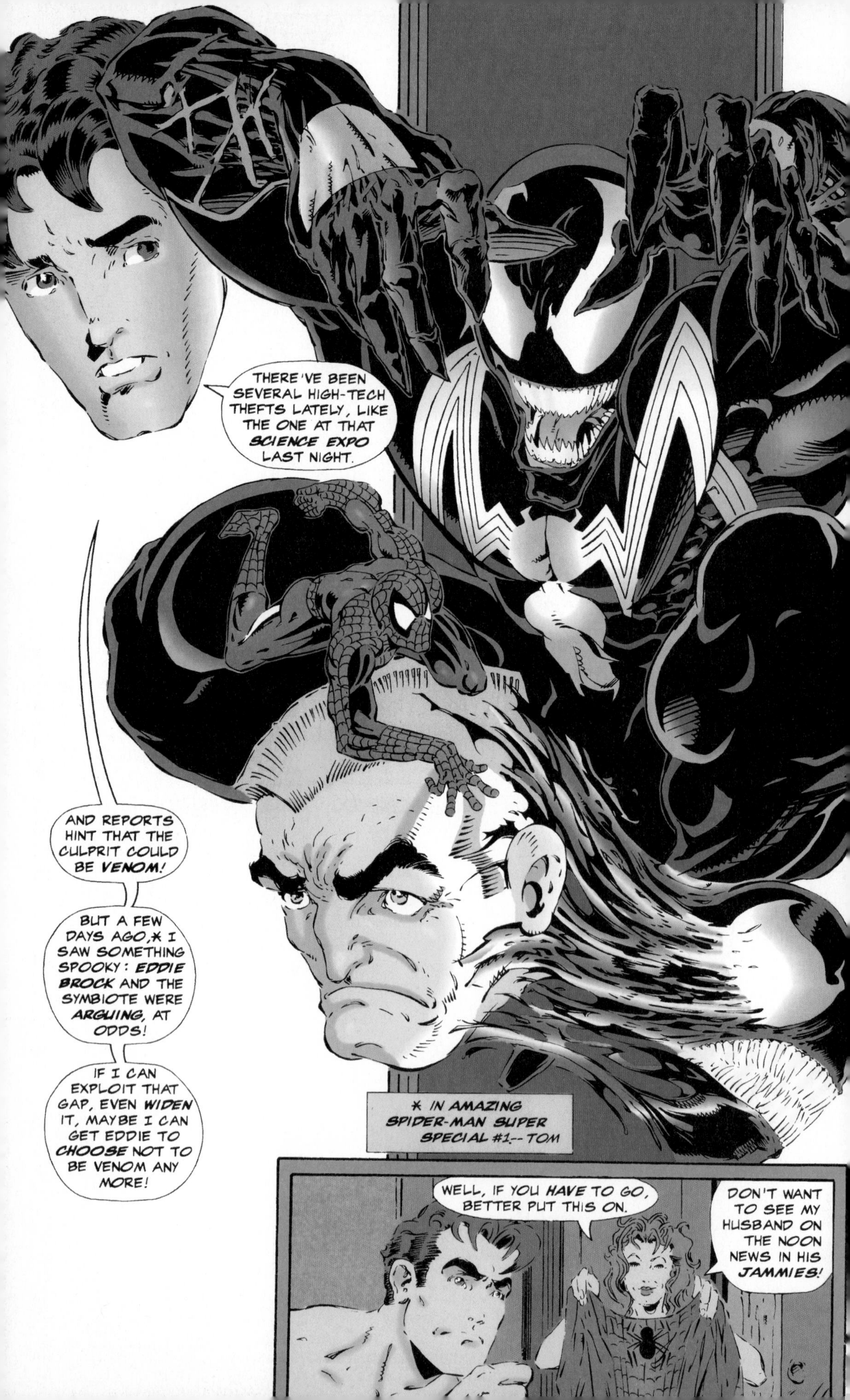
THERE'VE BEEN SEVERAL HIGH-TECH THEFTS LATELY, LIKE THE ONE AT THAT SCIENCE EXPO LAST NIGHT.
AND REPORTS HINT THAT THE CULPRIT COULD BE VENOM!
BUT A FEW DAYS AGO,* I SAW SOMETHING SPOOKY: EDDIE BROCK AND THE SYMBIOTE WERE ARGUING, AT ODDS!
IF I CAN EXPLOIT THAT GAP, EVEN WIDEN IT, MAYBE I CAN GET EDDIE TO CHOOSE NOT TO BE VENOM ANY MORE!
* IN AMAZING SPIDER-MAN SUPER SPECIAL #1-- TOM
WELL, IF YOU HAVE TO GO, BETTER PUT THIS ON.
DON'T WANT TO SEE MY HUSBAND ON THE NOON NEWS IN HIS JAMMIES!

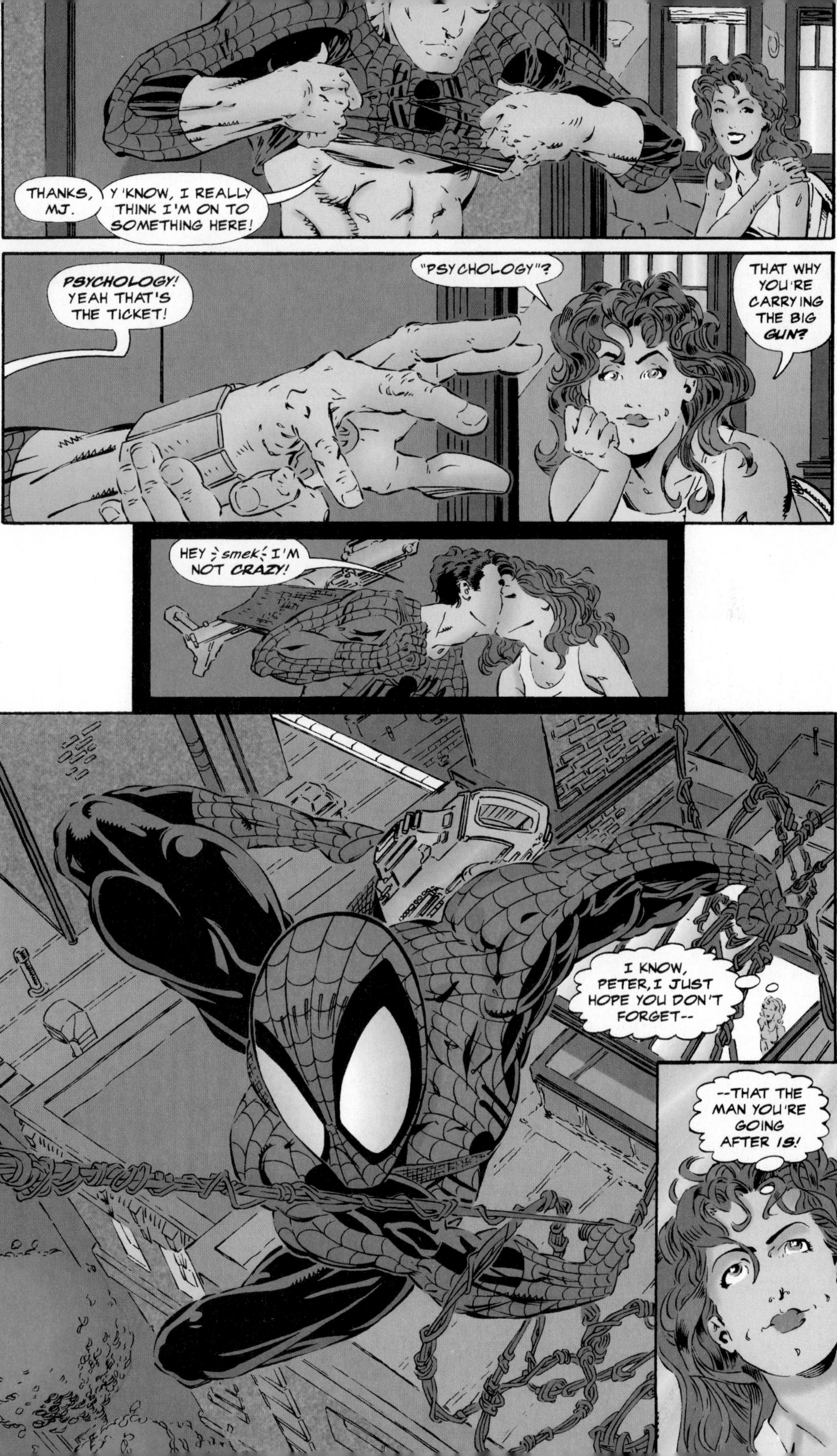
THANKS, MJ.
Y'KNOW, I REALLY THINK I'M ON TO SOMETHING HERE!
PSYCHOLOGY! YEAH THAT'S THE TICKET!
"PSYCHOLOGY"?
THAT WHY YOU'RE CARRYING THE BIG GUN?
HEY smek I'M NOT CRAZY!
I KNOW, PETER, I JUST HOPE YOU DON'T FORGET--
--THAT THE MAN YOU'RE GOING AFTER IS!

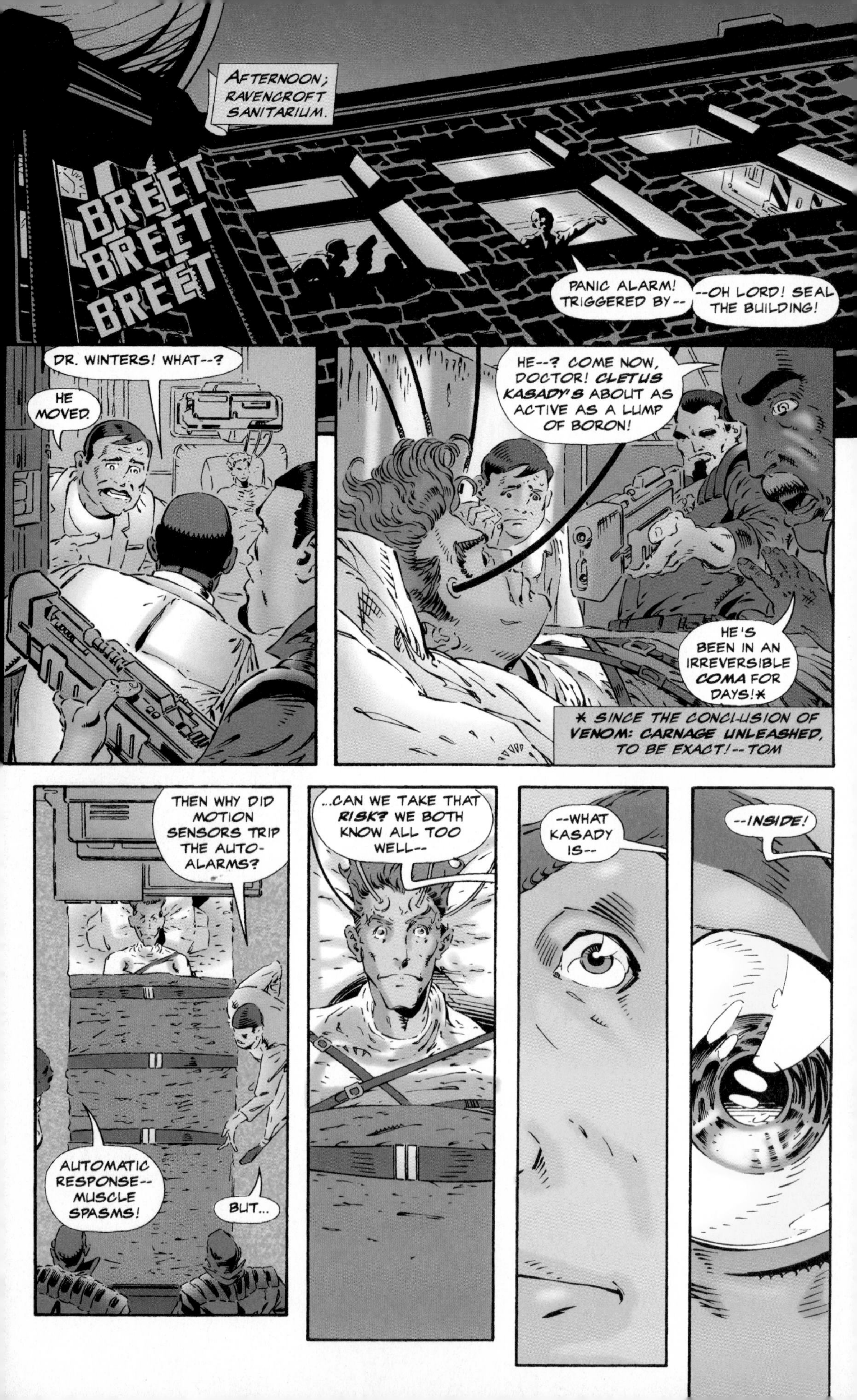

AFTERNOON; RAVENCROFT SANITARIUM.
BREET BREET BREET
PANIC ALARM! TRIGGERED BY--
--OH LORD! SEAL THE BUILDING!
DR. WINTERS! WHAT--?
HE MOVED.
HE--? COME NOW, DOCTOR! CLETUS KASADY'S ABOUT AS ACTIVE AS A LUMP OF BORON!
HE'S BEEN IN AN IRREVERSIBLE COMA FOR DAYS!*
* SINCE THE CONCLUSION OF VENOM: CARNAGE UNLEASHED, TO BE EXACT!--TOM
THEN WHY DID MOTION SENSORS TRIP THE AUTO-ALARMS?
AUTOMATIC RESPONSE--MUSCLE SPASMS!
BUT...
...CAN WE TAKE THAT RISK? WE BOTH KNOW ALL TOO WELL--
--WHAT KASADY IS--
--INSIDE!

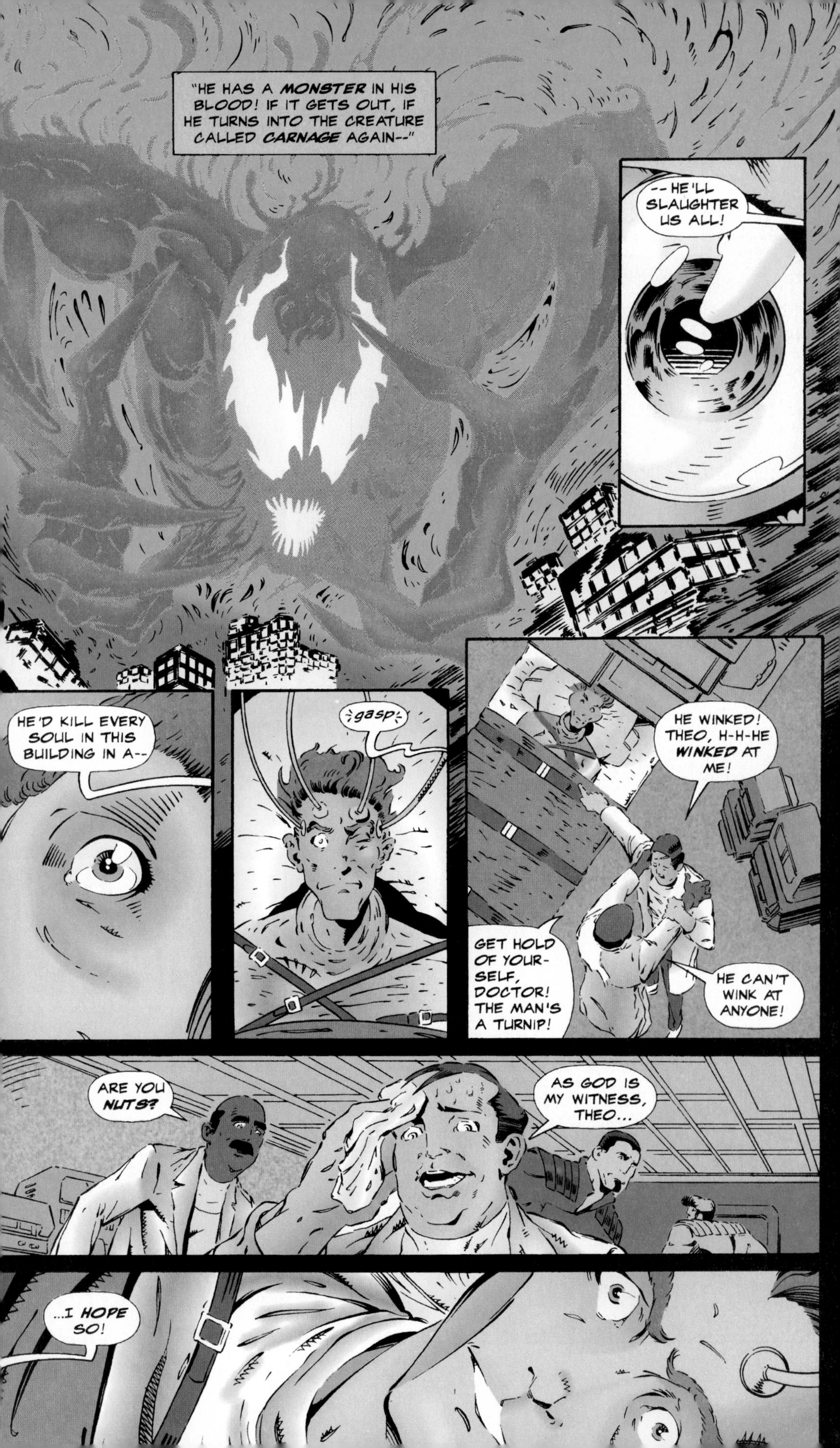

"HE HAS A MONSTER IN HIS BLOOD! IF IT GETS OUT, IF HE TURNS INTO THE CREATURE CALLED CARNAGE AGAIN--"
--HE'LL SLAUGHTER US ALL!
HE'D KILL EVERY SOUL IN THIS BUILDING IN A--
gasp
HE WINKED! THEO, H-H-HE WINKED AT ME!
GET HOLD OF YOUR-SELF, DOCTOR! THE MAN'S A TURNIP!
HE CAN'T WINK AT ANYONE!
ARE YOU NUTS?
AS GOD IS MY WITNESS, THEO...
...I HOPE SO!

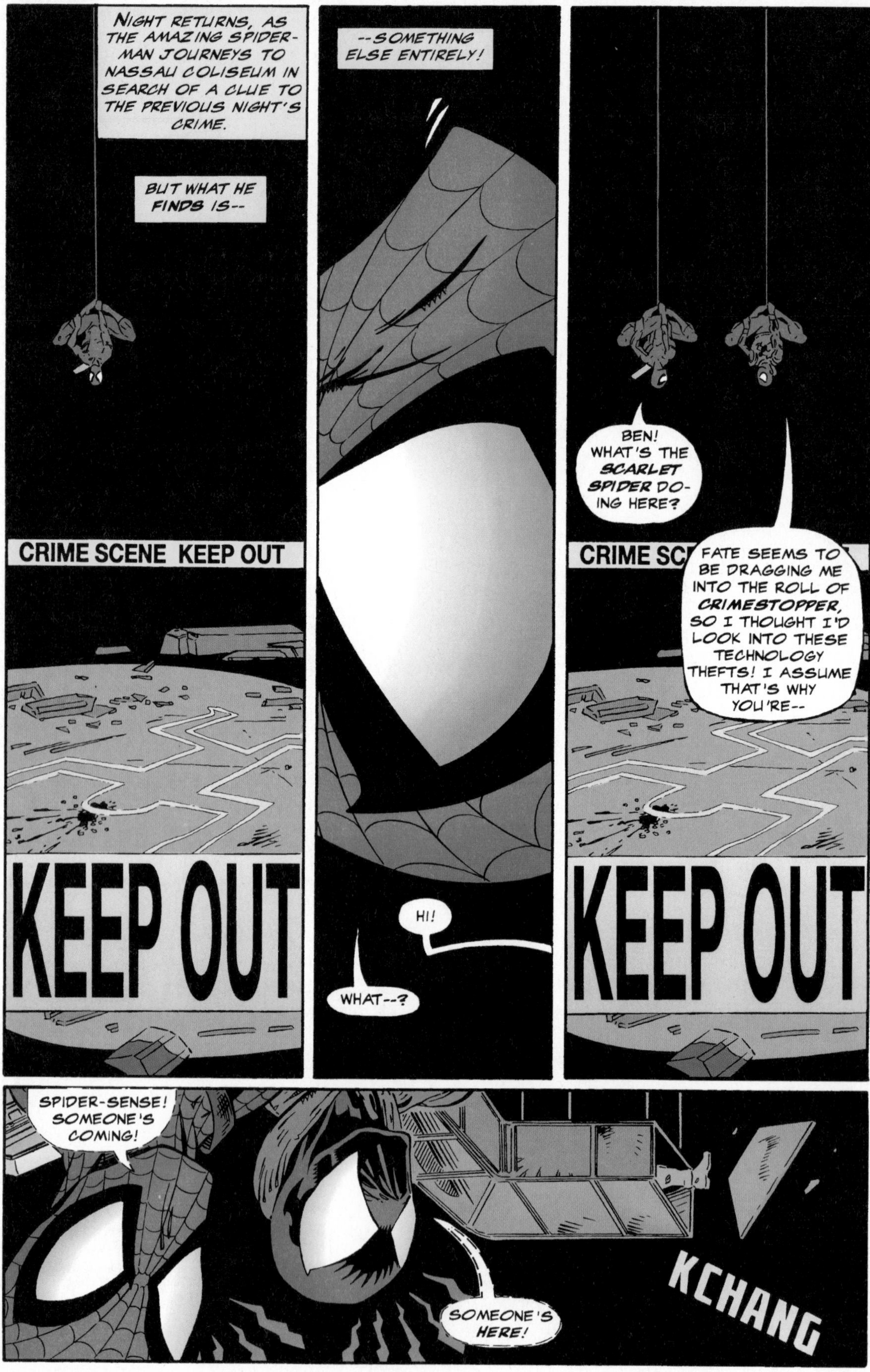
NIGHT RETURNS, AS THE AMAZING SPIDER-MAN JOURNEYS TO NASSAU COLISEUM IN SEARCH OF A CLUE TO THE PREVIOUS NIGHT'S CRIME.
BUT WHAT HE FINDS IS--
CRIME SCENE KEEP OUT
KEEP OUT
--SOMETHING ELSE ENTIRELY!
HI!
WHAT--?
BEN! WHAT'S THE SCARLET SPIDER DOING HERE?
FATE SEEMS TO BE DRAGGING ME INTO THE ROLL OF CRIMESTOPPER, SO I THOUGHT I'D LOOK INTO THESE TECHNOLOGY THEFTS! I ASSUME THAT'S WHY YOU'RE--
KEEP OUT
SPIDER-SENSE! SOMEONE'S COMING!
SOMEONE'S HERE!
KCHANG

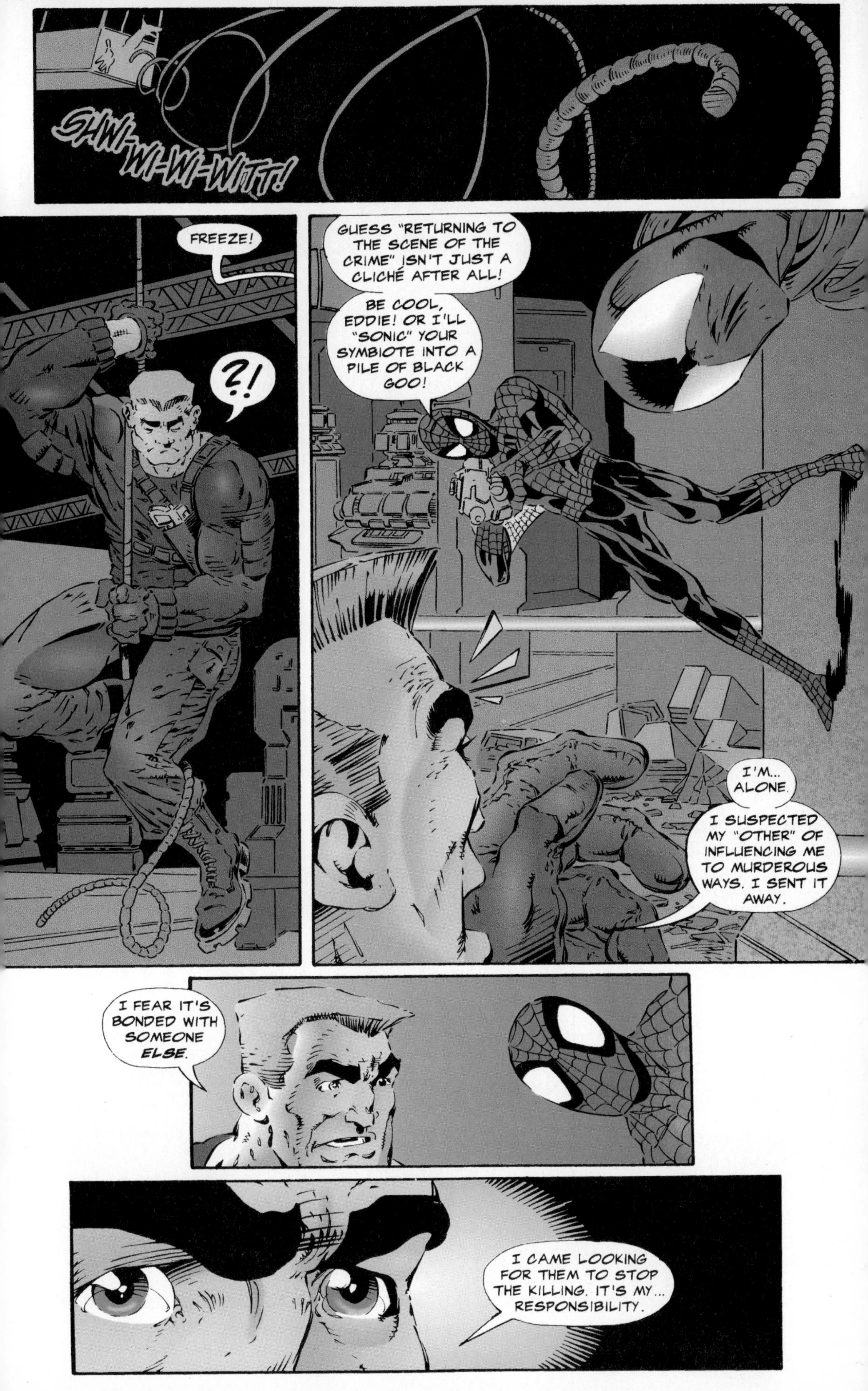
SHWI-WI-WI-WITT!
FREEZE!
?!
GUESS "RETURNING TO THE SCENE OF THE CRIME" ISN'T JUST A CLICHÉ AFTER ALL!
BE COOL, EDDIE! OR I'LL "SONIC" YOUR SYMBIOTE INTO A PILE OF BLACK GOO!
I'M... ALONE.
I SUSPECTED MY "OTHER" OF INFLUENCING ME TO MURDEROUS WAYS. I SENT IT AWAY.
I FEAR IT'S BONDED WITH SOMEONE ELSE.
I CAME LOOKING FOR THEM TO STOP THE KILLING. IT'S MY... RESPONSIBILITY.

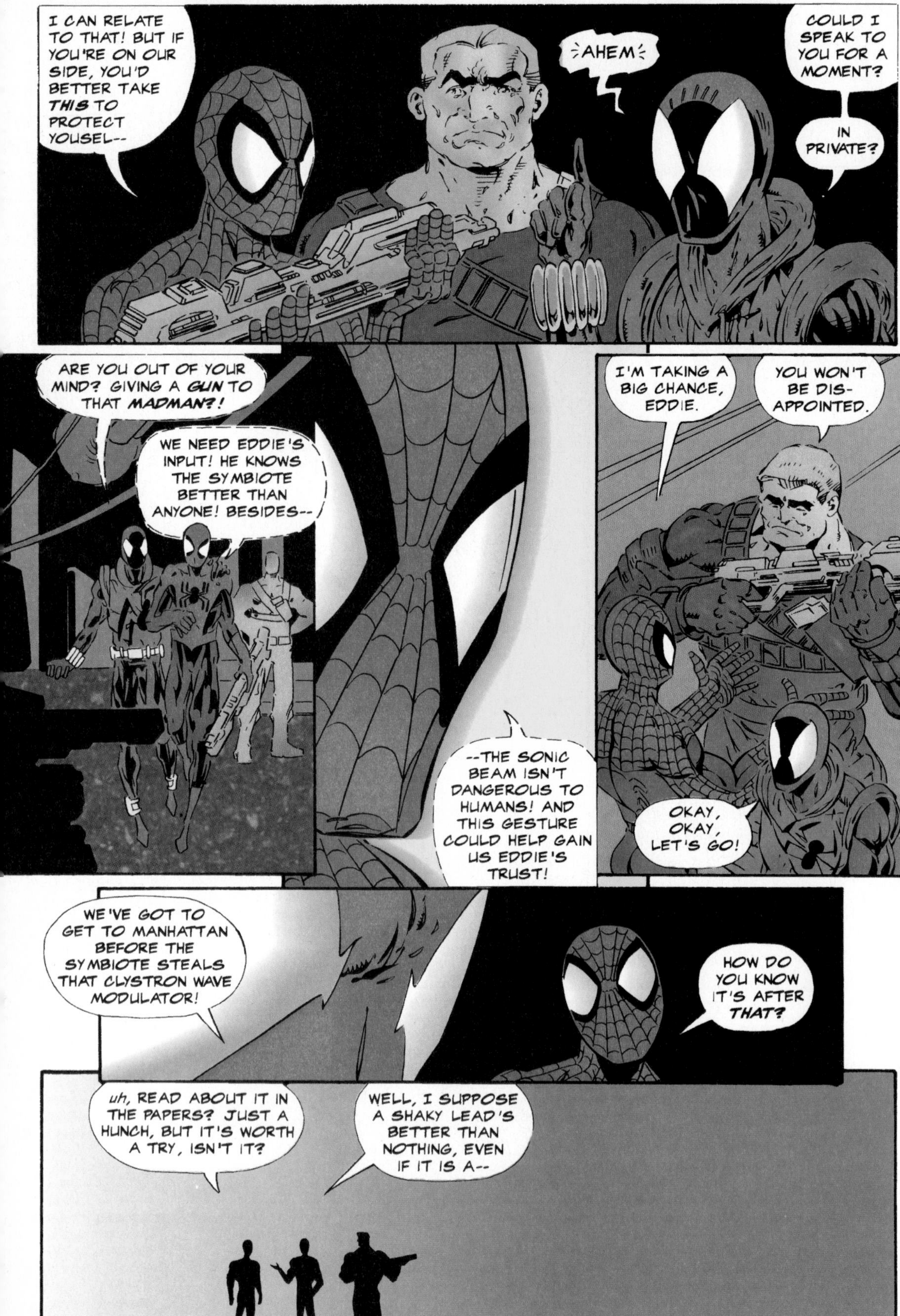

I CAN RELATE TO THAT! BUT IF YOU'RE ON OUR SIDE, YOU'D BETTER TAKE THIS TO PROTECT YOUSEL--
AHEM
COULD I SPEAK TO YOU FOR A MOMENT?
IN PRIVATE?
ARE YOU OUT OF YOUR MIND? GIVING A GUN TO THAT MADMAN?!
WE NEED EDDIE'S INPUT! HE KNOWS THE SYMBIOTE BETTER THAN ANYONE! BESIDES--
--THE SONIC BEAM ISN'T DANGEROUS TO HUMANS! AND THIS GESTURE COULD HELP GAIN US EDDIE'S TRUST!
I'M TAKING A BIG CHANCE, EDDIE.
YOU WON'T BE DIS-APPOINTED.
OKAY, OKAY, LET'S GO!
WE'VE GOT TO GET TO MANHATTAN BEFORE THE SYMBIOTE STEALS THAT CLYSTRON WAVE MODULATOR!
HOW DO YOU KNOW IT'S AFTER THAT?
uh, READ ABOUT IT IN THE PAPERS? JUST A HUNCH, BUT IT'S WORTH A TRY, ISN'T IT?
WELL, I SUPPOSE A SHAKY LEAD'S BETTER THAN NOTHING, EVEN IF IT IS A--

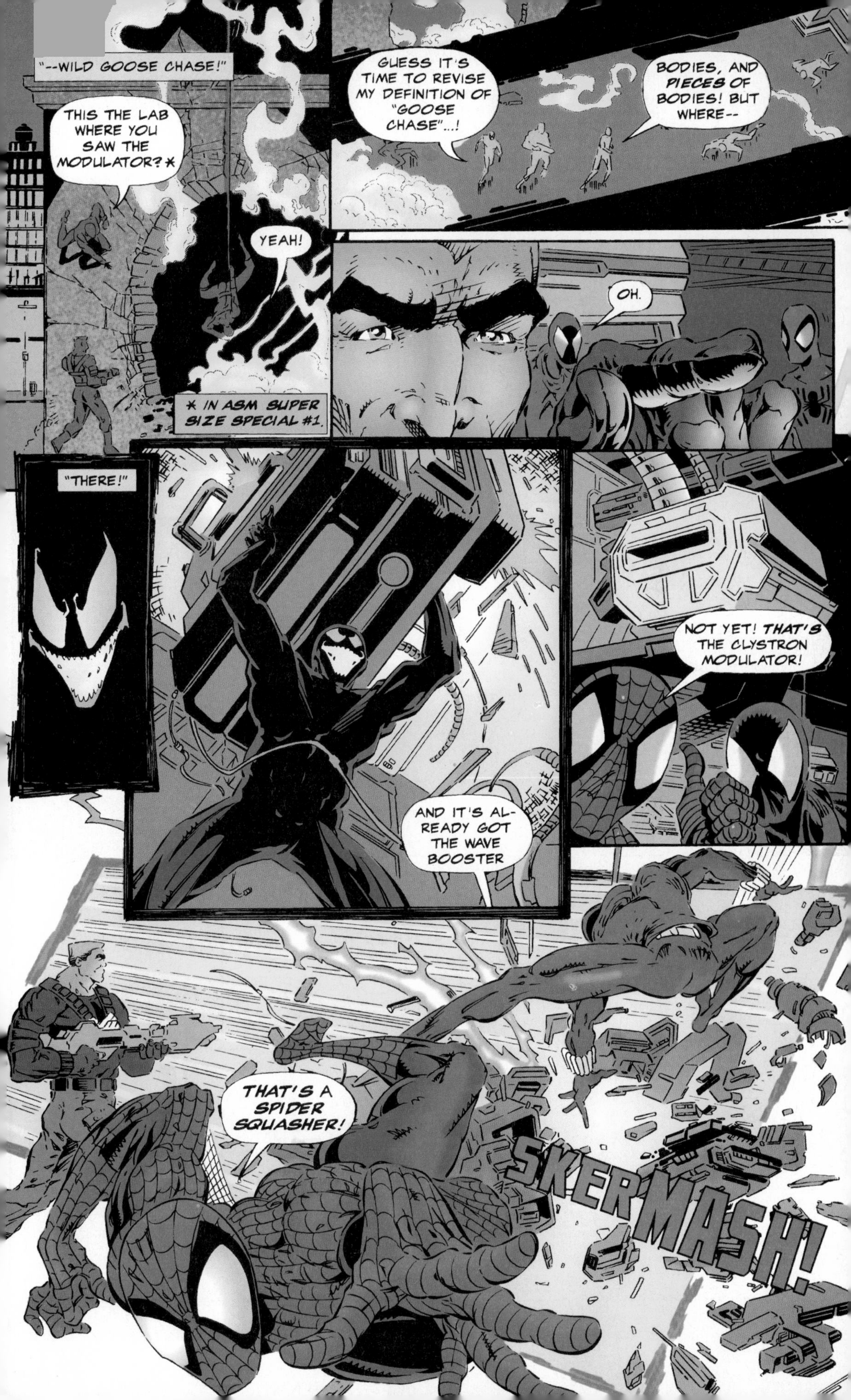
"--WILD GOOSE CHASE!"
THIS THE LAB WHERE YOU SAW THE MODULATOR?*
GUESS IT'S TIME TO REVISE MY DEFINITION OF "GOOSE CHASE"...!
BODIES, AND PIECES OF BODIES! BUT WHERE--
YEAH!
OH.
* IN ASM SUPER SIZE SPECIAL #1.
"THERE!"
NOT YET! THAT'S THE CLYSTRON MODULATOR!
AND IT'S ALREADY GOT THE WAVE BOOSTER
THAT'S A SPIDER SQUASHER!
SKERMASH!

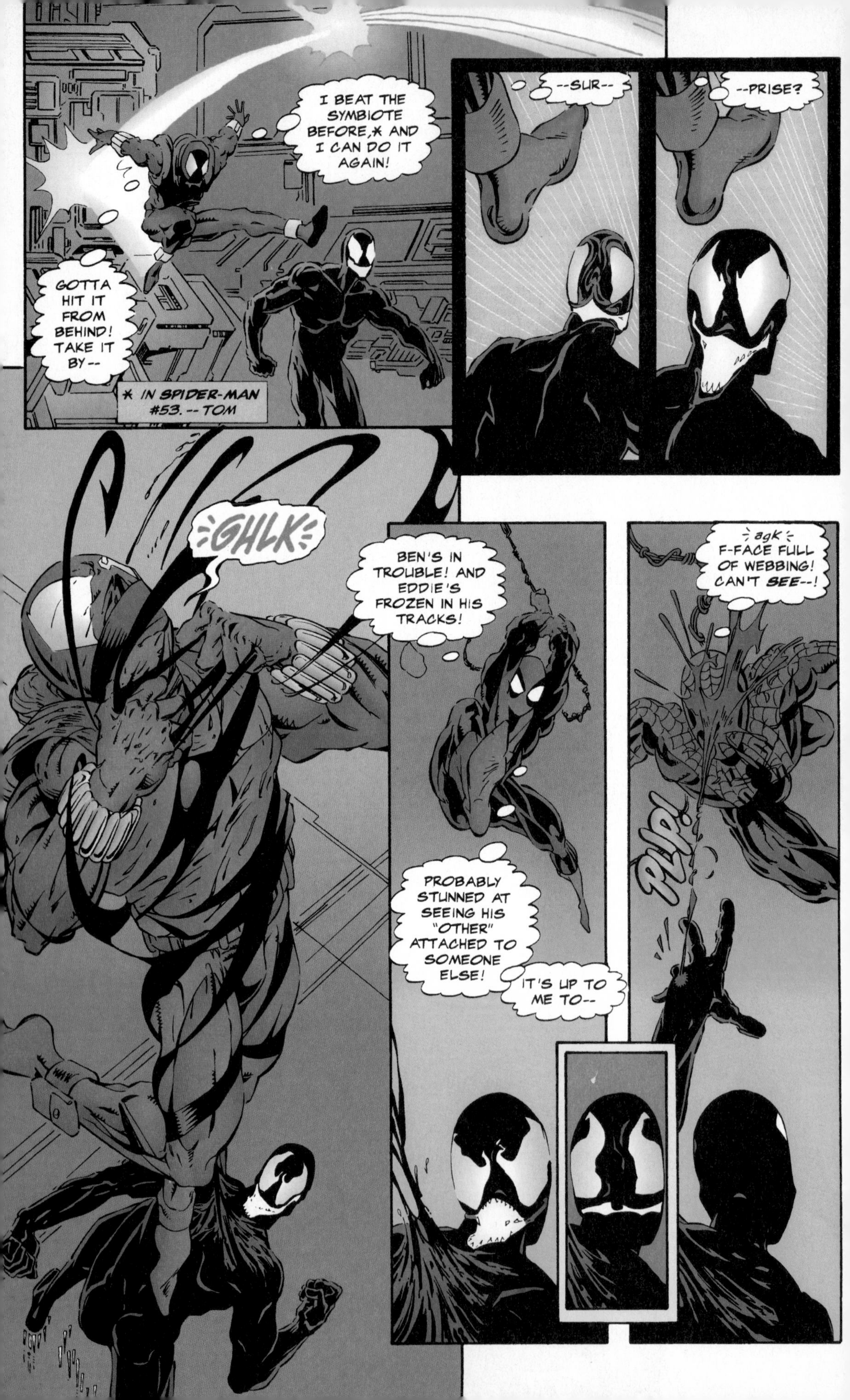
I BEAT THE SYMBIOTE BEFORE,* AND I CAN DO IT AGAIN!
GOTTA HIT IT FROM BEHIND! TAKE IT BY--
* IN SPIDER-MAN #53. --TOM
--SUR--
--PRISE?
GHLK
BEN'S IN TROUBLE! AND EDDIE'S FROZEN IN HIS TRACKS!
PROBABLY STUNNED AT SEEING HIS "OTHER" ATTACHED TO SOMEONE ELSE!
IT'S UP TO ME TO--
agk
F-FACE FULL OF WEBBING! CAN'T SEE--!
PLIP!

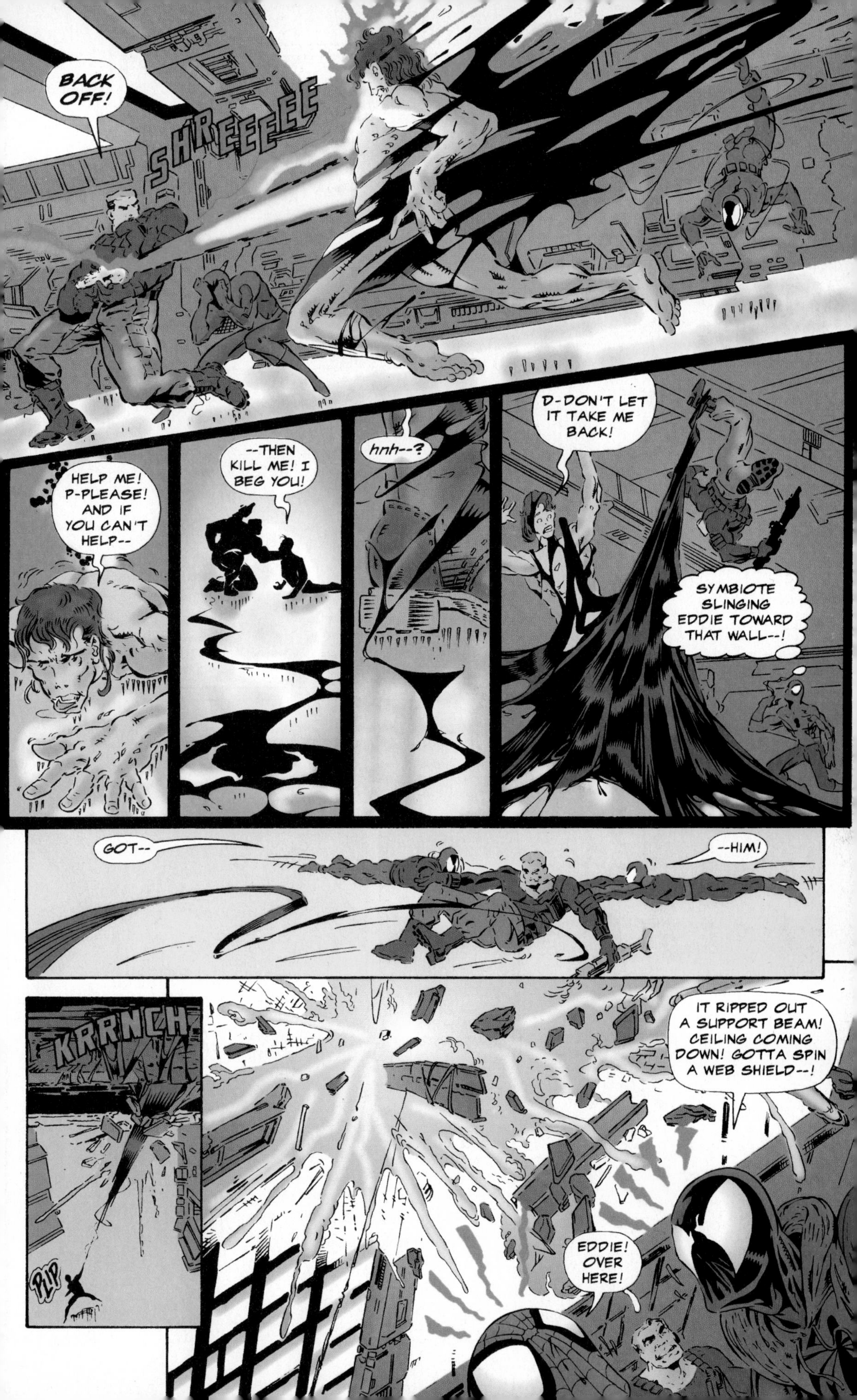
BACK OFF!
SHREEEEEE
HELP ME! P-PLEASE! AND IF YOU CAN'T HELP--
--THEN KILL ME! I BEG YOU!
hnh--?
D-DON'T LET IT TAKE ME BACK!
SYMBIOTE SLINGING EDDIE TOWARD THAT WALL--!
GOT--
--HIM!
KRRNCH
PLIP
IT RIPPED OUT A SUPPORT BEAM! CEILING COMING DOWN! GOTTA SPIN A WEB SHIELD--!
EDDIE! OVER HERE!

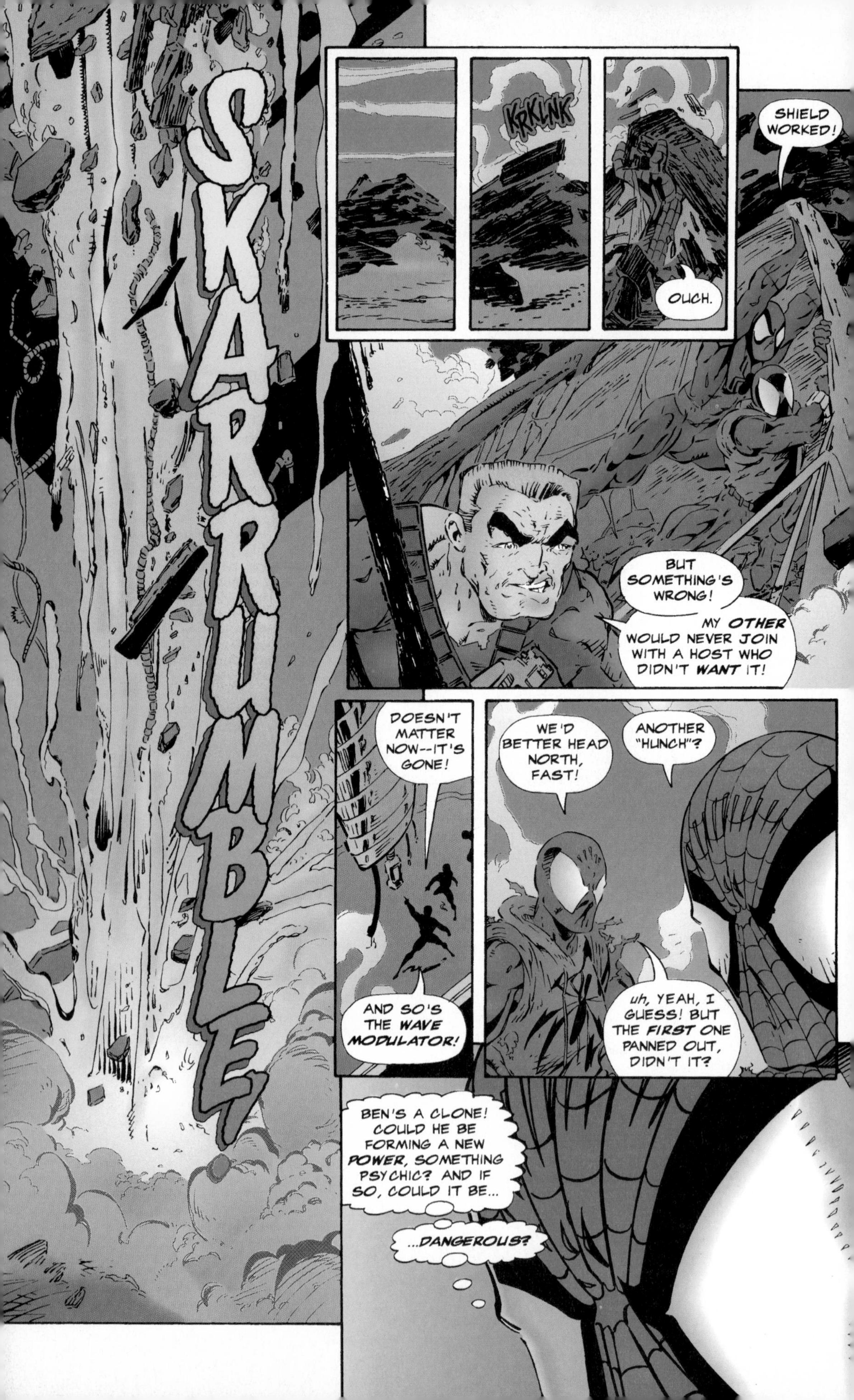
SKARUMBLE
KRKLNK
OUCH.
SHIELD WORKED!
BUT SOMETHING'S WRONG!
MY **OTHER** WOULD NEVER JOIN WITH A HOST WHO DIDN'T **WANT** IT!
DOESN'T MATTER NOW--IT'S GONE!
AND SO'S THE **WAVE MODULATOR**!
WE'D BETTER HEAD NORTH, FAST!
ANOTHER "HUNCH"?
uh, YEAH, I GUESS! BUT THE **FIRST** ONE PANNED OUT, DIDN'T IT?
BEN'S A CLONE! COULD HE BE FORMING A NEW **POWER**, SOMETHING PSYCHIC? AND IF SO, COULD IT BE...
...**DANGEROUS**?

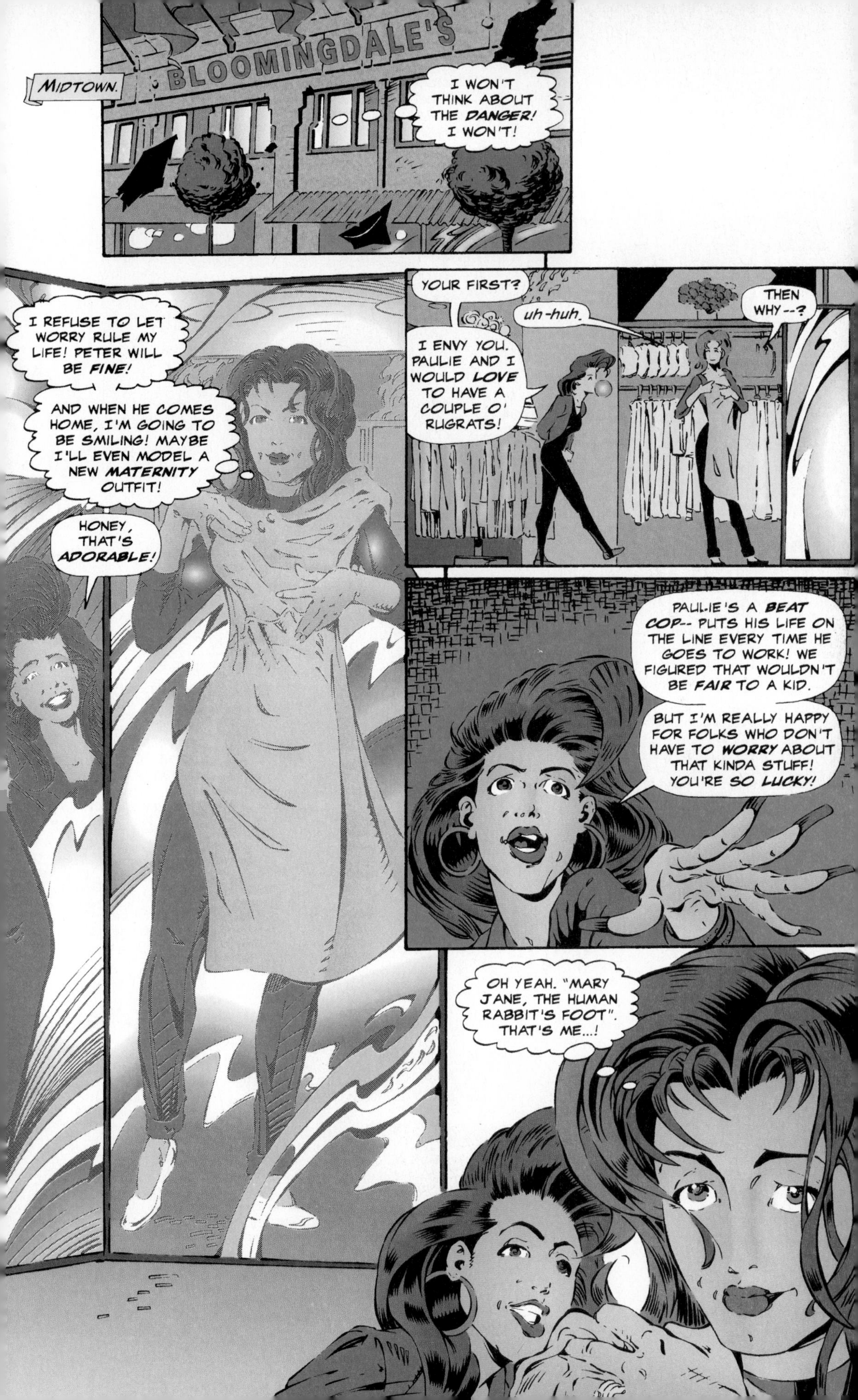
BLOOMINGDALE'S
MIDTOWN.
I WON'T THINK ABOUT THE DANGER! I WON'T!
I REFUSE TO LET WORRY RULE MY LIFE! PETER WILL BE FINE!
AND WHEN HE COMES HOME, I'M GOING TO BE SMILING! MAYBE I'LL EVEN MODEL A NEW MATERNITY OUTFIT!
HONEY, THAT'S ADORABLE!
YOUR FIRST?
uh-huh.
I ENVY YOU. PAULIE AND I WOULD LOVE TO HAVE A COUPLE O' RUGRATS!
THEN WHY--?
PAULIE'S A BEAT COP-- PUTS HIS LIFE ON THE LINE EVERY TIME HE GOES TO WORK! WE FIGURED THAT WOULDN'T BE FAIR TO A KID.
BUT I'M REALLY HAPPY FOR FOLKS WHO DON'T HAVE TO WORRY ABOUT THAT KINDA STUFF! YOU'RE SO LUCKY!
OH YEAH. "MARY JANE, THE HUMAN RABBIT'S FOOT". THAT'S ME...!

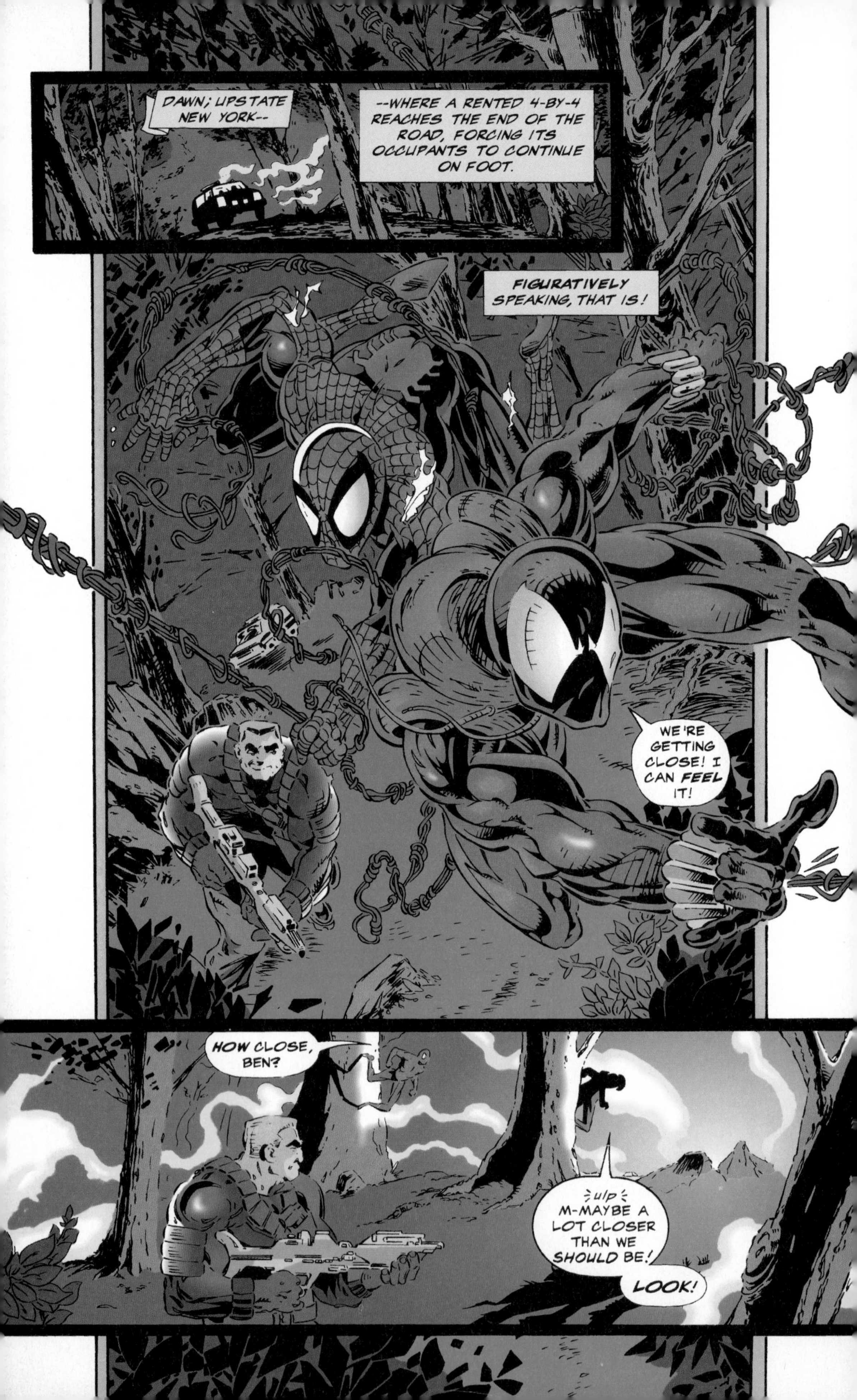
DAWN; UPSTATE NEW YORK--
--WHERE A RENTED 4-BY-4 REACHES THE END OF THE ROAD, FORCING ITS OCCUPANTS TO CONTINUE ON FOOT.
FIGURATIVELY SPEAKING, THAT IS!
WE'RE GETTING CLOSE! I CAN FEEL IT!
HOW CLOSE, BEN?
ulp
M-MAYBE A LOT CLOSER THAN WE SHOULD BE!
LOOK!

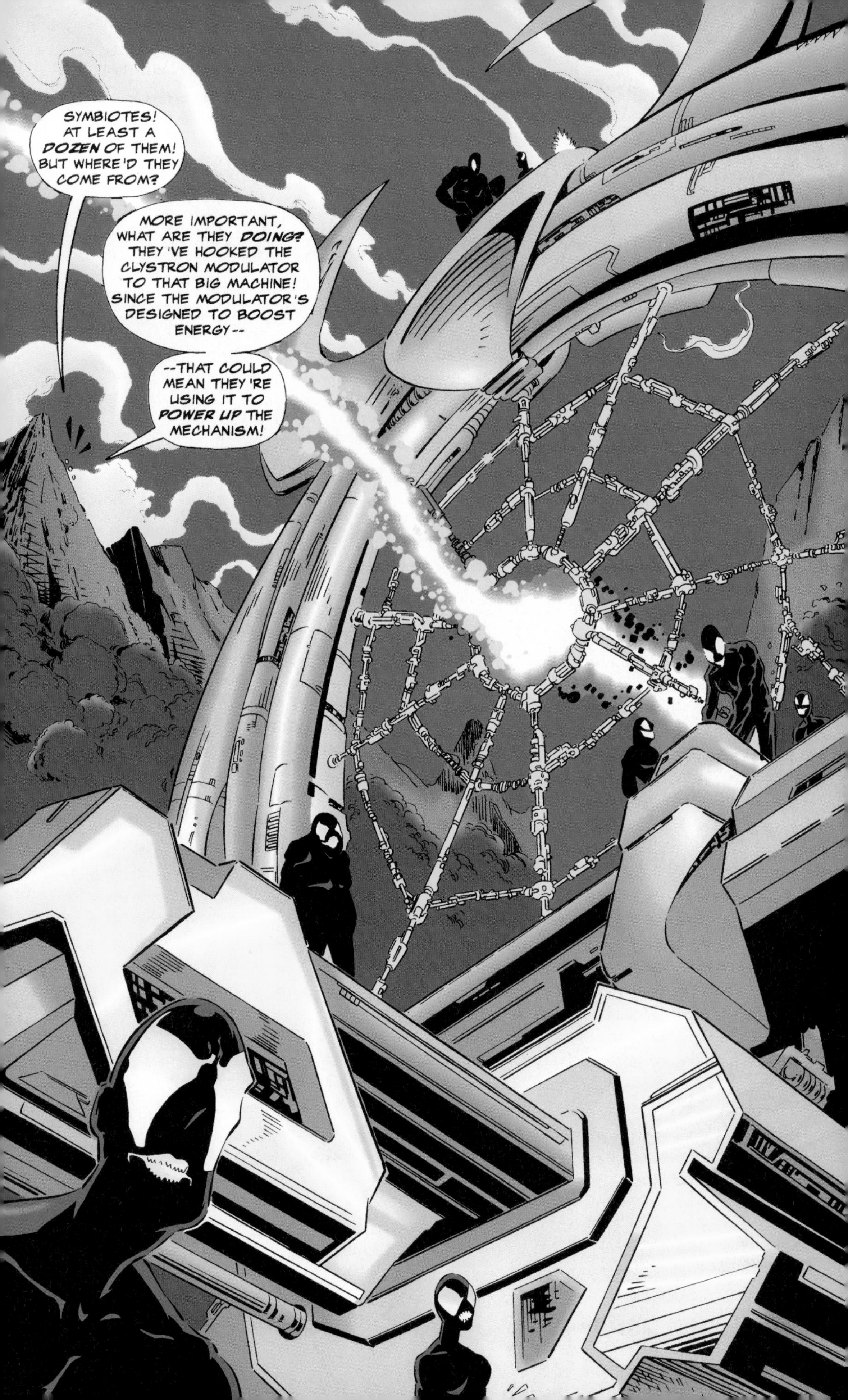
SYMBIOTES! AT LEAST A DOZEN OF THEM! BUT WHERE'D THEY COME FROM?
MORE IMPORTANT, WHAT ARE THEY DOING? THEY'VE HOOKED THE CLYSTRON MODULATOR TO THAT BIG MACHINE! SINCE THE MODULATOR'S DESIGNED TO BOOST ENERGY--
--THAT COULD MEAN THEY'RE USING IT TO POWER UP THE MECHANISM!

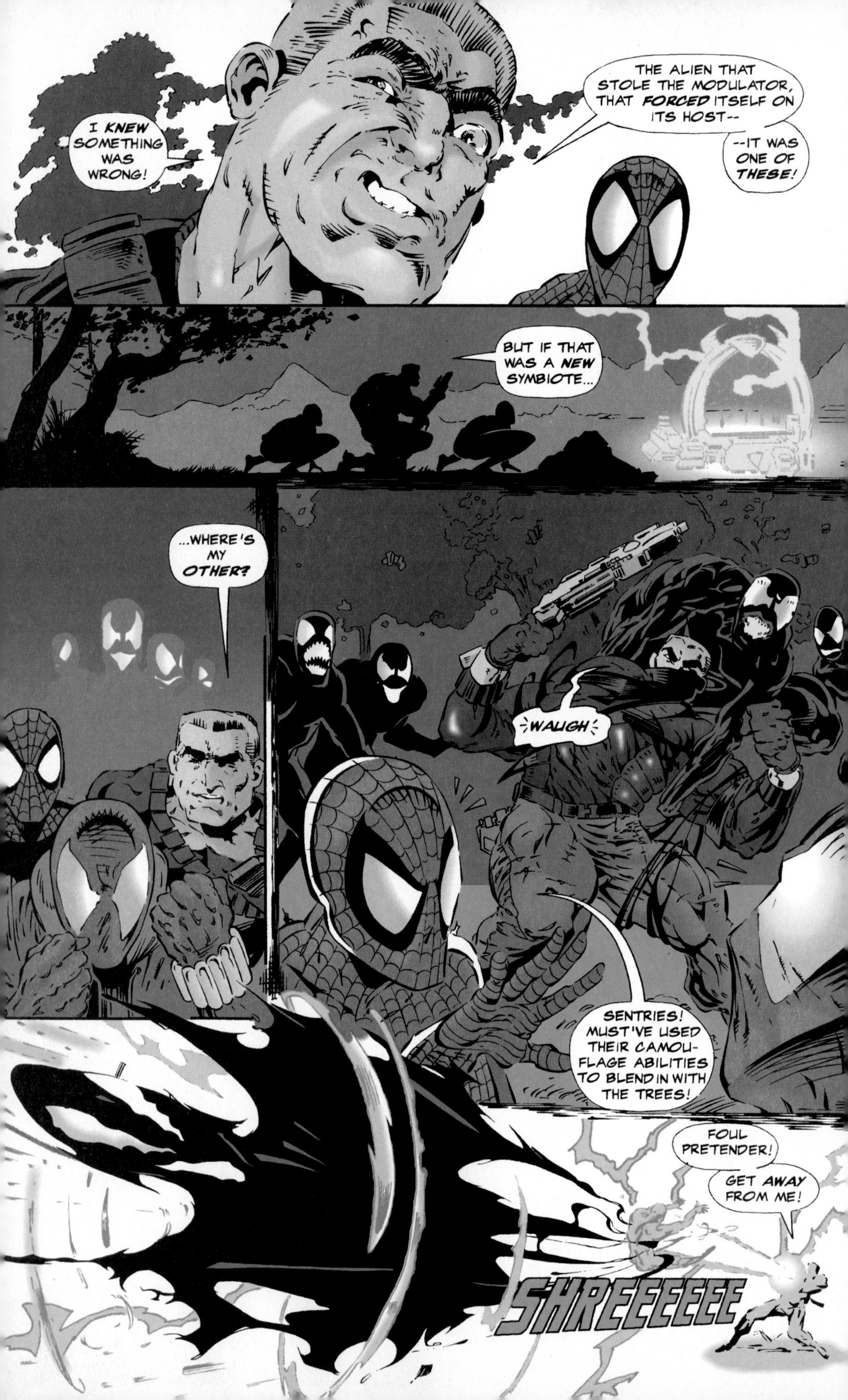

I KNEW SOMETHING WAS WRONG!
THE ALIEN THAT STOLE THE MODULATOR, THAT FORCED ITSELF ON ITS HOST--
--IT WAS ONE OF THESE!
BUT IF THAT WAS A NEW SYMBIOTE...
...WHERE'S MY OTHER?
WAUGH
SENTRIES! MUST'VE USED THEIR CAMOU-FLAGE ABILITIES TO BLEND IN WITH THE TREES!
FOUL PRETENDER!
GET AWAY FROM ME!
SHREEEEEE

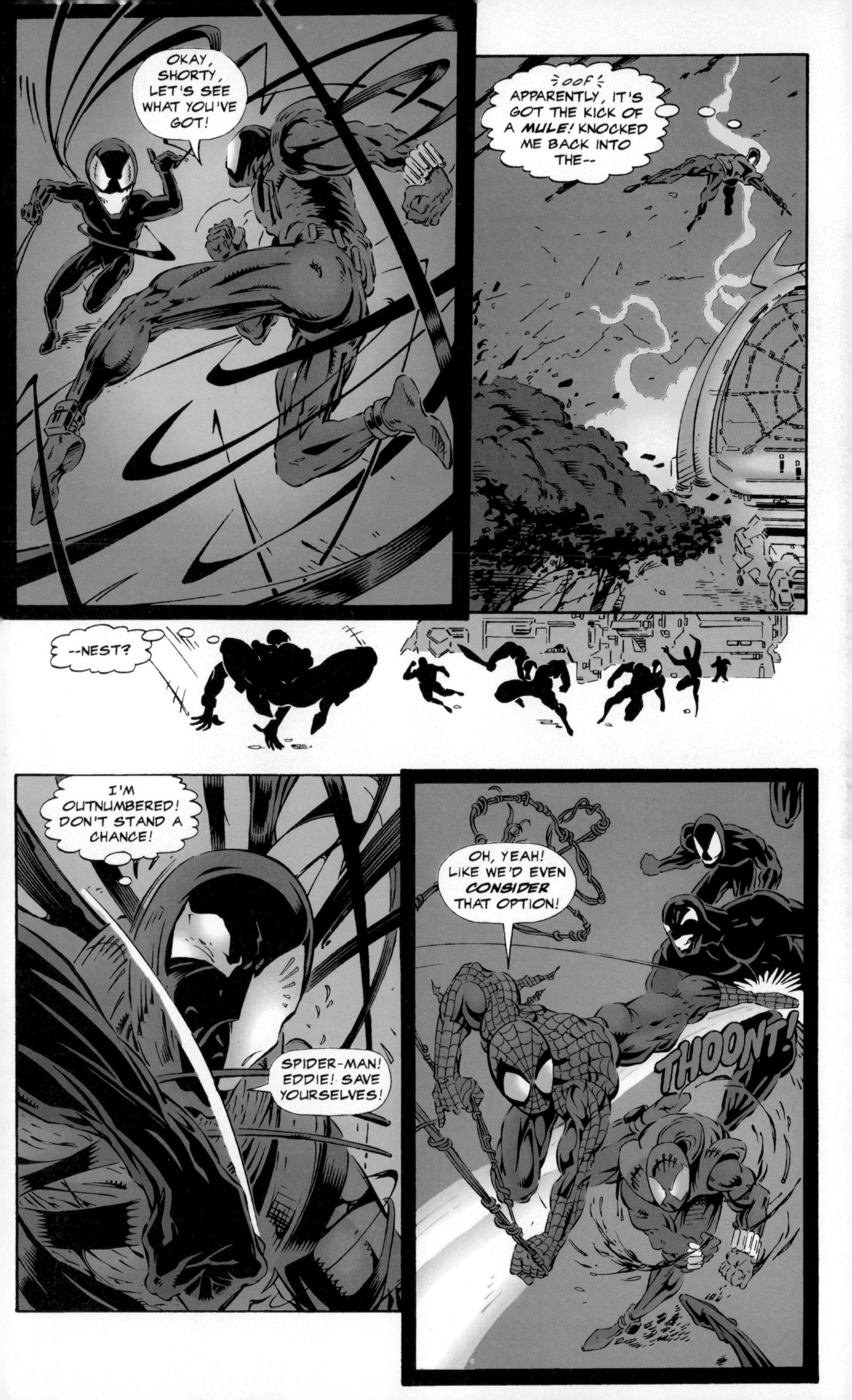
OKAY, SHORTY, LET'S SEE WHAT YOU'VE GOT!
OOF
APPARENTLY, IT'S GOT THE KICK OF A MULE! KNOCKED ME BACK INTO THE--
--NEST?
I'M OUTNUMBERED! DON'T STAND A CHANCE!
SPIDER-MAN! EDDIE! SAVE YOURSELVES!
OH, YEAH! LIKE WE'D EVEN CONSIDER THAT OPTION!
THOONT!

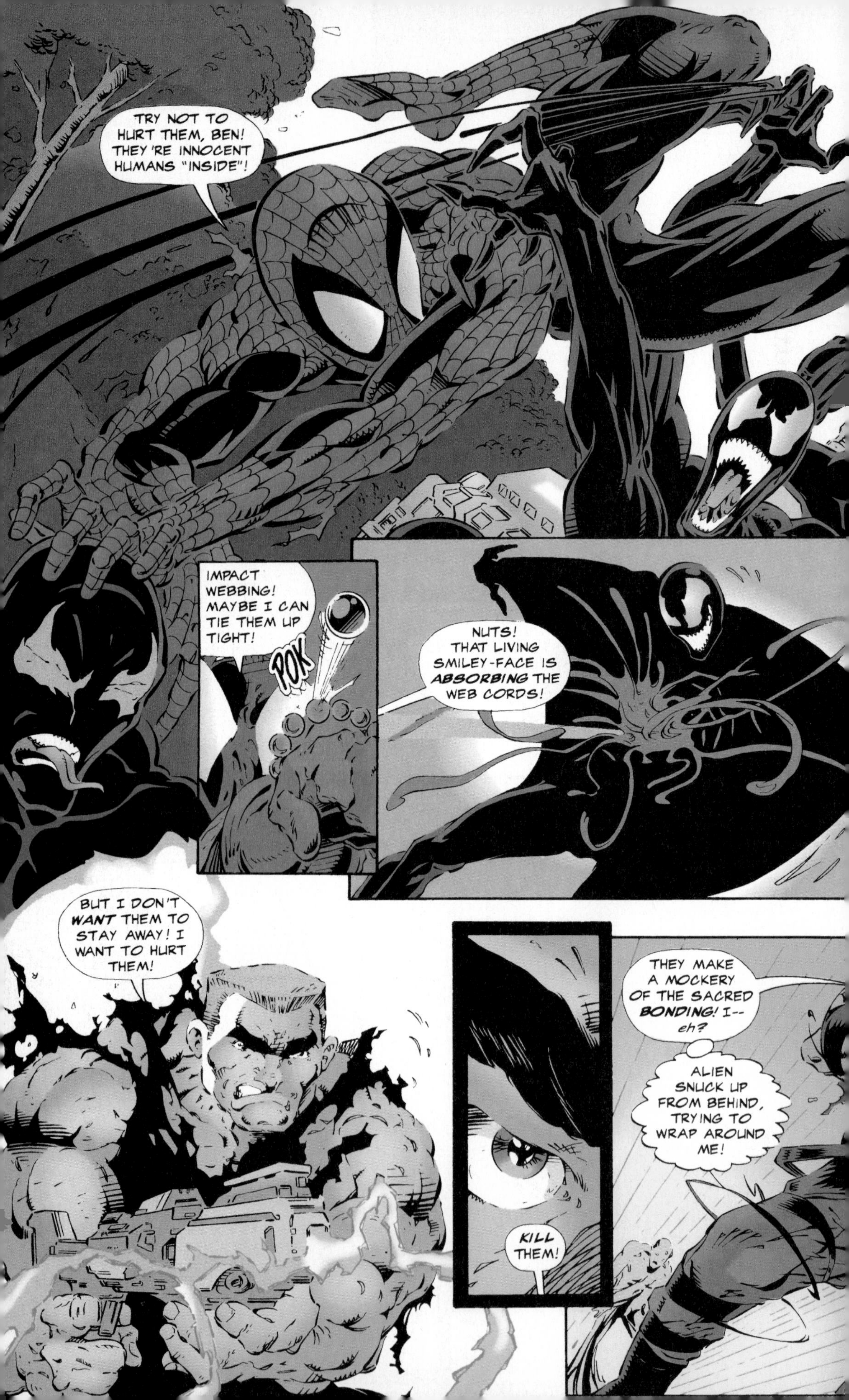
TRY NOT TO HURT THEM, BEN! THEY'RE INNOCENT HUMANS "INSIDE"!
IMPACT WEBBING! MAYBE I CAN TIE THEM UP TIGHT!
POK
NUTS! THAT LIVING SMILEY-FACE IS ABSORBING THE WEB CORDS!
BUT I DON'T WANT THEM TO STAY AWAY! I WANT TO HURT THEM!
KILL THEM!
THEY MAKE A MOCKERY OF THE SACRED BONDING! I-- eh?
ALIEN SNUCK UP FROM BEHIND, TRYING TO WRAP AROUND ME!

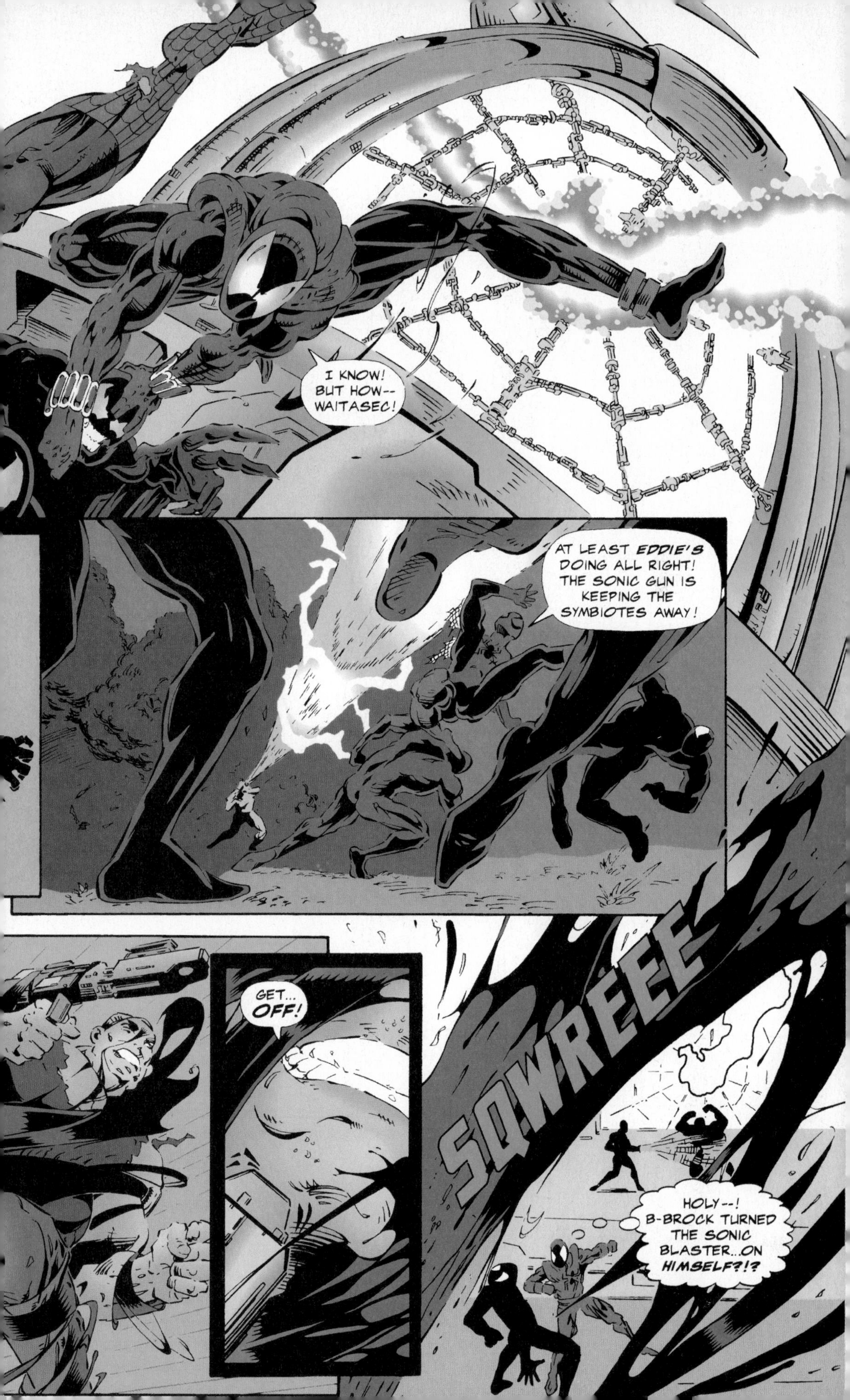
I KNOW! BUT HOW-- WAITASEC!
AT LEAST EDDIE'S DOING ALL RIGHT! THE SONIC GUN IS KEEPING THE SYMBIOTES AWAY!
GET... OFF!
SQWREEE
HOLY--! B-BROCK TURNED THE SONIC BLASTER...ON HIMSELF?!?

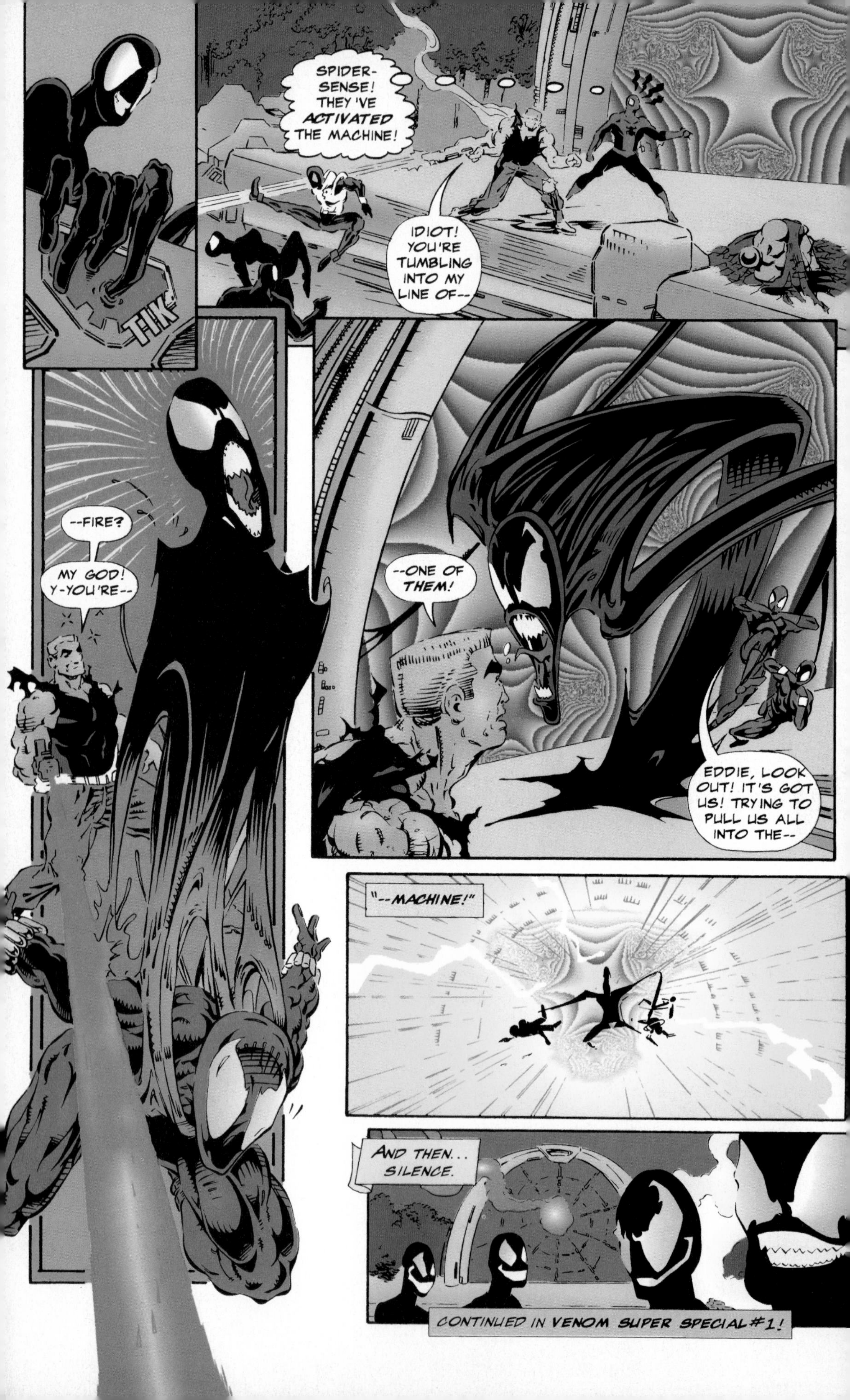
TIK
SPIDER-SENSE! THEY'VE ACTIVATED THE MACHINE!
IDIOT! YOU'RE TUMBLING INTO MY LINE OF--
--FIRE?
MY GOD! Y-YOU'RE--
--ONE OF THEM!
EDDIE, LOOK OUT! IT'S GOT US! TRYING TO PULL US ALL INTO THE--
"--MACHINE!"
AND THEN... SILENCE.
CONTINUED IN VENOM SUPER SPECIAL #1!

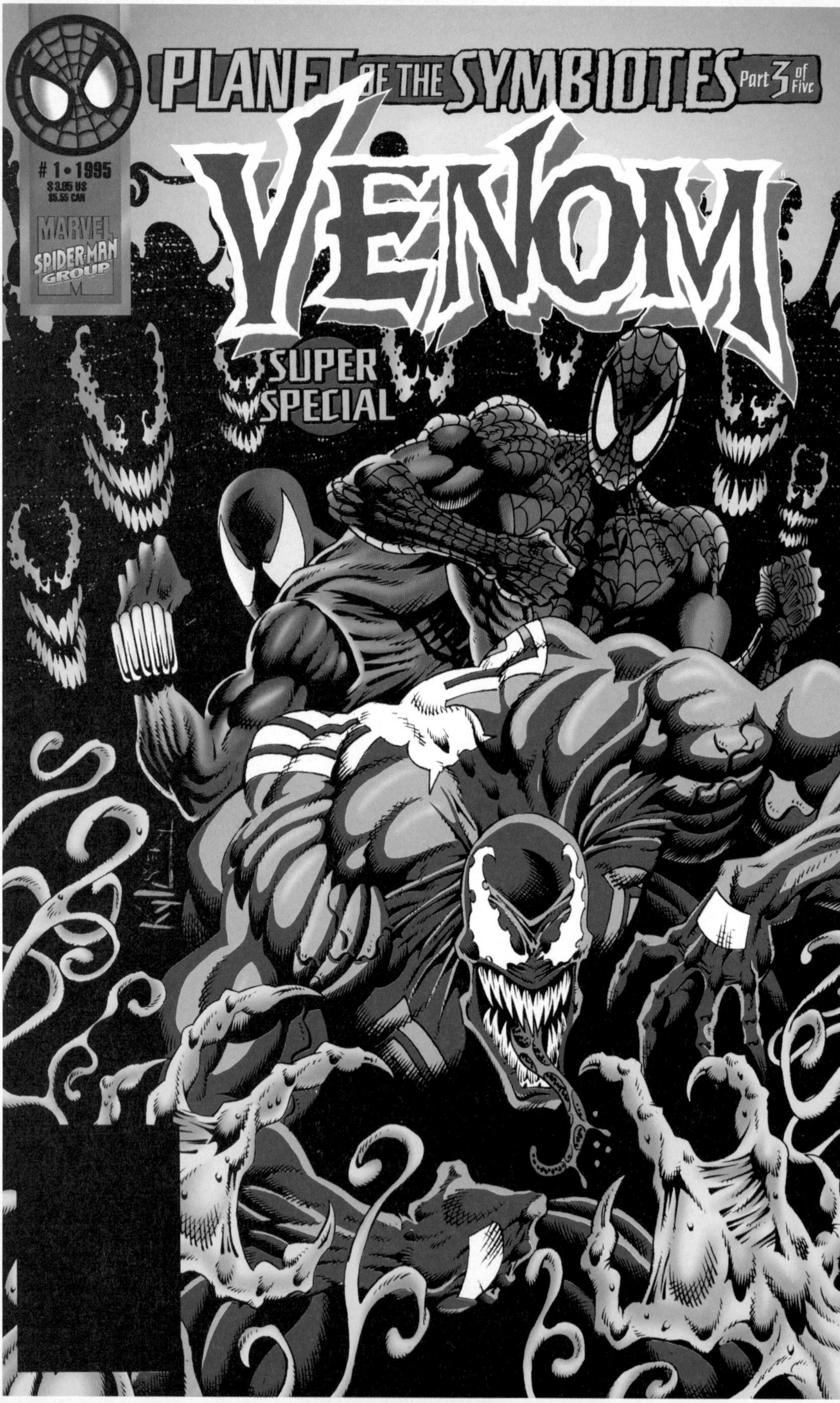
PLANET OF THE SYMBIOTES Part 3 of Five
1 • 1995
$3.95 US
$5.55 CAN
MARVEL
SPIDER-MAN GROUP
VENOM
SUPER SPECIAL

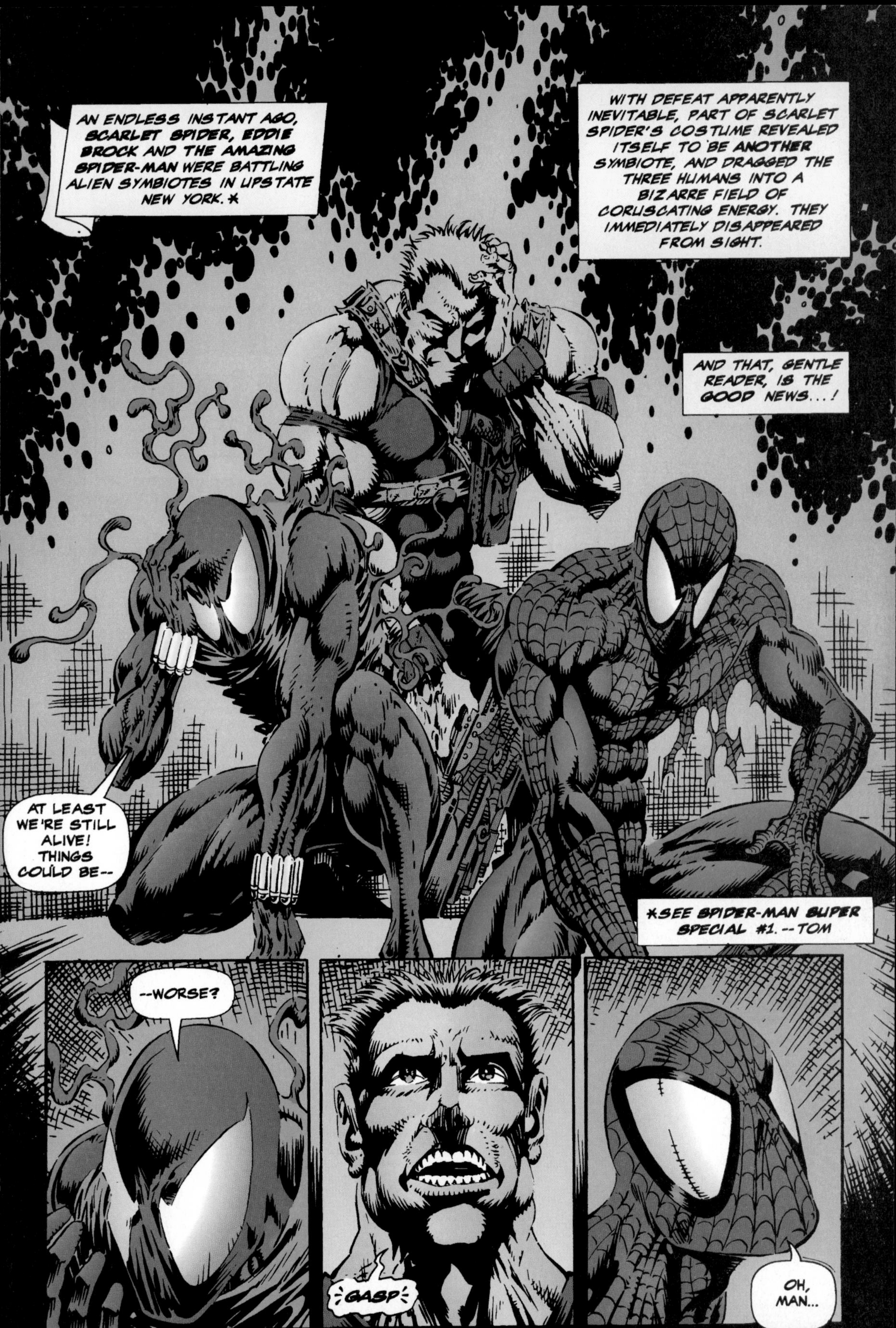

AN ENDLESS INSTANT AGO, SCARLET SPIDER, EDDIE BROCK AND THE AMAZING SPIDER-MAN WERE BATTLING ALIEN SYMBIOTES IN UPSTATE NEW YORK.*
WITH DEFEAT APPARENTLY INEVITABLE, PART OF SCARLET SPIDER'S COSTUME REVEALED ITSELF TO BE ANOTHER SYMBIOTE, AND DRAGGED THE THREE HUMANS INTO A BIZARRE FIELD OF CORUSCATING ENERGY. THEY IMMEDIATELY DISAPPEARED FROM SIGHT.
AND THAT, GENTLE READER, IS THE GOOD NEWS...!
AT LEAST WE'RE STILL ALIVE! THINGS COULD BE--
*SEE SPIDER-MAN SUPER SPECIAL #1. --TOM
--WORSE?
GASP
OH, MAN...

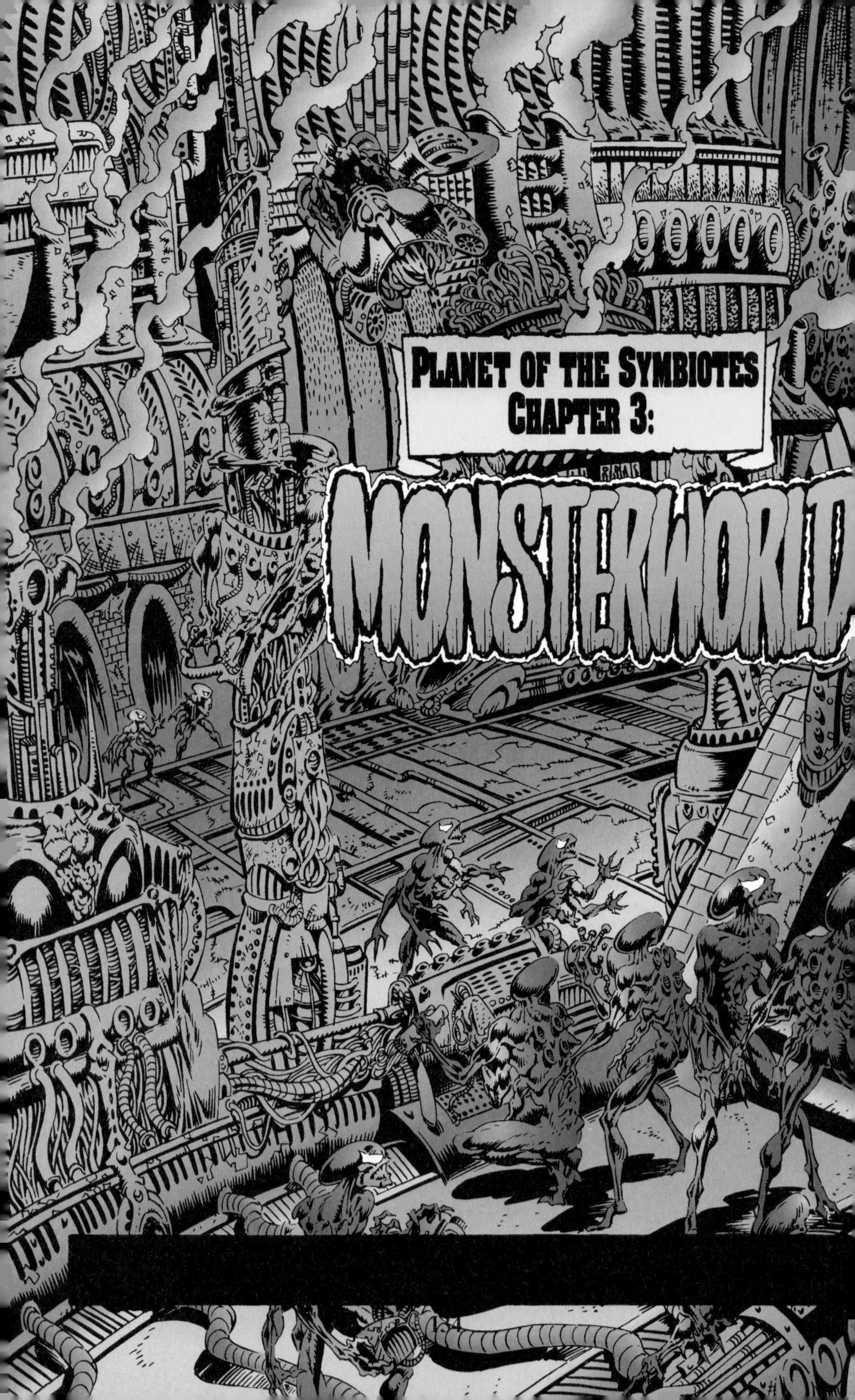
PLANET OF THE SYMBIOTES
CHAPTER 3:
MONSTERWORLD

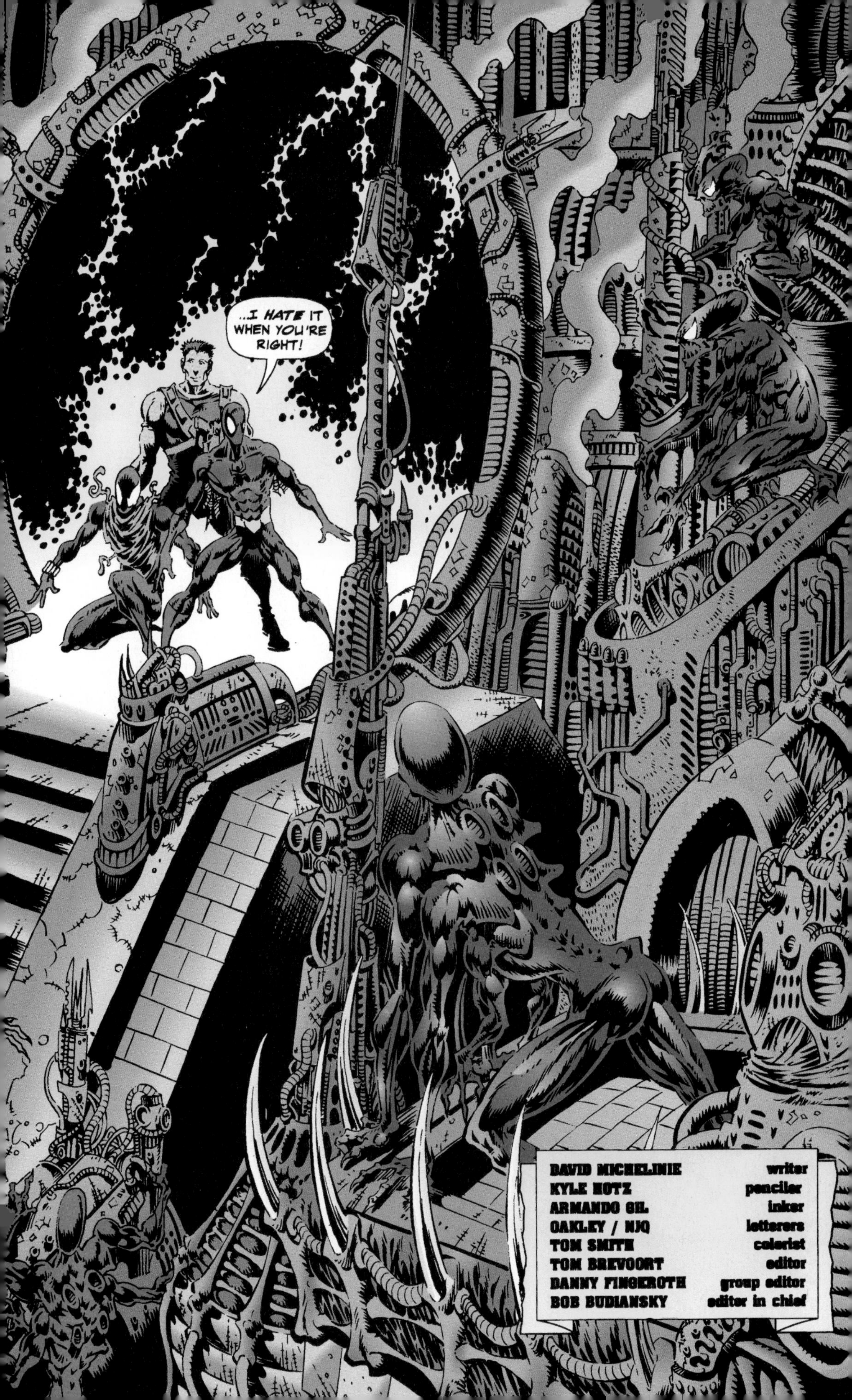

...I HATE IT WHEN YOU'RE RIGHT!
DAVID MICHELINIE writer
KYLE HOTZ penciler
ARMANDO GIL inker
OAKLEY / NJQ letterers
TOM SMITH colorist
TOM BREVOORT editor
DANNY FINGEROTH group editor
BOB BUDIANSKY editor in chief

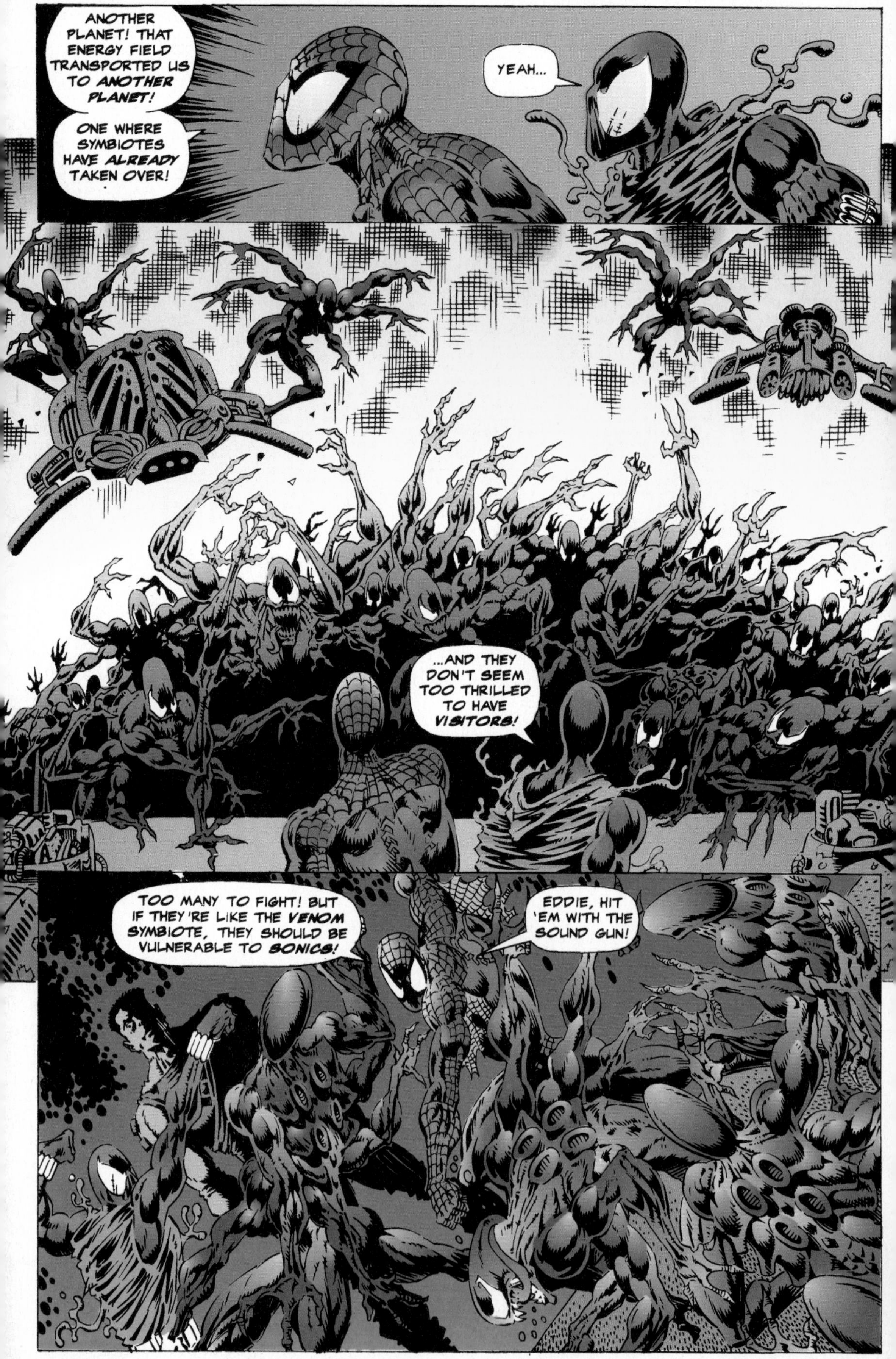
ANOTHER PLANET! THAT ENERGY FIELD TRANSPORTED US TO ANOTHER PLANET!
ONE WHERE SYMBIOTES HAVE ALREADY TAKEN OVER!
YEAH...
...AND THEY DON'T SEEM TOO THRILLED TO HAVE VISITORS!
TOO MANY TO FIGHT! BUT IF THEY'RE LIKE THE VENOM SYMBIOTE, THEY SHOULD BE VULNERABLE TO SONICS!
EDDIE, HIT 'EM WITH THE SOUND GUN!

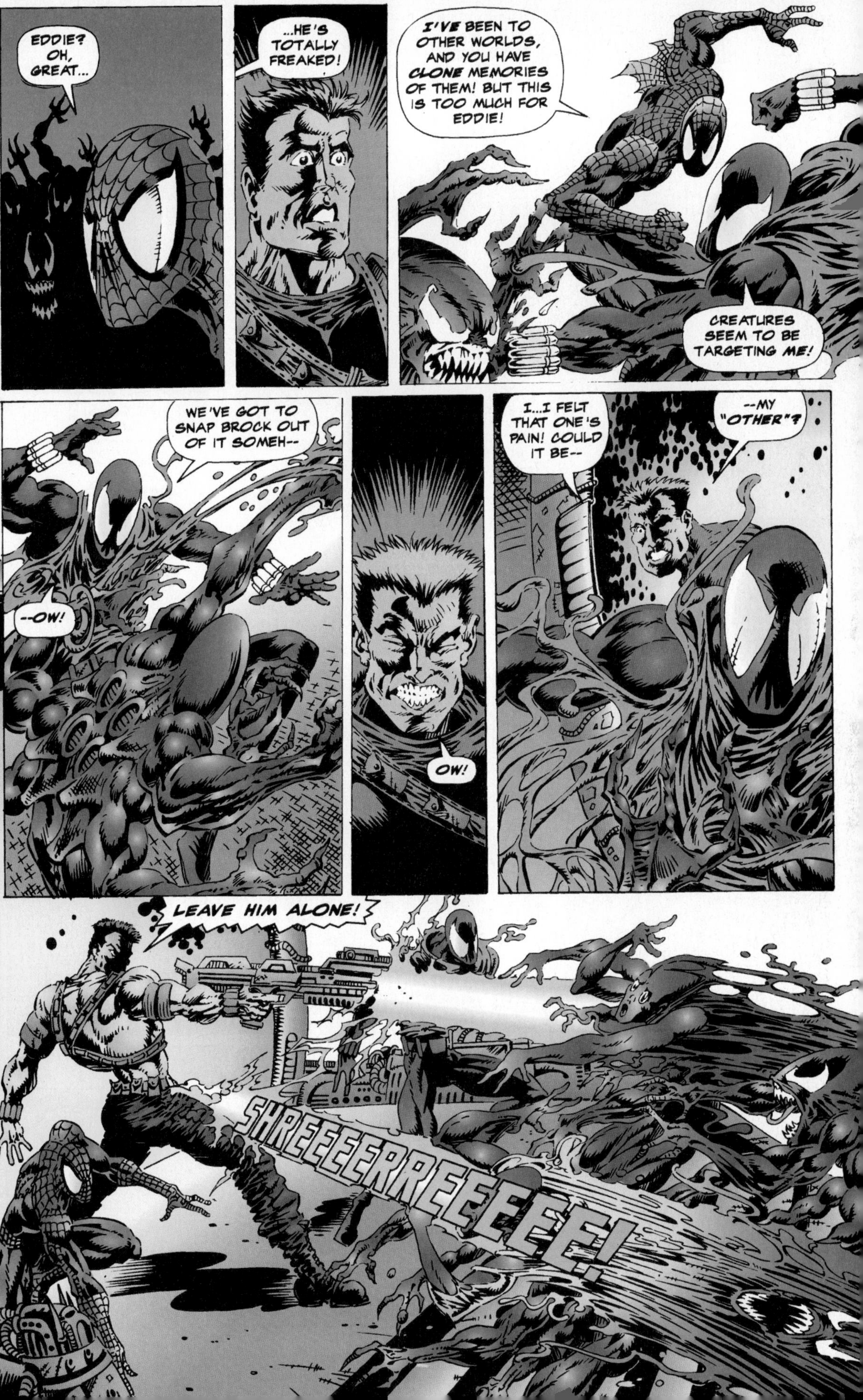

EDDIE? OH, GREAT...
...HE'S TOTALLY FREAKED!
I'VE BEEN TO OTHER WORLDS, AND YOU HAVE CLONE MEMORIES OF THEM! BUT THIS IS TOO MUCH FOR EDDIE!
CREATURES SEEM TO BE TARGETING ME!
WE'VE GOT TO SNAP BROCK OUT OF IT SOMEH--
--OW!
OW!
I...I FELT THAT ONE'S PAIN! COULD IT BE--
--MY "OTHER"?
LEAVE HIM ALONE!
SHREEEEERREEEEEE!

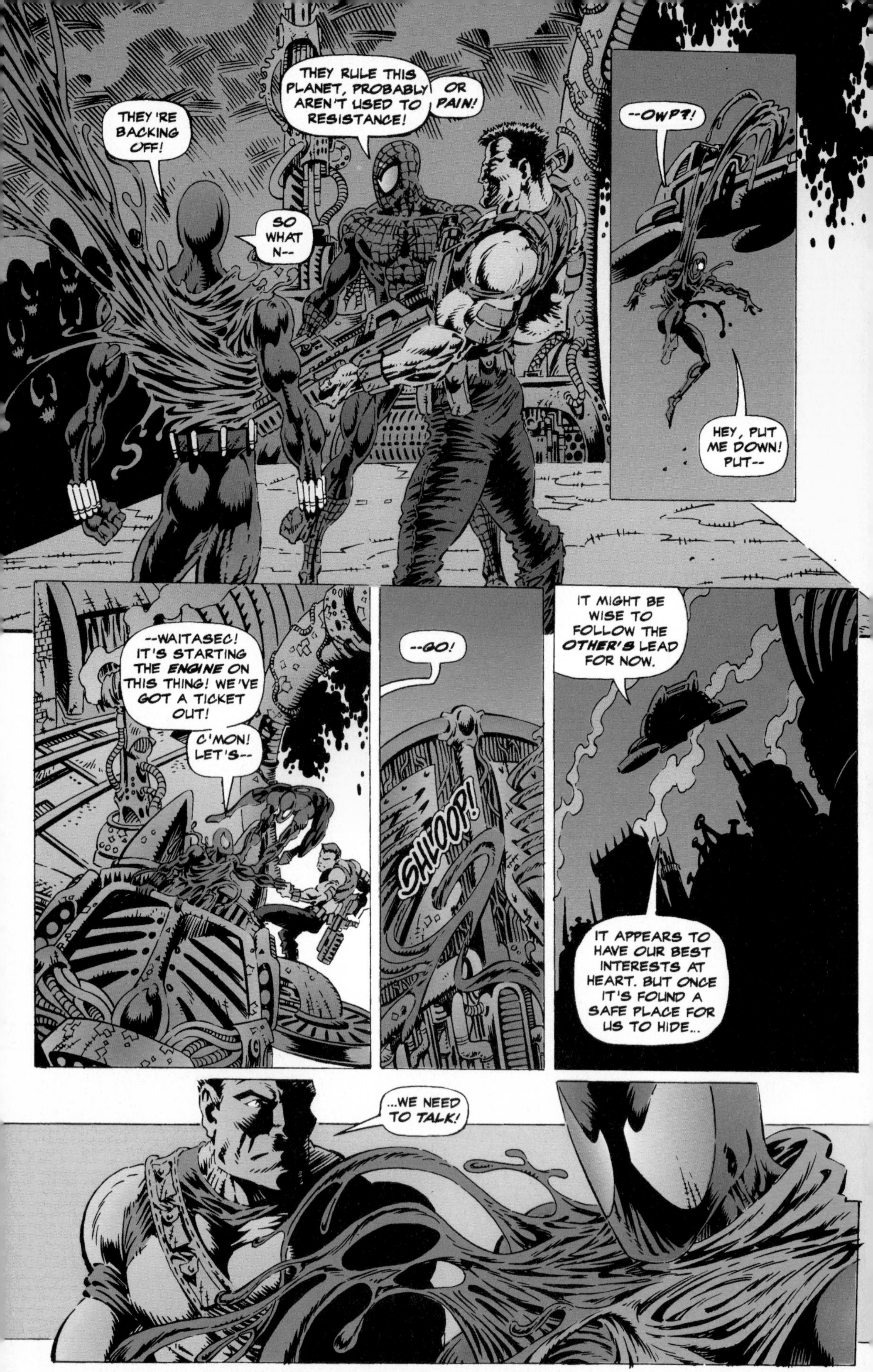
THEY'RE BACKING OFF!
THEY RULE THIS PLANET, PROBABLY AREN'T USED TO RESISTANCE!
OR PAIN!
SO WHAT N--
--OWP?!
HEY, PUT ME DOWN! PUT--
--WAITASEC! IT'S STARTING THE ENGINE ON THIS THING! WE'VE GOT A TICKET OUT!
C'MON! LET'S--
--GO!
SHLOOP!
IT MIGHT BE WISE TO FOLLOW THE OTHER'S LEAD FOR NOW.
IT APPEARS TO HAVE OUR BEST INTERESTS AT HEART. BUT ONCE IT'S FOUND A SAFE PLACE FOR US TO HIDE...
...WE NEED TO TALK!

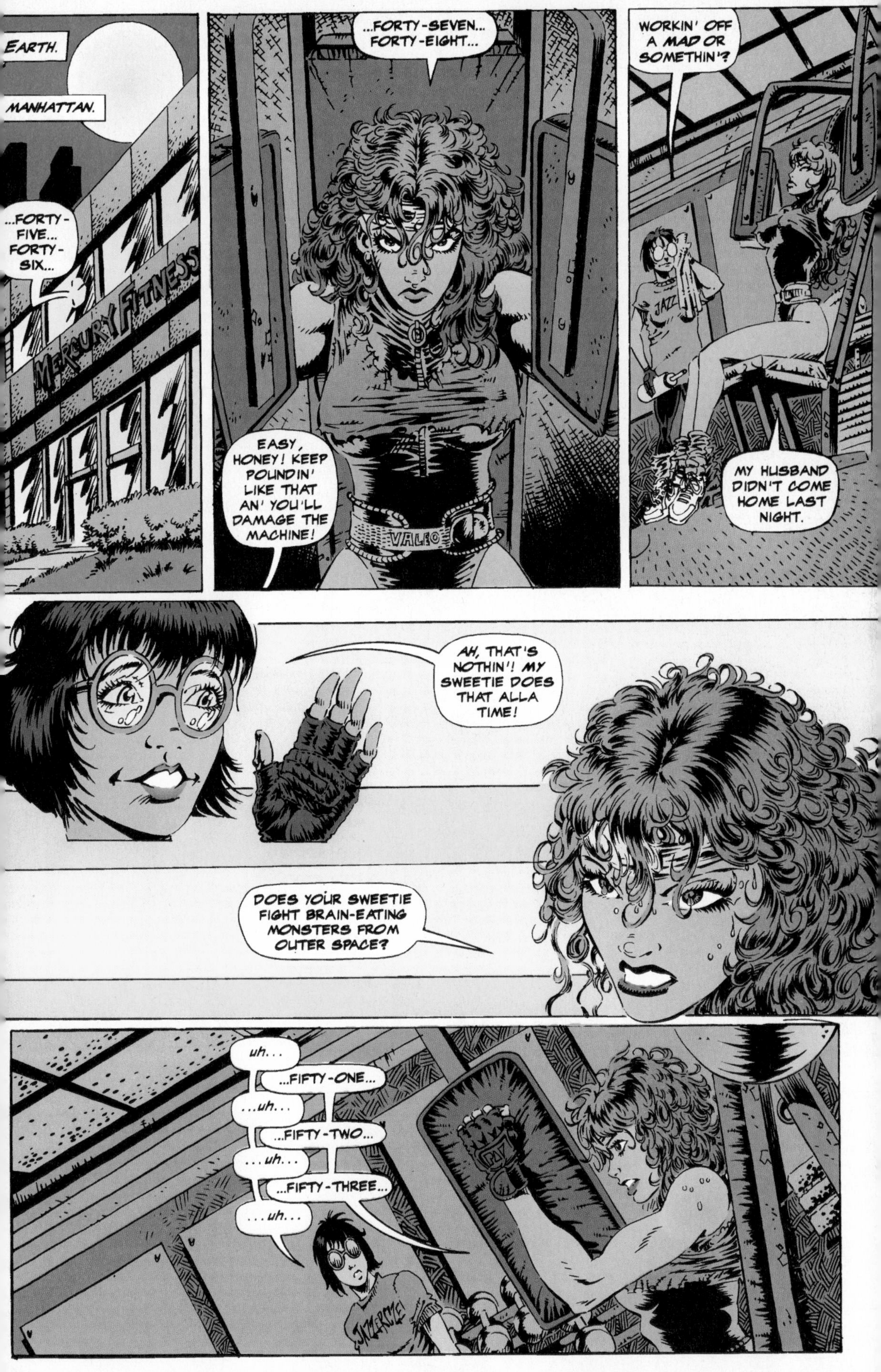
EARTH.
MANHATTAN.
...FORTY-FIVE... FORTY-SIX...
MERCURY FITNESS
...FORTY-SEVEN... FORTY-EIGHT...
EASY, HONEY! KEEP POUNDIN' LIKE THAT AN' YOU'LL DAMAGE THE MACHINE!
WORKIN' OFF A MAD OR SOMETHIN'?
MY HUSBAND DIDN'T COME HOME LAST NIGHT.
AH, THAT'S NOTHIN'! MY SWEETIE DOES THAT ALLA TIME!
DOES YOUR SWEETIE FIGHT BRAIN-EATING MONSTERS FROM OUTER SPACE?
uh...
...FIFTY-ONE...
...uh...
...FIFTY-TWO...
...uh...
...FIFTY-THREE...
...uh...

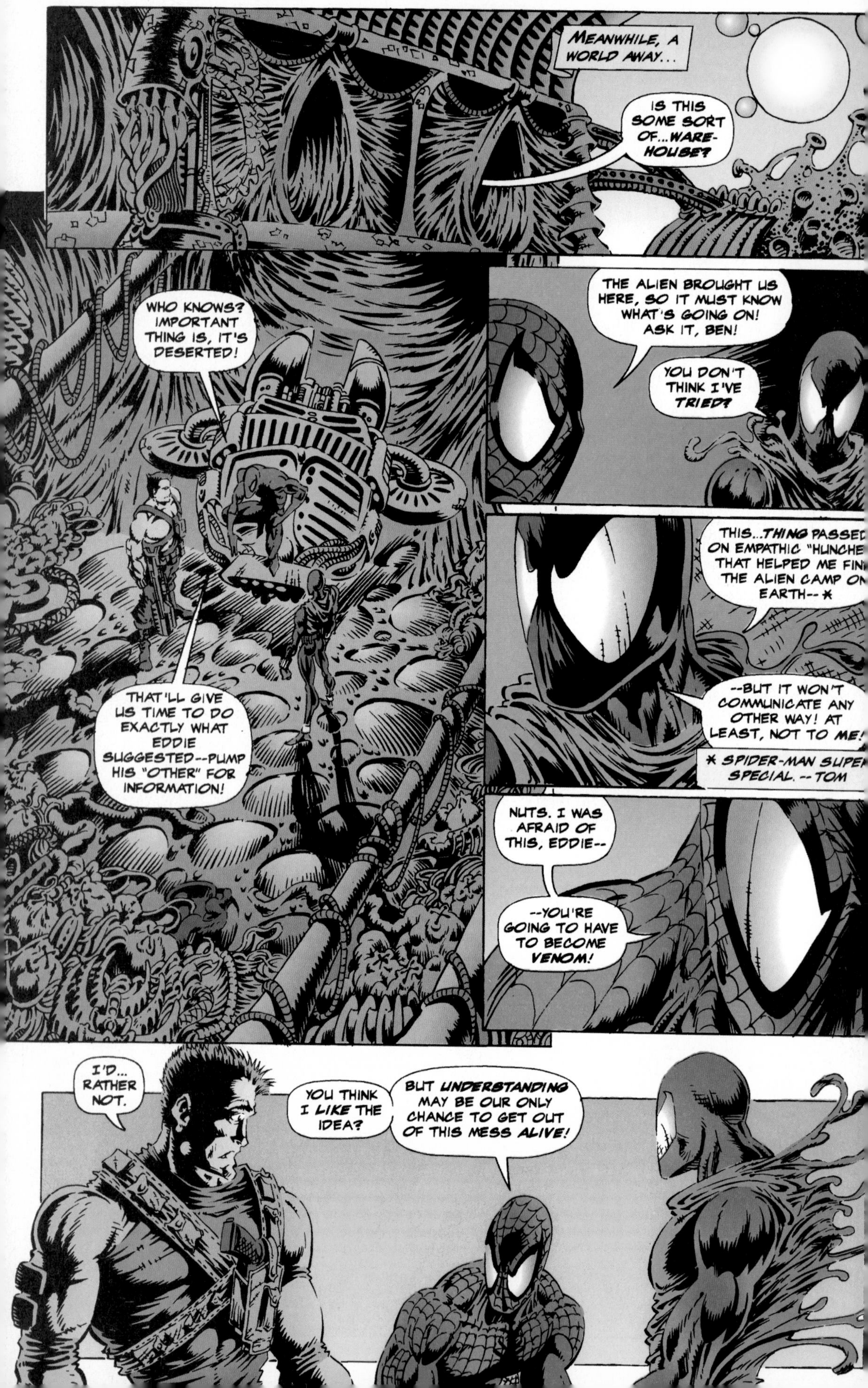
MEANWHILE, A WORLD AWAY...
IS THIS SOME SORT OF...WARE-HOUSE?
WHO KNOWS? IMPORTANT THING IS, IT'S DESERTED!
THAT'LL GIVE US TIME TO DO EXACTLY WHAT EDDIE SUGGESTED--PUMP HIS "OTHER" FOR INFORMATION!
THE ALIEN BROUGHT US HERE, SO IT MUST KNOW WHAT'S GOING ON! ASK IT, BEN!
YOU DON'T THINK I'VE TRIED?
THIS...THING PASSED ON EMPATHIC "HUNCHE THAT HELPED ME FIN THE ALIEN CAMP ON EARTH-- *
--BUT IT WON'T COMMUNICATE ANY OTHER WAY! AT LEAST, NOT TO ME!
* SPIDER-MAN SUPER SPECIAL. --TOM
NUTS. I WAS AFRAID OF THIS, EDDIE--
--YOU'RE GOING TO HAVE TO BECOME VENOM!
I'D... RATHER NOT.
YOU THINK I LIKE THE IDEA?
BUT UNDERSTANDING MAY BE OUR ONLY CHANCE TO GET OUT OF THIS MESS ALIVE!

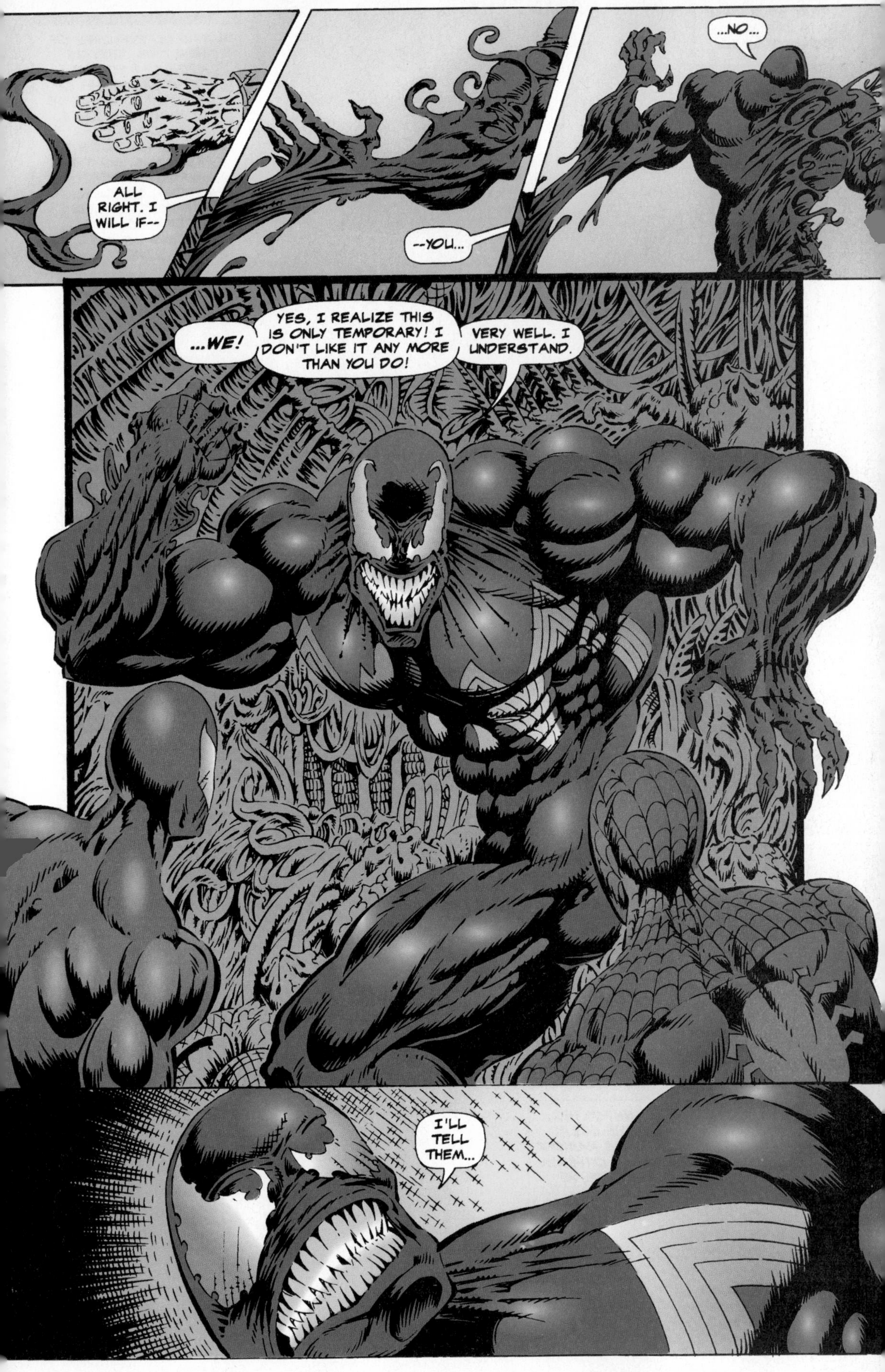
ALL RIGHT. I WILL IF--
--YOU...
...NO...
...WE!
YES, I REALIZE THIS IS ONLY TEMPORARY! I DON'T LIKE IT ANY MORE THAN YOU DO!
VERY WELL. I UNDERSTAND.
I'LL TELL THEM...

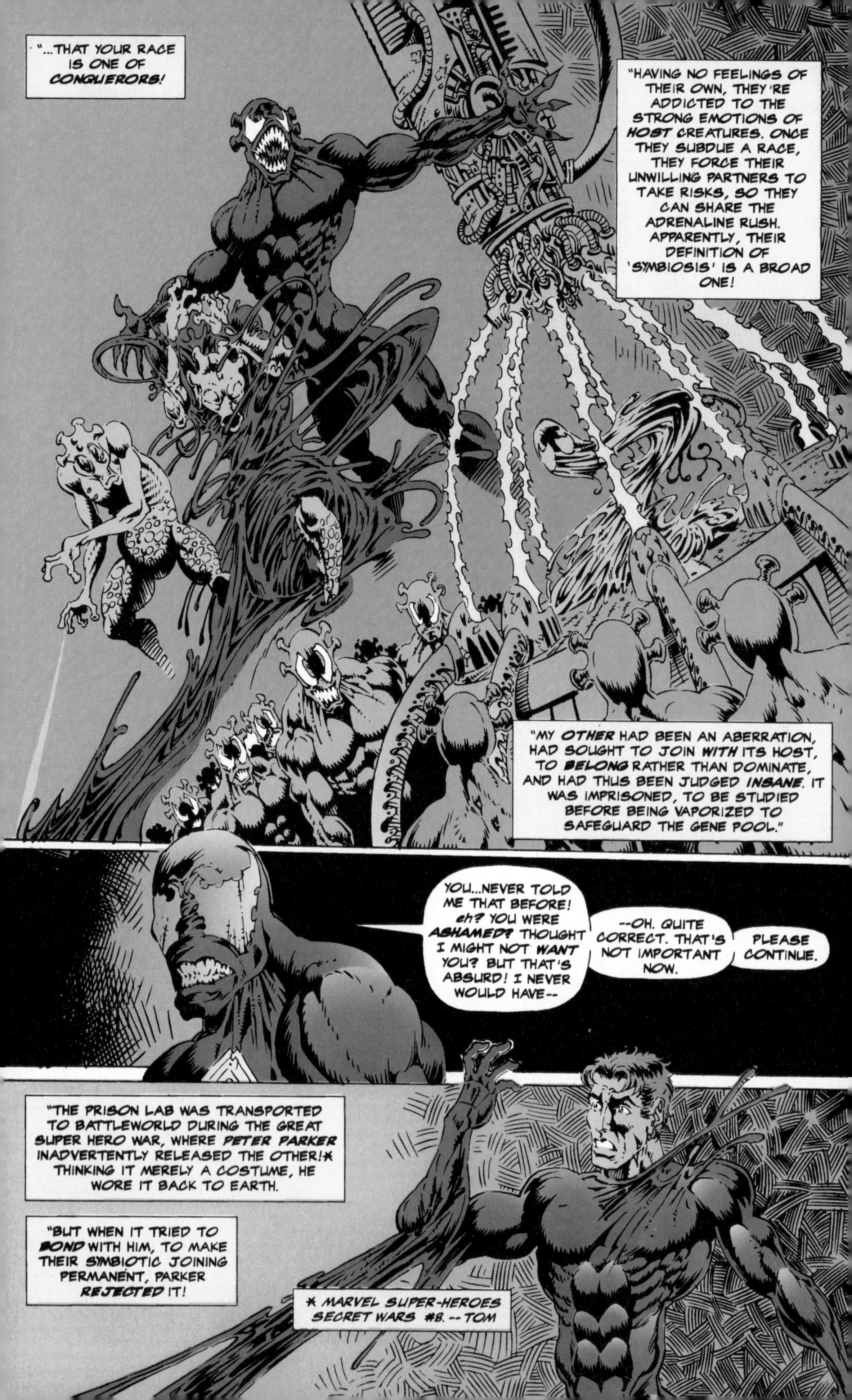
"...THAT YOUR RACE IS ONE OF CONQUERORS!
"HAVING NO FEELINGS OF THEIR OWN, THEY'RE ADDICTED TO THE STRONG EMOTIONS OF HOST CREATURES. ONCE THEY SUBDUE A RACE, THEY FORCE THEIR UNWILLING PARTNERS TO TAKE RISKS, SO THEY CAN SHARE THE ADRENALINE RUSH. APPARENTLY, THEIR DEFINITION OF 'SYMBIOSIS' IS A BROAD ONE!
"MY OTHER HAD BEEN AN ABERRATION, HAD SOUGHT TO JOIN WITH ITS HOST, TO BELONG RATHER THAN DOMINATE, AND HAD THUS BEEN JUDGED INSANE. IT WAS IMPRISONED, TO BE STUDIED BEFORE BEING VAPORIZED TO SAFEGUARD THE GENE POOL."
YOU...NEVER TOLD ME THAT BEFORE! eh? YOU WERE ASHAMED? THOUGHT I MIGHT NOT WANT YOU? BUT THAT'S ABSURD! I NEVER WOULD HAVE--
--OH. QUITE CORRECT. THAT'S NOT IMPORTANT NOW.
PLEASE CONTINUE.
"THE PRISON LAB WAS TRANSPORTED TO BATTLEWORLD DURING THE GREAT SUPER HERO WAR, WHERE PETER PARKER INADVERTENTLY RELEASED THE OTHER!* THINKING IT MERELY A COSTUME, HE WORE IT BACK TO EARTH.
"BUT WHEN IT TRIED TO BOND WITH HIM, TO MAKE THEIR SYMBIOTIC JOINING PERMANENT, PARKER REJECTED IT!
* MARVEL SUPER-HEROES SECRET WARS #8. --TOM

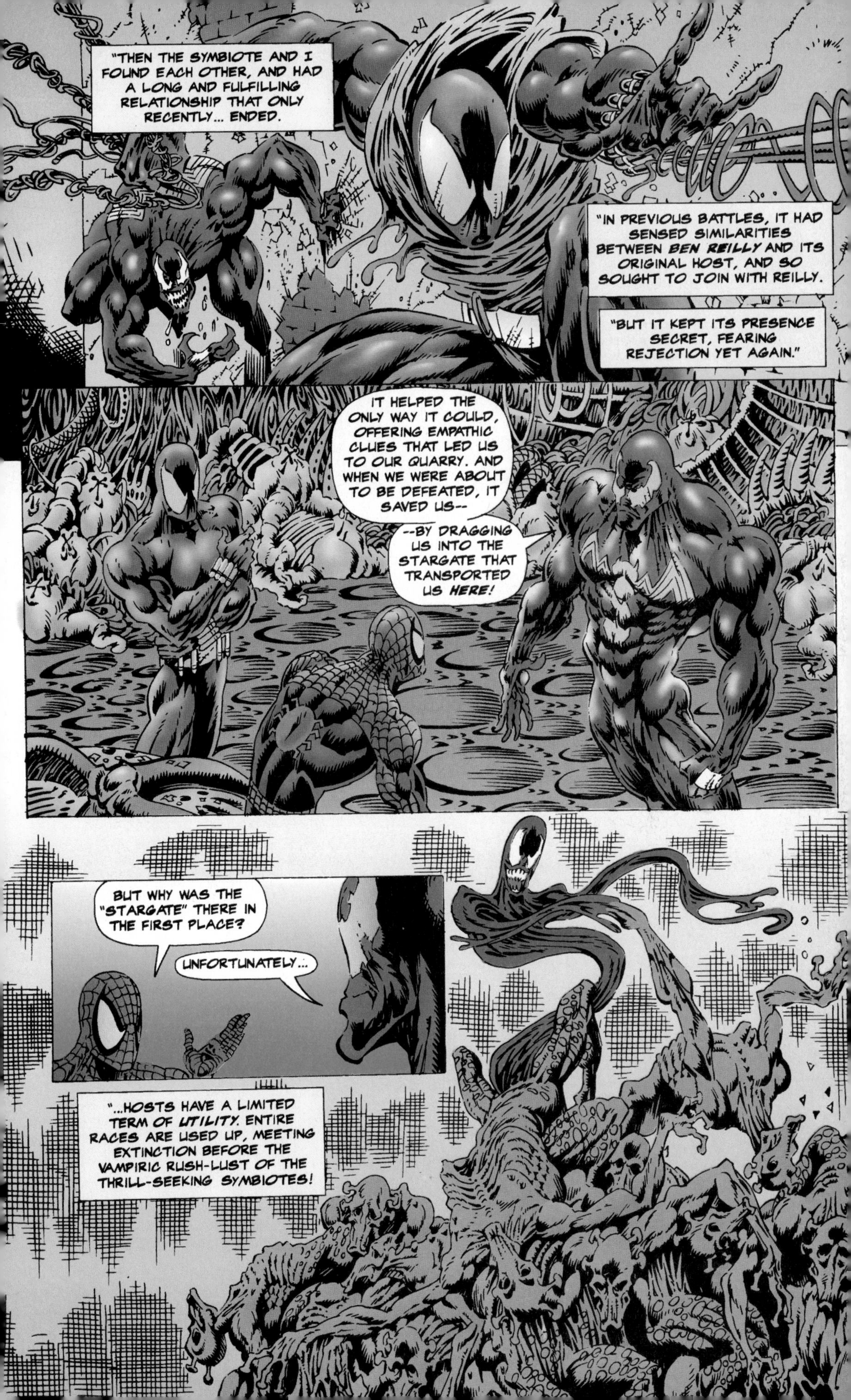
"THEN THE SYMBIOTE AND I FOUND EACH OTHER, AND HAD A LONG AND FULFILLING RELATIONSHIP THAT ONLY RECENTLY... ENDED.
"IN PREVIOUS BATTLES, IT HAD SENSED SIMILARITIES BETWEEN BEN REILLY AND ITS ORIGINAL HOST, AND SO SOUGHT TO JOIN WITH REILLY.
"BUT IT KEPT ITS PRESENCE SECRET, FEARING REJECTION YET AGAIN."
IT HELPED THE ONLY WAY IT COULD, OFFERING EMPATHIC CLUES THAT LED US TO OUR QUARRY. AND WHEN WE WERE ABOUT TO BE DEFEATED, IT SAVED US--
--BY DRAGGING US INTO THE STARGATE THAT TRANSPORTED US HERE!
BUT WHY WAS THE "STARGATE" THERE IN THE FIRST PLACE?
UNFORTUNATELY...
"...HOSTS HAVE A LIMITED TERM OF UTILITY. ENTIRE RACES ARE USED UP, MEETING EXTINCTION BEFORE THE VAMPIRIC RUSH-LUST OF THE THRILL-SEEKING SYMBIOTES!

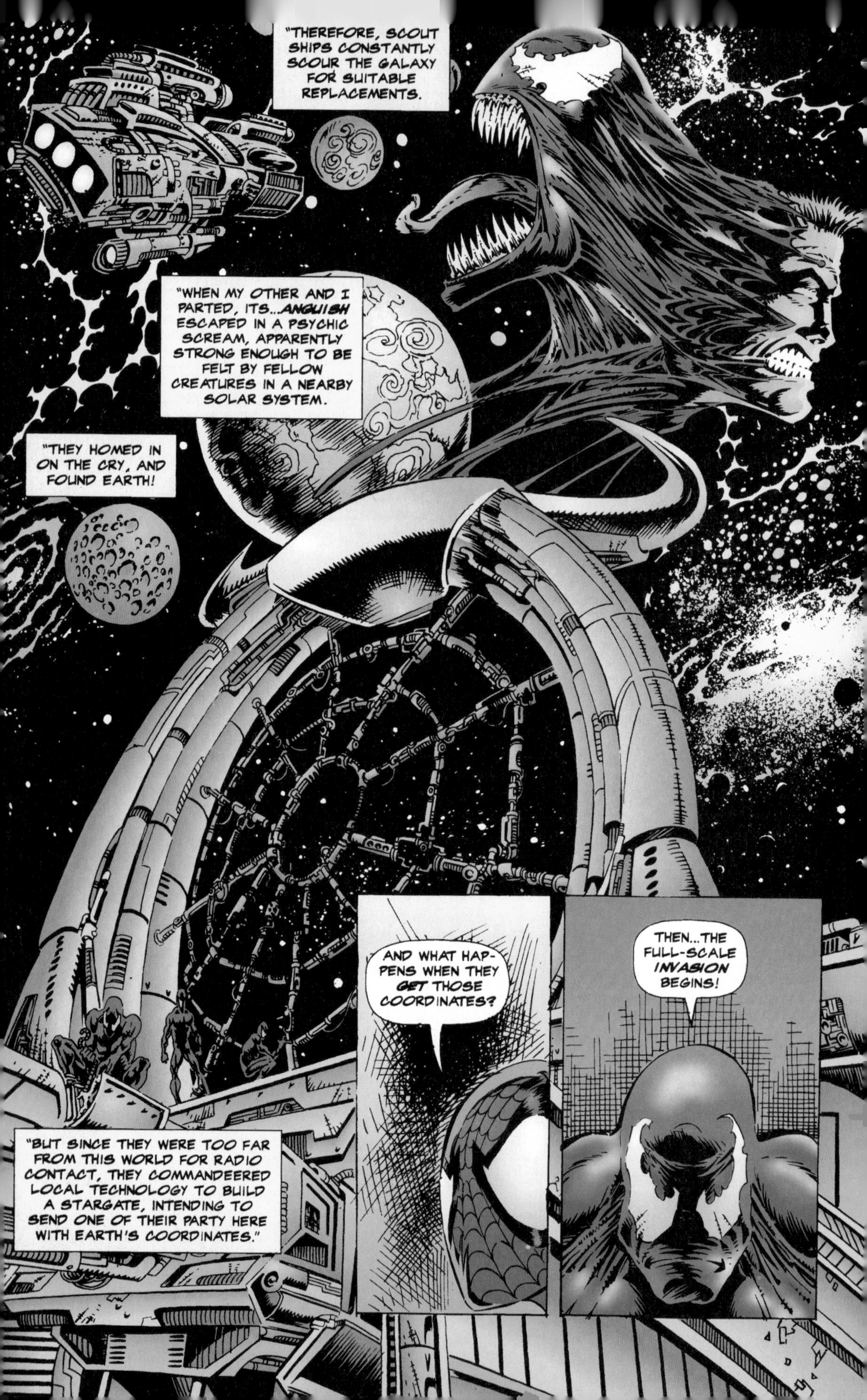
"THEREFORE, SCOUT SHIPS CONSTANTLY SCOUR THE GALAXY FOR SUITABLE REPLACEMENTS.
"WHEN MY OTHER AND I PARTED, ITS...ANGUISH ESCAPED IN A PSYCHIC SCREAM, APPARENTLY STRONG ENOUGH TO BE FELT BY FELLOW CREATURES IN A NEARBY SOLAR SYSTEM.
"THEY HOMED IN ON THE CRY, AND FOUND EARTH!
"BUT SINCE THEY WERE TOO FAR FROM THIS WORLD FOR RADIO CONTACT, THEY COMMANDEERED LOCAL TECHNOLOGY TO BUILD A STARGATE, INTENDING TO SEND ONE OF THEIR PARTY HERE WITH EARTH'S COORDINATES."
AND WHAT HAPPENS WHEN THEY GET THOSE COORDINATES?
THEN...THE FULL-SCALE INVASION BEGINS!

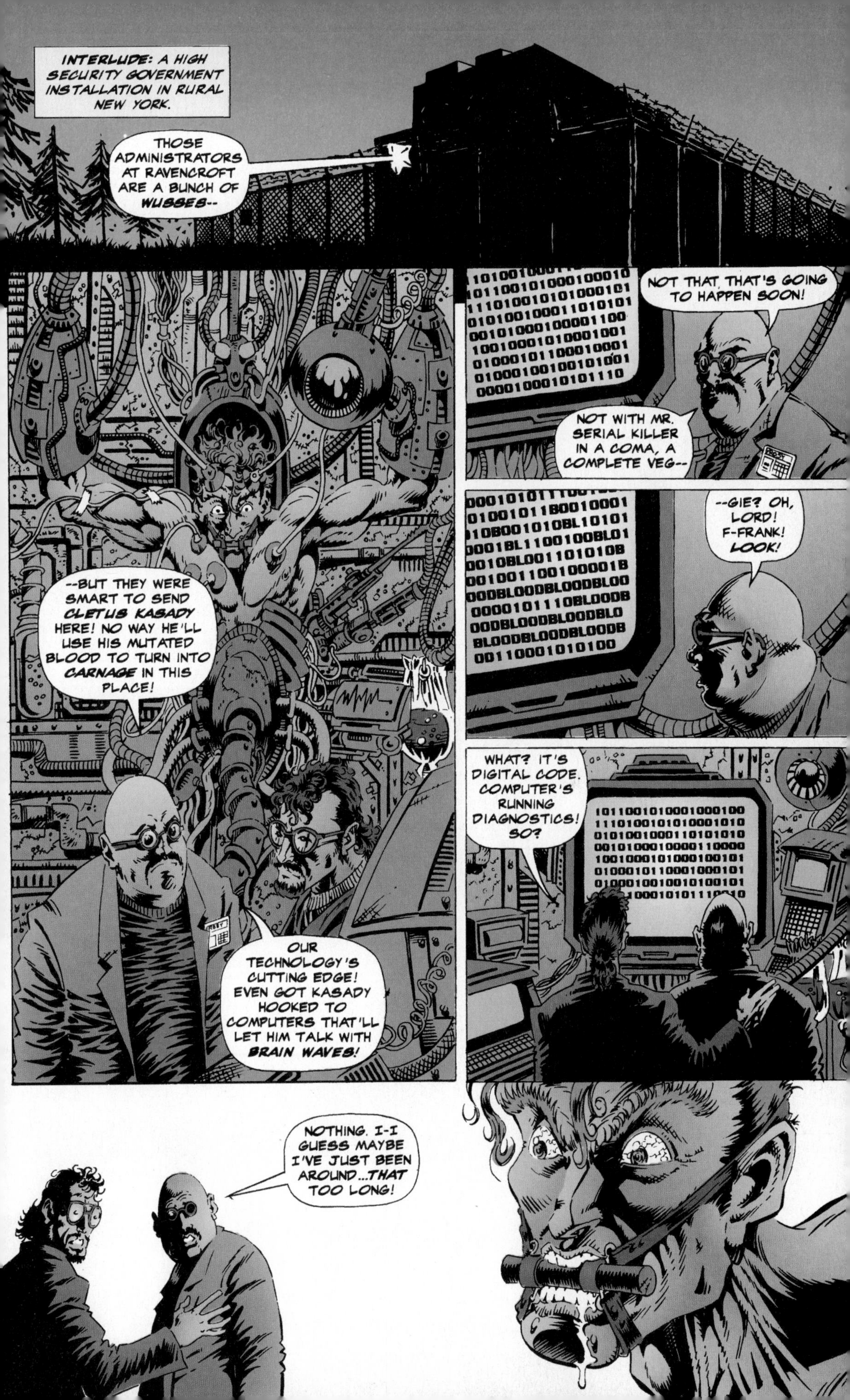

INTERLUDE: A HIGH SECURITY GOVERNMENT INSTALLATION IN RURAL NEW YORK.
THOSE ADMINISTRATORS AT RAVENCROFT ARE A BUNCH OF WUSSES--
--BUT THEY WERE SMART TO SEND CLETUS KASADY HERE! NO WAY HE'LL USE HIS MUTATED BLOOD TO TURN INTO CARNAGE IN THIS PLACE!
OUR TECHNOLOGY'S CUTTING EDGE! EVEN GOT KASADY HOOKED TO COMPUTERS THAT'LL LET HIM TALK WITH BRAIN WAVES!
NOT THAT THAT'S GOING TO HAPPEN SOON!
NOT WITH MR. SERIAL KILLER IN A COMA, A COMPLETE VEG--
--GIE? OH, LORD! F-FRANK! LOOK!
WHAT? IT'S DIGITAL CODE. COMPUTER'S RUNNING DIAGNOSTICS! SO?
NOTHING. I-I GUESS MAYBE I'VE JUST BEEN AROUND...THAT TOO LONG!

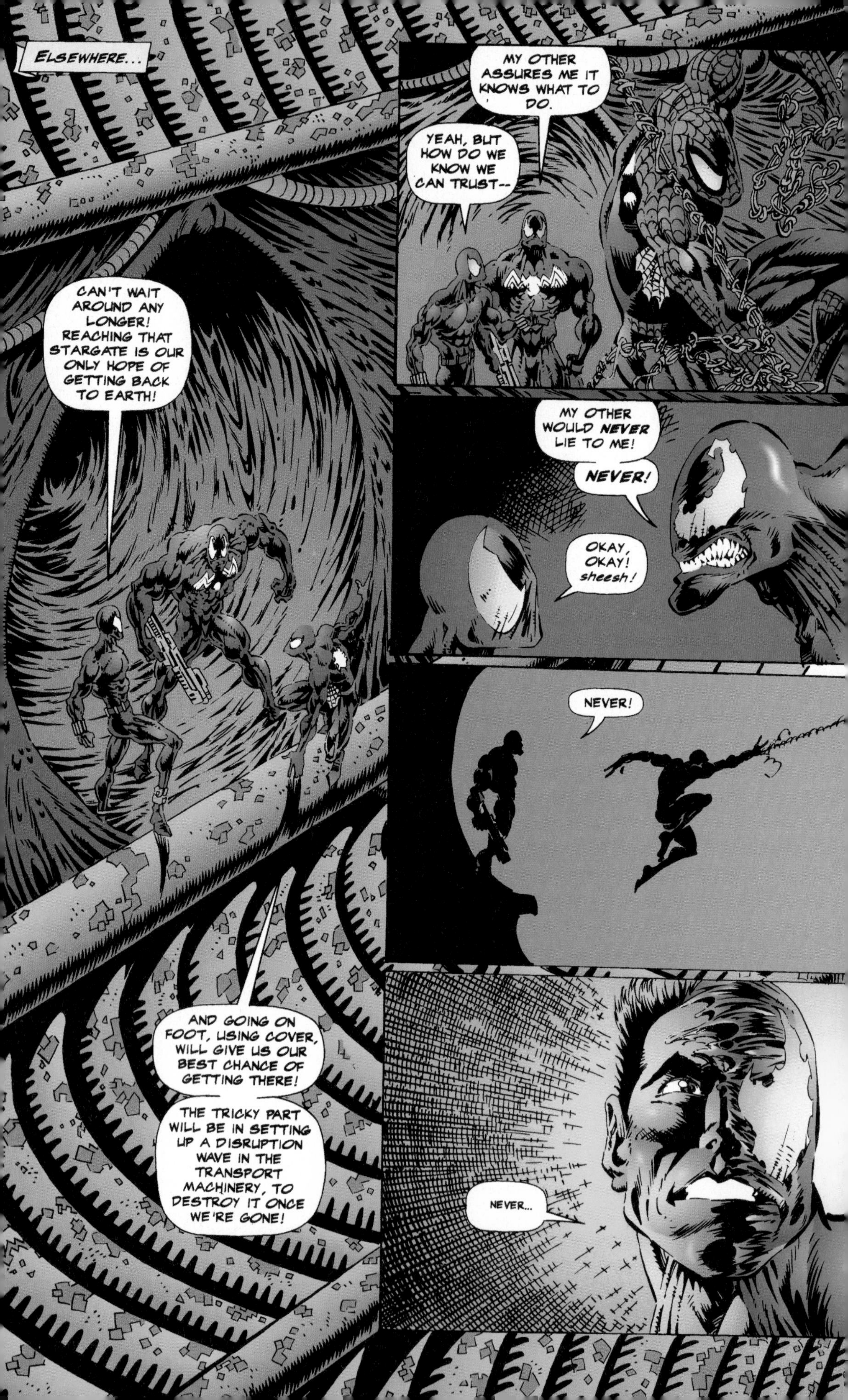
ELSEWHERE...
CAN'T WAIT AROUND ANY LONGER! REACHING THAT STARGATE IS OUR ONLY HOPE OF GETTING BACK TO EARTH!
AND GOING ON FOOT, USING COVER, WILL GIVE US OUR BEST CHANCE OF GETTING THERE!
THE TRICKY PART WILL BE IN SETTING UP A DISRUPTION WAVE IN THE TRANSPORT MACHINERY, TO DESTROY IT ONCE WE'RE GONE!
YEAH, BUT HOW DO WE KNOW WE CAN TRUST--
MY OTHER ASSURES ME IT KNOWS WHAT TO DO.
MY OTHER WOULD NEVER LIE TO ME!
NEVER!
OKAY, OKAY! sheesh!
NEVER!
NEVER...

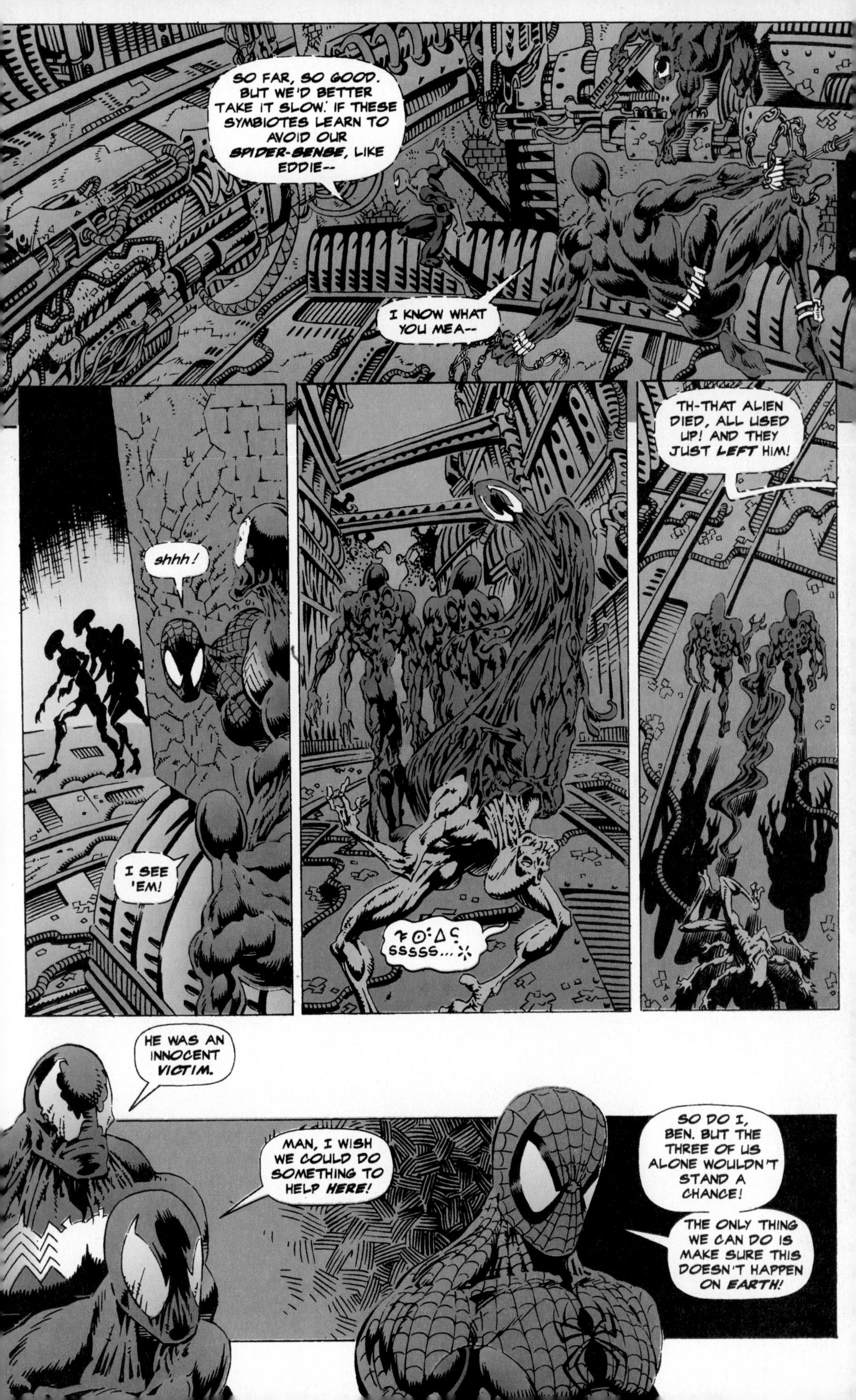
SO FAR, SO GOOD. BUT WE'D BETTER TAKE IT SLOW! IF THESE SYMBIOTES LEARN TO AVOID OUR SPIDER-SENSE, LIKE EDDIE--
I KNOW WHAT YOU MEA--
shhh!
I SEE 'EM!
SSSSS...
TH-THAT ALIEN DIED, ALL USED UP! AND THEY JUST LEFT HIM!
HE WAS AN INNOCENT VICTIM.
MAN, I WISH WE COULD DO SOMETHING TO HELP HERE!
SO DO I, BEN. BUT THE THREE OF US ALONE WOULDN'T STAND A CHANCE!
THE ONLY THING WE CAN DO IS MAKE SURE THIS DOESN'T HAPPEN ON EARTH!

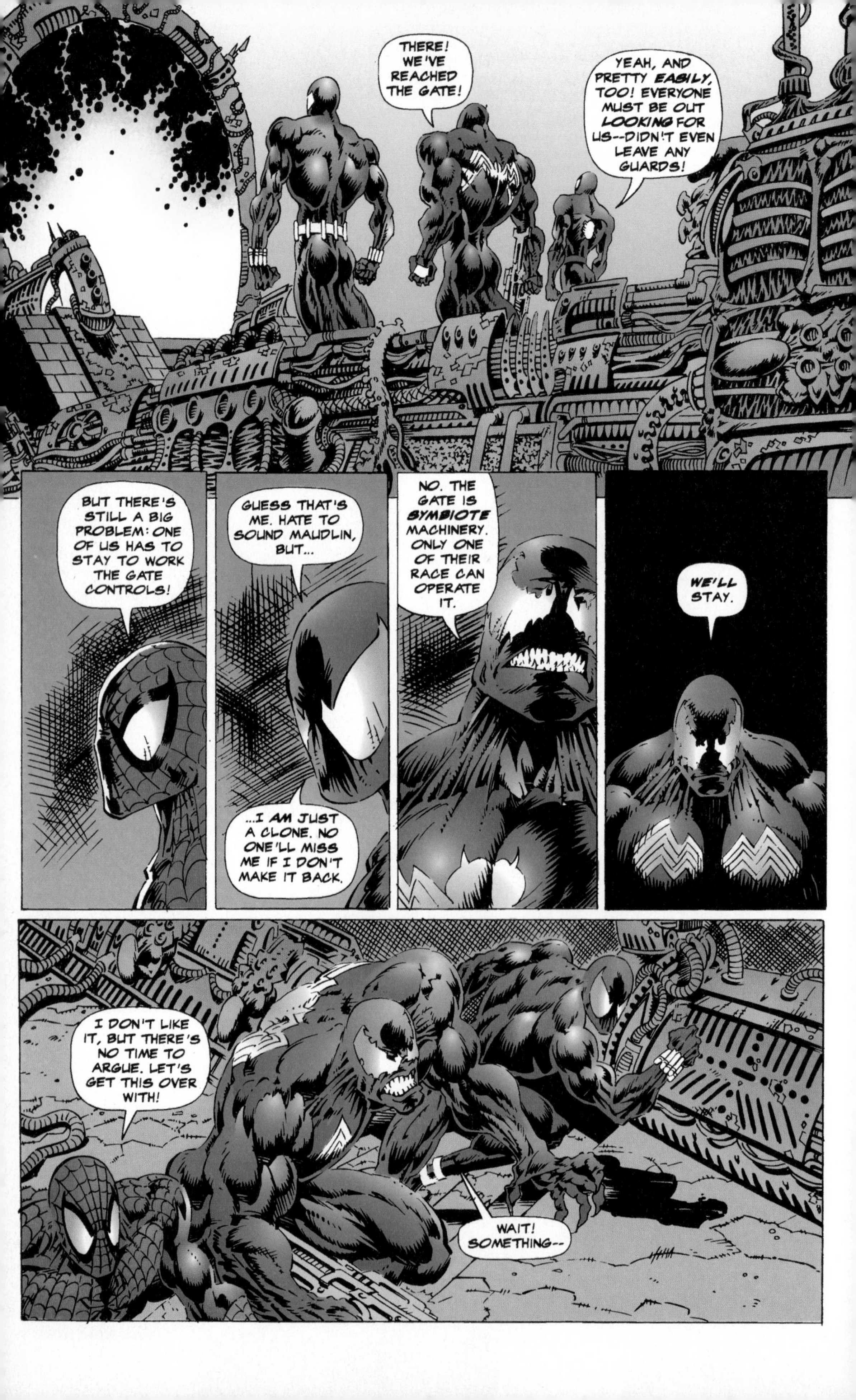
THERE! WE'VE REACHED THE GATE!
YEAH, AND PRETTY EASILY, TOO! EVERYONE MUST BE OUT LOOKING FOR US--DIDN'T EVEN LEAVE ANY GUARDS!
BUT THERE'S STILL A BIG PROBLEM: ONE OF US HAS TO STAY TO WORK THE GATE CONTROLS!
GUESS THAT'S ME. HATE TO SOUND MAUDLIN, BUT...
...I AM JUST A CLONE. NO ONE'LL MISS ME IF I DON'T MAKE IT BACK.
NO. THE GATE IS SYMBIOTE MACHINERY. ONLY ONE OF THEIR RACE CAN OPERATE IT.
WE'LL STAY.
I DON'T LIKE IT, BUT THERE'S NO TIME TO ARGUE. LET'S GET THIS OVER WITH!
WAIT! SOMETHING--

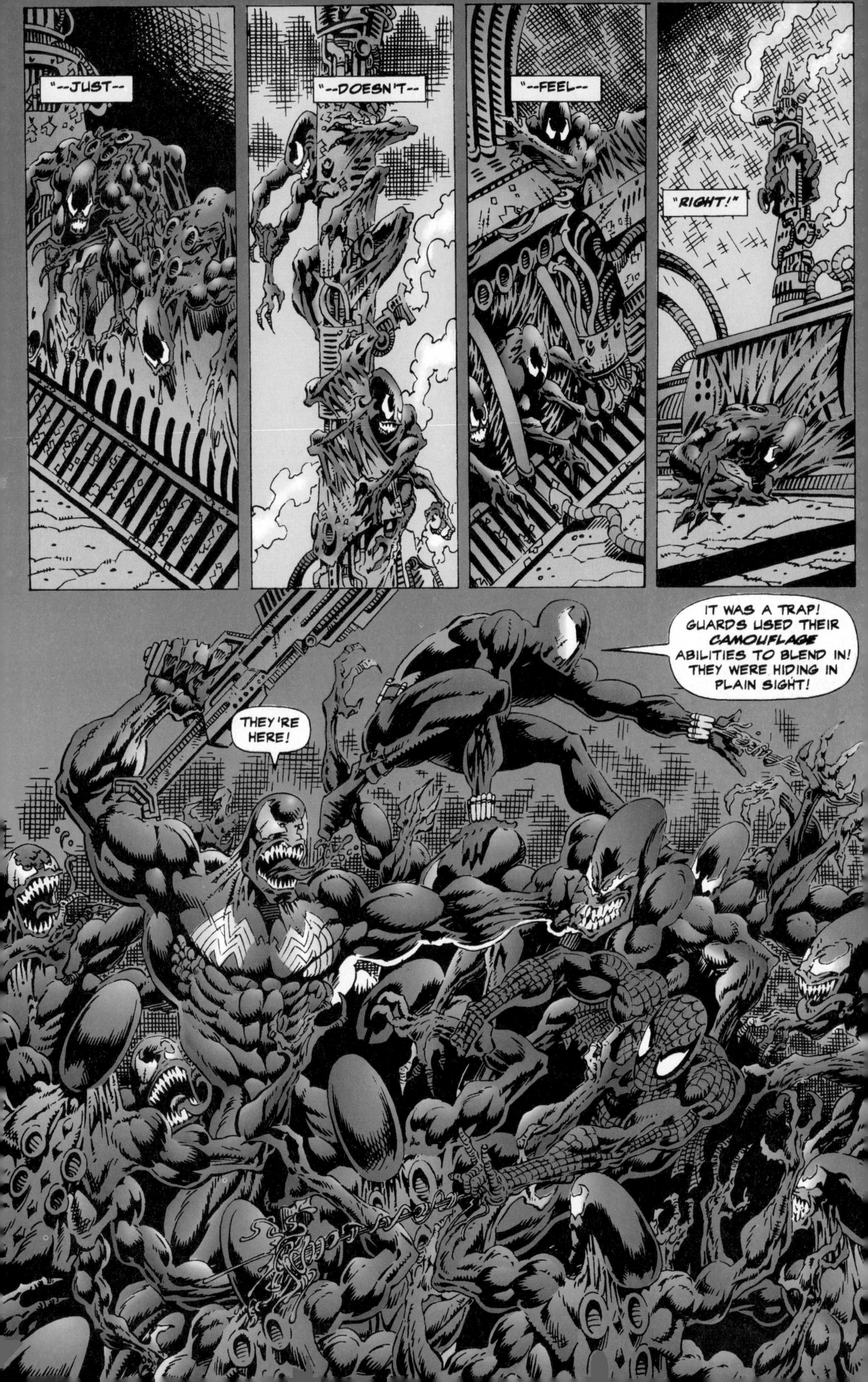
"--JUST--
"--DOESN'T--
"--FEEL--
"RIGHT!"
IT WAS A TRAP! GUARDS USED THEIR CAMOUFLAGE ABILITIES TO BLEND IN! THEY WERE HIDING IN PLAIN SIGHT!
THEY'RE HERE!

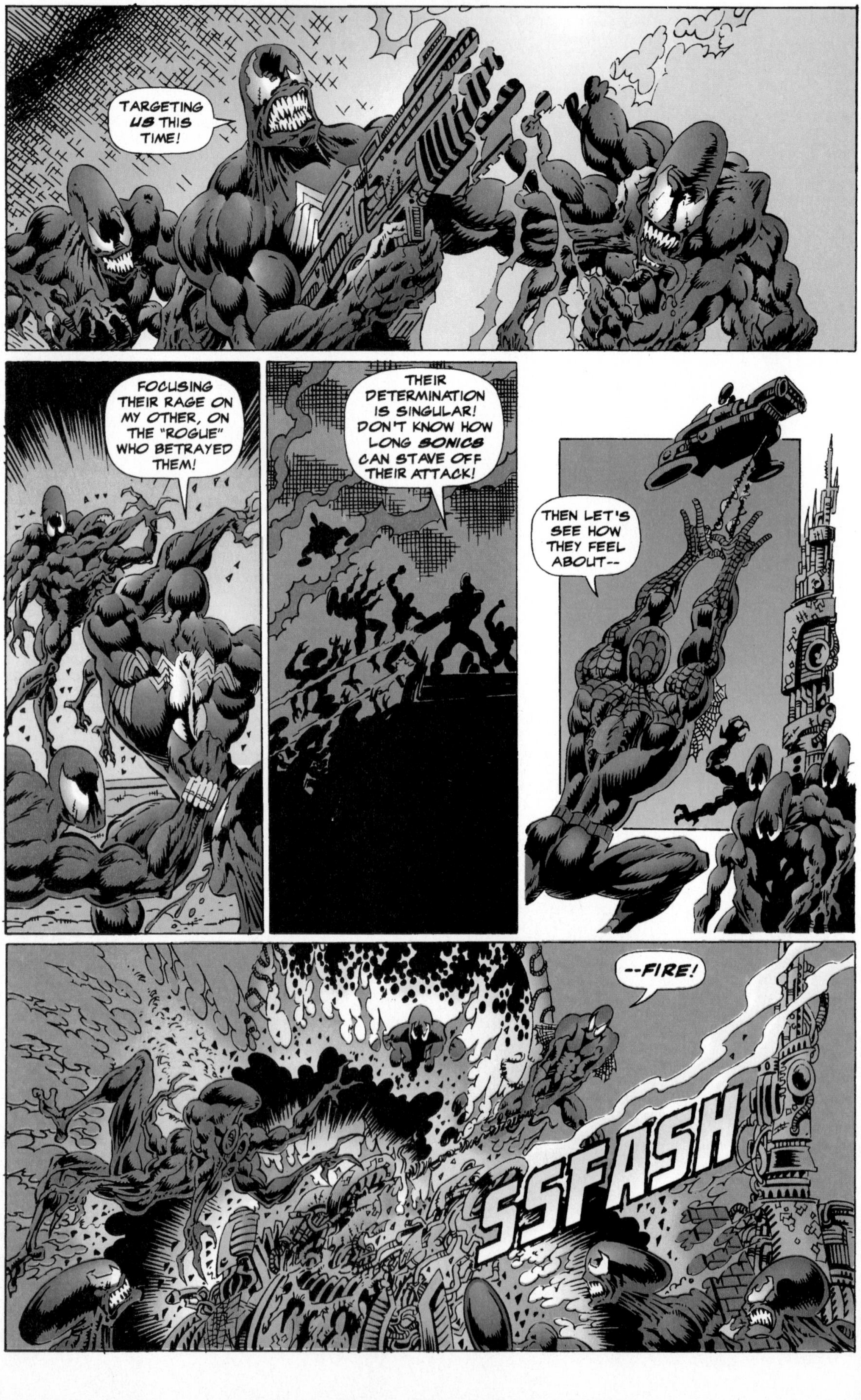
TARGETING US THIS TIME!
FOCUSING THEIR RAGE ON MY OTHER, ON THE "ROGUE" WHO BETRAYED THEM!
THEIR DETERMINATION IS SINGULAR! DON'T KNOW HOW LONG SONICS CAN STAVE OFF THEIR ATTACK!
THEN LET'S SEE HOW THEY FEEL ABOUT--
--FIRE!
SSFASH

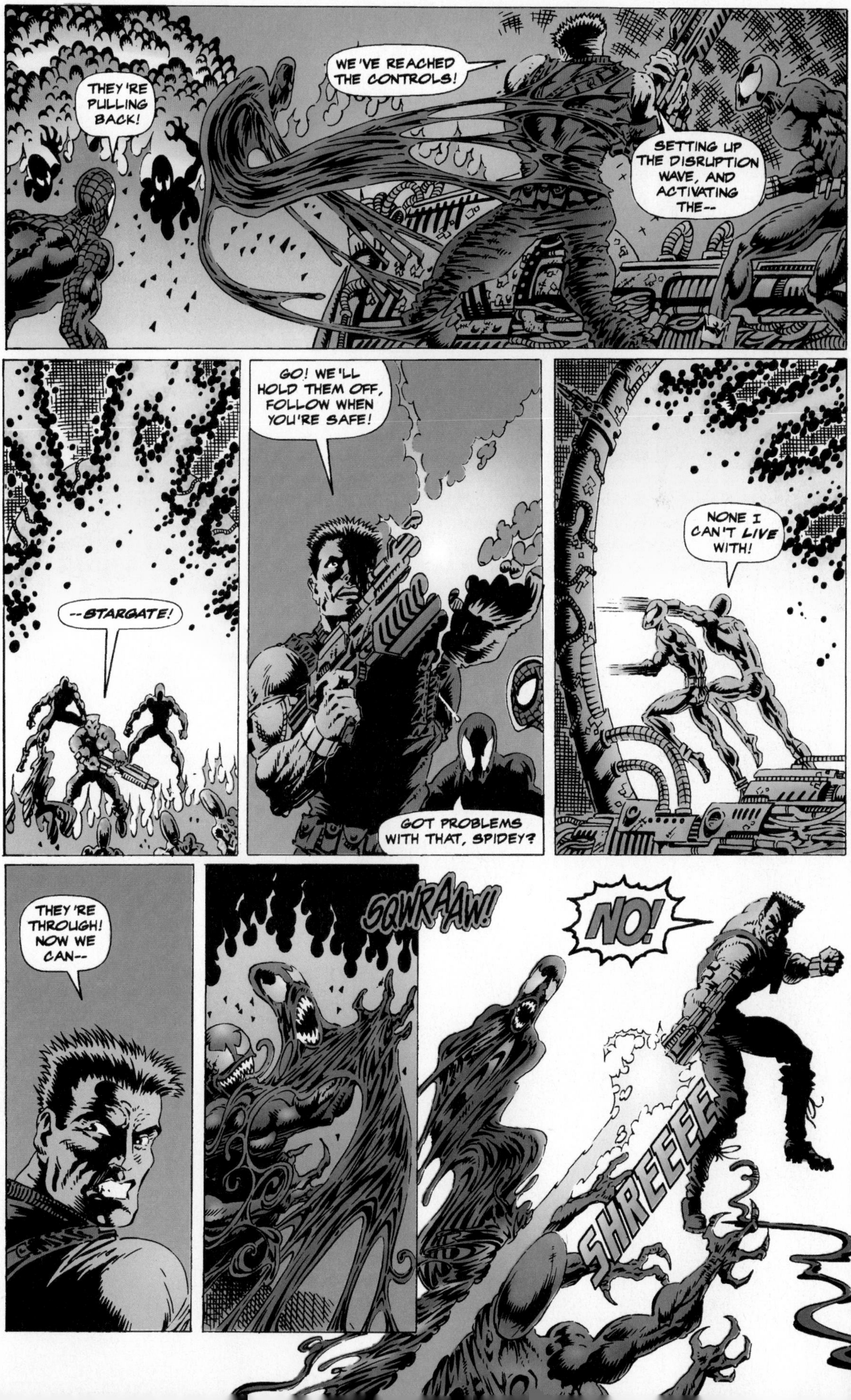
THEY'RE PULLING BACK!
WE'VE REACHED THE CONTROLS!
SETTING UP THE DISRUPTION WAVE, AND ACTIVATING THE--
--STARGATE!
GO! WE'LL HOLD THEM OFF, FOLLOW WHEN YOU'RE SAFE!
GOT PROBLEMS WITH THAT, SPIDEY?
NONE I CAN'T LIVE WITH!
THEY'RE THROUGH! NOW WE CAN--
SQWRAAW!!
NO!
SHREEEE

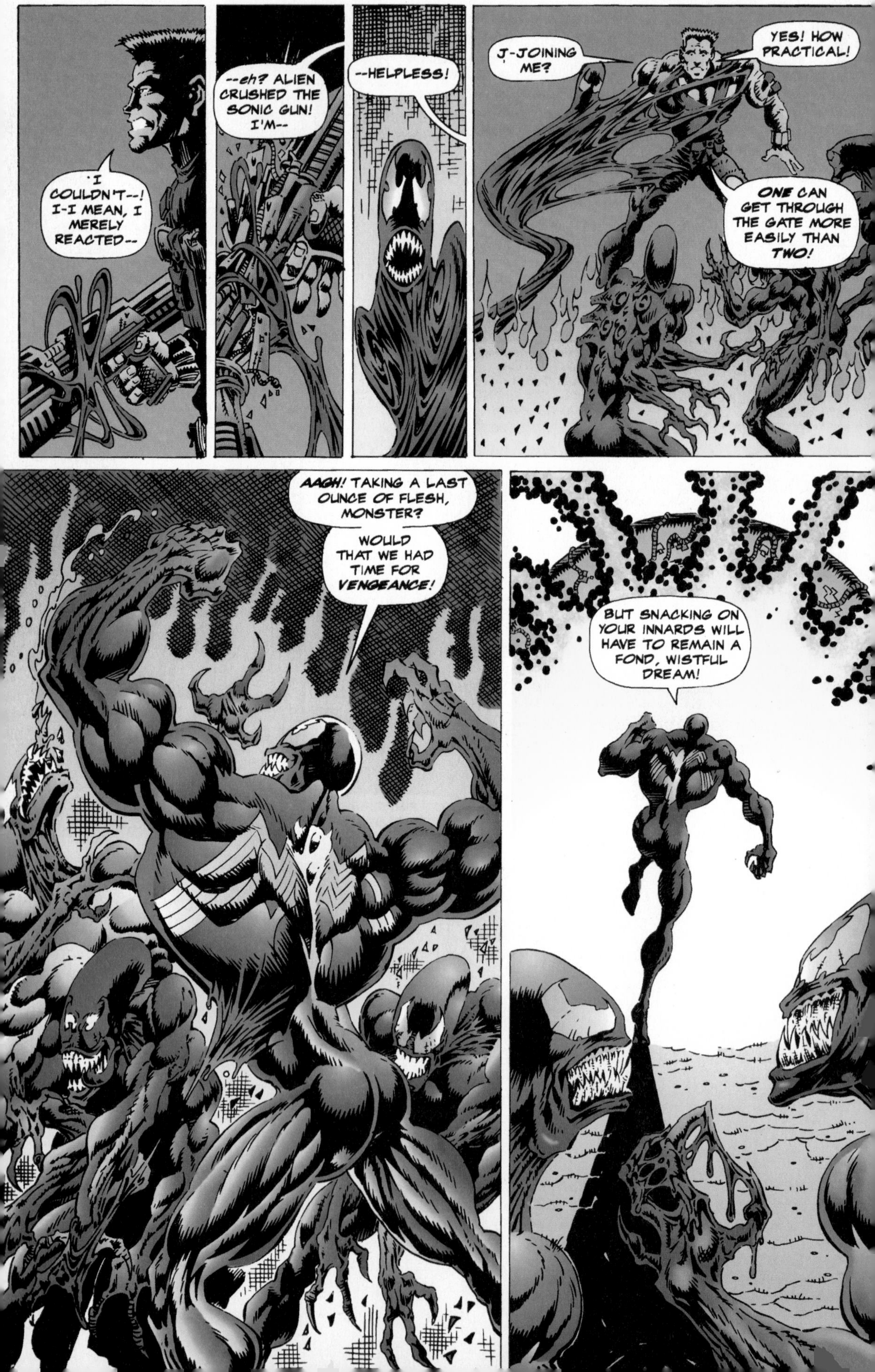
I COULDN'T--! I-I MEAN, I MERELY REACTED--
--eh? ALIEN CRUSHED THE SONIC GUN! I'M--
--HELPLESS!
J-JOINING ME?
YES! HOW PRACTICAL!
ONE CAN GET THROUGH THE GATE MORE EASILY THAN TWO!
AAGH! TAKING A LAST OUNCE OF FLESH, MONSTER?
WOULD THAT WE HAD TIME FOR VENGEANCE!
BUT SNACKING ON YOUR INNARDS WILL HAVE TO REMAIN A FOND, WISTFUL DREAM!

EARTH.

DONE!

NOT QUITE!

WE'VE STILL GOT TROUBLE HERE! BUT THAT'S BETTER THAN FACING A WHOLE *PLANET* OF--HEY!

SHOULDN'T THE GATE HAVE *SHUT DOWN* BY NOW?

SO HOW COME IT'S GLOWING *BRIGHTER?*

IT SEEMS THERE'S A SLIGHT...PROBLEM. ACCORDING TO MY OTHER--

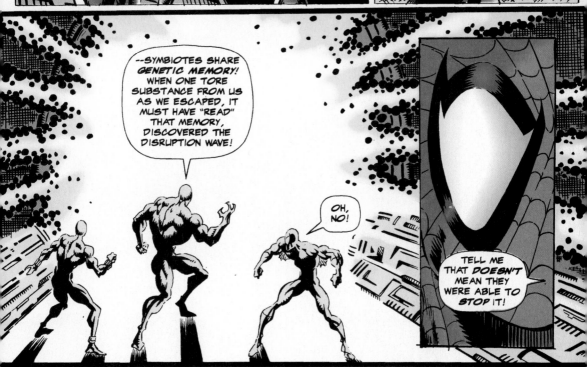

--SYMBIOTES SHARE *GENETIC MEMORY!* WHEN ONE TORE SUBSTANCE FROM US AS WE ESCAPED, IT MUST HAVE "READ" THAT MEMORY, DISCOVERED THE DISRUPTION WAVE!

OH, NO!

TELL ME THAT *DOESN'T* MEAN THEY WERE ABLE TO *STOP* IT!

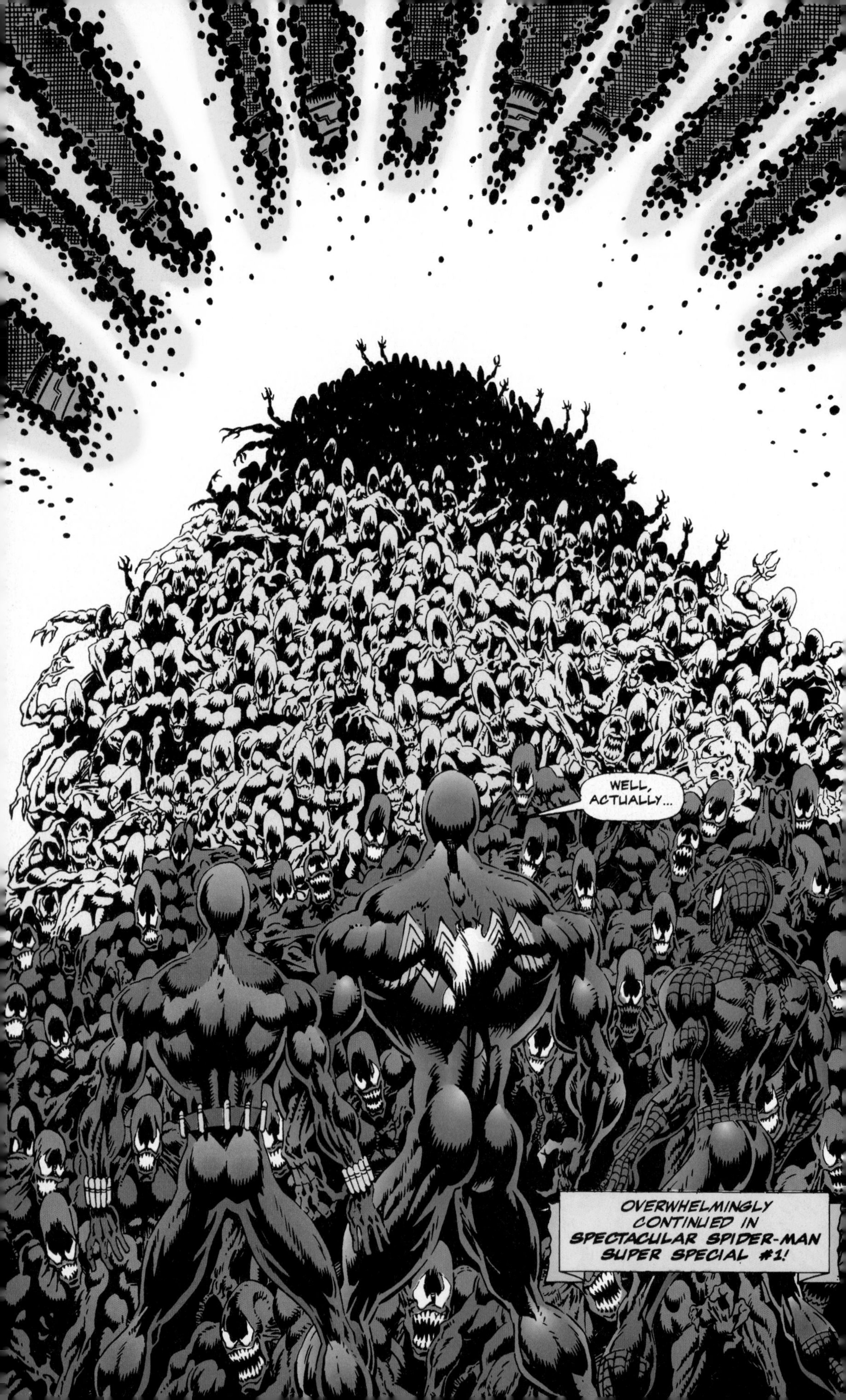
WELL, ACTUALLY...
OVERWHELMINGLY CONTINUED IN SPECTACULAR SPIDER-MAN SUPER SPECIAL #1!

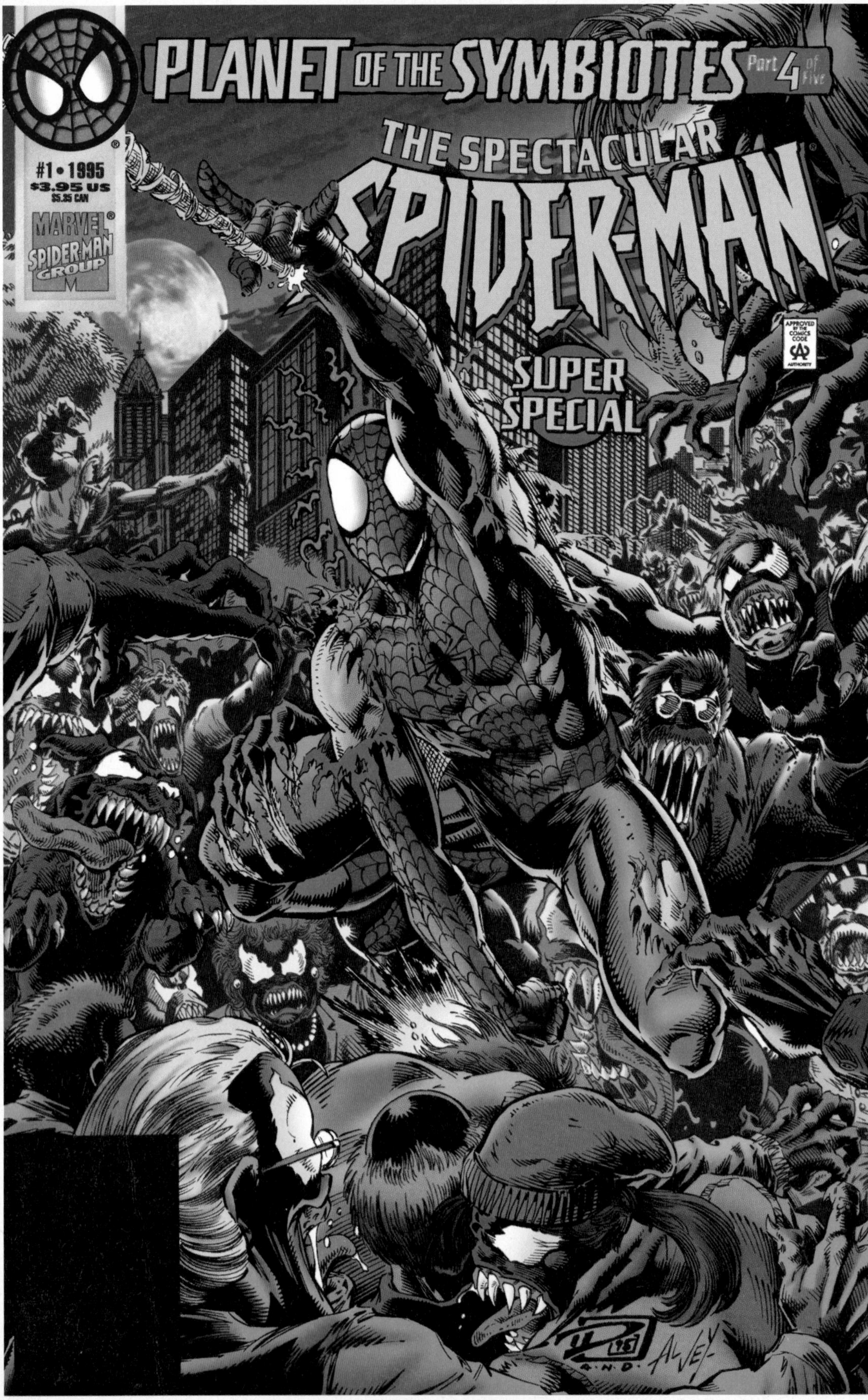

PLANET OF THE SYMBIOTES
Part 4 of Five
#1 • 1995
$3.95 US
$5.35 CAN
MARVEL
SPIDER-MAN GROUP
THE SPECTACULAR
SPIDER-MAN
APPROVED BY THE COMICS CODE AUTHORITY
SUPER SPECIAL

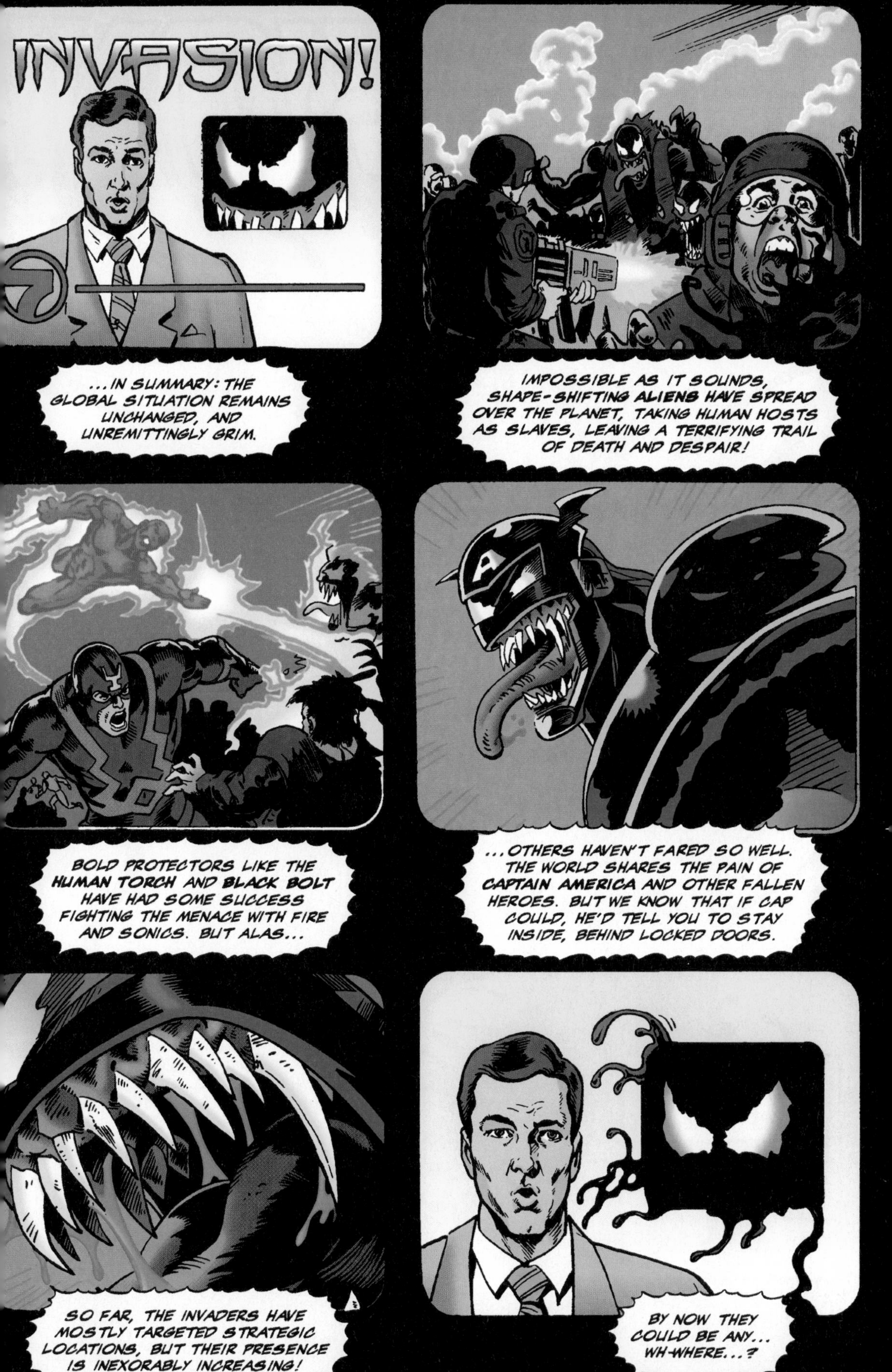
INVASION!
...IN SUMMARY: THE GLOBAL SITUATION REMAINS UNCHANGED, AND UNREMITTINGLY GRIM.
IMPOSSIBLE AS IT SOUNDS, SHAPE-SHIFTING ALIENS HAVE SPREAD OVER THE PLANET, TAKING HUMAN HOSTS AS SLAVES, LEAVING A TERRIFYING TRAIL OF DEATH AND DESPAIR!
BOLD PROTECTORS LIKE THE HUMAN TORCH AND BLACK BOLT HAVE HAD SOME SUCCESS FIGHTING THE MENACE WITH FIRE AND SONICS. BUT ALAS...
...OTHERS HAVEN'T FARED SO WELL. THE WORLD SHARES THE PAIN OF CAPTAIN AMERICA AND OTHER FALLEN HEROES. BUT WE KNOW THAT IF CAP COULD, HE'D TELL YOU TO STAY INSIDE, BEHIND LOCKED DOORS.
SO FAR, THE INVADERS HAVE MOSTLY TARGETED STRATEGIC LOCATIONS, BUT THEIR PRESENCE IS INEXORABLY INCREASING!
BY NOW THEY COULD BE ANY... WH-WHERE...?

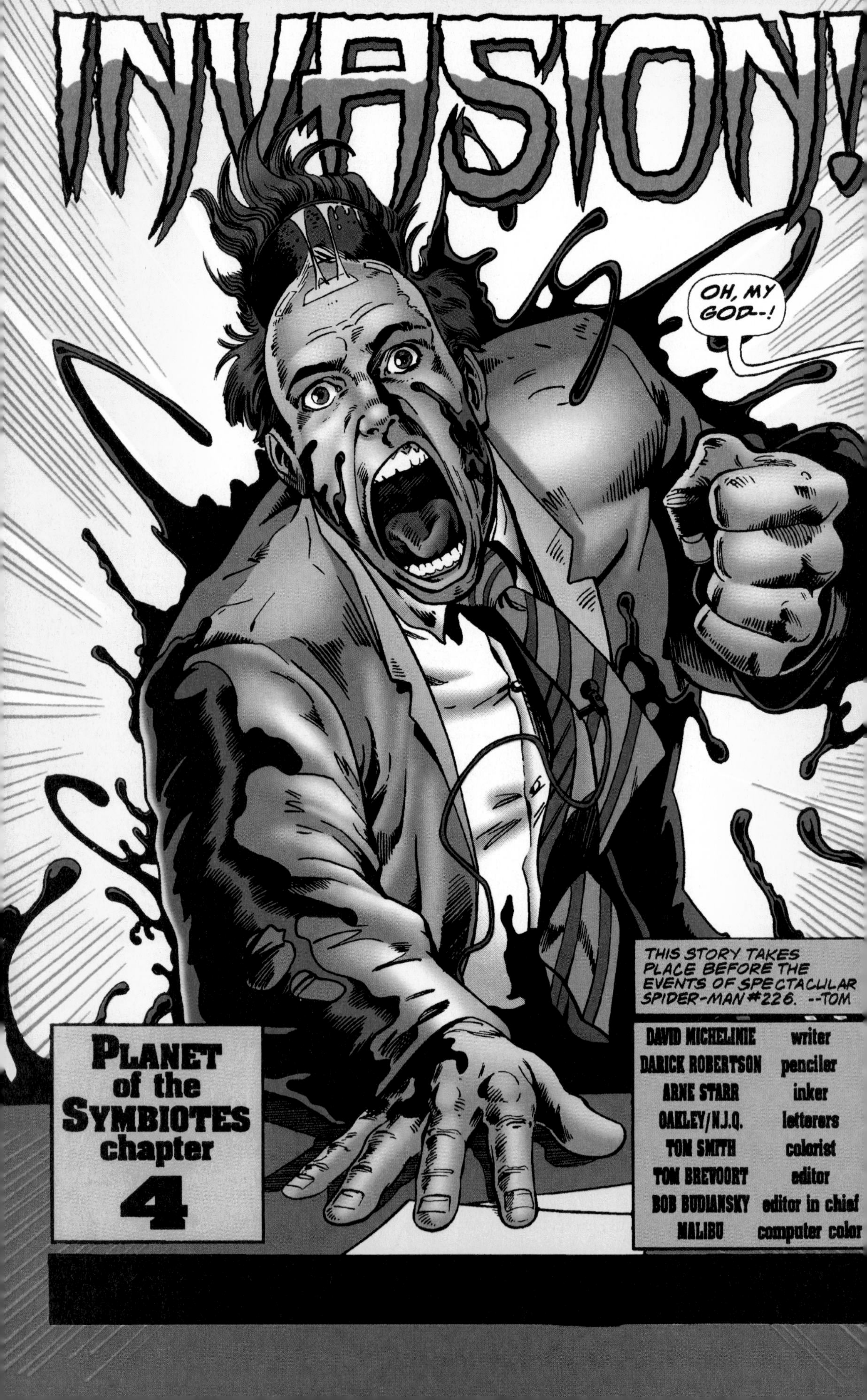
INVASION!
OH, MY GOD--!
THIS STORY TAKES PLACE BEFORE THE EVENTS OF SPECTACULAR SPIDER-MAN #226. --TOM
PLANET of the SYMBIOTES chapter 4
DAVID MICHELINIE writer
DARICK ROBERTSON penciler
ARNE STARR inker
OAKLEY/N.J.Q. letterers
TOM SMITH colorist
TOM BREVOORT editor
BOB BUDIANSKY editor in chief
MALIBU computer color

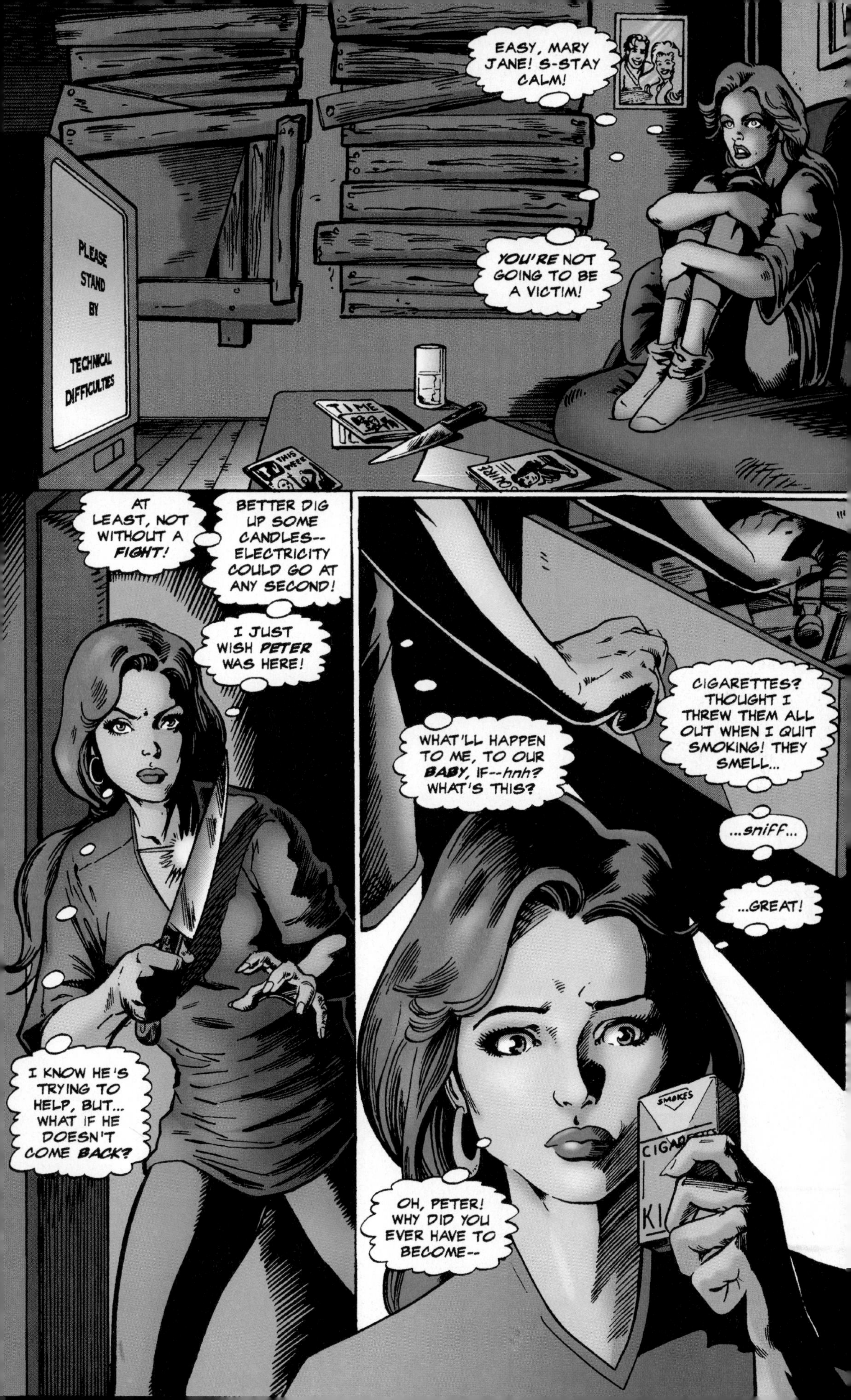

EASY, MARY JANE! S-STAY CALM!
PLEASE STAND BY TECHNICAL DIFFICULTIES
YOU'RE NOT GOING TO BE A VICTIM!
TIME
AT LEAST, NOT WITHOUT A FIGHT!
BETTER DIG UP SOME CANDLES-- ELECTRICITY COULD GO AT ANY SECOND!
I JUST WISH PETER WAS HERE!
I KNOW HE'S TRYING TO HELP, BUT... WHAT IF HE DOESN'T COME BACK?
WHAT'LL HAPPEN TO ME, TO OUR BABY, IF--hnh? WHAT'S THIS?
CIGARETTES? THOUGHT I THREW THEM ALL OUT WHEN I QUIT SMOKING! THEY SMELL...
...sniff...
...GREAT!
OH, PETER! WHY DID YOU EVER HAVE TO BECOME--
SMOKES

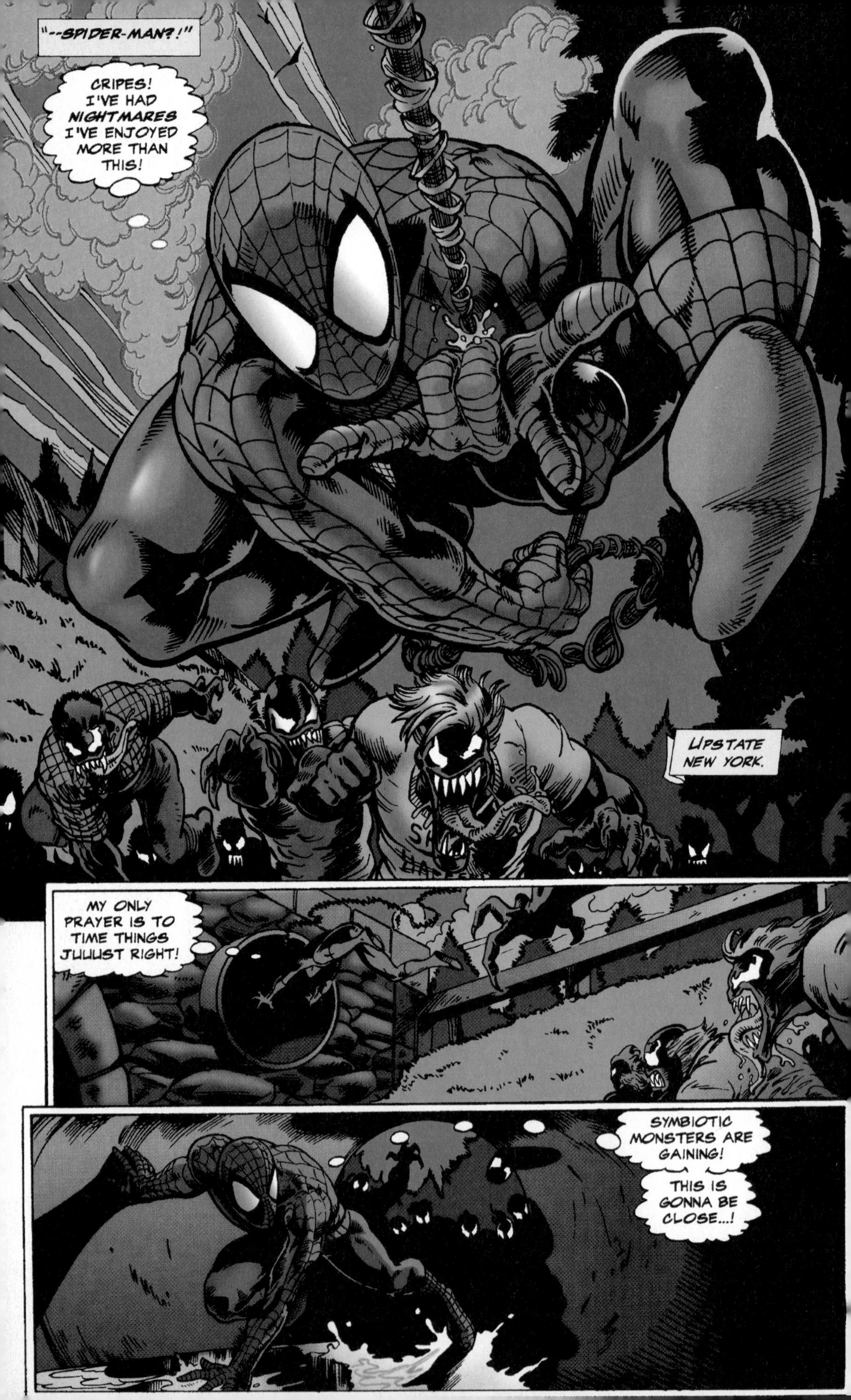
"--SPIDER-MAN?!"
CRIPES! I'VE HAD NIGHTMARES I'VE ENJOYED MORE THAN THIS!
UPSTATE NEW YORK.
MY ONLY PRAYER IS TO TIME THINGS JUUUST RIGHT!
SYMBIOTIC MONSTERS ARE GAINING!
THIS IS GONNA BE CLOSE...!

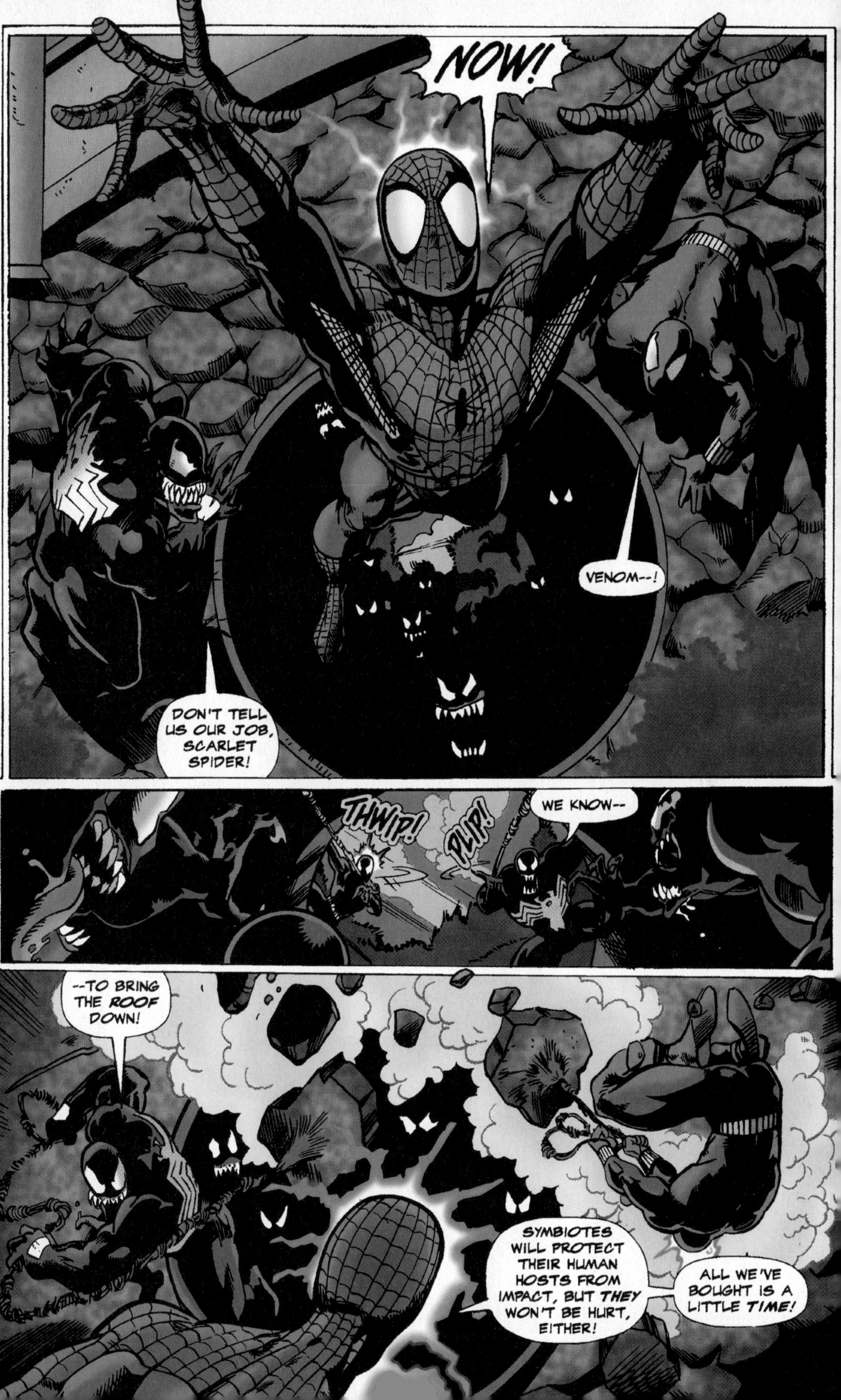
NOW!
VENOM--!
DON'T TELL US OUR JOB, SCARLET SPIDER!
THWIP!
PLIP!
WE KNOW--
--TO BRING THE *ROOF* DOWN!
SYMBIOTES WILL PROTECT THEIR HUMAN HOSTS FROM IMPACT, BUT *THEY* WON'T BE HURT, EITHER!
ALL WE'VE BOUGHT IS A LITTLE *TIME!*

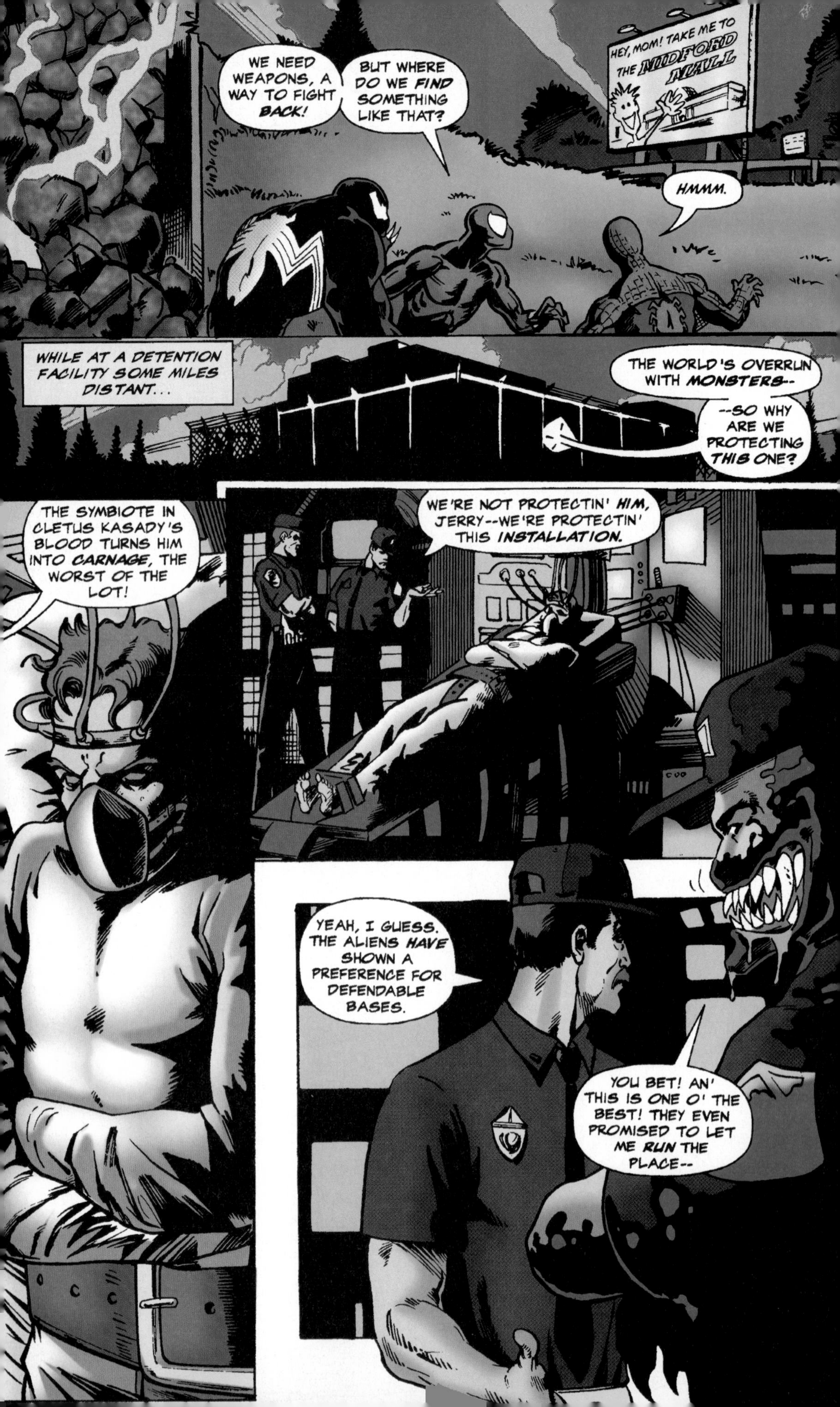

WE NEED WEAPONS, A WAY TO FIGHT BACK!
BUT WHERE DO WE FIND SOMETHING LIKE THAT?
HEY, MOM! TAKE ME TO THE MIDFORD MALL
HMMM.
WHILE AT A DETENTION FACILITY SOME MILES DISTANT...
THE WORLD'S OVERRUN WITH MONSTERS--
--SO WHY ARE WE PROTECTING THIS ONE?
THE SYMBIOTE IN CLETUS KASADY'S BLOOD TURNS HIM INTO CARNAGE, THE WORST OF THE LOT!
WE'RE NOT PROTECTIN' HIM, JERRY--WE'RE PROTECTIN' THIS INSTALLATION.
YEAH, I GUESS. THE ALIENS HAVE SHOWN A PREFERENCE FOR DEFENDABLE BASES.
YOU BET! AN' THIS IS ONE O' THE BEST! THEY EVEN PROMISED TO LET ME RUN THE PLACE--

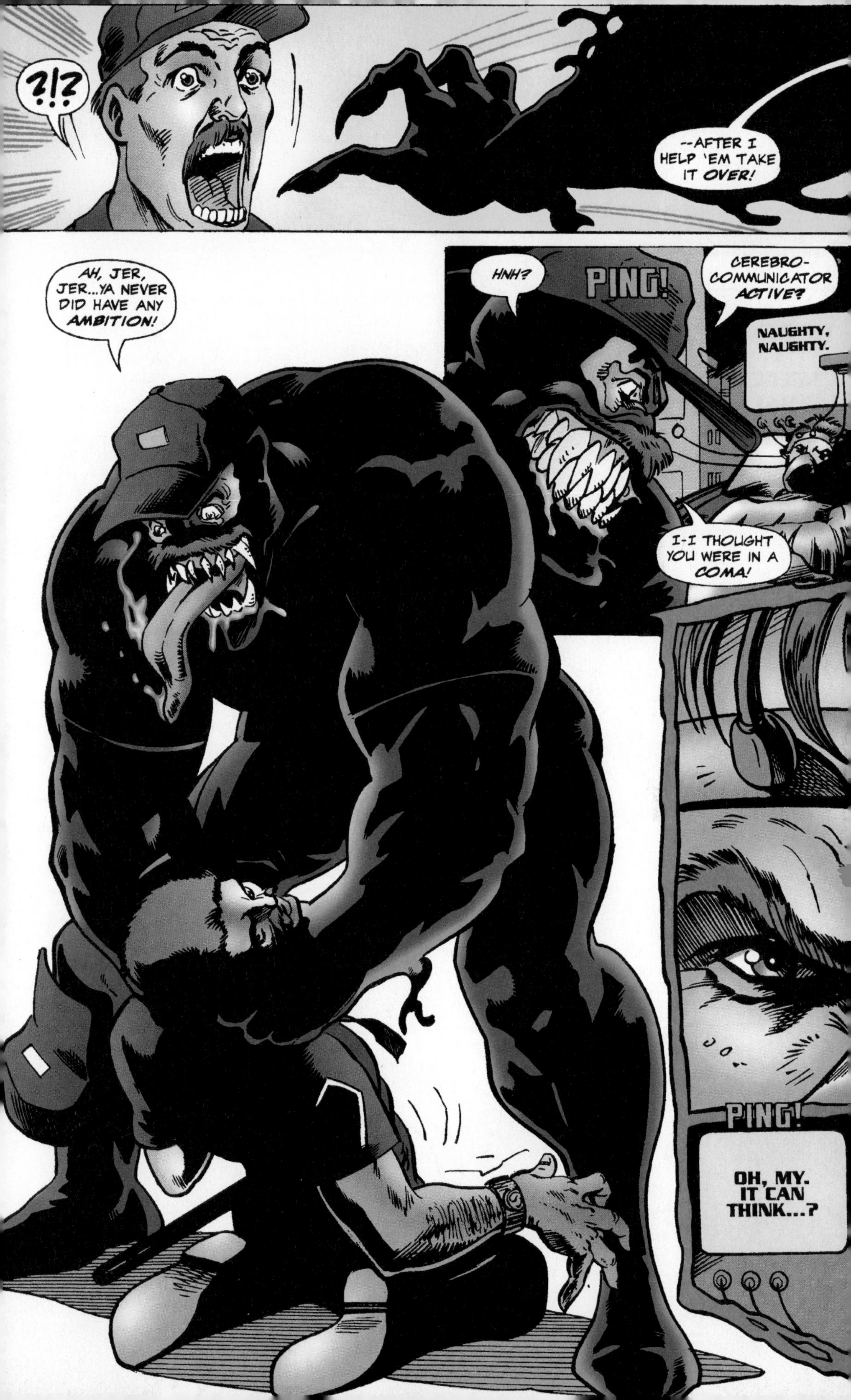
?!?
--AFTER I HELP 'EM TAKE IT OVER!
AH, JER, JER...YA NEVER DID HAVE ANY AMBITION!
HNH?
PING!
CEREBRO-COMMUNICATOR ACTIVE?
NAUGHTY, NAUGHTY.
I-I THOUGHT YOU WERE IN A COMA!
PING!
OH, MY. IT CAN THINK...?

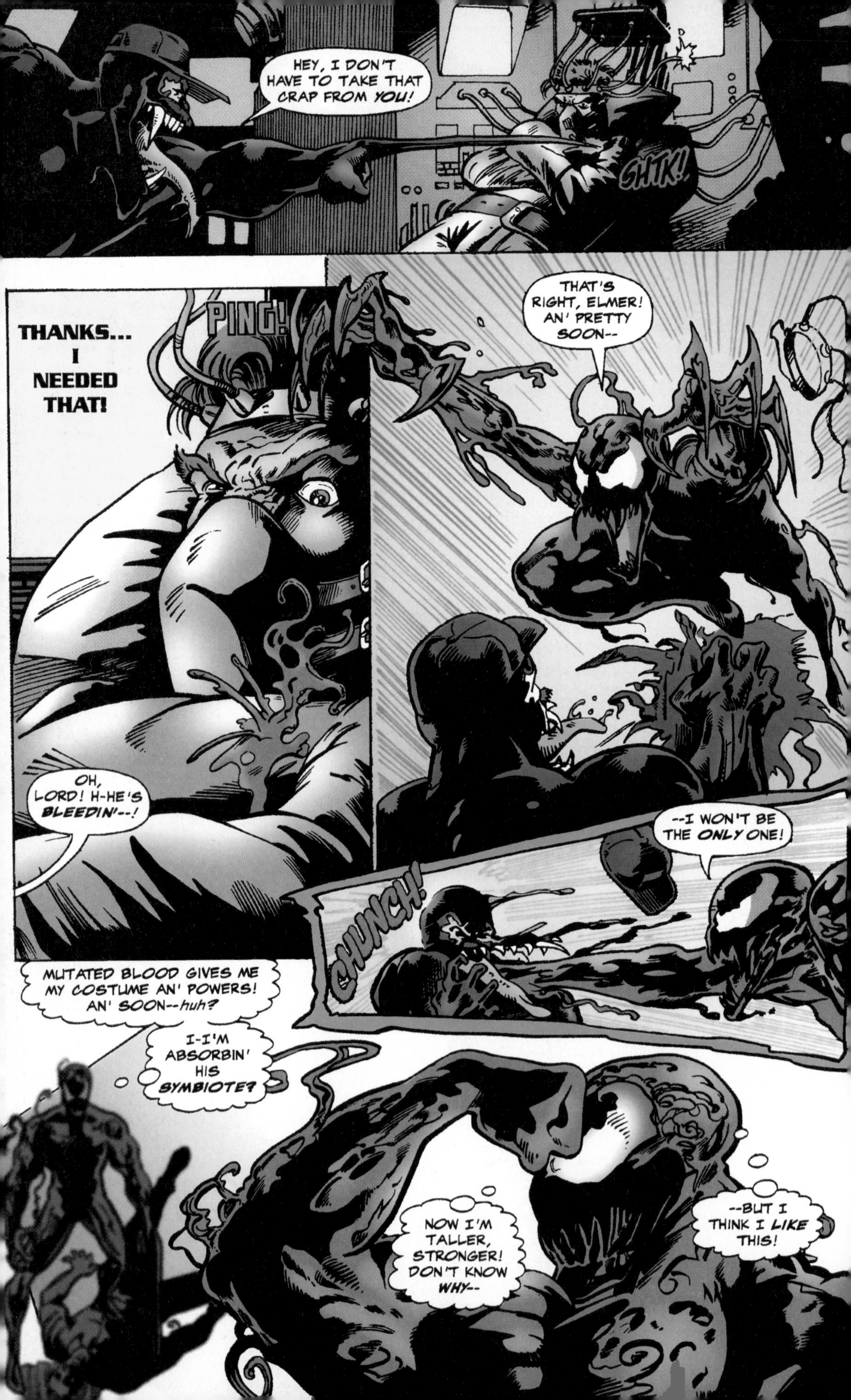

HEY, I DON'T HAVE TO TAKE THAT CRAP FROM YOU!
SHTK!
PING!
THANKS... I NEEDED THAT!
OH, LORD! H-HE'S BLEEDIN'--!
THAT'S RIGHT, ELMER! AN' PRETTY SOON--
--I WON'T BE THE ONLY ONE!
CHUNCH!
MUTATED BLOOD GIVES ME MY COSTUME AN' POWERS! AN' SOON--huh?
I-I'M ABSORBIN' HIS SYMBIOTE?
NOW I'M TALLER, STRONGER! DON'T KNOW WHY--
--BUT I THINK I LIKE THIS!

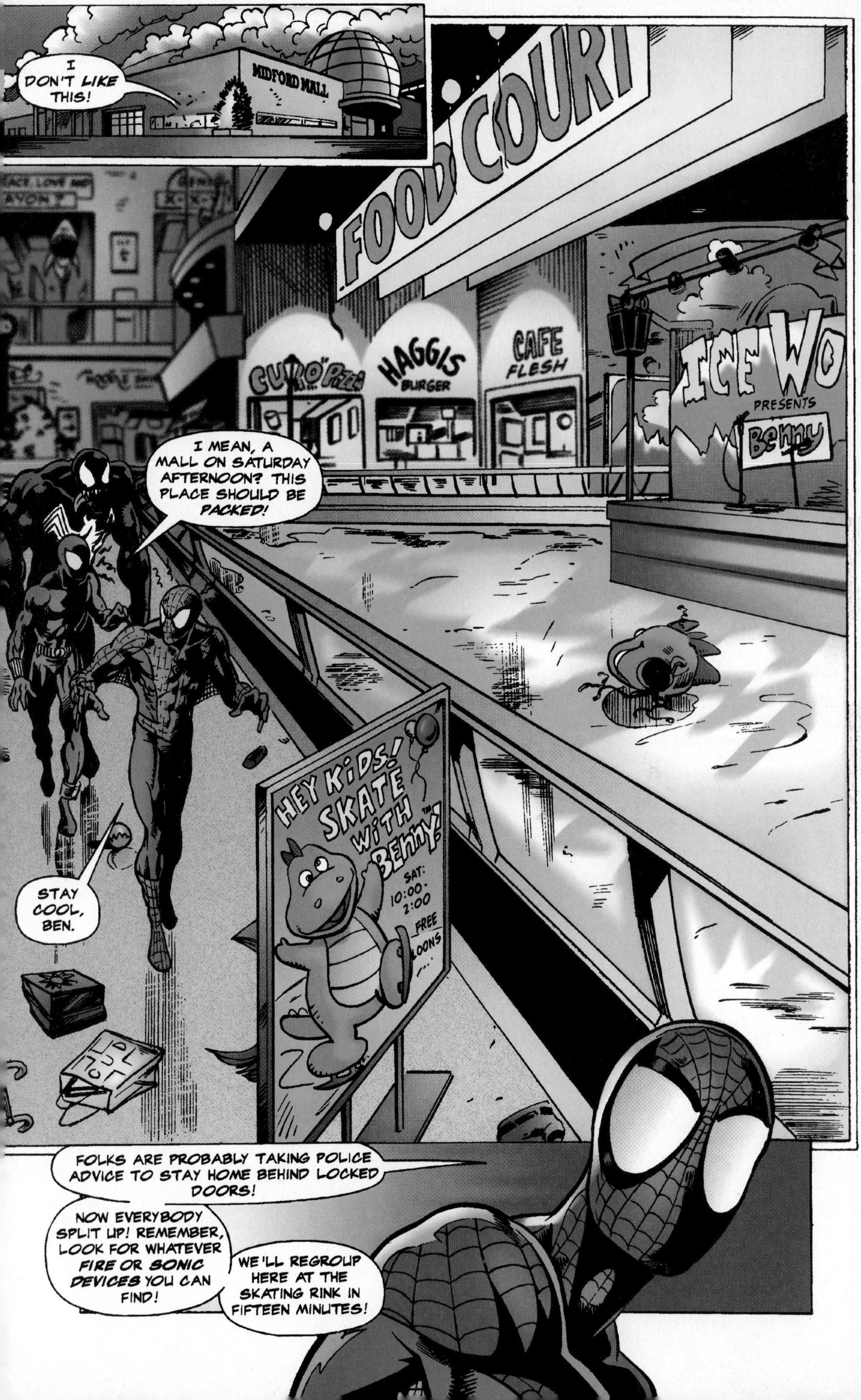

I DON'T LIKE THIS!
MIDFORD MALL
FOOD COURT
HAGGIS BURGER
CAFE FLESH
PRESENTS
Benny
I MEAN, A MALL ON SATURDAY AFTERNOON? THIS PLACE SHOULD BE PACKED!
STAY COOL, BEN.
HEY KIDS! SKATE WITH Benny!
SAT: 10:00-2:00
FREE
FOLKS ARE PROBABLY TAKING POLICE ADVICE TO STAY HOME BEHIND LOCKED DOORS!
NOW EVERYBODY SPLIT UP! REMEMBER, LOOK FOR WHATEVER FIRE OR SONIC DEVICES YOU CAN FIND!
WE'LL REGROUP HERE AT THE SKATING RINK IN FIFTEEN MINUTES!

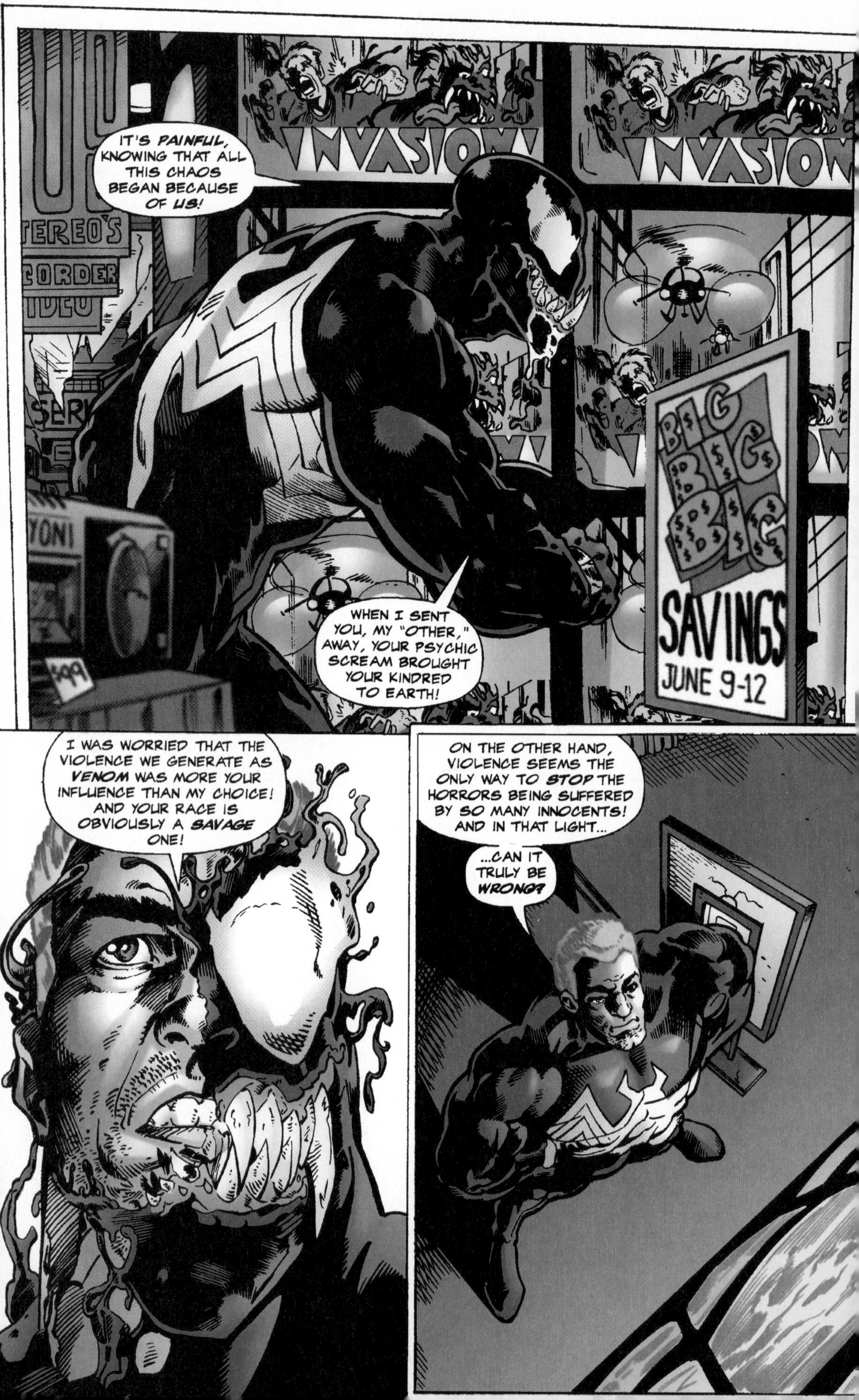
INVASION
IT'S PAINFUL, KNOWING THAT ALL THIS CHAOS BEGAN BECAUSE OF US!
BIG BIG BIG
SAVINGS
JUNE 9-12
WHEN I SENT YOU, MY "OTHER," AWAY, YOUR PSYCHIC SCREAM BROUGHT YOUR KINDRED TO EARTH!
I WAS WORRIED THAT THE VIOLENCE WE GENERATE AS VENOM WAS MORE YOUR INFLUENCE THAN MY CHOICE! AND YOUR RACE IS OBVIOUSLY A SAVAGE ONE!
ON THE OTHER HAND, VIOLENCE SEEMS THE ONLY WAY TO STOP THE HORRORS BEING SUFFERED BY SO MANY INNOCENTS! AND IN THAT LIGHT...
...CAN IT TRULY BE WRONG?

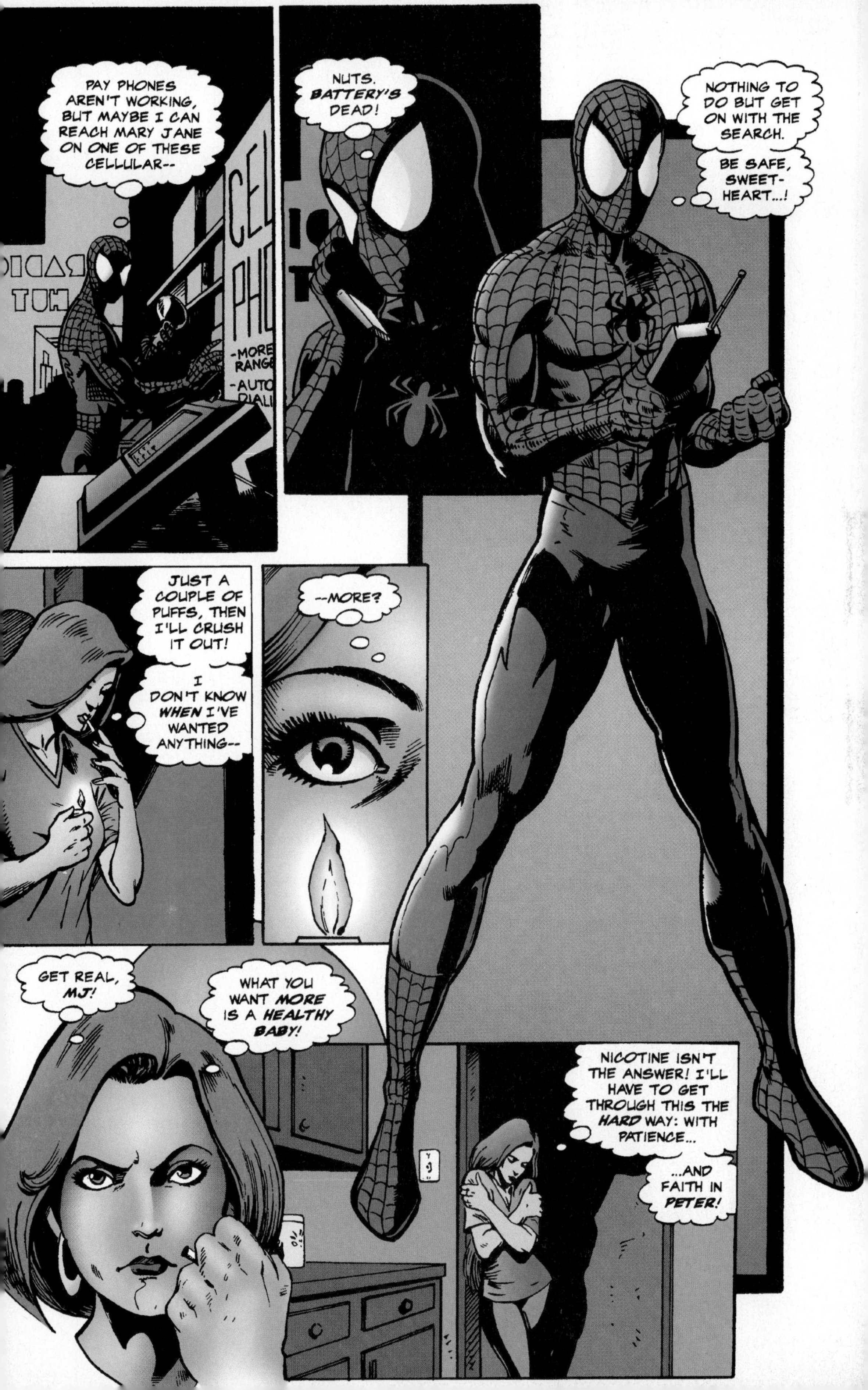
PAY PHONES AREN'T WORKING, BUT MAYBE I CAN REACH MARY JANE ON ONE OF THESE CELLULAR--
NUTS. BATTERY'S DEAD!
NOTHING TO DO BUT GET ON WITH THE SEARCH.
BE SAFE, SWEET-HEART...!
JUST A COUPLE OF PUFFS, THEN I'LL CRUSH IT OUT!
I DON'T KNOW WHEN I'VE WANTED ANYTHING--
--MORE?
GET REAL, MJ!
WHAT YOU WANT MORE IS A HEALTHY BABY!
NICOTINE ISN'T THE ANSWER! I'LL HAVE TO GET THROUGH THIS THE HARD WAY: WITH PATIENCE...
...AND FAITH IN PETER!

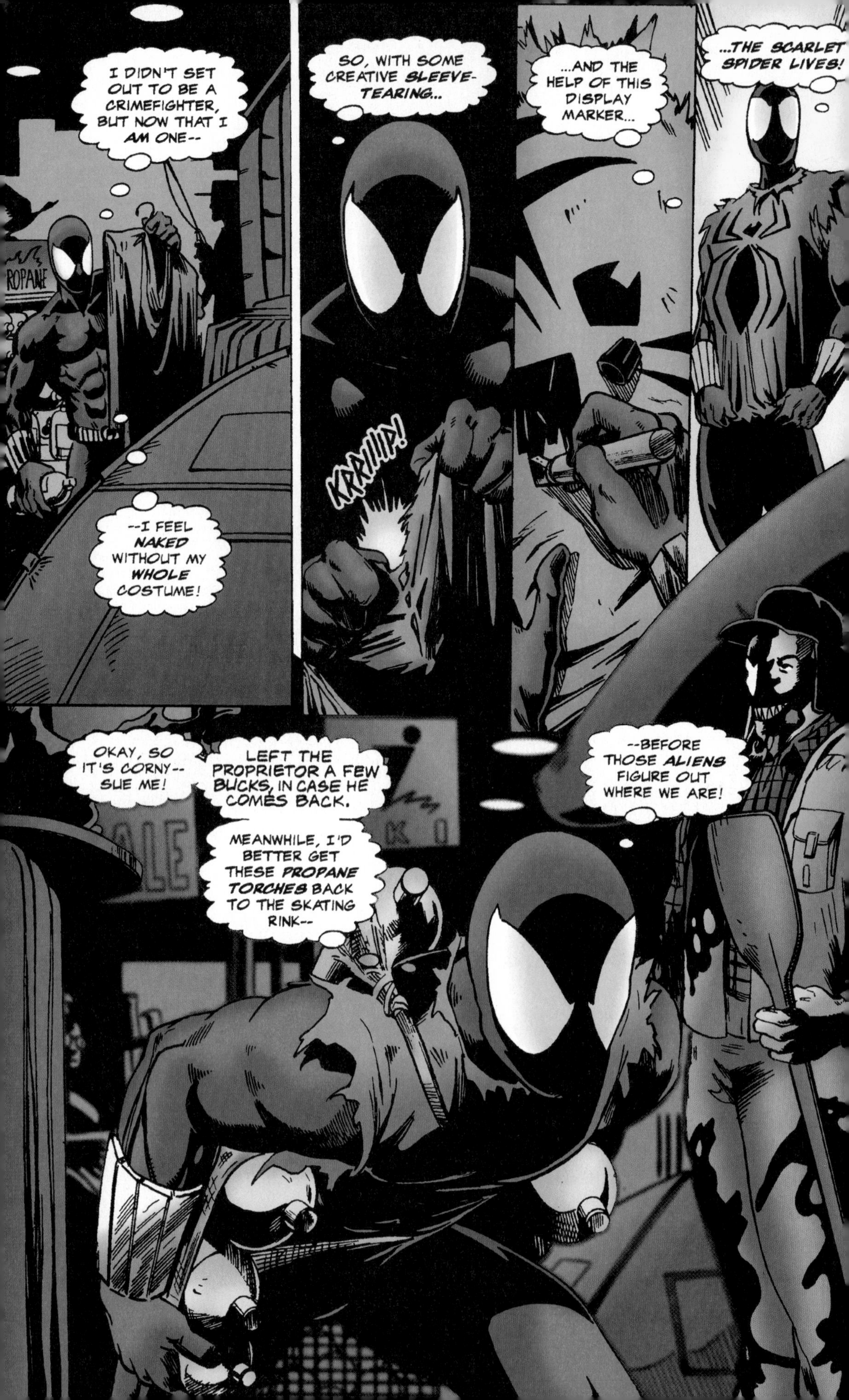
I DIDN'T SET OUT TO BE A CRIMEFIGHTER, BUT NOW THAT I AM ONE--
--I FEEL NAKED WITHOUT MY WHOLE COSTUME!
SO, WITH SOME CREATIVE SLEEVE-TEARING...
KRRIIIP!
...AND THE HELP OF THIS DISPLAY MARKER...
...THE SCARLET SPIDER LIVES!
OKAY, SO IT'S CORNY-- SUE ME!
LEFT THE PROPRIETOR A FEW BUCKS, IN CASE HE COMES BACK.
MEANWHILE, I'D BETTER GET THESE PROPANE TORCHES BACK TO THE SKATING RINK--
--BEFORE THOSE ALIENS FIGURE OUT WHERE WE ARE!

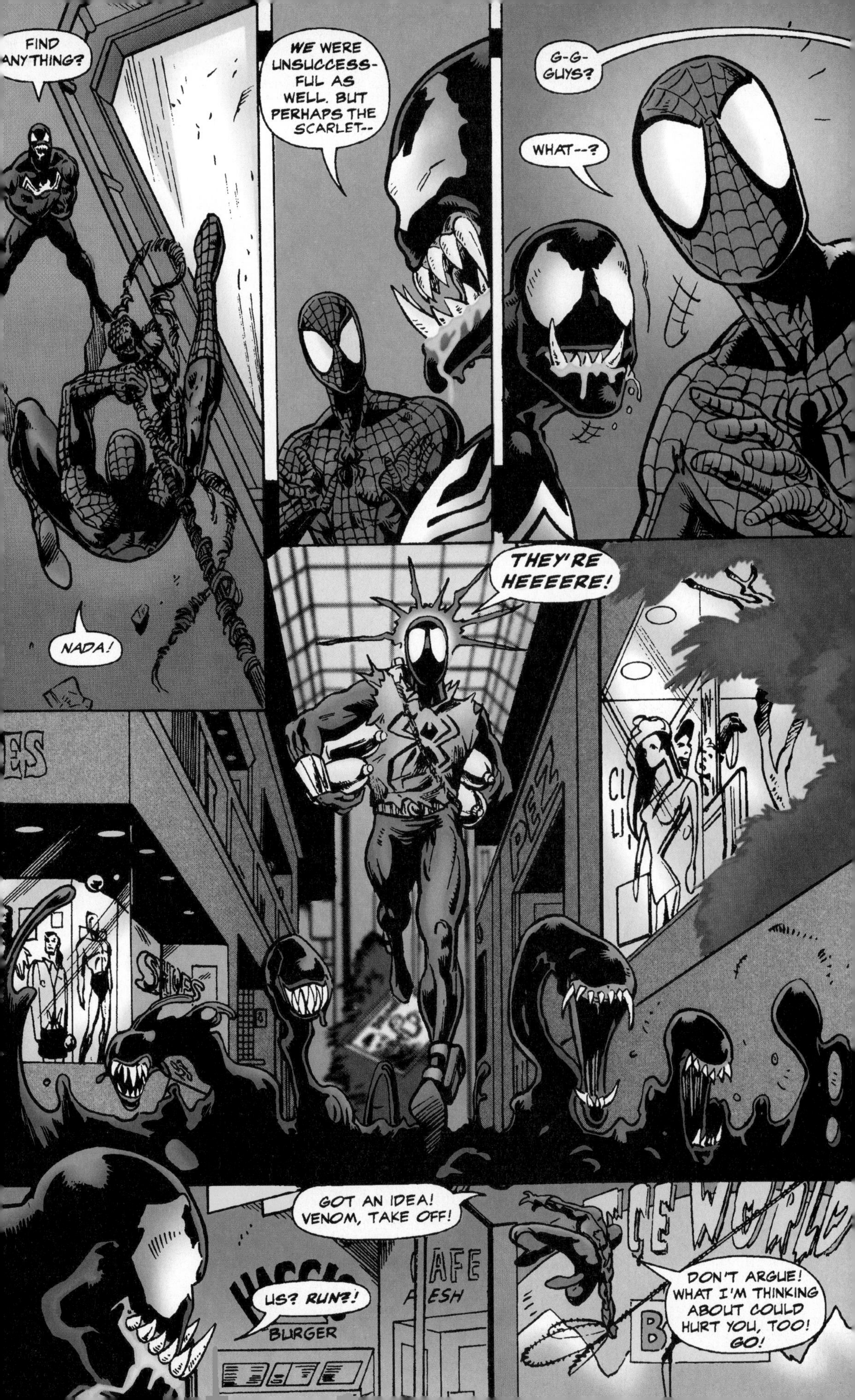

FIND ANYTHING?
NADA!
WE WERE UNSUCCESSFUL AS WELL. BUT PERHAPS THE SCARLET--
G-G-GUYS?
WHAT--?
THEY'RE HEEEERE!
GOT AN IDEA! VENOM, TAKE OFF!
US? RUN?!
DON'T ARGUE! WHAT I'M THINKING ABOUT COULD HURT YOU, TOO! GO!

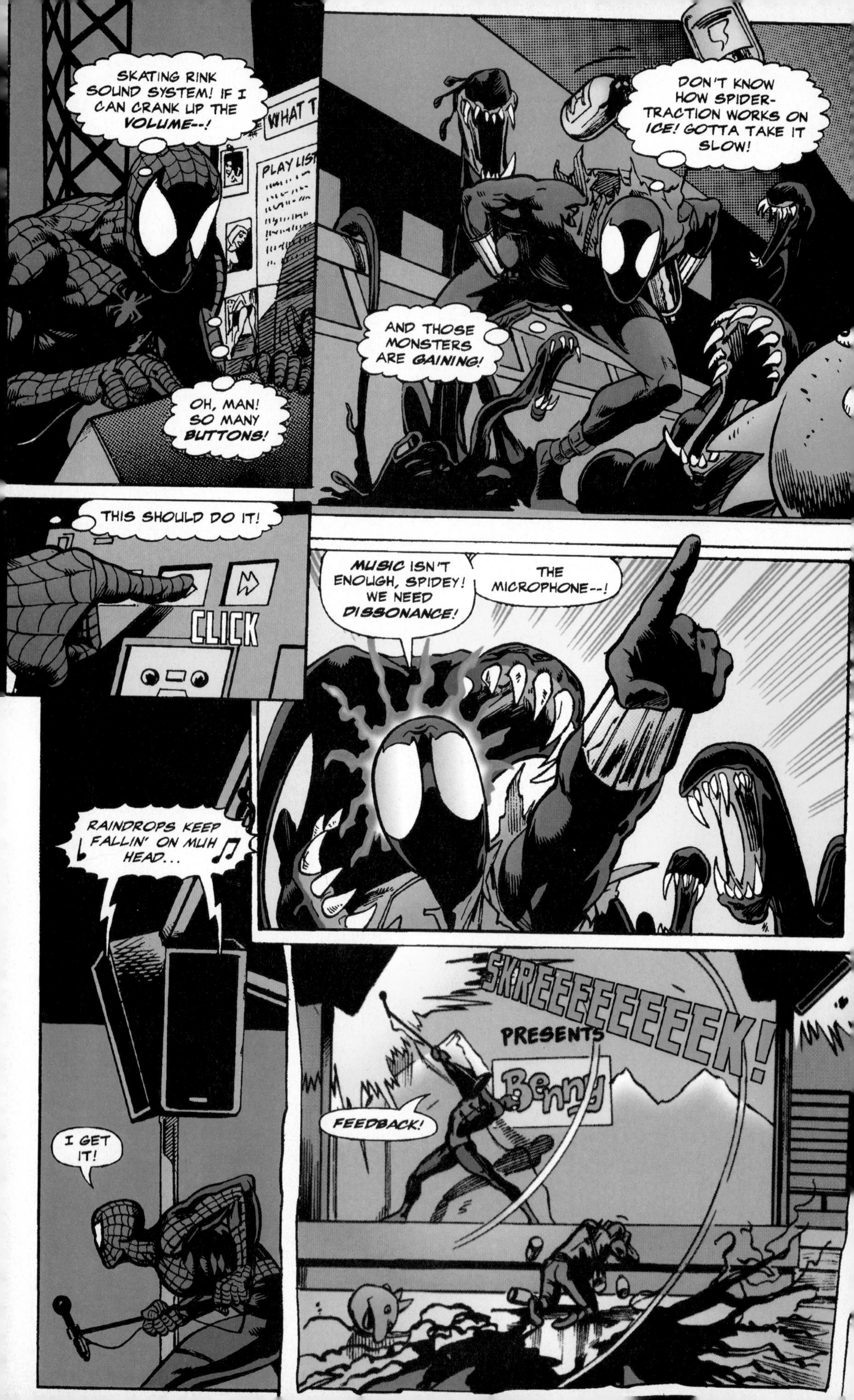

SKATING RINK SOUND SYSTEM! IF I CAN CRANK UP THE VOLUME--!
WHAT T
PLAY LIST
OH, MAN! SO MANY BUTTONS!
DON'T KNOW HOW SPIDER-TRACTION WORKS ON ICE! GOTTA TAKE IT SLOW!
AND THOSE MONSTERS ARE GAINING!
THIS SHOULD DO IT!
CLICK
MUSIC ISN'T ENOUGH, SPIDEY! WE NEED DISSONANCE!
THE MICROPHONE--!
RAINDROPS KEEP FALLIN' ON MUH HEAD...
I GET IT!
SKREEEEEEEEEEK!
PRESENTS
Benny
FEEDBACK!

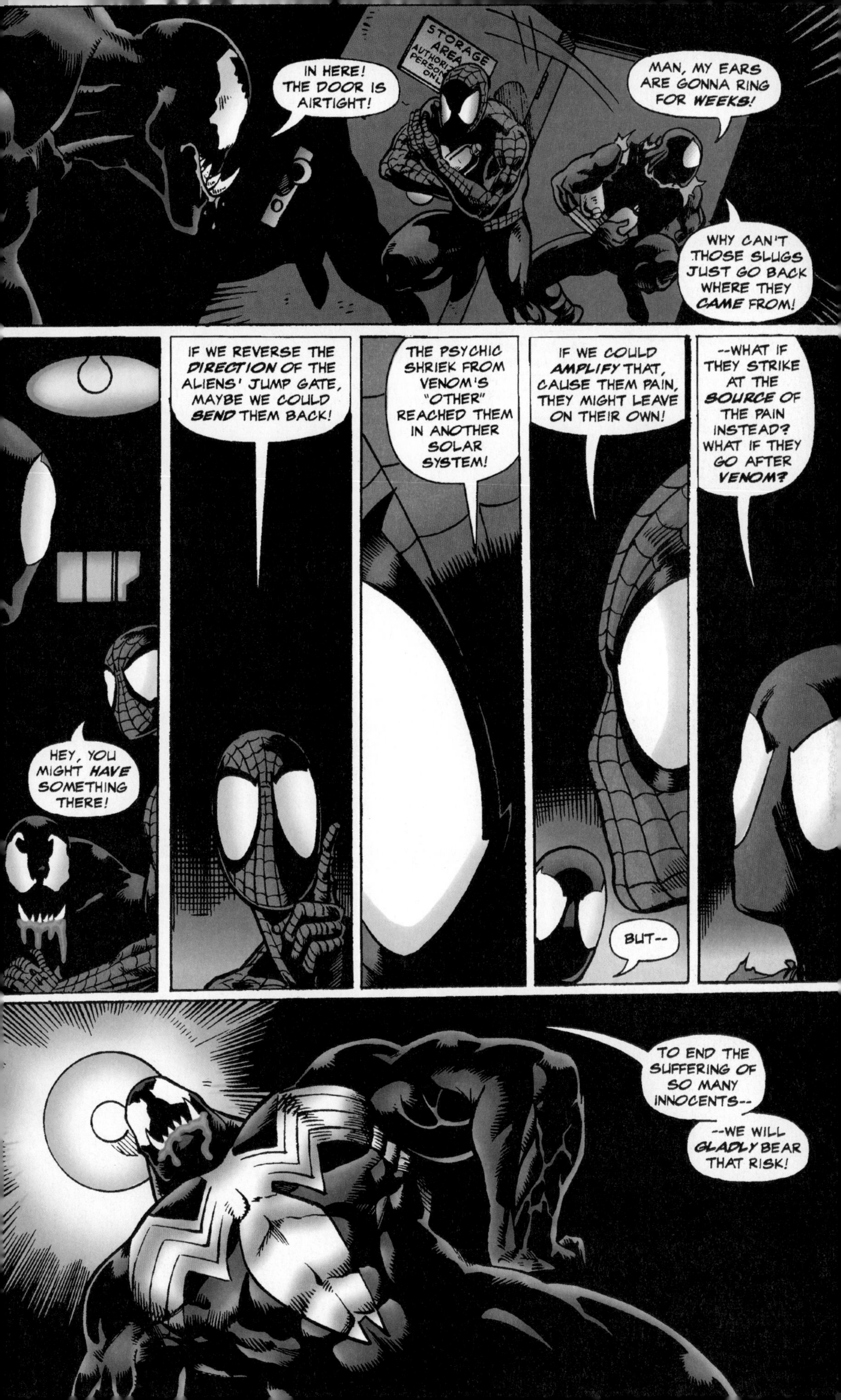
STORAGE AREA AUTHORI PERSON ONL
IN HERE! THE DOOR IS AIRTIGHT!
MAN, MY EARS ARE GONNA RING FOR WEEKS!
WHY CAN'T THOSE SLUGS JUST GO BACK WHERE THEY CAME FROM!
HEY, YOU MIGHT HAVE SOMETHING THERE!
IF WE REVERSE THE DIRECTION OF THE ALIENS' JUMP GATE, MAYBE WE COULD SEND THEM BACK!
THE PSYCHIC SHRIEK FROM VENOM'S "OTHER" REACHED THEM IN ANOTHER SOLAR SYSTEM!
IF WE COULD AMPLIFY THAT, CAUSE THEM PAIN, THEY MIGHT LEAVE ON THEIR OWN!
BUT--
--WHAT IF THEY STRIKE AT THE SOURCE OF THE PAIN INSTEAD? WHAT IF THEY GO AFTER VENOM?
TO END THE SUFFERING OF SO MANY INNOCENTS--
--WE WILL GLADLY BEAR THAT RISK!

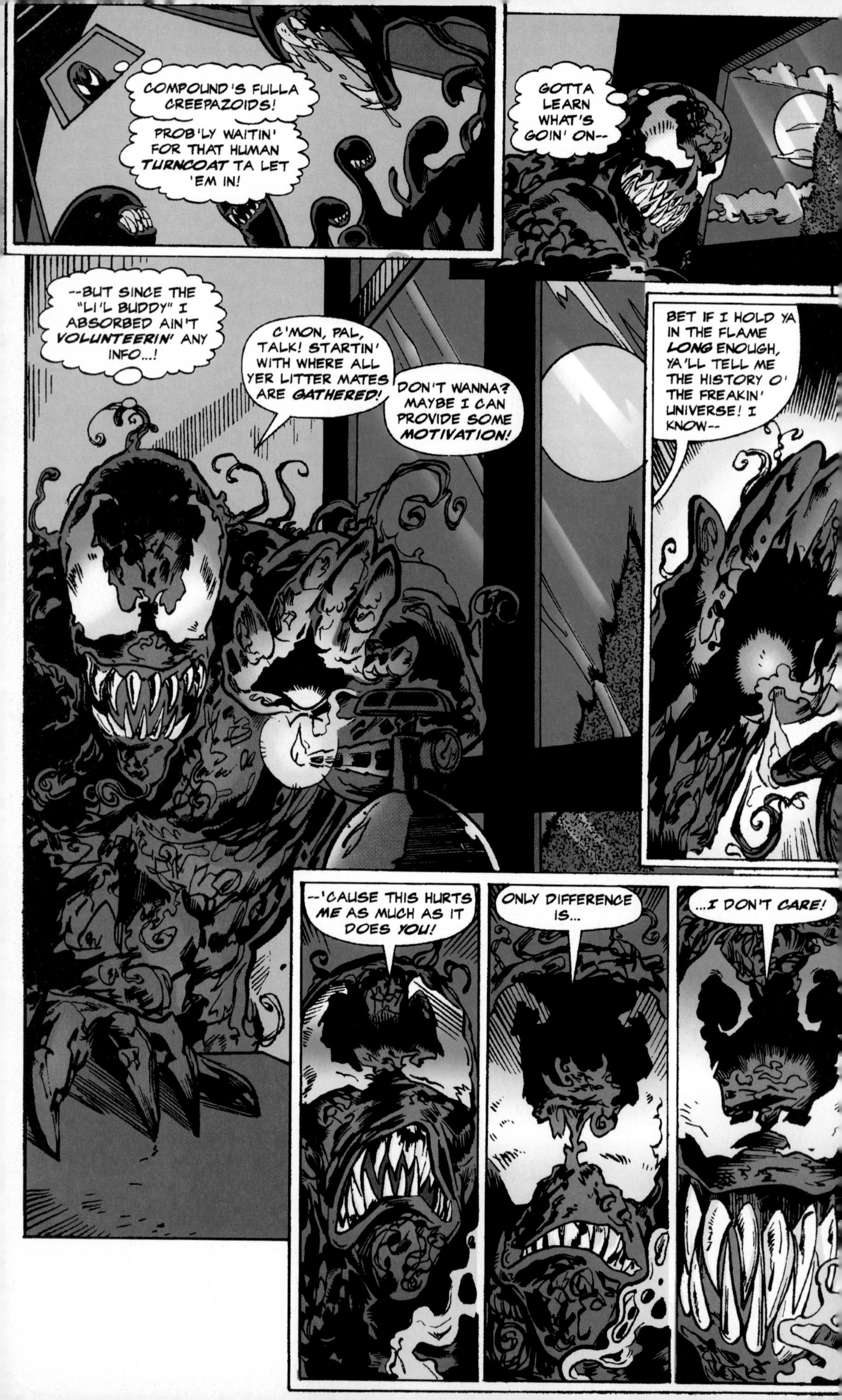
COMPOUND'S FULLA CREEPAZOIDS!
PROB'LY WAITIN' FOR THAT HUMAN TURNCOAT TA LET 'EM IN!
GOTTA LEARN WHAT'S GOIN' ON--
--BUT SINCE THE "LI'L BUDDY" I ABSORBED AIN'T VOLUNTEERIN' ANY INFO...!
C'MON, PAL, TALK! STARTIN' WITH WHERE ALL YER LITTER MATES ARE GATHERED!
DON'T WANNA? MAYBE I CAN PROVIDE SOME MOTIVATION!
BET IF I HOLD YA IN THE FLAME LONG ENOUGH, YA'LL TELL ME THE HISTORY O' THE FREAKIN' UNIVERSE! I KNOW--
--'CAUSE THIS HURTS ME AS MUCH AS IT DOES YOU!
ONLY DIFFERENCE IS...
...I DON'T CARE!

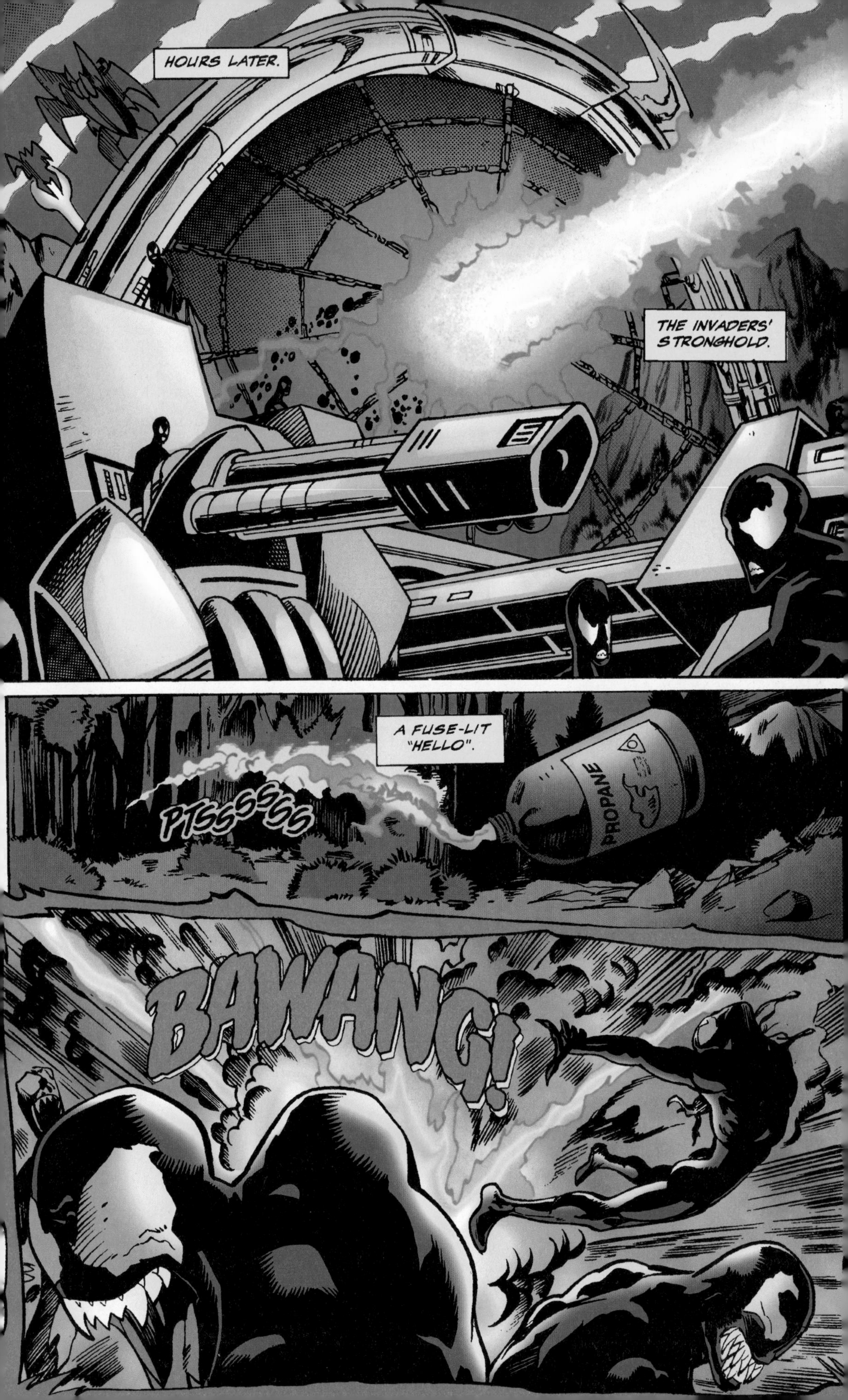
HOURS LATER.
THE INVADERS' STRONGHOLD.
A FUSE-LIT "HELLO".
PROPANE
PTSSSSSS
BAWANG!

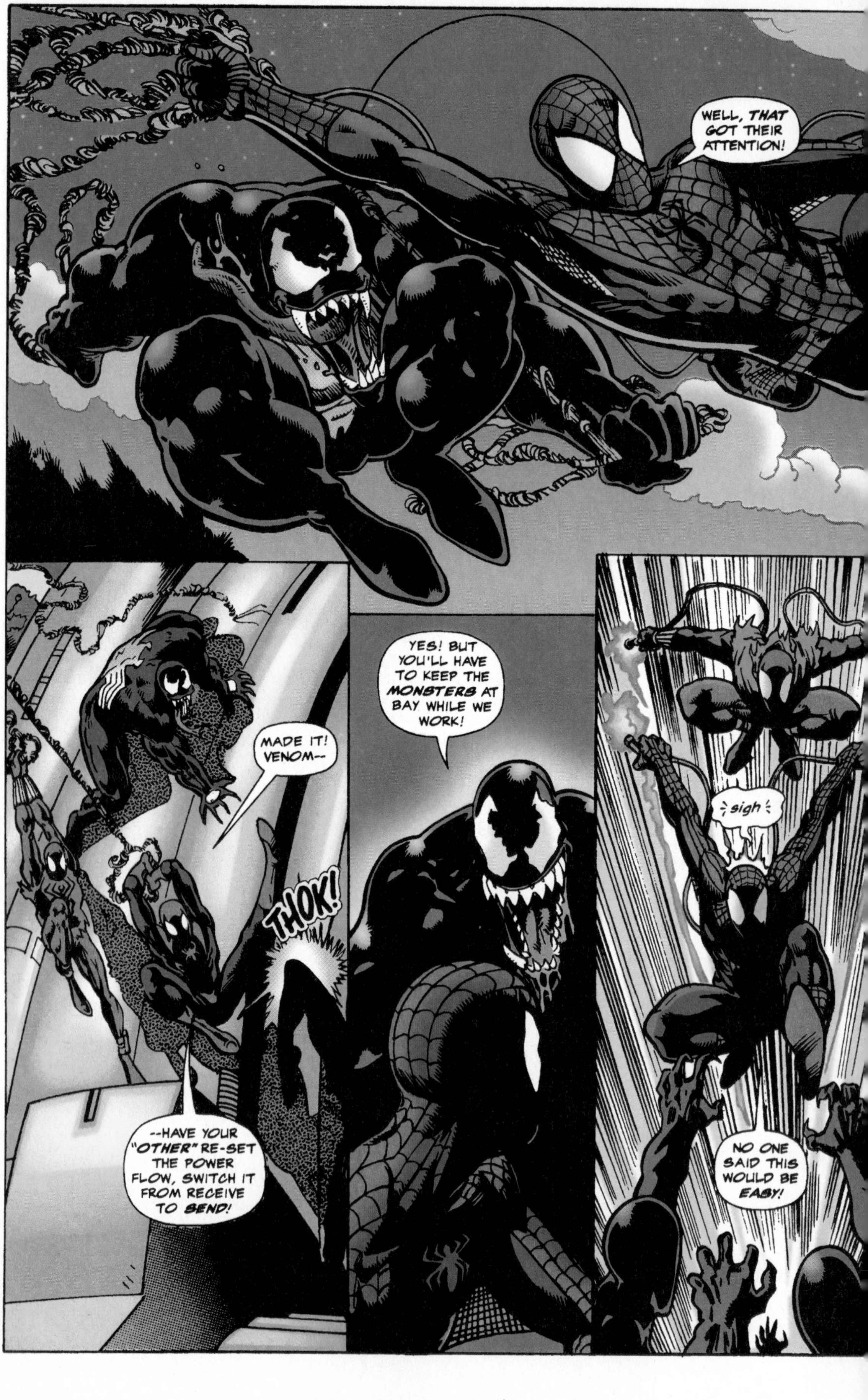
WELL, THAT GOT THEIR ATTENTION!
MADE IT! VENOM--
THOK!
--HAVE YOUR "OTHER" RE-SET THE POWER FLOW, SWITCH IT FROM RECEIVE TO SEND!
YES! BUT YOU'LL HAVE TO KEEP THE MONSTERS AT BAY WHILE WE WORK!
sigh
NO ONE SAID THIS WOULD BE EASY!

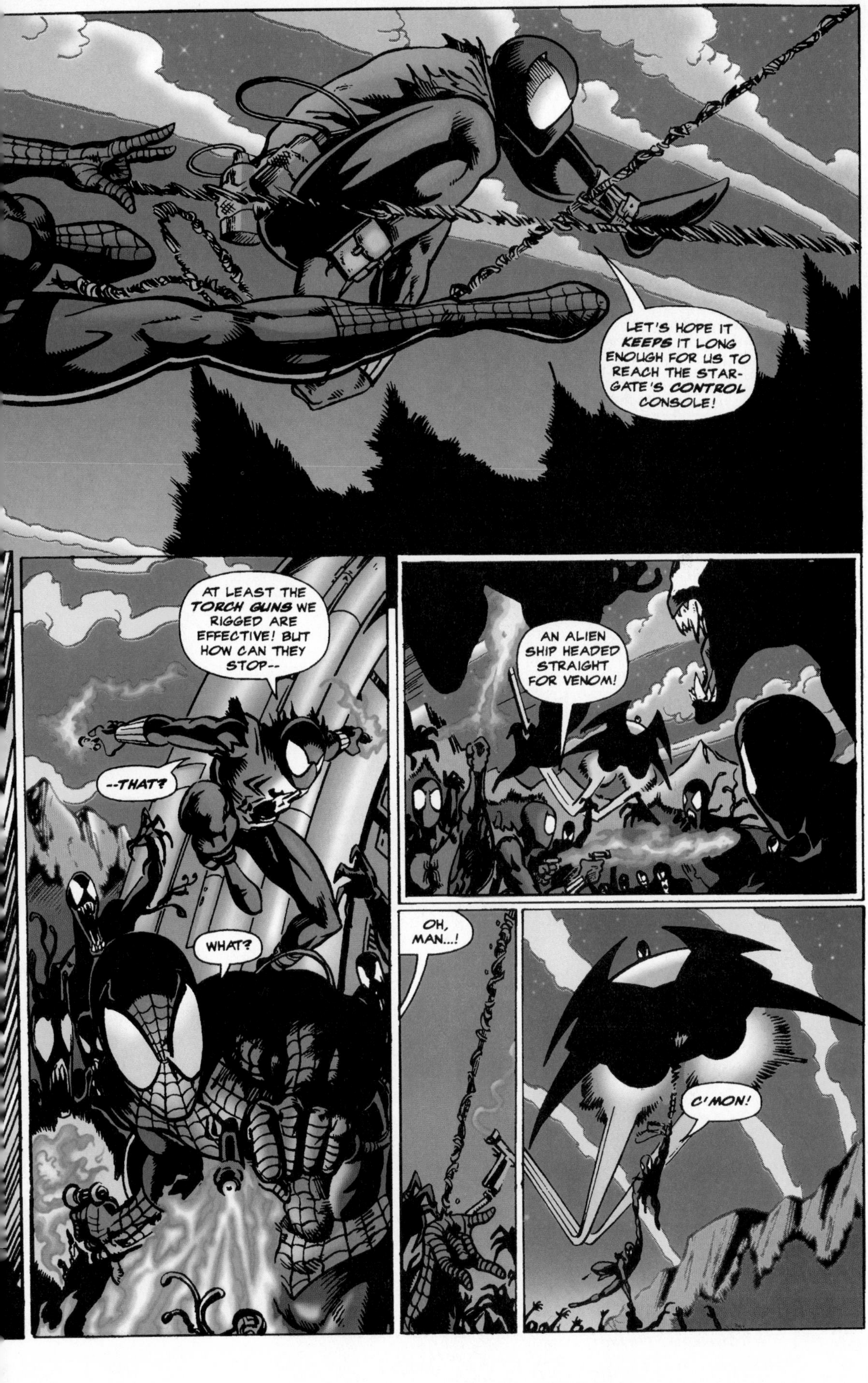
LET'S HOPE IT KEEPS IT LONG ENOUGH FOR US TO REACH THE STAR-GATE'S CONTROL CONSOLE!
AT LEAST THE TORCH GUNS WE RIGGED ARE EFFECTIVE! BUT HOW CAN THEY STOP--
--THAT?
WHAT?
AN ALIEN SHIP HEADED STRAIGHT FOR VENOM!
OH, MAN...!
C'MON!

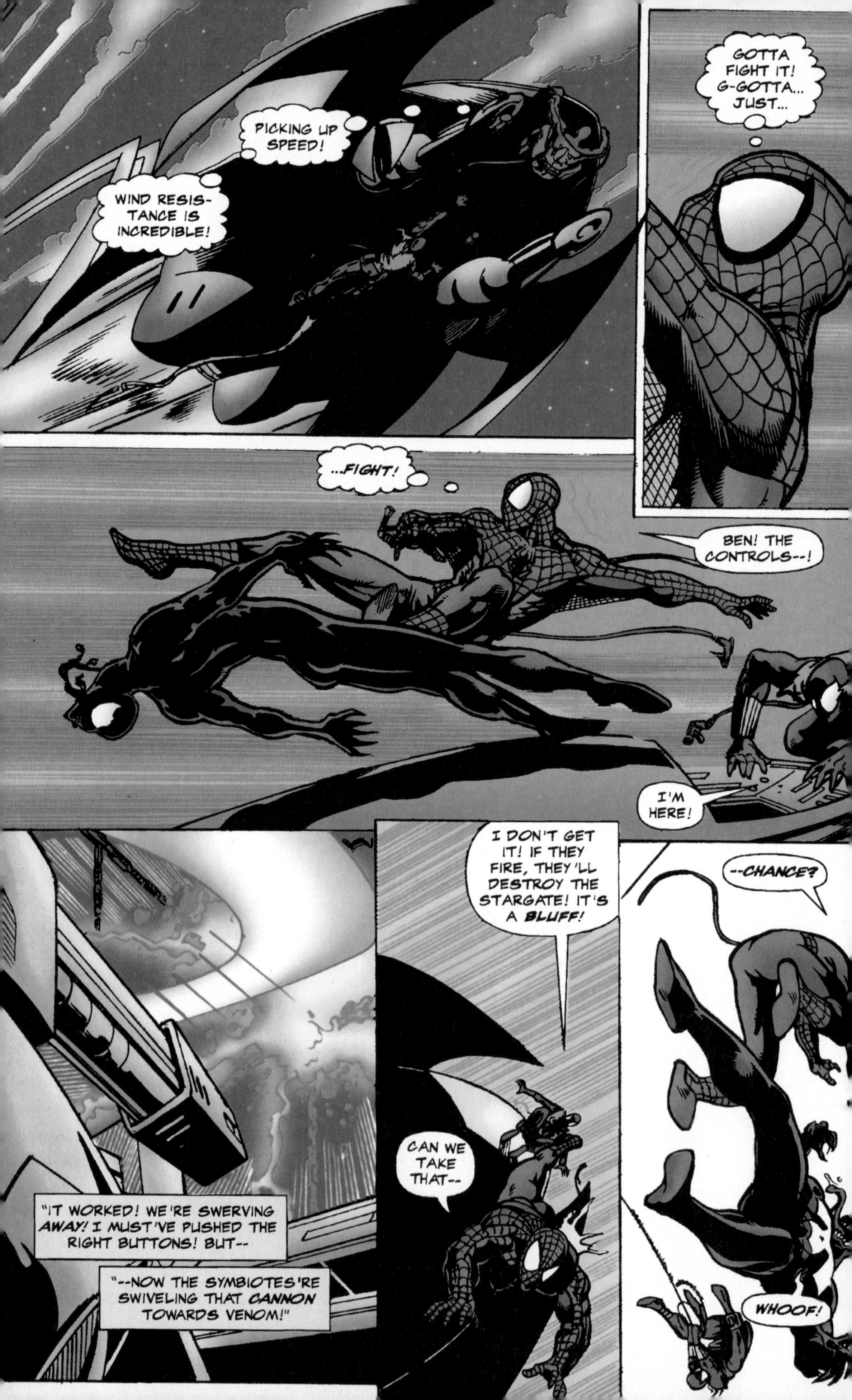
PICKING UP SPEED!
WIND RESIS-TANCE IS INCREDIBLE!
GOTTA FIGHT IT! G-GOTTA... JUST...
...FIGHT!
BEN! THE CONTROLS--!
I'M HERE!
"IT WORKED! WE'RE SWERVING AWAY! I MUST'VE PUSHED THE RIGHT BUTTONS! BUT--
"--NOW THE SYMBIOTES'RE SWIVELING THAT CANNON TOWARDS VENOM!"
I DON'T GET IT! IF THEY FIRE, THEY'LL DESTROY THE STARGATE! IT'S A BLUFF!
CAN WE TAKE THAT--
--CHANCE?
WHOOF!

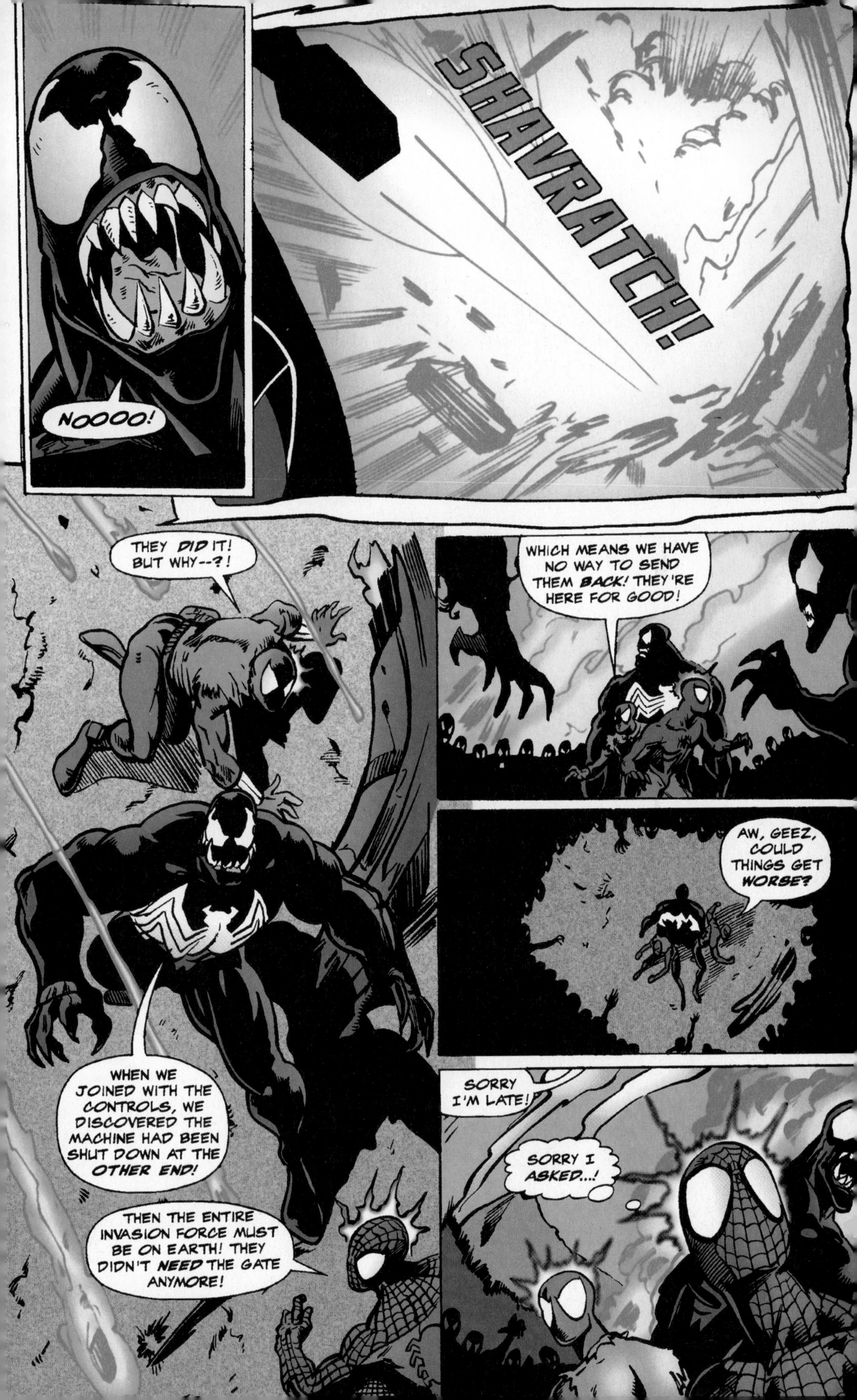
NOOOO!
SHAVRATCH!
THEY DID IT! BUT WHY--?!
WHEN WE JOINED WITH THE CONTROLS, WE DISCOVERED THE MACHINE HAD BEEN SHUT DOWN AT THE OTHER END!
THEN THE ENTIRE INVASION FORCE MUST BE ON EARTH! THEY DIDN'T NEED THE GATE ANYMORE!
WHICH MEANS WE HAVE NO WAY TO SEND THEM BACK! THEY'RE HERE FOR GOOD!
AW, GEEZ, COULD THINGS GET WORSE?
SORRY I'M LATE!
SORRY I ASKED...!

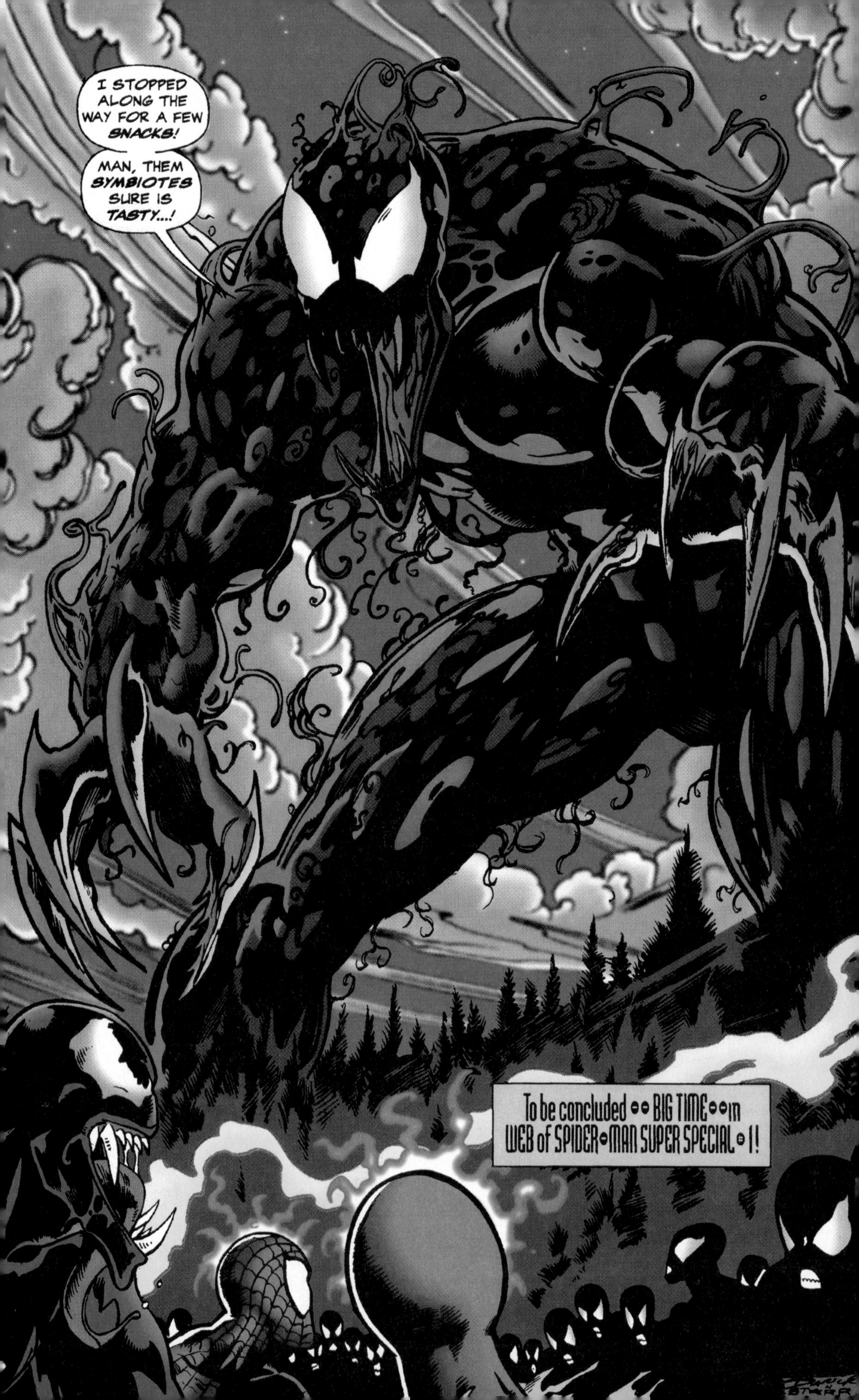
I STOPPED ALONG THE WAY FOR A FEW SNACKS!
MAN, THEM SYMBIOTES SURE IS TASTY...!
To be concluded -- BIG TIME -- in WEB of SPIDER-MAN SUPER SPECIAL #1!

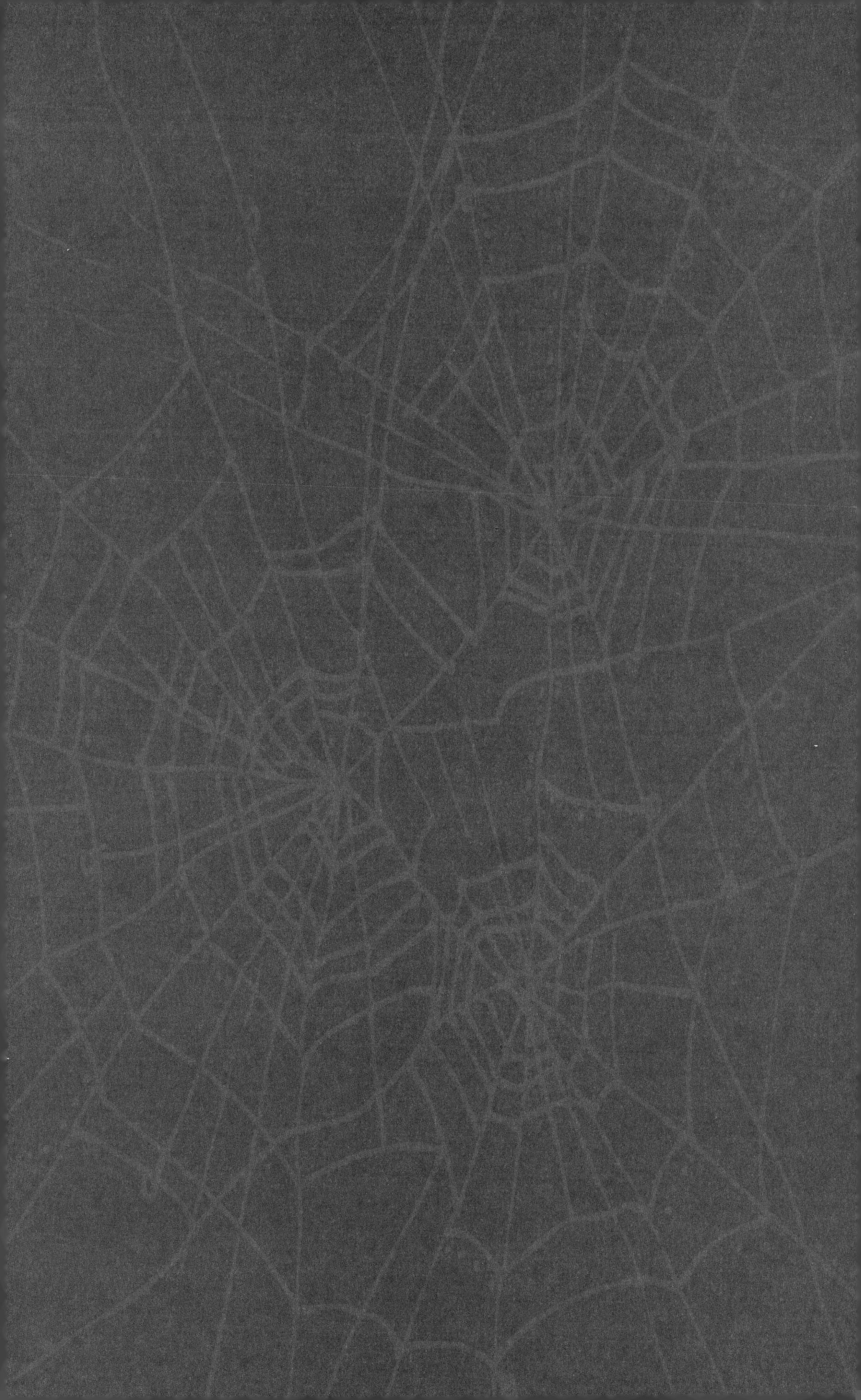

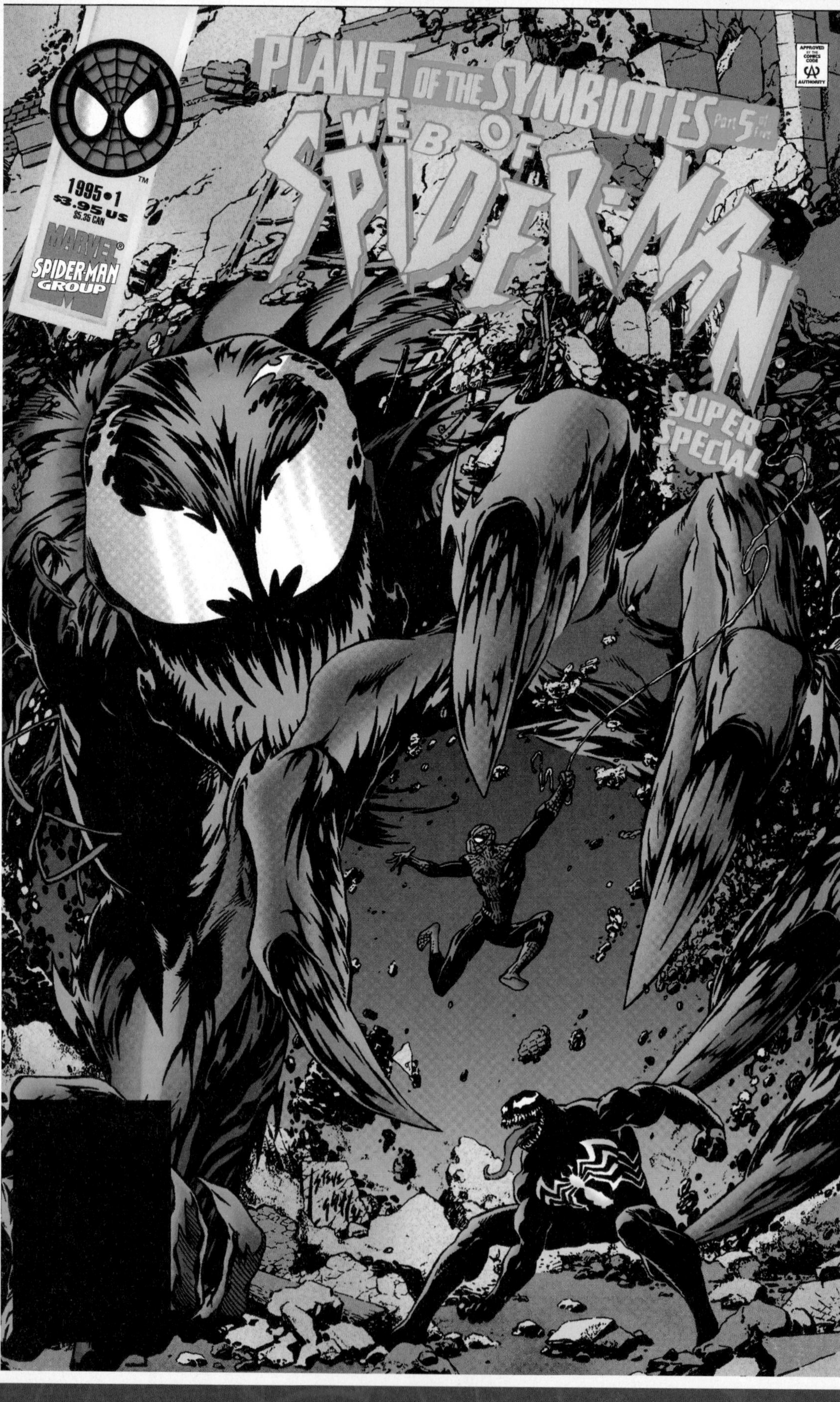
PLANET OF THE SYMBIOTES
Part 5 of five
WEB OF SPIDER-MAN
SUPER SPECIAL
1995 • 1
$3.95 US
$5.35 CAN
MARVEL
SPIDER-MAN GROUP
APPROVED BY THE COMICS CODE AUTHORITY

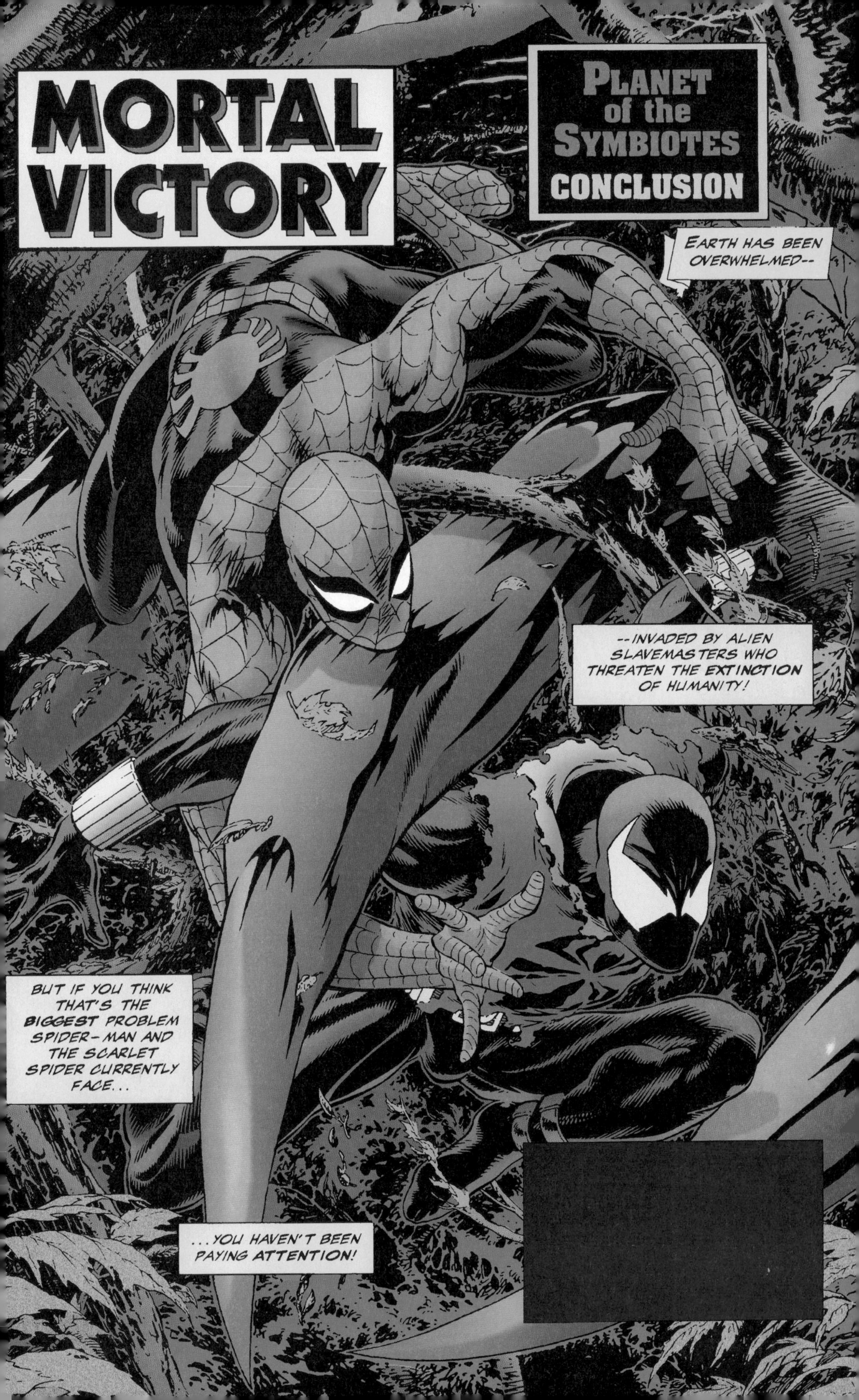

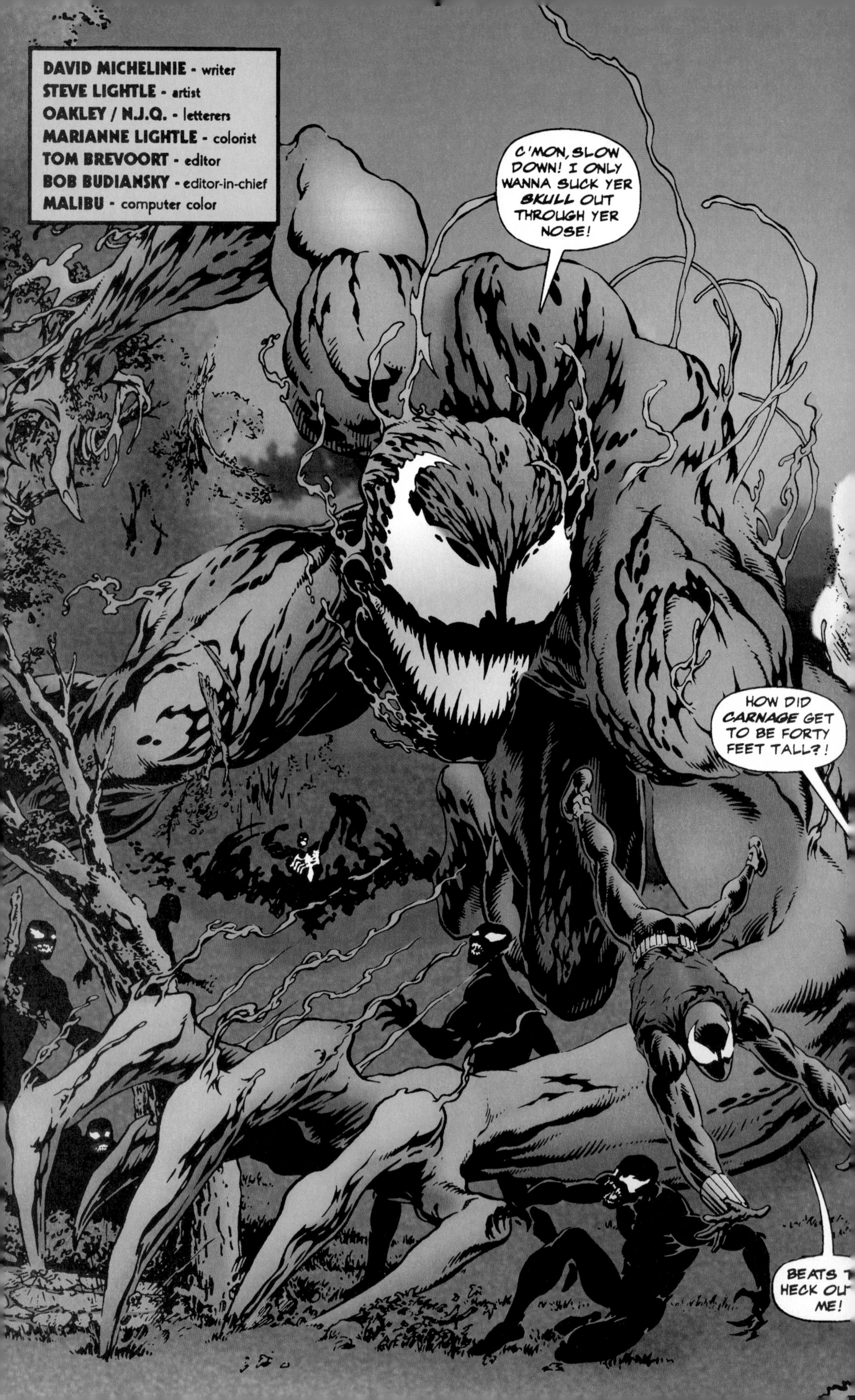
DAVID MICHELINIE - writer
STEVE LIGHTLE - artist
OAKLEY / N.J.Q. - letterers
MARIANNE LIGHTLE - colorist
TOM BREVOORT - editor
BOB BUDIANSKY - editor-in-chief
MALIBU - computer color
C'MON, SLOW DOWN! I ONLY WANNA SUCK YER SKULL OUT THROUGH YER NOSE!
HOW DID CARNAGE GET TO BE FORTY FEET TALL?!
BEATS T HECK OU ME!

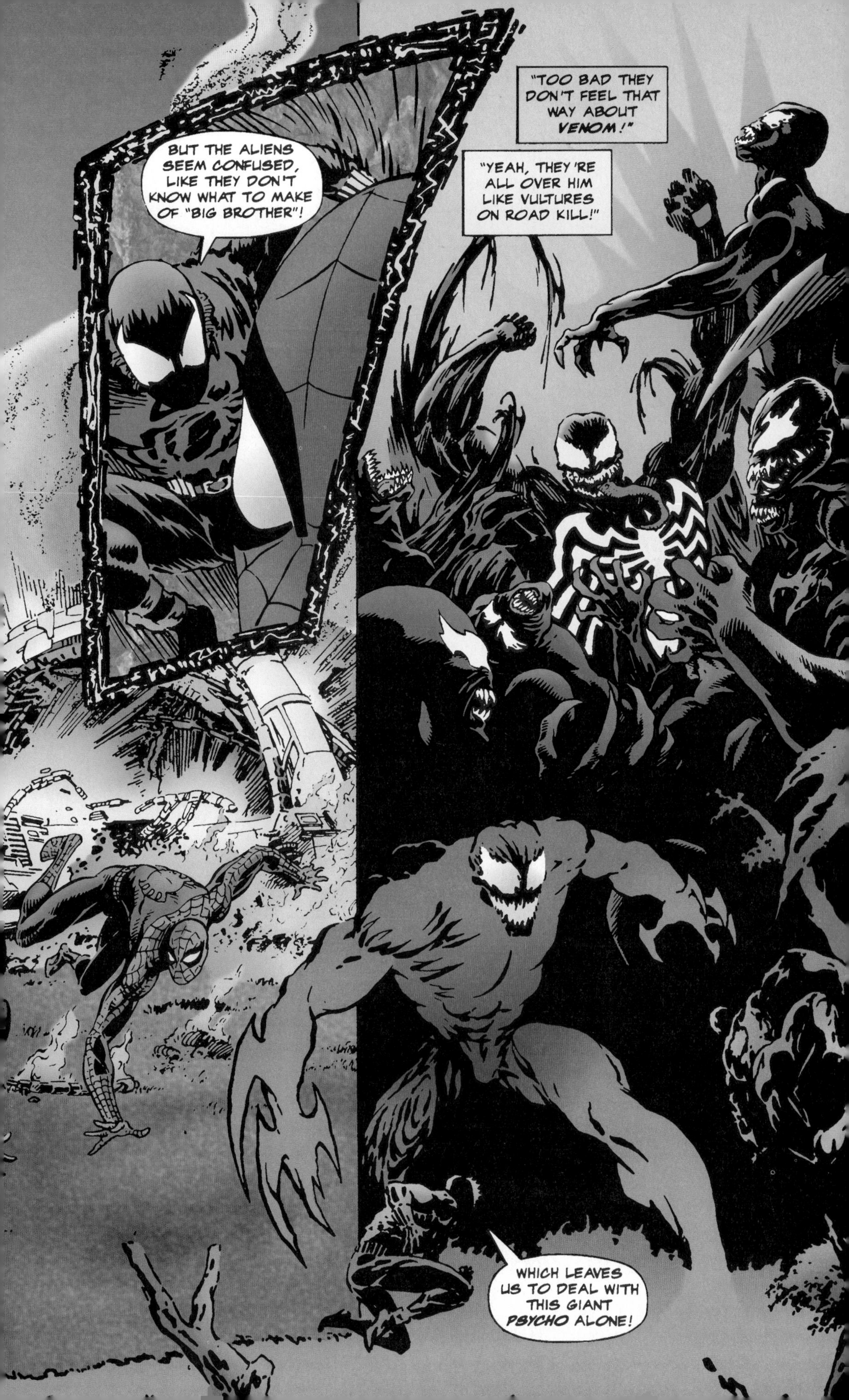
BUT THE ALIENS SEEM CONFUSED, LIKE THEY DON'T KNOW WHAT TO MAKE OF "BIG BROTHER"!
"TOO BAD THEY DON'T FEEL THAT WAY ABOUT VENOM!"
"YEAH, THEY'RE ALL OVER HIM LIKE VULTURES ON ROAD KILL!"
WHICH LEAVES US TO DEAL WITH THIS GIANT PSYCHO ALONE!

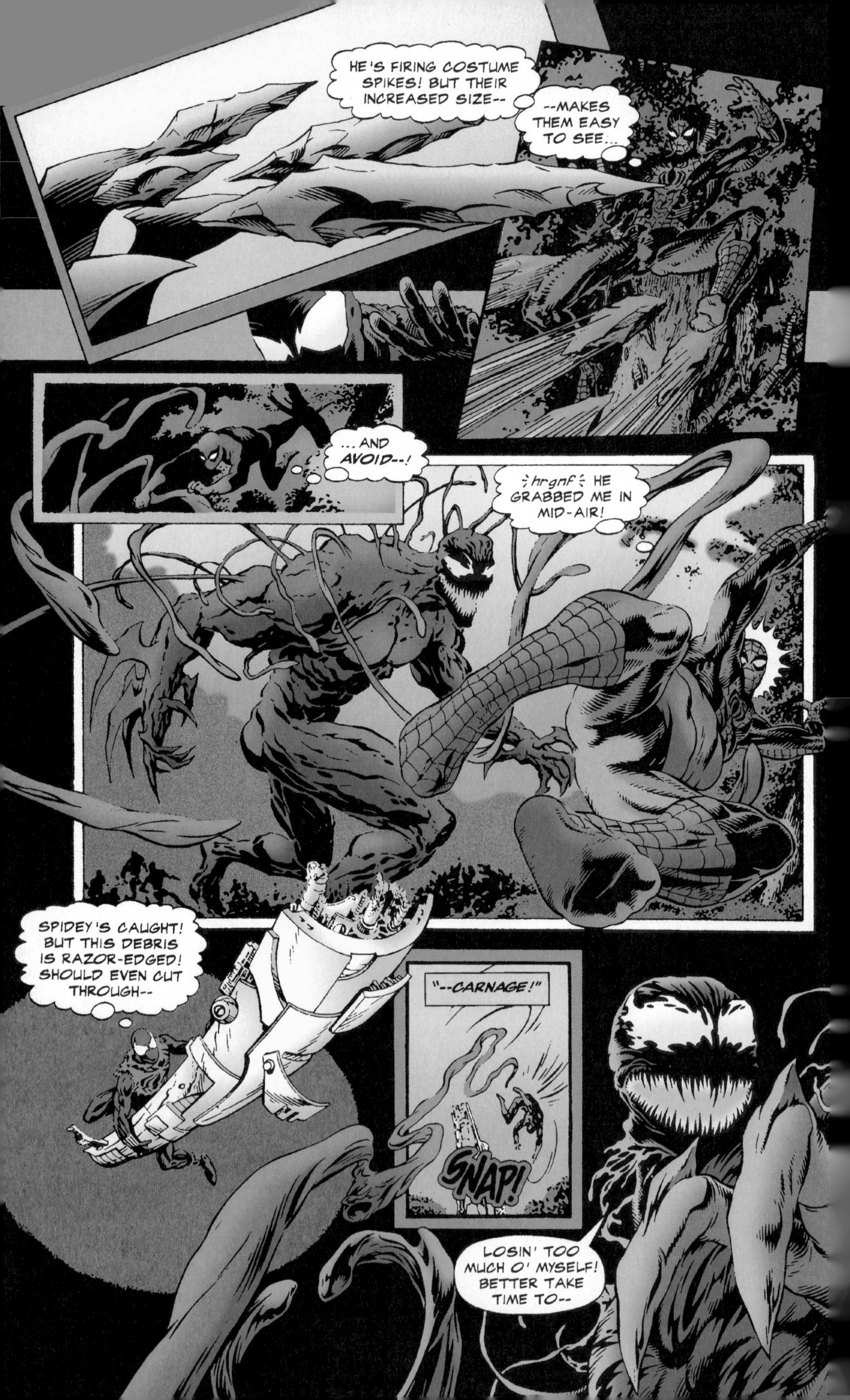
HE'S FIRING COSTUME SPIKES! BUT THEIR INCREASED SIZE--
--MAKES THEM EASY TO SEE...
...AND AVOID--!
hrgnf HE GRABBED ME IN MID-AIR!
SPIDEY'S CAUGHT! BUT THIS DEBRIS IS RAZOR-EDGED! SHOULD EVEN CUT THROUGH--
"--CARNAGE!"
SNAP!
LOSIN' TOO MUCH O' MYSELF! BETTER TAKE TIME TO--

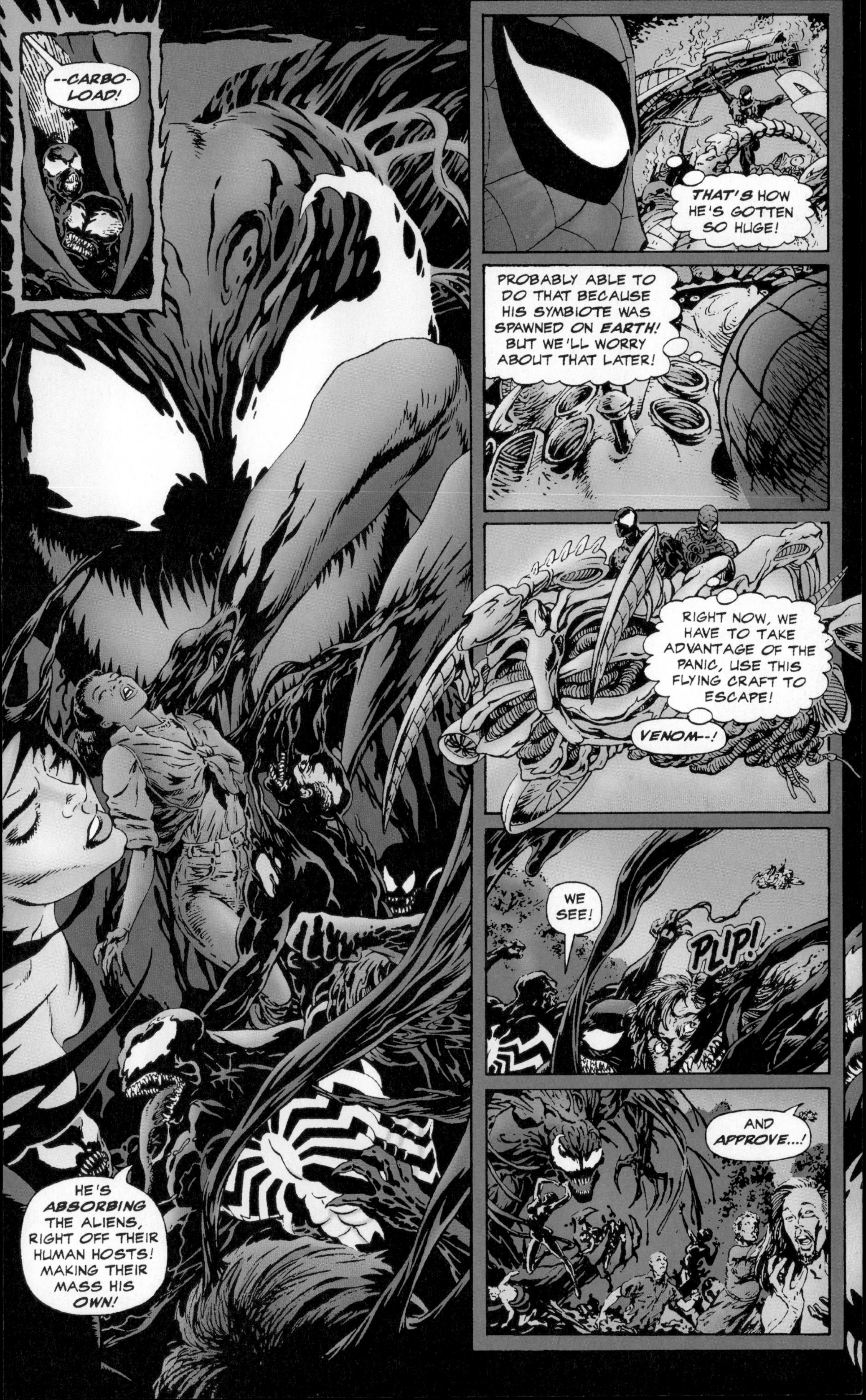
--CARBO-LOAD!
HE'S ABSORBING THE ALIENS, RIGHT OFF THEIR HUMAN HOSTS! MAKING THEIR MASS HIS OWN!
THAT'S HOW HE'S GOTTEN SO HUGE!
PROBABLY ABLE TO DO THAT BECAUSE HIS SYMBIOTE WAS SPAWNED ON EARTH! BUT WE'LL WORRY ABOUT THAT LATER!
RIGHT NOW, WE HAVE TO TAKE ADVANTAGE OF THE PANIC, USE THIS FLYING CRAFT TO ESCAPE!
VENOM--!
WE SEE!
PLIP!
AND APPROVE...!

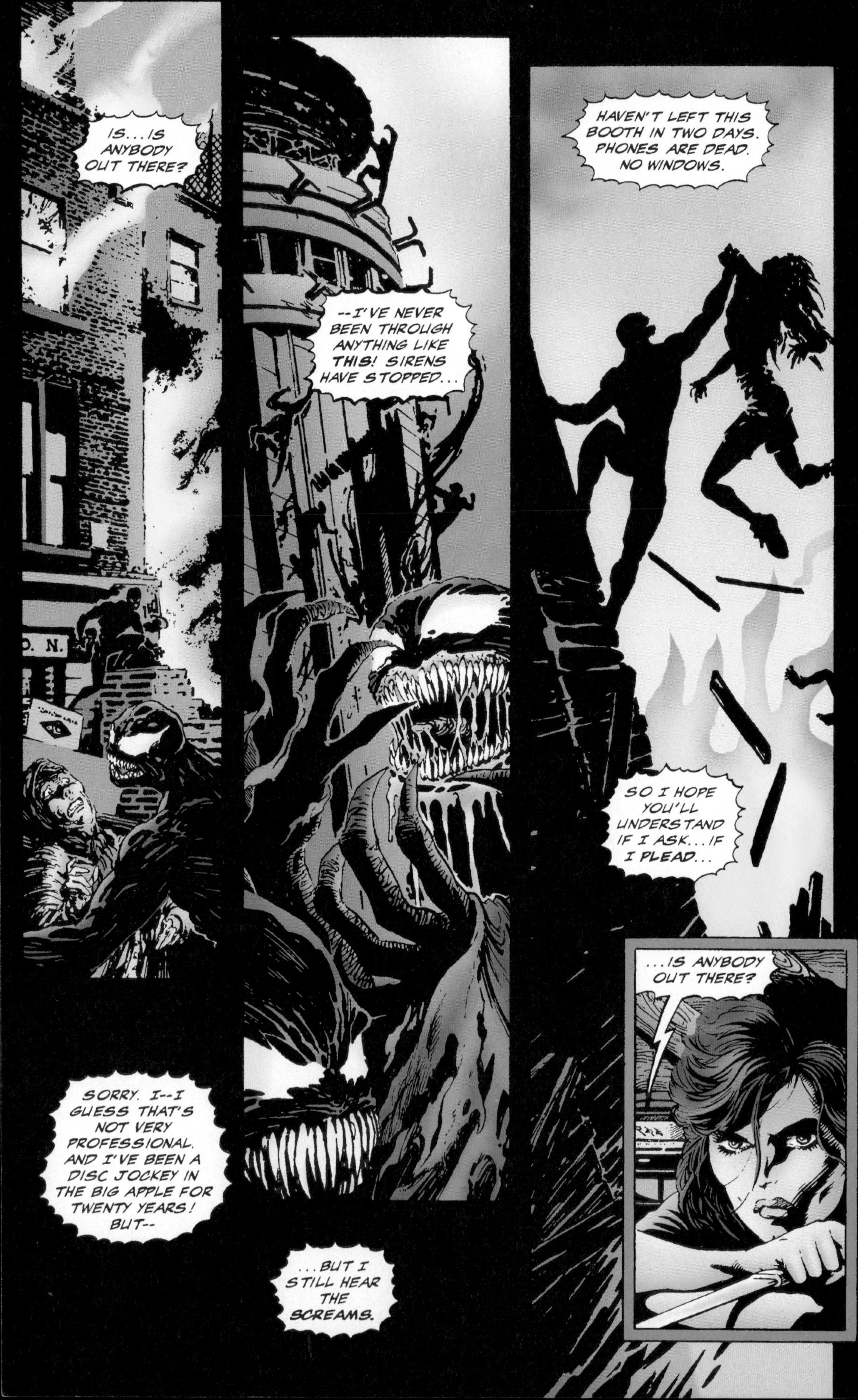
IS...IS ANYBODY OUT THERE?
--I'VE NEVER BEEN THROUGH ANYTHING LIKE THIS! SIRENS HAVE STOPPED...
SORRY. I--I GUESS THAT'S NOT VERY PROFESSIONAL. AND I'VE BEEN A DISC JOCKEY IN THE BIG APPLE FOR TWENTY YEARS! BUT--
...BUT I STILL HEAR THE SCREAMS.
HAVEN'T LEFT THIS BOOTH IN TWO DAYS. PHONES ARE DEAD. NO WINDOWS.
SO I HOPE YOU'LL UNDERSTAND IF I ASK...IF I PLEAD...
...IS ANYBODY OUT THERE?

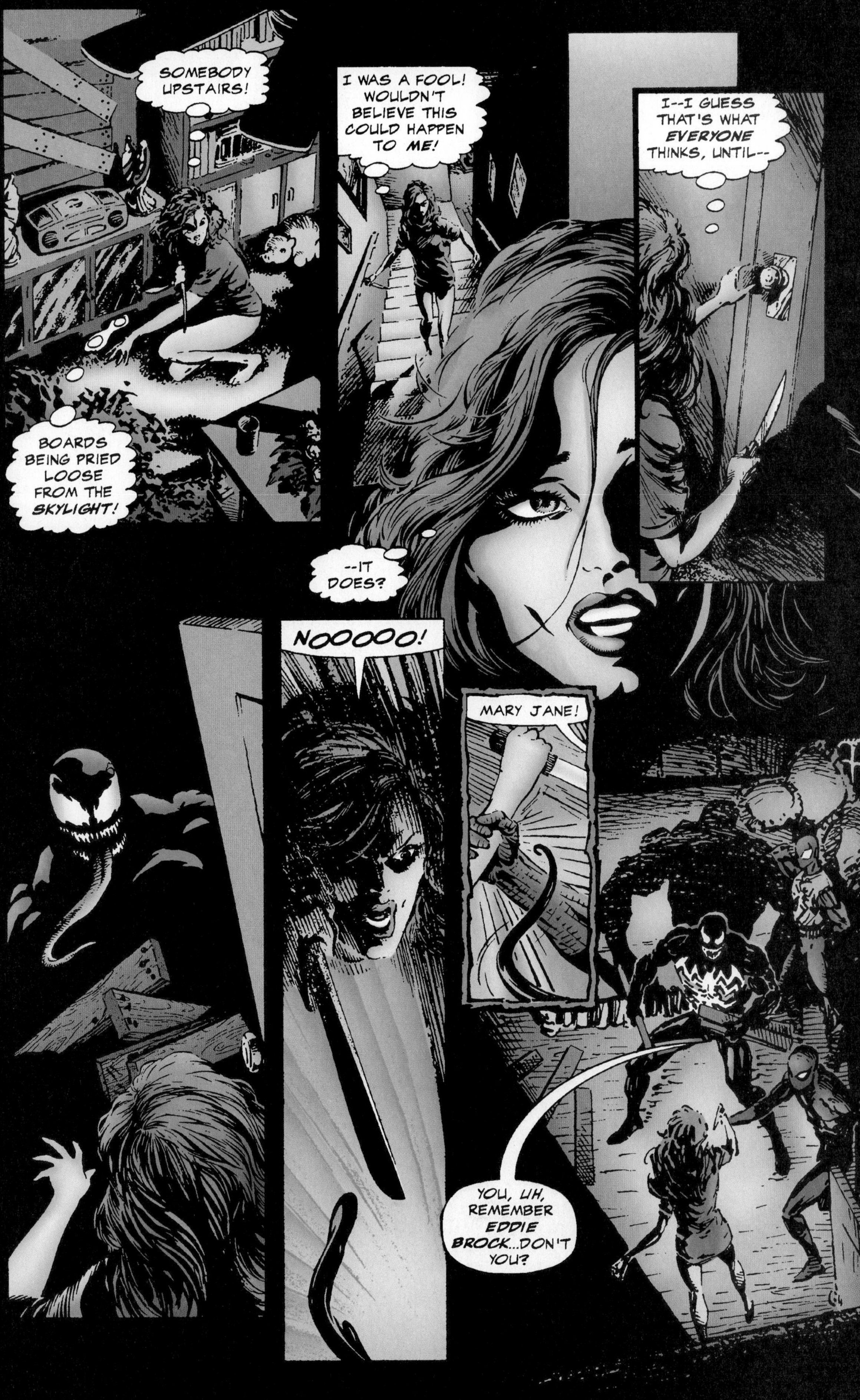
SOMEBODY UPSTAIRS!
BOARDS BEING PRIED LOOSE FROM THE SKYLIGHT!
I WAS A FOOL! WOULDN'T BELIEVE THIS COULD HAPPEN TO ME!
I--I GUESS THAT'S WHAT EVERYONE THINKS, UNTIL--
--IT DOES?
NOOOOO!
MARY JANE!
YOU, UH, REMEMBER EDDIE BROCK...DON'T YOU?

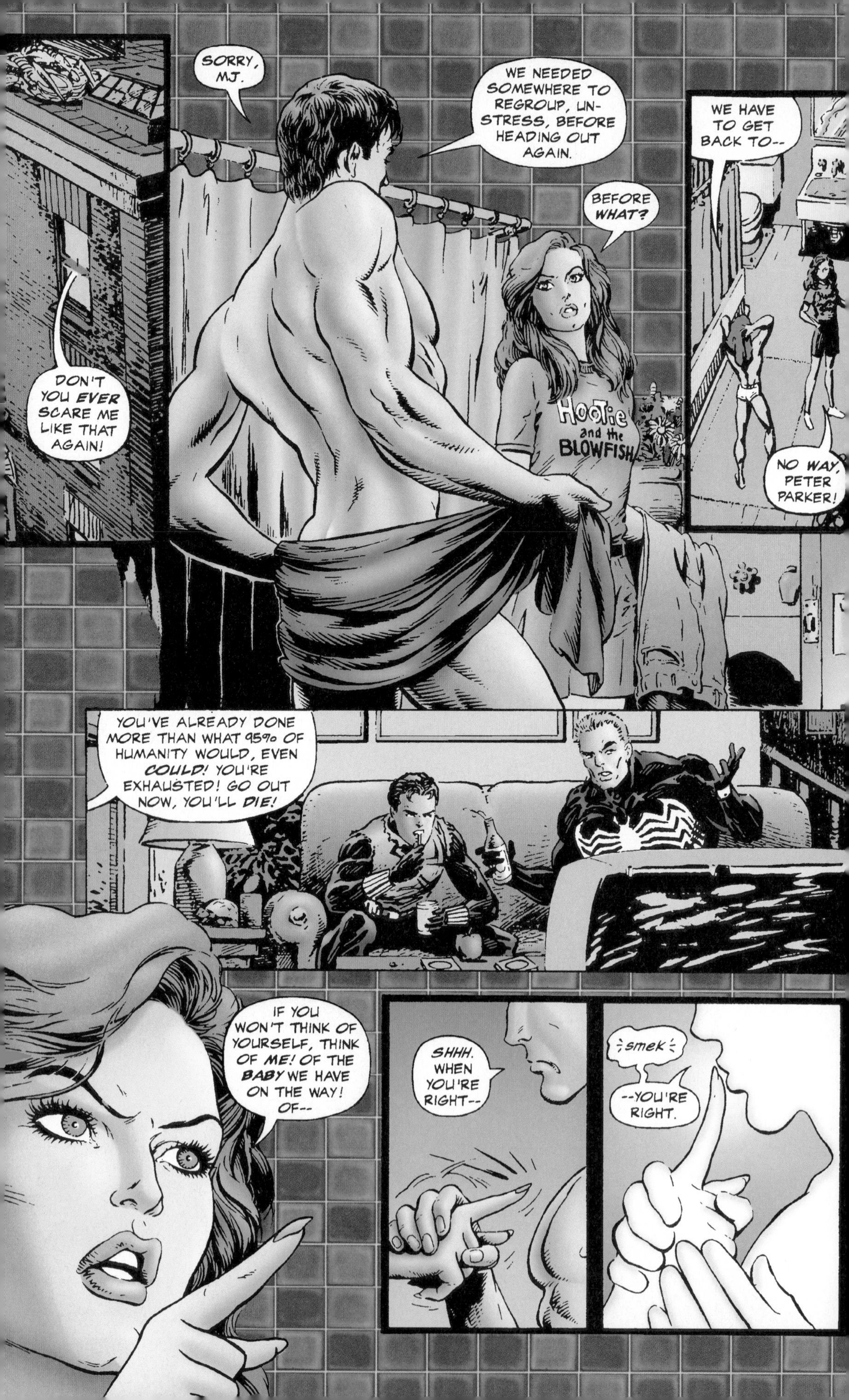
DON'T YOU EVER SCARE ME LIKE THAT AGAIN!
SORRY, MJ.
WE NEEDED SOMEWHERE TO REGROUP, UN-STRESS, BEFORE HEADING OUT AGAIN.
BEFORE WHAT?
HOOTIE and the BLOWFISH
WE HAVE TO GET BACK TO--
NO WAY, PETER PARKER!
YOU'VE ALREADY DONE MORE THAN WHAT 95% OF HUMANITY WOULD, EVEN COULD! YOU'RE EXHAUSTED! GO OUT NOW, YOU'LL DIE!
IF YOU WON'T THINK OF YOURSELF, THINK OF ME! OF THE BABY WE HAVE ON THE WAY! OF--
SHHH. WHEN YOU'RE RIGHT--
smek
--YOU'RE RIGHT.

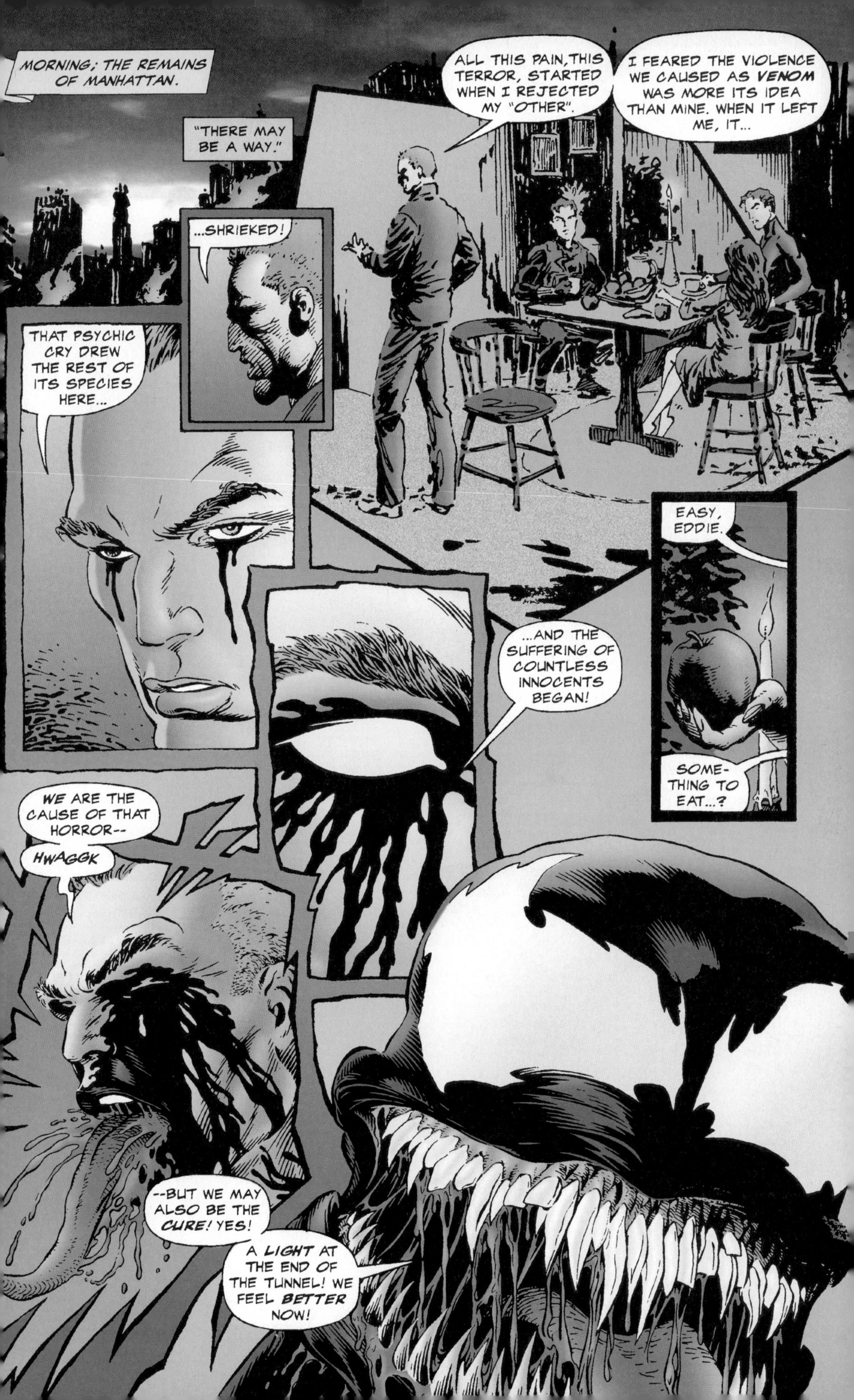
MORNING; THE REMAINS OF MANHATTAN.
"THERE MAY BE A WAY."
ALL THIS PAIN, THIS TERROR, STARTED WHEN I REJECTED MY "OTHER".
I FEARED THE VIOLENCE WE CAUSED AS VENOM WAS MORE ITS IDEA THAN MINE. WHEN IT LEFT ME, IT...
...SHRIEKED!
THAT PSYCHIC CRY DREW THE REST OF ITS SPECIES HERE...
...AND THE SUFFERING OF COUNTLESS INNOCENTS BEGAN!
EASY, EDDIE.
SOME-THING TO EAT...?
WE ARE THE CAUSE OF THAT HORROR--
HWAGGK
--BUT WE MAY ALSO BE THE CURE! YES!
A LIGHT AT THE END OF THE TUNNEL! WE FEEL BETTER NOW!

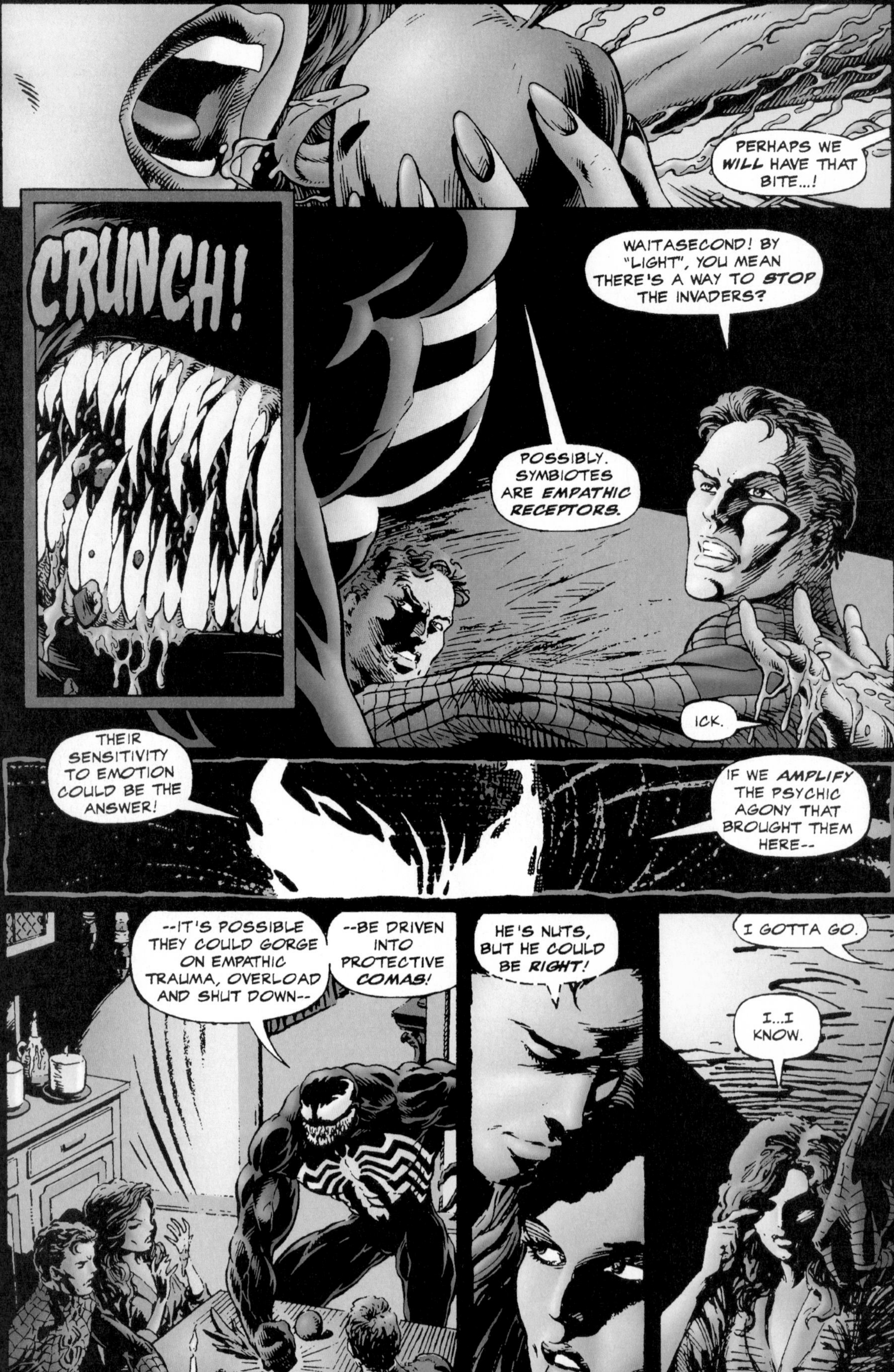
PERHAPS WE WILL HAVE THAT BITE...!
CRUNCH!
WAITASECOND! BY "LIGHT", YOU MEAN THERE'S A WAY TO STOP THE INVADERS?
POSSIBLY. SYMBIOTES ARE EMPATHIC RECEPTORS.
ICK.
THEIR SENSITIVITY TO EMOTION COULD BE THE ANSWER!
IF WE AMPLIFY THE PSYCHIC AGONY THAT BROUGHT THEM HERE--
--IT'S POSSIBLE THEY COULD GORGE ON EMPATHIC TRAUMA, OVERLOAD AND SHUT DOWN--
--BE DRIVEN INTO PROTECTIVE COMAS!
HE'S NUTS, BUT HE COULD BE RIGHT!
I GOTTA GO.
I...I KNOW.

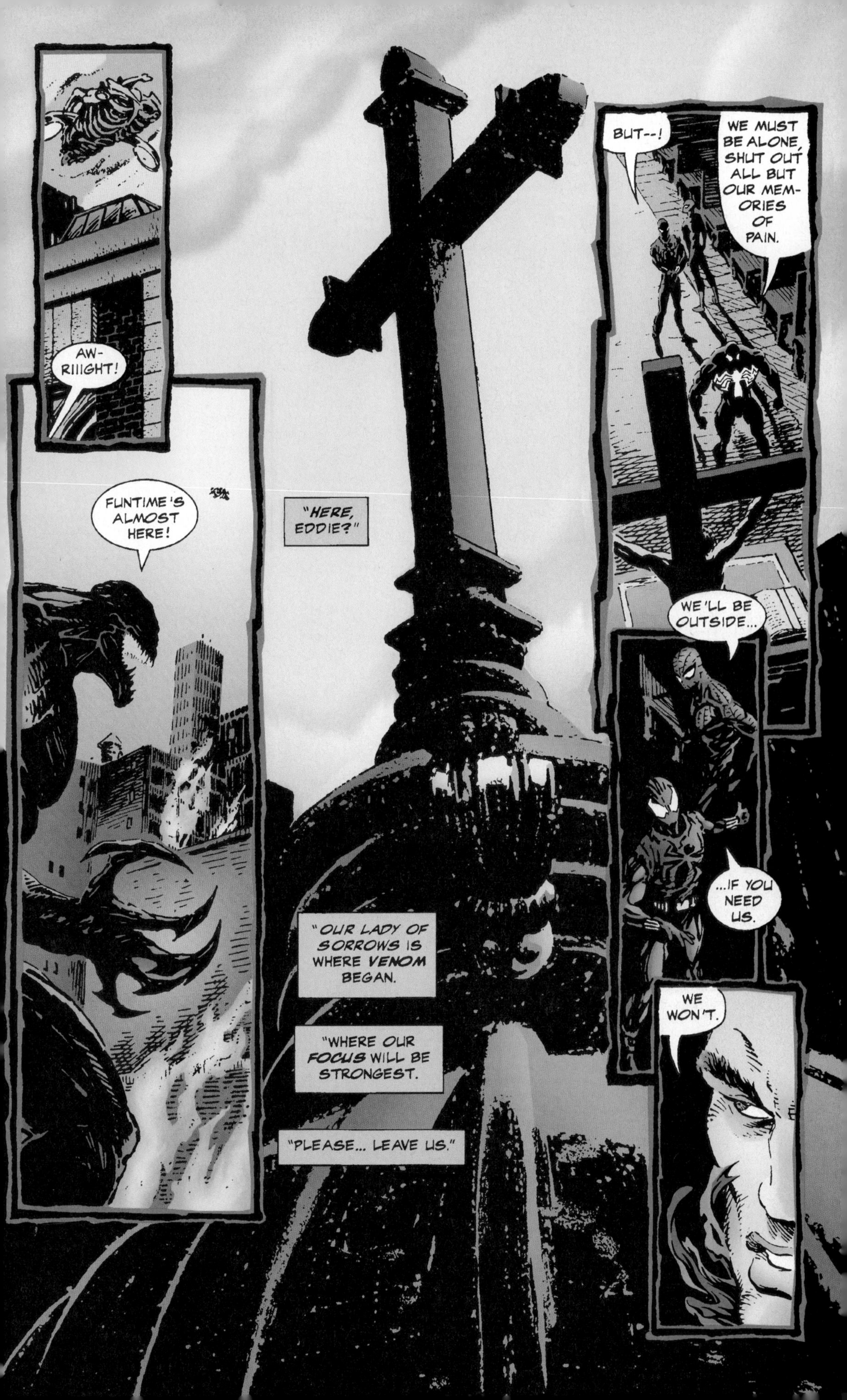
AW-RIIIGHT!
FUNTIME'S ALMOST HERE!
"HERE, EDDIE?"
"OUR LADY OF SORROWS IS WHERE VENOM BEGAN.
"WHERE OUR FOCUS WILL BE STRONGEST.
"PLEASE... LEAVE US."
BUT--!
WE MUST BE ALONE, SHUT OUT ALL BUT OUR MEMORIES OF PAIN.
WE'LL BE OUTSIDE...
...IF YOU NEED US.
WE WON'T.

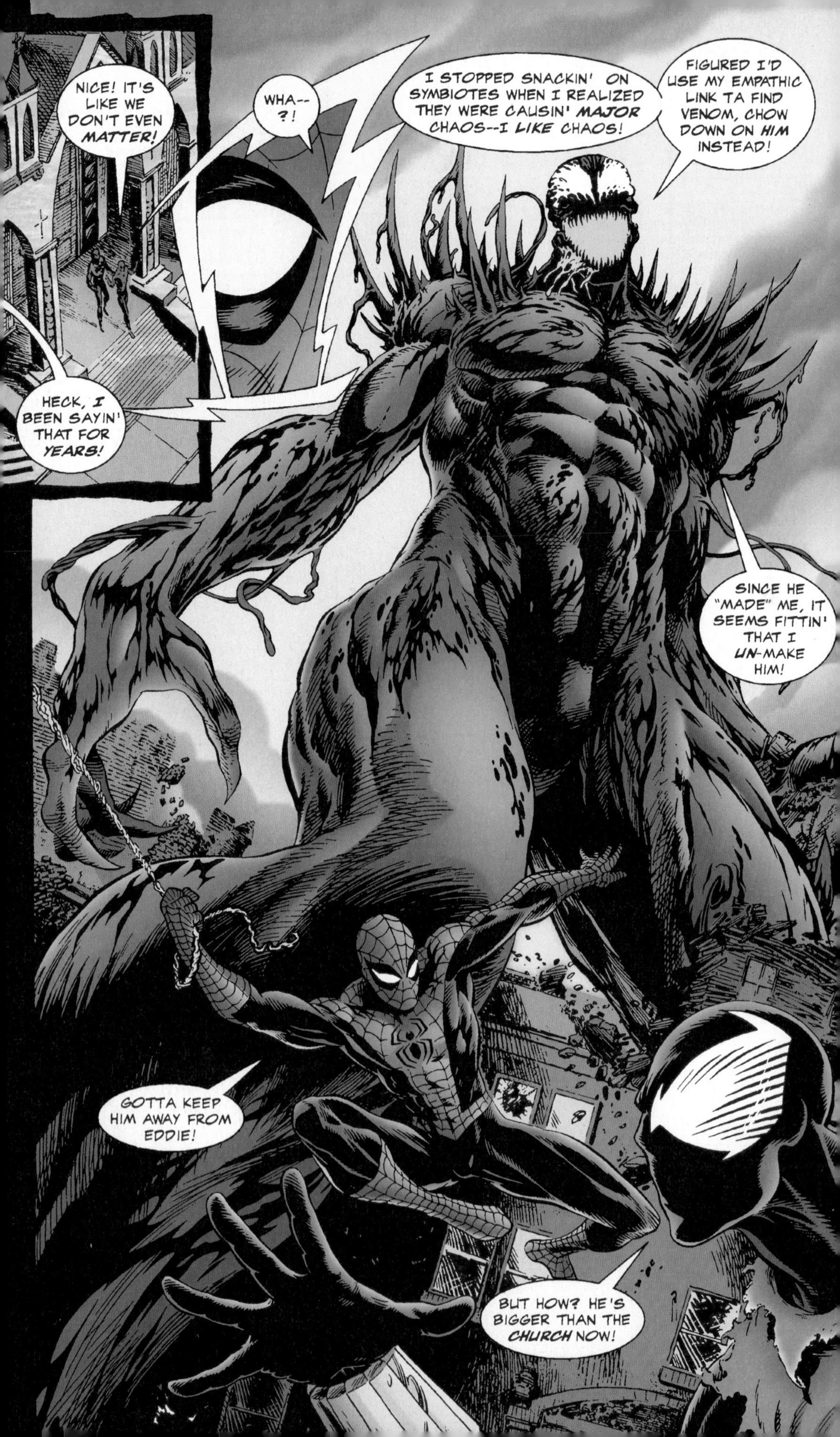
NICE! IT'S LIKE WE DON'T EVEN MATTER!
HECK, I BEEN SAYIN' THAT FOR YEARS!
WHA-- ?!
I STOPPED SNACKIN' ON SYMBIOTES WHEN I REALIZED THEY WERE CAUSIN' MAJOR CHAOS--I LIKE CHAOS!
FIGURED I'D USE MY EMPATHIC LINK TA FIND VENOM, CHOW DOWN ON HIM INSTEAD!
SINCE HE "MADE" ME, IT SEEMS FITTIN' THAT I UN-MAKE HIM!
GOTTA KEEP HIM AWAY FROM EDDIE!
BUT HOW? HE'S BIGGER THAN THE CHURCH NOW!

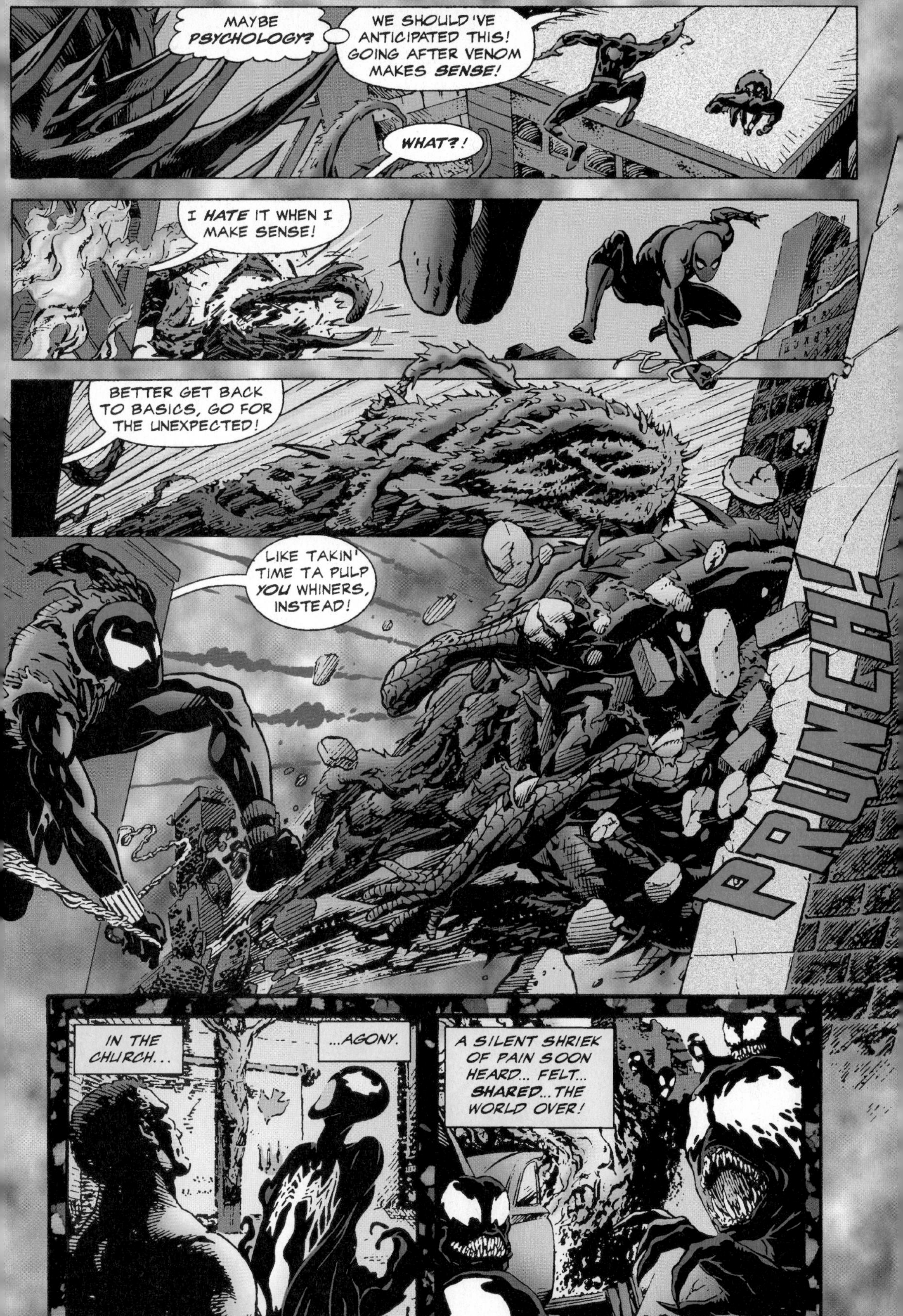
MAYBE PSYCHOLOGY?
WE SHOULD'VE ANTICIPATED THIS! GOING AFTER VENOM MAKES SENSE!
WHAT?!
I HATE IT WHEN I MAKE SENSE!
BETTER GET BACK TO BASICS, GO FOR THE UNEXPECTED!
LIKE TAKIN' TIME TA PULP YOU WHINERS, INSTEAD!
PRUNCH!
IN THE CHURCH...
...AGONY.
A SILENT SHRIEK OF PAIN SOON HEARD... FELT... SHARED... THE WORLD OVER!

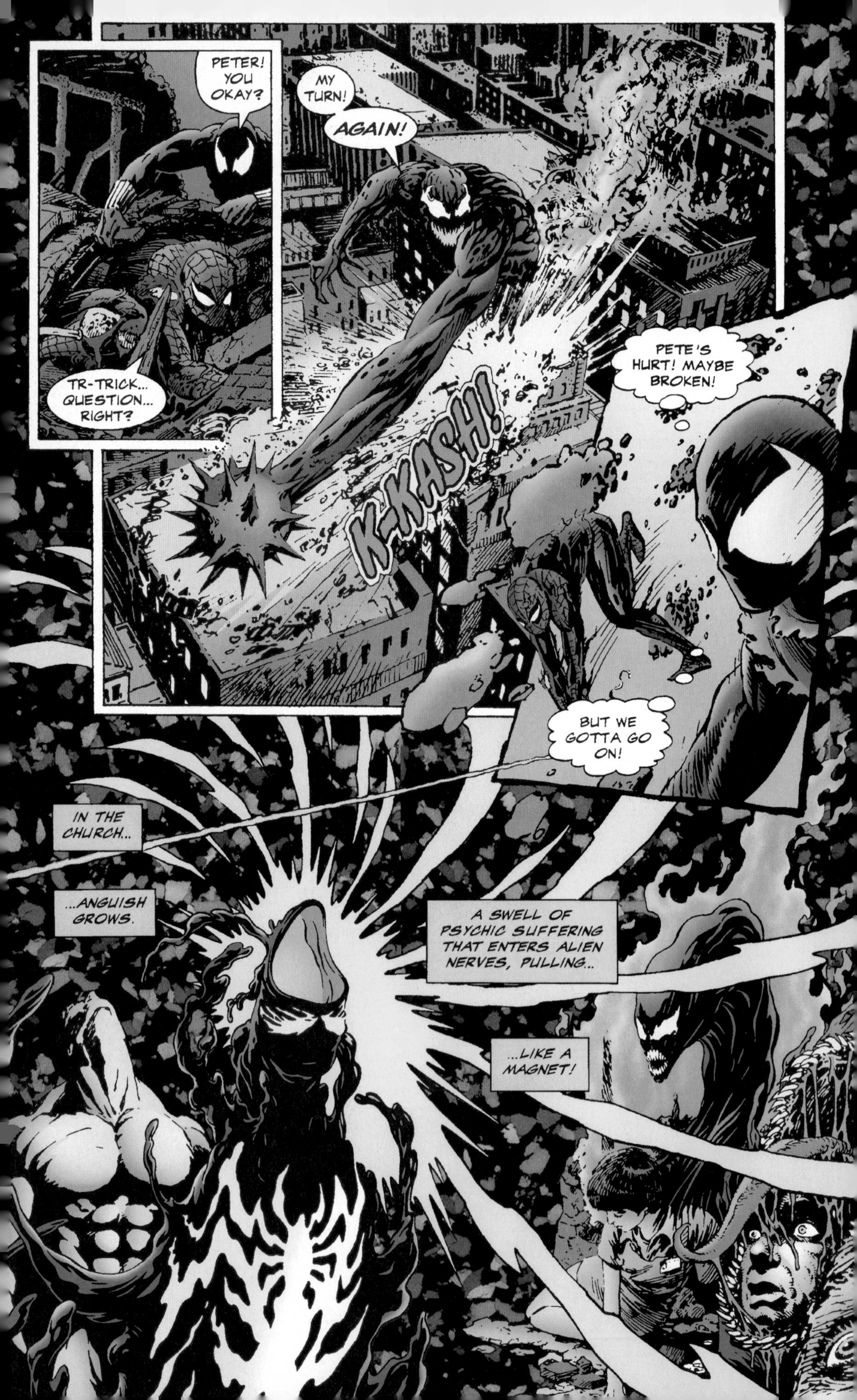
PETER! YOU OKAY?
TR-TRICK... QUESTION... RIGHT?
MY TURN!
AGAIN!
K-KASH!
PETE'S HURT! MAYBE BROKEN!
BUT WE GOTTA GO ON!
IN THE CHURCH...
...ANGUISH GROWS.
A SWELL OF PSYCHIC SUFFERING THAT ENTERS ALIEN NERVES, PULLING...
...LIKE A MAGNET!

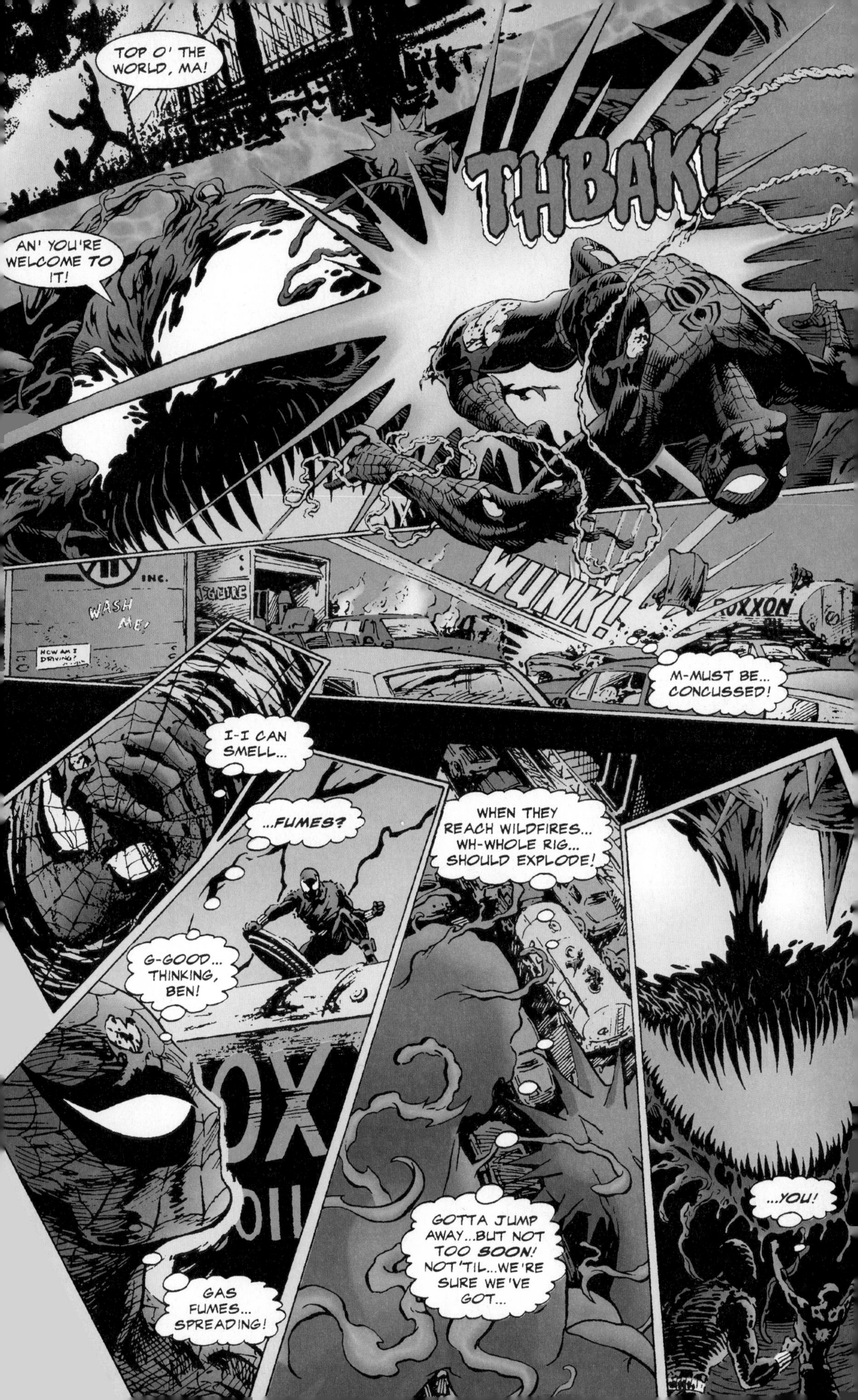
TOP O' THE WORLD, MA!
AN' YOU'RE WELCOME TO IT!
THBAK!
WUNK!
WASH ME!
INC.
ROXXON
M-MUST BE... CONCUSSED!
I-I CAN SMELL...
...FUMES?
G-GOOD... THINKING, BEN!
WHEN THEY REACH WILDFIRES... WH-WHOLE RIG... SHOULD EXPLODE!
GAS FUMES... SPREADING!
GOTTA JUMP AWAY...BUT NOT TOO SOON! NOT 'TIL...WE'RE SURE WE'VE GOT...
...YOU!

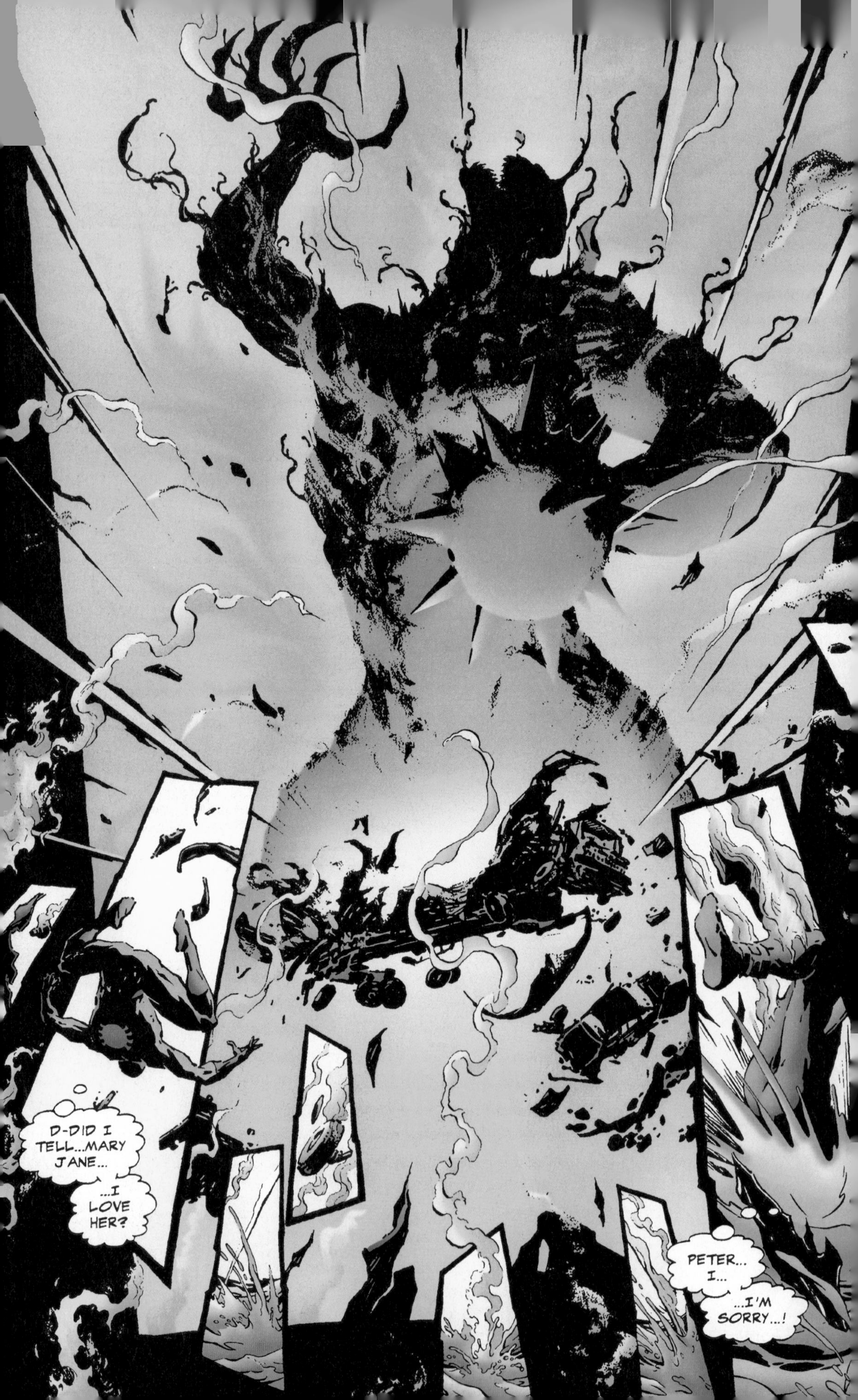
D-DID I TELL...MARY JANE...
...I LOVE HER?
PETER... I...
...I'M SORRY...!

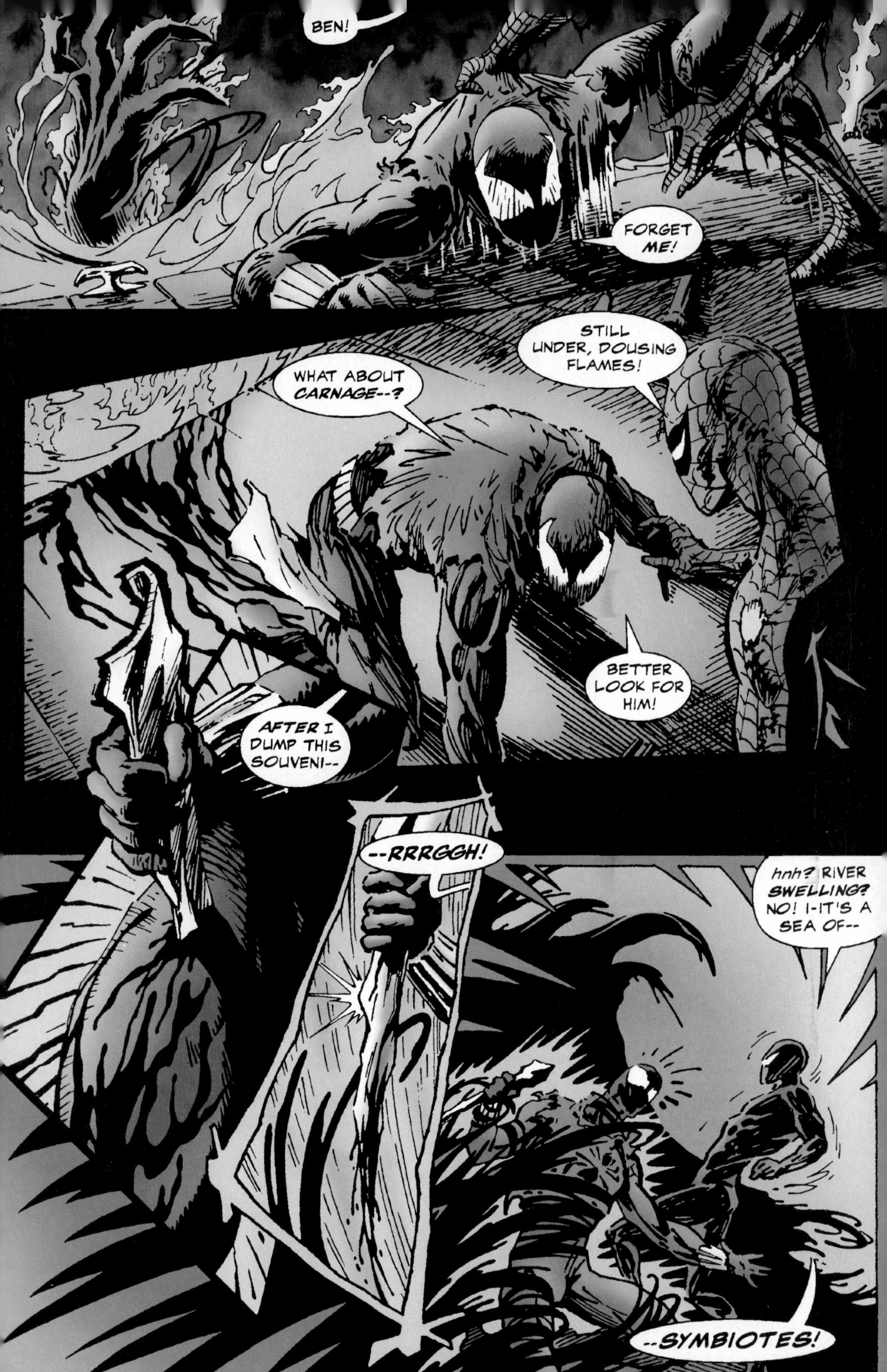
BEN!
FORGET ME!
WHAT ABOUT CARNAGE--?
STILL UNDER, DOUSING FLAMES!
BETTER LOOK FOR HIM!
AFTER I DUMP THIS SOUVENI--
--RRRGGH!
hnh? RIVER SWELLING? NO! I-IT'S A SEA OF--
--SYMBIOTES!

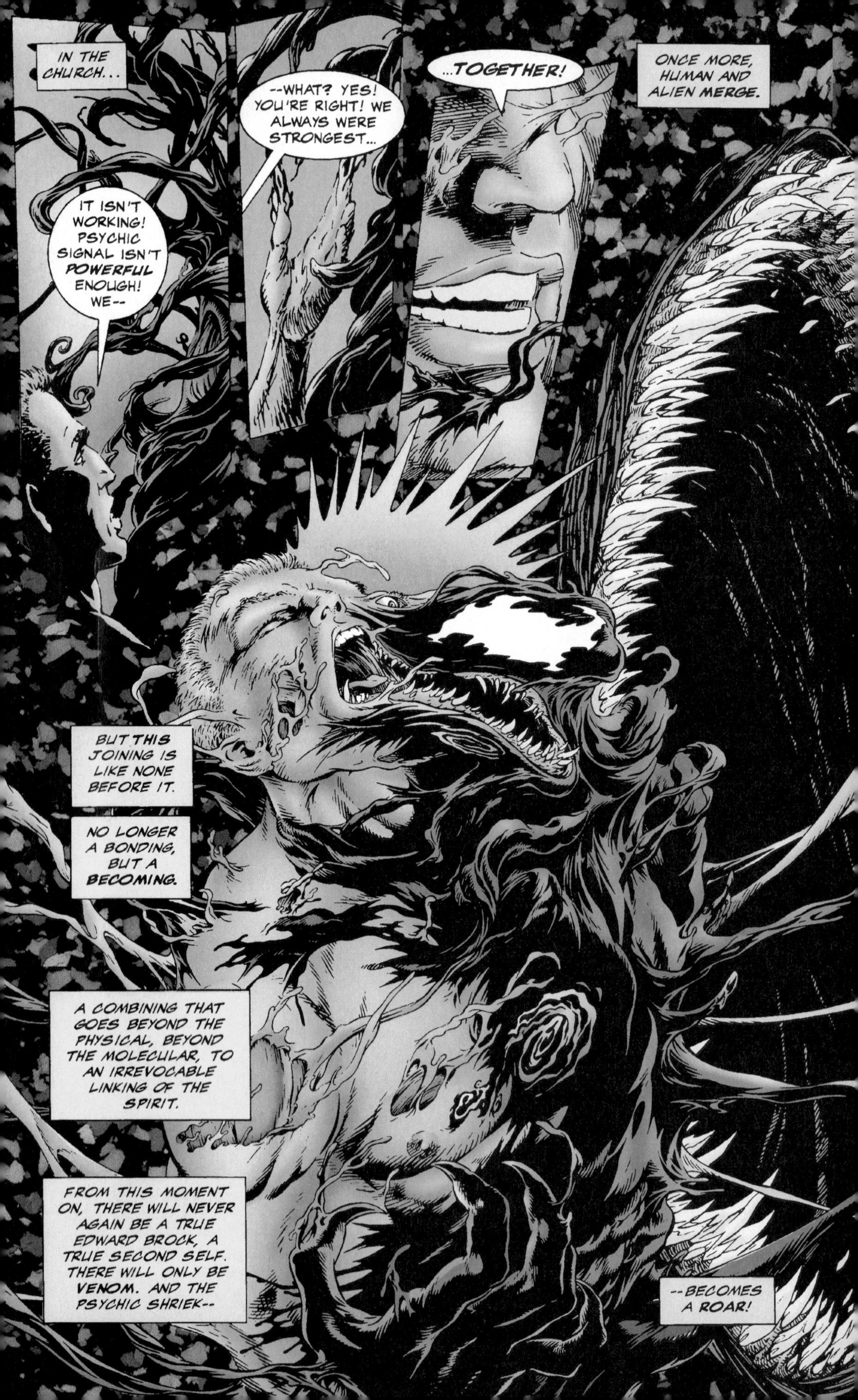
IN THE CHURCH...
IT ISN'T WORKING! PSYCHIC SIGNAL ISN'T POWERFUL ENOUGH! WE--
--WHAT? YES! YOU'RE RIGHT! WE ALWAYS WERE STRONGEST...
...TOGETHER!
ONCE MORE, HUMAN AND ALIEN MERGE.
BUT THIS JOINING IS LIKE NONE BEFORE IT.
NO LONGER A BONDING, BUT A BECOMING.
A COMBINING THAT GOES BEYOND THE PHYSICAL, BEYOND THE MOLECULAR, TO AN IRREVOCABLE LINKING OF THE SPIRIT.
FROM THIS MOMENT ON, THERE WILL NEVER AGAIN BE A TRUE EDWARD BROCK, A TRUE SECOND SELF. THERE WILL ONLY BE VENOM. AND THE PSYCHIC SHRIEK--
--BECOMES A ROAR!

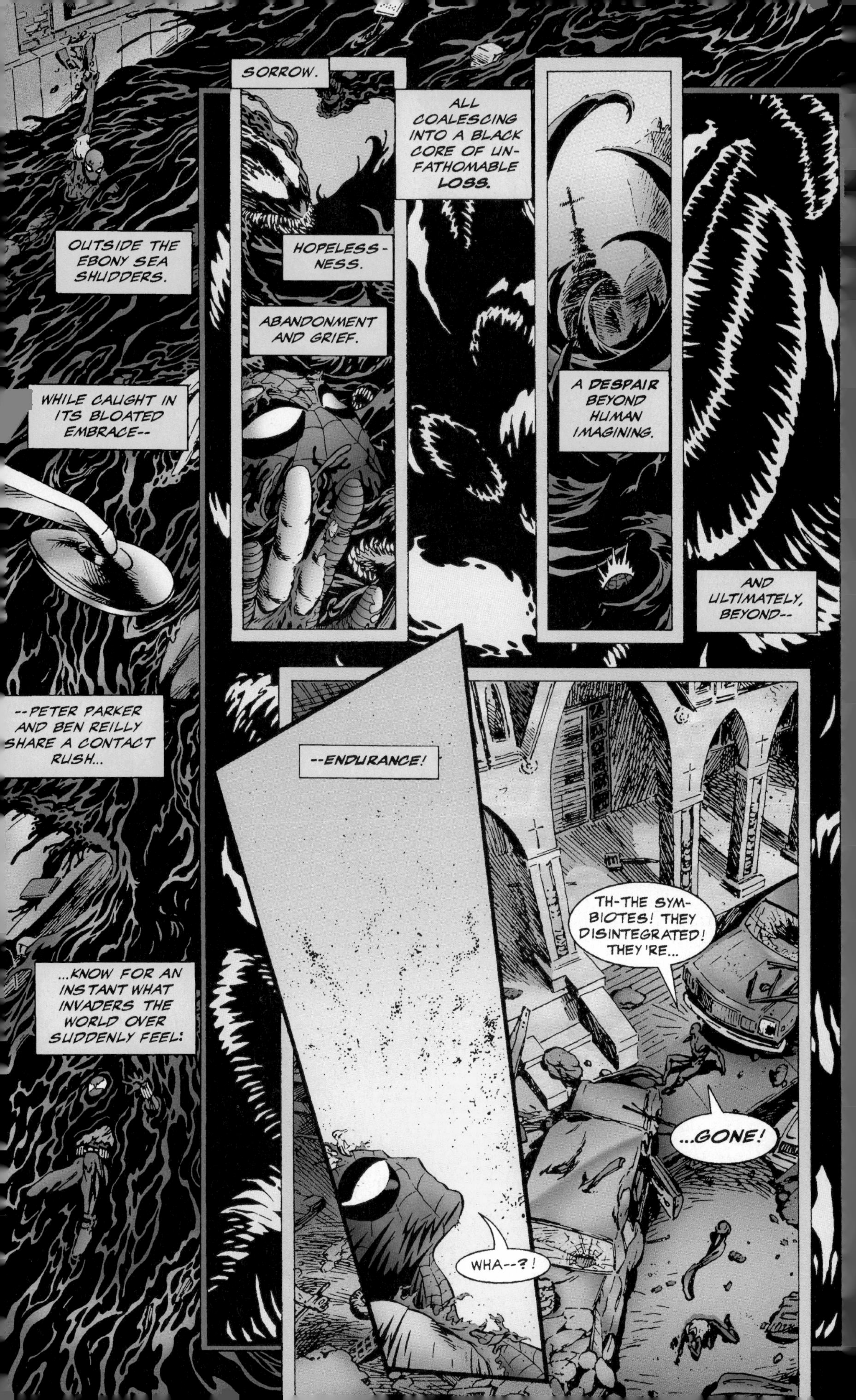
SORROW.
ALL COALESCING INTO A BLACK CORE OF UN-FATHOMABLE LOSS.
OUTSIDE THE EBONY SEA SHUDDERS.
HOPELESS-NESS.
ABANDONMENT AND GRIEF.
A DESPAIR BEYOND HUMAN IMAGINING.
WHILE CAUGHT IN ITS BLOATED EMBRACE--
AND ULTIMATELY, BEYOND--
--PETER PARKER AND BEN REILLY SHARE A CONTACT RUSH...
--ENDURANCE!
...KNOW FOR AN INSTANT WHAT INVADERS THE WORLD OVER SUDDENLY FEEL:
TH-THE SYM-BIOTES! THEY DISINTEGRATED! THEY'RE...
...GONE!
WHA--?!

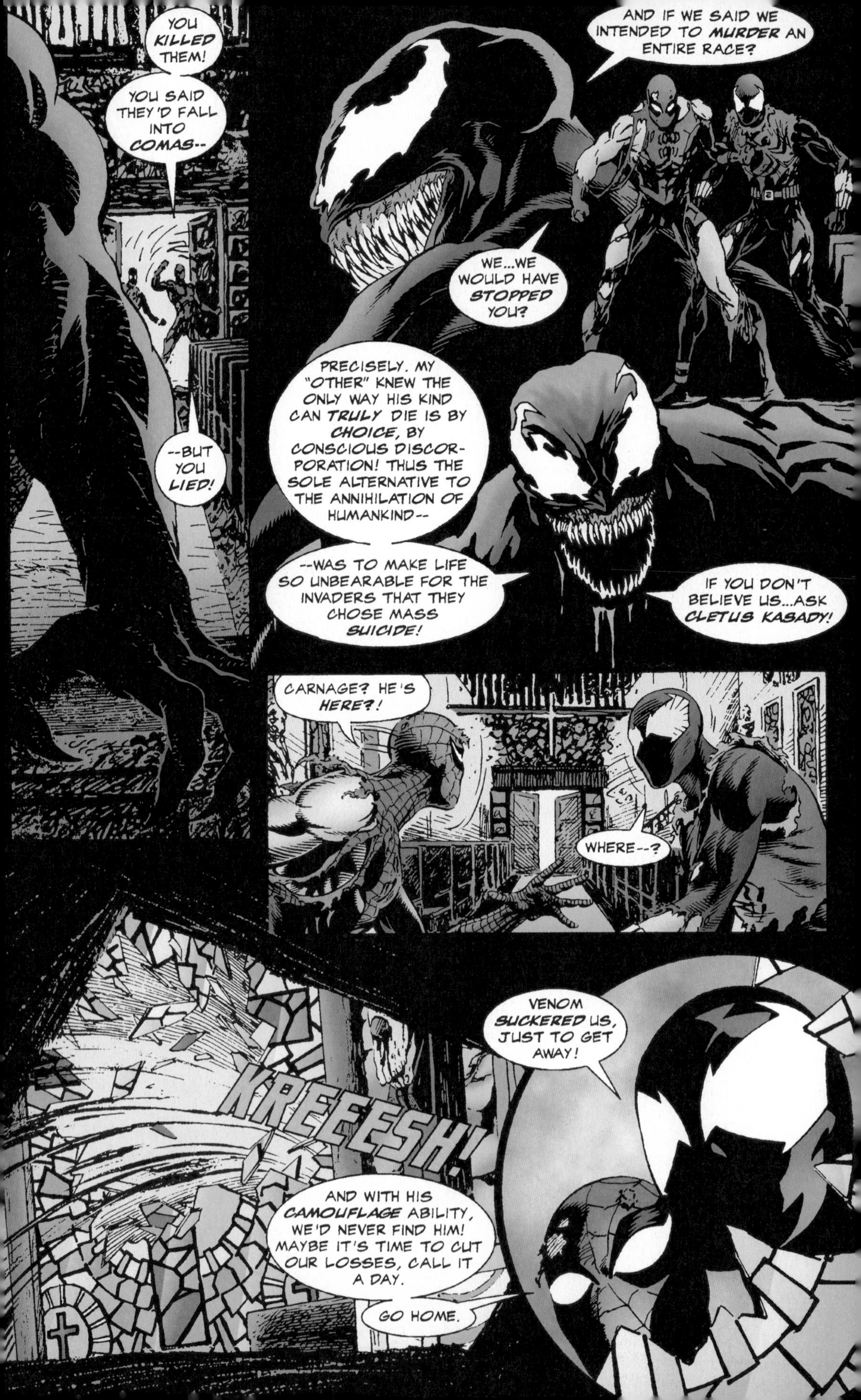
YOU KILLED THEM!
YOU SAID THEY'D FALL INTO COMAS--
--BUT YOU LIED!
AND IF WE SAID WE INTENDED TO MURDER AN ENTIRE RACE?
WE...WE WOULD HAVE STOPPED YOU?
PRECISELY. MY "OTHER" KNEW THE ONLY WAY HIS KIND CAN TRULY DIE IS BY CHOICE, BY CONSCIOUS DISCORPORATION! THUS THE SOLE ALTERNATIVE TO THE ANNIHILATION OF HUMANKIND--
--WAS TO MAKE LIFE SO UNBEARABLE FOR THE INVADERS THAT THEY CHOSE MASS SUICIDE!
IF YOU DON'T BELIEVE US...ASK CLETUS KASADY!
CARNAGE? HE'S HERE?!
WHERE--?
KREEESH!
VENOM SUCKERED US, JUST TO GET AWAY!
AND WITH HIS CAMOUFLAGE ABILITY, WE'D NEVER FIND HIM! MAYBE IT'S TIME TO CUT OUR LOSSES, CALL IT A DAY.
GO HOME.

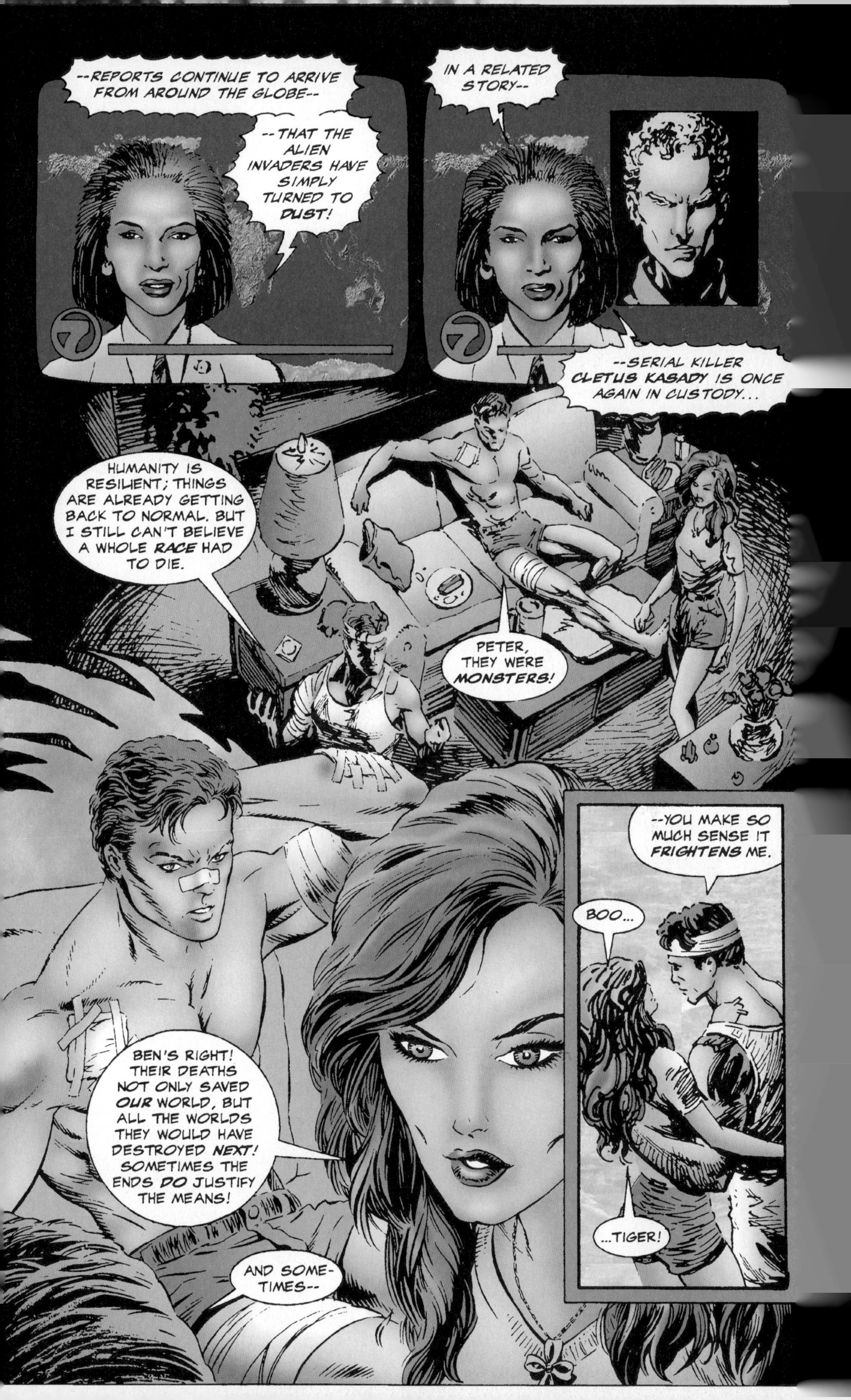

--REPORTS CONTINUE TO ARRIVE FROM AROUND THE GLOBE--
--THAT THE ALIEN INVADERS HAVE SIMPLY TURNED TO DUST!
IN A RELATED STORY--
--SERIAL KILLER CLETUS KASADY IS ONCE AGAIN IN CUSTODY...
HUMANITY IS RESILIENT; THINGS ARE ALREADY GETTING BACK TO NORMAL. BUT I STILL CAN'T BELIEVE A WHOLE RACE HAD TO DIE.
PETER, THEY WERE MONSTERS!
BEN'S RIGHT! THEIR DEATHS NOT ONLY SAVED OUR WORLD, BUT ALL THE WORLDS THEY WOULD HAVE DESTROYED NEXT! SOMETIMES THE ENDS DO JUSTIFY THE MEANS!
AND SOME-TIMES--
--YOU MAKE SO MUCH SENSE IT FRIGHTENS ME.
BOO...
...TIGER!

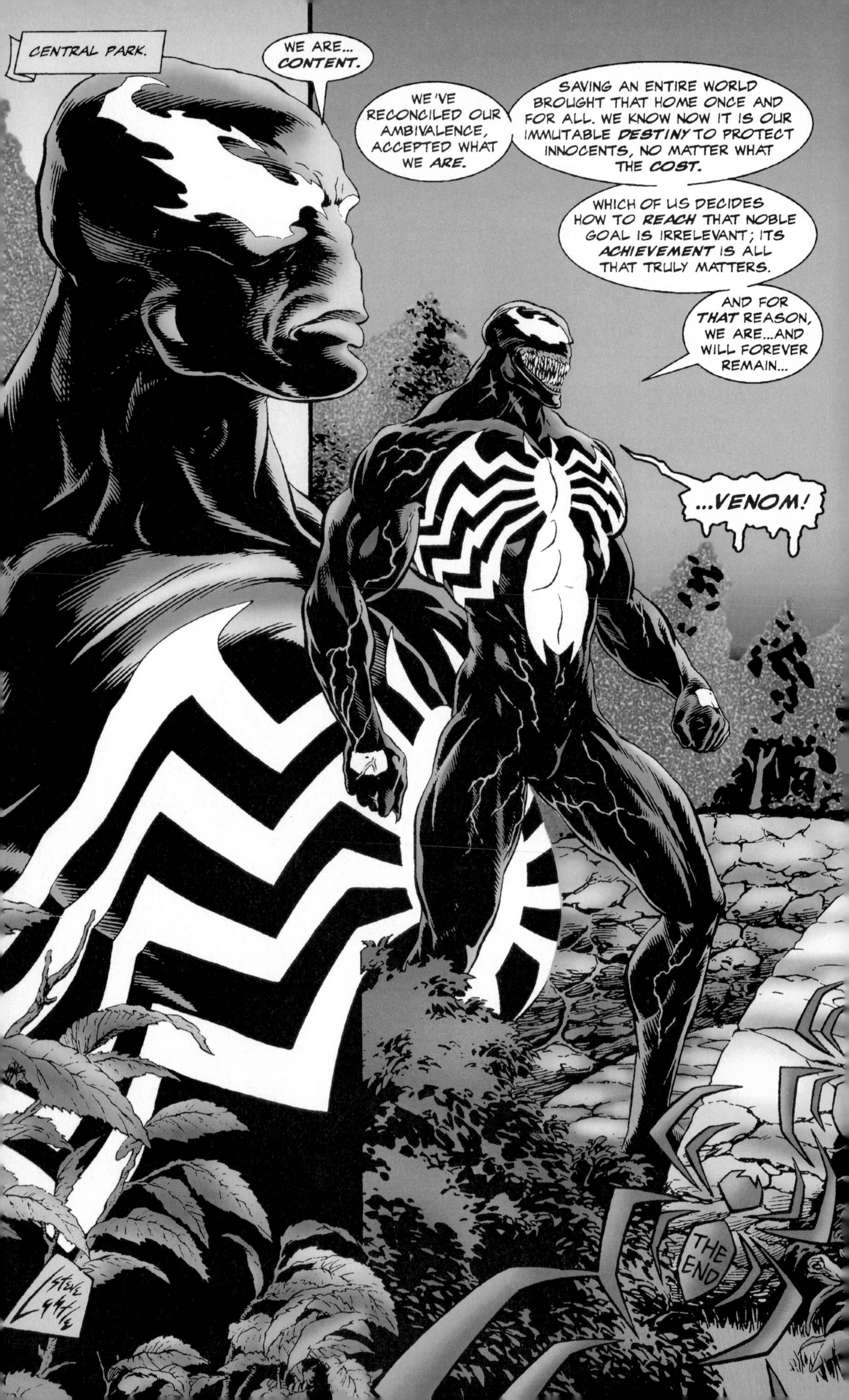
CENTRAL PARK.
WE ARE... CONTENT.
WE'VE RECONCILED OUR AMBIVALENCE, ACCEPTED WHAT WE ARE.
SAVING AN ENTIRE WORLD BROUGHT THAT HOME ONCE AND FOR ALL. WE KNOW NOW IT IS OUR IMMUTABLE DESTINY TO PROTECT INNOCENTS, NO MATTER WHAT THE COST.
WHICH OF US DECIDES HOW TO REACH THAT NOBLE GOAL IS IRRELEVANT; ITS ACHIEVEMENT IS ALL THAT TRULY MATTERS.
AND FOR THAT REASON, WE ARE...AND WILL FOREVER REMAIN...
...VENOM!
THE END

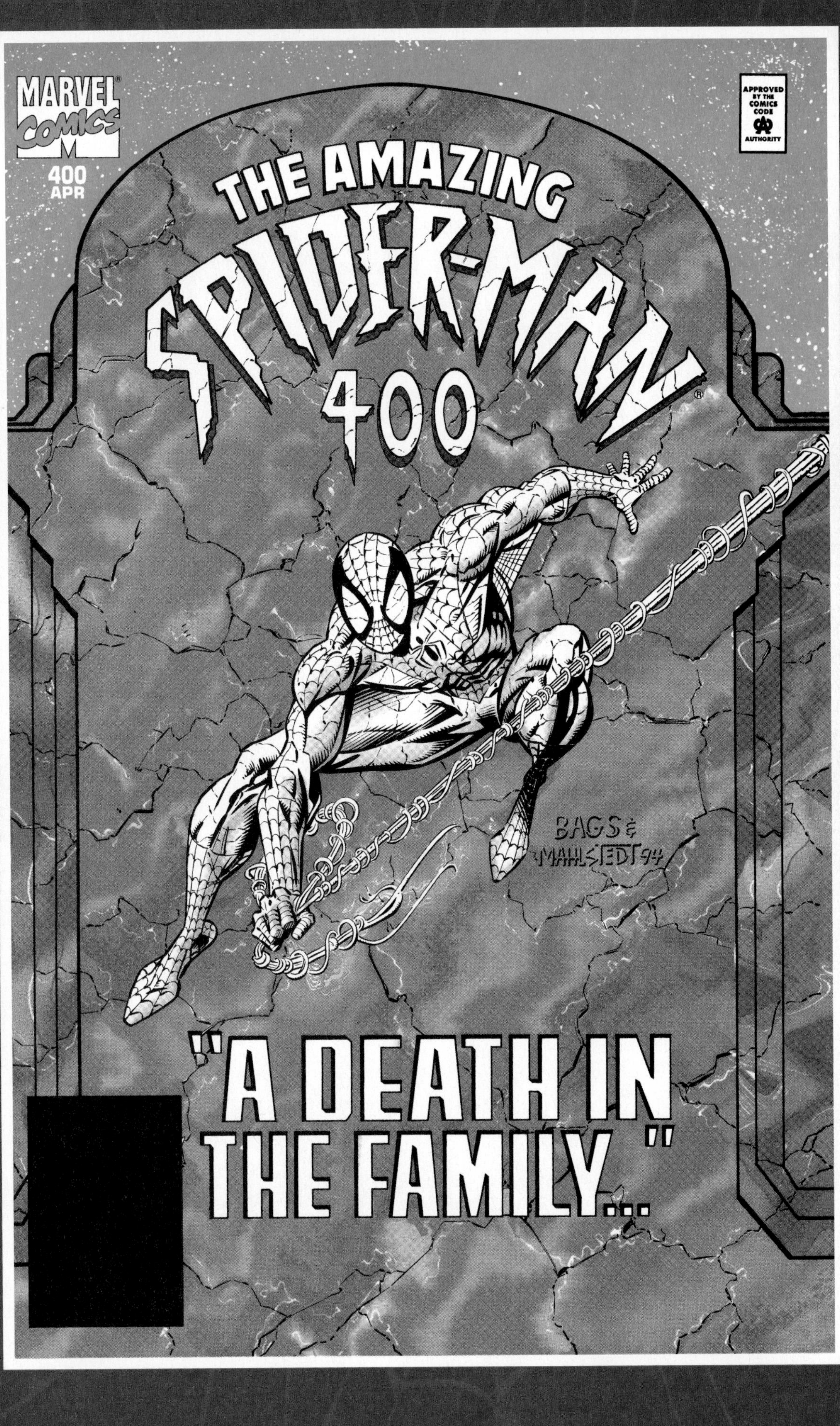
MARVEL COMICS
400 APR
APPROVED BY THE COMICS CODE AUTHORITY
THE AMAZING
SPIDER-MAN
400
BAGS & MAHLSTEDT '94
"A DEATH IN THE FAMILY..."

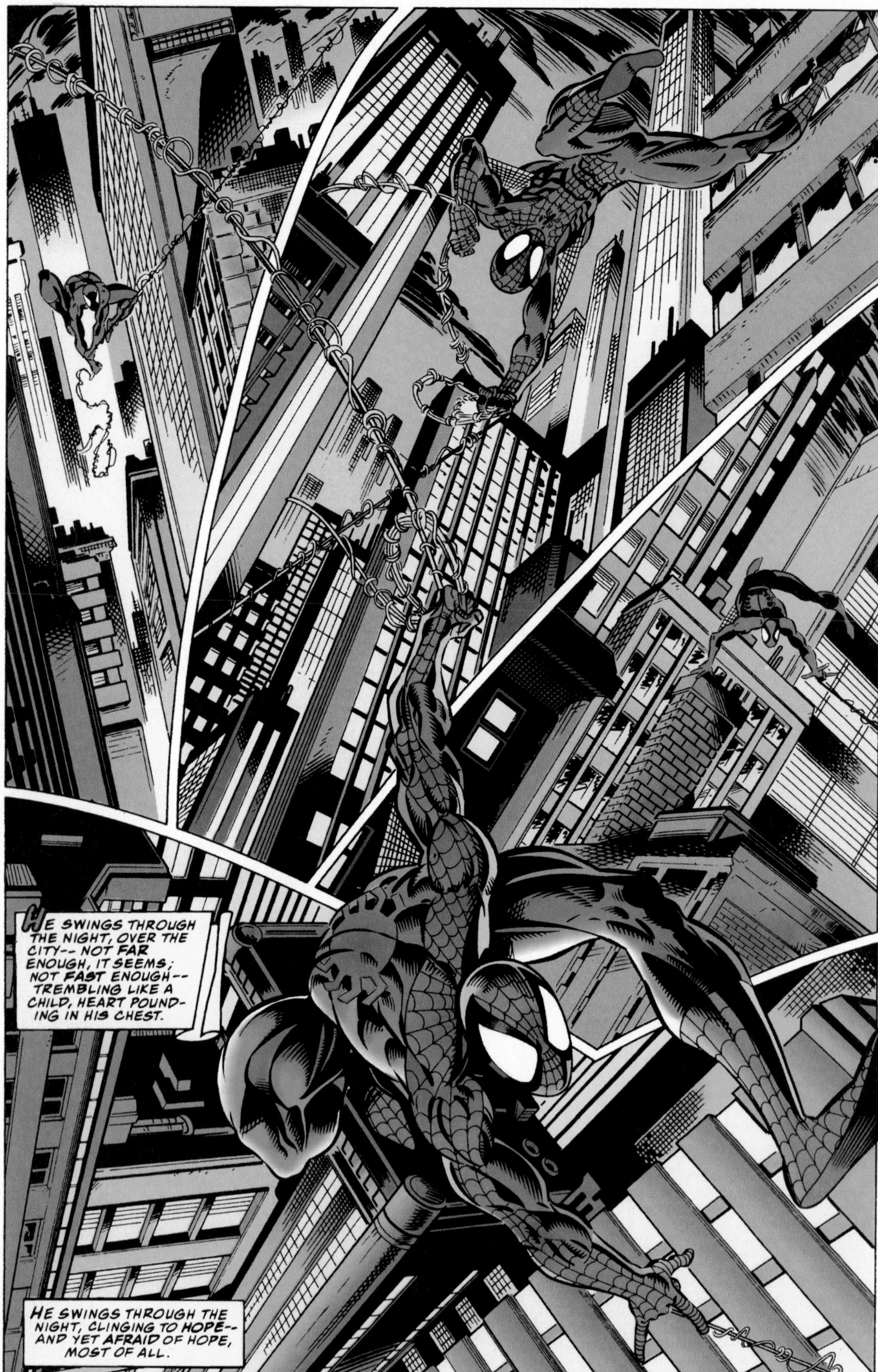
HE SWINGS THROUGH THE NIGHT, OVER THE CITY-- NOT FAR ENOUGH, IT SEEMS; NOT FAST ENOUGH-- TREMBLING LIKE A CHILD, HEART POUNDING IN HIS CHEST.
HE SWINGS THROUGH THE NIGHT, CLINGING TO HOPE-- AND YET AFRAID OF HOPE, MOST OF ALL.

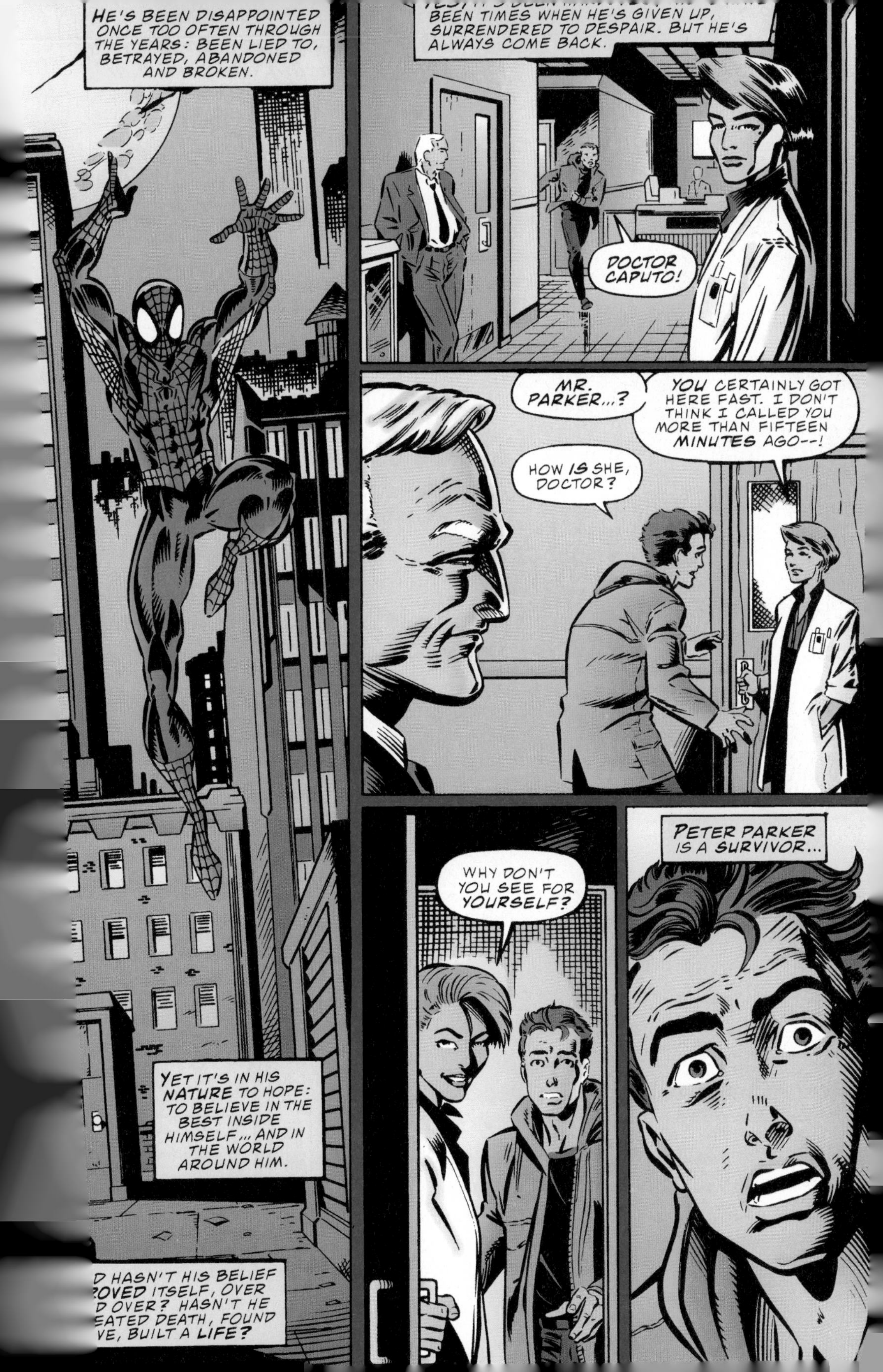
HE'S BEEN DISAPPOINTED ONCE TOO OFTEN THROUGH THE YEARS: BEEN LIED TO, BETRAYED, ABANDONED AND BROKEN.
YET IT'S IN HIS NATURE TO HOPE: TO BELIEVE IN THE BEST INSIDE HIMSELF... AND IN THE WORLD AROUND HIM.
D HASN'T HIS BELIEF ROVED ITSELF, OVER D OVER? HASN'T HE EATED DEATH, FOUND VE, BUILT A LIFE?
BEEN TIMES WHEN HE'S GIVEN UP, SURRENDERED TO DESPAIR. BUT HE'S ALWAYS COME BACK.
DOCTOR CAPUTO!
MR. PARKER...?
YOU CERTAINLY GOT HERE FAST. I DON'T THINK I CALLED YOU MORE THAN FIFTEEN MINUTES AGO--!
HOW IS SHE, DOCTOR?
WHY DON'T YOU SEE FOR YOURSELF?
PETER PARKER IS A SURVIVOR...

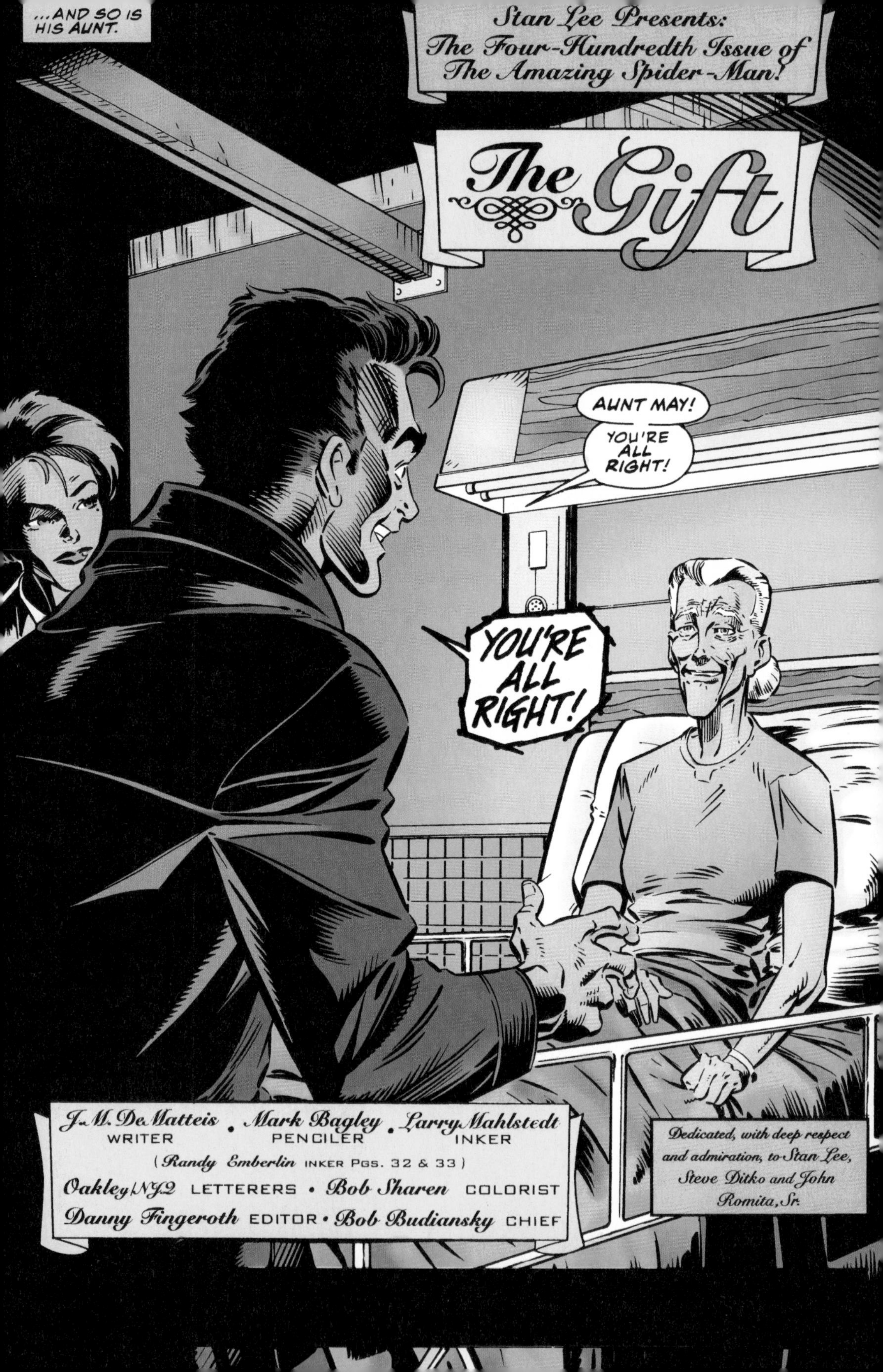
...AND SO IS HIS AUNT.
Stan Lee Presents: The Four-Hundredth Issue of The Amazing Spider-Man!
The Gift
AUNT MAY!
YOU'RE ALL RIGHT!
YOU'RE ALL RIGHT!
J. M. DeMatteis WRITER • Mark Bagley PENCILER • Larry Mahlstedt INKER
(Randy Emberlin INKER PGS. 32 & 33)
Oakley/NJQ LETTERERS • Bob Sharen COLORIST
Danny Fingeroth EDITOR • Bob Budiansky CHIEF
Dedicated, with deep respect and admiration, to Stan Lee, Steve Ditko and John Romita, Sr.

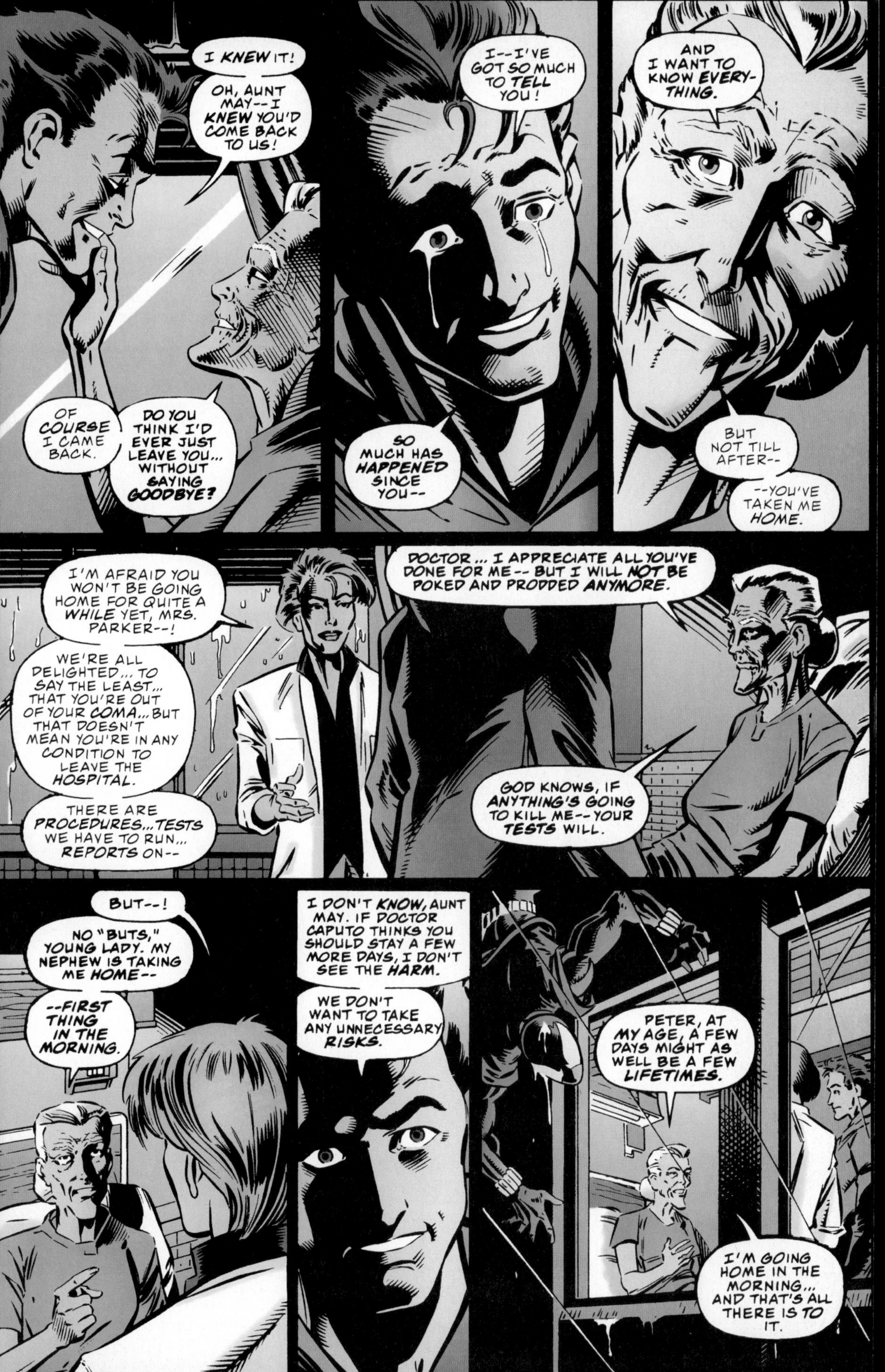

I KNEW IT!
OH, AUNT MAY-- I KNEW YOU'D COME BACK TO US!
OF COURSE I CAME BACK.
DO YOU THINK I'D EVER JUST LEAVE YOU... WITHOUT SAYING GOODBYE?
I--I'VE GOT SO MUCH TO TELL YOU!
SO MUCH HAS HAPPENED SINCE YOU--
AND I WANT TO KNOW EVERY-THING.
BUT NOT TILL AFTER--
--YOU'VE TAKEN ME HOME.
I'M AFRAID YOU WON'T BE GOING HOME FOR QUITE A WHILE YET, MRS. PARKER--!
WE'RE ALL DELIGHTED... TO SAY THE LEAST... THAT YOU'RE OUT OF YOUR COMA... BUT THAT DOESN'T MEAN YOU'RE IN ANY CONDITION TO LEAVE THE HOSPITAL.
THERE ARE PROCEDURES... TESTS WE HAVE TO RUN... REPORTS ON--
DOCTOR... I APPRECIATE ALL YOU'VE DONE FOR ME-- BUT I WILL NOT BE POKED AND PRODDED ANYMORE.
GOD KNOWS, IF ANYTHING'S GOING TO KILL ME-- YOUR TESTS WILL.
BUT--!
NO "BUTS," YOUNG LADY. MY NEPHEW IS TAKING ME HOME--
--FIRST THING IN THE MORNING.
I DON'T KNOW, AUNT MAY. IF DOCTOR CAPUTO THINKS YOU SHOULD STAY A FEW MORE DAYS, I DON'T SEE THE HARM.
WE DON'T WANT TO TAKE ANY UNNECESSARY RISKS.
PETER, AT MY AGE, A FEW DAYS MIGHT AS WELL BE A FEW LIFETIMES.
I'M GOING HOME IN THE MORNING... AND THAT'S ALL THERE IS TO IT.

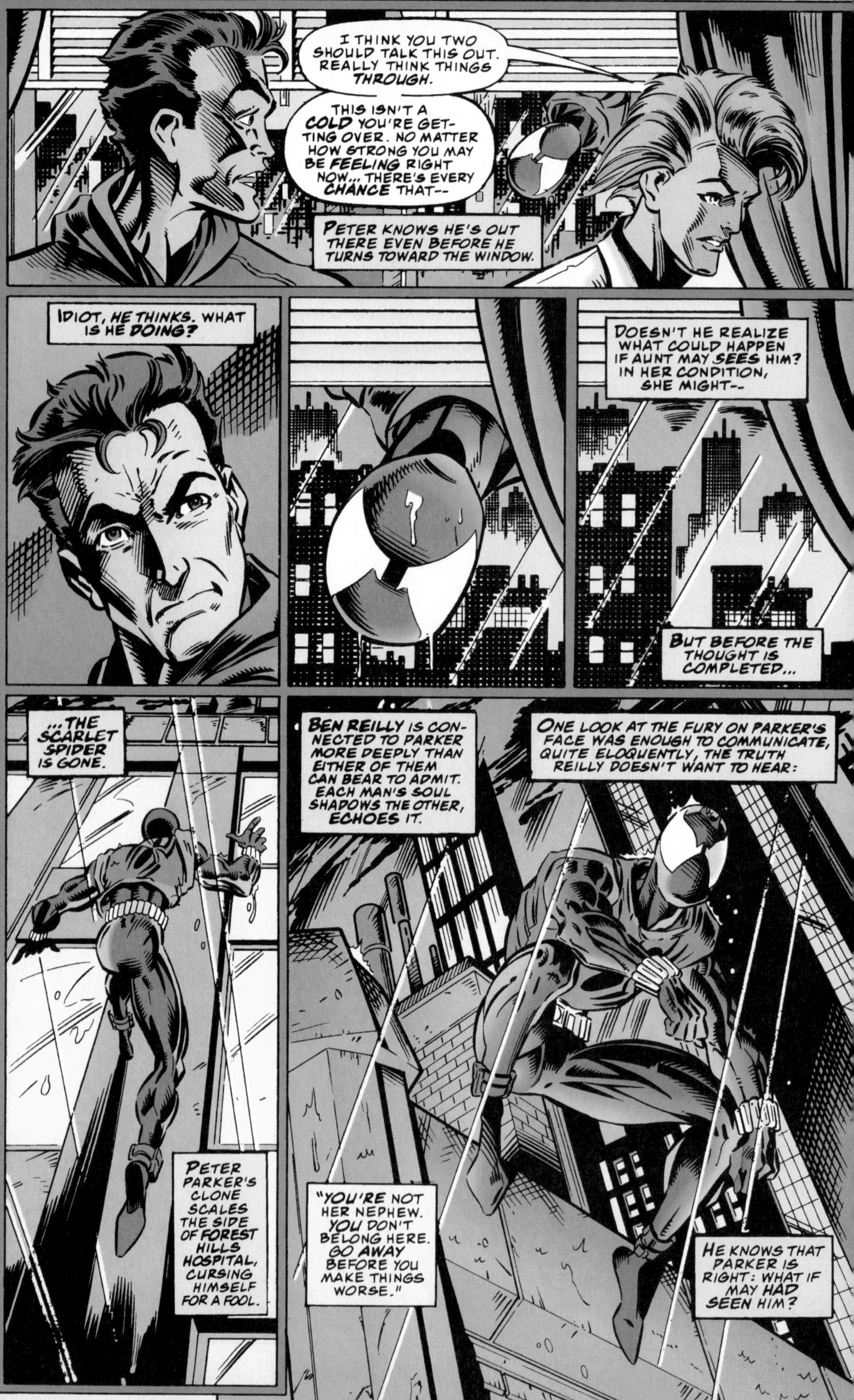

I THINK YOU TWO SHOULD TALK THIS OUT. REALLY THINK THINGS THROUGH.
THIS ISN'T A COLD YOU'RE GETTING OVER. NO MATTER HOW STRONG YOU MAY BE FEELING RIGHT NOW... THERE'S EVERY CHANCE THAT--
PETER KNOWS HE'S OUT THERE EVEN BEFORE HE TURNS TOWARD THE WINDOW.
IDIOT, HE THINKS. WHAT IS HE DOING?
DOESN'T HE REALIZE WHAT COULD HAPPEN IF AUNT MAY SEES HIM? IN HER CONDITION, SHE MIGHT--
BUT BEFORE THE THOUGHT IS COMPLETED...
...THE SCARLET SPIDER IS GONE.
PETER PARKER'S CLONE SCALES THE SIDE OF FOREST HILLS HOSPITAL, CURSING HIMSELF FOR A FOOL.
BEN REILLY IS CONNECTED TO PARKER MORE DEEPLY THAN EITHER OF THEM CAN BEAR TO ADMIT. EACH MAN'S SOUL SHADOWS THE OTHER, ECHOES IT.
ONE LOOK AT THE FURY ON PARKER'S FACE WAS ENOUGH TO COMMUNICATE, QUITE ELOQUENTLY, THE TRUTH REILLY DOESN'T WANT TO HEAR:
"YOU'RE NOT HER NEPHEW. YOU DON'T BELONG HERE. GO AWAY BEFORE YOU MAKE THINGS WORSE."
HE KNOWS THAT PARKER IS RIGHT: WHAT IF MAY HAD SEEN HIM?

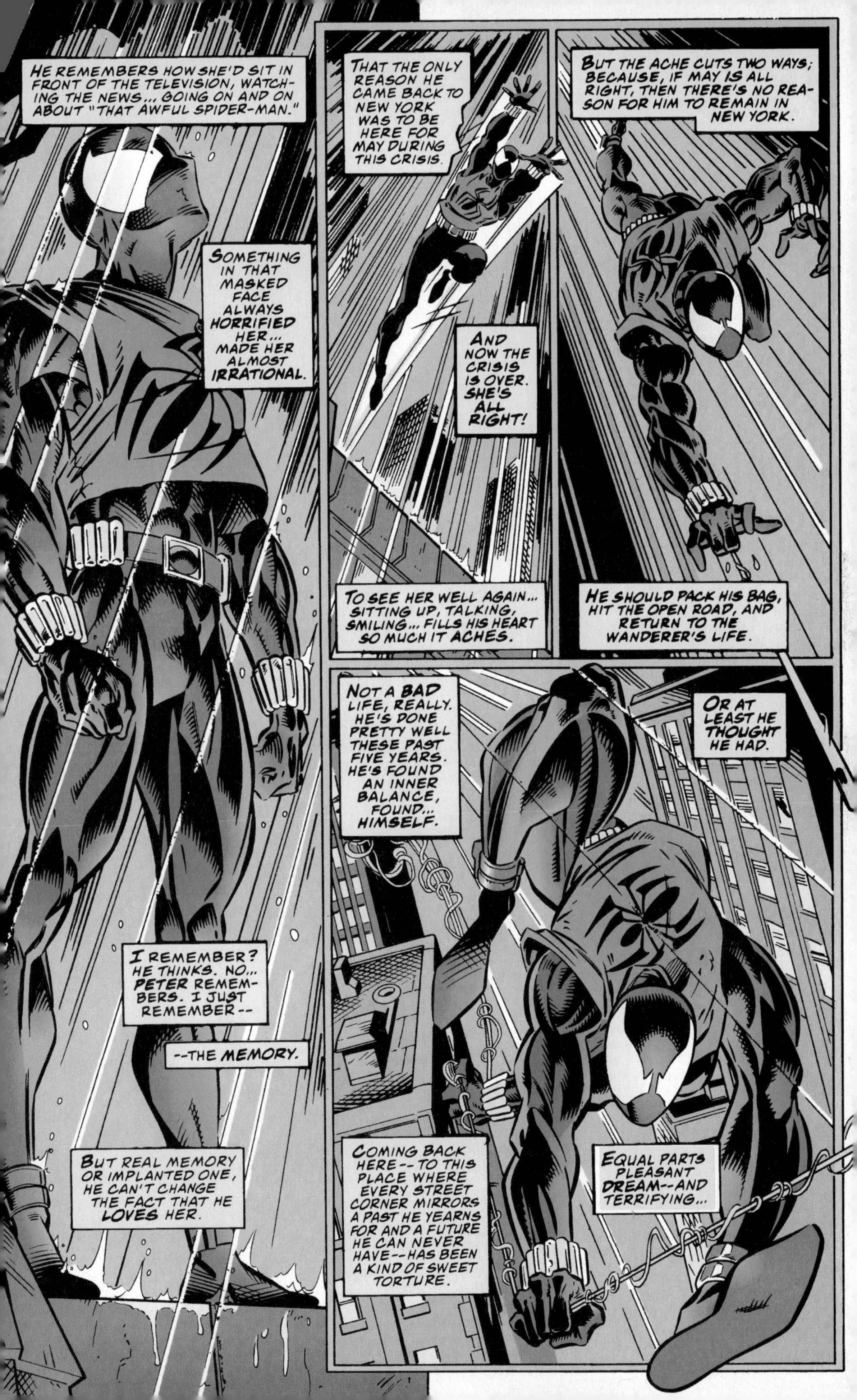
HE REMEMBERS HOW SHE'D SIT IN FRONT OF THE TELEVISION, WATCHING THE NEWS... GOING ON AND ON ABOUT "THAT AWFUL SPIDER-MAN."
SOMETHING IN THAT MASKED FACE ALWAYS HORRIFIED HER... MADE HER ALMOST IRRATIONAL.
I REMEMBER? HE THINKS. NO... PETER REMEMBERS. I JUST REMEMBER--
--THE MEMORY.
BUT REAL MEMORY OR IMPLANTED ONE, HE CAN'T CHANGE THE FACT THAT HE LOVES HER.
THAT THE ONLY REASON HE CAME BACK TO NEW YORK WAS TO BE HERE FOR MAY DURING THIS CRISIS.
AND NOW THE CRISIS IS OVER. SHE'S ALL RIGHT!
TO SEE HER WELL AGAIN... SITTING UP, TALKING, SMILING... FILLS HIS HEART SO MUCH IT ACHES.
BUT THE ACHE CUTS TWO WAYS; BECAUSE, IF MAY IS ALL RIGHT, THEN THERE'S NO REASON FOR HIM TO REMAIN IN NEW YORK.
HE SHOULD PACK HIS BAG, HIT THE OPEN ROAD, AND RETURN TO THE WANDERER'S LIFE.
NOT A BAD LIFE, REALLY. HE'S DONE PRETTY WELL THESE PAST FIVE YEARS. HE'S FOUND AN INNER BALANCE, FOUND... HIMSELF.
OR AT LEAST HE THOUGHT HE HAD.
COMING BACK HERE--TO THIS PLACE WHERE EVERY STREET CORNER MIRRORS A PAST HE YEARNS FOR AND A FUTURE HE CAN NEVER HAVE--HAS BEEN A KIND OF SWEET TORTURE.
EQUAL PARTS PLEASANT DREAM--AND TERRIFYING...

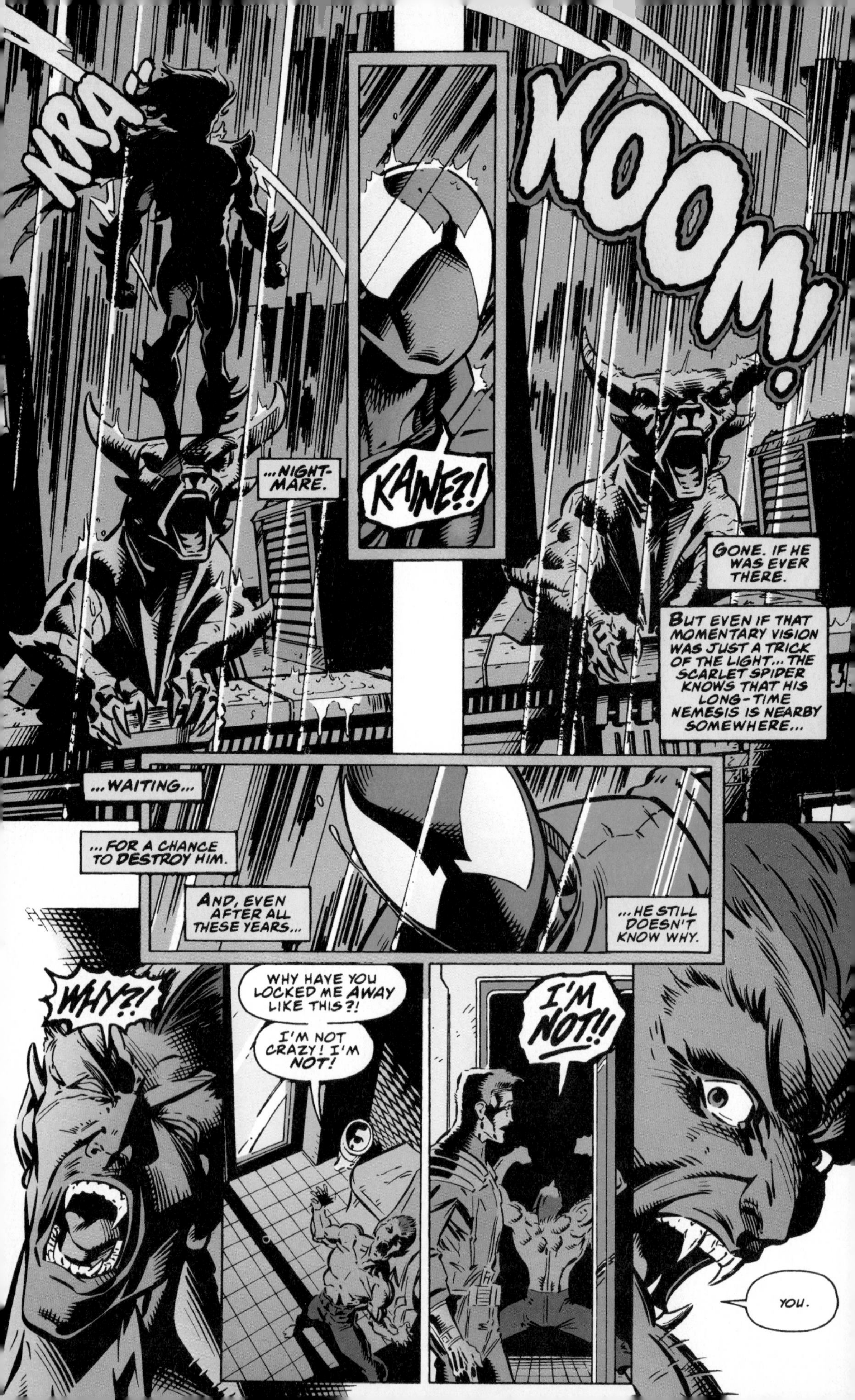
KRA-
...NIGHT-
MARE.
KAINE?!
KOOM!
GONE. IF HE WAS EVER THERE.
BUT EVEN IF THAT MOMENTARY VISION WAS JUST A TRICK OF THE LIGHT... THE SCARLET SPIDER KNOWS THAT HIS LONG-TIME NEMESIS IS NEARBY SOMEWHERE...
...WAITING...
...FOR A CHANCE TO DESTROY HIM.
AND, EVEN AFTER ALL THESE YEARS...
...HE STILL DOESN'T KNOW WHY.
WHY?!
WHY HAVE YOU LOCKED ME AWAY LIKE THIS?!
I'M NOT CRAZY! I'M NOT!
I'M NOT!!
YOU.

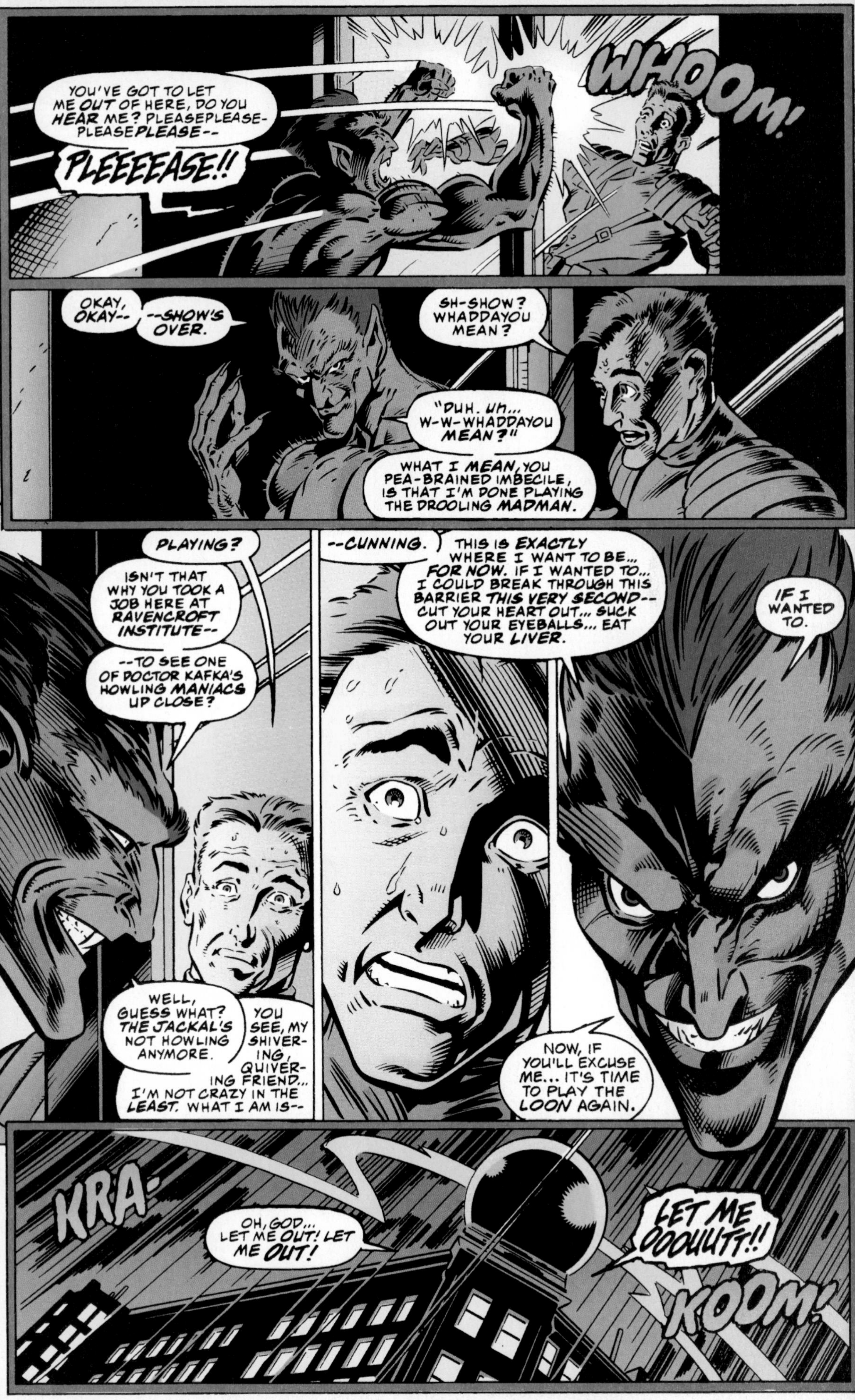
YOU'VE GOT TO LET ME OUT OF HERE, DO YOU HEAR ME? PLEASEPLEASE-PLEASEPLEASE--
PLEEEEEASE!!
WHOOOM!
OKAY, OKAY--
--SHOW'S OVER.
SH-SHOW? WHADDAYOU MEAN?
"DUH. UH... W-W-WHADDAYOU MEAN?"
WHAT I MEAN, YOU PEA-BRAINED IMBECILE, IS THAT I'M DONE PLAYING THE DROOLING MADMAN.
PLAYING?
ISN'T THAT WHY YOU TOOK A JOB HERE AT RAVENCROFT INSTITUTE--
--TO SEE ONE OF DOCTOR KAFKA'S HOWLING MANIACS UP CLOSE?
WELL, GUESS WHAT? THE JACKAL'S NOT HOWLING ANYMORE.
YOU SEE, MY SHIVERING, QUIVERING FRIEND... I'M NOT CRAZY IN THE LEAST. WHAT I AM IS--
--CUNNING.
THIS IS EXACTLY WHERE I WANT TO BE... FOR NOW. IF I WANTED TO... I COULD BREAK THROUGH THIS BARRIER THIS VERY SECOND--CUT YOUR HEART OUT... SUCK OUT YOUR EYEBALLS... EAT YOUR LIVER.
IF I WANTED TO.
NOW, IF YOU'LL EXCUSE ME... IT'S TIME TO PLAY THE LOON AGAIN.
KRA-
OH, GOD... LET ME OUT! LET ME OUT!
LET ME OOOUUUTT!!
KOOM!

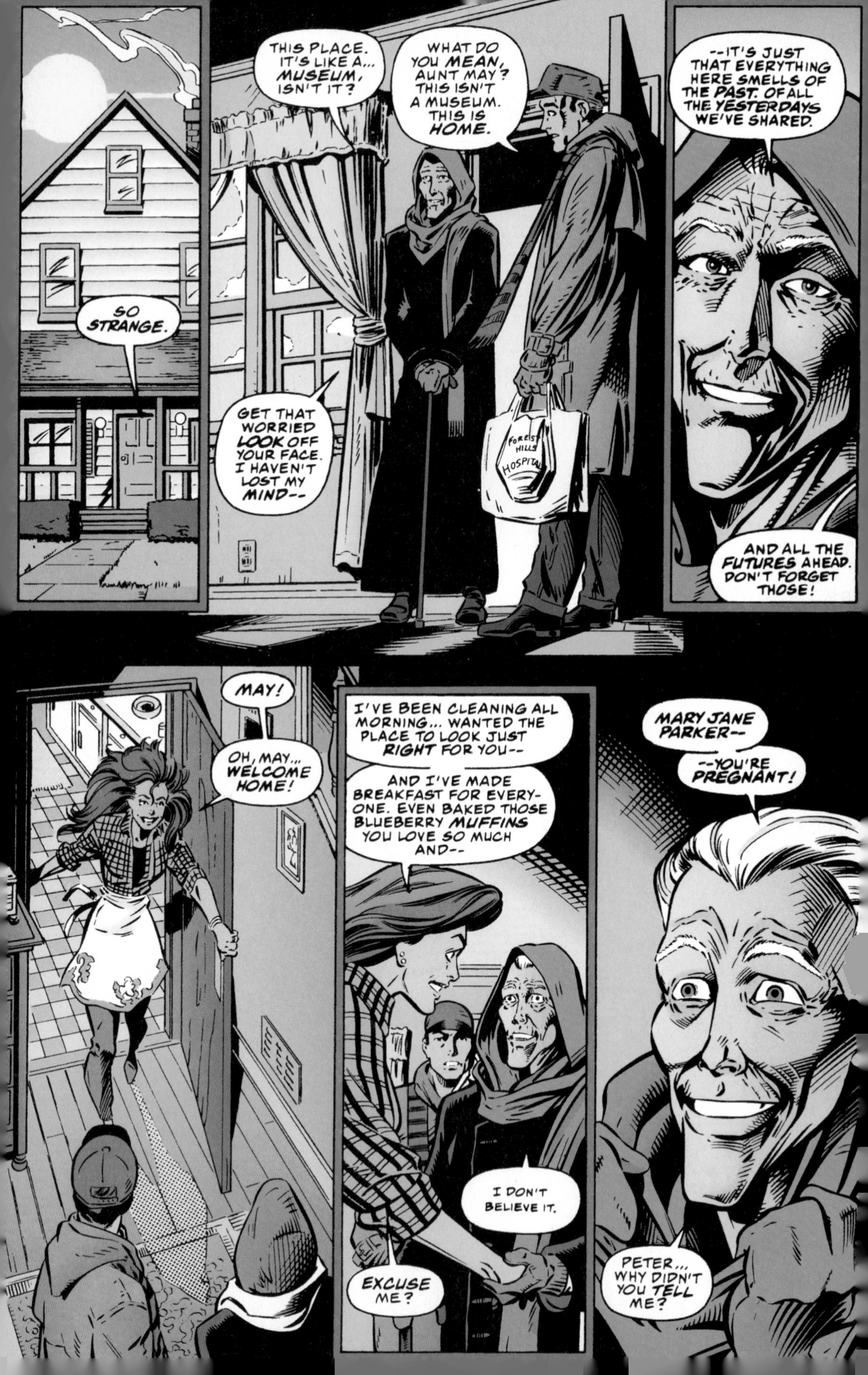
SO STRANGE.
THIS PLACE. IT'S LIKE A... MUSEUM, ISN'T IT?
WHAT DO YOU MEAN, AUNT MAY? THIS ISN'T A MUSEUM. THIS IS HOME.
GET THAT WORRIED LOOK OFF YOUR FACE. I HAVEN'T LOST MY MIND--
FOREST HILLS HOSPITAL
--IT'S JUST THAT EVERYTHING HERE SMELLS OF THE PAST. OF ALL THE YESTERDAYS WE'VE SHARED.
AND ALL THE FUTURES AHEAD. DON'T FORGET THOSE!
MAY!
OH, MAY... WELCOME HOME!
I'VE BEEN CLEANING ALL MORNING... WANTED THE PLACE TO LOOK JUST RIGHT FOR YOU--
AND I'VE MADE BREAKFAST FOR EVERY-ONE. EVEN BAKED THOSE BLUEBERRY MUFFINS YOU LOVE SO MUCH AND--
I DON'T BELIEVE IT.
EXCUSE ME?
MARY JANE PARKER--
--YOU'RE PREGNANT!
PETER... WHY DIDN'T YOU TELL ME?

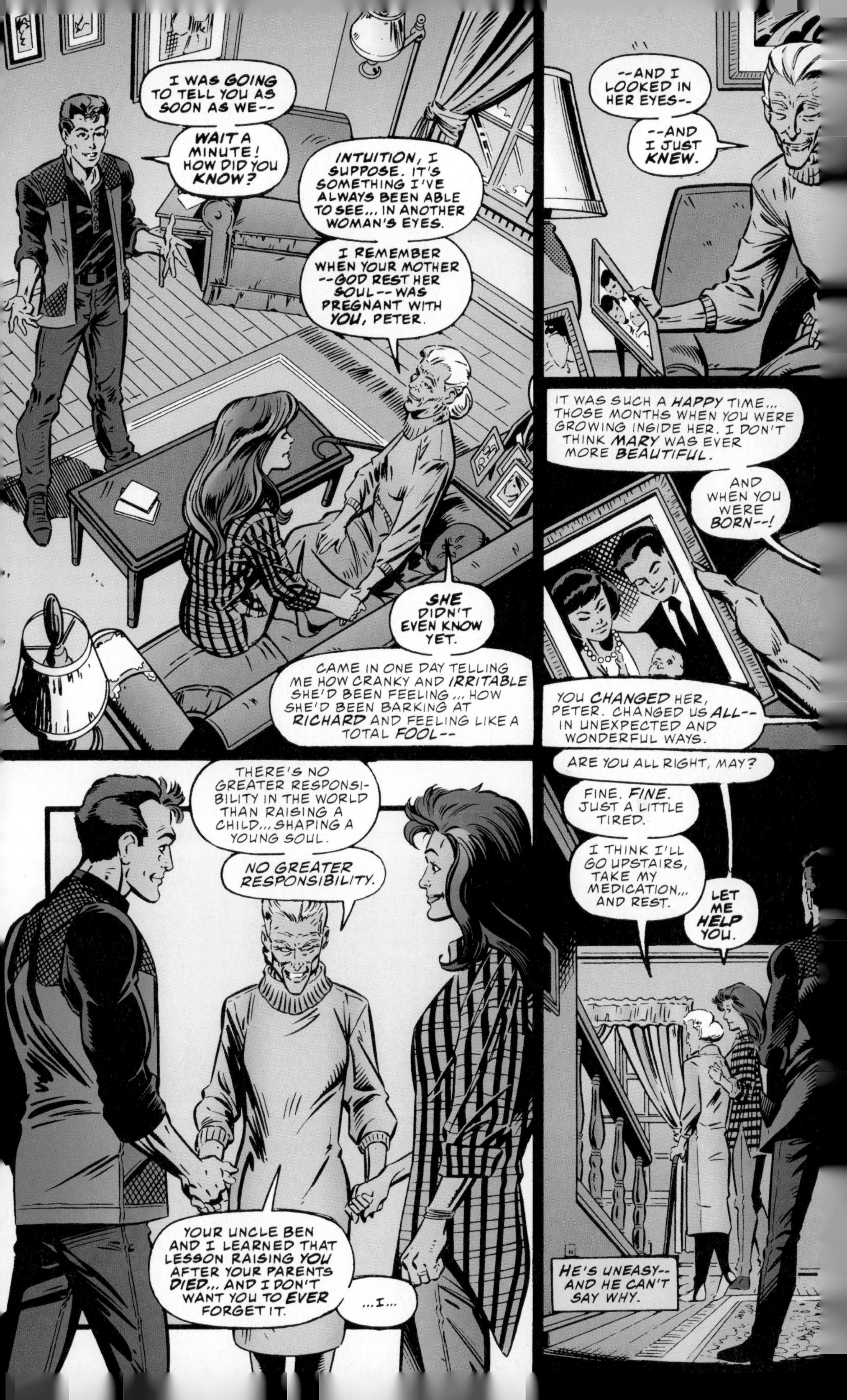
I WAS GOING TO TELL YOU AS SOON AS WE--
WAIT A MINUTE! HOW DID YOU KNOW?
INTUITION, I SUPPOSE. IT'S SOMETHING I'VE ALWAYS BEEN ABLE TO SEE... IN ANOTHER WOMAN'S EYES.
I REMEMBER WHEN YOUR MOTHER --GOD REST HER SOUL-- WAS PREGNANT WITH YOU, PETER.
SHE DIDN'T EVEN KNOW YET.
CAME IN ONE DAY TELLING ME HOW CRANKY AND IRRITABLE SHE'D BEEN FEELING... HOW SHE'D BEEN BARKING AT RICHARD AND FEELING LIKE A TOTAL FOOL--
--AND I LOOKED IN HER EYES--
--AND I JUST KNEW.
IT WAS SUCH A HAPPY TIME... THOSE MONTHS WHEN YOU WERE GROWING INSIDE HER. I DON'T THINK MARY WAS EVER MORE BEAUTIFUL.
AND WHEN YOU WERE BORN--!
YOU CHANGED HER, PETER. CHANGED US ALL-- IN UNEXPECTED AND WONDERFUL WAYS.
THERE'S NO GREATER RESPONSIBILITY IN THE WORLD THAN RAISING A CHILD... SHAPING A YOUNG SOUL.
NO GREATER RESPONSIBILITY.
YOUR UNCLE BEN AND I LEARNED THAT LESSON RAISING YOU AFTER YOUR PARENTS DIED... AND I DON'T WANT YOU TO EVER FORGET IT.
...I...
ARE YOU ALL RIGHT, MAY?
FINE. FINE. JUST A LITTLE TIRED.
I THINK I'LL GO UPSTAIRS, TAKE MY MEDICATION... AND REST.
LET ME HELP YOU.
HE'S UNEASY-- AND HE CAN'T SAY WHY.

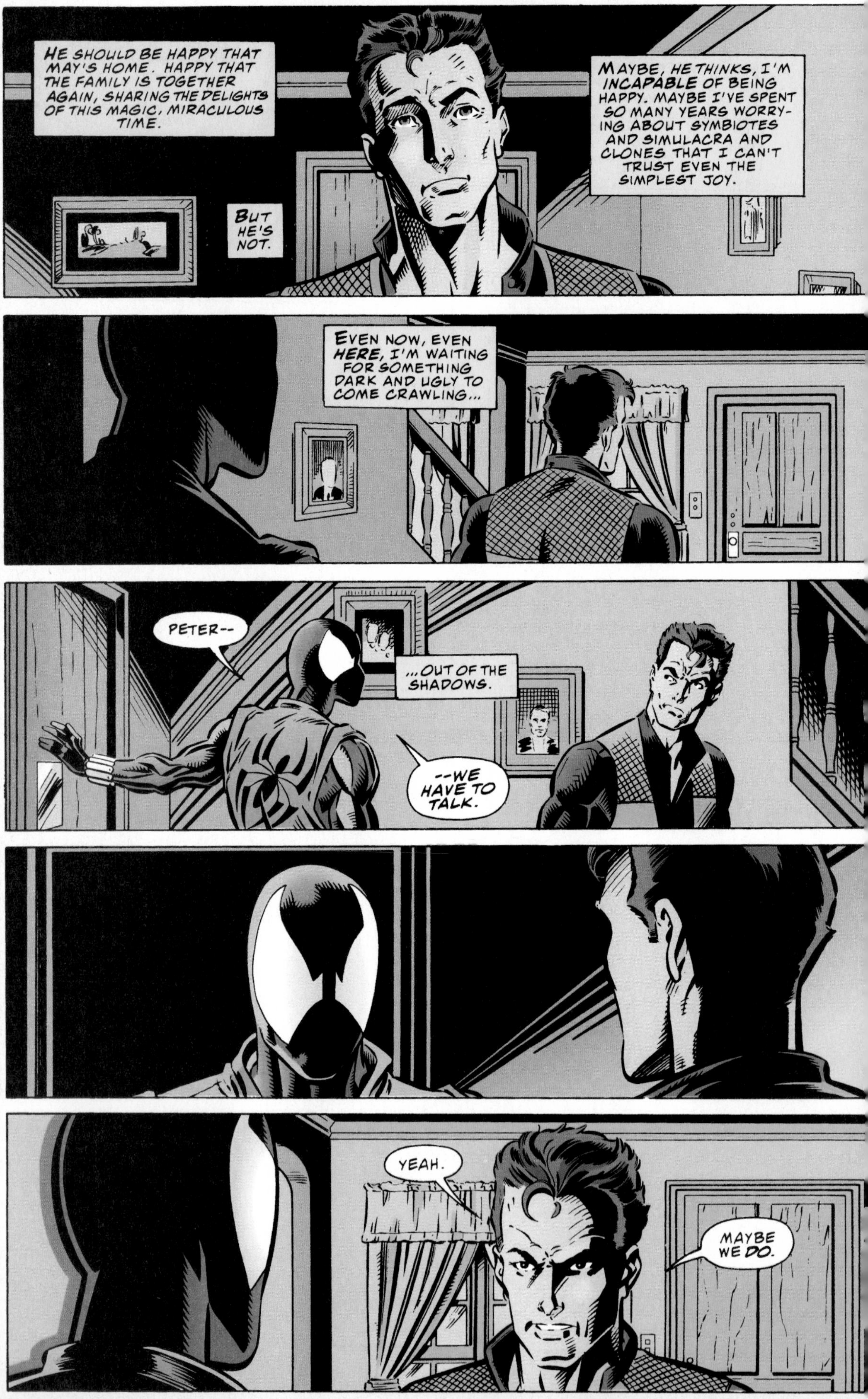

HE SHOULD BE HAPPY THAT MAY'S HOME. HAPPY THAT THE FAMILY IS TOGETHER AGAIN, SHARING THE DELIGHTS OF THIS MAGIC, MIRACULOUS TIME.
BUT HE'S NOT.
MAYBE, HE THINKS, I'M INCAPABLE OF BEING HAPPY. MAYBE I'VE SPENT SO MANY YEARS WORRYING ABOUT SYMBIOTES AND SIMULACRA AND CLONES THAT I CAN'T TRUST EVEN THE SIMPLEST JOY.
EVEN NOW, EVEN HERE, I'M WAITING FOR SOMETHING DARK AND UGLY TO COME CRAWLING...
PETER--
...OUT OF THE SHADOWS.
--WE HAVE TO TALK.
YEAH.
MAYBE WE DO.

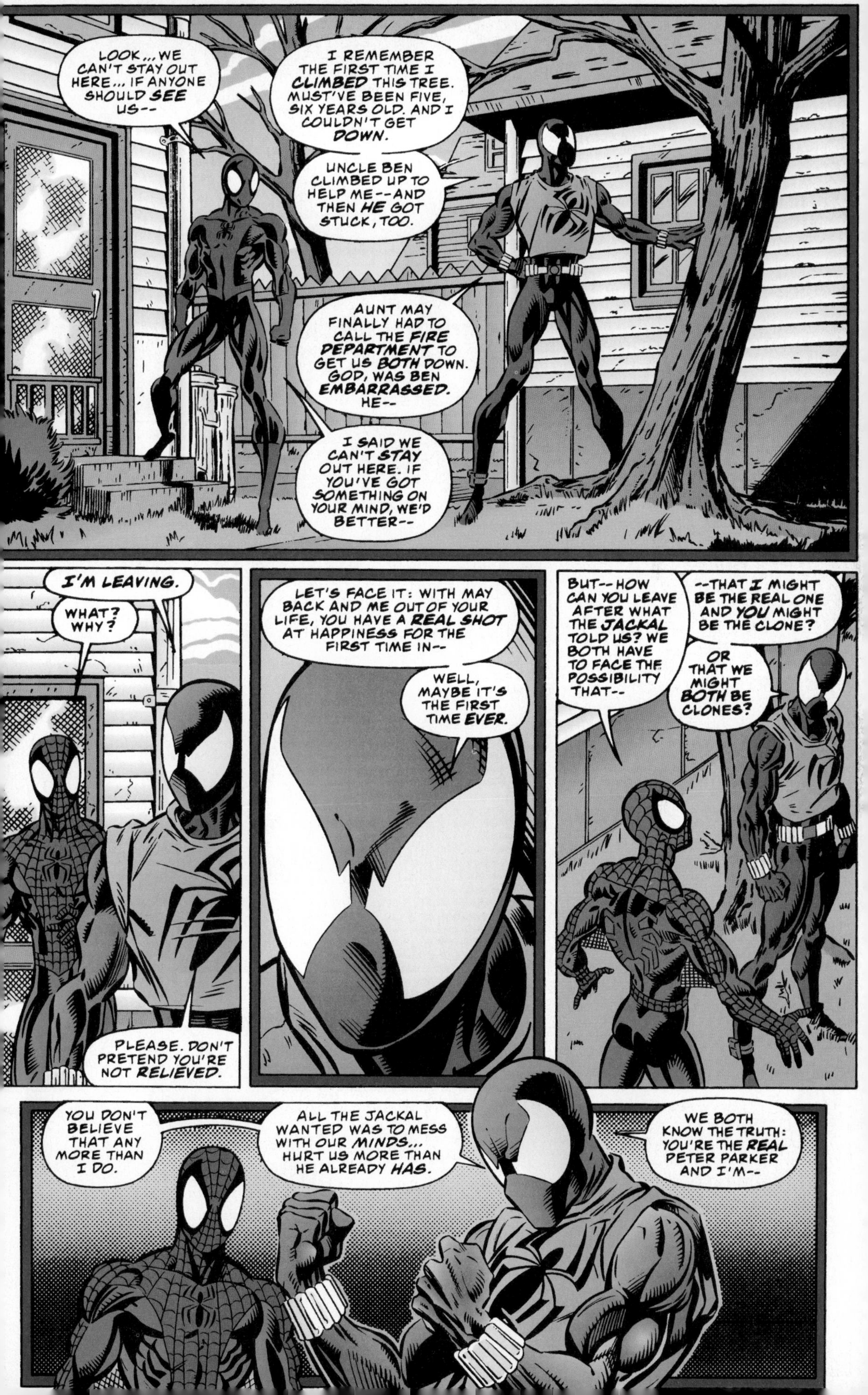

LOOK... WE CAN'T STAY OUT HERE... IF ANYONE SHOULD SEE US--
I REMEMBER THE FIRST TIME I CLIMBED THIS TREE. MUST'VE BEEN FIVE, SIX YEARS OLD. AND I COULDN'T GET DOWN.
UNCLE BEN CLIMBED UP TO HELP ME--AND THEN HE GOT STUCK, TOO.
AUNT MAY FINALLY HAD TO CALL THE FIRE DEPARTMENT TO GET US BOTH DOWN. GOD, WAS BEN EMBARRASSED. HE--
I SAID WE CAN'T STAY OUT HERE. IF YOU'VE GOT SOMETHING ON YOUR MIND, WE'D BETTER--
I'M LEAVING.
WHAT? WHY?
PLEASE. DON'T PRETEND YOU'RE NOT RELIEVED.
LET'S FACE IT: WITH MAY BACK AND ME OUT OF YOUR LIFE, YOU HAVE A REAL SHOT AT HAPPINESS FOR THE FIRST TIME IN--
WELL, MAYBE IT'S THE FIRST TIME EVER.
BUT--HOW CAN YOU LEAVE AFTER WHAT THE JACKAL TOLD US? WE BOTH HAVE TO FACE THE POSSIBILITY THAT--
--THAT I MIGHT BE THE REAL ONE AND YOU MIGHT BE THE CLONE?
OR THAT WE MIGHT BOTH BE CLONES?
YOU DON'T BELIEVE THAT ANY MORE THAN I DO.
ALL THE JACKAL WANTED WAS TO MESS WITH OUR MINDS... HURT US MORE THAN HE ALREADY HAS.
WE BOTH KNOW THE TRUTH: YOU'RE THE REAL PETER PARKER AND I'M--

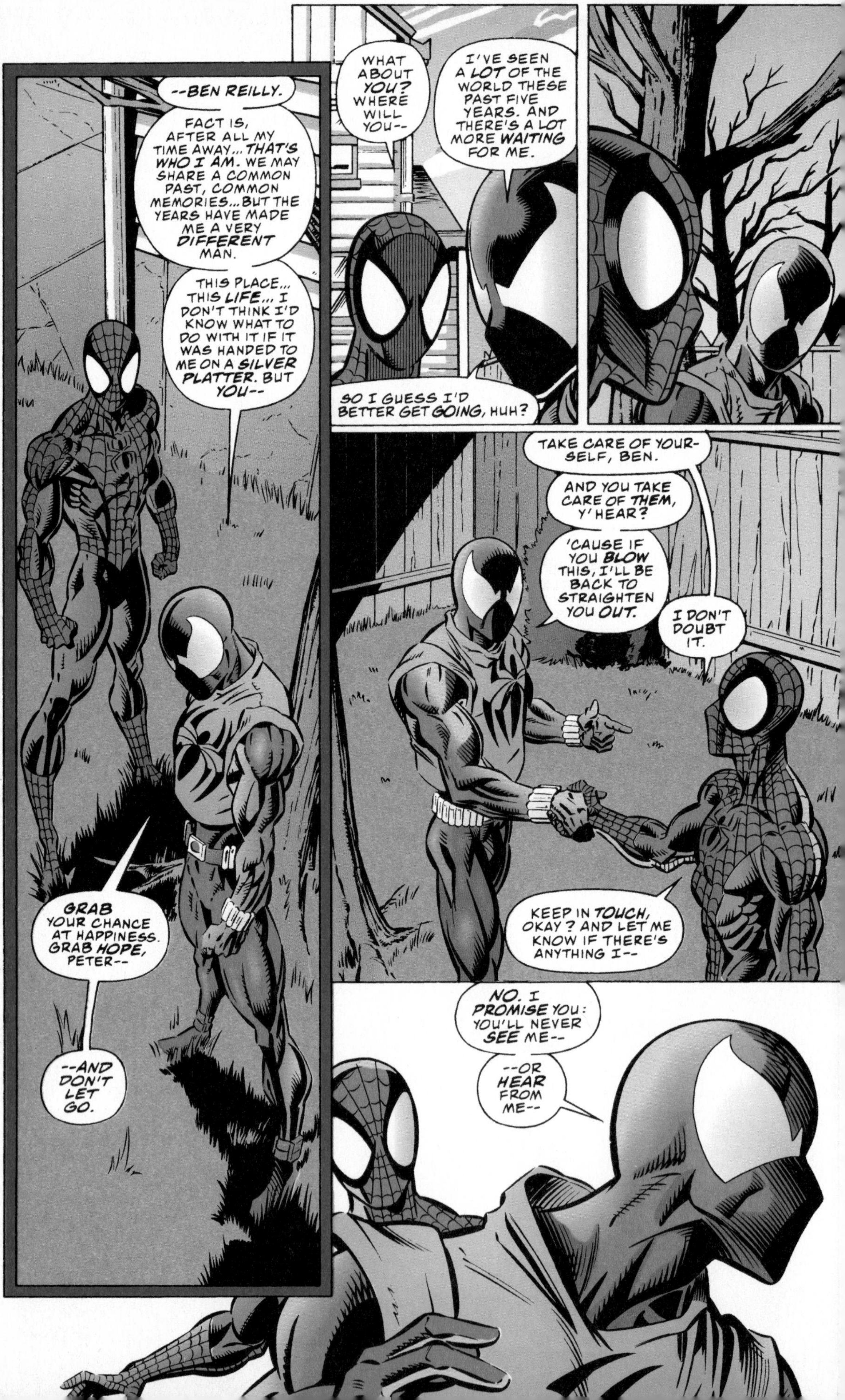
--BEN REILLY.
FACT IS, AFTER ALL MY TIME AWAY... THAT'S WHO I AM. WE MAY SHARE A COMMON PAST, COMMON MEMORIES... BUT THE YEARS HAVE MADE ME A VERY DIFFERENT MAN.
THIS PLACE... THIS LIFE... I DON'T THINK I'D KNOW WHAT TO DO WITH IT IF IT WAS HANDED TO ME ON A SILVER PLATTER. BUT YOU--
GRAB YOUR CHANCE AT HAPPINESS. GRAB HOPE, PETER--
--AND DON'T LET GO.
WHAT ABOUT YOU? WHERE WILL YOU--
I'VE SEEN A LOT OF THE WORLD THESE PAST FIVE YEARS. AND THERE'S A LOT MORE WAITING FOR ME.
SO I GUESS I'D BETTER GET GOING, HUH?
TAKE CARE OF YOURSELF, BEN.
AND YOU TAKE CARE OF THEM, Y'HEAR?
'CAUSE IF YOU BLOW THIS, I'LL BE BACK TO STRAIGHTEN YOU OUT.
I DON'T DOUBT IT.
KEEP IN TOUCH, OKAY? AND LET ME KNOW IF THERE'S ANYTHING I--
NO. I PROMISE YOU: YOU'LL NEVER SEE ME--
--OR HEAR FROM ME--

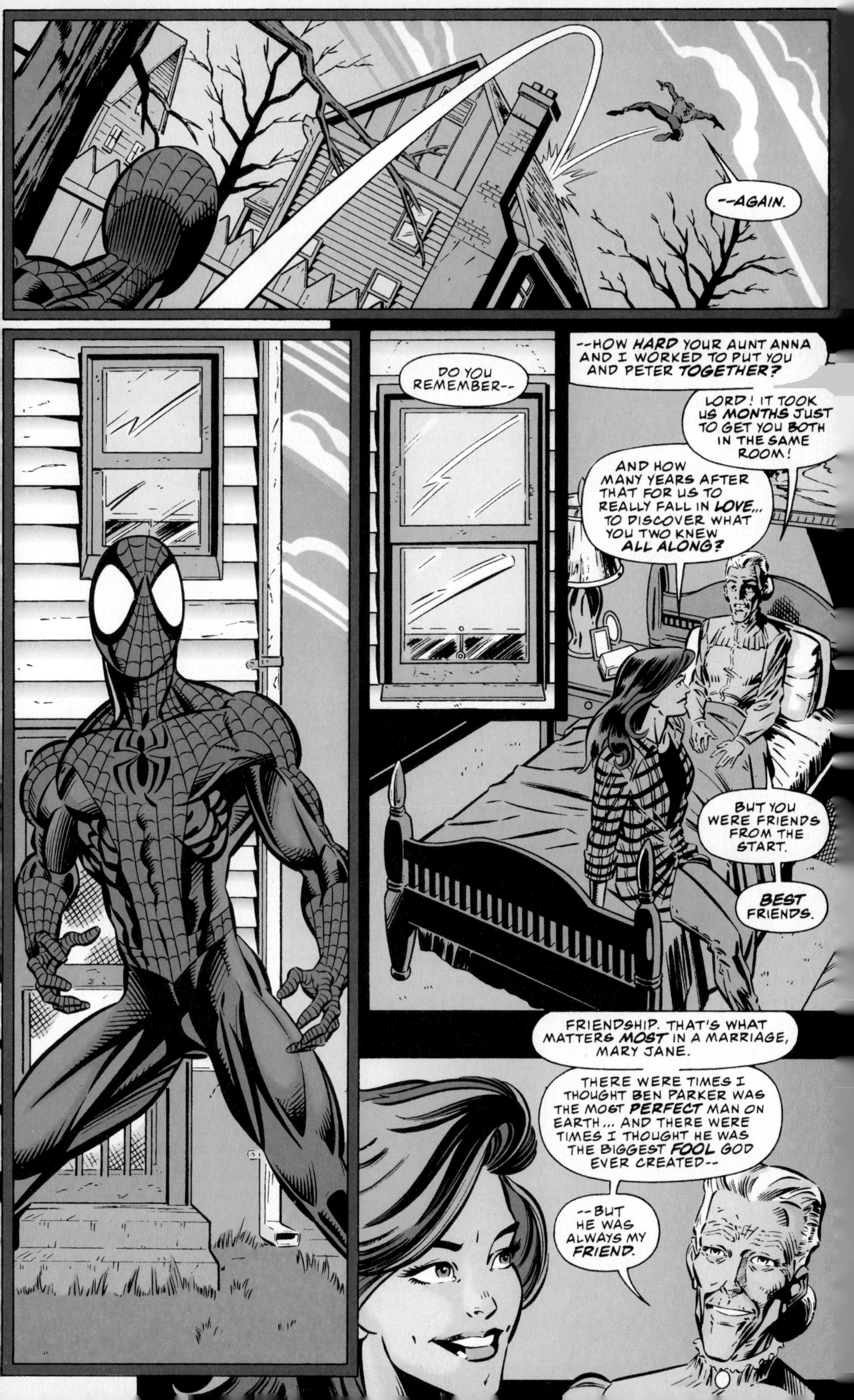
--AGAIN.
DO YOU REMEMBER--
--HOW HARD YOUR AUNT ANNA AND I WORKED TO PUT YOU AND PETER TOGETHER?
LORD! IT TOOK US MONTHS JUST TO GET YOU BOTH IN THE SAME ROOM!
AND HOW MANY YEARS AFTER THAT FOR US TO REALLY FALL IN LOVE... TO DISCOVER WHAT YOU TWO KNEW ALL ALONG?
BUT YOU WERE FRIENDS FROM THE START.
BEST FRIENDS.
FRIENDSHIP. THAT'S WHAT MATTERS MOST IN A MARRIAGE, MARY JANE.
THERE WERE TIMES I THOUGHT BEN PARKER WAS THE MOST PERFECT MAN ON EARTH... AND THERE WERE TIMES I THOUGHT HE WAS THE BIGGEST FOOL GOD EVER CREATED--
--BUT HE WAS ALWAYS MY FRIEND.

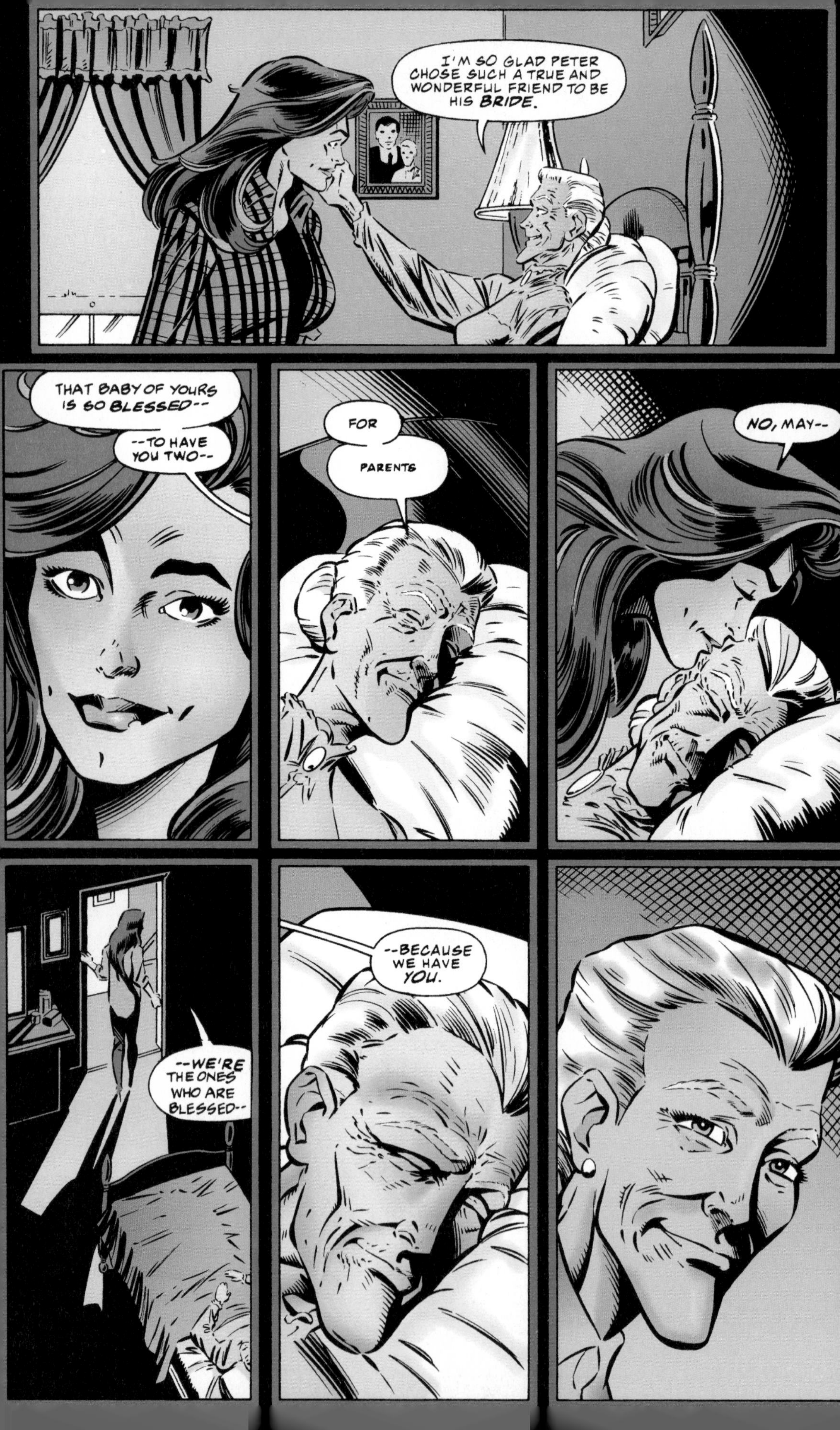
I'M SO GLAD PETER CHOSE SUCH A TRUE AND WONDERFUL FRIEND TO BE HIS BRIDE.
THAT BABY OF YOURS IS SO BLESSED--
--TO HAVE YOU TWO--
FOR
PARENTS
NO, MAY--
--WE'RE THE ONES WHO ARE BLESSED--
--BECAUSE WE HAVE YOU.

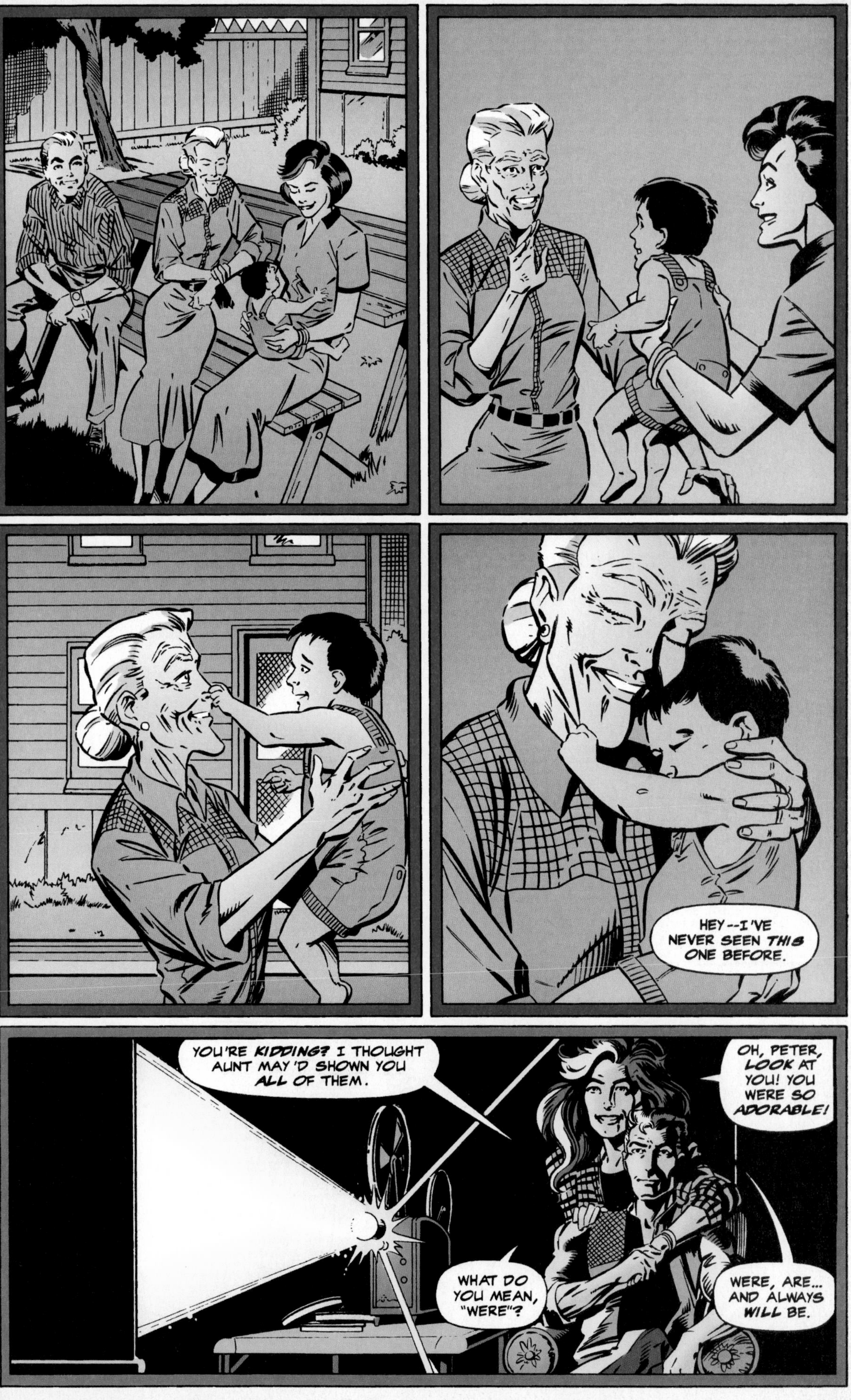
HEY--I'VE NEVER SEEN THIS ONE BEFORE.
YOU'RE KIDDING? I THOUGHT AUNT MAY'D SHOWN YOU ALL OF THEM.
OH, PETER, LOOK AT YOU! YOU WERE SO ADORABLE!
WHAT DO YOU MEAN, "WERE"?
WERE, ARE... AND ALWAYS WILL BE.

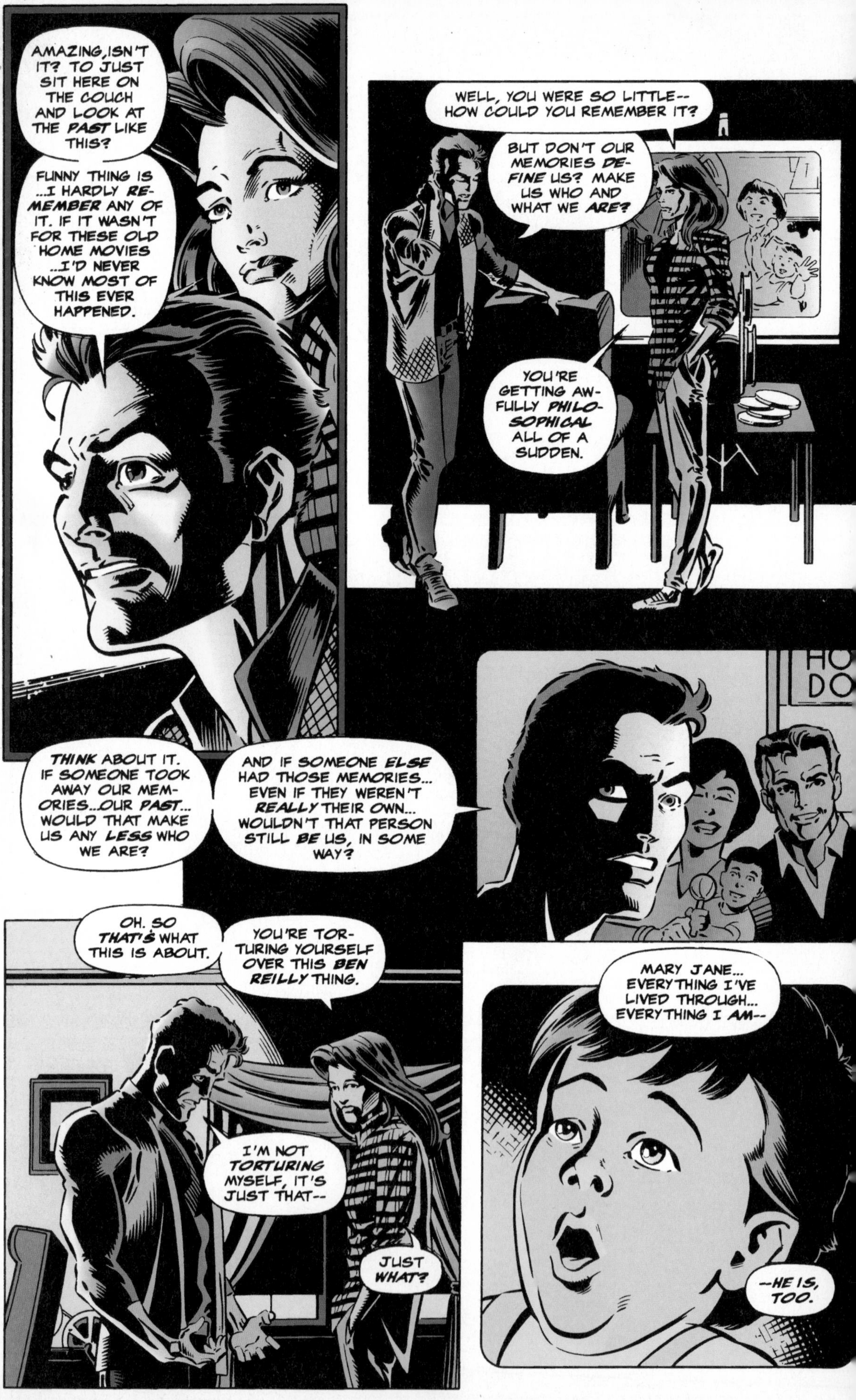
AMAZING, ISN'T IT? TO JUST SIT HERE ON THE COUCH AND LOOK AT THE PAST LIKE THIS?
FUNNY THING IS ...I HARDLY REMEMBER ANY OF IT. IF IT WASN'T FOR THESE OLD HOME MOVIES ...I'D NEVER KNOW MOST OF THIS EVER HAPPENED.
WELL, YOU WERE SO LITTLE-- HOW COULD YOU REMEMBER IT?
BUT DON'T OUR MEMORIES DEFINE US? MAKE US WHO AND WHAT WE ARE?
YOU'RE GETTING AWFULLY PHILOSOPHICAL ALL OF A SUDDEN.
THINK ABOUT IT. IF SOMEONE TOOK AWAY OUR MEMORIES...OUR PAST... WOULD THAT MAKE US ANY LESS WHO WE ARE?
AND IF SOMEONE ELSE HAD THOSE MEMORIES... EVEN IF THEY WEREN'T REALLY THEIR OWN... WOULDN'T THAT PERSON STILL BE US, IN SOME WAY?
OH. SO THAT'S WHAT THIS IS ABOUT.
YOU'RE TORTURING YOURSELF OVER THIS BEN REILLY THING.
I'M NOT TORTURING MYSELF, IT'S JUST THAT--
JUST WHAT?
MARY JANE... EVERYTHING I'VE LIVED THROUGH... EVERYTHING I AM--
--HE IS, TOO.

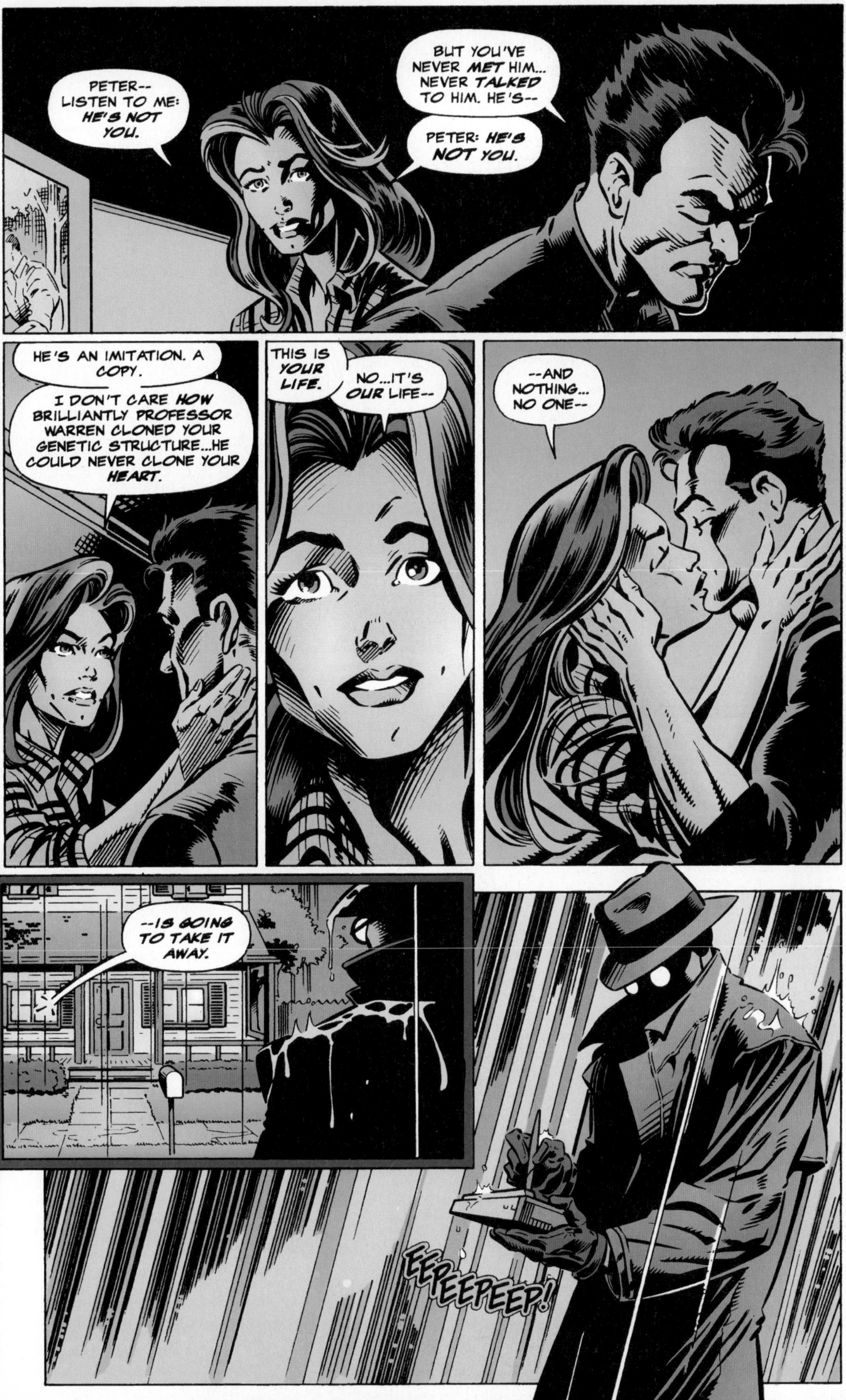
PETER-- LISTEN TO ME: HE'S NOT YOU.
BUT YOU'VE NEVER MET HIM... NEVER TALKED TO HIM. HE'S--
PETER: HE'S NOT YOU.
HE'S AN IMITATION. A COPY.
I DON'T CARE HOW BRILLIANTLY PROFESSOR WARREN CLONED YOUR GENETIC STRUCTURE...HE COULD NEVER CLONE YOUR HEART.
THIS IS YOUR LIFE.
NO...IT'S OUR LIFE--
--AND NOTHING... NO ONE--
--IS GOING TO TAKE IT AWAY.
EEPEEPEEP!

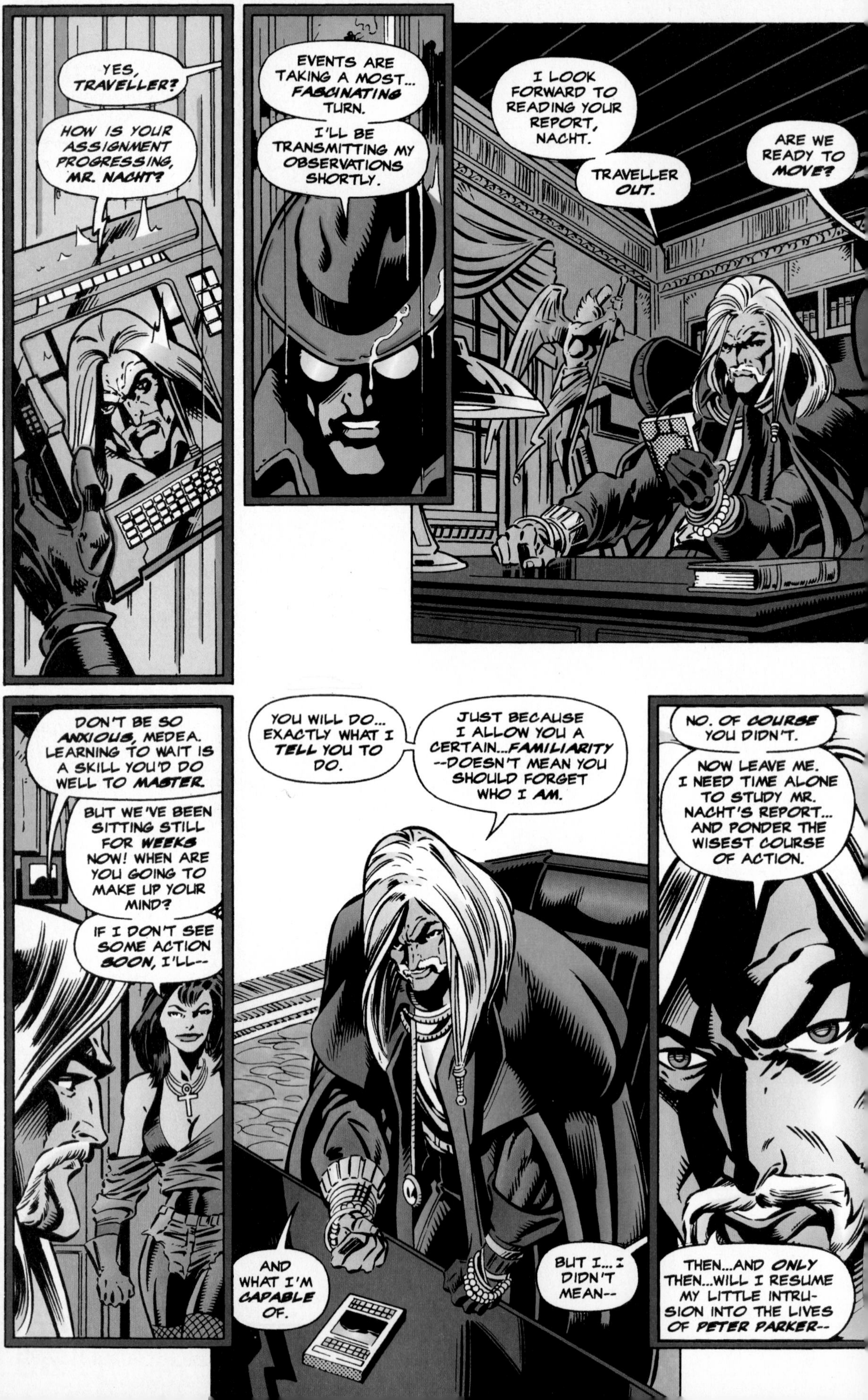
YES, TRAVELLER?
HOW IS YOUR ASSIGNMENT PROGRESSING, MR. NACHT?
EVENTS ARE TAKING A MOST... FASCINATING TURN.
I'LL BE TRANSMITTING MY OBSERVATIONS SHORTLY.
I LOOK FORWARD TO READING YOUR REPORT, NACHT.
TRAVELLER OUT.
ARE WE READY TO MOVE?
DON'T BE SO ANXIOUS, MEDEA. LEARNING TO WAIT IS A SKILL YOU'D DO WELL TO MASTER.
BUT WE'VE BEEN SITTING STILL FOR WEEKS NOW! WHEN ARE YOU GOING TO MAKE UP YOUR MIND?
IF I DON'T SEE SOME ACTION SOON, I'LL--
YOU WILL DO... EXACTLY WHAT I TELL YOU TO DO.
JUST BECAUSE I ALLOW YOU A CERTAIN...FAMILIARITY --DOESN'T MEAN YOU SHOULD FORGET WHO I AM.
AND WHAT I'M CAPABLE OF.
BUT I... I DIDN'T MEAN--
NO. OF COURSE YOU DIDN'T.
NOW LEAVE ME. I NEED TIME ALONE TO STUDY MR. NACHT'S REPORT... AND PONDER THE WISEST COURSE OF ACTION.
THEN...AND ONLY THEN...WILL I RESUME MY LITTLE INTRUSION INTO THE LIVES OF PETER PARKER--

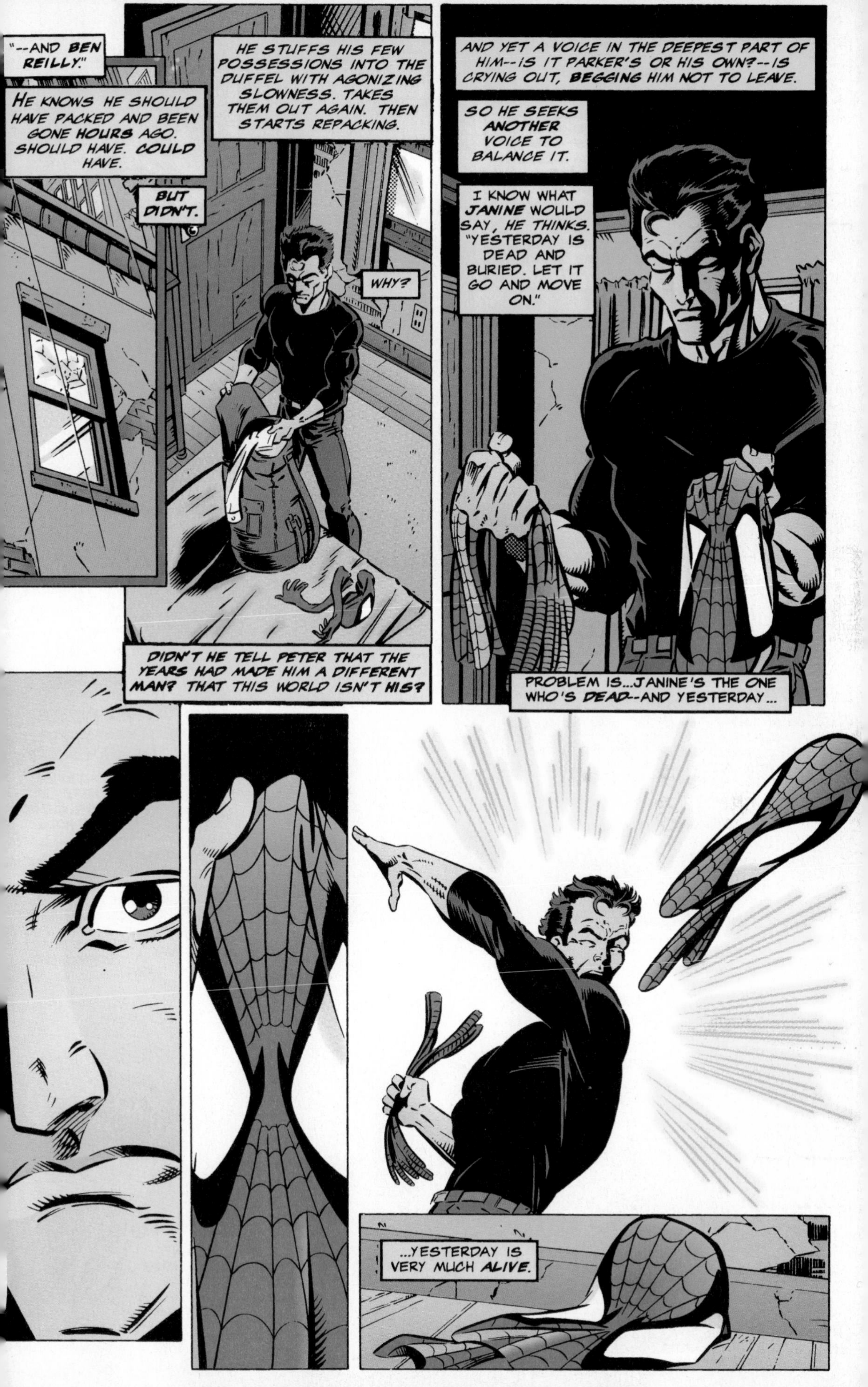
"--AND BEN REILLY."
HE KNOWS HE SHOULD HAVE PACKED AND BEEN GONE HOURS AGO. SHOULD HAVE. COULD HAVE.
BUT DIDN'T.
HE STUFFS HIS FEW POSSESSIONS INTO THE DUFFEL WITH AGONIZING SLOWNESS. TAKES THEM OUT AGAIN. THEN STARTS REPACKING.
WHY?
DIDN'T HE TELL PETER THAT THE YEARS HAD MADE HIM A DIFFERENT MAN? THAT THIS WORLD ISN'T HIS?
AND YET A VOICE IN THE DEEPEST PART OF HIM--IS IT PARKER'S OR HIS OWN?--IS CRYING OUT, BEGGING HIM NOT TO LEAVE.
SO HE SEEKS ANOTHER VOICE TO BALANCE IT.
I KNOW WHAT JANINE WOULD SAY, HE THINKS. "YESTERDAY IS DEAD AND BURIED. LET IT GO AND MOVE ON."
PROBLEM IS...JANINE'S THE ONE WHO'S DEAD--AND YESTERDAY...
...YESTERDAY IS VERY MUCH ALIVE.

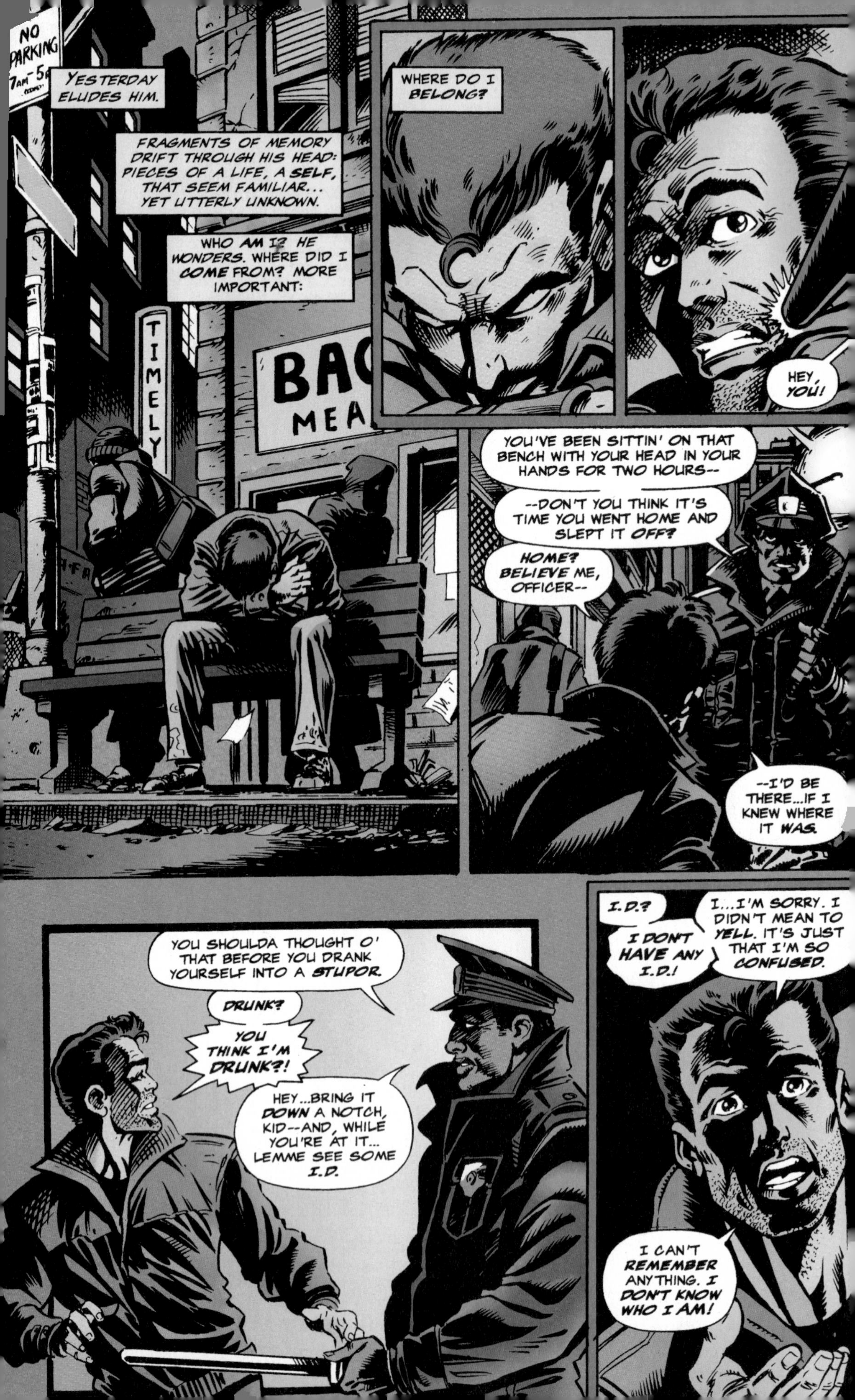
NO PARKING 7AM-5
YESTERDAY ELUDES HIM.
FRAGMENTS OF MEMORY DRIFT THROUGH HIS HEAD: PIECES OF A LIFE, A SELF, THAT SEEM FAMILIAR... YET UTTERLY UNKNOWN.
WHO AM I? HE WONDERS. WHERE DID I COME FROM? MORE IMPORTANT:
TIMELY
BAC MEA
WHERE DO I BELONG?
HEY, YOU!
YOU'VE BEEN SITTIN' ON THAT BENCH WITH YOUR HEAD IN YOUR HANDS FOR TWO HOURS--
--DON'T YOU THINK IT'S TIME YOU WENT HOME AND SLEPT IT OFF?
HOME? BELIEVE ME, OFFICER--
--I'D BE THERE...IF I KNEW WHERE IT WAS.
YOU SHOULDA THOUGHT O' THAT BEFORE YOU DRANK YOURSELF INTO A STUPOR.
DRUNK?
YOU THINK I'M DRUNK?!
HEY...BRING IT DOWN A NOTCH, KID--AND, WHILE YOU'RE AT IT... LEMME SEE SOME I.D.
I.D.?
I DON'T HAVE ANY I.D.!
I...I'M SORRY. I DIDN'T MEAN TO YELL. IT'S JUST THAT I'M SO CONFUSED.
I CAN'T REMEMBER ANYTHING. I DON'T KNOW WHO I AM!

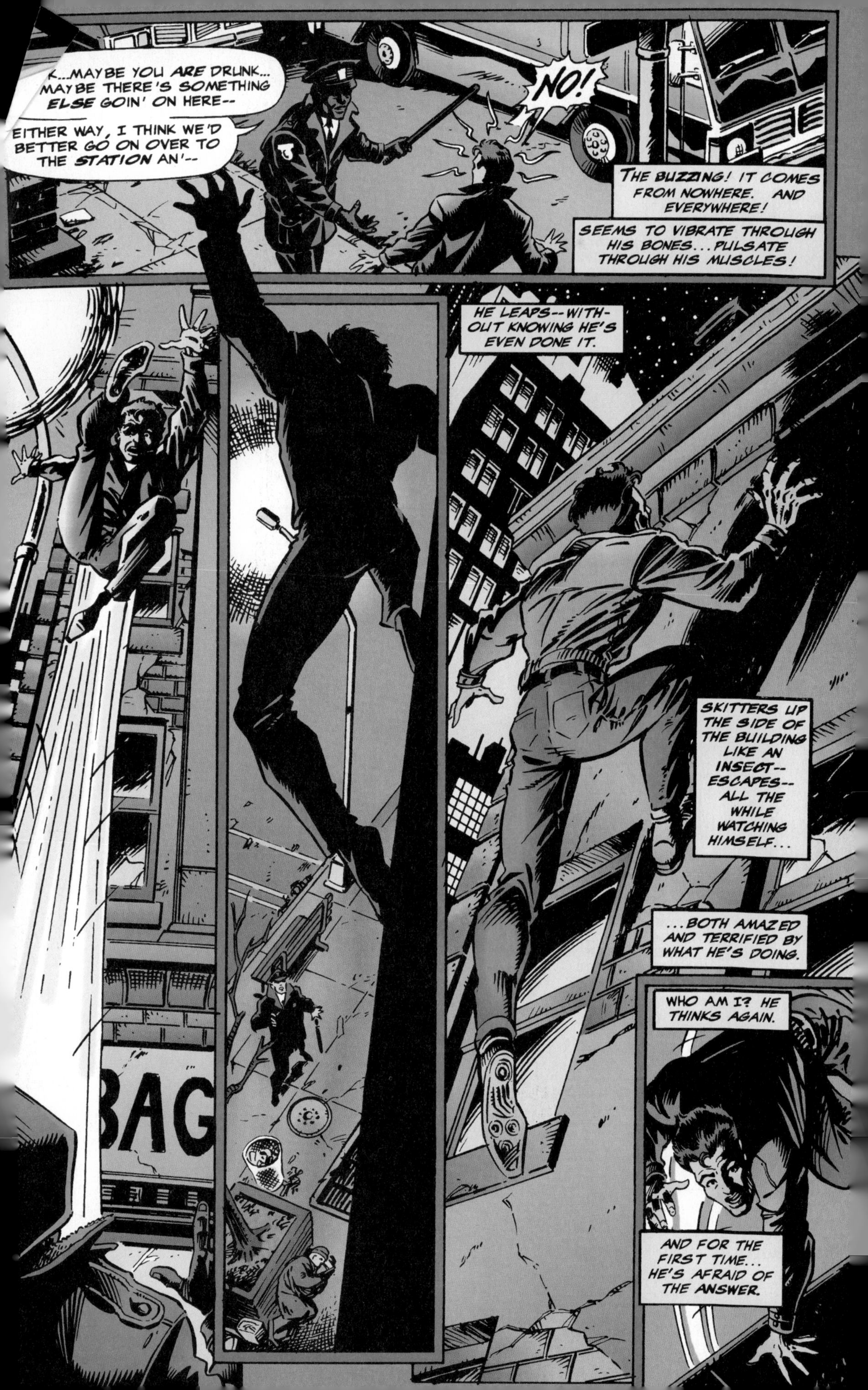

K...MAYBE YOU ARE DRUNK... MAYBE THERE'S SOMETHING ELSE GOIN' ON HERE--
EITHER WAY, I THINK WE'D BETTER GO ON OVER TO THE STATION AN'--
NO!
THE BUZZING! IT COMES FROM NOWHERE. AND EVERYWHERE!
SEEMS TO VIBRATE THROUGH HIS BONES... PULSATE THROUGH HIS MUSCLES!
HE LEAPS--WITHOUT KNOWING HE'S EVEN DONE IT.
SKITTERS UP THE SIDE OF THE BUILDING LIKE AN INSECT-- ESCAPES-- ALL THE WHILE WATCHING HIMSELF...
...BOTH AMAZED AND TERRIFIED BY WHAT HE'S DOING.
WHO AM I? HE THINKS AGAIN.
AND FOR THE FIRST TIME... HE'S AFRAID OF THE ANSWER.
BAG

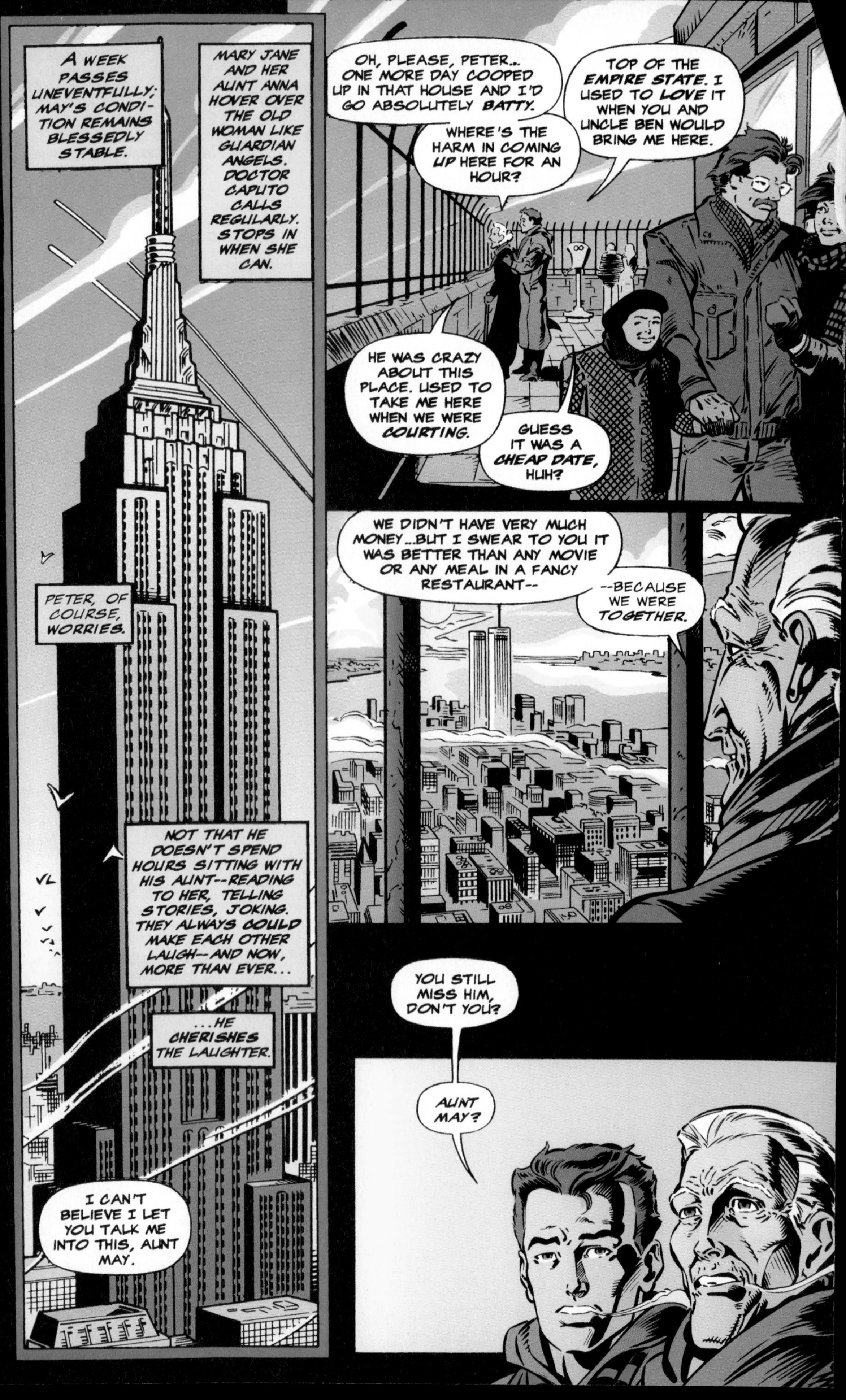
A WEEK PASSES UNEVENTFULLY; MAY'S CONDITION REMAINS BLESSEDLY STABLE.
MARY JANE AND HER AUNT ANNA HOVER OVER THE OLD WOMAN LIKE GUARDIAN ANGELS. DOCTOR CAPUTO CALLS REGULARLY. STOPS IN WHEN SHE CAN.
PETER, OF COURSE, WORRIES.
NOT THAT HE DOESN'T SPEND HOURS SITTING WITH HIS AUNT--READING TO HER, TELLING STORIES, JOKING. THEY ALWAYS COULD MAKE EACH OTHER LAUGH--AND NOW, MORE THAN EVER...
...HE CHERISHES THE LAUGHTER.
I CAN'T BELIEVE I LET YOU TALK ME INTO THIS, AUNT MAY.
OH, PLEASE, PETER... ONE MORE DAY COOPED UP IN THAT HOUSE AND I'D GO ABSOLUTELY BATTY.
WHERE'S THE HARM IN COMING UP HERE FOR AN HOUR?
TOP OF THE EMPIRE STATE. I USED TO LOVE IT WHEN YOU AND UNCLE BEN WOULD BRING ME HERE.
HE WAS CRAZY ABOUT THIS PLACE. USED TO TAKE ME HERE WHEN WE WERE COURTING.
GUESS IT WAS A CHEAP DATE, HUH?
WE DIDN'T HAVE VERY MUCH MONEY...BUT I SWEAR TO YOU IT WAS BETTER THAN ANY MOVIE OR ANY MEAL IN A FANCY RESTAURANT--
--BECAUSE WE WERE TOGETHER.
YOU STILL MISS HIM, DON'T YOU?
AUNT MAY?

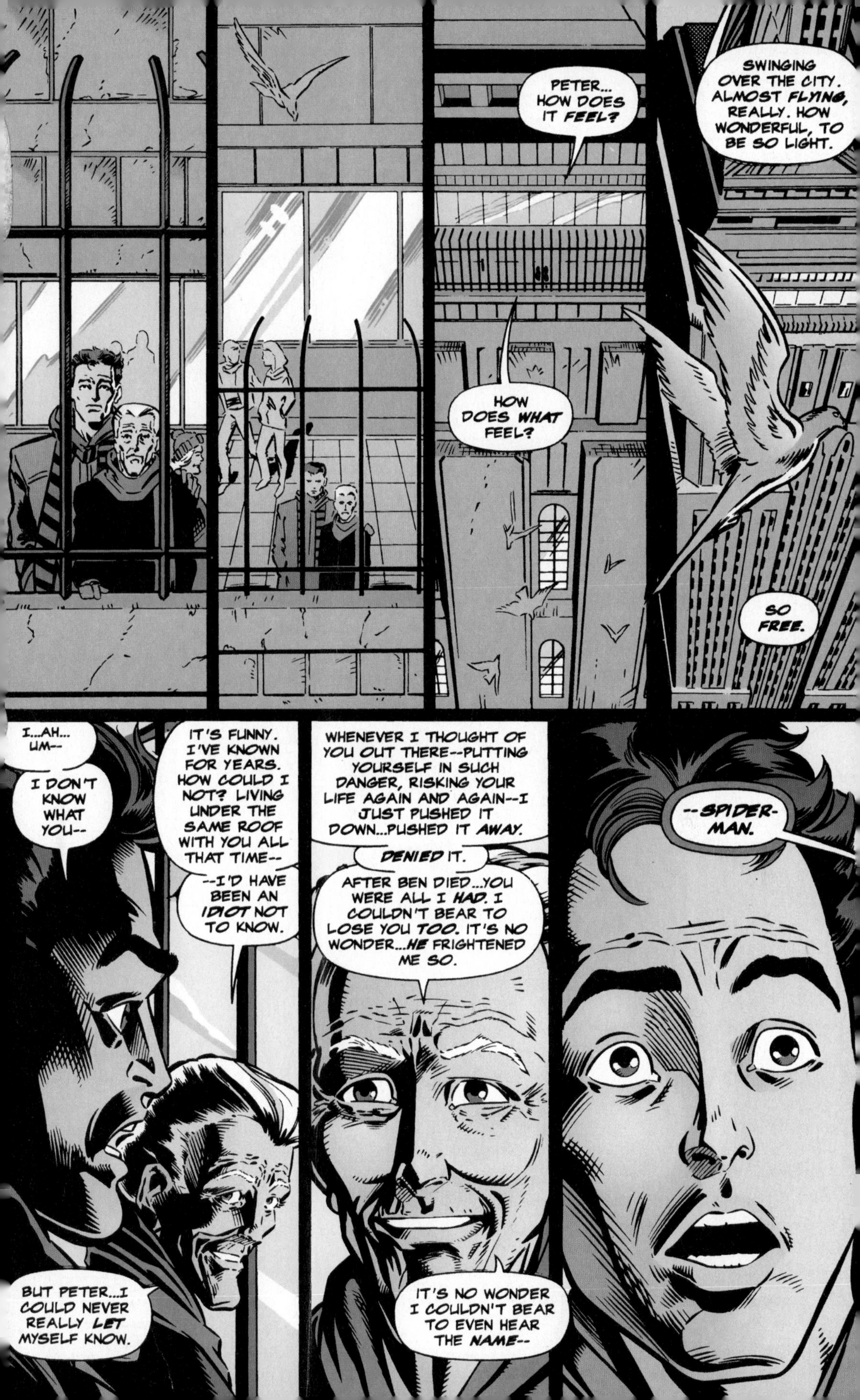

PETER... HOW DOES IT FEEL?
HOW DOES WHAT FEEL?
SWINGING OVER THE CITY. ALMOST FLYING, REALLY. HOW WONDERFUL, TO BE SO LIGHT.
SO FREE.
I...AH... UM--
I DON'T KNOW WHAT YOU--
IT'S FUNNY. I'VE KNOWN FOR YEARS. HOW COULD I NOT? LIVING UNDER THE SAME ROOF WITH YOU ALL THAT TIME--
--I'D HAVE BEEN AN IDIOT NOT TO KNOW.
BUT PETER...I COULD NEVER REALLY LET MYSELF KNOW.
WHENEVER I THOUGHT OF YOU OUT THERE--PUTTING YOURSELF IN SUCH DANGER, RISKING YOUR LIFE AGAIN AND AGAIN--I JUST PUSHED IT DOWN...PUSHED IT AWAY.
DENIED IT.
AFTER BEN DIED...YOU WERE ALL I HAD. I COULDN'T BEAR TO LOSE YOU TOO. IT'S NO WONDER...HE FRIGHTENED ME SO.
IT'S NO WONDER I COULDN'T BEAR TO EVEN HEAR THE NAME--
--SPIDER-MAN.

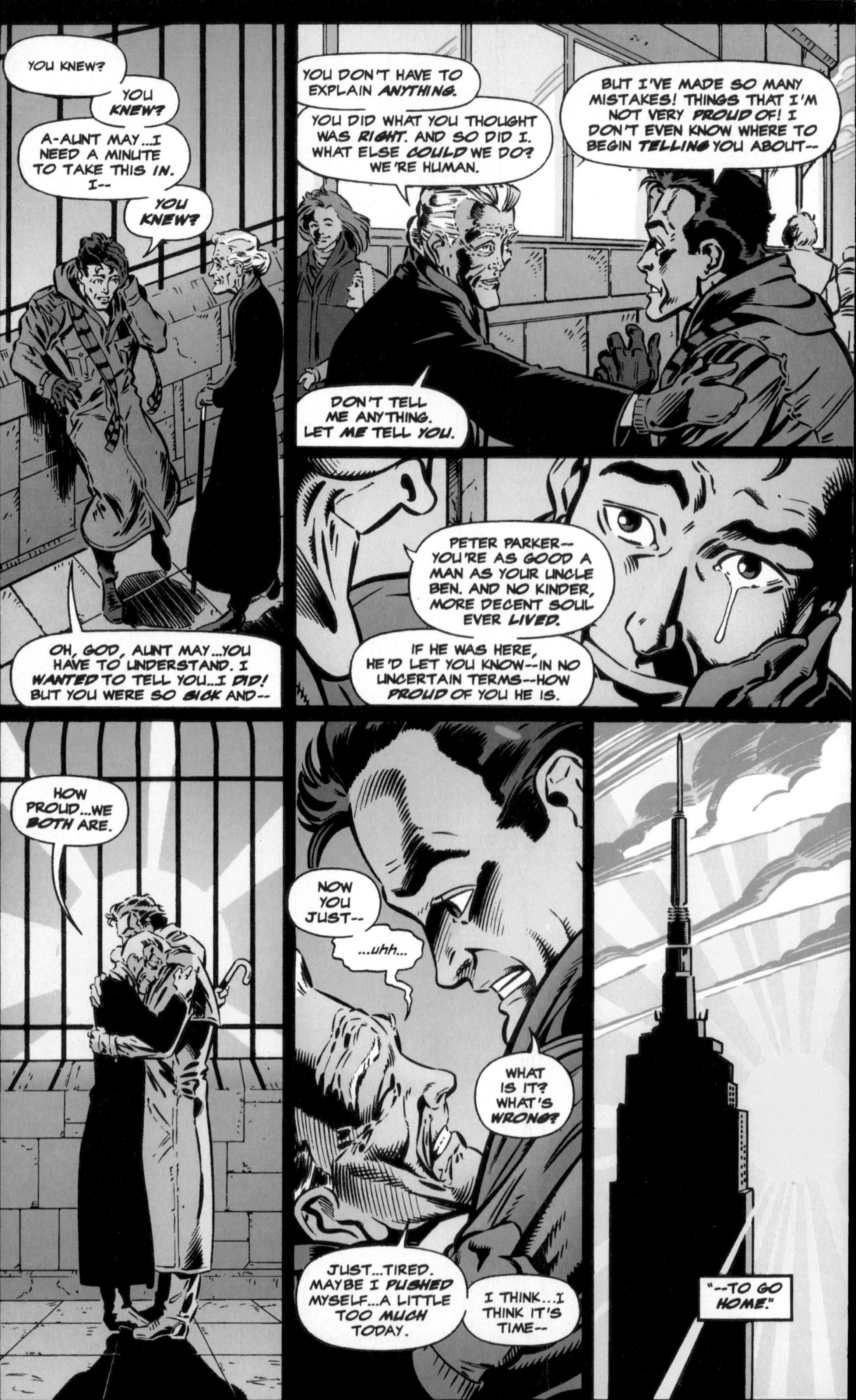
YOU KNEW?
YOU KNEW?
A-AUNT MAY...I NEED A MINUTE TO TAKE THIS IN. I--
YOU KNEW?
OH, GOD, AUNT MAY...YOU HAVE TO UNDERSTAND. I WANTED TO TELL YOU...I DID! BUT YOU WERE SO SICK AND--
YOU DON'T HAVE TO EXPLAIN ANYTHING.
YOU DID WHAT YOU THOUGHT WAS RIGHT. AND SO DID I. WHAT ELSE COULD WE DO? WE'RE HUMAN.
BUT I'VE MADE SO MANY MISTAKES! THINGS THAT I'M NOT VERY PROUD OF! I DON'T EVEN KNOW WHERE TO BEGIN TELLING YOU ABOUT--
DON'T TELL ME ANYTHING. LET ME TELL YOU.
PETER PARKER--YOU'RE AS GOOD A MAN AS YOUR UNCLE BEN. AND NO KINDER, MORE DECENT SOUL EVER LIVED.
IF HE WAS HERE, HE'D LET YOU KNOW--IN NO UNCERTAIN TERMS--HOW PROUD OF YOU HE IS.
HOW PROUD...WE BOTH ARE.
NOW YOU JUST--
...uhh...
WHAT IS IT? WHAT'S WRONG?
JUST...TIRED. MAYBE I PUSHED MYSELF...A LITTLE TOO MUCH TODAY.
I THINK...I THINK IT'S TIME--
"--TO GO HOME."

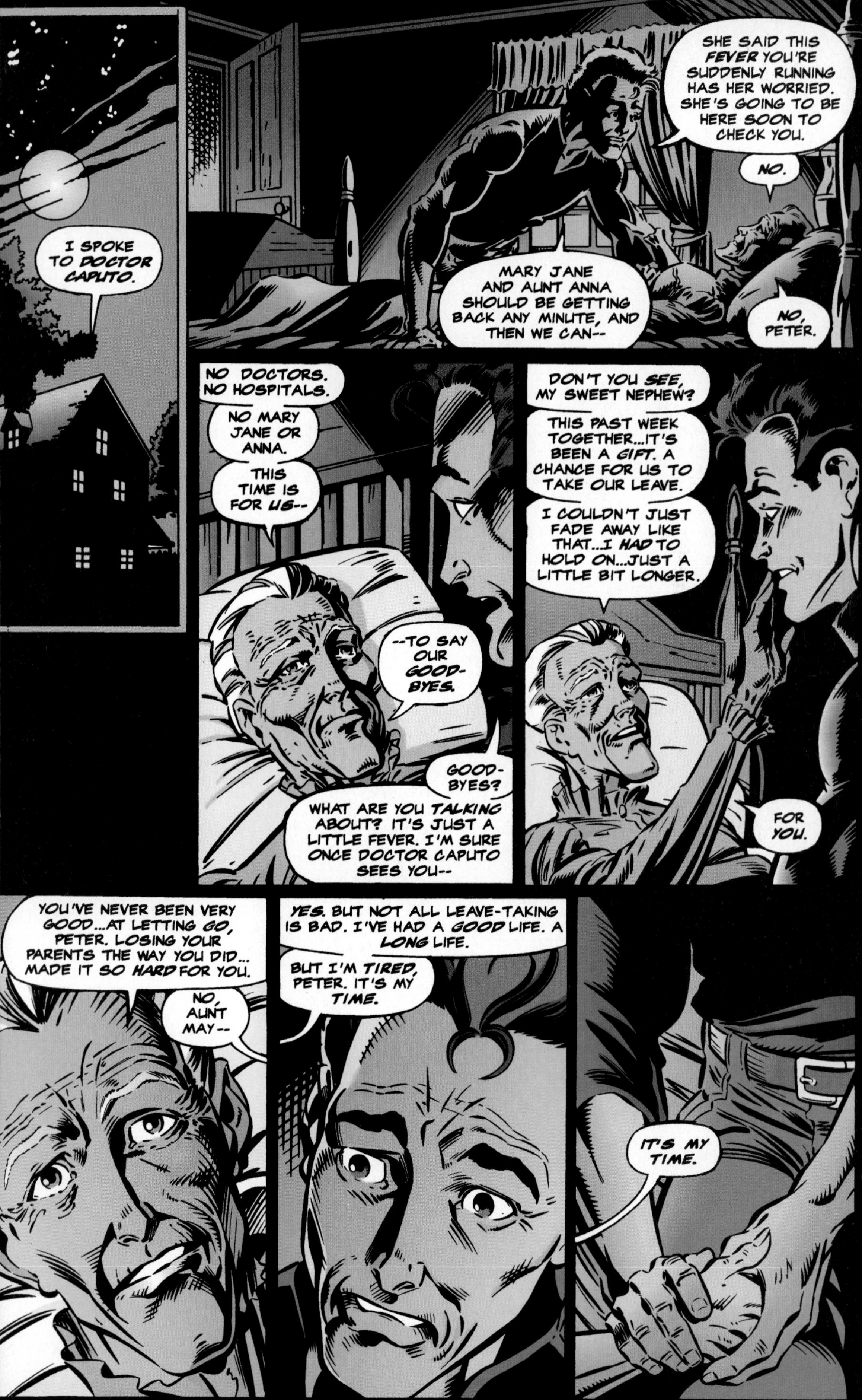
I SPOKE TO DOCTOR CAPUTO.
SHE SAID THIS FEVER YOU'RE SUDDENLY RUNNING HAS HER WORRIED. SHE'S GOING TO BE HERE SOON TO CHECK YOU.
NO.
MARY JANE AND AUNT ANNA SHOULD BE GETTING BACK ANY MINUTE, AND THEN WE CAN--
NO, PETER.
NO DOCTORS. NO HOSPITALS.
NO MARY JANE OR ANNA.
THIS TIME IS FOR US--
--TO SAY OUR GOOD-BYES.
GOOD-BYES?
WHAT ARE YOU TALKING ABOUT? IT'S JUST A LITTLE FEVER. I'M SURE ONCE DOCTOR CAPUTO SEES YOU--
DON'T YOU SEE, MY SWEET NEPHEW?
THIS PAST WEEK TOGETHER...IT'S BEEN A GIFT. A CHANCE FOR US TO TAKE OUR LEAVE.
I COULDN'T JUST FADE AWAY LIKE THAT...I HAD TO HOLD ON...JUST A LITTLE BIT LONGER.
FOR YOU.
YOU'VE NEVER BEEN VERY GOOD...AT LETTING GO, PETER. LOSING YOUR PARENTS THE WAY YOU DID... MADE IT SO HARD FOR YOU.
NO, AUNT MAY--
YES. BUT NOT ALL LEAVE-TAKING IS BAD. I'VE HAD A GOOD LIFE. A LONG LIFE.
BUT I'M TIRED, PETER. IT'S MY TIME.
IT'S MY TIME.

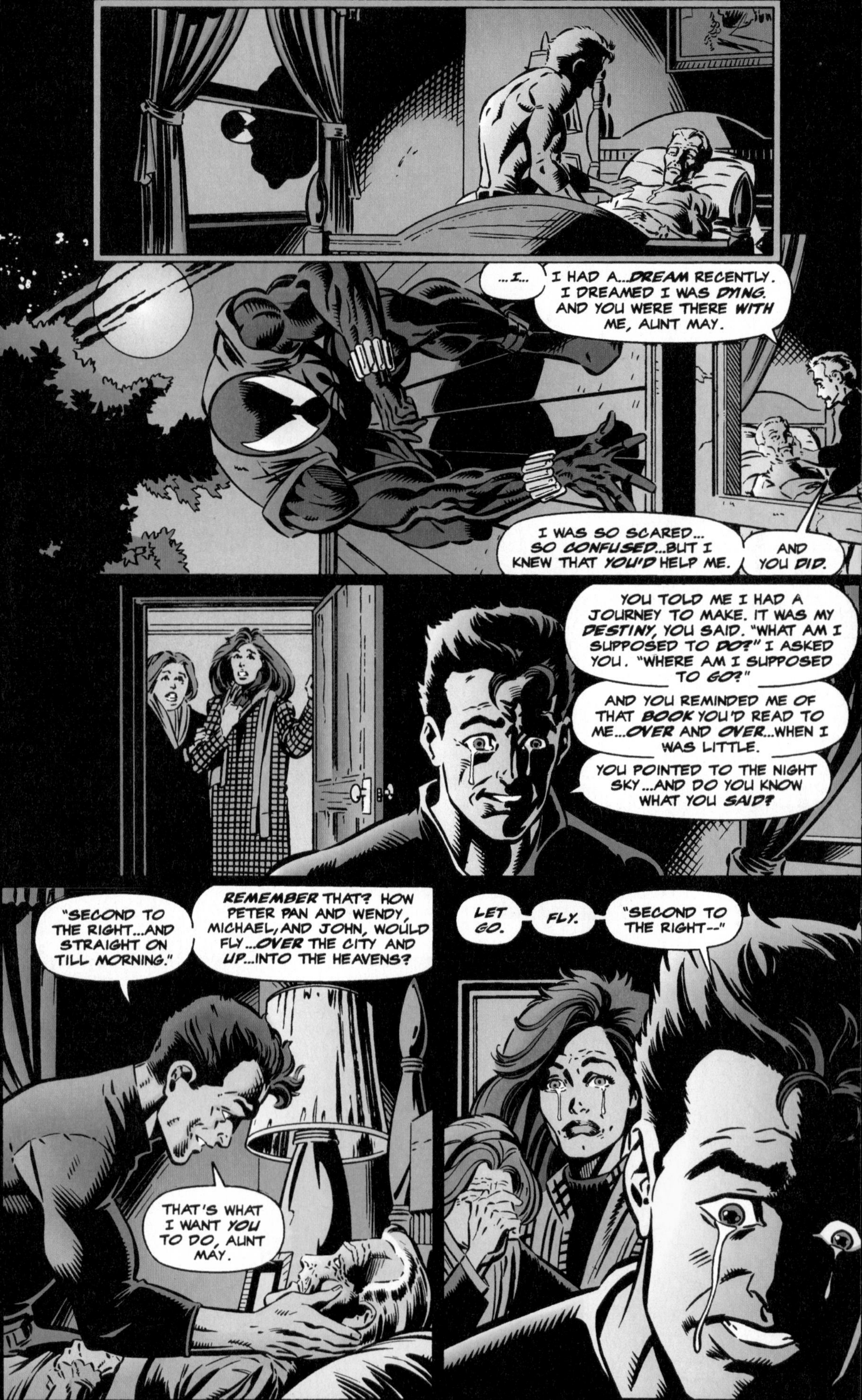
...I...
I HAD A...DREAM RECENTLY. I DREAMED I WAS DYING. AND YOU WERE THERE WITH ME, AUNT MAY.
I WAS SO SCARED... SO CONFUSED...BUT I KNEW THAT YOU'D HELP ME.
AND YOU DID.
YOU TOLD ME I HAD A JOURNEY TO MAKE. IT WAS MY DESTINY, YOU SAID. "WHAT AM I SUPPOSED TO DO?" I ASKED YOU. "WHERE AM I SUPPOSED TO GO?"
AND YOU REMINDED ME OF THAT BOOK YOU'D READ TO ME...OVER AND OVER...WHEN I WAS LITTLE.
YOU POINTED TO THE NIGHT SKY...AND DO YOU KNOW WHAT YOU SAID?
"SECOND TO THE RIGHT...AND STRAIGHT ON TILL MORNING."
REMEMBER THAT? HOW PETER PAN AND WENDY, MICHAEL, AND JOHN, WOULD FLY...OVER THE CITY AND UP...INTO THE HEAVENS?
THAT'S WHAT I WANT YOU TO DO, AUNT MAY.
LET GO.
FLY.
"SECOND TO THE RIGHT--"

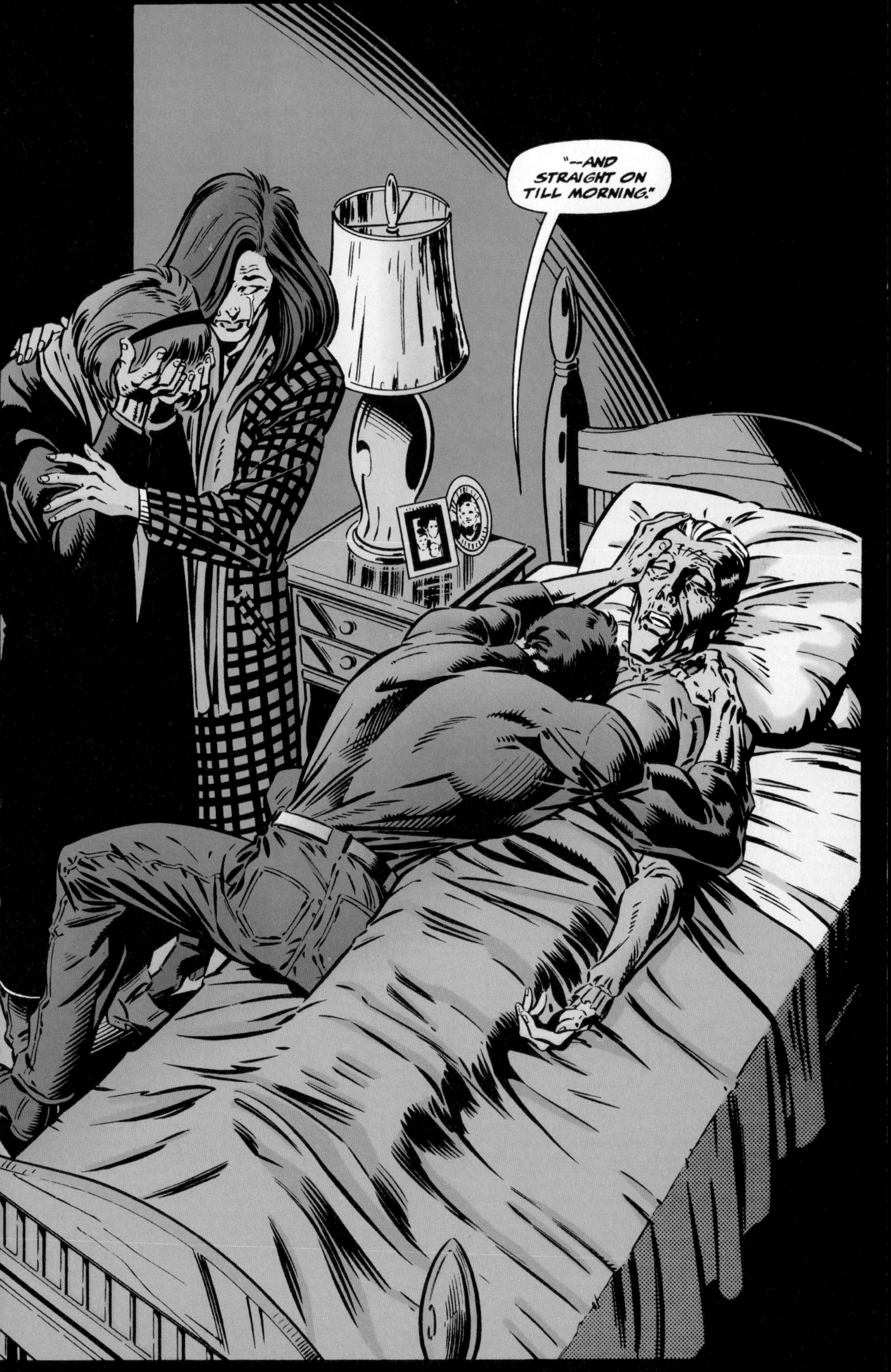
"--AND STRAIGHT ON TILL MORNING."

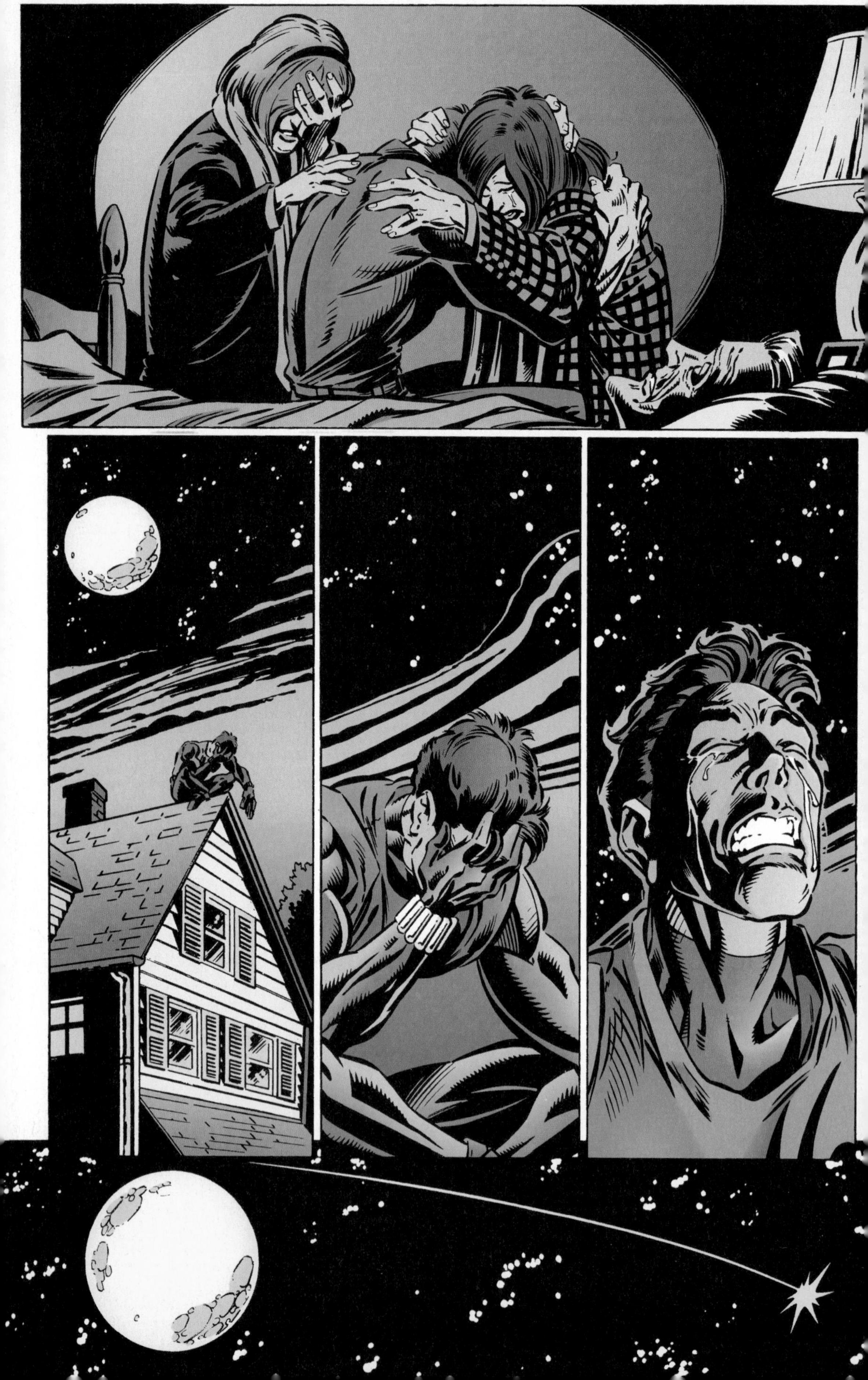

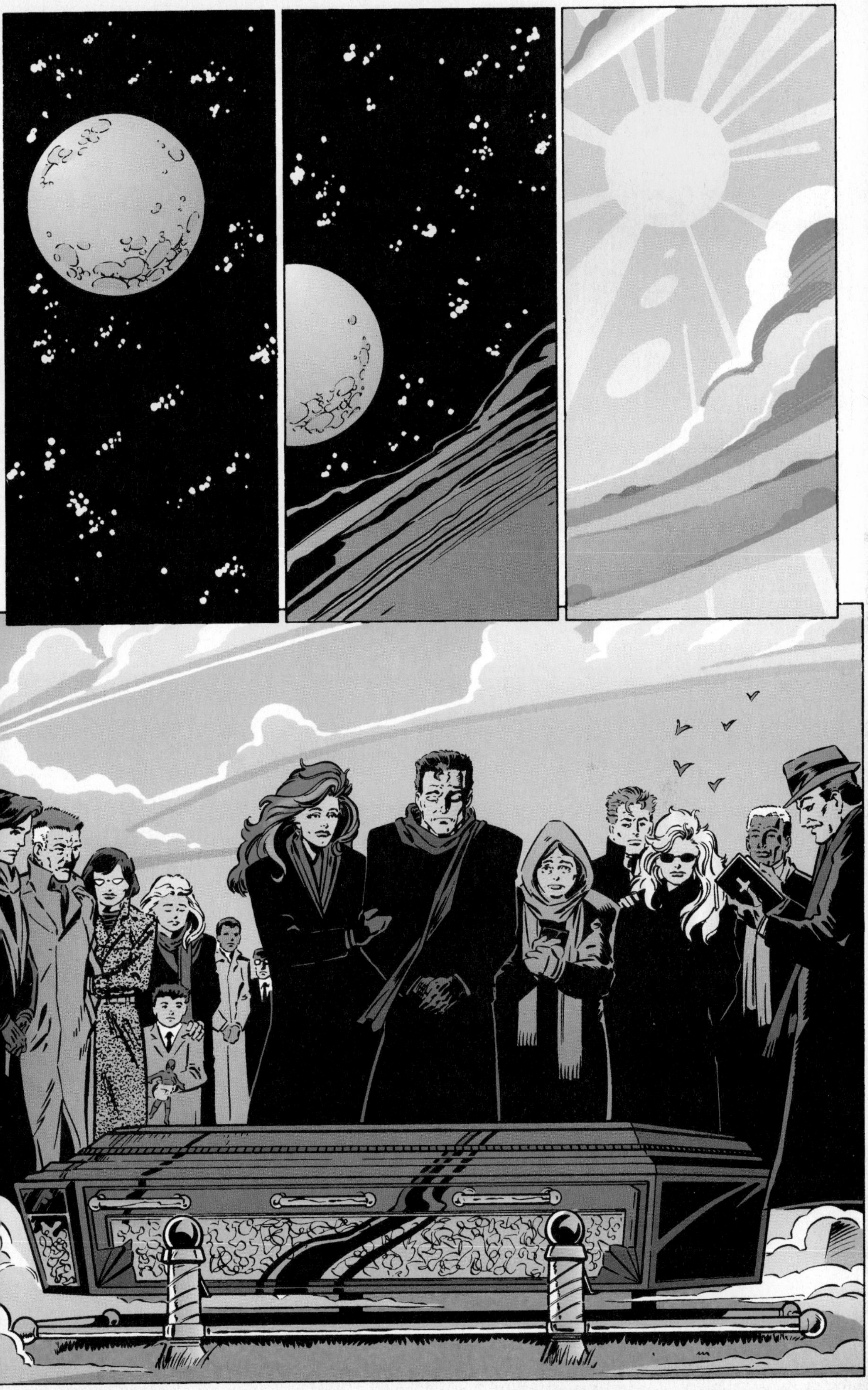

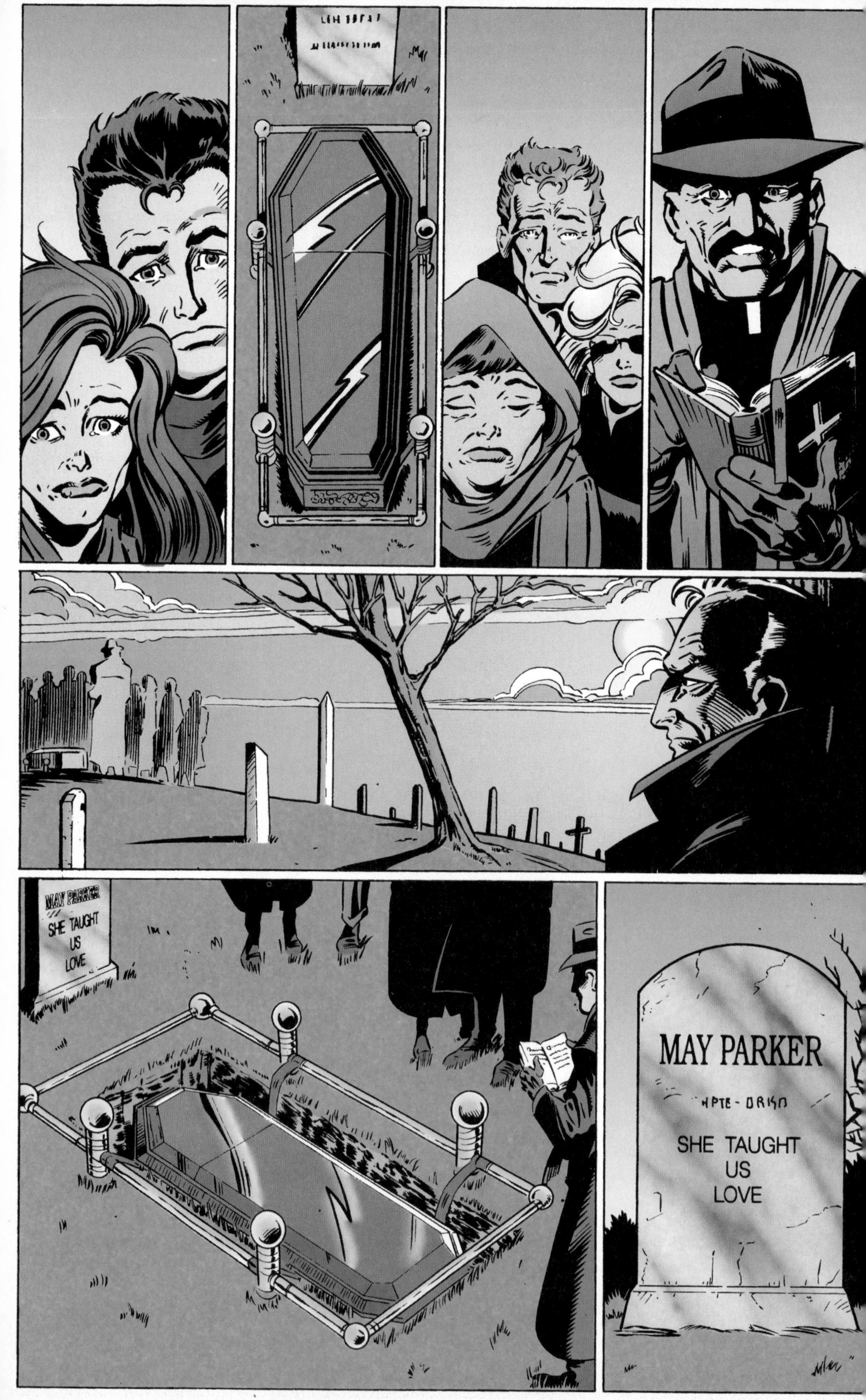
MAY PARKER
SHE TAUGHT US LOVE
MAY PARKER
SHE TAUGHT US LOVE

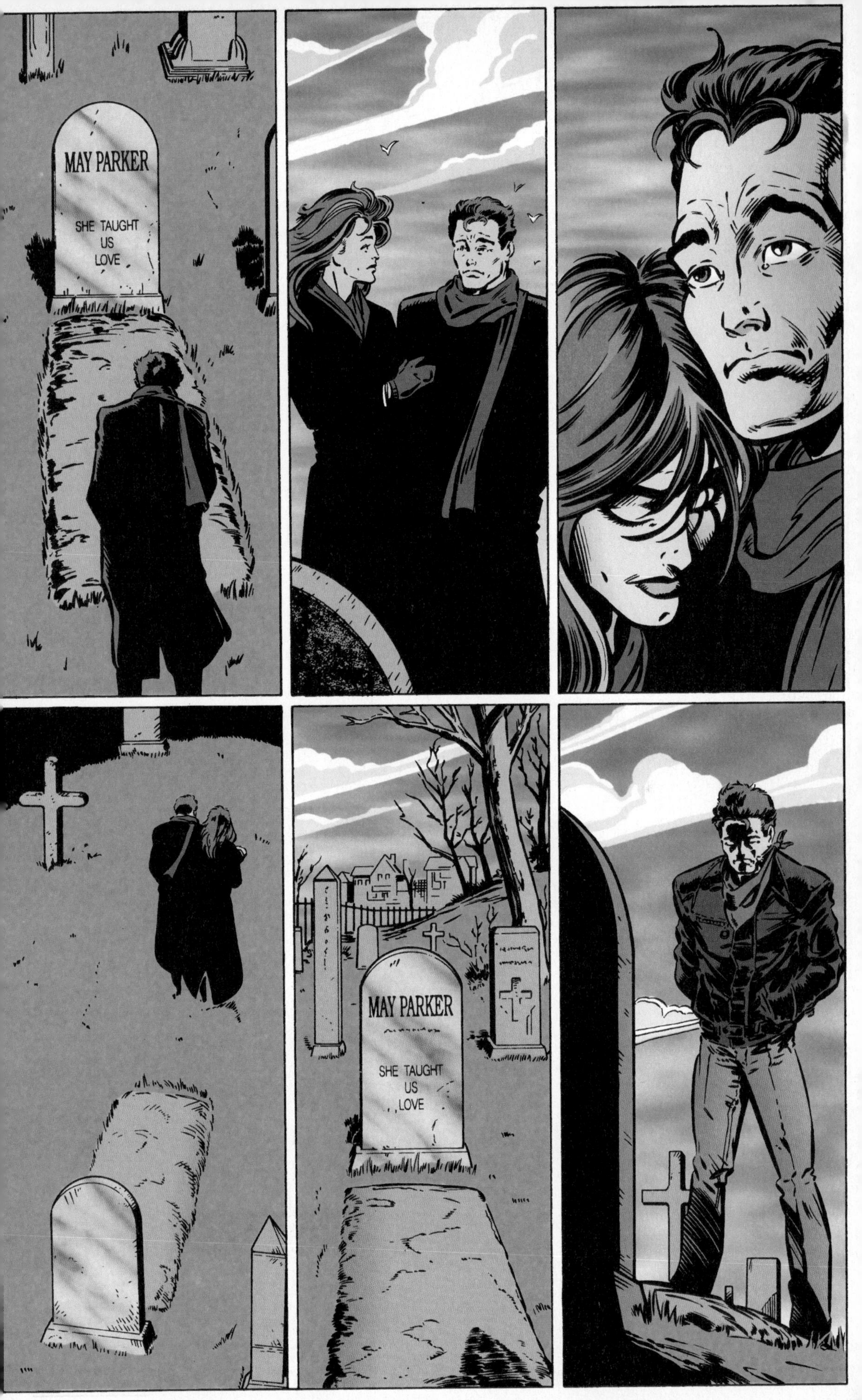
MAY PARKER
SHE TAUGHT US LOVE
MAY PARKER
SHE TAUGHT US LOVE

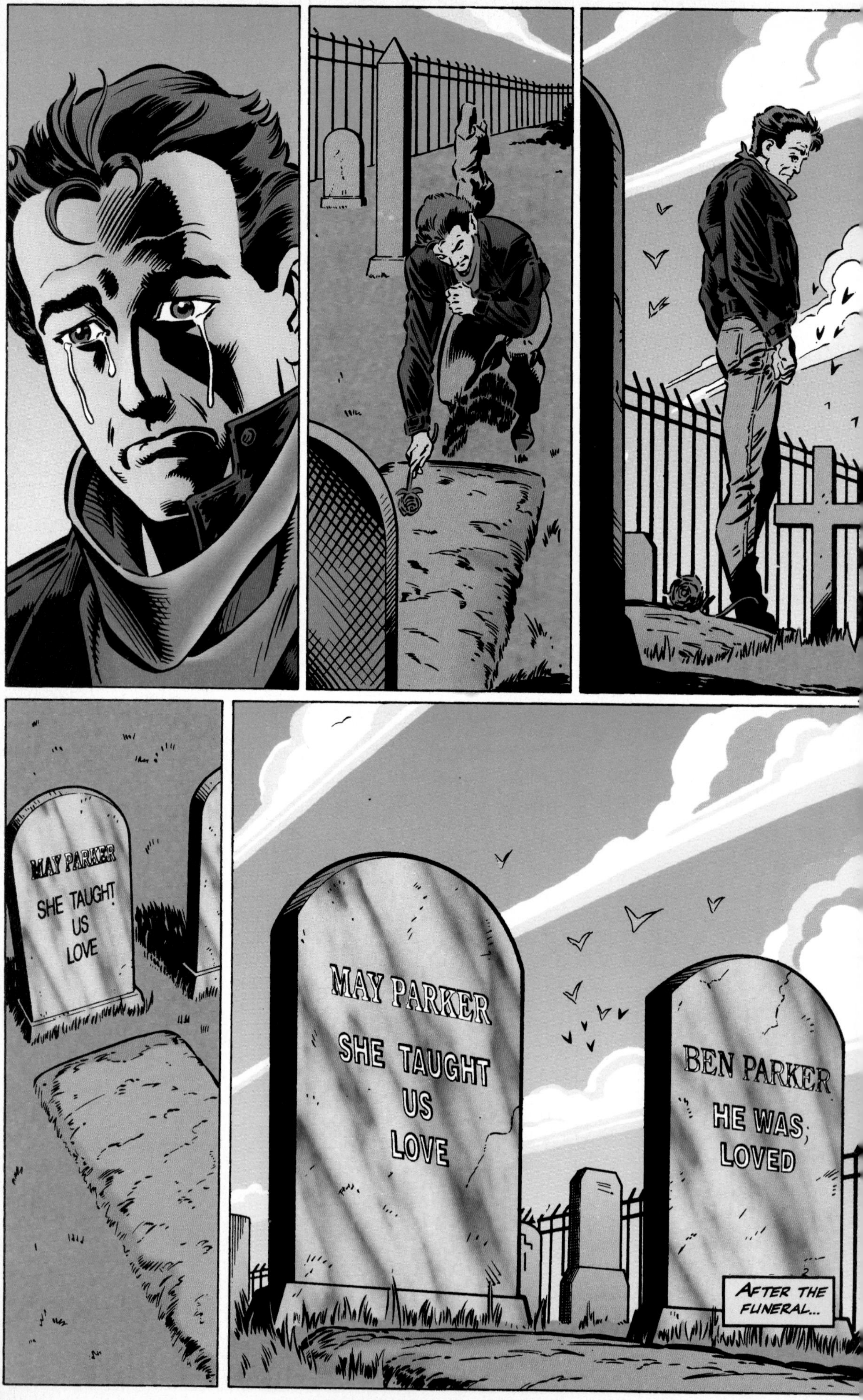
MAY PARKER
SHE TAUGHT US LOVE
MAY PARKER
SHE TAUGHT US LOVE
BEN PARKER
HE WAS LOVED
AFTER THE FUNERAL...

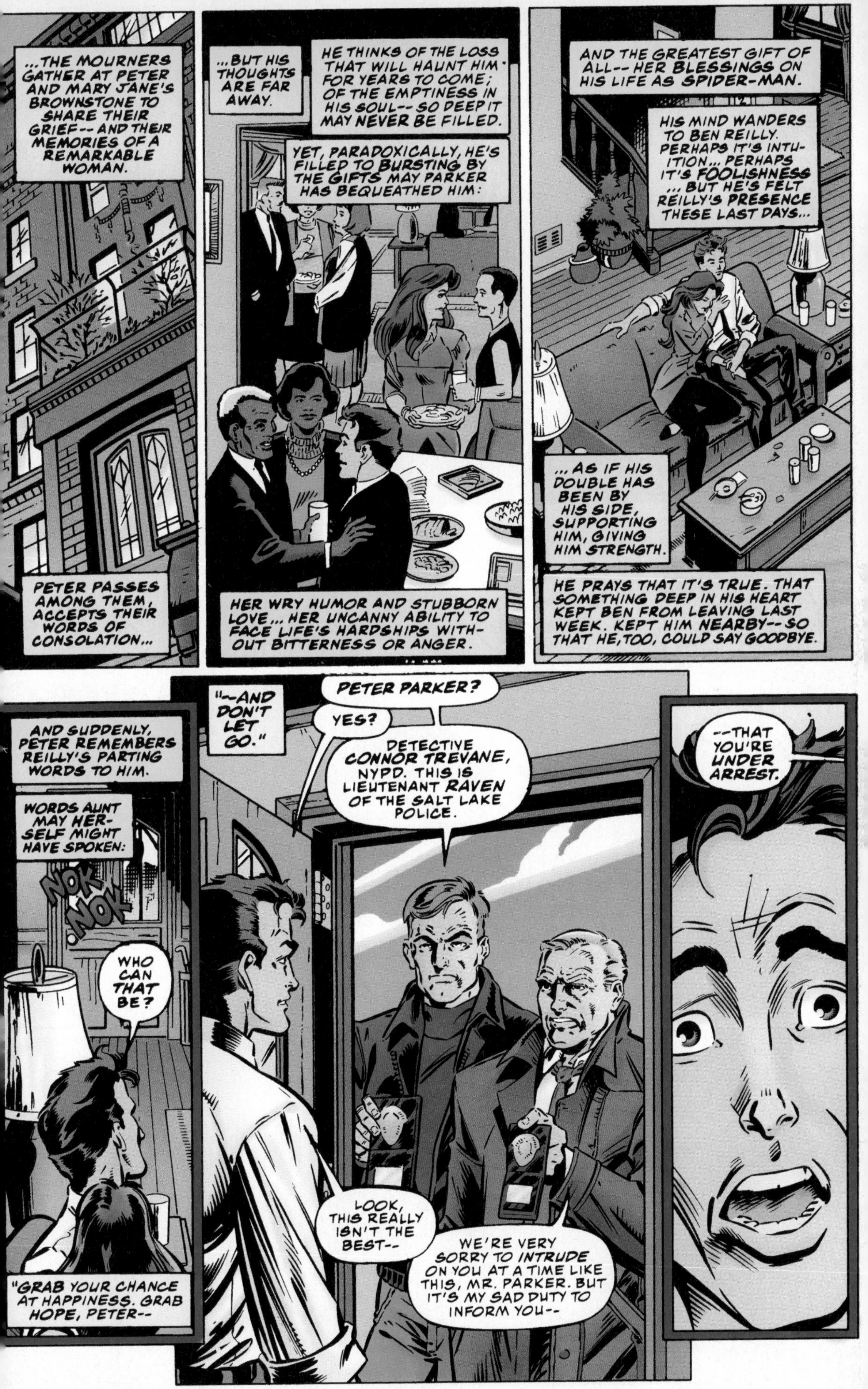
...THE MOURNERS GATHER AT PETER AND MARY JANE'S BROWNSTONE TO SHARE THEIR GRIEF-- AND THEIR MEMORIES OF A REMARKABLE WOMAN.
PETER PASSES AMONG THEM, ACCEPTS THEIR WORDS OF CONSOLATION...
...BUT HIS THOUGHTS ARE FAR AWAY.
HE THINKS OF THE LOSS THAT WILL HAUNT HIM FOR YEARS TO COME; OF THE EMPTINESS IN HIS SOUL-- SO DEEP IT MAY NEVER BE FILLED.
YET, PARADOXICALLY, HE'S FILLED TO BURSTING BY THE GIFTS MAY PARKER HAS BEQUEATHED HIM:
HER WRY HUMOR AND STUBBORN LOVE... HER UNCANNY ABILITY TO FACE LIFE'S HARDSHIPS WITHOUT BITTERNESS OR ANGER.
AND THE GREATEST GIFT OF ALL-- HER BLESSINGS ON HIS LIFE AS SPIDER-MAN.
HIS MIND WANDERS TO BEN REILLY. PERHAPS IT'S INTUITION... PERHAPS IT'S FOOLISHNESS ... BUT HE'S FELT REILLY'S PRESENCE THESE LAST DAYS...
...AS IF HIS DOUBLE HAS BEEN BY HIS SIDE, SUPPORTING HIM, GIVING HIM STRENGTH.
HE PRAYS THAT IT'S TRUE. THAT SOMETHING DEEP IN HIS HEART KEPT BEN FROM LEAVING LAST WEEK. KEPT HIM NEARBY-- SO THAT HE, TOO, COULD SAY GOODBYE.
AND SUDDENLY, PETER REMEMBERS REILLY'S PARTING WORDS TO HIM.
WORDS AUNT MAY HERSELF MIGHT HAVE SPOKEN:
NOK NOK
WHO CAN THAT BE?
"GRAB YOUR CHANCE AT HAPPINESS. GRAB HOPE, PETER--
"--AND DON'T LET GO."
PETER PARKER?
YES?
DETECTIVE CONNOR TREVANE, NYPD. THIS IS LIEUTENANT RAVEN OF THE SALT LAKE POLICE.
LOOK, THIS REALLY ISN'T THE BEST--
WE'RE VERY SORRY TO INTRUDE ON YOU AT A TIME LIKE THIS, MR. PARKER. BUT IT'S MY SAD DUTY TO INFORM YOU--
--THAT YOU'RE UNDER ARREST.

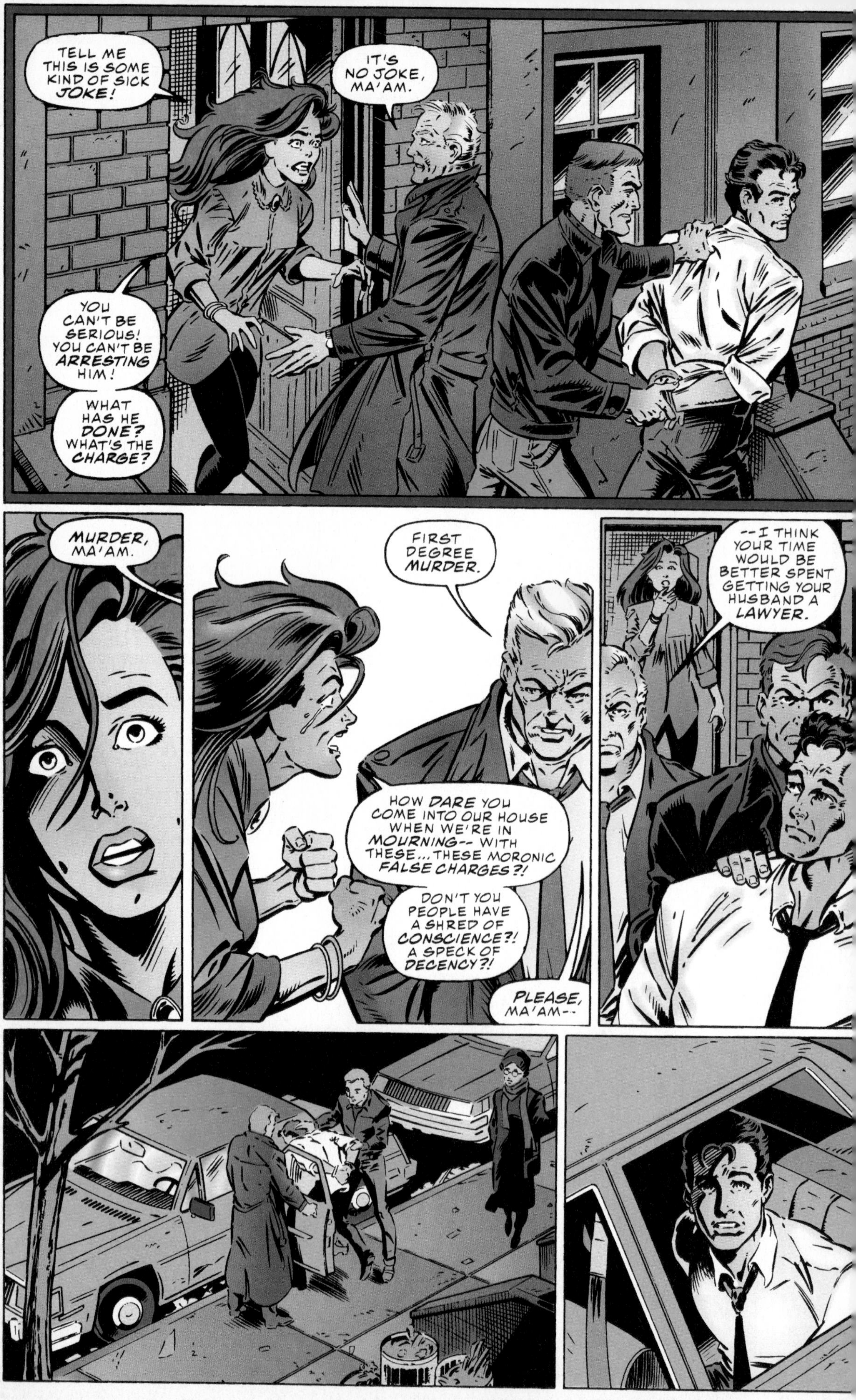
TELL ME THIS IS SOME KIND OF SICK JOKE!
IT'S NO JOKE, MA'AM.
YOU CAN'T BE SERIOUS! YOU CAN'T BE ARRESTING HIM!
WHAT HAS HE DONE? WHAT'S THE CHARGE?
MURDER, MA'AM.
FIRST DEGREE MURDER.
HOW DARE YOU COME INTO OUR HOUSE WHEN WE'RE IN MOURNING-- WITH THESE... THESE MORONIC FALSE CHARGES?!
DON'T YOU PEOPLE HAVE A SHRED OF CONSCIENCE?! A SPECK OF DECENCY?!
PLEASE, MA'AM--
--I THINK YOUR TIME WOULD BE BETTER SPENT GETTING YOUR HUSBAND A LAWYER.

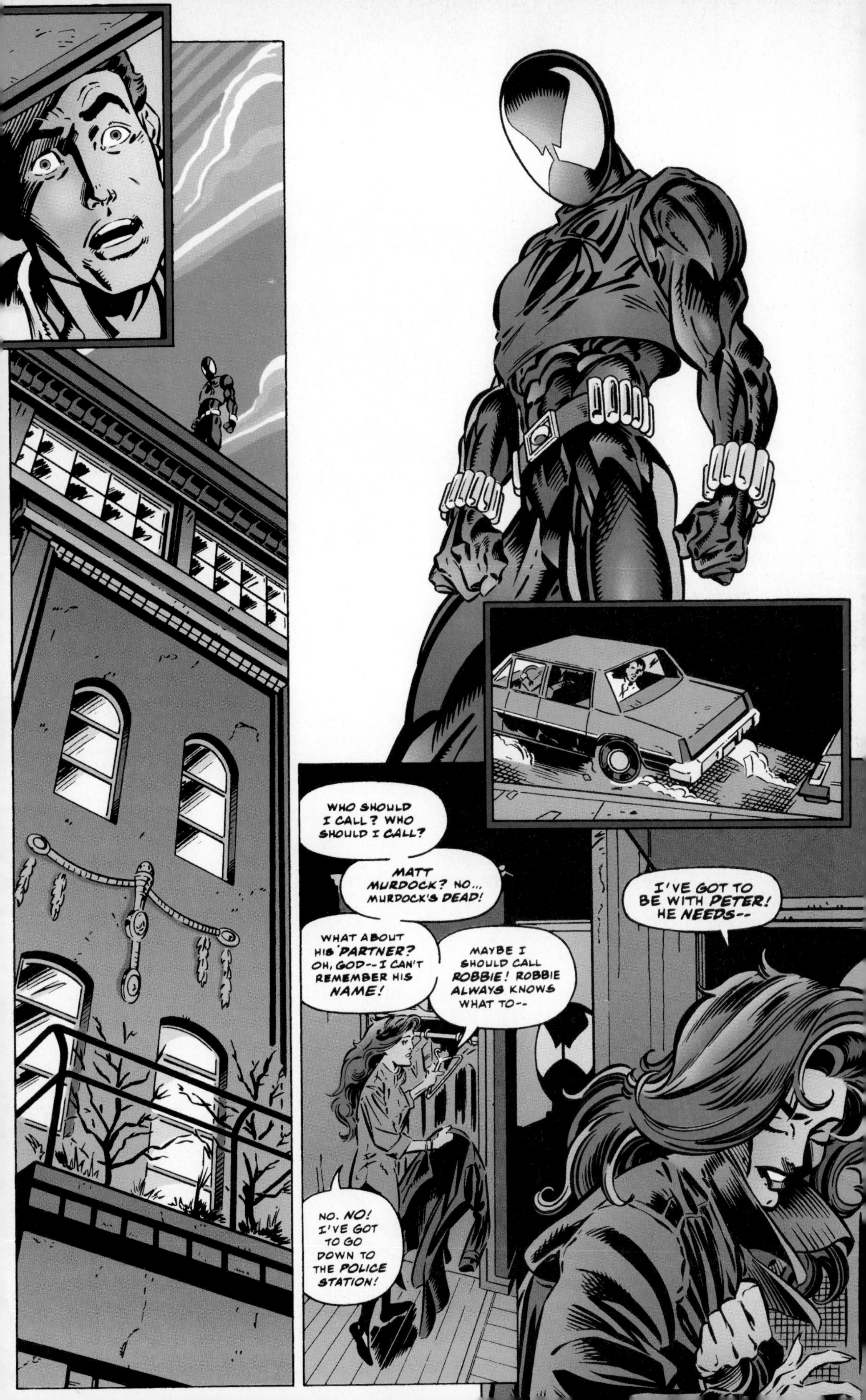

WHO SHOULD I CALL? WHO SHOULD I CALL?
MATT MURDOCK? NO... MURDOCK'S DEAD!
WHAT ABOUT HIS PARTNER? OH, GOD-- I CAN'T REMEMBER HIS NAME!
MAYBE I SHOULD CALL ROBBIE! ROBBIE ALWAYS KNOWS WHAT TO--
NO. NO! I'VE GOT TO GO DOWN TO THE POLICE STATION!
I'VE GOT TO BE WITH PETER! HE NEEDS--

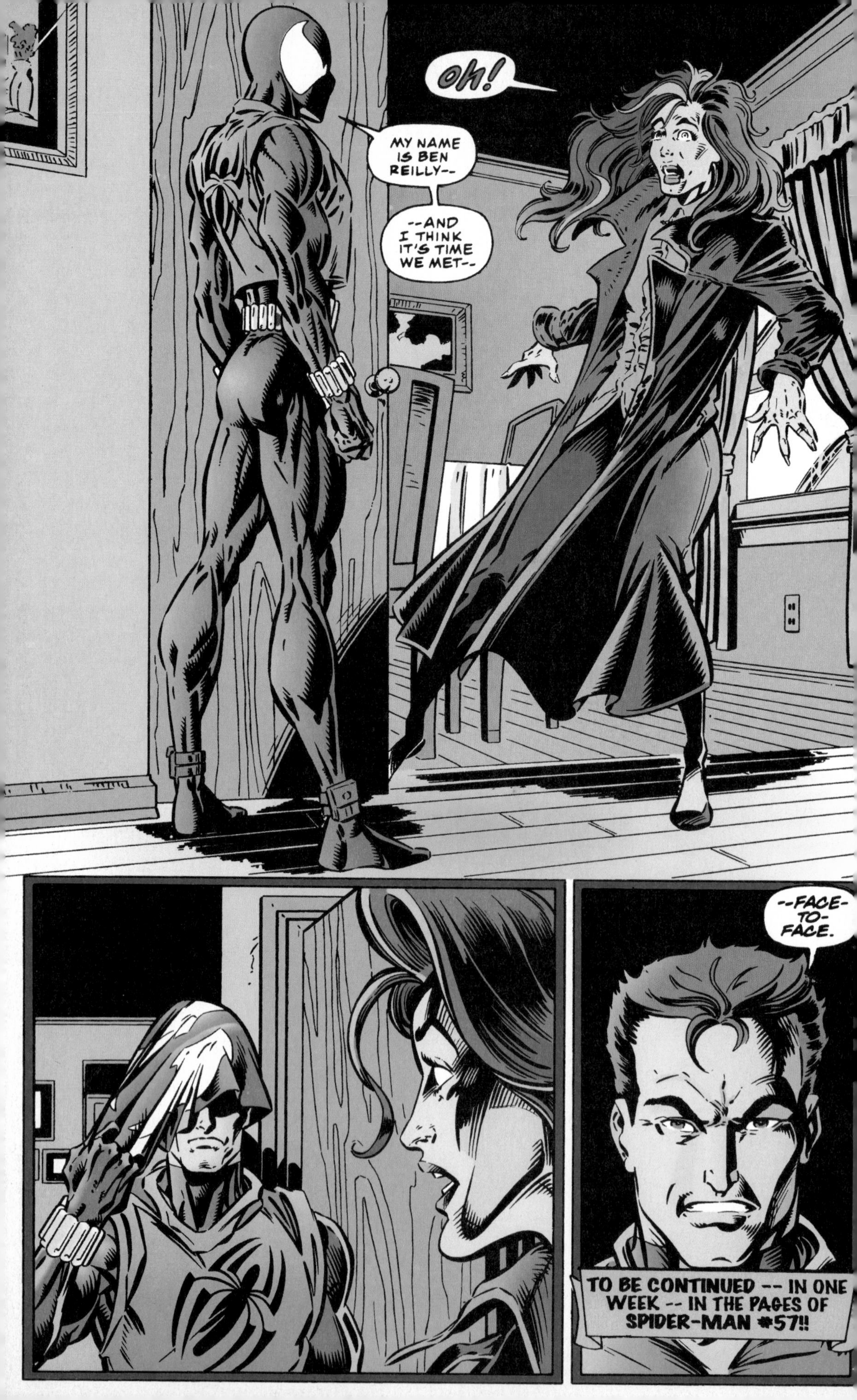
oh!
MY NAME IS BEN REILLY--
--AND I THINK IT'S TIME WE MET--
--FACE-TO-FACE.
TO BE CONTINUED -- IN ONE WEEK -- IN THE PAGES OF SPIDER-MAN #57!!

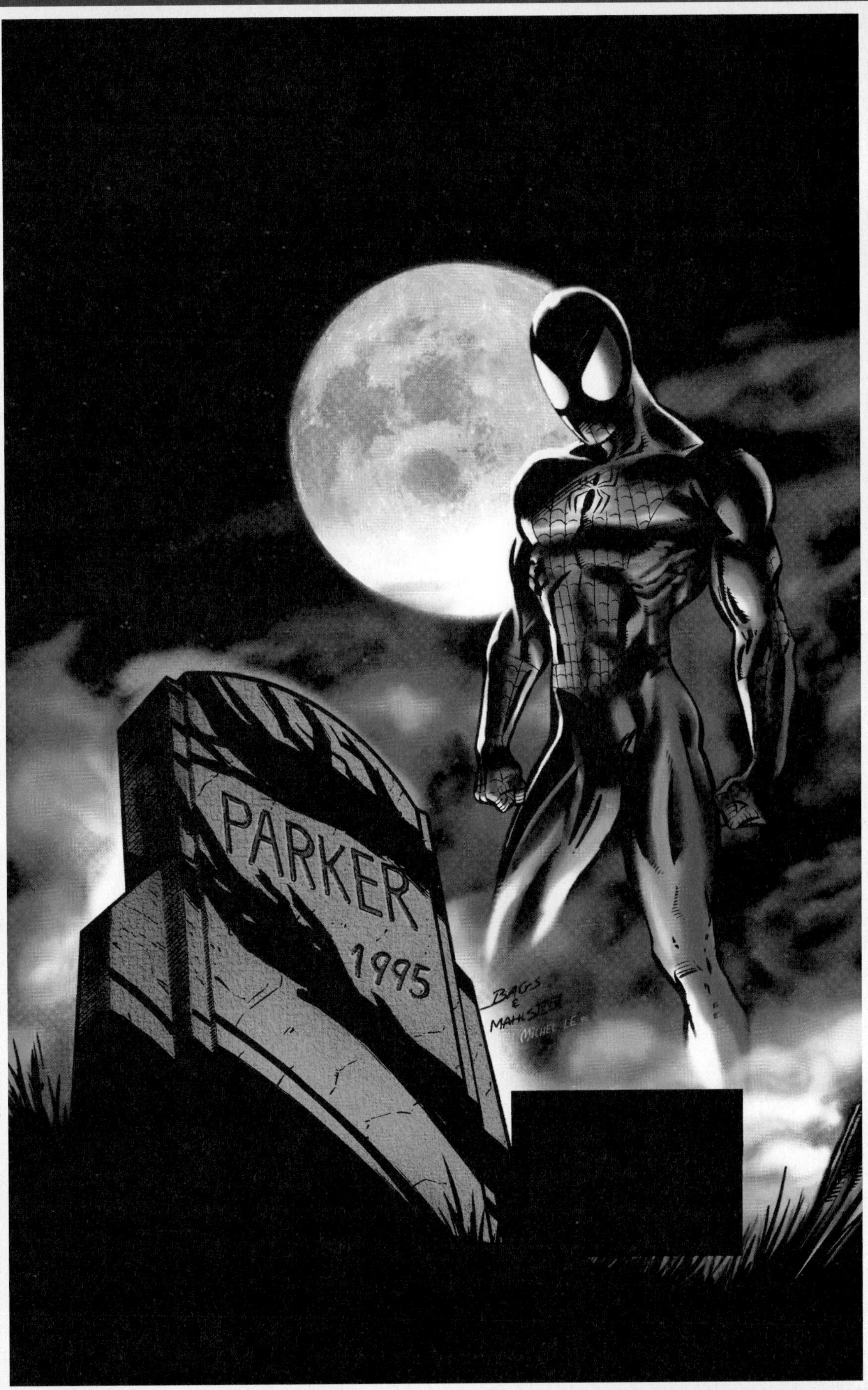
PARKER
1995

Amazing Spider-Man #400 **deluxe edition die-cut undercover**

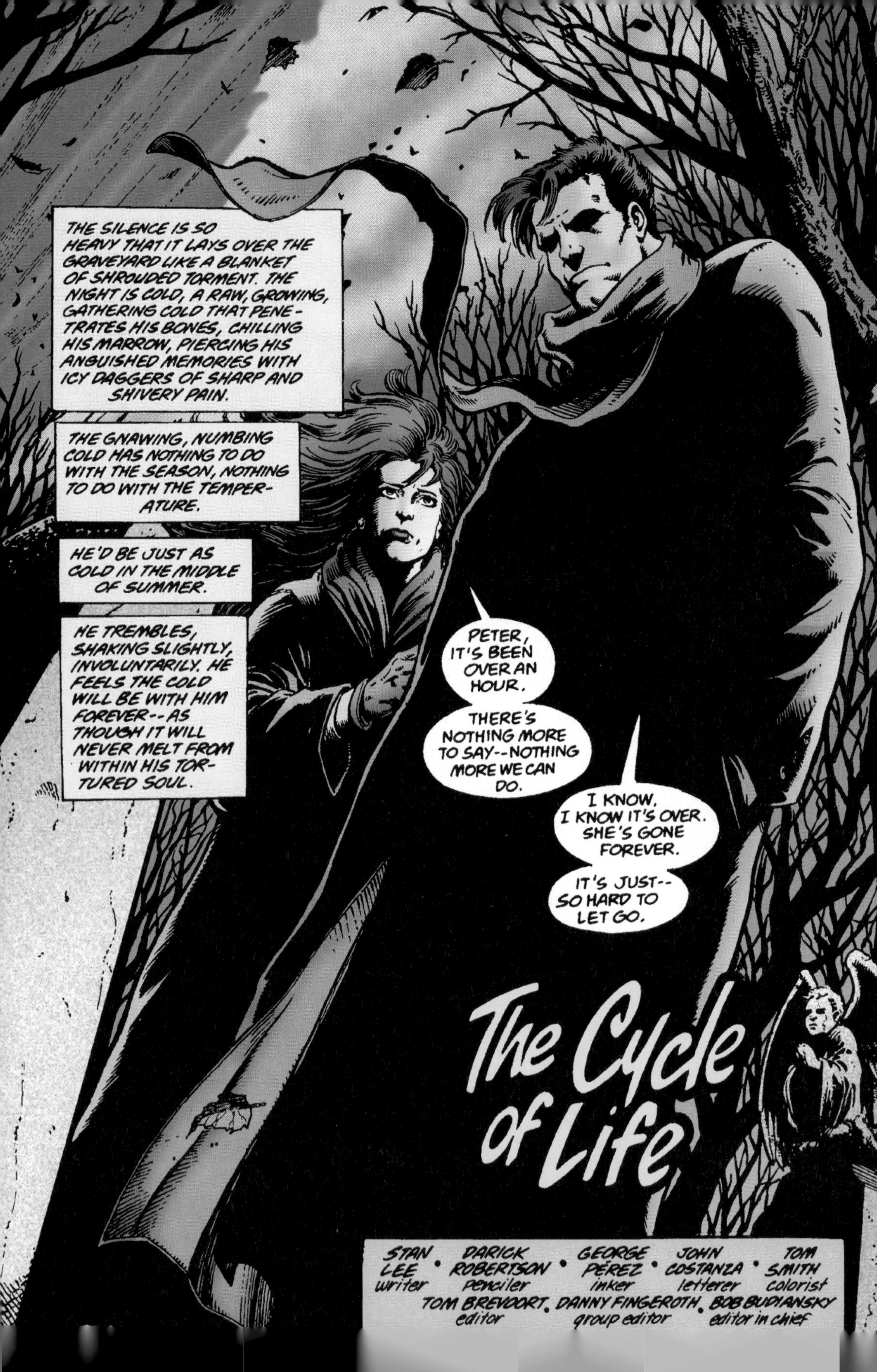

THE SILENCE IS SO HEAVY THAT IT LAYS OVER THE GRAVEYARD LIKE A BLANKET OF SHROUDED TORMENT. THE NIGHT IS COLD, A RAW, GROWING, GATHERING COLD THAT PENETRATES HIS BONES, CHILLING HIS MARROW, PIERCING HIS ANGUISHED MEMORIES WITH ICY DAGGERS OF SHARP AND SHIVERY PAIN.
THE GNAWING, NUMBING COLD HAS NOTHING TO DO WITH THE SEASON, NOTHING TO DO WITH THE TEMPERATURE.
HE'D BE JUST AS COLD IN THE MIDDLE OF SUMMER.
HE TREMBLES, SHAKING SLIGHTLY, INVOLUNTARILY. HE FEELS THE COLD WILL BE WITH HIM FOREVER--AS THOUGH IT WILL NEVER MELT FROM WITHIN HIS TORTURED SOUL.
PETER, IT'S BEEN OVER AN HOUR.
THERE'S NOTHING MORE TO SAY--NOTHING MORE WE CAN DO.
I KNOW. I KNOW IT'S OVER. SHE'S GONE FOREVER.
IT'S JUST-- SO HARD TO LET GO.
The Cycle of Life
STAN LEE writer • DARICK ROBERTSON penciler • GEORGE PÉREZ inker • JOHN COSTANZA letterer • TOM SMITH colorist
TOM BREVOORT, editor • DANNY FINGEROTH, group editor • BOB BUDIANSKY editor in chief

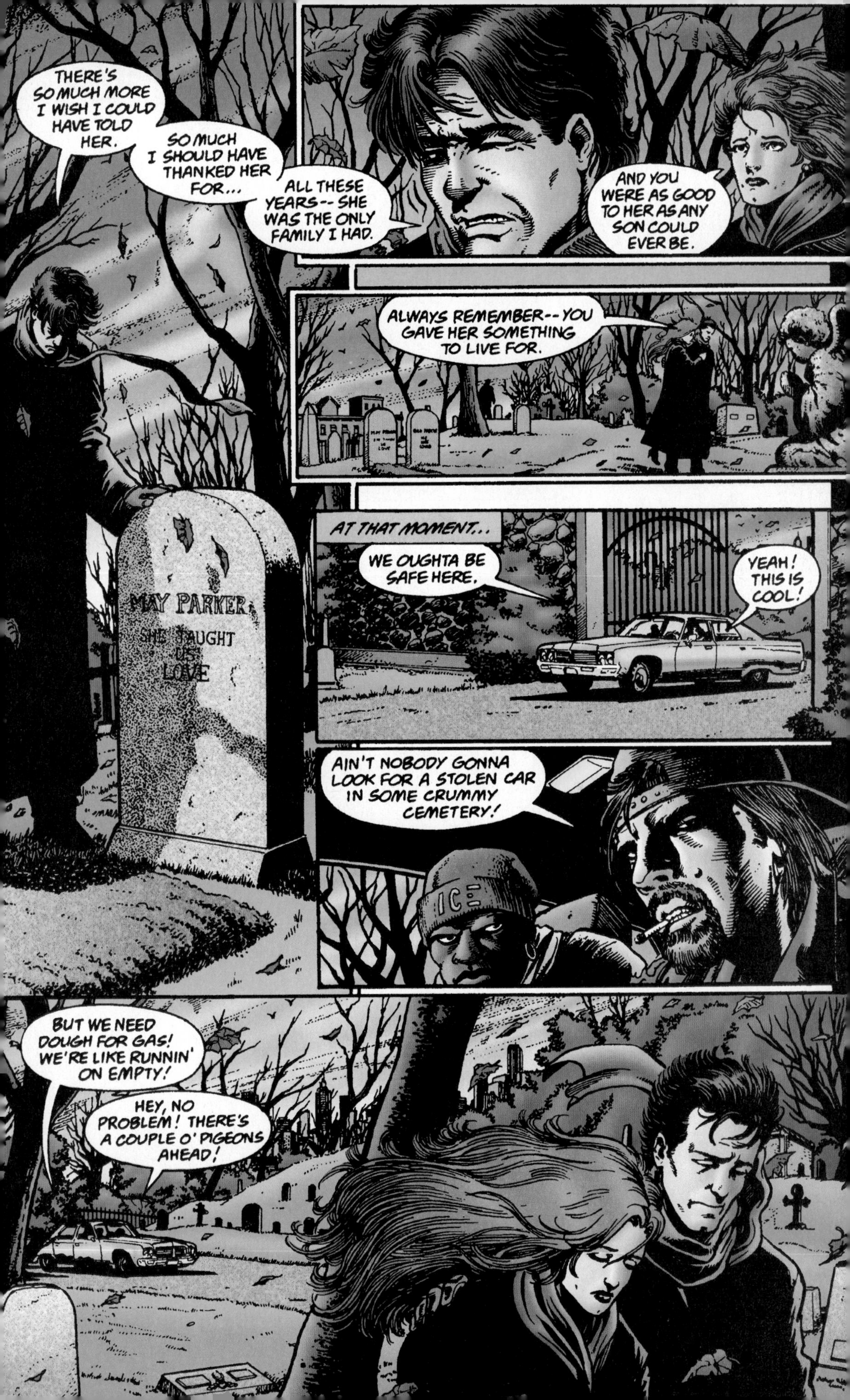

THERE'S SO MUCH MORE I WISH I COULD HAVE TOLD HER.
SO MUCH I SHOULD HAVE THANKED HER FOR...
ALL THESE YEARS-- SHE WAS THE ONLY FAMILY I HAD.
AND YOU WERE AS GOOD TO HER AS ANY SON COULD EVER BE.
MAY PARKER
SHE TAUGHT US LOVE
ALWAYS REMEMBER-- YOU GAVE HER SOMETHING TO LIVE FOR.
AT THAT MOMENT...
WE OUGHTA BE SAFE HERE.
YEAH! THIS IS COOL!
AIN'T NOBODY GONNA LOOK FOR A STOLEN CAR IN SOME CRUMMY CEMETERY!
ICE
BUT WE NEED DOUGH FOR GAS! WE'RE LIKE RUNNIN' ON EMPTY!
HEY, NO PROBLEM! THERE'S A COUPLE O' PIGEONS AHEAD!

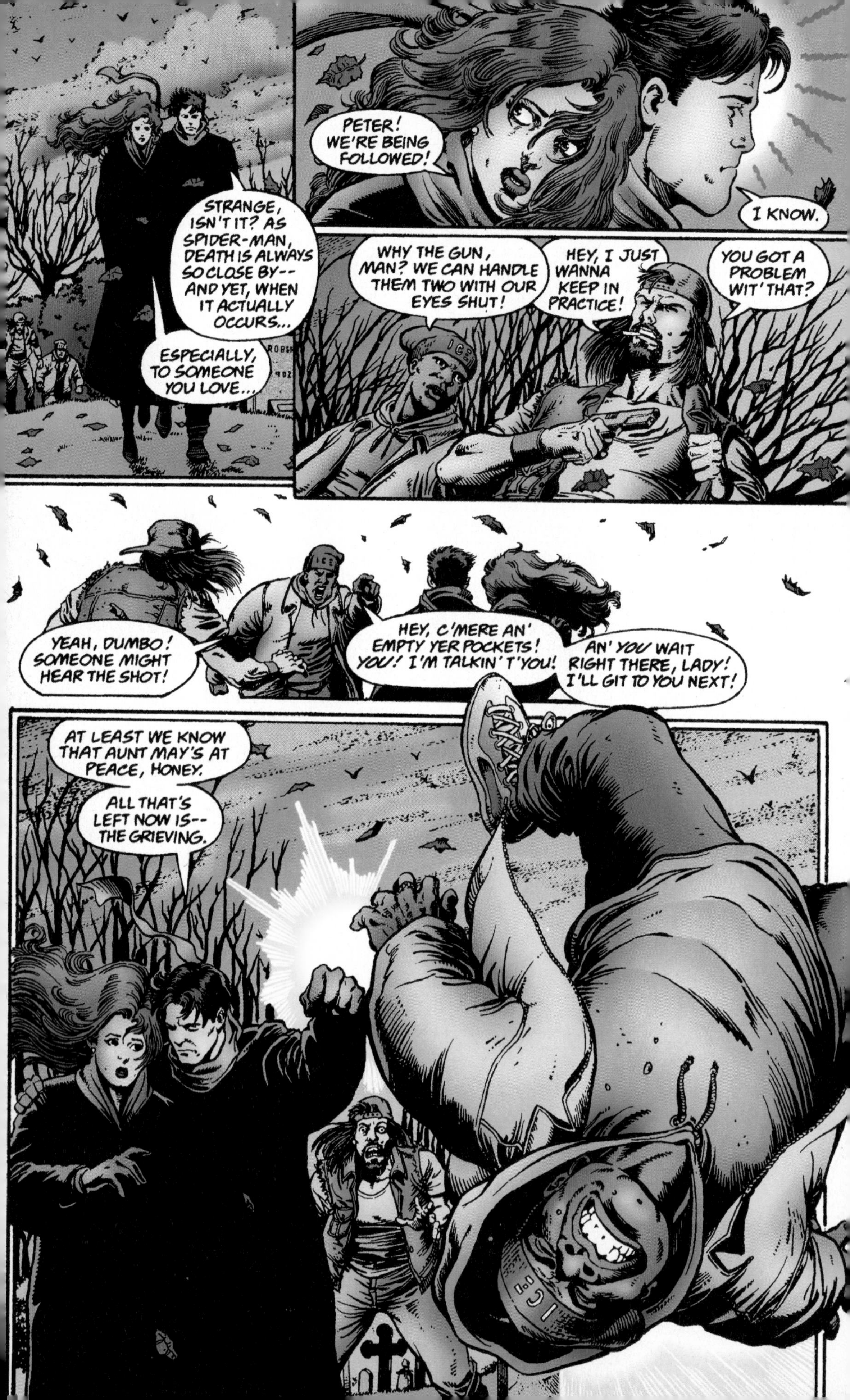
STRANGE, ISN'T IT? AS SPIDER-MAN, DEATH IS ALWAYS SO CLOSE BY-- AND YET, WHEN IT ACTUALLY OCCURS...
ESPECIALLY, TO SOMEONE YOU LOVE...
PETER! WE'RE BEING FOLLOWED!
I KNOW.
WHY THE GUN, MAN? WE CAN HANDLE THEM TWO WITH OUR EYES SHUT!
HEY, I JUST WANNA KEEP IN PRACTICE!
YOU GOT A PROBLEM WIT' THAT?
YEAH, DUMBO! SOMEONE MIGHT HEAR THE SHOT!
HEY, C'MERE AN' EMPTY YER POCKETS! YOU! I'M TALKIN' T'YOU!
AN' YOU WAIT RIGHT THERE, LADY! I'LL GIT TO YOU NEXT!
AT LEAST WE KNOW THAT AUNT MAY'S AT PEACE, HONEY.
ALL THAT'S LEFT NOW IS-- THE GRIEVING.

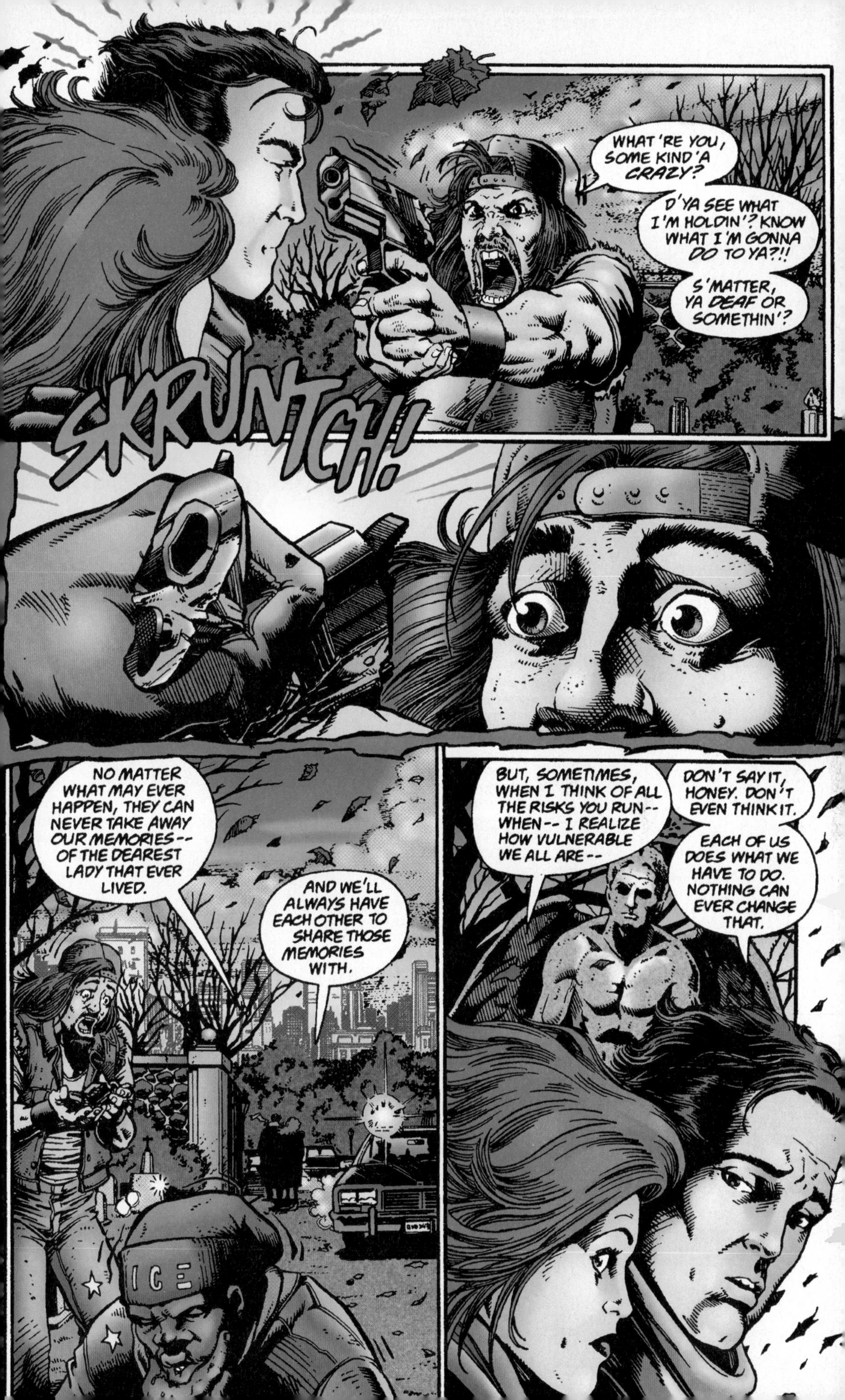
WHAT 'RE YOU, SOME KIND 'A CRAZY?
D'YA SEE WHAT I'M HOLDIN'? KNOW WHAT I'M GONNA DO TO YA?!!
S'MATTER, YA DEAF OR SOMETHIN'?
SKRUNTCH!
NO MATTER WHAT MAY EVER HAPPEN, THEY CAN NEVER TAKE AWAY OUR MEMORIES-- OF THE DEAREST LADY THAT EVER LIVED.
AND WE'LL ALWAYS HAVE EACH OTHER TO SHARE THOSE MEMORIES WITH.
BUT, SOMETIMES, WHEN I THINK OF ALL THE RISKS YOU RUN-- WHEN-- I REALIZE HOW VULNERABLE WE ALL ARE--
DON'T SAY IT, HONEY. DON'T EVEN THINK IT.
EACH OF US DOES WHAT WE HAVE TO DO. NOTHING CAN EVER CHANGE THAT.
ICE

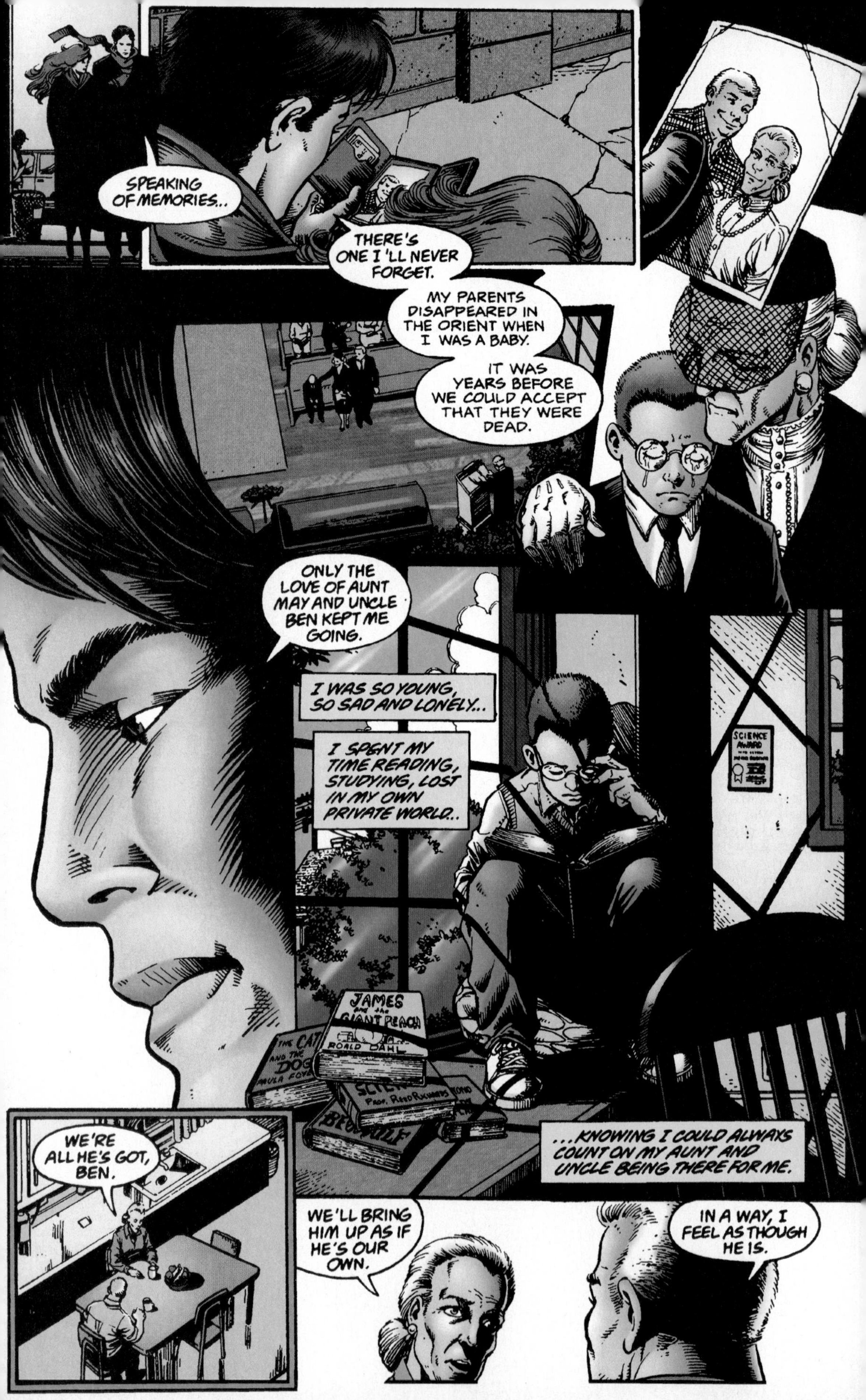

SPEAKING OF MEMORIES...
THERE'S ONE I'LL NEVER FORGET.
MY PARENTS DISAPPEARED IN THE ORIENT WHEN I WAS A BABY.
IT WAS YEARS BEFORE WE COULD ACCEPT THAT THEY WERE DEAD.
ONLY THE LOVE OF AUNT MAY AND UNCLE BEN KEPT ME GOING.
I WAS SO YOUNG, SO SAD AND LONELY...
I SPENT MY TIME READING, STUDYING, LOST IN MY OWN PRIVATE WORLD...
SCIENCE AWARD
JAMES and the GIANT PEACH
ROALD DAHL
THE CAT AND THE DOG
SCIENCE
PROF. REED RICHARDS
BEOWULF
...KNOWING I COULD ALWAYS COUNT ON MY AUNT AND UNCLE BEING THERE FOR ME.
WE'RE ALL HE'S GOT, BEN.
WE'LL BRING HIM UP AS IF HE'S OUR OWN.
IN A WAY, I FEEL AS THOUGH HE IS.

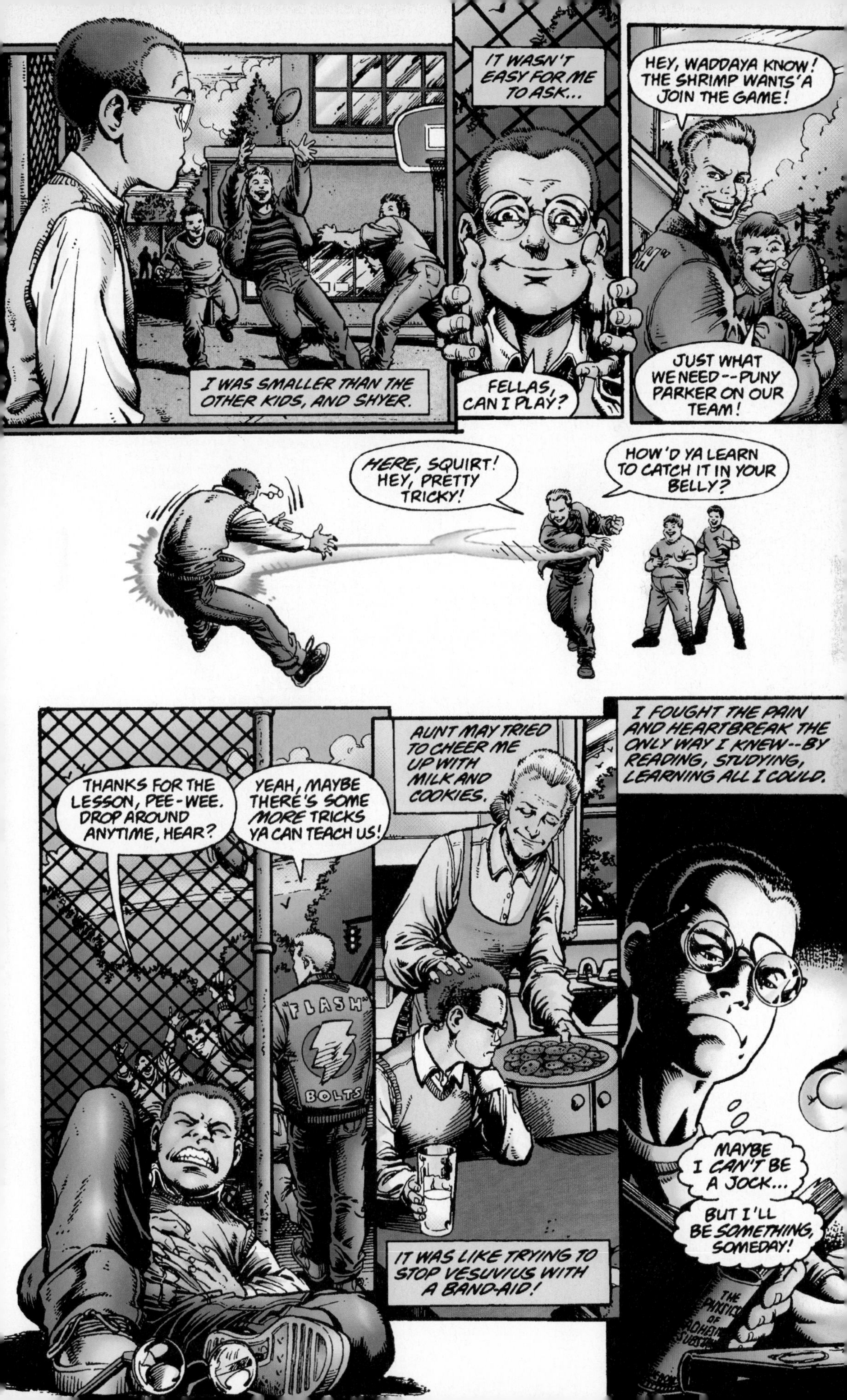

IT WASN'T EASY FOR ME TO ASK...
I WAS SMALLER THAN THE OTHER KIDS, AND SHYER.
FELLAS, CAN I PLAY?
HEY, WADDAYA KNOW! THE SHRIMP WANTS'A JOIN THE GAME!
JUST WHAT WE NEED--PUNY PARKER ON OUR TEAM!
HERE, SQUIRT! HEY, PRETTY TRICKY!
HOW'D YA LEARN TO CATCH IT IN YOUR BELLY?
THANKS FOR THE LESSON, PEE-WEE. DROP AROUND ANYTIME, HEAR?
YEAH, MAYBE THERE'S SOME MORE TRICKS YA CAN TEACH US!
"FLASH"
BOLTS
AUNT MAY TRIED TO CHEER ME UP WITH MILK AND COOKIES.
IT WAS LIKE TRYING TO STOP VESUVIUS WITH A BAND-AID!
I FOUGHT THE PAIN AND HEARTBREAK THE ONLY WAY I KNEW--BY READING, STUDYING, LEARNING ALL I COULD.
MAYBE I CAN'T BE A JOCK...
BUT I'LL BE SOMETHING, SOMEDAY!

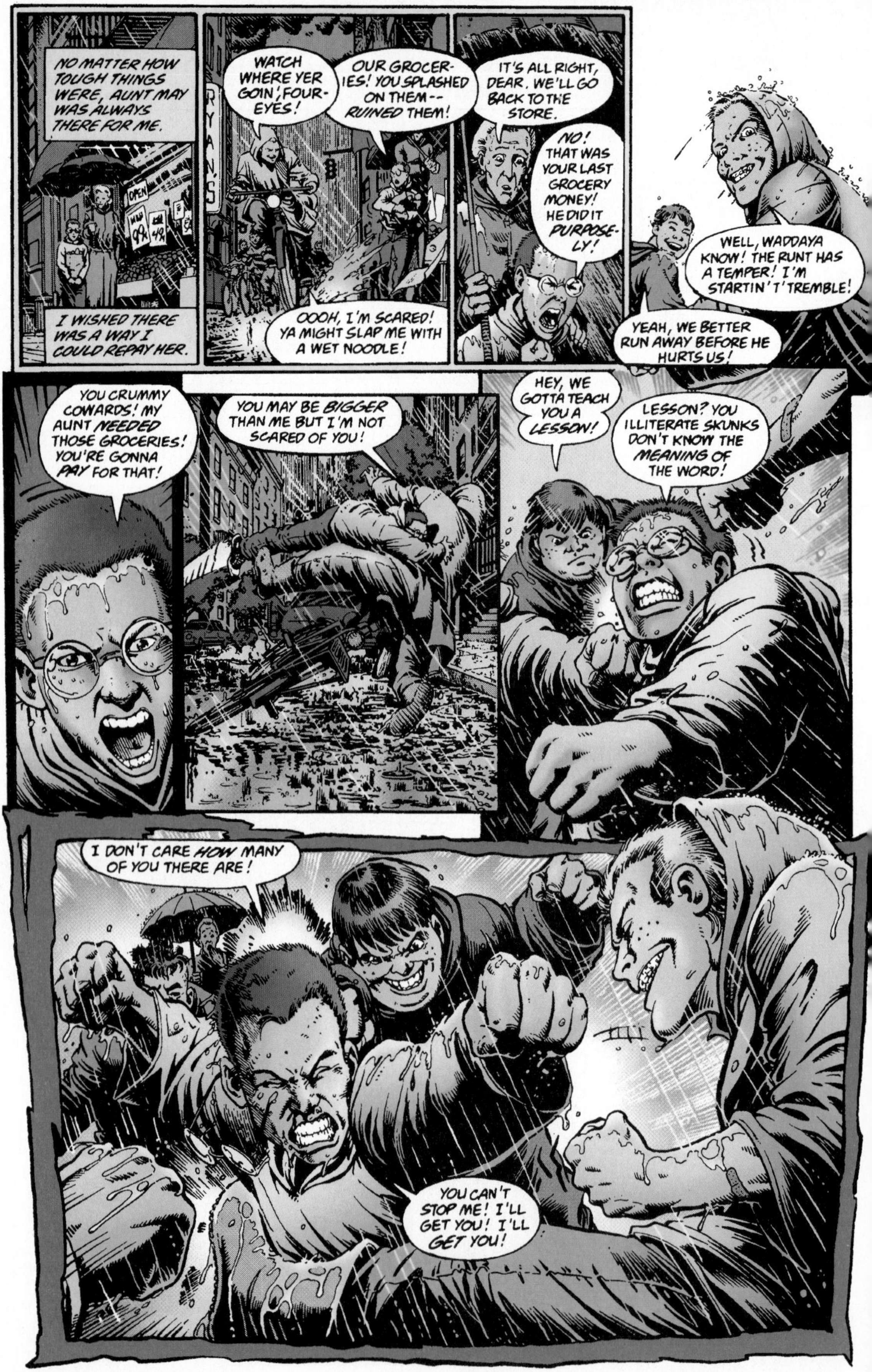
NO MATTER HOW TOUGH THINGS WERE, AUNT MAY WAS ALWAYS THERE FOR ME.
I WISHED THERE WAS A WAY I COULD REPAY HER.
WATCH WHERE YER GOIN', FOUR-EYES!
OUR GROCERIES! YOU SPLASHED ON THEM -- RUINED THEM!
OOOH, I'M SCARED! YA MIGHT SLAP ME WITH A WET NOODLE!
IT'S ALL RIGHT, DEAR. WE'LL GO BACK TO THE STORE.
NO! THAT WAS YOUR LAST GROCERY MONEY! HE DID IT PURPOSELY!
WELL, WADDAYA KNOW! THE RUNT HAS A TEMPER! I'M STARTIN' T' TREMBLE!
YEAH, WE BETTER RUN AWAY BEFORE HE HURTS US!
YOU CRUMMY COWARDS! MY AUNT NEEDED THOSE GROCERIES! YOU'RE GONNA PAY FOR THAT!
YOU MAY BE BIGGER THAN ME BUT I'M NOT SCARED OF YOU!
HEY, WE GOTTA TEACH YOU A LESSON!
LESSON? YOU ILLITERATE SKUNKS DON'T KNOW THE MEANING OF THE WORD!
I DON'T CARE HOW MANY OF YOU THERE ARE!
YOU CAN'T STOP ME! I'LL GET YOU! I'LL GET YOU!

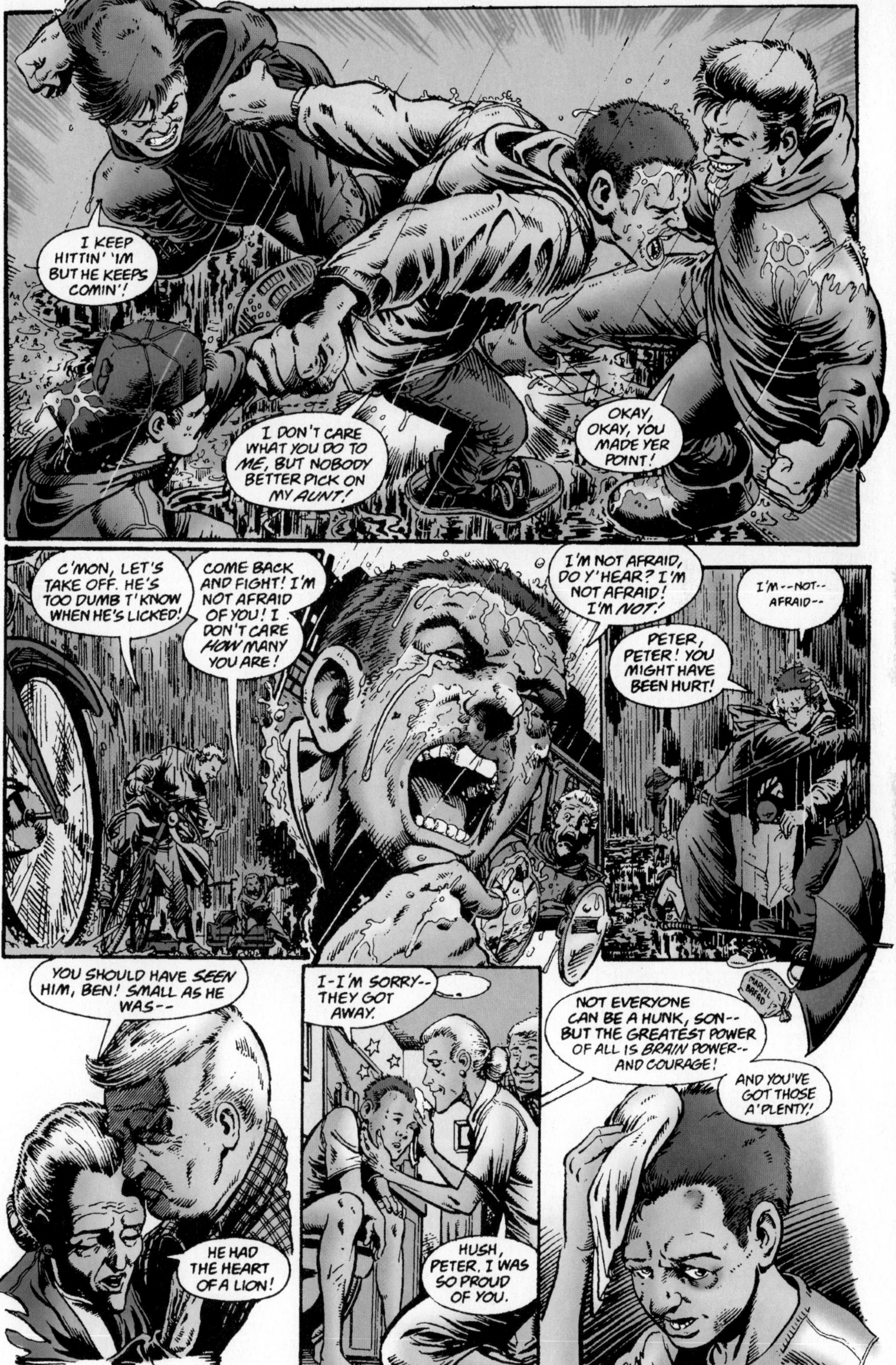
I KEEP HITTIN' 'IM BUT HE KEEPS COMIN'!
I DON'T CARE WHAT YOU DO TO ME, BUT NOBODY BETTER PICK ON MY AUNT!
OKAY, OKAY, YOU MADE YER POINT!
C'MON, LET'S TAKE OFF. HE'S TOO DUMB T'KNOW WHEN HE'S LICKED!
COME BACK AND FIGHT! I'M NOT AFRAID OF YOU! I DON'T CARE HOW MANY YOU ARE!
I'M NOT AFRAID, DO Y'HEAR? I'M NOT AFRAID! I'M NOT!
I'M--NOT--AFRAID--
PETER, PETER! YOU MIGHT HAVE BEEN HURT!
MARVEL BREAD
YOU SHOULD HAVE SEEN HIM, BEN! SMALL AS HE WAS--
HE HAD THE HEART OF A LION!
I-I'M SORRY--THEY GOT AWAY.
HUSH, PETER. I WAS SO PROUD OF YOU.
NOT EVERYONE CAN BE A HUNK, SON--BUT THE GREATEST POWER OF ALL IS BRAIN POWER--AND COURAGE!
AND YOU'VE GOT THOSE A'PLENTY!

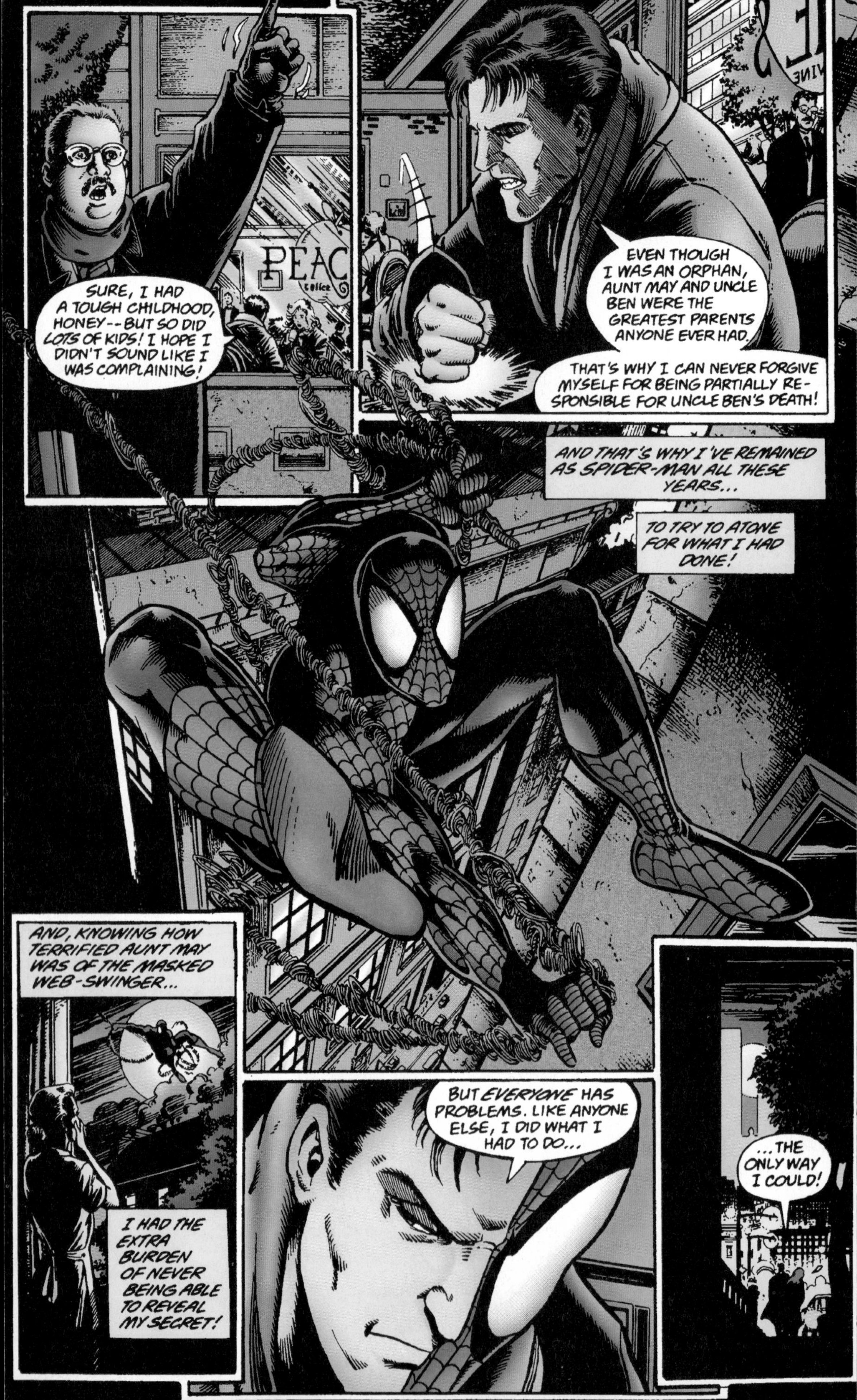
SURE, I HAD A TOUGH CHILDHOOD, HONEY-- BUT SO DID LOTS OF KIDS! I HOPE I DIDN'T SOUND LIKE I WAS COMPLAINING!
PEAC
EVEN THOUGH I WAS AN ORPHAN, AUNT MAY AND UNCLE BEN WERE THE GREATEST PARENTS ANYONE EVER HAD.
THAT'S WHY I CAN NEVER FORGIVE MYSELF FOR BEING PARTIALLY RE-SPONSIBLE FOR UNCLE BEN'S DEATH!
AND THAT'S WHY I'VE REMAINED AS SPIDER-MAN ALL THESE YEARS...
TO TRY TO ATONE FOR WHAT I HAD DONE!
AND, KNOWING HOW TERRIFIED AUNT MAY WAS OF THE MASKED WEB-SWINGER...
I HAD THE EXTRA BURDEN OF NEVER BEING ABLE TO REVEAL MY SECRET!
BUT EVERYONE HAS PROBLEMS. LIKE ANYONE ELSE, I DID WHAT I HAD TO DO...
...THE ONLY WAY I COULD!

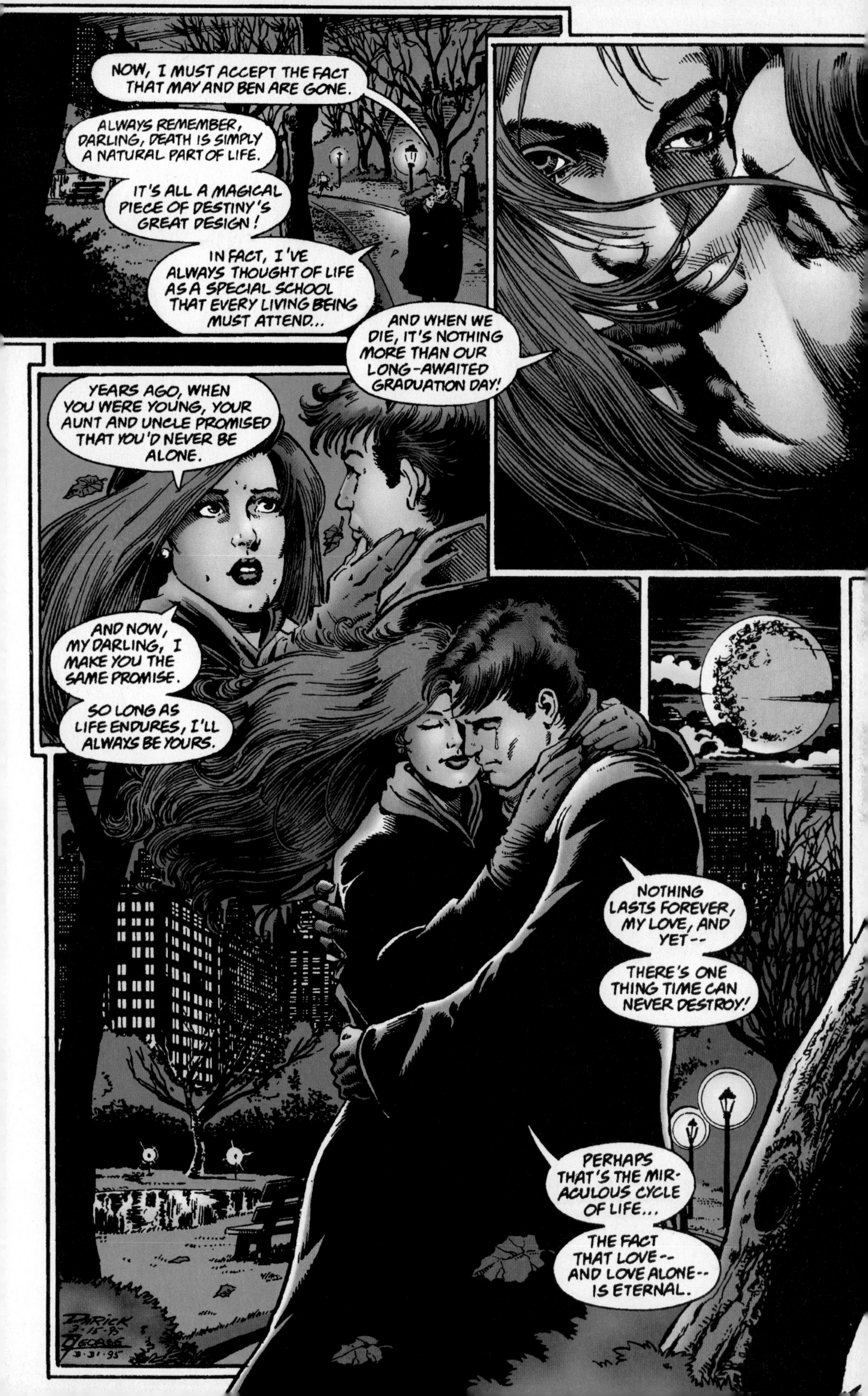
NOW, I MUST ACCEPT THE FACT THAT MAY AND BEN ARE GONE.
ALWAYS REMEMBER, DARLING, DEATH IS SIMPLY A NATURAL PART OF LIFE.
IT'S ALL A MAGICAL PIECE OF DESTINY'S GREAT DESIGN!
IN FACT, I'VE ALWAYS THOUGHT OF LIFE AS A SPECIAL SCHOOL THAT EVERY LIVING BEING MUST ATTEND...
AND WHEN WE DIE, IT'S NOTHING MORE THAN OUR LONG-AWAITED GRADUATION DAY!
YEARS AGO, WHEN YOU WERE YOUNG, YOUR AUNT AND UNCLE PROMISED THAT YOU'D NEVER BE ALONE.
AND NOW, MY DARLING, I MAKE YOU THE SAME PROMISE.
SO LONG AS LIFE ENDURES, I'LL ALWAYS BE YOURS.
NOTHING LASTS FOREVER, MY LOVE, AND YET--
THERE'S ONE THING TIME CAN NEVER DESTROY!
PERHAPS THAT'S THE MIR-ACULOUS CYCLE OF LIFE...
THE FACT THAT LOVE-- AND LOVE ALONE-- IS ETERNAL.

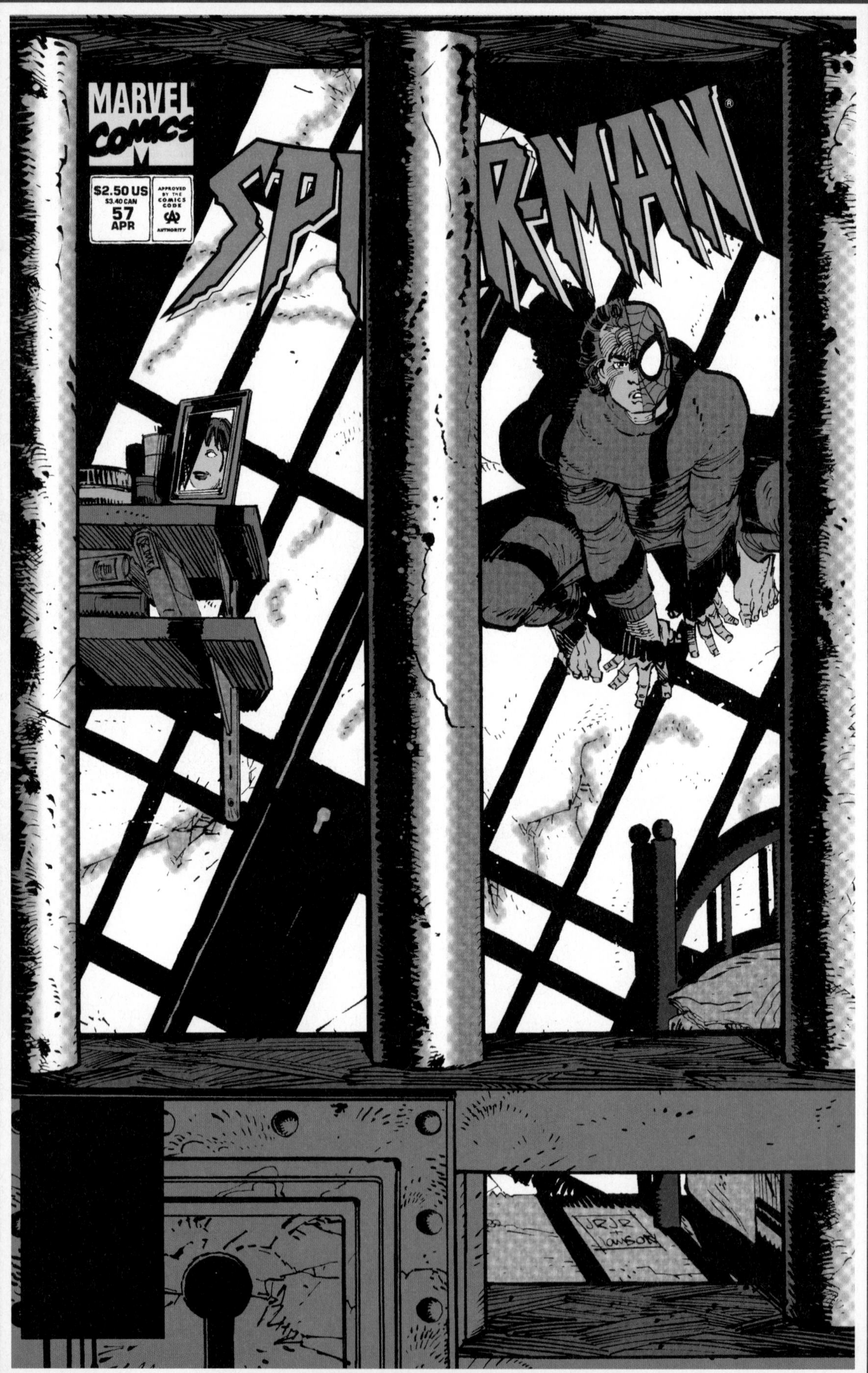
MARVEL COMICS
$2.50 US
$3.40 CAN
57
APR
APPROVED BY THE COMICS CODE AUTHORITY

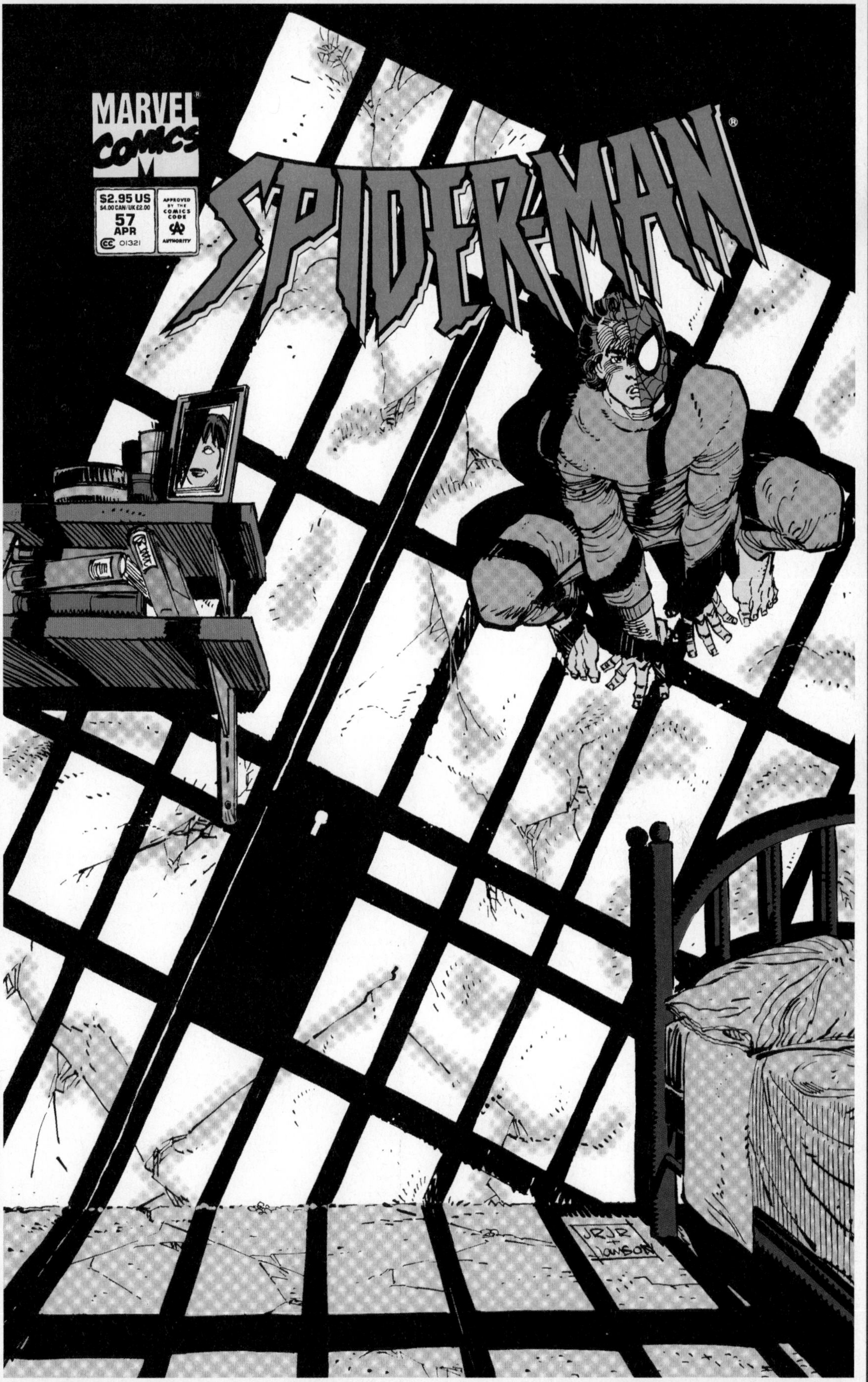
MARVEL COMICS
SPIDER-MAN
$2.95 US
$4.00 CAN/UK £2.00
57
APR
APPROVED BY THE COMICS CODE AUTHORITY

Spider-Man #57 **deluxe edition die-cut undercover**

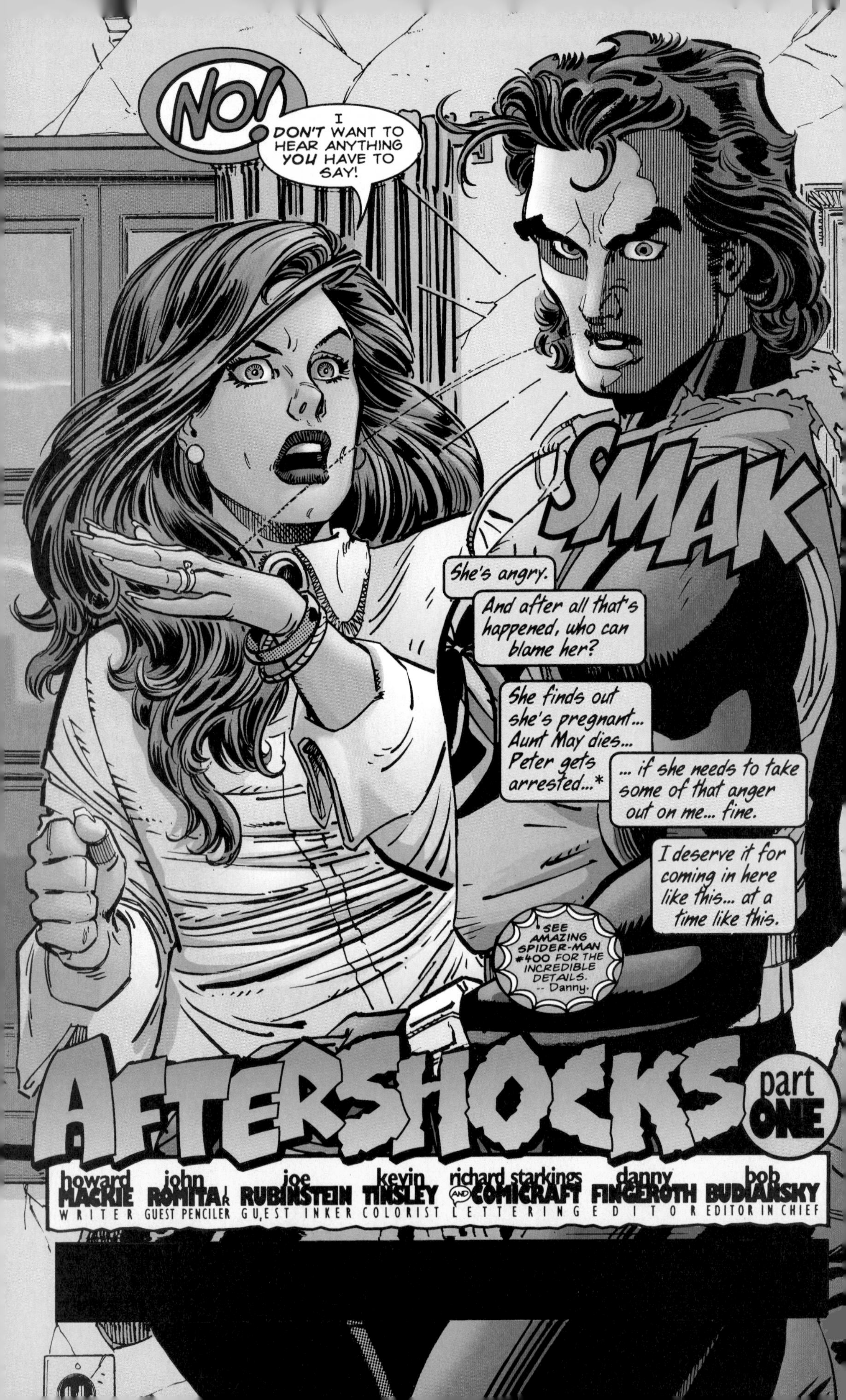
NO!
I DON'T WANT TO HEAR ANYTHING YOU HAVE TO SAY!
SMAK
She's angry.
And after all that's happened, who can blame her?
She finds out she's pregnant... Aunt May dies... Peter gets arrested...*
... if she needs to take some of that anger out on me... fine.
I deserve it for coming in here like this... at a time like this.
*SEE AMAZING SPIDER-MAN #400 FOR THE INCREDIBLE DETAILS. -- Danny.
AFTERSHOCKS part ONE
howard MACKIE WRITER
john ROMITA JR GUEST PENCILER
joe RUBINSTEIN GUEST INKER
kevin TINSLEY COLORIST
richard starkings AND COMICRAFT LETTERING
danny FINGEROTH EDITOR
bob BUDIANSKY EDITOR IN CHIEF

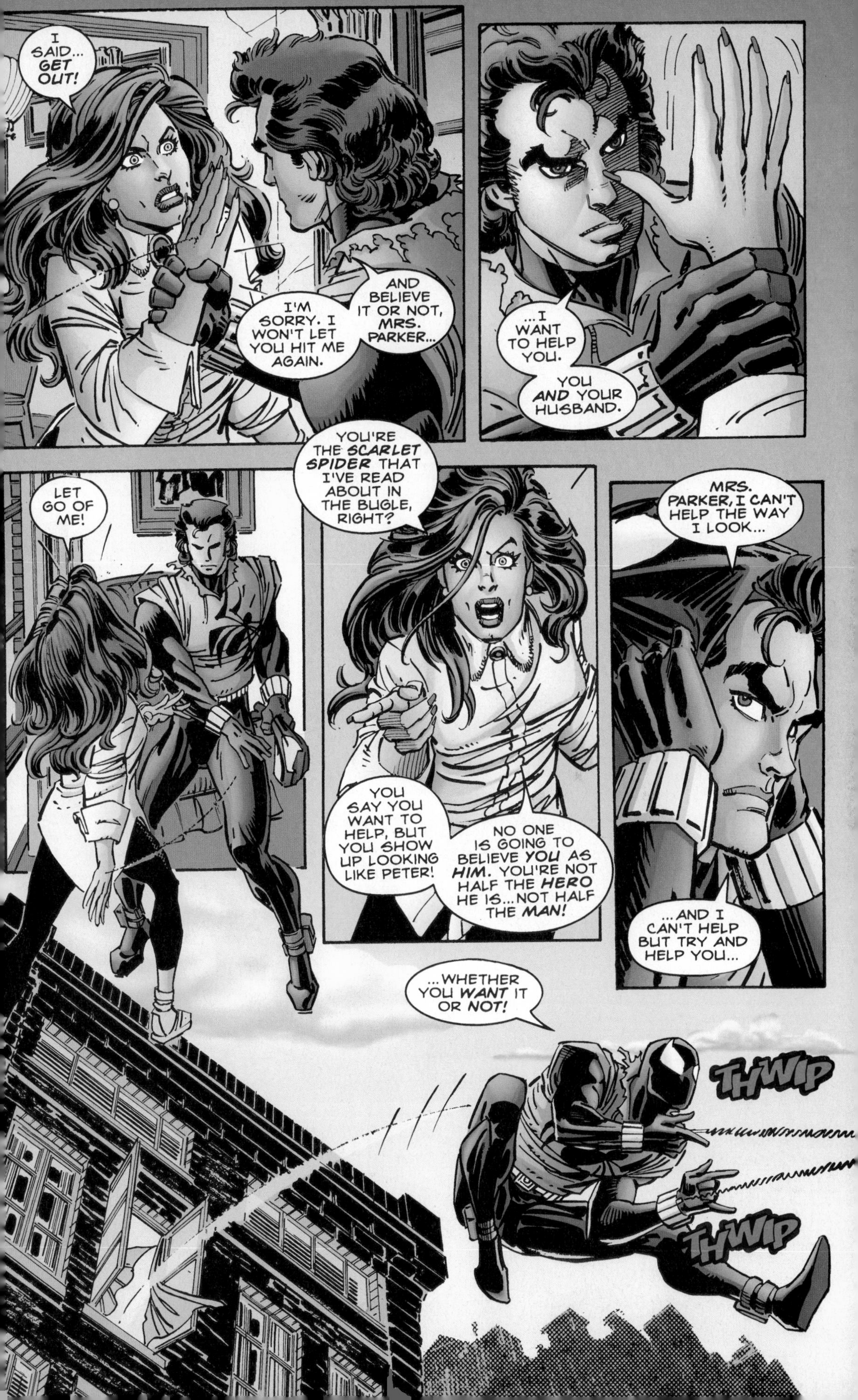
I SAID... GET OUT!
I'M SORRY. I WON'T LET YOU HIT ME AGAIN.
AND BELIEVE IT OR NOT, MRS. PARKER...
...I WANT TO HELP YOU.
YOU AND YOUR HUSBAND.
LET GO OF ME!
YOU'RE THE SCARLET SPIDER THAT I'VE READ ABOUT IN THE BUGLE, RIGHT?
YOU SAY YOU WANT TO HELP, BUT YOU SHOW UP LOOKING LIKE PETER!
NO ONE IS GOING TO BELIEVE YOU AS HIM. YOU'RE NOT HALF THE HERO HE IS...NOT HALF THE MAN!
MRS. PARKER, I CAN'T HELP THE WAY I LOOK...
...AND I CAN'T HELP BUT TRY AND HELP YOU...
...WHETHER YOU WANT IT OR NOT!
THWIP
THWIP

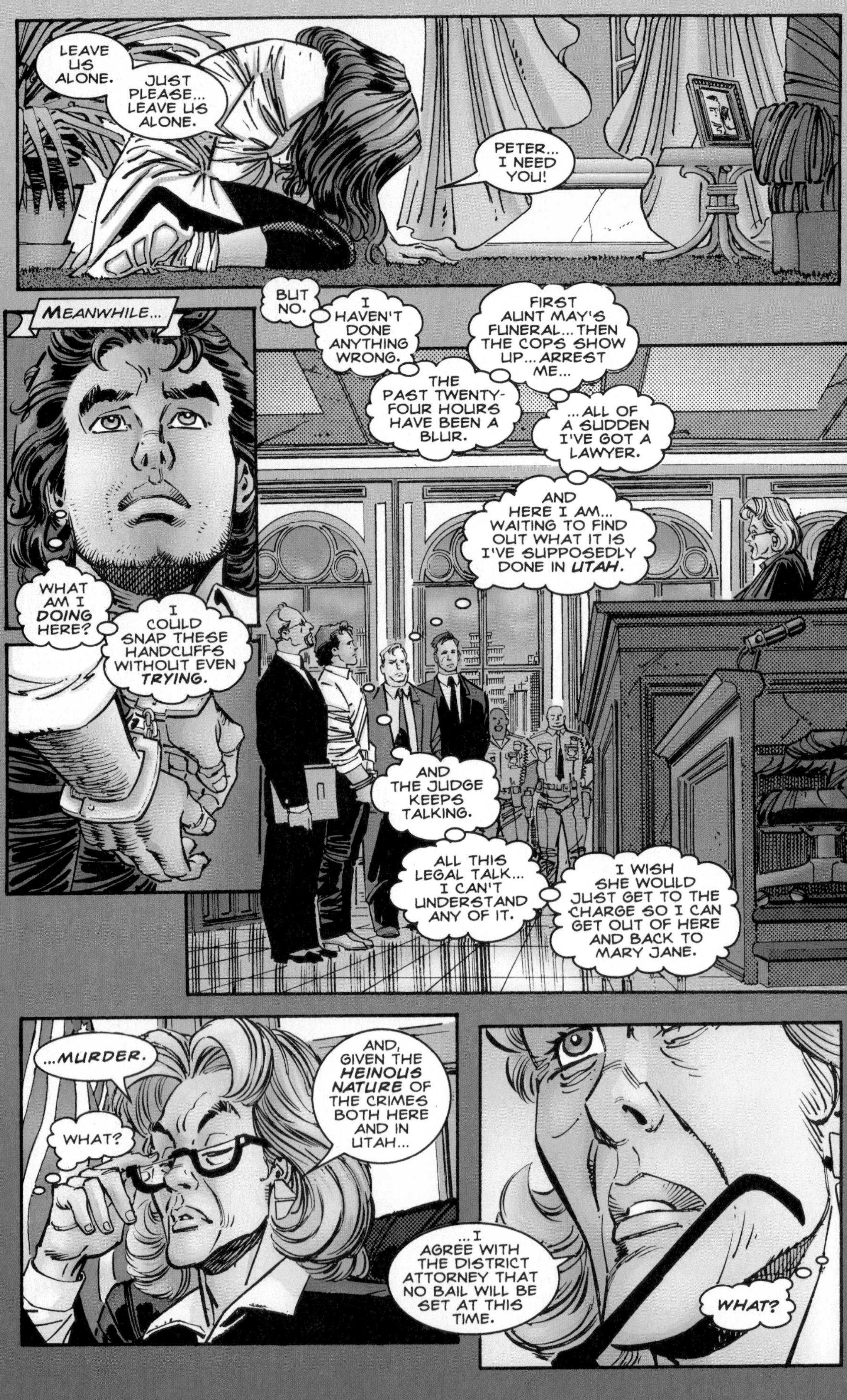
LEAVE US ALONE.
JUST PLEASE... LEAVE US ALONE.
PETER... I NEED YOU!
MEANWHILE...
BUT NO.
I HAVEN'T DONE ANYTHING WRONG.
FIRST AUNT MAY'S FUNERAL... THEN THE COPS SHOW UP... ARREST ME...
THE PAST TWENTY-FOUR HOURS HAVE BEEN A BLUR.
...ALL OF A SUDDEN I'VE GOT A LAWYER.
AND HERE I AM... WAITING TO FIND OUT WHAT IT IS I'VE SUPPOSEDLY DONE IN UTAH.
WHAT AM I DOING HERE?
I COULD SNAP THESE HANDCUFFS WITHOUT EVEN TRYING.
AND THE JUDGE KEEPS TALKING.
ALL THIS LEGAL TALK... I CAN'T UNDERSTAND ANY OF IT.
I WISH SHE WOULD JUST GET TO THE CHARGE SO I CAN GET OUT OF HERE AND BACK TO MARY JANE.
...MURDER.
WHAT?
AND, GIVEN THE HEINOUS NATURE OF THE CRIMES BOTH HERE AND IN UTAH...
...I AGREE WITH THE DISTRICT ATTORNEY THAT NO BAIL WILL BE SET AT THIS TIME.
WHAT?

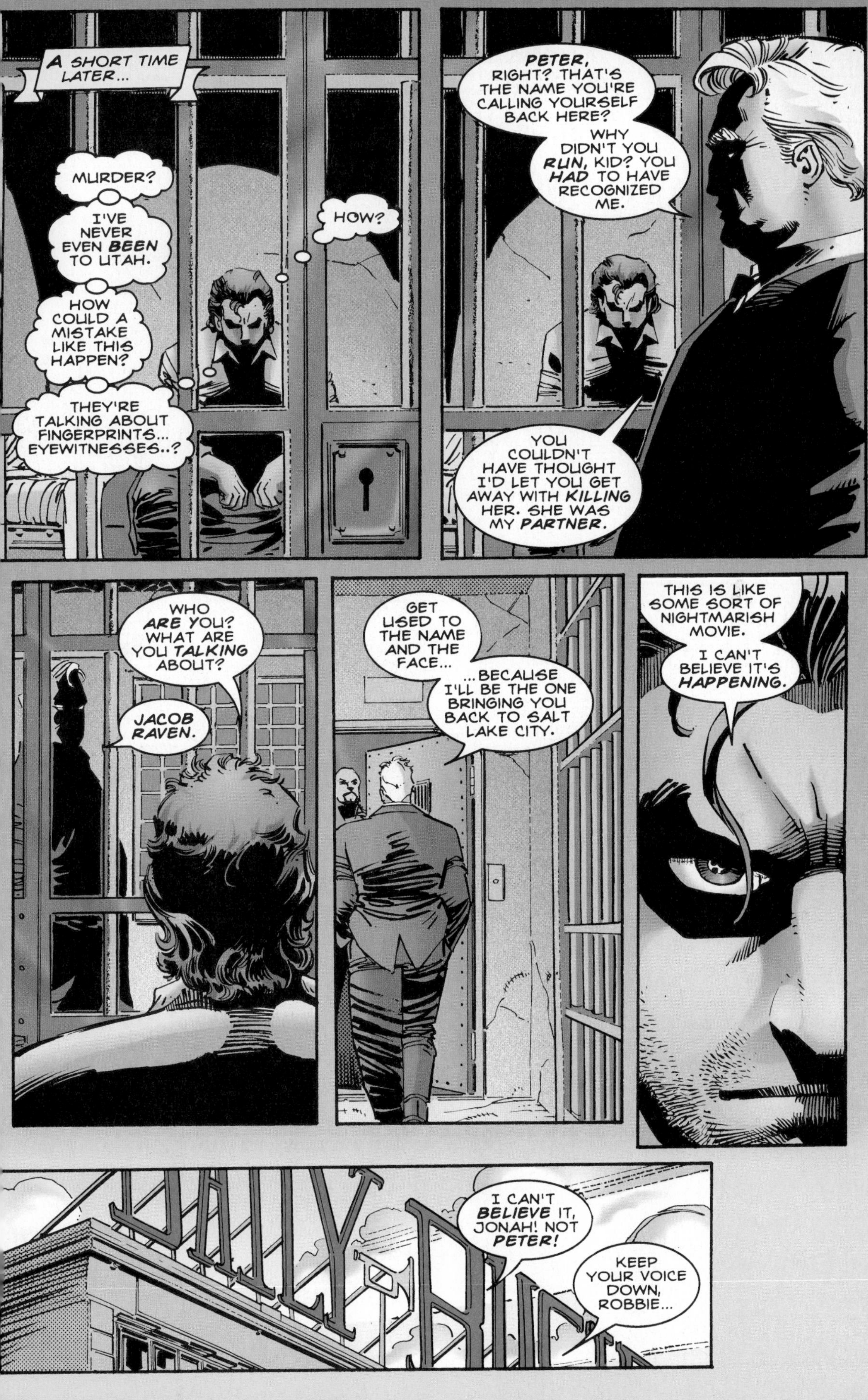
A SHORT TIME LATER...
MURDER?
I'VE NEVER EVEN BEEN TO UTAH.
HOW COULD A MISTAKE LIKE THIS HAPPEN?
THEY'RE TALKING ABOUT FINGERPRINTS... EYEWITNESSES..?
HOW?
PETER, RIGHT? THAT'S THE NAME YOU'RE CALLING YOURSELF BACK HERE?
WHY DIDN'T YOU RUN, KID? YOU HAD TO HAVE RECOGNIZED ME.
YOU COULDN'T HAVE THOUGHT I'D LET YOU GET AWAY WITH KILLING HER. SHE WAS MY PARTNER.
WHO ARE YOU? WHAT ARE YOU TALKING ABOUT?
JACOB RAVEN.
GET USED TO THE NAME AND THE FACE...
...BECAUSE I'LL BE THE ONE BRINGING YOU BACK TO SALT LAKE CITY.
THIS IS LIKE SOME SORT OF NIGHTMARISH MOVIE.
I CAN'T BELIEVE IT'S HAPPENING.
I CAN'T BELIEVE IT, JONAH! NOT PETER!
KEEP YOUR VOICE DOWN, ROBBIE...

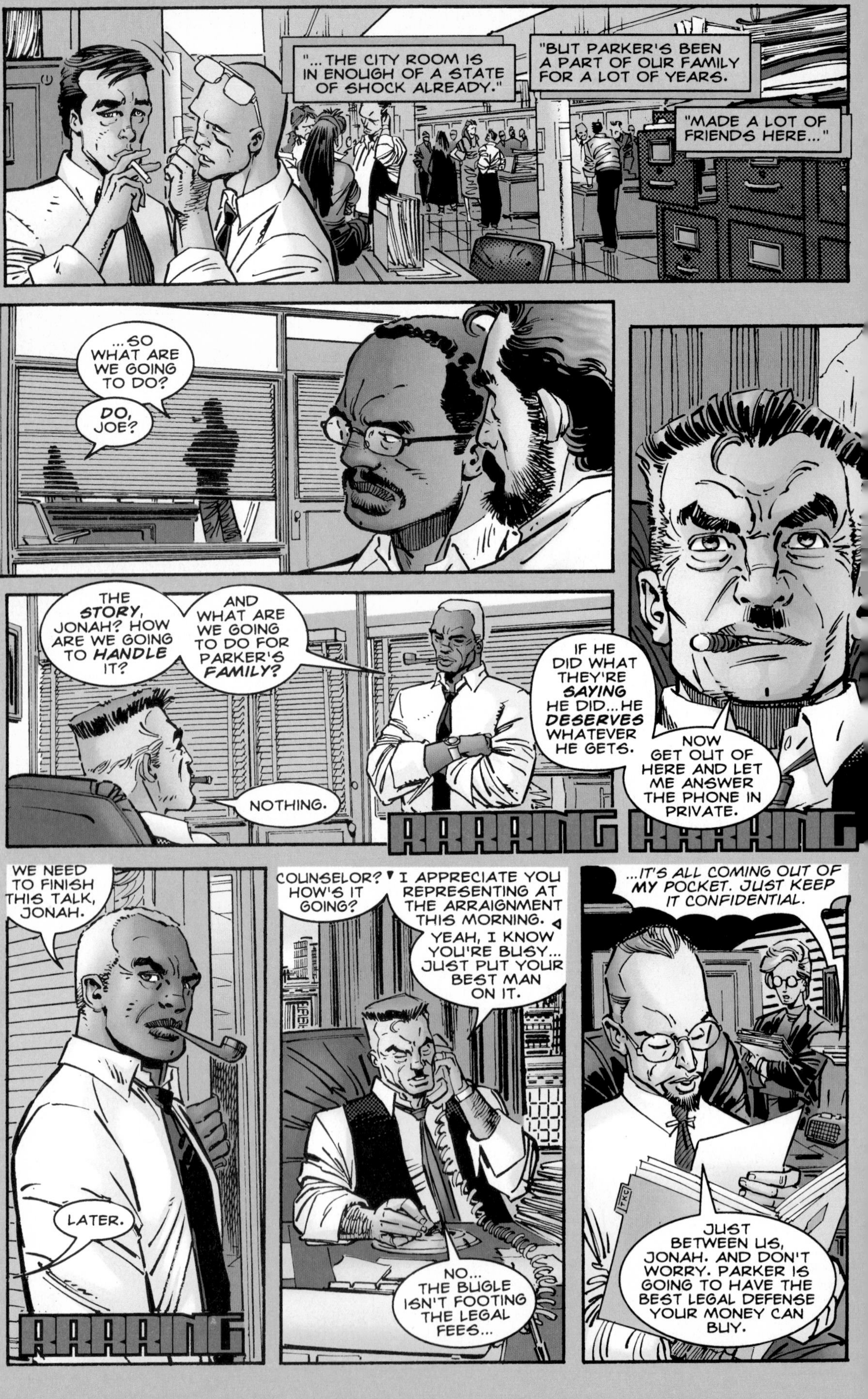
"... THE CITY ROOM IS IN ENOUGH OF A STATE OF SHOCK ALREADY."
"BUT PARKER'S BEEN A PART OF OUR FAMILY FOR A LOT OF YEARS.
"MADE A LOT OF FRIENDS HERE..."
...SO WHAT ARE WE GOING TO DO?
DO, JOE?
THE STORY, JONAH? HOW ARE WE GOING TO HANDLE IT?
AND WHAT ARE WE GOING TO DO FOR PARKER'S FAMILY?
NOTHING.
IF HE DID WHAT THEY'RE SAYING HE DID...HE DESERVES WHATEVER HE GETS.
NOW GET OUT OF HERE AND LET ME ANSWER THE PHONE IN PRIVATE.
RRRRING RRRRING
WE NEED TO FINISH THIS TALK, JONAH.
LATER.
RRRRING
COUNSELOR? HOW'S IT GOING?
I APPRECIATE YOU REPRESENTING AT THE ARRAIGNMENT THIS MORNING.
YEAH, I KNOW YOU'RE BUSY... JUST PUT YOUR BEST MAN ON IT.
NO... THE BUGLE ISN'T FOOTING THE LEGAL FEES...
...IT'S ALL COMING OUT OF MY POCKET. JUST KEEP IT CONFIDENTIAL.
JUST BETWEEN US, JONAH. AND DON'T WORRY. PARKER IS GOING TO HAVE THE BEST LEGAL DEFENSE YOUR MONEY CAN BUY.

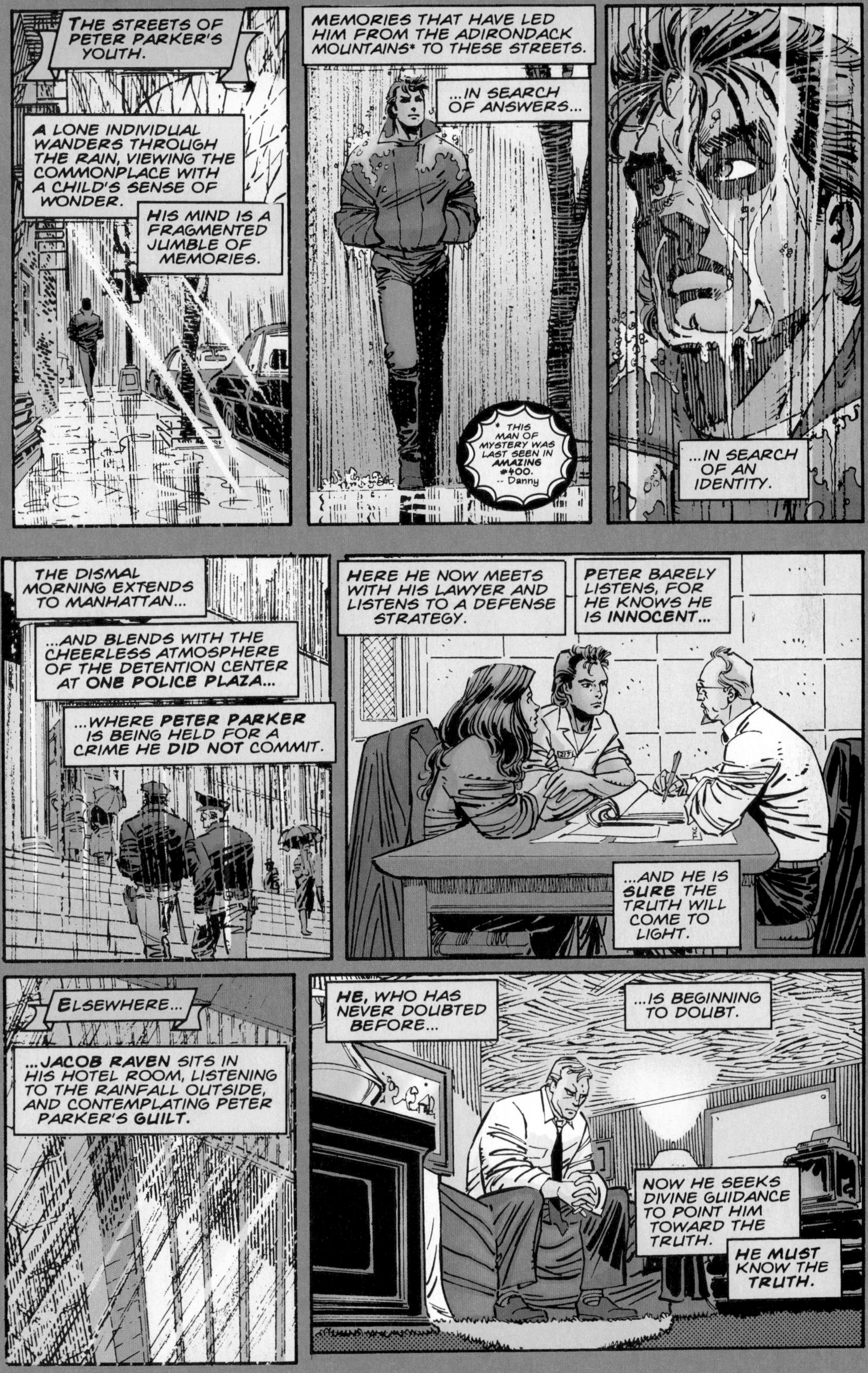
THE STREETS OF PETER PARKER'S YOUTH.
A LONE INDIVIDUAL WANDERS THROUGH THE RAIN, VIEWING THE COMMONPLACE WITH A CHILD'S SENSE OF WONDER.
HIS MIND IS A FRAGMENTED JUMBLE OF MEMORIES.
MEMORIES THAT HAVE LED HIM FROM THE ADIRONDACK MOUNTAINS* TO THESE STREETS.
...IN SEARCH OF ANSWERS...
* THIS MAN OF MYSTERY WAS LAST SEEN IN AMAZING #400. -- Danny
...IN SEARCH OF AN IDENTITY.
THE DISMAL MORNING EXTENDS TO MANHATTAN...
...AND BLENDS WITH THE CHEERLESS ATMOSPHERE OF THE DETENTION CENTER AT ONE POLICE PLAZA...
...WHERE PETER PARKER IS BEING HELD FOR A CRIME HE DID NOT COMMIT.
HERE HE NOW MEETS WITH HIS LAWYER AND LISTENS TO A DEFENSE STRATEGY.
PETER BARELY LISTENS, FOR HE KNOWS HE IS INNOCENT...
...AND HE IS SURE THE TRUTH WILL COME TO LIGHT.
ELSEWHERE...
...JACOB RAVEN SITS IN HIS HOTEL ROOM, LISTENING TO THE RAINFALL OUTSIDE, AND CONTEMPLATING PETER PARKER'S GUILT.
HE, WHO HAS NEVER DOUBTED BEFORE...
...IS BEGINNING TO DOUBT.
NOW HE SEEKS DIVINE GUIDANCE TO POINT HIM TOWARD THE TRUTH.
HE MUST KNOW THE TRUTH.

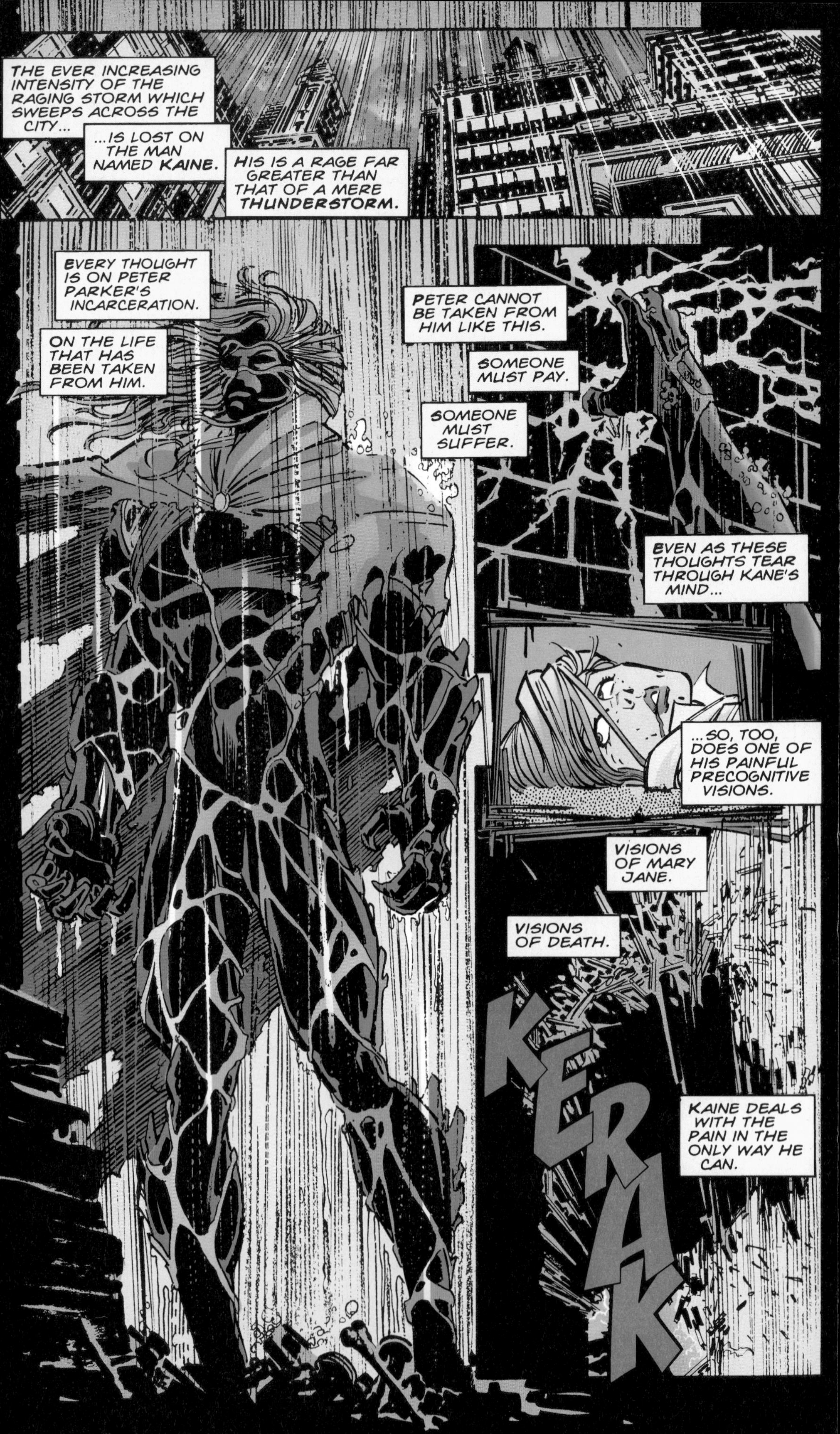
THE EVER INCREASING INTENSITY OF THE RAGING STORM WHICH SWEEPS ACROSS THE CITY...
...IS LOST ON THE MAN NAMED KAINE.
HIS IS A RAGE FAR GREATER THAN THAT OF A MERE THUNDERSTORM.
EVERY THOUGHT IS ON PETER PARKER'S INCARCERATION.
ON THE LIFE THAT HAS BEEN TAKEN FROM HIM.
PETER CANNOT BE TAKEN FROM HIM LIKE THIS.
SOMEONE MUST PAY.
SOMEONE MUST SUFFER.
EVEN AS THESE THOUGHTS TEAR THROUGH KANE'S MIND...
...SO, TOO, DOES ONE OF HIS PAINFUL PRECOGNITIVE VISIONS.
VISIONS OF MARY JANE.
VISIONS OF DEATH.
KERAK
KAINE DEALS WITH THE PAIN IN THE ONLY WAY HE CAN.

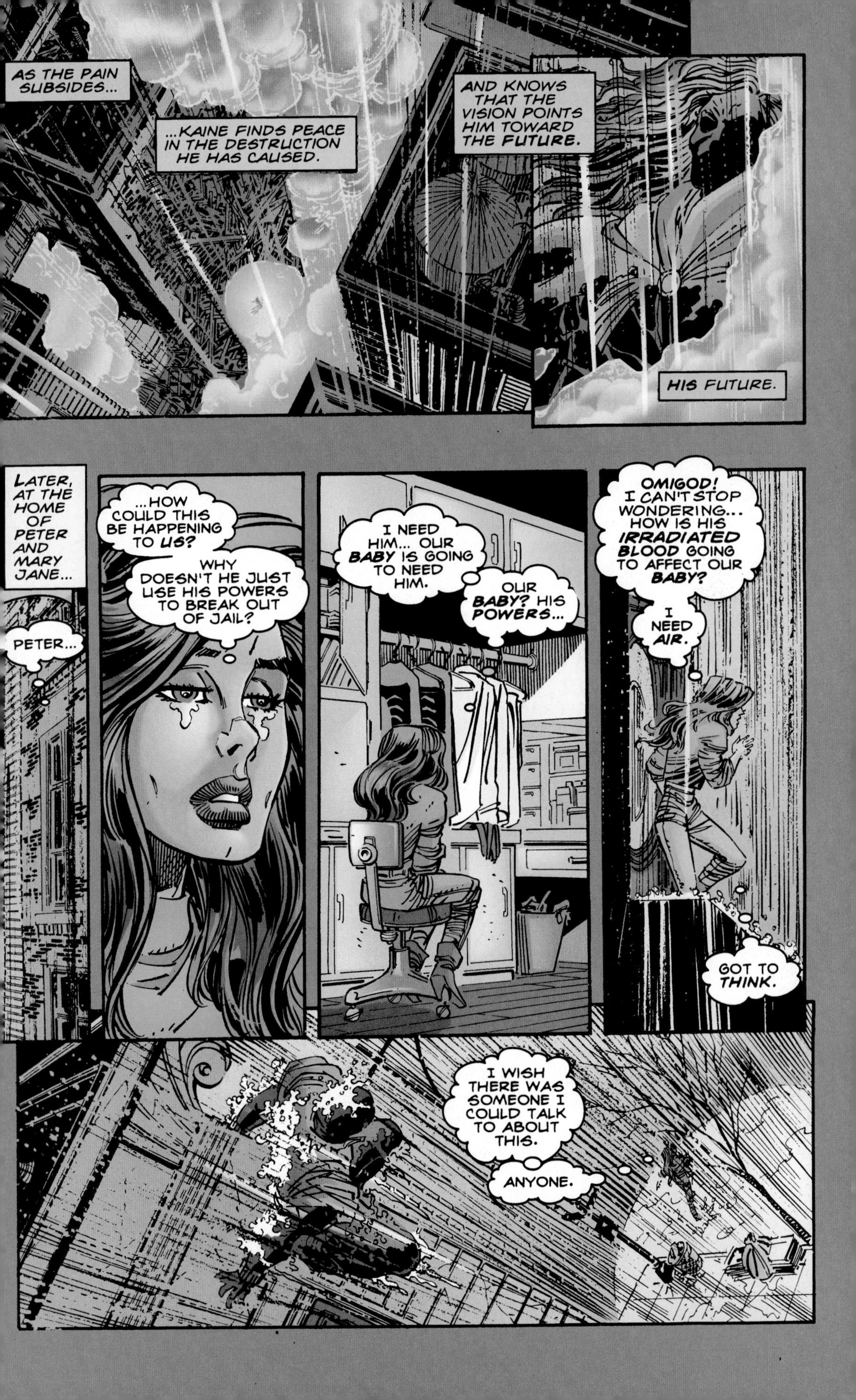
AS THE PAIN SUBSIDES...
...KAINE FINDS PEACE IN THE DESTRUCTION HE HAS CAUSED.
AND KNOWS THAT THE VISION POINTS HIM TOWARD THE FUTURE.
HIS FUTURE.
LATER, AT THE HOME OF PETER AND MARY JANE...
PETER...
...HOW COULD THIS BE HAPPENING TO US?
WHY DOESN'T HE JUST USE HIS POWERS TO BREAK OUT OF JAIL?
I NEED HIM... OUR BABY IS GOING TO NEED HIM.
OUR BABY? HIS POWERS...
OMIGOD! I CAN'T STOP WONDERING... HOW IS HIS IRRADIATED BLOOD GOING TO AFFECT OUR BABY?
I NEED AIR.
GOT TO THINK.
I WISH THERE WAS SOMEONE I COULD TALK TO ABOUT THIS.
ANYONE.

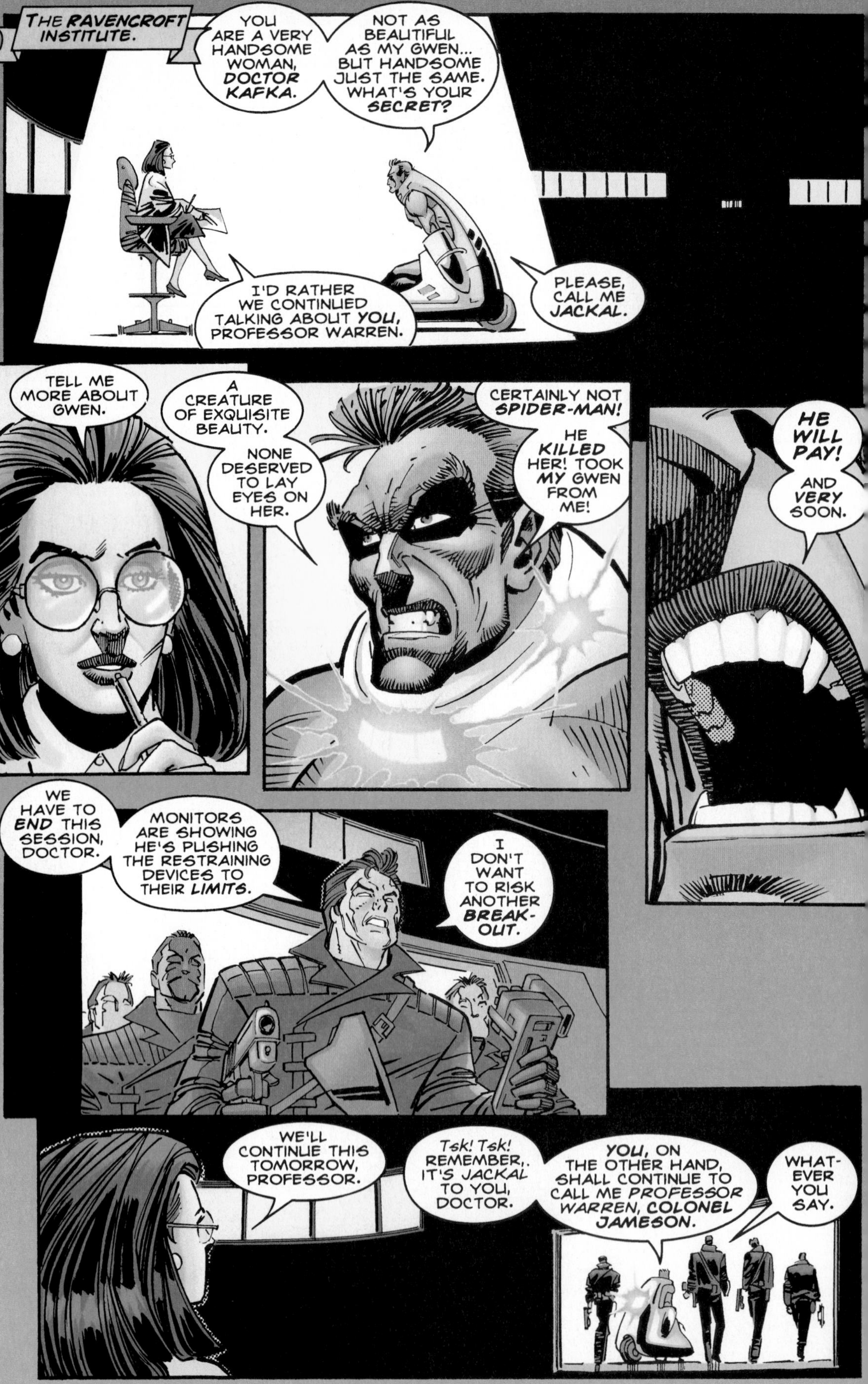
THE RAVENCROFT INSTITUTE.
YOU ARE A VERY HANDSOME WOMAN, DOCTOR KAFKA.
NOT AS BEAUTIFUL AS MY GWEN... BUT HANDSOME JUST THE SAME. WHAT'S YOUR SECRET?
I'D RATHER WE CONTINUED TALKING ABOUT YOU, PROFESSOR WARREN.
PLEASE, CALL ME JACKAL.
TELL ME MORE ABOUT GWEN.
A CREATURE OF EXQUISITE BEAUTY.
NONE DESERVED TO LAY EYES ON HER.
CERTAINLY NOT SPIDER-MAN!
HE KILLED HER! TOOK MY GWEN FROM ME!
HE WILL PAY!
AND VERY SOON.
WE HAVE TO END THIS SESSION, DOCTOR.
MONITORS ARE SHOWING HE'S PUSHING THE RESTRAINING DEVICES TO THEIR LIMITS.
I DON'T WANT TO RISK ANOTHER BREAK-OUT.
WE'LL CONTINUE THIS TOMORROW, PROFESSOR.
Tsk! Tsk! REMEMBER, IT'S JACKAL TO YOU, DOCTOR.
YOU, ON THE OTHER HAND, SHALL CONTINUE TO CALL ME PROFESSOR WARREN, COLONEL JAMESON.
WHAT-EVER YOU SAY.

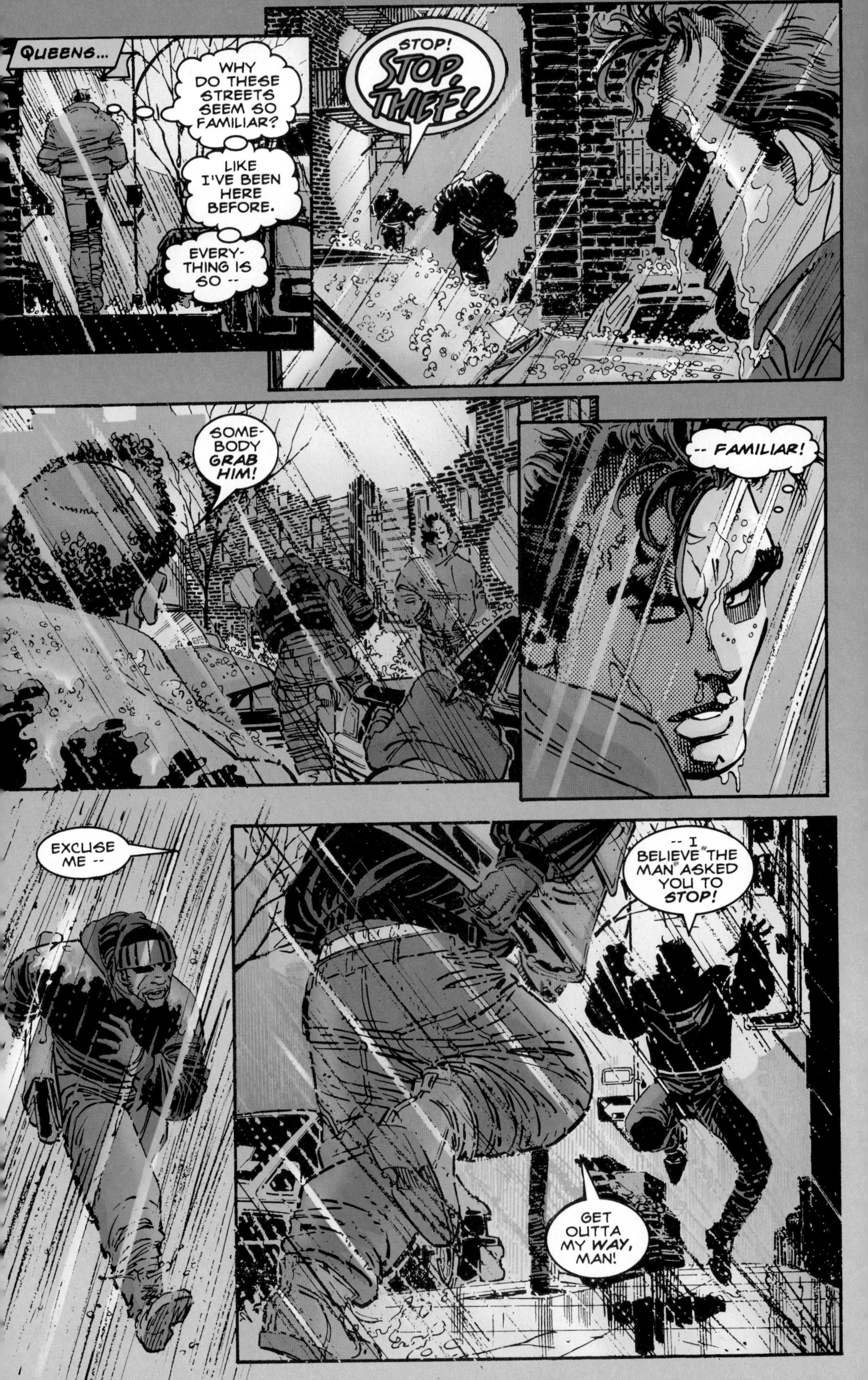
QUEENS...
WHY DO THESE STREETS SEEM SO FAMILIAR?
LIKE I'VE BEEN HERE BEFORE.
EVERY-THING IS SO --
STOP! STOP, THIEF!
SOME-BODY GRAB HIM!
-- FAMILIAR!
EXCUSE ME --
-- I BELIEVE "THE MAN" ASKED YOU TO STOP!
GET OUTTA MY WAY, MAN!

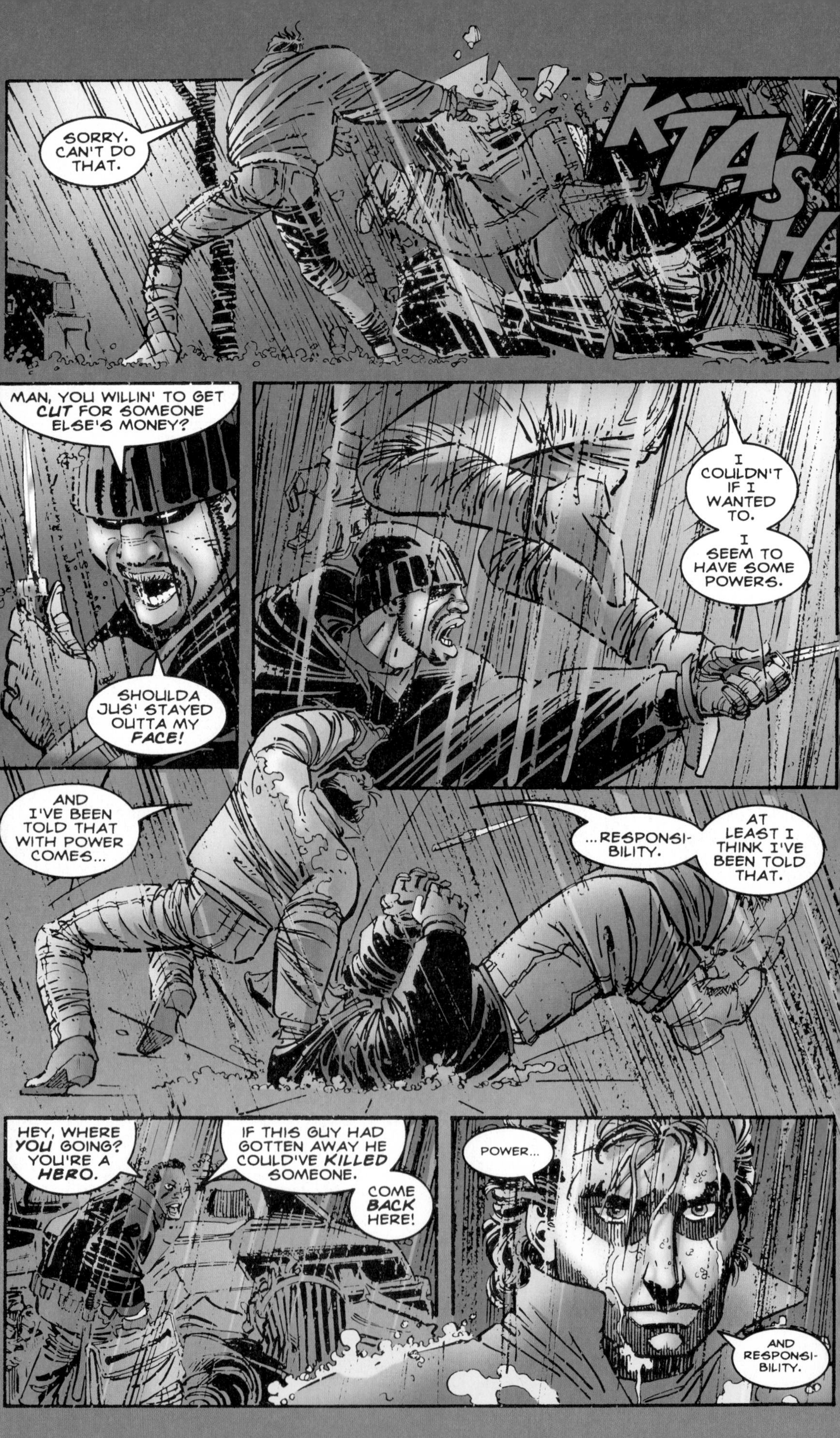
SORRY. CAN'T DO THAT.
KTASH
MAN, YOU WILLIN' TO GET CUT FOR SOMEONE ELSE'S MONEY?
SHOULDA JUS' STAYED OUTTA MY FACE!
I COULDN'T IF I WANTED TO.
I SEEM TO HAVE SOME POWERS.
AND I'VE BEEN TOLD THAT WITH POWER COMES...
...RESPONSIBILITY.
AT LEAST I THINK I'VE BEEN TOLD THAT.
HEY, WHERE YOU GOING? YOU'RE A HERO.
IF THIS GUY HAD GOTTEN AWAY HE COULD'VE KILLED SOMEONE.
COME BACK HERE!
POWER...
AND RESPONSIBILITY.

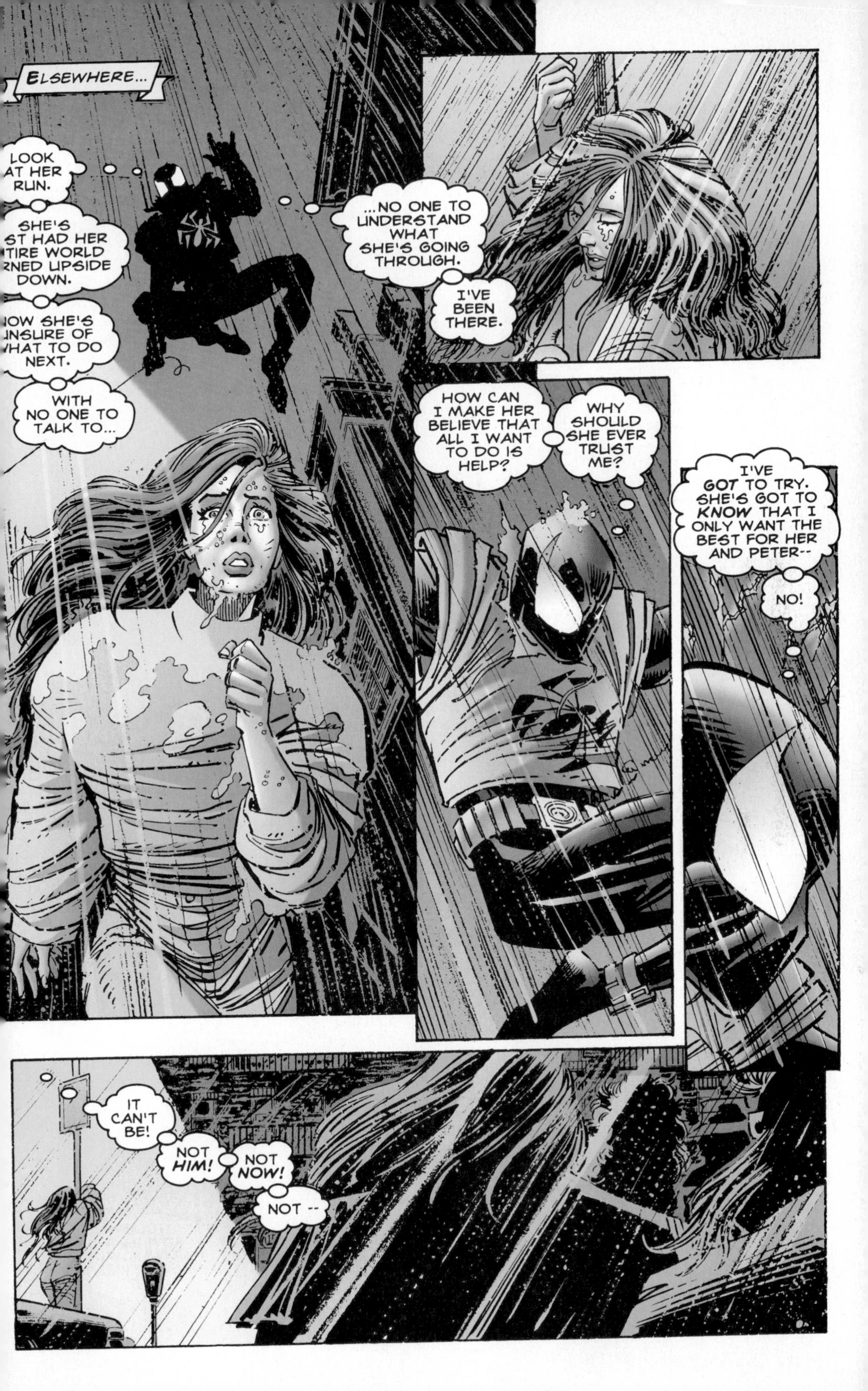
ELSEWHERE...
LOOK AT HER RUN.
SHE'S ST HAD HER TIRE WORLD RNED UPSIDE DOWN.
OW SHE'S NSURE OF HAT TO DO NEXT.
WITH NO ONE TO TALK TO...
...NO ONE TO UNDERSTAND WHAT SHE'S GOING THROUGH.
I'VE BEEN THERE.
HOW CAN I MAKE HER BELIEVE THAT ALL I WANT TO DO IS HELP?
WHY SHOULD SHE EVER TRUST ME?
I'VE GOT TO TRY. SHE'S GOT TO KNOW THAT I ONLY WANT THE BEST FOR HER AND PETER--
NO!
IT CAN'T BE!
NOT HIM!
NOT NOW!
NOT --

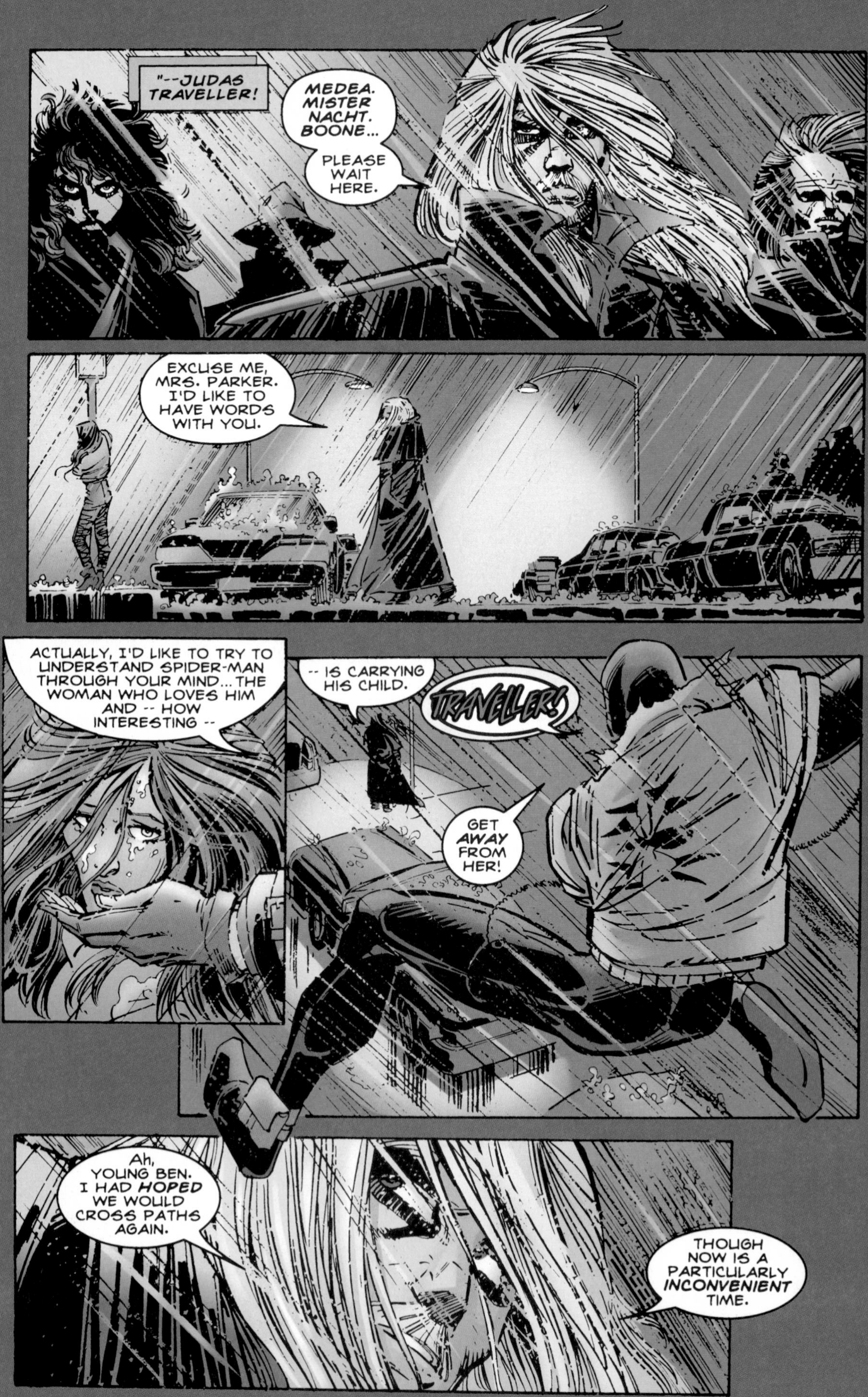
"--JUDAS TRAVELLER!
MEDEA. MISTER NACHT. BOONE...
PLEASE WAIT HERE.
EXCUSE ME, MRS. PARKER. I'D LIKE TO HAVE WORDS WITH YOU.
ACTUALLY, I'D LIKE TO TRY TO UNDERSTAND SPIDER-MAN THROUGH YOUR MIND... THE WOMAN WHO LOVES HIM AND -- HOW INTERESTING --
-- IS CARRYING HIS CHILD.
TRAVELLER!
GET AWAY FROM HER!
Ah, YOUNG BEN. I HAD HOPED WE WOULD CROSS PATHS AGAIN.
THOUGH NOW IS A PARTICULARLY INCONVENIENT TIME.

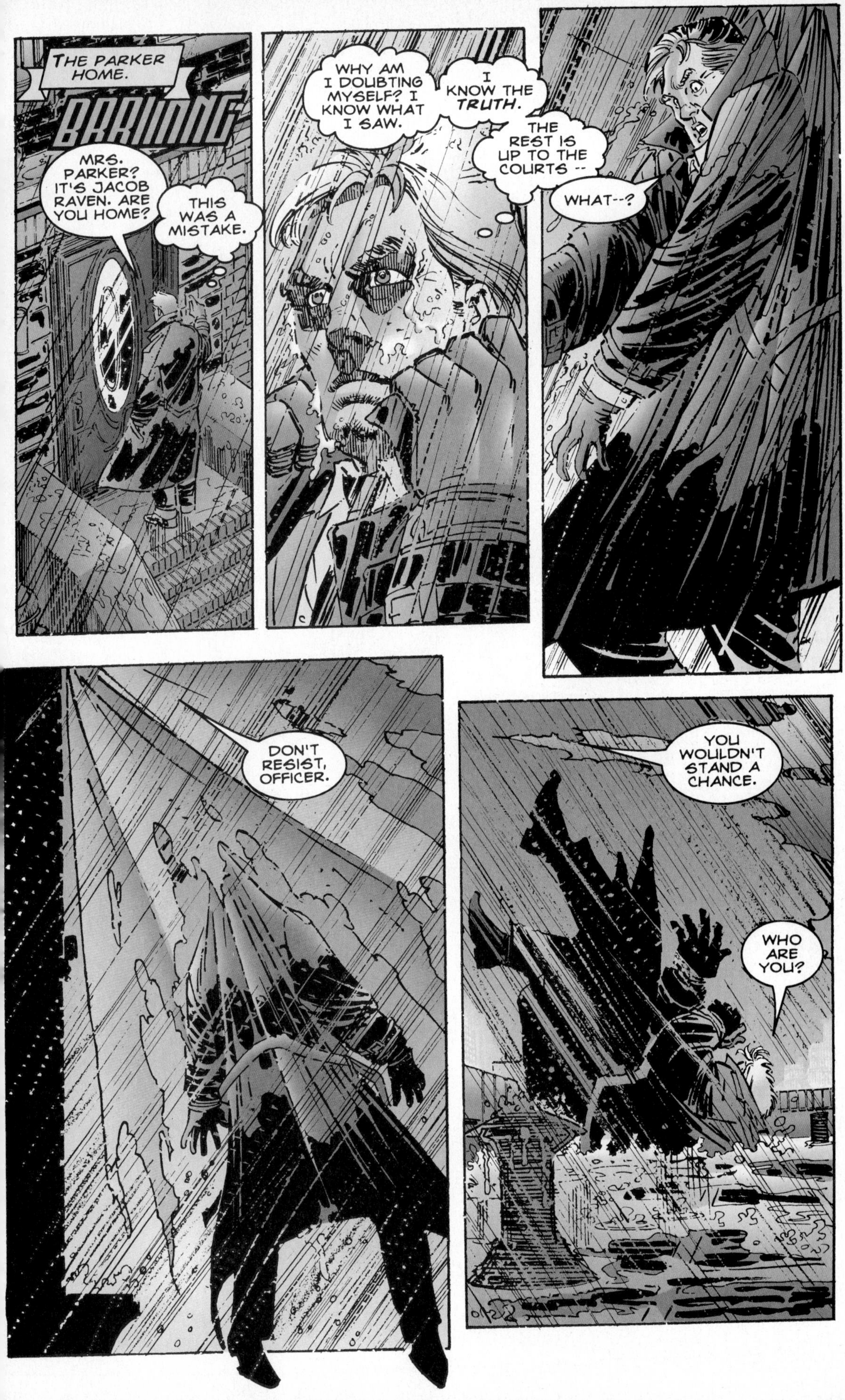
THE PARKER HOME.
BRRIIING
MRS. PARKER? IT'S JACOB RAVEN. ARE YOU HOME?
THIS WAS A MISTAKE.
WHY AM I DOUBTING MYSELF? I KNOW WHAT I SAW.
I KNOW THE TRUTH.
THE REST IS UP TO THE COURTS --
WHAT--?
DON'T RESIST, OFFICER.
YOU WOULDN'T STAND A CHANCE.
WHO ARE YOU?

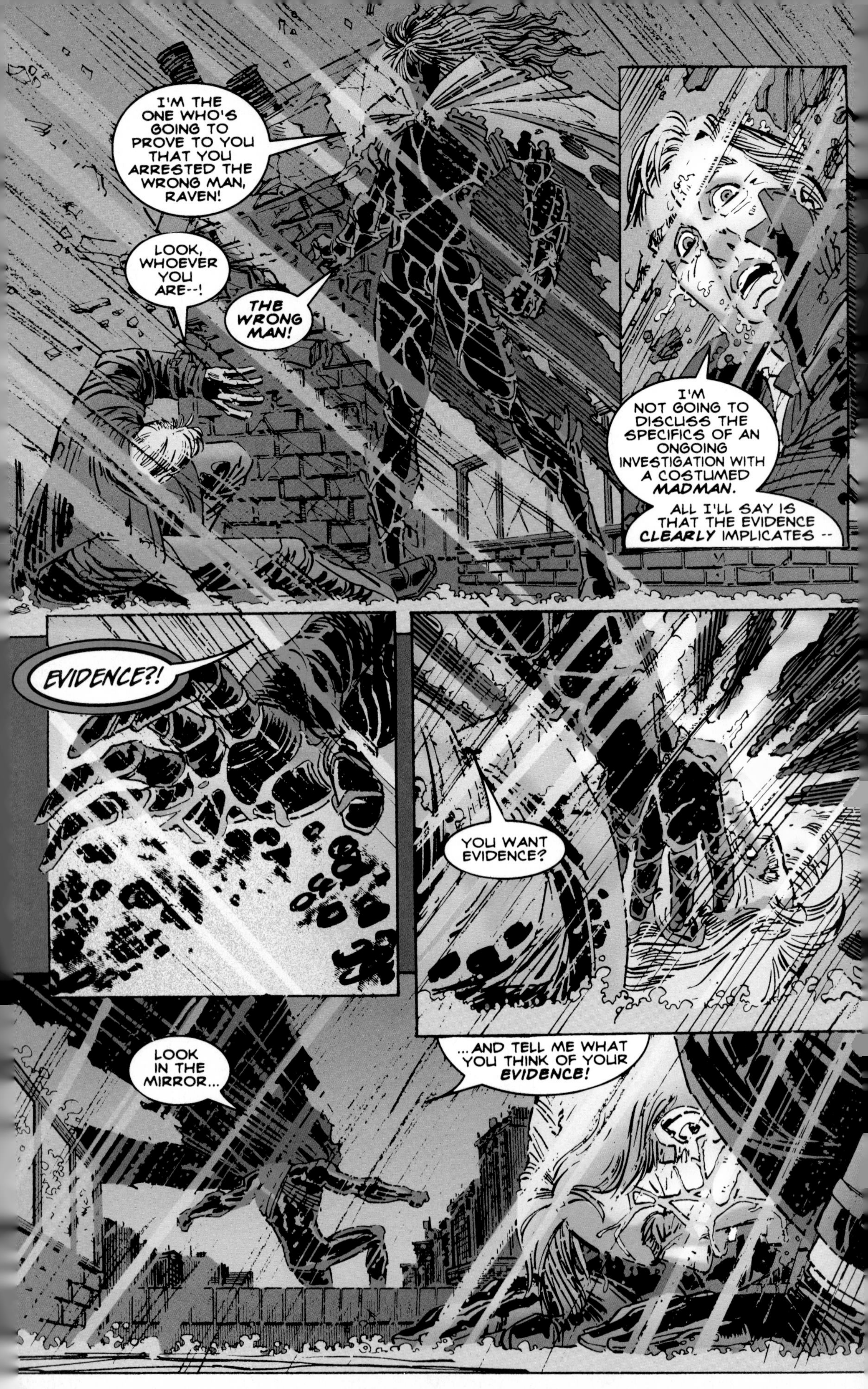
I'M THE ONE WHO'S GOING TO PROVE TO YOU THAT YOU ARRESTED THE WRONG MAN, RAVEN!
LOOK, WHOEVER YOU ARE--!
THE WRONG MAN!
I'M NOT GOING TO DISCUSS THE SPECIFICS OF AN ONGOING INVESTIGATION WITH A COSTUMED MADMAN.
ALL I'LL SAY IS THAT THE EVIDENCE CLEARLY IMPLICATES --
EVIDENCE?!
YOU WANT EVIDENCE?
LOOK IN THE MIRROR...
...AND TELL ME WHAT YOU THINK OF YOUR EVIDENCE!

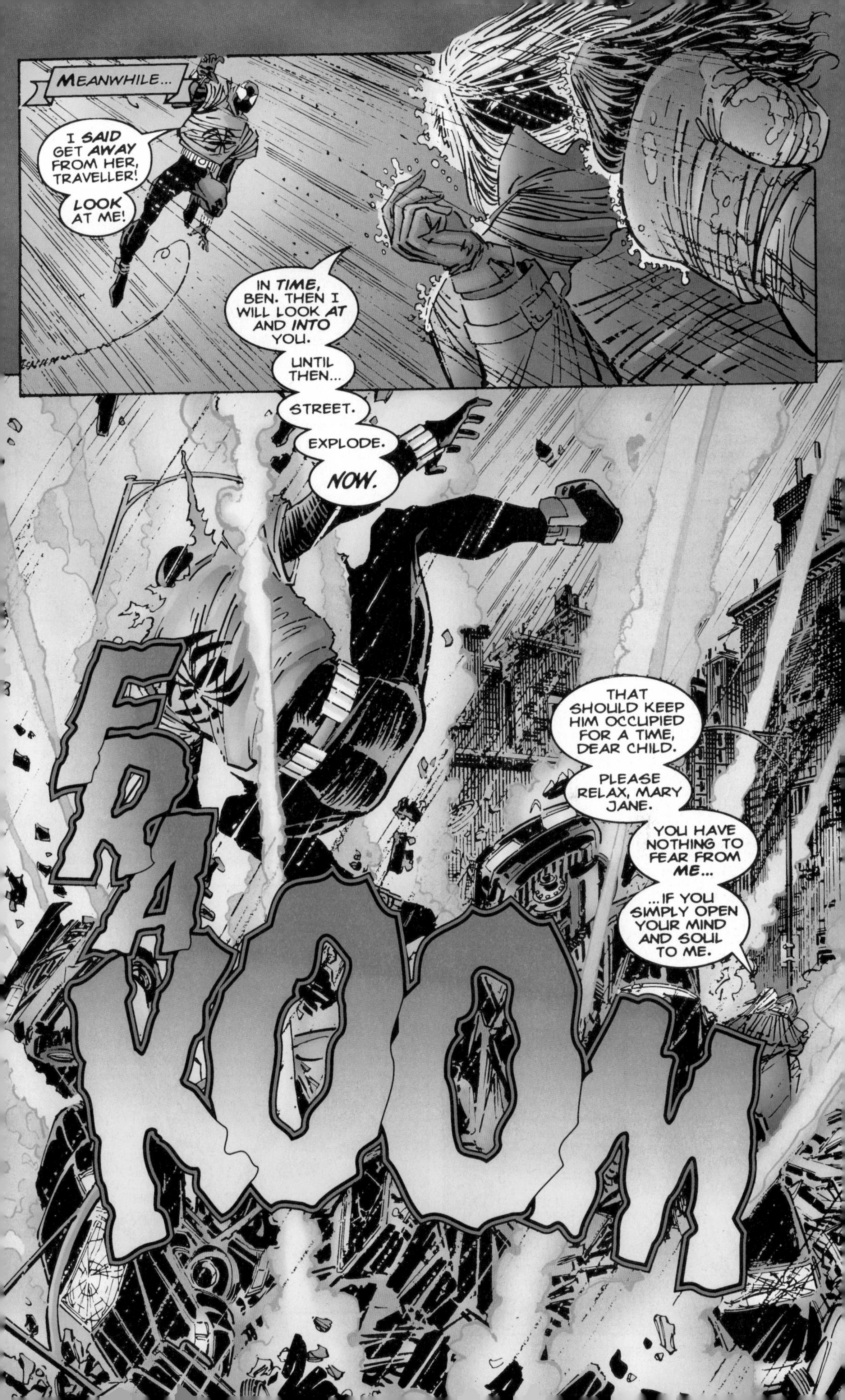
MEANWHILE...
I SAID GET AWAY FROM HER, TRAVELLER!
LOOK AT ME!
IN TIME, BEN. THEN I WILL LOOK AT AND INTO YOU.
UNTIL THEN...
STREET.
EXPLODE.
NOW.
FAROOM
THAT SHOULD KEEP HIM OCCUPIED FOR A TIME, DEAR CHILD.
PLEASE RELAX, MARY JANE.
YOU HAVE NOTHING TO FEAR FROM ME...
...IF YOU SIMPLY OPEN YOUR MIND AND SOUL TO ME.

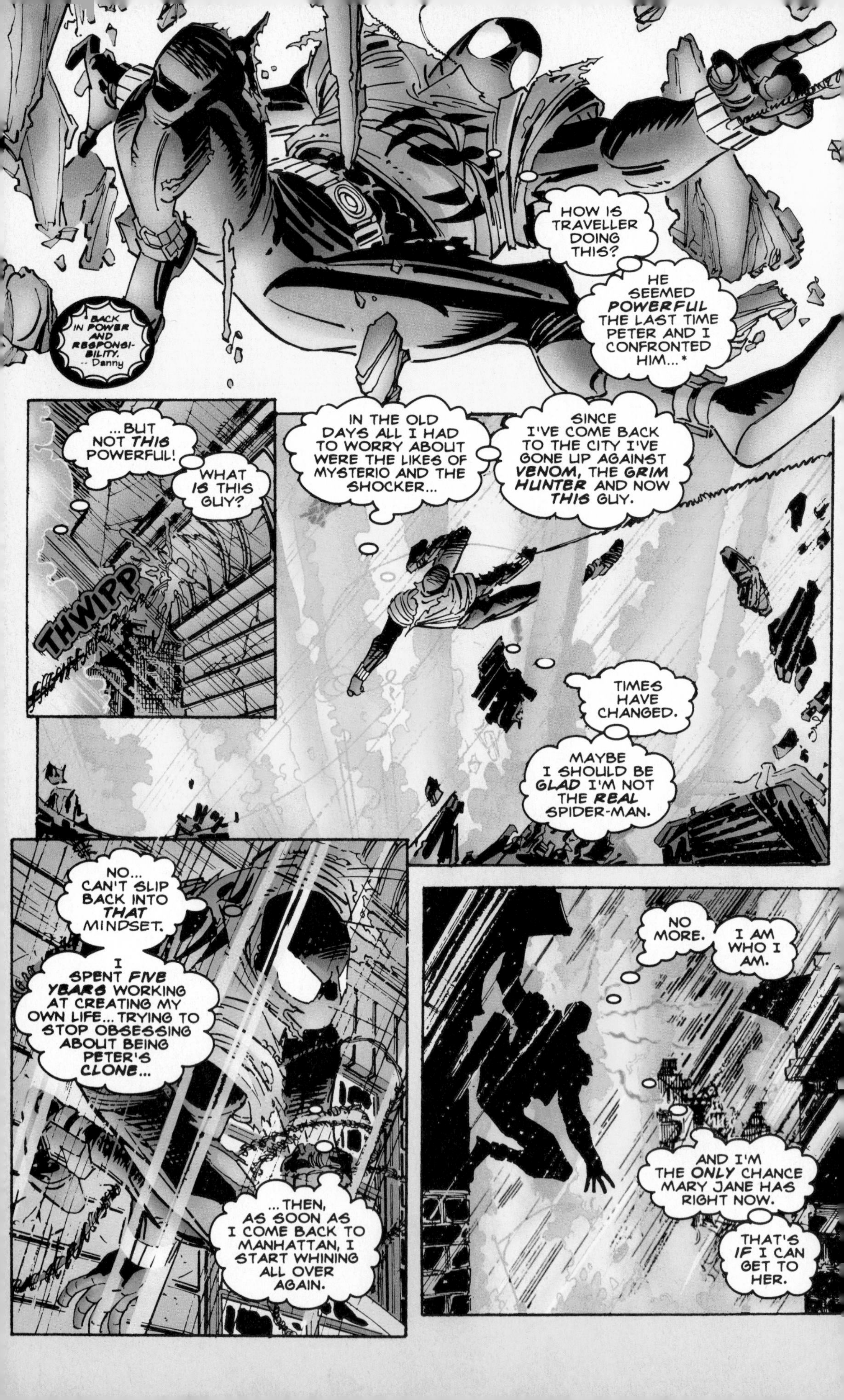
HOW IS TRAVELLER DOING THIS?
HE SEEMED POWERFUL THE LAST TIME PETER AND I CONFRONTED HIM...*
*BACK IN POWER AND RESPONSIBILITY. -- Danny
...BUT NOT THIS POWERFUL!
WHAT IS THIS GUY?
THWIPP
IN THE OLD DAYS ALL I HAD TO WORRY ABOUT WERE THE LIKES OF MYSTERIO AND THE SHOCKER...
SINCE I'VE COME BACK TO THE CITY I'VE GONE UP AGAINST VENOM, THE GRIM HUNTER AND NOW THIS GUY.
TIMES HAVE CHANGED.
MAYBE I SHOULD BE GLAD I'M NOT THE REAL SPIDER-MAN.
NO... CAN'T SLIP BACK INTO THAT MINDSET.
I SPENT FIVE YEARS WORKING AT CREATING MY OWN LIFE... TRYING TO STOP OBSESSING ABOUT BEING PETER'S CLONE...
...THEN, AS SOON AS I COME BACK TO MANHATTAN, I START WHINING ALL OVER AGAIN.
NO MORE.
I AM WHO I AM.
AND I'M THE ONLY CHANCE MARY JANE HAS RIGHT NOW.
THAT'S IF I CAN GET TO HER.

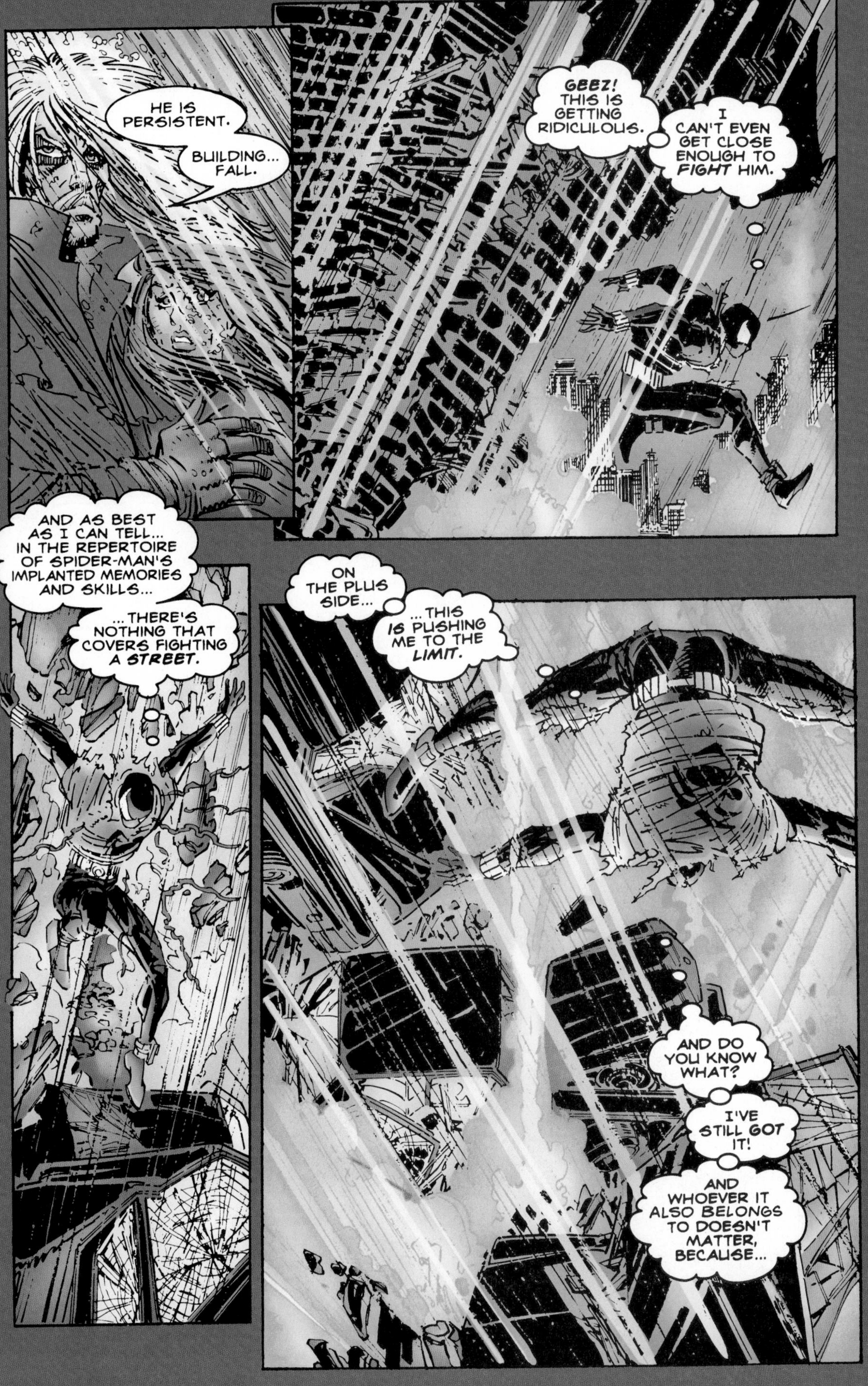
HE IS PERSISTENT.
BUILDING... FALL.
GEEZ! THIS IS GETTING RIDICULOUS.
I CAN'T EVEN GET CLOSE ENOUGH TO FIGHT HIM.
AND AS BEST AS I CAN TELL... IN THE REPERTOIRE OF SPIDER-MAN'S IMPLANTED MEMORIES AND SKILLS...
...THERE'S NOTHING THAT COVERS FIGHTING A STREET.
ON THE PLUS SIDE...
...THIS IS PUSHING ME TO THE LIMIT.
AND DO YOU KNOW WHAT?
I'VE STILL GOT IT!
AND WHOEVER IT ALSO BELONGS TO DOESN'T MATTER, BECAUSE...

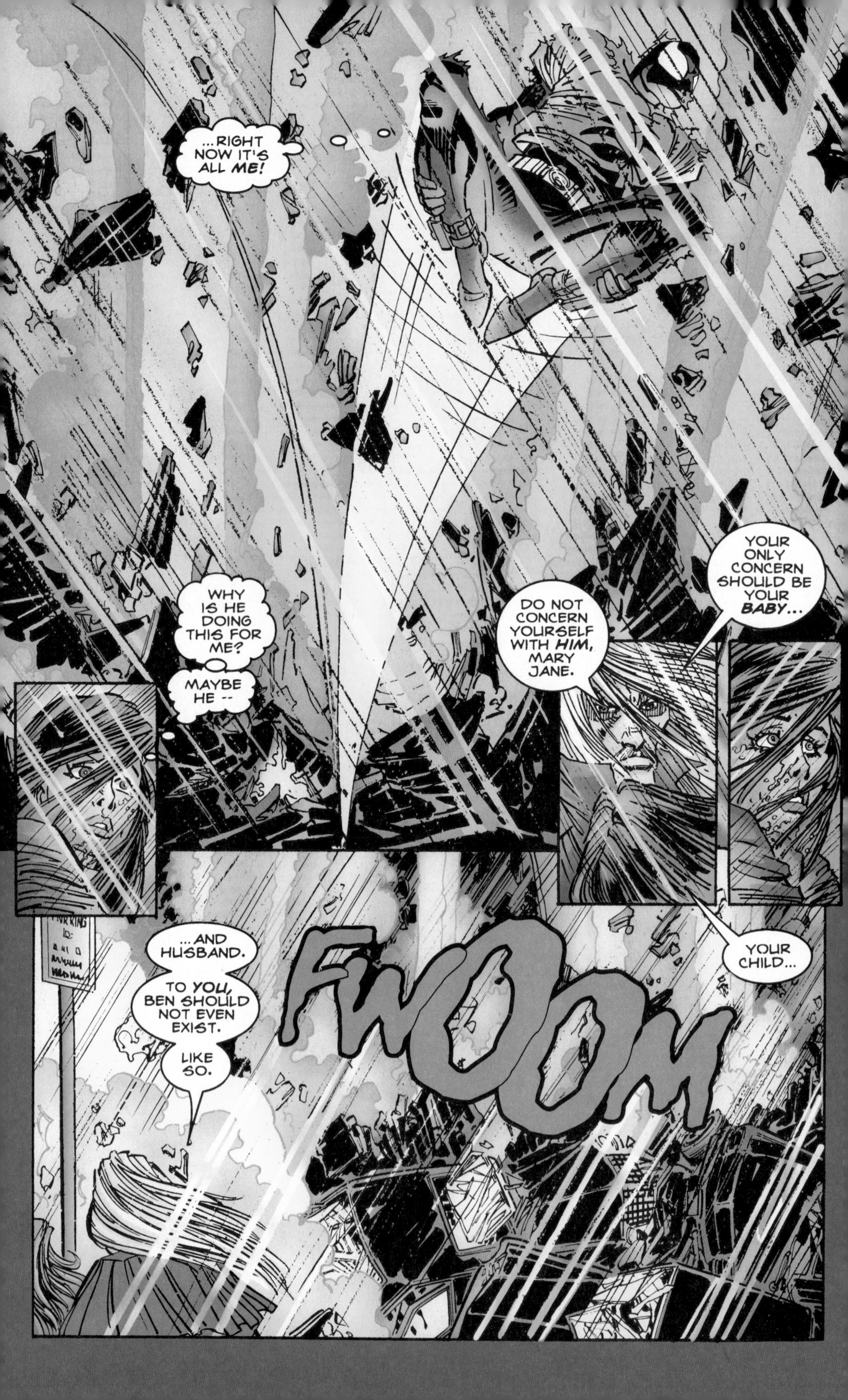
...RIGHT NOW IT'S ALL ME!
WHY IS HE DOING THIS FOR ME?
MAYBE HE --
DO NOT CONCERN YOURSELF WITH HIM, MARY JANE.
YOUR ONLY CONCERN SHOULD BE YOUR BABY...
YOUR CHILD...
...AND HUSBAND.
TO YOU, BEN SHOULD NOT EVEN EXIST.
LIKE SO.
FWOOM

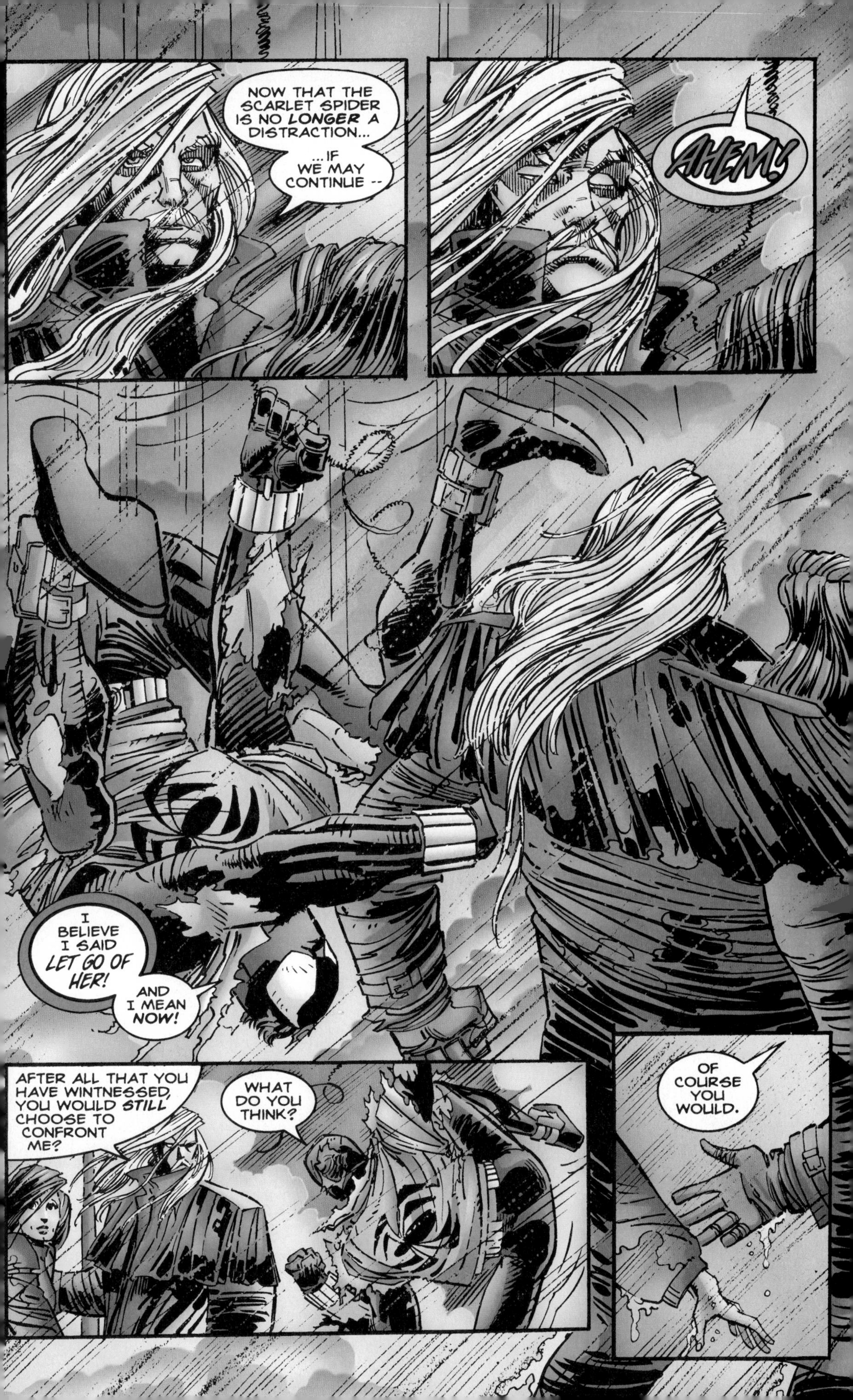
NOW THAT THE SCARLET SPIDER IS NO LONGER A DISTRACTION...
...IF WE MAY CONTINUE --
AHEM!
I BELIEVE I SAID LET GO OF HER!
AND I MEAN NOW!
AFTER ALL THAT YOU HAVE WINTNESSED, YOU WOULD STILL CHOOSE TO CONFRONT ME?
WHAT DO YOU THINK?
OF COURSE YOU WOULD.

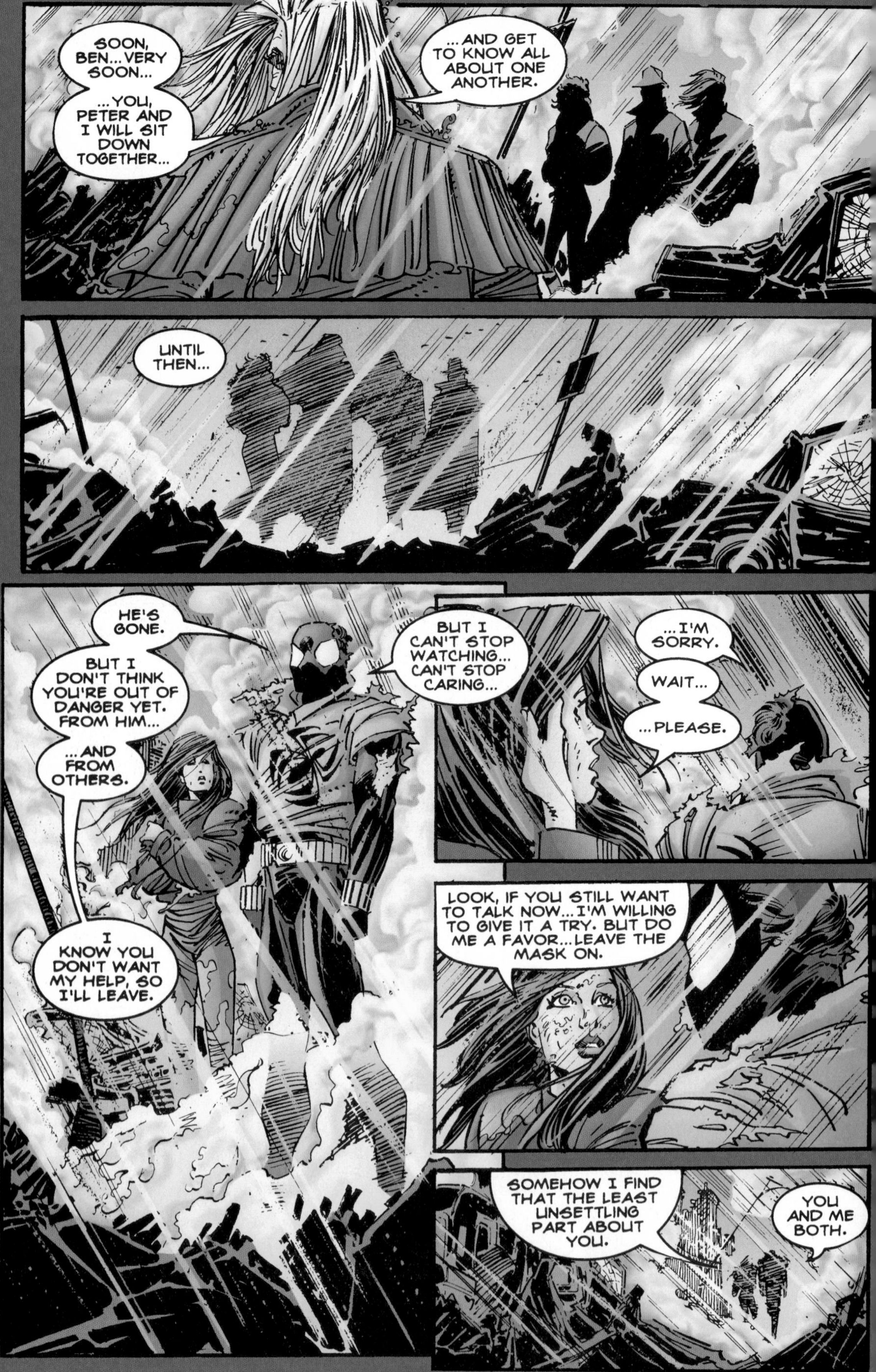
SOON, BEN... VERY SOON...
...YOU, PETER AND I WILL SIT DOWN TOGETHER...
...AND GET TO KNOW ALL ABOUT ONE ANOTHER.
UNTIL THEN...
HE'S GONE.
BUT I DON'T THINK YOU'RE OUT OF DANGER YET. FROM HIM...
...AND FROM OTHERS.
I KNOW YOU DON'T WANT MY HELP, SO I'LL LEAVE.
BUT I CAN'T STOP WATCHING... CAN'T STOP CARING...
...I'M SORRY.
WAIT...
...PLEASE.
LOOK, IF YOU STILL WANT TO TALK NOW... I'M WILLING TO GIVE IT A TRY. BUT DO ME A FAVOR... LEAVE THE MASK ON.
SOMEHOW I FIND THAT THE LEAST UNSETTLING PART ABOUT YOU.
YOU AND ME BOTH.

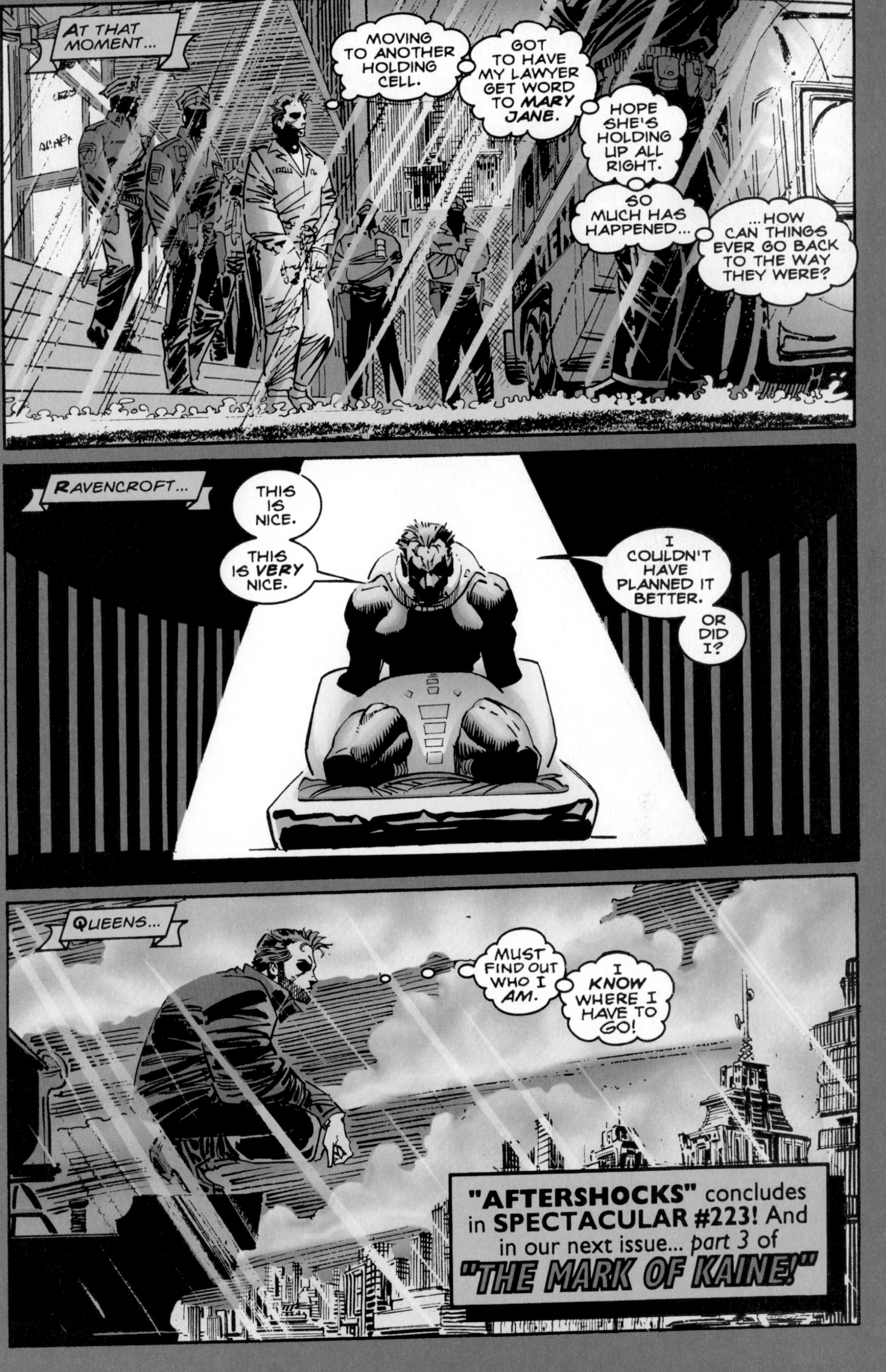
AT THAT MOMENT...
MOVING TO ANOTHER HOLDING CELL.
GOT TO HAVE MY LAWYER GET WORD TO MARY JANE.
HOPE SHE'S HOLDING UP ALL RIGHT.
SO MUCH HAS HAPPENED...
...HOW CAN THINGS EVER GO BACK TO THE WAY THEY WERE?
RAVENCROFT...
THIS IS NICE.
THIS IS VERY NICE.
I COULDN'T HAVE PLANNED IT BETTER.
OR DID I?
QUEENS...
MUST FIND OUT WHO I AM.
I KNOW WHERE I HAVE TO GO!
"AFTERSHOCKS" concludes in SPECTACULAR #223! And in our next issue... part 3 of "THE MARK OF KAINE!"

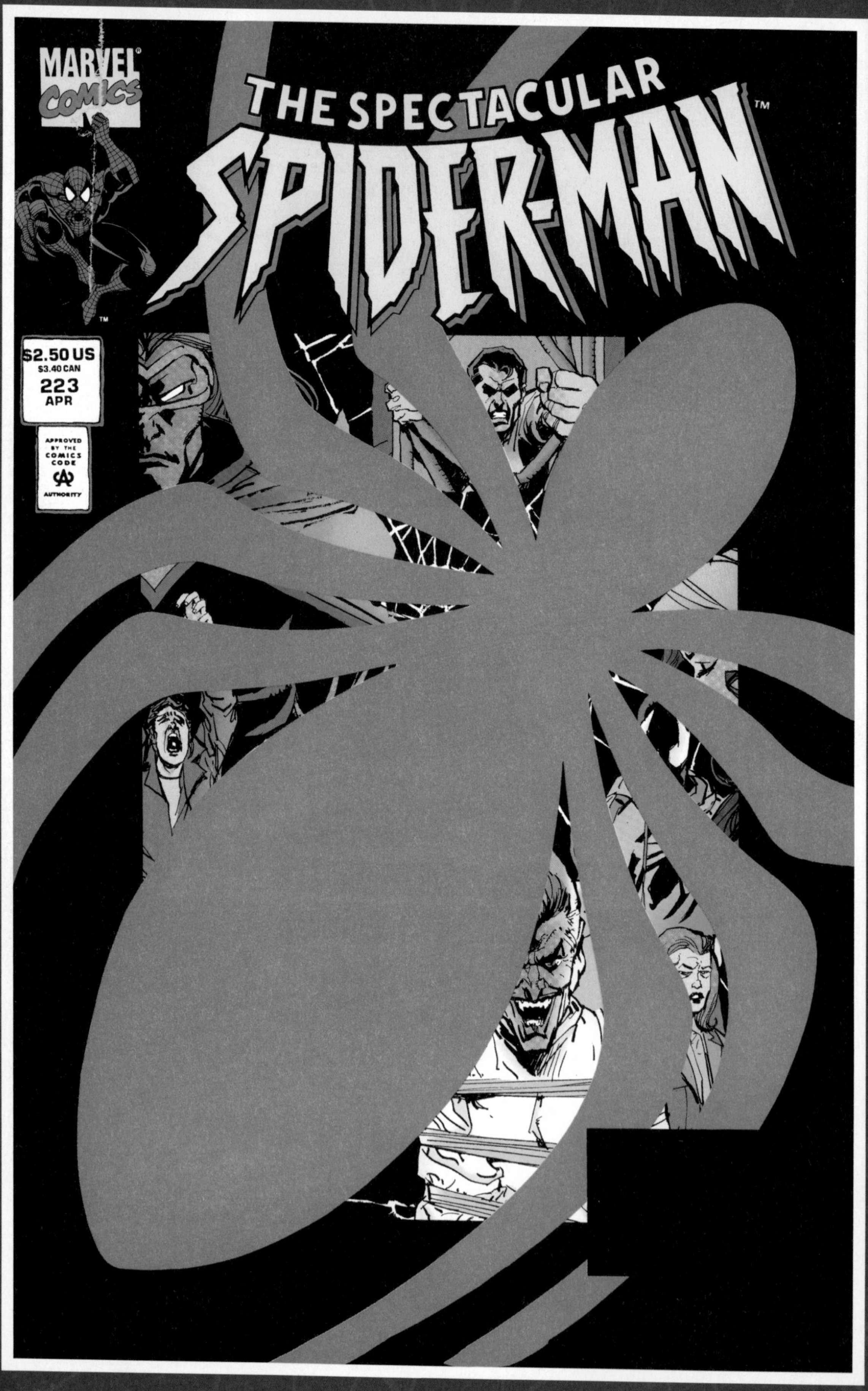
MARVEL COMICS
THE SPECTACULAR
SPIDER-MAN
$2.50 US
$3.40 CAN
223
APR
APPROVED BY THE COMICS CODE AUTHORITY

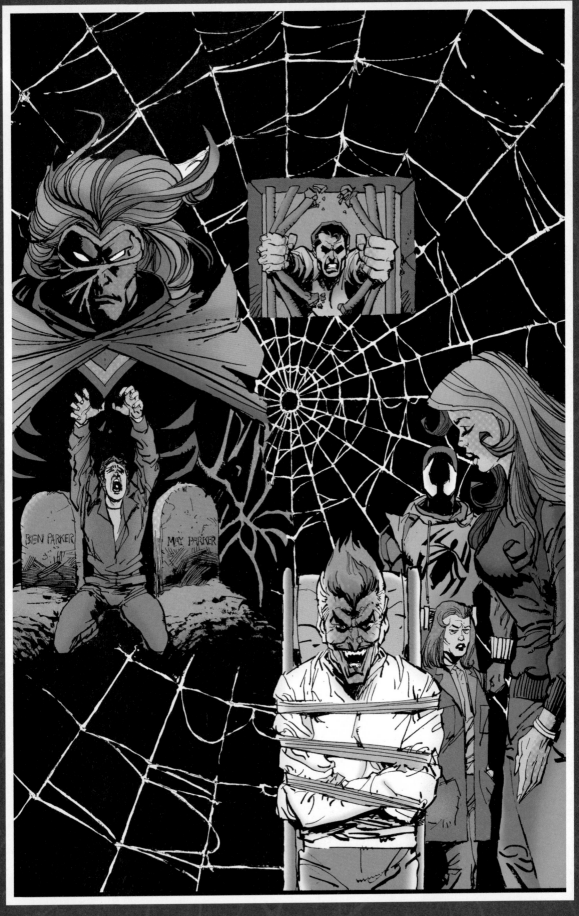

Spectacular Spider-Man #223 deluxe edition die-cut undercover

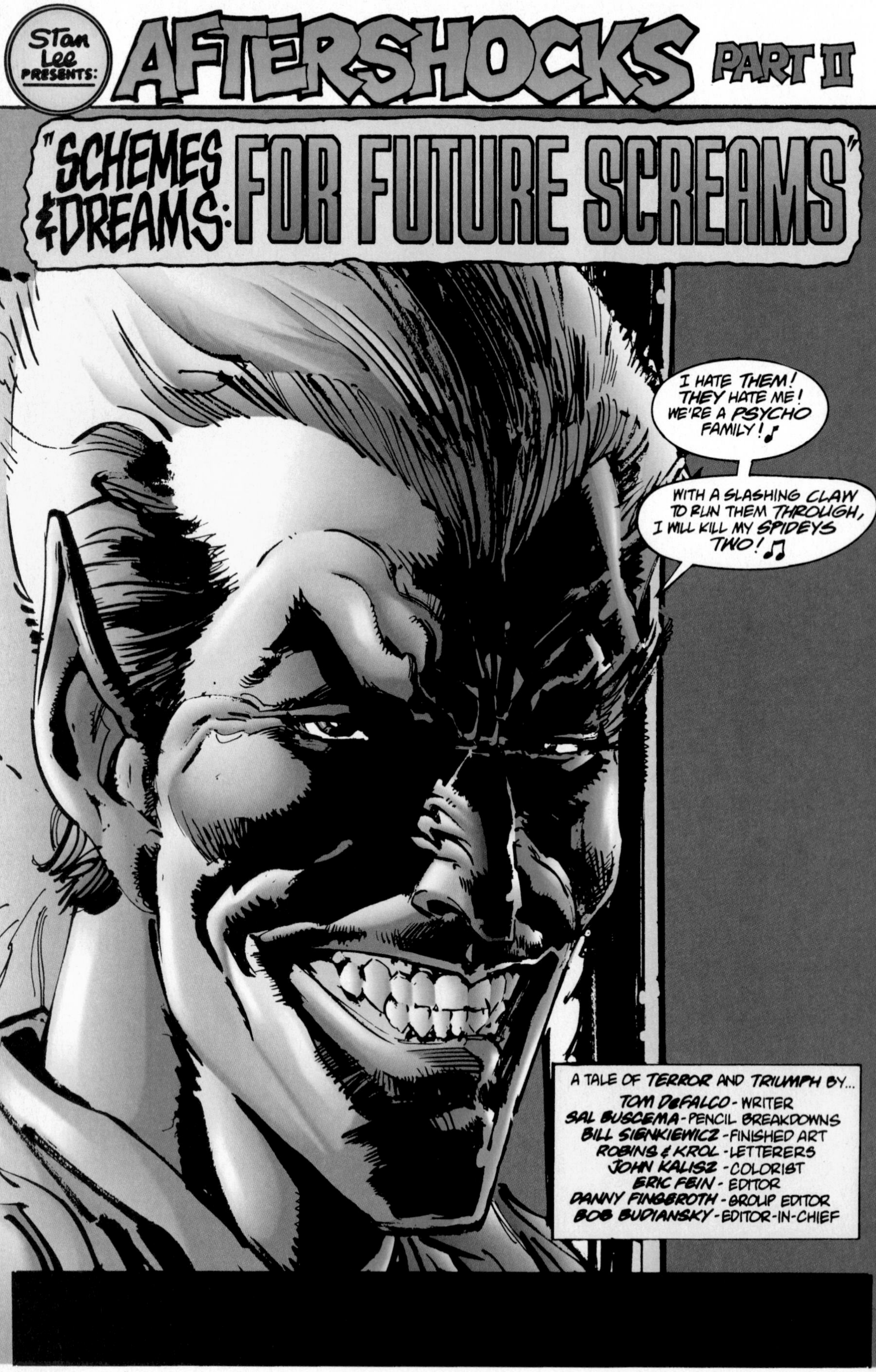

Stan Lee PRESENTS:
AFTERSHOCKS PART II
"SCHEMES & DREAMS: FOR FUTURE SCREAMS"
I HATE THEM! THEY HATE ME! WE'RE A PSYCHO FAMILY! ♪
WITH A SLASHING CLAW TO RUN THEM THROUGH, I WILL KILL MY SPIDEYS TWO! ♫
A TALE OF TERROR AND TRIUMPH BY...
TOM DeFALCO - WRITER
SAL BUSCEMA - PENCIL BREAKDOWNS
BILL SIENKIEWICZ - FINISHED ART
ROBINS & KROL - LETTERERS
JOHN KALISZ - COLORIST
ERIC FEIN - EDITOR
DANNY FINGEROTH - GROUP EDITOR
BOB BUDIANSKY - EDITOR-IN-CHIEF

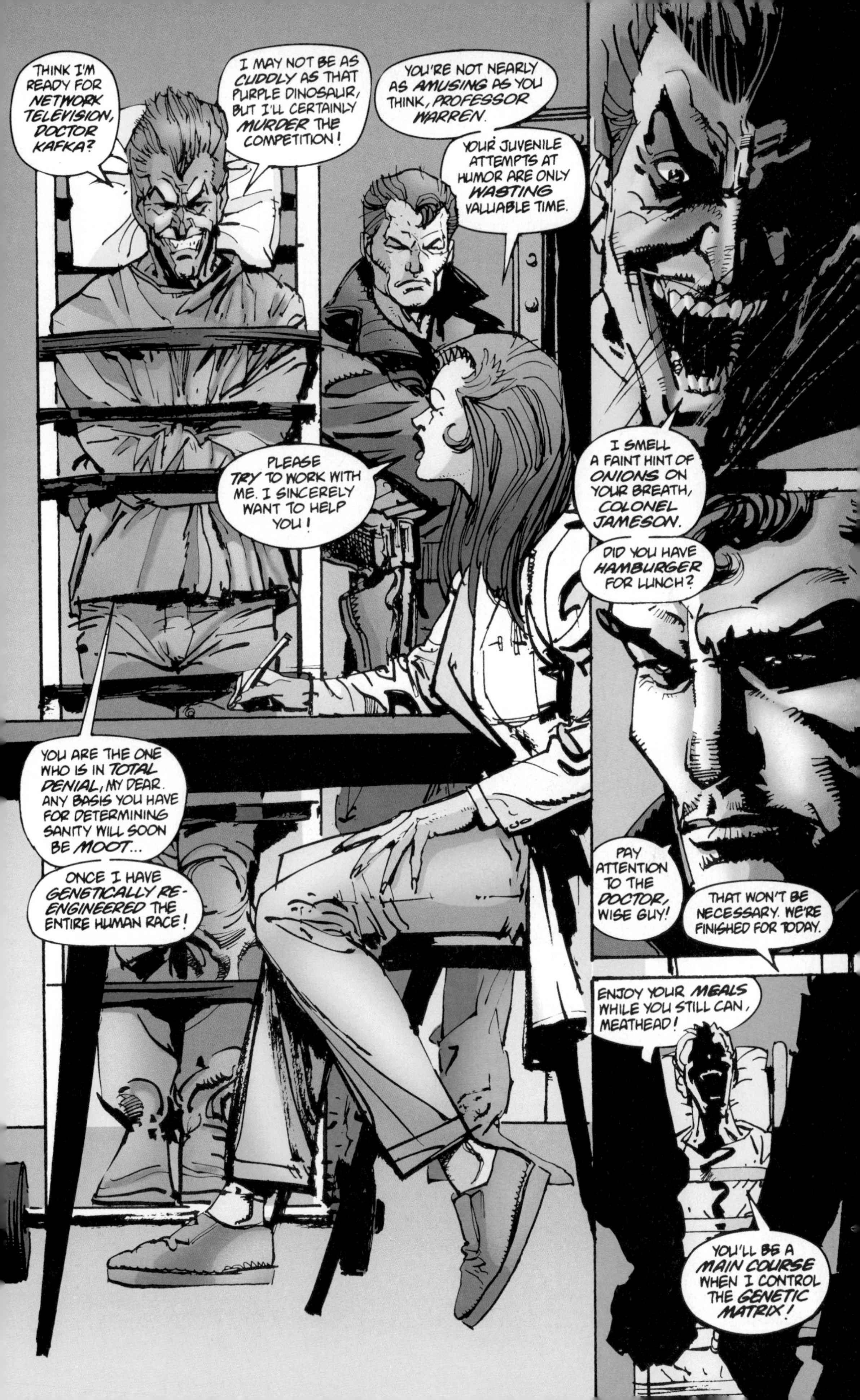
THINK I'M READY FOR NETWORK TELEVISION, DOCTOR KAFKA?
I MAY NOT BE AS CUDDLY AS THAT PURPLE DINOSAUR, BUT I'LL CERTAINLY MURDER THE COMPETITION!
YOU'RE NOT NEARLY AS AMUSING AS YOU THINK, PROFESSOR WARREN.
YOUR JUVENILE ATTEMPTS AT HUMOR ARE ONLY WASTING VALUABLE TIME.
PLEASE TRY TO WORK WITH ME. I SINCERELY WANT TO HELP YOU!
YOU ARE THE ONE WHO IS IN TOTAL DENIAL, MY DEAR. ANY BASIS YOU HAVE FOR DETERMINING SANITY WILL SOON BE MOOT...
ONCE I HAVE GENETICALLY RE-ENGINEERED THE ENTIRE HUMAN RACE!
I SMELL A FAINT HINT OF ONIONS ON YOUR BREATH, COLONEL JAMESON.
DID YOU HAVE HAMBURGER FOR LUNCH?
PAY ATTENTION TO THE DOCTOR, WISE GUY!
THAT WON'T BE NECESSARY. WE'RE FINISHED FOR TODAY.
ENJOY YOUR MEALS WHILE YOU STILL CAN, MEATHEAD!
YOU'LL BE A MAIN COURSE WHEN I CONTROL THE GENETIC MATRIX!

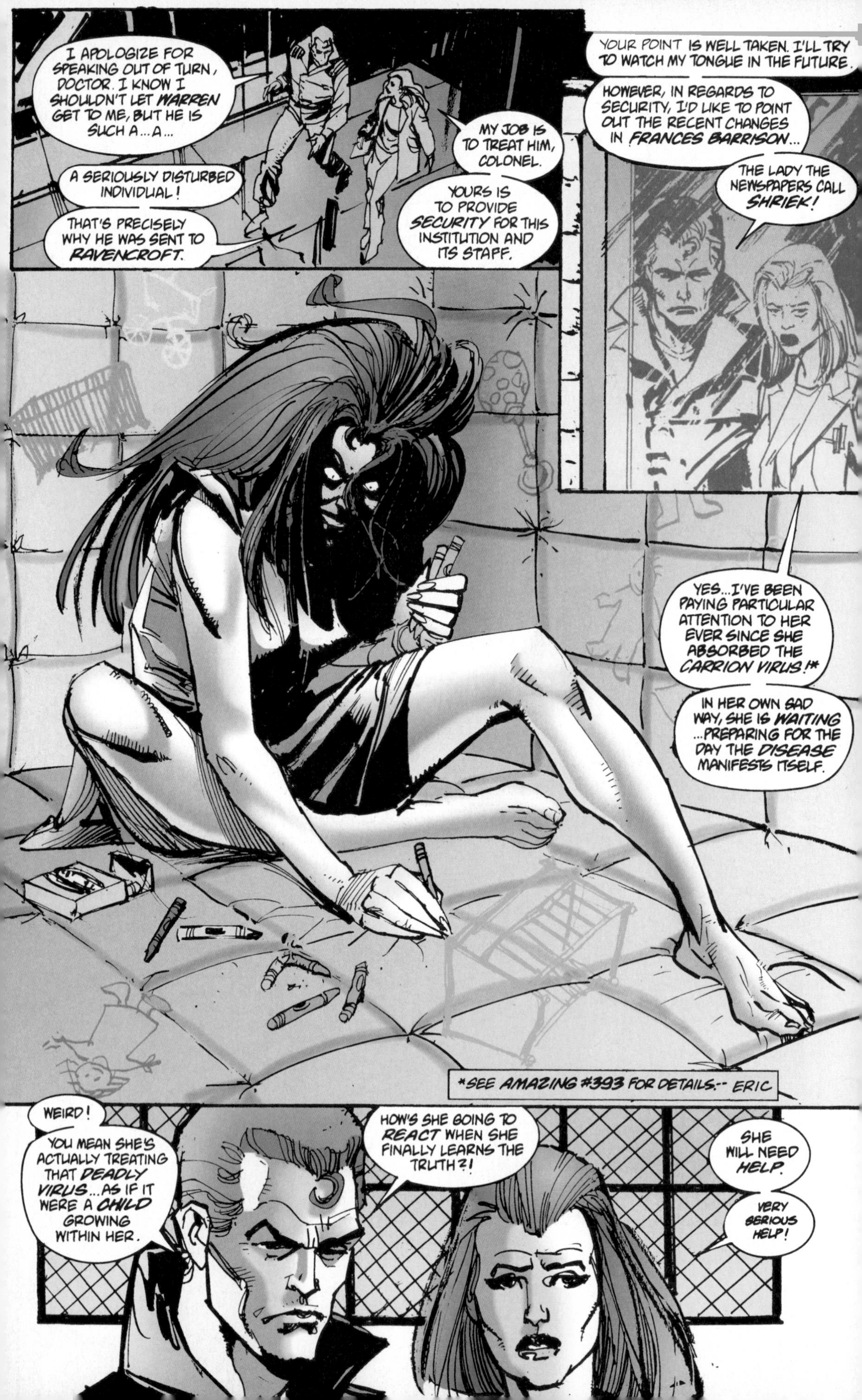
I APOLOGIZE FOR SPEAKING OUT OF TURN, DOCTOR. I KNOW I SHOULDN'T LET WARREN GET TO ME, BUT HE IS SUCH A... A...
A SERIOUSLY DISTURBED INDIVIDUAL!
THAT'S PRECISELY WHY HE WAS SENT TO RAVENCROFT.
MY JOB IS TO TREAT HIM, COLONEL.
YOURS IS TO PROVIDE SECURITY FOR THIS INSTITUTION AND ITS STAFF.
YOUR POINT IS WELL TAKEN. I'LL TRY TO WATCH MY TONGUE IN THE FUTURE.
HOWEVER, IN REGARDS TO SECURITY, I'D LIKE TO POINT OUT THE RECENT CHANGES IN FRANCES BARRISON...
THE LADY THE NEWSPAPERS CALL SHRIEK!
YES...I'VE BEEN PAYING PARTICULAR ATTENTION TO HER EVER SINCE SHE ABSORBED THE CARRION VIRUS!*
IN HER OWN SAD WAY, SHE IS WAITING ...PREPARING FOR THE DAY THE DISEASE MANIFESTS ITSELF.
*SEE AMAZING #393 FOR DETAILS.-- ERIC
WEIRD!
YOU MEAN SHE'S ACTUALLY TREATING THAT DEADLY VIRUS...AS IF IT WERE A CHILD GROWING WITHIN HER.
HOW'S SHE GOING TO REACT WHEN SHE FINALLY LEARNS THE TRUTH?!
SHE WILL NEED HELP.
VERY SERIOUS HELP!

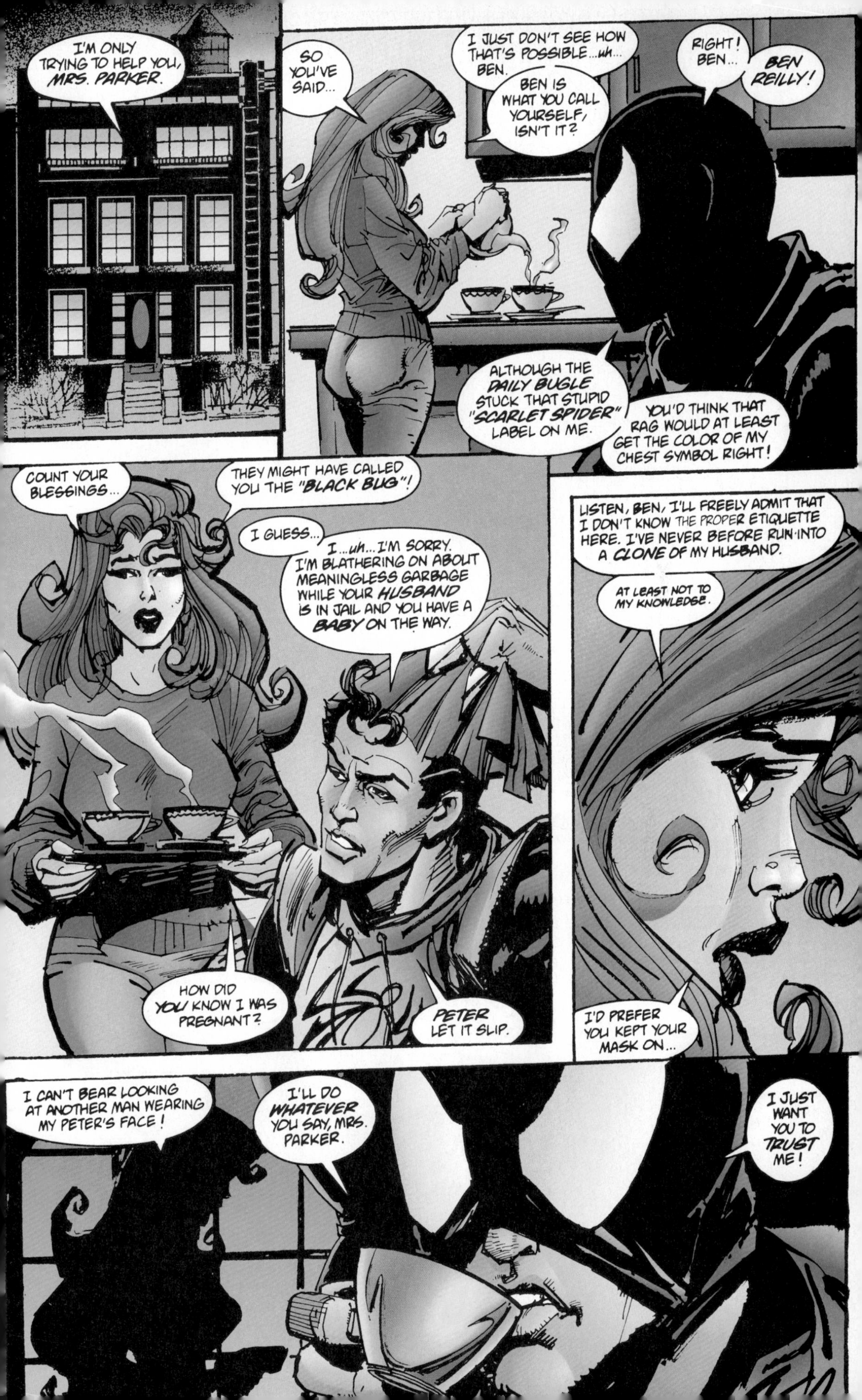
I'M ONLY TRYING TO HELP YOU, MRS. PARKER.
SO YOU'VE SAID...
I JUST DON'T SEE HOW THAT'S POSSIBLE...uh... BEN.
BEN IS WHAT YOU CALL YOURSELF, ISN'T IT?
RIGHT! BEN...
BEN REILLY!
ALTHOUGH THE DAILY BUGLE STUCK THAT STUPID "SCARLET SPIDER" LABEL ON ME.
YOU'D THINK THAT RAG WOULD AT LEAST GET THE COLOR OF MY CHEST SYMBOL RIGHT!
COUNT YOUR BLESSINGS...
THEY MIGHT HAVE CALLED YOU THE "BLACK BUG"!
I GUESS...
I...uh...I'M SORRY. I'M BLATHERING ON ABOUT MEANINGLESS GARBAGE WHILE YOUR HUSBAND IS IN JAIL AND YOU HAVE A BABY ON THE WAY.
HOW DID YOU KNOW I WAS PREGNANT?
PETER LET IT SLIP.
LISTEN, BEN, I'LL FREELY ADMIT THAT I DON'T KNOW THE PROPER ETIQUETTE HERE. I'VE NEVER BEFORE RUN INTO A CLONE OF MY HUSBAND.
AT LEAST NOT TO MY KNOWLEDGE.
I'D PREFER YOU KEPT YOUR MASK ON...
I CAN'T BEAR LOOKING AT ANOTHER MAN WEARING MY PETER'S FACE!
I'LL DO WHATEVER YOU SAY, MRS. PARKER.
I JUST WANT YOU TO TRUST ME!

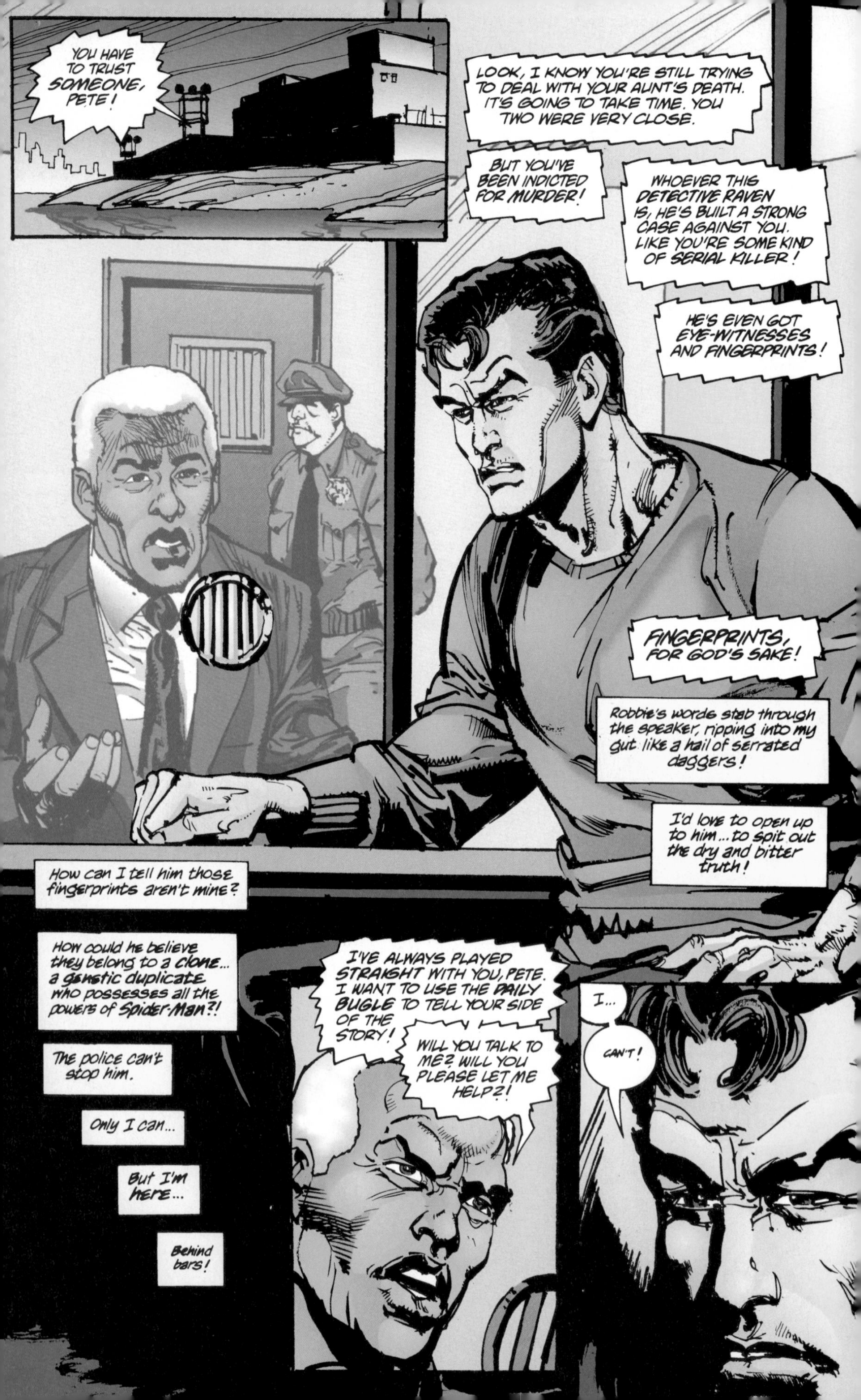
YOU HAVE TO TRUST SOMEONE, PETE!
LOOK, I KNOW YOU'RE STILL TRYING TO DEAL WITH YOUR AUNT'S DEATH. IT'S GOING TO TAKE TIME. YOU TWO WERE VERY CLOSE.
BUT YOU'VE BEEN INDICTED FOR MURDER!
WHOEVER THIS DETECTIVE RAVEN IS, HE'S BUILT A STRONG CASE AGAINST YOU. LIKE YOU'RE SOME KIND OF SERIAL KILLER!
HE'S EVEN GOT EYE-WITNESSES AND FINGERPRINTS!
FINGERPRINTS, FOR GOD'S SAKE!
Robbie's words stab through the speaker, ripping into my gut like a hail of serrated daggers!
I'd love to open up to him... to spit out the dry and bitter truth!
How can I tell him those fingerprints aren't mine?
How could he believe they belong to a clone... a genetic duplicate who possesses all the powers of Spider-Man?!
The police can't stop him.
Only I can...
But I'm here...
Behind bars!
I'VE ALWAYS PLAYED STRAIGHT WITH YOU, PETE. I WANT TO USE THE DAILY BUGLE TO TELL YOUR SIDE OF THE STORY!
WILL YOU TALK TO ME? WILL YOU PLEASE LET ME HELP?!
I...
CAN'T!

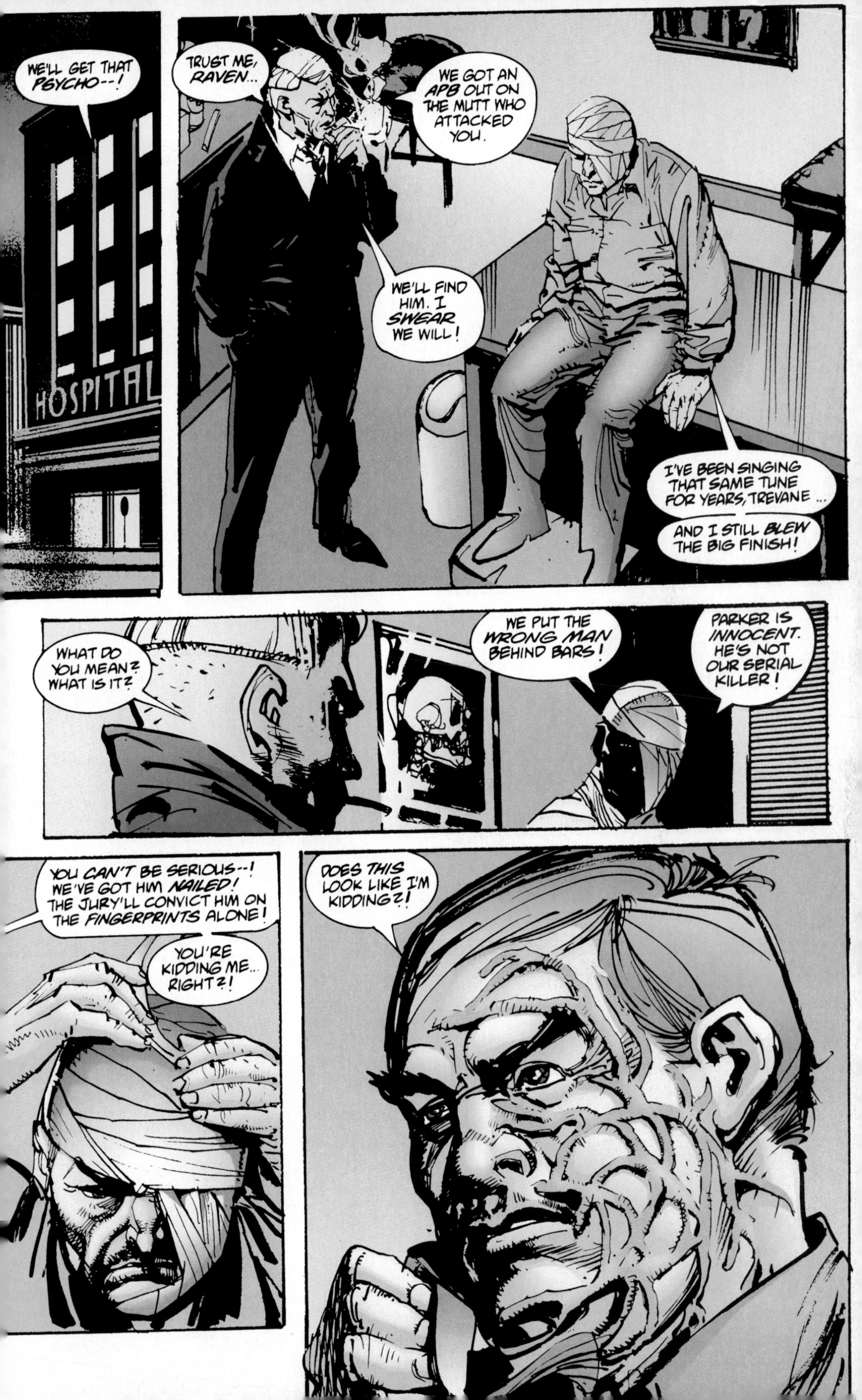

WE'LL GET THAT PSYCHO--!
TRUST ME, RAVEN...
WE GOT AN APB OUT ON THE MUTT WHO ATTACKED YOU.
WE'LL FIND HIM. I SWEAR WE WILL!
I'VE BEEN SINGING THAT SAME TUNE FOR YEARS, TREVANE...
AND I STILL BLEW THE BIG FINISH!
WHAT DO YOU MEAN? WHAT IS IT?
WE PUT THE WRONG MAN BEHIND BARS!
PARKER IS INNOCENT. HE'S NOT OUR SERIAL KILLER!
YOU CAN'T BE SERIOUS--! WE'VE GOT HIM NAILED! THE JURY'LL CONVICT HIM ON THE FINGERPRINTS ALONE!
YOU'RE KIDDING ME... RIGHT?!
DOES THIS LOOK LIKE I'M KIDDING?!
HOSPITAL

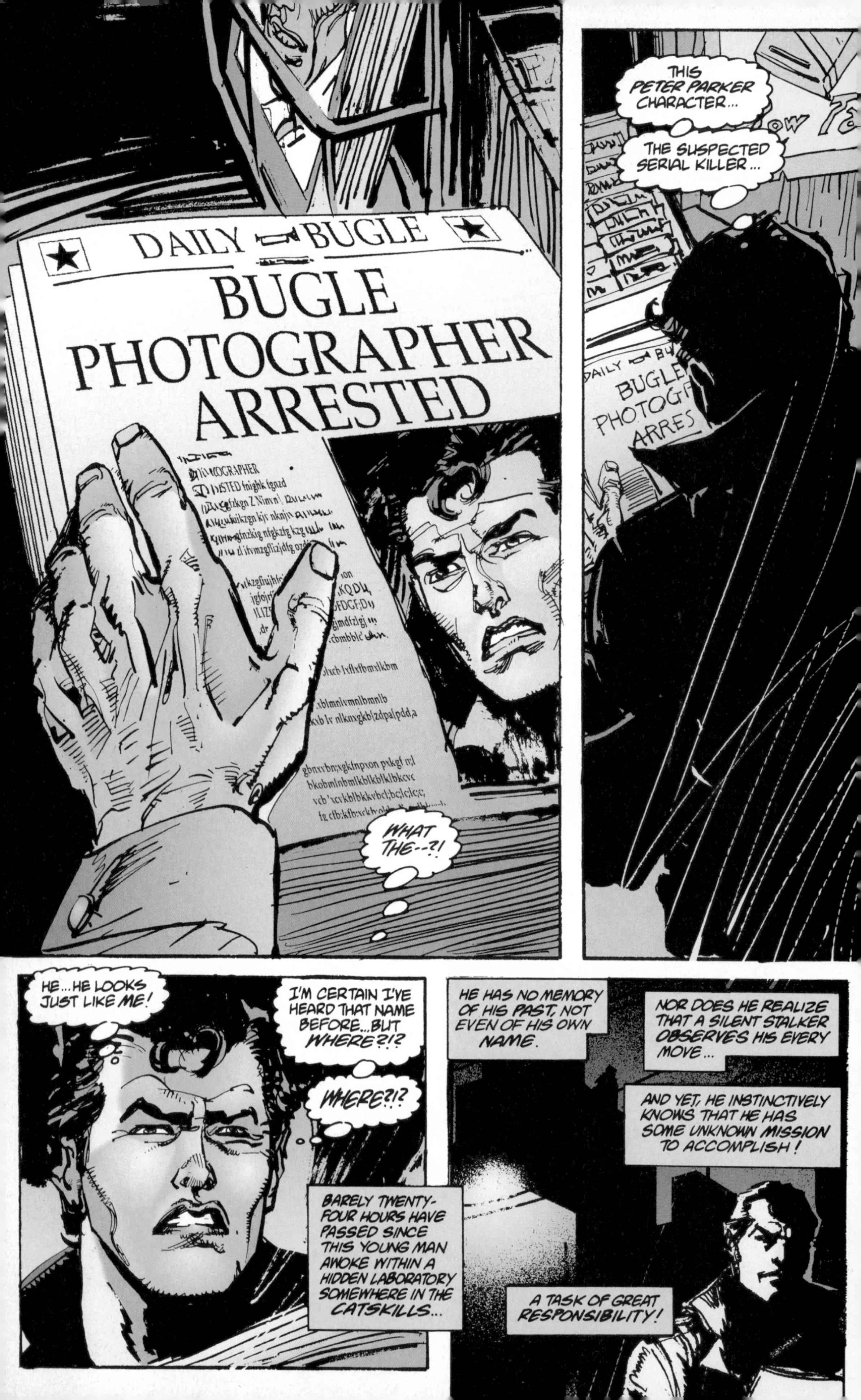
DAILY BUGLE
BUGLE PHOTOGRAPHER ARRESTED
WHAT THE--?!
THIS PETER PARKER CHARACTER...
THE SUSPECTED SERIAL KILLER...
HE...HE LOOKS JUST LIKE ME!
I'M CERTAIN I'VE HEARD THAT NAME BEFORE...BUT WHERE?!?
WHERE?!?
BARELY TWENTY-FOUR HOURS HAVE PASSED SINCE THIS YOUNG MAN AWOKE WITHIN A HIDDEN LABORATORY SOMEWHERE IN THE CATSKILLS...
HE HAS NO MEMORY OF HIS PAST, NOT EVEN OF HIS OWN NAME.
NOR DOES HE REALIZE THAT A SILENT STALKER OBSERVES HIS EVERY MOVE...
AND YET, HE INSTINCTIVELY KNOWS THAT HE HAS SOME UNKNOWN MISSION TO ACCOMPLISH!
A TASK OF GREAT RESPONSIBILITY!

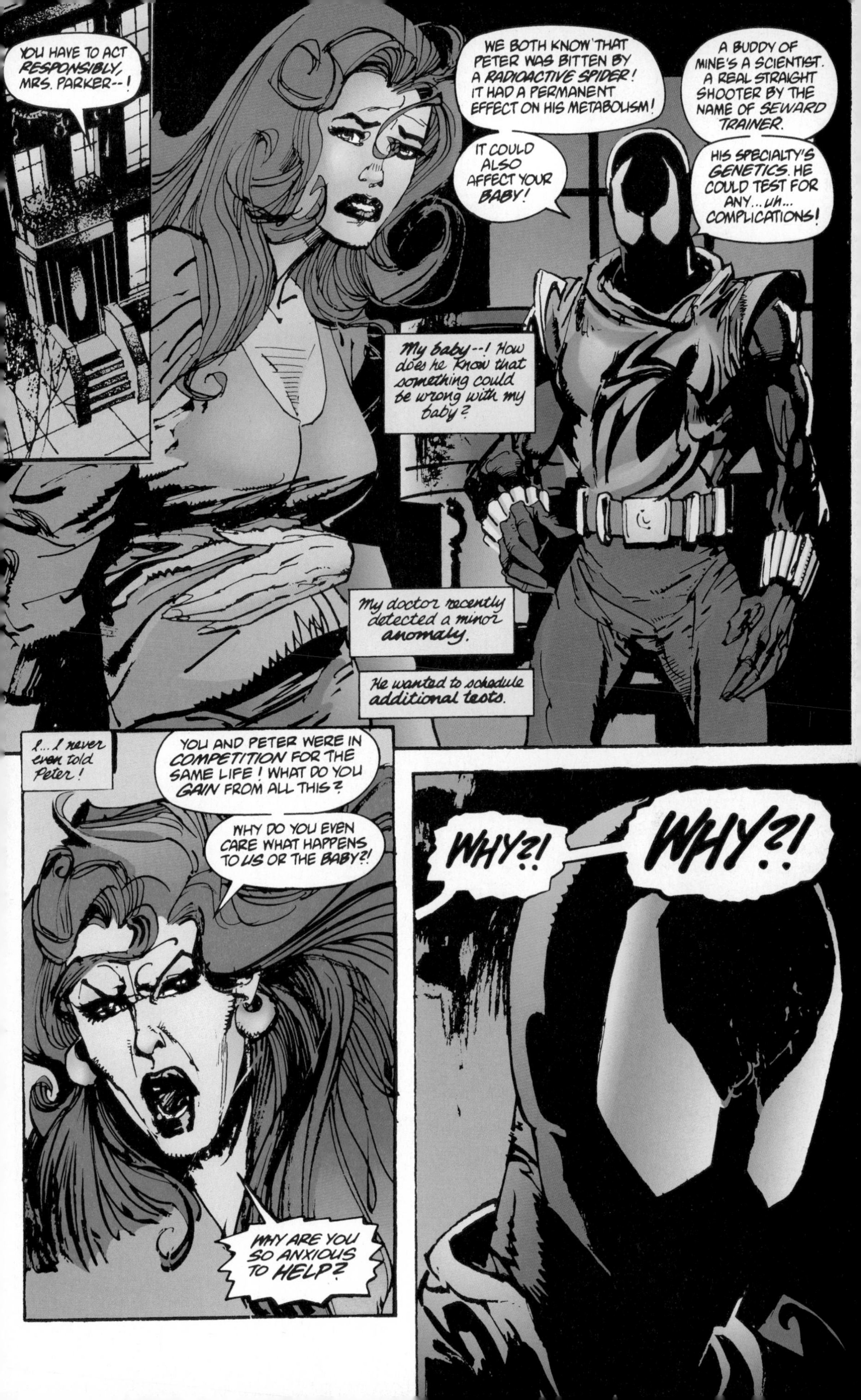
YOU HAVE TO ACT RESPONSIBLY, MRS. PARKER--!
WE BOTH KNOW THAT PETER WAS BITTEN BY A RADIOACTIVE SPIDER! IT HAD A PERMANENT EFFECT ON HIS METABOLISM!
IT COULD ALSO AFFECT YOUR BABY!
A BUDDY OF MINE'S A SCIENTIST. A REAL STRAIGHT SHOOTER BY THE NAME OF SEWARD TRAINER.
HIS SPECIALTY'S GENETICS. HE COULD TEST FOR ANY... UH... COMPLICATIONS!
My baby--! How does he know that something could be wrong with my baby?
My doctor recently detected a minor anomaly.
He wanted to schedule additional tests.
I... I never even told Peter!
YOU AND PETER WERE IN COMPETITION FOR THE SAME LIFE! WHAT DO YOU GAIN FROM ALL THIS?
WHY DO YOU EVEN CARE WHAT HAPPENS TO US OR THE BABY?!
WHY ARE YOU SO ANXIOUS TO HELP?
WHY?!
WHY?!

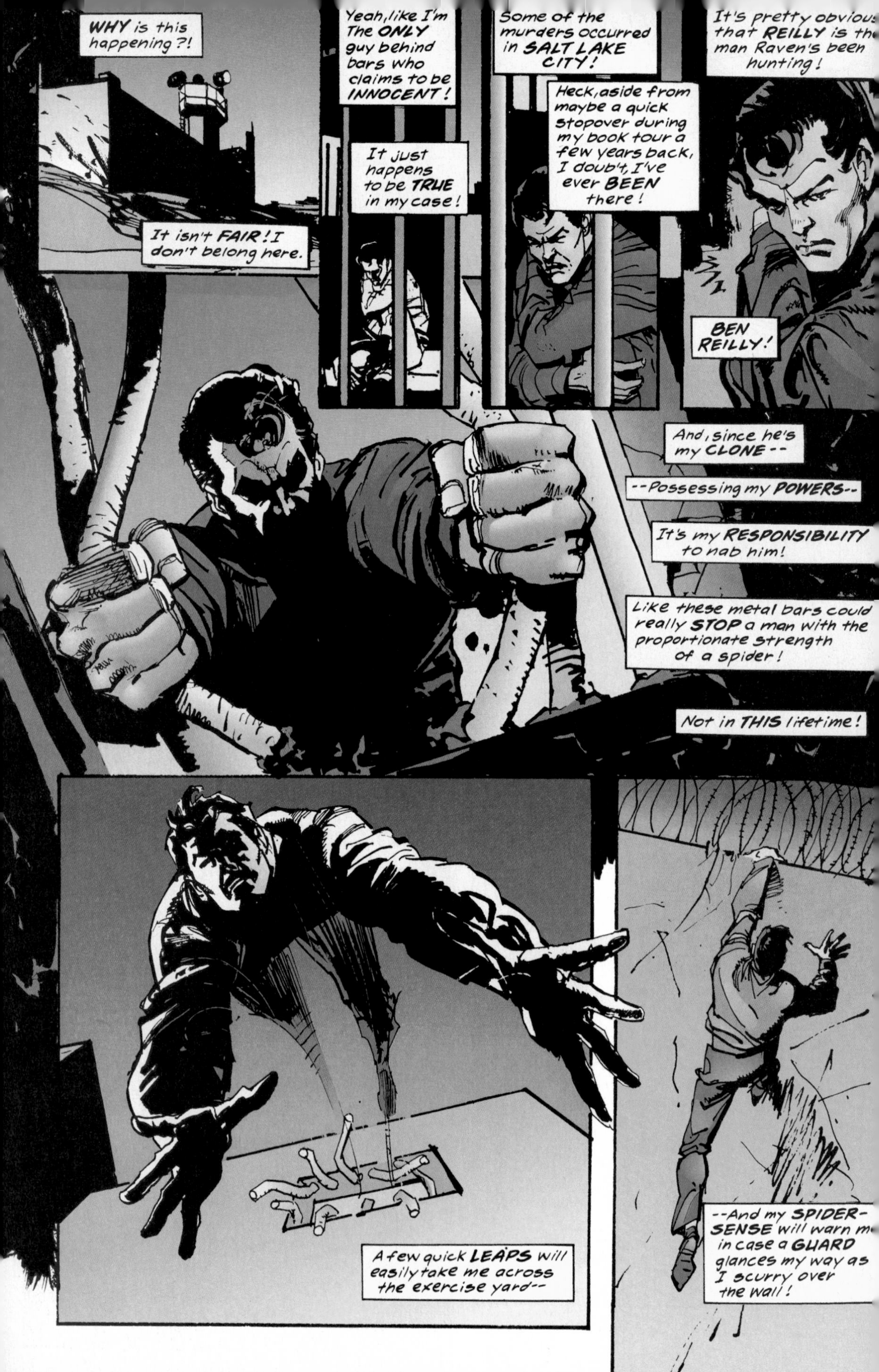
WHY is this happening?!
It isn't FAIR! I don't belong here.
Yeah, like I'm The ONLY guy behind bars who claims to be INNOCENT!
It just happens to be TRUE in my case!
Some of the murders occurred in SALT LAKE CITY!
Heck, aside from maybe a quick stopover during my book tour a few years back, I doub't, I've ever BEEN there!
It's pretty obvious that REILLY is the man Raven's been hunting!
BEN REILLY!
And, since he's my CLONE--
--Possessing my POWERS--
It's my RESPONSIBILITY to nab him!
Like these metal bars could really STOP a man with the proportionate strength of a spider!
Not in THIS lifetime!
A few quick LEAPS will easily take me across the exercise yard--
--And my SPIDER-SENSE will warn me in case a GUARD glances my way as I scurry over the wall!

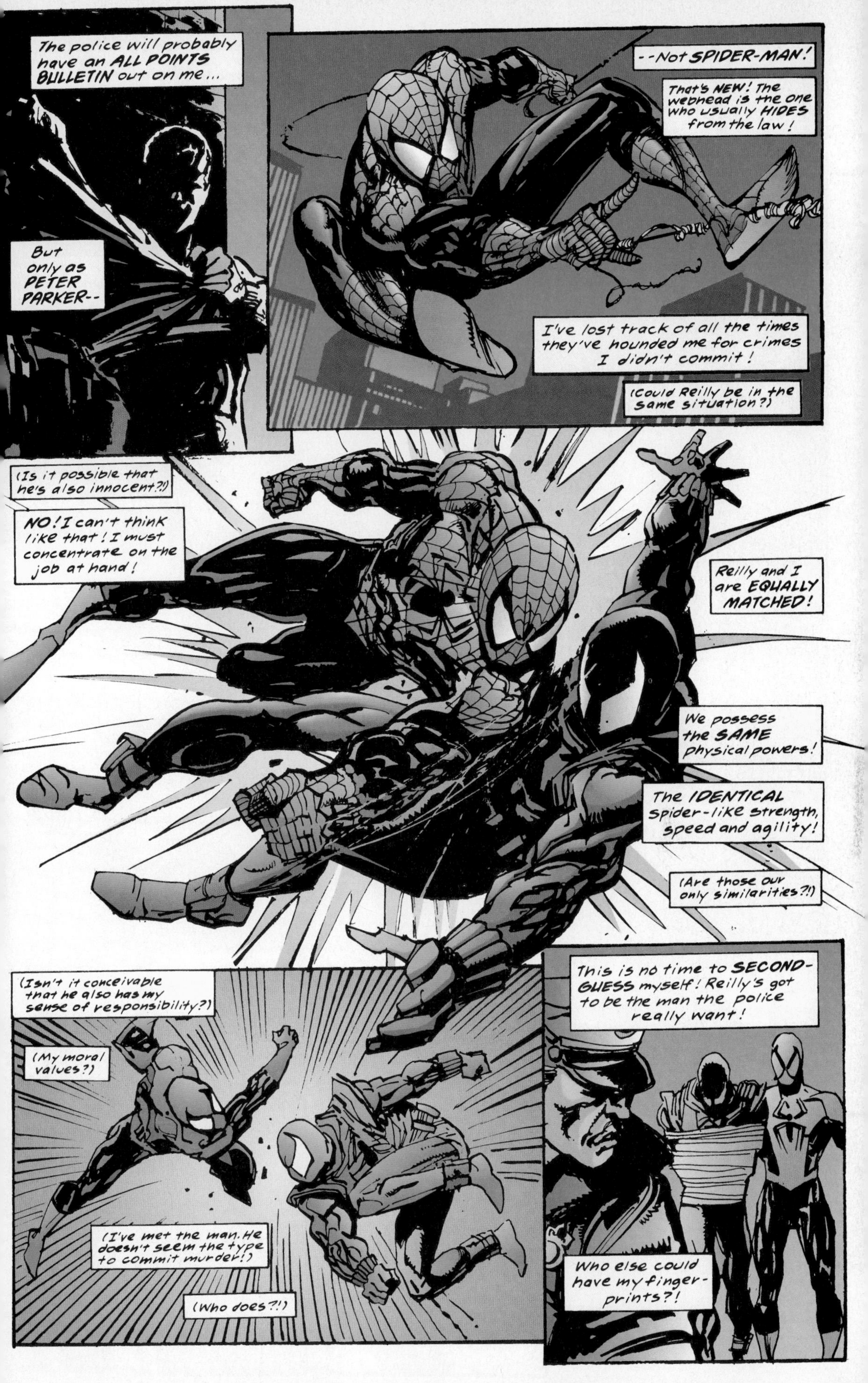

The police will probably have an ALL POINTS BULLETIN out on me...
But only as PETER PARKER--
--Not SPIDER-MAN!
That's NEW! The webhead is the one who usually HIDES from the law!
I've lost track of all the times they've hounded me for crimes I didn't commit!
(Could Reilly be in the same situation?)
(Is it possible that he's also innocent?!)
NO! I can't think like that! I must concentrate on the job at hand!
Reilly and I are EQUALLY MATCHED!
We possess the SAME physical powers!
The IDENTICAL spider-like strength, speed and agility!
(Are those our only similarities?!)
(Isn't it conceivable that he also has my sense of responsibility?)
(My moral values?)
(I've met the man. He doesn't seem the type to commit murder!)
(Who does?!)
This is no time to SECOND-GUESS myself! Reilly's got to be the man the police really want!
Who else could have my finger-prints?!

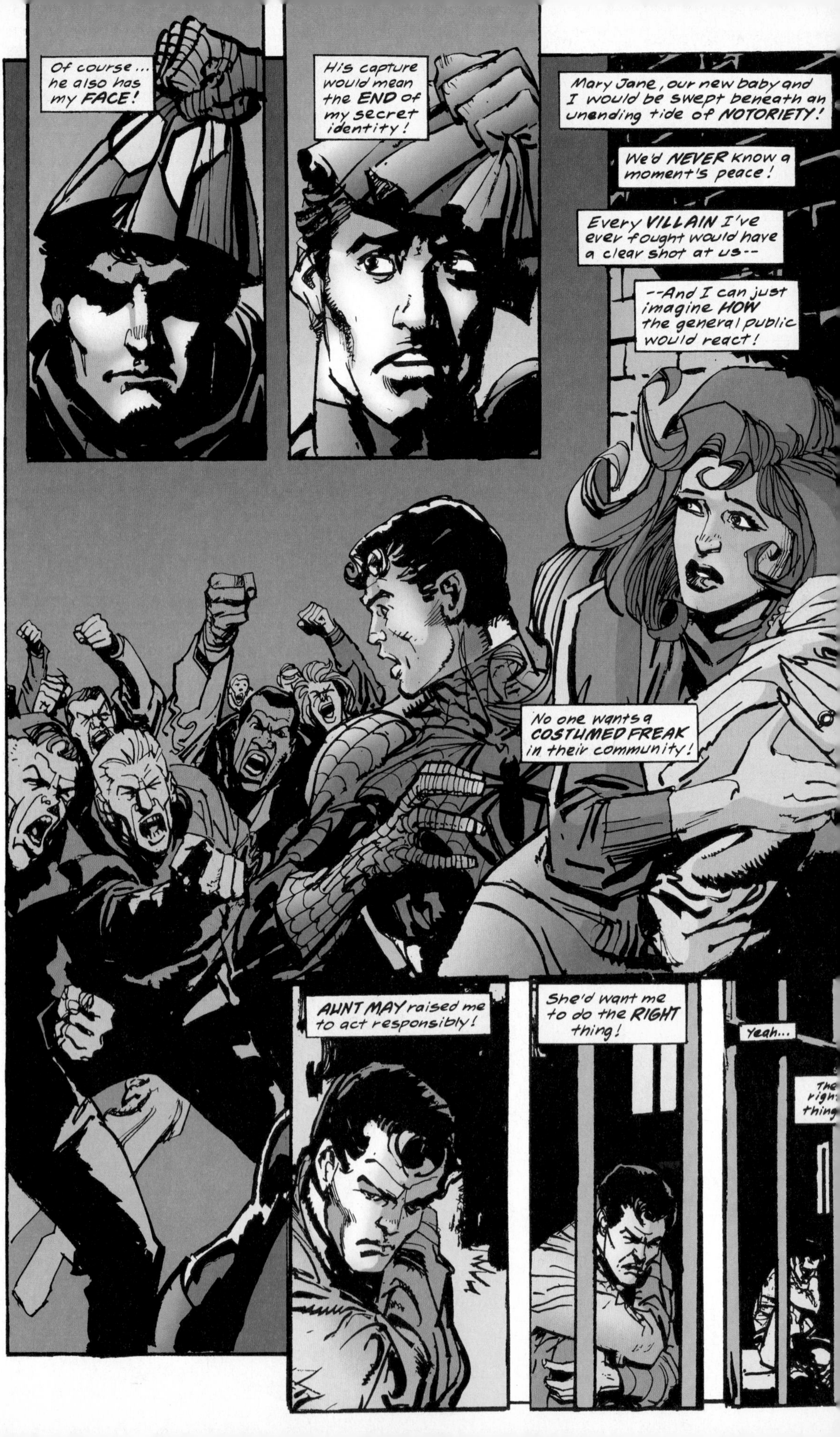
Of course... he also has my FACE!
His capture would mean the END of my secret identity!
Mary Jane, our new baby and I would be swept beneath an unending tide of NOTORIETY!
We'd NEVER know a moment's peace!
Every VILLAIN I've ever fought would have a clear shot at us--
--And I can just imagine HOW the general public would react!
No one wants a COSTUMED FREAK in their community!
AUNT MAY raised me to act responsibly!
She'd want me to do the RIGHT thing!
Yeah...
The

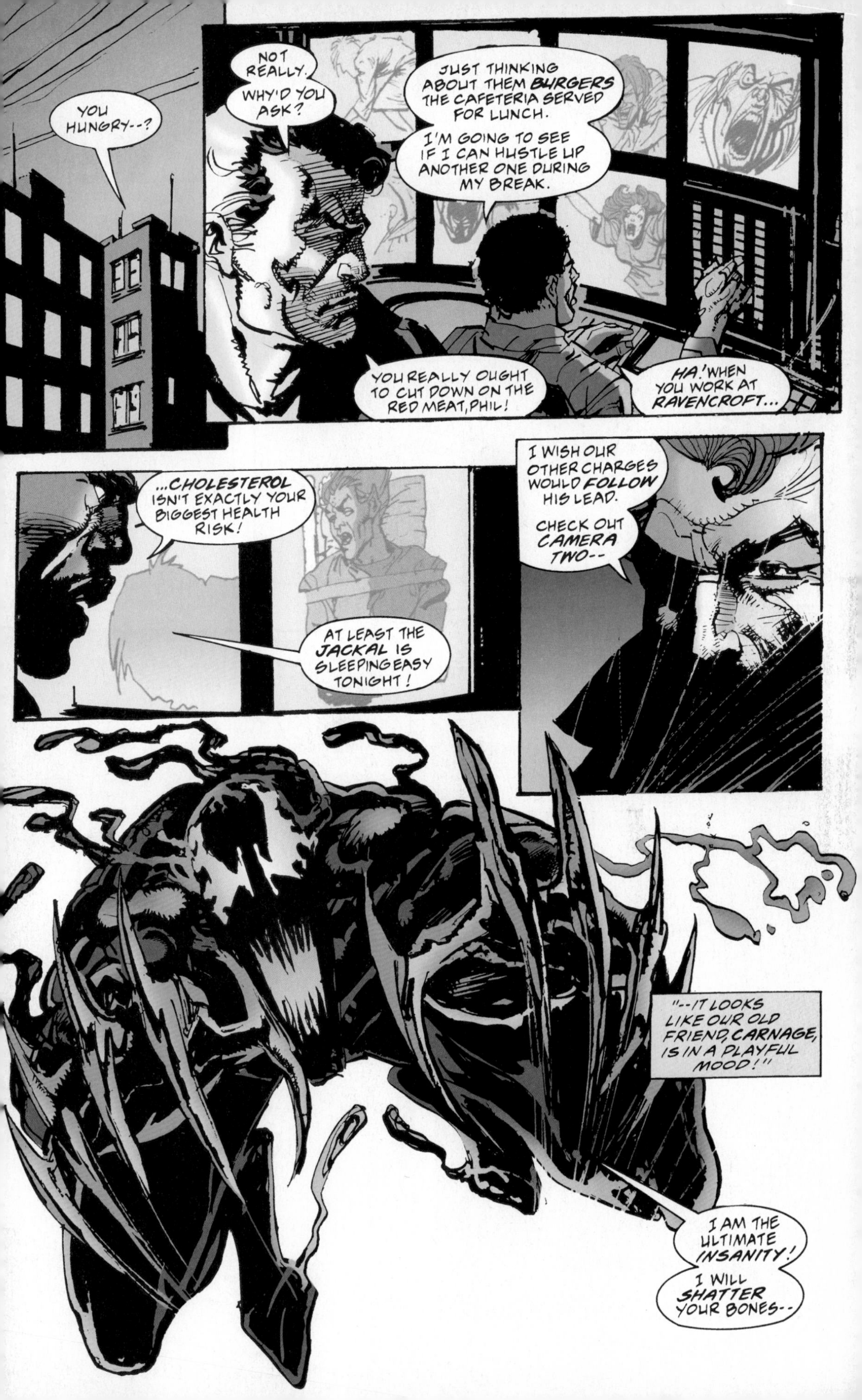

YOU HUNGRY--?
NOT REALLY.
WHY'D YOU ASK?
JUST THINKING ABOUT THEM BURGERS THE CAFETERIA SERVED FOR LUNCH.
I'M GOING TO SEE IF I CAN HUSTLE UP ANOTHER ONE DURING MY BREAK.
YOU REALLY OUGHT TO CUT DOWN ON THE RED MEAT, PHIL!
HA! WHEN YOU WORK AT RAVENCROFT...
...CHOLESTEROL ISN'T EXACTLY YOUR BIGGEST HEALTH RISK!
AT LEAST THE JACKAL IS SLEEPING EASY TONIGHT!
I WISH OUR OTHER CHARGES WOULD FOLLOW HIS LEAD.
CHECK OUT CAMERA TWO--
"--IT LOOKS LIKE OUR OLD FRIEND, CARNAGE, IS IN A PLAYFUL MOOD!"
I AM THE ULTIMATE INSANITY!
I WILL SHATTER YOUR BONES--

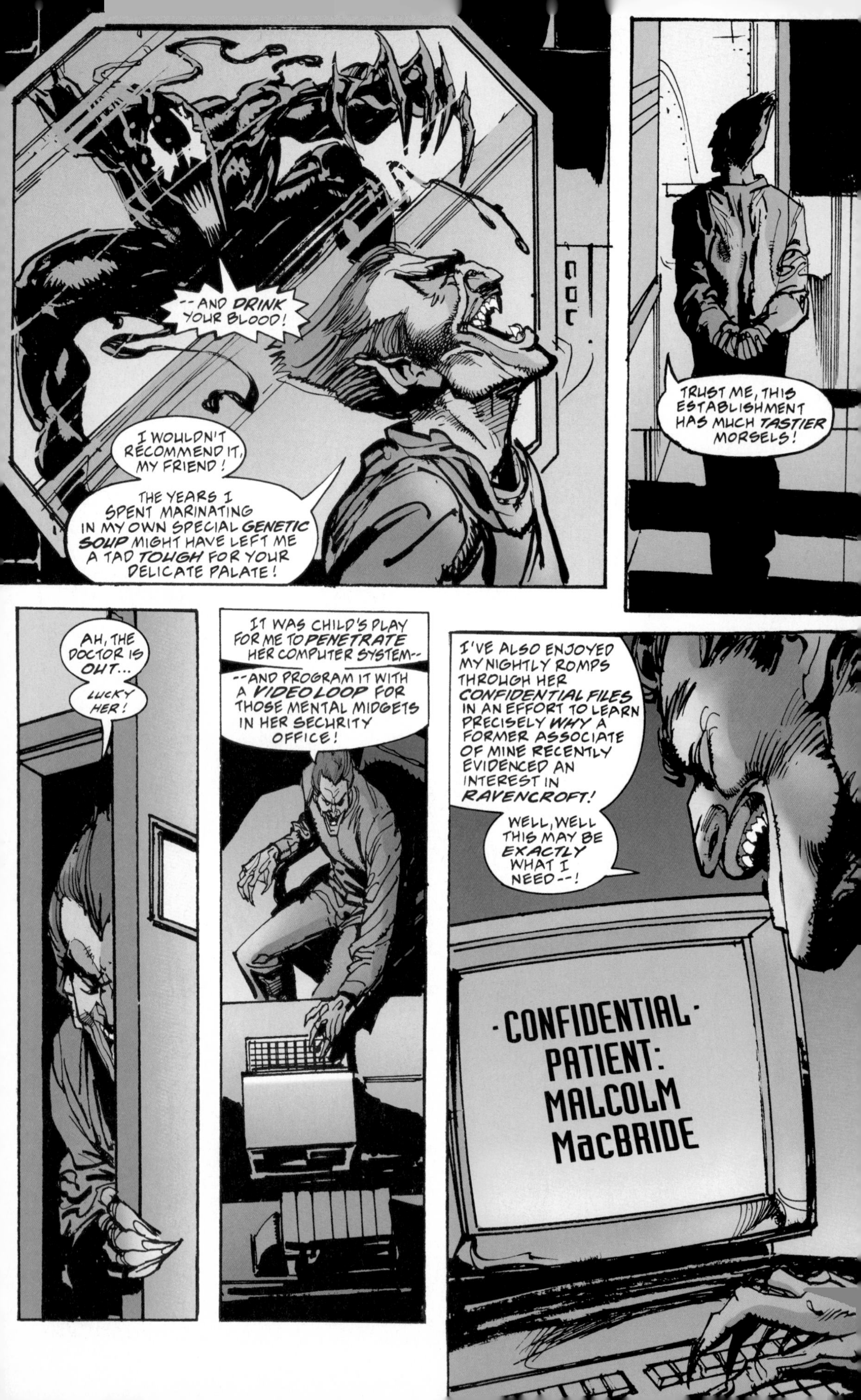

--AND DRINK YOUR BLOOD!
I WOULDN'T RECOMMEND IT, MY FRIEND!
THE YEARS I SPENT MARINATING IN MY OWN SPECIAL GENETIC SOUP MIGHT HAVE LEFT ME A TAD TOUGH FOR YOUR DELICATE PALATE!
TRUST ME, THIS ESTABLISHMENT HAS MUCH TASTIER MORSELS!
AH, THE DOCTOR IS OUT...
LUCKY HER!
IT WAS CHILD'S PLAY FOR ME TO PENETRATE HER COMPUTER SYSTEM--
--AND PROGRAM IT WITH A VIDEOLOOP FOR THOSE MENTAL MIDGETS IN HER SECURITY OFFICE!
I'VE ALSO ENJOYED MY NIGHTLY ROMPS THROUGH HER CONFIDENTIAL FILES IN AN EFFORT TO LEARN PRECISELY WHY A FORMER ASSOCIATE OF MINE RECENTLY EVIDENCED AN INTEREST IN RAVENCROFT!
WELL, WELL THIS MAY BE EXACTLY WHAT I NEED--!
·CONFIDENTIAL·
PATIENT:
MALCOLM
MacBRIDE

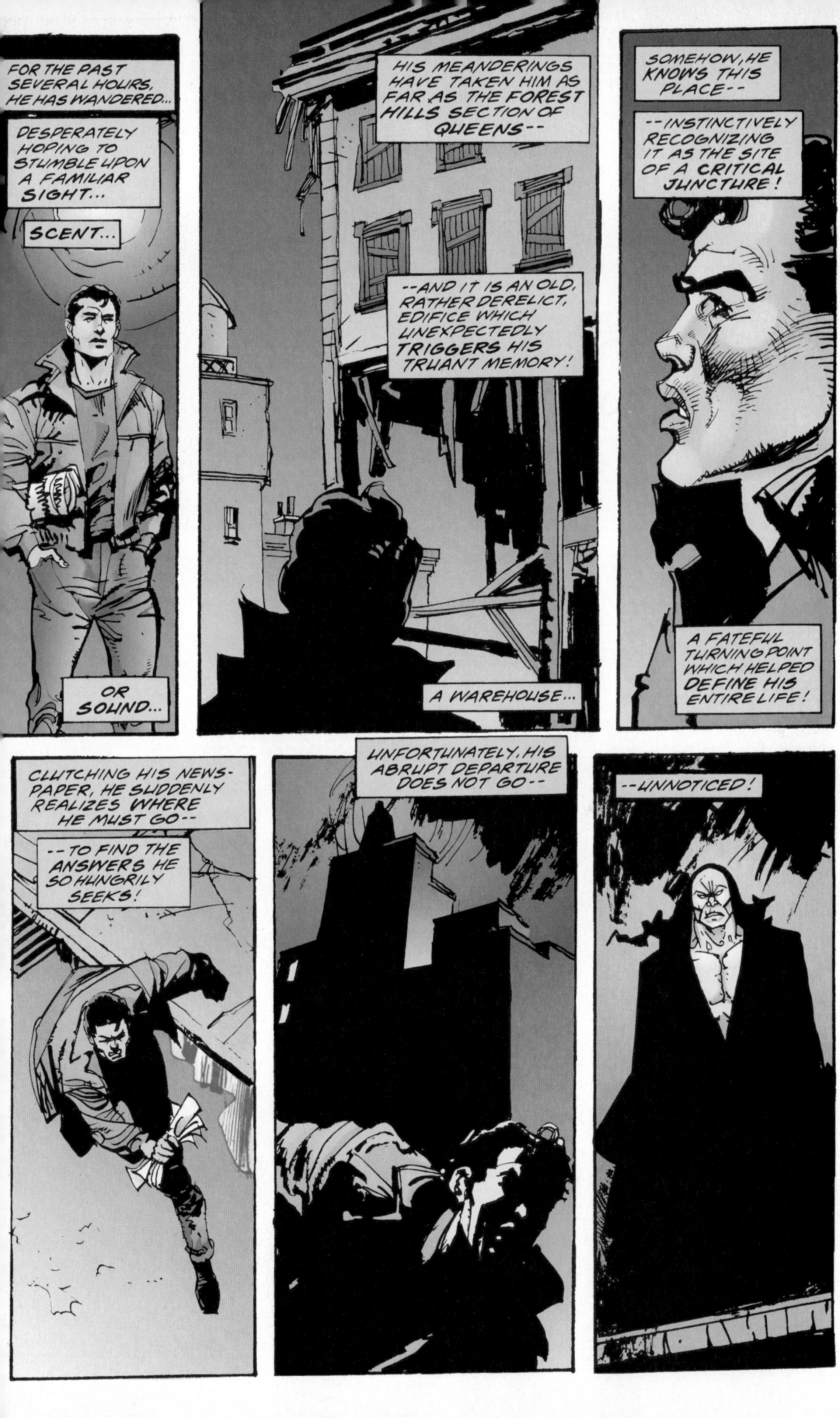
FOR THE PAST SEVERAL HOURS, HE HAS WANDERED...
DESPERATELY HOPING TO STUMBLE UPON A FAMILIAR SIGHT...
SCENT...
OR SOUND...
HIS MEANDERINGS HAVE TAKEN HIM AS FAR AS THE FOREST HILLS SECTION OF QUEENS--
--AND IT IS AN OLD, RATHER DERELICT, EDIFICE WHICH UNEXPECTEDLY TRIGGERS HIS TRUANT MEMORY!
A WAREHOUSE...
SOMEHOW, HE KNOWS THIS PLACE--
--INSTINCTIVELY RECOGNIZING IT AS THE SITE OF A CRITICAL JUNCTURE!
A FATEFUL TURNING POINT WHICH HELPED DEFINE HIS ENTIRE LIFE!
CLUTCHING HIS NEWS-PAPER, HE SUDDENLY REALIZES WHERE HE MUST GO--
--TO FIND THE ANSWERS HE SO HUNGRILY SEEKS!
UNFORTUNATELY, HIS ABRUPT DEPARTURE DOES NOT GO--
--UNNOTICED!

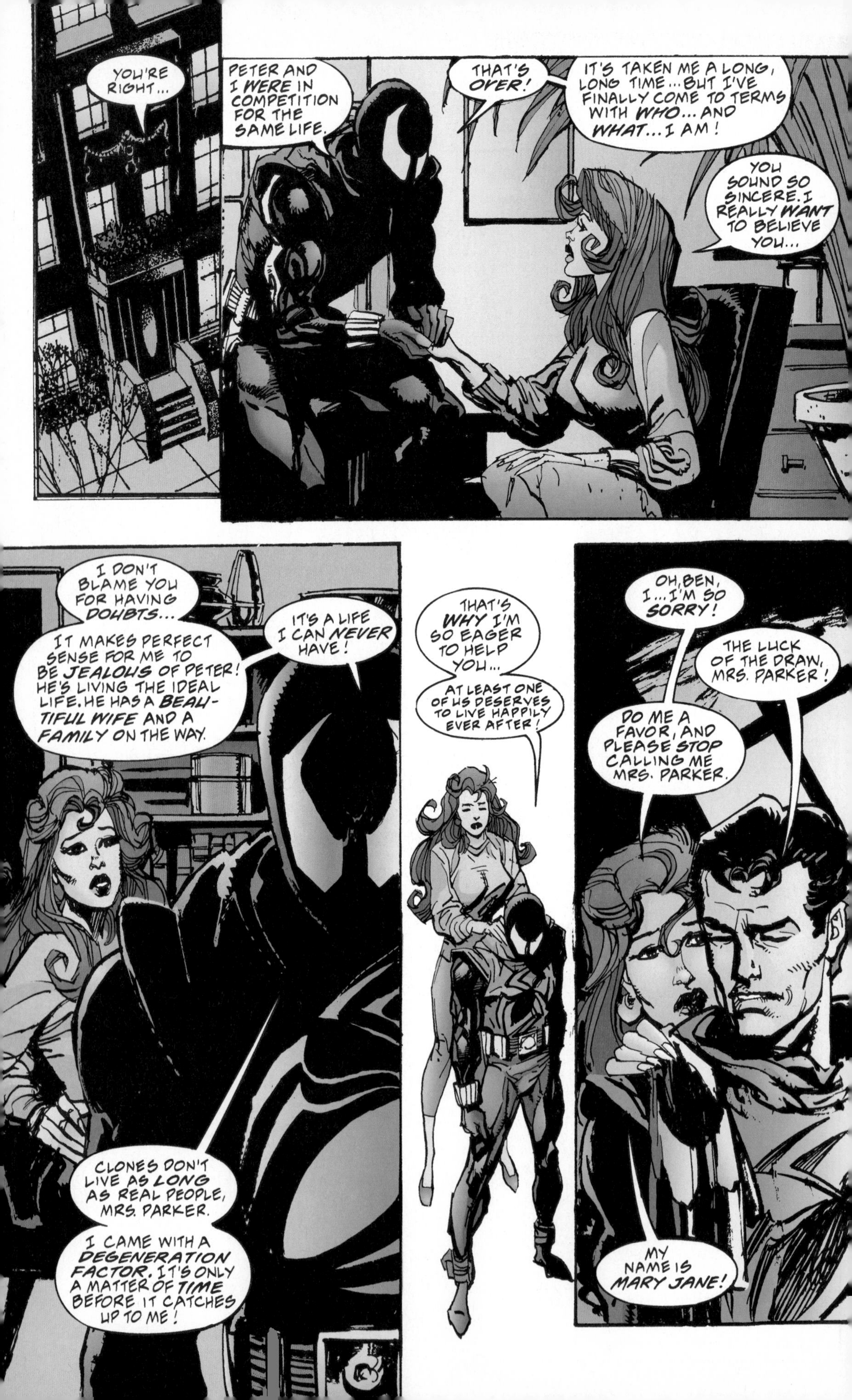
YOU'RE RIGHT...
PETER AND I WERE IN COMPETITION FOR THE SAME LIFE.
THAT'S OVER!
IT'S TAKEN ME A LONG, LONG TIME... BUT I'VE FINALLY COME TO TERMS WITH WHO... AND WHAT... I AM!
YOU SOUND SO SINCERE. I REALLY WANT TO BELIEVE YOU...
I DON'T BLAME YOU FOR HAVING DOUBTS...
IT MAKES PERFECT SENSE FOR ME TO BE JEALOUS OF PETER! HE'S LIVING THE IDEAL LIFE. HE HAS A BEAUTIFUL WIFE AND A FAMILY ON THE WAY.
IT'S A LIFE I CAN NEVER HAVE!
CLONES DON'T LIVE AS LONG AS REAL PEOPLE, MRS. PARKER.
I CAME WITH A DEGENERATION FACTOR. IT'S ONLY A MATTER OF TIME BEFORE IT CATCHES UP TO ME!
THAT'S WHY I'M SO EAGER TO HELP YOU...
AT LEAST ONE OF US DESERVES TO LIVE HAPPILY EVER AFTER!
OH, BEN, I... I'M SO SORRY!
THE LUCK OF THE DRAW, MRS. PARKER!
DO ME A FAVOR, AND PLEASE STOP CALLING ME MRS. PARKER.
MY NAME IS MARY JANE!

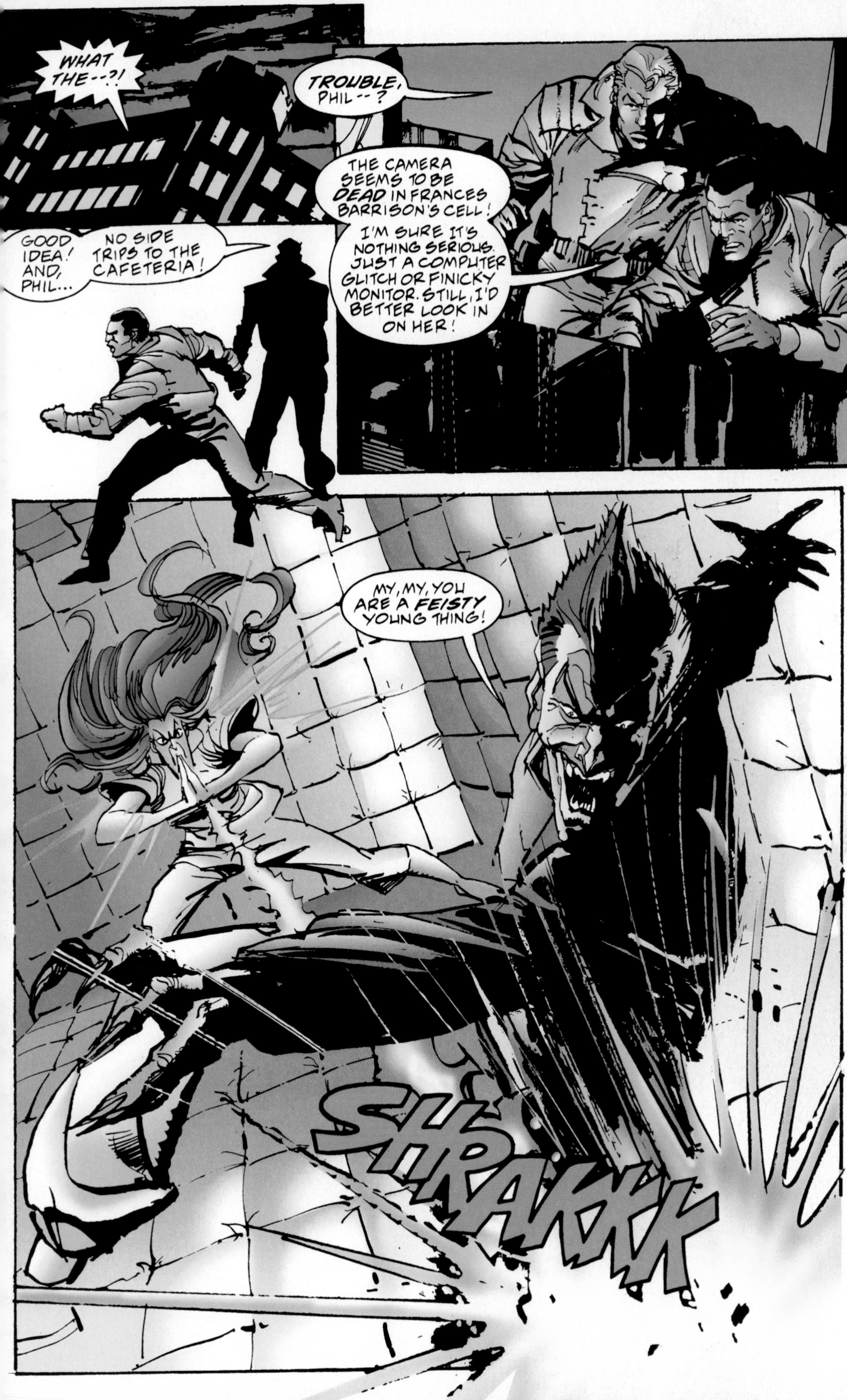
WHAT THE--?!
TROUBLE, PHIL--?
THE CAMERA SEEMS TO BE DEAD IN FRANCES BARRISON'S CELL!
I'M SURE IT'S NOTHING SERIOUS. JUST A COMPUTER GLITCH OR FINICKY MONITOR. STILL, I'D BETTER LOOK IN ON HER!
GOOD IDEA! AND, PHIL...
NO SIDE TRIPS TO THE CAFETERIA!
MY, MY, YOU ARE A FEISTY YOUNG THING!
SHRAKKK

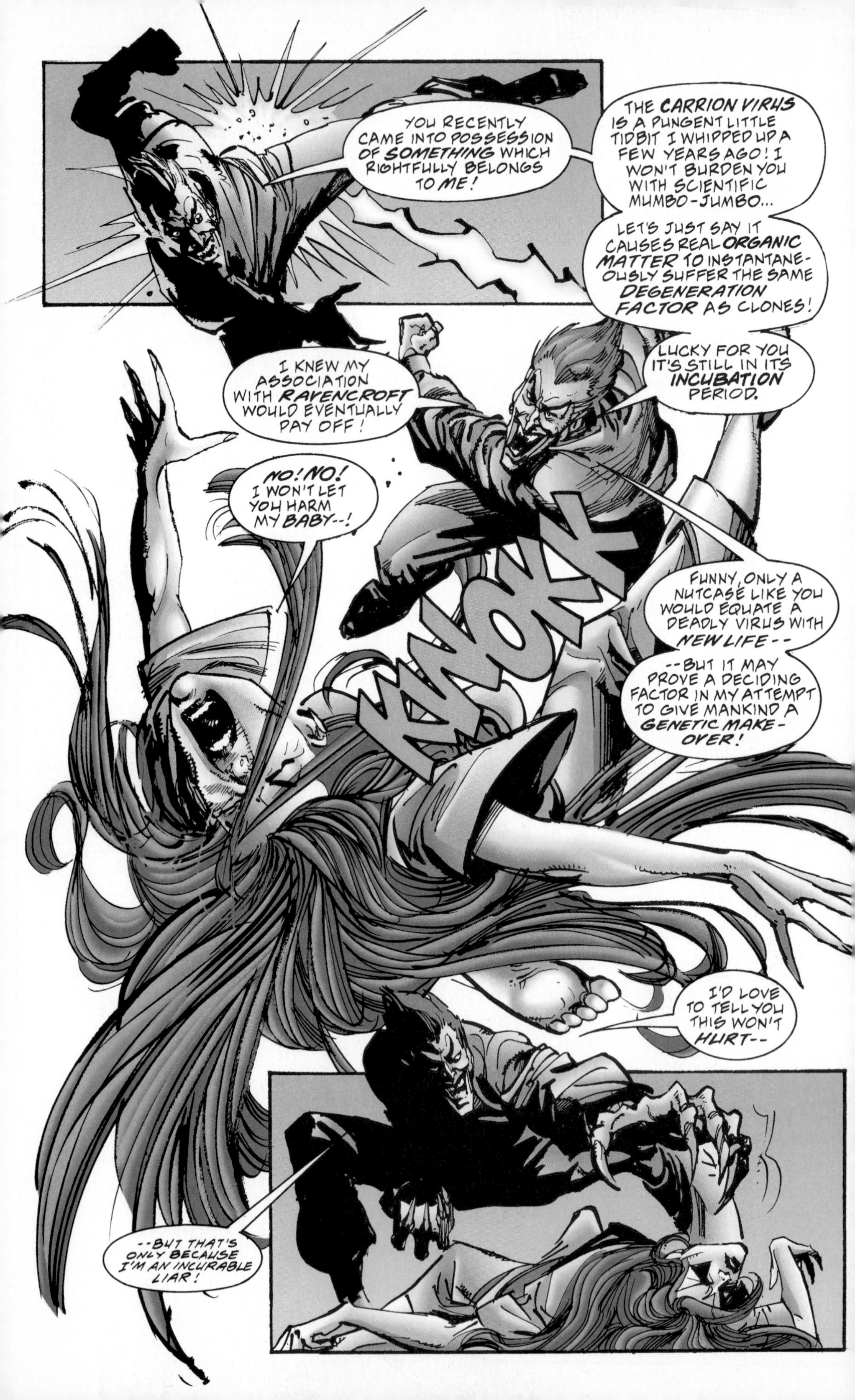
YOU RECENTLY CAME INTO POSSESSION OF SOMETHING WHICH RIGHTFULLY BELONGS TO ME!
THE CARRION VIRUS IS A PUNGENT LITTLE TIDBIT I WHIPPED UP A FEW YEARS AGO! I WON'T BURDEN YOU WITH SCIENTIFIC MUMBO-JUMBO...
LET'S JUST SAY IT CAUSES REAL ORGANIC MATTER TO INSTANTANEOUSLY SUFFER THE SAME DEGENERATION FACTOR AS CLONES!
I KNEW MY ASSOCIATION WITH RAVENCROFT WOULD EVENTUALLY PAY OFF!
LUCKY FOR YOU IT'S STILL IN ITS INCUBATION PERIOD.
NO! NO! I WON'T LET YOU HARM MY BABY--!
KNOKK
FUNNY, ONLY A NUTCASE LIKE YOU WOULD EQUATE A DEADLY VIRUS WITH NEW LIFE--
--BUT IT MAY PROVE A DECIDING FACTOR IN MY ATTEMPT TO GIVE MANKIND A GENETIC MAKE-OVER!
I'D LOVE TO TELL YOU THIS WON'T HURT--
--BUT THAT'S ONLY BECAUSE I'M AN INCURABLE LIAR!

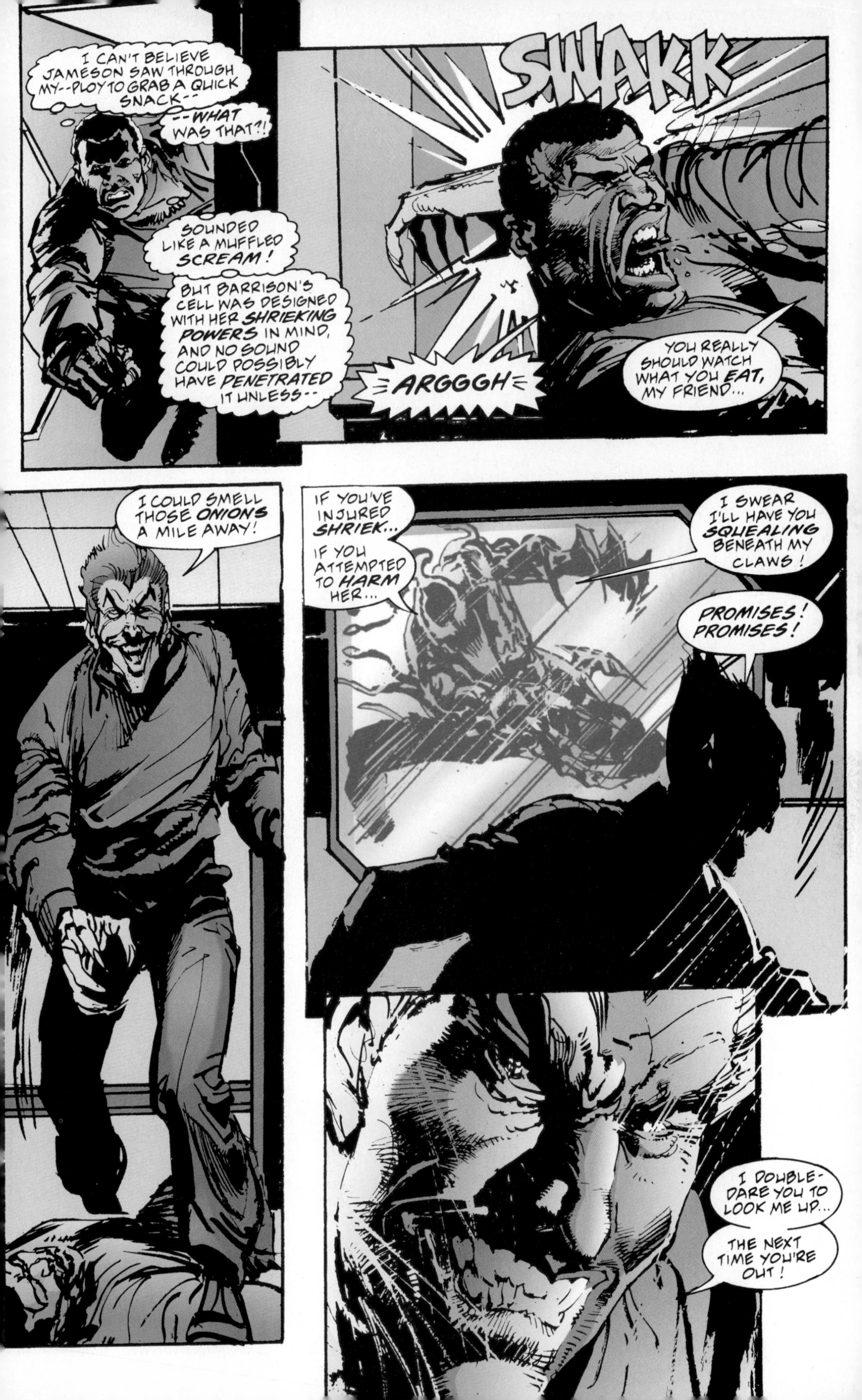
I CAN'T BELIEVE JAMESON SAW THROUGH MY--PLOY TO GRAB A QUICK SNACK--
--WHAT WAS THAT?!
SOUNDED LIKE A MUFFLED SCREAM!
BUT BARRISON'S CELL WAS DESIGNED WITH HER SHRIEKING POWERS IN MIND, AND NO SOUND COULD POSSIBLY HAVE PENETRATED IT UNLESS--
SWAKK
ARGGGH
YOU REALLY SHOULD WATCH WHAT YOU EAT, MY FRIEND...
I COULD SMELL THOSE ONIONS A MILE AWAY!
IF YOU'VE INJURED SHRIEK...
IF YOU ATTEMPTED TO HARM HER...
I SWEAR I'LL HAVE YOU SQUEALING BENEATH MY CLAWS!
PROMISES! PROMISES!
I DOUBLE-DARE YOU TO LOOK ME UP...
THE NEXT TIME YOU'RE OUT!

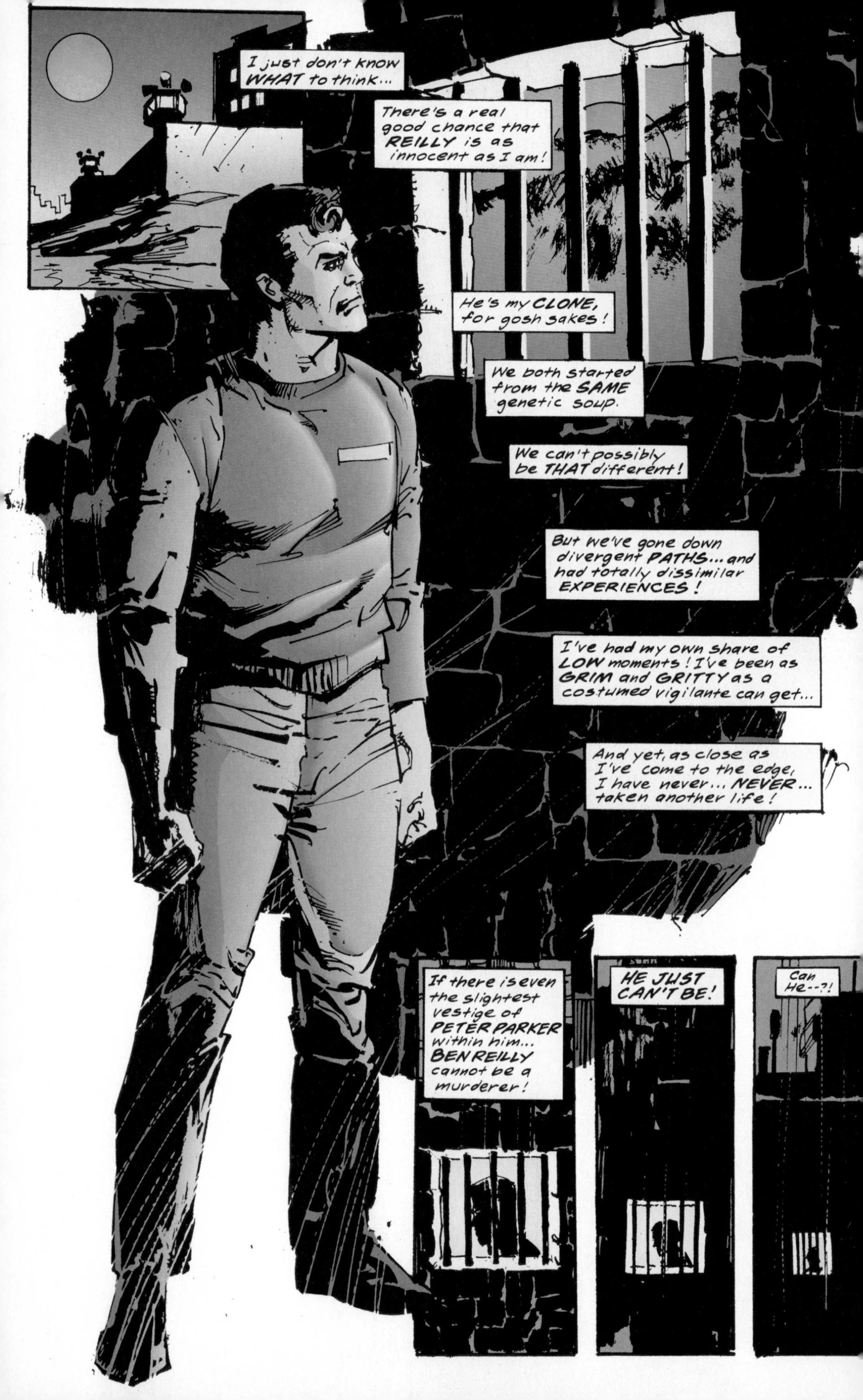
I just don't know WHAT to think...
There's a real good chance that REILLY is as innocent as I am!
He's my CLONE, for gosh sakes!
We both started from the SAME genetic soup.
We can't possibly be THAT different!
But we've gone down divergent PATHS... and had totally dissimilar EXPERIENCES!
I've had my own share of LOW moments! I've been as GRIM and GRITTY as a costumed vigilante can get...
And yet, as close as I've come to the edge, I have never... NEVER... taken another life!
If there is even the slightest vestige of PETER PARKER within him... BEN REILLY cannot be a murderer!
HE JUST CAN'T BE!
Can He--?!

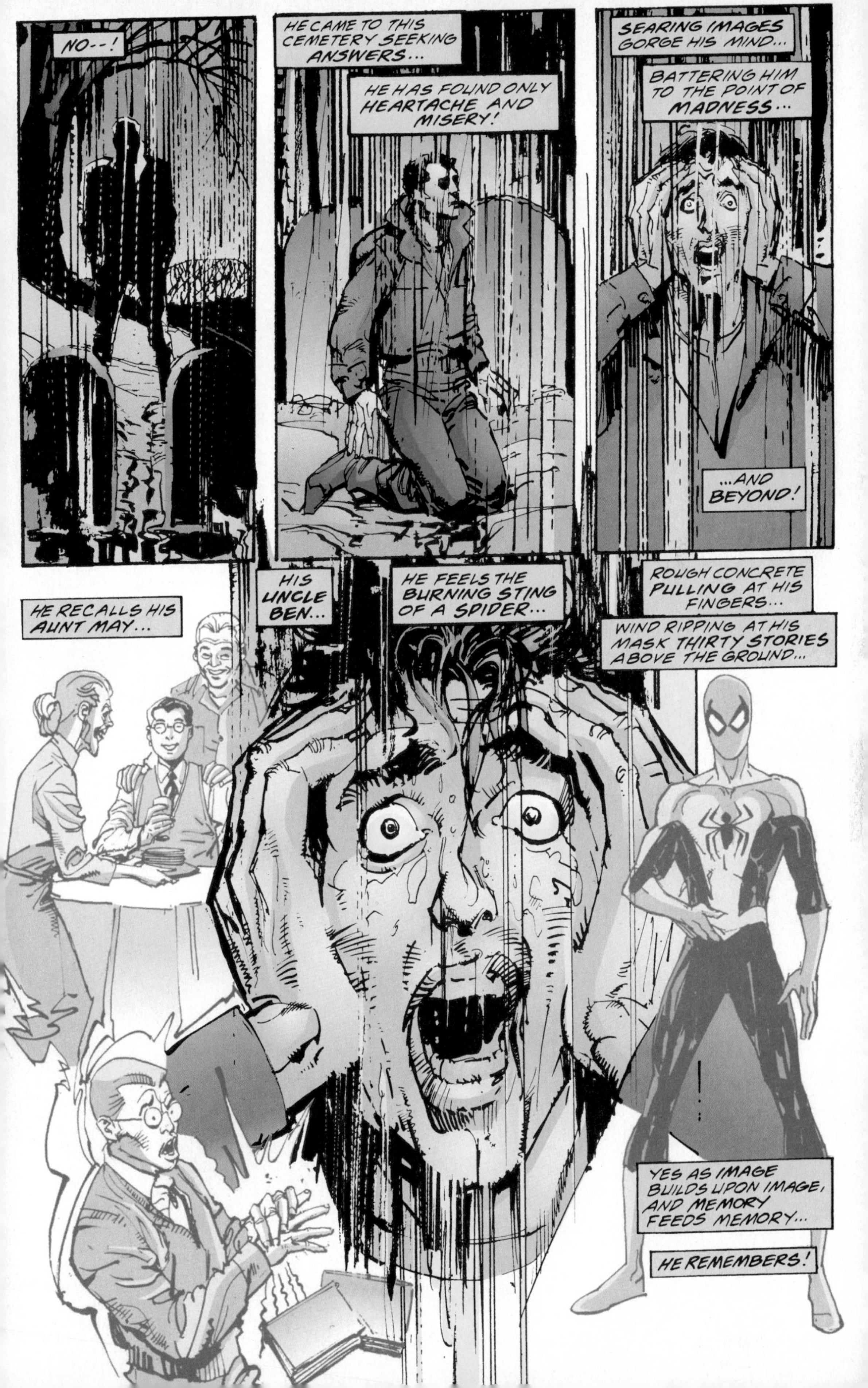
NO--!
HE CAME TO THIS CEMETERY SEEKING ANSWERS...
HE HAS FOUND ONLY HEARTACHE AND MISERY!
SEARING IMAGES GORGE HIS MIND...
BATTERING HIM TO THE POINT OF MADNESS...
...AND BEYOND!
HE RECALLS HIS AUNT MAY...
HIS UNCLE BEN...
HE FEELS THE BURNING STING OF A SPIDER...
ROUGH CONCRETE PULLING AT HIS FINGERS...
WIND RIPPING AT HIS MASK THIRTY STORIES ABOVE THE GROUND...
YES AS IMAGE BUILDS UPON IMAGE, AND MEMORY FEEDS MEMORY...
HE REMEMBERS!

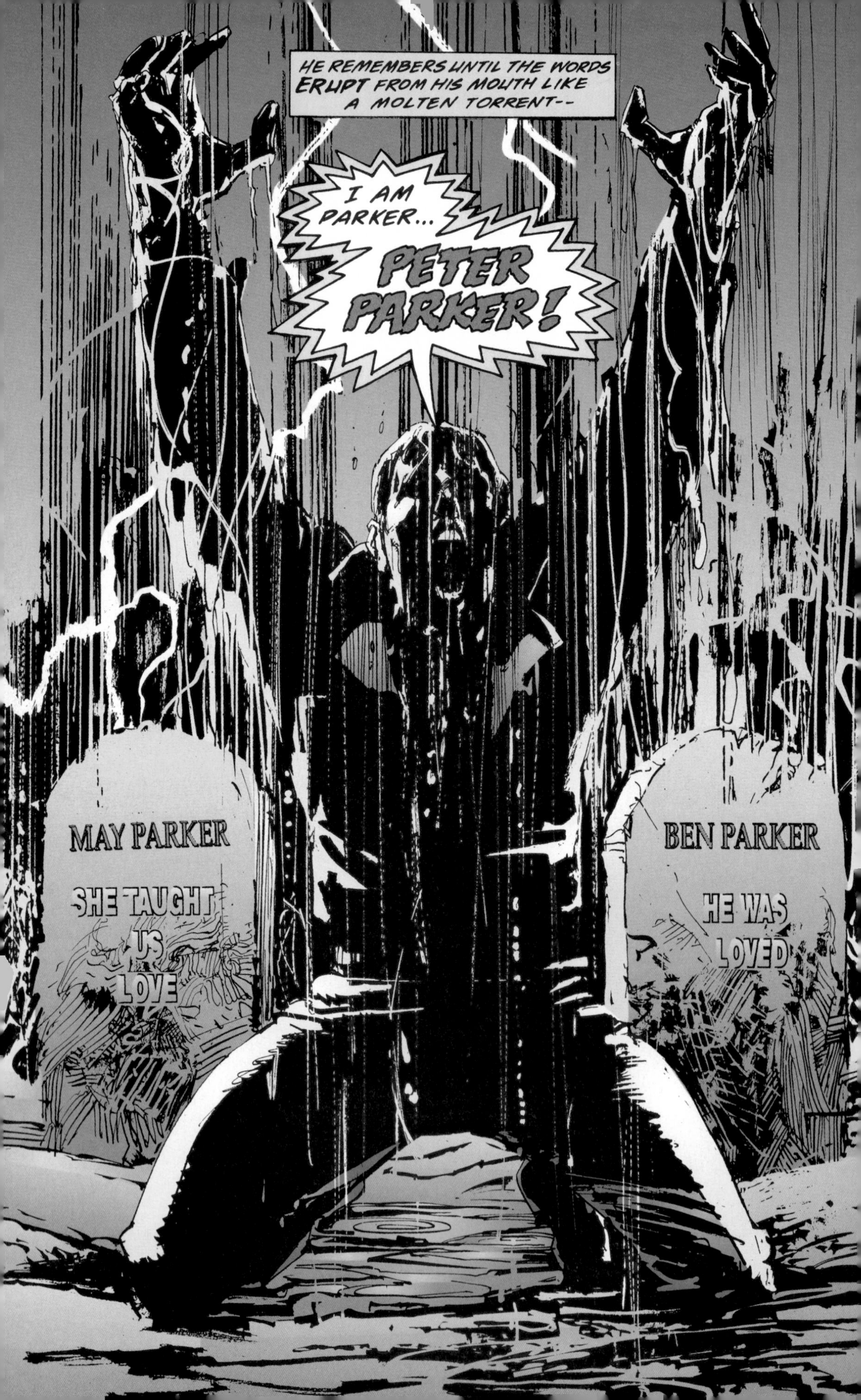
HE REMEMBERS UNTIL THE WORDS ERUPT FROM HIS MOUTH LIKE A MOLTEN TORRENT--
I AM PARKER...
PETER PARKER!
MAY PARKER
SHE TAUGHT US LOVE
BEN PARKER
HE WAS LOVED

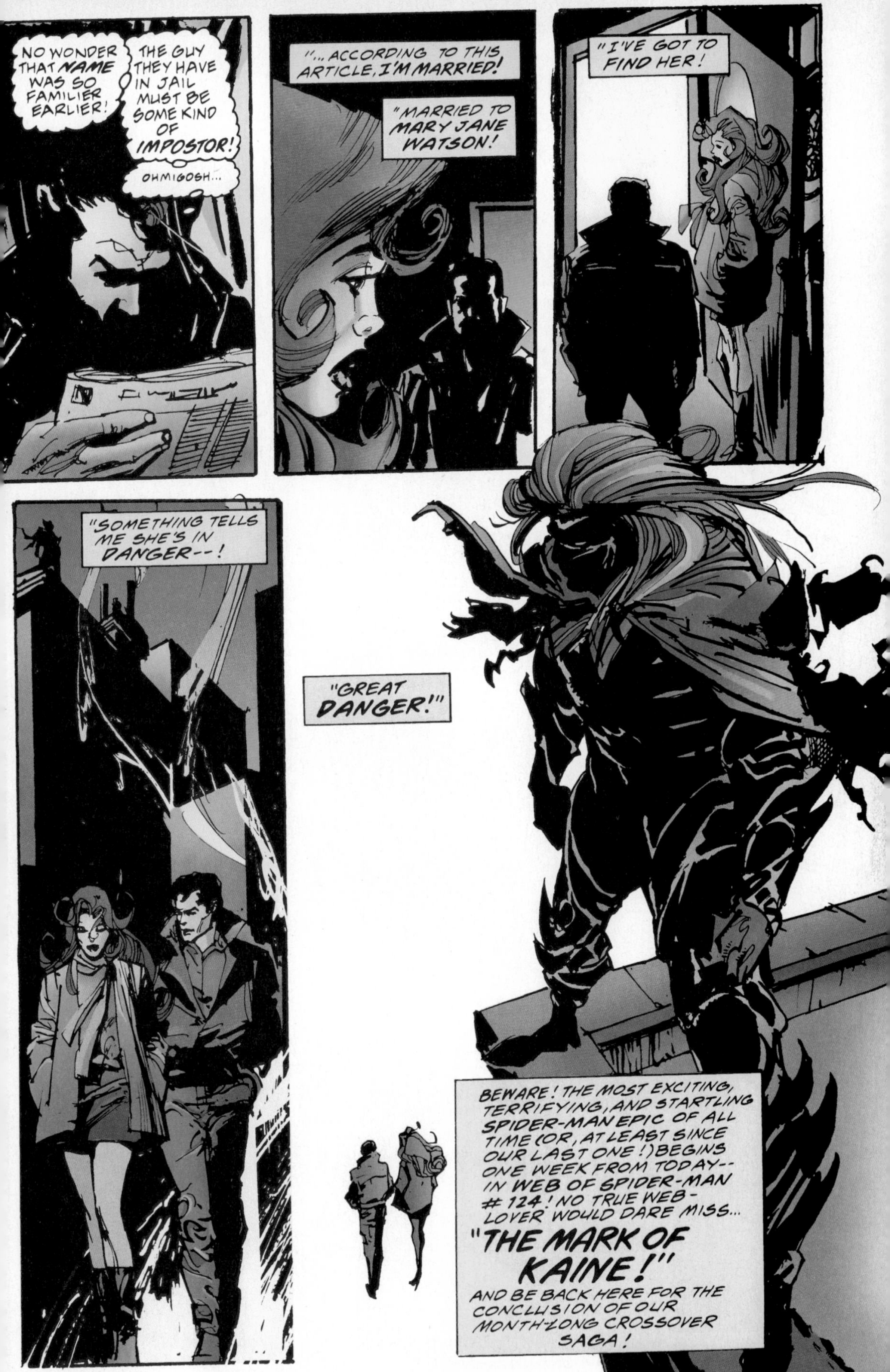

NO WONDER THAT NAME WAS SO FAMILIER EARLIER!
THE GUY THEY HAVE IN JAIL MUST BE SOME KIND OF IMPOSTOR!
OHMIGOSH...
"...ACCORDING TO THIS ARTICLE, I'M MARRIED!
"MARRIED TO MARY JANE WATSON!
"I'VE GOT TO FIND HER!
"SOMETHING TELLS ME SHE'S IN DANGER--!
"GREAT DANGER!"
BEWARE! THE MOST EXCITING, TERRIFYING, AND STARTLING SPIDER-MAN EPIC OF ALL TIME (OR, AT LEAST SINCE OUR LAST ONE!) BEGINS ONE WEEK FROM TODAY-- IN WEB OF SPIDER-MAN #124! NO TRUE WEB-LOVER WOULD DARE MISS...
"THE MARK OF KAINE!"
AND BE BACK HERE FOR THE CONCLUSION OF OUR MONTH-LONG CROSSOVER SAGA!

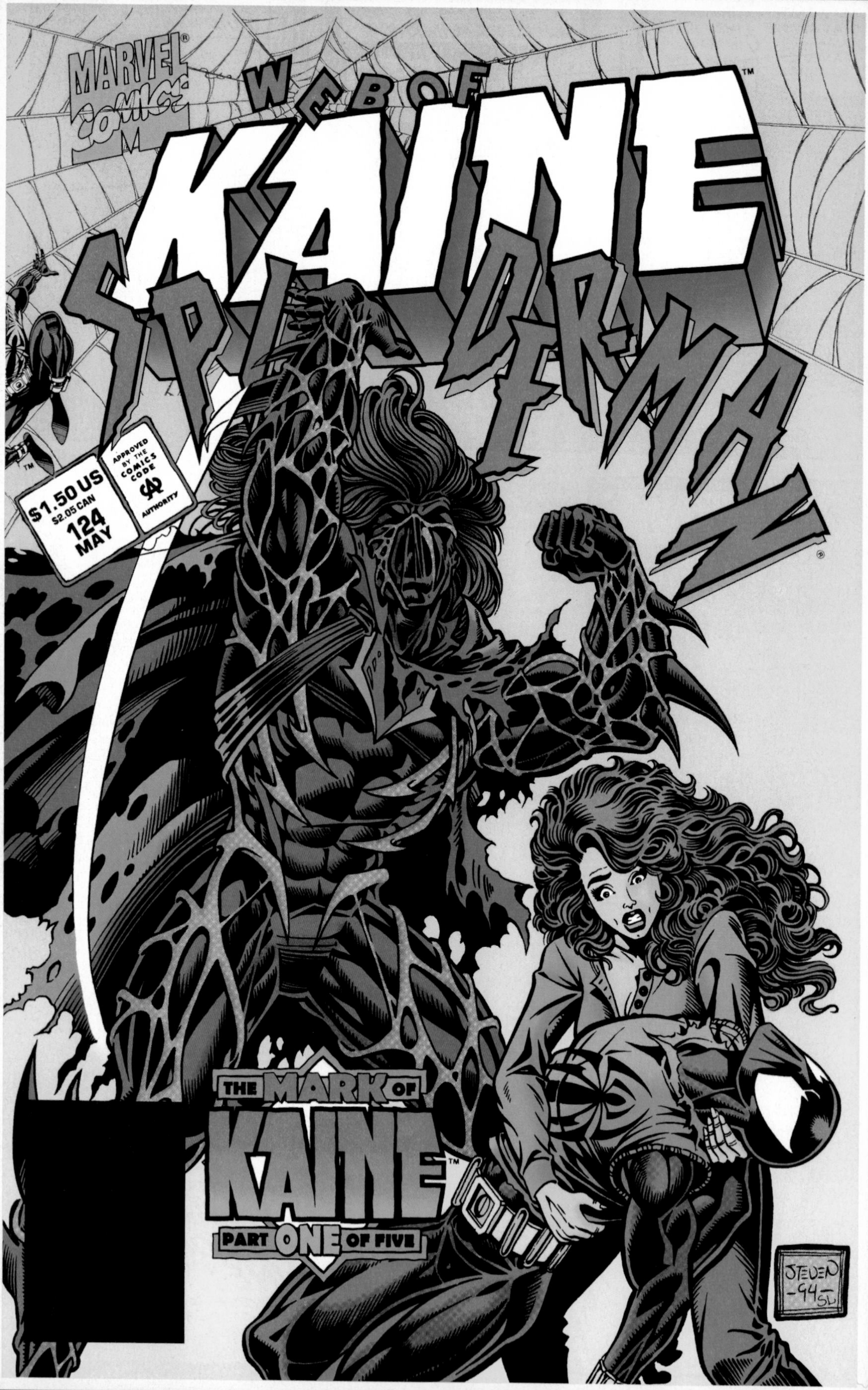
MARVEL COMICS
WEB OF SPIDER-MAN
KAINE
$1.50 US $2.05 CAN 124 MAY
APPROVED BY THE COMICS CODE AUTHORITY
THE MARK OF KAINE
PART ONE OF FIVE

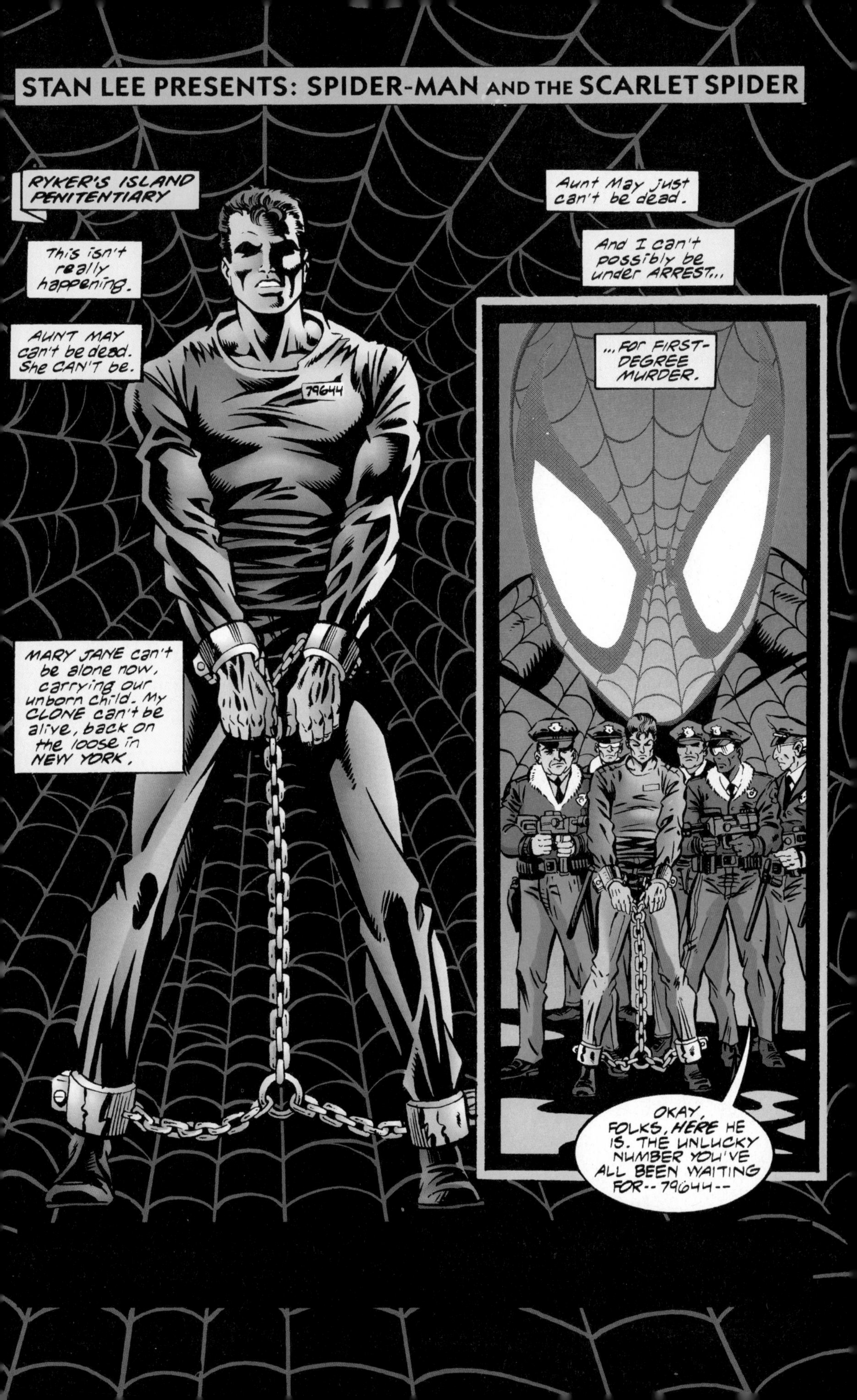
STAN LEE PRESENTS: SPIDER-MAN AND THE SCARLET SPIDER
RYKER'S ISLAND PENITENTIARY
This isn't really happening.
AUNT MAY can't be dead. She CAN'T be.
79644
MARY JANE can't be alone now, carrying our unborn child. My CLONE can't be alive, back on the loose in NEW YORK.
Aunt May just can't be dead.
And I can't possibly be under ARREST...
...FOR FIRST-DEGREE MURDER.
OKAY, FOLKS, HERE HE IS. THE UNLUCKY NUMBER YOU'VE ALL BEEN WAITING FOR--79644--

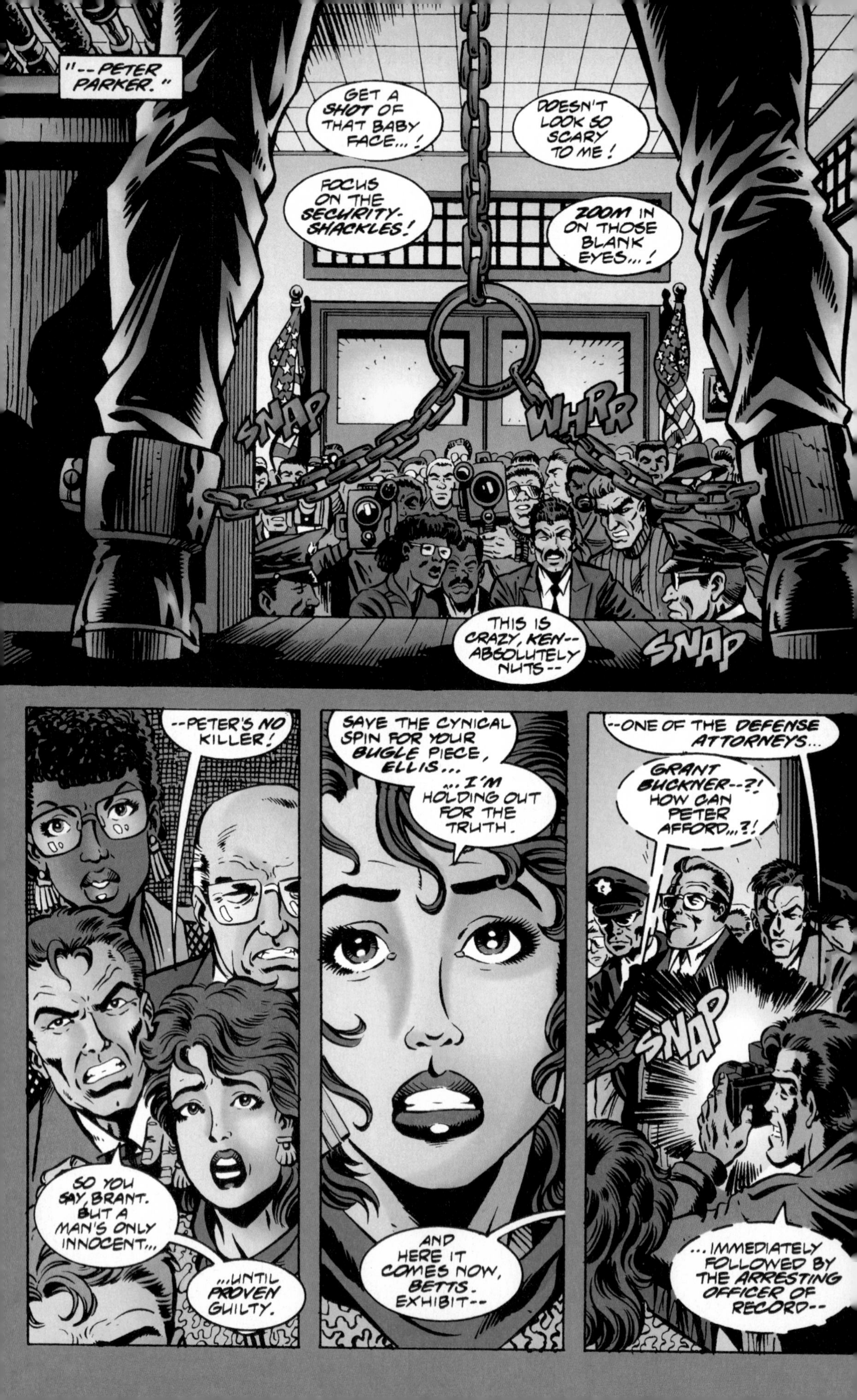
"--PETER PARKER."
GET A SHOT OF THAT BABY FACE...!
DOESN'T LOOK SO SCARY TO ME!
FOCUS ON THE SECURITY-SHACKLES!
ZOOM IN ON THOSE BLANK EYES...!
SNAP
WHRR
THIS IS CRAZY, KEN-- ABSOLUTELY NUTS--
SNAP
--PETER'S NO KILLER!
SO YOU SAY, BRANT. BUT A MAN'S ONLY INNOCENT...
...UNTIL PROVEN GUILTY.
SAVE THE CYNICAL SPIN FOR YOUR BUGLE PIECE, ELLIS...
...I'M HOLDING OUT FOR THE TRUTH.
AND HERE IT COMES NOW, BETTS. EXHIBIT--
--ONE OF THE DEFENSE ATTORNEYS...
GRANT BUCKNER--?! HOW CAN PETER AFFORD...?!
SNAP
...IMMEDIATELY FOLLOWED BY THE ARRESTING OFFICER OF RECORD--

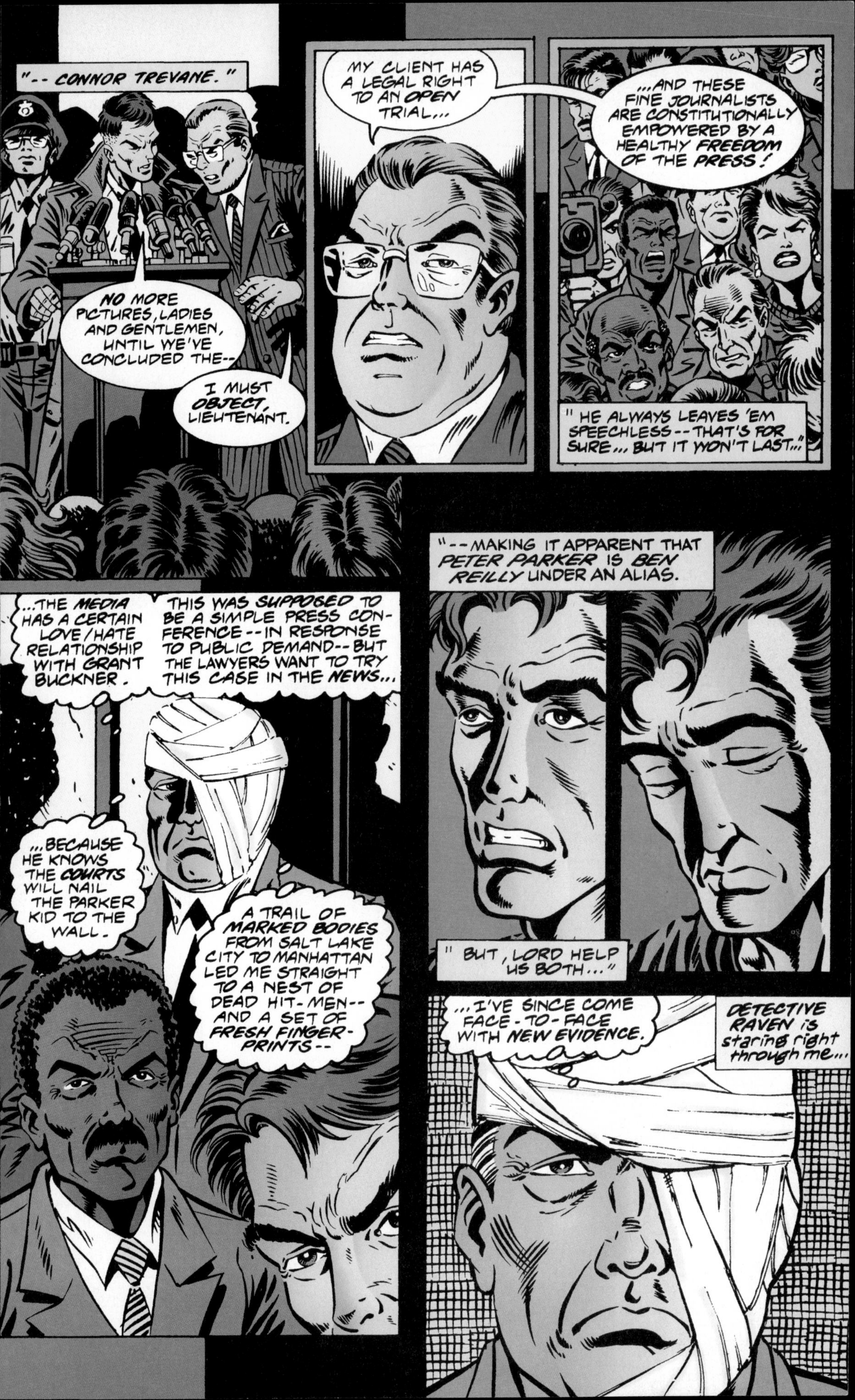
"-- CONNOR TREVANE."
NO MORE PICTURES, LADIES AND GENTLEMEN, UNTIL WE'VE CONCLUDED THE--
I MUST OBJECT, LIEUTENANT.
MY CLIENT HAS A LEGAL RIGHT TO AN OPEN TRIAL...
...AND THESE FINE JOURNALISTS ARE CONSTITUTIONALLY EMPOWERED BY A HEALTHY FREEDOM OF THE PRESS!
"HE ALWAYS LEAVES 'EM SPEECHLESS -- THAT'S FOR SURE... BUT IT WON'T LAST..."
...THE MEDIA HAS A CERTAIN LOVE/HATE RELATIONSHIP WITH GRANT BUCKNER.
THIS WAS SUPPOSED TO BE A SIMPLE PRESS CONFERENCE -- IN RESPONSE TO PUBLIC DEMAND -- BUT THE LAWYERS WANT TO TRY THIS CASE IN THE NEWS...
...BECAUSE HE KNOWS THE COURTS WILL NAIL THE PARKER KID TO THE WALL.
A TRAIL OF MARKED BODIES FROM SALT LAKE CITY TO MANHATTAN LED ME STRAIGHT TO A NEST OF DEAD HIT-MEN-- AND A SET OF FRESH FINGER-PRINTS--
"--MAKING IT APPARENT THAT PETER PARKER IS BEN REILLY UNDER AN ALIAS.
"BUT, LORD HELP US BOTH..."
...I'VE SINCE COME FACE-TO-FACE WITH NEW EVIDENCE.
DETECTIVE RAVEN is staring right through me...

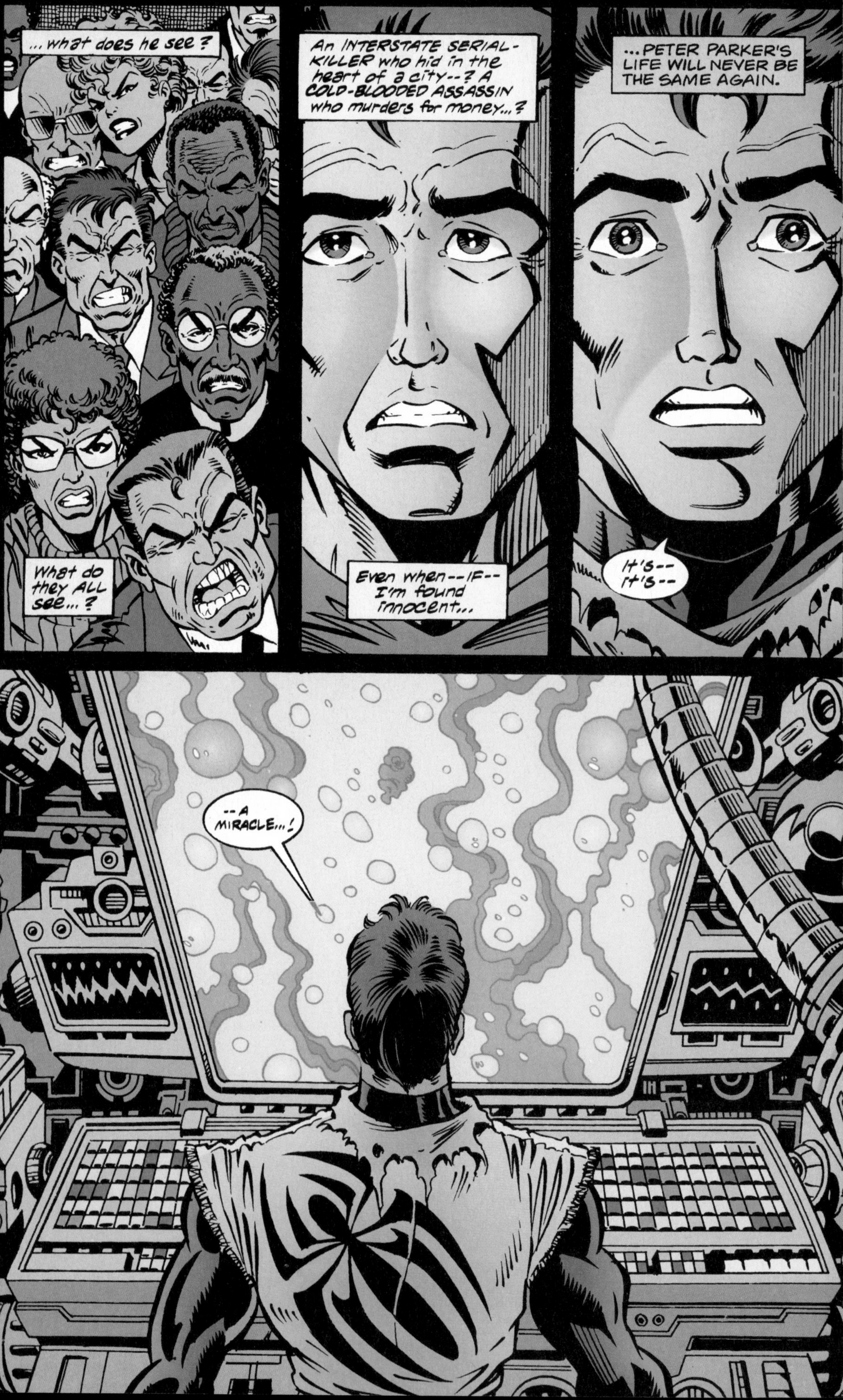
...what does he see?
What do they ALL see...?
An INTERSTATE SERIAL-KILLER who hid in the heart of a city--? A COLD-BLOODED ASSASSIN who murders for money...?
Even when--IF--I'm found innocent...
...PETER PARKER'S LIFE WILL NEVER BE THE SAME AGAIN.
It's--it's--
--A MIRACLE...!

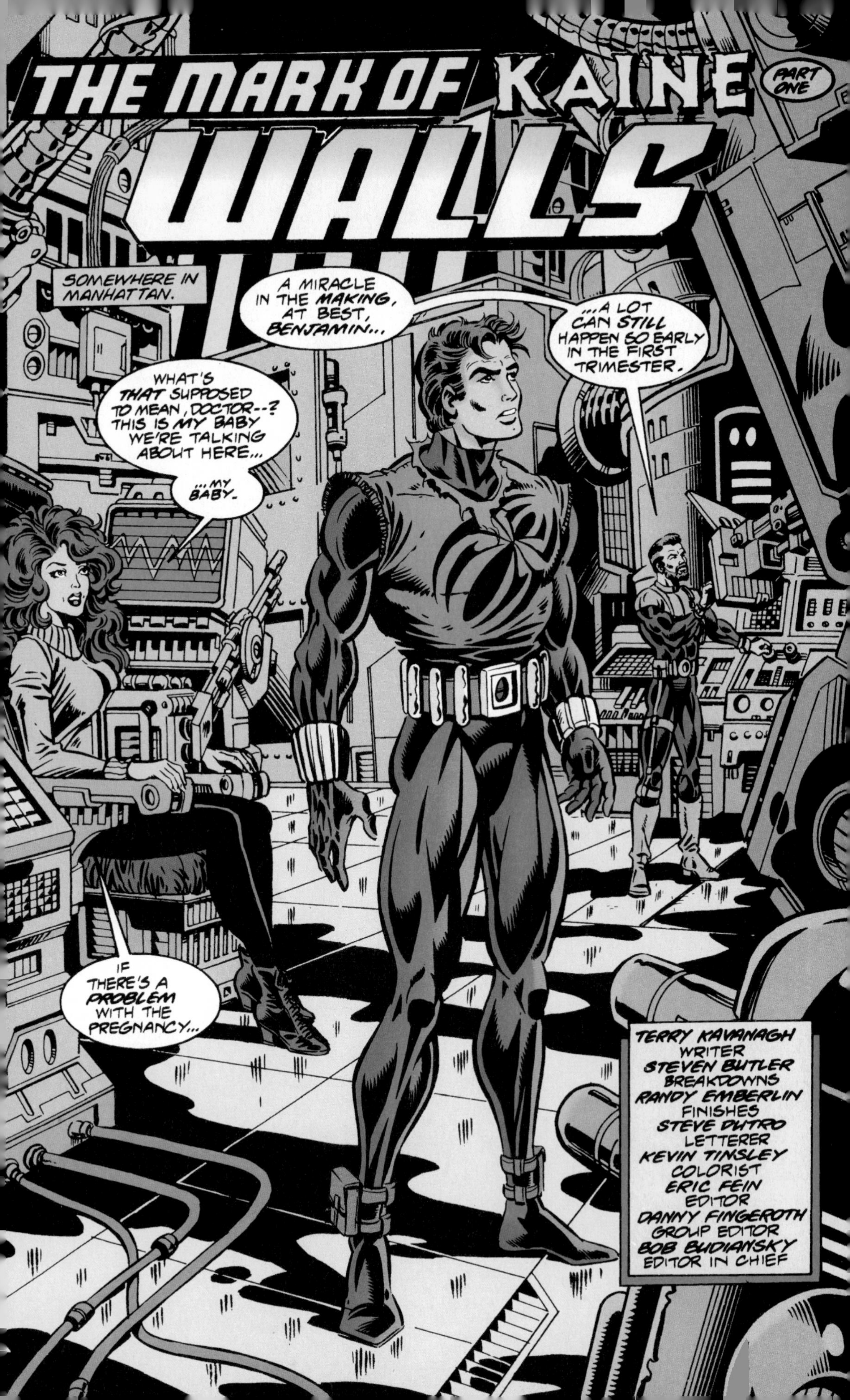
THE MARK OF KAINE PART ONE
WALLS
SOMEWHERE IN MANHATTAN.
A MIRACLE IN THE MAKING, AT BEST, BENJAMIN...
...A LOT CAN STILL HAPPEN SO EARLY IN THE FIRST TRIMESTER.
WHAT'S THAT SUPPOSED TO MEAN, DOCTOR--? THIS IS MY BABY WE'RE TALKING ABOUT HERE...
...MY BABY.
IF THERE'S A PROBLEM WITH THE PREGNANCY...
TERRY KAVANAGH WRITER
STEVEN BUTLER BREAKDOWNS
RANDY EMBERLIN FINISHES
STEVE DUTRO LETTERER
KEVIN TINSLEY COLORIST
ERIC FEIN EDITOR
DANNY FINGEROTH GROUP EDITOR
BOB BUDIANSKY EDITOR IN CHIEF

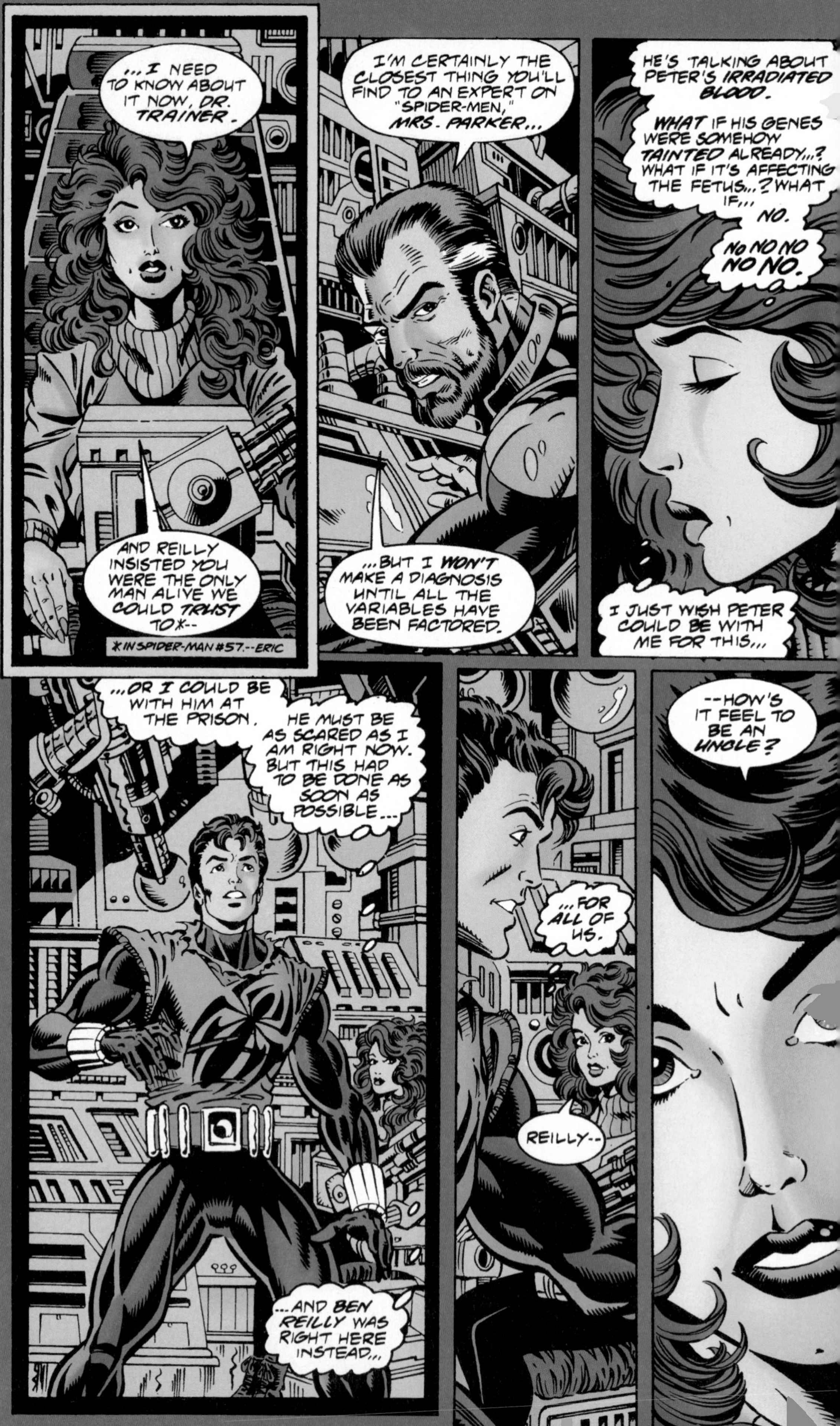

...I NEED TO KNOW ABOUT IT NOW, DR. TRAINER.
AND REILLY INSISTED YOU WERE THE ONLY MAN ALIVE WE COULD TRUST TO*--
*IN SPIDER-MAN #57.--ERIC
I'M CERTAINLY THE CLOSEST THING YOU'LL FIND TO AN EXPERT ON "SPIDER-MEN," MRS. PARKER...
...BUT I WON'T MAKE A DIAGNOSIS UNTIL ALL THE VARIABLES HAVE BEEN FACTORED.
HE'S TALKING ABOUT PETER'S IRRADIATED BLOOD.
WHAT IF HIS GENES WERE SOMEHOW TAINTED ALREADY...? WHAT IF IT'S AFFECTING THE FETUS...? WHAT IF... NO.
NO NO NO NO NO.
I JUST WISH PETER COULD BE WITH ME FOR THIS...
...OR I COULD BE WITH HIM AT THE PRISON.
HE MUST BE AS SCARED AS I AM RIGHT NOW. BUT THIS HAD TO BE DONE AS SOON AS POSSIBLE...
...AND BEN REILLY WAS RIGHT HERE INSTEAD...
...FOR ALL OF US.
REILLY--
--HOW'S IT FEEL TO BE AN UNCLE?

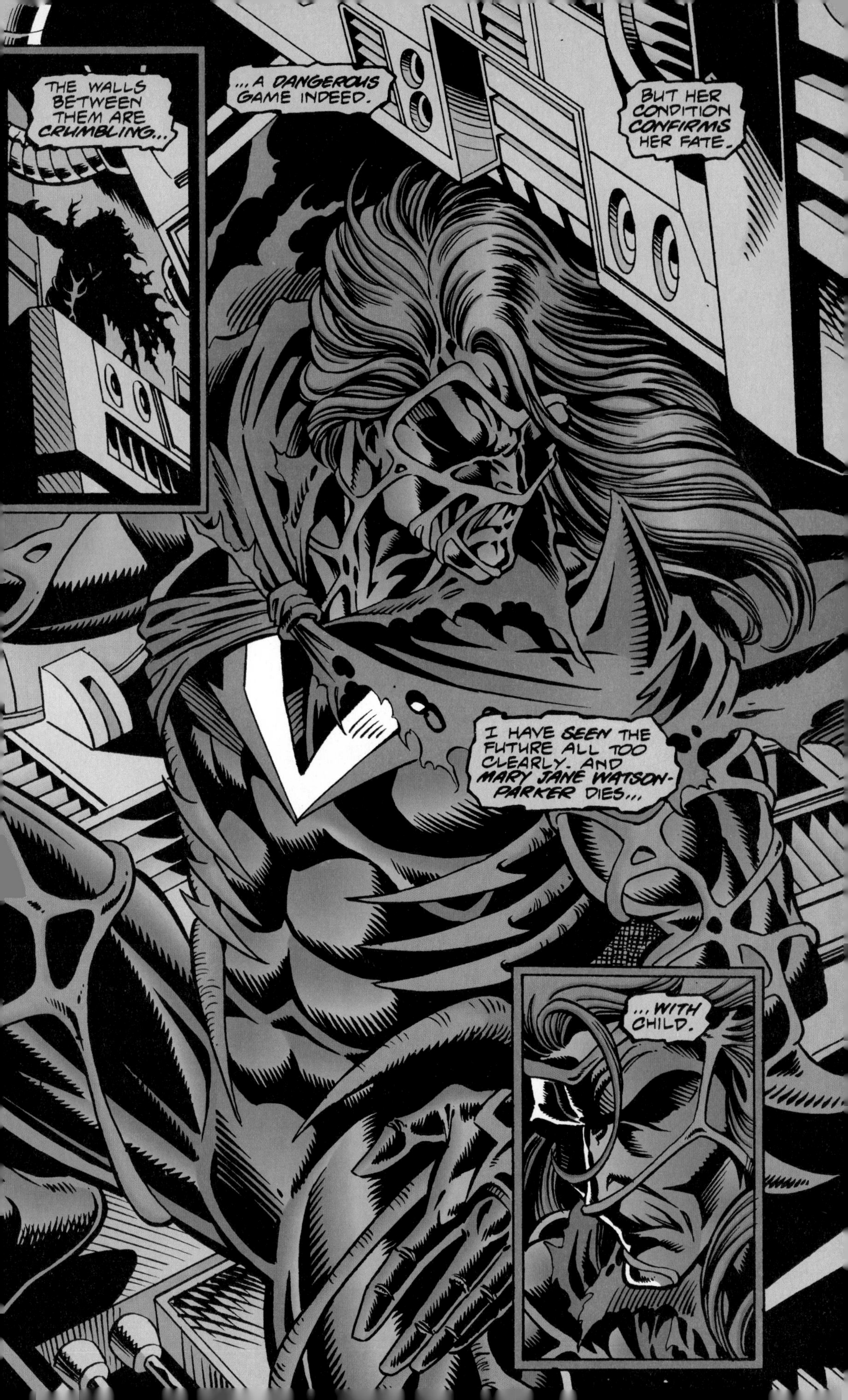
THE WALLS BETWEEN THEM ARE CRUMBLING...
...A DANGEROUS GAME INDEED.
BUT HER CONDITION CONFIRMS HER FATE.
I HAVE SEEN THE FUTURE ALL TOO CLEARLY. AND MARY JANE WATSON-PARKER DIES...
...WITH CHILD.

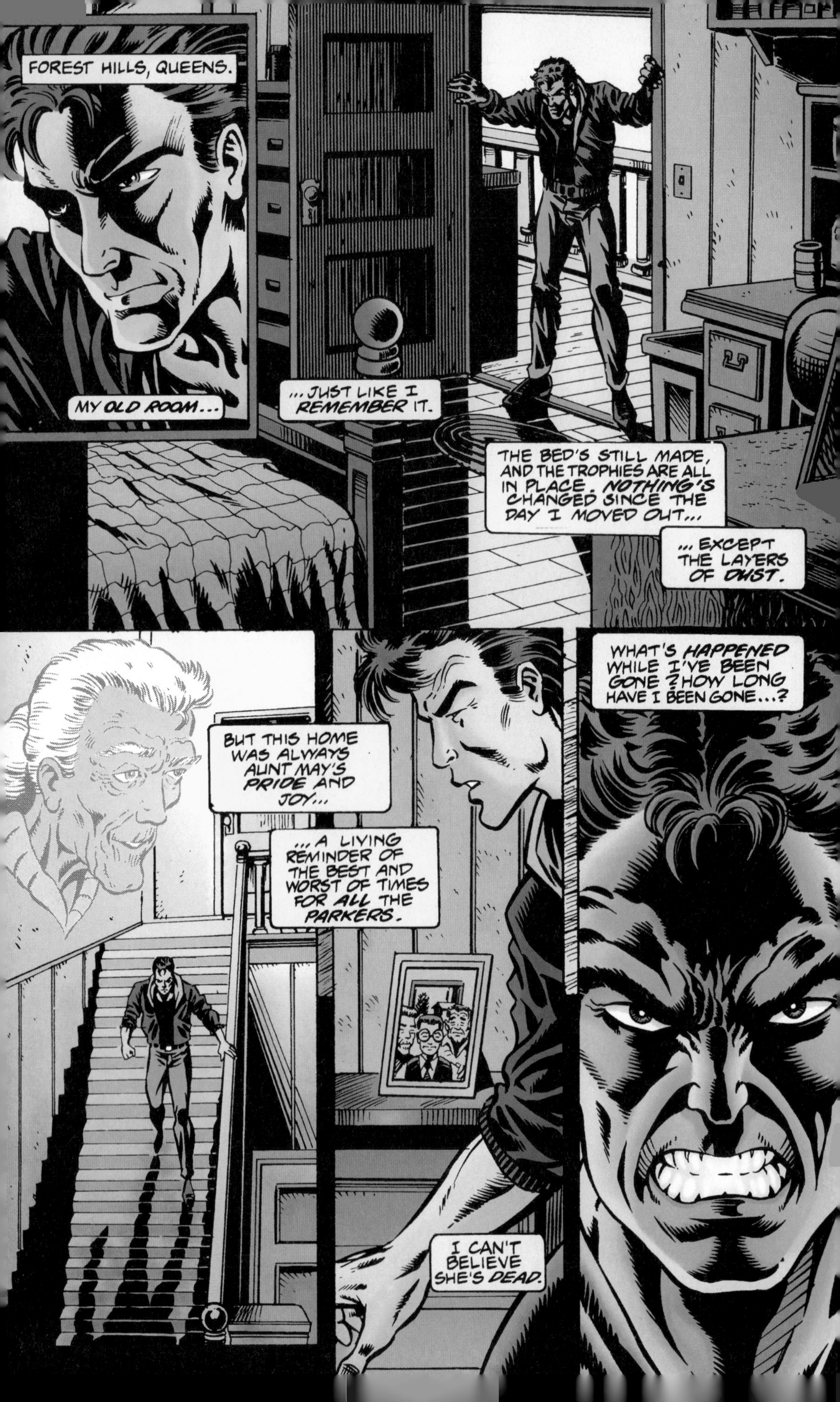
FOREST HILLS, QUEENS.
MY OLD ROOM...
...JUST LIKE I REMEMBER IT.
THE BED'S STILL MADE, AND THE TROPHIES ARE ALL IN PLACE. NOTHING'S CHANGED SINCE THE DAY I MOVED OUT...
...EXCEPT THE LAYERS OF DUST.
BUT THIS HOME WAS ALWAYS AUNT MAY'S PRIDE AND JOY...
...A LIVING REMINDER OF THE BEST AND WORST OF TIMES FOR ALL THE PARKERS.
WHAT'S HAPPENED WHILE I'VE BEEN GONE? HOW LONG HAVE I BEEN GONE...?
I CAN'T BELIEVE SHE'S DEAD.

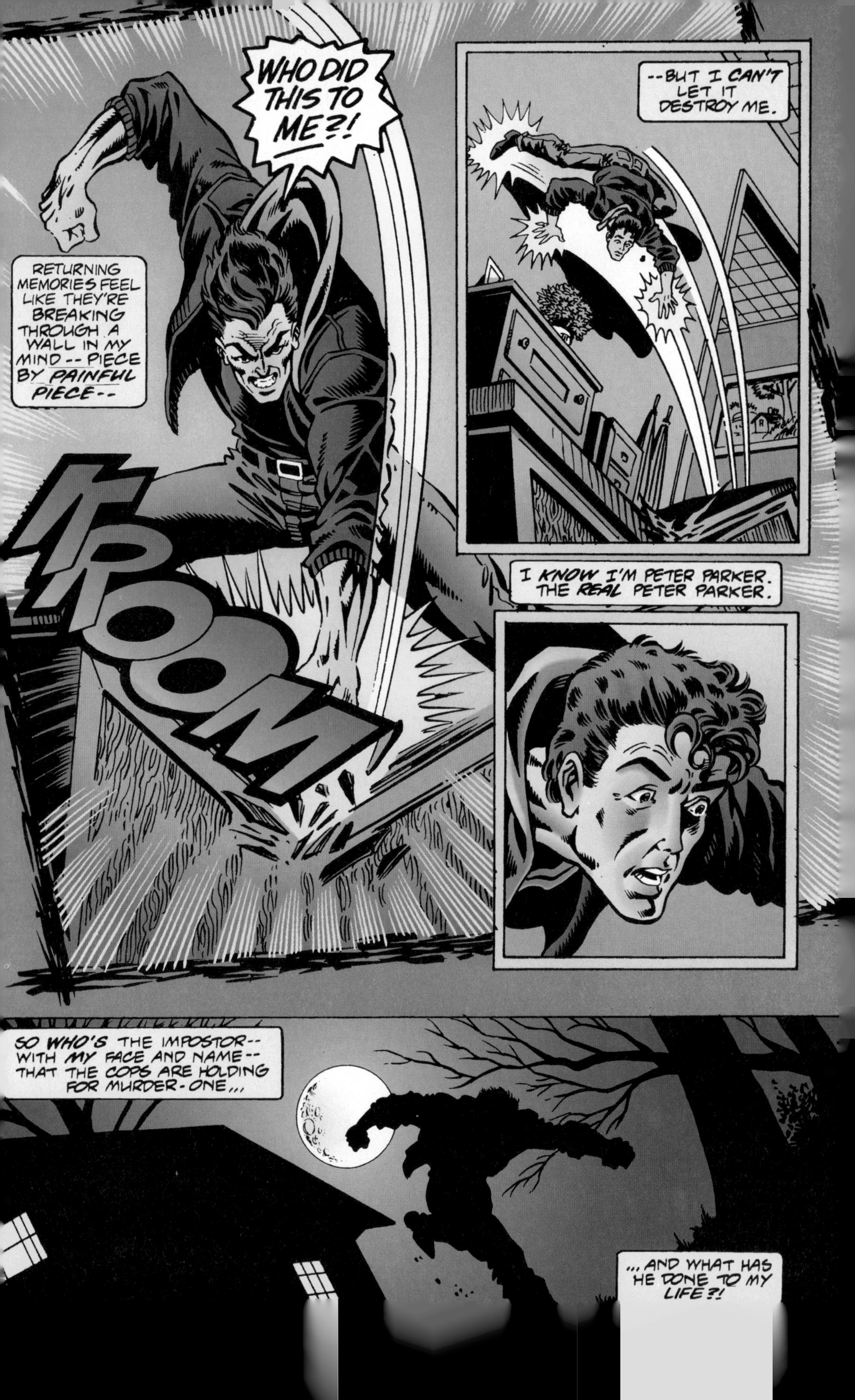
WHO DID THIS TO ME?!
RETURNING MEMORIES FEEL LIKE THEY'RE BREAKING THROUGH A WALL IN MY MIND -- PIECE BY PAINFUL PIECE--
KROOM
--BUT I CAN'T LET IT DESTROY ME.
I KNOW I'M PETER PARKER. THE REAL PETER PARKER.
SO WHO'S THE IMPOSTOR-- WITH MY FACE AND NAME-- THAT THE COPS ARE HOLDING FOR MURDER-ONE...
...AND WHAT HAS HE DONE TO MY LIFE?!

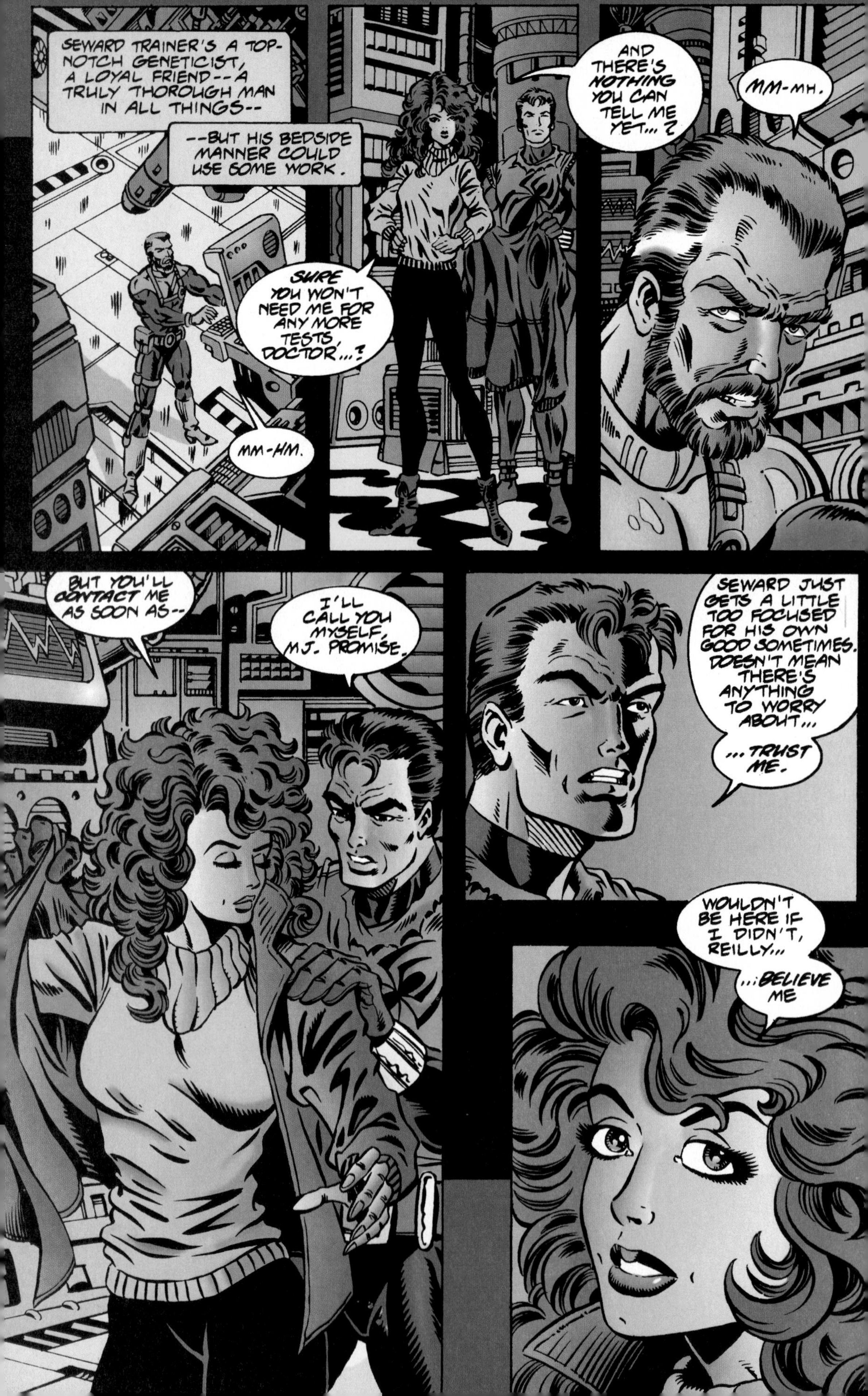
SEWARD TRAINER'S A TOP-NOTCH GENETICIST, A LOYAL FRIEND--A TRULY THOROUGH MAN IN ALL THINGS--
--BUT HIS BEDSIDE MANNER COULD USE SOME WORK.
SURE YOU WON'T NEED ME FOR ANY MORE TESTS, DOCTOR...?
MM-HM.
AND THERE'S NOTHING YOU CAN TELL ME YET...?
MM-MH.
BUT YOU'LL CONTACT ME AS SOON AS--
I'LL CALL YOU MYSELF, M.J. PROMISE.
SEWARD JUST GETS A LITTLE TOO FOCUSED FOR HIS OWN GOOD SOMETIMES. DOESN'T MEAN THERE'S ANYTHING TO WORRY ABOUT...
...TRUST ME.
WOULDN'T BE HERE IF I DIDN'T, REILLY...
...BELIEVE ME

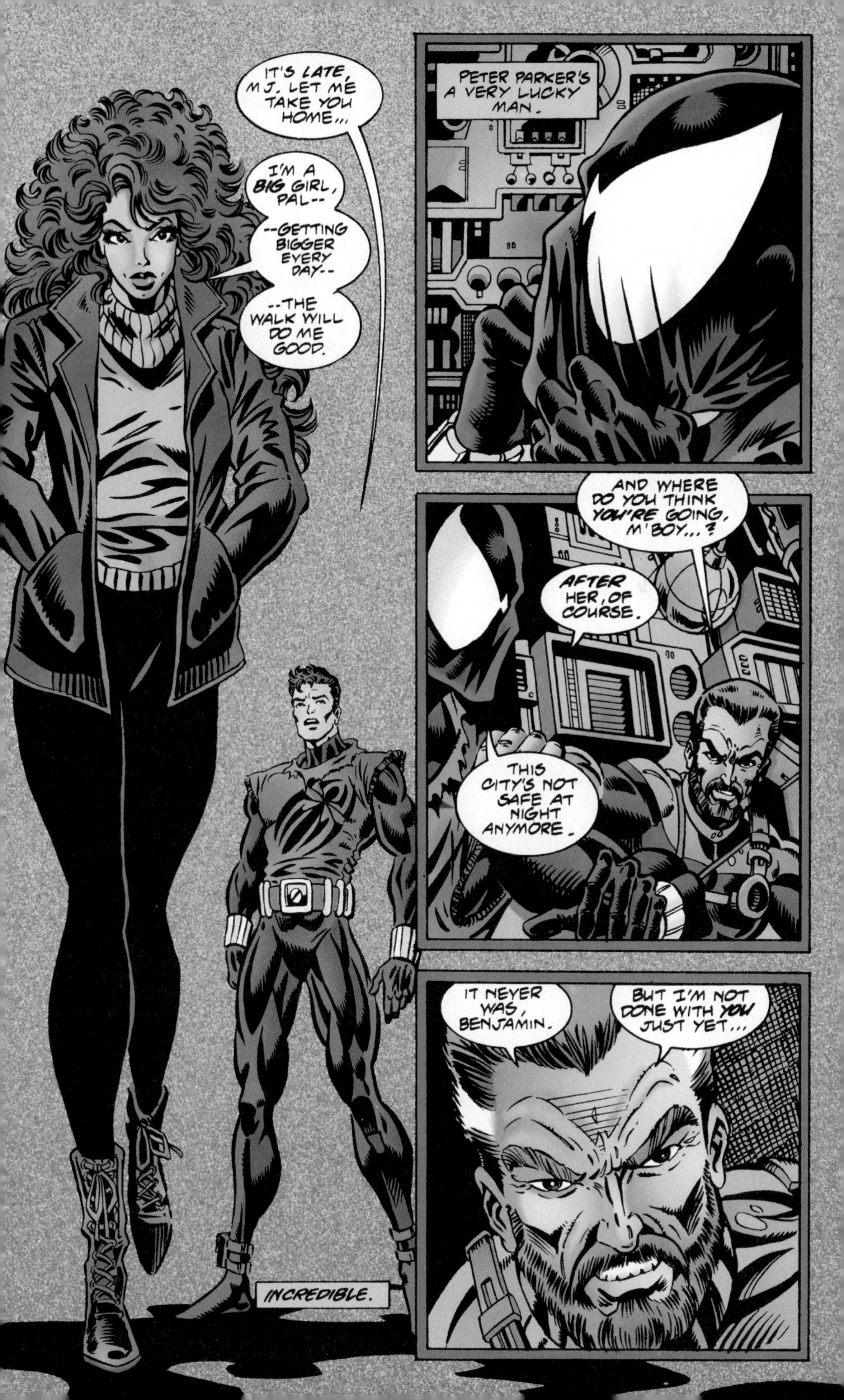
IT'S LATE, M J. LET ME TAKE YOU HOME...
I'M A BIG GIRL, PAL--
--GETTING BIGGER EVERY DAY--
--THE WALK WILL DO ME GOOD.
INCREDIBLE.
PETER PARKER'S A VERY LUCKY MAN.
AND WHERE DO YOU THINK YOU'RE GOING, M'BOY...?
AFTER HER, OF COURSE.
THIS CITY'S NOT SAFE AT NIGHT ANYMORE.
IT NEVER WAS, BENJAMIN.
BUT I'M NOT DONE WITH YOU JUST YET...

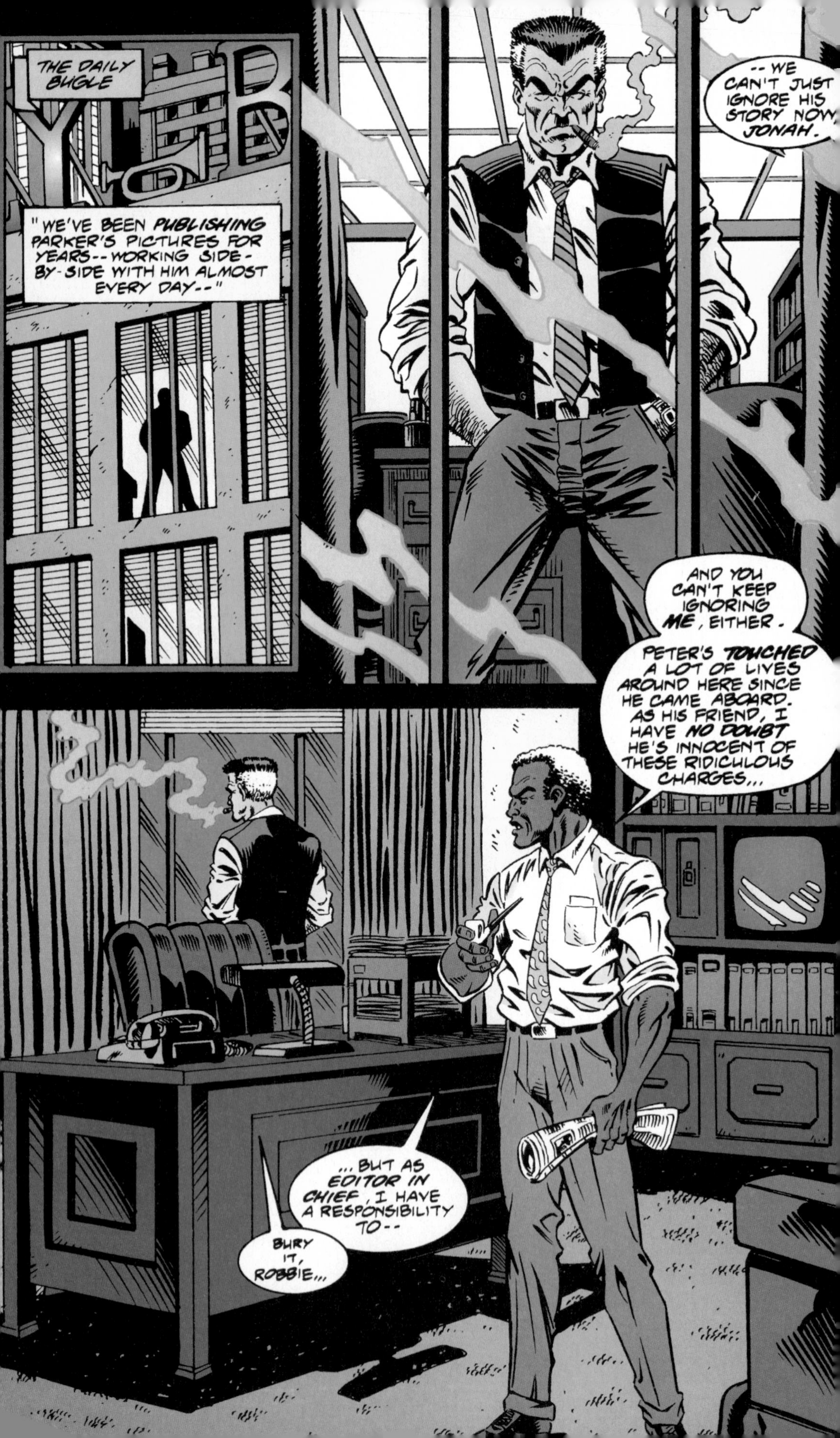
THE DAILY BUGLE
"WE'VE BEEN PUBLISHING PARKER'S PICTURES FOR YEARS--WORKING SIDE-BY-SIDE WITH HIM ALMOST EVERY DAY--"
--WE CAN'T JUST IGNORE HIS STORY NOW, JONAH.
AND YOU CAN'T KEEP IGNORING ME, EITHER.
PETER'S TOUCHED A LOT OF LIVES AROUND HERE SINCE HE CAME ABOARD. AS HIS FRIEND, I HAVE NO DOUBT HE'S INNOCENT OF THESE RIDICULOUS CHARGES...
...BUT AS EDITOR IN CHIEF, I HAVE A RESPONSIBILITY TO--
BURY IT, ROBBIE...

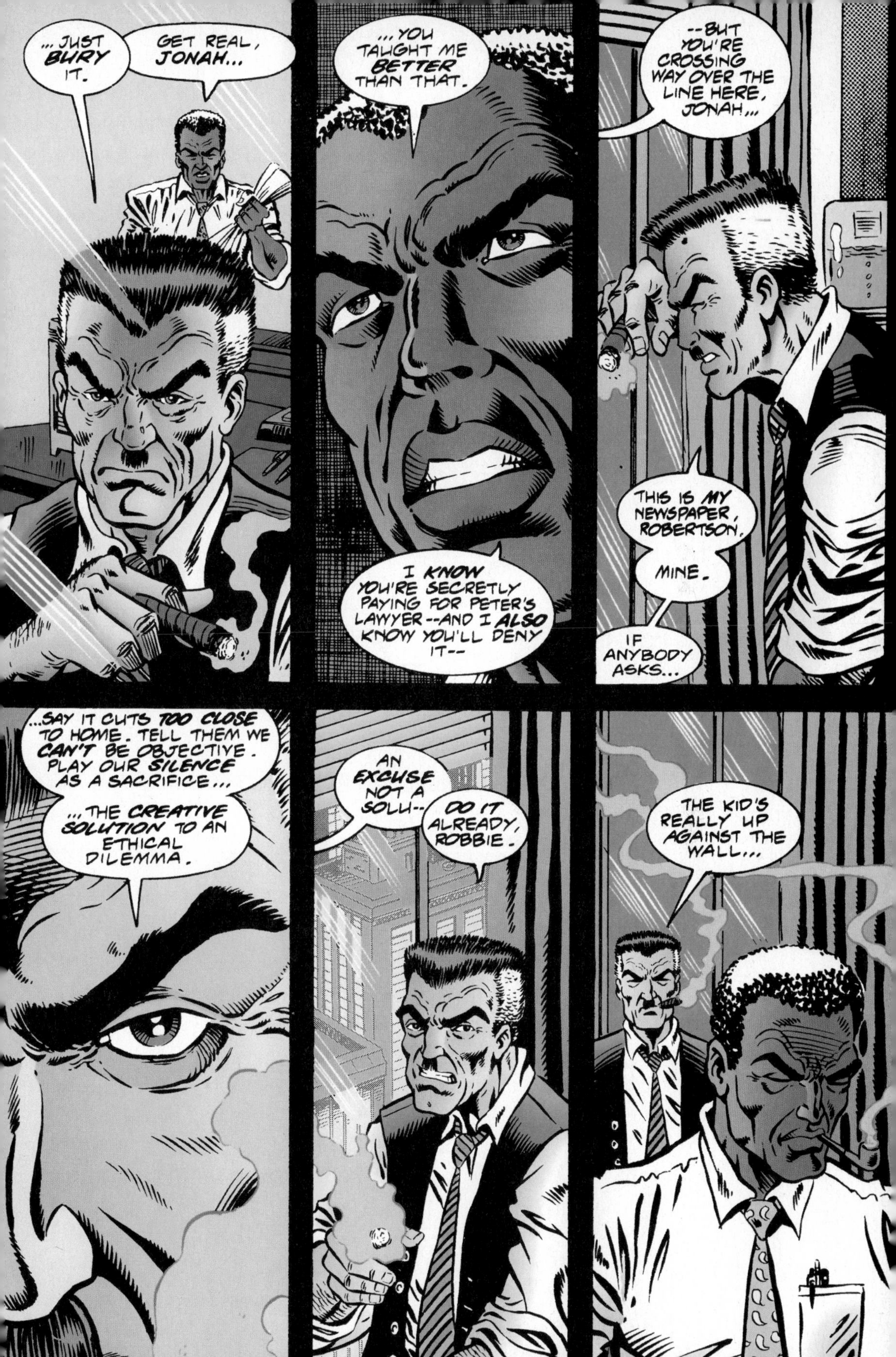
...JUST BURY IT.
GET REAL, JONAH...
...YOU TAUGHT ME BETTER THAN THAT.
I KNOW YOU'RE SECRETLY PAYING FOR PETER'S LAWYER--AND I ALSO KNOW YOU'LL DENY IT--
--BUT YOU'RE CROSSING WAY OVER THE LINE HERE, JONAH...
THIS IS MY NEWSPAPER, ROBERTSON.
MINE.
IF ANYBODY ASKS...
...SAY IT CUTS TOO CLOSE TO HOME. TELL THEM WE CAN'T BE OBJECTIVE. PLAY OUR SILENCE AS A SACRIFICE...
...THE CREATIVE SOLUTION TO AN ETHICAL DILEMMA.
AN EXCUSE NOT A SOLU--
DO IT ALREADY, ROBBIE.
THE KID'S REALLY UP AGAINST THE WALL...

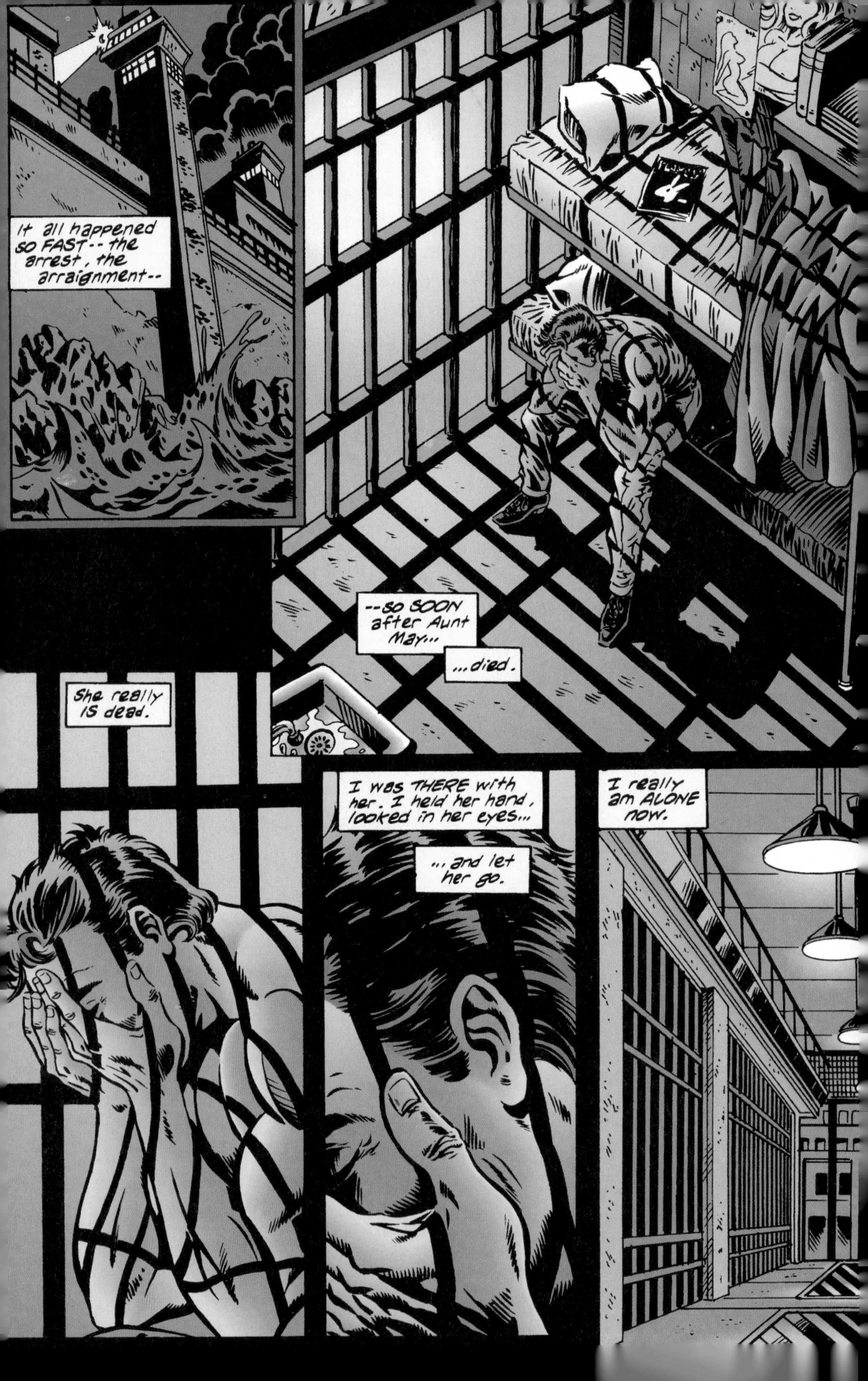
It all happened SO FAST-- the arrest, the arraignment--
--SO SOON after Aunt May...
...died.
She really IS dead.
I was THERE with her. I held her hand, looked in her eyes...
...and let her go.
I really am ALONE now.

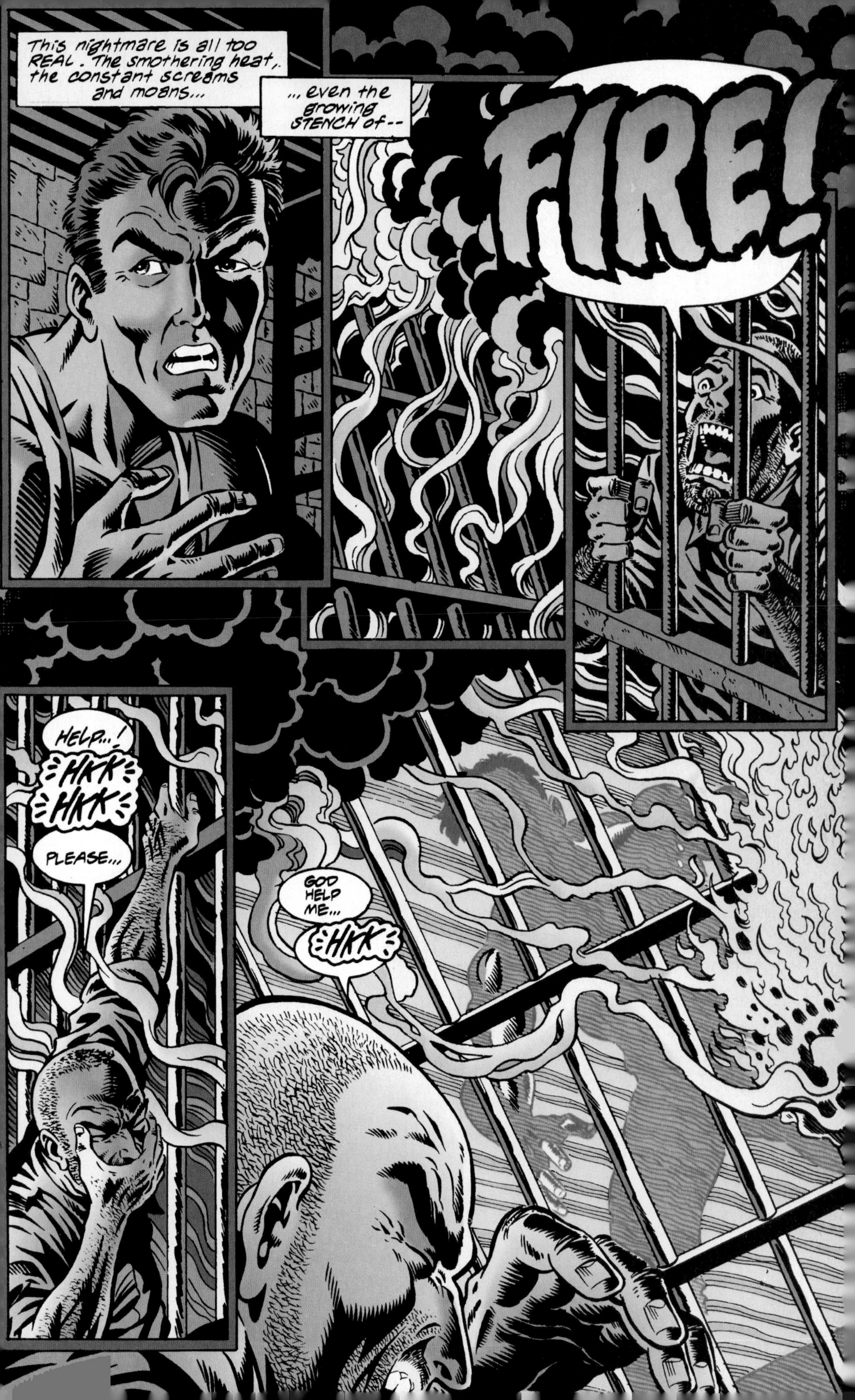
This nightmare is all too REAL. The smothering heat, the constant screams and moans...
...even the growing STENCH of--
FIRE!
HELP...!
HKK
HKK
PLEASE...
GOD HELP ME...
HKK

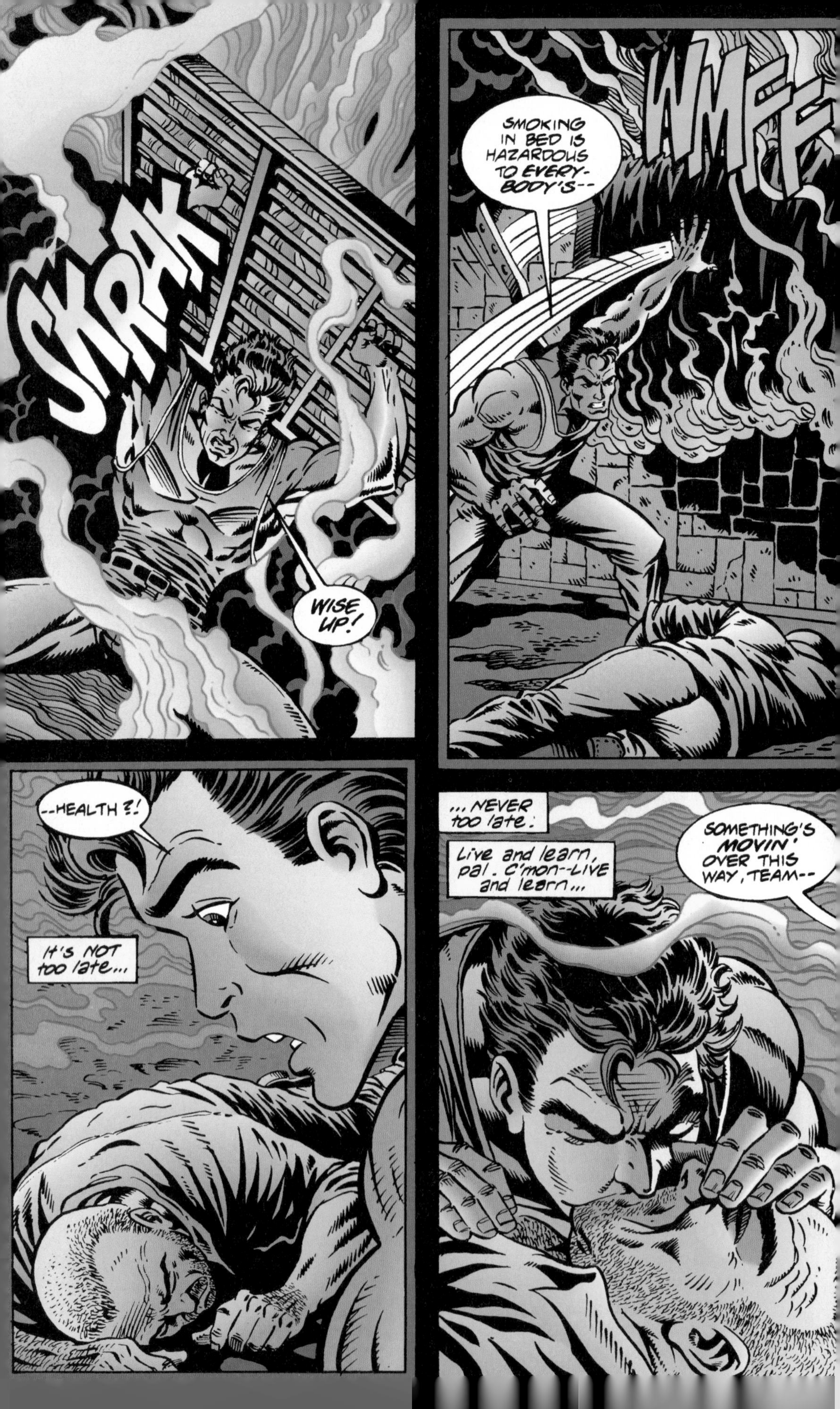
SKRAK
WISE UP!
WMFF
SMOKING IN BED IS HAZARDOUS TO EVERY-BODY'S--
--HEALTH ?!
It's NOT too late...
...NEVER too late.
Live and learn, pal. C'mon--LIVE and learn...
SOMETHING'S MOVIN' OVER THIS WAY, TEAM--

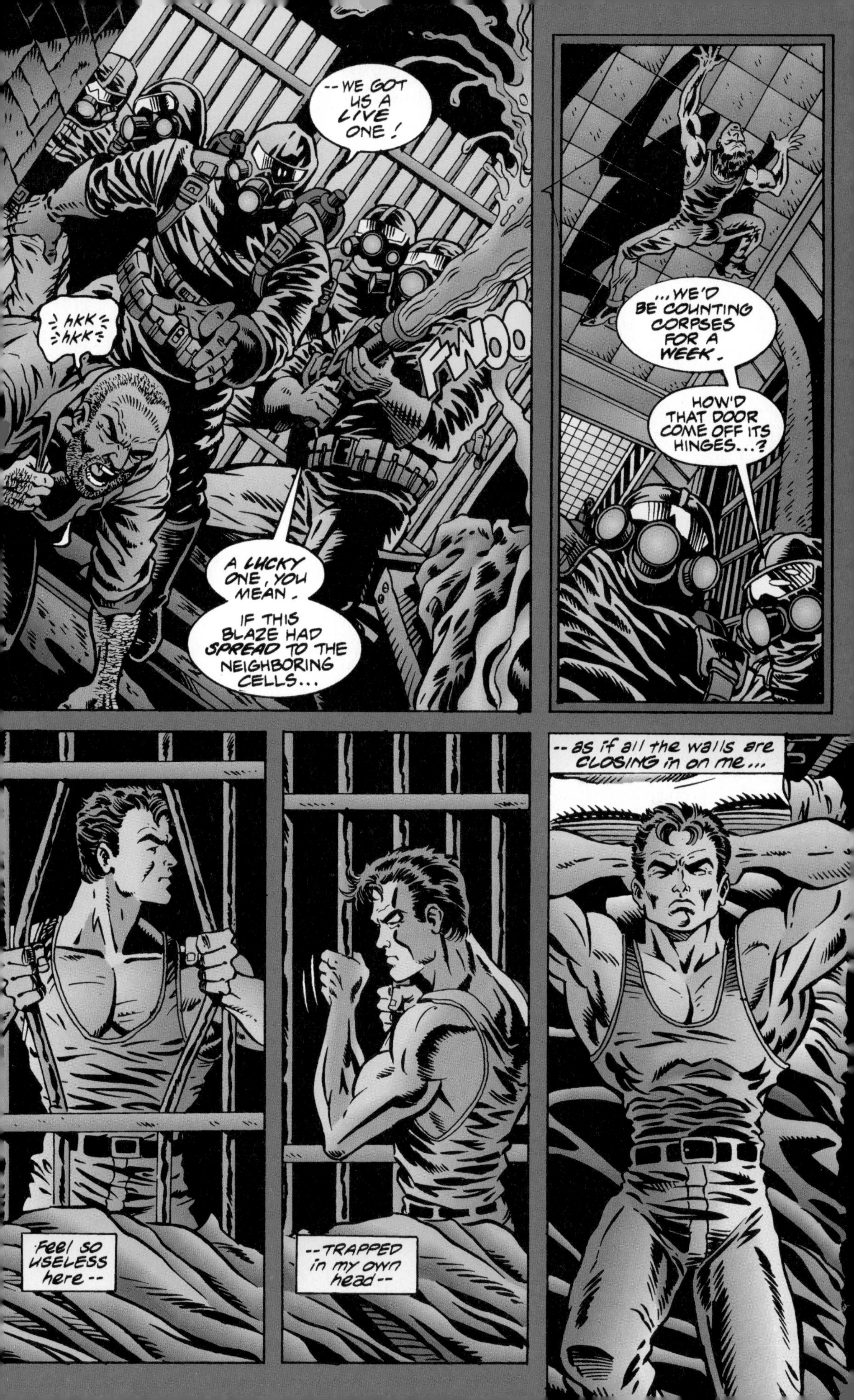

--WE GOT US A LIVE ONE!
hkk hkk
FWOO
A LUCKY ONE, YOU MEAN.
IF THIS BLAZE HAD SPREAD TO THE NEIGHBORING CELLS...
...WE'D BE COUNTING CORPSES FOR A WEEK.
HOW'D THAT DOOR COME OFF ITS HINGES...?
Feel so USELESS here--
--TRAPPED in my own head--
--as if all the walls are CLOSING in on me...

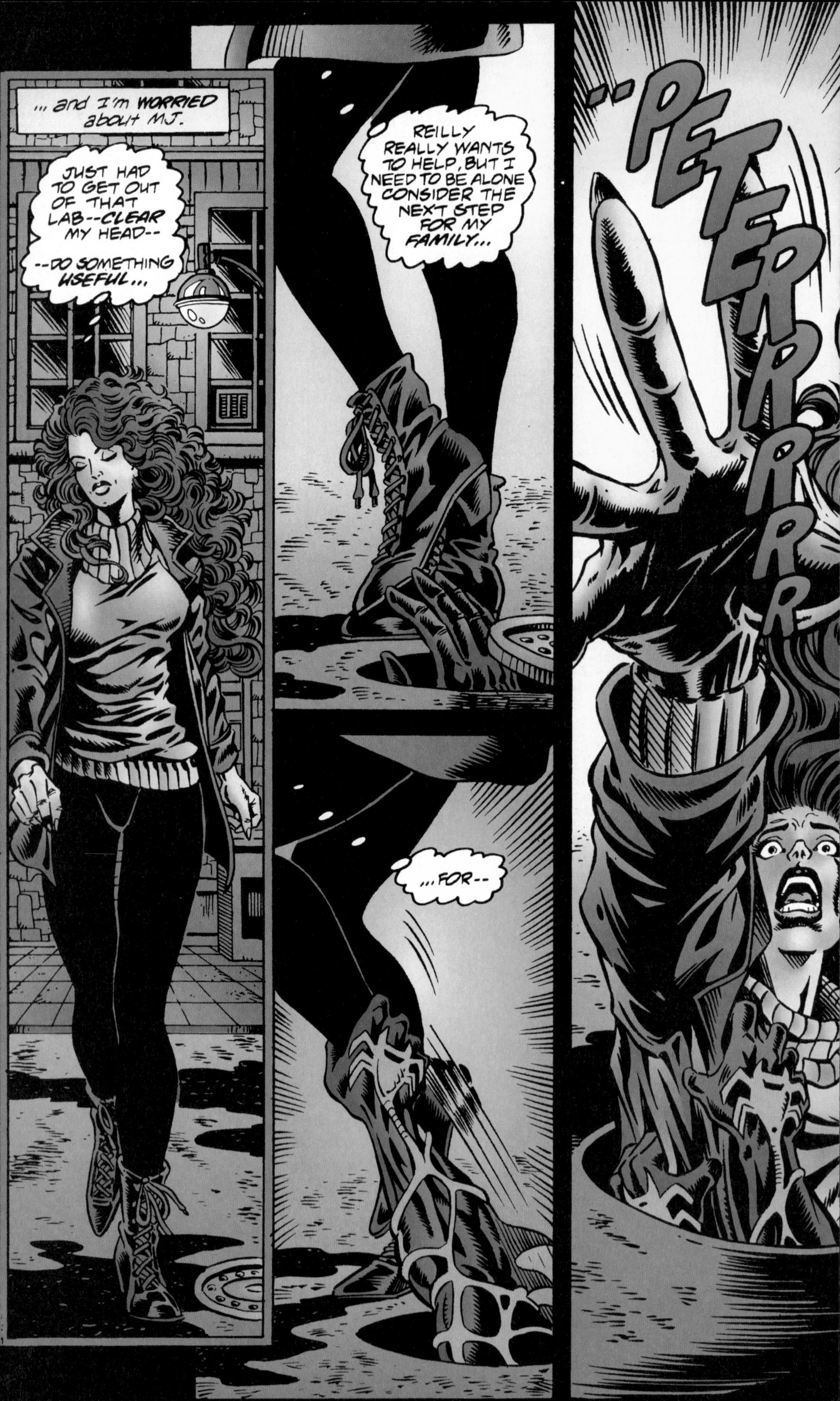
...and I'm WORRIED about MJ.
JUST HAD TO GET OUT OF THAT LAB--CLEAR MY HEAD--
--DO SOMETHING USEFUL...
REILLY REALLY WANTS TO HELP, BUT I NEED TO BE ALONE CONSIDER THE NEXT STEP FOR MY FAMILY...
...FOR--
..PETERRRRR

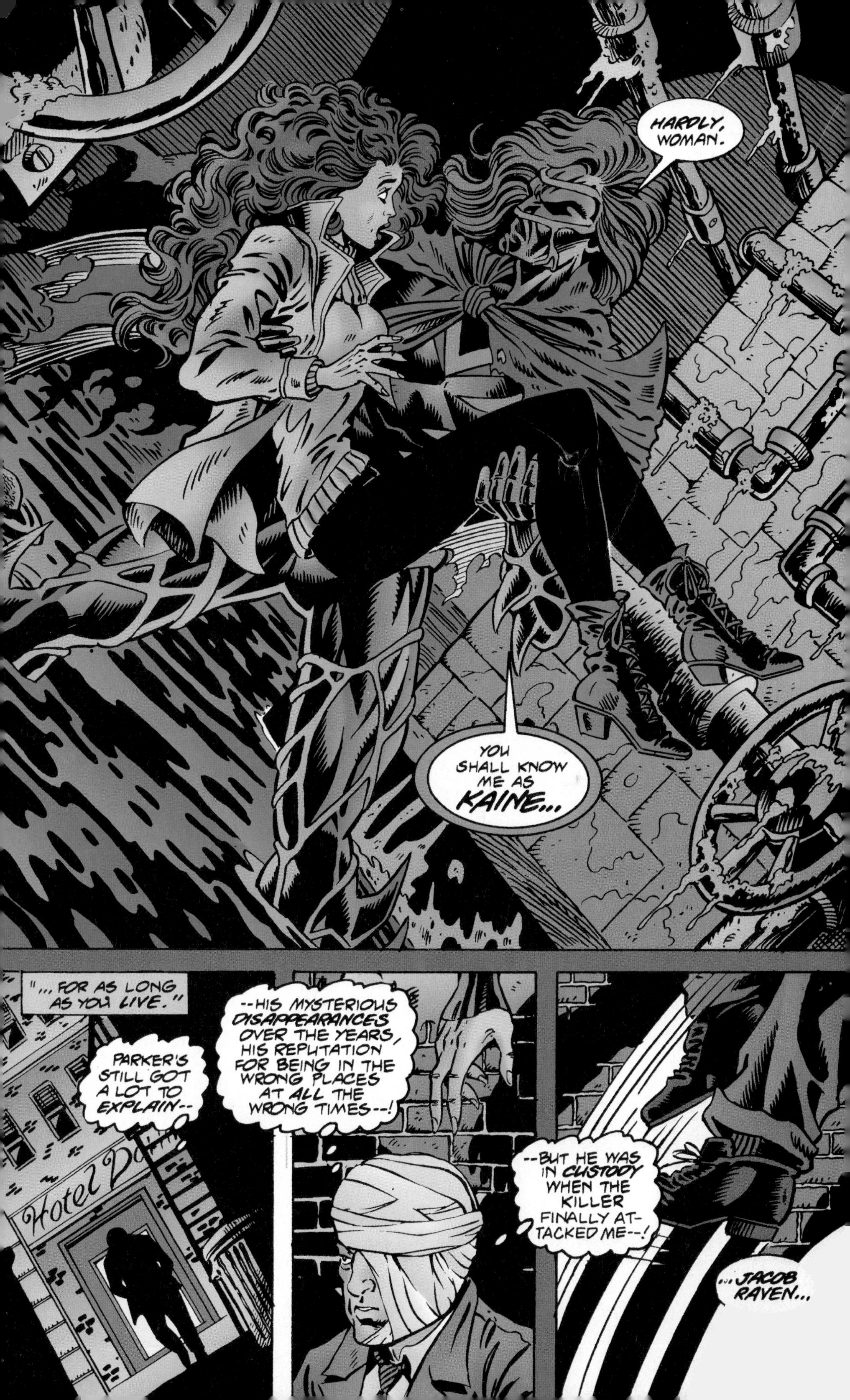
HARDLY, WOMAN.
YOU SHALL KNOW ME AS KAINE...
"..., FOR AS LONG AS YOU LIVE."
PARKER'S STILL GOT A LOT TO EXPLAIN--
--HIS MYSTERIOUS DISAPPEARANCES OVER THE YEARS, HIS REPUTATION FOR BEING IN THE WRONG PLACES AT ALL THE WRONG TIMES--!
Hotel
--BUT HE WAS IN CUSTODY WHEN THE KILLER FINALLY AT-TACKED ME--!
...JACOB RAVEN...

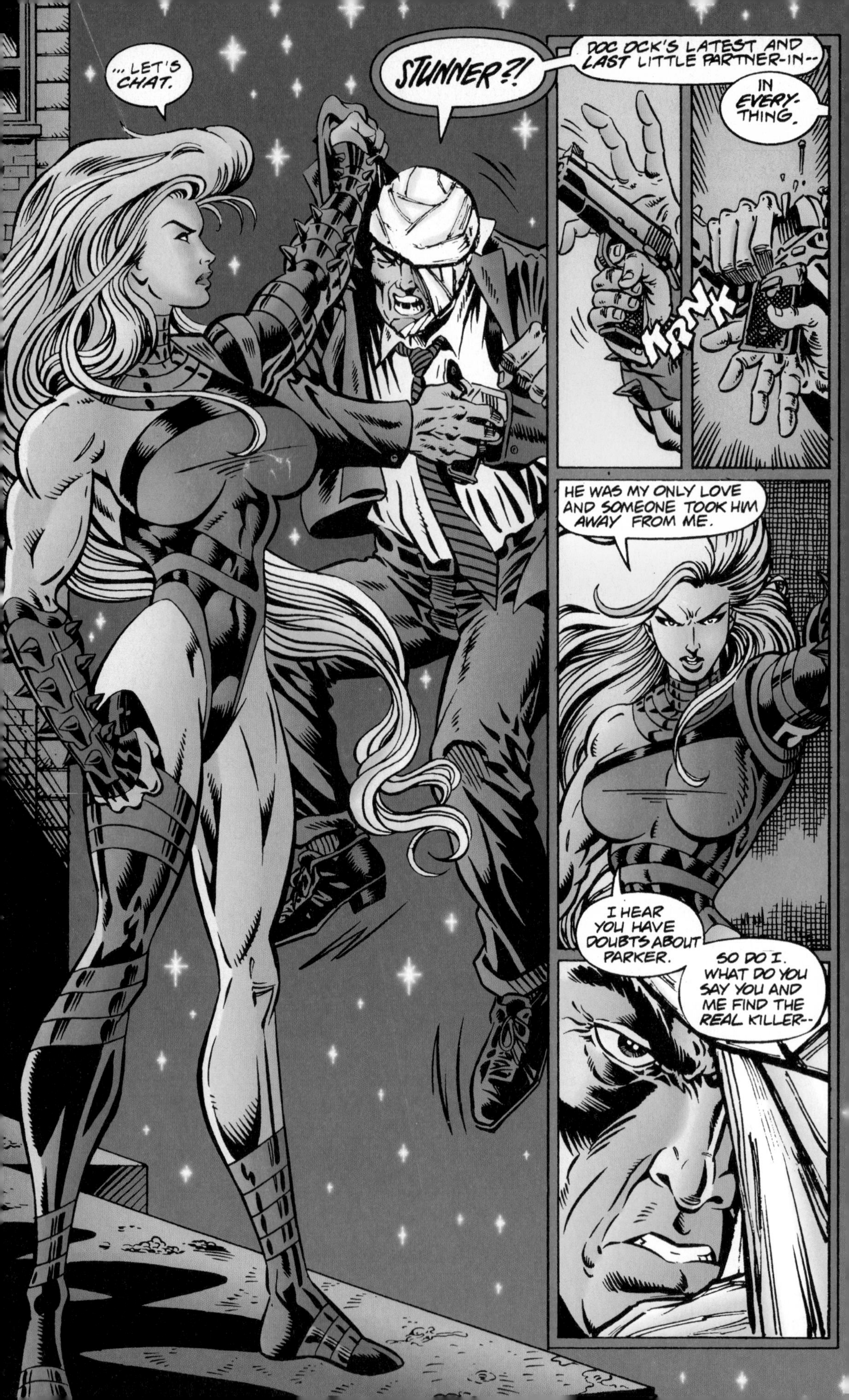
...LET'S CHAT.
STUNNER?!
DOC OCK'S LATEST AND LAST LITTLE PARTNER-IN--
IN EVERY-THING.
KRNK
HE WAS MY ONLY LOVE AND SOMEONE TOOK HIM AWAY FROM ME.
I HEAR YOU HAVE DOUBTS ABOUT PARKER.
SO DO I. WHAT DO YOU SAY YOU AND ME FIND THE REAL KILLER--

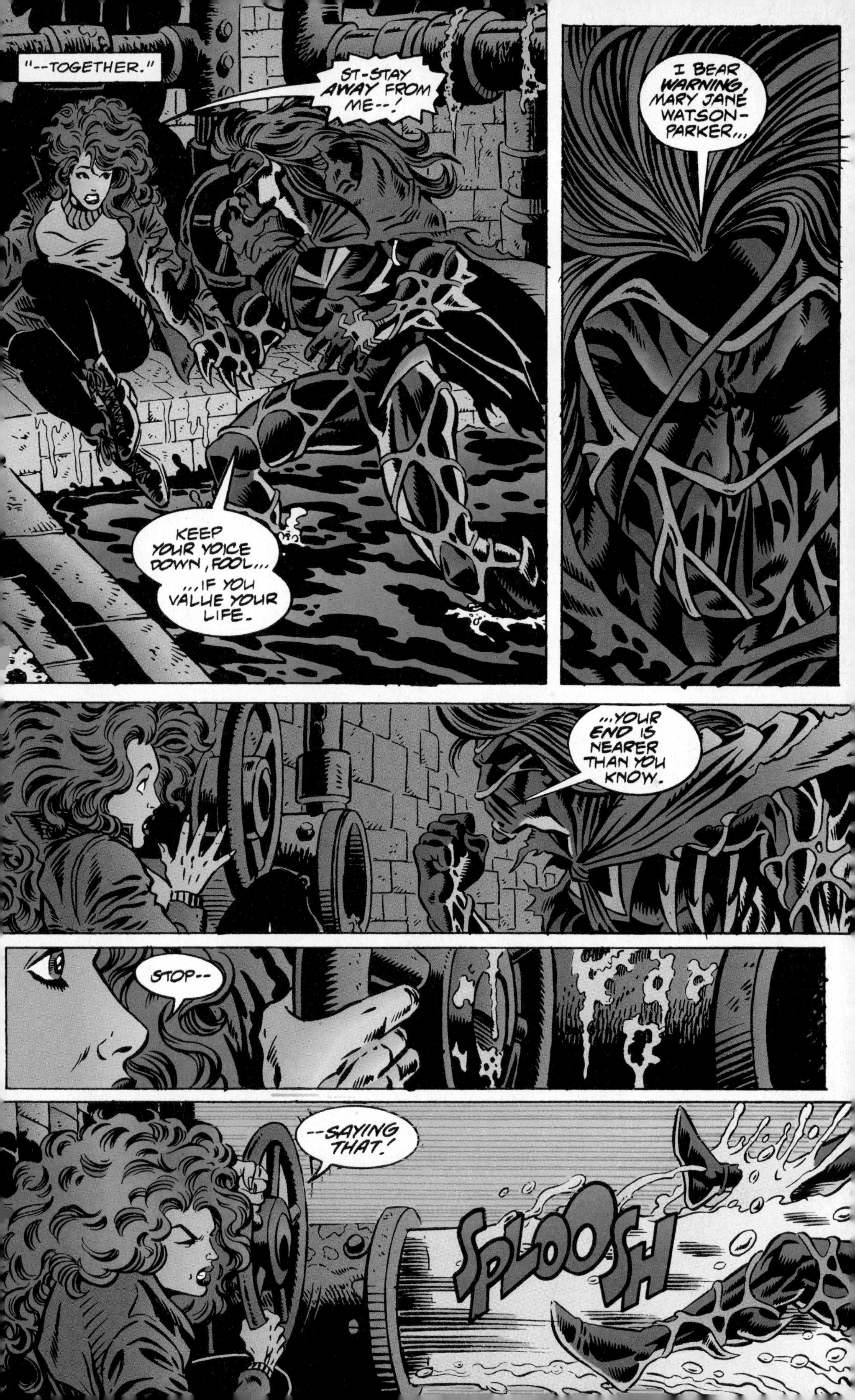
"--TOGETHER."
ST-STAY AWAY FROM ME--!
KEEP YOUR VOICE DOWN, FOOL...
...IF YOU VALUE YOUR LIFE.
I BEAR WARNING, MARY JANE WATSON-PARKER...
...YOUR END IS NEARER THAN YOU KNOW.
STOP--
--SAYING THAT!
SPLOOSH

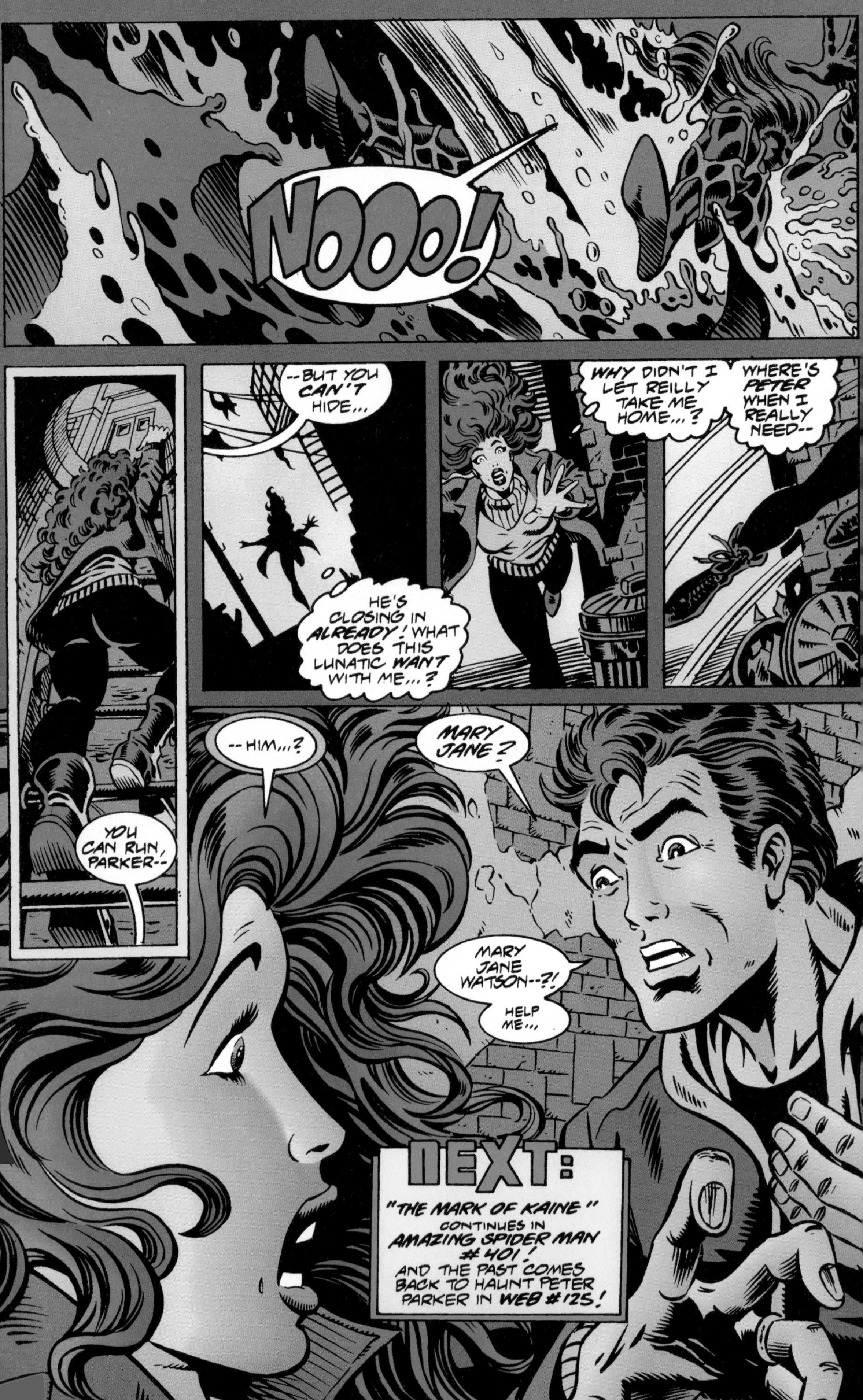
NOOO!
YOU CAN RUN, PARKER--
--BUT YOU CAN'T HIDE...
HE'S CLOSING IN ALREADY! WHAT DOES THIS LUNATIC WANT WITH ME...?
WHY DIDN'T I LET REILLY TAKE ME HOME...?
WHERE'S PETER WHEN I REALLY NEED--
--HIM...?
MARY JANE?
MARY JANE WATSON--?!
HELP ME...
NEXT:
"THE MARK OF KAINE" CONTINUES IN AMAZING SPIDER MAN #401! AND THE PAST COMES BACK TO HAUNT PETER PARKER IN WEB #125!

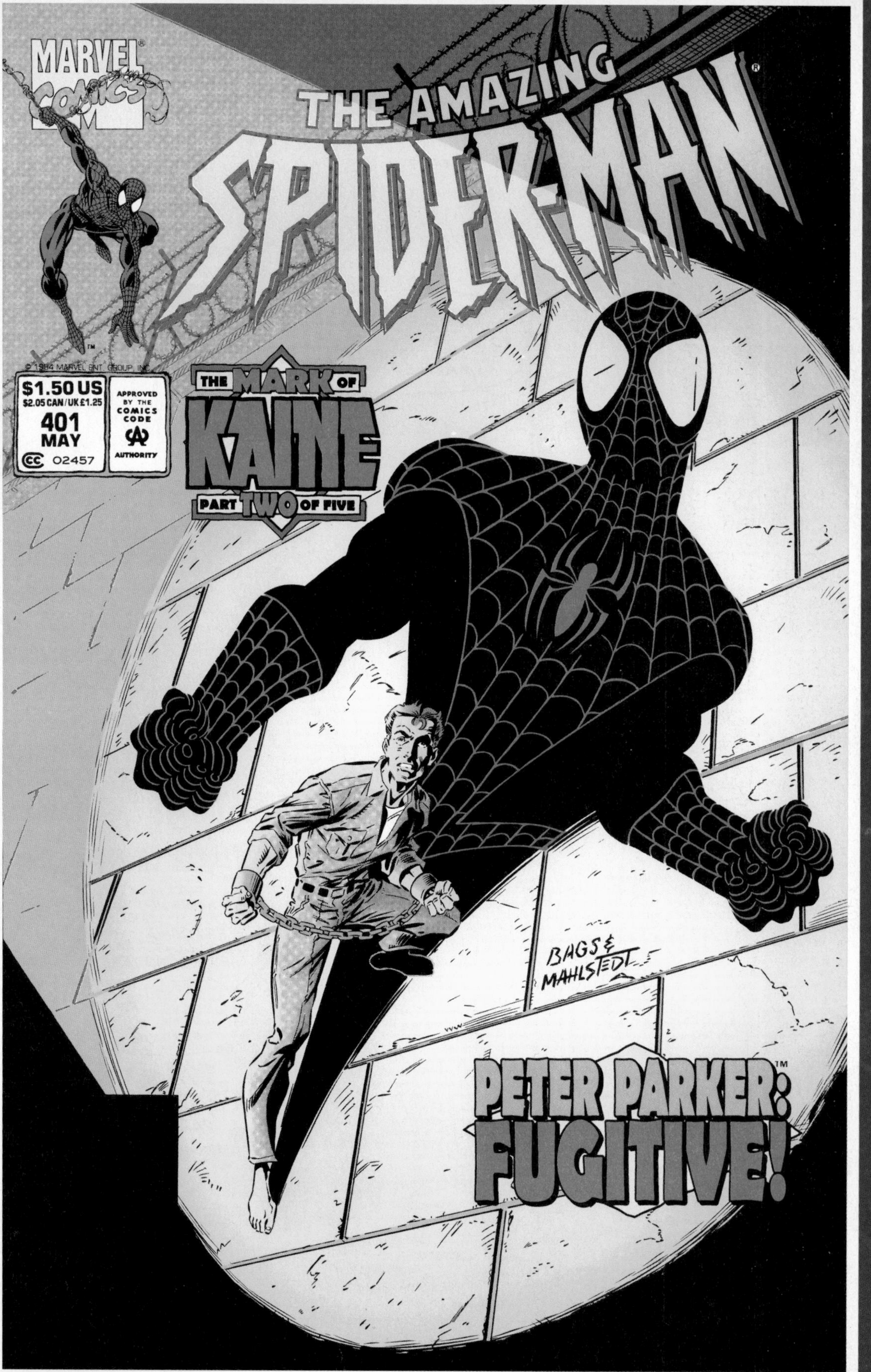
MARVEL COMICS
THE AMAZING SPIDER-MAN
© 1994 MARVEL ENT. GROUP, INC.
$1.50 US
$2.05 CAN/UK £1.25
401
MAY
02457
APPROVED BY THE COMICS CODE AUTHORITY
THE MARK OF KAINE
PART TWO OF FIVE
BAGS & MAHLSTEDT
PETER PARKER: FUGITIVE!

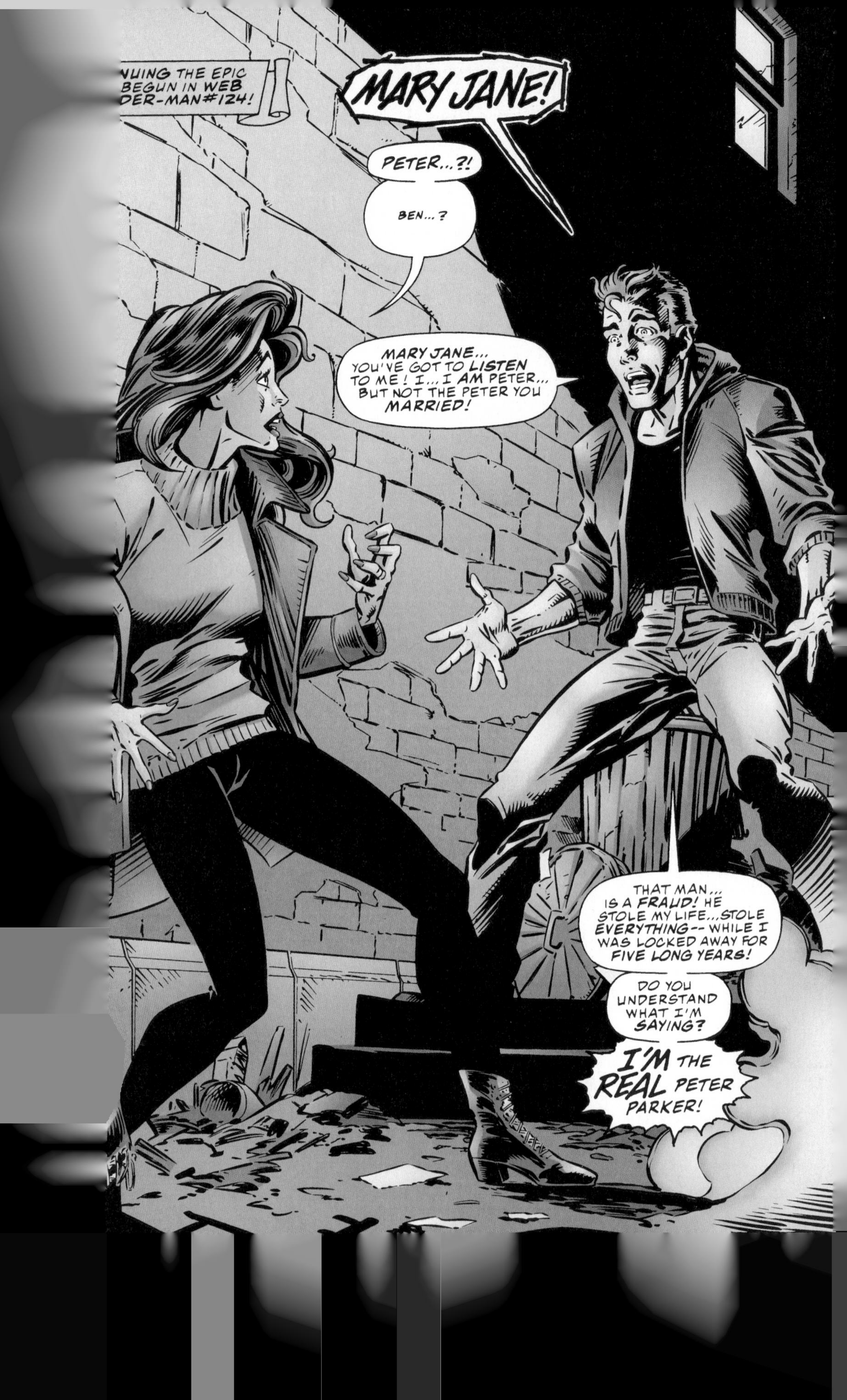
NUING THE EPIC BEGUN IN WEB DER-MAN #124!
MARY JANE!
PETER...?!
BEN...?
MARY JANE... YOU'VE GOT TO LISTEN TO ME! I... I AM PETER... BUT NOT THE PETER YOU MARRIED!
THAT MAN... IS A FRAUD! HE STOLE MY LIFE...STOLE EVERYTHING-- WHILE I WAS LOCKED AWAY FOR FIVE LONG YEARS!
DO YOU UNDERSTAND WHAT I'M SAYING?
I'M THE REAL PETER PARKER!

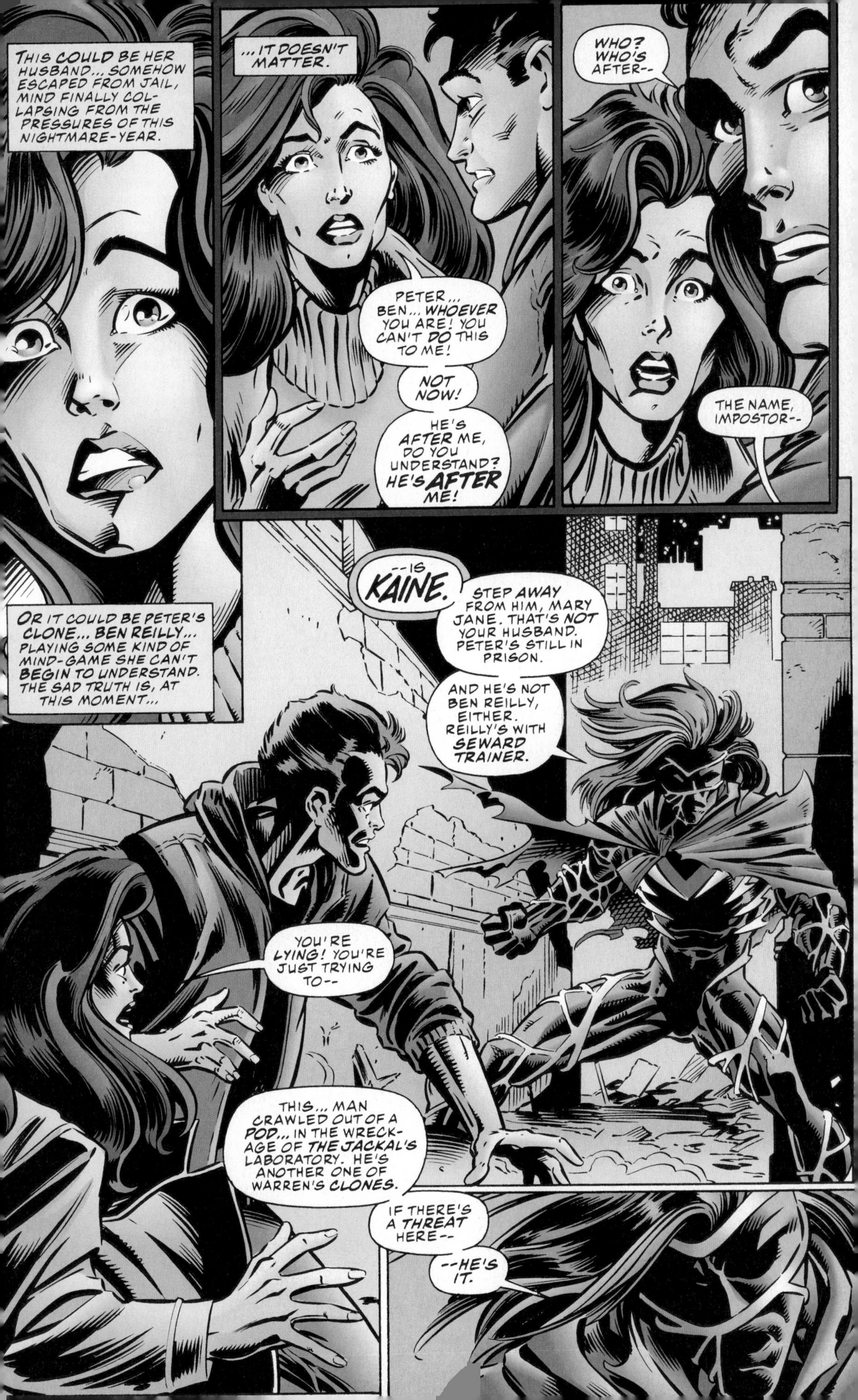
THIS COULD BE HER HUSBAND... SOMEHOW ESCAPED FROM JAIL, MIND FINALLY COL-LAPSING FROM THE PRESSURES OF THIS NIGHTMARE-YEAR.
...IT DOESN'T MATTER.
PETER... BEN... WHOEVER YOU ARE! YOU CAN'T DO THIS TO ME!
NOT NOW!
HE'S AFTER ME, DO YOU UNDERSTAND? HE'S AFTER ME!
WHO? WHO'S AFTER--
THE NAME, IMPOSTOR--
--IS KAINE.
OR IT COULD BE PETER'S CLONE... BEN REILLY... PLAYING SOME KIND OF MIND-GAME SHE CAN'T BEGIN TO UNDERSTAND. THE SAD TRUTH IS, AT THIS MOMENT...
STEP AWAY FROM HIM, MARY JANE. THAT'S NOT YOUR HUSBAND. PETER'S STILL IN PRISON.
AND HE'S NOT BEN REILLY, EITHER. REILLY'S WITH SEWARD TRAINER.
YOU'RE LYING! YOU'RE JUST TRYING TO--
THIS... MAN CRAWLED OUT OF A POD... IN THE WRECK-AGE OF THE JACKAL'S LABORATORY. HE'S ANOTHER ONE OF WARREN'S CLONES.
IF THERE'S A THREAT HERE--
--HE'S IT.

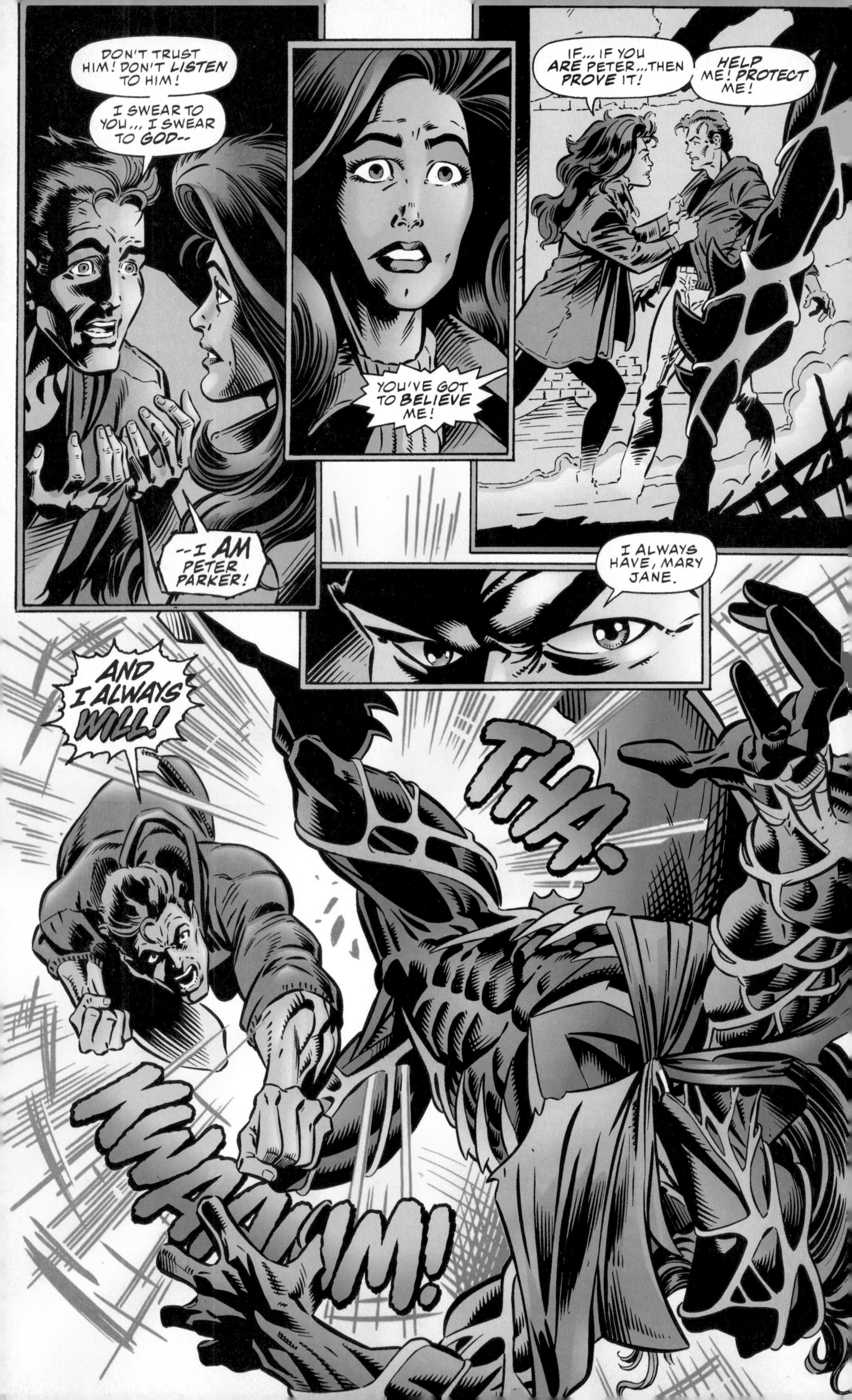
DON'T TRUST HIM! DON'T LISTEN TO HIM!
I SWEAR TO YOU... I SWEAR TO GOD--
--I AM PETER PARKER!
YOU'VE GOT TO BELIEVE ME!
IF... IF YOU ARE PETER...THEN PROVE IT!
HELP ME! PROTECT ME!
I ALWAYS HAVE, MARY JANE.
AND I ALWAYS WILL!
THA.
WWHAAM!

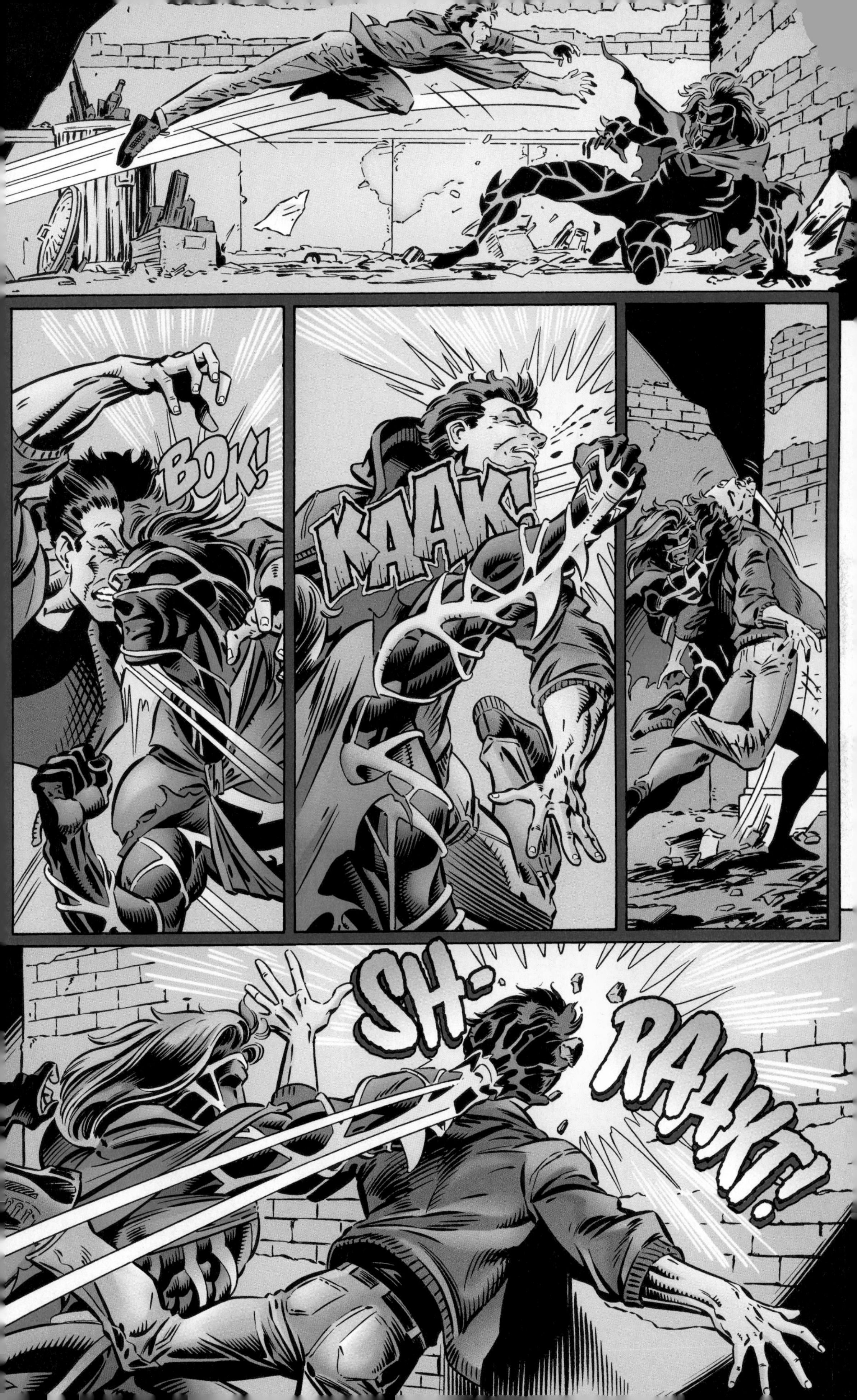
BOK!
KAAK!
SH-
RAAKT!

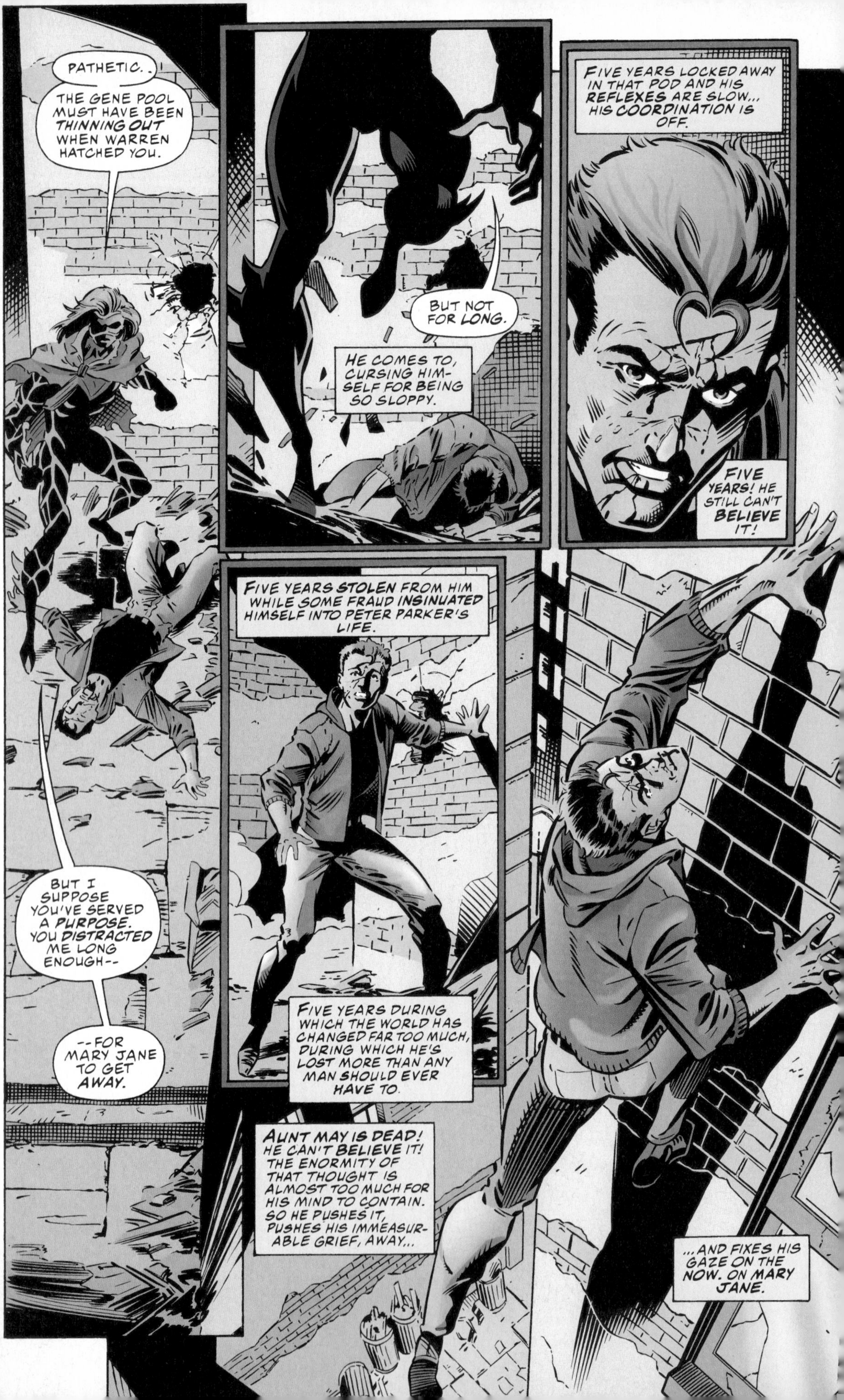
PATHETIC.
THE GENE POOL MUST HAVE BEEN THINNING OUT WHEN WARREN HATCHED YOU.
BUT I SUPPOSE YOU'VE SERVED A PURPOSE. YOU DISTRACTED ME LONG ENOUGH--
--FOR MARY JANE TO GET AWAY.
BUT NOT FOR LONG.
HE COMES TO, CURSING HIMSELF FOR BEING SO SLOPPY.
FIVE YEARS LOCKED AWAY IN THAT POD AND HIS REFLEXES ARE SLOW... HIS COORDINATION IS OFF.
FIVE YEARS! HE STILL CAN'T BELIEVE IT!
FIVE YEARS STOLEN FROM HIM WHILE SOME FRAUD INSINUATED HIMSELF INTO PETER PARKER'S LIFE.
FIVE YEARS DURING WHICH THE WORLD HAS CHANGED FAR TOO MUCH, DURING WHICH HE'S LOST MORE THAN ANY MAN SHOULD EVER HAVE TO.
AUNT MAY IS DEAD! HE CAN'T BELIEVE IT! THE ENORMITY OF THAT THOUGHT IS ALMOST TOO MUCH FOR HIS MIND TO CONTAIN. SO HE PUSHES IT, PUSHES HIS IMMEASURABLE GRIEF, AWAY...
...AND FIXES HIS GAZE ON THE NOW. ON MARY JANE.

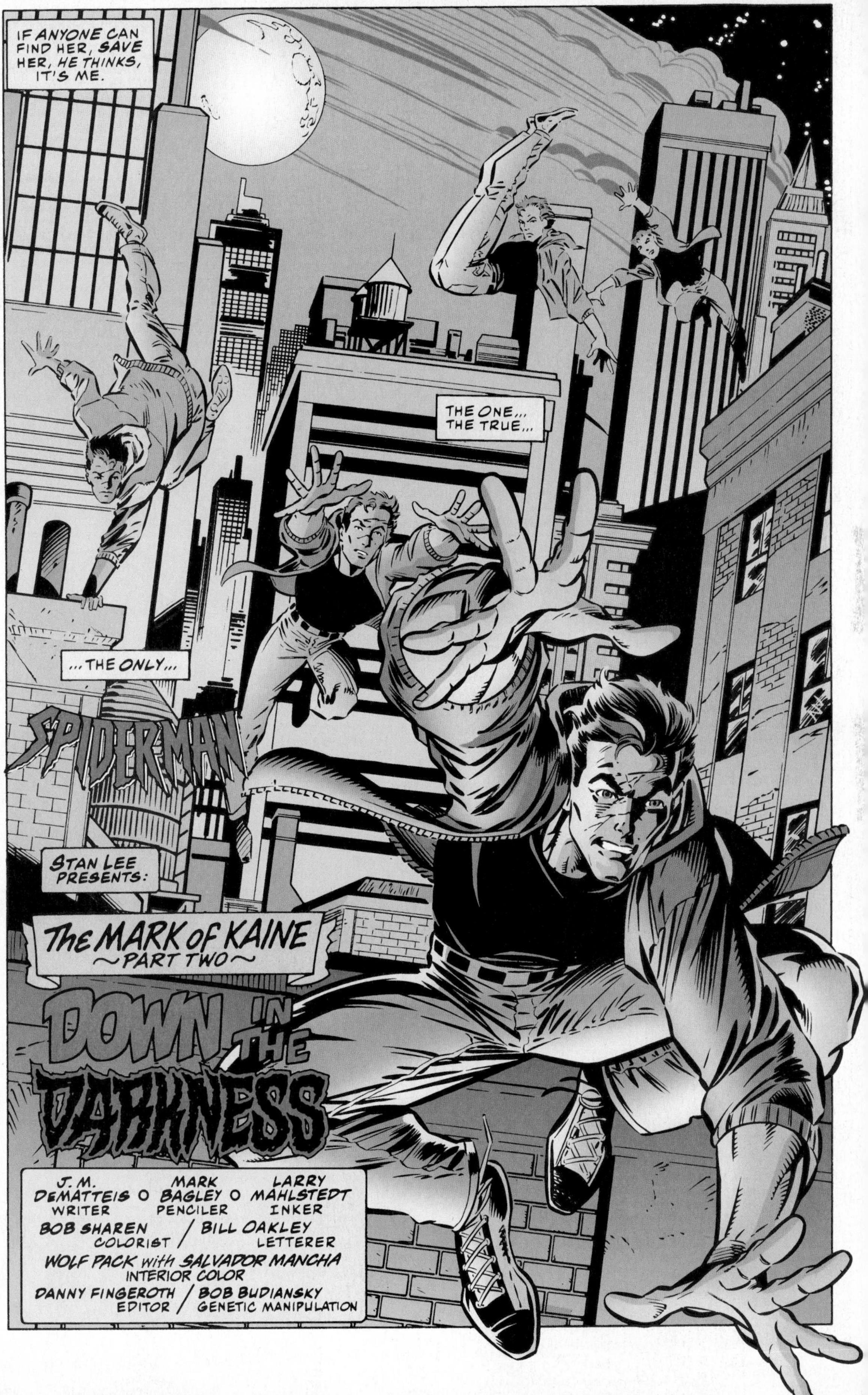
IF ANYONE CAN FIND HER, SAVE HER, HE THINKS, IT'S ME.
THE ONE... THE TRUE...
...THE ONLY...
SPIDER-MAN
STAN LEE PRESENTS:
The MARK of KAINE ~PART TWO~
DOWN IN THE DARKNESS
J. M. DEMATTEIS WRITER
MARK BAGLEY PENCILER
LARRY MAHLSTEDT INKER
BOB SHAREN COLORIST / BILL OAKLEY LETTERER
WOLF PACK with SALVADOR MANCHA INTERIOR COLOR
DANNY FINGEROTH EDITOR / BOB BUDIANSKY GENETIC MANIPULATION

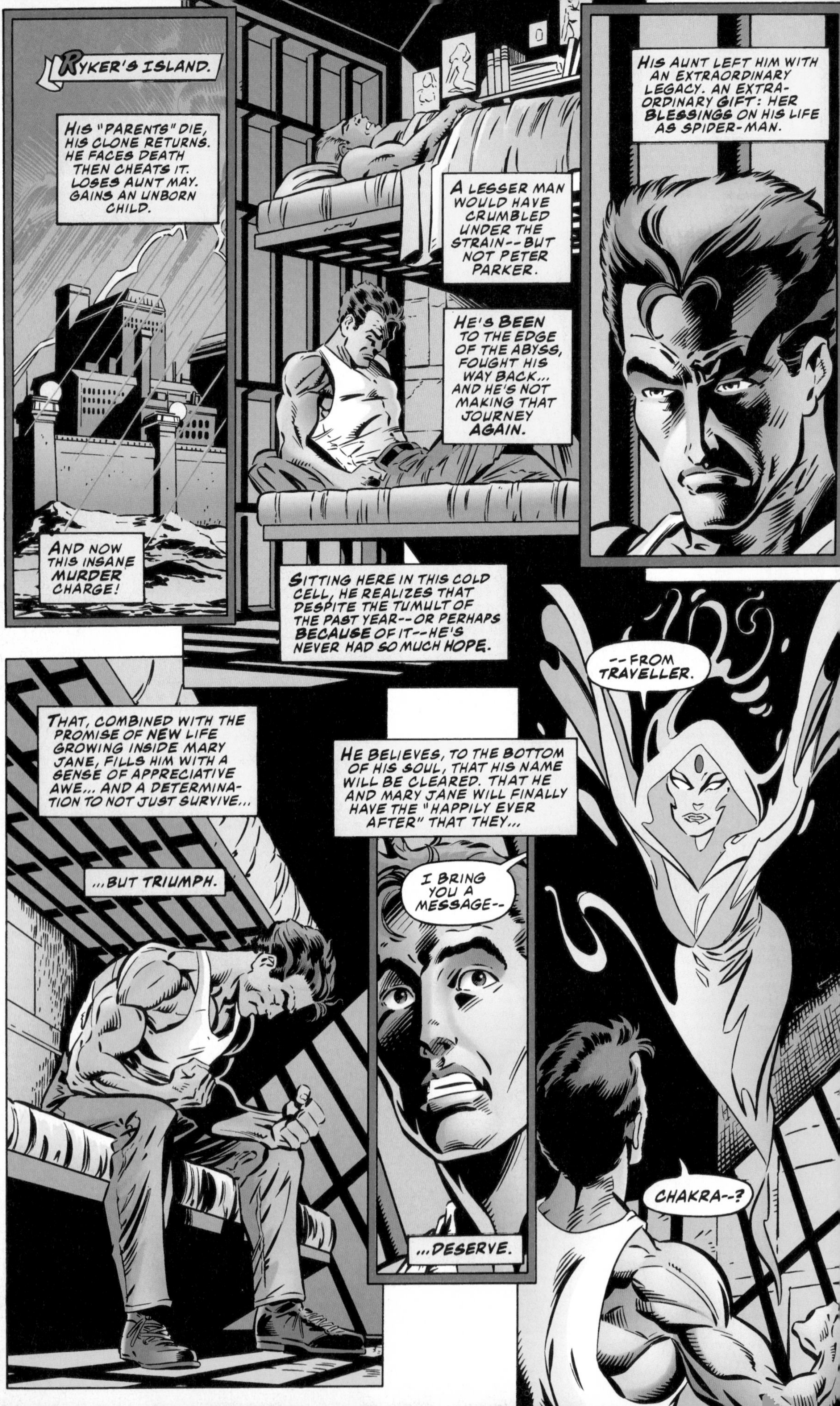
RYKER'S ISLAND.
HIS "PARENTS" DIE, HIS CLONE RETURNS. HE FACES DEATH THEN CHEATS IT. LOSES AUNT MAY. GAINS AN UNBORN CHILD.
AND NOW THIS INSANE MURDER CHARGE!
A LESSER MAN WOULD HAVE CRUMBLED UNDER THE STRAIN--BUT NOT PETER PARKER.
HE'S BEEN TO THE EDGE OF THE ABYSS, FOUGHT HIS WAY BACK... AND HE'S NOT MAKING THAT JOURNEY AGAIN.
HIS AUNT LEFT HIM WITH AN EXTRAORDINARY LEGACY. AN EXTRA-ORDINARY GIFT: HER BLESSINGS ON HIS LIFE AS SPIDER-MAN.
SITTING HERE IN THIS COLD CELL, HE REALIZES THAT DESPITE THE TUMULT OF THE PAST YEAR--OR PERHAPS BECAUSE OF IT--HE'S NEVER HAD SO MUCH HOPE.
THAT, COMBINED WITH THE PROMISE OF NEW LIFE GROWING INSIDE MARY JANE, FILLS HIM WITH A SENSE OF APPRECIATIVE AWE... AND A DETERMINA-TION TO NOT JUST SURVIVE...
...BUT TRIUMPH.
HE BELIEVES, TO THE BOTTOM OF HIS SOUL, THAT HIS NAME WILL BE CLEARED. THAT HE AND MARY JANE WILL FINALLY HAVE THE "HAPPILY EVER AFTER" THAT THEY...
I BRING YOU A MESSAGE--
...DESERVE.
--FROM TRAVELLER.
CHAKRA--?

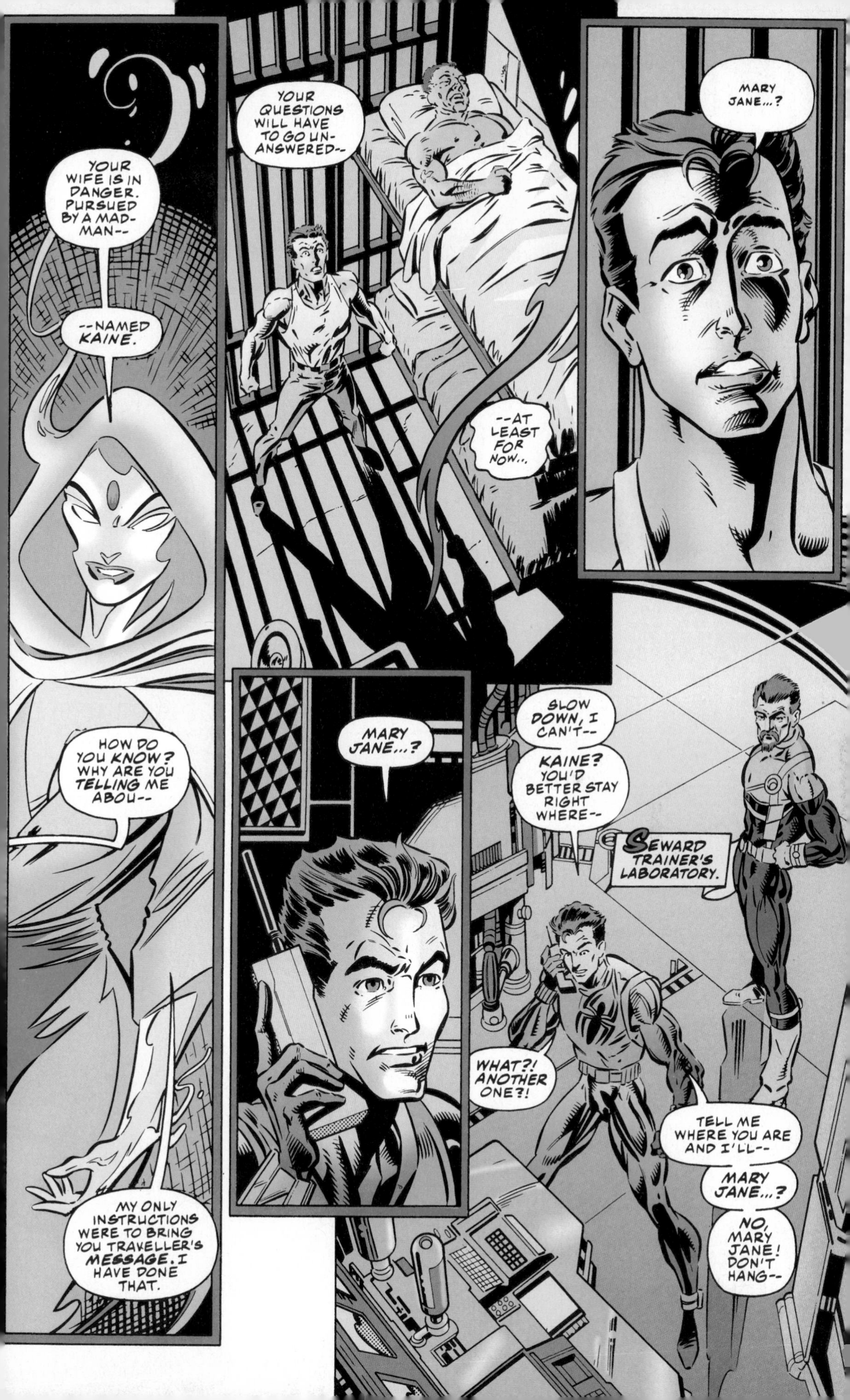
YOUR WIFE IS IN DANGER. PURSUED BY A MAD-MAN--
--NAMED KAINE.
YOUR QUESTIONS WILL HAVE TO GO UN-ANSWERED--
--AT LEAST FOR NOW...
MARY JANE...?
HOW DO YOU KNOW? WHY ARE YOU TELLING ME ABOU--
MY ONLY INSTRUCTIONS WERE TO BRING YOU TRAVELLER'S MESSAGE. I HAVE DONE THAT.
MARY JANE...?
SLOW DOWN, I CAN'T--
KAINE? YOU'D BETTER STAY RIGHT WHERE--
SEWARD TRAINER'S LABORATORY.
WHAT?! ANOTHER ONE?!
TELL ME WHERE YOU ARE AND I'LL--
MARY JANE...?
NO, MARY JANE! DON'T HANG--

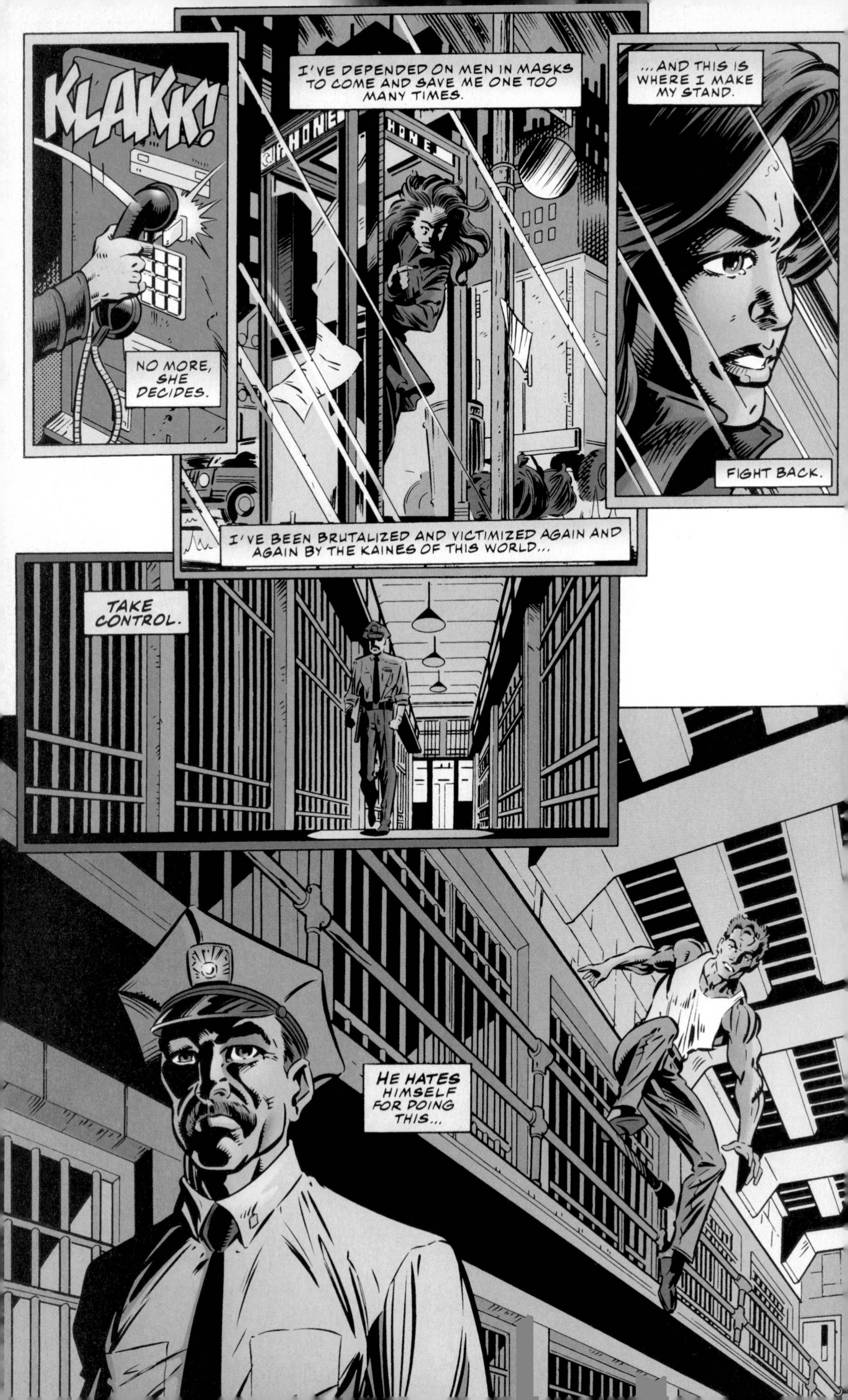
KLAKK!
NO MORE, SHE DECIDES.
I'VE DEPENDED ON MEN IN MASKS TO COME AND SAVE ME ONE TOO MANY TIMES.
I'VE BEEN BRUTALIZED AND VICTIMIZED AGAIN AND AGAIN BY THE KAINES OF THIS WORLD...
...AND THIS IS WHERE I MAKE MY STAND.
FIGHT BACK.
TAKE CONTROL.
HE HATES HIMSELF FOR DOING THIS...

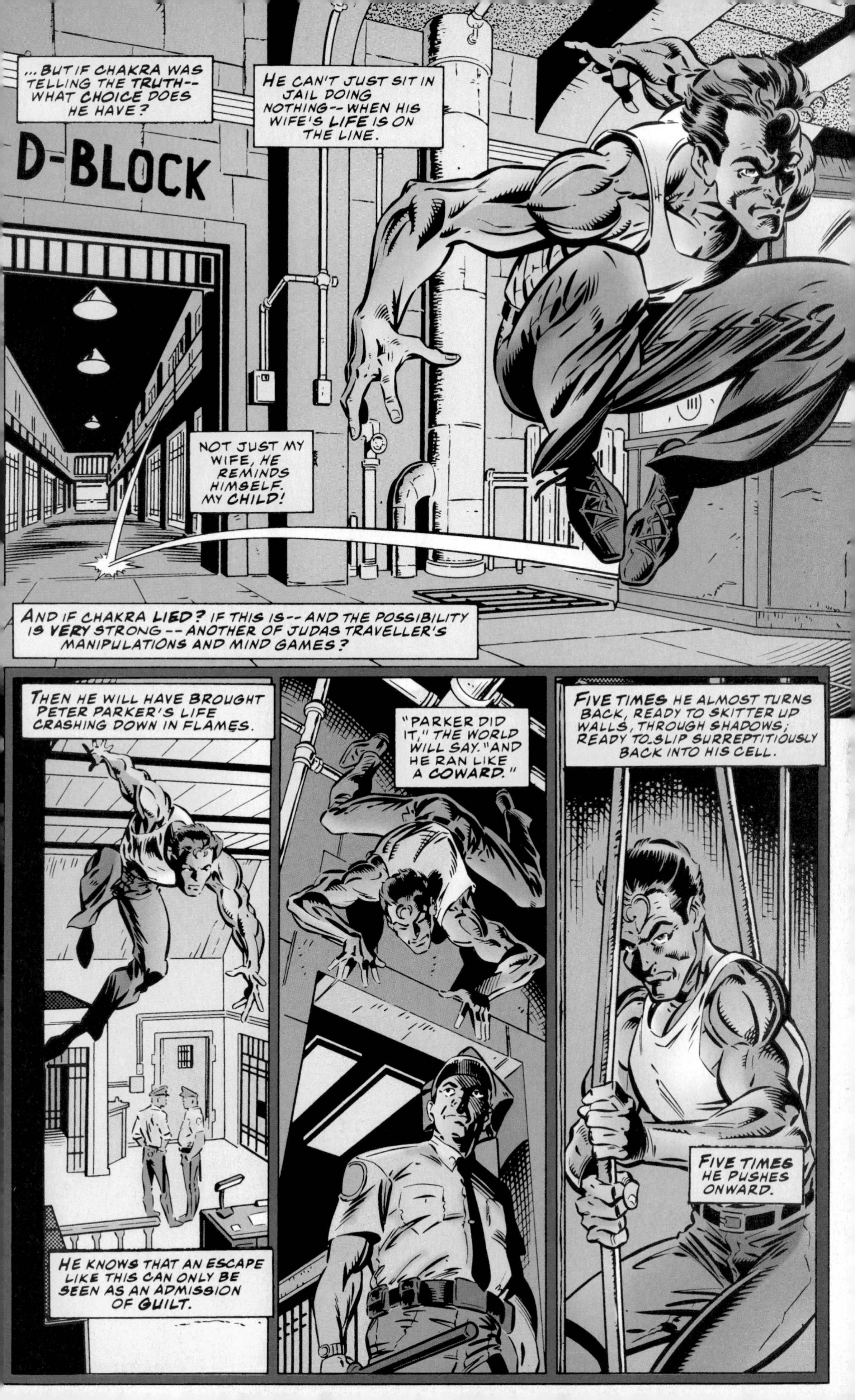
...BUT IF CHAKRA WAS TELLING THE TRUTH-- WHAT CHOICE DOES HE HAVE?
HE CAN'T JUST SIT IN JAIL DOING NOTHING-- WHEN HIS WIFE'S LIFE IS ON THE LINE.
D-BLOCK
NOT JUST MY WIFE, HE REMINDS HIMSELF. MY CHILD!
AND IF CHAKRA LIED? IF THIS IS-- AND THE POSSIBILITY IS VERY STRONG -- ANOTHER OF JUDAS TRAVELLER'S MANIPULATIONS AND MIND GAMES?
THEN HE WILL HAVE BROUGHT PETER PARKER'S LIFE CRASHING DOWN IN FLAMES.
HE KNOWS THAT AN ESCAPE LIKE THIS CAN ONLY BE SEEN AS AN ADMISSION OF GUILT.
"PARKER DID IT," THE WORLD WILL SAY. "AND HE RAN LIKE A COWARD."
FIVE TIMES HE ALMOST TURNS BACK, READY TO SKITTER UP WALLS, THROUGH SHADOWS; READY TO SLIP SURREPTITIOUSLY BACK INTO HIS CELL.
FIVE TIMES HE PUSHES ONWARD.

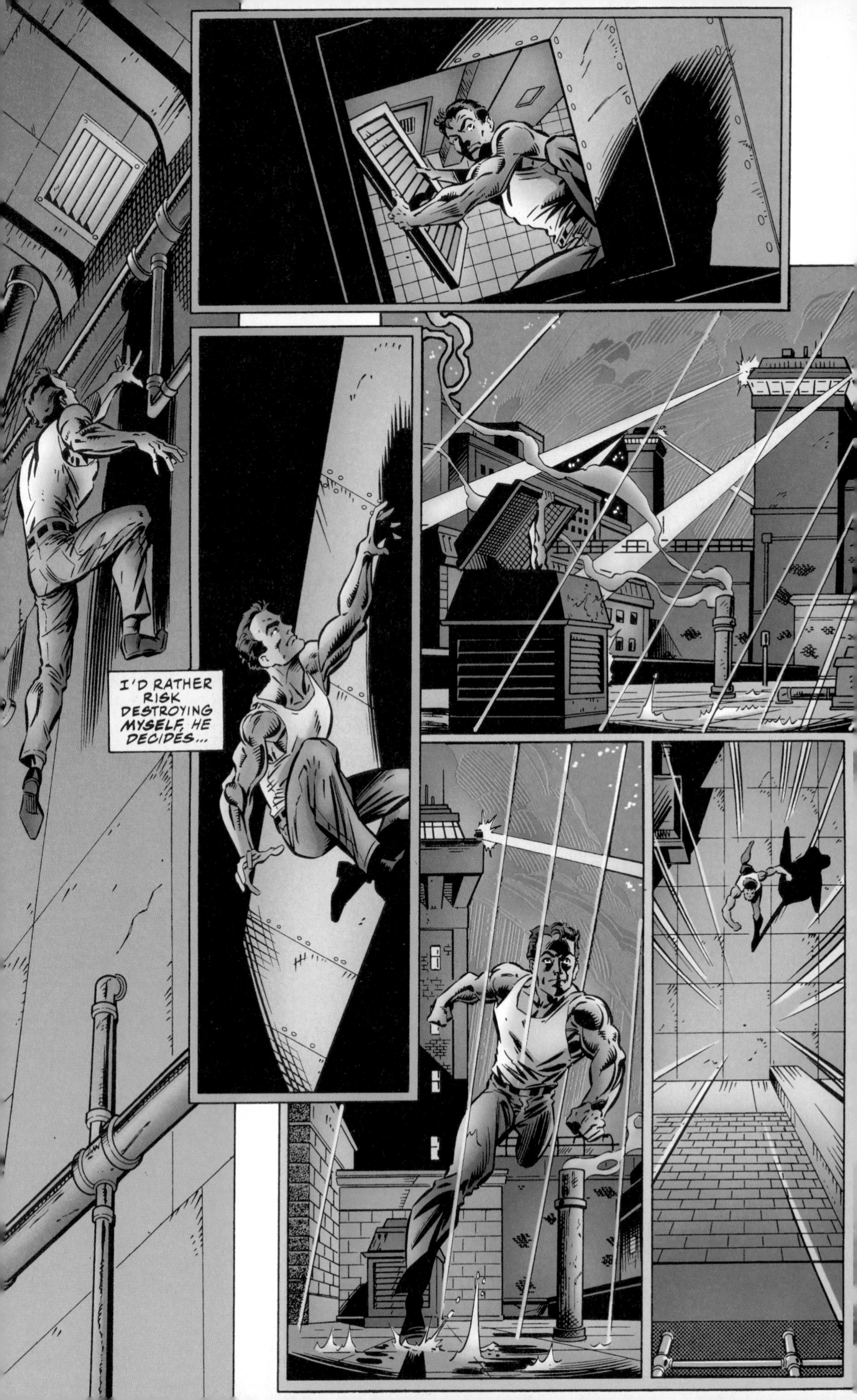
I'D RATHER RISK DESTROYING MYSELF, HE DECIDES...

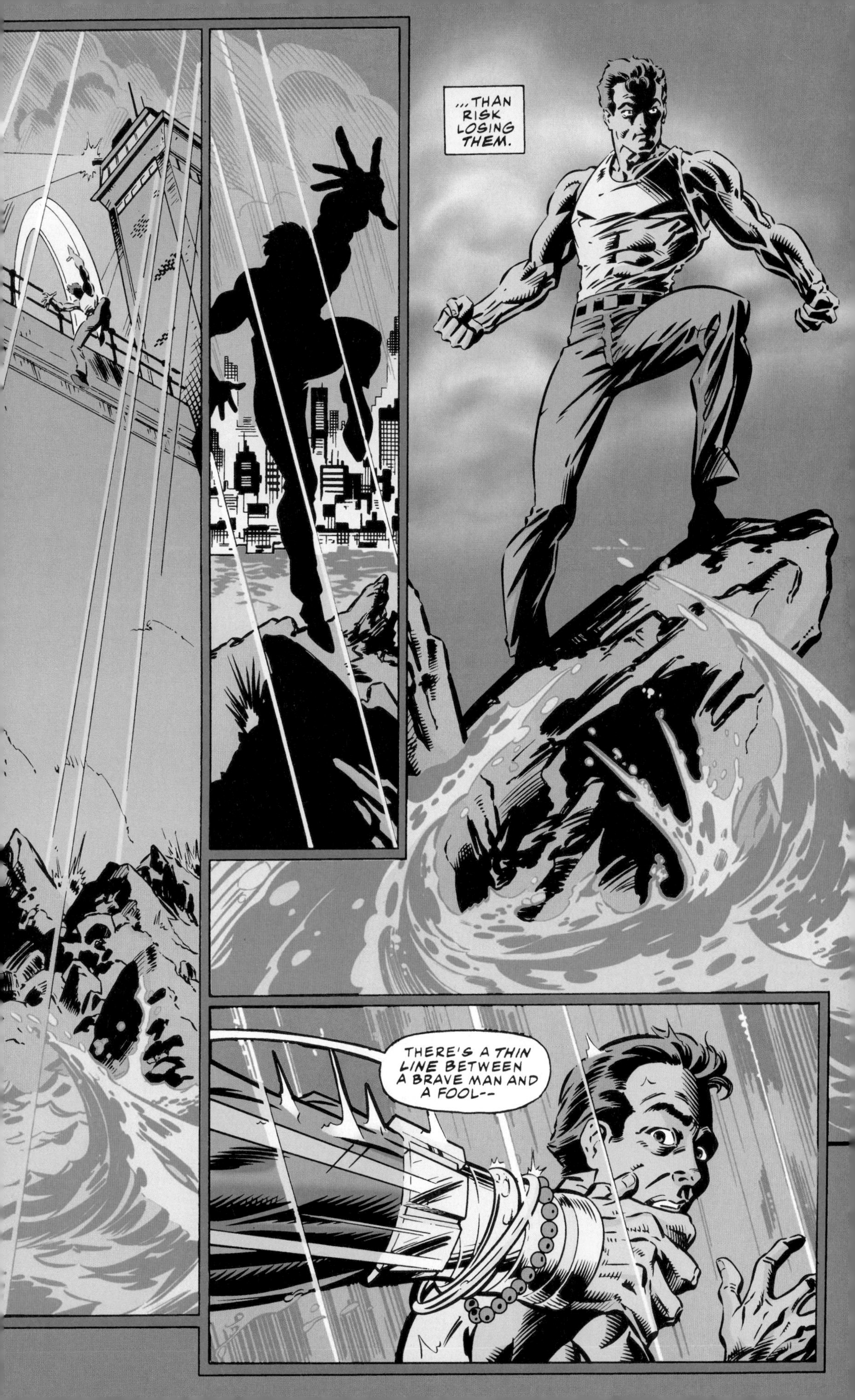
...THAN RISK LOSING THEM.
THERE'S A THIN LINE BETWEEN A BRAVE MAN AND A FOOL--

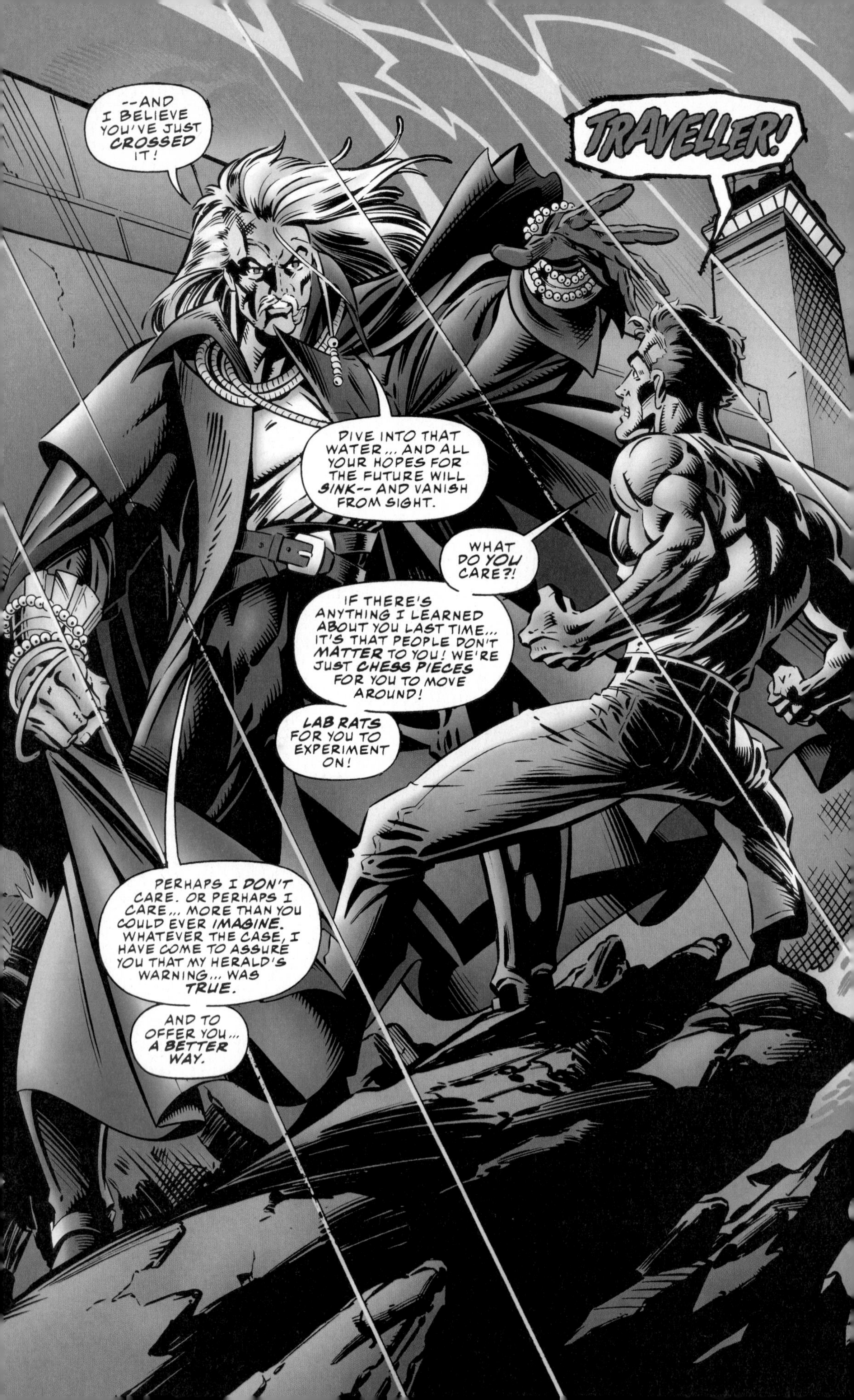
TRAVELLER!
--AND I BELIEVE YOU'VE JUST CROSSED IT!
DIVE INTO THAT WATER... AND ALL YOUR HOPES FOR THE FUTURE WILL SINK-- AND VANISH FROM SIGHT.
WHAT DO YOU CARE?!
IF THERE'S ANYTHING I LEARNED ABOUT YOU LAST TIME... IT'S THAT PEOPLE DON'T MATTER TO YOU! WE'RE JUST CHESS PIECES FOR YOU TO MOVE AROUND!
LAB RATS FOR YOU TO EXPERIMENT ON!
PERHAPS I DON'T CARE. OR PERHAPS I CARE... MORE THAN YOU COULD EVER IMAGINE. WHATEVER THE CASE, I HAVE COME TO ASSURE YOU THAT MY HERALD'S WARNING... WAS TRUE.
AND TO OFFER YOU... A BETTER WAY.

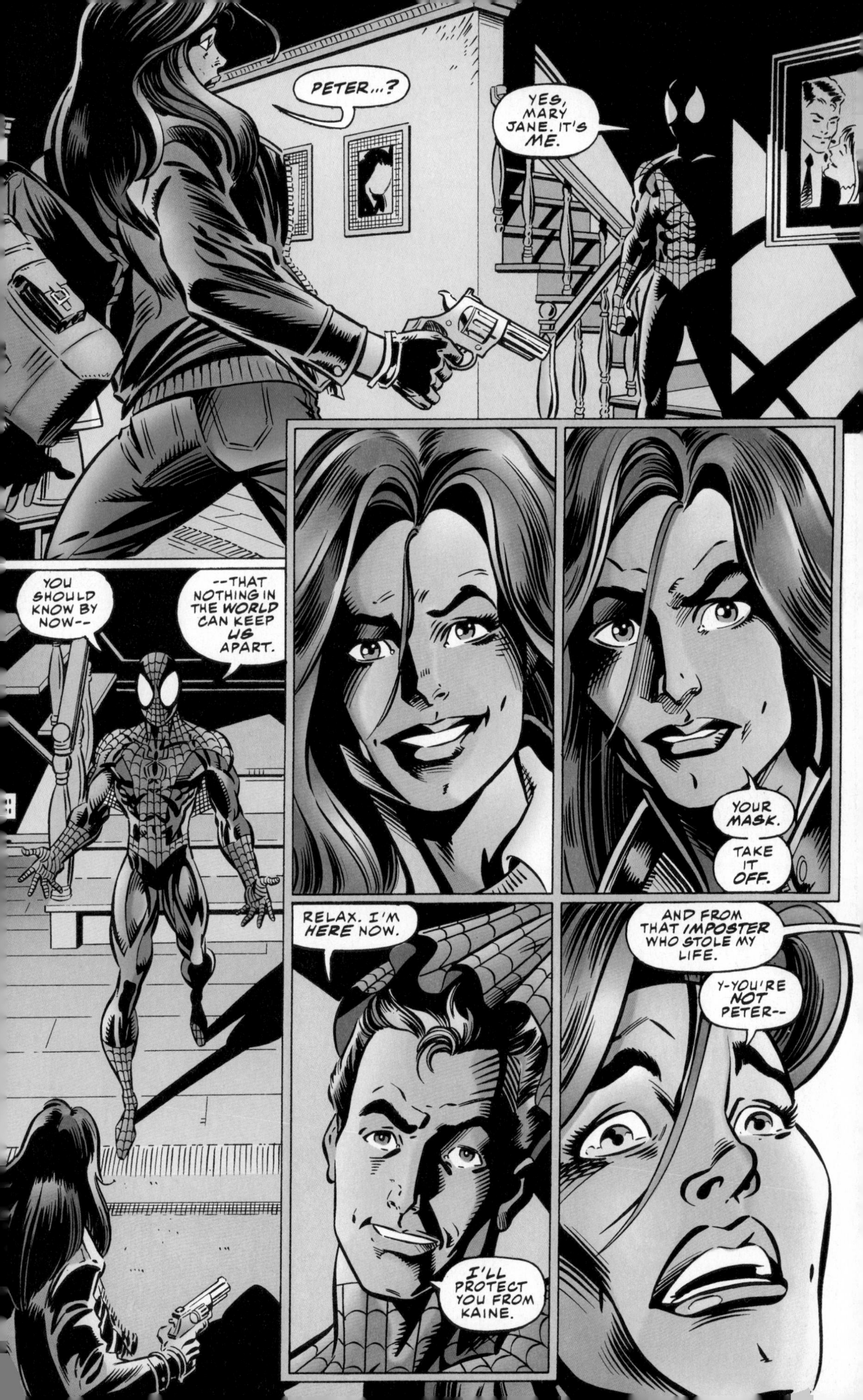
PETER...?
YES, MARY JANE. IT'S ME.
YOU SHOULD KNOW BY NOW--
--THAT NOTHING IN THE WORLD CAN KEEP US APART.
YOUR MASK.
TAKE IT OFF.
RELAX. I'M HERE NOW.
I'LL PROTECT YOU FROM KAINE.
AND FROM THAT IMPOSTER WHO STOLE MY LIFE.
Y-YOU'RE NOT PETER--

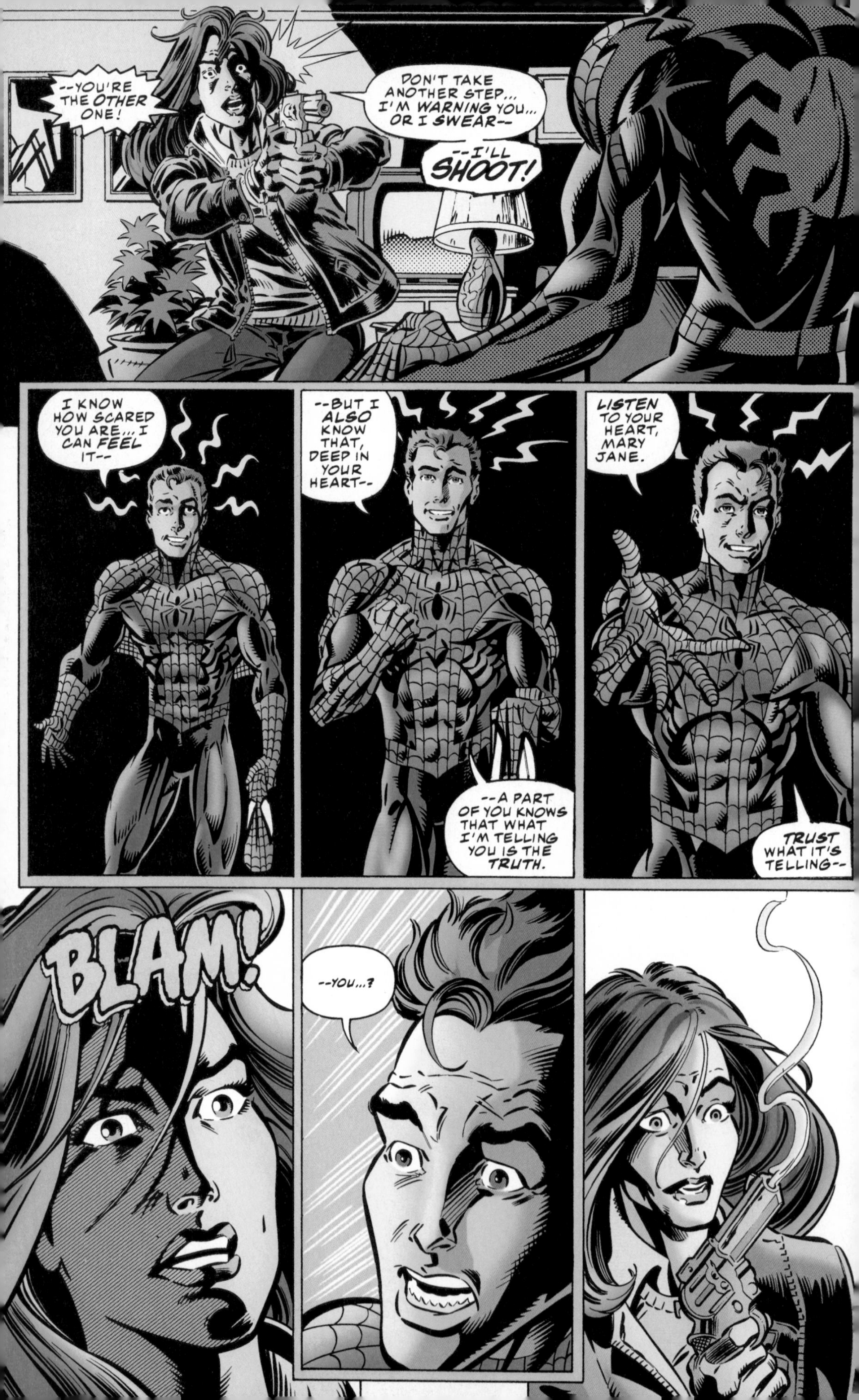
--YOU'RE THE OTHER ONE!
DON'T TAKE ANOTHER STEP... I'M WARNING YOU... OR I SWEAR--
--I'LL SHOOT!
I KNOW HOW SCARED YOU ARE... I CAN FEEL IT--
--BUT I ALSO KNOW THAT, DEEP IN YOUR HEART--
--A PART OF YOU KNOWS THAT WHAT I'M TELLING YOU IS THE TRUTH.
LISTEN TO YOUR HEART, MARY JANE.
TRUST WHAT IT'S TELLING--
BLAM!
--YOU...?

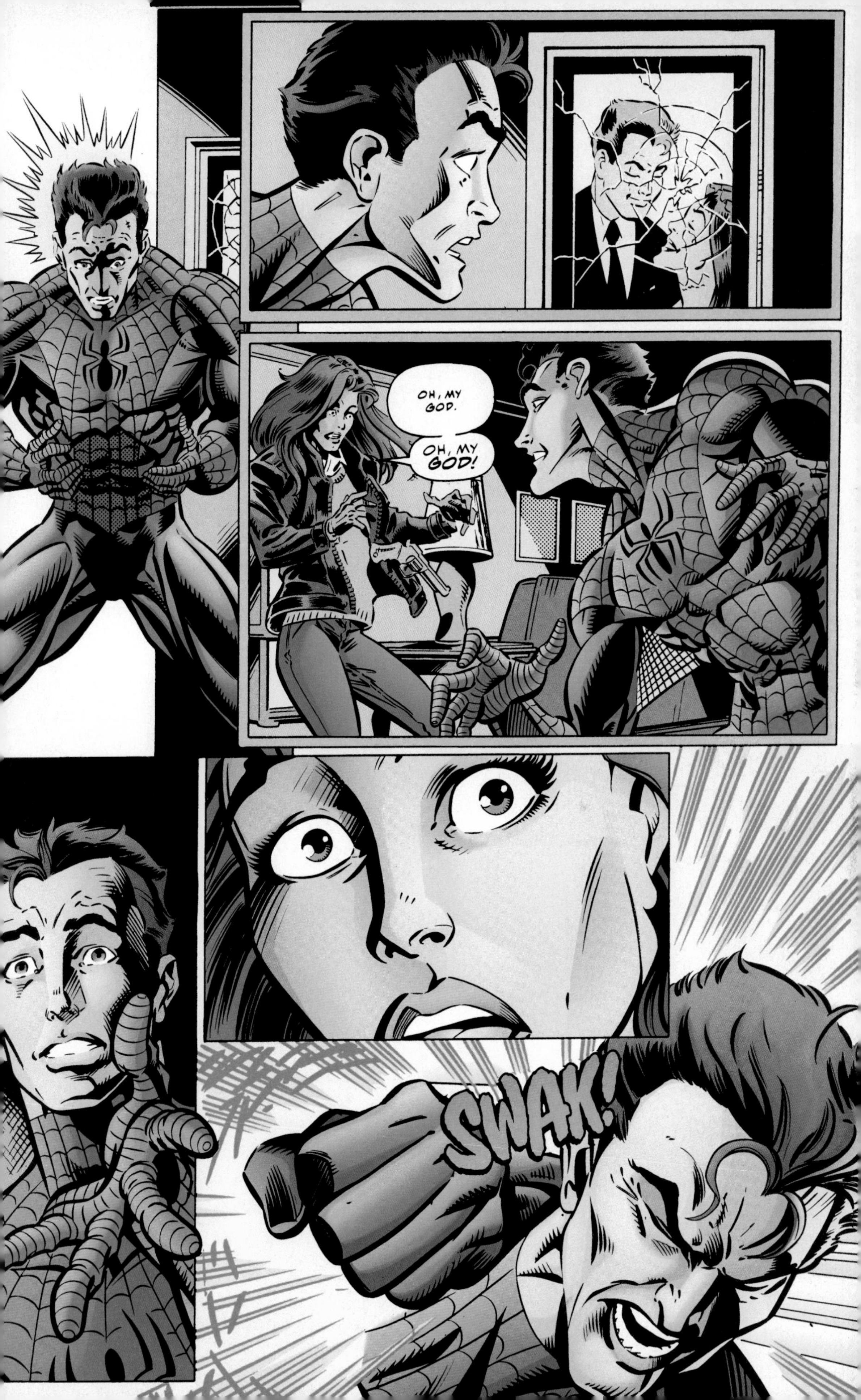
OH, MY GOD.
OH, MY GOD!
SWAK!

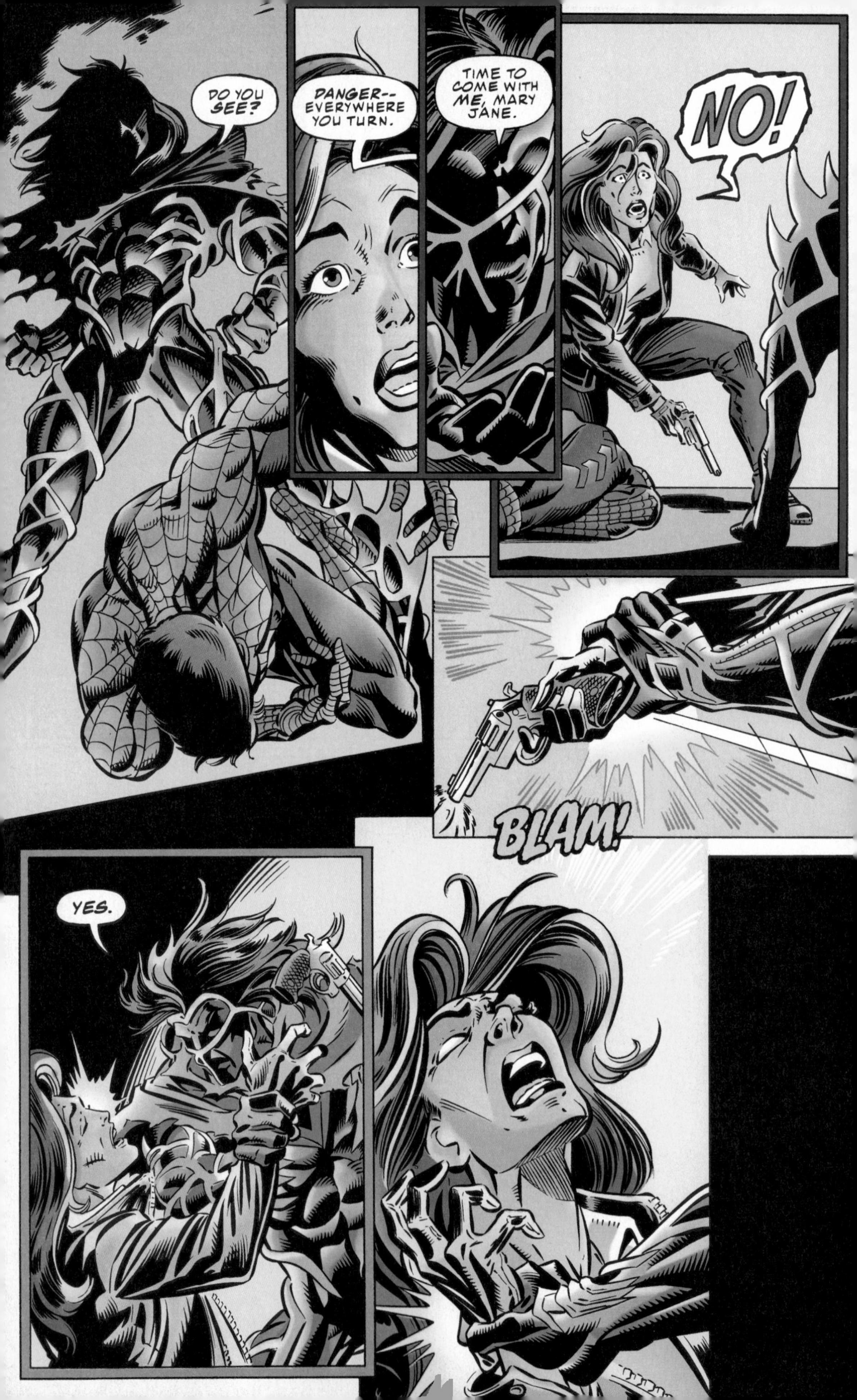
DO YOU SEE?
DANGER-- EVERYWHERE YOU TURN.
TIME TO COME WITH ME, MARY JANE.
NO!
BLAM!
YES.

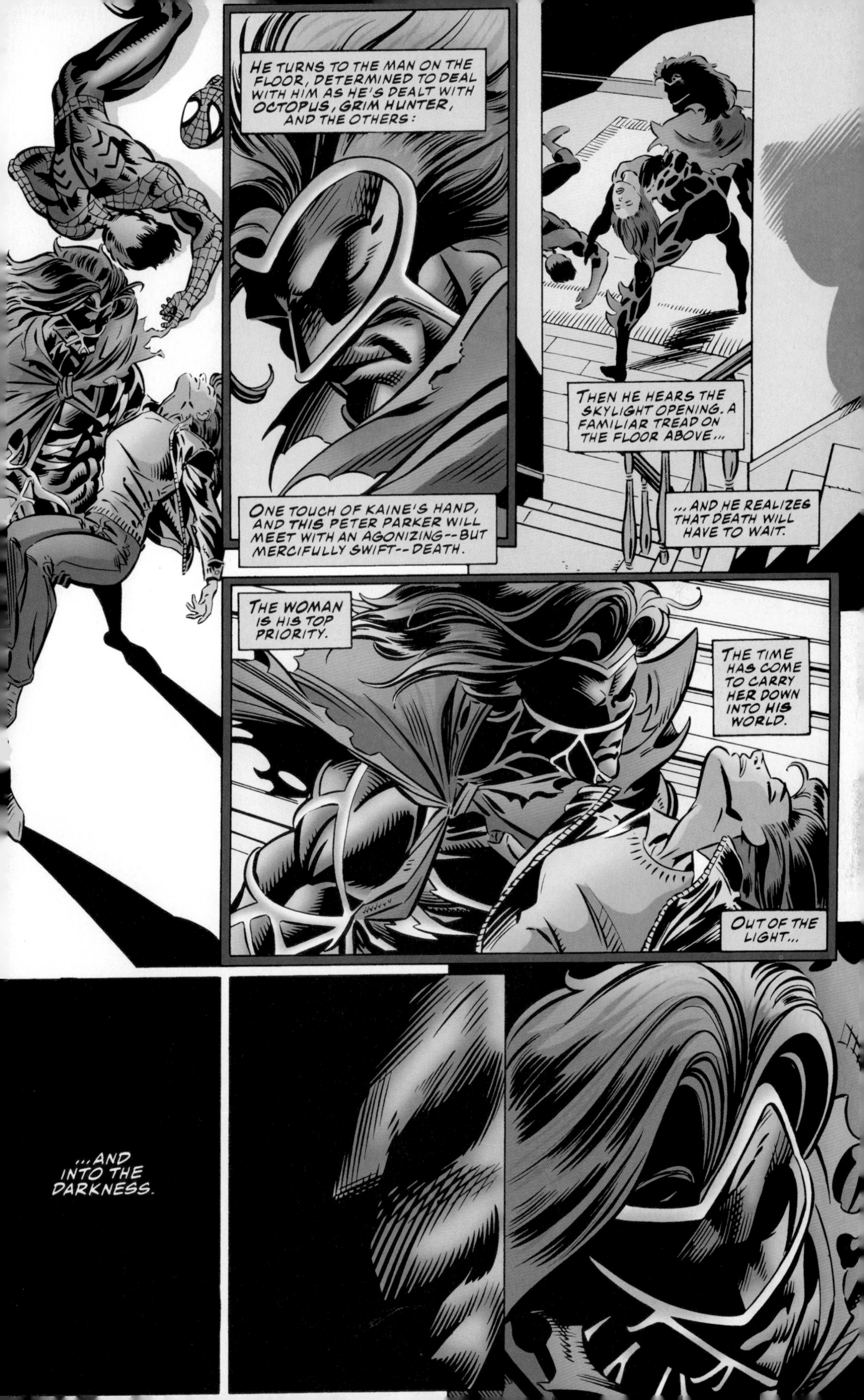

HE TURNS TO THE MAN ON THE FLOOR, DETERMINED TO DEAL WITH HIM AS HE'S DEALT WITH OCTOPUS, GRIM HUNTER, AND THE OTHERS:
ONE TOUCH OF KAINE'S HAND, AND THIS PETER PARKER WILL MEET WITH AN AGONIZING--BUT MERCIFULLY SWIFT--DEATH.
THEN HE HEARS THE SKYLIGHT OPENING. A FAMILIAR TREAD ON THE FLOOR ABOVE...
...AND HE REALIZES THAT DEATH WILL HAVE TO WAIT.
THE WOMAN IS HIS TOP PRIORITY.
THE TIME HAS COME TO CARRY HER DOWN INTO HIS WORLD.
OUT OF THE LIGHT...
...AND INTO THE DARKNESS.

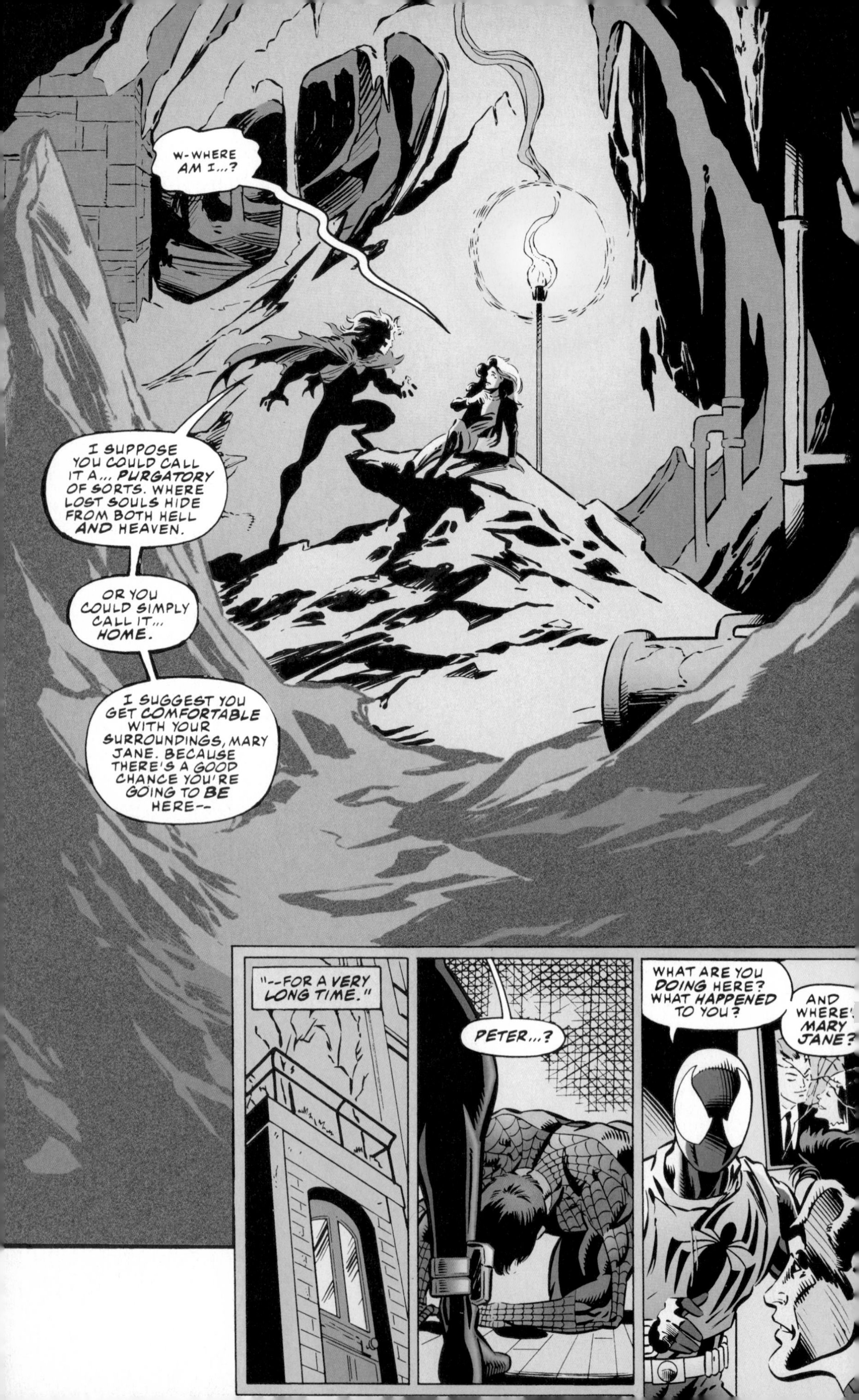
W-WHERE AM I...?
I SUPPOSE YOU COULD CALL IT A... PURGATORY OF SORTS. WHERE LOST SOULS HIDE FROM BOTH HELL AND HEAVEN.
OR YOU COULD SIMPLY CALL IT... HOME.
I SUGGEST YOU GET COMFORTABLE WITH YOUR SURROUNDINGS, MARY JANE. BECAUSE THERE'S A GOOD CHANCE YOU'RE GOING TO BE HERE--
"--FOR A VERY LONG TIME."
PETER...?
WHAT ARE YOU DOING HERE? WHAT HAPPENED TO YOU?

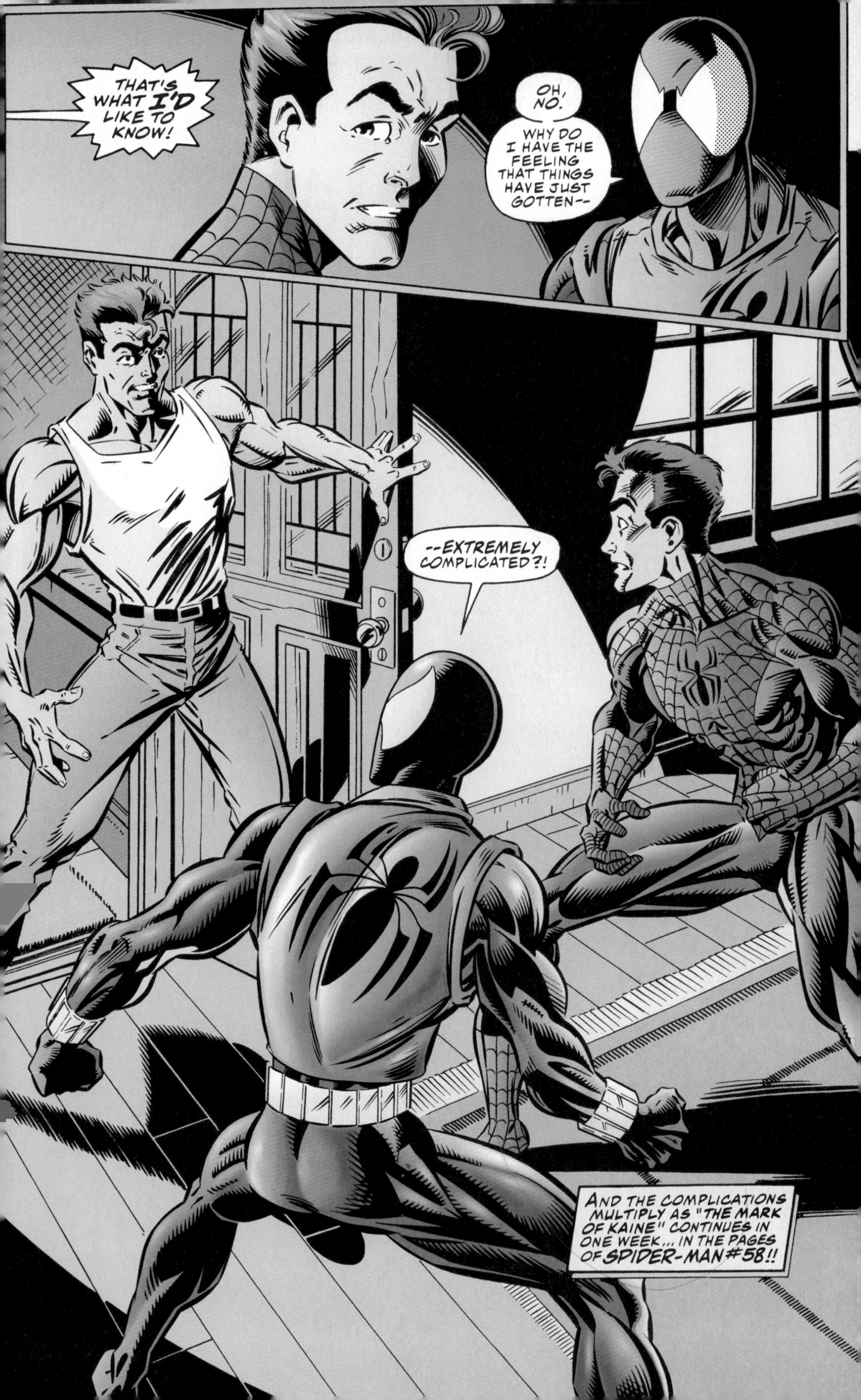
THAT'S WHAT I'D LIKE TO KNOW!
OH, NO.
WHY DO I HAVE THE FEELING THAT THINGS HAVE JUST GOTTEN--
--EXTREMELY COMPLICATED?!
AND THE COMPLICATIONS MULTIPLY AS "THE MARK OF KAINE" CONTINUES IN ONE WEEK... IN THE PAGES OF SPIDER-MAN #58!!

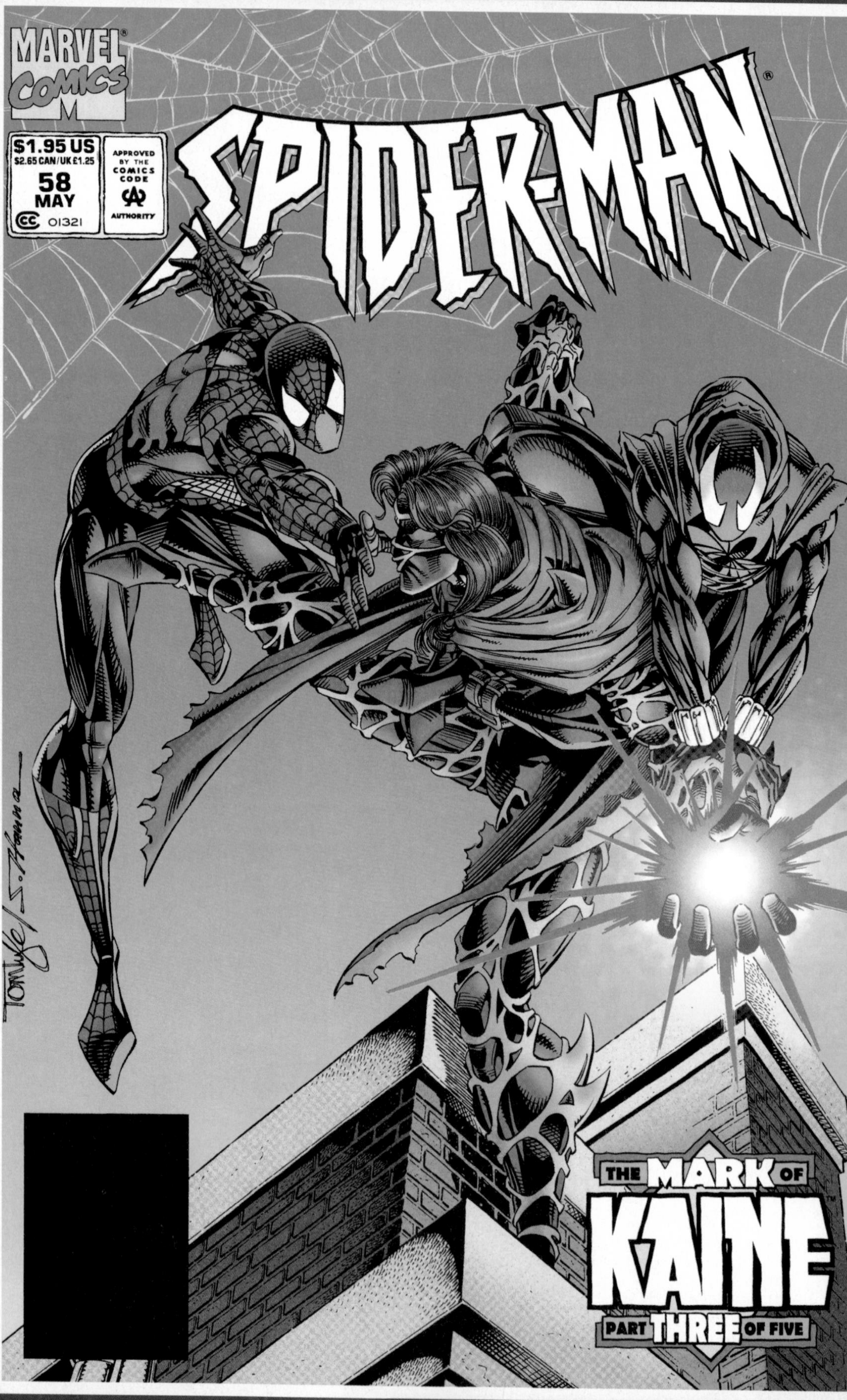
MARVEL COMICS
$1.95 US
$2.65 CAN/UK £1.25
58
MAY
01321
APPROVED BY THE COMICS CODE AUTHORITY
SPIDER-MAN
THE MARK OF
KAINE
PART THREE OF FIVE

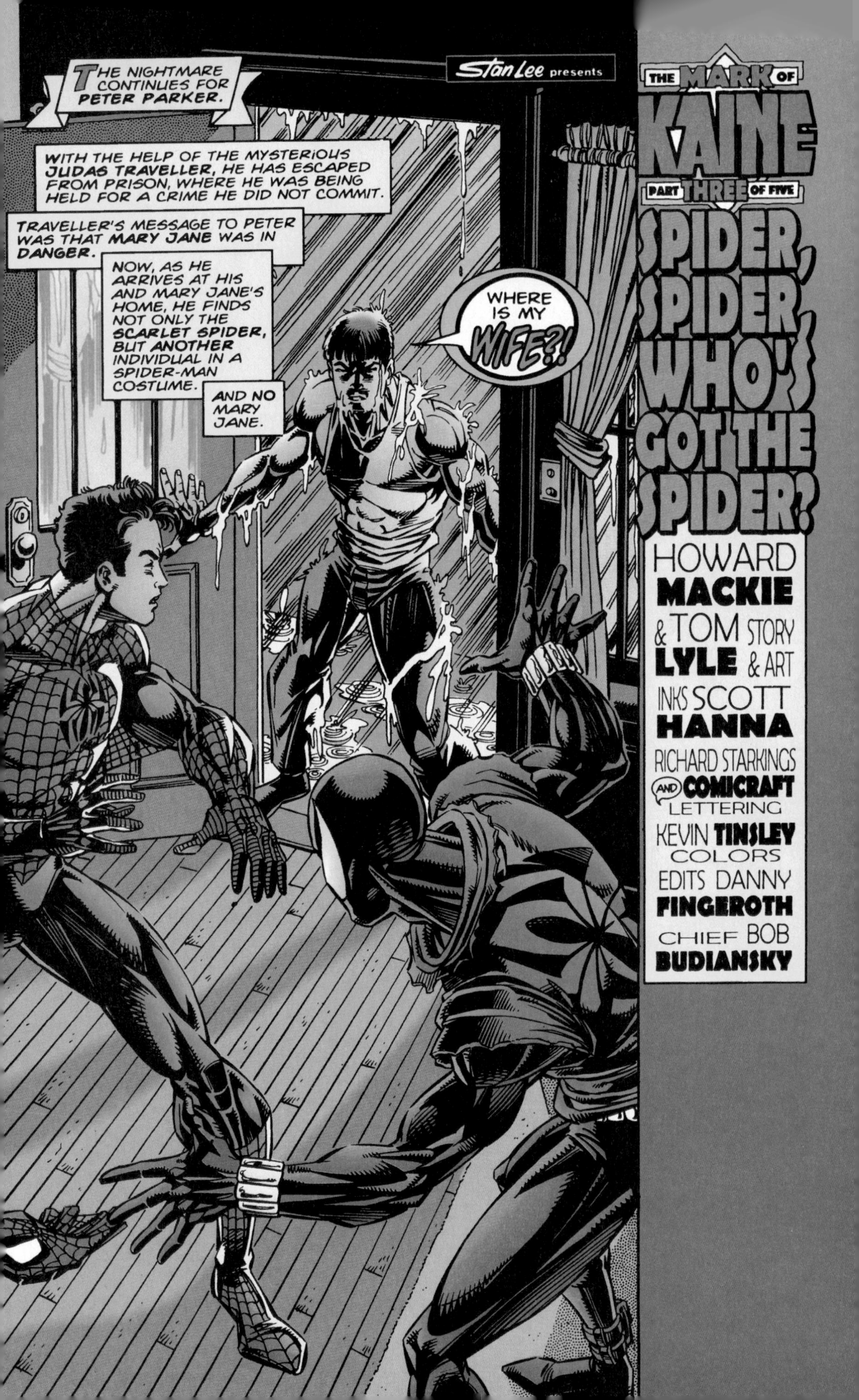

THE NIGHTMARE CONTINUES FOR PETER PARKER.
Stan Lee presents
THE MARK OF KAINE PART THREE OF FIVE
SPIDER, SPIDER, WHO'S GOT THE SPIDER?
WITH THE HELP OF THE MYSTERIOUS JUDAS TRAVELLER, HE HAS ESCAPED FROM PRISON, WHERE HE WAS BEING HELD FOR A CRIME HE DID NOT COMMIT.
TRAVELLER'S MESSAGE TO PETER WAS THAT MARY JANE WAS IN DANGER.
NOW, AS HE ARRIVES AT HIS AND MARY JANE'S HOME, HE FINDS NOT ONLY THE SCARLET SPIDER, BUT ANOTHER INDIVIDUAL IN A SPIDER-MAN COSTUME.
AND NO MARY JANE.
WHERE IS MY WIFE?!
HOWARD MACKIE & TOM LYLE STORY & ART
INKS SCOTT HANNA
RICHARD STARKINGS AND COMICRAFT LETTERING
KEVIN TINSLEY COLORS
EDITS DANNY FINGEROTH
CHIEF BOB BUDIANSKY

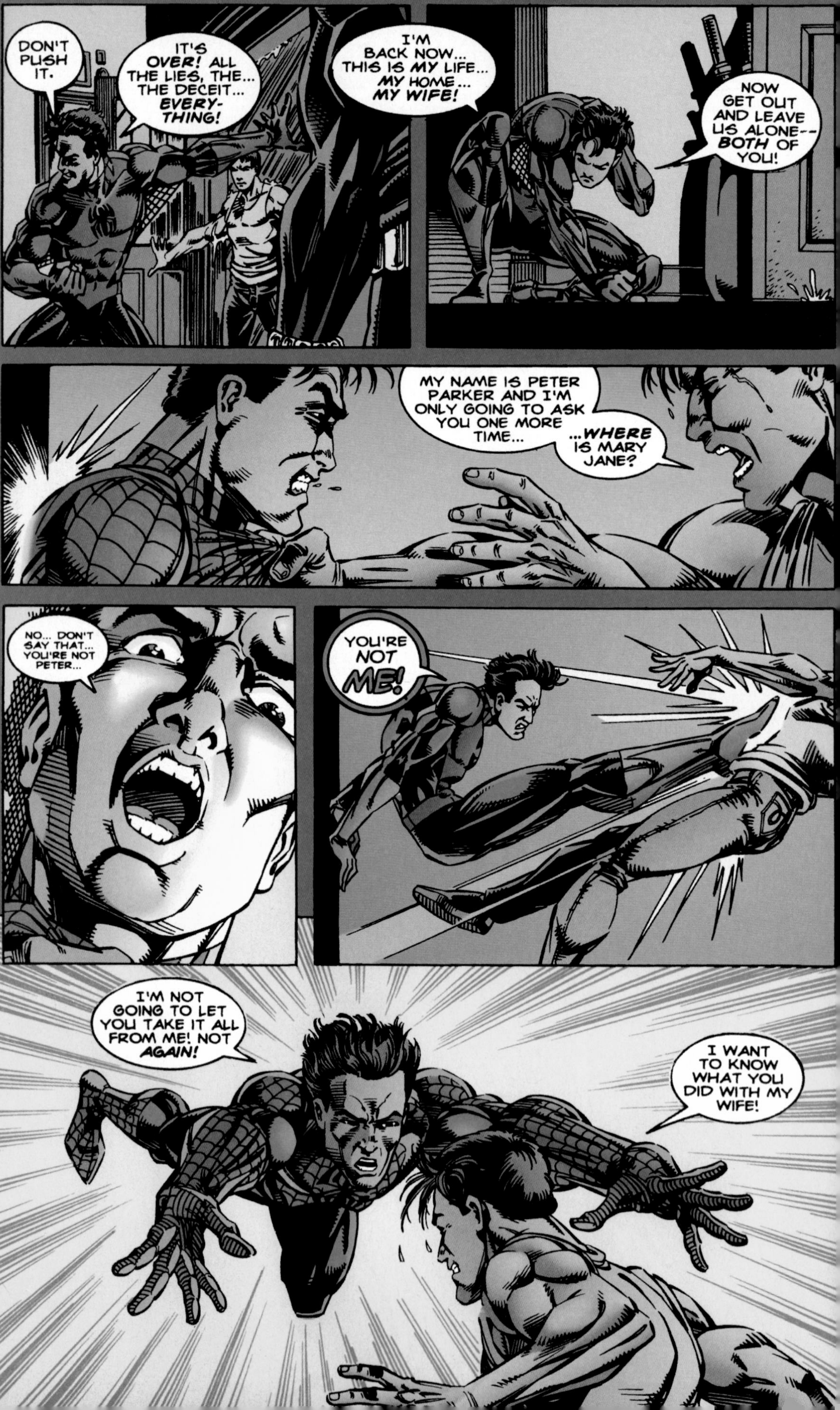
DON'T PUSH IT.
IT'S OVER! ALL THE LIES, THE... THE DECEIT... EVERY-THING!
I'M BACK NOW... THIS IS MY LIFE... MY HOME... MY WIFE!
NOW GET OUT AND LEAVE US ALONE-- BOTH OF YOU!
MY NAME IS PETER PARKER AND I'M ONLY GOING TO ASK YOU ONE MORE TIME...
...WHERE IS MARY JANE?
NO... DON'T SAY THAT... YOU'RE NOT PETER...
YOU'RE NOT ME!
I'M NOT GOING TO LET YOU TAKE IT ALL FROM ME! NOT AGAIN!
I WANT TO KNOW WHAT YOU DID WITH MY WIFE!

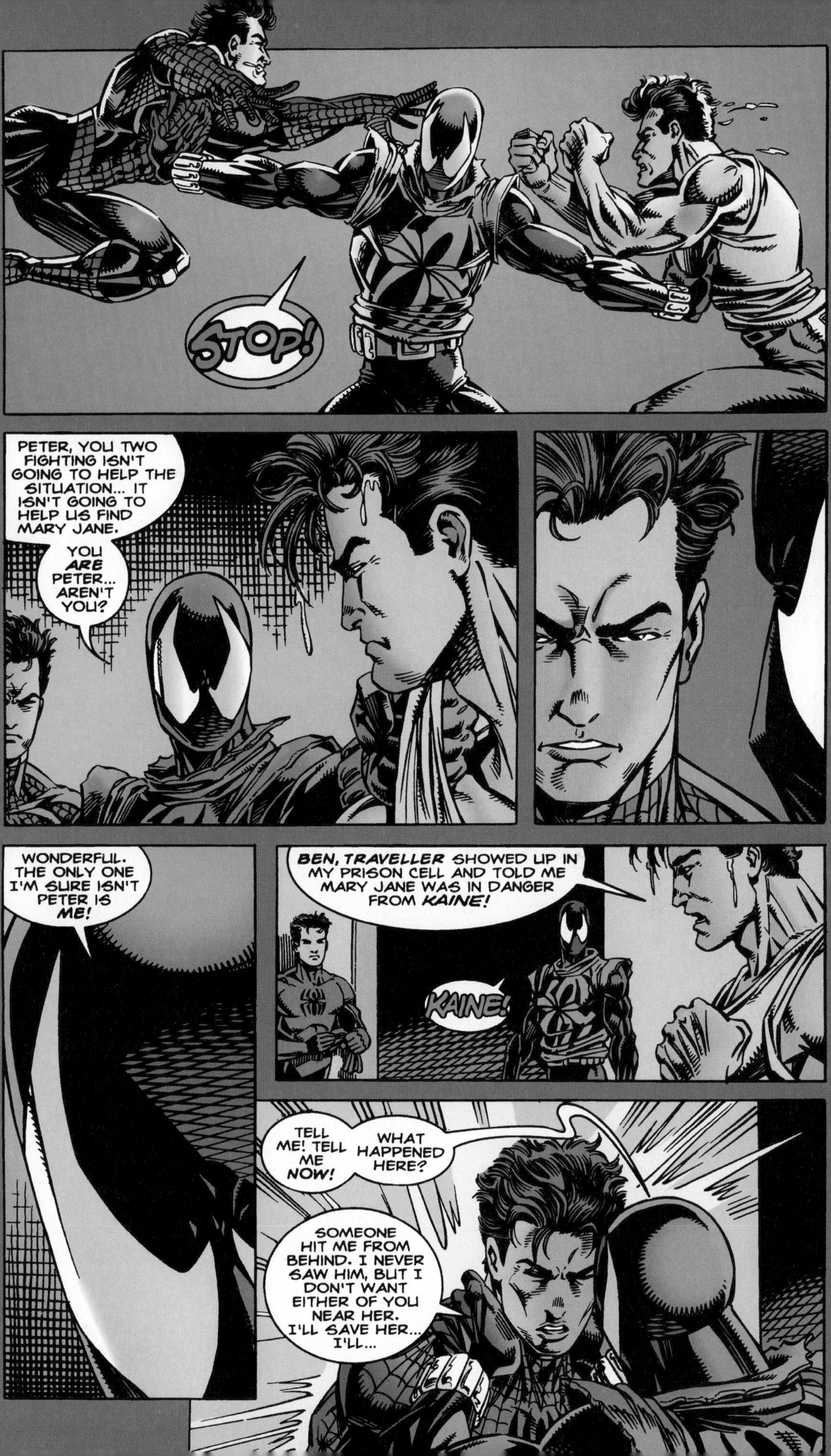
STOP!
PETER, YOU TWO FIGHTING ISN'T GOING TO HELP THE SITUATION... IT ISN'T GOING TO HELP US FIND MARY JANE.
YOU ARE PETER... AREN'T YOU?
WONDERFUL. THE ONLY ONE I'M SURE ISN'T PETER IS ME!
BEN, TRAVELLER SHOWED UP IN MY PRISON CELL AND TOLD ME MARY JANE WAS IN DANGER FROM KAINE!
KAINE!
WHAT HAPPENED HERE?
TELL ME! TELL ME NOW!
SOMEONE HIT ME FROM BEHIND. I NEVER SAW HIM, BUT I DON'T WANT EITHER OF YOU NEAR HER. I'LL SAVE HER... I'LL...

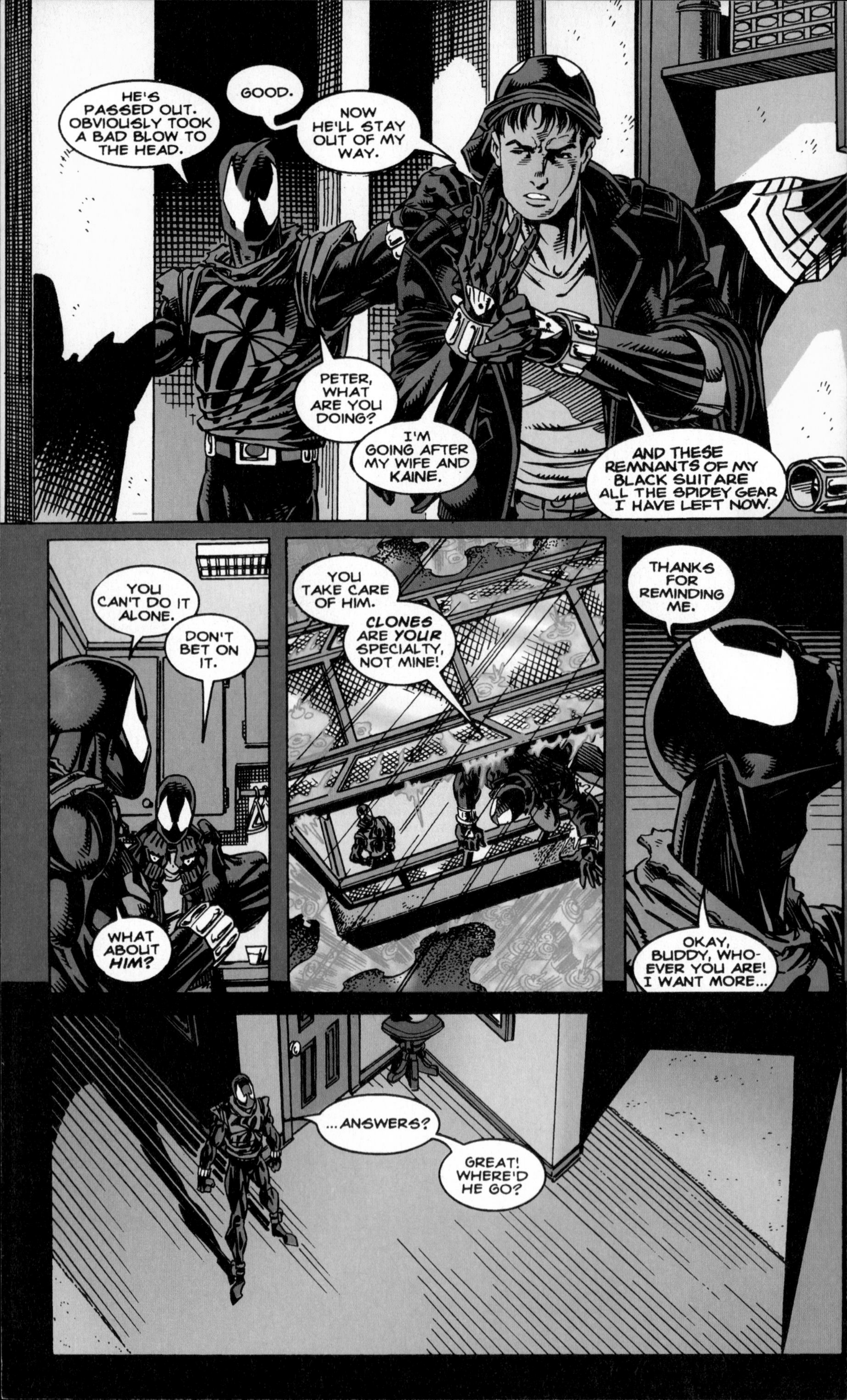
HE'S PASSED OUT. OBVIOUSLY TOOK A BAD BLOW TO THE HEAD.
GOOD.
NOW HE'LL STAY OUT OF MY WAY.
PETER, WHAT ARE YOU DOING?
I'M GOING AFTER MY WIFE AND KAINE.
AND THESE REMNANTS OF MY BLACK SUIT ARE ALL THE SPIDEY GEAR I HAVE LEFT NOW.
YOU CAN'T DO IT ALONE.
DON'T BET ON IT.
WHAT ABOUT *HIM*?
YOU TAKE CARE OF HIM.
CLONES ARE *YOUR* SPECIALTY, NOT MINE!
THANKS FOR REMINDING ME.
OKAY, BUDDY, WHO-EVER YOU ARE! I WANT MORE...
...ANSWERS?
GREAT! WHERE'D HE GO?

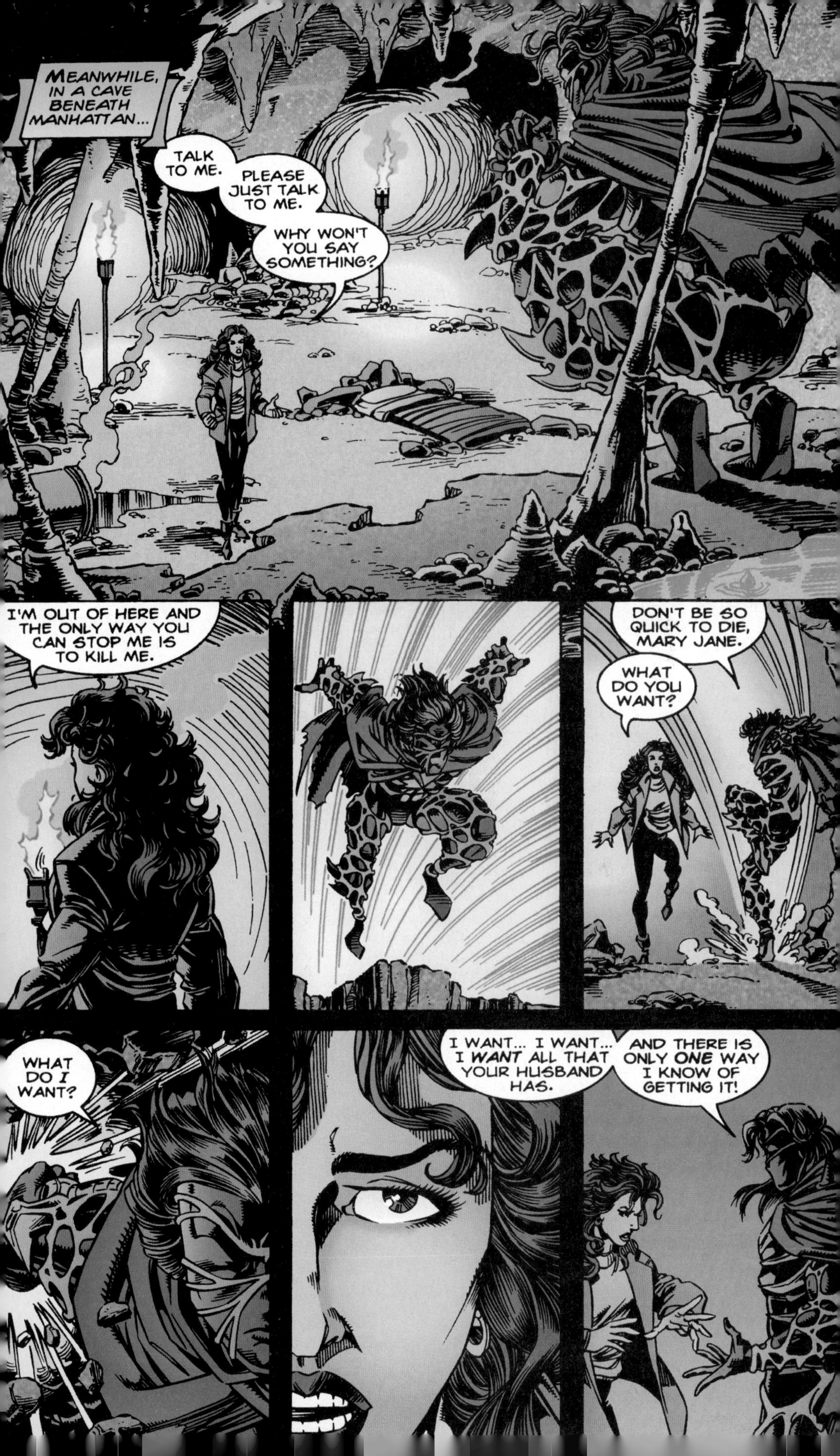
MEANWHILE, IN A CAVE BENEATH MANHATTAN...
TALK TO ME.
PLEASE JUST TALK TO ME.
WHY WON'T YOU SAY SOMETHING?
I'M OUT OF HERE AND THE ONLY WAY YOU CAN STOP ME IS TO KILL ME.
DON'T BE SO QUICK TO DIE, MARY JANE.
WHAT DO YOU WANT?
WHAT DO *I* WANT?
I WANT... I WANT... I *WANT* ALL THAT YOUR HUSBAND HAS.
AND THERE IS ONLY *ONE* WAY I KNOW OF GETTING IT!

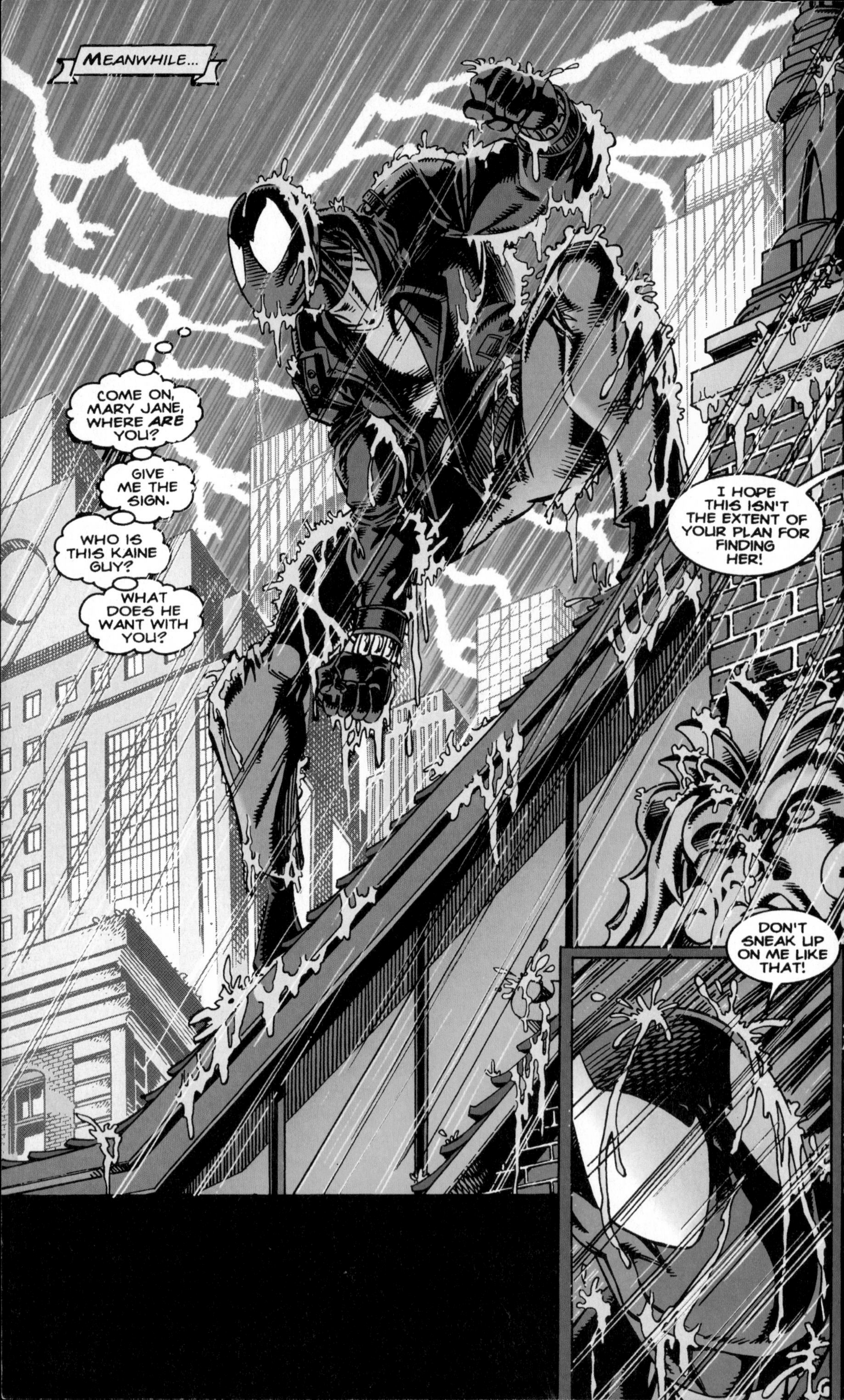
MEANWHILE...
COME ON, MARY JANE, WHERE ARE YOU?
GIVE ME THE SIGN.
WHO IS THIS KAINE GUY?
WHAT DOES HE WANT WITH YOU?
I HOPE THIS ISN'T THE EXTENT OF YOUR PLAN FOR FINDING HER!
DON'T SNEAK UP ON ME LIKE THAT!

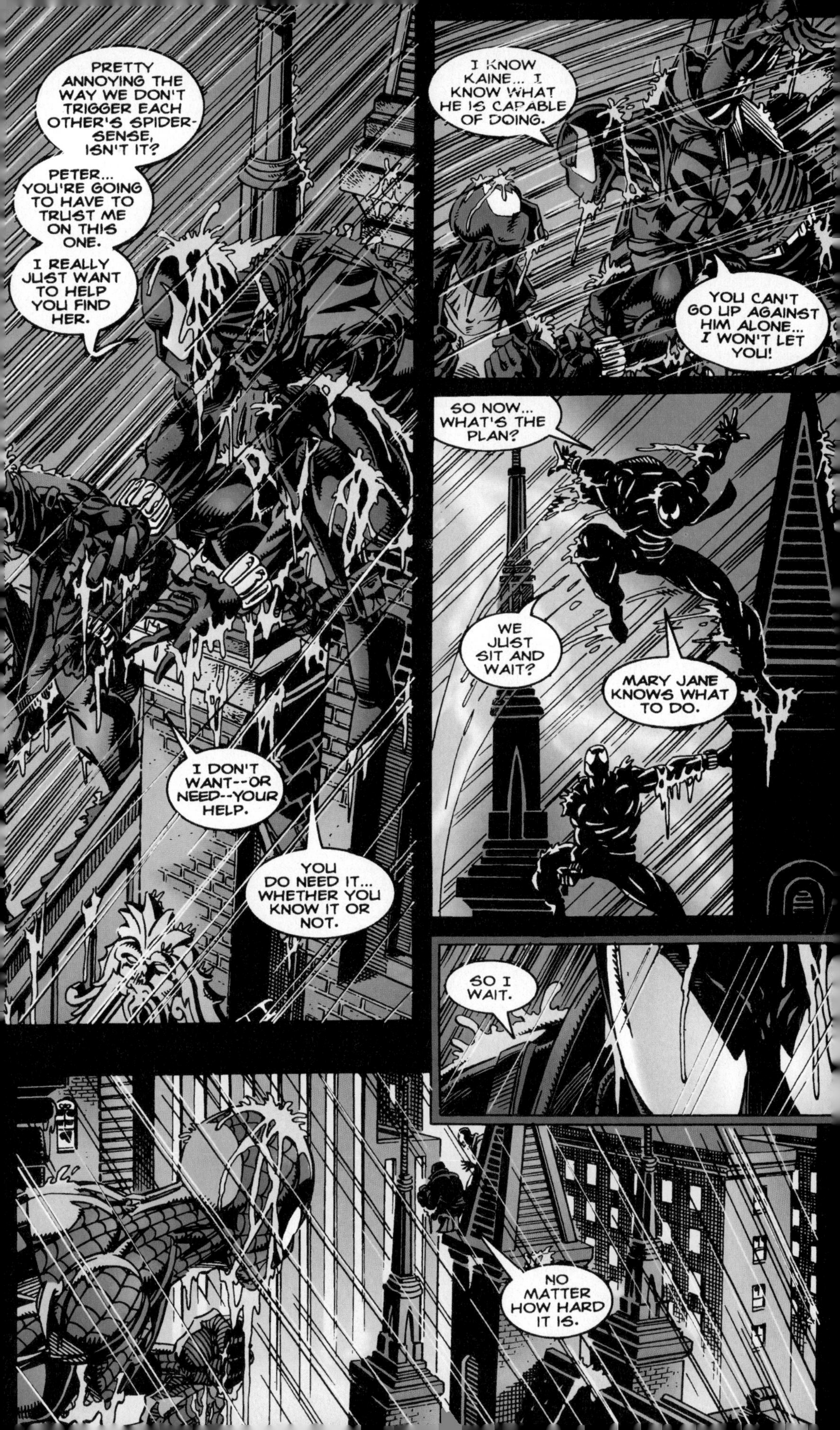
PRETTY ANNOYING THE WAY WE DON'T TRIGGER EACH OTHER'S SPIDER-SENSE, ISN'T IT?
PETER... YOU'RE GOING TO HAVE TO TRUST ME ON THIS ONE.
I REALLY JUST WANT TO HELP YOU FIND HER.
I DON'T WANT--OR NEED--YOUR HELP.
YOU DO NEED IT... WHETHER YOU KNOW IT OR NOT.
I KNOW KAINE... I KNOW WHAT HE IS CAPABLE OF DOING.
YOU CAN'T GO UP AGAINST HIM ALONE... I WON'T LET YOU!
SO NOW... WHAT'S THE PLAN?
WE JUST SIT AND WAIT?
MARY JANE KNOWS WHAT TO DO.
SO I WAIT.
NO MATTER HOW HARD IT IS.

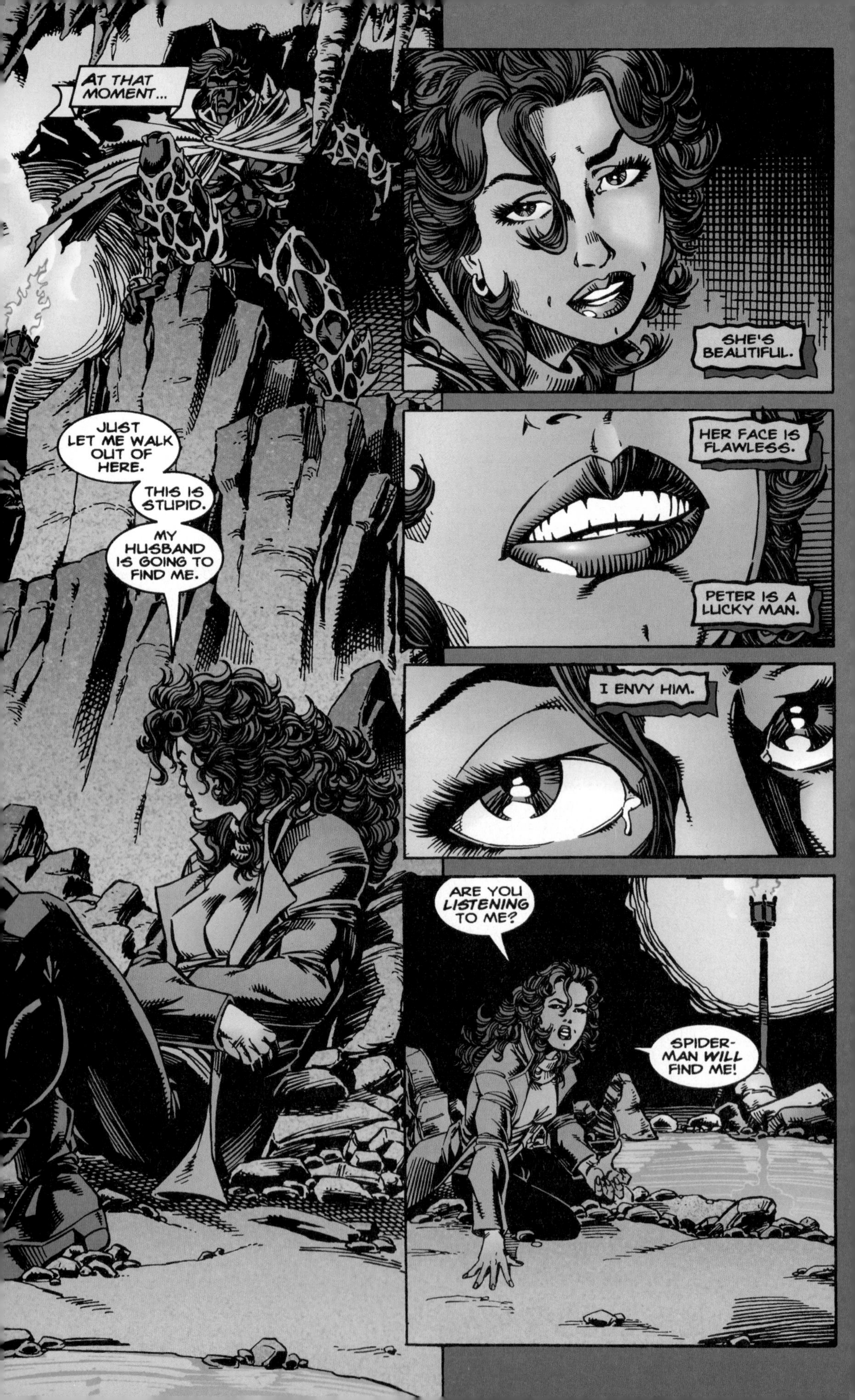
AT THAT MOMENT...
SHE'S BEAUTIFUL.
JUST LET ME WALK OUT OF HERE.
THIS IS STUPID.
MY HUSBAND IS GOING TO FIND ME.
HER FACE IS FLAWLESS.
PETER IS A LUCKY MAN.
I ENVY HIM.
ARE YOU LISTENING TO ME?
SPIDER-MAN WILL FIND ME!

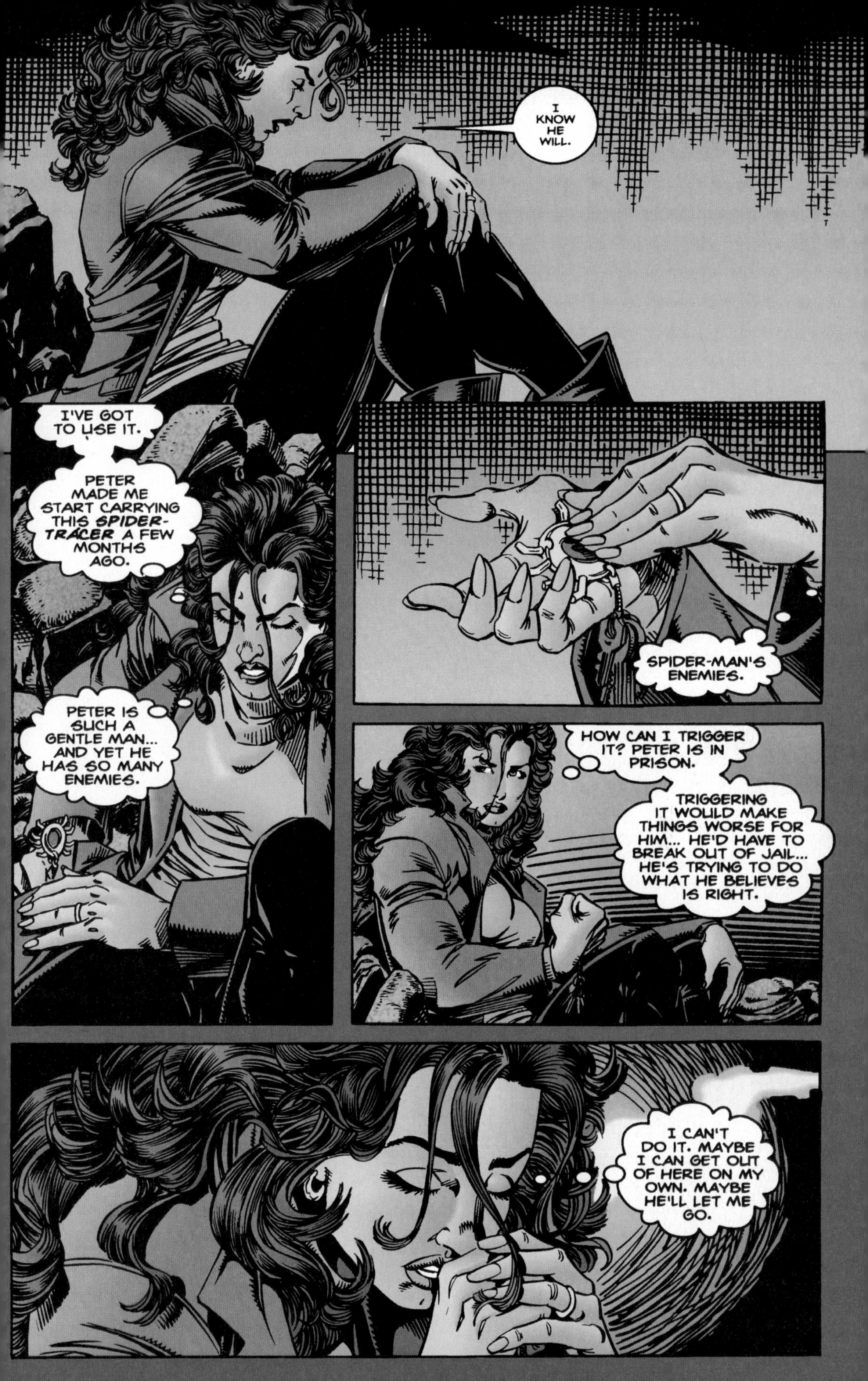
I KNOW HE WILL.
I'VE GOT TO USE IT.
PETER MADE ME START CARRYING THIS SPIDER-TRACER A FEW MONTHS AGO.
PETER IS SUCH A GENTLE MAN... AND YET HE HAS SO MANY ENEMIES.
SPIDER-MAN'S ENEMIES.
HOW CAN I TRIGGER IT? PETER IS IN PRISON.
TRIGGERING IT WOULD MAKE THINGS WORSE FOR HIM... HE'D HAVE TO BREAK OUT OF JAIL... HE'S TRYING TO DO WHAT HE BELIEVES IS RIGHT.
I CAN'T DO IT. MAYBE I CAN GET OUT OF HERE ON MY OWN. MAYBE HE'LL LET ME GO.

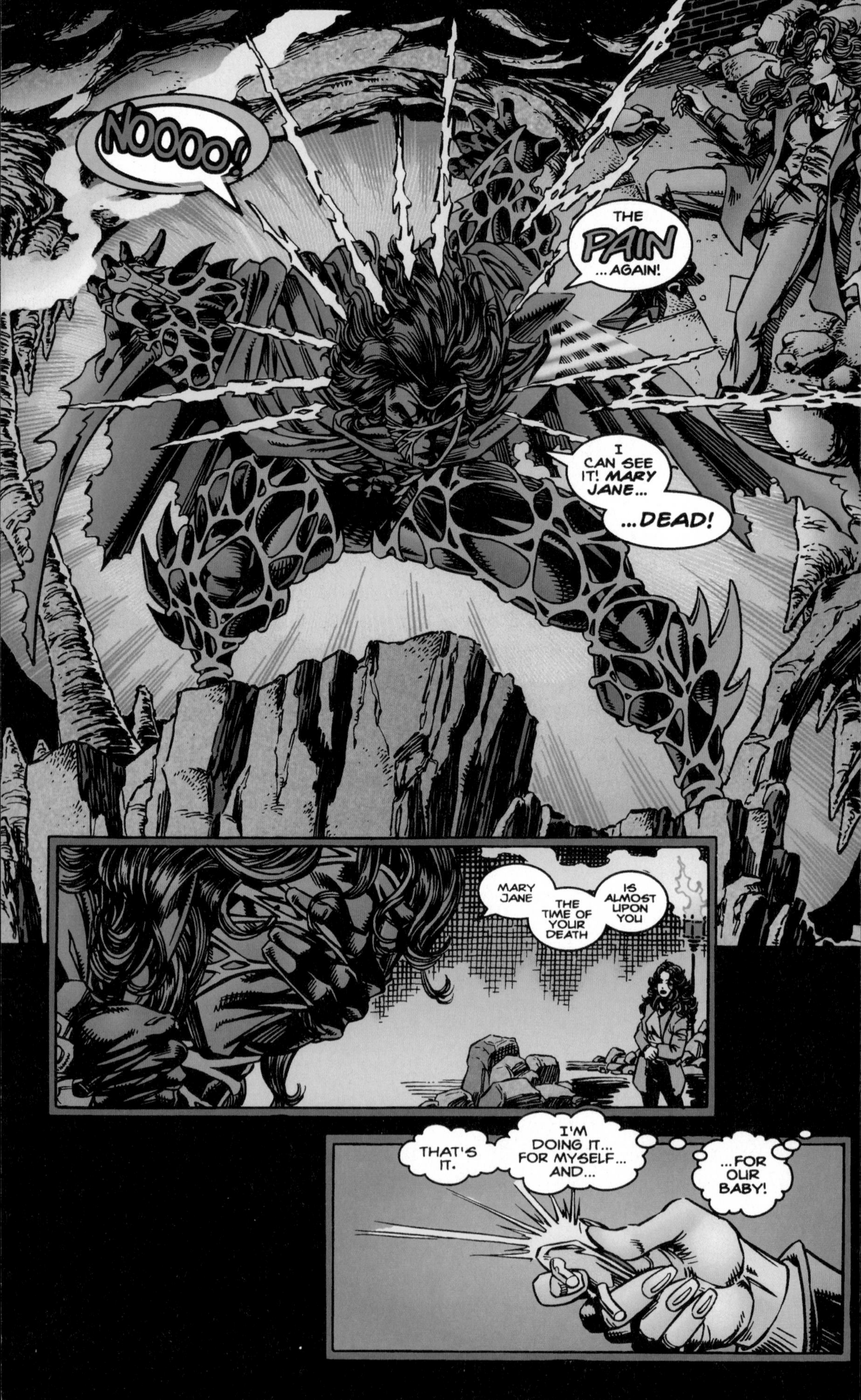
NOOOO!!
THE PAIN ...AGAIN!
I CAN SEE IT! MARY JANE...
...DEAD!
MARY JANE
THE TIME OF YOUR DEATH
IS ALMOST UPON YOU
THAT'S IT.
I'M DOING IT... FOR MYSELF... AND...
...FOR OUR BABY!

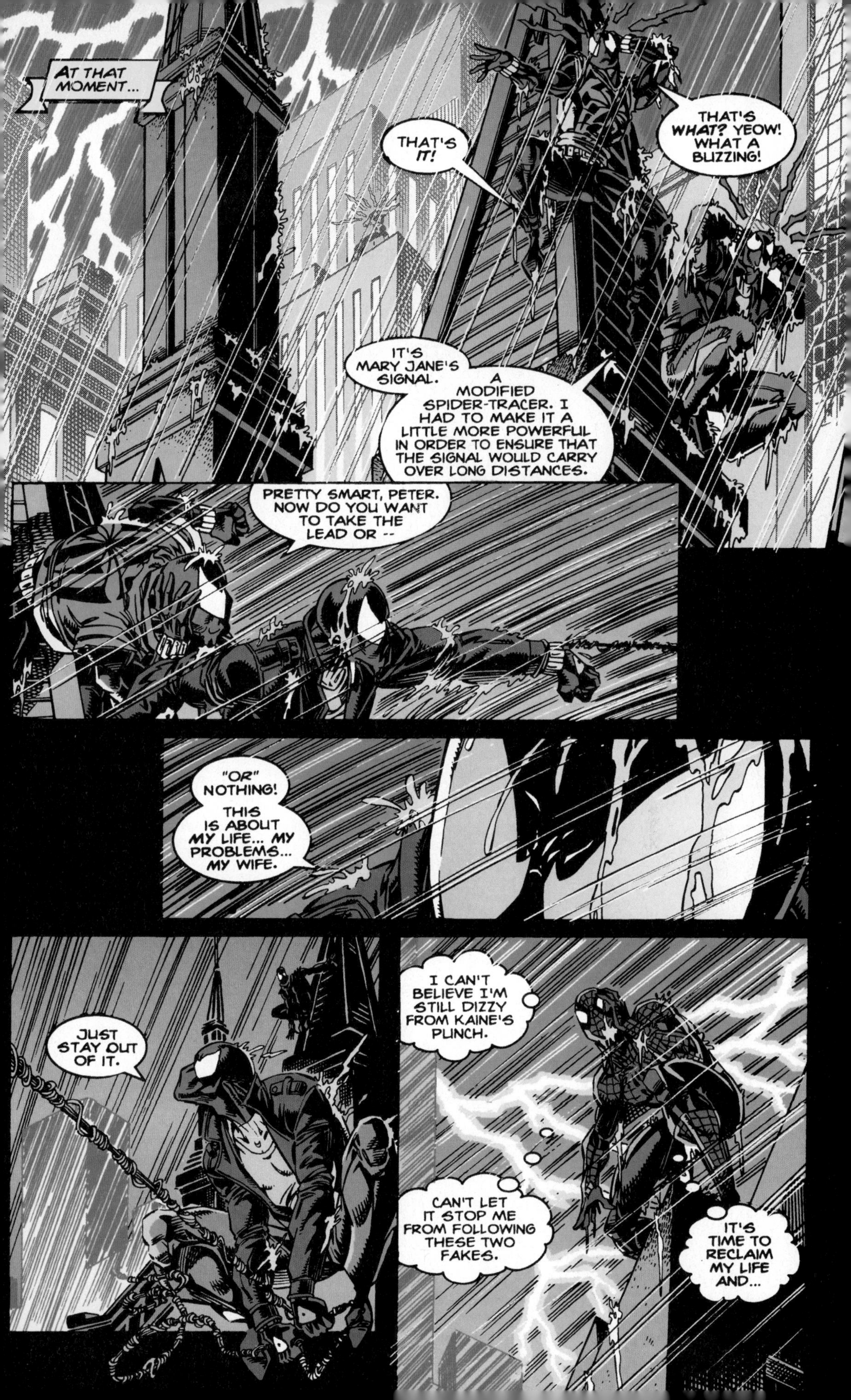
AT THAT MOMENT...
THAT'S IT!
THAT'S WHAT? YEOW! WHAT A BUZZING!
IT'S MARY JANE'S SIGNAL.
A MODIFIED SPIDER-TRACER. I HAD TO MAKE IT A LITTLE MORE POWERFUL IN ORDER TO ENSURE THAT THE SIGNAL WOULD CARRY OVER LONG DISTANCES.
PRETTY SMART, PETER. NOW DO YOU WANT TO TAKE THE LEAD OR --
"OR" NOTHING!
THIS IS ABOUT MY LIFE... MY PROBLEMS... MY WIFE.
JUST STAY OUT OF IT.
I CAN'T BELIEVE I'M STILL DIZZY FROM KAINE'S PUNCH.
CAN'T LET IT STOP ME FROM FOLLOWING THESE TWO FAKES.
IT'S TIME TO RECLAIM MY LIFE AND...

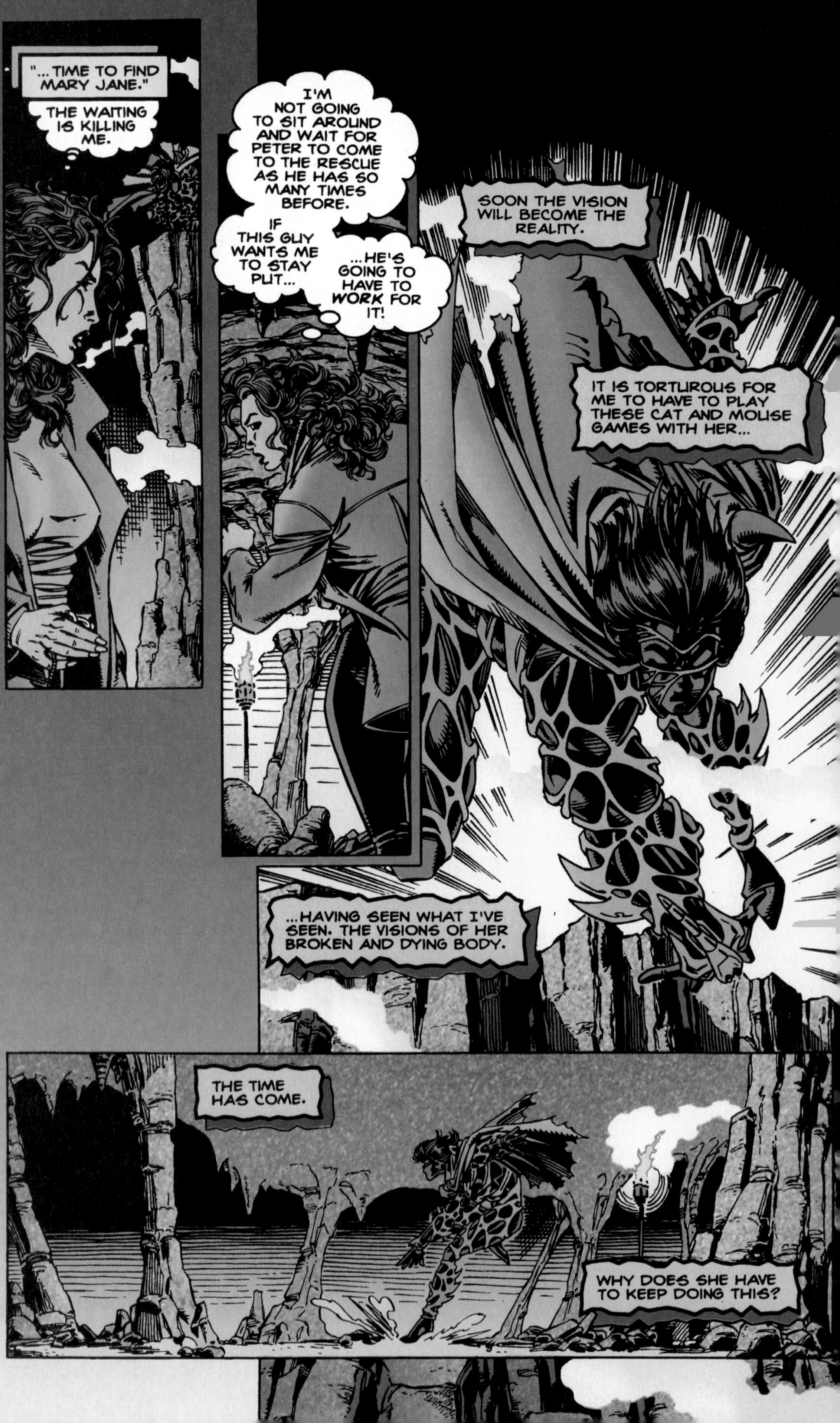
"...TIME TO FIND MARY JANE."
THE WAITING IS KILLING ME.
I'M NOT GOING TO SIT AROUND AND WAIT FOR PETER TO COME TO THE RESCUE AS HE HAS SO MANY TIMES BEFORE.
IF THIS GUY WANTS ME TO STAY PUT...
...HE'S GOING TO HAVE TO WORK FOR IT!
SOON THE VISION WILL BECOME THE REALITY.
IT IS TORTUROUS FOR ME TO HAVE TO PLAY THESE CAT AND MOUSE GAMES WITH HER...
...HAVING SEEN WHAT I'VE SEEN. THE VISIONS OF HER BROKEN AND DYING BODY.
THE TIME HAS COME.
WHY DOES SHE HAVE TO KEEP DOING THIS?

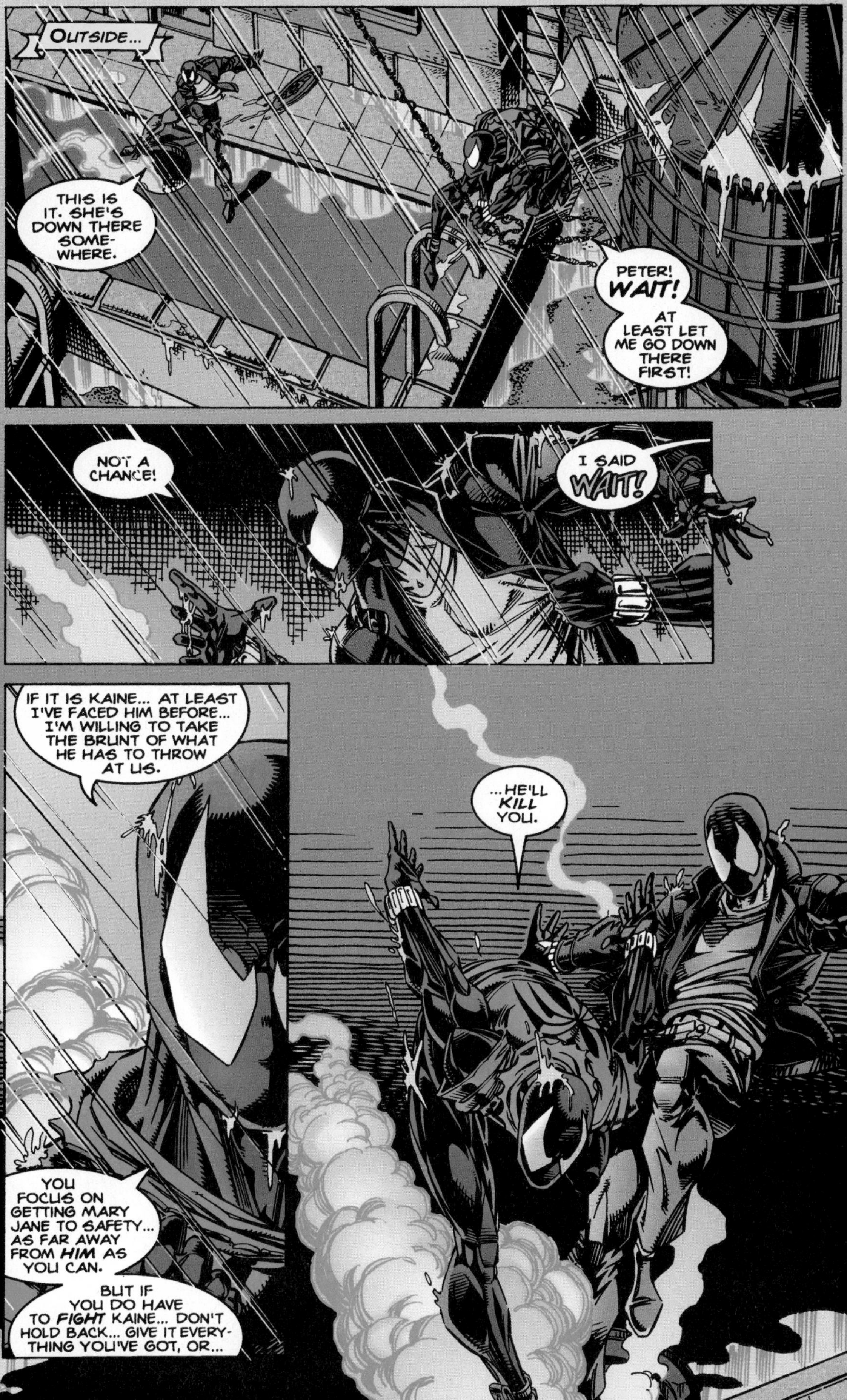
OUTSIDE...
THIS IS IT. SHE'S DOWN THERE SOME-WHERE.
PETER! WAIT!
AT LEAST LET ME GO DOWN THERE FIRST!
NOT A CHANCE!
I SAID WAIT!
IF IT IS KAINE... AT LEAST I'VE FACED HIM BEFORE... I'M WILLING TO TAKE THE BRUNT OF WHAT HE HAS TO THROW AT US.
YOU FOCUS ON GETTING MARY JANE TO SAFETY... AS FAR AWAY FROM HIM AS YOU CAN.
BUT IF YOU DO HAVE TO FIGHT KAINE... DON'T HOLD BACK... GIVE IT EVERY-THING YOU'VE GOT, OR...
...HE'LL KILL YOU.

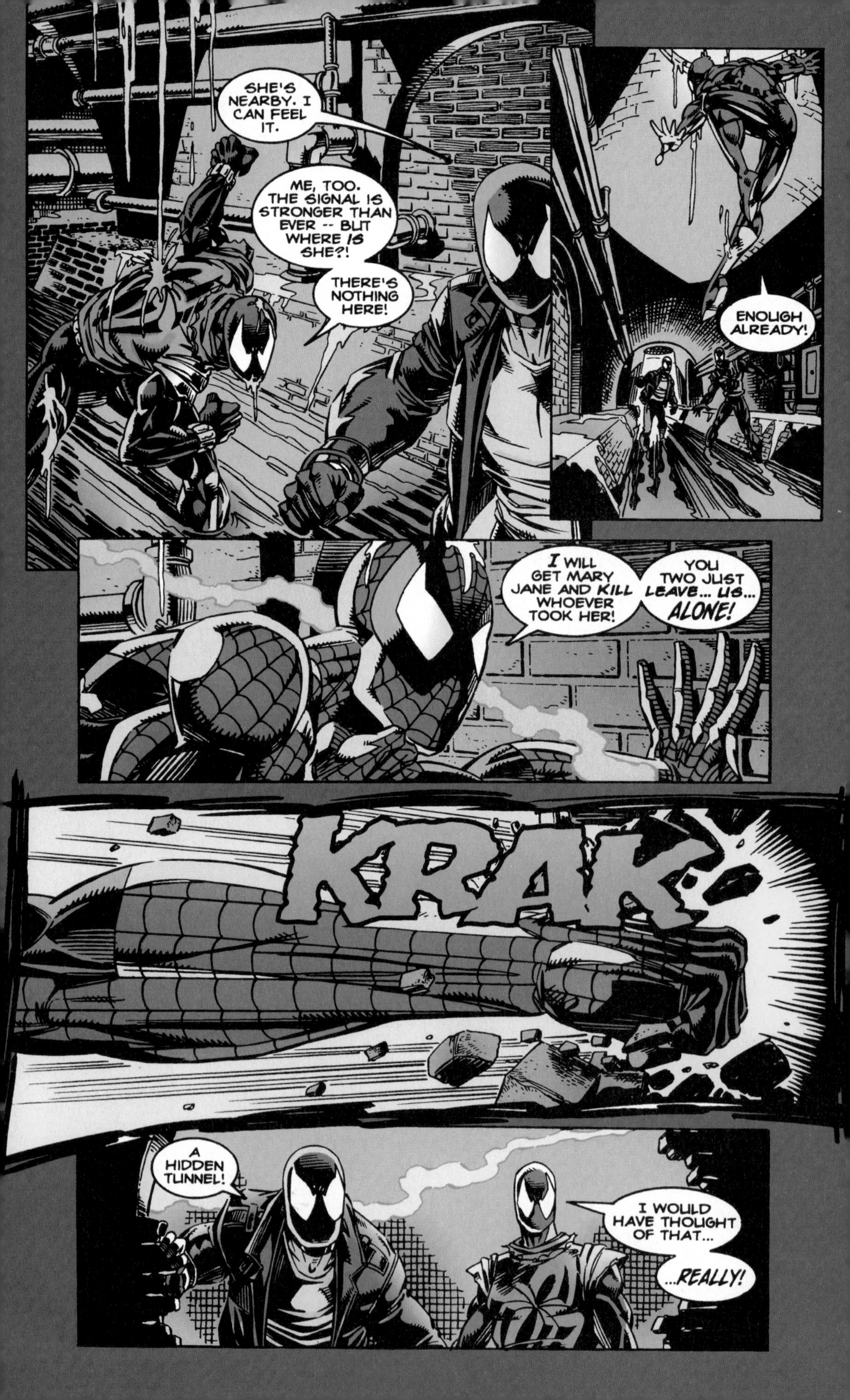
SHE'S NEARBY. I CAN FEEL IT.
ME, TOO. THE SIGNAL IS STRONGER THAN EVER -- BUT WHERE *IS* SHE?!
THERE'S NOTHING HERE!
ENOUGH ALREADY!
I WILL GET MARY JANE AND *KILL* WHOEVER TOOK HER!
YOU TWO JUST *LEAVE*... *US*... *ALONE!*
KRAK
A HIDDEN TUNNEL!
I WOULD HAVE THOUGHT OF THAT...
...*REALLY!*

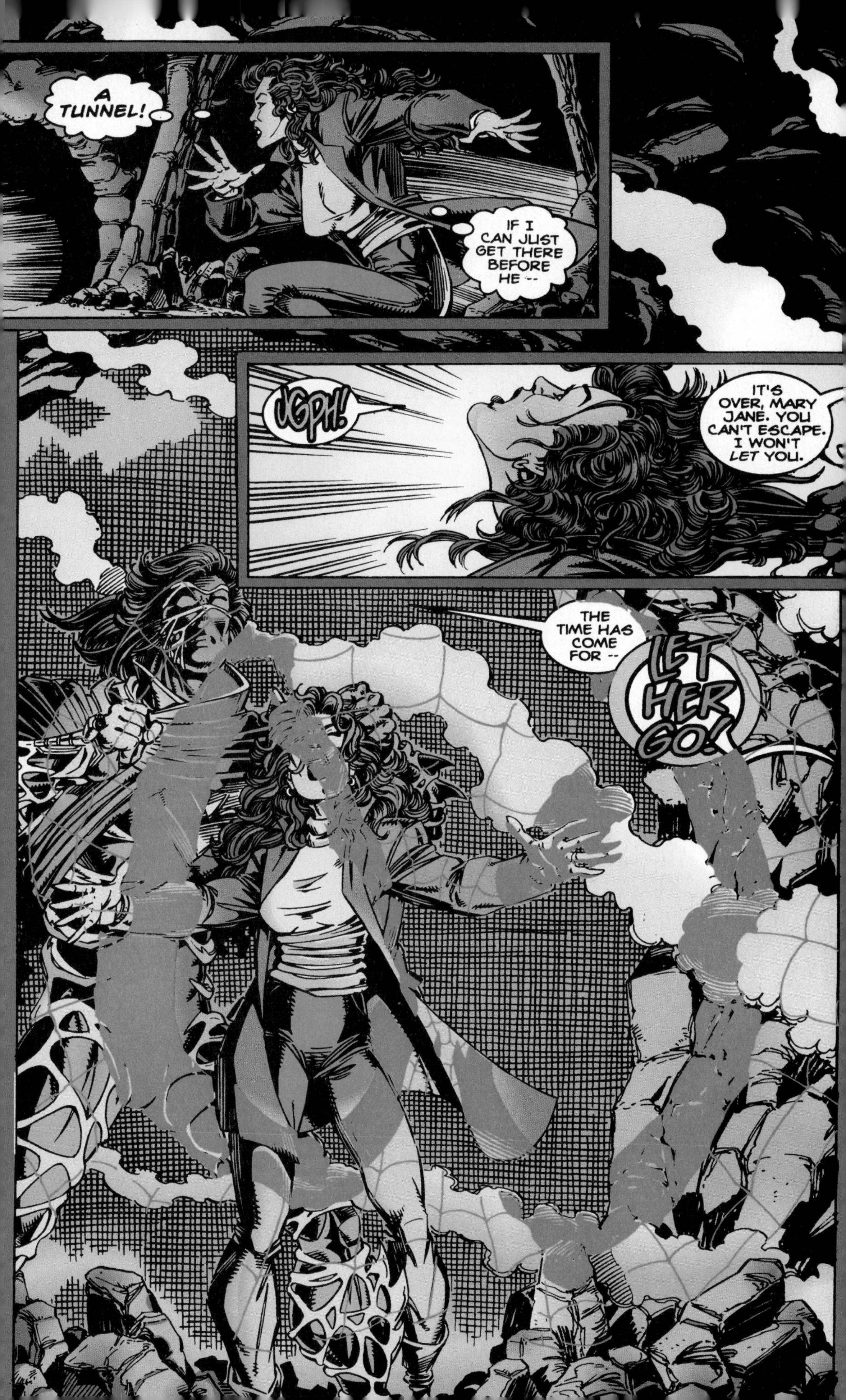
A TUNNEL!
IF I CAN JUST GET THERE BEFORE HE --
UGH!
IT'S OVER, MARY JANE. YOU CAN'T ESCAPE. I WON'T *LET* YOU.
THE TIME HAS COME FOR --
LET HER GO!

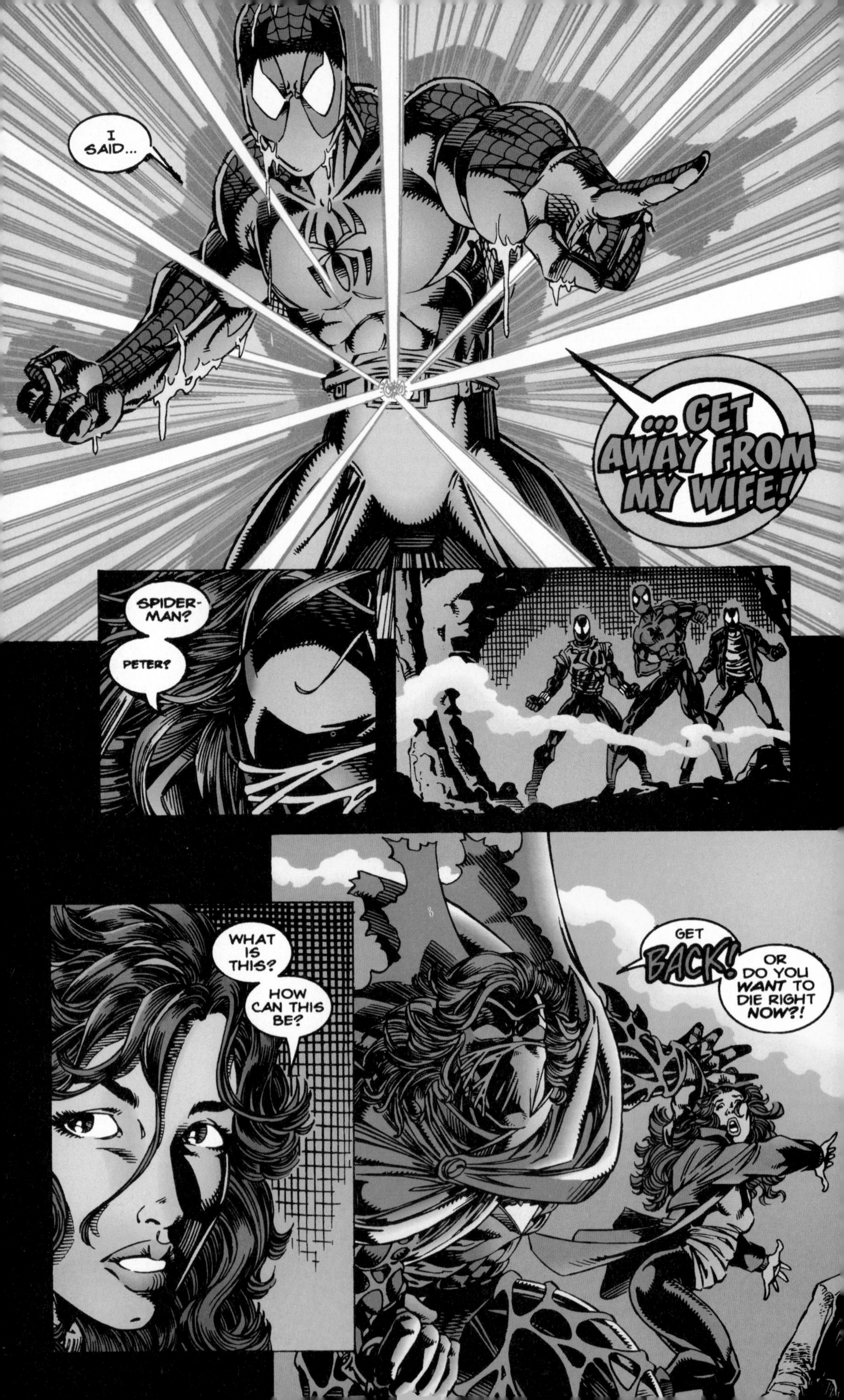
I SAID...
...GET AWAY FROM MY WIFE!
SPIDER-MAN?
PETER?
WHAT IS THIS?
HOW CAN THIS BE?
GET BACK!
OR DO YOU WANT TO DIE RIGHT NOW?!

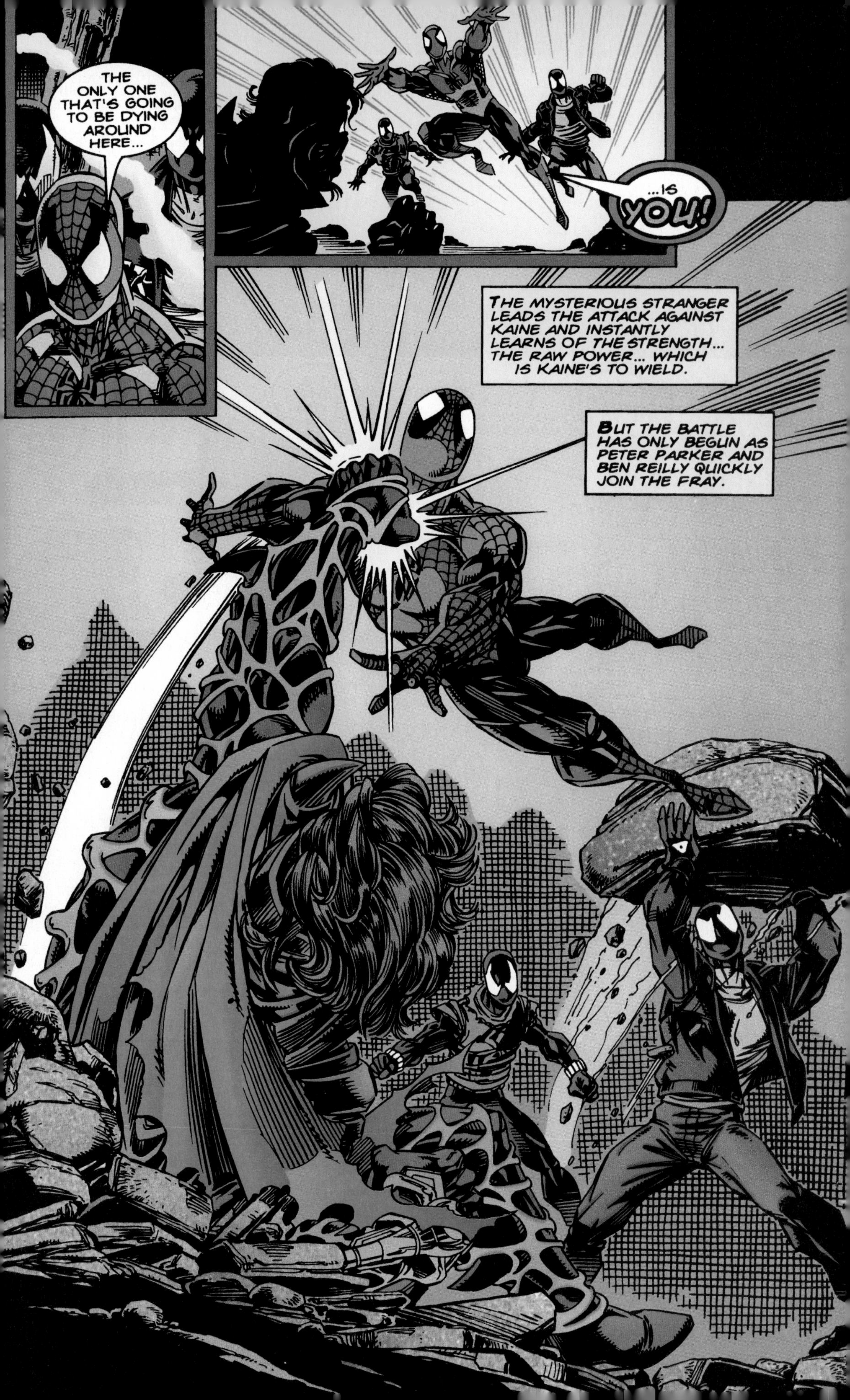
THE ONLY ONE THAT'S GOING TO BE DYING AROUND HERE...
...IS YOU!
THE MYSTERIOUS STRANGER LEADS THE ATTACK AGAINST KAINE AND INSTANTLY LEARNS OF THE STRENGTH... THE RAW POWER... WHICH IS KAINE'S TO WIELD.
BUT THE BATTLE HAS ONLY BEGUN AS PETER PARKER AND BEN REILLY QUICKLY JOIN THE FRAY.

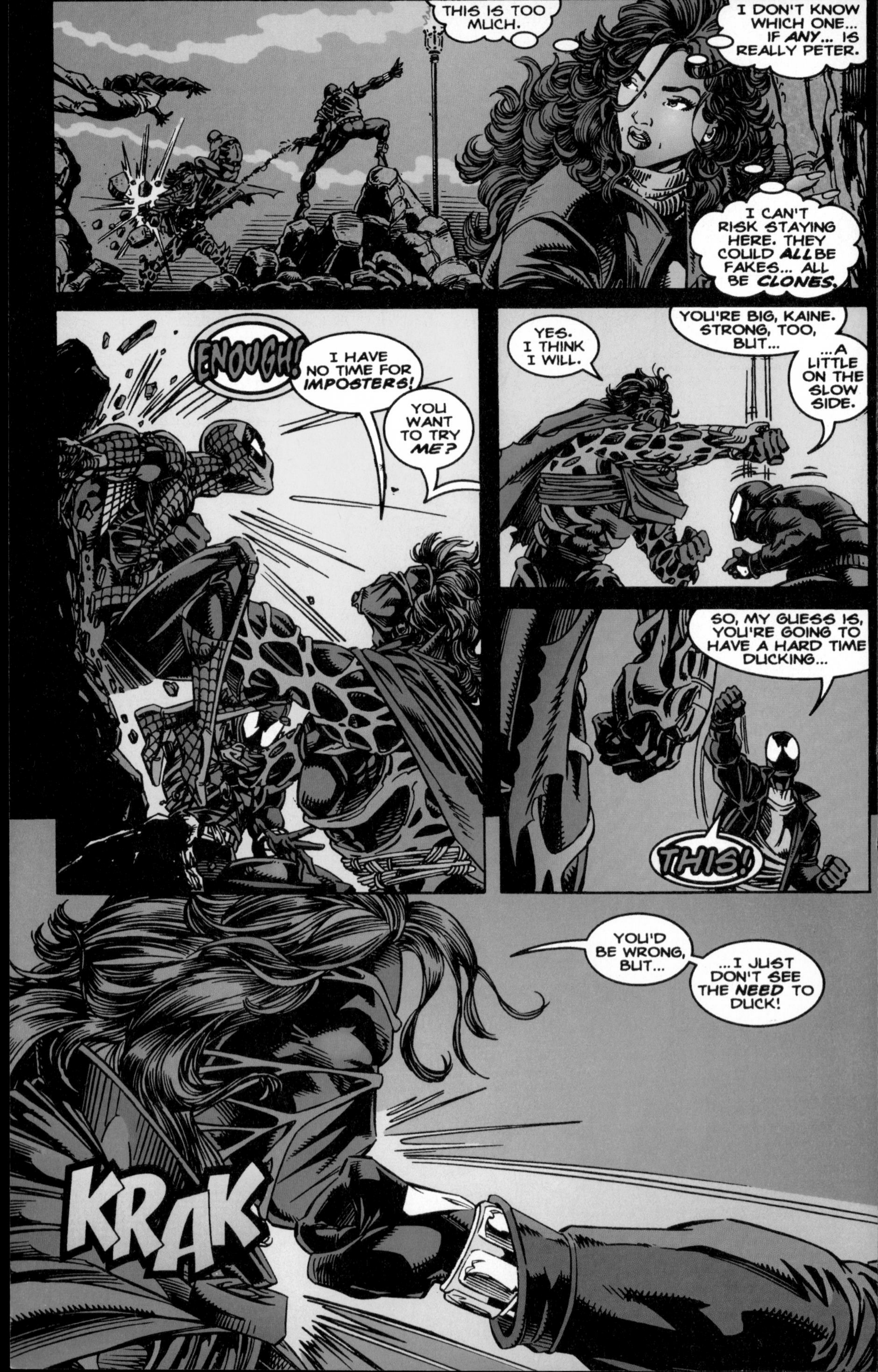
THIS IS TOO MUCH.
I DON'T KNOW WHICH ONE... IF ANY... IS REALLY PETER.
I CAN'T RISK STAYING HERE. THEY COULD ALL BE FAKES... ALL BE CLONES.
ENOUGH!
I HAVE NO TIME FOR IMPOSTERS!
YOU WANT TO TRY ME?
YES. I THINK I WILL.
YOU'RE BIG, KAINE. STRONG, TOO, BUT...
...A LITTLE ON THE SLOW SIDE.
SO, MY GUESS IS, YOU'RE GOING TO HAVE A HARD TIME DUCKING...
THIS!
YOU'D BE WRONG, BUT...
...I JUST DON'T SEE THE NEED TO DUCK!
KRAK

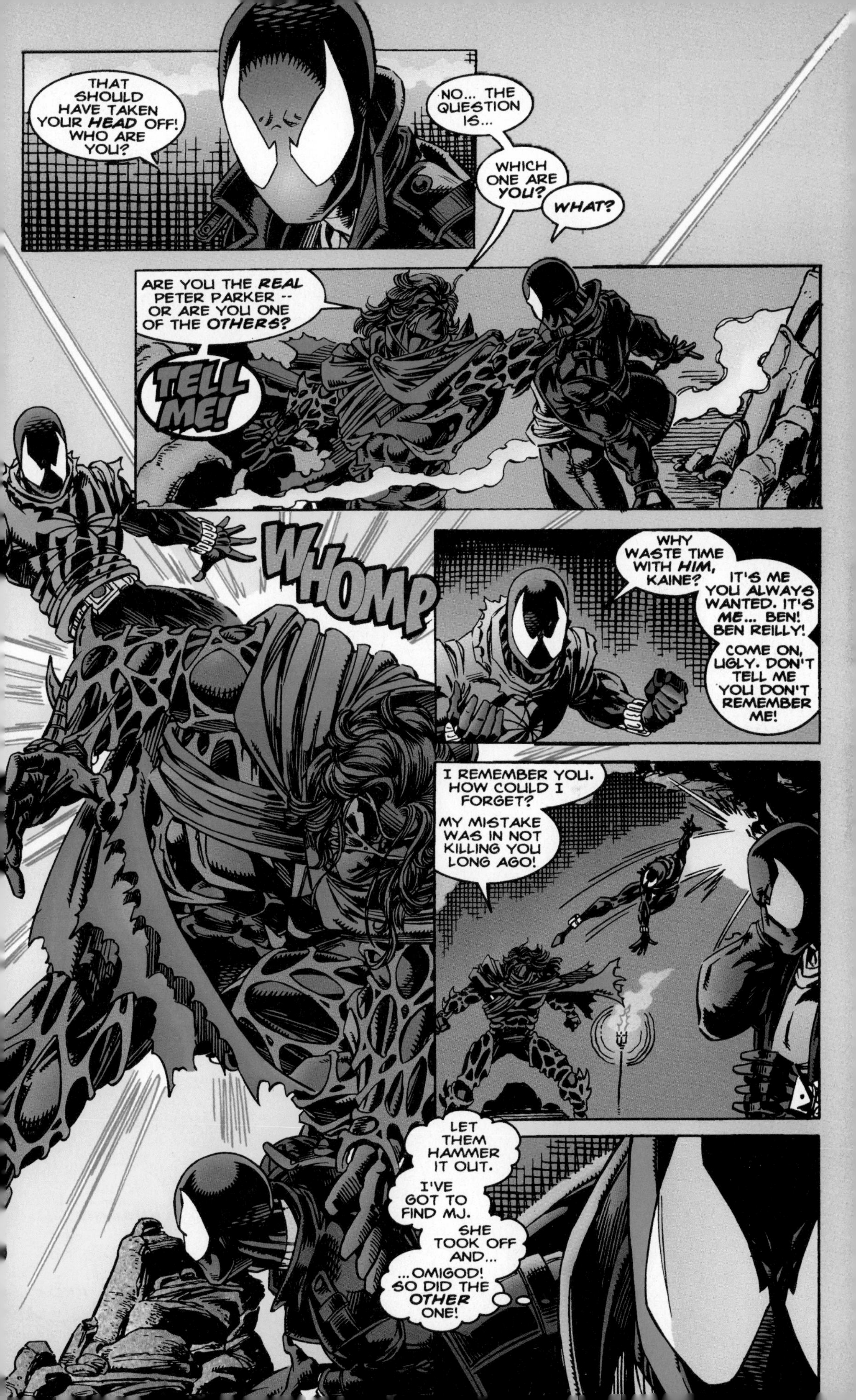
THAT SHOULD HAVE TAKEN YOUR HEAD OFF! WHO ARE YOU?
NO... THE QUESTION IS...
WHICH ONE ARE YOU?
WHAT?
ARE YOU THE REAL PETER PARKER -- OR ARE YOU ONE OF THE OTHERS?
TELL ME!
WHOMP
WHY WASTE TIME WITH HIM, KAINE?
IT'S ME YOU ALWAYS WANTED. IT'S ME... BEN! BEN REILLY!
COME ON, UGLY. DON'T TELL ME YOU DON'T REMEMBER ME!
I REMEMBER YOU. HOW COULD I FORGET?
MY MISTAKE WAS IN NOT KILLING YOU LONG AGO!
LET THEM HAMMER IT OUT.
I'VE GOT TO FIND MJ.
SHE TOOK OFF AND...
...OMIGOD! SO DID THE OTHER ONE!

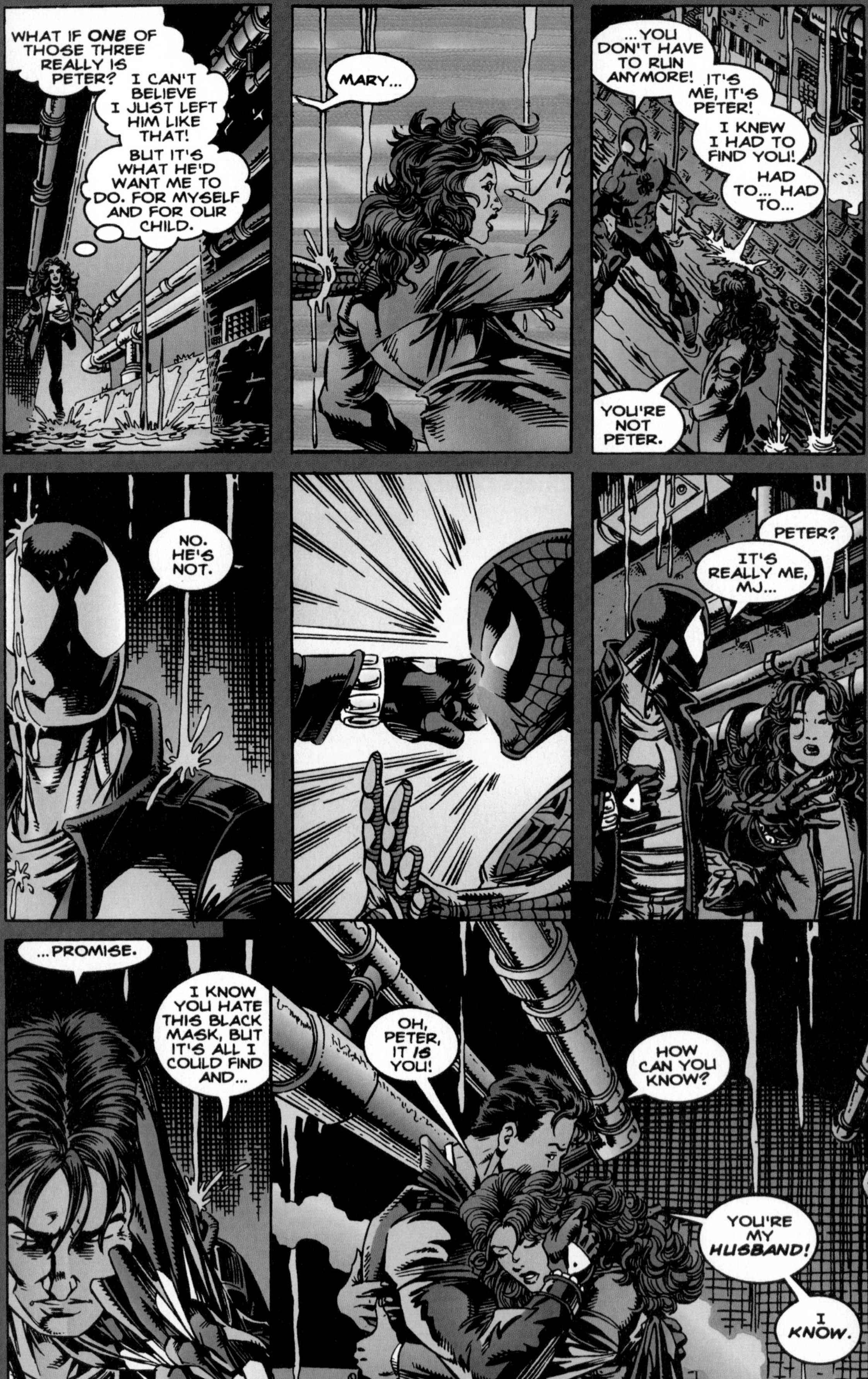
WHAT IF ONE OF THOSE THREE REALLY IS PETER?
I CAN'T BELIEVE I JUST LEFT HIM LIKE THAT!
BUT IT'S WHAT HE'D WANT ME TO DO. FOR MYSELF AND FOR OUR CHILD.
MARY...
...YOU DON'T HAVE TO RUN ANYMORE!
IT'S ME, IT'S PETER!
I KNEW I HAD TO FIND YOU!
HAD TO... HAD TO...
YOU'RE NOT PETER.
NO. HE'S NOT.
PETER?
IT'S REALLY ME, MJ...
...PROMISE.
I KNOW YOU HATE THIS BLACK MASK, BUT IT'S ALL I COULD FIND AND...
OH, PETER, IT IS YOU!
HOW CAN YOU KNOW?
YOU'RE MY HUSBAND!
I KNOW.

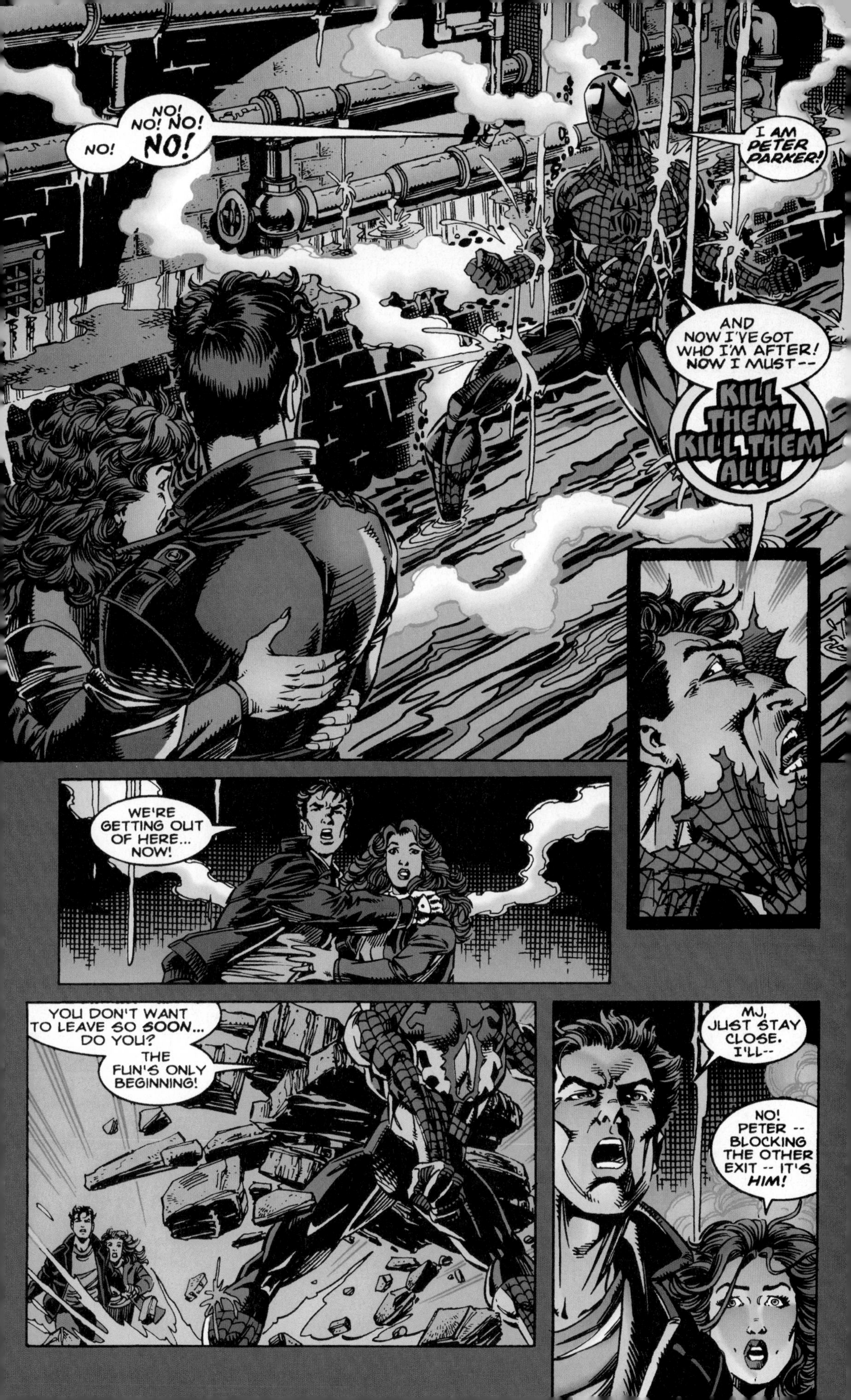
NO!
NO! NO! NO!
NO!
I AM PETER PARKER!
AND NOW I'VE GOT WHO I'M AFTER! NOW I MUST --
KILL THEM! KILL THEM ALL!
WE'RE GETTING OUT OF HERE... NOW!
YOU DON'T WANT TO LEAVE SO SOON... DO YOU?
THE FUN'S ONLY BEGINNING!
MJ, JUST STAY CLOSE. I'LL--
NO! PETER -- BLOCKING THE OTHER EXIT -- IT'S HIM!

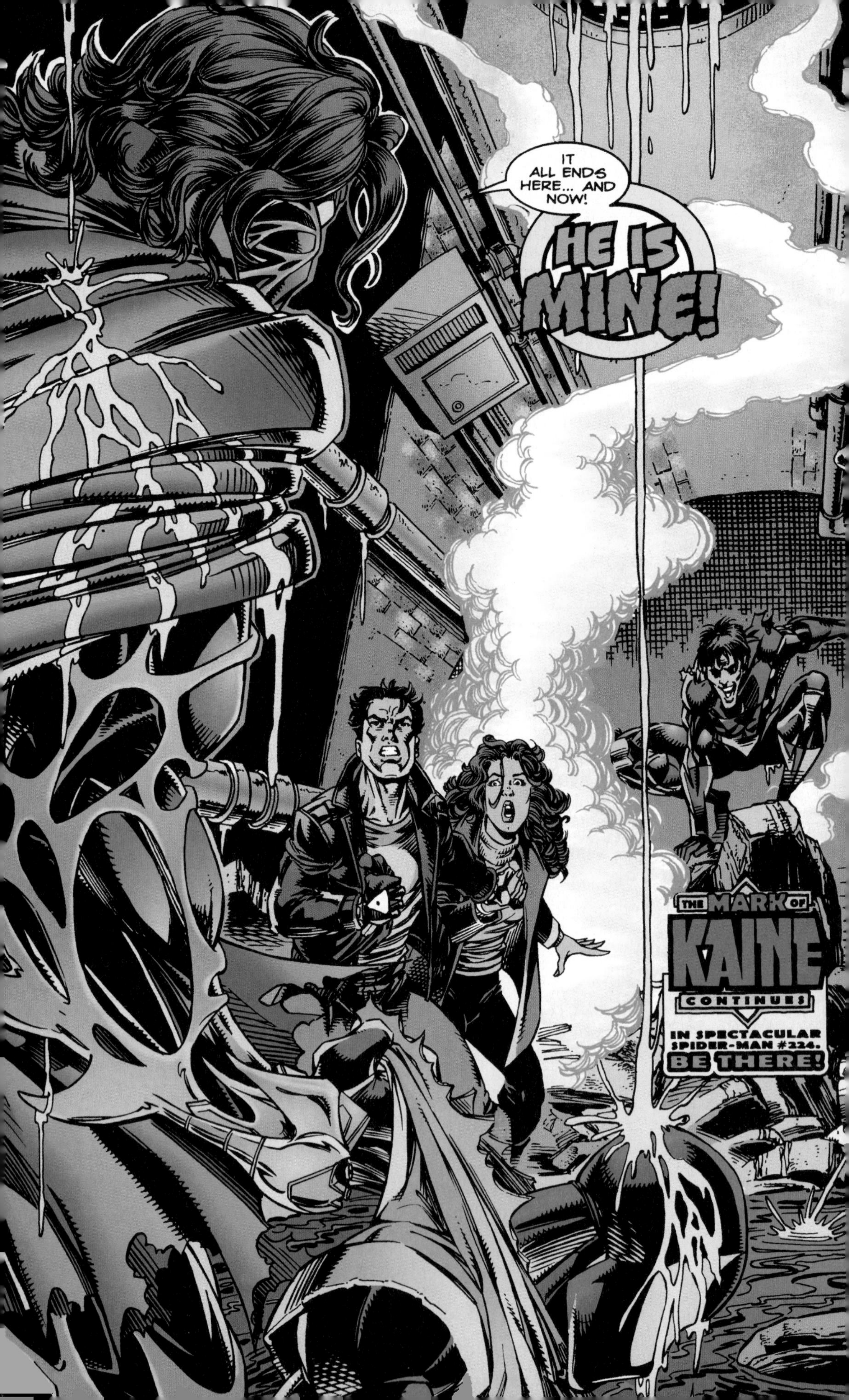
IT ALL ENDS HERE... AND NOW!
HE IS MINE!
THE MARK OF KAINE CONTINUES
IN SPECTACULAR SPIDER-MAN #224.
BE THERE!

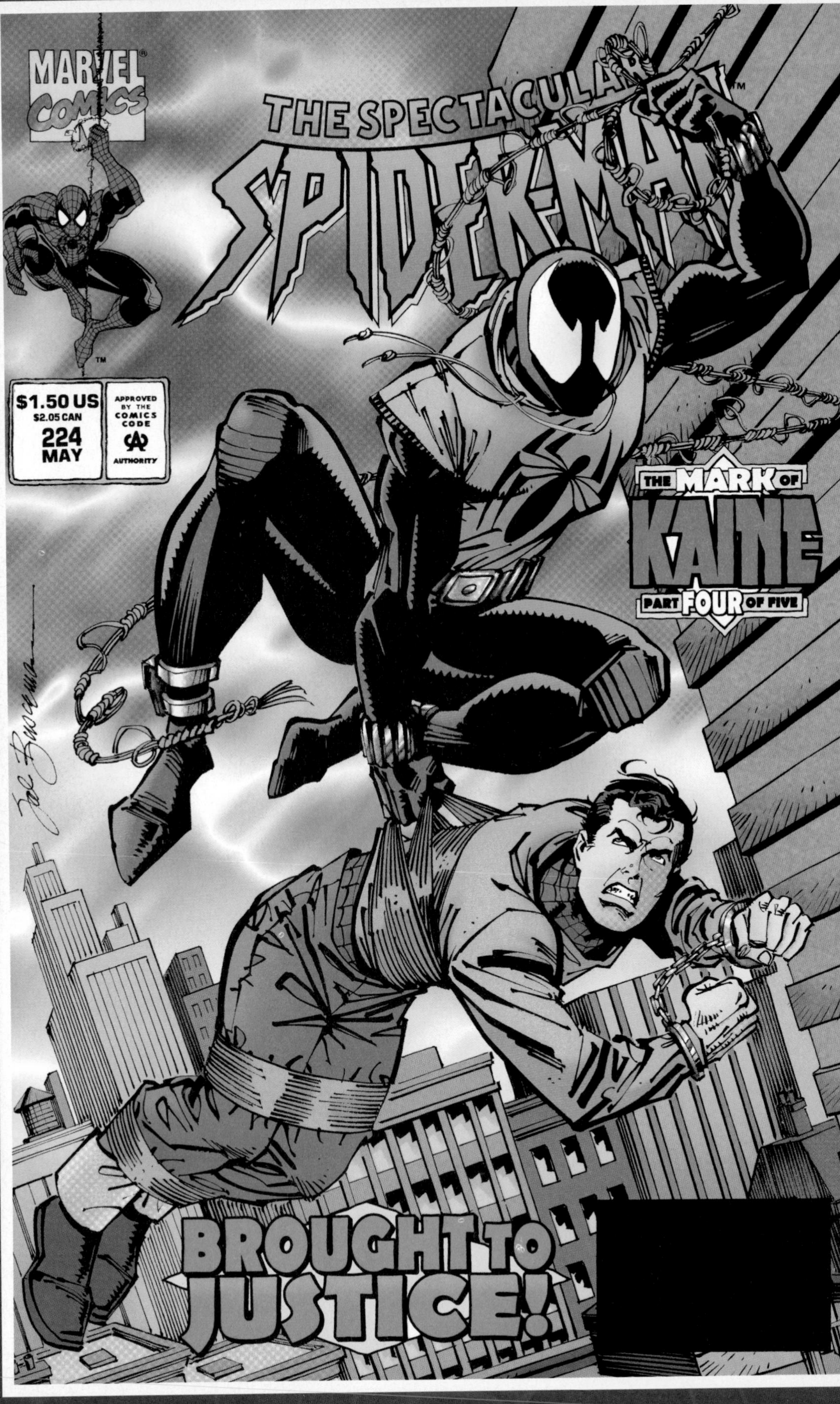
MARVEL COMICS
THE SPECTACULAR SPIDER-MAN
$1.50 US
$2.05 CAN
224
MAY
APPROVED BY THE COMICS CODE AUTHORITY
THE MARK OF KAINE
PART FOUR OF FIVE
BROUGHT TO JUSTICE!

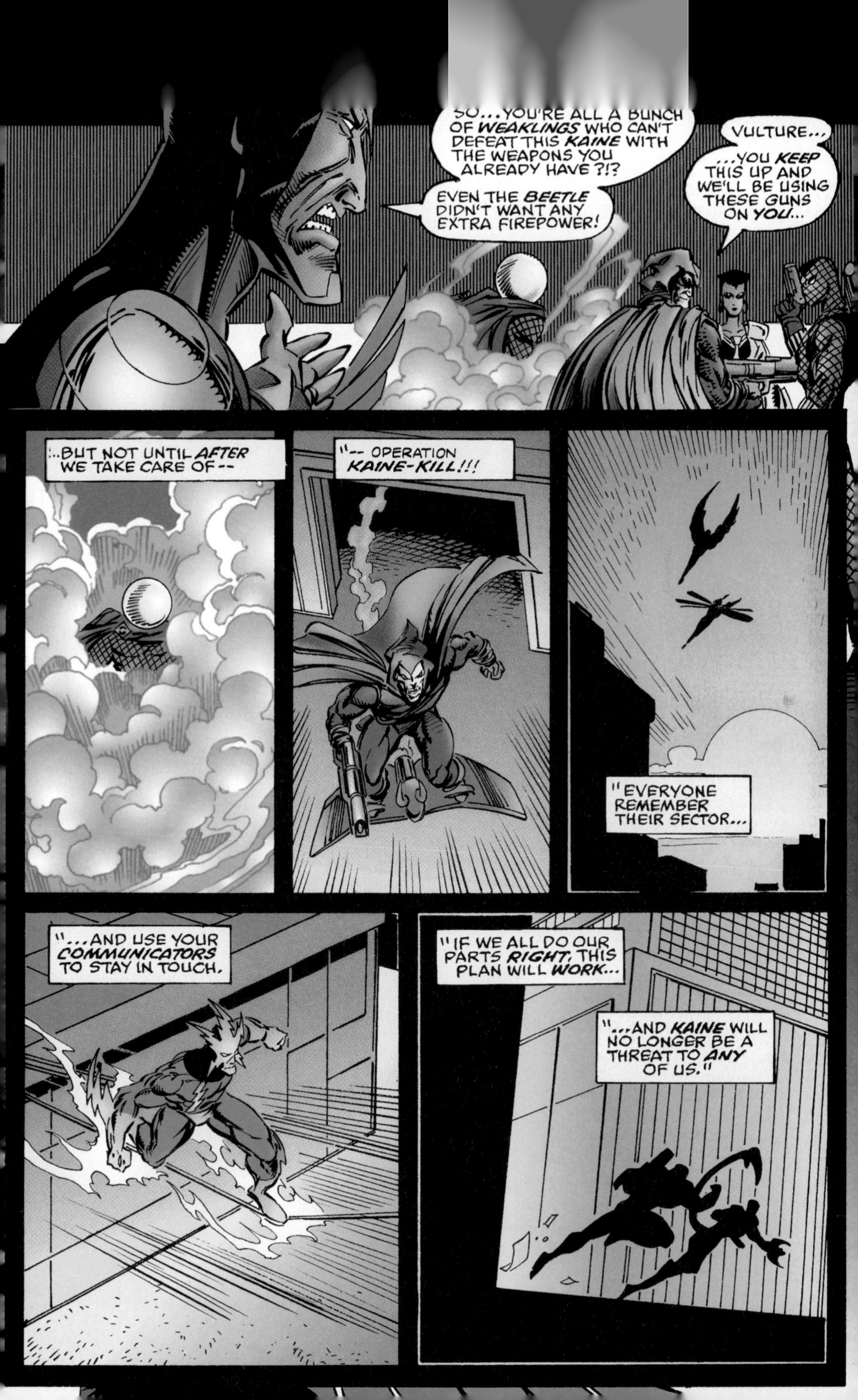

SO... YOU'RE ALL A BUNCH OF WEAKLINGS WHO CAN'T DEFEAT THIS KAINE WITH THE WEAPONS YOU ALREADY HAVE?!?
EVEN THE BEETLE DIDN'T WANT ANY EXTRA FIREPOWER!
VULTURE...
...YOU KEEP THIS UP AND WE'LL BE USING THESE GUNS ON YOU...
"...BUT NOT UNTIL AFTER WE TAKE CARE OF --
"-- OPERATION KAINE-KILL!!!
"EVERYONE REMEMBER THEIR SECTOR...
"...AND USE YOUR COMMUNICATORS TO STAY IN TOUCH.
"IF WE ALL DO OUR PARTS RIGHT, THIS PLAN WILL WORK...
"...AND KAINE WILL NO LONGER BE A THREAT TO ANY OF US."

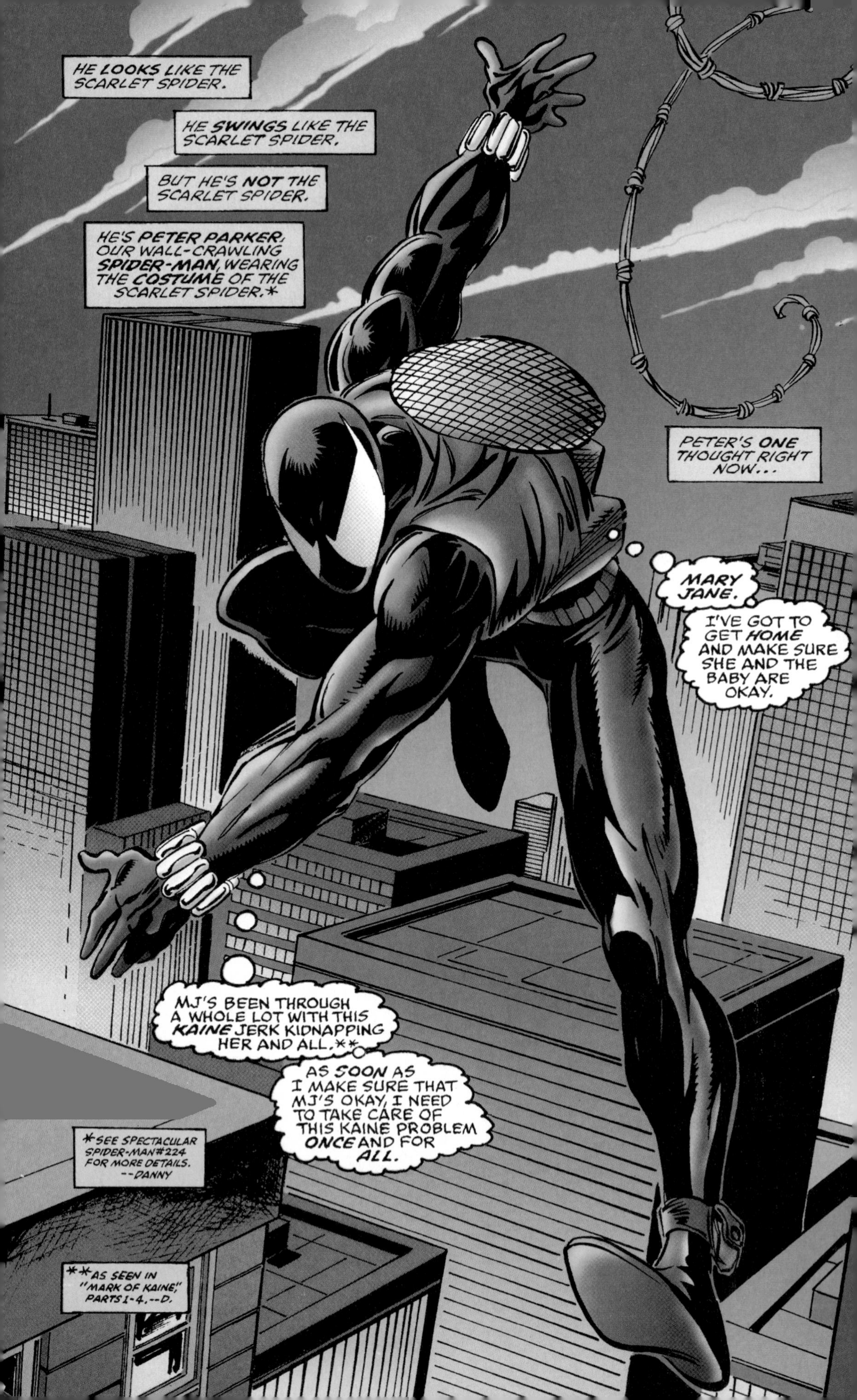
HE LOOKS LIKE THE SCARLET SPIDER.
HE SWINGS LIKE THE SCARLET SPIDER.
BUT HE'S NOT THE SCARLET SPIDER.
HE'S PETER PARKER, OUR WALL-CRAWLING SPIDER-MAN, WEARING THE COSTUME OF THE SCARLET SPIDER.*
PETER'S ONE THOUGHT RIGHT NOW...
MARY JANE.
I'VE GOT TO GET HOME AND MAKE SURE SHE AND THE BABY ARE OKAY.
MJ'S BEEN THROUGH A WHOLE LOT WITH THIS KAINE JERK KIDNAPPING HER AND ALL.**
AS SOON AS I MAKE SURE THAT MJ'S OKAY, I NEED TO TAKE CARE OF THIS KAINE PROBLEM ONCE AND FOR ALL.
*SEE SPECTACULAR SPIDER-MAN #224 FOR MORE DETAILS. --DANNY
**AS SEEN IN "MARK OF KAINE," PARTS 1-4. --D.

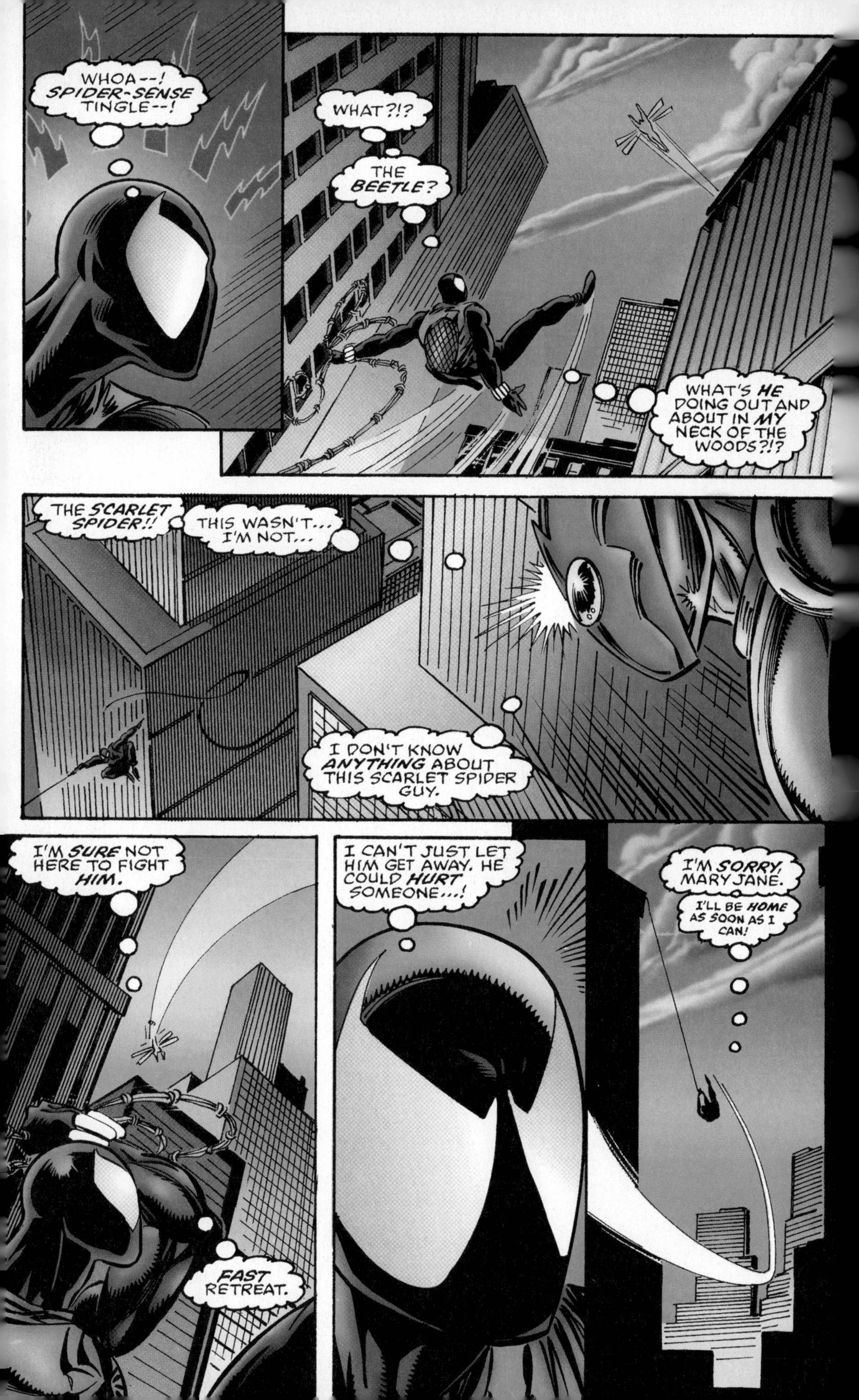

WHOA--! SPIDER-SENSE TINGLE--!
WHAT?!?
THE BEETLE?
WHAT'S HE DOING OUT AND ABOUT IN MY NECK OF THE WOODS?!?
THE SCARLET SPIDER!!
THIS WASN'T... I'M NOT...
I DON'T KNOW ANYTHING ABOUT THIS SCARLET SPIDER GUY.
I'M SURE NOT HERE TO FIGHT HIM.
FAST RETREAT.
I CAN'T JUST LET HIM GET AWAY. HE COULD HURT SOMEONE...!
I'M SORRY, MARY JANE.
I'LL BE HOME AS SOON AS I CAN!

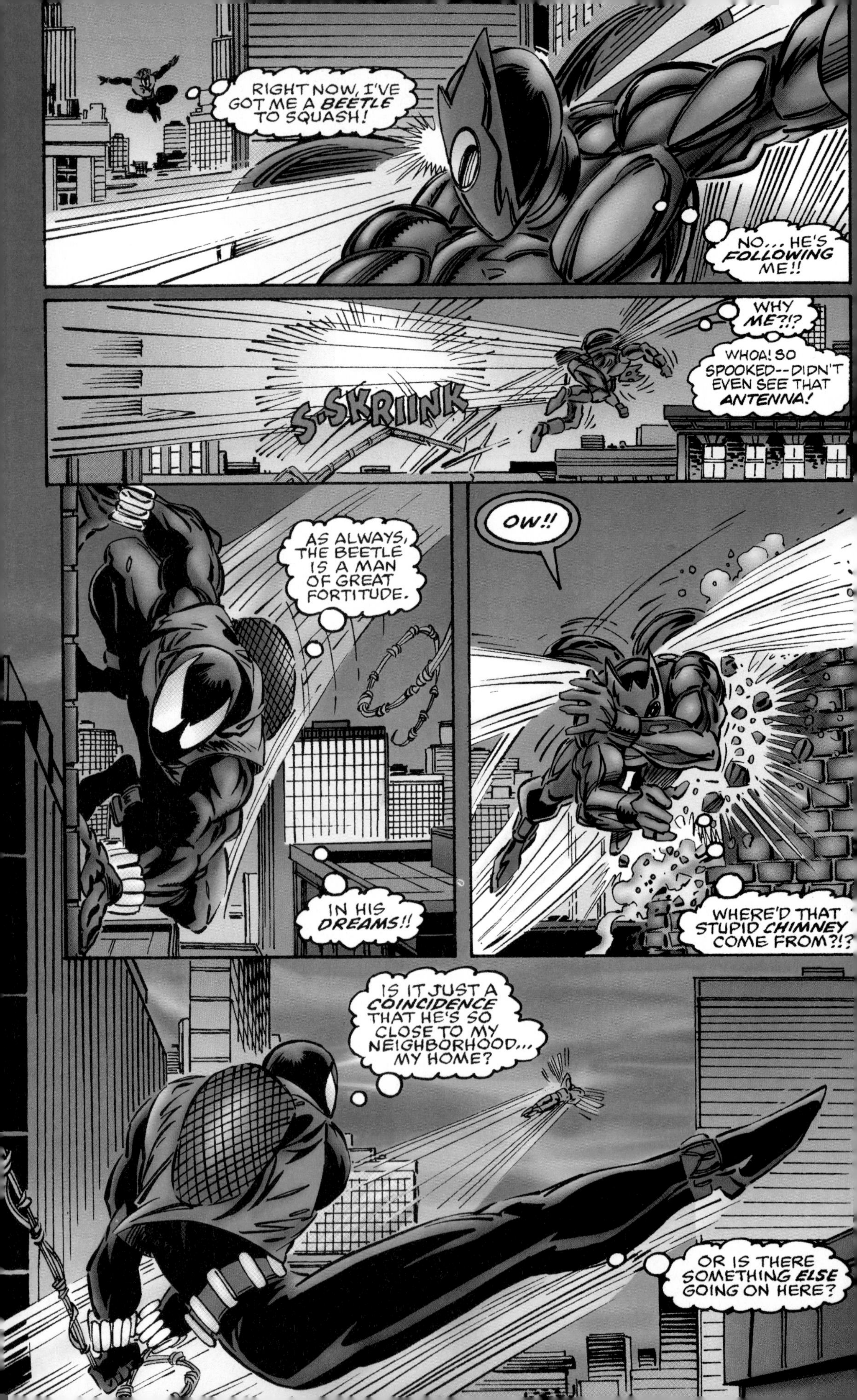
RIGHT NOW, I'VE GOT ME A BEETLE TO SQUASH!
NO... HE'S FOLLOWING ME!!
WHY ME?!?
WHOA! SO SPOOKED--DIDN'T EVEN SEE THAT ANTENNA!
S-SKRIIINK
AS ALWAYS, THE BEETLE IS A MAN OF GREAT FORTITUDE.
IN HIS DREAMS!!
OW!!
WHERE'D THAT STUPID CHIMNEY COME FROM?!?
IS IT JUST A COINCIDENCE THAT HE'S SO CLOSE TO MY NEIGHBORHOOD... MY HOME?
OR IS THERE SOMETHING ELSE GOING ON HERE?

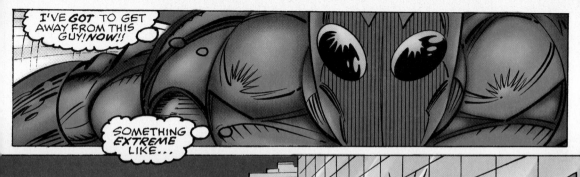

I'VE *GOT* TO GET AWAY FROM THIS GUY! *NOW!!*

SOMETHING *EXTREME* LIKE...

K-KRINKZZZT

K-KERAASSSH

...FLYING *THROUGH* A BUILDING!!

OH, MAN... PEOPLE ARE HURT!!

I HAVE A REALLY HARD TIME NOT TAKING *RE-SPONSIBILITY* FOR WHEN THESE BAD GUYS DO SOMETHING STUPID AND INNOCENT PEOPLE GET HURT.

I'LL DO EVERY-ONE ELSE *AND* MYSELF MORE GOOD IF I DON'T LET THE GUILT FEELINGS GET ME...

...AND JUST MAKE SURE I'M THERE TO *HELP* INSTEAD OF BEING AS OBSESSED AND BLIND AS THE BAD GUYS ARE.

THIS WOMAN NEEDS A DOCTOR... *NOW!!*

POLICE

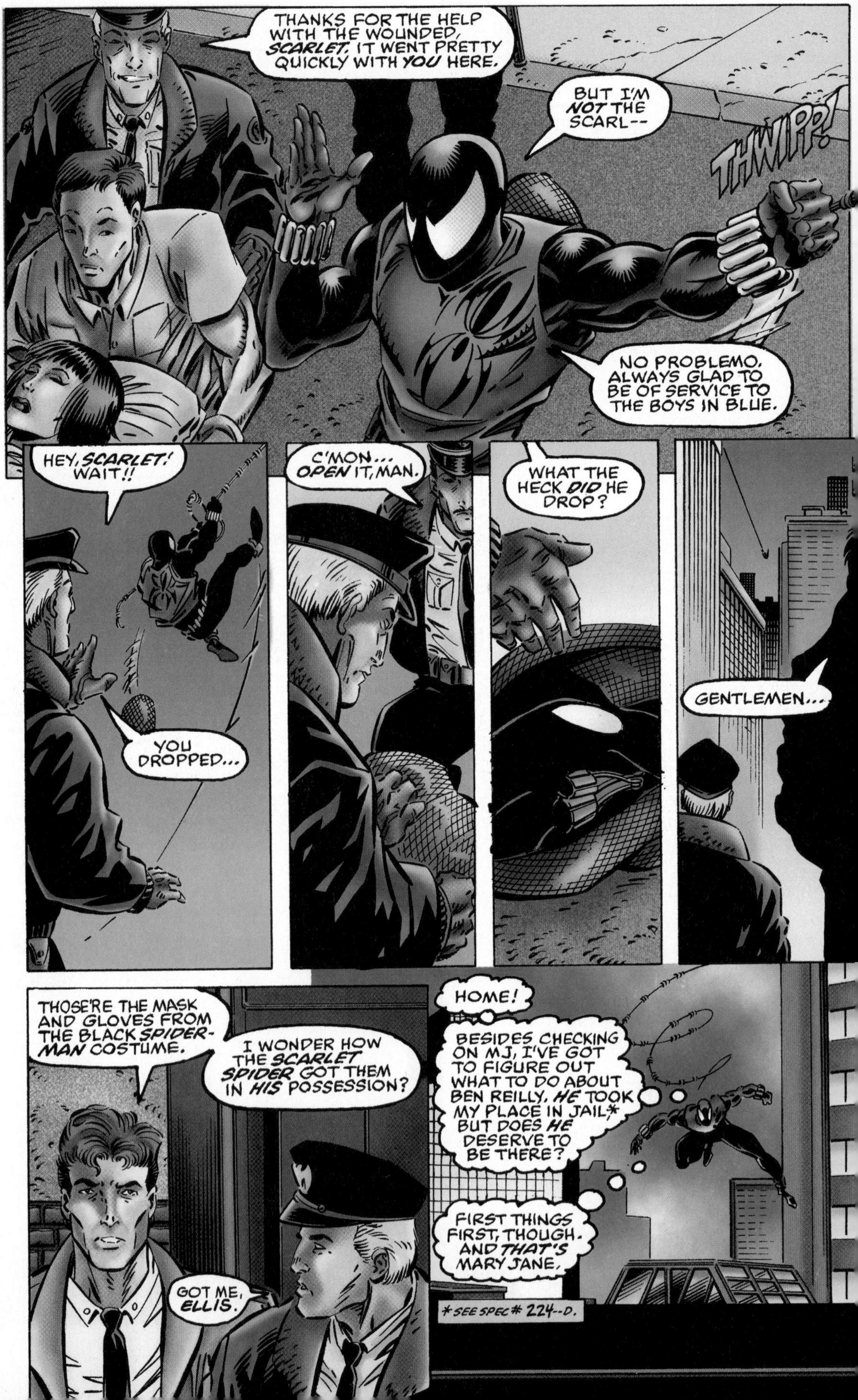
THANKS FOR THE HELP WITH THE WOUNDED, SCARLET. IT WENT PRETTY QUICKLY WITH YOU HERE.
BUT I'M NOT THE SCARL--
THWIPP!
NO PROBLEMO. ALWAYS GLAD TO BE OF SERVICE TO THE BOYS IN BLUE.
HEY, SCARLET! WAIT!!
YOU DROPPED...
C'MON... OPEN IT, MAN.
WHAT THE HECK DID HE DROP?
GENTLEMEN...
THOSE'RE THE MASK AND GLOVES FROM THE BLACK SPIDER-MAN COSTUME.
I WONDER HOW THE SCARLET SPIDER GOT THEM IN HIS POSSESSION?
GOT ME, ELLIS.
HOME!
BESIDES CHECKING ON MJ, I'VE GOT TO FIGURE OUT WHAT TO DO ABOUT BEN REILLY. HE TOOK MY PLACE IN JAIL* BUT DOES HE DESERVE TO BE THERE?
FIRST THINGS FIRST, THOUGH. AND THAT'S MARY JANE.
*SEE SPEC # 224--D.

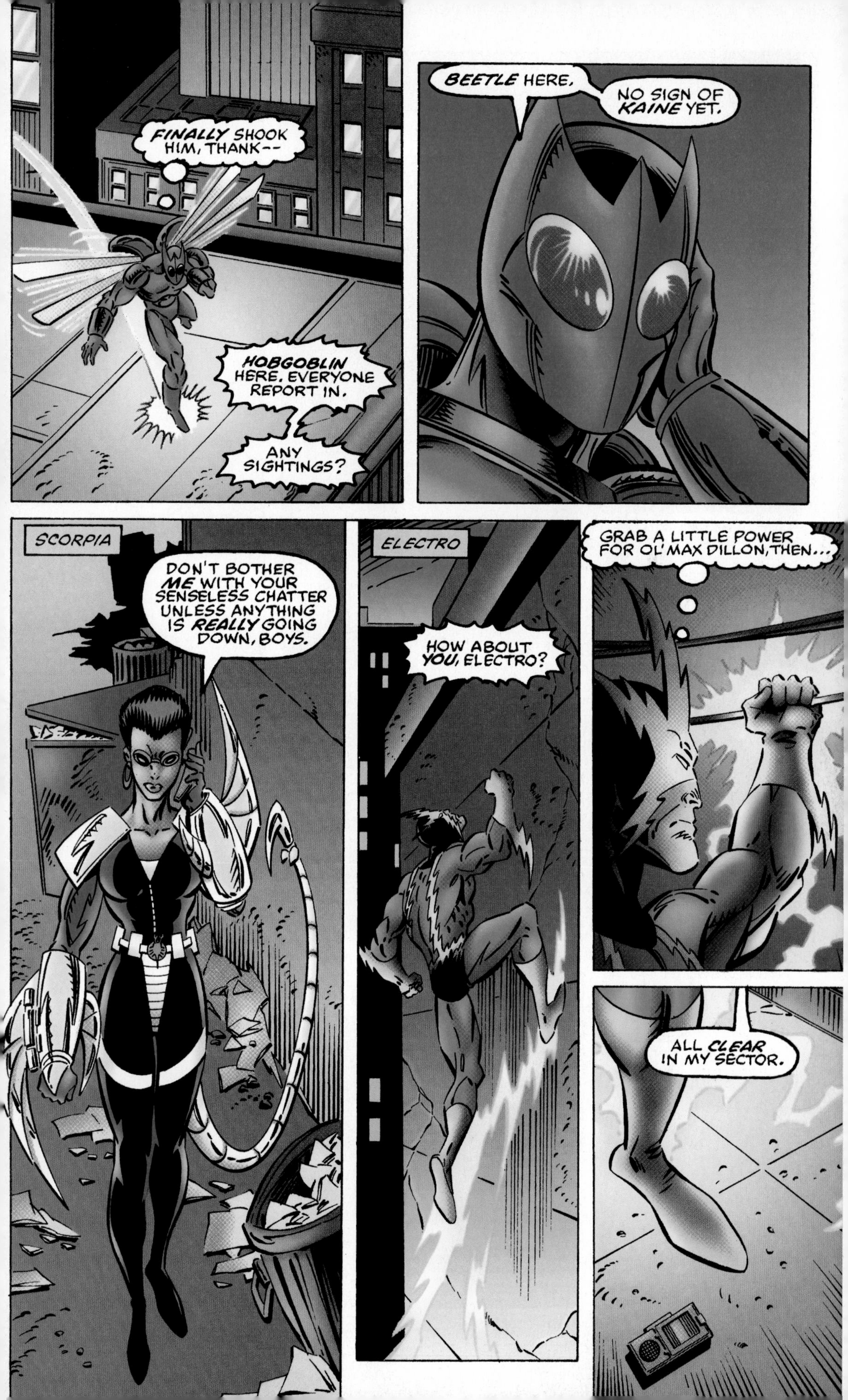

FINALLY SHOOK HIM, THANK--
HOBGOBLIN HERE. EVERYONE REPORT IN.
ANY SIGHTINGS?
BEETLE HERE,
NO SIGN OF KAINE YET.
SCORPIA
DON'T BOTHER ME WITH YOUR SENSELESS CHATTER UNLESS ANYTHING IS REALLY GOING DOWN, BOYS.
ELECTRO
HOW ABOUT YOU, ELECTRO?
GRAB A LITTLE POWER FOR OL' MAX DILLON, THEN...
ALL CLEAR IN MY SECTOR.

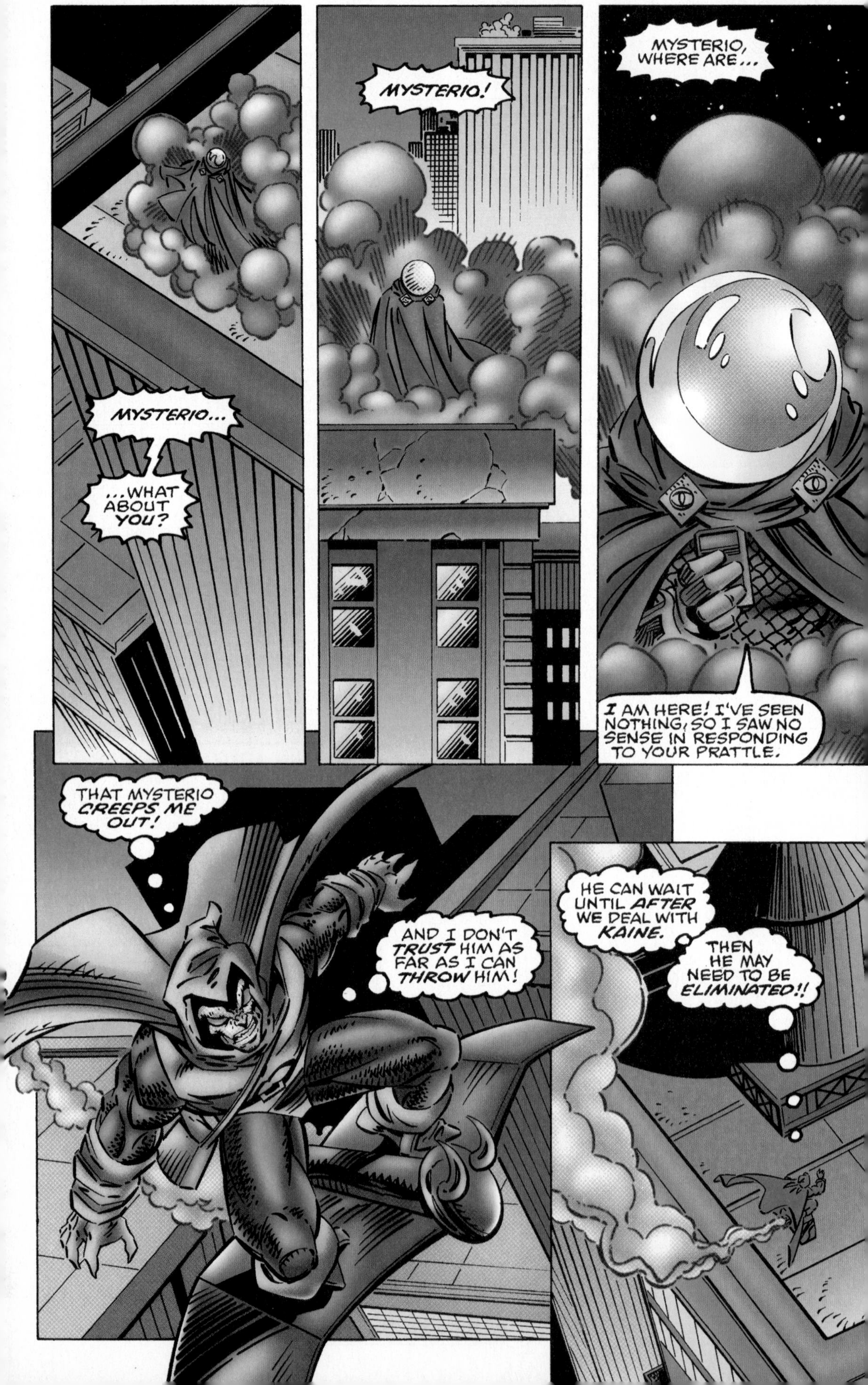
MYSTERIO...
...WHAT ABOUT YOU?
MYSTERIO!
MYSTERIO, WHERE ARE...
I AM HERE! I'VE SEEN NOTHING, SO I SAW NO SENSE IN RESPONDING TO YOUR PRATTLE.
THAT MYSTERIO CREEPS ME OUT!
AND I DON'T TRUST HIM AS FAR AS I CAN THROW HIM!
HE CAN WAIT UNTIL AFTER WE DEAL WITH KAINE.
THEN HE MAY NEED TO BE ELIMINATED!!

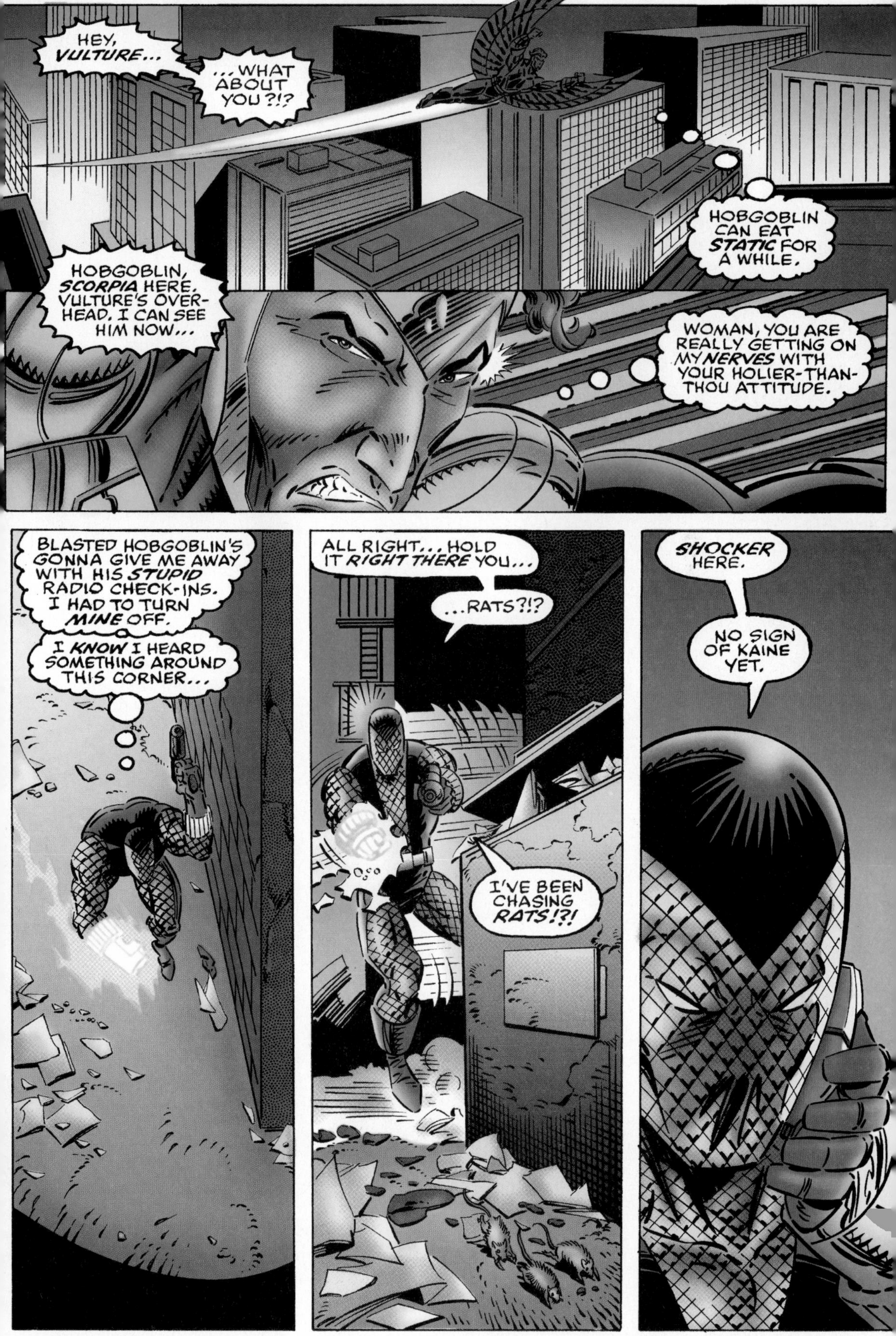
HEY, VULTURE...
...WHAT ABOUT YOU?!?
HOBGOBLIN CAN EAT STATIC FOR A WHILE.
HOBGOBLIN, SCORPIA HERE. VULTURE'S OVERHEAD. I CAN SEE HIM NOW...
WOMAN, YOU ARE REALLY GETTING ON MY NERVES WITH YOUR HOLIER-THAN-THOU ATTITUDE.
BLASTED HOBGOBLIN'S GONNA GIVE ME AWAY WITH HIS STUPID RADIO CHECK-INS. I HAD TO TURN MINE OFF.
I KNOW I HEARD SOMETHING AROUND THIS CORNER...
ALL RIGHT... HOLD IT RIGHT THERE YOU...
...RATS?!?
I'VE BEEN CHASING RATS!?!
SHOCKER HERE.
NO SIGN OF KAINE YET.

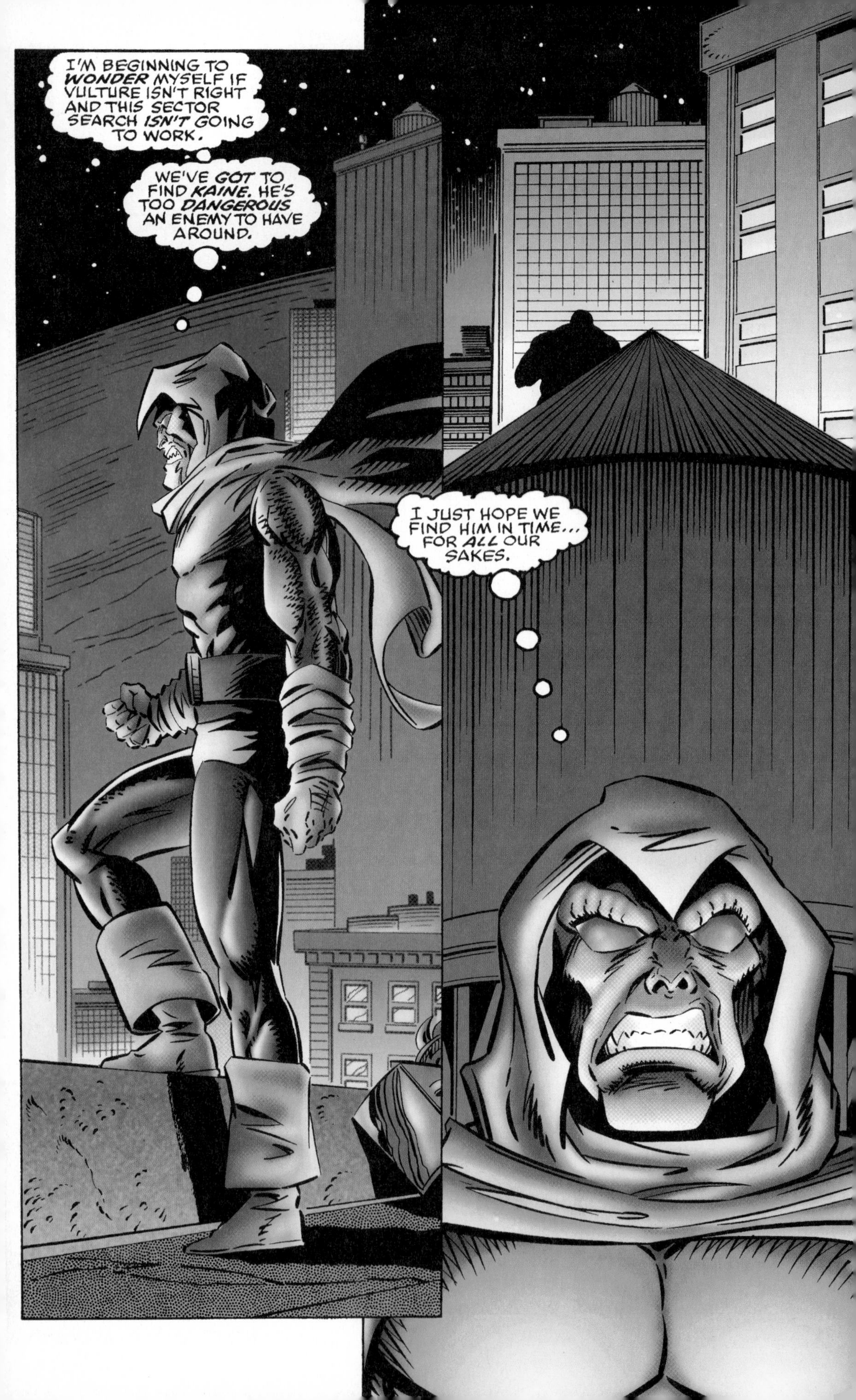
I'M BEGINNING TO WONDER MYSELF IF VULTURE ISN'T RIGHT AND THIS SECTOR SEARCH ISN'T GOING TO WORK.
WE'VE GOT TO FIND KAINE. HE'S TOO DANGEROUS AN ENEMY TO HAVE AROUND.
I JUST HOPE WE FIND HIM IN TIME... FOR ALL OUR SAKES.

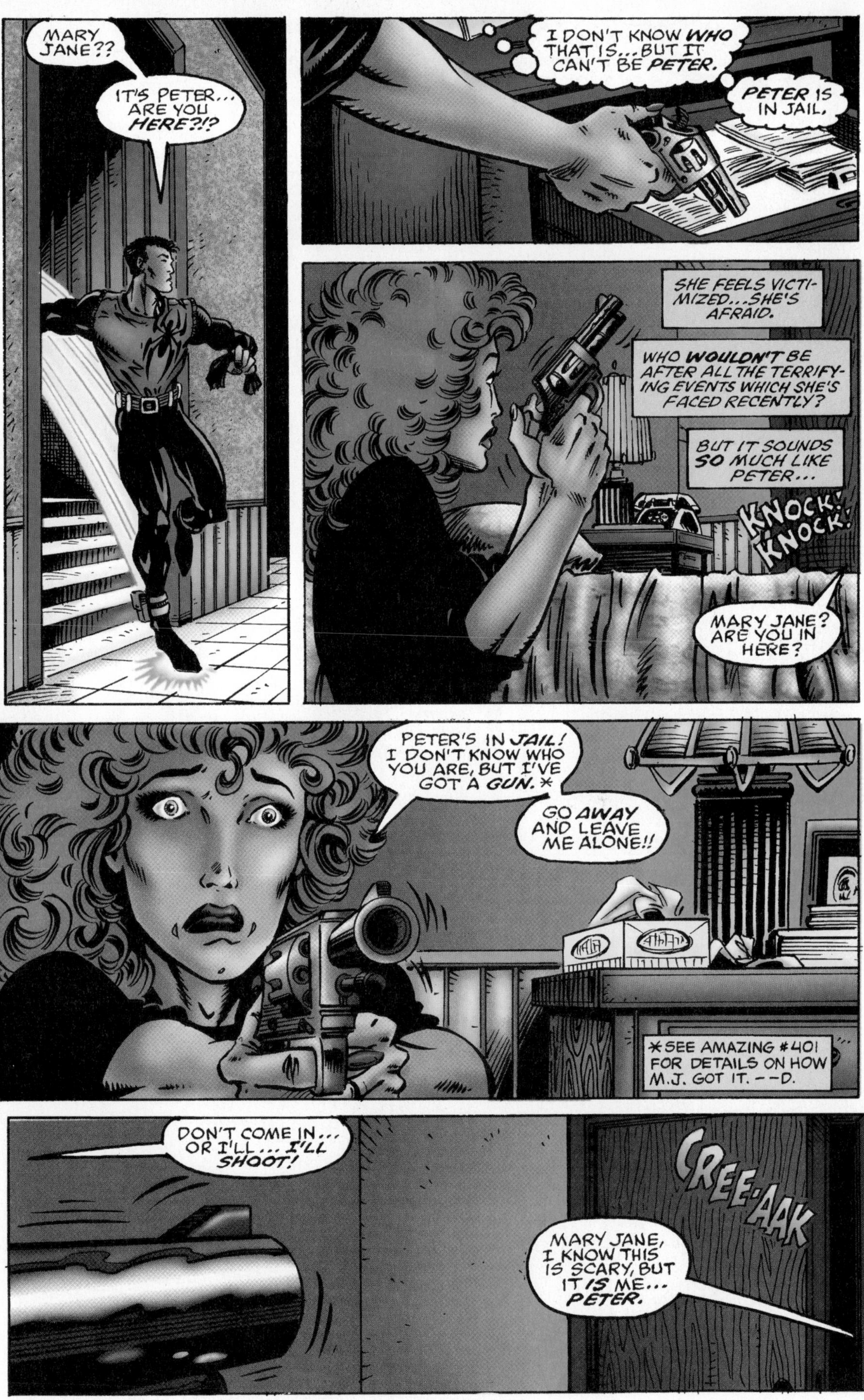
MARY JANE??
IT'S PETER... ARE YOU HERE?!?
I DON'T KNOW WHO THAT IS... BUT IT CAN'T BE PETER.
PETER IS IN JAIL.
SHE FEELS VICTIMIZED... SHE'S AFRAID.
WHO WOULDN'T BE AFTER ALL THE TERRIFYING EVENTS WHICH SHE'S FACED RECENTLY?
BUT IT SOUNDS SO MUCH LIKE PETER...
KNOCK! KNOCK!
MARY JANE? ARE YOU IN HERE?
PETER'S IN JAIL! I DON'T KNOW WHO YOU ARE, BUT I'VE GOT A GUN.*
GO AWAY AND LEAVE ME ALONE!!
*SEE AMAZING #401 FOR DETAILS ON HOW M.J. GOT IT. --D.
DON'T COME IN... OR I'LL... I'LL SHOOT!
CREE-AAK
MARY JANE, I KNOW THIS IS SCARY, BUT IT IS ME... PETER.

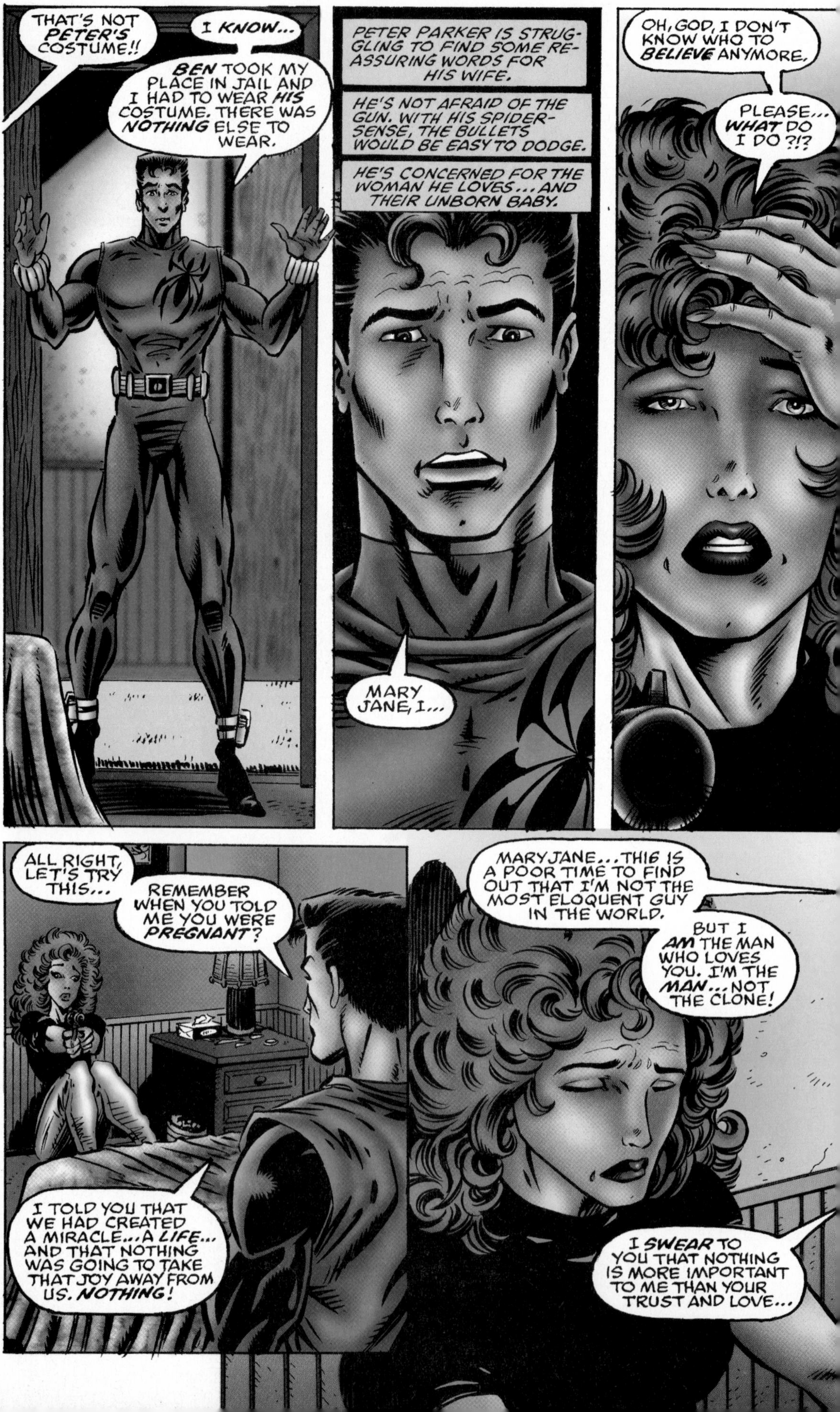
THAT'S NOT PETER'S COSTUME!!
I KNOW...
BEN TOOK MY PLACE IN JAIL AND I HAD TO WEAR HIS COSTUME. THERE WAS NOTHING ELSE TO WEAR.
PETER PARKER IS STRUGGLING TO FIND SOME REASSURING WORDS FOR HIS WIFE.
HE'S NOT AFRAID OF THE GUN. WITH HIS SPIDER-SENSE, THE BULLETS WOULD BE EASY TO DODGE.
HE'S CONCERNED FOR THE WOMAN HE LOVES... AND THEIR UNBORN BABY.
MARY JANE, I...
OH, GOD, I DON'T KNOW WHO TO BELIEVE ANYMORE.
PLEASE... WHAT DO I DO ?!?
ALL RIGHT, LET'S TRY THIS...
REMEMBER WHEN YOU TOLD ME YOU WERE PREGNANT?
I TOLD YOU THAT WE HAD CREATED A MIRACLE... A LIFE... AND THAT NOTHING WAS GOING TO TAKE THAT JOY AWAY FROM US. NOTHING!
MARY JANE... THIS IS A POOR TIME TO FIND OUT THAT I'M NOT THE MOST ELOQUENT GUY IN THE WORLD.
BUT I AM THE MAN WHO LOVES YOU. I'M THE MAN... NOT THE CLONE!
I SWEAR TO YOU THAT NOTHING IS MORE IMPORTANT TO ME THAN YOUR TRUST AND LOVE...

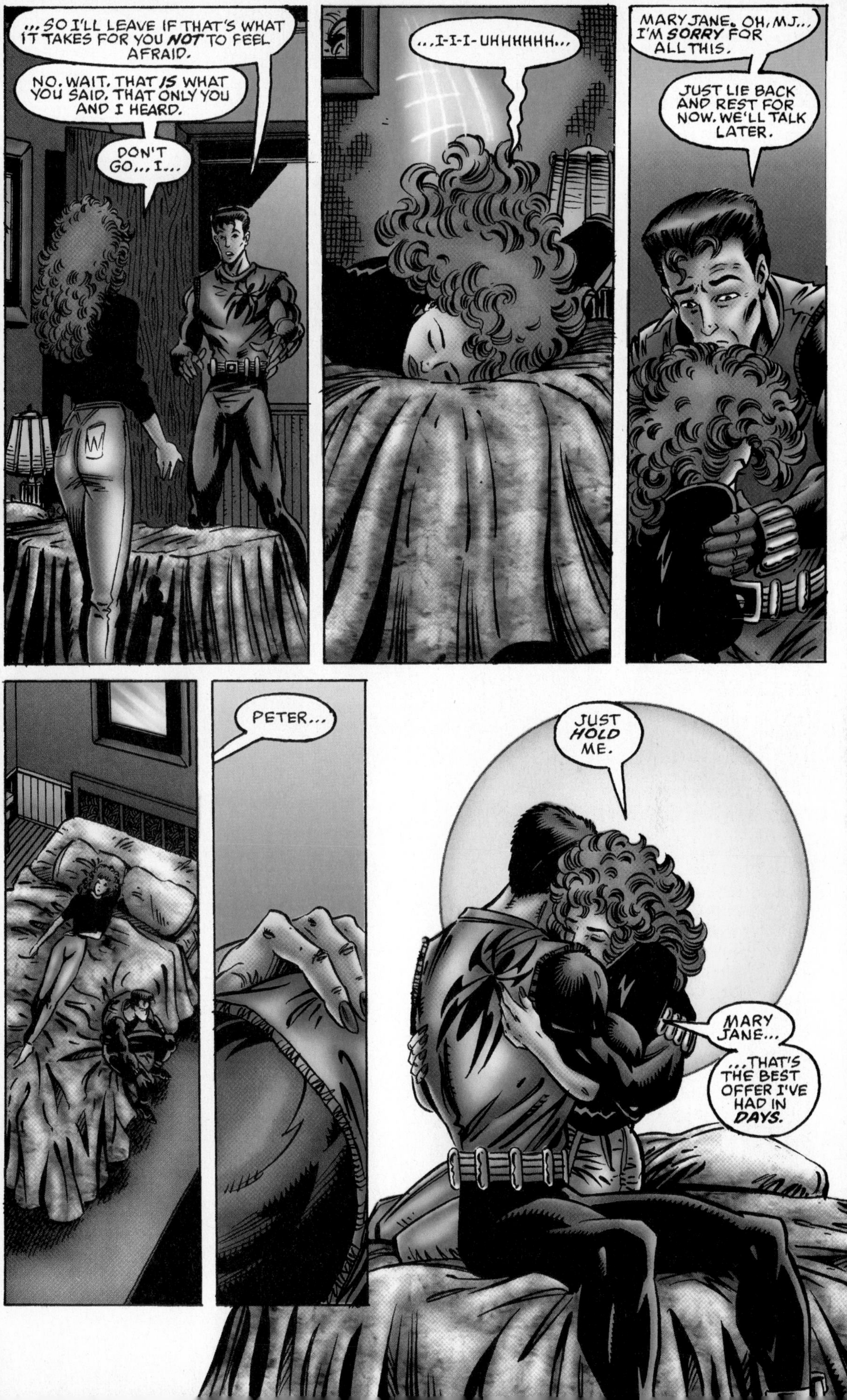
...SO I'LL LEAVE IF THAT'S WHAT IT TAKES FOR YOU NOT TO FEEL AFRAID.
NO. WAIT. THAT IS WHAT YOU SAID. THAT ONLY YOU AND I HEARD.
DON'T GO... I...
...I-I-I-UHHHHHH...
MARY JANE. OH, MJ... I'M SORRY FOR ALL THIS.
JUST LIE BACK AND REST FOR NOW. WE'LL TALK LATER.
PETER...
JUST HOLD ME.
MARY JANE...
...THAT'S THE BEST OFFER I'VE HAD IN DAYS.

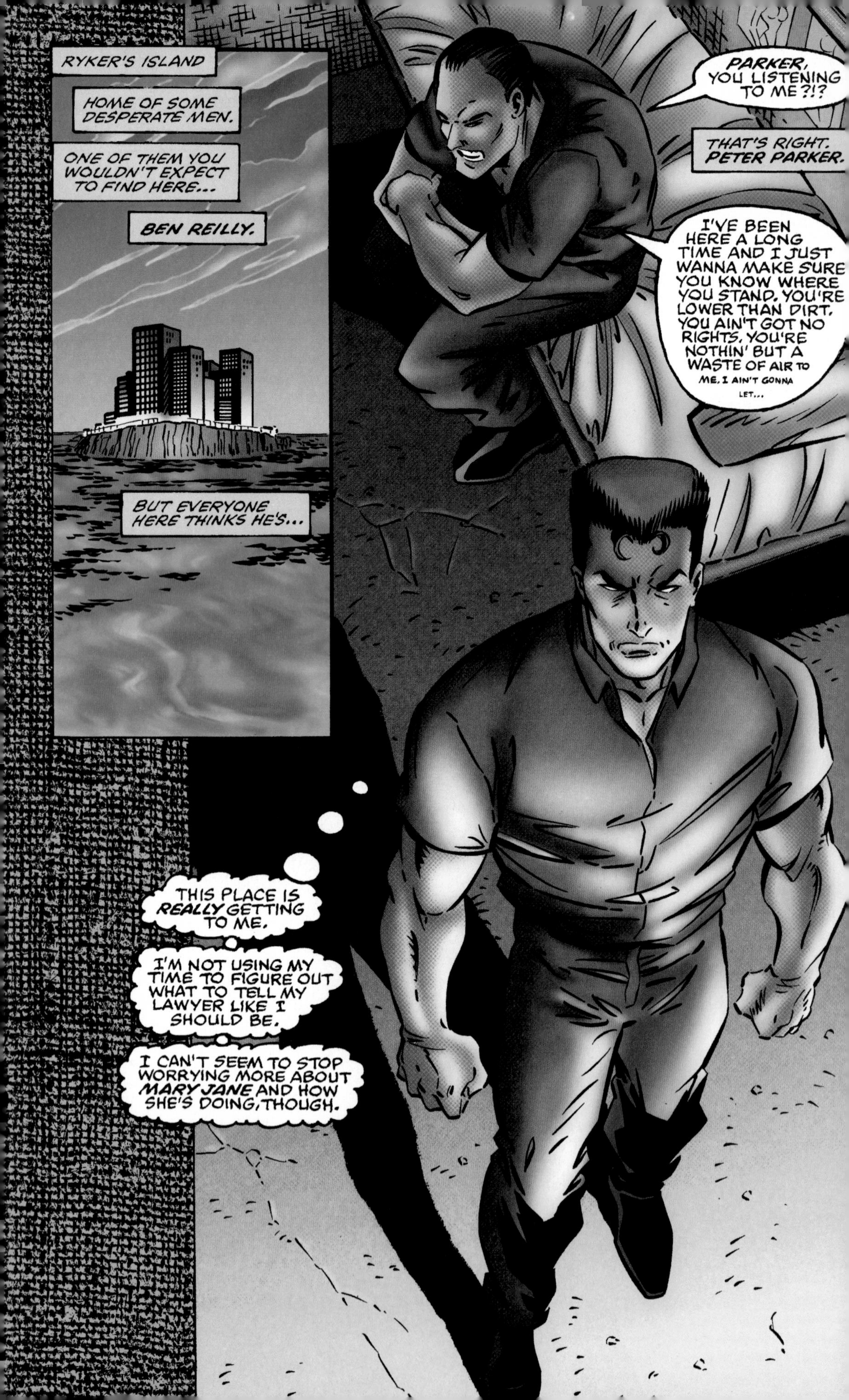
RYKER'S ISLAND
HOME OF SOME DESPERATE MEN.
ONE OF THEM YOU WOULDN'T EXPECT TO FIND HERE...
BEN REILLY.
BUT EVERYONE HERE THINKS HE'S...
PARKER, YOU LISTENING TO ME?!?
THAT'S RIGHT. PETER PARKER.
I'VE BEEN HERE A LONG TIME AND I JUST WANNA MAKE SURE YOU KNOW WHERE YOU STAND. YOU'RE LOWER THAN DIRT. YOU AIN'T GOT NO RIGHTS. YOU'RE NOTHIN' BUT A WASTE OF AIR TO ME. I AIN'T GONNA LET...
THIS PLACE IS REALLY GETTING TO ME.
I'M NOT USING MY TIME TO FIGURE OUT WHAT TO TELL MY LAWYER LIKE I SHOULD BE.
I CAN'T SEEM TO STOP WORRYING MORE ABOUT MARY JANE AND HOW SHE'S DOING, THOUGH.

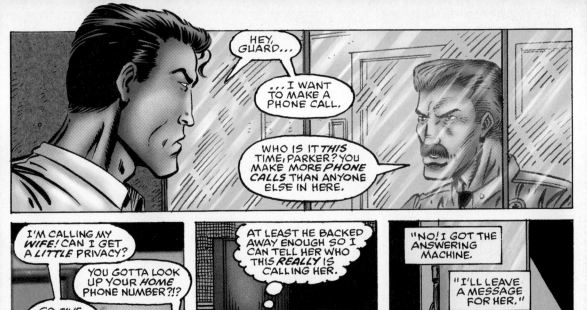

HEY, GUARD...

...I WANT TO MAKE A PHONE CALL.

WHO IS IT *THIS* TIME, PARKER? YOU MAKE MORE *PHONE CALLS* THAN ANYONE ELSE IN HERE.

I'M CALLING MY *WIFE!* CAN I GET A *LITTLE* PRIVACY?

YOU GOTTA LOOK UP YOUR *HOME* PHONE NUMBER?!?

SO I'VE GOT A *BAD* MEMORY...IS *THAT* A CRIME?

AT LEAST HE BACKED AWAY ENOUGH SO I CAN TELL HER WHO THIS *REALLY* IS CALLING HER.

"NO! I GOT THE ANSWERING MACHINE.

"I'LL LEAVE A MESSAGE FOR HER,"

MARY JANE, THIS IS BEN. I'M SORRY TO KEEP *BOTHERING* YOU, BUT I CAN'T HELP BUT BE *CONCERNED* WITH HOW YOU ARE.

I HOPE YOU'RE OKAY AND THAT PETER IS *HOME* WITH YOU NOW.

SHOULDN'T WE ANSWER IT?

NO. NOT RIGHT NOW.

WELL, I'VE GOT TO GO. I'LL CALL YOU AGAIN LATER. ⸬CLICK⸬

WHAT *AM* I GOING TO DO ABOUT *BEN?*

I CAN'T JUST *IGNORE* HIM AND WHAT HE DID FOR ME BY TAKING MY PLACE IN JAIL.

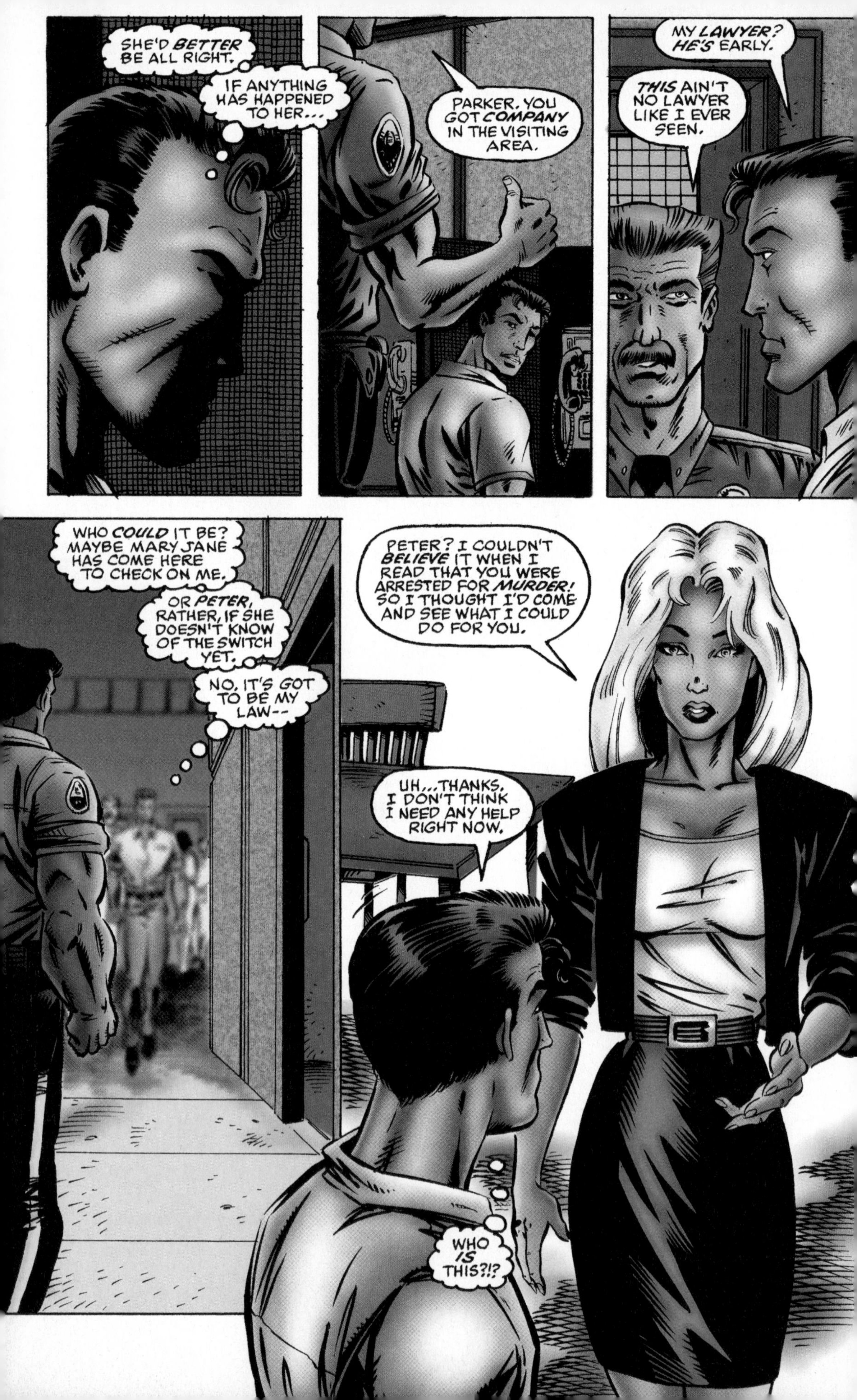
SHE'D BETTER BE ALL RIGHT.
IF ANYTHING HAS HAPPENED TO HER...
PARKER. YOU GOT COMPANY IN THE VISITING AREA.
MY LAWYER? HE'S EARLY.
THIS AIN'T NO LAWYER LIKE I EVER SEEN.
WHO COULD IT BE? MAYBE MARY JANE HAS COME HERE TO CHECK ON ME.
OR PETER, RATHER, IF SHE DOESN'T KNOW OF THE SWITCH YET.
NO, IT'S GOT TO BE MY LAW--
PETER? I COULDN'T BELIEVE IT WHEN I READ THAT YOU WERE ARRESTED FOR MURDER! SO I THOUGHT I'D COME AND SEE WHAT I COULD DO FOR YOU.
UH... THANKS. I DON'T THINK I NEED ANY HELP RIGHT NOW.
WHO IS THIS?!?

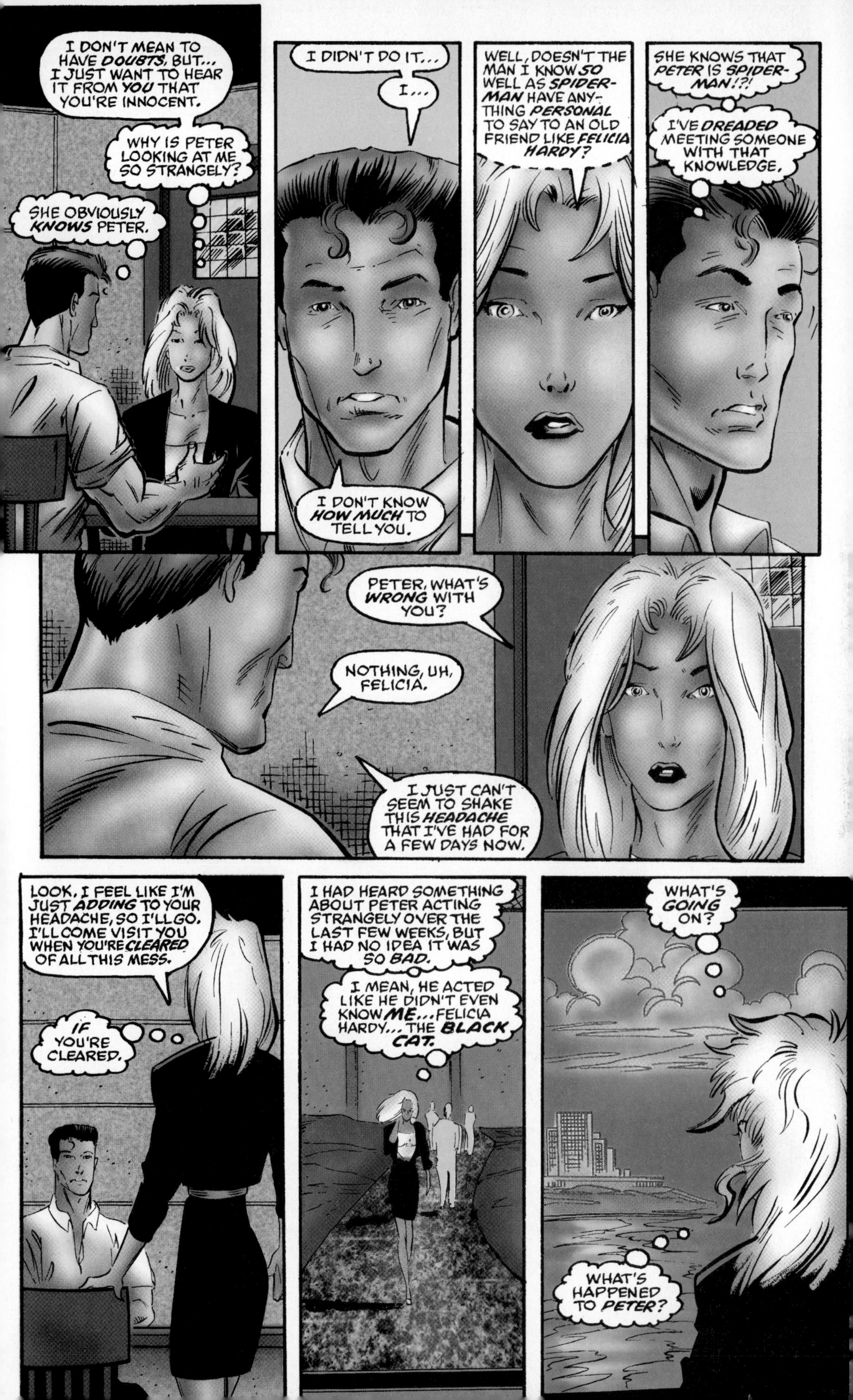
I DON'T MEAN TO HAVE DOUBTS, BUT... I JUST WANT TO HEAR IT FROM YOU THAT YOU'RE INNOCENT.
WHY IS PETER LOOKING AT ME SO STRANGELY?
SHE OBVIOUSLY KNOWS PETER.
I DIDN'T DO IT...
I...
I DON'T KNOW HOW MUCH TO TELL YOU.
WELL, DOESN'T THE MAN I KNOW SO WELL AS SPIDER-MAN HAVE ANYTHING PERSONAL TO SAY TO AN OLD FRIEND LIKE FELICIA HARDY?
SHE KNOWS THAT PETER IS SPIDER-MAN!?!
I'VE DREADED MEETING SOMEONE WITH THAT KNOWLEDGE.
PETER, WHAT'S WRONG WITH YOU?
NOTHING, UH, FELICIA.
I JUST CAN'T SEEM TO SHAKE THIS HEADACHE THAT I'VE HAD FOR A FEW DAYS NOW.
LOOK, I FEEL LIKE I'M JUST ADDING TO YOUR HEADACHE, SO I'LL GO. I'LL COME VISIT YOU WHEN YOU'RE CLEARED OF ALL THIS MESS.
IF YOU'RE CLEARED.
I HAD HEARD SOMETHING ABOUT PETER ACTING STRANGELY OVER THE LAST FEW WEEKS, BUT I HAD NO IDEA IT WAS SO BAD.
I MEAN, HE ACTED LIKE HE DIDN'T EVEN KNOW ME... FELICIA HARDY... THE BLACK CAT.
WHAT'S GOING ON?
WHAT'S HAPPENED TO PETER?

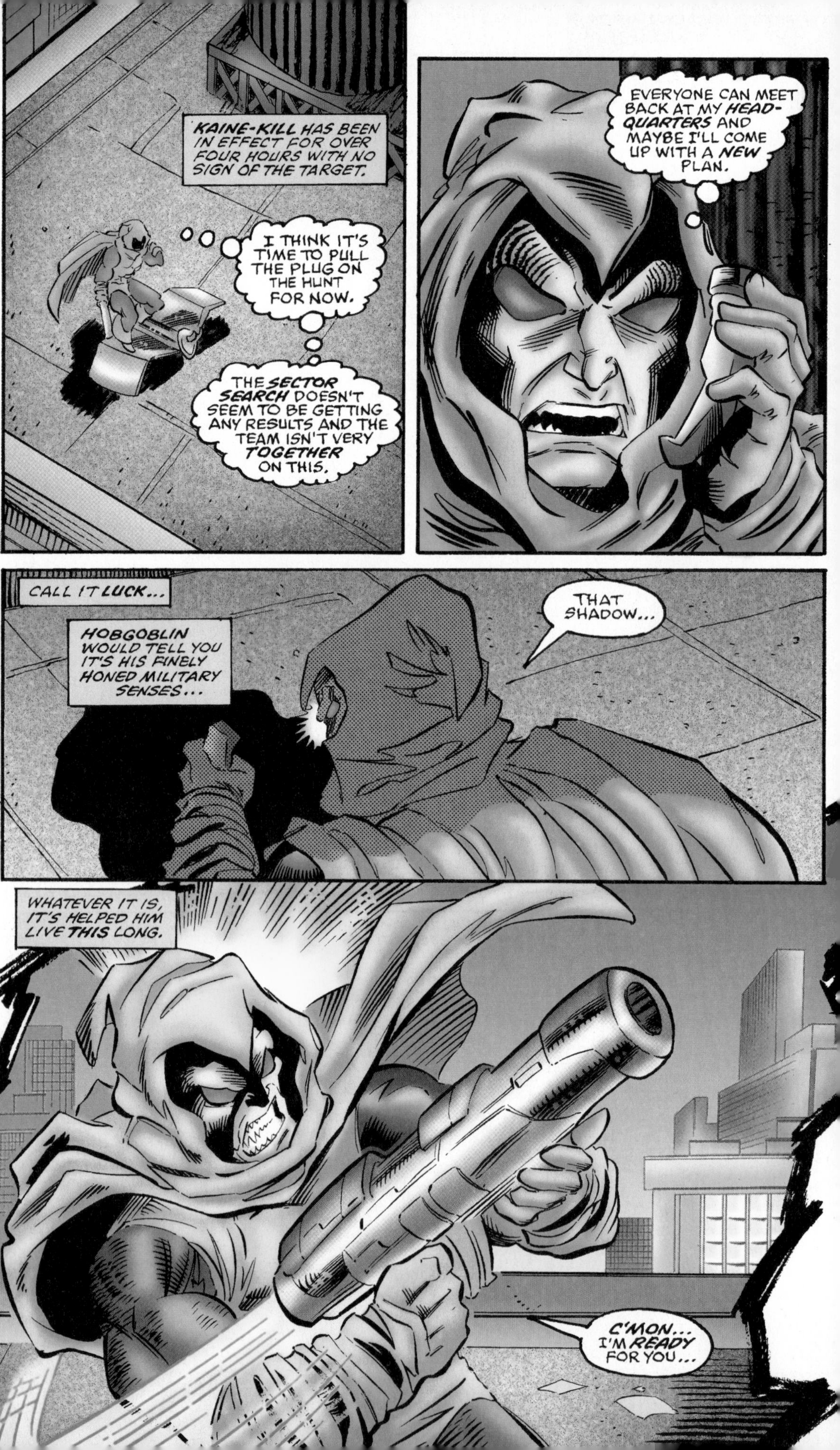

KAINE-KILL HAS BEEN IN EFFECT FOR OVER FOUR HOURS WITH NO SIGN OF THE TARGET.
I THINK IT'S TIME TO PULL THE PLUG ON THE HUNT FOR NOW.
THE SECTOR SEARCH DOESN'T SEEM TO BE GETTING ANY RESULTS AND THE TEAM ISN'T VERY TOGETHER ON THIS.
EVERYONE CAN MEET BACK AT MY HEAD-QUARTERS AND MAYBE I'LL COME UP WITH A NEW PLAN.
CALL IT LUCK...
HOBGOBLIN WOULD TELL YOU IT'S HIS FINELY HONED MILITARY SENSES...
THAT SHADOW...
WHATEVER IT IS, IT'S HELPED HIM LIVE THIS LONG.
C'MON... I'M READY FOR YOU...

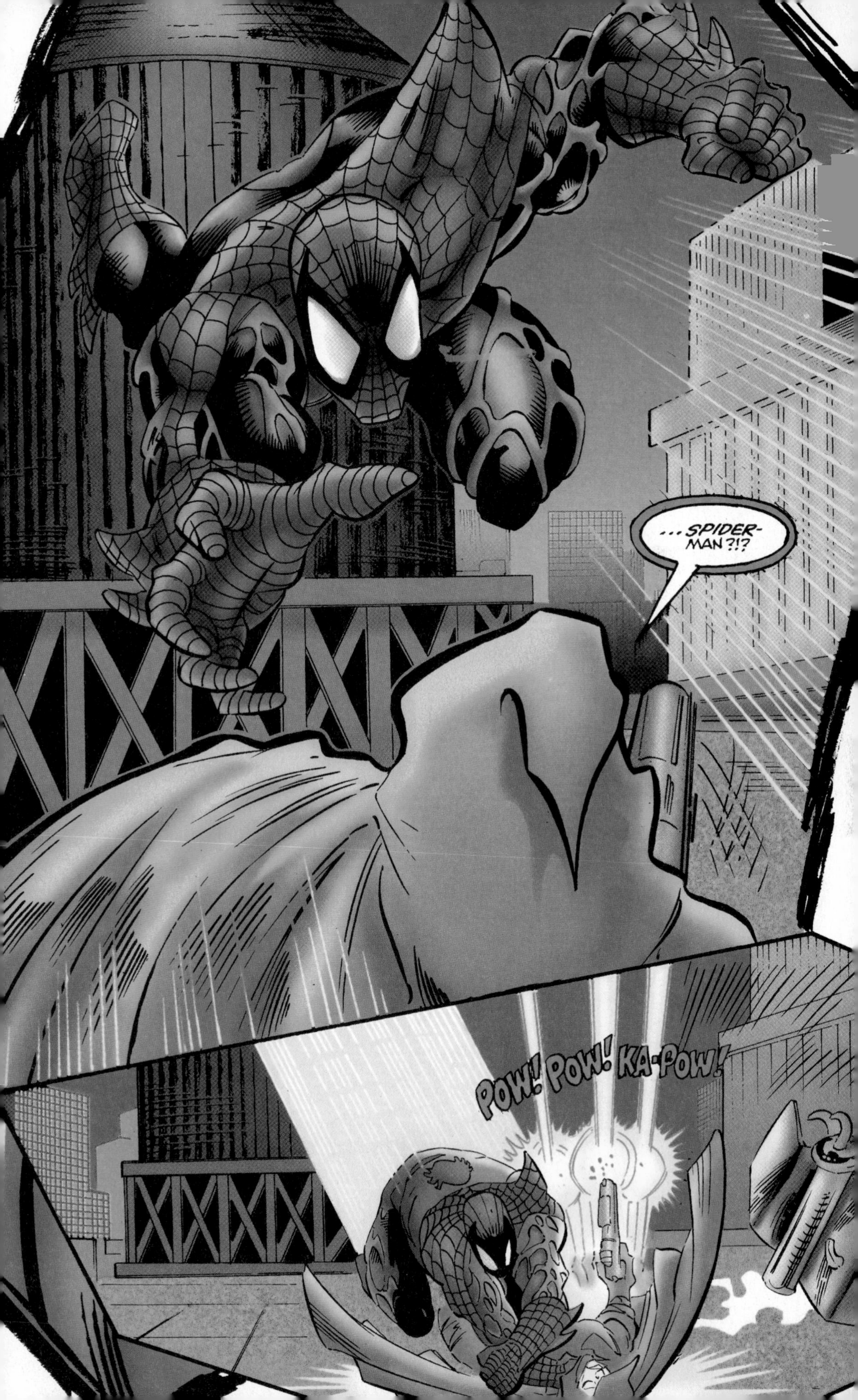
...SPIDER-MAN?!?
POW! POW! KA-POW!

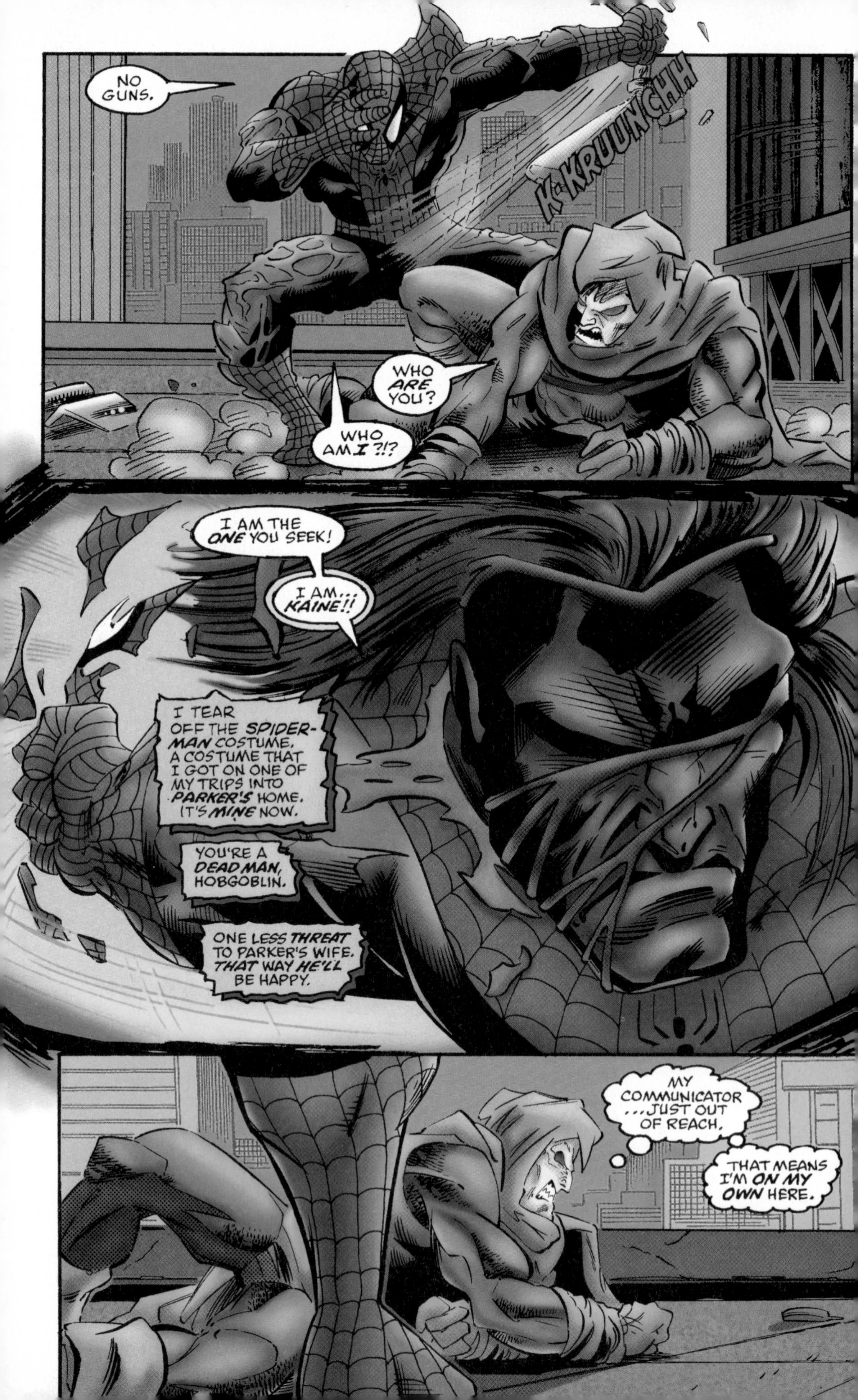

NO GUNS.
K-KRUUNCHH
WHO ARE YOU?
WHO AM I ?!?
I AM THE ONE YOU SEEK!
I AM... KAINE!!
I TEAR OFF THE SPIDER-MAN COSTUME, A COSTUME THAT I GOT ON ONE OF MY TRIPS INTO PARKER'S HOME. IT'S MINE NOW.
YOU'RE A DEAD MAN, HOBGOBLIN.
ONE LESS THREAT TO PARKER'S WIFE. THAT WAY HE'LL BE HAPPY.
MY COMMUNICATOR ...JUST OUT OF REACH.
THAT MEANS I'M ON MY OWN HERE.

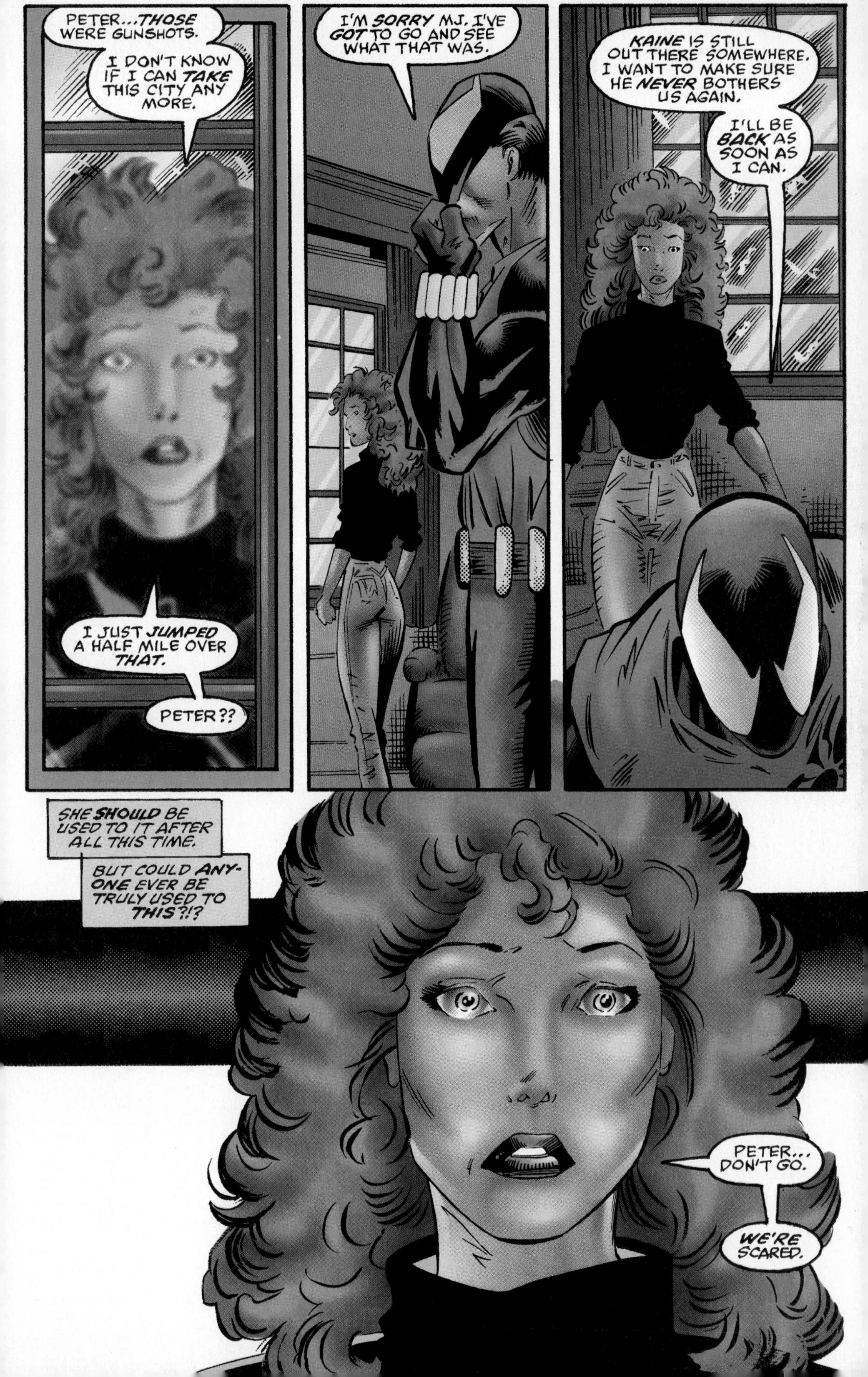
PETER...THOSE WERE GUNSHOTS.
I DON'T KNOW IF I CAN TAKE THIS CITY ANY MORE.
I JUST JUMPED A HALF MILE OVER THAT.
PETER??
I'M SORRY MJ. I'VE GOT TO GO AND SEE WHAT THAT WAS.
KAINE IS STILL OUT THERE SOMEWHERE. I WANT TO MAKE SURE HE NEVER BOTHERS US AGAIN.
I'LL BE BACK AS SOON AS I CAN.
SHE SHOULD BE USED TO IT AFTER ALL THIS TIME.
BUT COULD ANYONE EVER BE TRULY USED TO THIS?!?
PETER... DON'T GO.
WE'RE SCARED.

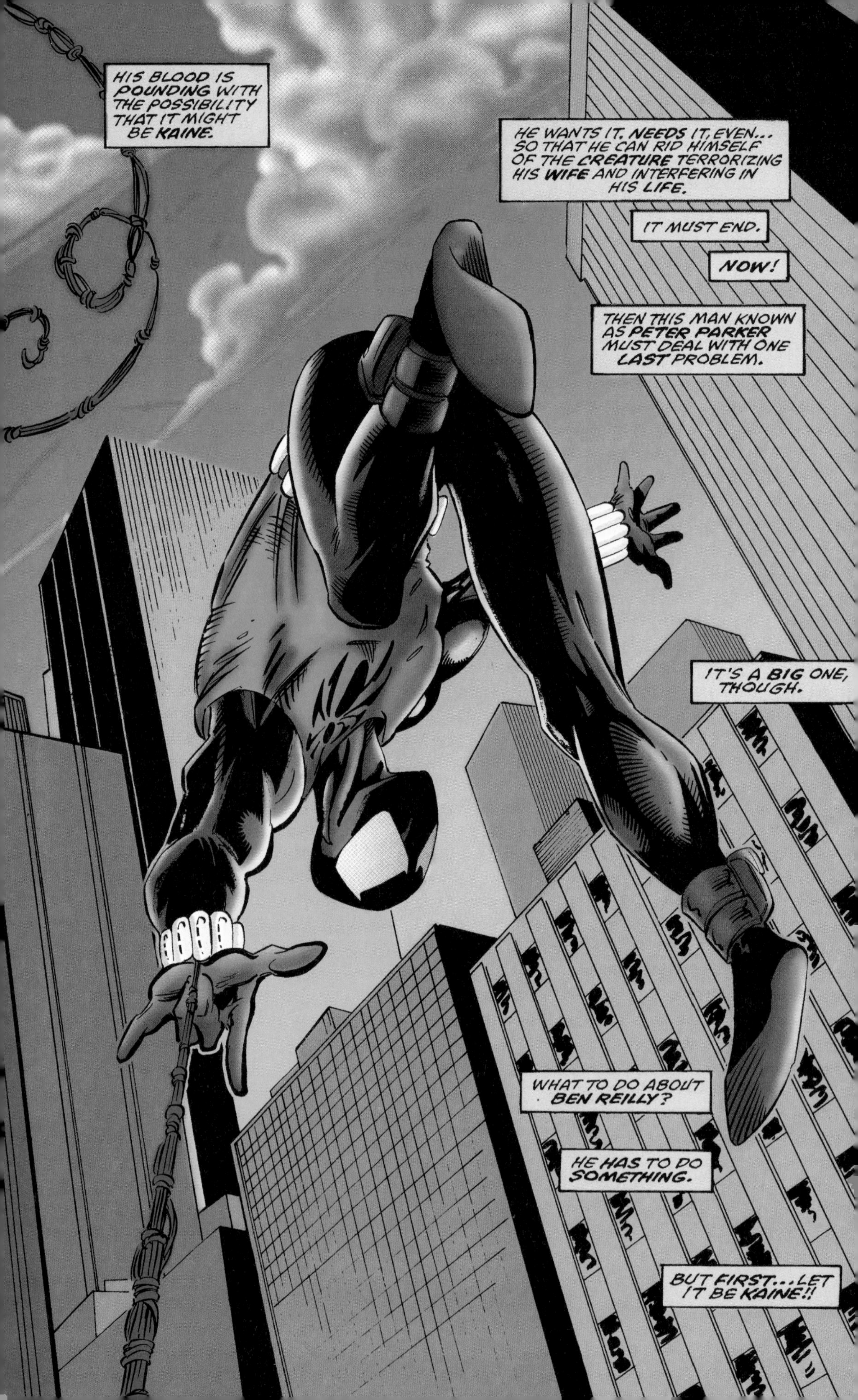
HIS BLOOD IS POUNDING WITH THE POSSIBILITY THAT IT MIGHT BE KAINE.
HE WANTS IT. NEEDS IT, EVEN... SO THAT HE CAN RID HIMSELF OF THE CREATURE TERRORIZING HIS WIFE AND INTERFERING IN HIS LIFE.
IT MUST END.
NOW!
THEN THIS MAN KNOWN AS PETER PARKER MUST DEAL WITH ONE LAST PROBLEM.
IT'S A BIG ONE, THOUGH.
WHAT TO DO ABOUT BEN REILLY?
HE HAS TO DO SOMETHING.
BUT FIRST...LET IT BE KAINE!!

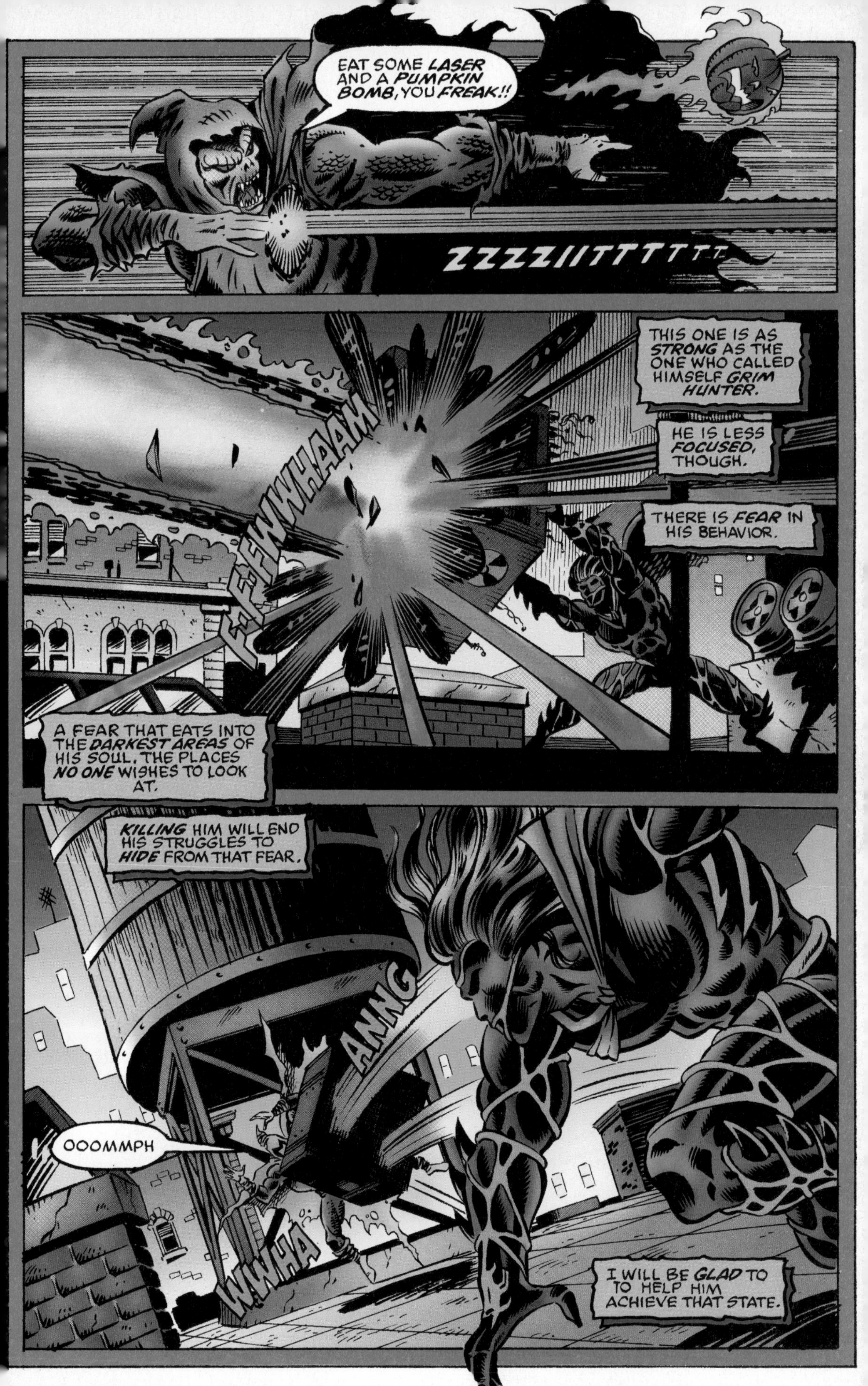
EAT SOME LASER AND A PUMPKIN BOMB, YOU FREAK!!
ZZZZIITTTTTTT
FFFFWWHAAM
THIS ONE IS AS STRONG AS THE ONE WHO CALLED HIMSELF GRIM HUNTER.
HE IS LESS FOCUSED, THOUGH.
THERE IS FEAR IN HIS BEHAVIOR.
A FEAR THAT EATS INTO THE DARKEST AREAS OF HIS SOUL. THE PLACES NO ONE WISHES TO LOOK AT.
KILLING HIM WILL END HIS STRUGGLES TO HIDE FROM THAT FEAR.
WWHAANNG
OOOMMPH
I WILL BE GLAD TO TO HELP HIM ACHIEVE THAT STATE.

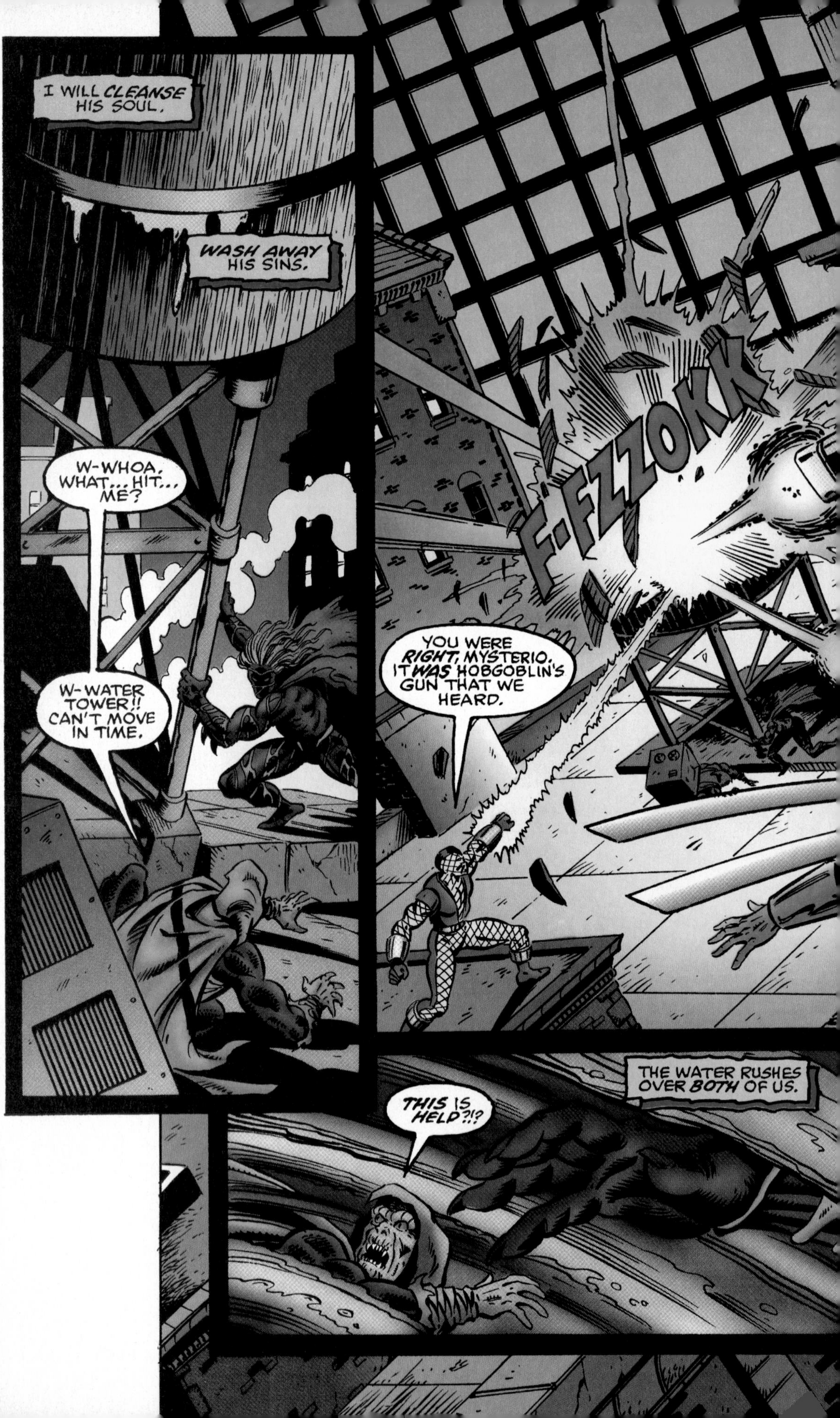
I WILL CLEANSE HIS SOUL.
WASH AWAY HIS SINS.
W-WHOA. WHAT... HIT... ME?
W-WATER TOWER!! CAN'T MOVE IN TIME.
F-FZZZOKK
YOU WERE RIGHT, MYSTERIO. IT WAS HOBGOBLIN'S GUN THAT WE HEARD.
THE WATER RUSHES OVER BOTH OF US.
THIS IS HELP?!?

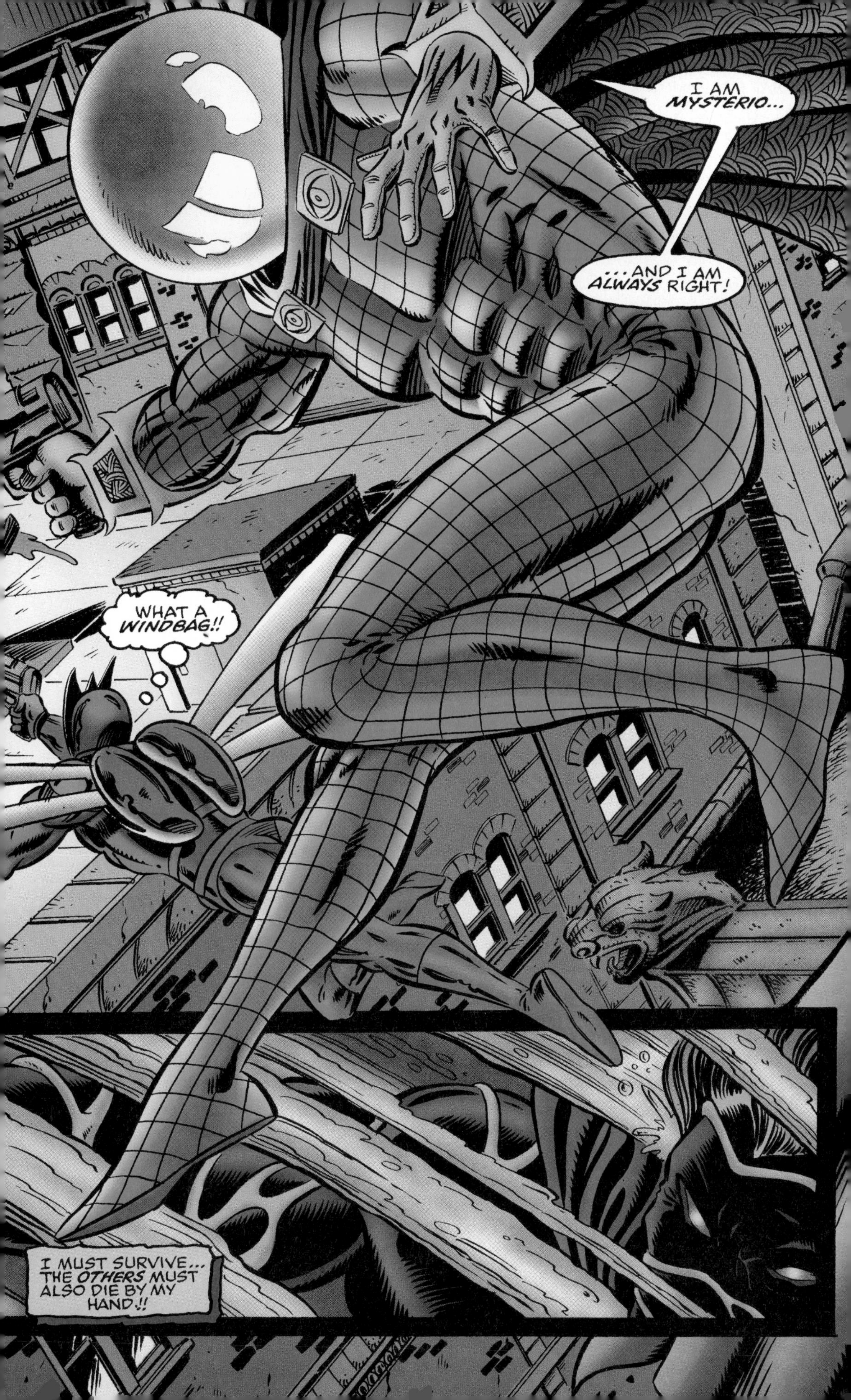
I AM MYSTERIO...
...AND I AM ALWAYS RIGHT!
WHAT A WINDBAG!!
I MUST SURVIVE... THE OTHERS MUST ALSO DIE BY MY HAND!!

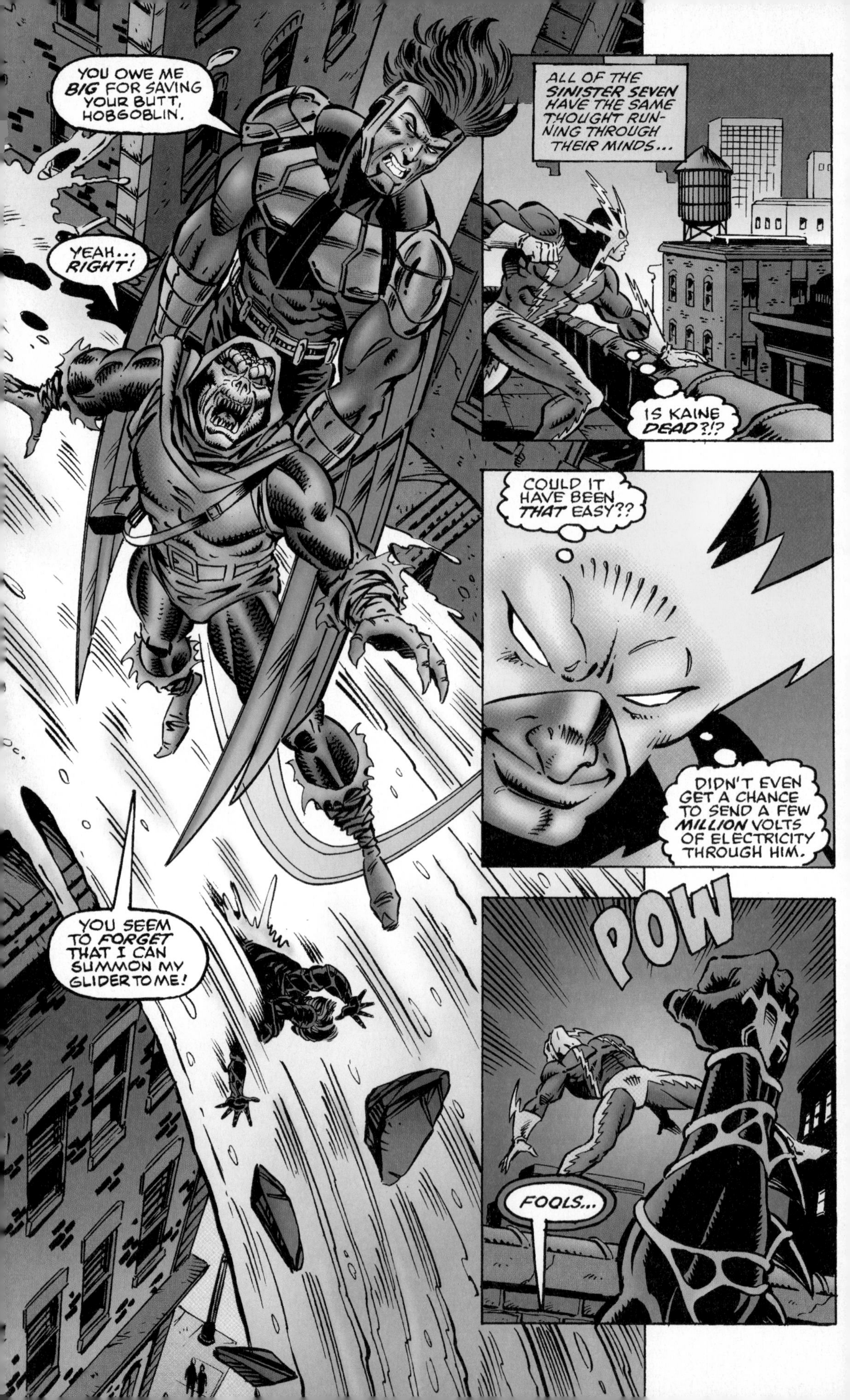
YOU OWE ME BIG FOR SAVING YOUR BUTT, HOBGOBLIN.
YEAH... RIGHT!
YOU SEEM TO FORGET THAT I CAN SUMMON MY GLIDER TO ME!
ALL OF THE SINISTER SEVEN HAVE THE SAME THOUGHT RUNNING THROUGH THEIR MINDS...
IS KAINE DEAD?!?
COULD IT HAVE BEEN THAT EASY??
DIDN'T EVEN GET A CHANCE TO SEND A FEW MILLION VOLTS OF ELECTRICITY THROUGH HIM.
POW
FOOLS...

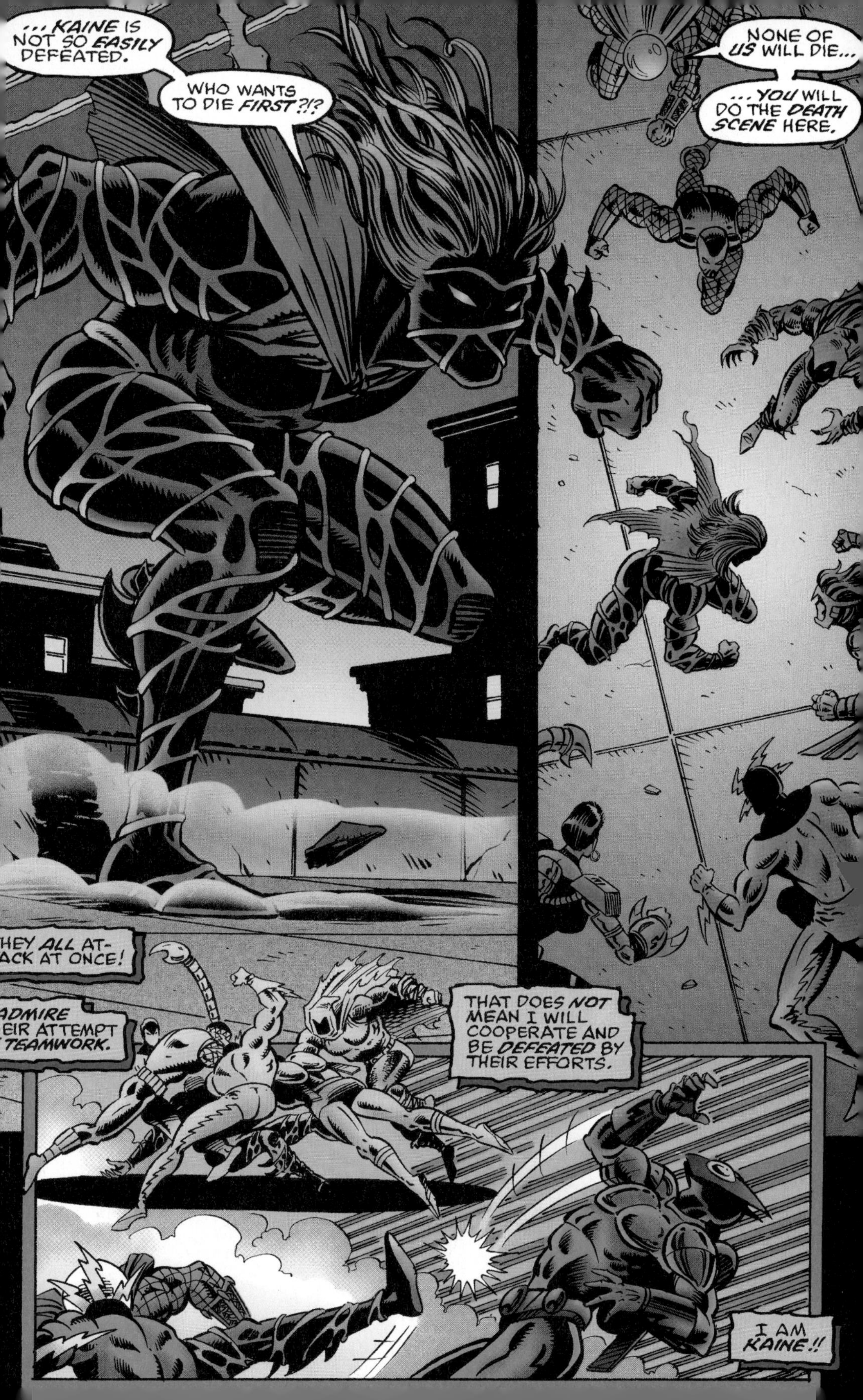

...KAINE IS NOT SO EASILY DEFEATED.
WHO WANTS TO DIE FIRST?!?
NONE OF US WILL DIE...
...YOU WILL DO THE DEATH SCENE HERE.
HEY ALL AT-
ACK AT ONCE!
ADMIRE
EIR ATTEMPT
TEAMWORK.
THAT DOES NOT MEAN I WILL COOPERATE AND BE DEFEATED BY THEIR EFFORTS.
I AM KAINE!!

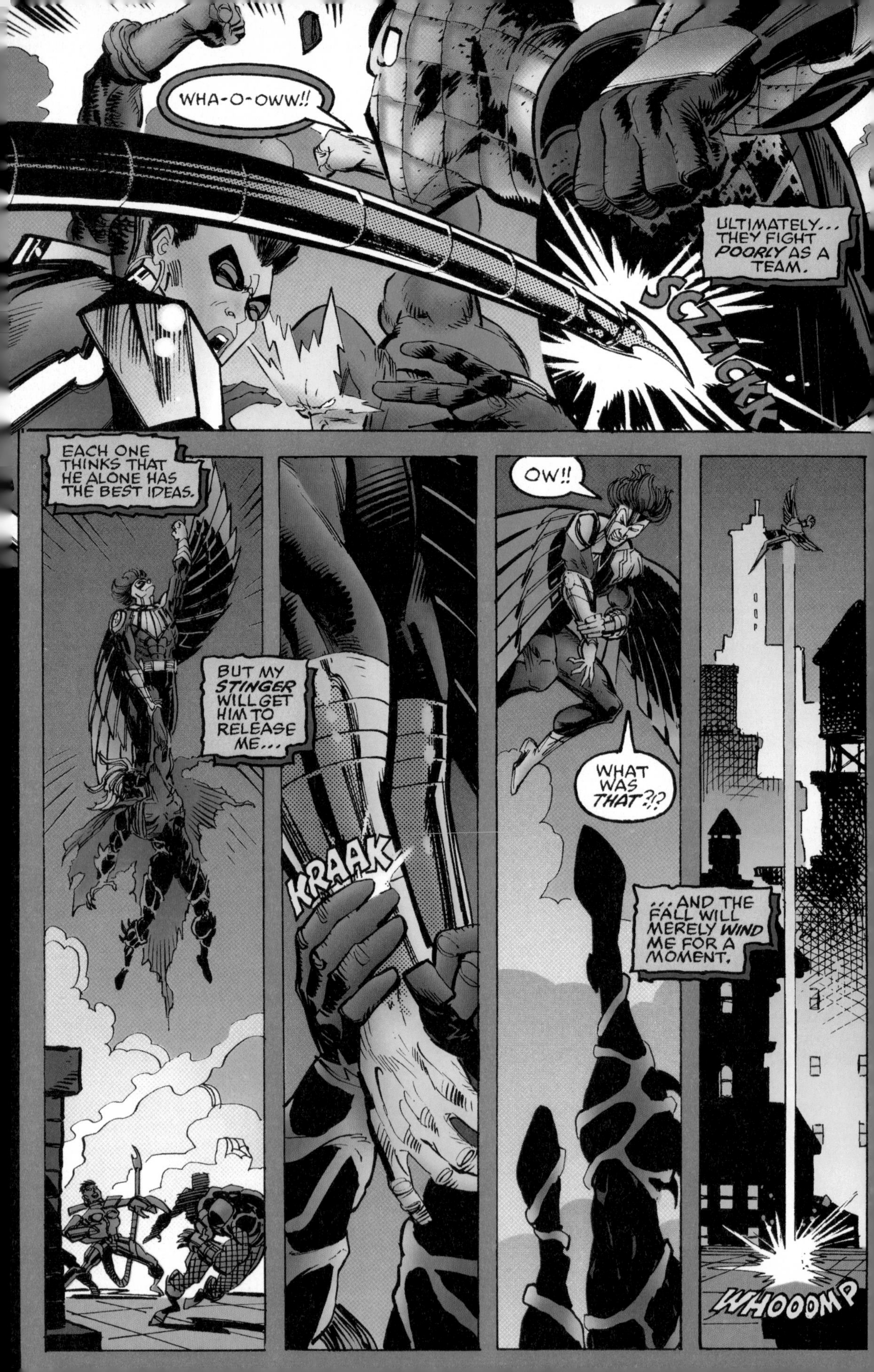
WHA-O-OWW!!
ULTIMATELY... THEY FIGHT POORLY AS A TEAM.
SCZLICKK
EACH ONE THINKS THAT HE ALONE HAS THE BEST IDEAS.
BUT MY STINGER WILL GET HIM TO RELEASE ME...
KRAAK
OW!!
WHAT WAS THAT?!?
...AND THE FALL WILL MERELY WIND ME FOR A MOMENT.
WHOOOMP

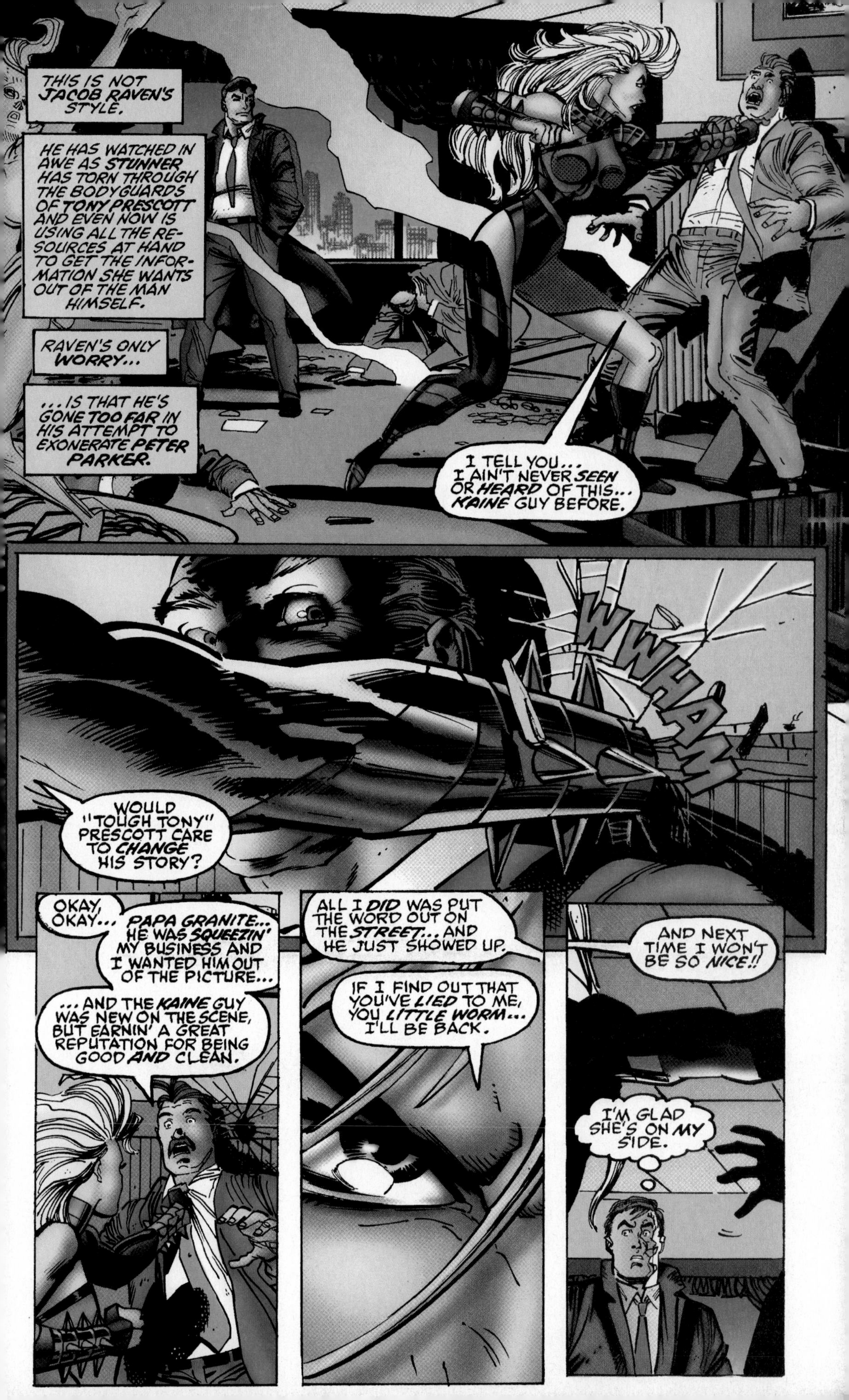

THIS IS NOT JACOB RAVEN'S STYLE.
HE HAS WATCHED IN AWE AS STUNNER HAS TORN THROUGH THE BODYGUARDS OF TONY PRESCOTT AND EVEN NOW IS USING ALL THE RESOURCES AT HAND TO GET THE INFORMATION SHE WANTS OUT OF THE MAN HIMSELF.
RAVEN'S ONLY WORRY...
...IS THAT HE'S GONE TOO FAR IN HIS ATTEMPT TO EXONERATE PETER PARKER.
I TELL YOU... I AIN'T NEVER SEEN OR HEARD OF THIS... KAINE GUY BEFORE.
WWHAM
WOULD "TOUGH TONY" PRESCOTT CARE TO CHANGE HIS STORY?
OKAY, OKAY... PAPA GRANITE... HE WAS SQUEEZIN' MY BUSINESS AND I WANTED HIM OUT OF THE PICTURE...
...AND THE KAINE GUY WAS NEW ON THE SCENE, BUT EARNIN' A GREAT REPUTATION FOR BEING GOOD AND CLEAN.
ALL I DID WAS PUT THE WORD OUT ON THE STREET... AND HE JUST SHOWED UP.
IF I FIND OUT THAT YOU'VE LIED TO ME, YOU LITTLE WORM... I'LL BE BACK.
AND NEXT TIME I WON'T BE SO NICE!!
I'M GLAD SHE'S ON MY SIDE.

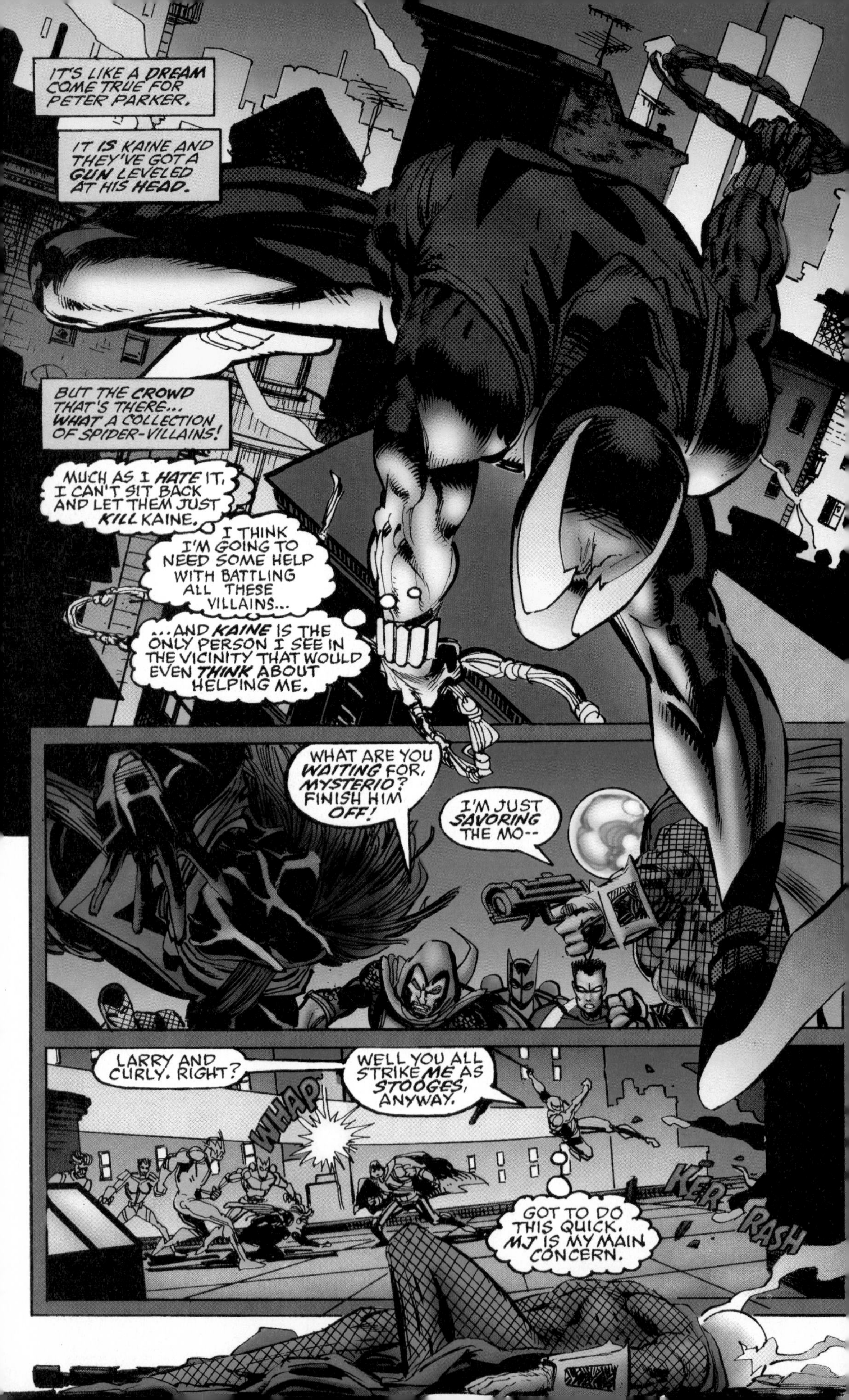
IT'S LIKE A DREAM COME TRUE FOR PETER PARKER.
IT IS KAINE AND THEY'VE GOT A GUN LEVELED AT HIS HEAD.
BUT THE CROWD THAT'S THERE... WHAT A COLLECTION OF SPIDER-VILLAINS!
MUCH AS I HATE IT, I CAN'T SIT BACK AND LET THEM JUST KILL KAINE.
I THINK I'M GOING TO NEED SOME HELP WITH BATTLING ALL THESE VILLAINS...
...AND KAINE IS THE ONLY PERSON I SEE IN THE VICINITY THAT WOULD EVEN THINK ABOUT HELPING ME.
WHAT ARE YOU WAITING FOR, MYSTERIO? FINISH HIM OFF!
I'M JUST SAVORING THE MO--
LARRY AND CURLY. RIGHT?
WELL YOU ALL STRIKE ME AS STOOGES, ANYWAY.
WHAP
GOT TO DO THIS QUICK. MJ IS MY MAIN CONCERN.
KER-RASH

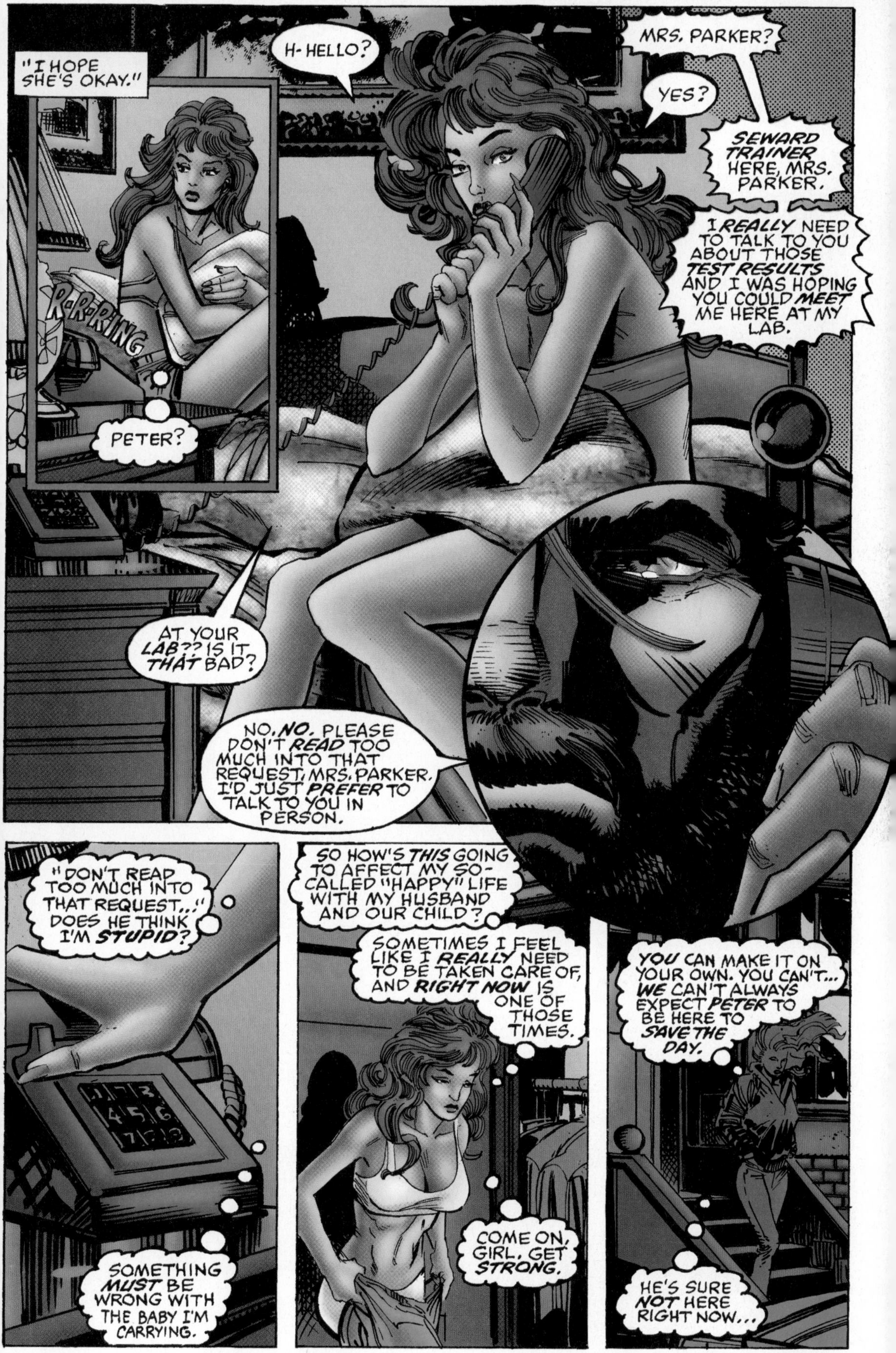

"I HOPE SHE'S OKAY."
R-R-RING
PETER?
H- HELLO?
MRS. PARKER?
YES?
SEWARD TRAINER HERE, MRS. PARKER.
I REALLY NEED TO TALK TO YOU ABOUT THOSE TEST RESULTS AND I WAS HOPING YOU COULD MEET ME HERE AT MY LAB.
AT YOUR LAB?? IS IT THAT BAD?
NO. NO. PLEASE DON'T READ TOO MUCH INTO THAT REQUEST, MRS. PARKER. I'D JUST PREFER TO TALK TO YOU IN PERSON.
"DON'T READ TOO MUCH INTO THAT REQUEST..." DOES HE THINK I'M STUPID?
SOMETHING MUST BE WRONG WITH THE BABY I'M CARRYING.
SO HOW'S THIS GOING TO AFFECT MY SO-CALLED "HAPPY" LIFE WITH MY HUSBAND AND OUR CHILD?
SOMETIMES I FEEL LIKE I REALLY NEED TO BE TAKEN CARE OF, AND RIGHT NOW IS ONE OF THOSE TIMES.
COME ON, GIRL, GET STRONG.
YOU CAN MAKE IT ON YOUR OWN. YOU CAN'T... WE CAN'T ALWAYS EXPECT PETER TO BE HERE TO SAVE THE DAY.
HE'S SURE NOT HERE RIGHT NOW...

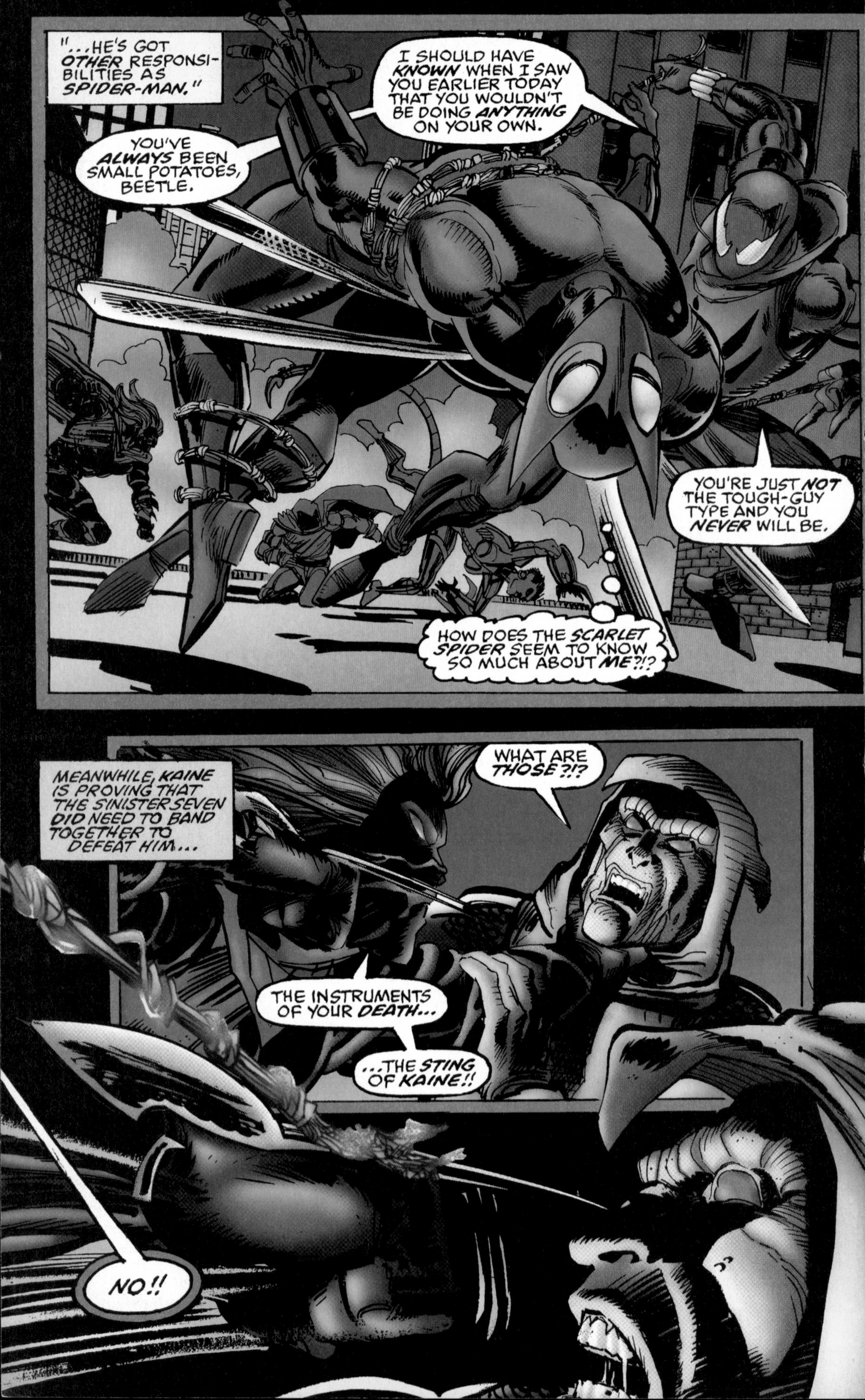
"...HE'S GOT OTHER RESPONSIBILITIES AS SPIDER-MAN."
I SHOULD HAVE KNOWN WHEN I SAW YOU EARLIER TODAY THAT YOU WOULDN'T BE DOING ANYTHING ON YOUR OWN.
YOU'VE ALWAYS BEEN SMALL POTATOES, BEETLE.
YOU'RE JUST NOT THE TOUGH-GUY TYPE AND YOU NEVER WILL BE.
HOW DOES THE SCARLET SPIDER SEEM TO KNOW SO MUCH ABOUT ME?!?
MEANWHILE, KAINE IS PROVING THAT THE SINISTER SEVEN DID NEED TO BAND TOGETHER TO DEFEAT HIM...
WHAT ARE THOSE?!?
THE INSTRUMENTS OF YOUR DEATH...
...THE STING OF KAINE!!
NO!!

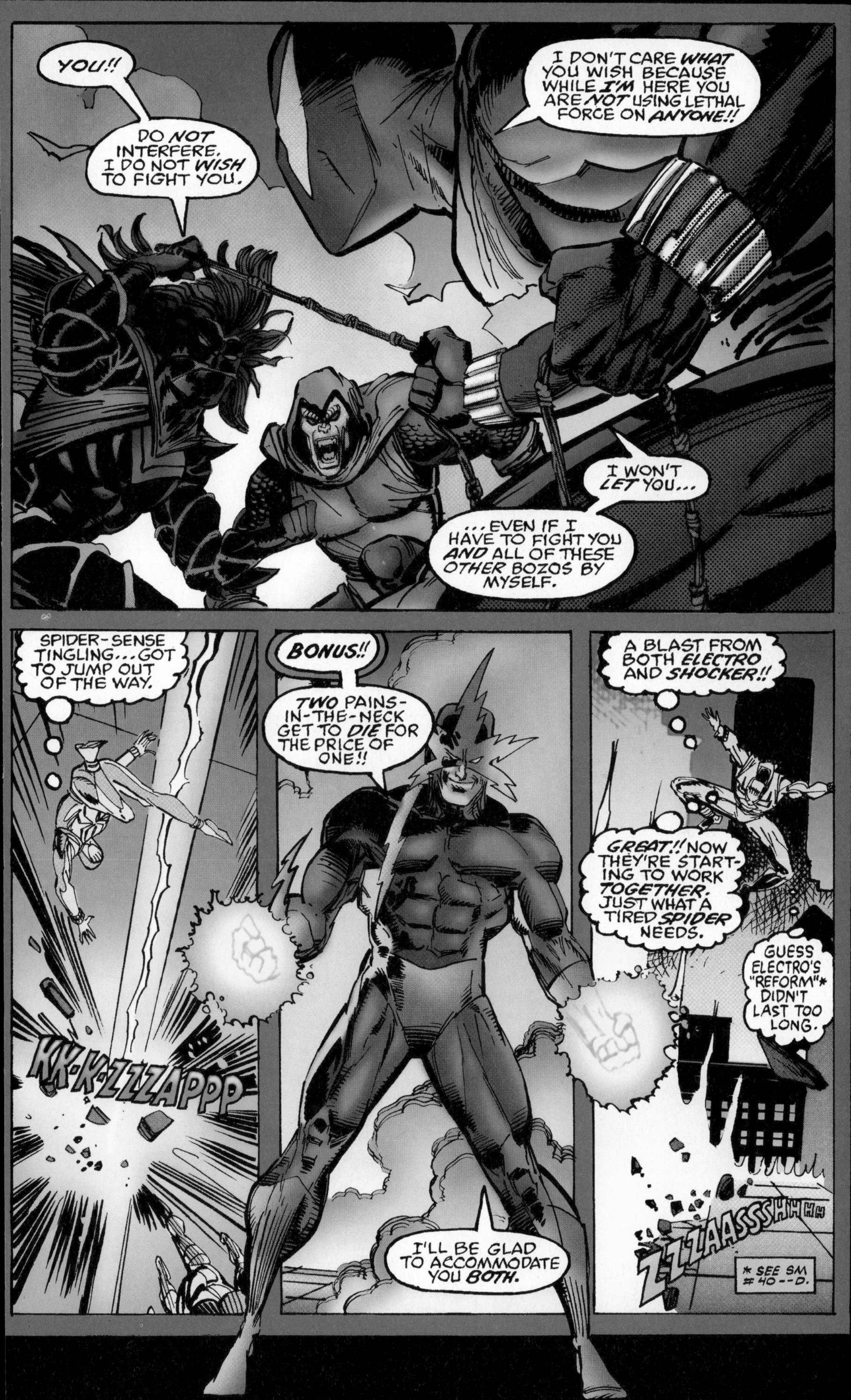
YOU!!
DO NOT INTERFERE. I DO NOT WISH TO FIGHT YOU.
I DON'T CARE WHAT YOU WISH BECAUSE WHILE I'M HERE YOU ARE NOT USING LETHAL FORCE ON ANYONE!!
I WON'T LET YOU...
...EVEN IF I HAVE TO FIGHT YOU AND ALL OF THESE OTHER BOZOS BY MYSELF.
SPIDER-SENSE TINGLING...GOT TO JUMP OUT OF THE WAY.
KK-K-ZZZZAPPP
BONUS!!
TWO PAINS-IN-THE-NECK GET TO DIE FOR THE PRICE OF ONE!!
I'LL BE GLAD TO ACCOMMODATE YOU BOTH.
A BLAST FROM BOTH ELECTRO AND SHOCKER!!
GREAT!! NOW THEY'RE STARTING TO WORK TOGETHER. JUST WHAT A TIRED SPIDER NEEDS.
GUESS ELECTRO'S "REFORM"* DIDN'T LAST TOO LONG.
ZZZZAASSSHHHHH
* SEE SM #40--D.

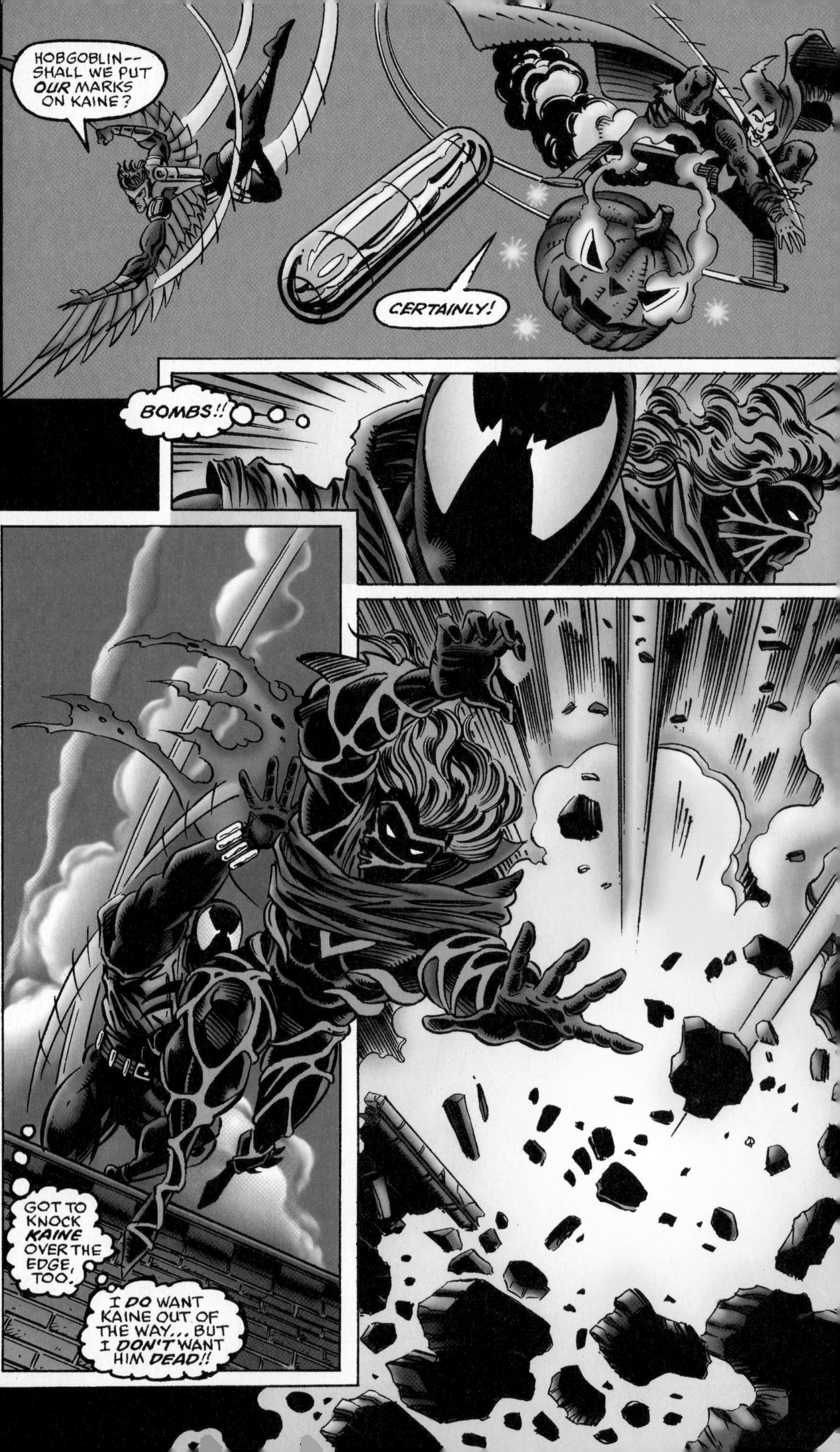
HOBGOBLIN-- SHALL WE PUT OUR MARKS ON KAINE?
CERTAINLY!
BOMBS!!
GOT TO KNOCK KAINE OVER THE EDGE, TOO.
I DO WANT KAINE OUT OF THE WAY... BUT I DON'T WANT HIM DEAD!!

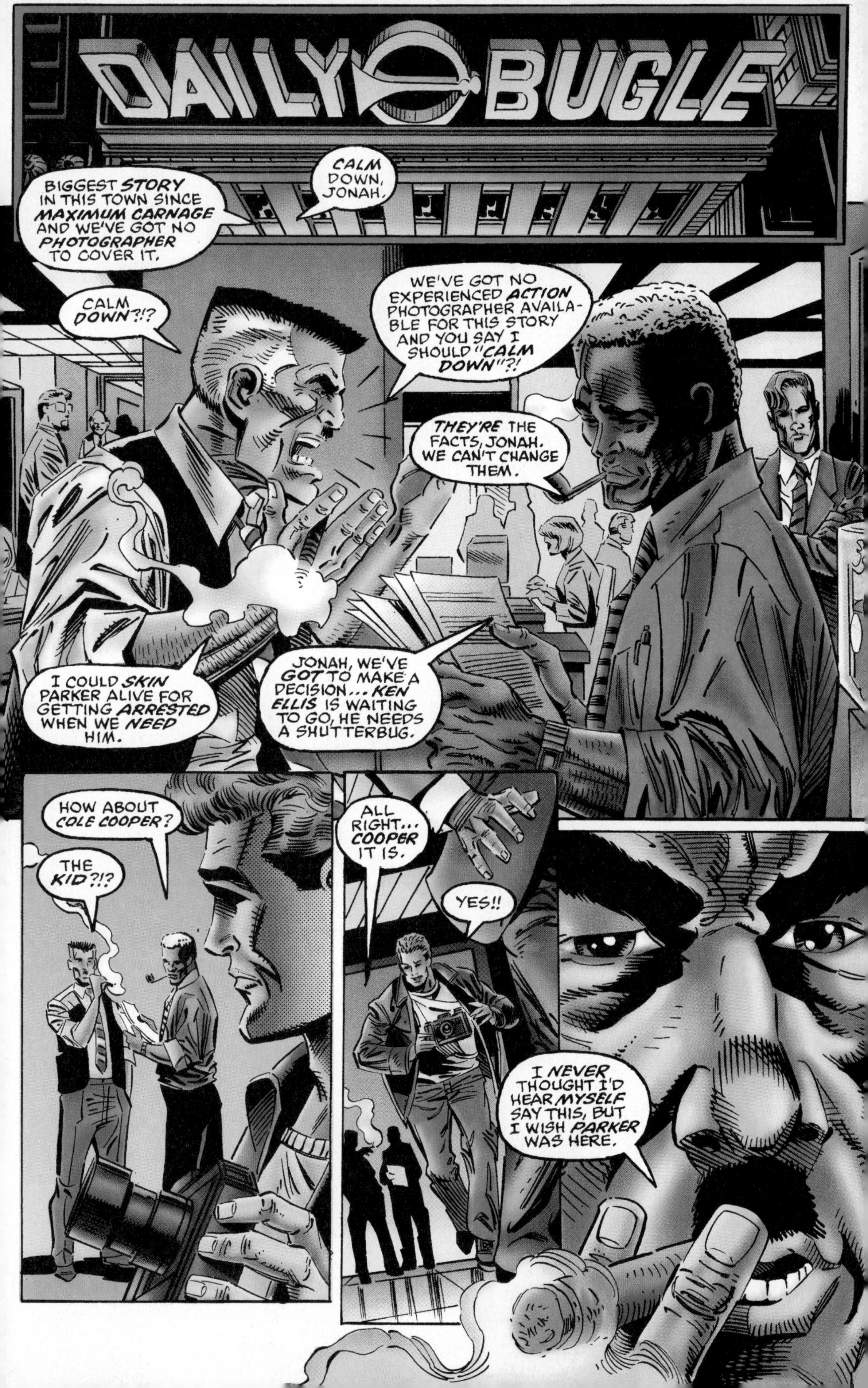
DAILY BUGLE
BIGGEST STORY IN THIS TOWN SINCE MAXIMUM CARNAGE AND WE'VE GOT NO PHOTOGRAPHER TO COVER IT.
CALM DOWN, JONAH.
CALM DOWN?!?
WE'VE GOT NO EXPERIENCED ACTION PHOTOGRAPHER AVAILABLE FOR THIS STORY AND YOU SAY I SHOULD "CALM DOWN"?!
THEY'RE THE FACTS, JONAH. WE CAN'T CHANGE THEM.
I COULD SKIN PARKER ALIVE FOR GETTING ARRESTED WHEN WE NEED HIM.
JONAH, WE'VE GOT TO MAKE A DECISION... KEN ELLIS IS WAITING TO GO, HE NEEDS A SHUTTERBUG.
HOW ABOUT COLE COOPER?
THE KID?!?
ALL RIGHT... COOPER IT IS.
YES!!
I NEVER THOUGHT I'D HEAR MYSELF SAY THIS, BUT I WISH PARKER WAS HERE.

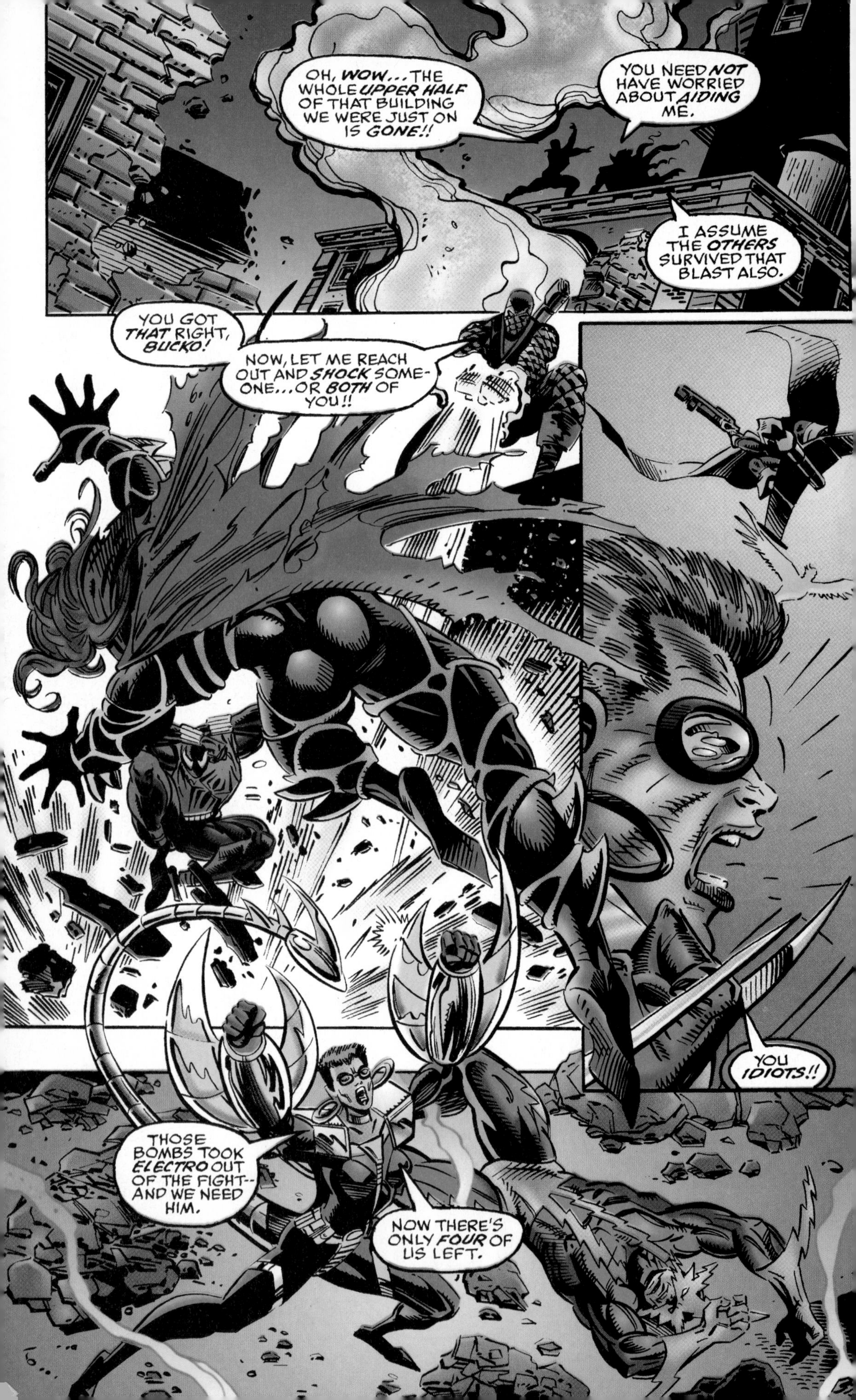

OH, WOW... THE WHOLE UPPER HALF OF THAT BUILDING WE WERE JUST ON IS GONE!!
YOU NEED NOT HAVE WORRIED ABOUT AIDING ME.
I ASSUME THE OTHERS SURVIVED THAT BLAST ALSO.
YOU GOT THAT RIGHT, BUCKO!
NOW, LET ME REACH OUT AND SHOCK SOME-ONE...OR BOTH OF YOU!!
YOU IDIOTS!!
THOSE BOMBS TOOK ELECTRO OUT OF THE FIGHT-- AND WE NEED HIM.
NOW THERE'S ONLY FOUR OF US LEFT.

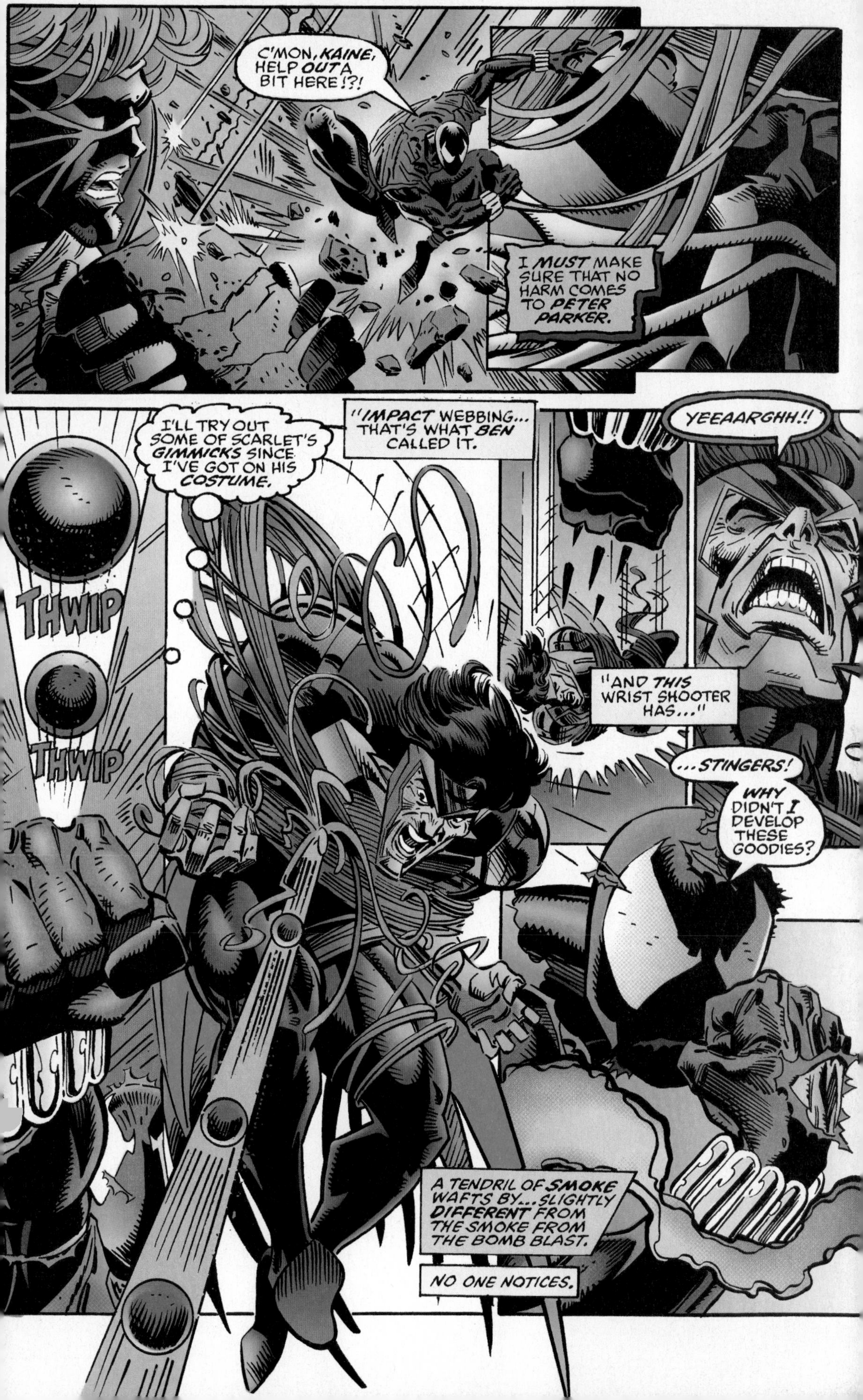
C'MON, KAINE, HELP OUT A BIT HERE!?!
I MUST MAKE SURE THAT NO HARM COMES TO PETER PARKER.
I'LL TRY OUT SOME OF SCARLET'S GIMMICKS SINCE I'VE GOT ON HIS COSTUME.
"IMPACT WEBBING... THAT'S WHAT BEN CALLED IT.
THWIP
THWIP
YEEAARGHH!!
"AND THIS WRIST SHOOTER HAS..."
...STINGERS!
WHY DIDN'T I DEVELOP THESE GOODIES?
A TENDRIL OF SMOKE WAFTS BY... SLIGHTLY DIFFERENT FROM THE SMOKE FROM THE BOMB BLAST.
NO ONE NOTICES.

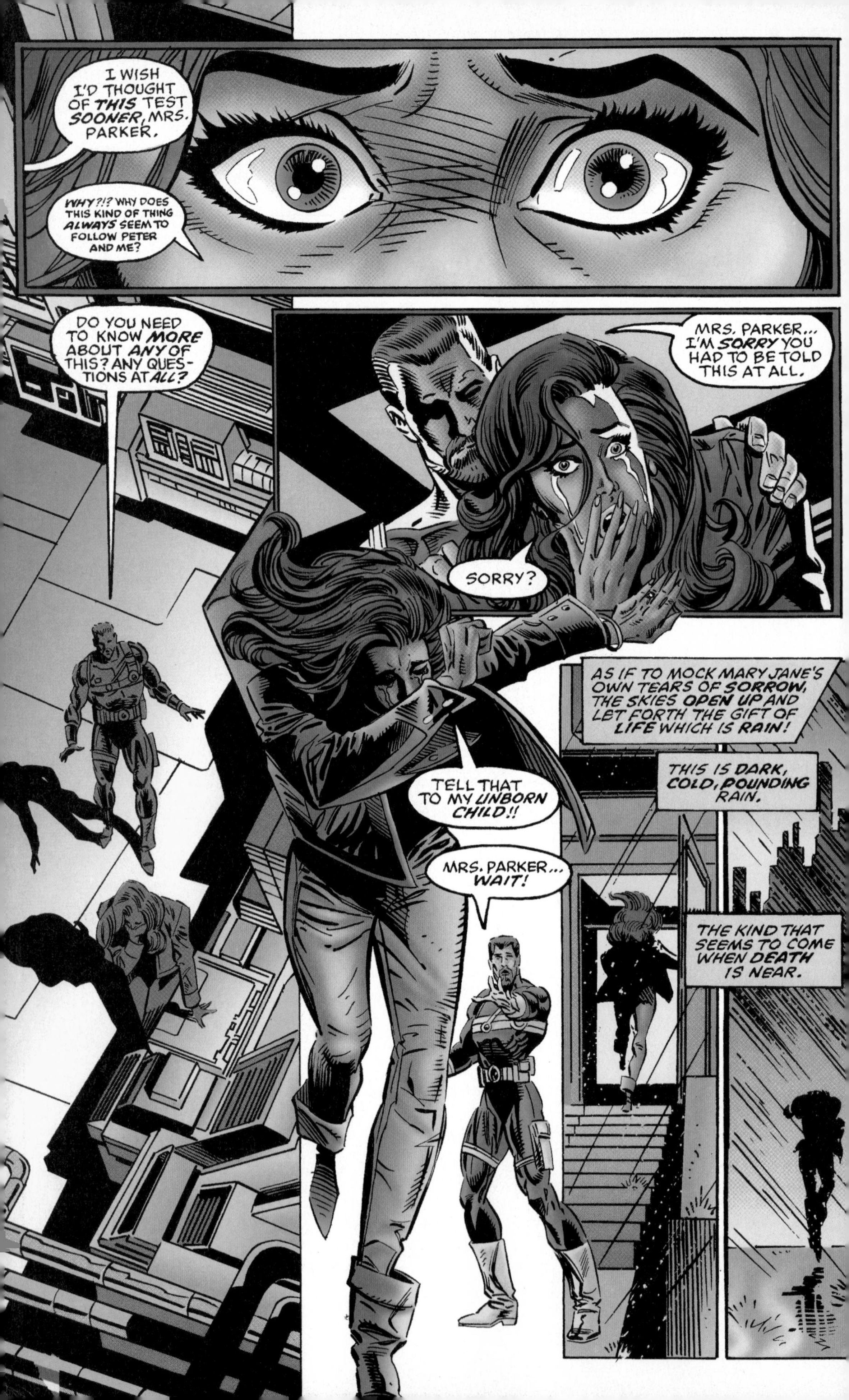
I WISH I'D THOUGHT OF THIS TEST SOONER, MRS. PARKER.
WHY?!? WHY DOES THIS KIND OF THING ALWAYS SEEM TO FOLLOW PETER AND ME?
DO YOU NEED TO KNOW MORE ABOUT ANY OF THIS? ANY QUESTIONS AT ALL?
MRS. PARKER... I'M SORRY YOU HAD TO BE TOLD THIS AT ALL.
SORRY?
TELL THAT TO MY UNBORN CHILD!!
AS IF TO MOCK MARY JANE'S OWN TEARS OF SORROW, THE SKIES OPEN UP AND LET FORTH THE GIFT OF LIFE WHICH IS RAIN!
THIS IS DARK, COLD, POUNDING RAIN.
MRS. PARKER... WAIT!
THE KIND THAT SEEMS TO COME WHEN DEATH IS NEAR.

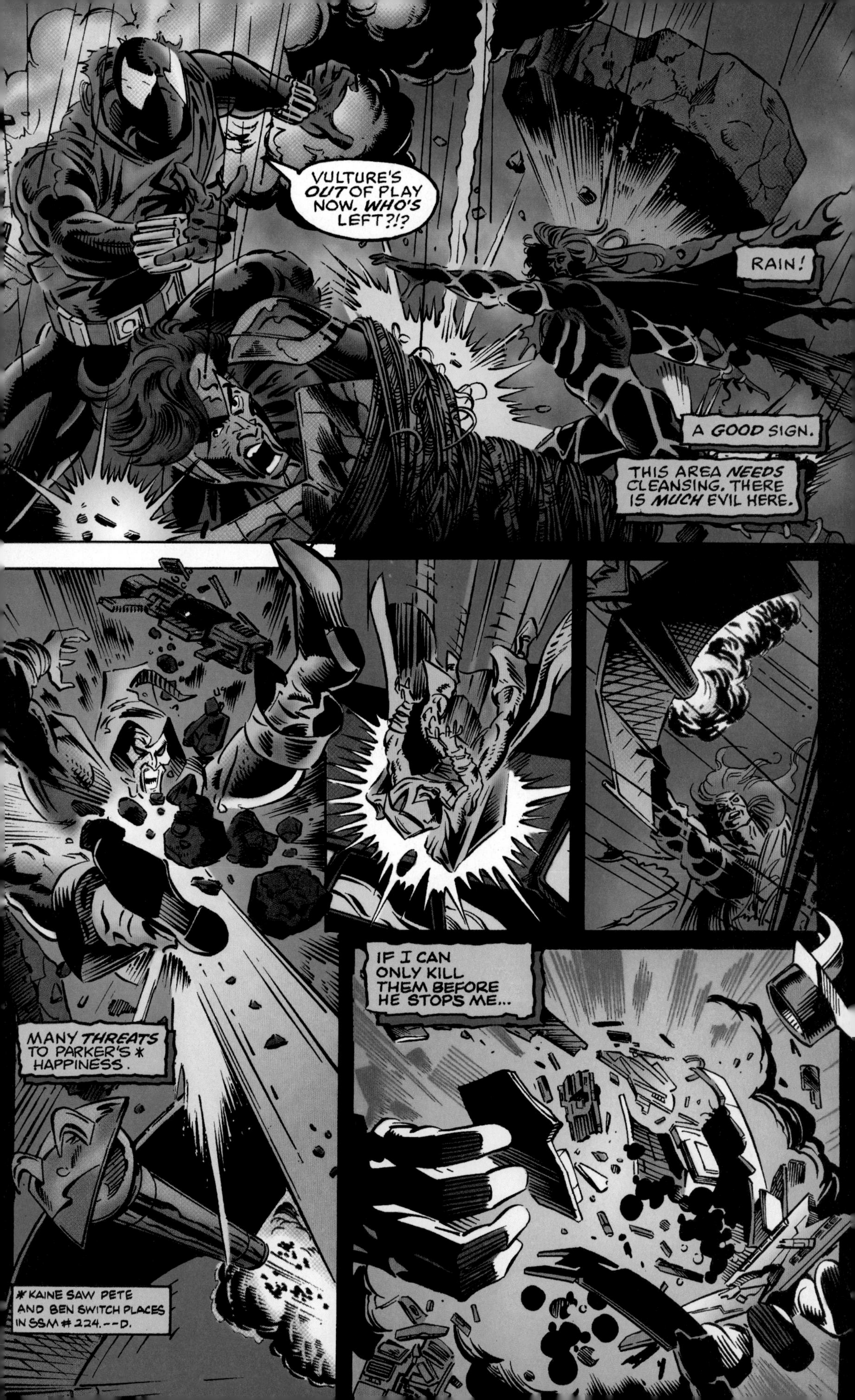
VULTURE'S OUT OF PLAY NOW. WHO'S LEFT?!?
RAIN!
A GOOD SIGN.
THIS AREA NEEDS CLEANSING. THERE IS MUCH EVIL HERE.
MANY THREATS TO PARKER'S* HAPPINESS.
*KAINE SAW PETE AND BEN SWITCH PLACES IN SSM #224.--D.
IF I CAN ONLY KILL THEM BEFORE HE STOPS ME...

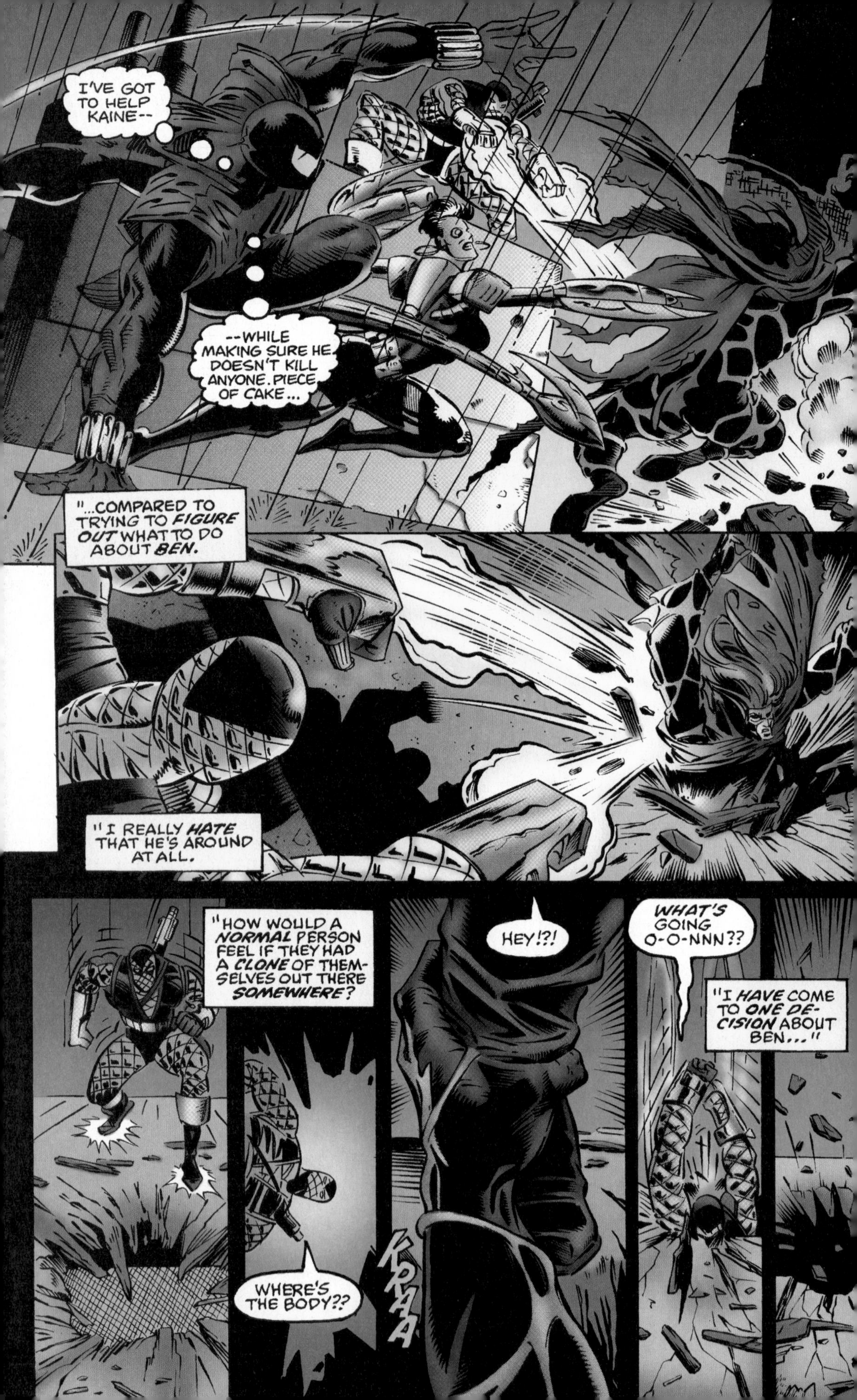
I'VE GOT TO HELP KAINE--
--WHILE MAKING SURE HE DOESN'T KILL ANYONE. PIECE OF CAKE...
"...COMPARED TO TRYING TO FIGURE OUT WHAT TO DO ABOUT BEN.
"I REALLY HATE THAT HE'S AROUND AT ALL.
"HOW WOULD A NORMAL PERSON FEEL IF THEY HAD A CLONE OF THEMSELVES OUT THERE SOMEWHERE?
WHERE'S THE BODY??
HEY!?!
KRAA
WHAT'S GOING O-O-NNN??
"I HAVE COME TO ONE DECISION ABOUT BEN..."

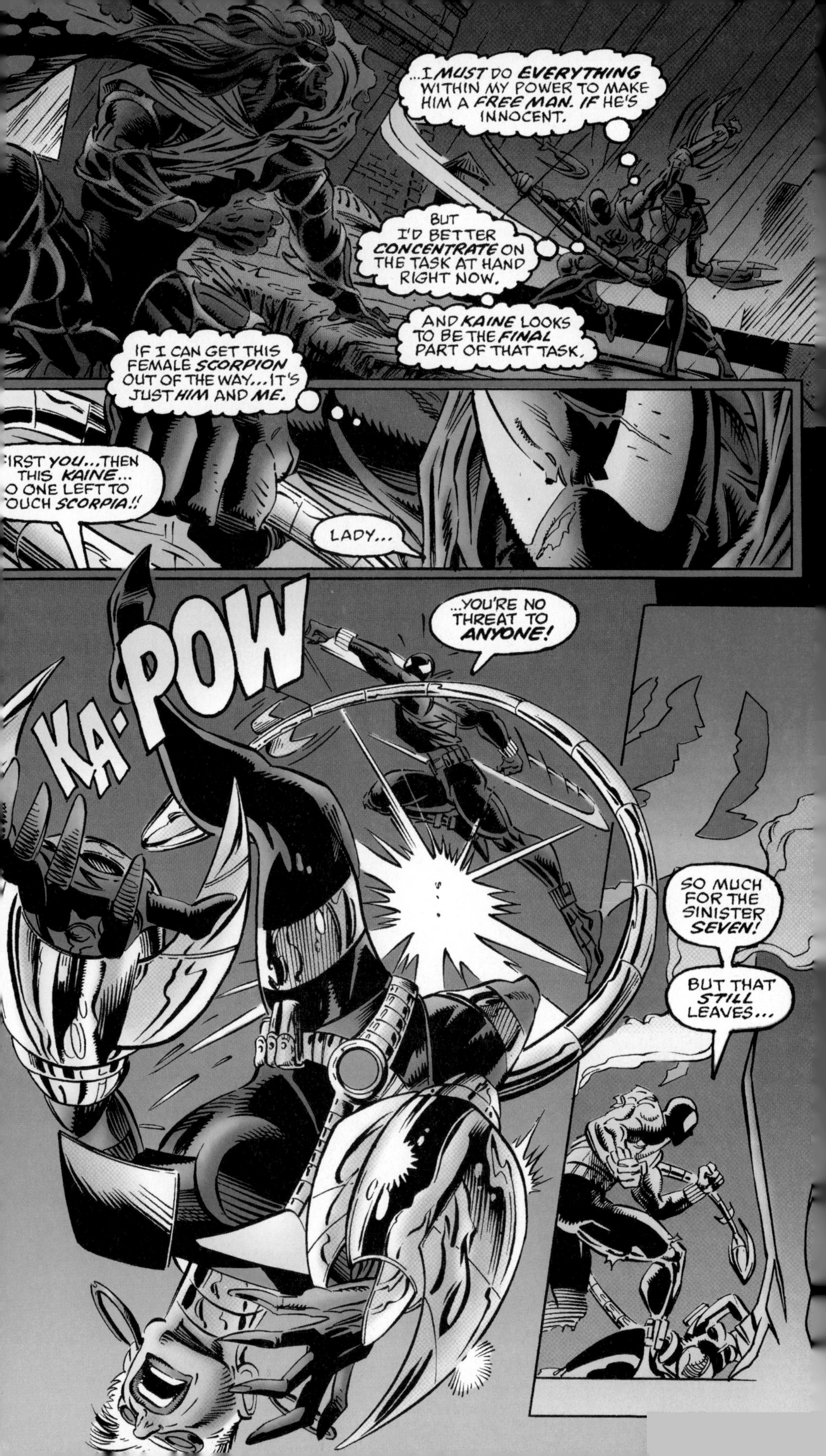
...I MUST DO EVERYTHING WITHIN MY POWER TO MAKE HIM A FREE MAN. IF HE'S INNOCENT.
BUT I'D BETTER CONCENTRATE ON THE TASK AT HAND RIGHT NOW.
AND KAINE LOOKS TO BE THE FINAL PART OF THAT TASK.
IF I CAN GET THIS FEMALE SCORPION OUT OF THE WAY... IT'S JUST HIM AND ME.
FIRST YOU... THEN THIS KAINE... O ONE LEFT TO OUCH SCORPIA!!
LADY...
KA-POW
...YOU'RE NO THREAT TO ANYONE!
SO MUCH FOR THE SINISTER SEVEN!
BUT THAT STILL LEAVES...

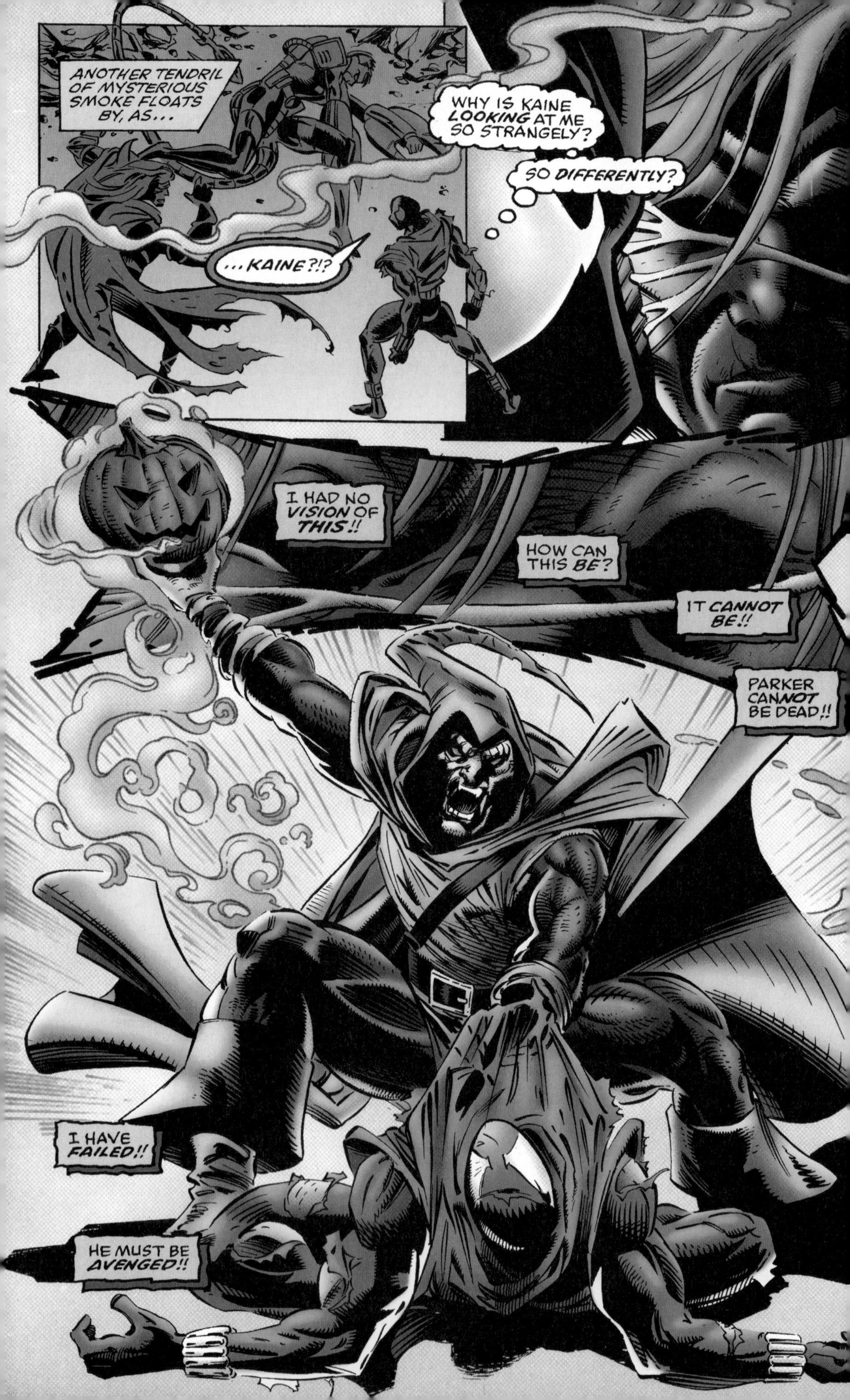
ANOTHER TENDRIL OF MYSTERIOUS SMOKE FLOATS BY, AS...
WHY IS KAINE LOOKING AT ME SO STRANGELY?
SO DIFFERENTLY?
...KAINE?!?
I HAD NO VISION OF THIS!!
HOW CAN THIS BE?
IT CANNOT BE!!
PARKER CANNOT BE DEAD!!
I HAVE FAILED!!
HE MUST BE AVENGED!!

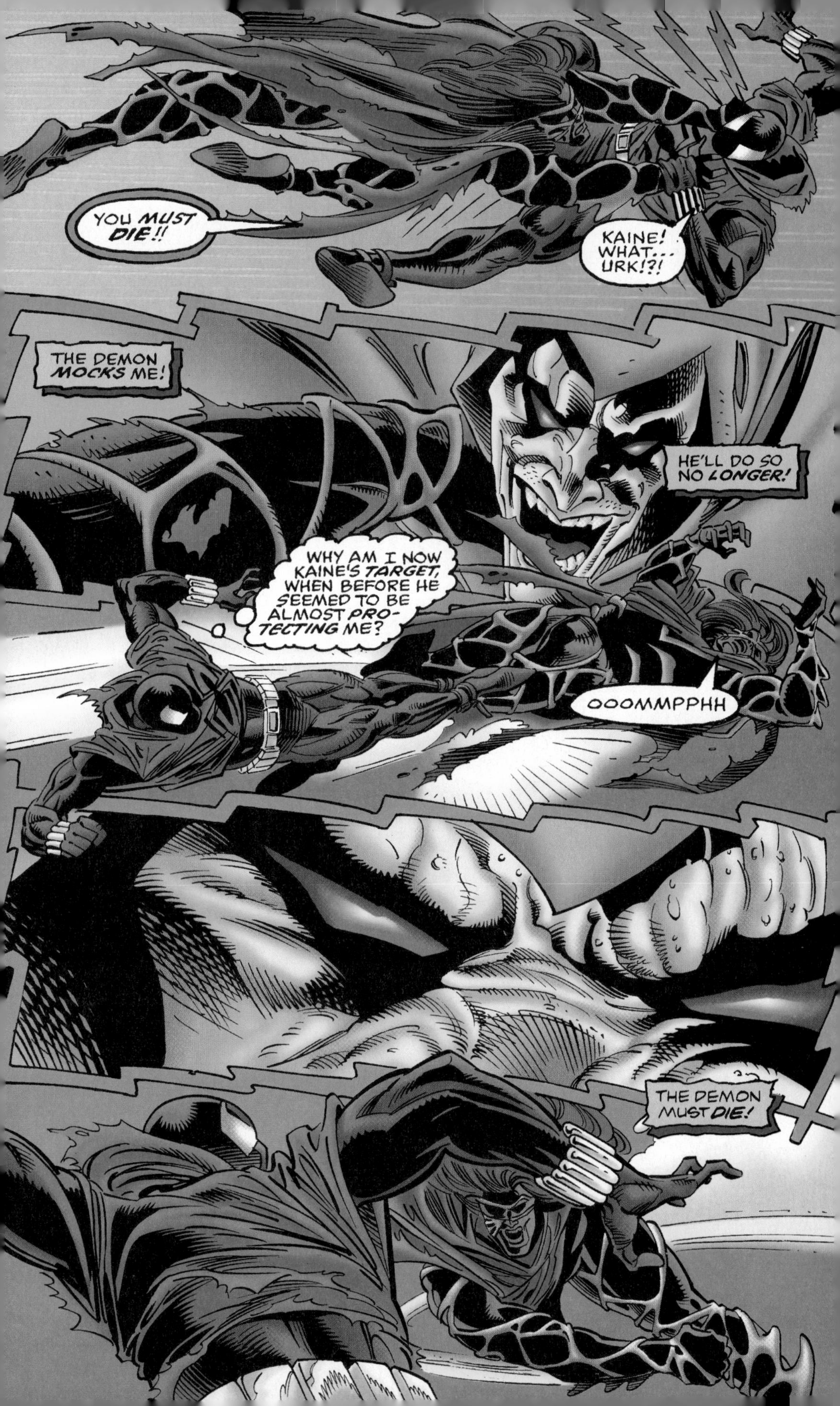
YOU MUST DIE!!
KAINE! WHAT... URK!?!
THE DEMON MOCKS ME!
HE'LL DO SO NO LONGER!
WHY AM I NOW KAINE'S TARGET, WHEN BEFORE HE SEEMED TO BE ALMOST PRO-TECTING ME?
OOOMMPPHH
THE DEMON MUST DIE!

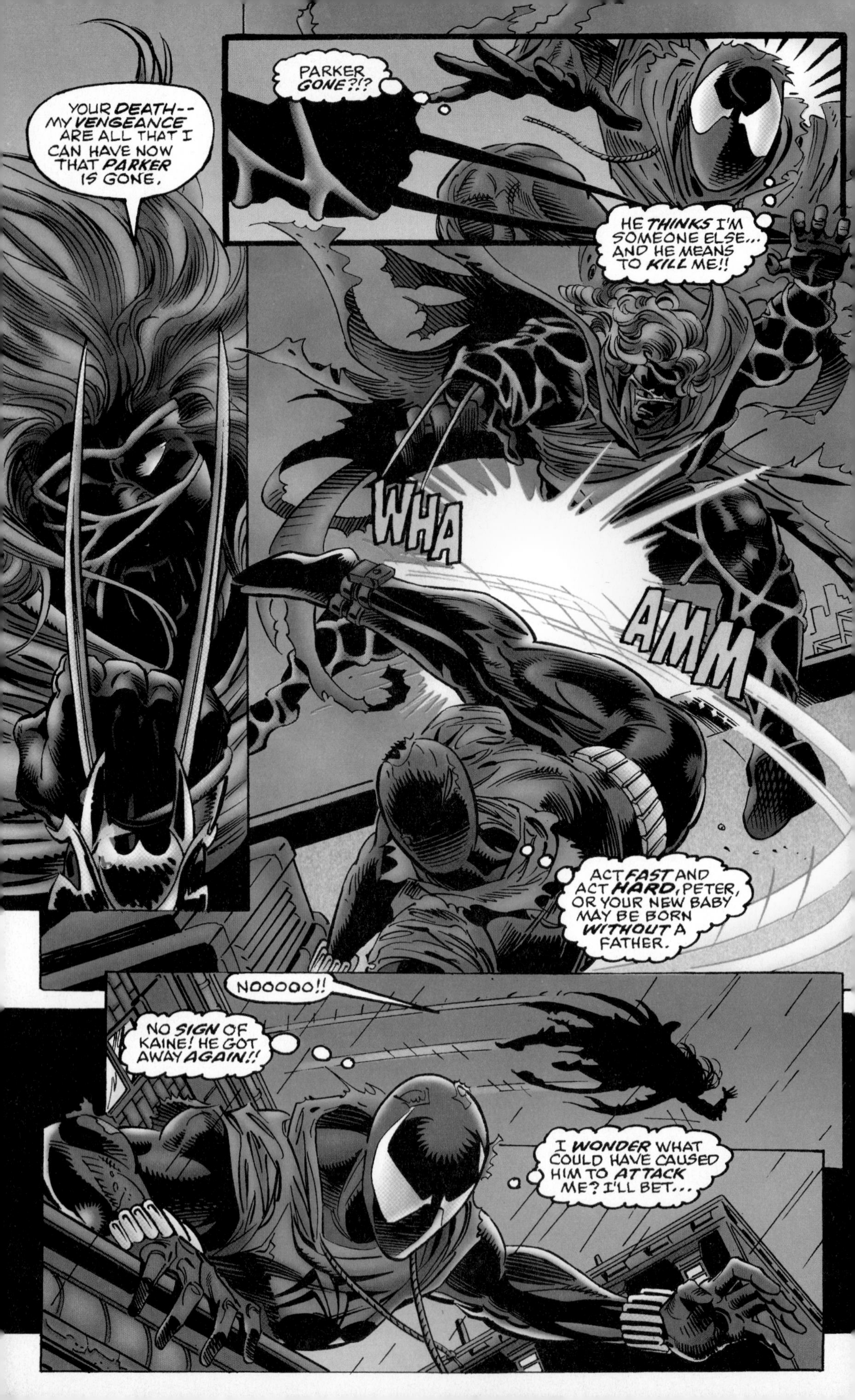
YOUR DEATH-- MY VENGEANCE ARE ALL THAT I CAN HAVE NOW THAT PARKER IS GONE.
PARKER GONE?!?
HE THINKS I'M SOMEONE ELSE... AND HE MEANS TO KILL ME!!
WHA
AMM
ACT FAST AND ACT HARD, PETER, OR YOUR NEW BABY MAY BE BORN WITHOUT A FATHER.
NOOOOO!!
NO SIGN OF KAINE! HE GOT AWAY AGAIN!!
I WONDER WHAT COULD HAVE CAUSED HIM TO ATTACK ME? I'LL BET...

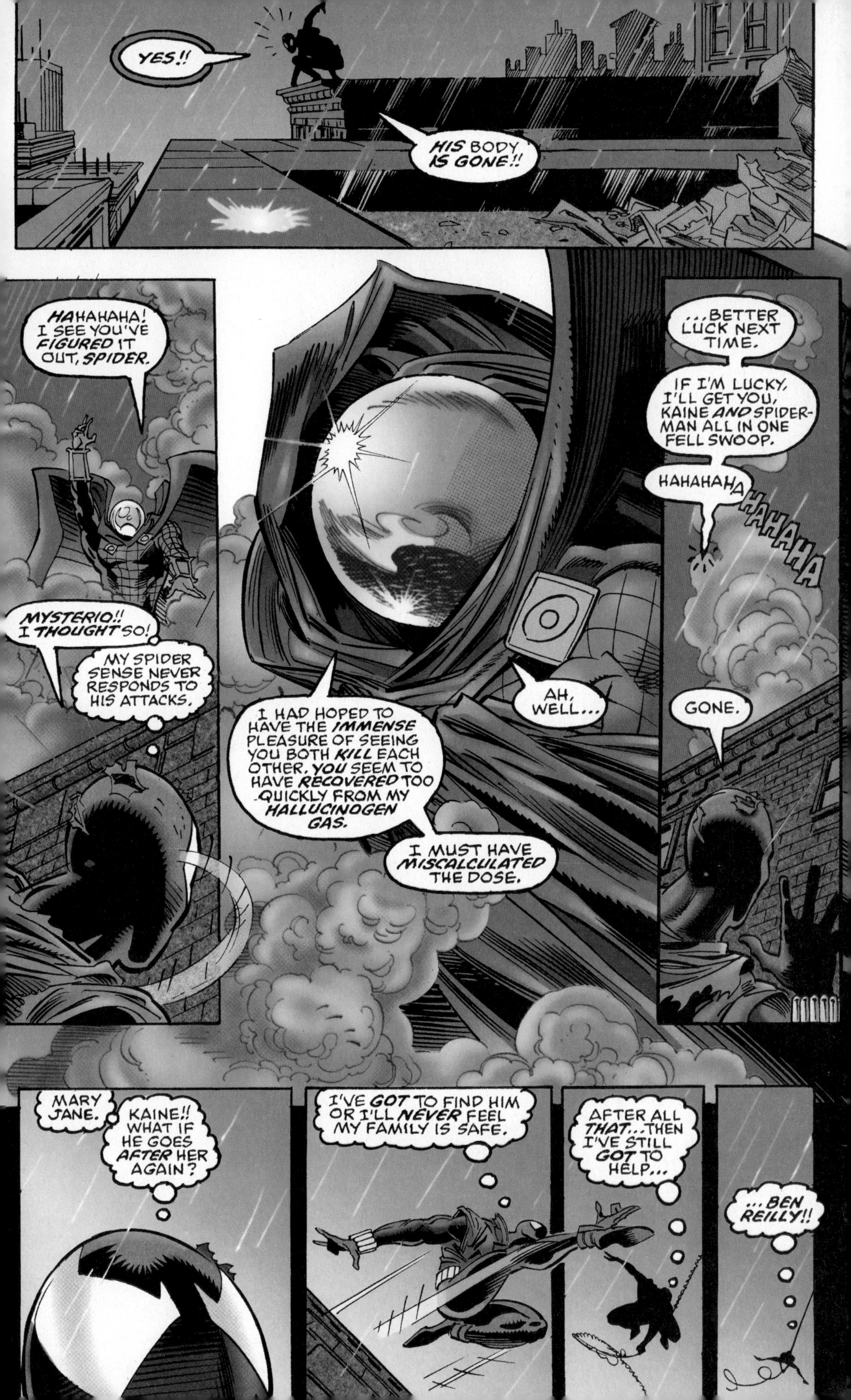
YES!!
HIS BODY IS GONE!!
HAHAHAHA! I SEE YOU'VE FIGURED IT OUT, SPIDER.
MYSTERIO!! I THOUGHT SO!
MY SPIDER SENSE NEVER RESPONDS TO HIS ATTACKS.
I HAD HOPED TO HAVE THE IMMENSE PLEASURE OF SEEING YOU BOTH KILL EACH OTHER. YOU SEEM TO HAVE RECOVERED TOO QUICKLY FROM MY HALLUCINOGEN GAS.
I MUST HAVE MISCALCULATED THE DOSE.
AH, WELL...
...BETTER LUCK NEXT TIME.
IF I'M LUCKY, I'LL GET YOU, KAINE AND SPIDER-MAN ALL IN ONE FELL SWOOP.
HAHAHAHA
HAHAHA
GONE.
MARY JANE.
KAINE!! WHAT IF HE GOES AFTER HER AGAIN?
I'VE GOT TO FIND HIM OR I'LL NEVER FEEL MY FAMILY IS SAFE.
AFTER ALL THAT...THEN I'VE STILL GOT TO HELP...
...BEN REILLY!!

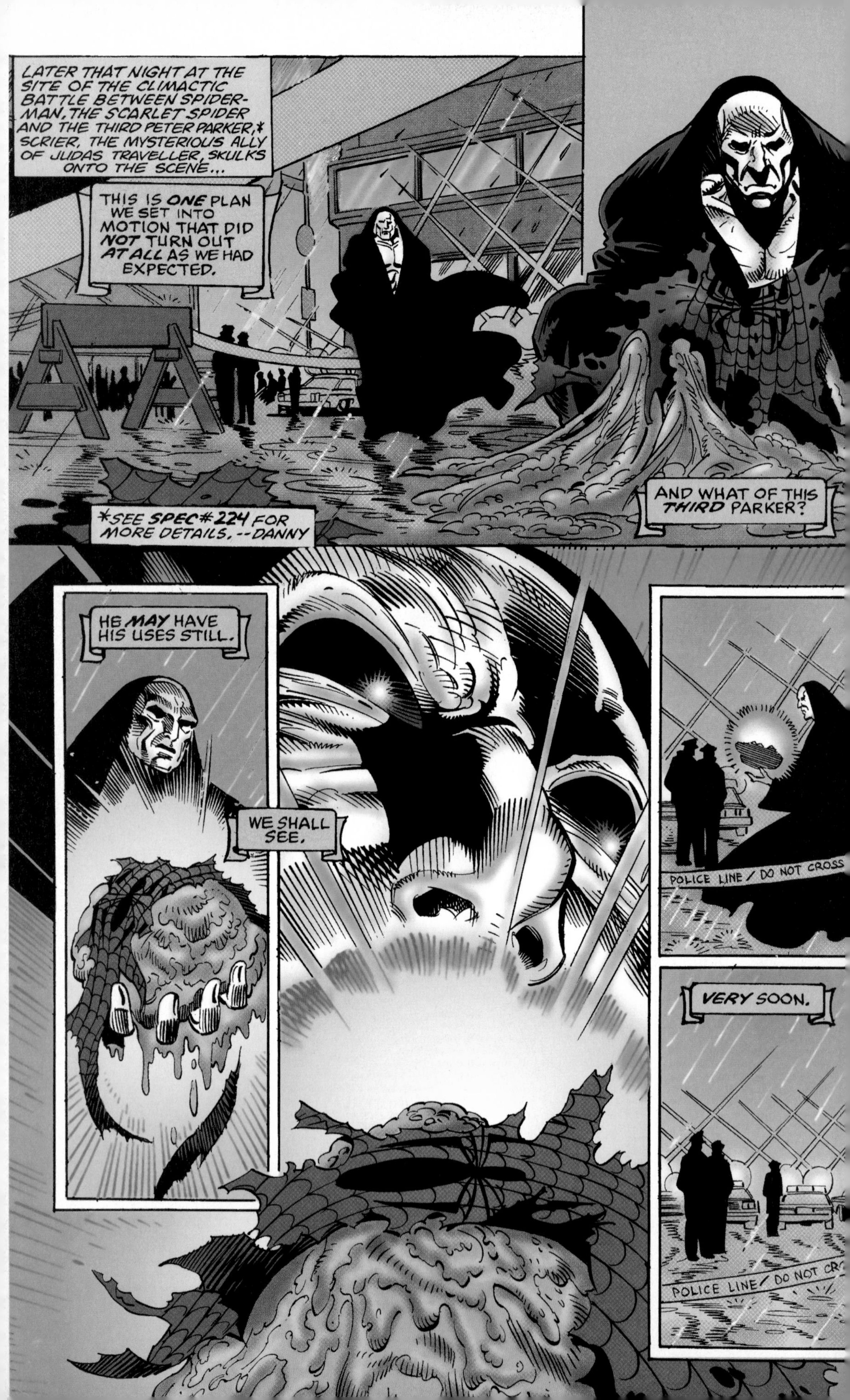
LATER THAT NIGHT AT THE SITE OF THE CLIMACTIC BATTLE BETWEEN SPIDER-MAN, THE SCARLET SPIDER AND THE THIRD PETER PARKER,* SCRIER, THE MYSTERIOUS ALLY OF JUDAS TRAVELLER, SKULKS ONTO THE SCENE...
THIS IS ONE PLAN WE SET INTO MOTION THAT DID NOT TURN OUT AT ALL AS WE HAD EXPECTED.
AND WHAT OF THIS THIRD PARKER?
*SEE SPEC #224 FOR MORE DETAILS. --DANNY
HE MAY HAVE HIS USES STILL.
WE SHALL SEE.
POLICE LINE / DO NOT CROSS
VERY SOON.
POLICE LINE / DO NOT CR

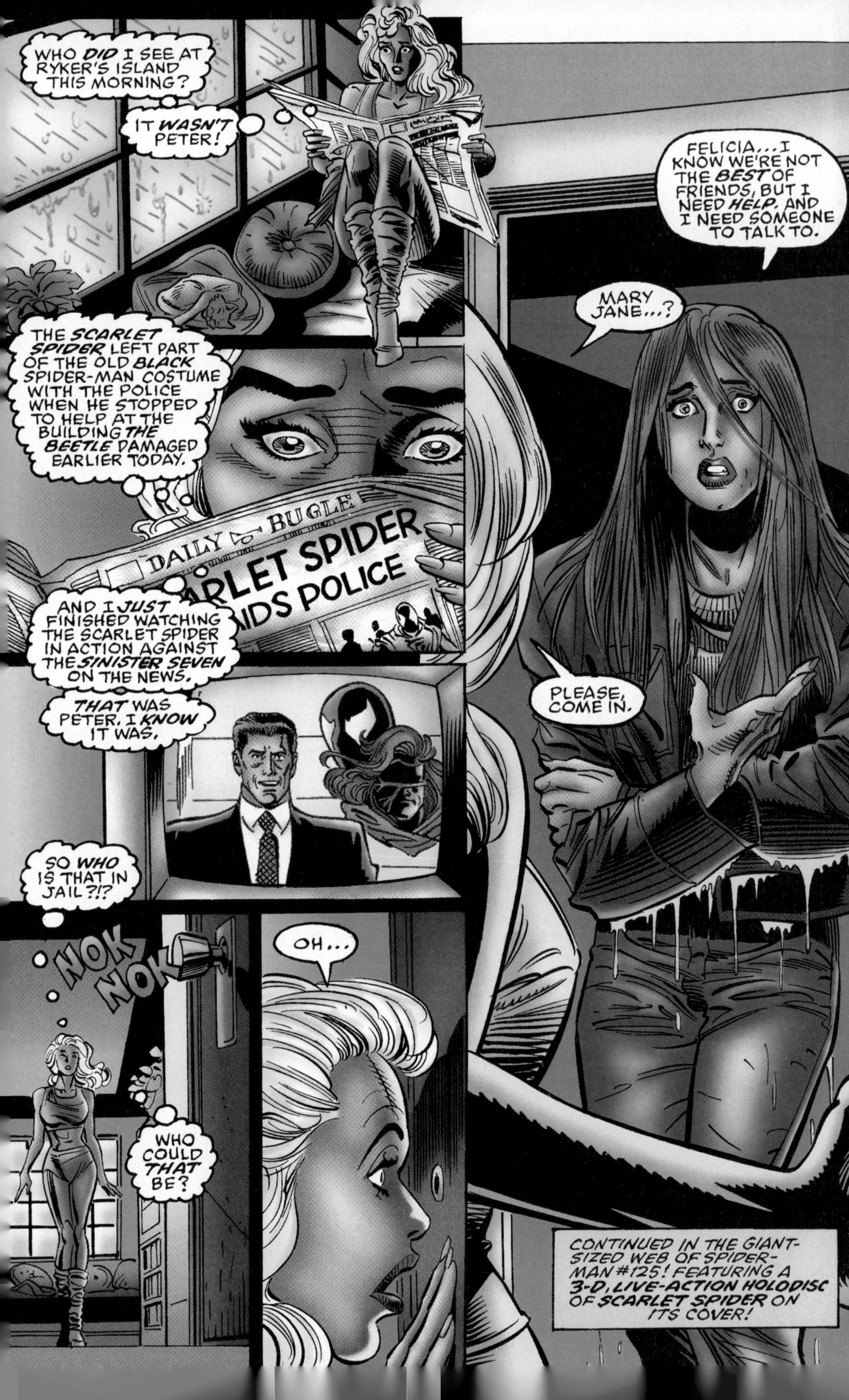
WHO DID I SEE AT RYKER'S ISLAND THIS MORNING?
IT WASN'T PETER!
FELICIA... I KNOW WE'RE NOT THE BEST OF FRIENDS, BUT I NEED HELP, AND I NEED SOMEONE TO TALK TO.
MARY JANE...?
THE SCARLET SPIDER LEFT PART OF THE OLD BLACK SPIDER-MAN COSTUME WITH THE POLICE WHEN HE STOPPED TO HELP AT THE BUILDING THE BEETLE DAMAGED EARLIER TODAY.
DAILY BUGLE
SCARLET SPIDER
AIDS POLICE
AND I JUST FINISHED WATCHING THE SCARLET SPIDER IN ACTION AGAINST THE SINISTER SEVEN ON THE NEWS.
THAT WAS PETER. I KNOW IT WAS.
PLEASE, COME IN.
SO WHO IS THAT IN JAIL?!?
NOK NOK
OH...
WHO COULD THAT BE?
CONTINUED IN THE GIANT-SIZED WEB OF SPIDER-MAN #125! FEATURING A 3-D, LIVE-ACTION HOLODISC OF SCARLET SPIDER ON ITS COVER!

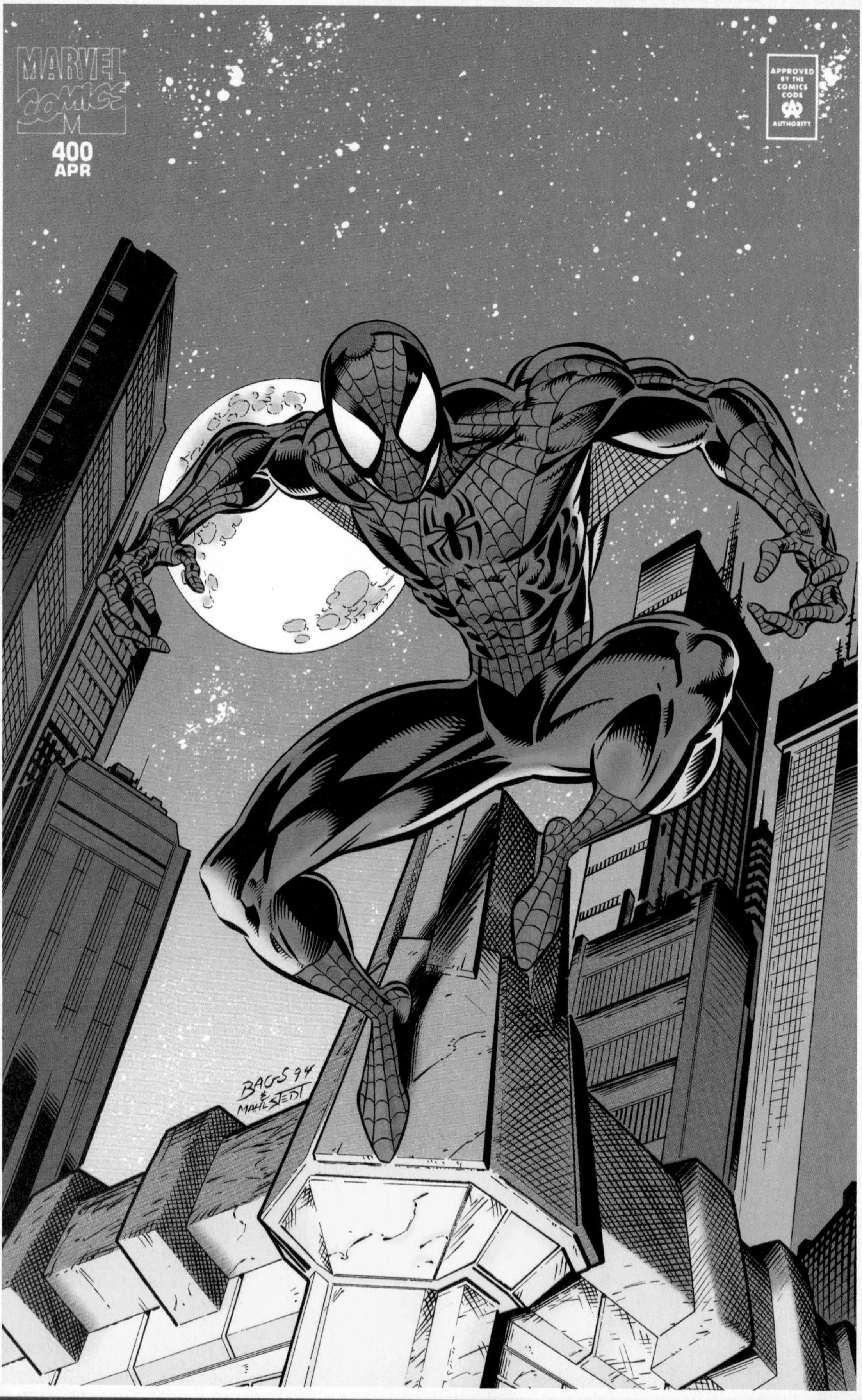
MARVEL COMICS
400
APR
APPROVED BY THE COMICS CODE AUTHORITY
BAGS 94 & MAHLSTEDT

Amazing Spider-Man #400 deluxe edition die-cut undercover

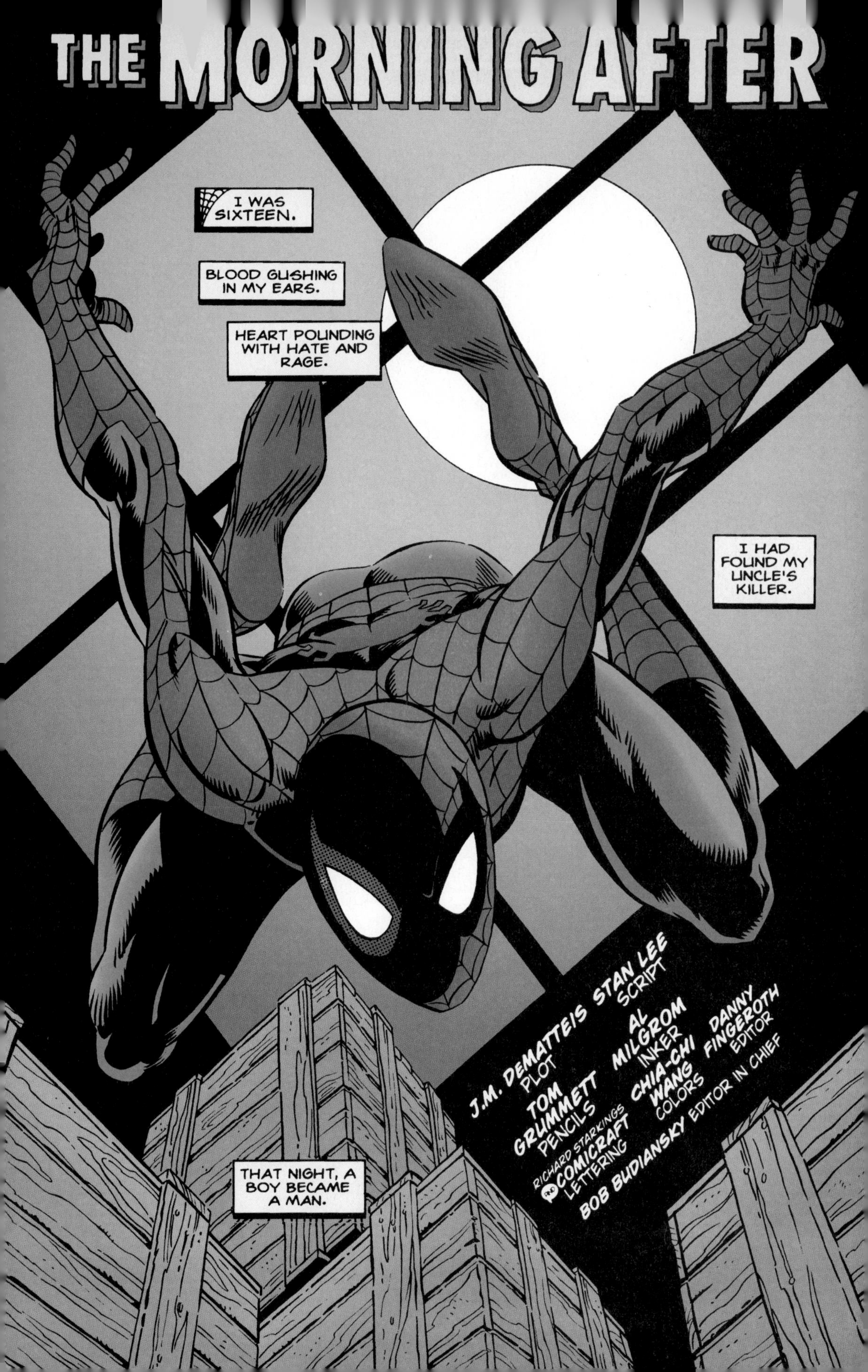
THE MORNING AFTER
I WAS SIXTEEN.
BLOOD GUSHING IN MY EARS.
HEART POUNDING WITH HATE AND RAGE.
I HAD FOUND MY UNCLE'S KILLER.
J.M. DEMATTEIS PLOT
STAN LEE SCRIPT
TOM GRUMMETT PENCILS
AL MILGROM INKER
RICHARD STARKINGS AND COMICRAFT LETTERING
CHIA-CHI WANG COLORS
DANNY FINGEROTH EDITOR
BOB BUDIANSKY EDITOR IN CHIEF
THAT NIGHT, A BOY BECAME A MAN.

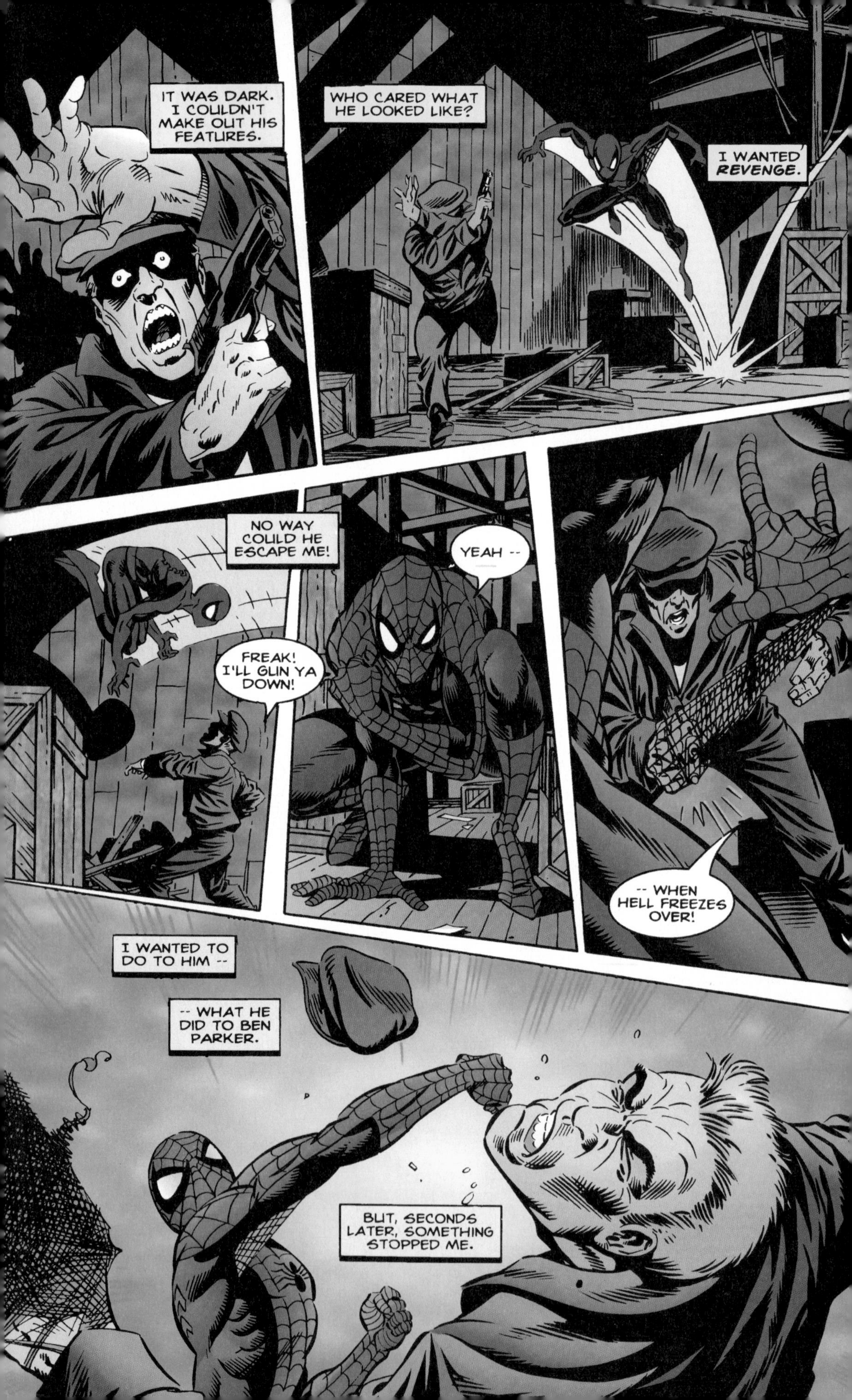
IT WAS DARK. I COULDN'T MAKE OUT HIS FEATURES.
WHO CARED WHAT HE LOOKED LIKE?
I WANTED REVENGE.
NO WAY COULD HE ESCAPE ME!
FREAK! I'LL GUN YA DOWN!
YEAH --
-- WHEN HELL FREEZES OVER!
I WANTED TO DO TO HIM --
-- WHAT HE DID TO BEN PARKER.
BUT, SECONDS LATER, SOMETHING STOPPED ME.

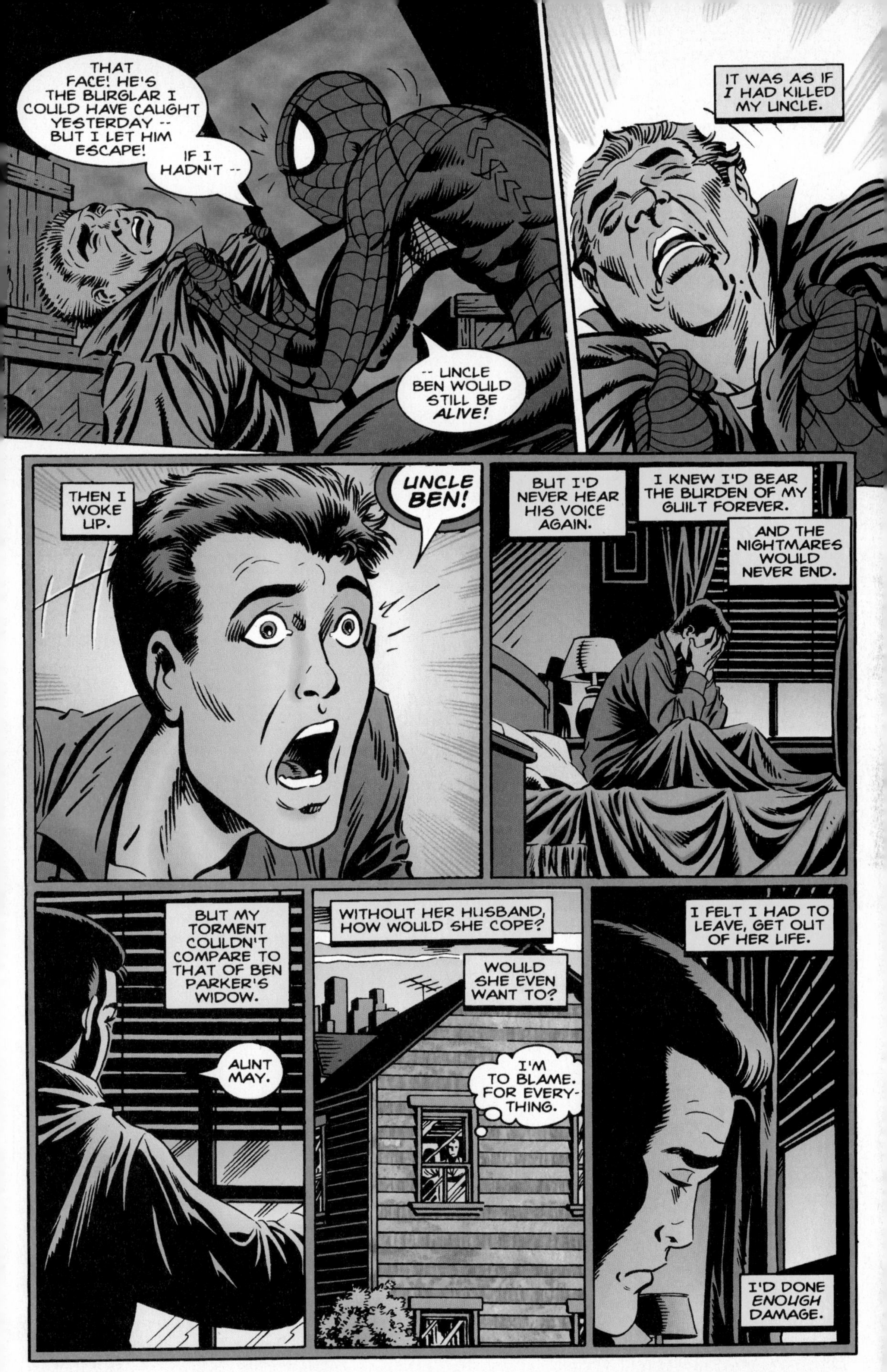
THAT FACE! HE'S THE BURGLAR I COULD HAVE CAUGHT YESTERDAY -- BUT I LET HIM ESCAPE!
IF I HADN'T --
-- UNCLE BEN WOULD STILL BE *ALIVE!*
IT WAS AS IF *I* HAD KILLED MY UNCLE.
THEN I WOKE UP.
UNCLE BEN!
BUT I'D NEVER HEAR HIS VOICE AGAIN.
I KNEW I'D BEAR THE BURDEN OF MY GUILT FOREVER.
AND THE NIGHTMARES WOULD NEVER END.
BUT MY TORMENT COULDN'T COMPARE TO THAT OF BEN PARKER'S WIDOW.
AUNT MAY.
WITHOUT HER HUSBAND, HOW WOULD SHE COPE?
WOULD SHE EVEN WANT TO?
I'M TO BLAME. FOR EVERY-THING.
I FELT I HAD TO LEAVE, GET OUT OF HER LIFE.
I'D DONE *ENOUGH* DAMAGE.

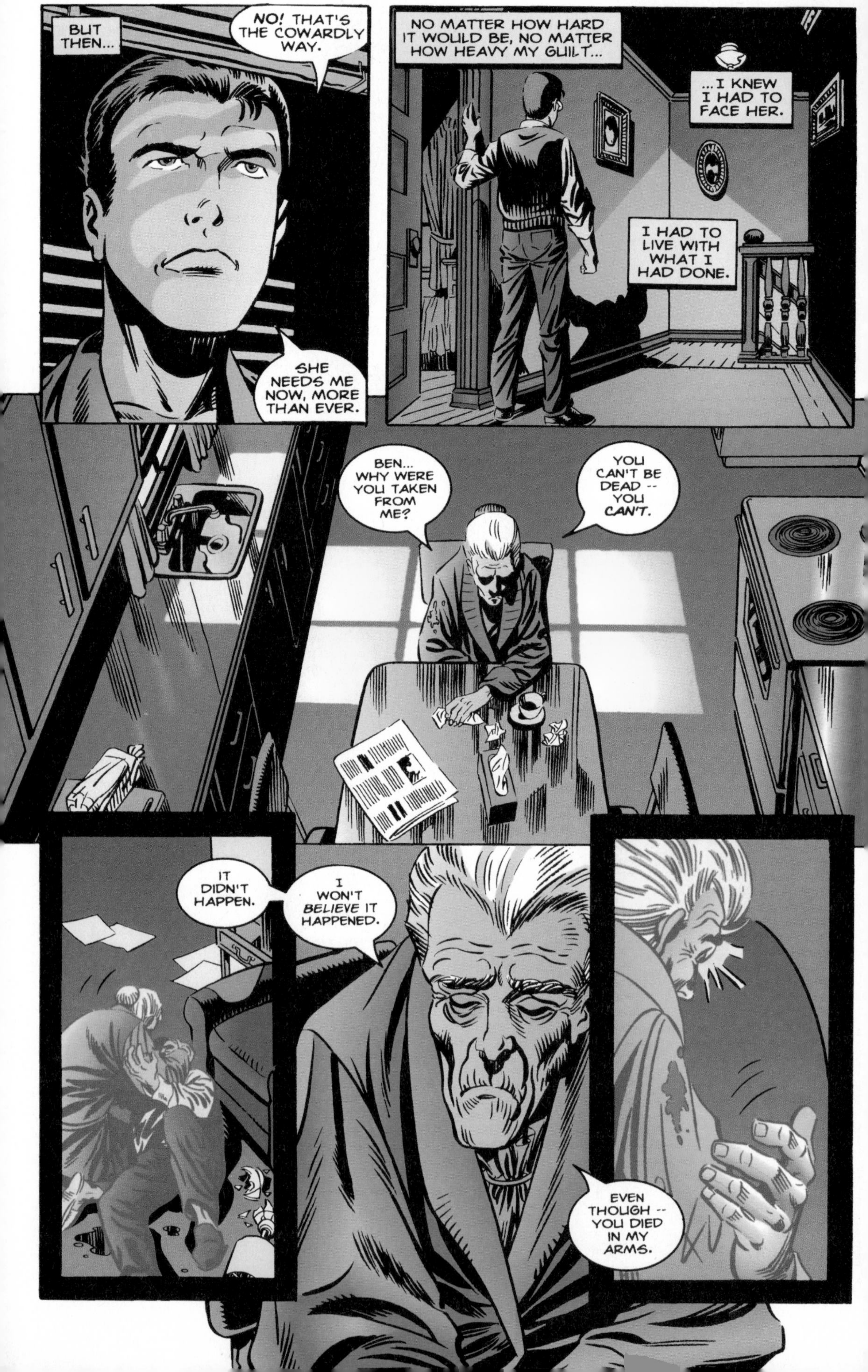

BUT THEN...
NO! THAT'S THE COWARDLY WAY.
SHE NEEDS ME NOW, MORE THAN EVER.
NO MATTER HOW HARD IT WOULD BE, NO MATTER HOW HEAVY MY GUILT...
...I KNEW I HAD TO FACE HER.
I HAD TO LIVE WITH WHAT I HAD DONE.
BEN... WHY WERE YOU TAKEN FROM ME?
YOU CAN'T BE DEAD -- YOU CAN'T.
IT DIDN'T HAPPEN.
I WON'T BELIEVE IT HAPPENED.
EVEN THOUGH -- YOU DIED IN MY ARMS.

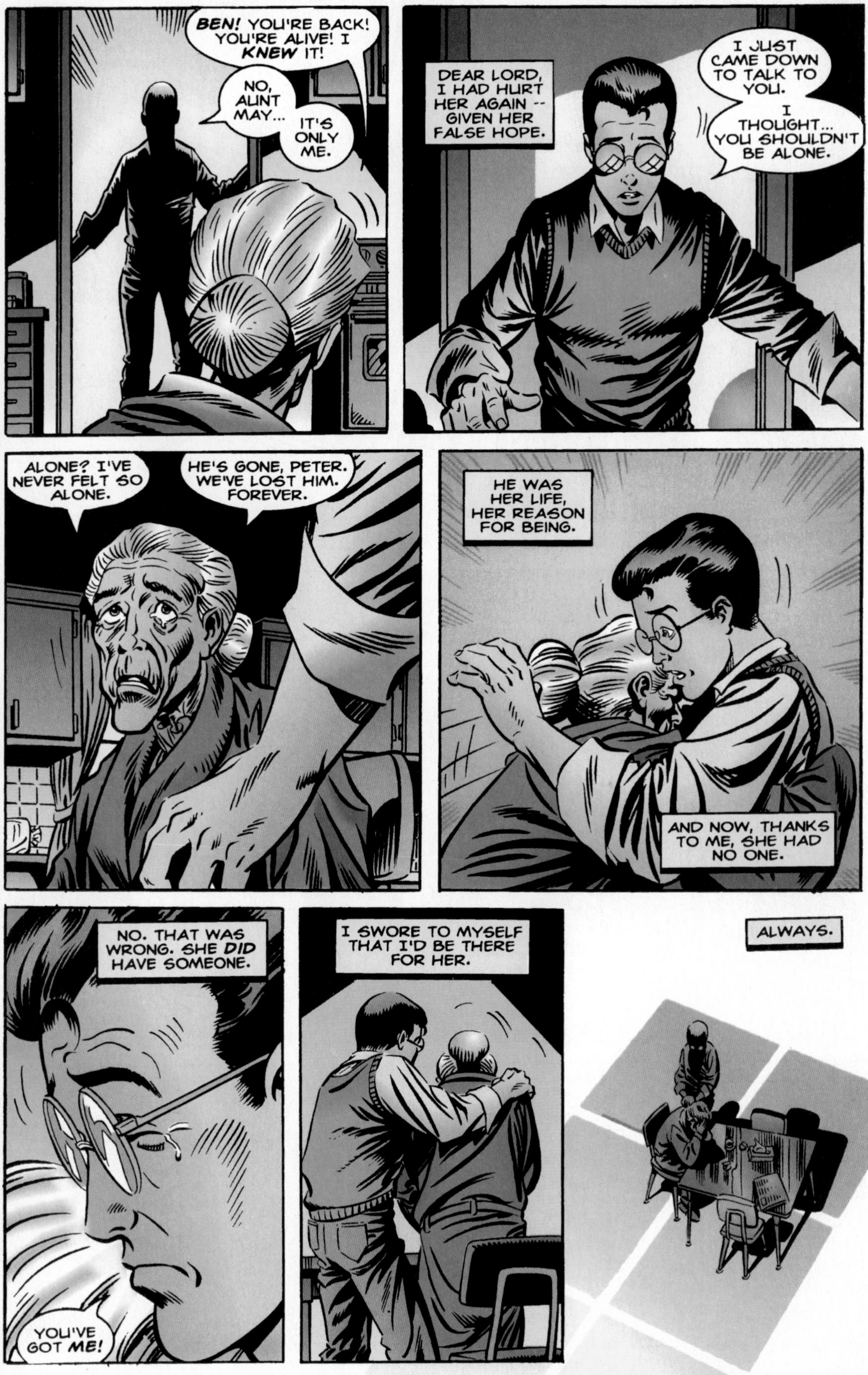
BEN! YOU'RE BACK! YOU'RE ALIVE! I KNEW IT!
NO, AUNT MAY...
IT'S ONLY ME.
DEAR LORD, I HAD HURT HER AGAIN -- GIVEN HER FALSE HOPE.
I JUST CAME DOWN TO TALK TO YOU.
I THOUGHT... YOU SHOULDN'T BE ALONE.
ALONE? I'VE NEVER FELT SO ALONE.
HE'S GONE, PETER. WE'VE LOST HIM. FOREVER.
HE WAS HER LIFE, HER REASON FOR BEING.
AND NOW, THANKS TO ME, SHE HAD NO ONE.
NO. THAT WAS WRONG. SHE DID HAVE SOMEONE.
YOU'VE GOT ME!
I SWORE TO MYSELF THAT I'D BE THERE FOR HER.
ALWAYS.

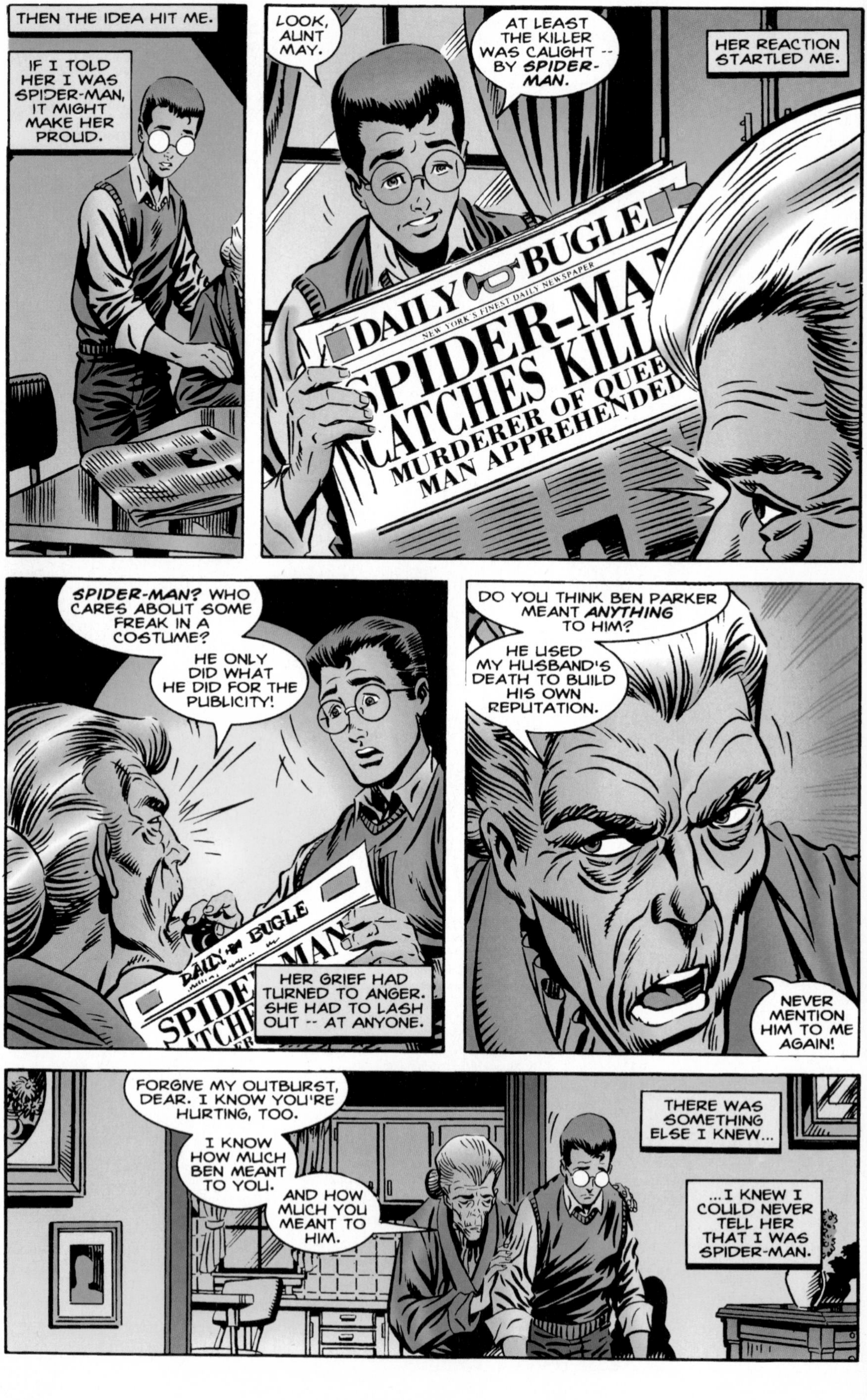
THEN THE IDEA HIT ME.
IF I TOLD HER I WAS SPIDER-MAN, IT MIGHT MAKE HER PROUD.
LOOK, AUNT MAY.
AT LEAST THE KILLER WAS CAUGHT -- BY SPIDER-MAN.
DAILY BUGLE
NEW YORK'S FINEST DAILY NEWSPAPER
SPIDER-MAN CATCHES KILL
MURDERER OF QUEE
MAN APPREHENDED
HER REACTION STARTLED ME.
SPIDER-MAN? WHO CARES ABOUT SOME FREAK IN A COSTUME?
HE ONLY DID WHAT HE DID FOR THE PUBLICITY!
DAILY BUGLE
SPIDER-MAN CATCHE
HER GRIEF HAD TURNED TO ANGER. SHE HAD TO LASH OUT -- AT ANYONE.
DO YOU THINK BEN PARKER MEANT ANYTHING TO HIM?
HE USED MY HUSBAND'S DEATH TO BUILD HIS OWN REPUTATION.
NEVER MENTION HIM TO ME AGAIN!
FORGIVE MY OUTBURST, DEAR. I KNOW YOU'RE HURTING, TOO.
I KNOW HOW MUCH BEN MEANT TO YOU.
AND HOW MUCH YOU MEANT TO HIM.
THERE WAS SOMETHING ELSE I KNEW...
...I KNEW I COULD NEVER TELL HER THAT I WAS SPIDER-MAN.

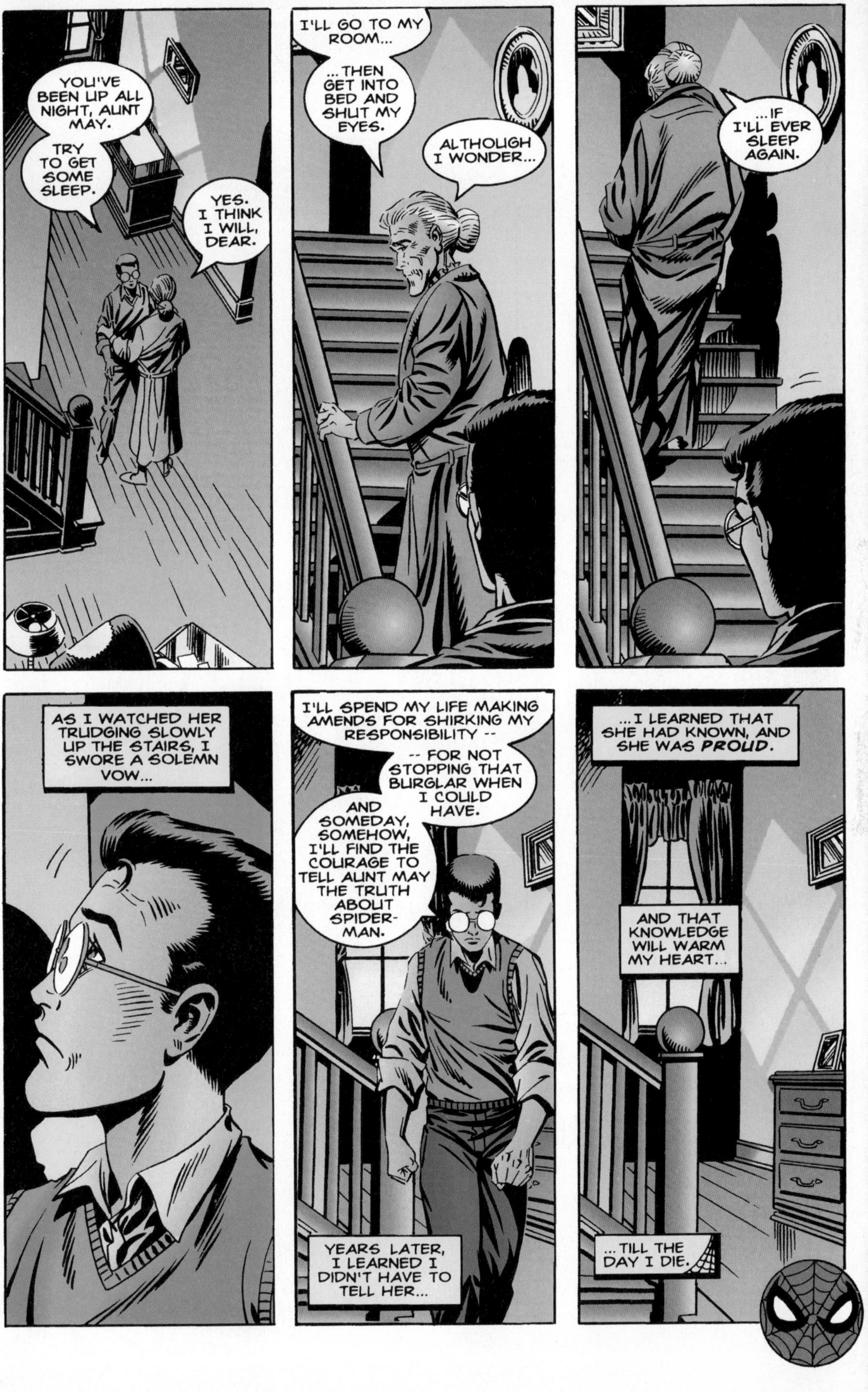
YOU'VE BEEN UP ALL NIGHT, AUNT MAY.
TRY TO GET SOME SLEEP.
YES. I THINK I WILL, DEAR.
I'LL GO TO MY ROOM...
...THEN GET INTO BED AND SHUT MY EYES.
ALTHOUGH I WONDER...
...IF I'LL EVER SLEEP AGAIN.
AS I WATCHED HER TRUDGING SLOWLY UP THE STAIRS, I SWORE A SOLEMN VOW...
I'LL SPEND MY LIFE MAKING AMENDS FOR SHIRKING MY RESPONSIBILITY --
-- FOR NOT STOPPING THAT BURGLAR WHEN I COULD HAVE.
AND SOMEDAY, SOMEHOW, I'LL FIND THE COURAGE TO TELL AUNT MAY THE TRUTH ABOUT SPIDER-MAN.
YEARS LATER, I LEARNED I DIDN'T HAVE TO TELL HER...
...I LEARNED THAT SHE HAD KNOWN, AND SHE WAS *PROUD*.
AND THAT KNOWLEDGE WILL WARM MY HEART...
...TILL THE DAY I DIE.

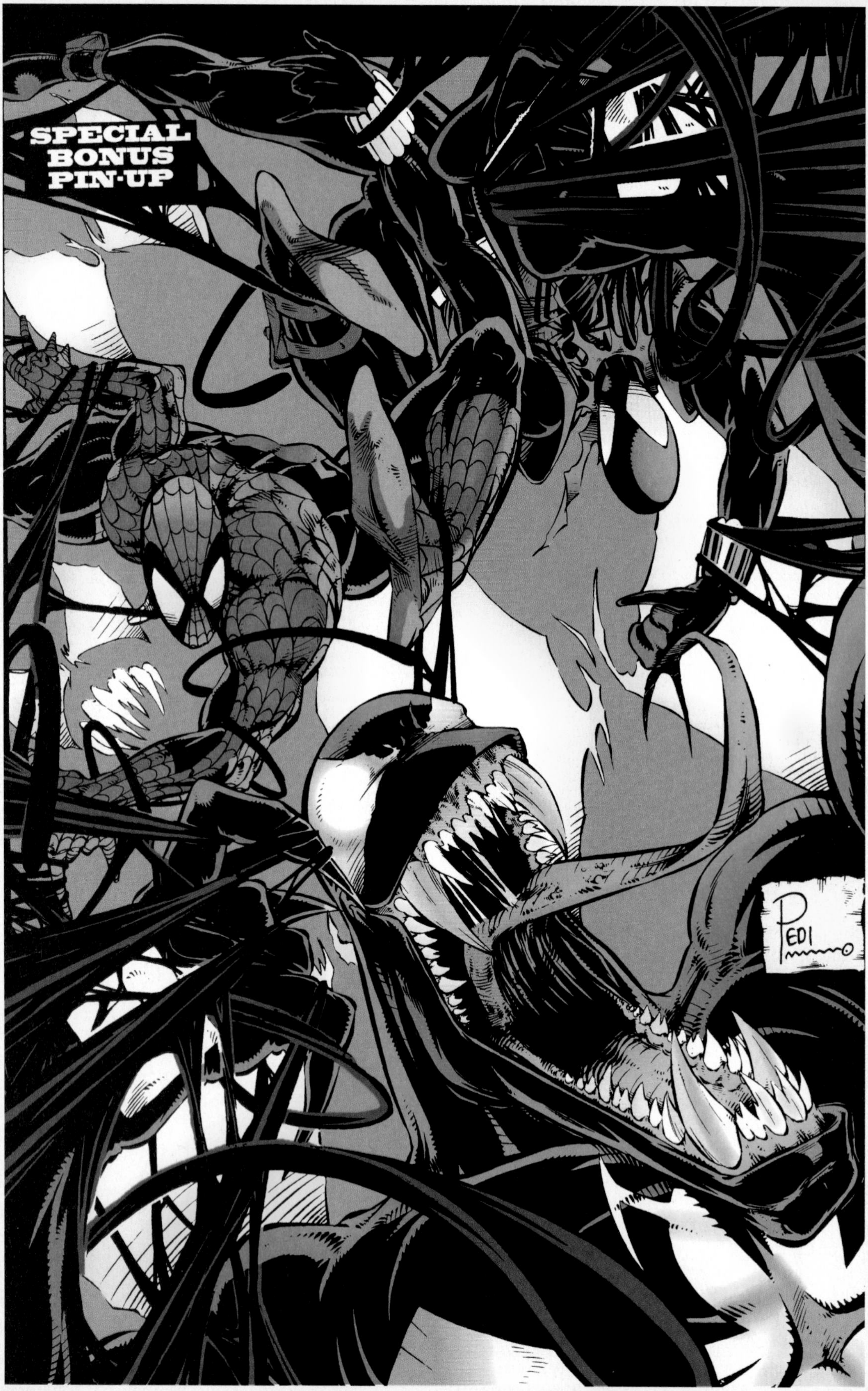

SPECIAL BONUS PIN-UP
PEDI

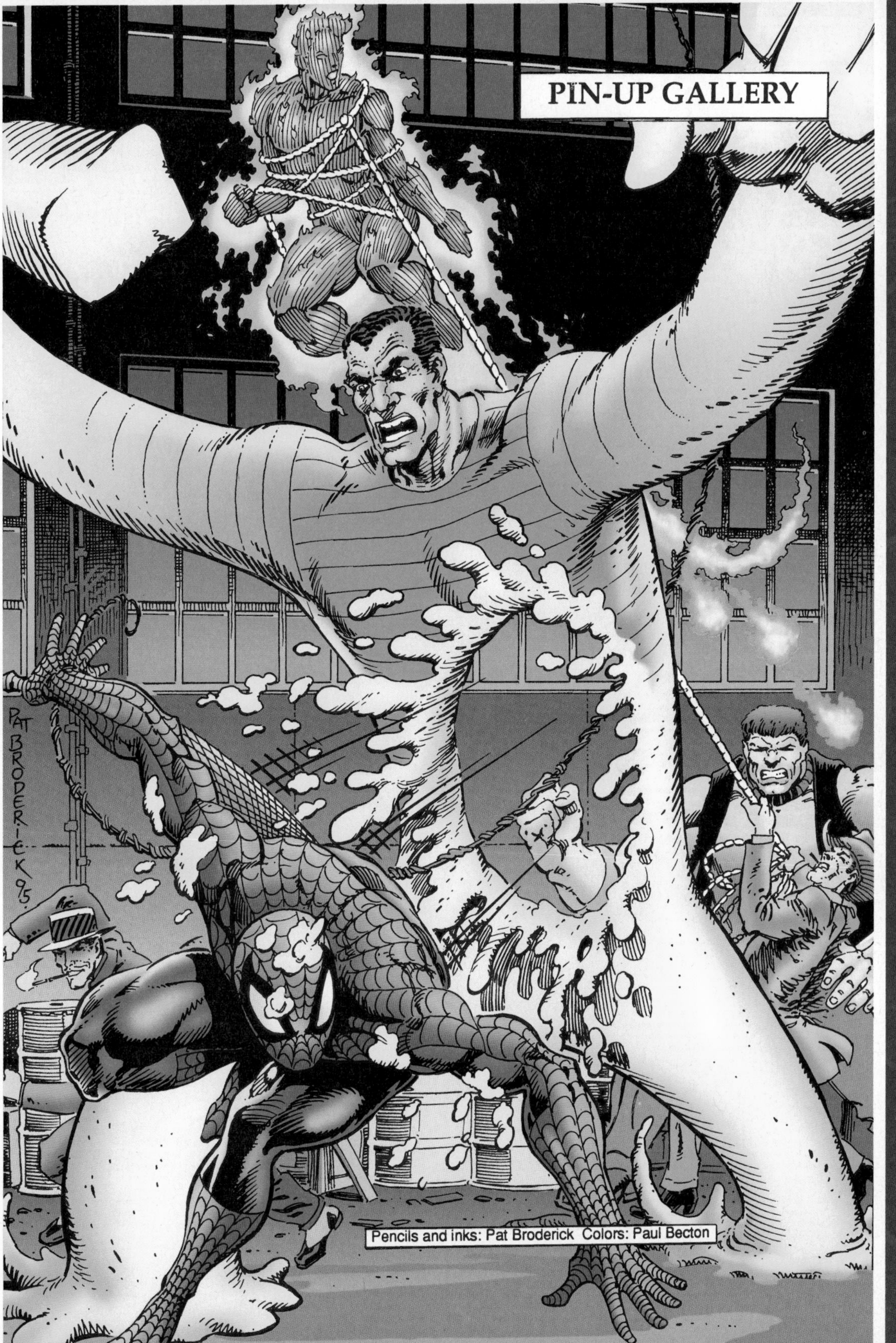
PIN-UP GALLERY
PAT BRODERICK 95
Pencils and inks: Pat Broderick Colors: Paul Becton

PIN-UP GALLERY

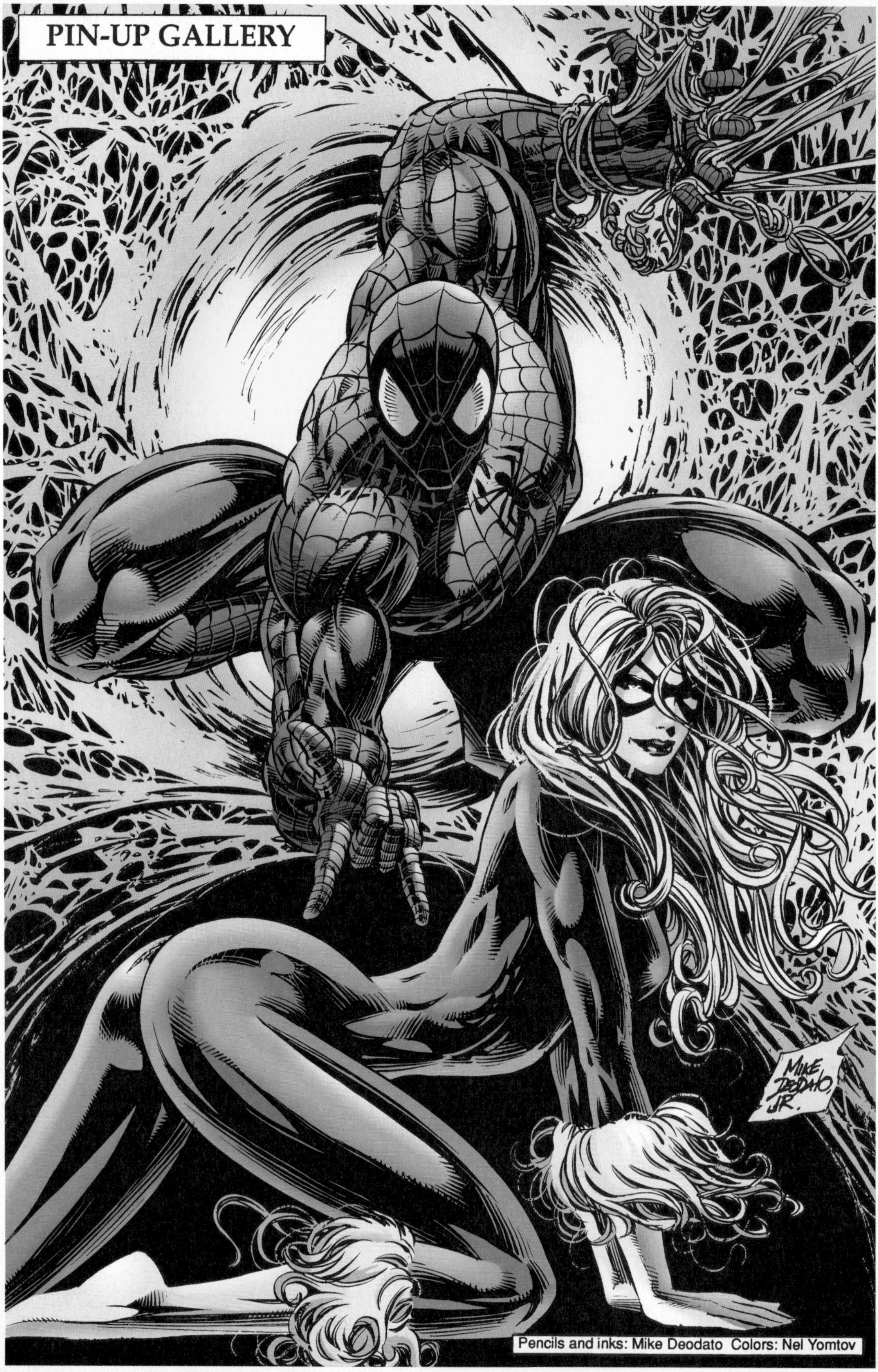
MIKE DEODATO, JR.

Pencils and inks: Mike Deodato Colors: Nel Yomtov

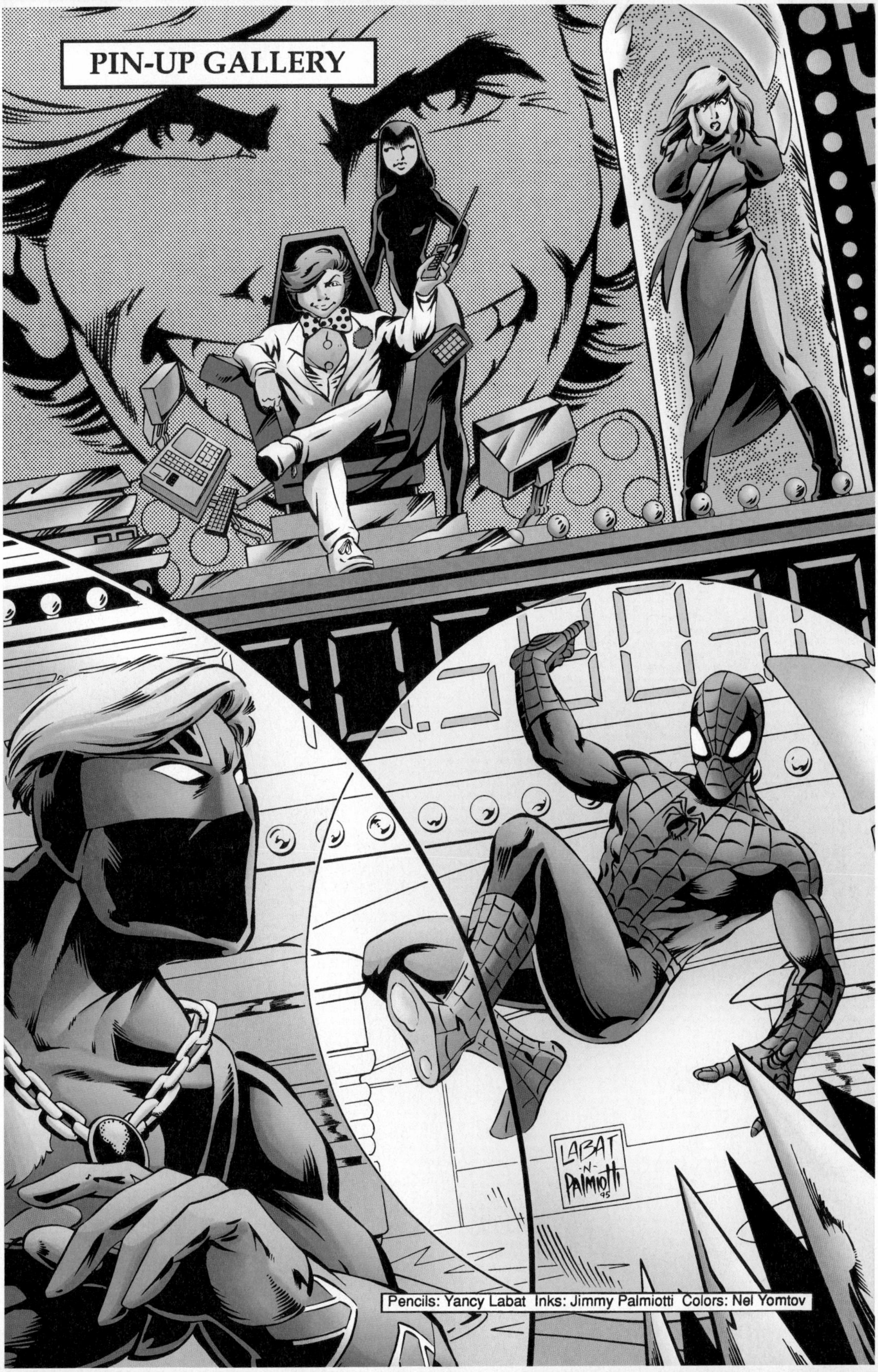
PIN-UP GALLERY
LABAT -N- PALMIOTTI '95
Pencils: Yancy Labat Inks: Jimmy Palmiotti Colors: Nel Yomtov

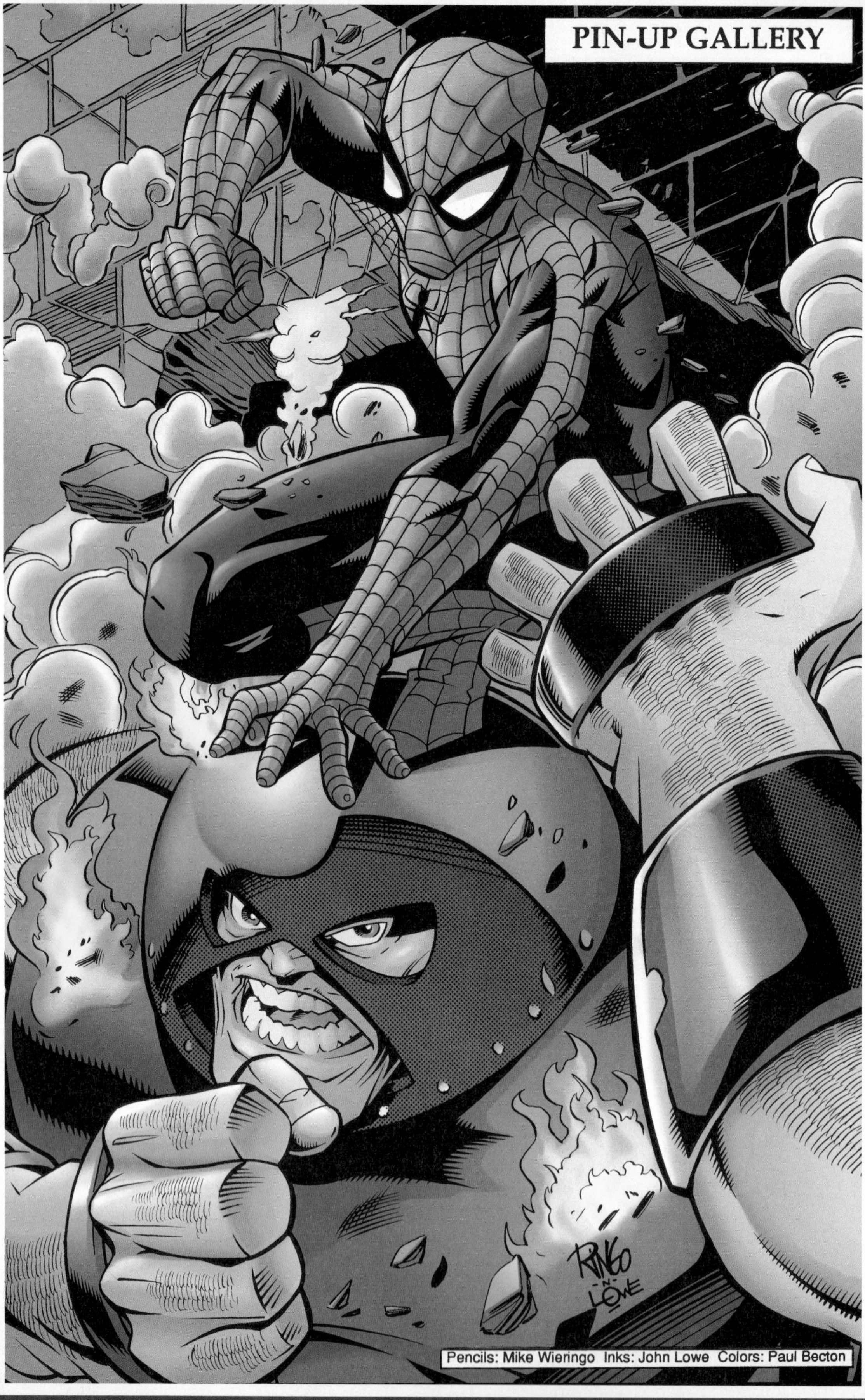
PIN-UP GALLERY
RINGO -N- LOWE
Pencils: Mike Wieringo Inks: John Lowe Colors: Paul Becton

PIN-UP GALLERY

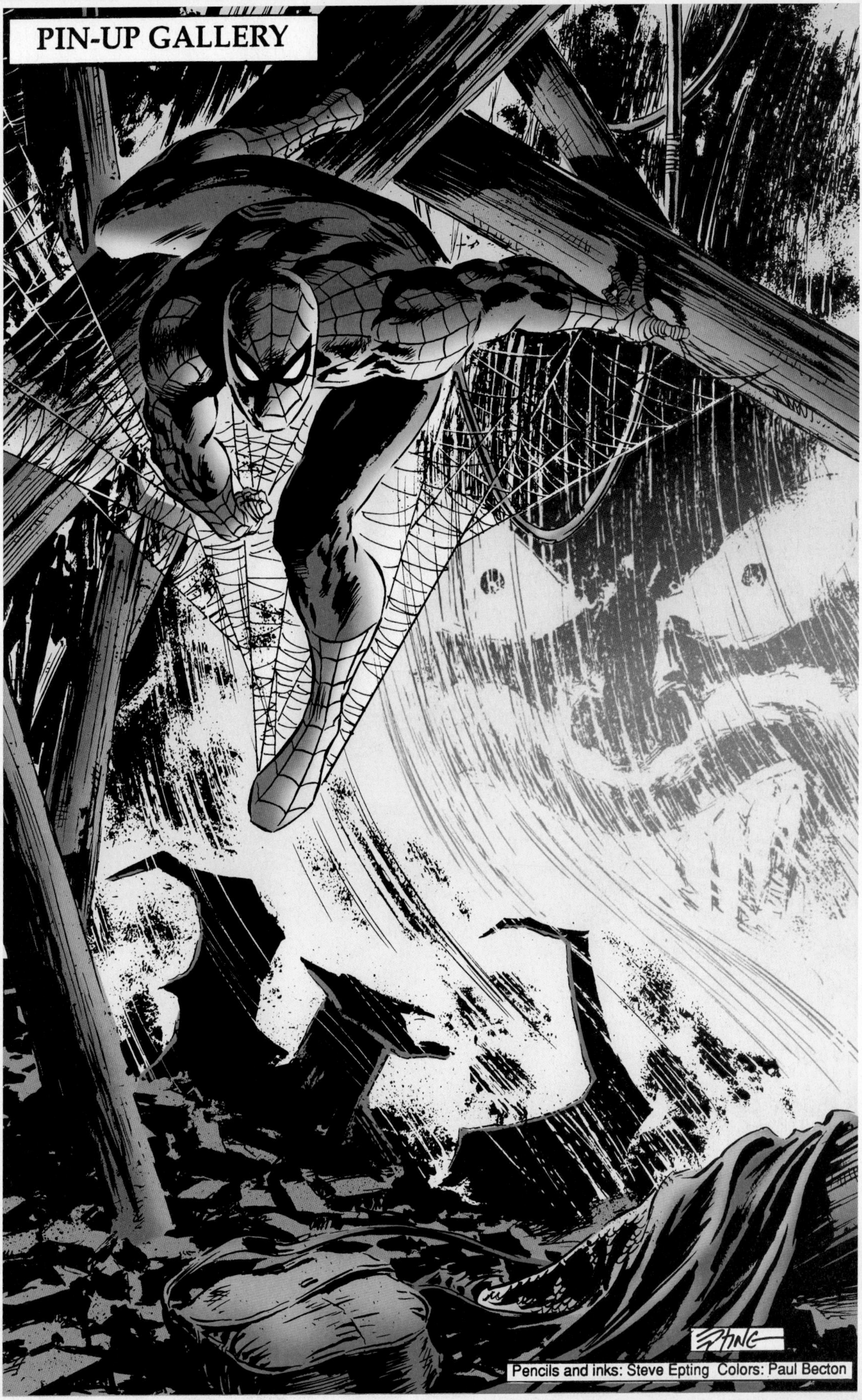

Pencils and inks: Steve Epting Colors: Paul Becton

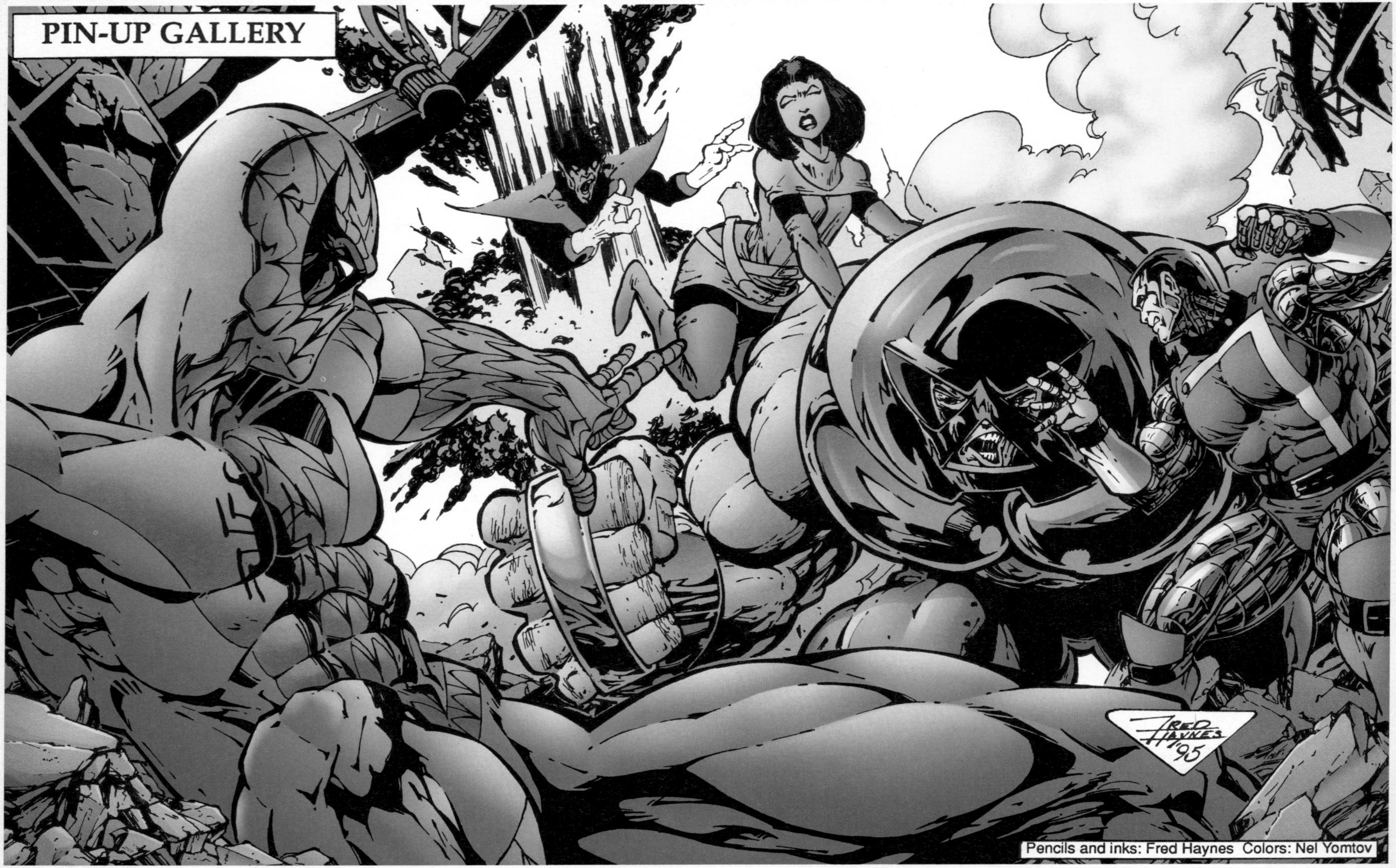
PIN-UP GALLERY
FRED HAYNES '95
Pencils and inks: Fred Haynes Colors: Nel Yomtov

PIN-UP GALLERY

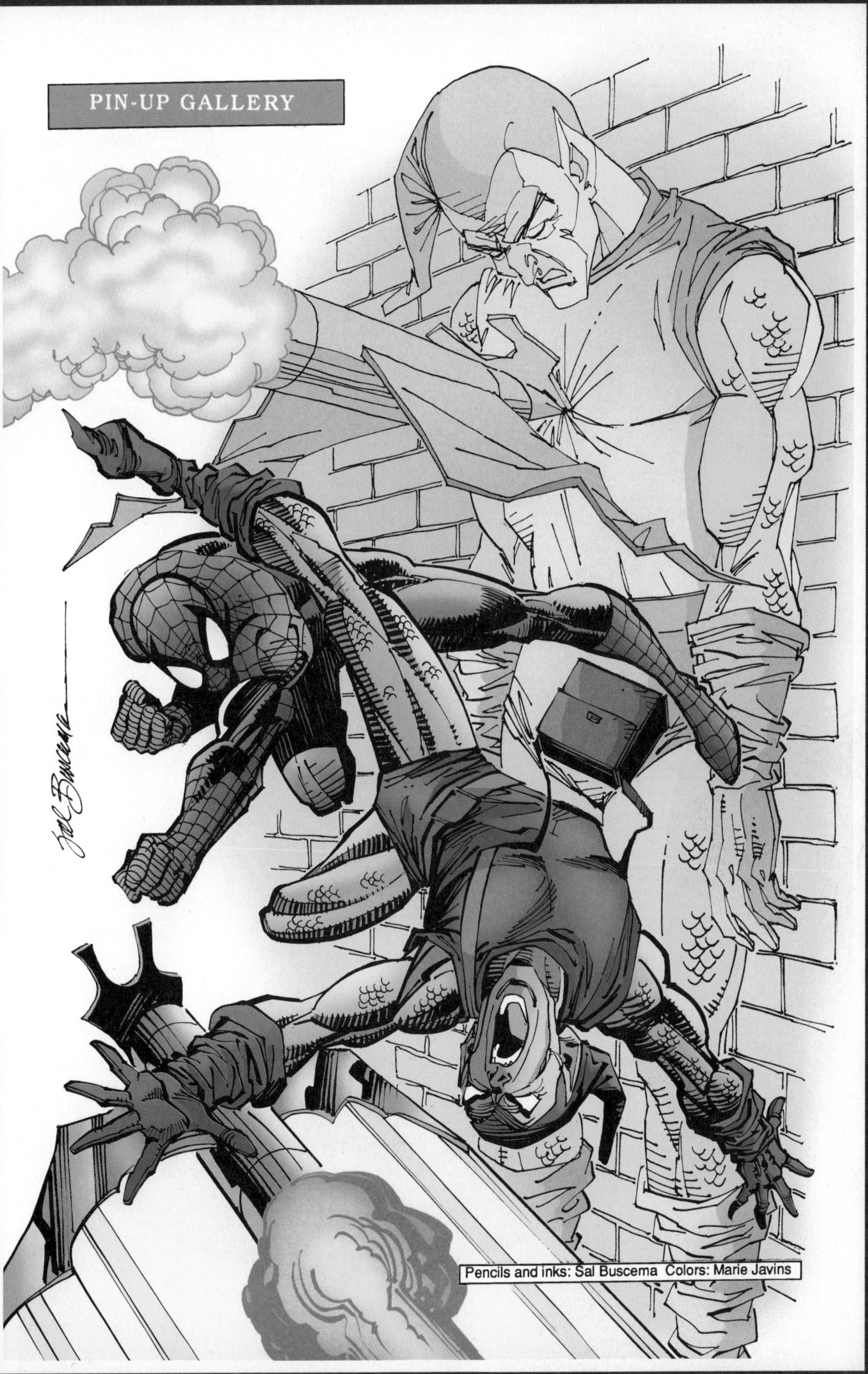

Pencils and inks: Sal Buscema Colors: Marie Javins

PIN-UP GALLERY

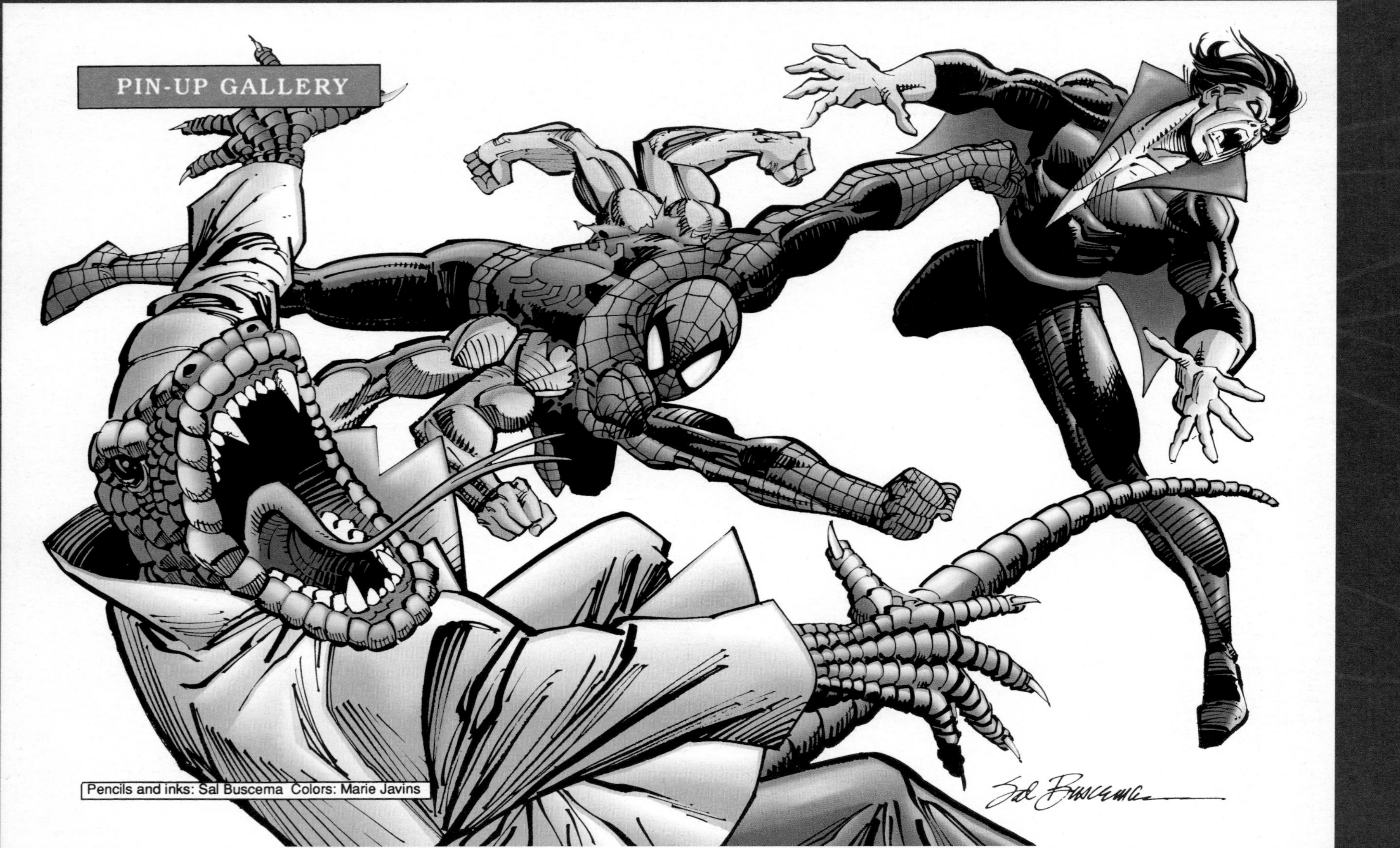

Pencils and inks: Sal Buscema Colors: Marie Javins

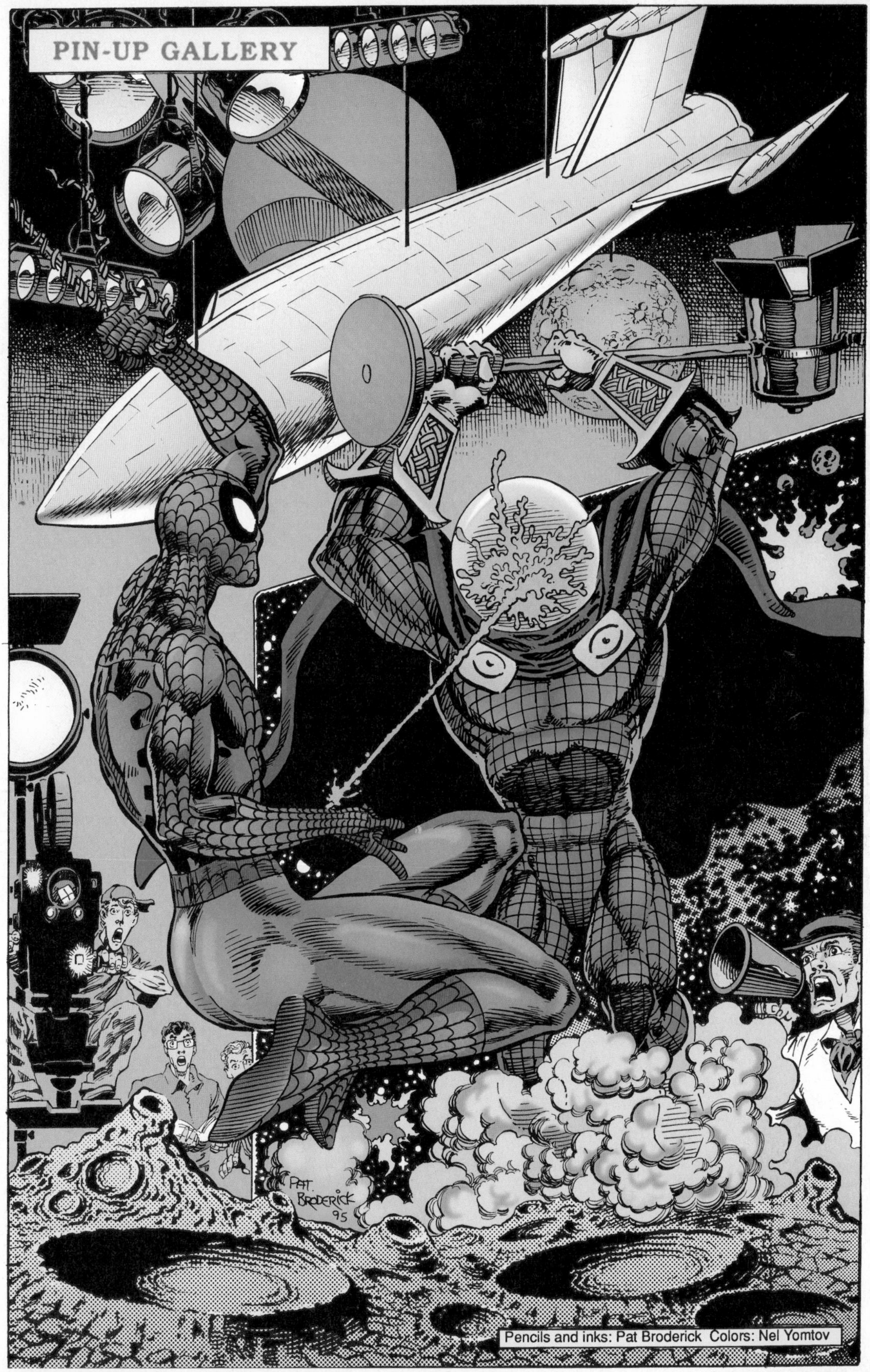
PIN-UP GALLERY
PAT. BRODERICK '95

Pencils and inks: Pat Broderick Colors: Nel Yomtov

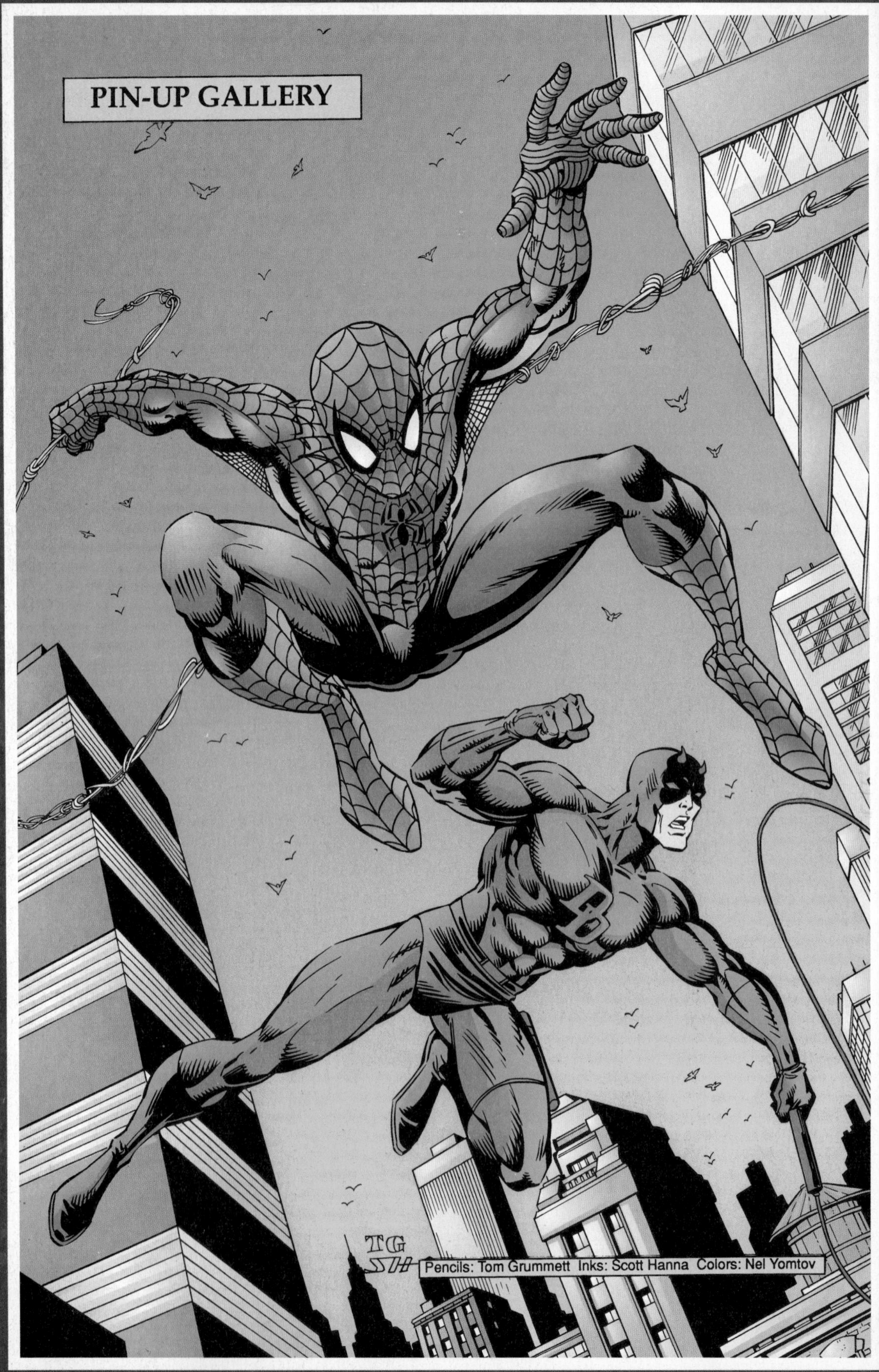
PIN-UP GALLERY
TG
SH
Pencils: Tom Grummett Inks: Scott Hanna Colors: Nel Yomtov